READINGS IN

American History

READINGS IN

American History

EDITED BY OSCAR HANDLIN

PROFESSOR OF HISTORY, HARVARD UNIVERSITY

NEW YORK   ALFRED A. KNOPF *1966*

ACKNOWLEDGMENTS

I WISH TO ACKNOWLEDGE with gratitude the permission of the following publishers and individuals to reprint in this book extracts from the following copyright works controlled by them. Unless otherwise indicated, the copyright claimant in every case was the person or organization who has given permission to reprint the selection.

American Economic Association: from *American Economic Review*, © 1940 (No. 356).

American Historical Association: from L. W. Labaree, ed., *Royal Instructions to British Colonial Governors*, © 1935 (Nos. 30, 44, 63).

Anderson House: from Maxwell Anderson, *Winterset*, © 1935 by Anderson House and Maxwell Anderson (No. 405).

Appleton-Century-Crofts: from M. B. Chesnut, *Diary from Dixie*, © 1905 by D. Appleton & Company; renewed 1932 by Myra Lockett Avary (No. 227).

Atlantic Monthly: from Oscar Handlin, "Second Chance for the South" and "Payroll Prosperity," © 1953 (Nos. 452, 454); and from A. E. Sutherland, "Segregation," © 1954 by the Atlantic Monthly Company, Boston 16, Massachusetts (No. 461).

Barnes and Noble: from G. L. Burr, ed., *Narratives of the Witchcraft Cases*, © 1914, 1942 (No. 61); and J. F. Jameson, ed., Edward Johnson, *Wonder-Working Providence*, © 1910, 1937 (No. 28).

Bobbs-Merrill Company, Inc.: from Herbert Quick, *One Man's Life*, © 1925, 1953 by Ella Corey Quick (No. 273); and from Robert Lansing, *War Memoirs*, © 1935 (No. 320).

Estate of Louis D. Brandeis: from Brandeis, *Other People's Money*, © 1913 by The McClure Publications; 1914, 1932 by Louis D. Brandeis (No. 245).

W. J. Bryan, Jr.: from William Jennings Bryan, *Speeches*, © 1909 by William Jennings Bryan, Vol. I (No. 296).

Business Week: from "Twenty-Five Years That Remade America," © 1954 (No. 455).

University of California Press: from M. F. Williams, *History of the San Francisco Committee of Vigilance*, © 1921 by Mary Flloyd Williams (No. 179).

Carnegie Endowment for International Peace: from James Madison, *Debates in the Federal Convention*, © 1920 (Nos. 119, 121).

Emmett K. Carver: from Thomas N. Carver, *Present Economic Revolution in the United States*, © 1925 by Thomas Nixon Carver (No. 360).

University of Chicago Press: from B. A. Botkin, ed., *Lay My Burden Down*, © 1945 (No. 234).

Chicago Tribune: from *A Century of Tribune Editorials*, © 1947 (No. 340).

Arthur H. Clark Company: from *Documentary History of American Industrial Society*, Vol. I, © 1910 (Nos. 47, 48, 52, 214).

Mrs. Mina Curtiss: from *Letters Home*, © 1944 (No. 419).

Dodd, Mead & Company, Inc.: from *This Is Wendell Willkie*, © 1940 (No. 440).

Doubleday & Co., Inc.: from J. M. Beck, *Constitution of the United States*, © 1924 (No. 361); from Frank Norris, *A Deal in Wheat*, © 1928 (No. 240); from Henry Ford, *My Life and Work*, © 1922 (No. 238).

W. E. B. DuBois: from *Souls of Black Folk*, © 1903 by A. C. McClurg and Company; renewed 1953 by W. E. B. DuBois (No. 283).

E. P. Dutton & Co., Inc.: from Samuel Gompers, *Seventy Years of Life and Labor*, © 1925 by Samuel Gompers; renewed 1952 by Mrs. Gertrude G. Gompers (No. 256); and from J. L. Heaton, *Cobb of The World*, © 1924 (No. 323).

James A. Farley: from *Jim Farley's Story—The Roosevelt Years*, Whittlesey House, McGraw-Hill Book Company, Inc., © 1948 (No. 380).

Fortune: from R. W. Davenport, *U.S.A., The Permanent Revolution*, © 1951 by Time Inc. (No. 451); and "No One Has Starved," © 1932 by Time Inc. (No. 357).

Harcourt, Brace and Company: from D. M. Nelson, *Arsenal of Democracy,* © 1946 by Donald M. Nelson (No. 421); from A. M. Lindbergh, *Wave of the Future,* © 1940 by Anne Morrow Lindbergh (No. 406); and from Sinclair Lewis, *Babbitt,* © 1922 by Harcourt, Brace and Company, Inc.; renewed 1950 by Sinclair Lewis (No. 397). All abridged and reprinted by permission.

Harper & Brothers: from R. E. Sherwood, *Roosevelt and Hopkins,* © 1948 (No. 424); from R. H. Conwell, *Acres of Diamonds,* © 1915 (No. 286); from R. B. Fosdick, *Story of the Rockefeller Foundation,* © 1952 by Raymond B. Fosdick (No. 400); from S. I. Rosenman, *Working with Roosevelt,* © 1952 (No. 386); from D. E. Lilienthal, *TVA—Democracy on the March,* © 1944 by David E. Lilienthal (No. 376); and from J. F. Byrnes, *Speaking Frankly,* © 1947 by James F. Byrnes (No. 428).

Harvard University Press: from Theodore Roosevelt, *Letters,* © 1952 by The President and Fellows of Harvard College (No. 297); from A. W. Williams, *Work, Wages and Education,* © 1940 by The President and Fellows of Harvard College (No. 375); from *General Education in a Free Society,* © 1945 by The President and Fellows of Harvard College (No. 464); from K. B. Murdock, ed., *Handkerchiefs from Paul,* © 1927 by The President and Fellows of Harvard College (No. 26); from Handlin, *This Was America,* © 1949 by The President and Fellows of Harvard College (Nos. 101, 103); and from Peter Wraxall, *Abridgment of Indian Affairs,* © 1915 by The President and Fellows of Harvard College (Nos. 38, 43).

Hermitage House, Inc.: from Margaret Anderson, *Little Review Anthology,* © 1953 by Margaret Anderson (No. 399).

Henry Holt and Company: from Ernie Pyle, *Brave Men,* © 1943, 1944, by Scripps-Howard Newspaper Alliance. © 1944 by Henry Holt and Company, Inc. By permission of the publishers (No. 418); and from John Dewey, *Influence of Darwinism on Philosophy,* © 1910, 1937 by John Dewey (No. 292).

Houghton Mifflin Company: from Charles Seymour, *Intimate Papers of Colonel House,* © 1926 (No. 331); from J. C. Grew, *Turbulent Era,* © 1952 by Joseph C. Grew (Nos. 412, 415); from Henry Adams, *Letters,* © 1938 by Worthington C. Ford (No. 279); from Andrew Carnegie, *Autobiography,* © 1920 by Louise Whitfield Carnegie (No. 237); and from A. H. Vandenberg, *Private Papers of Senator Vandenberg,* © 1952 by Arthur H. Vandenberg, Jr. (Nos. 417, 433).

International Publishers: from *Bill Haywood's Book,* © 1929 (No. 261).

Charles H. Kerr & Co.: from M. H. Jones, *Autobiography of Mother Jones,* © 1925 (No. 259).

Alfred A. Knopf, Inc.: from Alistair Cooke, *A Generation on Trial,* © 1950 by Alistair Cooke (No. 444); and from Marriner S. Eccles, *Beckoning Frontiers,* © 1950, 1951 by Marriner S. Eccles (No. 423).

Labor (Newspaper): from its issue © November 17, 1923 (No. 370).

J. B. Lippincott Company: from Carey McWilliams, *North from Mexico,* © 1949 by Carey McWilliams (No. 457).

Little, Brown & Co.: from Sumner Slichter, *What's Ahead for American Business,* © 1950, 1951 by Sumner Slichter (No. 450).

Longmans, Green and Company: from J. W. Chase, ed., *Years of the Modern,* © 1949 (Nos. 453, 465); and from J. K. Polk, *Diary of a President,* © 1929 (No. 165).

Samuel Lubell: from "Who Elected Eisenhower?" © 1953, by The Curtis Publishing Company (No. 447).

The Macmillan Company: from Jane Addams, *Twenty Years at Hull House,* © 1910 by The Phillips Publishing Company; 1911 by the Macmillan Company (No. 267); from Jesse Jones, *Fifty Billion Dollars,* © 1951 by The Chronicle Company (No. 422); from Cordell Hull, *Memoirs,* © 1948 by Cordell Hull (No. 408); from Herbert Hoover, *Memoirs,* © 1952 by Herbert Hoover (No. 381); from W. A. White, *Autobiography,* © 1946 (No. 377); from Maxine Davis, *Lost Generation,* © 1936 (No. 391); from Herbert Croly, *Promise of American Life,* © 1909 (No. 299); and from James Bryce, *American Commonwealth,* © 1893 by Macmillan & Company; 1910 by The Macmillan Company; 1914 by The Macmillan Company; 1920 by The Rt. Hon. Viscount Bryce (No. 302).

The Manning Association: from William Manning, *Key of Libberty* © 1922 by Warren H. Manning (No. 138).

McBride Company, Inc.: from A. M. Landon, *America at the Crossroads,* © 1936 by Dodge Publishing Co. (No. 384).

McGraw-Hill, Inc.: from *Recent Economic Changes,* © 1929 by The Committee on Recent Economic Changes of the President's Conference on Unemployment (No. 354); and from *Recent Social Trends,* © 1933 (Nos. 390, 393).

Mrs. Roger Merrill: from William Manning, *Key of Libberty,* © 1922 (No. 138).

Guy S. Métraux: from his translation of Dr. Kaspar Koepfli's address (No. 145).

Mount Vernon Ladies' Association: from George Washington, *Diaries,* © 1929 (No. 51).

National Society of Colonial Dames of America: from J. F. Jameson, *Privateering and Piracy in the Colonial Period* © 1923 by The Macmillan Company (Nos. 36, 37, 42).

The New York Sun, Inc.: from "Theater Review of Mrs. Warren's Profession," © 1905 (No. 280).

University of North Carolina Press: from Robert Beverley, *History and Present State of Virginia,* © 1947 (No. 62); and from E. W. Knight, ed., *Documentary History of Education,* © 1952 (No. 191).

W. W. Norton & Co.: from Grace Overmyer, *Government and the Arts,* © 1939 by Grace Overmyer (No. 401).

Partisan Review: from Sidney Hook, "New Failure of Nerve," © 1943 (No. 458); and from "Situation in American Writing," © 1939 (No. 403).

Westbrook Pegler: "Farewell to Mencken" from *Dissenting Opinions of Mr. Westbrook Pegler,* © 1938, published by Charles Scribner's Sons (No. 385).

Pennsylvania Magazine of History and Biography: from L. H. Harrison, "William Duane on Education," © 1949 (No. 194).

Pilgrim Press: from Washington Gladden, *Labor Question,* © 1911 by Washington Gladden (No. 251).

Mrs. Rutherford Platt: from A. D. Noyes, *The Market Place,* © 1938 by Little, Brown & Company (No. 281).

Princeton University Library: from Philip Freneau, *Poems,* F. L. Pattee, ed., © 1902 (No. 126).

Princeton University Press: from Hadley Cantril, *Invasion from Mars,* © 1947 (No. 395); and from Edward Taylor, *Poetical Works,* © 1939, Rocklands Editions; © 1943 (No. 24).

G. P. Putnam's Sons: from A. D. Noyes, *Forty Years of American Finance,* © 1909 (No. 241); and from George Creel, *Rebel at Large,* © 1947 by George Creel (No. 325).

Random House, Inc.: from Adlai E. Stevenson, *Major Campaign Speeches,* © 1953 (No. 445); and from *Public Papers and Addresses of Franklin D. Roosevelt,* © 1938–1950 by Franklin D. Roosevelt (Nos. 353, 364, 365, 371, 372).

Rinehart & Co., Inc.: from Ilya Ilf and Eugene Petrov, *Little Golden America*, © 1937 (No. 359).

Charles Scribner's Sons: from F. Scott Fitzgerald, *The Great Gatsby*, © 1925 (No. 404); from Clarence Darrow, *Story of My Life*, © 1932 (No. 389); from Herbert Hoover, *Challenge to Liberty*, © 1934 by The Curtis Publishing Co. & Charles Scribner's Sons (No. 363); and from Madison Grant, *Passing of the Great Race*, © 1918 by Charles Scribner's Sons; 1946 by De Forest Grant (No. 334).

Simon and Schuster, Inc.: from H. L. Ickes, *Secret Diary*, © 1954 (No. 407).

Society of Colonial Wars in the State of New York: from L. E. deForest, ed., *Louisbourg Journals 1745*, © 1932 (No. 45).

Spectator (London): from "Eisenhower the Pawn?" © 1952 (No. 446).

Swedish Colonial Society: from Amandus Johnson, ed., *Instruction for Johan Printz*, © 1930 by Amandus Johnson (No. 8).

Twentieth Century Fund, Inc.: from J. F. Dewhurst *et al.*, *America's Needs and Resources*, © 1955 (No. 456).

United States Catholic Historical Society: from Archbishop John Hughes, "Reminiscences," © 1952 (No. 173).

The Viking Press, Inc.: from *Letters of Sacco and Vanzetti*, M. D. Frankfurter and Gardner Jackson, eds., © 1928 (No. 339); from Alfred E. Smith, *Up to Now*, © 1929 by Alfred E. Smith (No. 379); from Frances Perkins, *The Roosevelt I Knew*, © 1946 by Frances Perkins (No. 442); from E. J. Flynn, *You're the Boss*, © 1947 (No. 438); and from Walter White, *A Man Called White*, © 1948 by Walter White (No. 394).

Henry H. Villard: from O. G. Villard, *Fighting Years*, © 1939 by Harcourt Brace and Company (Nos. 319, 327, 328).

Harry R. Warfel: from Noah Webster, *Letters*, © 1953 by Library Publishers (No. 128).

Louis Waldman: from *Labor Lawyer*, © 1944 (No. 387).

Washington Post Company: from its editorials, © 1918, 1919, (Nos. 329, 330, 337).

Michael Williams: from *Shadow of the Pope*, © 1932 (No. 335).

Edmund Wilson: from *Travels in Two Democracies*, © 1936 by Harcourt Brace and Company (No. 398).

Wilson-Erickson, Inc.: from Durand de Dauphiné, *Huguenot Exile in Virginia*, © 1934 (Nos. 29, 46).

George Wittenborn, Inc.: from L. H. Sullivan, *Kindergarten Chats,* Documents of Modern Art, Vol. 4, Director Robert Mathews, ed., © 1947 by Wittenborn, Schultz, Inc. (No. 282).

World Publishing Co.: from Abraham Lincoln, *Speeches*, R. P. Basler, ed., © 1946 (No. 224).

Frank Lloyd Wright: from *An Autobiography*, © 1943, published by Duell, Sloan and Pierce (No. 402).

Yale University Press: from W. G. Sumner, *War and Other Essays*, © 1911 (No. 310).

TO PAUL H. BUCK

PREFACE

THIS IS A TEXTBOOK. It aims to bring together in convenient and usable form a body of texts that will serve as an effective tool in introductory college courses in American history and in the social sciences. It is directed particularly at the needs of today's students who are concerned with their nation's past and who seek a mature yet easily comprehensible understanding of it.

The American college sophomore or freshman who enters a course in American history has usually covered the outlines of his subject at least twice before; however much or little he may have brought away from those courses, the essential story seems familiar, even repetitious. "It is like seeing an old movie," a student has said to me. "The plot has been forgotten, but the memory gradually comes back as the successive scenes unfold." The successful teacher must impart vividness, excitement, and meaning to the subject, lest it seem stale and unoriginal. This volume aims to help him do so.

There has been no effort here to survey the whole span of American history, nor to compress within these pages even its essential facts. The unifying themes, the trends of development, and the outline of the story will be supplied by the teacher himself in lectures and discussions. This volume may also, where the situation dictates, be used in conjunction with one or another of the excellent narrative survey histories now available; or, alternatively, it may be combined with a succession of supplementary readings in monographs and secondary works that will supply both details and interpretation.

In any case, this work itself does not aim to cover the story. Its purpose is, rather, to furnish the student with a body of documents contemporary to the events with which they deal, documents which are themselves the materials of history. It hopes, by bringing the reader into direct contact with the sources, to illustrate, as no secondary writing can, the complexities and vividness of the American past.

These objectives have shaped the character of the collection. Given the interest of today's teachers and students, it has seemed advisable to broaden the scope of the collection. The introductory course is no longer exclusively political in its emphasis. It now touches also upon the fields of social, economic, cultural, and intellectual history. The critical political documents have found a place here. But there has also been a conscious effort to include in this collection usable materials that illustrate the development of those wider fields.

That has called for a high degree of selectivity. It has not seemed necessary to include more material than the student, to whom it is directed, could use profitably. Consequently there has been no effort to assemble a complete collection of the important documents of American history. The aim has been to choose those which most graphically illustrate its meaning as it has unfolded.

The function this volume is intended to serve has also shaped the form of its presentation. These are not documents edited from manuscripts for the use of other scholars. They are sources meant to be read and understood by undergraduates. Therefore it has not seemed desirable to preserve archaic mis-spellings and the individual aberrations of punctuation and paragraphing characteristic of the earlier centuries of our writing. Rather, the principles of modernization developed by Samuel Eliot Morison and explained in the *Harvard Guide to American History*, section twenty-eight, have, as far as possible, been applied to these documents. This may entail a loss in authenticity. Nothing—not even a photographic reproduction —can convey the sense of the past that an original manuscript can. But the gains in readability and usability will more than offset that loss.

Effort has been made to present texts at sufficient length to be understood in their wholeness; yet it has not seemed necessary to preserve long repetitious passages or the digressions that interrupt the flow of the meaning. In editing, the needs and interests of the students were kept constantly in view; and often brevity proved a virtue. Above all, it was intended that these selections be as readable as possible, so that they may be read and not merely assigned.

The volume was also designed to be teachable. Within broad chronological limits, the materials have been organized into fifty coherent units. Each represents a convenient week's work for the average student, who will also be occupied with other types of reading at the same time. Each teacher will no doubt wish to omit some of these units and to rearrange their order of presentation in accord with the special needs of his own course. The organization of the volume readily lends itself to such use.

The introductory comments and the notes merely supply a framework for the documents in each section. There was no intention to have them interpret the material; that must remain the function of the teacher. Nor did the compiler wish to have this book dictate any particular mold for the organization of the course, which in the last analysis depends entirely upon the teacher. The textbook can only be a convenient tool that assists the instructor in bringing to students the drama and the deep meaning of the past of the nation.

Harvard University   OSCAR HANDLIN

CONTENTS

PART FOUR: *Young America, 1820–70*

READINGS IN
American History

PART ONE

First Settlers 1600-80

NORTH from Florida along the Atlantic, a thousand miles of coastline lay, in 1600 empty and unexplored. For more than a century the Spaniards had passed that region by in favor of the more attractive areas to the southward; and other Europeans who now and then ventured into the forbidding forests that swept down to the very shore always withdrew and left no permanent settlement there.

In the early decades of the seventeenth century, this virgin land haltingly, but steadily, welcomed a succession of colonizing expeditions. Little clusters of Europeans dotted the ocean's edge; they developed the forms and the institutions of a civil society; and from them evolved the United States.

The first plantations were the products of movements created by the disturbed condition of Western Europe. In the sixteenth century a massive disturbance in the ancient routes of trade with the East had shifted commerce away from the Mediterranean powers and into the hands of the Atlantic states. After the age of discovery the rich goods of the Indies moved through the markets of Spain and Portugal rather than through the Italian cities. The vast empires of the Iberian powers, in the East and in the West, awakened the avarice and the ambition of the other trading nations—France, England, the Netherlands, and Sweden. The opportunities for gain stirred the restless merchants and gentry throughout the continent. Quickened by the political objectives of the newly developed national state, these interests drew men on to new colonial ventures in every part of the globe.

The most effective instrument of overseas trade was the chartered commercial company. This was an association of merchants and others interested in the distant and dangerous trades. To pursue its ends, the company received from the state, through a charter, a grant of political power that permitted it to govern its stations or plantations overseas. Since it could also draw together large sums in its joint stock, it united effectively the capital of its individual members with the political power of the state. In all the nations of western Europe such corporations were formed for trade with every part of the world.

The adventurers who risked their capital were often associated with enterprising men willing to risk their lives. Operating at a great distance from home, the corporation needed fighters to protect its ships against pirates and to defend its plantations against enemies abroad. The planters, often gentlemen in reduced circumstances, were men anxious to make their fortune and willing to face any danger in its pursuit.

Such trading companies formed the first permanent establishments in the territory that later became the United States. But the corporation was not as effective in Virginia or Delaware or New Netherlands as it had been in India and Turkey. In America, it could not exploit available surface resources or an economy already functioning. Instead, the company early found it necessary to people its colony to keep it in existence, and to do so, resorted to a number of desperate expedients that quickly changed the character of the settlements.

There was some hope thus that little feudal enterprises or proprieties, as in New Netherlands or in Maryland, might add to the population. Outsiders, driven by religious motives, were tolerated, as were the Pilgrims in Plymouth; free land was held forth as an attraction; and servants were carried across without charge if they agreed to labor a number of years for those who paid their way. Through such varied means the population grew steadily despite the harshness of life in the wilderness. But in that growth the character of the colonies was transformed.

The change was partly economic. The early conception of the settlements as trading posts which would simply funnel goods to the mother country collapsed. Instead, the colonies became societies of yeomen who depended for their livelihood mainly on agriculture with peripheral interests in the fisheries, in trapping, and in trade.

The change also touched the basic assumptions of the society. As the decades passed, it became clear that these were not plantations of Europeans who lived temporarily in exile while awaiting a future return to their home. Rather, these people were permanent residents of the New World, cut off from the places of their birth and resolved to adjust themselves, with no return, to the conditions of their homes in the wilderness. That adjustment presented material and spiritual difficulties. But after eight decades, as the first generation of settlers passed away, it was on the verge of creating a new kind of society in America.

The documents which follow illustrate the political, economic, and social aspects of these changes.

I ❧ *Government Policy and the Colonies*

THE MOTIVES that united the Crown with private investors in furthering colonization are expressed in the "Reasons for Raising a Public Stock" (No. 1), an early plea for the support of English settlement in America. Such motives produced the joint-stock corporation, the basic structure of which may be observed in the charters of Virginia and Massachusetts. The Massachusetts charter (No. 2) remained the frame of government of that territory until 1691. It reveals the outlines of political forms that would remain important long thereafter.

The company, however, could not remain unchanged in America. Within its general forms there quickly intruded a variety of significant innovations that met the special needs of the groups actually migrating to the New World. The Mayflower Compact (No. 3) was the voluntary association of the members of an enterprise worried as to the legality of their patent. The Cambridge Agreement (No. 4) reflects the intention of some of the promoters of the Massachusetts Bay Company to use its charter for purposes other than commercial. The Fundamental Orders of Connecticut (No. 5) brought a government into being by the action of the settlers without the benefit of charter.

Added to such forces for change was the continuing pressure for concessions to attract new settlers. The privileges granted the patroons in New Netherland (No. 6) and the inducements to settlers in Maryland (No. 7) each in their way illustrate the force of that pressure. By the end of the period the colonies were far removed from the company plantations they had been at the start.

1. *"Reasons for Raising a Public Stock," 1605–07*

"Reasons to Move the High Court of Parliament to Raise a Stock for Maintaining a Colony in Virginia." From a manuscript in the British Museum, dated January 5, 1607. The actual date has variously been given as the fall of 1605 and January 5, 1608. The version given is taken from that printed in Alexander Brown, ed., *Genesis of the United States* (Boston, 1890), I, 36–43.

REASONS or motives for the raising of a public stock to be employed for the peopling and discovering of such countries as may be found most convenient for the supply of those defects which this realm of England most requireth.

1. All kingdoms are maintained by rents or traffic, but especially by the latter, which in maritime places most flourishes by means of navigation.

2. The realm of England is an island impossible to be otherwise fortified than by strong ships and able mariners and is secluded from all corners...of the main continent; therefore fit abundance of vessels [must] be prepared to export and import merchandise.

3. The furniture of shipping consists in masts, cordage, pitch, tar, rosin, that of which England is by nature unprovided

and at this present enjoys them only by the favor of foreign potency.

4. The life of shipping rests in [the] number of able mariners and worthy chieftains, which cannot be maintained without assurance of reward of honorable means to be employed and sufficient second of their adventures.

5. Private purses are cold comforts to adventurers and have ever been found fatal to all enterprises hitherto undertaken by the English by reason of delays, jealousies and unwillingness to back that project which succeeded not at the first attempt.

6. The example of Hollanders is very pregnant. . . .

7. It is honorable for a state rather to back an exploit by a public consent than by a private monopoly.

8. Where colonies are founded for a public-weal, [they] may continue in better obedience, and become more industrious, than where private men are absolute . . . for as much as better men . . . will engage themselves in a public service, which carries more reputation with it, than a private, which is for the most part ignominious in the end, as being presumed to aim at a lucre. . . .

9. The manifest decay of shipping and mariners and of many borough and post towns and havens cannot be relieved by private increase. . . .

10. It is publicly known that traffic with our neighbor countries begin to be of small request, the game seldom answering the merchants' adventure. . . .

11. That realm is most complete and wealthy which either has sufficient to serve itself or can find the means to export of the natural commodities than [if] it has occasion necessarily to import. Consequently it must ensue that by a public consent, a colony transported into a good and plentiful climate able to furnish our wants, our monies and wares that now run into the hands of our adversaries or cold friends shall pass unto our friends and natural kinsmen and from them like-

wise we shall receive such things as shall be most available to our necessities, which intercourse of trade may rather be called a home bred traffic than a foreign exchange. . . .

13. Experience teaches us that it is dangerous to our state to enterprise a discovery and not to proceed therein even to the very sifting it to the uttermost, for . . . disreputation grows thereby, . . . [betraying] our own idleness and want of counsel to manage our enterprises. . . .

14. The want of our fresh . . . discoveries has in manner taken away the title which the law of nations gives us unto the coast first found out by our industry, forasmuch as whatsoever a man relinquishes may be claimed by the next finder as his own property. Neither is it sufficient to set foot in a country but to possess and hold it, in defense of an invading force. [For want whereof] the King of Denmark intends into the northwest passage (as it is reported), and it is also reported that the French intend to inhabit Virginia. . . .

The circumstances necessary to back a colony sent out are these:

1. Reputation and opinion of the enterprise.

2. A competent sum of money raised aforehand to supply all accidents, that distrust hereby may be wrought in foreign states to attempt anything in prejudice of our colonies; because they may well be assured that where there is not a public purse, and a common consent to prosecute an action it is but hopeless to hope of advantage to be gotten without revenge.

3. As [states] are most apt to make a conquest so are public weals fitter to hold what is gotten and skillfuller by industry to enrich it.

4. It is probable that if the whole state be engaged in these adventures it will be no hard matter when apparent ground of profit is laid to persuade every county according to the proportion of bigness and ability to build barks and ships of a component size and to maintain them, when

gentlemen's youngest sons and other men of quality may be employed.

5. Also it importeth much that no man be suffered to venture more than he may be deemed able to spare out of his own superfluity, or if he go in person [than] he would idly spend at home, lest such men entering into a rage of repentance, ... thereby discourage others and scandalize the enterprise.

2. *Massachusetts Bay Company Charter, 1629*

Founding of Massachusetts. A Selection from the Sources of the History of the Settlement. 1628–31. (Boston, 1930), 27–49.

CHARLES, by the grace of God King of England, Scotland, France and Ireland, Defender of the Faith, etc. To all to whom these presents shall come. Greeting.

Whereas our most dear and royal father King James ... hath ... granted unto the council established at Plymouth ... all that part of America lying ... from forty degrees of northerly latitude ... to forty-eight degrees of the said northerly latitude inclusively, and ... from sea to sea....

And whereas the said council established at Plymouth ... have ... given ... to Sir Henry Rosewell ... [and others] all that part of New England ... which lies ... between a great river there commonly called ... Merrimack, and a certain other river there called Charles River being in the bottom of a certain bay there commonly called Massachusetts ... Bay. And also, all ... lands ... lying within ... three English miles on the south part of the said Charles River ... and also, all ... lands ... lying ... within ... three English miles to the southward of ... Massachusetts Bay. And also all ... lands ... which lie ... within ... three English miles to the northward of the said river called Merrimack ... from the Atlantic ... Sea on the east, to the South Sea on the west.... And also all mines and minerals ..., and all jurisdictions, rights, royalties, liberties, freedoms, immunities, privileges, franchises, preeminences and commodities whatsoever which ... the ... council established at Plymouth then had.... To be

holden of us ... as of our manor of East Greenwich in the county of Kent, in free and common soccage, and not in capite, nor by knights' service. Yielding and paying therefore unto us ... the fifth part of the ore of gold and silver which shall ... be found, ... in any of the said lands ... in satisfaction of all manner duties ... to be done ... to us....

Now know ye that we, at the humble suit and petition of the said Sir Henry Rosewell, ... and of others, ... by this present ... do grant and confirm ... all the said part of New England ... to them....

And forasmuch as the good and prosperous success of the plantation of the said parts of New England aforesaid ..., cannot but chiefly depend, next under the blessing of almighty God, and the support of our royal authority upon the good government of the same, to the end that the affairs ... concerning the said lands and the plantation ... may be the better managed and ordered, we have further hereby ... granted and confirmed ... unto our said trusty and well beloved subjects [named] that they ... and all such others as shall hereafter be ... made free of the company ..., shall ... be ... one body corporate and politic ... by the name of the Governor and Company of the Massachusetts Bay in New England. ... And ... by that name they shall have perpetual succession, and ... shall ... be ... enabled ... to implead and to be impleaded ... in all ... suits ... and actions. ... And also to have, take, possess, acquire and purchase any lands, tenements or hereditaments or any goods or chattels, and the same to lease, grant, demise, alien, bargain, sell and dispose of, as other our liege people of this our realm of England, or any other corporation or body politic of the same may lawfully do. And further that the said governor and company and their successors may have forever one common seal to be used in all causes and occasions. . . .

And our will and pleasure is ... that from henceforth forever there shall be one governor, one deputy governor and eighteen asistants of the same company to be from time to time ... chosen out of the freemen of the said company ... ; which said officers shall apply themselves to take care for the best disposing and ordering of the general business ... of ... the said lands and premises ... and the government of the people there. . . .

[First officers named]

And further, we ... do ordain ... that the governor ... or in his absence ... the deputy governor ... shall have authority ... to give order for the assembling of the said company, and calling them together to consult and advise of the businesses ... of the said company, and that the said governor, deputy governor and assistants ... shall or may once every month or oftener ... assemble, and hold ... a court or assembly ... for the better ordering and directing of their affairs, and that any seven or more persons of the assistants together with the governor or deputy governor so assembled shall be ... a full and sufficient court or assembly of the said company. . . . And that there shall ... be held ... by the governor or deputy governor of the said company and seven or more of the said assistants ... upon every last Wednesday in Hillary, Easter, Trinity and Michas Terms respectively forever, one great general and solemn assembly; which four general assemblies shall be styled and called the four great and general courts of the said company. In all and every, or any of which said great and general courts so assembled ... the governor, or in his absence the deputy governor ... and such of the assistants and freemen ... as shall be present, or the greater number of them ... shall have full power ... to choose, ... such ... others as they shall think fit ... to be free of the said company; ... and to elect and constitute such officers as they shall think fit and requisite; ... and to make laws and ordinances ... for the government and ordering of the said lands and plantation, and the people inhabiting ... the same, as to them from time to time shall be thought meet. So as such laws and ordinances be not contrary or repugnant to the laws and statutes of this our realm of England. And our will and pleasure is ... that ... the last Wednesday in Easter Term yearly, the governor, deputy governor and assistants of the said company, and all other officers ... shall be in the general court or assembly ... newly chosen for the year ensuing. . . . And if ... the ... governor, deputy governor and assistants ... or any other of the officers to be appointed for the said company ... die, or ... be removed from his or their several offices ... before the said general day of election ... , then ... it shall... be lawful ... for the governor, deputy governor, assistants and company aforesaid ... in any of their assemblies to proceed to a new election. . . . Provided ... that ... all ... officers to be appointed ... shall before they undertake the execution of their said offices ... take their corporal oaths for the ... faithful performance of their duties in their several offices. . . .

And we do further ... give and grant to the said governor and company ... that it shall be lawful ... for them ... out of any our ... dominions whatsoever, to take ... into their voyages, and for and towards the said plantation in New England ... so many of our loving subjects or any other strangers that will become our loving subjects ... as shall willingly accompany them ... and also shipping, armor, weapons, ordinance, munition, powder, shot, corn, victuals, and all manner of clothing, implements, furniture, beasts, cattle, horses, mares, merchandises, and all other things necessary for the said plantation ... without paying ... any custom or subsidy either inward or outward to us ... for the same, by the space of seven years from the ... date of these presents. ... And for their further encouragement, ... we do ... yield and grant to the said governor and company ... that they ... shall be free and quit from all taxes, subsidies and customs in New England for the like space of seven years, and from all taxes and impositions for the space of twenty and one years upon all goods and merchandises at any time or times hereafter, either upon importation thither, or exportation from thence into our realm of England, or into any other [of] our dominions ... except only the five pounds per centum due for custom ... after the said seven years shall be expired. ... Which five pounds per centum only being paid, it shall be thenceforth lawful and free for the said adventurers the same goods and merchandises to export and carry out of our said dominions into foreign parts, without any custom, tax or other duty. ...

[Mode of paying customs]. ...

And further ... we do hereby ... grant to the said governor and company ... that all ... the subjects of us, our heirs or successors which shall go to ... the said lands ... and ... their children ... born there, or on the seas in going thither, or returning from thence, shall ... enjoy all liberties and immunities of free and natural subjects within any of the dominions of us, our heirs or successors to all intents, constructions and purposes whatsoever, as if they ... were born within the realm of England. And that the governor and deputy governor of the said company ... and any two or more of such of the said assistants, as shall be thereunto appointed by the said governor and company at any

of their courts or assemblies ... may at all times ... have full power and authority to minister and give the ... oaths of supremacy and allegiance ... to all ... persons which shall at any time ... hereafter go ... to the lands ... hereby mentioned to be granted. ...

And we do ... grant to the said governor and company ... that it shall ... be lawful ... for the governor or deputy governor and such of the assistants and freemen of the said company ... as shall be assembled in any of their general courts ... or the greater part of them ... from time to time to make ... all manner of wholesome and reasonable orders, laws, statutes and ordinances ... not contrary to the laws of this our realm of England, as well for settling of the forms and ceremonies of government and magistracy fit and necessary for the said plantation and the inhabitants there, and for naming and styling all sorts of officers ... which they shall find needful ... , and the distinguishing, and setting forth of the several duties, powers and limits of every such office and place, and the forms of such oaths ... as shall be respectively ministered unto them for the execution of the said several offices and places, as also for the disposing and ordering of the elections of such of the said officers as shall be annual, ... and ministering the said oaths to the new elected officers and for impositions of lawful fines, mulcts, imprisonment or other lawful correction, according to the course of other corporations in this our realm of England. And for the directing, ruling and disposing of all other matters and things whereby our said people inhabitants there may be so religiously, peaceably and civilly governed, as their good life and orderly conversation may win and incite the natives of country to the knowledge and obedience of the only true God and Saviour of mankind, and the Christian faith, which is ... the principal end of this plantation. Willing, commanding and requiring ... that all such orders, laws, statutes and ordinances ...

as shall be so made ... and published in writing ..., shall be carefully and duly observed ... and put in execution according to the true intent and meaning of the same. And these our letters patents ... shall be ... for the putting of the same orders, laws, statutes, and ordinances ... a sufficient warrant and discharge.

And we do further ... grant to the said governor and company ... that all ... such ... officers and ministers, as ... shall be ... employed either in the government of the said inhabitants and plantation, or in the way by sea thither, or from thence ... shall ... have full and absolute power and authority to correct, punish, pardon, govern and rule all such ... subjects ... as shall from time to time adventure themselves in any voyage thither or from thence, or that shall at any time hereafter inhabit ... New England ..., according to the orders, laws, ordinances, instructions and directions aforesaid, not being repugnant to the laws and statutes of our realm of England. ...

And we do further ... grant to the said governor and company ... that it shall ... be lawful ... for the chief commanders, governors and officers of the said company ... for their special defense and safety to encounter, expulse, repel and resist by force of arms as well by sea as by land, and by all fitting ways and means whatsoever all such person and persons as shall at any time hereafter attempt or enterprise the destruction, invasion, detriment or annoyance to the said plantation or inhabitants. ... Nevertheless ... if any ... persons ... of the said company or plantation ... shall ... rob or spoil by sea or land ... any of the subjects of any prince or state being then in league and amity with us, ... we ... shall make open proclamation ... that the ... persons having committed any such robbery or spoil, shall ... make full restitution or satisfaction of all such injuries done, and that if the said ... persons ... shall not make or cause to be made satisfaction accordingly ... that then it shall be lawful for us ... to put the said ... persons out of our allegiance and protection. ...

Provided also ... that these presents shall not in any manner ... be taken to abridge, bar, or hinder any of our loving subjects ... to ... exercise the trade of fishing upon that coast of New England ... but that they ... shall have full ... liberty to continue and use their said trade of fishing upon the said coast ... where they have been wont to fish, and to build ... upon the lands by these presents granted such wharves, stages and workhouses as shall be necessary for the salting, drying, keeping and packing up of their fish ... in such manner and form as they have been ... accustomed to do, without making any willful waste or spoil. ...

And we do further ... ordain ... that these our letters patent ... shall be construed ... in all cases most favorably on the behalf ... of the said governor and company. ...

3. *Mayflower Compact, 1620 (Plymouth Colonists)*

B. P. Poore, compiler, *Federal and State Constitutions* (Washington, 1878), Part I, 931.

IN THE NAME OF GOD, AMEN. We, whose names are underwritten, the loyal subjects of our dread Sovereign Lord King James, by the Grace of God, of Great Britain, France, and Ireland, King, Defender of the Faith, &c. Having undertaken for the glory of God and advancement of the Christian faith, and the honor of our king and country, a voyage to plant the first colony in the northern parts of Virginia; do by these presents, solemnly and mutually, in the presence of

God and one another, covenant and combine ourselves together into a civil body politic, for our better ordering and preservation, and furtherance of the ends aforesaid: And by virtue hereof do enact, constitute, and frame, such just and equal laws, ordinances, acts, constitutions, and officers, from time to time, as shall be thought most meet and convenient for the general good of the colony; unto which we promise all due submission and obedience. IN WITNESS whereof we have hereunto subscribed our names at Cape Cod the eleventh of November, . . . Anno Domini, 1620.

4. *Cambridge Agreement, 1629 (Massachusetts Settlers)*

Founding of Massachusetts, 55–6.

Upon due consideration of the state of the plantation now in hand for New England, wherein we . . . have engaged ourselves: and having weighed the greatness of the work in regard of the consequence, God's glory and the churches' good: as also in regard of the difficulties and discouragements which in all probabilities must be forecast upon the prosecution of this business: Considering withal that this whole adventure grows upon the joint confidence we have in each other's fidelity and resolution herein, so as no man of us would have adventured it without assurance of the rest.

Now for the better encouragement of ourselves and others that shall join with us in this action, and to the end that every man may without scruple dispose of his estate and affairs as may best fit his preparation for this voyage, it is fully and faithfully agreed amongst us, and every of us doth hereby freely and sincerely promise and bind himself in the word of a Christian and in the presence of God who is the searcher of all hearts, that we will so really endeavor the prosecution of this work, as by God's assistance we will be ready in our persons, and with such of our several families as are to go with us and such provision as we are able conveniently to furnish ourselves withal, to embark for the said plantation by the first of March next, at such port or ports of this land as shall be agreed upon by the company, to the end to pass the seas (under God's protection) to inhabit and continue in New England.

Provided, always that before the last of September next the whole government together with the patent for the said plantation be first by an order of court legally transferred and established to remain with us and others which shall inhabit upon the said plantation. And provided also that if any shall be hindered by such just and inevitable let or other cause to be allowed by three parts of four of these whose names are hereunto subscribed, then such persons for such times and during such lets to be discharged of this bond. And we do further promise every one for himself that shall fail to be ready through his own default by the day appointed, to pay for every day's default the sum of £3 to the use of the rest of the company who shall be ready by the same day and time.

5. *Fundamental Orders of Connecticut, 1639*

Poore, Federal and State Constitutions, Part I, 249 ff.

FORASMUCH as it hath pleased the Almighty God by the wise disposition of his divine providence so to order and dispose of things that we the inhabitants and residents of Windsor, Hartford and Wethersfield are now cohabiting and dwelling in and upon the River of Connecticut and the lands thereunto adjoining; and well knowing where a people are gathered together the word of God requires that to maintain the peace and union of such a people there should be an orderly and decent government established according to God, to order and dispose of the affairs of the people at all seasons as occasion shall require: do therefore associate and conjoin ourselves to be as one public state of commonwealth; and do, for ourselves and our successors and such as shall be adjoined to us at any time hereafter, enter into combination and confederation together, to maintain and preserve the liberty and purity of the gospel of our Lord Jesus, which we now profess, as also the discipline of the churches, which according to the truth of the said gospel is now practised amongst us; as also in our civil affairs to be guided and governed according to such laws, rules, orders and decrees as shall be made, ordered and decreed, as followeth:

1. It is ordered, sentenced and decreed, that there shall be yearly two general assemblies or courts, the one the second Thursday in April, the other the second Thursday in September, following; the first shall be called the Court of Election, wherein shall be yearly chosen ... so many magistrates and other public officers as shall be found requisite: whereof one to be chosen governor for the year ensuing ... (and no other magistrate to be chosen for more than one year), provided always there be six chosen beside the governor; which being chosen and sworn ... shall have power to administer justice according to the laws here established, and for want thereof according to the rule of the word of God; which choice shall be made by all that are admitted freemen and have taken the oath of fidelity, and do cohabit within this jurisdiction (having been admitted inhabitants by the major part of the town wherein they live) or the major part of such as shall be then present.

2. It is ordered, sentenced and decreed, that the election of the aforesaid magistrates shall be on this manner. Every person present and qualified for choice shall bring in (to the persons deputed to receive them) one single paper with the name of him written in it whom he desires to have governor, and he that hath the greatest number of papers shall be governor for that year. And the rest of the magistrates or public officers to be chosen in this manner: The secretary ... shall first read the names of all that are to be put to choice and then shall severally nominate them distinctly, and every one that would have the person nominated to be chosen shall bring in one single paper written upon, and he that would not have him chosen shall bring in a blank. And every one that hath more written papers than blanks shall be a magistrate for that year. . . . But in case there should not be six chosen as aforesaid, beside the governor ... then he or they which have the most written papers shall be a magistrate or magistrates for the ensuing year, to make up the aforesaid number.

3. It is ordered, sentenced and decreed, that the Secretary shall not nominate any person ... which was not propounded in some General Court before, to be nominated the next election; and to that end it shall be lawful for each of the towns aforesaid by their deputies to nominate any two who they conceive fit to be put to election; and the Court may add so many more as they judge requisite.

4. It is ordered, sentenced and decreed that no person be chosen governor above once in two years, and that the governor be always a member of some approved congregation, and formerly of the magistracy within this jurisdiction; and all the magistrates freemen of this Commonwealth: and that no magistrate or other public officer shall execute any part of his or their office before they are severally sworn. . . .

5. It is ordered, sentenced, and decreed, that to the aforesaid court of elec-

tion the several towns shall send their deputies, and when the elections are ended they may proceed in any public service as at other courts. Also the other General Court in September shall be for making of laws, and any other public occasion, which concerns the good of the Commonwealth.

6. It is ordered, sentenced and decreed, that the governor shall ... send out summons to the constables of every town for the calling of these two standing courts, one month at least before their several times. And also if the governor and the greatest part of the magistrates see cause upon any special occasion to call a General Court, they may give order to the secretary so to do within fourteen days warning; and if urgent necessity so require, upon a shorter notice, giving sufficient grounds for it to the deputies when they meet, or else be questioned for the same. And if the governor and major part of magistrates shall either neglect or refuse to call the two General standing Courts ..., as also at other times when the occasions of the Commonwealth require, the freemen thereof, or the major part of them, shall petition to them so to do. If then it be either denied or neglected the said freemen ... shall have power to give order to the constables of the several towns to do the same, and so may meet together, and choose to themselves a moderator, and may proceed to do any act of power, which any other General Court may.

7. It is ordered, sentenced and decreed that after there are warrants given out for any of the said General Courts, the constable or constables of each town shall forthwith give notice distinctly to the inhabitants of the same, in some public assembly or by going or sending from house to house, that at a place and time by him or them limited and set, they meet and assemble themselves together to elect and choose certain deputies to be at the General Court then following to agitate the affairs of the Commonwealth; which said

deputies shall be chosen by all that are admitted inhabitants in the several towns and have taken the oath of fidelity; provided that none be chosen a deputy for any General Court which is not a freeman of this Commonwealth....

8. It is ordered, sentenced and decreed, that Windsor, Hartford, and Wethersfield shall have power, each town, to send four of their freemen as deputies to every General Court; and whatsoever other towns shall be hereafter added to this jurisdiction, they shall send so many deputies as the Court shall judge meet, a reasonable proportion to the number of freemen that are in the said towns being to be attended therein; which deputies shall have the power of the whole town to give their votes and allowance to all such laws and orders as may be for the public good, and unto which the said towns are to be bound.

9. It is ordered and decreed, that the deputies thus chosen shall have power and liberty to appoint a time and a place of meeting together before any General Court to advise and consult of all such things as may concern the good of the public, as also to examine their own elections ... and if they or the greatest part of them find any election to be illegal they may seclude such for present from their meeting, and return the same and their reasons to the Court. And if it prove true, the Court may fine the party or parties so intruding and the town ... and give out a warrant to go to a new election in a legal way.... Also the said deputies shall have power to fine any that shall be disorderly at their meetings, or for not coming in due time or place according to appointment....

10. It is ordered, sentenced and decreed, that every General Court (except such as through neglect of the governor and the greatest part of magistrates the freemen themselves do call) shall consist of the governor, or some one chosen to moderate the Court, and four other magistrates at least, with the major part of

the deputies of the several towns legally chosen. And in case the freemen or major part of them, through neglect or refusal of the governor and . . . the magistrates, shall call a Court, it shall consist of the major part of freemen that are present or their deputies, with a moderator chosen by them. In which said General Courts shall consist the supreme power of the Commonwealth, and they only shall have power to make laws or repeal them, to grant levies, to admit of freemen, dispose of lands . . . , and also shall have power to call either Court or magistrate or any other person whatsoever into question for any misdemeanor, and may for just causes displace or deal otherwise according to the nature of the offense; and also may deal in any other matter that concerns the good of this Commonwealth, except election of magistrates, which shall

be done by the whole body of freemen.

In which Court the governor or moderator shall have power to order the Court to give liberty of speech, and silence unseasonable and disorderly speakings, to put all things to vote, and in case the vote be equal to have the casting voice. But none of these Courts shall be adjourned or dissolved without the consent of the major part of the Court.

11. It is ordered, sentenced and decreed, that when any General Court upon the occasions of the Commonwealth have agreed upon any sum . . . to be levied upon the several towns within this jurisdiction, that a committee be chosen to set out and appoint what shall be the proportion of every town to pay . . . , provided the committees be made up of an equal number out of each town.

6. *Freedoms and Exemptions to Dutch Patroons, New Netherland, 1629*

E. B. O'Callaghan, ed., *Documents Relative to the Colonial History of the State of New York* (Albany, 1856), II, 553 ff.

ALL SUCH shall be acknowledged Patroons of New Netherland who shall, within the space of four years next after they have given notice to any of the Chambers of the Company here, or to the Commander or Council there, undertake to plant a colony there of fifty souls, upwards of fifteen years old; one-fourth part within one year, and within three years after the sending of the first, making together four years, the remainder, to the full number of fifty persons. . . .

They shall, from the time they make known the situation of the places where they propose to settle colonies, have the preference to all others of the absolute property of such lands as they have there chosen; but in case the situation should not afterwards please them, . . . they may, after remonstrating concerning the same

to the Commander and Council there, be at liberty to choose another place. . . .

They shall forever possess and enjoy all the lands lying within the aforesaid limits, together with the fruits, rights, minerals, rivers and fountains thereof; as also the chief command and lower jurisdictions, fishing, fowling and grinding, to the exclusion of all others, to be holden from the Company as a perpetual inheritance. . . . And further, no person or persons whatsoever shall be privileged to fish and hunt but the Patroons and such as they shall permit. And in case any one should in time prosper so much as to found one or more cities, he shall have power and authority to establish officers and magistrates there, and to make use of the title of his colony, according to his pleasure and to the quality of the persons. . . .

The Patroons and colonists shall be privileged to send their people and effects thither, in ships belonging to the Company, provided they take the oath, and pay to the Company for bringing over the people. . . .

Inasmuch as it is intended to people the Island of the Manhattes first, all fruits and wares that are produced on the lands situate on the North River, and lying thereabout, shall, for the present, be brought there before being sent elsewhere. . . .

All the Patroons of colonies in New Netherland, and of colonies on the Island of Manhattes, shall be at liberty to sail and traffic all along the coast, from Florida to Terra Neuf, provided that they do again return with all such goods as they shall get in trade to the Island of Manhattes, and pay five per cent duty to the Company, in order, if possible, that, after the necessary inventory of the goods shipped be taken, the same may be sent hither. . . .

All coarse wares that the colonists of the Patroons there shall consume, such as pitch, tar, weed-ashes, wood, grain, fish, salt, hearthstone and such like things shall be conveyed in the Company's ships, at the rate of eighteen guilders per last. . . .

The Company promises the colonists of the Patroons that they shall be free from customs, taxes, excise, imposts or any other contributions for the space of ten years; and after the expiration of the said ten years, at the highest, such customs as the goods pay here for the present. . . .

From all judgments given by the Courts of the Patroons for upwards of fifty guilders, there may be an appeal to the Company's Commander and Council in New Netherland. . . .

In regard to such private persons as on their own account, . . . shall be inclined to go thither and settle, they shall, with the approbation of the Director and Council there, be at liberty to take up . . . as much land as they shall be able properly to improve. . . .

Whosoever . . . shall discover any shores, bays or other fit places for erecting fisheries, or the making of salt ponds . . . may take possession thereof, and begin to work on them as their own absolute property. . . . And it is consented to that the Patroons of colonists may send ships along the coast of New Netherland, on the cod fishery. . . .

Whoever shall settle any colony out of the limits of the Manhattes Island, shall be obliged to satisfy the Indians for the land they shall settle upon, and they may extend or enlarge the limits of their colonies if they settle a proportionate number of colonists thereon.

The Patroons and colonists shall . . . in the speediest manner, endeavor to find out ways and means whereby they may support a minister and schoolmaster, that thus the service of God and zeal for religion may not grow cool and be neglected among them, and they shall, for the first, procure a comforter of the sick there. . . .

The colonists shall not be permitted to make any woolen, linen or cotton cloth, nor weave any other stuffs there, on pain of being banished, and as perjurers, to be arbitrarily punished. . . .

The Company will use their endeavors to supply the colonists with as many Blacks as they conveniently can, on the conditions hereafter to be made, in such manner, however, that they shall not be bound to do it for a longer time than they shall think proper. . . .

The Company promises to finish the fort on the Island of the Manhattes, and to put it in a posture of defense without delay.

7. *Conditions for Settlers in Maryland, 1633*

A Relation of Maryland (London, 1635; Harvard College Library copy), 38–40. The tract was reprinted in C. C. Hall, ed., *Narratives of Early Maryland* (New York, 1910), 63 ff.

WHAT person soever, subject to our sovereign lord the King of England, shall be at the charge to transport into the province of Maryland, himself or his deputy, with any number of able men, between the ages of sixteen and fifty, . . . there shall be assigned unto every such adventurer, for every five men which he shall so transport thither, a proportion of good land within the said province, containing in quantity 1000 acres of English measure, which shall be erected into a manor, and be conveyed to him . . . forever, with all such royalties and privileges as are usually belonging to manors in England; rendering and paying yearly unto his lordship, and his heirs for every such manor, a quit rent of twenty shillings . . . and such other services as shall be generally agreed upon for public uses, and the common good.

What person soever, as aforesaid, shall transport himself, or any less number of servants than five, (aged and provided as aforesaid) he shall have assigned to him . . . one hundred acres of good land within the said province; and for and in respect of every such servant, one hundred acres more, he beholden of his lordship in freehold, paying therefore a yearly quit rent of two shillings for every hundred acres, in the commodities of the country.

Any married man that shall transport himself, his wife and children, shall have assigned unto him . . . in freehold, (as aforesaid) for himself one hundred acres, and for his wife one hundred acres, and for every child that he shall carry over, under the age of sixteen years, fifty acres; paying for a quit rent twelve pence for every fifty acres.

Any woman that shall transport herself or any children, under the age of six years, shall have the like conditions as aforesaid.

Anyone that shall carry over any women servants, under the age of forty years, shall have for and in respect of every such woman servant, fifty acres; paying only a quit rent as aforesaid.

II 🧩 *Colonial Economy*

As THE ORIGINAL conception of what the plantation should be changed in the face of the realities of American life, the colonial system of production took on new forms. The old aspirations were still reflected in the instructions sent from Sweden to Governor Printz (No. 8). But John Smith's experience (No. 9) shows it was necessary to make even gentlemen adventurers work; and William Bradford's account (No. 10) reveals the transition from a communal to an individual economy. Secretary van Tienhoven's "Information" (No. 11), a little later, reflects the stable agricultural order then developing.

Meanwhile the colonies were also exerting themselves in the production of staples that could enter readily into overseas trade. In Virginia and Maryland tobacco solved the problem for a time. Although the colonies were troubled by overproduction, the crop remained important. Alsop's description (No. 12) shows its central place in the economy of the Chesapeake region. New England's staple came from the sea. Josselyn (No. 13) described various aspects of the development of the fisheries.

In addition the opportunities for trade, particularly with the West Indies, brought prosperity to commercial towns such as Boston (No. 14). By the end of the period these colonies boasted a well-rounded economic life.

Economic growth depended upon a steady increase in the number of laborers. But the only new hands available were the servants brought over under indenture and bound for a period of years to work for those who paid their passage. They became an important element of society; and it was soon necessary carefully to regulate their condition (No. 15). Their growing independence often confused relations with their masters. But while the status of those who had the freedom to decide whether they would migrate or not improved, the lot of the Negroes declined. After 1660, they were held as slaves for life (No. 16).

8. *Instructions for Governor Printz, the Swedes on the Delaware, 1643*

Amandus Johnson, ed., *The Instruction for Johan Printz* (Philadelphia, 1930), 82–92.

AND IF THE Governor does not find it ... necessary at once ... to fortify another new place, but can for the present properly get along with Fort Christina, then he shall so much the more urge and arrange about agriculture and the cultivation of the land, setting and urging the people thereto with zeal and energy, exerting himself, before all other things, that so much seed-corn may be committed to the ground that the tenants may derive therefrom their necessary food. . . .

Next to this, he shall pay good and close attention to the cultivation of tobacco and appoint thereto a certain number of laborers, pressing the matter so that that cultivation may increase ... so that he can send over a good quantity of tobacco on all ships coming hither. . . .

That it may be better arranged for [the increase of] cattle and all kinds of live stock ... the Governor shall in the beginning exert himself to obtain a good breed of all kinds of cattle, and above or besides that which is sent out from here, also seek to purchase necessary additions from the neighboring ... English, distributing all such [cattle] among those who use and take care of fields, in exchange for grain, and in the manner he may find most serviceable to the stockholders. . . .

Among and above other things, he shall direct his attention to sheep, to obtain them of good breed, and gradually seek to establish as many sheepfolds as he possibly can, so that in the future a good and considerable quantity of wool may be shipped over here.

The peltry-trade with the wild [people] he shall also, so far as possible, seek to keep in a good state, exercise and keep inspection over the commissioners appointed for the purpose of trading with the Indians, to prevent all frauds, and take care that [Her] Roy[al] Maj[esty] and her subjects, and the members interested in this Company, may have reason to expect good returns from their cargoes. Likewise he shall see to it that no one ... may be permitted to traffic with the natives in peltries; but such trade shall alone be carried on by persons thereto appointed in the name of the whole Company and on its behalf.

Whatever else of useful things is, gradually, to be done in that country, time and circumstances there on the spot will best give the Governor advice. Especially as this land, New Sweden, is situated in a climate with Portugal; so ... it is to be supposed that salt-works might be established on the sea-coast. But in case the salt could not be perfectly evaporated by the ... sun, yet, at the least, the salt water might thereby so far be improved that it might afterwards be perfectly condensed by means of fire, without great labor and expense; which the Governor must have in mind and try. ...

And as almost everywhere on the ground wild grapevines and grapes are found, and the climate seems to be favorable to wine culture, therefore the Governor shall also direct his thoughts in that direction, that, as time goes on, such culture, and what further belongs to it, may be established and improved.

He can also have close and careful search made in all places as to whether any metals or minerals are to be found in the country, and, if there are any and can be discovered, send hither all full information about it. ...

Out of the over-abundant forests, the Governor shall consider and try how and in what manner profit may be made from the good trees of the country; especially what sort of positive advantage may be expected from oak-trees and walnut-trees, since one also could send over here a good quality as ballast. So it might also be tried, whether oil might not advantageously be pressed out of the walnuts.

How and where fisheries might best and with good advantage be established for profit, the Governor shall there likewise take into consideration and let himself be correctly informed; especially as it is reported that in ... Godin's Bay, and thereabouts, at a certain season of the year, whale fishery can be advantageously prosecuted and arranged. Therefore, he shall have an eye upon this and send over hither all needed information. ...

The Governor shall also diligently proceed, and inform himself, if [there are] good sustenance and convenience for keeping in that country a large quantity of silkworms, wherewith some manufacture might be carried on. And if he perceives and finds that something useful might therewith be accomplished, he shall have in mind that for such purpose every proper arrangement might gradually be made.

9. *Learning to Labor in Virginia, 1609*

John Smith, *Works.* Edward Arber, ed. (Westminster, 1895), II, 465–6, 471–3.

WHEN the ships departed, all the provision of the store ... was so rotten with the last summer's rain, and eaten with rats and worms as the hogs would scarcely eat it. Yet it was the soldiers' diet till our return ..., so that we found nothing

done, but our victuals spent; and the most part of our tools and a good part of our arms conveyed to the savages.

But now casting up the store and finding sufficient till the next harvest, the fear of starving was abandoned, and the company divided into tens, fifteens or as the business required. Six hours each day was spent in work, the rest in pastime and merry exercises.

But the untowardness of the greatest number caused the President to advise as follows:

"Countrymen, the long experience of our late miseries, I hope is sufficient to persuade every one to a present correction of himself, and think not that either my pains, nor the Adventurers' purses, will ever maintain you in idleness and sloth. ... The greater part must be more industrious, or starve.... You see now that power rests wholly in my self; you must obey this now for a law, that he that will not work shall not eat (except by sickness he be disabled) for the labors of thirty or forty honest and industrious men shall not be consumed to maintain an hundred and fifty idle loiterers.... Therefore he that offendeth, let him assuredly expect his due punishment.

He also made a table [notice board], as a public memorial of every man's deserts, to encourage the good, and with shame to spur on the rest to amendment. By this, many became very industrious, yet more by punishment performed their business, for all were so tasked, that there was no excuse could prevail to deceive him....

Now, we so quietly followed our business, that in three months ... we made three or four last of tar, pitch, and soap ashes; produced a trial of glass; made a well in the fort of excellent sweet water, which till then was wanting; built some twenty houses; re-covered our church; provided nets and weirs for fishing; and to stop the disorders of our disorderly thieves, and the savages, built a blockhouse in the neck of our isle, kept by a garrison to entertain the savages' trade, and none to pass or repass savage or Christian without the President's order. Thirty or forty acres of ground we dug and planted. Of three sows in eighteen months, increased sixty and odd pigs. And nearly five hun-

dred chickens brought up themselves without having any meat given them. But the hogs were transported to Hog Isle, where also we built a blockhouse with a garrison to give us notice of any shipping, and for their exercise they made clapboard and wainscot, and cut down trees.

We also built a fort for a retreat near a convenient river upon a high commanding hill, very hard to be assaulted and easy to be defended; but ere it was finished this defect caused a stay.

In searching our casked corn..., we found it half rotten, and the rest so consumed with so many thousands of rats that increased so fast, but their original was from the ships, as we knew not how to keep that little we had. This did drive us all to our wits' end, for there was nothing in the country but what nature afforded....

This want of corn occasioned the end of all our works, it being work sufficient to provide victuals. Sixty or eighty with Ensign Laxon were sent down the river to live upon oysters, and twenty with Lieutenant Percy to try for fishing at Point Comfort, but in six weeks they would not agree once to cast out the net, he being sick and burnt sore with gunpowder. Master West with as many went up to the falls, but nothing could be found but a few acorns; of that in store every man had his equal proportion.

Till this present, by the hazard and endeavors of some thirty or forty, this whole colony had ever been fed. We had more sturgeon than could be devoured by dog and man; of which the industrious by drying and pounding, mingling with caviar, sorell and other wholesome herbs, would make good bread and meat. Others would gather as much ... roots in a day as would make them bread a week, so that of those wild fruits and what we caught, we lived very well in regard of such a diet.

But such was the strange condition of some one hundred and fifty, that had they not been forced *nolens, volens,* perforce to gather and prepare their victuals they would all have starved or have eaten one another. Of those wild fruits the savages often brought us, and for that the President would not fulfill the unreasonable desire of those distracted gluttonous loiterers, to sell not only our kettles, hoes, tools and iron, nay, swords, pieces and the very ordnance and houses, might they have prevailed to have been but idle. For those savage fruits, they would have imparted all to the savages. . . . Thousands were their exclamations, suggestions and devices to force him to those base inventions to have made it an occasion to abandon the country.

Want perforce constrained him to endure their exclaiming follies till he found out the author, one Dyer, a most crafty fellow and his ancient maligner, whom he worthily punished. And with the rest he argued the case in this manner:

"Fellow soldiers, I did little think any so false to report, or so many to be so simple to be persuaded, that I . . . intend to starve you. . . . Neither did I think any so malicious as now I see a great many. But dream no longer . . . that I will longer forbear to force you from your idleness, and punish you if you rail. . . . You cannot deny but that by the hazard of my life many a time I have saved yours, when (might your own wills have prevailed) you would have starved; and will do still whether I will or no. But I protest by God that made me, since necessity has not power to force you to gather for yourselves those fruits the earth does yield, you shall not only gather for yourselves, but [for] those that are sick. As yet I never had more from the store than the worst of you, and all my English extraordinary provision that I have, you shall see me divide it amongst the sick.

"And this savage trash you so scornfully repine at; being put in your mouths your stomachs can digest. If you would have better, you should have brought it; therefore I will take a course you shall provide what is to be had. The sick shall not starve, but equally share of all our labors; and he that gathereth not every day as much as I do, the next day shall be set beyond the river, and be banished from the fort as a drone, till he amend his conditions or starve.". . .

This order many murmured was very cruel, but it caused the most part so well to bestir themselves, that of two hundred (except they were drowned) there died not past seven.

10. *Changes in the Plymouth Economy, 1623–38*

William Bradford, *Of Plymouth Plantation 1620–1647.* Samuel Eliot Morison, ed. (New York, 1953), 120–3, 144–5, 181–3, 252–3, 301–2.

ALL THIS while [1623] no supply was heard of, neither knew they when they might expect any. So they began to think how they might raise as much corn as they could, and obtain a better crop than they had done, that they might not still thus languish in misery. At length, after much debate of things, the Governor (with the advice of the chieftest amongst them) gave way that they should set corn every man for his own particular, and in that regard trust to themselves; in all other things to go on in the general way as before. And so assigned to every family a parcel of land, according to the proportion of their number, for that end, only for present use (but made no division for inheritance) and ranged all boys and youth under some family. This had very good success, for it made all hands very industrious, so as much more corn was planted than otherwise would have been by any means the Governor or any other could use, and saved him a great deal of trouble, and gave far better content. The women now went willingly into the field, and took their little ones with them to set corn; which before would allege weakness and inability. . . .

The experience that was had in this common course and condition, tried sundry years and that amongst godly and sober men, may well evince the vanity of that conceit of Plato's and other ancients applauded by some of later times; that the taking away of property and bringing in community into a commonwealth would make them happy and flourishing. . . . For this community (so far as it was) was found to breed much confusion and discontent and retard much employment that would have been to their benefit and comfort. For the young men, that were most able and fit for labor and service, did repine that they should spend their time and strength to work for other men's wives and children without any recompense. The strong, or man of parts, had no more in division of victuals and clothes than he that was weak and not able to do a quarter the other could; this was thought injustice. The aged and graver men to be ranked and equalized in labors and victuals, clothes, etc., with the meaner and younger sort, thought it some indignity and disrespect unto them. And for men's wives to be commanded to do service for other men, as dressing their meat, washing their clothes, etc., they deemed it a kind of slavery, neither could many husbands well brook it. Upon the point all being to have alike, and all to do alike, they thought themselves in the like condition, and one as good as another; and so, if it did not cut off those relations that God hath set amongst men, yet it did at least much diminish and take off the mutual respects that should be preserved amongst them. . . .

After this course settled, and by that their corn was planted, all their victuals were spent and they were only to rest on God's providence; at night not many times knowing where to have a bit of any-

thing the next day. . . . Yet they bore these wants with great patience and alacrity of spirit; and that for so long a time as for the most part of two years. . . .

They having but one boat left and she not over-well fitted, they were divided into several companies, six or seven to a gang or company, and so went out, with a net they had bought, to take bass and such like fish by course, every company knowing their turn. No sooner was the boat discharged of what she brought, but the next company took her and went out with her. Neither did they return till they had caught something, though it were five or six days before, for they knew there was nothing at home, and to go home empty would be a great discouragement to the rest. Yea, they strive who should do best. If she stayed long or got little, then all went to seeking of shellfish, which at low water they digged out of the sands. And this was their living in the summer time, till God sent them better; and in winter they were helped with ground nuts and fowl. Also in the summer they got now and then a deer, for one or two of the fittest were appointed to range the woods for that end, and what was got that way was divided amongst them. . . .

They began now [1624] highly to prize corn as more precious than silver, and those that had some to spare began to trade one with another for small things, by the quart, pottle and peck, etc.; for money they had none, and if any had, corn was preferred before it. That they might therefore increase their tillage to better advantage, they made suit to the Governor to have some portion of land given them for continuance, and not by yearly lot. For by that means, that which the more industrious had brought into good culture (by much pains) one year, came to leave it the next, and often another might enjoy it; so as the dressing of their lands were the more slighted over, and to less profit. Which being well considered, their request was granted. And to every person was given only one acre of land, to them and theirs, as near the town as might be; and they had no more till the seven years were expired. The reason was that they might be kept close together, both for more safety and defense, and the better improvement of the general employments. . . .

Having now [1626] no fishing business or other things to intend, but only their trading and planting, they set themselves to follow the same with the best industry they could. The Planters finding their corn . . . to be a commodity . . . used great diligence in planting the same. And the Governor and such as were designed to manage the trade (for it was retained for the general good and none were to trade in particular) they followed it to the best advantage they could. And wanting trading goods, they understood that a plantation which was at Monhegan and belonged to some merchants of Plymouth, was to break up and divers useful goods was there to be sold. The Governor and Mr. Winslow took a boat and some hands and went thither. But Mr. David Thompson, who lived at Piscataqua, understanding their purpose, took opportunity to go with them, which was some hindrance to them both. For they, perceiving their joint desires to buy, held their goods at higher rates, and not only so, but would not sell a parcel of their trading goods except they sold all. So lest they should further prejudice one another, they agreed to buy all and divide them equally between them. They bought also a parcel of goats which they distributed at home as they saw need and occasion, and took corn for them of the people, which gave them good content; their moiety of the goods came to above £400 sterling.

There was also that spring a French ship cast away at Sagadahoc, in which were many Biscay rugs and other commodities, which were fallen into these men's hands, and some other fishermen at Damariscove; which were also bought in partnership and made their part arise to above £500. This they made shift to pay for,

for the most part, with the beaver and commodities they had got the winter before, and what they had gathered up that summer. Mr. Thompson having something overcharged himself, desired they would take some of his, but they refused except he would let them have his French goods only, and the merchant (who was one of Bristol) would take their bill for to be paid the next year. They were both willing, so they became engaged for them and took them. By which means, they became very well furnished for trade. . . .

With these goods and their corn after harvest, they got good store of trade, so as they were enabled to pay their engagements against the time, and to get some clothing for the people, and had some commodities beforehand. But now they began to be envied, and others went and filled the Indians with corn and beat down the price, giving them twice as much as they had done, and undertraded them in other commodities also. . . .

And finding they ran a great hazard to go so long voyages in a small open boat, especially in the winter season, they began to think how they might get a small pinnace, as for the reason aforesaid; so also because others had raised the price with the Indians above the half of what they had formerly given, so as in such a boat they could not carry a quantity sufficient to answer their ends. They had no ship carpenter amongst them, neither knew how to get one at present; but they having an ingenious man that was a house carpenter, who also had wrought with the ship carpenter that was dead when he built their boats; at their request he put forth himself to make a trial that way of his skill. And took one of the biggest of their shallops and sawed her in the middle, and so lengthened her some five or six foot, and strengthened her with timbers, and so built her up and laid a deck on her. And so made her a convenient and wholesome vessel, very fit and comfortable for their use, which did them service seven years after. And they got

her finished and fitted with sails and an-
chors the ensuing year. . . .

Also [by 1632] the people of the Plantation began to grow in their outward estates, by reason of the flowing of many
people into the country, especially into
the Bay of the Massachusetts. By which
means corn and cattle rose to a great
price, by which many were much enriched
and commodities grew plentiful. And yet
in other regards this benefit turned to their
hurt, and this accession of strength to
their weakness. For now as their stocks
increased and the increase vendible, there
was no longer any holding them together,
but now they must of necessity go to their
great lots. They could not otherwise keep
their cattle, and having oxen grown they
must have land for plowing and tillage.
And no man now thought he could live
except he had cattle and a great deal of
ground to keep them, all striving to increase their stocks. By which means they
were scattered all over the Bay quickly
and the town in which they lived com-
pactly till now was left very thin and in
a short time almost desolate. . . .

It pleased God in these times [1638]

to bless the country with such access and
confluence of people into it, as it was
thereby much enriched, and cattle of all
kinds stood at a high rate for divers years
together. Kine were sold at £20 and some
at £25 apiece; yea, sometimes at £28; a
cow calf usually at £10. A milch goat
at £3 and some at £4, and female kids
at 30s and often at 40s apiece. By which
means the ancient planters which had any
stock, began to grow in their estates. Corn
also went at a round rate; viz. 6s a bushel,
so as other trading began to be neglected,
and the old partners . . . broke off their
trade at Kennebec and, as things stood,
would follow it no longer. But some of
them, with others they joined with, being
loath it should be lost by discontinu-
ance, agreed with the company for it and
gave them about the sixth part of their
gains for it, with the first fruits of which
they built a house for a prison. And the
trade there hath been since continued to
the great benefit of the place. For some
well foresaw that these high prices of corn
and cattle would not long continue, and
that then the commodities there raised
would be much missed.

11. *Farming in New Netherland, 1650*

"Secretary van Tienhoven's Information," O'Callaghan, *Documents Relative to the Colonial History of
New York*, I, 365 ff.

Boors and others who are obliged to work
at first in colonies ought to sail from this
country in the fore or latter part of winter,
in order to arrive with God's help in New
Netherland early in the spring, in March,
or at latest in April, so as to be able to
plant, during that summer, garden vegetables, maize and beans, and moreover
employ the whole summer in clearing land
and building cottages. . . .

All then who arrive in New Netherland
must immediately set about preparing the
soil, so as to be able, if possible to plant
some winter grain, and to proceed the
next winter to cut and clear the timber.

The trees are usually felled from the
stump, cut up and burnt in the field, unless such as are suitable for building, for
palisades, posts and rails, which must be
prepared during the winter, so as to be
set up in the spring on the new made
land which is intended to be sown, in
order that the cattle may not in any wise
injure the crops. In most lands is found a
certain root, called red wortel, which must
before ploughing, be extirpated with a
hoe, expressly made for that purpose. This
being done in the winter, some plough
right around the stumps, should time or
circumstances not allow these to be re-

moved; others plant tobacco, maize and beans, at first. The soil even thus becomes very mellow, and they sow winter grain the next fall. From tobacco, can be realized some of the expenses incurred in clearing the land. The maize and beans help to support both men and cattle. The farmer having thus begun, must endeavor, every year, to clear as much new land as he possibly can, and sow it with as much seed as he considers most suitable.

It is not necessary that the husbandmen should take up much stock in the beginning, since clearing land and other necessary labor do not permit him to save much hay and to build barns for stabling. One pair of draft horses or a yoke of oxen only is necessary, to ride the planks for buildings, or palisades or rails from the land to the place where they are to be set.

The farmer can get all sorts of cattle in the course of the second summer, when he will have more leisure to cut and bring home hay, also to build houses and barns for men and cattle.

Before beginning to build, it will above all things be necessary to select a well located spot, either on some river or bay, suitable for the settlement of a village or hamlet. This is previously properly surveyed and divided into lots, with good streets according to the situation of the place. This hamlet can be fenced all around with high palisades or long boards and closed with gates, which is advantageous in case of attack by the natives, who heretofore used to exhibit their insolence in new plantations.

Outside the village or hamlet, other land must be laid out which can in general be fenced and prepared at the most trifling expense.

Those in New Netherland and especially in New England, who have no means to build farm-houses at first according to their wishes, dig a square pit in the ground, cellar fashion, six or seven feet deep, as long and as broad as they think proper, case the earth inside all round the wall with timber, which they line with the bark of trees or something else to prevent the caving in of the earth; floor this cellar with plank and wainscot it overhead for a ceiling, raise a roof of spars clear up and cover the spars with bark or green sods, so that they can live dry and warm in these houses with their entire families for two, three and four years, it being understood that partitions are run through those cellars which are adapted to the size of the family.

The wealthy and principal men in New England, in the beginning of the colonies, commenced their first dwelling-houses in this fashion for two reasons; first, in order not to waste time building and not to want food the next season; secondly, in order not to discourage poorer laboring people whom they brought over in numbers. . . . In the course of three and four years, when the country became adapted to agriculture, they built themselves handsome houses, spending on them several thousands.

After the houses are built, . . . gardens are made and planted in season with all sorts of pot-herbs, principally parsnips, carrots and cabbage, which bring great plenty into the husbandman's dwelling. The maize can serve as bread for men and food for cattle.

The hogs, after having picked up their food for some months in the woods, are crammed with corn in the fall; when fat they are killed and furnish a very hard and clean pork; a good article for the husbandman who gradually and in time begins to purchase horses and cows with the produce of his grain and the increase of his hogs, and instead of a cellar as aforesaid, builds good farm-houses and barns.

The cattle necessary in a colony or private bouwery in New Netherland, are: good mares and sound stallions; yoke-oxen for the plough, inasmuch as in new lands, full of roots, oxen go forward steadily under the plough, and horses stand still, or with a start break the harness in pieces; milch-cows of kindly disposition; and good bulls, sheep, sows, etc. Fowls are well adapted to bouweries.

These cattle are abundant in New Netherland, and especially in New England, and to be had at a reasonable price, except sheep, which the English do not sell, and are rare in New Netherland.

All this being arranged it must be noted what description of people are best adapted for agriculture in New Netherland, and to perform the most service and return the most profit in the beginning.

First, a person is necessary to superintend the working men; he ought to be acquainted with farming.

Industrious country people, conversant with the working and cultivation of land, and possessing a knowledge of cattle.

It would not be unprofitable to add to these some Highland boors. . . . Northerners are a people adapted to cutting down trees and clearing land, inasmuch as they are very laborious and accustomed to work in the woods. Northerners can do almost anything; some can build much, others a little, and construct small craft which they call yawls.

Carpenters who can lay brick.

Smiths conversant with heavy work, curing cattle and provided with suitable medicines.

One or more surgeons, according to the number of the people, with a chest well supplied with all sorts of drugs.

One or more coopers.

A clergyman, comforter of the sick, or precentor who could also act as schoolmaster.

A wheelwright.

All other tradesmen would follow in time; the above mentioned mechanics are the most necessary at first.

In order to promote population through such and other means, the people must be provided with freedoms and privileges so as to induce them to quit their Fatherland, and emigrate with their families beyond the sea to this far distant New Netherland. And as poor people have no means to defray the cost of passage and other expenses, it were desirable that wealthy individuals would expend some capital, to people this country, or like the English of New England, at their own expense remove themselves with funds and a large body of working men, and provide those without means with land, dwelling, cattle, tools and necessary support; and that, until they could derive the necessary maintenance from the soil and the increase of cattle, after which time they would be able to pay yearly a reasonable quit-rent to their lords and masters from the effects in their possession.

By the population and cultivation of the aforesaid lands those who will have disbursed funds for the removal of the laboring classes, the purchase of cattle and all other expenses, would, in process of some years, after God had blessed the tillage and the increase of the cattle, derive a considerable revenue in grain, beef, pork, butter and tobacco, which form at first the earliest returns, and in time can be improved by industry, such as making pot and pearl ashes, clapboards, knees for ship building, staves, all sorts of pine and oak plank, masts for large ships, square timber and ash and hickory planks; in which a staple trade could be established. The English of New England put this in practice, as is to be seen, after the land had been first brought to proper condition; they sell their provisions at the Caribbean Islands, staves at Madeira and the Canaries, masts and fish in Spain and Portugal and bring in return all sorts of commodities; so much of these returns as they do not consume, are again distributed by them throughout all the islands known and inhabited in the northern part of America. Thus, through the variety of the returns which of necessity were received, a profitable trade is already established in New England, which can also be right well set on foot by the Netherlanders, if the population of the country were promoted.

12. *Tobacco and Trade in Maryland, 1666*

George Alsop, *A Character of the Province of Mary-land*. N. D. Mereness, ed. (Cleveland, 1902), 68–72.

THE THREE main commodities this country affords for traffic are tobacco, furs and flesh. Furs and skins, as beavers, otters, muskrats, raccoons, wildcats, and elk or buffalo, with divers others, which were first made vendible by the Indians of the country, and sold to the inhabitant, and by them to the merchant, and so transported into England and other places where it becomes most commodious.

Tobacco is the only solid staple commodity of this province. The use of it was first found out by the Indians many ages ago, and transferred into Christendom by that great discoverer of America, Columbus. It is generally made by all the inhabitants of this province; and between the months of March and April they sow the seed . . . in small beds and patches dug up and made so by art. About May the plants commonly appear green in those beds. In June they are transplanted from their beds, and set in little hillocks in distant rows, dug up for the same purpose. Some twice or thrice they are weeded, and succored from their illegitimate leaves that would be peeping out from the body of the stalk. They top the several plants as they find occasion in their predominating rankness. About the middle of September they cut the tobacco down, and carry it into houses (made for that purpose) to bring it to its purity; and after it has attained, by a convenient attendance upon time, to its perfection, it is then tied up in bundles and packed into hogsheads, and then laid by for the trade.

Between November and January there arrives in this province shipping to the number of twenty sail and upwards, all merchantmen laden with commodities to traffic and dispose of, trucking with the planter for silks, Hollands, serges and broadcloths, with other necessary goods, prized at such and such rates as shall be judged on is fair and legal, for tobacco at so much the pound, and advantage on both sides considered:—the planter for his work, and the merchant for adventuring himself and his commodity into so far a country. Thus is the trade on both sides driven with a fair and honest decorum.

The inhabitants of this province are seldom or never put to the affrightment of being robbed of their money, nor to dirty their fingers by telling of vast sums. They have more bags to carry corn, than coin. . . . The very effects of the dirt of this province afford as great a profit to the general inhabitant as the gold of Peru does to the straight-breeched commonalty of the Spaniard.

Our shops and exchanges of Maryland are the merchants' storehouses, where with few words and protestations goods are bought and delivered; not like those shopkeepers' boys in London that continually cry, "What do ye lack, sir? What do ye buy?" yelping with so wide a mouth, as if some apothecary had hired their mouths to stand open to catch gnats and vagabond flies in.

Tobacco is the current coin of Maryland and will sooner purchase commodities from the merchant, than money. I must confess the New England men that trade into this province had rather have fat pork for their goods than tobacco or furs, which I conceive is, because their bodies being fast bound up with the cords of restringent zeal, they are fain to make use of the lineaments of this non-Canaanite creature physically to loosen them; for a bit of a pound on a two-penny rye loaf, according to the original receipt, will bring the costiv'st red-eared zealot in some three hours' time to a fine stool, if methodically observed.

Madeira wines, sugars, salt, wicker chairs and tin candlesticks are the most of the commodities they bring in. They arrive in Maryland about September, being most of them ketches and barks and such small vessels, and those disperse themselves into several small creeks of this province to sell and dispose of their commodities, where they know the market is most fit for their small adventures.

Barbadoes, together with the several adjacent islands, has much provision yearly from this province. And though these sunburnt Phaetons think to outvie Maryland in their silks and puffs, daily speaking against her whom their necessity makes them beholden to, and ... cock their felts and look big upon it; yet if a man could go down into their infernals and see how it fares with them there, I believe he would hardly find any other spirit to buoy them up, than the ill-visaged ghost of want, that continually wanders from gut to gut to feed upon the undigested rinds of potatoes.

13. *The Massachusetts Fisheries, 1663*

John Josselyn, *An Account of Two Voyages to New-England* (Boston, 1865), 160–2.

THE FISHERMEN take yearly upon the coasts many hundred quintals of cod, hake, haddock, pollack, etc., which they split, salt and dry at their stages, making three voyages in a year. When they share their fish ... at the end of every voyage they separate the best from the worst. The first they call merchantable fish, being sound, full-grown fish and well made up, which is known when it is clear like a Lanthorn horn and without spots; the second sort they call refuse fish, that is such as is salt burned, spotted, rotten and carelessly ordered. These they put off to the Massachusetts merchants, the merchantable for thirty and two and thirty rials a quintal ... ; the refuse for nine shillings and ten shillings. ... The merchant sends the merchantable fish to Lisbon, Bilbao, Bordeaux, Marseilles, Toulon, Rochelle, Rouen and other cities of France, and to the Canaries with clapboard and pipe-staves, which is there and at the Caribes a prime commodity; the refuse fish they put off at the Carib Islands, Barbadoes, Jamaica, etc., who feed their Negroes with it.

To every shallop belong four fishermen, a master or steersman, a midshipman, ... a foremast-man, and a shore man who washes it out of the salt and dries it upon hurdles pitched upon stakes breast high, and tends their cookery. These often get in one voyage eight or nine pounds a man for their shares. But it does some of them little good, for the merchant to increase his gains ... comes in with a walking tavern, a bark laden with the legitimate blood of the rich grape ... with brandy, rum, the Barbadoes strong-water, and tobacco. Coming ashore he gives them a taste or two, which so charms them that for no persuasions that their employers can use will they go out to sea, although fair and seasonable weather, for two or three days, nay sometimes a whole week, till they are wearied with drinking. ... If a man of quality chance to come near where they are roistering and gulling in wine ... , he must be sociable and roly-poly with them ... or else be gone. ... For when wine in their guts is at full tide, they quarrel, fight and do one another mischief. ...

When the day of payment comes, they may justly complain of their costly sin of drunkenness, for their shares will do no more than pay the reckoning. If they save a quintal or two to buy shoes and stockings, shirts and waistcoats with, it is well; otherwise they must enter into the merchant's books for such things as they stand in need of, becoming thereby the merchant's slaves, and when it rises to a big sum are constrained to mortgage their plantation, if they have any. The merchant, when the time is expired, is sure to seize upon their plantation and flock of cattle, turning them out of house and home, poor creatures, to look out for a new habitation in some remote place where they begin the world again.

14. *Opportunities for Boston Trade with the West Indies, 1645*

Sir George Downing to John Winthrop, Jr., *Winthrop Papers.* A. B. Forbes, ed. (Boston, 1947), V, 42 ff.

As NEAR as I am able I have set down the state of the Indies. We were there from the 12th of February to the 27th of July, in which time I endeavored . . . to understand the state of things in all kinds. . . . If you go to Barbadoes you shall see a flourishing island. . . . I believe they have bought this year no less than a thousand Negroes; and the more they buy, the better able they are to buy, for in a year and a half they will earn . . . as much as they cost. . . .

The certainest commodities you can carry for those parts . . . will be fish as mackerel, bass, dry fish, beef, pork, if you can procure them at reasonable rates, and if you be there in the Spring,—it's the best time because the fewest ships are there.

Linen cloth is a certain commodity, but that is dear in New England. We sold linen which 10½ d the Portugal vare (which is within two inches of an English ell) for twelve pounds of tobacco or a pound of indigo the yard.

A man that will settle there must look to procure servants which, if you could get out of England for six or eight or nine years time only paying their passages or at the most but some small above, it would do very well. For so thereby you shall be able to do something upon a plantation, and in short time be able with good husbandry to procure Negroes (the life of this place) out of the increase of your own plantation.

15. *A Direction for Choice of Servants for Maryland, 1635*

A Relation of Maryland, 52–4.

IN THE taking of servants, he may do well to furnish himself with as many as he can, of useful and necessary arts: a carpenter, of all others the most necessary; a millwright; shipwright; boatwright; wheelwright; brickmaker; bricklayer; potter; one that can cleave lath and pale, and make pipestaves, etc.; a joiner; cooper; turner; sawyer; smith; cutler; leatherdresser; miller; fisherman; and gardener. These will be of most use; but any lusty young able man that is willing to labor and take pains, although he have no particular trade, will be beneficial enough to his master.

And in case any adventurer shall be unprovided of such men to supply his number, he may have directions at the place where these books are to be had, how and where he may provide himself of as many as he please.

The form of binding a servant.

THIS INDENTURE made the ⸻ day of ⸻ in the ⸻ year of our sovereign lord King Charles, etc. between of the one party, and   on the other party, Witnesseth, that the said   doth hereby covenant, promise, and grant, to and with the said   his executors and assignes, to serve him from the day of the date hereof, until his first and next arrival in Maryland; and after for and during the term of   years, in such service and employment, as he the said or his assignes shall there employ him, according to the custom of the country in the like kind. In consideration whereof, the said   doth promise and grant, to and with the said to pay for his passing, and to find him meat, drink, apparel and lodging, with other necessaries during the said term; and at the end of the said term, to give him one whole year's provision of corn and fifty acres of land, according to the order of the country. In witness whereof, the said   hath hereunto put his hand and seal, the day and year above written.

Sealed and delivered in
the presence of

The usual term of binding a servant, is for five years; but for any artificer, or one that shall deserve more than ordinary, the adventurer shall do well to shorten that time, and add encouragements of another nature ... rather than to want such useful men.

16. *Maryland Act Concerning Negroes and Other Slaves, 1664*

Maryland Archives, I, 533–4.

BE IT enacted by the right honorable the Lord Proprietary by the advice and consent of the upper and lower house of this present General Assembly that all Negroes or other slaves already within the Province and all Negroes and other slaves to be hereafter imported into the Province shall serve Durante Vita. And all children born of any Negro or other slave shall be slaves as their fathers were for the term of their lives. And forasmuch as divers freeborn English women forgetful of their free condition and to the disgrace of our nation do intermarry with Negro slaves, by which also divers suits may arise touching the issue of such women and a great damage doth befall the masters of such Negroes; ... be it further enacted ... that whatsoever free born woman shall intermarry with any slave from and after the last day of this present Assembly shall serve the master of such slave during the life of her husband, and that all the issue of such free born women so married shall be slaves as their fathers were. And be it further enacted that all the issues of English or other free born women that have already married Negroes shall serve the masters of their parents till they be thirty years of age and no longer.

III 🎔 *A Wilderness Society*

THE CHANGES in the character of the colonies were in themselves disturbing. But, in addition, the people involved were unsettled by the extremely harsh conditions of life in the early years of the migration. The reflections of the Virginia General

Assembly (No. 17), some years after the event, recall the problems of simple survival the first planters faced. William Bradford's account (No. 18) touches on the same difficulties, but also points to the personal and social disorders that followed upon removal from the homeland. Even later, the lack of amenities is prominent in the consciousness of a minister who came to serve the people of New Netherland (No. 19).

In the wilderness, to many persons the old moral and social assumptions seemed less binding than at home. Contact with the Indians (No. 20) and later with the helpless Negroes (No. 21) encouraged dissolute behavior; and the uncertainty of social sanctions made it difficult to preserve the traditional institutions of marriage (No. 22). In the life of these raw settlements there seemed no discernible place for the life of the intellect (No. 23).

Yet the colonists did not despair; they had at least the security of knowing that their experience was not the product of random accidents. God's infinity was assurance that nothing happened without design (No. 24). Even the death of an innocent child had a meaning and was part of a plan (No. 25).

On the basis of this faith, it was possible to find dignity in the hard round of daily life. A woman was not merely a drudge bound to strenuous labor but a soul triumphant (No. 26). And a man of humble beginnings, who rose in station, gained not only material rewards but also election to the company of saints (No. 27). So too, the very difficulties of the task of settlement were signs of the importance of the task. All these sufferings were evidence of a Divine Providence that had singled out the Americans for a mission of epochal importance to all humanity (No. 28). That was the meaning the first settlers gave to their experience in the New World.

17. *Hardships in Early Virginia, 1624*

H. R. McIlwaine, ed., *Journals of the House of Burgesses of Virginia* (Richmond, 1915), I, 21–2.

THE ANSWER of the General Assembly in Virginia to a declaration of the state of the colony in the twelve years of Sir Thomas Smith's government. . . .

Holding it a sin against God . . . to suffer the world to be abused with untrue reports, and to give unto vice the reward of virtue, we, in the name of the whole colony of Virginia, in our general assembly, many of us having been eyewitnesses and patients of those times, have framed out of our duty to this country, and love unto truth, this dismasking of those praises which are contained in the foresaid declarations.

In those twelve years of Sir Thomas Smith's government, we aver that the colony for the most part remained in great want and misery under most severe and cruel laws . . . (contrary to the express letter of the King in his most gracious charter), and as mercilessly executed, oftentimes without trial or judgment. The allowance in those times for a man was only eight ounces of meal and half a pint of peas for a day, the one and the other moldy, rotten, full of cobwebs and maggots, loathsome to man and not fit for beasts, which forced many to flee for relief to the savage enemy, who, being taken again, were put to sundry deaths as by hanging, shooting and breaking upon the wheel. And others were forced by famine to filch for their bellies, of whom one, for stealing two or three pints of oatmeal, had a bodkin thrust through his tongue and was tied with a chain to a tree until he starved. If a man, through his sickness had not been able to work, he had no allowance at all; and so consequently perished many through these extremities. Being weary of life [they] dug holes in the earth and hid themselves till they famished.

We cannot for this, our scarcity, blame our commanders here, in respect that our sustenance was to come from England, for had they at that time given us no better allowance we had perished in general. So lamentable was our scarcity that we were constrained to eat dogs, cats, rats, snakes, toadstools, horsehides and what not. One man, out of the misery he endured, killing his wife, powdered her up to eat her, for which he was burned. Many besides fed on the corpses of dead men, and one who had gotten insatiable out of custom to that food could not be restrained, until such time as he was executed for it. And indeed, so miserable was our estate that the happiest day that ever some of them hoped to see was when the Indians had killed a mare, they wishing while she was boiling that Sir Thomas Smith was upon her back in the kettle.

And whereas it is affirmed that there were very few of His Majesty's subjects left in those days, and those of the meanest rank, we answer that for one that now

dies there then perished five, many being of ancient houses. . . . Those who survived . . . were constrained to serve the colony as if they had been slaves, seven or eight years for their freedoms, who underwent as hard and servile labor as the basest fellow that was brought out of Newgate. . . .

For our houses and churches in those times, they were so mean and poor by reason of those calamities that they could not stand above one or two years; the people never going to work but out of the bitterness of their spirits, threatening execrable curses upon Sir Thomas Smith. Neither could a blessing from God be hoped for in those buildings which were founded upon the blood of so many Christians. . . .

If through the aforesaid calamities many had not perished we doubt not but there might have been many more than one thousand people in the land when Sir Thomas Smith left the government. But we conceive that when Sir George Yardley arrived governor he found not above four hundred, most of those in want of corn, nearly destitute of cattle, swine, poultry and other necessary provisions to nourish them. . . .

To what growth of perfection the colony hath attained at the end of those [twelve] years we conceive may easily be judged by what we have formerly said. And rather than to be reduced to live under the like government we desire His Majesty that commissioners may be sent over, with authority to hang us.

18. *Social Disorder in Plymouth*, 1620–42

Bradford, *Of Plymouth Plantation*, 77–9, 316–17, 320–2.

BUT THAT which was most sad and lamentable was, that in two or three months' time half of their company died, especially in January and February, being the depth of winter, and wanting houses and other comforts; being infected with the scurvy

and other diseases which this long voyage and their inaccommodate condition had brought upon them. So as there died sometimes two or three of a day in the foresaid time, that of the one hundred and odd persons, scarce fifty remained. And of these, in the time of most distress, there was but six or seven sound persons who . . . spared no pains night nor day, but with abundance of toil and hazard of their own health, fetched them wood, made them fires, dressed them meat, made their beds, washed their loathsome clothes, clothed and unclothed them. In a word, did all the homely and necessary offices for them which dainty and queasy stomachs cannot endure to hear named; and all this willingly and cheerfully. . . . And yet the Lord so upheld these persons as in this general calamity they were not at all infected either with sickness or lameness. And what I have said of these I may say of many others who died in this general visitation, and others yet living; that whilst they had health, yea, or any strength continuing, they were not wanting to any that had need of them. And I doubt not but their recompense is with the Lord. . . .

Marvelous it may be to see and consider how some kind of wickedness did grow and break forth here, in a land where the same was so much witnessed against and so narrowly looked unto, and severely punished when it was known. . . . And yet all this could not suppress the breaking out of sundry notorious sins . . . especially drunkenness and uncleanness. Not only incontinency between persons unmarried, for which many both men and women have been punished sharply enough, but some married persons also. But that which is worse, even sodomy and buggery (things fearful to name) have broke forth in this land oftener than once.

I say it may be justly marveled at and cause us to fear and tremble at the consideration of our corrupt natures, which are so hardly bridled, subdued and mortified; nay, cannot by any other means but the powerful work and grace of God's spirit. But (besides this) one reason may be that the Devil may carry a greater spite against the churches of Christ and the gospel here . . . that he might cast a blemish and stain upon them in the eyes of [the] world. . . .

Another reason may be, that it may be in this case as it is with waters when their streams are stopped or dammed up. When they get passage they flow with more violence and make more noise and disturbance than when they are suffered to run quietly in their own channels. So wickedness being here more stopped by strict laws, . . . it searches everywhere and at last breaks out where it gets vent.

A third reason may be, here . . . is not more evils in this kind, . . . but they are here more discovered and seen and made public. . . . Besides, here the people are but few in comparison of other places which are full and populous and lie hid, as it were, in a wood or thicket, and many horrible evils by that means are never seen nor known; whereas here they are, as it were, brought out into the light and . . . made conspicuous to the view of all. . . .

There was a youth whose name was Thomas Granger. He was servant to an honest man of Duxbury, being about sixteen or seventeen years of age. . . . He was this year detected of buggery, and indicted for the same, with a mare, a cow, two goats, five sheep, two calves and a turkey. Horrible it is to mention, but the truth of the history requires it.

He was first discovered by one that accidentally saw his lewd practice towards the mare. . . . Being upon it examined and committed, in the end he not only confessed the fact with that beast at that time, but sundry times before and at several times with all the rest of the forenamed in his indictment. And this his free confession was not only in private to the magistrates . . . but to sundry, both ministers and others; and afterwards, upon his indictment, to the whole Court and jury; and confirmed it at his execution. And whereas some of the sheep could not so well be known by his description of them, others with them were brought before him and he declared which were they and which were not. And accordingly he was cast by the jury and condemned, and after executed about the 8th of September, 1642. A very sad spectacle it was. For, first the mare and then the cow and the rest of the lesser cattle were killed before his face, according to the law, Leviticus XX. 15, and then he himself was executed. The cattle were all cast into a great and large pit that was digged of purpose for them, and no use made of any part of them. . . .

But it may be demanded how it came to pass that so many wicked persons . . . should so quickly come over into this land . . . seeing it was religious men that began the work and they came for religion's sake? I confess this may be marveled at, at least in time to come, when the reasons thereof should not be known; and the more because here was so many hardships and wants met withal. I shall therefore endeavor to give some answer hereunto.

And first, according to that in the gospel it is ever to be remembered that where the Lord begins to sow good seed, there the envious man will endeavor to sow tares.

Men being to come over in a wilderness, in which much labor and service was to be done about building and planting, etc., such as wanted help in that respect, when they could not have such as they would, were glad to take such as they could; and so, many untoward servants sundry of

them proved, that were thus brought over, both men and womenkind who, when their times were expired, became families of themselves, which gave increase hereunto.

Another and a main reason hereof was that men, finding so many godly disposed persons willing to come into these parts, some began to make a trade of it, to transport passengers and their goods, and hired ships for that end. And then, to make up their freight and advance their profit, cared not who the persons were, so they had money to pay them. And by this means the country became pestered with many unworthy persons who, being come over, crept into one place or other.

Again, the Lord's blessing usually following His people as well in outward as spiritual things . . . do make many to adhere to the People of God, as many followed Christ for the loaves' sake . . . (John vi. 26) and a "mixed multitude" came into the wilderness with the People of God out of Egypt of old. . . . (Exodus xii. 38). So also there were sent by their friends, some under hope that they would be made better; others that they might be eased of such burthens, and they kept from shame at home, that would necessarily follow their dissolute courses. And thus, by one means or other, in twenty years' time it is a question whether the greater part be not grown the worser?

19. *A Letter from Manhattan, 1628*

Reverend Jonas Michaëlius to Reverend Adrianus Smoutius, O'Callaghan, *Documents Relative to the Colonial History of New York*, II, 763–70.

It HAS pleased the Lord, seven weeks after we arrived in this country, to take from me my good partner, who has been to me for more than sixteen years, a virtuous, faithful and in every respect amiable yoke-fellow, and I find myself with three children very much discommoded, without her society and assistance. But what have I to say? The Lord himself has done this, in which

no one can oppose Him. . . . I hope therefore to bear my cross patiently, and by the grace and help of the Lord, not to let the courage fail me which I stand in need of in my particular duties.

The voyage continued long, namely, from the 24th of January till the 7th of April, when we first set our foot upon this land. Of storm and tempest we have had no lack, particularly about the Bermudas and the rough coasts of this country, the which fell hard upon the good wife and children, but they bore it better as regards sea-sickness and fear, than I had expected. Our fare in the ship was very poor and scanty, so that my blessed wife and children, not eating with us in the cabin, on account of the little room in it, had a worse lot than the sailors themselves; and that by reason of a wicked cook who annoyed them in every way; but especially by reason of the captain himself who, although I frequently complained of it in the most courteous manner, did not concern himself in the least, about correcting the rascal. . . .

As to the natives of this country I find them entirely savage and wild, strangers to all decency, yea, uncivil and stupid as posts, proficient in all wickedness and godlessness, devilish men, who serve nobody but the Devil, that is the spirit, which, in their language, they call *Manetto:* under which title they comprehend everything that is subtle and crafty and beyond human skill and power. They have so much witchcraft, divination, sorcery and and wicked tricks that they cannot be held in by any bands or locks. They are as thievish and treacherous as they are tall; and in cruelty they are more inhuman than the people of Barbary and far exceed the Africans. . . . How these people can best be led to the true knowledge of God and of the Mediator, Christ, is hard to say. I cannot myself wonder enough who it is who has imposed so much upon you, Right Reverend, and many others in Fatherland concerning the docility of these people and their good nature . . . , in whom I have as yet been able to discover hardly a single good point, except that they do not speak so jeeringly and so scoffingly of the godlike and glorious majesty of their Creator, as the Africans dare to do. . . . Now, by what means are we to make an inroad or practicable breach for the salvation of this people? . . . .

As to what concerns myself and my household: I find myself by the loss of my good and helping partner very much hindered and distressed,—for my two little daughters are yet small; maidservants are not here to be had, at least none whom they advise me to take; and the Angola slaves are thievish, lazy and useless trash. The young man whom I took with me, I discharged after Whitsuntide, for the reason that I could not employ him out of doors at any working of the land and, indoors, he was a burden to me instead of an assistance. . . .

The promise which the Lords Masters of the Company had made me of some acres or surveyed lands for me to make myself a home . . . is wholly of no avail. For their Honors well know that there are no horses, cows nor laborers to be obtained here for money. . . . The expense would not trouble me, if an opportunity only offered, as it would be for our own accommodation, although there were no profit from it . . . ; for there is here no refreshment of butter, milk, etc., to be obtained, although a very high price be offered for them; for the people who bring them and bespeak them are suspicious of each other. So I will be compelled to pass through the winter without butter and other necessaries which the ships did not bring with them to be sold here. The rations, which are given out and charged for high enough, are all hard stale food, as they are used to on board ship, and frequently this is not very good, and there cannot be obtained as much of it as may be desired. I began to get some strength through the grace of the Lord, but in consequence of this hard fare of beans and grey peas, which are hard enough, barley, stockfish, etc. without much change, I cannot become well as I otherwise would. The summer yields something, but what of that for any one who has no strength? The Indians also bring some things, but one who has no wares, such as knives, beads and the like . . . , cannot have any good of them. . . .

The business of furs is dull on account

of a new war of the ... [Mohawks] against the Mohicans. ... There have occurred cruel murders on both sides. The Mohicans have fled and their lands are unoccupied, and are very fertile and pleasant. It grieves us that there are no people, and that there is no regulation of the Lords Managers to occupy the same.

20. *Indian Entertainment, 1608*

Smith, *Works*, II, 436.

POWHATAN being thirty miles off, was presently sent for; in the meantime, Pocahontas and her women entertained Captain Smith in this manner.

In a fair plain field they made a fire, before which, he sitting upon a mat, suddenly amongst the woods was heard such a hideous noise and shrieking, that the five English betook themselves to their arms, and seized on two or three old men by them, supposing Powhatan with all his power was come to surprise them. But presently Pocahontas came, willing him to kill her if any hurt were intended; and the beholders, which were men, women and children, satisfied the Captain there was no such matter.

Then presently they were presented with this antic; thirty young women came naked out of the woods, only covered behind and before with a few green leaves, their bodies all painted, some of one color, some of another, all differing. Their leader had a fair pair of buck's horns on her head, and an otter's skin at her girdle, and another at her arm, a quiver of arrows at her back, a bow and arrows in her hand. The next had in her hand a sword, another a club, another a pot-stick; the rest, every one, with their several devices.

These fiends with most hellish shouts and cries, rushing from among the trees, cast themselves in a ring about the fire, singing and dancing with most excellent ill variety, oft falling into their infernal passions, and solemnly again to sing and dance. Having spent nearly an hour in this masquerade, as they entered, in like manner they departed.

Having reaccommodated themselves, they solemnly invited him to their lodgings, where he was no sooner within the house, but all these nymphs more tormented him than ever, with crowding, pressing and hanging about him, most tediously crying, "Love you not me? Love you not me?"

This salutation ended, the feast was set, consisting of all the savage dainties they could devise; some attending, others singing and dancing about them; which mirth being ended, with fire-brands instead of torches they conducted him to his lodging.

21. *A Breed of Negroes, 1663*

Josselyn, *Two Voyages to New-England*, 26.

THE SECOND of October, about nine of the clock in the morning, Mr. Maverick's Negro woman came to my chamber window, and in her own country language and tune sang very loud and shrill. Going out to her, she used a great deal of respect towards me, and willingly would have expressed her grief in English. But I apprehended it by her countenance and deportment, whereupon I repaired to my host, to learn of him the cause, and resolved to entreat him in her behalf, for that I understood before that she had been a queen in her own country, and observed a very humble and dutiful garb used towards her by another Negro who was her maid. Mr. Maverick was desirous to have a breed of Negroes, and therefore seeing she would not yield by persuasions to company with a young Negro man he had in his house, he commanded him, willed she nilled she, to go to bed to her, which was no sooner done but she kicked him out again. This she took in high disdain beyond her slavery, and this was the cause of her grief.

22. *Improper Contracts of Marriage, Virginia, 1624*

McIlwaine, *Journals of the House of Burgesses*, I, 121.

WHEREAS to the great contempt of the Majesty of God and ill example to others, certain women within this colony have of late, contrary to the laws ecclesiastical of the Realm of England, contracted themselves to several men at one time, whereby much trouble does grow between parties. ... To prevent the like offense in others hereafter, it is by the Governor and Council ordered in court, that every minister give notice in his church to his parishoners, that what man or woman soever shall hereafter use any word or speech tending to a contract of marriage unto two several persons at one time (though not precise and legal yet so as may entangle and breed struggle in their consciences) shall for such their offense undergo either corporal punishment (as whipping, etc.) or other punishment by fine, or otherwise, according to the quality of the person so offending.

23. *A Governor, on Education, 1671*

W. W. Hening, *Statutes at Large . . . of Virginia* (New York, 1823) II, 511–17.

ENQUIRY: What course is taken about the instructing the people within your government in the Christian religion; and what provision is there made for the paying of your ministry?

Answer: The same course that is taken in England out of towns; every man according to his ability instructing his children. We have forty eight parishes, and our ministers are well paid, and by my consent should be better if they would pray oftener and preach less. But of all other commodities, so of this, the worst are sent us, and we had few that we could boast of, since the persecution in Cromwell's tyranny drove divers worthy men hither. But, I thank God, there are no free schools nor printing, and I hope we shall not have these hundred years; for learning has brought disobedience, and heresy, and sects into the world, and printing has divulged them, and libels against the best government. God keep us from both!

24. *The Infinity of God*

Edward Taylor, *Poetical Works*. T. H. Johnson, ed. (New York, 1939), 31–2.

INFINITY, when all things it beheld,
In Nothing, and of Nothing all did build,

Upon what Base was fixed the Lath,
  wherein

He turned this Globe, and rigalled it so
  trim?
Who blew the Bellows of his Furnace
  Vast?
Or held the Mould wherein the world was
  Cast?
Who laid its Corner Stone? Or whose
  Command?
Where stand the Pillars upon which it
  stands?
Who Lac'de and Fillitted the earth so fine,
With Rivers like green Ribbons Smarag-
  dine?
Who made the Sea's its Selvedge, and it
  locks
Like a Quilt Ball within a Silver Box?
Who Spread its Canopy? Or Curtains
  Spun?
Who in this Bowling Alley Bowld the Sun?
Who made it always when it rises set:
To go at once both down, and up to get?
Who th' curtain rods made for this Tapis-
  try?
Who hung the twinckling Lanthorns in the
  Sky?

Who? who did this? or who is he? Why,
  know
It's Only Might Almighty this did do.
His Hand hath made this noble work
  which Stands
His Glorious Handywork not made by
  hands. . . .
Oh! what a might is this! Whose single
  frown
Doth shake the world as it would shake it
  down?
Which All from Nothing fet, from Noth-
  ing, All:
Hath All on Nothing set, lets Nothing fall.
Gave All to nothing Man indeed, whereby
Through nothing man all might him Glo-
  rify.
In Nothing is embossed the brightest Gem
More precious than all preciousness in
  them.
But Nothing man did throw down all by
  sin:
And darkened that lightsome Gem in him,
    That now his Brightest Diamond is
    Grown
    Darker by far than any Coalpit Stone.

25. *In Memory of a Grandchild, Aged a Year and a Half, 1665*

"In Memory of a Grandchild, Aged a Year and a
Half," 1665, Anne Bradstreet, *Works.* J. H. Ellis,
ed. (New York, edition of 1867; reprinted 1932),
404.

FAREWELL dear babe, my hearts too
  much content,
Farewell sweet babe, the pleasure of mine
  eye,
Farewell fair flower that for a space was
  lent,
Then ta'en away unto Eternity.
Blest babe why should I once bewail thy
  fate,
Or sigh the days so soon were terminate;
Sith thou art settled in an Everlasting
  state.

2.

By nature Trees do rot when they are
  grown.
And plums and apples thoroughly ripe do
  fall,
And corn and grass are in their season
  mown,
And time brings down what is both strong
  and tall.
But plants new set to be eradicate,
And buds new blown, to have so short a
  date,
Is by his hand alone that guides nature
  and fate.

26. *Memorial for a Wife, 1679*

"Memorial for a Wife," 1679, by Joseph Tompson,
in K. B. Murdock, ed., *Handkerchiefs from Paul*
(Cambridge, 1927), 3–5. Reprinted by permission
of the publishers. Copyright by the President and
Fellows of Harvard College.

OF ALL the treasure which this world doth
hold,
True saints are best, whose price tran-
scendeth gold;
And of all comforts which concern this life,
None to be found like to a virtuous wife.
Our proto-parent was environed round
With rarest things, yet no content he found
Till such an one was formed by his side,
With whom he might converse, in whom
confide,
Without which comfort all our sweets are
sours
And families bear thistles without flowers.
And here if anywhere it may be said
Lies the content of her lamenting head,
His dearest choice, his credit and his
crown,
A sweet example to a Christian town,
Whose life was made of innocence and
love,
Whose death doth all to great compassion
move.
Tis hard to tell, where love did bear such
sway,
Who twas commanded or who did obey.
The sweetest titles ever passed between
A Christian pair, and deeds, might here
be seen.
A choicer spirit hardly could be found
For universal virtue on the ground:
One who betimes gave up her virgin heart
To Christ, with solemn vows never to part,
And when she changed her state she did
attend
Such duties as concerned the marriage
end.
With lovely clusters round on every side
The house of God, and hers, she beauti-
fied;
Zeal to whose worship in her constant ways

Makes her an object of transcendent
praise.
What intercourse twixt heaven and her I
guess,
Besides what others did to me confess,
Makes me enroll her real saint indeed,
For whom her turtle may both weep and
bleed.
Ask but the neighborhood and they will
tell
She was a Dorcas in our Israel,
Ready on every hand to run or spend,
To sick and poor to minister and lend,
So amiable in her whole converse,
The least we can is to lament her hearse.
But twas a stock in hand only in trust,
Which to return upon demand is just;
Our interest holds no longer; heaven's de-
cree
Must give a supersedeas unto thee,
Her wedded consort, from those bitter
sighs;
She is above, a mortal that ne'er dies.
Tis true she might have lived many a year
And still have shone in her domestic
sphere; . . .
You might have lived both long and sweet
as ever—
Yet in the end the sword of death must
sever.
The faster love is twisted in the heart,
With roots confirmed, the harder tis to
part.
She might have pined away with tedious
moan,
But her dispatch is quick, she's quickly
gone. . . .
Well may her consort call this Mary's day;
Death's bitterness hath swept his joys away
But let in hers, at once, or let her in
Such chambers where never entered sin.

No tears or pains, nor what brings cross
or woe,
The climate where she is shall ever know.
Should soul and body both possess one
grave,
Relations then could small refreshment
have;
While we discharge poor duties to the
dust,
Her soul triumphant is among the just.
Could heaven one glimpse of passion
once retain,

She'd chide those tears of, and make you
refrain. . . .
Let her example as a copy stand
To childrens' children upon every hand;
Talk of her sayings, one to another tell
What in her life you have observed well;
Follow her steps and imitate her life,
Who was a virtuous virgin, mother, wife.
So when death's summons treats you in
such wise,
You may, with greatest comfort, close your
eyes.

27. *Life of William Phips, 1650–*

Cotton Mather, *Pietas in Patriam, the Life of His Excellency Sir William Phips* (London, 1697), 4–7, 28–30; extracts may be found in K. B. Murdock, ed., *Selections from Cotton Mather* (New York, 1926), 158–62, 187–9.

OUR PHIPS was born February 2, 1650 at a despicable plantation on the river of Kennebec, and almost the furthest village of the eastern settlement of New England. . . . A gunsmith, namely James Phips, once of Bristol, had the honor of being the father to him, whom we shall presently see, made by the God of Heaven as great a blessing to New England, as that country could have had. . . . His fruitful mother, yet living, had no less than twenty-six children, whereof twenty-one were sons; but equivalent to them all was William, one of the youngest, whom, his father dying, left young with his mother, and with her he lived, keeping of sheep in the wilderness, until he was eighteen years old; at which time he began to feel some further dispositions of mind from that providence of God which took him from the sheepfolds . . . and brought him to feed his people. . . .

His friends earnestly solicited him to settle among them in a plantation of the east; but he had an unaccountable impulse upon his mind, persuading him . . . that he was born to greater matters. To come at those greater matters, his first contrivance was to bind himself an apprentice unto a ship-carpenter for four years;

in which time, he became a master of the trade. . . . He then betook himself an hundred and fifty miles further afield, even to Boston, the chief town of New England; which being a place of the most business and resort in those parts of the world, he expected there more commodiously to pursue the . . . hopes [of greater things] which had inspired him. At Boston, where . . . he now learned . . . to read and write, he followed his trade for about a year; and by a laudable deportment, so recommended himself, that he married a young gentlewoman of good repute, who was the widow of one Mr. John Hull, a well-bred merchant. . . .

Within a little while after his marriage he indented with several persons in Boston to build them a ship at Sheepscoat River, two or three leagues eastward of Kennebec, where, having launched the ship, he also provided a lading of lumber to bring with him, which would have been to the advantage of all concerned. But just as the ship was hardly finished, the barbarous Indians on that river broke forth into an open and cruel war upon the English; and the miserable people, surprised by so sudden a storm of blood, had no refuge from the infidels, but the ship now finishing in the harbor. Whereupon he left his intended lading behind him, and instead thereof, carried with him his old neighbors and their families, free of all charges, to Boston. So the first action that he did, after he was his own man, was to save his father's house, with the rest of the neighborhood, from ruin. But the disappointment which befell him from the loss of his other lading, plunged his affairs into greater embarrassments with such as had employed him.

But he was hitherto no more than beginning to make scaffolds for further and higher actions! He would frequently tell the gentlewoman his wife, that he should yet be captain of a King's Ship; that he should come to have the command of better men than he was now accounted himself; and that he should be owner of a fair brick-house in the Green Lane of North Boston; and that, it may be, this would not be all that the providence of God would bring him to. . . . He was of an enterprising genius, and naturally disdained littleness. . . . He would prudently contrive a weighty undertaking and then patiently pursue it unto the end. He was of an inclination, cutting rather like a hatchet than like a razor; he would propose very considerable matters to himself, and then so cut through them that no difficulties could put by the edge of his resolutions.

Being thus of the true temper for doing of great things, he betakes himself to the sea, the right scene for such things; and upon advice of a Spanish wreck about the Bahamas he took a voyage thither; but with little more success than what just served him a little to furnish him for a voyage to England. . . . Having first informed himself that there was another Spanish wreck, wherein was lost a mighty treasure, hitherto undiscovered, he had a strong impression on his mind that he must be the discoverer; and he made such representations of his design at Whitehall, that by the year 1683 he became the captain of a King's Ship, and arrived at New England, commander of the *Algier Rose,* a frigate of eighteen guns and ninety-five men. . . .

[Phips gained his fortune. His own account of his conversion is then quoted.]

The first of God's making me sensible of my sins, was in the year 1674, by hearing . . . [Increase Mather] preach concerning *The Day of Trouble Near.* It pleased Almighty God to smite me with a deep sense of my miserable condition, who had lived until then in the world, and had done nothing for God. I did then begin to think, what I should do to be saved. And did bewail my youthful days, which I had spent in vain: I did think that I would begin to mind the things of God.

Being then some time . . . much troubled with my burden, but thinking on that Scripture, "Come unto me, you that are weary and heavy laden, and I will give you rest," I had some thoughts of drawing as near to the communion of the Lord Jesus as I could. But the ruins which the Indian wars brought on my affairs, and the entanglements which my following the sea laid upon me, hindered my pursuing the welfare of my own soul, as I ought to have done.

At length God was pleased to smile upon my outward concerns. The various providences, both merciful and afflictive, which attended me in my travels, were sanctified unto me, to make me acknowledge God in all my ways. I have divers times been in danger of my life, and I have been brought to see that I owe my life to him that has given a life so often to me. I thank God, he hath brought me to see myself altogether unhappy, without an interest in the Lord Jesus Christ, and to close heartily with him, desiring him to execute all his offices on my behalf. I have now, for some time, been under serious resolutions, that I would avoid whatever I should know to be displeasing unto God, and that I would serve him all the days of my life. I believe no man will repent the service of such a master. . . .

God hath done so much for me, that I

am sensible I owe myself to Him; to Him would I give myself, and all that he has given to me. I can't express His mercies to me. But as soon as ever God had smiled upon me with a turn of my affairs, I had laid myself under the VOWS of the Lord, that I would set myself to serve his people, and churches here, unto the utmost of my capacity.... I knew, that if God had a people anywhere, it was here: and I resolved to rise and fall in with them....

It has been my trouble, that since I came home I have made no more haste to get into the House of God, where I desire to be.... My being born in a part of the country, where I had not in my infancy enjoyed the first sacrament of the New Testament, has been something of a stumbling-block unto me. But though I have had proffers of baptism elsewhere made unto me, I resolved rather to defer it, until I might enjoy it in the communion of these churches; and I have had awful impressions from those words of the Lord Jesus in Matth. 8.38., "Whosoever shall be ashamed of me, and of my words, of him also shall the Son of Man be ashamed." When God had blessed me with something of the world, I had no trouble so great as this, lest it should not be in mercy; and I trembled at nothing more than being put off with a portion here. That I may make sure of better things, I now offer myself unto the communion of this church of the Lord JESUS.

28. A *Wonder-Working Providence, 1630–38*

Edward Johnson, *Wonder-Working Providence 1628–1651* (1654). J. F. Jameson, ed. (New York, 1910), 58–61, 77–8, 85, 187, 198–202.

THOSE honored persons who were now in places of government, having the propagation of the churches of Christ in their eye, labored by all means to make room for inhabitants, knowing well that where the dead carcass is, thither will the eagles resort. But herein they were much opposed by certain persons, whose greedy desire for land much hindered the work for a time.... And let such take notice how these were cured of this distemper; some were taken away by death, and then to be sure they had land enough; others fearing poverty and famishment, supposing the present scarcity would never be turned into plenty, removed themselves away, and so never beheld the great good the Lord hath done for His people.

But the valiant of the Lord waited with patience, and in the miss of beer supplied themselves with water, even the most honored as well as others, contentedly rejoicing in a cup of cold water, blessing the Lord that had given them the taste of that living water.

The women once a day, as the tide gave way, resorted to the mussels and clam banks ... where they daily gathered their families' food with much heavenly discourse of the provisions Christ had formerly made for many thousands of His followers in the wilderness. Quoth one, "My husband hath traveled as far as Plymouth" (which is near forty miles) "and hath with great toil brought a little corn home with him, and before that is spent the Lord will assuredly provide." Quoth the other, "Our last peck of meal is now in the oven at home a baking, and many of our godly neighbors have quite spent all, and we owe one loaf of that little we have.".... And as they were encouraging one another in Christ's careful providing for them, they lift up their eyes and saw two ships coming in, and presently this news came to their ears, that they were come from Ireland full of victuals; now their poor hearts were not so much refreshed in regard of the food they saw they were like to have, as their souls rejoiced in that Christ would now manifest Himself to be the commissary general of this His army, and that He should honor them so far as to be poor sutlers for His camp. . . .

The winter's frost being extracted forth the earth, they fell to tearing up the roots and bushes with their hoes; even such men as scarce ever set hand to labor before, men of good birth and breeding, but coming through the strength of Christ to war their warfare, readily rush through all difficulties. Cutting down of the woods, they enclose corn fields, the Lord having mitigated their labors by the Indians' frequent firing of the woods . . . which makes them thin of timber in many places, like our parks in England. The chiefest corn they planted before they had plows was Indian grain, whose increase is very much beyond all other, to the great refreshing of the poor servants of Christ in their low beginnings. . . .

[In 1638], although the estates of these pilgrim people were much wasted, yet seeing the benefit that would accrue to the churches of Christ and civil government, by the Lord's blessing, upon learning, they began to erect a college, the Lord by His provident hand giving His approbation to the work, in sending over a faithful and godly servant of His, the Reverend Mr. John Harvard, who, joining with the people of Christ at Charlestown, suddenly after departed this life, and gave near a thousand pound toward this work; wherefore the government thought it meet to call it Harvard College in remembrance of him. . . .

And verily, had not the Lord been pleased to furnish New Egnland with means for the attainment of learning, the work would have been carried on very heavily, and the hearts of godly parents would have vanished away with heaviness for their poor children, whom they must have left in a desolate wilderness, destitute of the means of grace.

It being a work . . . past the reach of a poor pilgrim people, who had expended

the greatest part of their estates on a long voyage, . . . knowing likewise, that young students could make but a poor progress in learning, by looking on the bare walls of their chambers, . . . amidst all these difficulties, it was thought meet learning should plead for itself, and . . . plod out a way to live. . . . Upon these resolutions, to work they go, and with thankful acknowledgment, readily take up all lawful means as they come to hand.

For place they fix their eye upon New-Town, which to tell their posterity whence they came, is now called Cambridge, and withal to make the whole world understand, that spiritual learning was the thing they chiefly desired . . . they chose this place, being then under the orthodox and soul-flourishing ministry of Mr. Thomas Shepheard. . . . The situation of this college is very pleasant, at the end of a spacious plain, more like a bowling green than a wilderness, near a fair navigable river, environed with many neighboring towns of note, being so near, that their houses join with her suburbs. . . . It hath the conveniences of a fair hall, comfortable studies and a good library, given by the liberal hand of some magistrates and ministers, with others. . . . The government hath endeavored to grant them all the privileges fit for a college, and accordingly the governor and magistrates, together with the president of the college . . . have a continual care of ordering all matters for the good of the whole. This college hath brought forth, and nursed up very hopeful plants, to the supplying some churches here. . . .

And now all you whose affections are taken with wonderful matters (attend) and you that think Christ hath forgotten his poor despised people (behold) and all you that hopefully long for Christ's appearing to confound antiChrist (consider). And rejoice all ye His churches the world throughout, for the Lamb is preparing His bride. And oh! ye the ancient beloved of Christ, whom He of old led by the hand from Egypt to Canaan, through that great and terrible wilderness, look here. Behold Him whom you have pierced, preparing to pierce your hearts with His Wonder-working Providence, and to provoke you by this little handful of His people to look on Him, and mourn. Yet let no man think these few weak worms would restrain the wonderful works of Christ, as only to themselves, but the quite contrary, these [are] but the porch of His glorious building in hand. . . .

The winter is past, the rain is changed and gone. Come out of the holes of the secret places; fear not because your number is but small. Gather into churches, and let Christ be your king. Ye presbytery, lord it not over them or any churches, but feed every one, that one flock over which Christ hath made you overseers. And ye people of Christ give your presbytery double honors, that they with you may keep the watch of the Lord over His churches. Ye Dutch, come out of your hodge-podge; the great mingle-mangle of religion among you hath caused the churches of Christ to increase so little with you, standing at a stay like corn among weeds. Oh, ye French! fear not the great swarms of locusts, nor the croaking frogs in your land; Christ is reaching out the hand to you; look what He hath done for these English. . . . Ye Germans that have had such a bloody bickering, Christ is now coming to your aid; then cast off your loose and careless kind of reformation, gather into churches and keep them pure, that Christ may delight to dwell among you. Oh Italy! the seat and center of the beast, Christ will now pick out a people from among you for Himself; see here what wonders He works in little time. Oh! ye Spaniards and Portugalls, Christ will show you the abominations of that beastly whore who hath made your nations drunk with the wine of her fornication. Dread not that cruel murderous inquisition, for Christ is now making inquisition for them. . . .

Finally, oh all ye nations of the world,

behold, great is the work of the glorious King of Heaven and Earth hath in hand; beware of neglecting the call of Christ. And you the seed of Israel both less and more, the rattling of your dead bones together is at hand. . . . If Christ hath done such great things for these low shrubs, what will His most admirable, excellent and wonderful work for you be, but as the resurrection from the dead, when all the miraculous acts of His wonderful power showed upon Pharaoh for your forefathers' deliverance shall be swallowed up with those far greater works that Christ shall show for your deliverance upon the whole world; by fires and blood destroying both Pope and Turk, when you shall see great smoke and flames ascending up on high, of that great whore. . . . Then oh! you people of Israel gather together as one man, and grow together as one tree. . . . For Christ the great King of all the earth is now going forth in His great wrath and terrible indignation to avenge the blood of His saints . . . ; and now for the great and bloody battle of Gog and Magog, rivers of blood, and up to the horse-bridles, even the blood of those [who] have drunk blood so long. Oh! dreadful day, when the patience and long-suffering of Christ that hath lasted so many hundreds of years, shall end. What wonderous works are now suddenly to be wrought for the accomplishment of these things!

Then judge all you . . . whether these poor New England people, be not the forerunners of Christ's army, and the marvelous providences which you shall now hear, be not the very finger of God, and whether the Lord hath not sent this people to preach in this wilderness, and to proclaim to all nations, the near approach of the most wonderful works that ever the sons of men saw.

Will you not believe that a nation can be born in a day? Here is a work come very near it. But if you will believe you shall see far greater things than these, and that in very little time.

PART TWO

Provincial Society, 1680-1760

A s THE last quarter of the seventeenth century got under way, a new generation assumed control over colonial affairs in America. The founders, who had been Europeans and thus, to some extent, always strangers in the New World, passed away. The native-born children who took their places viewed the world and themselves in the light of quite different assumptions. Products of the environment in which they lived, these Americans brought into being a new, provincial society.

The next eighty years were a period of constant change and exciting growth. The old established colonies thrived as their population rose and as their wealth increased. To those already in existence in 1680 were added, in the decade that followed, new settlements in Georgia, the Carolinas, and Pennsylvania. By 1760, the line of English colonies stretched from Maine to Georgia, secure, stable, self-confident.

Expansion proceeded along a variety of directions. The old agricultural system grew richer and more diversified. Increasingly its products entered into overseas trade. The coastal towns flourished as markets for these products and as the seats of a trade that enterprising merchants extended to many areas of the world. A strategic situation, and the long succession of European wars, gave the colonists opportunities that they did not forego.

Expansion was also territorial. The fur trade remained important and drew venturesome trappers and traders deep into the interior. The Indian barrier was still there; but steadily the settlers followed along, edging into the mountains and extending westward the areas under cultivation.

Such expansion involved the American colonies in a long series of bitter wars. In Europe through these decades France and England often confronted each other in struggles over dynastic and territorial quarrels. But in the New World these conflicts involved the clash of rival empires. In the North the border of English settlement touched the French establishment in Canada. In the South it encountered the Spaniards. And at its ill-defined western limits it ran into the the contending claims of both rival powers. Down through the middle of the eighteenth century these conflicts were indecisive. But, as the period drew to a close, the wars were approaching a climax that would ultimately expel the French from North America and push the Spaniards decisively southward.

In large measure the English victory was made possible by the vigorous internal development of the colonies which permitted them to supply themselves with some of the resources of war. In the North the free farming system followed trends already clear before 1680. In the South there was a radical shift to the plantation system. Virginia and Maryland had until then been primarily societies of yeoman farmers. Now they embarked upon the production of agricultural staples on large estates, using slaves as their labor force.

The change came first in the new colony of South Carolina and spread from there to the older Chesapeake settlements. The introduction from the West Indies of new tropical crops like rice called for substantial capital investments and therefore for large-scale production. The number of Negroes imported grew and at the same time their status as slaves was defined by law. The result was a highly rationalized mode of production, using large quantities of unskilled labor, subject to the discipline of the plantation. Quickly this system began to dominate the economy of the South. It brought prosperity to the region although, paradoxically, it often also left the planter in debt. More important, it saddled these sectors of American society with the burdens of a slave system, the cost of which was not to emerge for another century.

While the Negro was now more rigidly bound than ever before, other elements in the labor force were consolidating their freedom, and that conformed to the general trend of political development in the period. A variety of political forms could still be found throughout the colonies; some were proprietary, others royal, and still others functioned under their old charters. Nevertheless, certain features were almost universal. Legislative assemblies representing the people, popular local government, and a strong consciousness of personal rights had shown themselves to some degree everywhere. In these years there were few expressions of discontent with the connection with Britain; the Americans were loyal subjects of the Crown. But they were already prompt to resist arbitrary power, and they displayed frequently the inclination to question the authority of the governors as against that of the legislatures.

The political arguments were therefore linked to broad changes in culture which made Americans aware of the differences between the colonies and the mother country. Still healthily respectful of their European antecedents, the Americans were nevertheless increasingly adopting habits of thought and action that set them off from Englishmen.

These changes, even when analogous to those which spread at the same period in Europe, were marked by a distinctive confidence in man's ability to control his environment. Those who were born in the New World and had never known the restrictions of the Old were in awe neither of witches, nor of the devil, nor of the problems of taming the wilderness. All these seemed alike ready to yield to the force of the human will. Already therefore one could discern the outlines of intellectual assumptions that would grow in importance in the future; rationalism, pragmatism, and a willingness to question authority were already elements of the American character.

IV 🌿 *Colonial Expansion*

THE EIGHTY years after 1680 were a period of tremendous growth in the American economy. The productive system consistently displayed a capacity for expansion that was strengthened from a variety of sources.

The availability of land continued to amaze newcomers accustomed to the restrictions of Europe (No. 29). By the middle of the eighteenth century the potential value of the great tracts of empty land was attracting the interest of speculative companies, and the Crown was engaged in an effort to regulate and control land grants (No. 30). Despite the barrier created by powerful Indian tribes in the interior, settlement pushed steadily westward (*see below*, No. 44). The result was a steady rise in population. Although statistics are necessarily vague, every indication points to an upward trend; and contemporary opinion was confident that growth would continue (No. 31).

The rise in numbers was due partly to a high birth rate. It was due also to continued immigration from abroad. The number of indentured servants and Negroes still grew (*see below*, Nos. 47–50). But, in addition, many free men continued to come, as Franklin's Information indicates (No. 32). There were also well-integrated colonies, such as those of the Germans which Pastorius described (No. 33).

The colonial cities also grew, nurtured by thriving overseas commerce. The memorial of the Rhode Island legislature showed the nature of that trade viewed from the perspective of its merchants a few years later (No. 34). The only drawback, then as later, was the threat implicit in the British theories of trade, such as were embodied in the Molasses Act (No. 35). But in these years the necessities of a series of wars prevented the Crown from putting the theories effectively into practice. In any case, the venturesome colonial merchants were not inclined to limit their activities by strict scruples of law. Privateering offered them one kind of opportunity (*see below*, No. 42). Now and then piracy offered them another

(No. 36), in which even the most respectable may have engaged (No. 37). And the Indian trade held forth rich financial and political stakes (No. 38 and *below*, No. 43).

29. *Land in Virginia, 1680*

Durand de Dauphiné, *A Huguenot Exile in Virginia or Voyages of a Frenchman Exiled for His Religion with a Description of Virginia and Maryland.* Gilbert Chinard, ed. (New York, 1934), 143–4.

THE TABLE was immediately set, and after dinner his Excellency asked me what I thought of the country. I told him I considered it very fine and very beautiful, and if the preaching were in French, I would spend there the rest of my life; but that the difference of language would force me either to return to Europe, or to settle in the northern colonies. He replied that he had orders to give each foreigner wishing to settle in his "government" fifty acres of land, but inasmuch as I had left my country for the Religion, as well as because I was recommended by Monsieur Parker, he would give me five hundred. But I would have to settle further back and be among the savages, who, he added, are not greatly to be feared.

But there is some inconvenience owing to the fact that only small boats can sail up the rivers in the back country so one could not trade by water. For this reason, as there are vast tracts of land for sale very cheap, very good and among Christians, he advised me to buy there,

rather than further away. He believed this climate would suit Frenchmen better than Carolina which is too hot, or Pennsylvania and New England, because of the cold.

He had lately received news that there were great numbers [of French people] in England and more kept coming, so that if I wished to return and bring them with ministers, he would serve us to the best of his ability. And as for the pastors, provided that from time to time they preached in English and baptized and married the other Christians who might be among the French settlers, he would give benefices to two or three; and they would be required to read the book of common prayers when preaching, except when they preached to French people only. They could then do as they were accustomed in France.

There was nothing extraordinary in his offer of these lands, except the amount, for in all places under English rule they give each stranger fifty acres out of the land not yet taken up by the inhabitants.

30. *Procedures in Granting Land, 1753 ff*

General instructions to colonial governors, in L. W. Labaree, ed., *Royal Instructions to British Colonial Governors 1670–1776* (New York, 1935), II, 527–8.

AND WHEREAS nothing can more effectually tend to the further improving and settling the said province, the security of the property of our subjects, and the advancement of the revenue of quitrents, than the establishing a regular and proper method of proceeding with respect to the passing of grants of land within the same; it is therefore our will and pleasure that all and every person and persons who shall for the future apply to you for any grants of land shall previous to obtaining the same make it appear before you in council that they are in a condition to cultivate and improve the same by settling thereon in proportion to the quantity of acres a sufficient number of white persons or Negroes. And in case you shall upon a consideration of the circumstances of the person applying for such grants, think it advisable to pass the same, in such case you are to cause a warrant to be drawn up directed to the surveyor general or other proper officer empowering him or them to make a faithful and exact survey of the lands so petitioned for and to return the said warrant within six months at furthest from the date thereof with a plot or description of the land so surveyed thereunto annexed; provided that you do take care that before any such warrant is issued as aforesaid, a docket thereof be entered in the auditor's office; and then the warrant shall be returned by the said surveyor or other proper officer, the grant shall be made out in due form and the terms and conditions required by these our instructions be particularly and expressly mentioned in the respective grants; and it is our further will and pleasure that the said grants shall be registered within six months from the date thereof in our secretary's office there and a docket thereof be also entered in our auditor's office there, or that in default thereof such grants shall be void.

31. *The Increase of Population, 1755*

Benjamin Franklin, "Observations Concerning the Increase of Mankind and the Peopling of Countries," in *Works*. Jared Sparks, ed. (Boston, 1836), II, 313–14, 318–20.

LAND being thus plenty in America, and so cheap as that a laboring man, that understands husbandry, can in a short time save money enough to purchase a piece of new land sufficient for a plantation, whereon he may subsist a family; such are not afraid to marry; for if they even look far enough forward to consider how their children when grown up are to be provided for, they see that more land is to be had at rates equally easy, all circumstances considered.

Hence marriages in America are more general, and more generally early, than in Europe. And if it is reckoned there, that there is but one marriage *per annum* among one hundred persons, perhaps we may here reckon two; and if in Europe they have but four births to a marriage (many of their marriages being late) we may here reckon eight, of which if one half grow up, and other marriages are made, reckoning one with another at twenty years of age, our people must at least be doubled every tweny years.

But notwithstanding this increase, so vast is the territory of North America, that it will require many ages to settle it fully; and till it is fully settled, labor will never be cheap here, where no man continues long a laborer for others, but gets a plantation of his own, no man continues long a journeyman to a trade, but goes among those new settlers, and sets up for himself, etc. Hence labor is no cheaper now in Pennsylvania, than it was thirty years ago, though so many thousand laboring people have been imported. . . .

The importation of foreigners into a country that has as many inhabitants as the present employments and provisions for subsistence will bear, will be in the end no increase of people, unless the newcomers have more industry and frugality than the natives, and then they will provide more subsistence and increase in the country; but they will gradually eat the natives out. Nor is it necessary to bring in foreigners to fill up any occasional vacancy in a country; for such vacancy ... will soon be filled by natural generation. Who can now find the vacancy made in Sweden, France, or other warlike nations, by the plague of heroism forty years ago; in France, by the expulsion of the Protestants; in England, by the settlement of her colonies; or in Guinea, by one hundred years' exportation of slaves that has blackened half America?—The thinness of inhabitants in Spain, is owing to national pride and idleness, and other causes, rather than to the expulsion of the Moors, or to the making of new settlements.

There is, in short, no bound to the prolific nature of plants or animals, but what is made by their crowding and interfering with each other's means of subsistence. Was the face of the earth vacant of other plants, it might be gradually sowed and overspread with one kind only; as for instance, with fennel; and were it empty of other inhabitants, it might in a few ages be replenished from one nation only; as

for instance, with Englishmen. Thus there are supposed to be now upwards of one million English souls in North America, (though it is thought scarce eighty thousand have been brought over sea). And yet perhaps there is not one the fewer in Britain, but rather many more, on account of the employment the colonies afford to manufacturers at home.

This million doubling, suppose but once in twenty-five years, will in another century be more than the people of England, and the greatest number of Englishmen will be on this side the water. What an accession of power to the British Empire by sea as well as land! What increase of trade and navigation! What numbers of ships and seamen! We have been here but little more than one hundred years, and yet the force of our privateers in the late war, united, was greater, both in men and guns, than that of the whole British navy in Queen Elizabeth's time.—How important an affair then to Britain is the present treaty for settling the bounds between her colonies and the French, and how careful should she be to secure room enough, since on the room depends so much the increase of her people.

32. *Information for Immigrants, 1750*

Franklin, "Information to Those Who Would Remove to America," in Sparks, *Works*, II, 468, 469–72.

THE TRUTH is, that though there are in that country few people so miserable as the poor of Europe, there are also few that in Europe would be called rich. It is rather a general happy mediocrity that prevails. There are few great proprietors of the soil, and few tenants; most people cultivate their own lands, or follow some handicraft or merchandise; very few are rich enough to live idly upon their rents or incomes, or to pay the highest prices given in Europe for painting, statues,

architecture, and the other works of art, that are more curious than useful. ...

It can not be worth any man's while, who has a means of living at home, to expatriate himself, in hopes of obtaining a profitable civil office in America; and, as to military offices, they are at an end with the war, the armies being disbanded. Much less is it advisable for a person to go thither, who has no other quality to recommend him but his birth. In Europe it has indeed its value; but it is a commodity that cannot be carried to a worse market than that of America, where people do not inquire concerning a stranger, *What is he?* but, *What can he do?* If he has any useful art, he is welcome; and if he exercises it, and behaves well he will be respected by all that know him; but a mere man of quality who, on that account, wants to live upon the public, by some office or salary, will be despised and disregarded. The husbandman is in honor there, and even the mechanic, because their employments are useful. . . .

With regard to encouragements for strangers from government, they are really only what are derived from good laws and liberty. Strangers are welcome, because there is room enough for them all, and therefore the old inhabitants are not jealous of them; the laws protect them sufficiently, so that they have no need of the patronage of great men; and everyone will enjoy securely the profits of his industry. But, if he does not bring a fortune with him, he must work and be industrious to live. One or two years' residence gives him all the rights of a citizen; but the government does not, at present, whatever it may have done in former times, hire people to become settlers, by paying their passages, giving land, Negroes, utensils, stock, or any other kind of emolument whatsoever. In short, America is the land of labor, and by no means what the English call *Lubberland,* and the French *Pays de Cocagne,* where the streets are said to be paved with half-peck loaves, the houses tiled with pancakes, and where fowls fly about ready roasted, crying *Come eat me!*

Who then are the kind of persons to whom an emigration to America may be advantageous? And what are the advantages they may reasonably expect?

Land being cheap in that country, from the vast forests still void of inhabitants, and not likely to be occupied in an age to come, insomuch that the propriety of an hundred acres of fertile soil full of wood may be obtained near the frontiers,

in many places, for eight or ten guineas, hearty young laboring men, who understand the husbandry of corn and cattle, which is nearly the same in that country as in Europe, may easily establish themselves there. A little money saved of the good wages they receive there, while they work for others, enables them to buy the land and begin their plantation, in which they are assisted by the good-will of their neighbors, and some credit. Multitudes of poor people from England, Ireland, Scotland, and Germany, have by this means in a few years become wealthy farmers, who, in their own countries, where all the lands are fully occupied, and the wages of labor low, could never have emerged from the poor condition wherein they were born. . . .

The increase of inhabitants by natural generation is very rapid in America, and becomes still more so by the accession of strangers; hence there is a continual demand for more artisans of all the necessary and useful kinds, to supply those cultivators of the earth with houses, and with furniture and utensils of the grosser sorts, which cannot so well be brought from Europe. Tolerably good workmen in any of those mechanic arts are sure to find employ, and to be well paid for their work, there being no restraints preventing strangers from exercising any art they understand, nor any permission necessary. If they are poor, they begin first as servants or journeymen; and if they are sober, industrious, and frugal, they soon become masters, establish themselves in business, marry, raise families, and become respectable citizens.

Also, persons of moderate fortunes and capitals, who, having a number of children to provide for, are desirous of bringing them up to industry, and to secure estates for their posterity, have opportunities of doing it in America, which Europe does not afford. There they may be taught and practise profitable mechanic arts, without incurring disgrace on that account, but on the contrary acquiring respect by such abilities. There small capitals laid out in lands, which daily become more valuable by the increase of people, afford a solid prospect of ample fortunes thereafter for those children.

33. *The Germans in Pennsylvania, 1684*

F. D. Pastorius, "Description of Pennsylvania. 1700,"
Old South Leaflets, Vol. IV, No. 95, pp. 4–6, 7–8,
12–13, 15–16.

THE GERMAN SOCIETY commissioned myself, Francis Daniel Pastorius, as their licensed agent, to go to Pennsylvania and to superintend the purchase and survey of their lands. I set out from Frankfurt ..., went to London, where I made the purchase, and then embarked for America. Under the protection of the Almighty, I arrived safely at Philadelphia, and I was enabled to send my report home to Germany on the 7th of March, 1684....

Our first lot in the city is of the following dimensions. It has one hundred feet front, and is four hundred feet deep. Next to it is to be a street; adjoining it lies the second lot of the same size.... Then another street. Lot No. 3 joins this street, its size being the same as the other two. On these lots, we can build two dwellings at each end, making in all, twelve buildings with proper yards and gardens, and all of them fronting on the streets.

For the first few years, little or no profit can reasonably be expected to accrue from these lots, on account of the great scarcity of money in this province, and also, that as yet this country has no goods or productions of any kind to trade with or export to Europe.

Our Governor, William Penn, intends to establish and encourage the growing and manufactory of woolens; to introduce the cultivation of the vine, for which this country is peculiarly adapted, so that our Company had better send us a quantity of wine-barrels and vats of various sorts, also all kinds of farming and gardening implements. *Item,* several iron boilers of various sizes, and copper and brass kettles. *Item,* an iron stove, several blankets and mattresses, also a few pieces of *Barchet* and white linens, which might be sold in our trading-house here, to good advantage....

Another English Company have laid out the new town of *Frankfort,* five miles above Philadelphia, at which, now so flourishing and pleasant place, they have already established several good mills, a glass-house, pottery, and some stores and trading-houses. *New Castle* lies forty miles from the ocean, on the Dellavarra, and has a very good harbor. The town of *Uplandt* is twenty miles above New Castle, on the river, and is a fine large place inhabited mostly by Swedes.

On the twenty-fourth day of October 1685, have I, Francis Daniel Pastorius, with the wish and concurrence of our Governor, laid out and planned a new town, which we called Germantown or Germanopolis, in a very fine and fertile district, with plenty of springs of fresh water, being well supplied with oak, walnut and chestnut trees, and having besides excellent and abundant pasturage for the cattle. At the commencement, there were but twelve families of forty-one individuals, consisting mostly of German mechanics and weavers. The principal street of this, our town, I made sixty feet in width, and the cross street forty feet. The space or lot for each house and garden, I made three acres in size; for my own dwelling, however, six acres.

Before my laying out of this town, I

had already erected a small house in Philadelphia, thirty feet by fifteen in size. The windows, for the want of glass, were made of oiled paper. . . .

I have also obtained fifteen thousand acres of land for our Company, in one tract, with this condition,—that within one year at least thirty families should settle on it; and thus we may, by God's blessing, have a separate German province, where we can all live together in one. . . .

We Christians acknowledge as our Governor and chief magistrate the oft-named and excellent, the Honorable William Penn, to whom this region was granted and given as his own, by His Majesty of England, Charles II, with the express command that all the previous and future colonists should be subject to Penn's laws and jurisdiction.

This wise and truly pious ruler and governor did not, however, take possession of the province thus granted without having first conciliated, and at various councils and treaties duly purchased from the natives of this country the various regions of Pennsylvania. He, having by these means obtained good titles to the province, under the sanction and signature of the native chiefs, I therefore have purchased from him some thirty thousand acres for my German colony.

Now, although the oft-mentioned William Penn is one of the sect of Friends or Quakers, still he will compel no man to belong to his particular society, but he has granted to every one free and untrammeled exercise of their opinions, and the largest and most complete liberty of conscience. . . .

Our German society have in this place now established a lucrative trade in woolen and linen goods, together with a large assortment of other useful and necessary articles, and have entrusted this extensive business to my own direction; besides this they have now purchased and hold over thirty thousand acres of land, for the sake of establishing an entirely German colony. In my newly laid out Germantown, there are already sixty-four families in a very prosperous condition. Such persons, therefore, and all those who still arrive, have to fall to work and swing the axe most vigorously, for wherever you turn the cry is *Itur in antiquam sylvam,* nothing but endless forests; so that I have been often wishing for a number of stalwart Tyrolians, to throw down these gigantic oak and other forest trees, but which we will be obliged to cut down ourselves, by degrees, and with almost incredible labor and exertion; during which we can have a very forcible illustration of the sentence pronounced upon our poor old father Adam, that *in the sweat of his brow he should eat his bread.* To our successors, and others coming after us, we would say, that they must not only bring over money, but a firm determination to labor and make themselves useful to our infant colony. Upon the whole, we may consider that man blessed whom the devil does not find idling. In the meantime, we are employing the wild inhabitants as day-laborers, for which they are, however, not much inclined; and we ourselves are gradually learning their language, so as to instruct them in the religion of Christ, inviting them to attend our church services, and therefore have the pleasing hope that the spirit of God may be the means of enlightening many of these poor heathens unto their souls' salvation. To Him be honor, praise, thanks, and glory, forevermore. Amen.

34. *Rhode Island Remonstrance, 1764*

"Remonstrance of the Colony of Rhode Island to the Lords Commissioners of Trade and Plantations," in J. R. Bartlett, ed., *Records of the Colony of Rhode Island and Providence Plantations in New England* (Providence, 1861), VI, 378–81.

THE GOVERNOR and Company of the English colony of Rhode Island and Providence Plantations ... presume to offer some considerations drawn from the particular state and circumstances of said colony, against the renewal of ... [the sugar] act.

In doing this, it is hoped that the interest and advantage of the mother country, will be found to coincide with that of the colony, in the extinction of a law, conceived to be prejudicial to both.

The colony of Rhode Island included not a much larger extent of territory than about thirty miles square; and of this, a great part is a barren soil, not worth the expense of cultivation. The number of souls in it amount to forty-eight thousand, of which the two seaport towns of Newport and Providence, contain near one-third. The colony hath no staple commodity for exportation, and does not raise provisions sufficient for its own consumption. Yet, the goodness of its harbors, and its convenient situation for trade, agreeing with the spirit and industry of the people, hath in some measure supplied the deficiency of its natural produce, and provided the means of subsistence to its inhabitants.

By a moderate calculation, the quantity of British manufactures and other goods of every kind imported from Great Britain, and annually consumed in this colony, amount at least to £120,000 sterling, part of which is imported directly into the colony. But as remittances are more easily made to the neighboring provinces of the Massachusetts Bay, Pennsylvania and New York, than to Great Britain, a considerable part is purchased from them.

This sum of £120,000, sterling, may be considered as a debt due from the colony, the payment of which is the great object of every branch of commerce, carried on by its inhabitants, and exercises the skill and invention of every trader.

The only articles produced in the colony, suitable for a remittance to Europe, consist of some flax seed and oil, and some few ships built for sale; the whole amounting to about £5,000, sterling, per annum. The other articles furnished by the colony for exportation, are some lumber, cheese and horses; the whole amount of all which together bears but a very inconsiderable proportion to the debt contracted for British goods. It can therefore be nothing but commerce which enables us to pay it.

As there is no commodity raised in the colony suitable for the European market, but the few articles aforementioned; and as the other goods raised for exportation will answer at no market but in the West Indies, it necessarily follows that the trade thither must be the foundation of all our commerce; and it is undoubtedly true, that solely from the prosecution of this trade with the other branches that are pursued in consequence of it, arises the ability to pay for such quantities of British goods.

It appears from the customhouse books, in Newport, that from January, 1763, to January, 1764, there were one hundred and eighty-four sail of vessels bound on foreign voyages; that is, to Europe, Africa and the West Indies; and three hundred and fifty-two sail of vessels employed in the coasting trade; that is, between Georgia and Newfoundland, inclusive; which, with the fishing vessels, are navigated by at least twenty-two hundred seamen.

Of these foreign vessels, about one hundred and fifty are annually employed in the West India trade, which import into this colony about fourteen thousand hogsheads of molasses; whereof, a quantity, not exceeding twenty-five hundred hogsheads, come from all the English islands together.

It is this quantity of molasses which serves as an engine in the hands of the merchant to effect the great purpose of paying for British manufactures. For, part of it is exported to the Massachusetts Bay, to New York and Pennsylvania, to pay for British goods, for provisions and for many articles which compose our West India cargoes; and part to the other colonies, southward of these last mentioned, for such commodities as serve for a remittance immediately to Europe; such as rice, naval stores, etc., or such as are necessary to enable us to carry on our commerce; the remainder (besides what is consumed by the inhabitants) is distilled into rum, and exported to the coast of Africa; nor will this trade to Africa appear to be of little consequence, if the following account of it be considered.

Formerly, the Negroes upon the coast were supplied with large quantities of French brandies; but in the year 1723, some merchants in this colony first introduced the use of rum there, which, from small beginnings soon increased to the consumption of several thousand hogsheads yearly; by which the French are deprived of the sale of an equal quantity of brandy. And as the demand for rum is annually increasing upon the coast, there is the greatest reason to think, that in a few years, if this trade be not discouraged, the sale of French brandies there will be entirely destroyed. This little colony, only, for more than thirty years past, has annually sent about eighteen sail of vessels to the coast, which have carried about eighteen hundred hogsheads of rum, together with a small quantity of provisions

and some other articles, which have been sold for slaves, gold dust, elephant's teeth, camwood, etc. The slaves have been sold in the English islands, in Carolina and Virginia, for bills of exchange, and the other articles have been sent to Europe. And by this trade alone, remittances have been made from this colony to Great Britain, to the value of about £ 40,000, yearly; and this rum, carried to the coast, is so far from prejudicing the British trade thither, that it may be said rather to promote it; for as soon as our rum vessels arrive, they exchange away some of the rum with the traders from Britain, for a quantity of dry goods, with which each of them sort their cargoes to their mutual advantage.

Besides this method of remittance by the African trade, we often get bills of exchange from the Dutch colonies of Surinam, Barbice, etc.; and this happens when the sales of our cargoes amount to more than a sufficiency to load with molasses; so that, in this particular, a considerable benefit arises from the molasses trade, for these bills being paid in Holland, are the means of drawing from that republic so much cash yearly, into Great Britain, as these bills amount to.

From this deduction of the course of our trade, which is founded in exact truth, it appears that the whole trading stock of this colony, in its beginning, progress and end is uniformly directed to the payment of the debt contracted by the importation of British goods; and it also clearly appears, that without this trade, it would have been and always will be, utterly impossible for the inhabitants of this colony to subsist themselves, or to pay for any considerable quantity of British goods.

It hath been observed before, that of fourteen thousand hogsheads of molasses annually brought into this colony, not more than twenty-five hundred have been imported from the English islands; and it may be further added, that all these islands together do not make for exportation, more than two-thirds of the quantity of molasses annually imported into this colony for many years past. Of consequence, about eleven thousand five hundred hogsheads must have been brought from foreign plantations.

The present price of molasses is about twelve pence, sterling, per gallon; at which rate, only, it can be distilled into rum for exportation. Wherefore, if a duty should be laid on this article, the enhanced price may amount to a prohibition; and it may with truth be said, that there is not so large a sum of silver and gold circulating in the colony, as the duty imposed by the aforesaid act upon foreign molasses, would amount to in one year, which makes it absolutely impossible for the importers to pay it. . . .

Should the aforesaid act be revived and carried into execution, the colony will be reduced to the most deplorable condition.

There are upwards of thirty distil houses (erected at a vast expense; the principal materials of which, are imported from Great Britain), constantly employed in making rum from molasses. This distillery is the main hinge upon which the trade of the colony turns, and many hundreds of persons depend immediately upon it for a subsistence. These distil houses, for want of molasses, must be shut up, to the ruin of many families, and of our trade in general; particularly, of that to the coast of Africa, where the French will supply the natives with brandy, as they formerly did. Two-thirds of our vessels will become useless, and perish upon our hands. Our mechanics, and those who depend upon the merchant for employment, must seek for subsistence elsewhere. And what must very sensibly affect the present and future naval power and commerce of Great Britain, a nursery of seamen, at this time consisting of twenty-two hundred, in this colony only, will be in a manner destroyed. And as an end will be put to our commerce, the merchants cannot import any more British manufactures, nor will the people be able to pay for those they have already received.

35. *Molasses Act, 1733*

"An Act for the better securing and encouraging the Trade of His Majesty's Sugar Colonies in America," 6 Geo. II, c. 13 (1733), *Statutes at Large* (London, 1786), V, 616–18.

WHEREAS the welfare and prosperity of Your Majesty's sugar colonies in America are of the greatest consequence and importance to . . . this kingdom: and whereas the planters of the said sugar colonies . . . are unable to improve or carry on the sugar trade upon an equal footing with the foreign sugar colonies . . . : for remedy whereof . . . be it enacted . . . , That from and after the twenty-fifth day of December one thousand seven hundred and thirty-three, there shall be raised, levied, collected and paid, unto and for the use of His Majesty . . . , upon all rum or spirits of the produce or manufacture of any of the colonies or plantations in America, not in the possession or under the dominion of His Majesty . . . , which . . . shall be imported or brought into any of the colonies or plantations in America, which now are or hereafter may be in the possession or under the dominion of His Majesty . . . , the sum of nine pence, money of Great Britain, to be paid according to the proportion and value of five shillings and six pence the ounce in silver, for every gallon thereof, and after that rate for any greater or lesser quantity; and upon all molasses or syrups of such foreign produce or manufacture as aforesaid, which shall be imported or brought into any of the said colonies or plantations of or belonging to His Majesty, the sum of six pence of like money for every gallon thereof . . . ; and upon all sugars . . . of such foreign growth, produce or manufacture as aforesaid, which shall be imported into any of the said colonies or plantations of or belonging to His Majesty, a duty after the rate of five shillings of like money, for every hundred weight avoirdupois. . . .

And be it further enacted . . . , That from and after . . . (December 25, 1733) . . . , no sugars, paneles, syrups or molasses, of the growth, product and manufacture of any of the colonies or plantations in America, nor any rum or spirits of America, except of the growth or manufacture of His Majesty's sugar colonies there, shall be imported by any person or persons whatsoever into the Kingdom of Ireland, but such only as shall be fairly and bona fide loaden and shipped in Great Britain in ships navigated according to the several laws now in being in that behalf, under the penalty of forfeiting all such sugar, paneles, syrups or molasses, rum or spirits, or the value thereof, together with the ship or vessel in which the same shall be imported. . . .

And it is hereby further enacted . . . , That in case any sugar or paneles of the growth, produce or manufacture of any of the colonies or plantations belonging to or in the possession of His Majesty . . . , which shall have been imported into Great Britain after the twenty-fourth day of June one thousand seven hundred and thirty-three, shall at any time within one year after the importation thereof, be again exported out of Great Britain, and that due proof be first made, by certificate from the proper officers, of the due entry and payment of the subsidies or duties charged or payable upon the importation thereof, together with the oath of the merchant or his agent importing and exporting the same, or in case such merchant or agent shall be one of the people called Quakers, by his solemn affirmation to the truth thereof, and that all other requisites shall be performed that are by law to be performed in cases where any of the said subsidies or duties are to be paid by any former statute, all the residue and remainder of the subsidy or duty, by any former act or acts of parliament granted and charged on such sugar or paneles as aforesaid, shall without any delay or reward be repaid to such merchant or merchants, who do export the same, within one month after demand thereof.

36. *Piracy and Privateering,* 1691

"Declaration of Jeremiah Tay and Others. March, 1691 (?)," J. F. Jameson, *Privateering and Piracy in the Colonial Period: Illustrative Documents* (New York, 1923), 147–9.

Declaration of Jeremiah Tay and Others. March, 1691

AN ACCOUNT of the surprisal and taking of the ship *Good Hope* of Boston in New England, burthen about three hundred tons with twenty-two guns, Jeremiah Tay commander, which was acted and done in a most treacherous and piratical manner by certain rovers or pirates (most of them Their Majesties' subjects) in the Road of the Isle of May of the Cape de Verde Islands upon the fourth day of February Anno Domini 1690/1. . . .

Upon the twenty-eighth day of January 1690/1 we arrived from the Island of Madeira at said Island of May aforesaid and came to anchor in the road there. The next day our men went ashore and applied themselves to rake together of salt in the salt pounds in order to the loading our said ship and so continued working several days. And upon the first day of

February following there came into the aforesaid road a sloop wearing their Majesties' colors and anchored not far from our said ship, who told us they came from South Carolina, their captain one James Allison formerly of New York, and that they had a commission from the governor of Carolina aforesaid to take and indamage the French, for which end they were here arrived, expecting they might in a short time meet some of them.

The said Captain Allison and most part of his company were well known unto us, they having been logwood cutters in the Bay of Campeche [Yucatan] where we were with the said ship about twelve months since, loading logwood, part whereof we bought of them and fully satisfied them for, and during our stay there kept amicable correspondence with us, eating, drinking and lodging frequently on board our said ship, which we gladly consented unto in regard they might have been a defense and help to us if any enemy had assaulted us. By reason of which former friendship and good correspondence as also their specious pretense of a commission against our enemies (which we were in some fears of) we willingly continued the former kindness and amity between us, hoping if we were assaulted by the French we might by their assistance (they being thirty-five able men and our ship being of pretty good force) have been capable to make a good resistance, they often protesting and promising to stand by and help us to the utmost if there should be occasion.

We therefore, not doubting their honesty and sincerity, permitted them frequently to come on board our said ship, and sometimes some of us went on board their sloop, and believing ourselves secure and willing to make a quick dispatch as possible in loading our ship, we sent all [hands] to work in the pounds (as we [had done?] he[retof]ore) except our [carpenter]s, which were [then?] at work on our deck building a boat for the more convenient carriage of salt. Thus we continued

working, and upon the fourth day of February instant Capt. Allison and sundry of his men dined with us on board said ship in a friendly manner, as they were wont to do, and some time after dinner desired the said Commander Tay, with Mr. Edward Tyng the supercargo and James Meeres a passenger, to go on board their sloop to drink a glass of punch with them, which he did, and when we were come on board the said sloop they pretended their doctor (whom we left on board the ship talking with our men) had the keys where their sugar was, so they could not make the punch, and forthwith several of them stepped into the boat and rowed on board our ship to fetch the keys.

As soon as they entered our ship one of them ran to the steerage door and another to the round house and secured all our arms, the rest immediately seizing the carpenters who were at work on the boat. They then fired a gun as a signal to their sloop, who immediately seized us who were on board her (we being unarmed) and forthwith weighed anchor and laid our ship aboard, at the same time taking everything out of the sloop, excepting a little stinking brackish water, some flour, a little stinking beef and three or four bags of wheat, and then commanded us presently to put off from the ship about musket shot and then to come to anchor, which we were forced to comply with; after which they went on shore and fetched our men out of the pounds by force and arms, seventeen of whom they took with them, some whereof by force and threatenings and others of them went voluntarily, which we have good reason to believe were privy to the plot and surprisal of the ship, a list of whose names is hereto subjoined. Afterward they gave us our chests and some of our clothes and the next day commanded us to sail away with the said sloop (which they gave us), and upon the sixth day of February instant we sailed with said sloop for the Island of Barbados where we arrived the twenty-first day of the same.

37. *Captain Kidd's Complaint,* 1701

"William Kidd to the Speaker of the House of Commons, (Robert Harley), April (?), 1701," Jameson, *Privateering,* 250–2.

MAY IT PLEASE YOUR HONOR:

The long imprisonment I have undergone, or the trial I am to undergo, are not so great an affliction to me, as my not being able to give your Honorable House of Commons such satisfaction as was expected from me. I hope I have not offended against the law, but if I have, it was the fault of others who knew better, and made me the tool of their ambition and avarice, and who now perhaps think it their interest that I should be removed out of the world.

I did not seek the commission I undertook, but was partly cajoled, and partly menaced into it by the Lord Bellomont, and one Robert Livingston of New York, who was the projector, promoter and chief manager of that design, and who only can give your House a satisfactory account of all the transactions of my owners. He was the man admitted into their closets, and received their private instructions, which he kept in his own hands, and who encouraged me in their names to do more than I ever did, and to act without regard to my commission. I would not exceed my authority, and took no other ships than such as had French passes, which I brought with me to New England, and relied upon for my justification. But my Lord Bellomont seized upon them together with my cargo, and though he promised to send them into England, yet has he detained part of the effects, kept these passes wholly from me, and has stripped me of all the defense I have to make, which is such barbarous, as well as dishonorable usage, as I hope your Honorable House will not let an Englishman suffer, how unfortunate soever his circumstances are; but will intercede with His Majesty to defer my trial till I can have those passes, and that Livingston may be brought under your examination, and confronted by me.

I cannot be so unjust to myself, as to plead to an indictment till the French passes are restored to me, unless I would be accessory to my own destruction. For, though I can make proof that the ships I took had such passes, I am advised by Council, that it will little avail me without producing the passes themselves. I was in great consternation when I was before that great assembly, Your Honorable House, which with the disadvantages of a mean capacity, want of education, and a spirit cramped by long confinement, made me uncapable of representing my case; and I have therefore presumed to send Your Honor a short and true state of it, which I humbly beg Your Honor's perusal, and communication of to the House, if you think it worthy their notice.

I humbly crave leave to acquaint Your Honor that I was not privy to my being sent for up to your House the second time, nor to the paper lately printed in my name (both which may justly give offense to the House). But I owe the first to a coffeeman in the Court of Wards who designed to make a show of me, for his profit; and the latter was done by one Newy, a prisoner in Newgate, to get money for his support, at the hazard of my safety.

I humbly beg the compassion and protection of the Honorable House of Commons, and Your Honor's intercession with them on behalf of

Your Honor's
Most Dutiful and Distressed Servant
WM. KIDD

38. *Politics and Indian Trade, 1735*

Peter Wraxall, *An Abridgment of the Indian Affairs.*
C. H. McIlwain, ed. (Cambridge, 1915), 194–6. Reprinted by permission of the publisher. Copyright by
the President and Fellows of Harvard College.

GOVERNOR COSBY meets the Six Nations at Albany and speaks to them in manner following:

He pays them the compliments of condolence upon the loss of those of their people who are deceased since his last meeting them. He renews the covenant with them in behalf of all His Majesty's subjects in North America.

He repeats to them all the advantages they reap by the garrison at Oswego and tells them he expects they will on all occasions be ready to defend it. He exhorts them not to suffer the French to build any trading house or forts on their land, which he tells them they have put under the protection of the King of Great Britain.

He thanks them for their kindness to the traders, and tells them they must be sensible that when the King of Great Britain is at war with the King of France how unable the French are to supply them with goods; and says, "You very well know, that the French themselves in Canada could not have subsisted, had they not been supplied from Albany."

That he rejoices to hear of their inclination to peace with the southern Indians, he presses that matter upon them and desires they will name a time when they are willing to meet delegates from those Indians at Albany and he will write to the Governor near whose provinces they reside in order to bring this peace to a final issue.

He acquaints them with the treaty lately made by the Commissioners with the Canada Indians and delivers them the calumet which they left to be lodged at Onondaga.

He tells them the King has ordered him to give them several presents in his name, which they shall receive as soon as they give him their answer.

The Six Nations answer the Governor's speech. They return their compliments of condolence.

They promise the covenant shall be kept inviolable on their side. As to the garrison and trade at Oswego, they say when a number of traders are there goods are sold cheap, but when there is but a trader or two, they are cheated,—not only the Six Nations but the far Indians; and instead of pure rum they receive half water. This they say makes them appear as liars to the far Indians who come there upon their encouragement.

They say: "Brother, you told us that you would not suffer any French to go up the River Oswego. We suppose you are in a mistake in that affair. *For the trade and peace we take to be one thing* for here have lately been Indians from Canada to renew their old friendship. Therefore no passages ought to be stopped where messengers come through to make peace. Perhaps far Indians may want to come to Albany or to some of the Six Nations to make peace."

The Governor said he did not mean to hinder any Indians from coming to them, but to prevent the French from coming amongst them to infuse lies and prejudice them against this government.

They proceed and say: "You command that we should not suffer the French priest or any other French to live among us on this side of the Lake [Ontario]. Brother Corlaer, We take narrow notice of it, it's as if you on one side and the French on the other will press us out of our lands. We are like dumb people not knowing what ails us. But we promise we shall not consent to any French living among us or to settle on this side of the lake."

V 🪷 *International Conflicts in America*

A LONG SERIES of colonial wars occupied the great powers of Europe throughout this period. The battles for empire were fought in many parts of the world, but nowhere as bitterly as in North America. Here the westward surge of English settlement brought the colonists to points of occasional contact with the French, ambitious to unite the St. Lawrence with the Gulf of Mexico; and also with the Spaniards looking northward from Florida and Mexico. These rivalries were embittered by religious differences as well as by dynastic quarrels in Europe. By 1760, however, the English were approaching a victory that would give them dominance on the continent north of Mexico.

The colonists themselves were always involved. In New England they hated the French for their Catholicism, for their encouragement to Indians who raided the Yankee settlements, and for their rivalry in trade. These emotions were early expressed by Sir William Phips who himself led an expedition to the northward (No. 39). A half century later similar considerations still animated British policy (No. 40). In the South the Spaniards were the foe; a vivid Memorial from South Carolina exposes the bitterness of the colonists in the long struggle to hold on to their position (No. 41).

No means were disregarded in the wars. On the sea, provincial privateers were often active (No. 42). In the interior there were strenuous efforts to attract Indian allies (No. 43); and, in addition, the government attempted to control strategic sites with forts that might serve a trading as well as military purpose (No. 44; *see also above*, No. 38). But often the man power of the colonies was itself most useful, as in the capture of the great French post at Louisbourg (No. 45). In the process, the settlers acquired experience and self-confidence, the consequences of which became more important in later decades.

39. *Canada and New England's Miseries, 1690*

Cotton Mather, *Pietas in Patriam*, 33–5, 37, 38, 39–41; extracts in Murdock, *Mather*, 193–202.

IT WAS Canada that was the chief source of New England's miseries. There was the main strength of the French; there the Indians were mostly supplied with ammunition; thence issued parties of men, who uniting with the savages, barbarously murdered many innocent New Englanders, without any provocation on the New-English part, except this, that New England had proclaimed King William and Queen Mary, which they said were usurpers. And as Cato could make no speech in the Senate without that conclusion, *Delenda est Carthago* [Carthage must be destroyed], so it was the general conclusion of all that argued sensibly about the safety of that country, *Canada must be reduced*. It then became the concurring resolution of all

New England, with New York, to make a vigorous attack upon Canada at once, both by sea and land.

And a fleet was accordingly fitted out from Boston, under the command of Sir William Phips, to fall upon Quebec, the chief city of Canada. They waited until August for some stores of war from England. . . . But none at last arriving, and the season of the year being so far spent, Sir William could not, without many discouragements upon his mind, proceed in a voyage, for which he found himself so poorly provided. However, the ships being taken up, and the men on board, his usual courage would not permit him to desist from the enterprise; but he set sail from Hull near Boston, August 9, 1690, with a fleet of thirty-two ships and tenders. . . .

He so happily managed his charge, that they every one of them arrived safe at anchor before Quebec, although they had as dangerous, and almost untrodden a path, to take unpiloted, for the whole voyage, as ever any voyage was undertaken with. Some small French prizes he took by the way, and set up English colors upon the coast, here and there, as he went along. . . .

It was the fifth of October, when a fresh breeze coming up at east, carried them . . . up to the Isle of Orleans; and then haling southerly, they passed by the east end of that island, with the whole fleet approaching the city of Quebec. This loss of time, which made it so late before the fleet could get into the country, where a cold and fierce winter was already very far advanced, gave no very good prospect of success to the expedition. But that which gave a much worse, was a most horrid mismanagement, which had, the meanwhile, happened in the west. For a thousand English from New York and Albany and Connecticut, with fifteen hundred Indians, were to have gone overland to the west and fallen upon Montreal, while the fleet was to visit Quebec in the east; and no expedition could have been better laid than this, which was thus contrived. But those English companies in the west, marching as far as the great lake that was to be passed, found their canoes not provided according to expectation; and the Indians also were (How? God knows, and will one day judge!) dissuaded from joining with the English; and the army met with such discouragements, that they returned.

Had this western army done but so much as continued at the lake, the diversion thereby given to the French . . . would have rendered the conquest of Quebec easy and certain. But the governor of Canada being informed of the retreat made by the western army, had opportunity, by the cross winds that kept back the fleet, unhappily to get the whole strength of all the country into the city, before the fleet could come up into it. . . .

General Phips now saw that it must cost him dry blows, and that he must roar his persuasions out of the mouths of great guns, to make himself master of a city which had certainly surrendered itself unto him, if he had arrived but a little sooner. . . . Wherefore, on the seventh of October, the English, that were for the land service, went on board their lesser vessels, in order to land. . . . But so violent was the storm of wind all this day, that it was not possible for them to land until the eighth of October; when the English counting every hour to be a week until they were come to battle, vigorously got ashore, designing to enter the east end of the city.

The small-pox had got into the fleet, by which distemper prevailing, the number of effective men which now went ashore, under the command of Lieutenant-General Walley, did not amount unto more than fourteen hundred; but four companies of these were drawn out as forlorns [vanguards] whom, on every side, the enemy fired at. Nevertheless, the English rushing with a shout at once upon them, caused them to run as fast as legs could carry them: so that the whole English army . . . marched on until it was dark, having first killed many of the French, with the loss of but four men of their own; and frighted about seven or eight hundred more of the French from an ambuscado, where they lay ready to fall upon them.

But some thought, that by staying in the valley, they took the way never to get over the hill. And yet for them to stay where they were, till the smaller vessels came up the river before them, so far as by their guns to secure the passage of the army in their getting over, was what the council of war had ordered. . . .

This evening a French deserter coming to them, assured them . . . that Count Frontenac was come down to Quebec with no fewer than thirty hundred men to defend the city, having left but fifty soldiers to defend Montreal. . . . Notwithstanding this dispiriting information, the common soldiers did with much vehemency beg and pray, that they might be led on, professing, that they had rather lose their lives on the spot, than fail of taking the city. But the more wary commanders considered how rash a thing it would be, for about fourteen hundred raw men, tired with a long voyage, to assault more than twice as many expert soldiers, who were . . . cocks crowing on their own dunghill . . . ; look on one side or t'other, all was full of hostile difficulties. . . .

But in this time, General Phips and his men of war, with their canvas wings, flew close up unto the west end of the city, and there he behaved himself with the greatest bravery imaginable; nor did the other men of war forbear to follow his brave example. . . .

He lay within pistol-shot of the enemy's cannon, and beat them from thence, and very much battered the town, having his own ship shot through in almost an hundred places with four-and-twenty-pounders, and yet but one man was killed, and only two mortally wounded aboard him, in this hot engagement, which continued the greatest part of that night, and several hours of the day ensuing. But wondering that he saw no signal of any effective ac-

tion ashore at the east end of the city, he sent that he might know the condition of the army there; and received answer, that several of the men were so frozen in their hands and feet, as to be disabled from service, and others were apace falling sick of the small-pox. Whereupon he ordered them immediately to refresh themselves, and he intended then to have renewed his attack upon the city, in the method of landing his men in the face of it, under the shelter of his great guns; having to that purpose provided also a considerable number of well-shaped wheel-barrows, each of them carrying two petarraros [cannons] apiece, to march before the men and make the enemy fly. . . .

The army now on board continued still resolute and courageous, and on fire for the conquest of Quebec; or if they had missed of doing it by storm, they knew that they might, by possessing themselves of the Isle of Orleans, in a little while have starved them out. . . . And still they were loath to play for any lesser game than the immediate surrender of Quebec itself. But ere a full council of war could conclude the next steps to be taken, a violent storm arose that separated the fleet, and the snow and the cold became so extreme, that they could not continue in those quarters any longer.

Thus, by an evident Hand of Heaven, sending one unavoidable disaster after another, as well-formed an enterprise, as perhaps was ever made by the New Englanders, most unhappily miscarried; and General Phips underwent a very mortifying disappointment of a design, which his mind was, as much as ever any, set upon. He arrived November 19 at Boston, where . . . he had this to comfort him, that neither his courage nor his conduct could reasonably have been taxed. Nor could it be said that any man could have done any more than he did, under so many embarrassments of his business, as he was to fight withal.

40. *The Importance of Cape Breton to the British, 1744*

"A Memorial of Robert Auchmuty, Judge of His Majesty's Court of Vice-Admiralty for Massachusetts and New Hampshire, April 9, 1744." Massachusetts Historical Society, *Collections*, Vols. V–VI (1798), 202–5.

THIS island, situated between Newfoundland and Nova Scotia, the English exchanged with the French for Placentia, in the Treaty of Utrecht; and during the late peace between the two nations, the French, by the advantage of the place, carried on an unbounded fishery, annually employing at least a thousand sail . . . and twenty thousand men. . . . How dangerous a nursery of seamen this island, therefore, has been, and ever will be, while in their possession, is too obvious to a British constitution. And it is as demonstrable, the recovery of a place of this consequence will entirely break up their fishery, and destroy this formidable seminary of seamen. For, if they are happily removed from this advantageous shelter, no protection is left for them on the fishing ground nearer than Old France. Therefore they will not expose themselves to the frequent surprises and captures of the English . . . but finally will be obliged to quit the undertaking, leaving the English in the sole possession of this most valuable branch of trade, which annually will return to the English nation two millions sterling for the manufactures yearly shipped to her plantations, and constantly employ thousands of families, otherwise unserviceable to the public, and greatly increase shipping and navigation and mariners. It is further to be observed, while the English solely supply foreign markets with this commodity, Roman Catholic countries must have a sort of dependency on them.

Moreover, the acquisition of this important island cuts off all communication between France and Quebec . . . and must obstruct the French navigation through the Bay of St. Lawrence to the only possessions the French have upon the sea coast to the northward of Louisiana, in the great bay of Mexico. By this means, Quebec must, in the run of very little time, fall into the hands of the English; and the Indians, wanting the usual protection and supplies from France, will be obliged to court the English for both; and having once experienced the treatment of both nations, as the latter can supply them better and cheaper than the former, they will consequently be riveted in interest to her; and thus the English will render themselves entirely masters of the rich and profitable fur trade, at present chiefly engrossed by the French.

But the consideration alone, that the British navigation and settlements on the sea coasts, throughout North America, at present lie terribly exposed to men of war and privateers from this island, claims an attention to proper measures for immediately regaining possession of it. For from thence the French . . . may . . . intercept the navigation between England and all her plantations, and . . . between one plantation and another; . . . and from its vicinity with the continent may, with the like ease, surprise our settlements all along the coast, and take the mast ships when loaded out of Casco and Portsmouth harbors. Whereas, the accession of this island to the British dominions, will not only secure our navigation, and guard our coasts in America, but will be a safe retreat for our men of war in the hurricane months, or when threatened with a superior force. Besides, there they, with greater safety and less expense to the Crown, may refit, than in any other harbor in North America.

The expense and danger in taking this place will bear no proportion to the advantages and profits thereby resulting to the English nation and her plantations. To favor, therefore, an enterprise of so much consequence, it is humbly proposed that proper laws should be enacted, making it felony, without benefit of the clergy, in North America, to supply the enemy with warlike stores, provisions, etc.

And whereas Virginia, Maryland, New York, Massachusetts-Bay and Canso, in time of peace usually have each a station ship of twenty guns, it is humbly proposed to add to each, one of fifty guns, and they immediately to sail from home to their respective stations, with orders constantly to keep cruising on the fishing banks, and in latitudes proper to obstruct the French fishery and navigation, protect our own, and especially to intercept stores, provisions, etc. getting into Cape Breton.

It is likewise humbly proposed, that those men of war should carry clothing, arms, and all manner of warlike stores, necessary for a body of three thousand men, to be raised . . . in Virginia three hundred, in Maryland one hundred and fifty, Pennsylvania three hundred and fifty, New York two hundred and fifty, Jerseys one hundred and fifty, Connecticut three hundred and fifty, Rhode Island two hundred and fifty, Massachusetts-Bay one thousand, and New Hampshire one hundred and fifty; and instructions to these governments to encourage the speedy raising of their respective complements, in order to have the more time to discipline them, concealing the real design under the specious pretense that those troops are raised to defend the governments from invasion, or the surprise of an enemy.

It is also humbly proposed, that these levies should be formed into three regiments . . . and . . . that all the officers . . . should be gentlemen of interest in those several colonies. . . .

It is with great submission further proposed, that a squadron of six sail of the line, with two thousand regular troops, and all things necessary for a formal siege, should take their departure from hence the beginning of March next, so as to anchor in Gabarus bay, within four miles of the rampart of Louisbourg, by the middle of April following; there to be joined by the American troops under the convoy of the station ships. This may be executed without loss of men, no cannon commanding the entrance of this harbor. . . . It may be conceived advisable there to land the troops, and from thence to march and make regular approaches to the rampart. . . . If the rampart is taken the citadel and four other batteries that command the harbor must yield; and, what facilitates the design, there is no outworks, glacis, or covert-way.

41. *War on the Southern Frontier,* 1741

"Statements Made in the Introduction to the Report on General Oglethorpe's Expedition to St. Augustine," South Carolina House of Assembly, 1741, *Historical Collections of South Carolina* (New York, 1836), II, 349–59.

[The Spaniards in Florida] relying wholly on the King's pay for their subsistence, their thoughts never turned to trade or even agriculture, but depending on foreign supplies for the most common necessaries of life . . . spent their time in universal perpetual idleness. From such a state, mischievous inclinations naturally sprung up in such a people; and having leisure and opportunity ever since they had a neighbor, the fruits of whose industry excited their desires and envy, they have not failed to carry those inclinations into action as often as they could, without the

least regard to peace or war subsisting between the two crowns of Great Britain and
Spain. . . .

In 1686, peace still subsisting, the Lord
Cardoss who had obtained from the lords
proprietors a grant of a large tract of land
in Granville County, having just before
come over and settled at Beaufort on Port-
Royal with a number of north-Britons; the
Spaniards coming in three galleys from
Augustine landed upon them, killed and
whipped a great many, after taken, in a
most cruel and barbarous manner, plundered them all, and broke up that settlement. The same galleys going from thence
run up next to Bear Bluff on North Edisto
River, where those Spaniards again landed,
burned the houses, plundered the settlers,
and took Landgrave Morton's brother
prisoner. Their further progress was happily prevented by a hurricane, which
drove two of the galleys up so high on the
land that not being able to get one of them
off again . . . , they thought proper to make
a retreat; but first set fire to that galley
on board which Mr. Morton was actually
then in chains, and most inhumanly burned
in her.

In 1702, before Queen Anne's declaration of war was known in these parts, the
Spaniards formed another design to fall
upon our settlements by land, at the head
of nine hundred Apalatchee Indians from
thence. The Creek Indians, in friendship
with this province, coming at a knowledge
of it, . . . acquainted our traders . . . with
it. . . . The traders having thereupon encouraged the Creeks to get together an
army of five hundred men, headed the
same, and went out to meet the other.
Both armies met in an evening on the side
of Flint River. . . . In the morning . . . the
Creeks stirring up their fires drew back at
a little distance leaving their blankets by
the fires in the very same order as they
had slept. Immediately after the Spaniards and Apalatchees . . . coming on to attack them, fired and run in upon the blankets. Thereupon the Creeks rushing forth
fell on them, killed and took the greatest

part, and entirely routed them. To this
stratagem was owing the defeat of the
then intended design. . . .

In 1704, Colonel Moore was commissioned as Lieutenant General by Sir Nathaniel Johnson, who succeeded him in
the government, to make an expedition
against the Spaniards and Indians at
Apalatchee, about eighty miles to the west
of St. Augustine. . . . He marched up
thither at the head of fifty volunteers of
this province, and one thousand Indians.
The first fort he came to which had fifty
men in it, he took by storm, after a smart
resistance. The next day the Captain of
St. Lewisses fort . . . giving him battle,
Colonel Moore took him and eight of his
men prisoners, and killed two hundred of
the Indians. In two days after the king of
Attachooka . . . sent to him presents . . .
and made his peace. After which he
marched through all the rest of their
towns, . . . but all submitted, without conditions. . . . By this conquest of Apalachee
the province was freed from any danger
from that part during the whole war. And
this important service was effected without
putting this government to the least expense.

In 1706, the Spaniards at St. Augustine joined the French from Martinique,
in making up a fleet of ten sail . . . to invade this province. The ship on board
which the chief commander was, being
separated from the fleet, fell into Sewee
Bay, not knowing the place. The rest coming over Charlestown Bar, anchored just
within on a Sunday, where they remained . . . until Friday following. Captain
Fenwicke . . . attacked them, killed and
wounded about thirty, and took seventy
prisoners. The next day the ship which
had lost company, still not appearing, the
whole fleet set sail again.

In 1715, peace having been some time
concluded between the crowns, the Yamasee Indians . . . living contiguous to, and
in the most intimate manner with, the settlers in those parts, having been ill-used
by some of the traders amongst them,

were so far disgusted, that they broke out war with this province, by massacring on the fifteenth day of April above eighty of the inhabitants of Granville County. But it was manifest that they were prompted to severe resentment of their usage, whatever it was, by the Spaniards at St. Augustine.... And having ravaged the country, killing many more and doing all the mischief they could, so that all the southern parts were broke up, to about the distance of twenty miles from Charlestown, they themselves soon after retreated to St. Augustine also. There they were received, protected, and encouraged to make frequent incursions from thence into the settlements of this province; and being oftentimes headed by Spaniards, they cut off several of the settlers, and carried off their slaves. The slaves themselves at length, taking advantage of those things, deserted of their own accord to St. Augustine, and upon being demanded back by this government they were not returned....

In 1727, peace between the crowns continuing, fresh depradations were committed on this province from Augustine, both by land and water; which created the expense of two expeditions to prevent the progress of them. At that time this coast being infested by several Spanish vessels, who ... plundered and made prizes of all the English vessels they met with. A schooner fitted out from Augustine, on the like account, put in to North Edisto, where the men made a descent, and carried off the slaves of David Ferguson, which were never returned nor paid for. On this occasion Captain Mountjoy was fitted out by this government, who cleared the coast of those pirates, and retook a rich Virginian ship.

At the same time a party of Yamasee Indians, headed by Spaniards from St. Augustine, having murdered our outscouts, made an incursion into our settlements.... But being briskly pursued by the neighbors, who had notice of it, they were overtaken, routed, and obliged to quit their booty. The government judged

it necessary to chastise ... those Indians [and] commissioned Colonel Palmer for that purpose instantly; who with about one hundred whites, and the like number of our Indians, landed at St. Juan's, and having left a sufficient number to take care of the craft, marched undiscovered to the Yamasee town, within a mile of St. Augustine. He attacked it at once, killed several of those Indians, took several prisoners, and drove the rest into the very gates of St. Augustine Castle, where they were sheltered. And having destroyed their town, he returned....

In the latter end of 1737, still peace subsisting, great preparations were made to invade openly this province and Georgia. For that purpose a great body of men arrived at St. Augustine, in galleys from the Havana; which put this province to a very large expense to provide against. But happily they were countermanded just as they were ready to set off.

In 1738, although peace subsisted, ... another method was taken by the Spaniards to answer their ends. Hitherto the government of St. Augustine had not dared to acknowledge, much less to justify, the little villanies and violences offered to our properties. But now an edict of His Catholic Majesty himself, bearing date in November 1733, was published by beat of drum round the town of St. Augustine (where many Negroes belonging to English vessels that carried thither supplies of provisions, etc., had the opportunity of hearing it) promising liberty and protection to all slaves that should desert thither from any of the English colonies.... And ... secret measures were taken to make it known to our slaves in general. In consequence of which numbers of slaves did, from time to time, by land and water desert to St. Augustine; and, the better to facilitate their escape, carried off their masters' horses, boats, etc., some of them first committing murder, and were accordingly received and declared free.... The present governor of St. Augustine ... acknowledged those slaves to be there, yet ... declared that he could not deliver them up, without a positive order for that purpose from the King, and that he should continue to receive all others that should resort thither. . . .

In September 1739, our slaves made an insurrection at Stono, in the heart of our settlements not twenty miles from Charlestown, in which they massacred twenty-three whites, after the most cruel and barbarous manner. . . . Having got arms and ammunition out of a store, they bent their course to the southward, burning all the houses on the road. But they marched so slow, in full confidence of their own strength from their first success, that they gave time to a party of our militia to come up with them. The number was in a manner equal on both sides; and an engagement ensued, such as may be supposed in such a case. But by the blessing of God the Negroes were defeated, the greatest part being killed on the spot or taken; and those that then escaped were so closely pursued, and hunted day after day, that in the end all but two or three were killed or taken and executed. That the Negroes would not have made this insurrection had they not depended on St. Augustine for a place of reception afterwards, was very certain; and that the Spaniards had a hand in prompting them to this particular action, there was but little room to doubt. . . .

On this occasion every breast was filled with concern. Evil brought home to us, within our very doors, awakened the attention of the most unthinking. Every one that had any relation, any tie of nature, every one that had a life to lose, were in the most sensible manner shocked at such danger daily hanging over their heads. With regret we bewailed our peculiar case, that we could not enjoy the benefits of peace like the rest of mankind, and that our own industry should be the means of taking from us all the sweets of life, and of rendering us liable to the loss of our lives and fortunes. With indignation we looked at St. Augustine. . . . That den of thieves and ruffians! Receptacle of debtors, servants, and slaves! Bane of industry and society! And revolved in our minds all the injuries this province had received from thence, ever since its first settlement. . . . And what aggravated the same was, that this government (on the contrary) had never been wanting in its good offices with our Indians in their behalf. And even during Queen Anne's war had exercised so much humanity towards them that, in order to prevent those Indians from scalping them, according to their custom, when they should take any of them prisoners, a law was passed to give them five pounds proclamation money for every one they should bring in alive; and accordingly a great number of the Spaniards, by that means, were brought in alive, and the reward paid for them.

42. *Instructions to Privateers, 1739*

"Instructions of George II to Captains of Privateers, November 30, 1739," Jameson, *Privateering*, 347–53.

THAT it shall be lawful for the said . . . vessels . . . to set upon by force of arms and to subdue and take the men of war, ships and other vessels whatsoever, as also the goods, moneys and merchandises, belonging to the King of Spain, his vassals and subjects . . . and such other ships, vessels and goods, as are, or shall be, liable to confiscation; . . . but so as that no hostility be committed, nor prize attacked, seized or taken within the harbors of princes and states in amity with us. . . .

That all ships of what nation soever carrying any soldiers, arms, powder, ammunition or any other contraband goods, to any of the territories . . . of the King of Spain shall be seized as prizes.

That the . . . commanders of such . . . vessels shall bring such ships and goods, as they have seized . . . to such port . . . of our dominions as shall be most convenient for them, in order to have the same legally adjudged in our . . . admiralty courts as shall be lawfully authorized within our dominions. But if such prize be taken in the Mediterranean or within the Straits of Gibraltar, then the captor may . . . carry such ship and goods into the ports of such princes or states as are in alliance or amity with us.

That after such ships shall be taken and brought into any port the taker shall be obliged to bring or send, as soon as possible may be, three or four of the principal of the company (whereof the master and the pilot to be always two) of every ship so brought into port, before the judge . . . of such . . . admiralty courts, within our dominions, as shall be lawfully authorized as aforesaid . . . to be sworn and examined upon such interrogatories as shall tend to the discovery of the truth, touching the interest or property of such . . . ships. . . . And the taker shall be further obliged at the time he produceth the company to be examined, to bring and deliver . . . all such passes, sea briefs, charter-parties, bills of lading, cockets, letters and other documents and writings as shall be . . . found on board any such ship. . . .

That all such ships, goods and merchandises . . . shall be kept and preserved, and no part of them shall be sold, spoiled, wasted or diminished . . . before judgment to be given in . . . some . . . court of admiralty . . . that the said ships, goods and merchandises are lawful prize. And that no person or persons, taken or surprised in any ship or vessel as aforesaid, though known to be one of the enemy's party, shall be in cold blood killed, maimed, or by torture and cruelty inhumanly treated, contrary to the common usage and just permission of war. And whoever shall offend in any of the premises shall be severely punished.

That the said commanders . . . shall not do or attempt anything against the true meaning of any . . . treaty . . . between us, or any of our allies, touching the freedom of commerce in the time of war, and the authority of the passports or certificates under a certain form in some one of the articles or treaties so depending between us and our allies as aforesaid, when produced and shown by any of the subjects of our said allies, and shall not do or attempt anything against our loving subjects, or the subjects of any prince or state in amity with us, nor against their ships, vessels or goods, but only against the King of Spain, his vassals and subjects, and others inhabiting within his countries, territories or dominions, their ships, vessels and goods. . . .

That after condemnation of any prize, it shall . . . be lawful for the commanders of such merchant ships or vessels or the owners of the same, to keep such . . . ships, vessels, goods and merchandises as shall be condemned to them, for lawful prizes, in their own possession, to make sale or dispose thereof in open market or otherwise, to their best advantage . . . ; other than wrought silks, bengalls, and stuffs mixed with silk or [herbs] of the manufacture of Persia, China, or East India, or calicoes painted, dyed, printed or stained there, which are to be deposited for exportation, according to the directions of an act made in the eleventh year of the reign of the late King William. . . .

That if any ship or vessel, belonging to us or our subjects, or to our allies or their subjects, shall be found in distress, by being in fight, set upon, or taken by the enemy, the Captain, officers and company, who shall have such letters of marque or commission, as aforesaid, shall use their best endeavors to give aid and succor to all such ship or ships, and shall to the utmost of their power labor to free the same from the enemy.

That our subjects and all other persons

whatsoever, who shall . . . serve, or bear any charge or adventure . . . according to these articles, shall stand and be freed by virtue of the said commission. And that no person be in any wise reputed or challenged for an offender, against our laws, but shall be freed, under our protection, of and from all trouble and vexation that might in any wise grow thereby, in the same manner as any other our said subjects ought to be by law, in their aiding or assisting us, either in their own persons, or otherwise, in a lawful war against our declared enemies.

That the said commanders of such merchant ships and vessels or their owners or agents before the taking out commissions, shall give notice in writing, subscribed with their hands, to our High Admiral of Great Britain, for the time being . . . of the name of their ship, and of the tonnage and burthen, and the names of the captain, owners or setters out of the said ship, with the number of men, and the names of the officers in her, and for what time they are victualed, as also of their ordnance, furniture and ammunition: to the end the same may be registered in the said Court of Admiralty.

That those commanders of such merchant ships and vessels . . . shall hold and keep . . . a correspondence . . . with our High Admiral of Great Britain . . . , so as from time to time to render and give unto him or them not only an account and intelligence of their captures of proceedings . . . , but also of whatsoever else shall occur unto them . . . touching or concerning the designs of the enemy, or any of their fleets, ships, vessels or parties; and of the stations, seas, ports and places and of their intents therein; and of what merchant ships or vessels of the enemy, bound out or home, as they shall hear of; and of what else material in these cases may arrive to their knowledge, to the end such course may be thereupon taken, and such orders given as may be requisite.

43. *Indian Diplomacy, 1743–44*

Wraxall, *Abridgment*, 233–5.

OCTOBER 24, 1743. The Commissioners write a long letter to Governor Clinton [of New York] in which they lay before him a general state of the forts etc., relating to the Six Nations.

They say the fort at Oswego is the key of the Six Nations and that their fidelity and allegiance to His Majesty chiefly depends on our supporting the said fort; that at present it is garrisoned only with an officer and twenty men which though sufficient in time of peace is not so in a time of war. They say, should this place fall into the hands of the French all the Indian trade of this colony would go with it, by which means the French would gain over the Six Nations and all the other Indians wholly to their interest.

They say, the Senecas who are the most numerous of the Six Nations were formerly the most firmly attached to the British interest, are of late by the intrigues and management of the French become the most wavering, and without proper care be taken on our side for the time to come, they fear the French will get the greatest part of them over to their interest. The Commissioners propose that a fort should be built in their country and garrisoned with an officer and twenty men. Also that proper measures be fallen on to remove the French who reside in the Senecas country and who are constantly debauching their affections from us. If . . . the Assembly don't judge proper to support some such measures as these, they think the Six Nations will be lost to us, and of what fatal consequence that would be . . . those who have experienced what havoc a few Indians can make in time of war can well judge. . . .

June 18, 1744. Governor Clinton meets the Six Nations at Albany. His speech to them contains in substance:

His Majesty's orders to him to renew, strengthen and brighten the covenant chain which hath so long united the Six Nations and His Majesty's subjects together in union and friendship. . . .

He acquaints them that after several instances of treachery the French had declared war against the English and the latter against the French. He therefore recommends them to keep their warriors at home in readiness to withstand any attacks . . . from the French.

He promises in the King's name to . . . protect them from all assaults of the French and that [the] Commissioners are present from the colonies of Massachusetts and Connecticut to enter into the same engagements. . . .

In return he tells them he expects they shall at all times be ready . . . to assist . . . in the just prosecution of this war . . . against the French . . . whenever they shall be called upon so to do.

After recounting in general terms the great advantage and security of Oswego, . . . he acquaints them that he has strengthened that garrison with some cannon and reinforced it with more soldiers and expects that they will at all times be ready to defend it against . . . the French.

He exhorts them to live compact together in their castles which is absolutely necessary for their own security in this time of war.

He puts them in mind of their former promises not to suffer the French to live amongst them or to settle on any of their lands and expects they will at this time of war punctually fulfill those promises.

20 June the Six Nations return their answer:

They solemnly renew the covenant chain and say they will not put it in the power of the devil himself to break or injure it. . . .

They promise they will keep all their people at home and that they will be ready to do all the Governor expects or desires from them. But they say they desire to live in peace until the French begin an attack upon any of His Majesty's subjects when they will be ready to join in our defense. . . .

Concerning the house at Oswego, . . . they say the first two years after that trading house was settled goods were sold cheap and it was a pleasure to trade there; but they have since been sold so dear that they do not now think that place any advantage to them. However they are thankful the Governor has taken measures to strengthen and defend the fort. They take notice that the Governor has not exhorted them to endeavor to cultivate and extend a correspondence amongst the far Indians according to the custom of all former Governors but say, they shall however do all they can to keep friendship with those nations who are united with them and then they can overcome any enemy whatever. They say they are now busy in collecting themselves together in order to live in compact bodies.

As to their driving the French from amongst them, they say they have just now declared their desire of living in peace and should they deliver up the French who live amongst them they would be deemed the first aggressors and act contrary to their avowed principles, and therefore they will leave it to us to do with the French who come in their country as we think proper.

44. *Forts in the West, 1753*

"Instruction to Governor Dinwiddie," Labaree, *Royal Instructions*, I, 414–15.

WHEREAS you have represented . . . the utility of building some forts upon the Ohio in the western part of our colony of Virginia . . . , and have prayed that a sufficient number of cannon should be sent from hence to be placed in the said forts; we have thought it fit . . . to approve that proper forts should be erected on the said river for the defense and at the charge of the inhabitants of our said colony, agreeable to your proposal, and we have thereupon been pleased . . . to cause the necessary directions to be given that thirty cannon of four-pounders with a full proportion of stores be forthwith . . . consigned to you . . . for the uses above mentioned; and our will and pleasure is that you . . . erect the said forts as soon as the nature of the service will admit. . . .

And whereas we have received information of a number of Europeans not our subjects being assembled in a hostile manner upon the River Ohio, intending by force of arms to erect certain forts on the said river within our territory . . . , we do hereby strictly enjoin you to make diligent inquiry into the truth of this information, and if you shall find that any number of persons . . . shall presume to erect any fort or forts within the limits of our province of Virginia, you are first to require them peaceably to depart . . . and if notwithstanding your admonitions, they do still endeavor to carry on any such unlawful and unjustifiable designs, we do hereby strictly charge and command you to drive them off by force of arms.

45. *The Stronghold at Louisbourg, 1749*

From an anonymous journal reprinted in L. E. deForest, ed., *Louisbourg Journals, 1745* (New York, 1932), 30–1, 34, 50–1.

FRIDAY [June] 28: . . . This day I went into the city, and the more I view it, the more I admire it. Nor can I ever tell the strength, and cost of this place, and yet I can tell so much that perhaps I sha'n't be credited. Could I give a description of it in full I shouldn't expect to be believed. . . . While I was in the city I went to see the place where they buried their dead; and the French having occasion for earth to fortify themselves and it being easiest digging there, they had taken earth from that place which uncovered many coffins and bones etc. Since we besieged—there was such numbers killed and that died—with sickness, that they'd digged a hole about twelve feet square (and about as deep)

where they threw in all together, and without coffins, I was told.—

Thursday [July] 11: This day I went into the hospital to see the French people say Mass. I couldn't help wondering to see gentlemen who were men of learning (I supposed, and doubtless of good natural parts also) so led aside as to worship images, to bow down to a cross of wood, and to see so many of all ranks seemingly devout, when we've reason to think they never had any communion with God through the course of their lives, being ever so strict in the practice of their religion. It is now, and has been for some days, quite hot weather.

[October 17]: I shall mention a few remarkables in the city.... (1) the citadel, which was a very large house, being 23 rods long and about 45 feet wide, all built of stone and brick. It was defended by itself against the city, having a trench between it and the city, and the bridge on which we went over ... was easily hoisted up.... In the middle was a steeple where hung an excellent bell, the biggest (by far) that ever I see (although we broke it). At the east end it is three stories and several large rooms well-finished. There is also a chapel in it large enough to hold a large congregation. I trust a thousand men may live comfortably in said house. It was built in the year 1720....

(2) The Hopital du Roy or Royal Hospital—which is twenty rods long, the wall about two feet thick, built of stone and lime, two stories high, a great many large sash windows with iron grates to each of them. There is two large lower rooms for the sick, well-furnished with beds and curtains. There is the chambers over these, which are for the same use. There's also a great deal of linen, as also a great many vessels of pewter, etc. In the middle of said house is a steeple and a good bell hanging in the same.

VI ✻ *The Plantation Economy*

IN THE LAST decades of the seventeenth century, a new form of agricultural organization appeared in the mainland colonies. The introduction of such new tropical crops as rice encouraged large-scale cultivation; trade and speculation led to the accumulation of substantial sums of capital available for investment in land; and the legal definition of slavery as a status and the importation of large numbers of Negroes created a labor force, capable of being disciplined and controlled. The product of these developments was the plantation, adapted from West Indian models but with a distinctive character of its own on the continent.

At the start of the period the yeoman farm was still the typical agricultural unit in Virginia and in Maryland (No. 46). And such small farms continued to hold on in some parts of the South even in the middle of the eighteenth century. But their ability to expand was limited by the restricted free labor supply. Servants were difficult to come by and more difficult still to control and manage (No. 47). The labor shortage became more serious still as attractive opportunities for white servants who had freedom of choice opened up in the early eighteenth century in Pennsylvania and in New York (No. 48).

The Negro, on the other hand, was by now fixed decisively in the status of a slave, unfree for life. Although the slaves also were difficult to control and, at times, attempted to escape (*see above*, No. 41), they were more readily disciplined, within the law, and more economical. The demand of the planters for Black labor was therefore intense, as was evident in the development of Georgia, where slavery was at first prohibited (No. 49). The African slave trade brought growing numbers to America, under harsh conditions (No. 50).

Increasingly, therefore, Southern society revolved about the plantation. The problems of economic organization were substantial and time-occupying. The planter became a kind of business man preoccupied with the difficulties of management (No. 51) and with the problems of controlling large numbers of laborers through overseers (No. 52).

46. *Virginia Yeoman Farming in the 1680's*

Durand, *Huguenot Exile*, 115–27.

THEY usually plant tobacco, Indian corn, wheat, peas or beans, barley, sweet potatoes, turnips, which grow to a monstrous size and are very good to eat. They make gardens as we do in Europe. Hemp and flax grow very high, but ... they do not know how to prepare it or how to spin. Again the soil is so favorable for fruit trees that I saw orchards planted, I was told, only ten years before, with larger and better-grown trees than our twenty year old ones in Europe.

In the County of Gloucester wheat generally yields ten to one; Indian corn two hundred to one. The farmers reap only about a bushel of wheat each on their plantations for making pastries, because of the great abundance of game and apples which make very good pastries also. I asked why they did not grow more of it. They answered it yielded but ten to one, whereas Indian corn gave at least two hundred to one, and they were as healthy on this bread as they would be on that made of wheat. ...

They do not know what it is to plough the land with cattle, but just make holes into which they drop the seeds, although it would be easy to till and, there being no stones, a single horse could be used to plough anywhere. Some possess a hundred cows or oxen and thirty horses for riding only, except on a few plantations too far from the sea and the rivers, where they are used to draw carts. Wood is so handy their slaves always carry it on their shoulders, and I would like to state and aver that were I settled there, provided I

had two servants, a plough with two cows and another one with two horses, I could boast of accomplishing more work than anyone in the country with eight strong slaves.

So much timber have they that they build fences all around the land they cultivate. A man with fifty acres of ground, and others in proportion, will leave twenty-five wooded, and of the remaining twenty-five will cultivate half and keep the other as a pasture and paddock for his cattle. Four years later, he transfers his fences to this untilled half which meanwhile has had a period of rest and fertilization. ...

They sow wheat at the end of October and beginning of November, and corn at the end of April. This is the best grain to harvest, because those needing to, can commence using it for bread at the beginning of September; and the harvest is not over until the end of November. They only plant about a bushel, as otherwise the field would be too large, for this bushel takes up a lot of ground; they put four seeds close together under a small mound and every four feet apart sow four more. ... They transplant their tobacco in May, and leave three feet between each plant. Large quantities of it are used in this country, besides what they sell. Everyone smokes while working and idling. ...

Some people in this country are comfortably housed; the farmers' houses are built entirely of wood. ... Those who have some means, cover them inside with a coating of mortar in which they use oyster-shells for lime; it is as white as snow, so that although they look ugly from the outside, where only the wood can be seen, they are very pleasant inside, with convenient windows and openings. They have started making bricks in quantities, and I have seen several houses where the walls were entirely made of them. Whatever their rank, and I know not why, they build only two rooms with some closets on the ground floor, and two rooms in the attic above. . . . They build also a separate kitchen, a separate house for the Christian slaves, one for the Negro slaves, and several to dry the tobacco, so that when you come to the home of a person of some means, you think you are entering a fairly large village. There are no stables because they never lock up their cattle. Indeed few of the houses have a lock, for nothing is ever stolen. . . . In the same way all their cattle stay in the woods at night and they fear no thieves but wolves, against which they have faithful dogs. Then, too, if anyone kills a wolf the State gives him a barrel of tobacco, so for that reason they are very much sought for.

My host had only two young menservants, no maid; he had bought one of those shameless hussies who came over at the time I did, and she had been ill ever since from work. He gathered ten bushels of wheat, two hundred of corn, having sown a bushel of each; fifteen bushels of beans, a quantity of sweet potatoes, perhaps fifty bushels of turnips had they been measured, and twelve hogsheads of tobacco making seventy-five hundredweight, which I saw him sell for eleven écus a barrel, and it had never been so cheap.

47. *Recruiting and Managing Servants, 1724–39*

From Hugh Jones, *Present State of Virginia* (1724), quoted in J. R. Commons *et al.*, eds., *Documentary History of American Industrial Society* (Cleveland, 1910–11), I, 339–40, 346–8. Reprinted by permission of the publishers, The Arthur H. Clark Company.

THE SHIPS that transport these things often call at Ireland to victual, and bring over frequently white servants, which are of three kinds: such as come upon certain wages by agreement for a certain time; such as come bound by indenture, commonly called kids, who are usually to serve four or five years; and, those convicts or felons that are transported, whose room they had much rather have than their company, for abundance of them do great mischief, commit robbery and murder and spoil servants, that were before very good. But they frequently there meet with the end that they deserved at home, though indeed some of them prove indifferent good. Their being sent thither to work as slaves for punishment, is but a mere notion, for few of them ever lived so well and so easy before, especially if they are good for anything. These are to serve seven and sometimes fourteen years, and they and servants by indentures have an allowance of corn and clothes, when they are out of their time, that they may be therewith supported till they can be provided with services or otherwise settled. With these three sorts of servants are they supplied from England, Wales, Scotland, and Ireland, among which they that have a mind to it may serve their time with ease and satisfaction to themselves and their masters, especially if they fall into good hands.

These if they forsake their roguery together with the other kids . . . , when they are free, may work day-labor, or else rent a small plantation for a trifle almost, or else turn overseers, if they are expert, industrious and careful, or follow their trade, if they have been brought up to any, especially smiths, carpenters, tailors, sawyers, coopers and bricklayers. . . . The plenty of the country and the good wages given to work folks occasion very few poor, who are supported by the parish, being such as are lame, sick or decrepit through age, distempers, accidents, or some infirmities. For where there is a numerous family of poor children the vestry takes care to bind them out apprentices, till they are able to maintain themselves by their own labor; by which means they are never tormented with vagrant and vagabond beggars, there being a reward for taking up runaways, that are at a small distance from their home, if they are not known or are without a pass from their master and can give no good account of themselves, especially Negroes.

48. *Runaways, 1736–39*

From advertisements in *Virginia Gazette* and *South Carolina Gazette*, quoted in Commons, *Documentary History*, I, 346–8. Reprinted by permission of the publishers, The Arthur H. Clark Company.

RAN away some time in June last, from William Pierce of Nansemond County, near Mr. Theophilus Pugh's, merchant, a convict servant woman named Winifred Thomas. She is Welsh woman, short, black-haired and young; marked on the inside of her right arm with gunpowder, W.T., and the date of the year underneath. She knits and spins, and is supposed to be gone into North Carolina by the way of Cureatuck and Roanoke Inlet. Whoever brings her to her master shall be paid a pistole besides what the law allows, paid by

William Pierce.

Run away on the fifth instant from Robert William's plantation in Georgia, three men servants. One named James Powell, is a bricklayer by trade. About five feet nine inches high, a strong made man, born in Wiltshire, talks broad; and when he went away he wore his own short hair, with a white cap. Among his comrades he was called Alderman.

Another, named Charles Gastril, did formerly belong to the pilot boat at Pill, near Bristol; is by trade a sawyer. [He is] about 5 feet 10 inches high, of a thin, spare make, raw boned, and has a scar somewhere on his upper lip; aged about 25.

The third, named Jenkin James, a lusty young fellow, about the same height as Gastrill, had a good fresh complexion. Bred by trade a tailor, but of late has been used to sawing, talks very much Welshly, and had on when he went away a coarse red coat and waistcoat, the buttons and buttonholes of the coat black.

Any person or persons who apprehend them, or either of them, and bring them to Mr. Thomas Jenys in Charleston, or to the said Mr. Robert William in Savannah shall receive £10 currency of South Carolina for each.

Robert Williams

Besides the above mentioned reward, there is a considerable sum allowed by the trustees [of the colony of Georgia] for taking run away servants.

N.B. About a fortnight ago, three other of the said Robert William's servants run away, who are already advertised.

49. *The Demand for Negroes in Georgia, 1735*

Pat. Tailfer *et al.*, "A True and Historical Narrative of the Colony of Georgia, in America," in Peter Force, *Tracts* (Washington, 1835), I, No. IV, 20–3.

THE FIRST of February, 1732–3, Mr. Oglethorpe arrived at Georgia with the first embarkation, consisting of forty families, making upwards of one hundred persons, all brought over and supported at the public charge. The first thing he did after he arrived in Georgia, was to make a kind of solemn treaty with a parcel of fugitive Indians, . . . and all of them have been ever since maintained at the public charge, at vast expense, when many poor Christians were starving in the colony for want of bread; . . .

Secondly, he prohibited the importation of rum, under pretense, that it was destructive to the constitution, and an incentive to debauchery and idleness. However specious these pretenses might seem, a little experience soon convinced us, that this restriction was directly opposite to the well-being of the colony. . . .

The third thing he did, was regularly to set out to each freeholder in Savannah, lots of fifty acres, in three distinct divisions, viz. the eighth part of one acre for a house and garden in the town; four acres and seven-eighths, at a small distance from town; and forty-five acres at a considerable remove from thence. No regard was had to the quality of the ground in the divisions, so that some were altogether pine barren, and some swamp and morass, far surpassing the strength and ability of the planter: . . . But these and many other hardships were scarcely felt by the few people that came there, so long as Mr. Oglethorpe stayed, which was about fifteen months. They worked hard indeed, in building some houses in town; but then they labored in common, and were likewise assisted by Negroes from Carolina, who did the heaviest work.

But at Mr. Oglethorpe's going to England, the growing fame of the colony was thereby greatly increased, so that as it has been before observed, people, in abundance, from all parts of the world, flocked to Georgia. Then they began to consider and endeavor, every one according to his genius or abilities, how they might best subsist themselves. Some, with great labor and expense, essayed the making of tar; this, as 'tis well known to the trustees, never quitted costs. Others tried to make plank and saw boards, which, by the great price they were obliged to sell them at, by reason of the great expense of white servants, was the chief means of ruining those who thought to procure a living by their buildings in town; for boards of all kinds could always be bought in Carolina, for half the price that they were able to sell them at; but few were capable to commission them from thence, and those who were so, were prevented from doing it, upon pretense of discouraging the labor of white people in Georgia. Those who had numbers of servants and tracts of land in the county, went upon the planting of corn, peas, potatoes, etc., and the charge of these who succeeded the best, so far exceeded the value of the produce, that it would have saved three-fourths to have bought all from the Carolina market.

The falling of timber was a task very unequal to the strength and constitution of white servants; and the hoeing the ground, they being exposed to the sultry heat of the sun, insupportable. And it is well known, that this labor is one of the hardest upon the Negroes, even though their constitutions are much stronger than white people, and the heat no way disagreeable nor hurtful to them; but in us it created inflammatory fevers of various kinds, both continued and intermittent, wasting and tormenting fluxes, most excruciating colics, and dry-belly-aches; tremors, vertigoes, palsies, and a long train of painful and lingering nervous distempers; which brought on to many a cessation both from work and from life; especially as water without any qualification was the chief drink, and salt meat the only provisions that could be had or afforded.

And so general were these disorders, that during the hot season, which lasts from March to October, hardly one half of the servants and working people were ever able to do their masters or themselves the least service; and the yearly sickness

of each servant, generally speaking, cost his master as much as would have maintained a Negro for four years. These things were represented to the trustees in the summer of 1735, in a petition for the use of Negroes, signed by about seventeen of the better sort of people in Savannah. In this petition there was also set forth the great disproportion betwixt the maintenance and clothing of white servants and Negroes. This petition was carried to England and presented to the trustees, by Mr. Hugh Stirling, an experienced planter in the colony; but no regard was had to it.

50. *The Slave Trade*, 1700

From James Barbot's Voyage to the Congo River (August 28, 1700), in Elizabeth Donnan, *Documents Illustrative of the History of the Slave Trade to America* (Washington, 1930), Vol. I, Doc. No. 179, pp. 460–4.

I HAVE observed, that the great mortality, which so often happens in slave ships, proceeds as well from taking in too many, as from want of knowing how to manage them aboard, and how to order the course at sea so nicely, as not to overshoot their ports in America, as some bound to Cayenne with slaves, have done; attributing the tediousness of their passage, and their other mistakes, to wrong causes, as being becalmed about the line, etc., which only proceeded from their not observing the regular course, or not making due observations of land when they approached the American continent; or of the force and strength of the current of the Amazons. . . .

As to the management of our slaves aboard, we lodge the two sexes apart, by means of a strong partition at the main mast; the forepart is for men, the other behind the mast for the women. If it be in large ships carrying five or six hundred slaves, the deck in such ships ought to be at least five and a half or six foot high, which is very requisite for driving a continual trade of slaves. For the greater

height it has, the more airy and convenient it is for such a considerable number of human creatures; and consequently far the more healthy for them, and fitter to look after them. We build a sort of half-decks along the sides with deals and spars provided for that purpose in Europe, that half-deck extending no farther than the sides of our scuttles and so the slaves lie in two rows, one above the other, and as close together as they can be crowded. . . .

We are very nice in keeping the places where the slaves lie clean and neat, appointing some of the ship's crew to do that office constantly, and several of the slaves themselves to be assistant to them in that employment; and thrice a week we perfume betwixt decks with a quantity of good vinegar in pails, and red-hot iron bullets in them, to expel the bad air, after the place has been well washed and scrubbed with brooms. After which, the deck is cleaned with cold vinegar, and in the day-time, in good weather, we leave all the scuttles open, and shut them again at night.

It has been observed before, that some

slaves fancy they are carried to be eaten, which makes them desperate; and others are so on account of their captivity, so that if care be not taken, they will mutiny and destroy the ship's crew in hopes to get away.

To prevent such misfortunes, we use to visit them daily, narrowly searching every corner between decks, to see whether they have not found means, to gather any pieces of iron, or wood, or knives, about the ship, notwithstanding the great care we take not to leave any tools or nails, or other things in the way, which, however, cannot be always so exactly observed, where so many people are in the narrow compass of a ship.

We cause as many of our men as is convenient to lie in the quarter-deck and gun-room, and our principal officers in the great cabin, where we keep all our small arms in a readiness, with sentinels constantly at the door and avenues to it; being thus ready to disappoint any attempts our slaves might make on a sudden.

These precautions contribute very much to keep them in awe; and if all those who carry slaves duly observed them, we should not hear of so many revolts as have happened. Where I was concerned, we always kept our slaves in such order, that we did not perceive the least inclination in any of them to revolt, or mutiny, and lost very few of our number in the voyage. . . .

We messed the slaves twice a day. . . . The first meal was of our large beans boiled, with a certain quantity of Muscovy lard, which we have from Holland, well packed up in casks. The beans we have in great plenty at Rochel. The other meal was of pease, or of Indian wheat, and sometimes meal of Mandioca . . . boiled with either lard, or suet, or grease, by turns. . . . I found they had much better stomachs for beans, and it is a proper fattening food for captives; in my opinion far better to maintain them well, than Indian wheat, Mandioca or yams; though the Calabar slaves value this root above any other

food, as being used to it in their own country. But it is not at certain times of the year to be had in so great a quantity as is requisite to subsist such a number of people for several months; besides that they are apt to decay, and even to putrify as they grow old. Horse-beans are also very proper for slaves in lieu of large beans. There is good plenty of them in Great Britain, which, as well as the other beans, will keep, if put up in dry vats or casks.

We distributed them by ten in a mess, about a small flat tub, made for that use by our coopers, in which their victuals were served; each slave having a little wooden spoon to feed himself handsomely, and more cleanly than with their fingers, and they were well pleased with it.

At each meal we allowed every slave a full coconut shell of water, and from time to time a dram of brandy, to strengthen their stomachs. . . .

As for the sick and wounded, or those out of order, our surgeons, in their daily visits betwixt decks, finding any indisposed, caused them to be carried to the Lazaretto, under the fore-castle, a room reserved for a sort of hospital, where they were carefully looked after. Being out of the crowd, the surgeons had more conveniency and time to administer proper remedies; which they cannot do leisurely between decks, because of the great heat that is there continually, which is sometimes so excessive, that the surgeons would faint away, and the candles would not burn; besides, that in such a crowd of brutish people, there are always some very apt to annoy and hurt others, and all in general so greedy, that they will snatch from the sick slaves the fresh meat or liquor that is given them. It is no way advisable to put the sick slaves into the long-boat upon deck, as was very imprudently done in the *Albion* frigate, spoken of in the description of New Calabar. For they being thus exposed in the open air, and coming out of the excessive hot cold, and lying there in the cool of the nights, for some time just under the fall of the wind from the sails, were soon taken so ill of violent colics and bloody fluxes, that in a few days they died, and the owners lost above three hundred slaves in the passage from St. Tome to Barbadoes; and the two hundred and fifty that survived, were like skeletons, one half of them not yielding above four pounds a head there: an oversight, by which 50 per cent of the stock or outlet was lost.

Much more might be said relating to the preservation and maintenance of slaves in such voyages, which I leave to the prudence of the officers that govern aboard, if they value their own reputation and their owners' advantage; and shall only add these few particulars, that though we ought to be circumspect in watching the slaves narrowly, to prevent or disappoint their ill designs for our own conservation, yet must we not be too severe and haughty with them, but on the contrary, caress and humor them in every reasonable thing. Some commanders, of a morose peevish temper are perpetually beating and curbing them, even without the least offense, and will not suffer any upon deck but when unavoidable necessity to ease themselves does require; under pretense it hinders the work of the ship and sailors, and that they are troublesome by their nasty nauseous stench, or their noise; which makes those poor wretches desperate, and besides their falling into distempers through melancholy, often is the occasion of their destroying themselves.

Such officers should consider, those unfortunate creatures are men as well as themselves, though of a different color, and pagans; and that they ought to do to others as they would be done by in like circumstances; as it may be their turn, if they should have the misfortune to fall into the hands of Algerines or Sallee men, as it has happened to many after such voyages performed. They ought also to consider the interest of their owners, who put them into that employment; and, unless they have laid aside the sense of gratitude and credit, it may be an inducement to curb their brutish temper, and move them to a gentle humane carriage towards the poor slaves and to contribute as far as in them lies, to keep them clean, healthy and easy; to lessen the deep sense of their lamentable condition, which many are sensible enough of, whatever we may think of their stupidity. These methods will undoubtedly turn to the advantage of the adventurers, their masters, and is the least return they can reasonably expect from them.

51. *A Planter's Diary, 1760*

George Washington, *Diaries,* J. C. Fitzpatrick, ed. (Boston, 1925), I, 107–37.

JANUARY, Tuesday, 1. Visited my plantations and received an instance of Mr. French's great love of money in disappointing me of some pork, because the price had risen to 22/6 after he had engaged to let me have it at 20/.

Called at Mr. Possey's in my way home and desired him to engage me 100 barrels of corn upon the best terms he could in Maryland.

And found Mrs. Washington upon my arrival broke out with the measles. . . .

Wednesday, 2d. Fearing a disappointment elsewhere in pork I was fain to take Mr. French's upon his own terms and engaged them to be delivered at my house on Monday next. . . .

Thursday, 3d. Hauled the seine and got some fish, but was near being disappointed of my boat by means of an oyster man, who had lain at my landing and plagued me a good deal by his disorderly behavior.

Tuesday, 8th. Directed an indictment to be formed by Mr. Johnston against Jno. Ballendine for a fraud in some iron he sold me.

Got a little butter from Mr. Dalton, and wrote to Colonel West for pork.

In the evening eight of Mr. French's hogs from his Ravensworth Quarter came down, one being lost on the way—as the others might as well have been for their goodness. Nothing but the disappointments in this article of pork which he himself had caused and my necessities could possibly have obliged me to take them.

Carpenter Sam was taken with the measles.

Wednesday, 9th. Killed and dressed Mr. French's hogs, which weighed 751 lbs. neat.

Colonel West leaving me in doubt about his pork yesterday obliged me to send to him again today, and now no definitive answer was received—he purposing to send his overseer down tomorrow, to agree about it. . . .

Friday, 11th. Delivered Stephens' two hogs in part of his year's provisions weight, 69 [and] 90, [or] 159. He had one before of 100 lbs. weight. Two hogs were also reserved for Foster of the following weights

90		100
83		100
		97
173	which with	90
		387

that were cut out and salted makes up 719 lbs. and accounts for Mr. French's 8 hogs; showing the loss of weighing meat so soon killed, which cannot be less than 5 per cent.

Saturday, 12th. Set out with Mrs. Bassett on her journey . . . and lodged at Mr. McCrae's in Dumfries, sending the horses to the tavern.

Here I was informed that Colonel Cocke was disgusted at my house, and left be-

cause he see an old Negro there resembling his own image.

Sunday, 20th. My wagon, after leaving two hogsheads of tobacco at Alexandria, arrived here with three sides of sole leather and four of upper leather, two kegs of butter, one of which for Colonel Fairfax and fifteen bushels of salt which she took in at Alexandria.

Friday, 25th. Fine warm morning with wind at south till about 10 o'clock, when it came westerly and then northwest blowing exceeding hard till 3 in the afternoon.

Went to Alexandria and saw my tobacco as it came from the mountains, lying in an open shed, with the ends of the hogsheads out and in very bad order. Engaged the inspection of it on Monday.

Wrote to Doctor Ross to purchase me a joiner, bricklayer, and gardener, if any ship of servants was in.

Tuesday, 29th. White frost, and wind at south till 9 o'clock then northwest, but not very cold. Clear all day.

Darcus, daughter to Phillis, died, which makes four Negroes lost this winter; viz., three dower Negroes namely—Beck,—appraised to £50, Doll's child born since, and Darcus . . . , and Belinda, a wench of mine, in Frederick.

[Tuesday, February 5th.] . . . Passing by my carpenters that were hewing I found that four of them viz. George, Tom, Mike and young Billy had only hewed 120 foot yesterday from 10 o'clock. Sat down therefore and observed. Tom and Mike in a less space than thirty minutes cleared the bushes from about a poplar, stocklined it ten foot long and hewed each their side twelve inches deep.

Then, letting them proceed their own way, they spent twenty-five minutes more in getting the cross-cut saw standing to consider what to do, sawing the stock off in two places, putting it on the blocks for hewing it, square lining it, etc. and from this time till they had finished the stock entirely required twenty minutes more; so that in the space of one hour and a quarter they each of them from the stump finished twenty feet of hewing. From hence it appears very clear, that allowing they work only from sun to sun and require two hours at breakfast, they ought to yield each his 125 feet while the days are at their present length and more in proportion as they increase.

While this was doing George and Billy sawed thirty foot of plank, so that it appears as clear, making the same allowance as before (but not for the time required in piling the stock, etc.) that they ought to saw 180 foot of plank.

It is to be observed here, that this hewing and sawing likewise was of poplar; what may be the difference therefore between the working of this wood and other, some future observations must make known.

Thursday, 7th. The hogs which arrived yesterday were killed—weighing, as follows—viz.

142	140	140	139
130	130	110	90
90	90	90	90
83	80	70	
445	440	410	319

Total.... 1614

Out of which Jno. Foster received the remainder of his year's provisions, viz. 177 lbs. He had before 173, making 350, the year's allow[ance]e.

Doctor Laurie's man attended the sick this day also.

I went to Mr. Craig's funeral sermon at Alexandria, and there met my wagons with four hogsheads tobacco more. Unloaded and sent them down to Mt. Vernon.

Thursday, 14th. Mr. Clifton came here and we conditioned for his land, viz. if he is not bound by some prior engagement, I am to have all his land in the Neck (500 acres about his house excepted) and the land commonly called

Brent's for £1600 currency. He getting Messrs. Digges, etc. to join in making me a good and sufficient title. But note, I am not bound to ratify this bargain unless Colonel Carlyle will let me have his land adjoining Brent's at half a pistole an acre.

Visited my quarters and saw a plant patch burnt at the mill.

Brought home 4003 lbs. of hay from Mr. Digges's. . . .

Friday, 15th. A small fine rain from northeast wet the top of my hay that had been landed last night. It was all carted up however to the barn and the wet and dry separated.

Went to a ball at Alexandria, where music and dancing was the chief entertainment. However in a convenient room detached for the purpose abounded great plenty of bread and butter, some biscuits with tea, and coffee which the drinkers of could not distinguish from hot water sweetened. Be it remembered that pockethandkerchiefs served the purposes of table cloths and napkins and that no apologies were made for either.

The proprietors of this ball were Messrs. Carlyle, Laurie and Robert Wilson, but the Doctor not getting it conducted agreeable to his own taste would claim no share of the merit of it.

I shall therefore distinguish this ball by the style and title of the Bread and Butter Ball.

[Tuesday 26th. . . .] Made an absolute agreement with Mr. Clifton for his land (so far as depended upon him) on the following terms, to wit; I am to give him £1150 sterling for his neck lands, containing 1806 acres, and to allow him the use of this plantation he lives on till fall twelve months.

He on his part is to procure the gentlemen of Maryland to whom his lands are under mortgage to join in a conveyance and is to put me into possession of the land so soon as this can be done; he is not to cut down any timber, nor clear any ground, nor to use more wood than what shall be absolutely necessary for fences and firing.

Neither is he to assent to any alterations of tenants transferring of leases, etc. but on the contrary is to discourage every practice that has a tendency to lessen the value of the land.

N.B. he is also to bring Mr. Mercer's opinion concerning the validity of a private sale made by himself.

Tuesday, [March] 11th. Visited at Colonel Fairfax's and was informed that Clifton had sold his land to Mr. Thompson Mason for £1200 sterling, which fully unraveled his conduct on the 2d, and convinced me that he was nothing less than a thorough-paced rascal, disregardful of any engagements of words or oaths not bound by penalties.

52. *Instructions to an Agent, 1759*

Richard Corbin, instructions to James Semple, his agent, Virginia, 1759. Commons, *Documentary History*, I, 109–12. Reprinted by permission of the publishers, The Arthur H. Clark Company.

As IT will be necessary to say something to you and to suggest to you my thoughts upon the business you have undertaken, I shall endeavor to be particular and circumstantial.

The care of Negroes is the first thing to be recommended that you give me timely notice of their wants that they may be provided with all necessaries. The breeding wenches more particularly you must instruct the overseers to be kind and indulgent to, and not force them when with child upon any service or hardship that will be injurious to them and that they have every necessary when in that condition that is needful for them, and the children to be well looked after and to give them every Spring and Fall the Jerusalem Oak seed for a week together and that none of them suffer in time of sickness for want of proper care.

Observe a prudent and watchful conduct over the overseers, that they attend their business with diligence, keep the Negroes in good order, and enforce obedience by the example of their own industry, which is a more effectual method in every respect of succeeding and making good crops than hurry and severity. The ways of industry are constant and regular, not to be in a hurry at one time and do nothing at another, but to be always usefully and

steadily employed. A man who carries on business in this manner will be prepared for every incident that happens. He will see what work may be proper at the distance of some time and be gradually and leisurely providing for it. By this foresight he will never be in confusion himself and his business, instead of a labor, will be a pleasure to him.

Next to the care of Negroes is the care of stock and, supposing the necessary care taken, I shall only here mention the use to be made of them for the improvement of the tobacco grounds. Let them be constantly and regularly penned. Let the size of the pens be one thousand tobacco hills for one hundred cattle, and so in proportion for a greater or less quantity, and the pens moved once a week. By this practice, steadily pursued, a convenient quantity of land may be provided at Moss's Neck without clearing. And as I intend this seat of land to be a settlement for one of my sons, I would be very sparing of the woods; and that piece of woods that lies on the left hand of the Ferry Road must not be cut down on any account. A proper use of the cattle will answer every purpose of making tobacco without the disturbance too commonly made of the timber land. And as you will see this estate once a fortnight, you may easily discover if they have been neglectful of penning the cattle and moving the cowpens.

Take an exact account of all the Negroes and stocks at each plantation and send to me; and though once a year may be sufficient to take this account, yet it will be advisable to see them once a month at least, as such an inspection will fix more closely the overseers' attentions to these points. As complaints have been made by the Negroes in respect to their provision of corn, I must desire you to put that matter under such a regulation as your own prudence will dictate to you. The allowance, to be sure, is plentiful, and they ought to have their belly full; but care must be taken with this plenty that no waste is committed. You must let Hampton know that the care of the Negroes' corn, sending it to mill, always to be provided with meal that everyone may have enough, and that regularly and at stated times, this is a duty as much incumbent upon him as any other. As the corn at Moss's Neck is always ready money it will not be advisable to be at much expense in raising hogs. The shattered corn will probably be enough for this purpose. When I receive your account of the spare corn at Moss's Neck and Richland, which I hope will be from King and Queen Court, I shall give orders to Colonel Tucker to send for it.

Let me be acquainted with every incident that happens and let me have timely notice of everything that is wanted, that it may be provided. To employ the Fall and Winter well is the foundation of a successful crop in the summer. You will therefore animate the overseers to great diligence that their work may be in proper forwardness and not have that to do in the Spring that ought to be done in the Winter. There is business sufficient for every season of the year and to prevent the work of one season from interfering with the work of another depends upon the care of the overseer.

The time of sowing tobacco seed, the order the plant patch ought to be in, and the use of the wheat straw I have not touched upon, it being too obvious to be overlooked.

Supposing the corn new laid and the tobacco ripe for housing: to cut the corn tops and gather the blades in proper time is included under the care of cattle, their preservation in the winter depending upon good fodder. I shall therefore confine myself to tobacco. Tobacco hogsheads should always be provided the first week in September; every morning of the month is fit for striking and stripping. Every morning, therefore, of this month they should strike as much tobacco as they can strip while the dew is upon the ground, and what they strip in the morning must be stemmed in the evening; this method constantly practiced, the tobacco will be all prised before Christmas, weigh well, and at least one hogshead in ten gained by finishing the tobacco thus early. You shall never want either for my advice or assistance. These instructions will hold good for Poplar Neck and Portobacco and perhaps Spotsylvania too.

I now send my two carpenters Mack and Abram to Moss's Neck to build a good barn, mend up the quarters and get as many staves and heading as will be sufficient for next year's tobacco hogsheads; I expect they will complete the whole that is necessary upon that estate by the last of March.

VII 🦋 *Political Development*

BETWEEN 1680 and 1760 the colonies enjoyed a long period of relative freedom from interference by the mother country. These years gave them the opportunity to develop political experience and to work out political ideas immensely significant in the future. Although each province retained its identity and followed a course peculiar to itself, the general outlines of governmental structure, habits, and assumptions were acquiring a characteristically American form.

In part these developments were stimulated by the emergence of such new colonies as Pennsylvania, whose charter emphasized unusual freedom for the settlers (No. 53). The revolutionary disturbances of 1688 in England also had an effect in the colonies. The revolt against Governor Andros (No. 54) opened the way to a freer regime in New England, although Massachusetts was soon to lose its old charter. And, despite the defeat of Jacob Leisler in New York (No. 55), the forces he represented made substantial gains in the decades that followed. Thereafter the preoccupation of England in the long series of wars with France (*see above*, Section V) offered the colonies substantial respite from imperial control.

The development of provincial society in these decades also gave the colonists a new conception of their own rights. Increasingly this conception diverged from that held by Englishmen in the mother country. In the Zenger case, for instance, a difference of views as to what constituted a libel opened up the whole issue of whether the liberties of the colonists were not more extensive than those of men in England (No. 56). The development of popularly elected legislatures gave the colonists a potent voice, as the long series of conflicts with provincial governors showed. On specific issues, such as paper money, the Americans persistently disagreed with the Crown. By mid-century Thomas Mayhew was setting forth a doctrine which made it their right, even duty, to resist tyranny (No. 57). Such views were encouraged by the effective independence of government, of which that of Rhode Island was an extreme example (No. 58).

Meanwhile, the colonies were also drawn closer together in interest. The Albany Plan of Union (No. 59) failed. But it reflected the strength of the ties that already held the provinces together.

53. *The Pennsylvania Charter of Privileges, 1701*

Poore, *Federal and State Constitutions*, Part II, 1536–40

WILLIAM PENN, Proprietary and Governor of the Province of Pennsylvania . . . , To all whom these presents shall come, sendeth greeting. Whereas King Charles the Second . . . in the year one thousand six hundred and eight-one, was graciously pleased to give and grant unto me, and my heirs and assigns for ever, this Province of Pennsylvania, with divers great powers and jurisdictions for the well government thereof. . . .

And whereas for the encouragement of all the freemen and planters, that might be concerned in the said Province and territories, and for the good government thereof, I the said William Penn, in the year one thousand six hundred eighty and three . . . did grant and confirm unto all the freemen, planters and adventurers therein, divers liberties, franchises and properties, as by the said grant, entitled, The Frame of the Government of the Province of Pennsylvania, and Territories thereunto belonging, in America, may appear; which . . . Frame . . . was . . . delivered up to me, by . . . the freemen of this Province . . . in General Assembly met. . . .

And whereas I was then pleased to promise, that I would restore the said Charter to them again, with necessary alterations. . . .

Know ye therefore, that for the further well-being and good government of the said Province . . . , I . . . do . . . grant . . . unto all the . . . inhabitants of this Province . . . these following liberties, franchises and privileges. . . .

Because no people can be truly happy, though under the greatest enjoyment of civil liberties, if abridged of the freedom of their consciences, as to their religious profession and worship; and Almighty God being the only Lord of Conscience . . . who only doth enlighten the minds, and persuade and convince the understandings of people, I do hereby grant and declare, that no person or persons, inhabiting in this Province or territories, who shall confess and acknowledge One almighty God, the Creator, Upholder and Ruler of the World; and profess . . . themselves obliged to live quietly under the civil government, shall be in any case molested or prejudiced, in . . . their person or estate, because of . . . their conscientious persuasion or practice, nor be compelled to frequent

or maintain any religious worship, place or ministry, contrary to . . . their mind, or to do or suffer any other act or thing, contrary to their religious persuasion.

And that all persons who also profess to believe in Jesus Christ, the Savior of the World, shall be capable . . . to serve this government in any capacity . . . they solemnly promising, when lawfully required, allegiance to the King as sovereign, and fidelity to the proprietary and governor. . . .

For the well governing of this Province and territories, there shall be an Assembly yearly chosen, by the freemen thereof, to consist of four persons out of each county, of most note for virtue, wisdom and ability . . . upon the first day of October for ever; and shall sit on the fourteenth day of the same month, at Philadelphia, unless the Governor and Council for the time being, shall see cause to appoint another place within the said Province or territories. Which assembly shall have power to choose a speaker and other their officers; and shall be judges of the qualifications and elections of their own members, sit upon their own adjournments, appoint committees, prepare bills in order to pass into laws, impeach criminals, and redress grievances; and shall have all other powers and privileges of an Assembly, according to the rights of the free-born subjects of England, and as is usual in any of the King's plantations in America.

And if any county or counties, shall refuse or neglect to choose their respective representatives . . . , those who are . . . chosen and met, shall have the full power of an Assembly, in as ample manner as if all the representatives had been chosen and met, provided they are not less than two-thirds of the whole number that ought to meet. . . .

That the freemen in each respective county, at the time and place of meeting for electing their representatives to serve in Assembly, may as often as there shall be occasion, choose a double number of persons to present to the Governor for sheriffs and coroners to serve for three years, if so long they behave themselves well; out of which respective elections and presentments, the Governor shall nominate and commissionate one for each of the said offices, the third day after such presentment, or else the first named in such presentment, for each office as aforesaid, shall stand and serve in that office for the time before respectively limited; and in case of death or default, such vacancies shall be supplied by the Governor, to serve to the end of the said term.

Provided always, that if the said freemen shall at any time neglect or decline to choose a person or persons for either or both the aforesaid offices, then and in such case, the persons that are or shall be in the respective offices of sheriffs or coroners, at the time of election, shall remain therein, until they shall be removed by another election as aforesaid.

And that the justices of the respective counties shall or may nominate and present to the Governor three persons, to serve for clerk of the peace for the said county, when there is a vacancy, one of which the Governor shall commissionate within ten days after such presentment, or else the first nominated shall serve in the said office during good behavior. . . .

That all criminals shall have the same privileges of witnesses and council as their prosecutors.

That no person or persons shall or may, at any time hereafter, be obliged to answer any complaint, matter or thing whatsoever, relating to property, before the Governor and Council, or in any other place, but in ordinary course of justice, unless appeals thereunto shall be hereafter by law appointed.

That no person within this government, shall be licensed by the Governor to keep an ordinary, tavern or house of public entertainment, but such who are first recommended to him, under the hands of the justices of the respective counties, signed in open court; which justices are and shall be hereby impowered, to suppress and forbid any person, keeping such public house as aforesaid, upon their misbehavior, on such penalties as the law doth . . . direct. . . .

If any person, through temptation or melancholy, shall destroy himself; his estate, real and personal, shall notwithstanding descend to his wife and children, or relations, as if he had died a natural death; and if any person shall be destroyed or killed by casualty or accident, there shall be no forfeiture to the Governor by reason thereof.

And no act, law or ordinance whatsoever, shall at any time hereafter, be made or done, to alter, change or diminish the form or effect of this charter, or of any part or clause therein, contrary to the true intent and meaning thereof, without the consent of the Governor for the time being, and six parts of seven of the Assembly met.

But because the happiness of mankind depends so much upon the enjoying of liberty of their consciences as aforesaid, I do hereby solemnly declare, promise and grant . . . that the first article of this charter relating to liberty of conscience . . . shall be kept and remain, without any alteration, inviolably for ever.

And lastly, I the said William Penn, Proprietary and Governor of the Province of Pennsylvania . . . have solemnly declared, granted and confirmed . . . that neither I, my heirs or assigns, shall procure or do any thing or things whereby the liberties in this charter contained and expressed . . . , shall be infringed or broken. And if anything shall be procured or done, by any person or persons, contrary to these presents, it shall be held of no force or effect.

54. *The Revolution in Massachusetts Against Andros, 1689*

"Letter from Mr. Thomas Danforth to the Rev. Mr. Increase Mather. Cambridge in N. E. July 30th, 1869," in Thomas Hutchinson, *A Collection of Original Papers Relative to the History of the Colony of Massachusetts-Bay* (Boston, 1769), 567–71. From the facsimile reprint of the Prince Society (Albany, 1865).

IT's now fourteen weeks since the revolution of the government here, the manner whereof, before these can reach you, will spread far and near. Future consequences we are ignorant of, yet we know that, at present, we are eased of those great oppressions that we groaned under, by the exercise of an arbitrary and illegal commission, some brief account whereof is contained in the declaration published the same day, a copy whereof I herewith send you.

The business was acted by the soldiers that came armed into Boston from all parts, to the great amazement of all beholders, being greatly animated by the Prince's declarations, which about that time came into the country, and heightened by the oppressions of the governor, judges, and the most wicked extortion of their debauched officers. The ancient magistrates and elders, although they had strenuously advised to further waiting for orders from England, and discouraged any attempts of that nature so far as they had opportunity, yet were they now compelled to assist with their presence and counsels for the prevention of bloodshed, which had most certainly been the issue if prudent counsel had not been given to both parties. A copy of that paper sent Sir Edmund Andros I have herewith sent you, upon which he forthwith came and surrendered himself.

The same day, about thirty more of the principal persons of that knot were secured, whereof some were quickly released, and some yet remain under restraint, eight of whom . . . the representatives of the people, at their last sessions, voted unbailable. Mr. Dudley in a peculiar manner is the object of the people's displeasure, even throughout all the colonies where he hath sat judge. They deeply resent his correspondence with that wicked man Mr. Randolph . . . and the manner of his procuring his presidentship, his extreme covetousness, getting to himself so many bags of money, to the ruinating of trade; and since Sir Edmund's arrival here, hath been his great instrument in the oppression of the people. . . .

I am deeply sensible that we have a wolf by the ears. This one thing being circumstanced with much difficulty, the people will not permit any inlargement, they having accused them of treason against their King and country. . . . I do therefore earnestly entreat of you to procure the best advice you can in this matter that, if possible, the good intents of the people and their loyalty to the Crown of England may not turn to their prejudice. The example of England, the declarations put forth by the Prince of Orange, now our King, the alteration of the government in England making the arbitrary commission of Sir Edmund null and void in the law; these considerations, in conjunction with the great oppressions they lay under, were so far prevalent in the minds of all, that although some could not advise to the enterprise, yet are hopeful that we shall not be greatly blamed, but shall have a pardon granted for any error the law will charge us with in this matter. . . .

I must also yet a little further acquaint you that sundry of those gentlemen and merchants that were very active in this matter on the day of the revolution yet, since ... are greatly discontented and speak highly against the representatives of the people and present government. And, as we are informed, sundry of them, mostly factors and strangers, have drawn a petition to the lords of the Committee for Foreign Plantations, pretending loyalty and advance of revenue to the Crown, and highly inveighing against the government and people. Whereas, in truth, they are the transgressors of those acts for trade and navigation, and those whom they complain against are generally unconcerned in either, and so uncapable to do the thing they accuse them of. If anything of this nature be presented, let me intreat you sedulously to divert the mischief intended and send me a copy thereof by the first opportunity.

Captain George, commander of the Rose frigate, was also the same day with the rest of that knot seized, reports being spread by sundry of his men, that he intended for France, there to wait on the late King James, and before his departure to show his spleen against Boston, so that the people were afraid of being murdered and burned up in their beds,—the lieutenant also a known papist. The sails of the frigate are brought on shore and se-

cured till the government here receive Their Majesty's order, for which deed it's hoped we shall not receive blame.

We do crave that the circumstances of our case and condition in all respects may be considered. Nature hath taught us self preservation. God commands it as being the rule of charity towards our neighbor. Our great remoteness from England denies us the opportunity of direction and order from thence for the regulating ourselves in all emergencies, nor have we means to know the laws and customs of our nation. These things are our great disadvantage. We have always endeavored to approve ourselves loyal to the Crown of England, and are well assured that none of our worst enemies dare to tax us in that matter. And we have also labored to attend the directions of our charter, under the security whereof were laid by our fathers the foundation of this His Majesty's colony; and we are not without hopes but that before you do receive these lines we shall receive from Their Royal Majesties the confirmation of our charter, with such addition of privileges as may advance the revenue of the Crown, and be an encouragement to Their Majesties' subjects here.

55. *A Hostile Account of Leisler's Rebellion, New York, 1689*

"A Letter from a Gentleman of the City of New York to Another" (New York, 1698) in E. B. O'Callaghan, *Documentary History of the State of New York* (Albany, 1849), II, 426–33.

I CANNOT but admire to hear that some gentlemen still have a good opinion of the late disorders committed by Captain Jacob Leisler and his accomplices, in New York, as if they had been for His Majesty's service. . . .

It was about the beginning of April, 1689, when the first reports arrived at New York, that the Prince of Orange, now His present Majesty, was arrived in England with considerable forces, and

that the late King James was fled into France. . . .

The Lieutenant Governor, Francis Nicholson, and the Council, being Protestants, resolved thereupon to suspend all Roman Catholics from command and places of trust in the government. . . . And because but three members of the Council were residing in New York, . . . it was resolved by the said Lieutenant Governor and Council, to call and convene to their assistance all the justices of the peace, and other civil magistrates, and the commission officers in the Province, for to consult and advise with them what might be proper for the preservation of the peace, and the safety of said Province [in] that conjuncture, till orders should arrive from England.

Whereupon the said justices, magistrates and officers were accordingly convened, and styled by the name of "The General Convention for the Province of New York"; and all matters of government were carried on and managed by the major vote of that convention.

And in the first place it was by them agreed and ordered, forthwith to fortify the City of New York. . . . But against expectation it soon happened, that on the last day of said month of May, Captain Leisler having a vessel with some wines in the road, for which he refused to pay the duty, did in a seditious manner stir up the meanest sort of the inhabitants (affirming that King James being fled the Kingdom, all manner of government was fallen in this Province) to rise in arms and forcibly possess themselves of the fort and stores. Which accordingly was effected while the Lieutenant Governor and Council, with the Convention, were met at the City Hall to consult what might be proper for the common good and safety; where a party of armed men came from the fort, and forced the Lieutenant Governor to deliver them the keys; and seized also in his chamber a chest with seven hundred seventy-three pounds, twelve shillings in money of the government. And though Colonel Bayard, with some others appointed by the Convention, used all endeavors to prevent those disorders, all proved vain; for most of those that appeared in arms were drunk, and cried out, *they disowned all manner of government.* Whereupon, by Captain Leisler's persuasion, they proclaimed him to be their commander, there being then no other commission officer amongst them.

Captain Leisler being in this manner possessed of the fort, took some persons to his assistance, which he called, "The Committee of Safety." And the Lieutenant Governor, Francis Nicholson, . . . for the safety of his person, . . . withdrew out of the Province. . . .

The said Captain Leisler finding almost every man of sense, reputation or estate in the place to oppose and discourage his irregularities, caused frequent false alarms to be made, and sent several parties of his armed men out of the fort, dragged into nasty gaols within said fort several of the principal magistrates, officers and gentlemen, and others, that would not own his power to be lawful, which he kept in close prison during will and pleasure, without any process, or allowing them to bail. And he further published several times, by beat of drums, that all those who would not come into the fort and sign their hands, and so . . . own his power to be lawful, should be deemed . . . enemies to His Majesty and the country, and be . . . treated accordingly. By which means many of the inhabitants, though they abhorred his actions, only to escape a nasty gaol and to secure their estates, were by fear and compulsion drove to comply . . . and sign to whatever he commanded. . . .

Upon the 10th of December following returned . . . Mr. John Riggs from England, with letters from His Majesty and the Lords, in answer to the letters sent by the Lieutenant Governor and Council. . . , directed, "To our trusty and well-beloved Francis Nicholson, Esq; our Lieutenant Governor and Commander in Chief of our Province of New York in America, and in his absence to such as for the time being, take care for the preservation of the peace and administering the laws in our said Province.". . .

Soon after the receipt of said letters, said Captain Leisler styled himself Lieutenant Governor, appointed a council, and presumed further to call a select number of his own party, who called themselves the General Assembly of the Province, and by their advice and assistance raised several taxes and great sums of money from Their Majesties' good subjects within this Province. Which taxes, together with that £773. 12, in money, which he had seized from the government, and the whole revenue, he applied to his own use, and to maintain said disorders, allowing his private men 18d. per day, and to others proportionally. . . .

None in the Province, but those of his faction, had any safety in their estates; for said Captain Leisler, at will and pleasure, sent to those who disapproved of his actions, to furnish him with money, provisions, and what else he wanted, and upon denial, sent armed men out of the fort, and forcibly broke open several houses, shops, cellars, vessels, and other places, where they expected to be supplied, and without any the least payment or satisfaction, carried their plunder to the fort. . . .

In this calamity, misery and confusion was this Province, by those disorders, enthralled near the space of two years, until the arrival of His Majesty's forces, under the command of Major Ingoldesby, who, with several gentlemen of the Council, arrived about the last day of January, 1690. Which said gentlemen of the Council, for the preservation of the peace, . . . offered to said Leisler, that he might stay and continue his command in the fort, only desiring for themselves and the King's forces quietly to quarter and refresh themselves in the city, till Governor Slaughter should arrive. But . . . the said Leisler proceeded to make war against them and the King's forces, and fired a vast number of great and small shot in the city, whereby several of His Majesty's subjects were killed and wounded. . . .

At this height of extremity was it when Governor Slaughter arrived on the 19th of March, 1691. Who having published his commission from the City Hall, with great signs of joy, by firing all the artillery within and round the city, sent thrice to demand the surrender of the fort from Captain Leisler and his accomplices which was thrice denied; but upon great threatenings, the following day surrendered to Governor Slaughter, who forthwith caused the said Captain Leisler, with some of the chief malefactors to be bound over to answer their crimes at the next Supreme Court of Judicature, where the said Leisler and his pretended secretary, Milborne, did appear but refused to plead to the indictment of the grand jury, or to own the jurisdiction of that Court; and so after several hearings, as mutes, were found guilty of high treason and murder, and executed accordingly.

56. *Liberty and the Press, New York, 1735*

A Brief Narrative of the Case and Tryal of John Peter Zenger (New York, 1736). From the version reprinted in Livingston Rutherfurd, *John Peter Zenger* (New York, 1904), 203–6.

Mr. Hamilton. . . . Is it not surprising to see a subject, upon his receiving a commission from the King to be a governor of a colony in America, immediately imagining himself to be vested with all the prerogatives belonging to the sacred person of his Prince? And which is yet more astonishing, to see that a people can be so wild as to allow of and acknowledge those prerogatives and exemptions, even to their own destruction? . . . And yet in all the cases which Mr. Attorney has cited, to show the duty and obedience we owe to the supreme magistrate, it is the King that is there meant and understood, though Mr. Attorney is pleased to urge them as authorities to prove the heinousness of Mr. Zenger's offense against the Governor of New York. . . . Let us not (while we are pretending to pay a great regard to our Prince and his peace) make bold to transfer that allegiance to a subject, which we owe to our King only.

What strange doctrine is it, to press every thing for law here which is so in England? I believe we should not think it a favor, at present at least, to establish this practice. In England so great a regard and reverence is had to the judges, that if any man strikes another in Westminster Hall, while the judges are sitting, he shall lose his right hand, and forfeit his land and goods, for so doing. And though the judges here claim all the powers and authorities within this government, that a court of King's Bench has in England, yet I believe Mr. Attorney will scarcely say, that such a punishment could be legally inflicted on a man for committing such an offense, in the presence of the judges sitting in any court within the Province of New York. . . .

MR. ATTORNEY. . . . The case before the court is, whether Mr. Zenger is guilty of libelling His Excellency the Governor of New York, and indeed the whole administration of the government? Mr. Hamilton has confessed the printing and publishing, and I think nothing is plainer, than that the words in the information are *scandalous*, and *tend to sedition, and to disquiet the minds of the people of this province.* And if such papers are not libels, I think it may be said, there can be no such thing as a libel.

MR. HAMILTON. May it please your honor; I cannot agree with Mr. Attorney. For though I freely acknowledge, that there are such things as libels, yet I must insist at the same time, that what my client is charged with, is not a libel; and

I observed just now, that Mr. Attorney in defining a libel, made use of the words, *scandalous, seditious,* and *tend to disquiet the people;* but (whether with design or not I will not say) he omitted the word *false.*

MR. ATTORNEY. I think I did not omit the word *false:* But it has been said already, that it may be a libel, notwithstanding it may be true.

MR. HAMILTON. In this I must still differ with Mr. Attorney; for I depend upon it, we are to be tried upon this information now before the court and the jury, and to which we have pleaded *not guilty,* and by it we are charged with printing and publishing *a certain false, malicious, seditious and scandalous libel.* This word *false* must have some meaning, or else how came it there? I hope Mr. Attorney will not say, he put it there by chance, and I am of opinion his information would not be good without it. But to show that it is the principal thing which, in my opinion, makes a libel, I put the case, the information had been for printing and publishing a certain *true* libel, would that be the same thing? Or could Mr. Attorney support such an information by any precedent in the *English* law? No, the falsehood makes the scandal, and both make the libel. And to show the court that I am in good earnest, and to save the court's time, and Mr. Attorney's trouble, I will agree, that if he can prove the facts charged upon us, to be *false,* I'll own them to be *scandalous, seditious,* and a *libel.* So the work seems now to be pretty much shortened, and Mr. Attorney has now only to prove the words *false,* in order to make us guilty.

57. *A Sermon on Politics, 1750*

Alden Bradford, *Memoir of the Life and Writings of Rev. Jonathan Mayhew* (Boston, 1838), 109–12.

THERE is nothing in scripture which supports . . . political despotism, or . . . arbitrary principles. The apostle does not con-

cern himself with the different forms of government. This he supposes to be left entirely to human prudence and discretion. Now, the consequence of this is, that unlimited and passive obedience is no more enjoined, in this passage, under monarchical government, or to the supreme power in a state, than under any other form of government.

The essence of government, I mean good government, and this is the government the apostle treats of, consists in making good laws, and in the wise and just execution of them—laws attempered to the common welfare of the governed. And if this be in fact done, it is evidently, in itself, a thing of no consequence what the particular form of government is; whether the legislative and executive power be lodged in one and the same person, or in different persons; whether in one person, which is called a monarchy; whether in a few—whether in many, so as to constitute a republic; or in three co-ordinate branches, in such manner as to make the government partake of each of these forms, and to be, at the same time, essentially different from them all. If the end be attained, it is enough. But no form of government seems to be so unlikely to accomplish this end as absolute monarchy. Nor is there any one which has so little pretense to a divine original, unless it be in this sense, that God first permitted it into, and thereby overturned, the Commonwealth of Israel, as a curse or punishment on that people, for their folly and wickedness particularly, in desiring such a government.

If we calmly consider the nature of the thing itself, nothing can well be imagined more directly contrary to common sense, than to suppose that millions of people should be subject to the arbitrary and precarious pleasure of a single man (who has, naturally, no superiority over them in point of authority), so that their estates and everything valuable in life, and even their lives also, shall be absolutely at his disposal, if he happens to be wanton and capricious enough to demand them. What unprejudiced man can think that God made all to be thus subservient to the law-less pleasure and frenzy of one, so that it shall always be a sin to resist him. Nothing but the most plain and express revelation from heaven, could make a sober, impartial man believe such a monstrous, unaccountable doctrine. And, indeed, the thing itself appears so shocking, so out of all proportion, that it may be questioned whether all the miracles ever wrought could make it credible that such a doctrine came from God. At present there is not a syllable in scripture which gives any countenance to it. The hereditary, indefeasible, divine right of kings, and the doctrine of non-resistance, which is built on the supposition of such a right, are altogether as fabulous and chimerical as transubstantiation, or any of the most absurd reveries of ancient or modern visionaries. These notions are fetched neither from divine revelation, nor from human reason; and if they are derived from neither of these sources, it is not much matter whence they come, or whither they go. Only it is a pity such doctrines should be propagated in society, to raise factions and rebellions, as we see they have, in fact, both in the last and present reign.

We may safely assert these two things, in general, without undermining civil government. One is, that no civil rulers are to be obeyed, when they enjoin things inconsistent with the word and commands of God. All disobedience, in such case, is lawful and glorious; particularly if people refuse to comply with any legal establishment of religion, because it is a gross perversion and corruption of a pure and divine religion, brought from God to man by the Son of God himself, the only head of the Christian church. All commands, running counter to the revealed will of God, are null or void; and disobedience to them is not a crime, but a duty.

Another thing may be asserted with equal truth and safety; which is, that no government is to be submitted to, at the expense of that which is the great and sole end of government, the common good and welfare of society. Because, to submit in such a case, if it should ever happen, would evidently be to set up means as more valuable and above the end; than which there cannot be a greater solecism and absurdity. The only reason of the institution of civil government, and the only rational ground of submission to it, is the common safety and utility. If, therefore, in any case, the common safety and utility would not be promoted by submission to the government, but extensive and lasting evil ensue, there is no ground or motive for submission and obedience, but for the contrary.

58. A Democratic Government, 1759

Andrew Burnaby, *Travels in the Middle Settlements in North-America* (London, 1775), 123–30.

THE GOVERNMENT of . . . [Rhode Island] is entirely democratical; every officer, except the collector of the customs, being appointed, I believe, either immediately by the people, or by the general assembly. The people choose annually a governor, lieutenant-governor, and ten assistants, which constitute an upper house. The representatives, or lower house, are elected every half year. These jointly have the appointment of all other public officers, (except the recorder, treasurer and attorney-general, which are appointed likewise annually by the people,) both military and civil; are invested with the powers of legislation, of regulating the militia, and of performing all other acts of government. The governor has no negative, but votes with the assistants, and in case of an equality has a casting voice. The assembly, or two houses united, are obliged to sit immediately after each election; at Newport in the summer, and in the winter alternately at Providence and South Kingston in Narragansett. They adjourn themselves, but may be called together, notwithstanding such adjournment, upon any urgent occasion by the governor. No assistant, or representative is allowed any salary or pay for his attendance or service.

There are several courts of judicature. The assembly nominates annually so many justices for each township, as are judged necessary. These have power to join people in matrimony, and to exercise other acts of authority usually granted to this order of magistrates. Any two of them may hear cases concerning small debts and trespasses; and three may even try criminals for thefts, not exceeding ten pounds currency. Appeals in civil cases are allowed to the inferior Court of Common Pleas; in criminal ones to the sessions of the peace; and in these the determinations are final.

The sessions are held in each county twice every year by five or more justices; they adjudge all matters relative to the preservation of the peace, and the punishment of criminals, except in cases of death. Appeals are allowed from this court, in all cases that have originated in it, to the superior one. . . . The dernier resort is to the King in Council, but this only in cases of £300 value, new tenor. The people have the power of pardoning criminals, except in cases of piracy, murder or high treason; and then it is doubted whether they can even reprieve.

There is no established form of religion here; but Church of England men, Independents, Quakers, Anabaptists, Moravians, Jews and all other sects whatsoever, have liberty to exercise their several professions. The Society for the Propagation of the Gospel sends only four missionaries.

Arts and sciences are almost unknown, except to some few individuals; and there are no public seminaries of learning. Nor do the Rhode Islanders in general seem to regret the want of them. The institution of a library society, which has lately taken place, may possibly in time produce a change in these matters.

The character of the Rhode Islanders is by no means engaging, or amiable: a circumstance principally owing to their form of government. Their men in power, from the highest to the lowest, are dependent upon the people, and frequently act without that strict regard to probity and honor.... The private people are cunning, deceitful and selfish: they live almost entirely by unfair and illicit trading. Their magistrates are partial and corrupt; and it is folly to expect justice in their courts of judicature. For he, who has the greatest influence, is generally found to have the fairest cause. Were the governor to interpose his authority, were he to refuse to grant flags of truce, or not to wink at abuses, he would at the expiration of the year be excluded from his office, the only thing perhaps which he has to subsist upon. Were the judges to act with impartiality, and to decide a case to the prejudice or disadvantage of any great or popular leader, they would probably never be reelected. Indeed, they are incapable in general of determining the merits of a suit, for they are exceedingly illiterate, and, where they have nothing to make them partial, are managed almost entirely by the lawyers....

It is needless, after this, to observe that [this colony] is in a very declining state; for it is impossible that it should prosper under such abuses. Its West Indian trade has diminished; owing indeed, in some measure, to the other colonies having entered more largely into this lucrative branch of commerce. It has lost during the war, by the enemy, above one hundred and fifty vessels. Its own privateers ... have had very ill success. Having kept up a regiment of provincial troops, it has also been loaded with taxes, and many of the people have been oppressed by the mode of collecting them. For, ... the inhabitants have been assessed by the town council, consisting of the assistants residing there, the justices of the town, and a few free-holders elected annually by the freemen; and these have been generally partial in their assessments, as must necessarily happen under a combination of such circumstances.

59. *Albany Plan of Union,* 1754

F. N. Thorpe, ed., *Federal and State Constitutions* (Washington, 1909), I, 83–6.

THAT humble application be made for an act of [the] Parliament of Great Britain, by virtue of which, one general government may be formed in America, including all the said colonies, within and under which government each colony may retain its present constitution, except in the particulars wherein a change may be directed by the said act, as hereafter follows.

That the general government be administered by a President General, to be appointed and supported by the Crown, and a Grand Council to be chosen by the representatives of the people of the several colonies ... in their respective assemblies.

That within   months after the passing of such act, the House of Representatives [in the several assemblies], that happens to be sitting within that time or that shall be especially for that purpose convened, may and shall choose, members for the Grand Council in the following proportion ... :

Massachusetts Bay	7
New Hampshire	2
Connecticut	5
Rhode Island	2
New York	4

New Jerseys........... 3
Pennsylvania........... 6
Maryland 4
Virginia............... 7
North Carolina......... 4
South Carolina......... 4
—
48

Who shall meet for the present time at the city of Philadelphia in Pennsylvania, being called by the President General as soon as conveniently may be after his appointment.

That there shall be a new election of the members of the Grand Council every three years, and on the death or resignation of any member, his place should be supplied by a new choice at the next sitting of the assembly of the colony he represented.

That after the first three years, when the proportion of money arising out of each colony to the general treasury can be known, the number of members to be chosen for each colony shall from time to time in all ensuing elections be regulated by that proportion, yet so as that the number to be chosen by any one province be not more than seven nor less than two.

That the Grand Council shall meet once in every year, and oftener if occasion require, at such time and place as they shall adjourn to at the last preceding meeting, or as they shall be called to meet [at] by the President General, on any emergency, he having first obtained in writing the consent of seven of the members to such call, and sent due and timely notice to the whole.

That the Grand Council have power to choose their speaker, and shall neither be dissolved, prorogued, nor continue sitting longer than six weeks at one time without their own consent, or the special command of the Crown. . . .

That the assent of the President General be requisite to all acts of the Grand Council, and that it be his office and duty to cause them to be carried into execution. That the President General with the ad-

vice of the Grand Council, hold or direct all Indian treaties in which the general interest of the colonies may be concerned; and make peace or declare war with Indian nations. That they make such laws as they judge necessary for the regulating all Indian trade. That they make all purchases from Indians for the Crown, of lands not now within the bounds of particular colonies, or that shall not be within their bounds when some of them are reduced to more convenient dimensions. That they make new settlements on such purchases by granting lands, . . . reserving a quit rent to the Crown, for the use of the general treasury. That they make laws for regulating and governing such new settlements, till the Crown shall think fit to form them into particular governments.

That they raise and pay soldiers, and build forts for the defense of any of the colonies, and equip vessels of force to guard the coasts and protect the trade on the ocean, lakes or great rivers; but they shall not impress men in any colony without the consent of the legislature. That for these purposes they have power to make laws and lay and levy such general duties, imposts or taxes, as to them shall appear most equal and just (considering the ability and other circumstances of the inhabitants in the several colonies), and such as may be collected with the least inconvenience to the people, rather discouraging luxury, than loading industry with unnecessary burthens.—That they may appoint a general treasurer and particular treasurer in each government when necessary, and from time to time may order the sums in the treasuries of each government into the general treasury or draw on them for special payments as they find most convenient. Yet no money to issue but by joint orders of the President General and Grand Council; except where sums have been appropriated to particular purposes, and the President General is previously empowered by an act to draw such sums. . . .

That a quorum of the Grand Council

empowered to act with the President General, do consist of twenty-five members, among whom there shall be one or more from a majority of the colonies. That the laws made by them for the purposes aforesaid, shall not be repugnant, but, as near as may be, agreeable to the laws of England, and shall be transmitted to the King in Council for approbation, as soon as may be after their passing; and if not disapproved within three years after presentation to remain in force. . . .

That all military commission officers, whether for land or sea service . . . shall be nominated by the President General; but the approbation of the Grand Council is to be obtained before they receive their commissions. And all civil officers are to be nominated by the Grand Council, and to receive the President General's approbation before they officiate. But in case of vacancy by death or removal of any officer civil or military under this constitution, the governor of the province in which such vacancy happens, may appoint till the pleasure of the President General and Grand Council can be known.—That the particular military as well as civil establishments in each colony remain in their present state, the general constitution notwithstanding; and that on sudden emergencies any colony may defend itself, and lay the accounts of expense thence arising before the President General and Grand Council, who may allow and order payment of the same as far as they judge such accounts just and reasonable.

VIII *New World Ideas*

THE NEW GENERATION of Americans developed patterns of thought significantly different both from those of their American ancestors and from those of their contemporaries in Europe. The colonists were not cut off from the dominant intellectual movements of the Old World; through this period there was a continuous and liberal exchange of ideas across the Atlantic, stimulated by travel, immigration, and the diffusion of English books and magazines. Nevertheless, distinctive problems and relative isolation gave provincial thought a special cast.

The contrast between ideas of the earlier generation and those of the later is striking. A noteworthy demonstration occurred early in the period in the case of the witchcraft delusion in Salem Village. It was not surprising that many Americans at the time should have believed in the existence of witches. The seventeenth-century man—in the New World and in the Old—had taken these spectral spirits for granted. More significant in the 1690's in Massachusetts was the appearance of a skeptical attitude. The conservative, Increase Mather, who continued to regard these beings as real, nevertheless insisted upon "scientific" methods of proof (No. 60); and a few men by now were ready to deny altogether that the existence of witches could be demonstrated (No. 61). In this context, perhaps the early reversal of views was more meaningful than the trials themselves.

The change of views on witchcraft was an indication that Americans no longer feared the visible and invisible world about them, but were acquiring confidence in their capacity to manage the environment. So too, the Indians were less often regarded as creatures of the devil. They were still a menace (*see above*, No. 41); but they were a human threat and capable of being conquered and subdued (No. 62).

This generation also displayed less religious zeal than did its predecessor. Church membership was no longer associated with civic privilege and no longer taken as the sole criterion of virtue. Indeed, toleration became almost universal and could be stated as a principle quite casually (No. 63). The most important virtues now were the effective ones that contributed to the success of the individual. The standards of the times were set forth in practical instructions that would have practical results (No. 64).

Yet problems of conscience remained and they erupted in the 1740's in the Great Awakening (No. 65). This series of religious revivals led some men to look back toward the past for inspiration. But for most Americans it involved a reordering of attitudes in terms of the rationalism and optimism of their own times. The revivalist argument that salvation was available to every man through an act of his own will undermined traditional authority and, before many decades more, gave a new cast to American religion.

60. *Tests for Witches, Massachusetts, 1692*

Increase Mather, *Cases of Conscience Concerning Evil Spirits Personating Men* (Boston, 1693), in Cotton Mather, *The Wonders of the Invisible World* (London, 1862), 221–4, 225, 229, 232, 233, 234, 247–8, 254, 255, 259–60, 262–3, 265, 269, 270, 273, 275, 276–7, 282, 283, 285–6.

So ODIOUS and abominable is the name of a witch . . . that it is apt to grow up into a scandal for any, so much as to enter some sober cautions against the over hasty suspecting, or too precipitant judging of persons on this account. But certainly, the more execrable the crime is, the more critical care is to be used in the exposing of the names, liberties and lives of men . . . to the imputation of it. The awful hand of God now upon us . . . hath put serious persons into deep musings, and upon curious inquiries what is to be done for the detecting and defeating of this tremendous design of the grand Adversary. . . .

That there are devils and witches, the Scripture asserts, and experience confirms. That they are common enemies of mankind, and set upon mischief, is not to be doubted. That the Devil . . . delights to have the concurrence of witches, and their

consent in harming men, is consonant to his native malice to man. . . . That witches, when detected and convinced, ought to be exterminated and cut off, we have God's warrant for. . . .

Only the same God who hath said, thou shalt not suffer a witch to live; hath also said, at the mouth of two witnesses, or three witnesses shall he that is worthy of death, be put to death: but at the mouth of one witness, he shall not be put to death. . . .

It is therefore exceeding necessary that in such a day as this, men be informed what is evidence and what is not. It concerns men in point of charity; . . . And it is of no less necessity in point of justice. . . . Evidence supposed to be in the testimony . . . is thoroughly to be weighed, and if it do not infallibly prove the crime against the person accused, it ought not to determine him guilty of it; for so a righteous man may be condemned unjustly. . . .

Among many arguments to evince this, that which is most under present debate, is that which refers to something vulgarly called Specter Evidence, and a certain sort of Ordeal or trial by the sight and touch. The principal plea to justify the convictive evidence in these, is fetched from the consideration of the wisdom and righteousness of God in governing the world, which they suppose would fail, if such things were permitted to befall an innocent person. But it is certain, that . . . God doth sometimes suffer such things to evene [happen], that we may thereby know how much we are beholden to Him, for that restraint which he lays upon the Infernal Spirits, who would else reduce a world into a chaos. That the resolutions of such cases as these is proper for the servants of Christ in the ministry cannot be denied; the seasonableness of doing it now, will be justified by the consideration of the necessity there is at this time of a right information of men's judgments about these things, and the danger of their being misinformed. . . .

The first case that I am desired to express my judgment in, is this: Whether it is not possible for the Devil to impose on the imaginations of persons bewitched, and to cause them to believe that an innocent, yea that a pious person does torment them, when the Devil himself doth it . . . ? The answer to the question must be affirmative. . . .

From hence we infer, that there is no outward affliction whatsoever but may befall a good man. Now to be represented by Satan as a tormentor of bewitched or possessed persons, is a sore affliction to a good man. To be tormented by Satan is a sore affliction, yet nothing but what befell Job, and a daughter of Abraham, whom we read of in the Gospel. To be represented by Satan as tormenting others, is an affliction like the former; the Lord may bring such extraordinary temptations on

his own children, to afflict and humble them, for some sin they have been guilty of before Him. . . .

This then I declare and testify, that to take away the life of anyone, merely because a specter or devil, in a bewitched or possessed person does accuse them, will bring the guilt of innocent blood on the land. . . . What does such an evidence amount unto more than this: Either such an one did afflict such an one, or the Devil in his likeness, or his eyes were bewitched. . . .

These things being premised, I answer the question affirmatively. There are proofs for the conviction of witches which jurors may with a safe conscience proceed upon, so as to bring them in guilty. . . . But then the inquiry is, what is sufficient proof? . . .

A free and voluntary confession of the crime made by the person suspected and accused after examination, is a sufficient ground of conviction. Indeed, if persons are distracted, or under the power of phrenetic melancholy, that alters the case; but the jurors that examine them, and their neighbors that know them, may easily determine that case; or if confession be extorted, the evidence is not so clear and convictive; but if any persons out of remorse of conscience, or from a touch of God in their spirits, confess and show their deeds . . . nothing can be more clear. . . .

If two credible persons shall affirm upon oath that they have seen the party accused speaking such words, or doing things which none but such as have familiarity with the Devil ever did or can do, that's a sufficient ground for conviction. . . . The Devil never assists men to do supernatural things undesired. When therefore such like things shall be testified against the accused party not by specters which are devils in the shape of persons . . . but by real men or women . . . , it is proof enough that such an one has that conversation and correspondence with the Devil, as that he or she, whoever they be, ought to be exterminated from amongst men. This notwithstanding I will add. It were better that ten suspected witches should escape, than that one innocent person should be condemned. . . . I had

rather judge a witch to be an honest woman, than judge an honest woman as a witch.

61. *No Test for Witches, Massachusetts, 1692*

Thomas Brattle, "Letter, 1692," in G. L. Burr, ed., *Narratives of the Witchcraft Cases 1648–1706* (New York, 1914), 170–90.

As TO the method which the Salem justices do take in their examinations, it is truly this. A warrant being issued out to apprehend the persons that are charged and complained of by the afflicted children, . . . said persons are brought before the justices (the afflicted being present). The justices ask the apprehended why they afflict those poor children; to which the apprehended answer, they do not afflict them. The justices order the apprehended to look upon the said children, which accordingly they do; and at the time of that look . . . the afflicted are cast into a fit. The apprehended are then blinded, and ordered to touch the afflicted; and at that touch, . . . the afflicted ordinarily do come out of their fits. The afflicted persons then declare and affirm, that the apprehended have afflicted them. Upon which the apprehended persons, though of never so good repute, are forthwith committed to prison, on suspicion for witchcraft. . . .

I cannot but condemn this method of the justices, of making this touch of the hand a rule to discover witchcraft; because I am fully persuaded that it is sorcery, and a superstitious method, and that which we have no rule for, either from reason or religion. . . . I would fain know of these Salem gentlemen, but as yet could never know, how it comes about, that if these apprehended persons are witches, and, by a look of the eye, do cast the afflicted into their fits by poisoning them, how it comes about, I say, that, by a look of their eye, they do not cast others into fits, and poison others by their looks; and in particular, tender, fearful women, who

often are beheld by them, and as likely as any in the whole world to receive an ill impression from them. This Salem philosophy, some men may call the new philosophy; but I think it rather deserves the name of Salem superstition and sorcery, and it is not fit to be named in the land of such light as New England is. . . .

But furthermore, I would fain know . . . what can the jury or judges desire more, to convict any man of witchcraft, than a plain demonstration, that the said man is a witch? Now if this look and touch, circumstanced as before, be a plain demonstration, (as their philosophy teaches), what need they seek for further evidences, when, after all, it can be but a demonstration? . . . Yet certain is it, that the reasonable part of the world, when acquainted herewith, will laugh at the demonstration, and conclude that the said Salem gentlemen are actually possessed, at least, with ignorance and folly. . . .

Secondly, with respect to . . . such as confess themselves to be witches, . . . there are now about fifty of them in prison; many of which I have again and again seen and heard; and I cannot but tell you, that my faith is strong concerning them, that they are deluded, imposed upon, and under the influence of some evil spirit; and therefore unfit to be evidences either against themselves, or anyone else. . . .

These confessors . . . do very often contradict themselves, as inconsistently as is usual for any crazed, distempered person to do. . . . Even the judges themselves have, at some times, taken these confessors in flat lies, or contradictions, even in the courts; by reason of which, one would have thought, that the judges would have frowned upon the said confessors, discarded them, and not minded one tittle of any thing that they said. But instead ... the judges vindicate these confessors, and salve their contradictions, by proclaiming, that the Devil takes away their memory, and imposes on their brain. . . .

In the next place, I proceed to the form of their indictments, and the trials thereupon.

The indictment runs for sorcery and witchcraft, acted upon the body of such an one ... at such a particular time. . . . Now for the proof of the said sorcery and witchcraft, the prisoner at the bar pleading not guilty.

1. The afflicted persons are brought into court; and after much patience and pains taken with them, do take their oaths, that the prisoner at the bar did afflict them. . . . Often, when the afflicted do mean and intend only the appearance and shape of such an one, (say Goodwife Proctor) yet they positively swear that Goodwife Proctor did afflict them; and they have been allowed so to do, as though there was no real difference between Goodwife Proctor and the shape of Goodwife Proctor. This ... may readily prove a stumbling block to the jury, lead them into a very fundamental error. . . .

2. The confessors do declare what they know of the said prisoner; and some of the confessors are allowed to give their oaths; a thing which I believe was never heard of in this world; that such as confess themselves to be witches, to have renounced God and Christ, and all that is sacred, should yet be allowed and ordered to swear by the name of the great God! . . .

3. Whoever can be an evidence against the prisoner at the bar is ordered to come into court. And here it scarce ever fails but that evidences, of one nature and another, are brought in, though, I think, all of them altogether alien to the matter of indictment; for they none of them do respect witchcraft upon the bodies of the afflicted, which is the lone matter of charge in the indictment.

4. They [the accused] are searched by a jury; and as to some of them, the jury brought in, that [on] such or such a place there was a preternatural excrescence. And I wonder what person there is, whether man or woman, of whom it cannot be said but that, in some part of their body or other, there is a preternatural excrescence. The term is a very general and inclusive term. . . .

In short, the prisoner at the bar is indicted for sorcery and witchcraft acted upon the bodies of the afflicted. Now, for the proof of this, I reckon that the only pertinent evidences brought in are the evidences of the said afflicted.

It is true, that over and above the evidences of the afflicted persons, there are many evidences brought in, against the prisoner at the bar: either that he was at a witch meeting, or that he performed things which could not be done by an ordinary natural power; or that she sold butter to a sailor, which proving bad at sea, and the seamen exclaiming against her, she appeared, and soon after there was a storm, or the like. But what if there were ten thousand evidences of this nature; how do they prove the matter of indictment! And if they do not reach the matter of indictment, then I think it is clear, that the prisoner at the bar is brought in guilty, and condemned, merely from the evidences of the afflicted persons. . . .

As to the late executions, I shall only tell you, that in the opinion of many unprejudiced, considerate and considerable spectators, some of the condemned went out of the world not only with as great protestations, but also with as good shows of innocency, as men could do.

They protested their innocency as in the presence of the great God, whom forthwith they were to appear before. They wished, and declared their wish, that their blood might be the last innocent blood shed upon that account. With great affection they entreated Mr. C[otton] M[ather] to pray with them. They prayed that God would discover what witch-crafts were among us; they forgave their accusers; they spoke without reflection on jury and judges, for bringing them in guilty, and condemning them. They prayed earnestly for pardon for all other sins, and for an interest in the precious blood of our dear Redeemer; and seemed to be very sincere, upright, and sensible of their circumstances on all accounts. . . .

I cannot but admire that the justices, whom I think to be well-meaning men, should so far give ear to the Devil, as merely upon his authority to issue out their warrants, and apprehend people. Liberty was evermore accounted the great privilege of an Englishman; but certainly, if the Devil will be heard against us, and his testimony taken, to the seizing and apprehending of us, our liberty vanishes, and we are fools if we boast of our liberty. Now, that the justices have thus far given ear to the Devil I think may be mathe-matically demonstrated to any man of common sense: And for the demonstra-tion and proof hereof, I desire, only, that these two things may be duly considered, viz.

1. That several persons have been ap-prehended purely upon the complaints of these afflicted, to whom the afflicted were perfect strangers, and had not the least knowledge of imaginable, before they were apprehended.

2. That the afflicted do own and as-sert, and the justices do grant, that the Devil does inform and tell the afflicted the names of those persons that are thus unknown unto them. Now these two things being duly considered, I think it will ap-pear evident to anyone, that the Devil's information is the fundamental testimony that is gone upon in the apprehending of the aforesaid people.

If I believe such or such an assertion as comes immediately from the minister of God in the pulpit, because it is the word of the everliving God, I build my faith on God's testimony: and if I practice upon it, this my practice is properly built on the word of God. Even so in the case before us, if I believe the afflicted per-sons as informed by the Devil, and act thereupon, this my act may properly be said to be grounded upon the testimony or information of the Devil. And now, if things are thus, I think it ought to be for a lamentation to you and me, and all such as would be accounted good Chris-tians. . . .

The chief judge is very zealous in these proceedings, and says, he is very clear as to all that hath as yet been acted by this court, and, as far as ever I could per-ceive, is very impatient in hearing any-thing that looks another way. I very highly honor and reverence the wisdom and in-tegrity of the said judge, and hope that this matter shall not diminish my venera-tion for his honor; however, I cannot but say, my great fear is, that wisdom and counsel are withheld from his honor as to this matter, which yet I look upon not so much as a judgment to his honor as to this poor land.

But although the chief judge, and some of the other judges, be very zealous in these proceedings, yet this you may take for a truth, that there are several about the Bay, men for understanding, judgment, and piety, inferior to few, (if any), in New England that do utterly condemn the said proceedings, and do freely de-liver their judgment in the case to be . . . that these methods will utterly ruin and undo poor New England. . . . Several of the late justices, viz. Thomas Graves, Esq., N. Byfield, Esq., Francis Foxcroft, Esq., are much dissatisfied; also several of the present justices; and in particular, some of the Boston justices, were resolved rather to throw up their commissions than be active in disturbing the liberty of Their Majesties' subjects, merely on the ac-cusations of these afflicted, possessed chil-dren.

Finally; the principal gentlemen in Bos-ton, and thereabout, are generally agreed that irregular and dangerous methods have been taken as to these matters. . . . Nineteen persons have now been executed, and one pressed to death for a mute: seven more are condemned; two of which are reprieved, because they pretend their being with child; one, viz. Mrs. Bradbury of Salisbury, from the intercession of some friends; and two or three more, because they are confessors.

The court is adjourned to the first Tuesday in November, then to be kept at Salem; between this and then will be [the] great assembly [the General Court], and this matter will be a peculiar matter of their agitation. I think it is matter of earnest supplication and prayer to Almighty God, that He would afford His Gracious Presence to the said assembly, and direct them aright in this weighty matter. . . . I am very sensible, that it is irksome and disagreeable to go back, when a man's doing so is an implication that he has been walking in a wrong path. However, nothing is more honorable than, upon due conviction, to retract and undo, so far as may be, what has been amiss and irregular. . . .

Many of these afflicted persons . . . do say . . . that they can see specters when their eyes are shut, as well as when they are open. This one thing I evermore accounted as very observable, and that which might serve as a good key to unlock the nature of these mysterious troubles, if duly improved by us. Can they see specters when their eyes are shut? I am sure they lie, at least speak falsely, if they say so; for the thing, in nature, is an utter impossibility. It is true, they may strongly fancy, or have things represented to their imagination, when their eyes are shut; and I think this is all which ought to be allowed to these blind, nonsensical girls. And if our officers and courts have apprehended, imprisoned, condemned, and executed our guiltless neighbors, certainly our error is great, and we shall rue it in the conclusion.

There are two or three other things that I have observed in and by these afflicted persons, which make me strongly suspect that the Devil imposes upon their brains, and deludes their fancy and imagination; and that the Devil's book (which they say has been offered them) is a mere fancy of theirs, and no reality; that the witches' meeting, the Devil's baptism, and mock sacraments, which they oft speak of, are nothing else but the effect of their fancy, depraved and deluded by the Devil, and not a reality to be regarded or minded by any wise man. And whereas the confessors have owned and asserted the said meetings, the said baptism, and mock sacrament, . . . I am very apt to think, that, did you know the circumstances of the said confessors, you would not be swayed thereby, any otherwise than to be confirmed, that all is perfect devilism, and an hellish design to ruin and destroy this poor land. For whereas there are of the said confessors fifty-five in number, some of them are known to be distracted, crazed women; . . . Others of them denied their guilt, and maintained their innocency for above eighteen hours, after most violent, distracting and dragooning methods had been used with them, to make them confess. Such methods they were, that more than one of the said confessors did since tell many, with tears in their eyes, that they thought their very lives would have gone out of their bodies; and wished that they might have been cast into the lowest dungeon, rather than be tortured with such repeated buzzings and chuckings and unreasonable urgings as they were treated withal. They soon recanted their confessions, acknowledging, with sorrow and grief, that it was an hour of great temptation with them. . . .

But, finally, as to about thirty of these fifty-five confessors, they are possessed (I reckon) with the Devil, and afflicted as the children are, and therefore not fit to be regarded as to anything they say of themselves or others. . . .

What will be the issue of these troubles, God only knows; I am afraid that ages will not wear off that reproach and those stains which these things will leave behind them upon our land. I pray God pity us, humble us, forgive us, and appear mercifully for us in this our mount of distress.

62. *The Indians and Civilization, 1705*

Robert Beverley, *History and Present State of Virginia*. L. B. Wright, ed. (Chapel Hill, 1947), 233.

THUS I have given a succinct account of the Indians; happy, I think, in their simple state of nature, and in their enjoyment of plenty, without the curse of labor. They have on several accounts reason to lament the arrival of the Europeans, by whose means they seem to have lost their felicity, as well as their innocence. The English have taken away great part of their country, and consequently made everything less plenty amongst them. They have introduced drunkenness and luxury amongst them, which have multiplied their wants, and put them upon desiring a thousand things, they never dreamt of before.

63. *Religious Liberty in New York, 1686*

Labaree, *Royal Instructions*, II, 494–5.

YOU shall permit all persons of what religion soever quietly to inhabit within your government without giving them any disturbance or disquiet whatsoever for or by reason of their differing opinions in matters of religion, provided they give no disturbance to the public peace nor do molest or disquiet others in the free exercise of their religion.

64. *Advice to a Young Tradesman, 1748*

Franklin, "Advice to a Young Tradesman" (1748), *Works*, II, 87–9.

To MY Friend, A.B.:

As you have desired it of me, I write the following hints, which have been of service to me, and may, if observed, be so to you.

Remember, that time is money. He that can earn ten shillings a day by his labor, and goes abroad, or sits idle, one half of that day, though he spends but sixpence during his diversion or idleness, ought not to reckon that the only expense; he has really spent, or rather thrown away, five shillings besides.

Remember, that credit is money. If a man lets his money lie in my hands after it is due, he gives me the interest, or so much as I can make of it during that time. This amounts to a considerable sum where a man has good and large credit, and makes good use of it.

Remember, that money is of the prolific, generating nature. Money can beget money, and its offspring can beget more, and so on. Five shillings turned is six, turned again it is seven and three-pence, and so on till it becomes an hundred pounds. The more there is of it, the more it produces every turning, so that the profits rise quicker and quicker. He that kills a breeding sow, destroys all her off-spring to the thousandth generation. He that murders a crown, destroys all that it might have produced, even scores of pounds.

Remember, that six pounds a year is but a groat a day. For this little sum (which may be daily wasted either in time or expense unperceived) a man of credit may, on his own security, have the constant possession and use of an hundred pounds. So much in stock, briskly turned by an industrious man, produces great advantage.

Remember this saying, "The good paymaster is lord of another man's purse." He that is known to pay punctually and exactly to the time he promises, may at any time, and on any occasion, raise all the money his friends can spare. This is sometimes of great use. After industry and frugality, nothing contributes more to the raising of a young man in the world than punctuality and justice in all his dealings; therefore never keep borrowed money an hour beyond the time you promised, lest a disappointment shut up your friend's purse forever.

The most trifling actions that affect a man's credit are to be regarded. The sound of your hammer at five in the morning, or nine at night, heard by a creditor, makes him easy six months longer; but, if he sees you at a billiard table, or hears your voice at a tavern, when you should be at work, he sends for his money the next day; demands it, before he can receive it, in a lump.

It shows, besides, that you are mindful of what you owe; it makes you appear a careful as well as an honest man, and that still increases your credit.

Beware of thinking all your own that you possess, and of living accordingly. It is a mistake that many people who have credit fall into. To prevent this, keep an exact account for some time, both of your expenses and your income. If you take the pains at first to mention particulars, it will have this good effect: you will discover how wonderfully small, trifling expenses mount up to large sums, and will discern what might have been, and may for the future be saved, without occasioning any great inconvenience.

In short, the way to wealth, if you desire it, is as plain as the way to market. It depends chiefly on two words, industry and frugality; that is, waste neither time nor money, but make the best use of both. Without industry and frugality nothing will do, and with them everything. He that gets all he can honestly, and saves all he gets (necessary expenses excepted), will certainly become rich, if that Being who governs the world, to whom all should look for a blessing on their honest endeavors, doth not, in his wise providence, otherwise determine.

An Old Tradesman

65. *The Effects of Revival, Massachusetts, 1743*

Rev. Jonathan Edwards to Rev. Prince, December 12, 1743, in *The Christian History 1743* (Boston, 1744), Nos. 46, 47 (January 14, 21, 1743), 367–8, 370–2.

EVER since the great work of God, that was wrought here about nine years ago, there has been a great abiding alteration in this town in many respects. There has been vastly more religion kept up in the town, among all sorts of persons, in religious exercises, and in common conversation. . . . There has been a great alteration among the youth of the town, with respect to reveling, frolicking, profane and unclean conversation, and lewd songs. Instances of fornication have been very rare.

There has also been a great alteration amongst both old and young, with respect to tavern-haunting. I suppose the town has been in no measure so free of vice in these respects, for any long time together, for these sixty years, as it has been these nine years past. There has also been an evident alteration, with respect to a charitable spirit to the poor; though I think with regard to this, we in this town, as well as the land in general, come far short of gospel rules. And though after that great work of nine years ago, there has been a very lamentable decay of religious affections, and the engagedness of people's spirit in religion; yet many societies for prayer and social religion, were all along kept up; and there were some few instances of awakening, and deep concern about the things of another world, even in the most dead time.

In the year 1740, in the spring, before Mr. Whitefield came to this town, there was a visible alteration. There was more seriousness and religious conversation, especially among young people. Those things that were of ill tendency among them, were foreborne; and it was a more frequent thing for persons to visit their minister upon soul accounts. And in some particular persons, there appeared a great alteration, about that time.

And thus it continued, till Mr. Whitefield came to town, which was about the middle of October following. He preached here four sermons in the meeting-house (besides a private lecture at my house), one on Friday, another on Saturday, and two upon the Sabbath. The congregation was extraordinarily melted by every sermon; almost the whole assembly being in tears for a great part of sermon time. Mr. Whitefield's sermons were suitable to the circumstances of the town; containing just reproofs of our backslidings, and in a most moving and affecting manner, making use of our great profession and great mercies as arguments with us to return to God, from whom we had departed. Immediately after this, the minds of the people

in general appeared more engaged in religion, showing a greater forwardness to make religion the subject of their conversation, and to meet frequently together for religious purposes, and to embrace all opportunities to hear the word preached.

The revival at first appeared chiefly among professors [the converted], and those that had entertained the hope that they were in a State of Grace, to whom Mr. Whitefield chiefly addressed himself. But in a very short time, there appeared an awakening and deep concern among some young persons, that looked upon themselves as in a Christless state; and there were some hopeful appearances of conversion, and some professors were greatly revived. In about a month or six weeks, there was a great alteration in the town, both as to the revivals of professors and awakenings of others. By the middle of December, a considerable work of God appeared among those that were very young; and the revival of religion continued to increase, so that in the spring an engagedness of spirit, about the things of religion, was become very general amongst young people and children, and religious subjects almost wholly took up their conversation, when they were together. . . .

About the middle of the summer [of 1741], I called together the young people that were communicants, from sixteen to twenty-six years of age, to my house; which proved to be a most happy meeting. Many seemed to be very greatly and most agreeably affected with those views, which excited humility, self-condemnation, self-abhorrence, love and joy; many fainted under these affections. We had several meetings that summer, of young people, attended with like appearances. It was about that time, that there first began to be cryings out in the meeting-house; which several times occasioned many of the congregation to stay in the house after the public exercise was over, to confer with those who seemed to be overcome with religious convictions and affections, which was found to tend much to the propagation of their impressions, with lasting effect upon many; conference being, at these times, commonly joined with prayer and singing. In the summer and fall, the children in various parts of the town had religious meetings by themselves, for prayer, sometimes joined with fasting; wherein many of them seemed to be greatly and properly affected, and I hope some of them savingly wrought upon.

The months of August and September were the most remarkable of any this year, for appearances of the conviction and conversion of sinners, and great revivings, quickenings, and comforts of professors, and for extraordinary external effects of these things. It was a very frequent thing, to see an house full of outcries, fainting, convulsions, and such like, both with distress and also with admiration and joy. It was not the manner here to hold meetings all night, as in some places, nor was it common to continue them till very late in the night. But it was pretty often so, that there were some that were so affected, and their bodies so overcome, that they could not go home, but were obliged to stay all night at the house where they were. There was no difference that I know of here, with regard to these extraordinary effects, in meetings in the night and in the daytime; the meetings in which these effects appeared in the evening, being commonly begun, and their extraordinary effects, in the day, and continued in the evening; and some meetings have been very remarkable for such extraordinary effects, that were both begun and finished in the daytime.

There was an appearance of a glorious progress of the work of God upon the hearts of sinners, in conviction and conversion, this summer and fall; and great numbers, I think we have reason to hope, were brought savingly home to Christ. But this was remarkable: the work of God in his influences of this nature, seemed to be almost wholly upon a new generation; those that were not come to years of dis-

cretion in that wonderful season, nine years ago, children, or those that were then children. Others that had enjoyed that former glorious opportunity, without any appearance of saving benefit, seemed now to be almost wholly passed over and let alone. But now we had the most wonderful work among children, that ever was in Northampton. The former outpouring of the spirit was remarkable for influences upon the minds of children, beyond all that ever been before; but this far exceeded that. Indeed, as to influences on the minds of professors, this work was by no means confined to a new generation. Many of all ages partook of it; but yet, in this respect, it was more general on those that were of the younger sort.

Many, that had formerly been wrought upon, that in the times of our declension had fallen into decays, and had in a great measure left God, and gone after the world, now passed under a very remarkable new work of the spirit of God, as if they had been the subjects of a second conversion. They were first led into the wilderness, and had a work of conviction, having much greater convictions of the sin of both nature and practice than ever before (though with some new circumstances, and something new in the kind of conviction) in some with great distress, beyond what they had felt before their first conversion. Under these convictions, they were excited to strive for salvation, and the Kingdom of Heaven suffered violence from some of them, in a far more remarkable manner than before; and after great convictions and humblings, and agonizings with God, they had Christ discovered to them anew, as an all-sufficient Savior, and in the glories of His grace, and in a far more clear manner than before; and with greater humility, self-emptiness and brokenness of heart, and a purer, a higher joy, and greater desires after holiness of life; but with greater self-diffidence and distrust of their treacherous hearts.

One circumstance wherein this work differed from that which had been in the towns five or six years before was, that conversions were frequently wrought more sensibly and visibly; the impressions stronger, and more manifest by external effects of them; and the progress of the spirit of God in conviction, from step to step, more apparent; and the transition from one state to another, more sensible and plain; so that it might, in many instances, be as it were seen by bystanders.

The preceding season had been very remarkable on this account, beyond what had been before; but this more remarkable than that. And in this season, these apparent or visible conversions (if I may so call them), were more frequently in the presence of others, at religious meetings, where the appearances of what was wrought on the heart, fell under public observation.

PART THREE

A Revolutionary Culture, 1760-1820

THE REVOLUTION marked the beginning of the existence of the United States as an independent nation and also the end of its experience as a colonial society.

Yet it can perhaps be viewed best as neither a total beginning nor a total end, but rather as a decisive point in a process that went back considerably before 1776, and extended considerably beyond that date. American nationality began to take form in the middle of the eighteenth century; and, paradoxically, aspects of American colonialism extended into the nineteenth century. The change was not abrupt, but gradual; and it can best be understood thus.

The grievances under which the colonies labored had roots in earlier problems of colonial administration. But the liquidation of the French Empire after the French and Indian War (1763) brought these complaints to a critical stage of development. The statesmen who shaped British imperial policy now attempted to fit the mainland colonies into a comprehensive scheme of development in the interest of the British Crown. This scheme called for a permanent defensive establishment in America. It depended upon the readiness of the colonies to assume some of the expenses of government, of defense, and of the wars which had just been fought. And it looked forward to a period when their economies would be so shaped by the Acts of Trade that the mother country would gain strength through their resources.

On each count the designs of the English statesmen came into conflict with the interests of important groups of colonists, who did not wish to be garrisoned, taxed, or regulated from overseas. Even more important, the methods by which the changes were imposed offended the sensibilities of the Americans who by then held distinctive ideas as to the relationship of the government to the governed. Increasingly, the Crown seemed to the colonists to be bent on seeking its own advantage through tyrannical methods.

The sense of grievance mounted steadily after 1763 and gained strength from the growing awareness of the separateness of American nationality. Already then many people were conscious of compelling cultural and social ties that bound together the settlements from Maine to Georgia; and they were aware also that they had grown different from the mother country. Hence the habit of referring to themselves as "Americans" even before there was a political state to which that designation applied. The Revolution was in part a result of this nationalism; but it also stimulated the sentiment. The political separation from England thereafter constituted a standing challenge to the citizens of the new nation to show by their achievements in every field of life that the Revolution had been justified. The men who responded to this challenge felt they were engaged in a mission significant for all mankind.

The War for Independence began therefore as a struggle for the remedy of specific grievances and ended as a struggle for national identity. The early fighting was not directed toward any broad goal until the Declaration of Independence formulated the relationship between the specific grievances of the colonists and general principles for which they hoped the new nation would stand. The war was bitterly fought and was conducted to a victorious conclusion with the aid of European alliances. The Treaty of 1783 brought the United States independence under highly favorable terms.

But independence created an imposing series of new problems. Cut apart from the empire, the United States found itself in a precarious economic position. There followed decades of effort to re-establish the commerce of the nation. To self-interest as an incentive was joined the desire to show by significant advances the beneficent effects of liberation from the restrictions of Great Britain. The Americans hoped that the power of the state might develop advanced financial institutions, stimulate commerce and manufacturing, and assist agriculture. Success did not always attend these efforts. But the enormous resources of the new continent nevertheless gave the productive system enough room in which to grow.

The Revolution also left the United States serious social problems. The emigration of the loyalists had removed an important stratum of society; and the disorders of the war period had confused all relationships. To re-establish order was a slow and difficult task and one complicated by the continued existence within the nation of substantial groups such as the Negroes and the Indians that seemed to have no consistent role within it. If the United States was a nation, why should part of its population remain unassimilated; if it was a democratic republic, why should not all its residents be equal in rights? Such problems were not to be resolved for many decades.

There was more success in political reorganization. Indeed, for the time being, the development of its forms of government was the most striking achievement of the new nation. Almost at once the rebels had set themselves the task of creating new polities. Their revolt had as an objective the formation of a new system, not merely the destruction of an old one. Having, as it seemed to them, reverted to a state of nature, they found it necessary, in new constitutions, to bring new states into being, and they did so with relative ease. Federation was more complicated for there was no precedent for a federal government on this scale in a democratic republic. A considerable period of experiment was required before the solutions arrived at in 1788 were finally effective. And it took several decades more before the ultimate forms of national government developed.

In the meantime the establishment of a durable pattern of international relations was an immediate concern of the Republic. It was necessary to make peace with England and to regularize the political and economic associations with the other nations of Europe and Africa. In addition, the diplomacy of the United States was directed toward wider interests. The vagueness of American boundaries led to negotiations that stretched over decades. Commerce, particularly after the outbreak of war between Britain and France, called for diplomatic protection. Questions arising out of the navigation of the Mississippi finally led to the acquisition of Louisiana. Toward the close of the period, expansive drives involved the naton in war with Britain.

Some Americans, at the opening of the nineteenth century, regarded these foreign affairs as distractions. The crowning achievement of the American Republic, after all, was to be a new culture that would embody its democratic spirit. Through these years there were repeated efforts to formulate the terms within which this culture would function. Yet the actual achievements often fell far behind the abstract statements of purpose, for the techniques to realize the aspirations of the new nation were as yet lacking.

IX 🪷 *The Grievances*

THE WAR with France was no sooner over in 1763 than the British government, in pursuance of its schemes of imperial reorganization, began to take a series of steps that seriously alienated many important groups of Americans. Already, during the war, the strategy of alliance with the Indians had encouraged policies that seemed to favor them over the settlers. Instructions to the royal governors showed this bias; and the proclamation line of 1763, although intended to be temporary, nevertheless erected a barrier in the way of the advance of settlement (No. 66). That barrier added to the sense of grievance and injury under which the frontiersmen already labored (No. 67).

At the same time the financial and military measures of the Crown antagonized other Americans. Even a respectable merchant, loyal to the government, found it difficult to stomach these proposals (No. 68). The Stamp Act evoked a Congress that drew together representative men from nine of the colonies in a concerted protest (No. 69); and the decade that followed was marked by one irritating incident after another.

The crisis came in 1774. Political pressures within England were making it difficult to put off a colonial settlement, and the defiant action of the Bostonians who resisted the importation of the East India Company's tea provided the occasion for decisive action. The four measures that came to be known as the Intolerable Acts (No. 70) were designed to bring the resistants to terms. Instead they called forth the united protests of all the colonies, and compelled Americans to make a choice between loyalty to the Crown and loyalty to their own communities (No. 71). Thereafter the break was open, although whether the result would be independence or not would remain unclear for almost two years.

Looking back at the crisis, an aging American described the means by which the empire had lost its hold on the colonies (No. 72).

66. The Proclamation of 1763

Annual Register (1763), VI, 208–13.

WHEREAS we have taken into our royal consideration the extensive and valuable acquisitions in America secured to our Crown by the late definitive treaty of peace concluded at Paris [on] the 10th day of February last; and being desirous that all our loving subjects, as well of our kingdom as of our colonies in America, may avail themselves, with all convenient speed, of the great benefits and advantages which must accrue therefrom to their commerce, manufactures, and navigation: we . . . hereby . . . publish and declare to all our loving subjects that we have, with the advice of our said Privy Council, granted our letters patent under our Great Seal of Great Britain, to erect within the countries and islands ceded and confirmed to us by the said treaty, four distinct and separate governments, styled and called by the names of Quebec, East Florida, West Florida, and Granada. . . .

And to the end that the open and free fishery of our subjects may be extended to, and carried on upon the coast of Labrador and the adjacent islands, we have thought fit . . . to put all that coast, from the River St. John's to Hudson's Straits, together with the islands of Anticosti and Madelaine, and all other smaller islands lying upon the said coast, under the care and inspection of our governor of Newfoundland. . . .

And . . . we have . . . given express power and direction to our governors of our said colonies respectively, that so soon as the state and circumstances of the said colonies will admit thereof, they shall, with the advice and consent of the members of our council, summon and call general assemblies within the said governments respectively, in such manner and form as is used and directed in those colonies and provinces in America, which are under our immediate government; and we have also given power to the said governors, with the consent of our said councils, and the representatives of the people, so to be summoned . . . to make . . . laws, statutes, and ordinances for the public peace, welfare, and good government of our said colonies . . . ; and in the meantime, and until such assemblies can be called . . . we have given power under our Great Seal to the governors of our said colonies respectively, to erect and constitute . . . courts of judicature and public justice . . . with liberty to all persons who may think themselves aggrieved by the sentence of such courts, in all civil cases, to appeal, under the usual limitations and restrictions, to us, in our Privy Council. . . .

And whereas it is just and reasonable, and essential to our interest and the security of our colonies, that the several nations or tribes of Indians with whom we are connected, and who live under our protection, should not be molested or disturbed in the possession of such parts of our dominions and territories as, not having been ceded to or purchased by us, are reserved to them, or any of them, as their hunting-grounds; we do therefore . . . declare it to be our royal will and pleasure, that no governor or commander in chief, in any of our colonies . . . or plantations in America do presume for the present . . . to grant warrants of survey or pass patents for any lands beyond the heads or sources of any of the rivers which fall into the Atlantic Ocean from the west or northwest; or upon any lands whatever, which, not having been ceded to or purchased by us, as aforesaid, are reserved to the said Indians, or any of them.

And we do further declare it to be our royal will and pleasure . . . to reserve under our sovereignty, protection, and dominion, for the use of the said Indians, all the land and territories not included within the limits of our said three new governments, or within the limits of the territory granted to the Hudson's Bay Company; as also all the land and territories lying to the westward of the sources of the rivers which fall into the sea from the west and northwest as aforesaid. And we do hereby strictly forbid, on pain of our displeasure, all our loving subjects from making any purchases or settlements whatever, or taking possession of any of the lands above reserved, without our special leave and license for that purpose first obtained.

And we do further strictly enjoin and require all persons whatever, who have either wilfully or inadvertently seated themselves upon any lands within the countries above described, or upon any other lands which, not having been ceded to or purchased by us, are still reserved to the said Indians as aforesaid, forthwith to remove themselves from such settlements.

And whereas great frauds and abuses have been committed in the purchasing lands of the Indians, to the great prejudice of our interests, and to the great dissatisfaction of the said Indians; in order, therefore, to prevent such irregularities for the future, and to the end that the Indians may be convinced of our justice and determined resolution to remove all reasonable cause of discontent, we do . . . strictly enjoin and require, that no private person do presume to make any purchase from the said Indians of any lands reserved to the said Indians within those parts of our colonies where we have thought proper to allow settlement. But that if at any time any of the said Indians should be inclined to dispose of the said lands, the same shall be purchased only for us, in our name, at some public meeting or assembly of the said Indians, to be held for that purpose by the governor or commander in chief of our colony respectively within which they shall lie. And in case they shall lie within the limits of any proprietaries, conformable to such directions and instructions as we or they shall think proper to give for that purpose. And we do . . . declare and enjoin, that the trade with the said Indians shall be free and open to all our subjects whatever, provided that every person who may incline to trade with the said Indians do take out a license for carrying on such trade, from the governor or commander in chief of any of our colonies respectively where such person shall reside, and also give security to observe such regulations as we shall at any time think fit . . . to direct and appoint for the benefit of the said trade. And we do hereby . . . require the governors . . . to grant such licenses without fee or reward, taking especial care to insert therein a condition that such license shall be void, and the security forfeited, in case the person to whom the same is granted shall refuse or neglect to observe such regulations. . . .

And we do further expressly enjoin and require all officers . . . to seize and apprehend all persons whatever who, standing charged with treasons, misprisions of treason, murders, or other felonies or misdemeanors, shall fly from justice and take refuge in the said territory, and to send them under a proper guard to the colony where the crime was committed of which they shall stand accused, in order to take their trial for the same.

67. *Frontier Grievances in Pennsylvania, 1764*

"Remonstrance from the Frontier Inhabitants," February 13, 1764, in *Minutes of the Provincial Council of Pennsylvania* (Harrisburg, 1852), 138–42.

THE INHABITANTS of the frontier counties of Lancaster, York, Cumberland, Berks and Northampton, humbly beg leave to remonstrate and [to] lay before you the following grievances . . . for redress.

First. We apprehend that as freemen and English subjects, we have an indisputable title to the same privileges and immunities with His Majesty's other subjects who reside in the interior counties of Philadelphia, Chester, and Bucks, and therefore ought not to be excluded from an equal share with them in the very important privilege of legislation. Nevertheless . . . our five counties are restrained from electing more than ten representatives . . . while the three counties and city of Philadelphia, Chester, and Bucks, elect twenty-six. This we humbly conceive is oppressive, unequal, and unjust, the cause of many of our grievances, and an infringement of our natural privileges of freedom and equality. Wherefore we humbly pray that we may be no longer deprived of an equal number with the three aforesaid counties, to represent us in Assembly.

Secondly. We understand that a bill is now before the House of Assembly, wherein it is provided that such persons as shall be charged with killing any Indians in Lancaster County, shall not be tried in the county where the fact was committed, but in the counties of Philadelphia, Chester, or Bucks. This is manifestly to deprive British subjects of their known privileges, to cast an eternal reproach upon whole counties, as if they were unfit to serve their country in the quality of jurymen, and to contradict the well-known laws of the British nation in a point whereon life, liberty, and security essentially depend, namely, that of being tried by their equals in the neighborhood where their own, their accusers', and the witnesses' character and credit, with the circumstances of the fact, are best known, and instead thereof putting their lives in the hands of strangers who may as justly be suspected of partiality to, as the frontier counties can be of prejudices against Indians; and this, too, in favor of Indians only, against His Majesty's faithful and loyal subjects. . . .

Thirdly. During the late and present Indian War, the frontiers of this province have been repeatedly attacked and ravaged by skulking parties of the Indians, who have with the most savage cruelty murdered men, women and children without distinction, and have reduced near a thousand families to the most extreme distress. It grieves us to the very heart to see such ... inhabitants ... left destitute by the public ... while upwards of an hundred and twenty of these savages, who are with great reason suspected of being guilty of these horrid barbarities ..., have procured themselves to be taken under the protection of the government, with a view to elude the fury of the brave relatives of the murdered, and are now maintained at the public expense. ...

Fourthly. ... It is contrary to the maxims of good policy, and extremely dangerous to our frontiers, to suffer any Indians of what tribe soever to live within the inhabited parts of this province while we are engaged in an Indian War, as experience has taught us that they are all perfidious, and their claim to freedom and independency, puts it in their power to act as spies, to entertain and give intelligence to our enemies, and to furnish them with provisions and warlike stores. ...

Fifthly. We cannot help lamenting that no provision has been hitherto made, that such of our frontier inhabitants as have been wounded in defense of the province,

their lives and liberties, may be taken care of and cured of their wounds at the public expense. We therefore pray that this grievance may be redressed.

Sixthly. In the late Indian War this province, with others of His Majesty's colonies, gave rewards for Indian scalps ... as the most likely means of destroying or reducing them to reason; but no such encouragement has been given in this war. ... We therefore pray that public rewards may be proposed for Indian scalps, which may be adequate to the dangers attending enterprises of this nature.

Seventhly. We daily lament that numbers of our nearest and dearest relatives are still in captivity among the savage heathen, to be trained up in all their ignorance and barbarity, or to be tortured to death with all the contrivances of Indian cruelty, for attempting to make their escape from bondage. We see they pay no regard to the many solemn promises which they have made to restore our friends who are in bondage amongst them. We therefore earnestly pray that no trade may hereafter be permitted to be carried on with them, until our brethren and relatives are brought home to us.

68. *An Indignant New York Merchant, 1765*

John Watts to James Napier, June 1, 1765, "Letter Book of John Watts," New York Historical Society, *Collections*, LXI (1925), 354–5.

THIS same billeting bill on the carpet is a new matter of serious speculation; people say they had rather part with their money, though rather unconstitutionally, than to have a parcel of military masters put by act of Parliament a bed to their wives and daughters.

I don't know where to begin or where to end in answer to your request about our government, taxation and trade. I should think they must be all as well understood in England where they are

chiefly if not all regulated, as they can be in America. We affect to imitate the mother country, and indeed are directed so to do as nearly as circumstance will admit of. The Crown, you know, appoints all the commissioned officers, civil and military, from the governor-in-chief down to the smallest clerk of the most inconsiderable county. The Assembly, of course, are chose[n]; so are the magistrates in the corporation towns and so are the servile officers, such as collectors, assessors, constables, etc. This seems to be the general system of government. All money raised by taxes are laid on estates both real and personal. The counties differ somewhat in their mode, but in general the assessor upon oath values the land and the stock, comparing one estate with another, both as to quantity and quality, which is executed equitably enough. The Assembly by act ascertains the quota of each county, when a sum is to be raised. New York pays invariably one third of such sum. The rents of houses and personal estates produce it; the first is easily fixed, the other guessed at, comparing one man's appearance or known substance with another. In these matters you cannot be over-nice; the circumstances of people in commerce, where the greater part live by credit, won't bear it.

As to trade, I have almost forgot it. Our provisions are generally carried to the West Indies among all nations who will encourage them to come. Some little goes to Portugal and Madeira, scarce anywhere else. The quantity of each species I don't know and might guess at wildly; the custom house could fix it best. I should imagine this port exports about eighty thousand barrels flour per annum, a great deal of the wheat brought from Maryland and Virginia and manufactured; besides, we export a moiety at least of the produce of Connecticut and New Jersey included in that number. Lumber is admitted to be shipped almost everywhere, till lately it was amazingly restrained, to Ireland. The duties on rum, wine and Negroes have heretofore supported our civil list; how it will operate under the new system, time must discover.

69. Resolutions of the Stamp Act Congress, 1765

Journal of the First Congress of the American Colonies ... 1765 (New York, 1845), 27–9.

THE MEMBERS of this Congress, sincerely devoted, with the warmest sentiments of affection and duty to His Majesty's person and government ... and with minds deeply impressed by a sense of the present and impending misfortunes of the British colonies on this continent; having considered as maturely as time will permit, the circumstances of the said colonies, esteem it our indispensable duty to make the following declarations of our humble opinion, respecting the most essential rights and liberties of the colonists, and of the grievances under which they labor, by reason of several late acts of Parliament.

I. That His Majesty's subjects in these colonies, owe the same allegiance to the crown of Great Britain, that is owing from his subjects born within the realm, and all due subordination to that august body the Parliament of Great Britain.

II. That His Majesty's liege subjects in these colonies are entitled to all the inherent rights and liberties of his natural born subjects, within the kingdom of Great Britain.

III. That it is inseparably essential to the freedom of a people, and the undoubted right of Englishmen, that no taxes be imposed on them but with their own consent, given personally, or by their representatives.

IV. That the people of these colonies are not, and, from their local circumstances, cannot be, represented in the House of Commons in Great Britain.

V. That the only representatives of the people of these colonies are persons chosen therein by themselves, and that no taxes ever have been, or can be constitutionally imposed on them, but by their respective legislatures.

VI. That all supplies to the crown being free gifts of the people, it is unreasonable and inconsistent with the principles and spirit of the British constitution, for the people of Great Britain to grant to His Majesty the property of the colonists.

VII. That trial by jury, is the inherent and invaluable right of every British subject in these colonies.

VIII. That the late act of Parliament, entitled, *An act for granting and supplying certain stamp duties, and other duties, in the British colonies and plantations in America, etc.,* by imposing taxes on the inhabitants of these colonies, and the said act, and several other acts, by extending the jurisdiction of the courts of admiralty beyond its ancient limits, have a manifest tendency to subvert the rights and liberties of the colonists.

IX. That the duties imposed by several late acts of Parliament, from the peculiar circumstances of these colonies, will be extremely burthensome and grievous; and from the scarcity of specie, the payment of them absolutely impracticable.

X. That as the profits of the trade of these colonies ultimately center in Great Britain, to pay for the manufactures which they are obliged to take from thence, they eventually contribute very largely to all supplies granted there to the crown.

XI. That the restrictions imposed by several late acts of Parliament on the trade of these colonies, will render them unable to purchase the manufactures of Great Britain. . . .

Lastly. That it is the indispensable duty of these colonies, to the best of sovereigns, to the mother country, and to themselves, to endeavor by a loyal and dutiful address to His Majesty, and humble applications to both houses of Parliament, to procure the repeal of the act for granting and applying certain stamp duties, of all clauses of any other acts of Parliament, whereby the jurisdiction of the admiralty is extended as aforesaid, and of the other late acts for the restriction of American commerce.

70. *The Intolerable Acts, 1774*

Boston Port Act, 14 Geo. III, ch. 19 (1774); Administration of Justice Act, 14 Geo. III, ch. 39 (1774); Massachusetts Government Act, 14 Geo. III, ch. 45 (1774); Quebec Act, 14 Geo. III, ch. 83 (1774). All from Peter Force, ed., *American Archives . . . Fourth Series* (Washington, 1837), I, 61–4, 104–7, 129–30, 217–19.

The Boston Port Act

WHEREAS dangerous commotions and insurrections have been fomented and raised in the town of Boston . . . by divers ill-affected persons . . . ; in which commotions and insurrections certain valuable cargoes of teas, being the property of the East India Company . . . were seized and destroyed. And whereas, in the present condition of the said town and harbor, the commerce of His Majesty's subjects cannot be safely carried on there, nor the customs payable to His Majesty duly collected; and it is therefore expedient that the officers of His Majesty's customs should be forthwith removed from the said town. . . .

Be it enacted . . . , that from and after the first day of June, 1774, it shall not be lawful for any person . . . to lade, put, or cause to procure to be laden or put, off or from any quay, wharf, or other place, within the said town of Boston . . . any goods, wares, or merchandise whatsoever . . . upon the pain of forfeiture of the said goods, . . . merchandise, and of the said boat. . . . And if any such goods, . . . shall, within the said town . . . be laden or taken in from the shore into any barge, . . . to be carried on board any ship or vessel outward-bound to any other country or province, . . . or be laden . . . into such barge, . . . or out of any ship or vessel coming ... from any other country, ... such barge, ... shall be forfeited and lost. ...

[These provisions are to continue] until ... full satisfaction hath been made by ... the inhabitants of ... Boston to the United Company of Merchants of England Trading to the East Indies, for the damages sustained ... by the destruction of their goods ... and until ... reasonable satisfaction hath been made to the officers of His Majesty's revenue, and others, who suffered by the riots and insurrections above mentioned. ...

Massachusetts Government Act

The ... method of electing ... counselors or assistants ... in which the appointment of the respective governors had been vested in the general courts or assemblies ..., hath, by repeated experience, been found to be extremely ill adapted to the plan of government established in the province of the Massachusetts Bay ..., and hath ... for some time past, been such as had the most manifest tendency to obstruct ... the execution of the laws; to weaken the attachment of His Majesty's well-disposed subjects in the said province to His Majesty's government, and to encourage the ill-disposed among them to proceed even to acts of direct resistance to, and defiance of, His Majesty's authority. And it hath accordingly happened, that an open resistance to the execution of the laws hath actually taken place in the town of Boston, and the neighborhood thereof, within the said Province. ... It is, under these circumstances, ... absolutely necessary, ... that the said method of annually electing the counselors or assistants of the said province should no longer be suffered to continue, but that the appointment of the said counselors or assistants should henceforth be put upon the like footing as is established in such other of His Majesty's colonies or plantations in America, the governors whereof are appointed by His Majesty's commission. ...

Be it therefore enacted ..., that from and after the first day of August, 1774, so much of the charter ... [of 1691] ... which relates to the time and manner of electing the assistants or counselors for the said province, be revoked. ... And that from and after the said first day of August, 1774, the council, or court of assistants ... for the time being, shall be composed of such of the inhabitants or proprietors of lands within the same as shall be thereunto nominated and appointed by His Majesty. ...

And it is hereby further enacted, that the said assistants or counselors ... shall hold their offices respectively, for and during the pleasure of His Majesty. ...

And be it further enacted ..., that ... after the first day of July, 1774, it shall ... be lawful for His Majesty's governor ... to nominate and appoint ... and also to remove, without the consent of the council, all judges of the inferior courts of common pleas, commissioners of *Oyer* and *Terminer*, the attorney general, provosts, marshals, justices of the peace, and other officers to the council or courts of justice. ...

And whereas, by several acts of the General Court, ... the freeholders and inhabitants of the several townships ... are authorized to assemble together annually, or occasionally, upon notice given ... for the choice of selectmen, constables, and other officers, and for the making and agreeing upon such necessary rules, orders, and by-laws, for the directing, managing, and ordering, the prudential affairs of such townships ... ; and whereas a great abuse has been made of the power of calling such meetings, and the inhabitants have, contrary to the design of their institution, been misled to treat upon matters of the most general concern, and to pass many dangerous and unwarrantable resolves. For remedy whereof ... be it enacted, that after the first day of August, 1774, no meeting shall be called ... without the leave of the governnor, ... in writing, expressing the special business of the said meeting, except the annual meeting in the months of

March or May, for the choice of select-men, constables, and other officers, ... and also, except any meeting for the election of ... representatives in the general court; and that no other matter shall be treated of at such meetings. ...

Administration of Justice Act

WHEREAS in His Majesty's province of Massachusetts Bay, ... an attempt hath lately been made to throw off the authority of the Parliament of Great Britain ... and ... resistance by open force to the execution of certain acts of Parliament, hath been suffered to take place. ... And whereas, in the present disordered state of the said province, it is of the utmost importance ... that neither the magistrates acting in support of the laws, nor any of His Majesty's subjects aiding and assisting them therein, ... should be discouraged from the proper discharge of their duty. ... In order therefore to remove every ... discouragement from the minds of His Majesty's subjects, and to induce them, upon all proper occasions, to exert themselves in support of the public peace of the province, and of the authority of the King and Parliament of Great Britain over the same; be it enacted ... , that if any ... indictment shall be found, or if any appeal shall be sued or preferred against any person, for murder, or other capital offence, in the province of the Massachusetts Bay, and it shall appear, by information given upon oath to the governor ... of the said province, that the fact was committed by the person against whom such ... indictment shall be found, or against whom such appeal shall be sued or preferred, as aforesaid, either in the execution of his duty as a magistrate, for the suppression of riots, or in the support of the laws of revenue, or in acting in his duty as an officer of revenue, or in acting under the direction and order of any magistrate, for the suppression of riots, or for the carrying into effect the laws of revenue ... ; and if it shall also appear, to the satisfaction of the said governor ... that an indifferent

trial cannot be had within the said province, in that case, it shall ... be lawful for the governor ... , to direct, with the advice and consent of the council, that the ... indictment, or appeal, shall be tried in some other of His Majesty's colonies, or in Great Britain; and for that purpose, to order the person against whom such ... indictment shall be found, ... to be sent ... to the place appointed for his trial, or to admit such person to bail, taking a recognizance ... from such a person, with sufficient sureties, ... in such sums of money as the said governor ... shall deem reasonable, for the personal appearance of such person ... at a time to be mentioned in such recognizances; and the governor, ... or court of King's Bench, where the trial is appointed to be had in Great Britain, upon the appearance of such person, according to such recognizance, or in custody, shall either commit such person, or admit him to bail, until such trial. ...

And, to prevent a failure of justice, from the want of evidence on the trial of any such inquisition, indictment or appeal, be it further enacted, that the governor ... is hereby authorized and required, to bind in recognizances to His Majesty all such witnesses as the prosecutor or person against whom such ... indictment shall be found, or appeal sued or preferred, shall desire to attend the trial of the said inquisition, ... for their personal appearance, at the time and place of such trial, to give evidence: and the said governor ... shall thereupon appoint a reasonable sum to be allowed for the expenses of every such witness. ...

The Quebec Act

[Boundaries defined to include territory west to the Mississippi and north to the frontiers of the Hudson's Bay territory.]

And whereas ... the inhabitants ... amounted at the conquest, to above ... [165,000] persons, professing the religion of the Church of Rome. ... It is hereby declared, that His Majesty's subjects professing the religion of the Church of Rome . . . in the said Province of Quebec, may have, hold, and enjoy, the free exercise of the religion of the Church of Rome, subject to the King's supremacy . . . ; and that the clergy of the said Church may hold, receive, and enjoy their accustomed dues and rights, with respect to such persons only as shall profess the said religion. Provided nevertheless, that it shall be lawful for His Majesty . . . to make such provisions out of the rest of the said accustomed dues and rights, for the encouragement of the Protestant religion, and for the maintenance and support of a Protestant clergy within the said province, as he . . . shall . . . think necessary and expedient. . . .

And be it further enacted . . . that all His Majesty's Canadian subjects within the Province of Quebec, the religious orders and communities only excepted, may also hold and enjoy their property and possessions, together with all customs and usages, relative thereto, and all other their civil rights, in as large, ample and beneficial manner, as . . . may consist with their allegiance to His Majesty, and subjection to the Crown and Parliament of Great Britain; and that in all matters of controversy relative to property and civil rights, resort shall be had to the laws of Canada, as the rule for the decision of the same; and all cases that shall hereafter be instituted in any of the courts of justice . . . shall, with respect to such property and rights, be determined agreeably to the said laws and customs of Canada. . . .

And whereas it may be necessary to ordain many regulations, for the future welfare and good government of the Province of Quebec, the occasions of which cannot now be foreseen, nor without much delay and inconvenience be provided for, without entrusting that authority for a certain time . . . to persons resident there. And whereas it is at present inexpedient to call an Assembly. Be it therefore enacted . . . that it shall . . . be lawful for His Majesty . . . to constitute and appoint a Council for the Affairs of the Province of Quebec, to consist of such persons resident there . . . as His Majesty, . . . shall be pleased to appoint . . . which Council, so appointed and nominated . . . shall have power and authority to make ordinances for the peace, welfare, and good government of the said province with the consent of His Majesty's Governor.

71. *The Association, 1774*

"The Association," October 20, 1774. *Journals of the Continental Congress.* W. C. Ford, ed. (Washington, 1904), I, 75–80.

WE, His Majesty's most loyal subjects, the delegates of the several colonies . . . in a continental congress, held in the city of Philadelphia, on the 5th day of September, 1774, avowing our allegiance to His Majesty, our affection and regard for our fellow-subjects in Great Britain and elsewhere, affected with the deepest anxiety, and most alarming apprehensions, at those grievances and distresses, with which His Majesty's American subjects are oppressed; and having taken under our most serious deliberation, the state of the whole continent, find, that the present unhappy situation of our affairs is occasioned by a ruinous system of colony administration, adopted by the British ministry about the year 1763, evidently calculated for inslaving these colonies, and, with them, the British empire. In prosecution of which system, various acts of Parliament have been passed, for raising a revenue in America, for depriving the American subjects, in many instances, of the constitutional trial by jury, exposing their lives to danger, by directing a new and illegal trial beyond the seas, for crimes alleged to have been committed in America. And in prosecution of the same system, several late, cruel, and oppressive acts have been passed, respecting the town of Boston and the Massachusetts Bay, and also an act for extending the Province of Quebec, so as to border on the western frontiers of these colonies, establishing an arbitrary government therein, and discouraging the settlement of British subjects in that wide extended country; thus, by the influence of civil principles and ancient prejudices, to dispose the inhabitants to act with hostility against the free Protestant colonies, whenever a wicked ministry shall choose so to direct them.

To obtain redress of these grievances, ... we are of opinion, that a non-importation, non-consumption, and non-exportation agreement ... will prove the most speedy, effectual, and peaceable measure. And, therefore, we do, for ourselves, and the inhabitants of the several colonies, whom we represent, firmly agree and associate, under the sacred ties of virtue, honor and love of our country, as follows:

1. That from and after the first day of December next, we will not import, into British America, from Great Britain or Ireland, any goods ... whatsoever, or from any other place, any such goods ... as shall have been exported from Great Britain or Ireland; nor will we, after that day, import any East India tea from any part of the world; nor any molasses, syrups, paneles, coffee, or pimento, from the British plantations or from Dominica; nor wines from Madeira, or the Western Islands; nor foreign indigo.

2. We will neither import nor purchase, any slave imported after the first day of December next; after which time, we will wholly discontinue the slave trade. ...

3. ... We will not purchase or use any tea, imported on account of the East India Company, or any on which a duty hath been ... paid; ... nor will we ... purchase or use any of those goods ... we have agreed not to import, which we ... have cause to suspect, were imported after the first day of December, except such as come under the rules and directions of the tenth article hereafter mentioned.

4. The earnest desire we have, not to injure our fellow-subjects in Great Britain, Ireland, or the West Indies, induces us to suspend a non-exportation, until the tenth day of September, 1775; at which time, if the said acts and parts of acts of the British Parliament hereinafter mentioned are not repealed, we will not, directly or indirectly, export any merchandise or commodity whatsoever to Great Britain, Ireland, or the West Indies, except rice to Europe.

5. Such as are merchants ... will give orders, as soon as possible, to their factors, agents and correspondents, in Great Britain and Ireland, not to ship any goods to them ...; and if any merchant, residing in Great Britain or Ireland, shall directly or indirectly ship any goods ... for America, in order to break the said non-importation agreement, or in any manner contravene the same, ... such unworthy conduct ... ought to be made public; and, on the same being so done, we will not, from thenceforth, have any commercial connection with such merchant.

6. That such as are owners of vessels will give positive orders to their captains, or masters, not to receive on board their vessels any goods prohibited by the said non-importation agreement, on pain of immediate dismission from their service.

7. We will use our utmost endeavors to improve the breed of sheep, and increase their number to the greatest extent; and to that end, we will kill them as seldom as may be ...; nor will we export any ...; and those of us, who ... can conveniently spare any sheep, will dispose of them to our neighbors, especially to the poorer sort, on moderate terms.

8. We will ... encourage frugality, economy, and industry, and promote agriculture, arts and the manufactures of this country, especially that of wool; and

will ... discourage every species of extravagance and dissipation, especially all horse-racing, and all kinds of gaming, cock-fighting, exhibitions of shows, plays, and other expensive diversions and entertainments; and on the death of any relation or friend, none of us, or any of our families, will go into any further mourning dress, than a black crepe or ribbon on the arm or hat, for gentlemen, and a black ribbon and necklace for ladies, and we will discontinue the giving of gloves and scarves at funerals.

9. Such as are venders of goods or merchandise will not take advantage of the scarcity of goods ... , but will sell the same at the rates we have been respectively accustomed to do, for twelve months last past.—And if any vender ... shall sell any such goods on higher terms, or shall, in any manner ... violate or depart from this agreement, no person ought ... deal with any such person ... at any time thereafter, for any commodity whatever.

10. In case any ... person shall import any goods ... after the first day of December, and before the first day of February next, the same ought forthwith ... to be either reshipped or delivered up to the committee of the county or town ... to be stored at the risk of the importer, until the non-importation agreement shall cease, or be sold under the direction of the committee aforesaid; and in the last-mentioned case, the owner or owners of such goods shall be reimbursed out of the sales, the first cost and charges, the profit, if any, to be applied towards relieving and employing such poor inhabitants of the town of Boston, as are immediate sufferers by the Boston Port Bill; and a particular account of all goods so returned, stored, or sold, to be inserted in the public papers....

11. That a committee be chosen in every county, city, and town, by those who are qualified to vote for representatives in the legislature, whose business it shall be attentively to observe the conduct of all persons touching this association; and

when ... any person ... has violated this association, [the committee shall] ... cause the truth of the case to be published in the gazette; to the end, that all such foes to the rights of British America may be publicly known, and universally contemned as the enemies of American liberty; and thenceforth we ... will break off all dealings with him or her.

12. That the committee of correspondence, in the respective colonies, do frequently inspect the entries of their customhouses, and inform each other, from time to time, of the true state thereof, and of every other material circumstance that may occur relative to this association.

13. That all manufactures of this country be sold at reasonable prices, so that no undue advantage be taken of a future scarcity of goods.

14. And we do further agree and resolve, that we will have no trade, commerce, dealings or intercourse whatsoever, with any colony or province, in North America, which shall not accede to, or which shall hereafter violate this association, but will hold them as unworthy of the rights of freemen, and as inimical to the liberties of their country.

And we do solemnly bind ourselves and our constituents, under the ties aforesaid, to adhere to this association, until such parts of the several acts of Parliament passed since the close of the last war, as impose or continue duties on tea, wine, molasses, syrups, paneles, coffee, sugar, pimento, indigo, foreign paper, glass, and painters' colors, imported into America, and extend the powers of the admiralty courts beyond their ancient limits, deprive the American subject of trial by jury, authorize the judge's certificate to indemnify the prosecutor from damages, that he might otherwise be liable to from a trial by his peers, require oppressive security from a claimant of ships or goods seized, before he shall be allowed to defend his property, are repealed.—And until that part of the act ... for the better securing His Majesty's dock-yards, ... by which any persons charged with committing any of the offenses therein described, in America, may be tried in any shire or county within the realm, is repealed.—And until the four [intolerable] acts ... are repealed. And we recommend it to the provincial conventions, and to the committees in the respective colonies, to establish such farther regulations as they may think proper, for carrying into execution this association.

72. *Rules by Which a Great Empire May Be Reduced to a Small One, 1773*

Franklin, *Works*, IV, 388–98

I ADDRESS myself to all ministers who have the management of extensive dominions, which from their very greatness have become troublesome to govern, because the multiplicity of their affairs leaves no time for fiddling.

I. In the first place, gentlemen, you are to consider that a great empire, like a great cake, is most easily diminished at the edges. Turn your attention, therefore, first to your remotest provinces; that, as you get rid of them, the next may follow in order.

II. That the possibility of this separation may always exist, take special care the provinces are never incorporated with the mother country; that they do not enjoy the same common rights, the same privileges in commerce; and that they are governed by severer laws, all of your enacting, without allowing them any share in the choice of the legislators. By carefully making and preserving such distinctions, you will (to keep my simile of the cake) act like a wise gingerbread-baker, who, to facilitate a division, cuts his dough half through in those places where, when baked, he would have it broken to pieces.

III. Those remote provinces have perhaps been acquired, purchased, or conquered at the sole expense of the settlers, or their ancestors, without the aid of the mother country. If this should happen to increase her strength, by their growing numbers, ready to join in her wars; her commerce, by their growing demand for her manufactures; or her naval power, by greater employment for her ships and seamen, they may probably suppose some merit in this, and that it entitles them to some favor; you are therefore to forget it all, or resent it, as if they had done you injury. If they happen to be zealous whigs, friends of liberty, nurtured in revolution principles, remember all that to their prejudice, and contrive to punish it. ...

IV. However peaceably your colonies have submitted to your government, shown their affection to your interests, and patiently borne their grievances; you are to suppose them always inclined to revolt, and treat them accordingly. Quarter troops among them, who by their insolence may provoke the rising of mobs. ... By this means, like the husband who uses his wife ill from suspicion, you may in time convert your suspicions into realities.

V. Remote provinces must have governors and judges, to represent the royal person, and execute everywhere the delegated parts of his office and authority. You ministers know, that much of the strength of the government depends on the opinion of the people; and much of that opinion on the choice of rulers placed immediately over them. ... You are therefore to be careful whom you recommend for those offices. If you can fine prodigals, who have ruined their fortunes, broken gamesters or stockjobbers, these may do well as governors; for they will probably be rapacious, and provoke the people by their extortions. Wrangling proctors and pettifogging lawyers, too, are not amiss;

for they will be forever disputing and quarreling with their little parliaments. If withal they should be ignorant, wrongheaded, and insolent, so much the better. Attorneys' clerks and Newgate solicitors will do for chief justices, especially if they hold their places during your pleasure; and all will contribute to impress those ideas of your government, that are proper for a people you would wish to renounce it.

VI. To confirm these impressions, and strike them deeper, whenever the injured come to the capital with complaints of maladministration, oppression or injustice, punish such suitors with long delay, enormous expense, and a final judgment in favor of the oppressor. . . .

VII. When such governors have crammed their coffers, and made themselves so odious to the people that they can no longer remain among them with safety to their person, recall and reward them with pensions. . . .

VIII. If, when you are engaged in war, your colonies should vie in liberal aids of men and money against the common enemy, upon your simple requisition, and give far beyond their abilities, reflect that a penny taken from them by your power is more honorable to you, than a pound presented by their benevolence; despise therefore their voluntary grants, and resolve to harass them with novel taxes. . . .

IX. In laying these taxes, never regard the heavy burdens those remote people already undergo, in defending their own frontiers, supporting their own provincial government, making new roads, building bridges, churches, and other public edifices, which in old countries have been done to your hands by your ancestors, but which occasion constant calls and demands on the purses of a new people. Forget the restraints you lay on their trade for your own benefit, and the advantage a monopoly of this trade gives your exacting merchants. Think nothing of the wealth those merchants and your manufacturers acquire by the colony commerce; their

increased ability thereby to pay taxes at home; . . . all this, and the employment and support of thousands of your poor by the colonists, you are entirely to forget. But remember to make your arbitrary tax more grievous to your provinces, by public declarations importing that your power of taxing them has no limits; so that when you take from them without their consent a shilling in the pound, you have a clear right to the other nineteen. This will probably weaken every idea of security in their property, and convince them, that under such a government they have nothing they can call their own; which can scarce fail of producing the happiest consequences!

X. Possibly, indeed, some of them might still comfort themselves, and say, "Though we have no property, we have yet something left that is valuable; we have constitutional liberty, both of person and of conscience. This King, these Lords, and these Commons, who it seems are too remote from us to know us, and feel for us, cannot take from us our habeas corpus right, or our right of trial by a jury of our neighbors; they cannot deprive us of the exercise of our religion, alter our ecclesiastical constitution, and compel us to be Papists, if they please, or Mahometans." To annihilate this comfort, begin by laws to perplex their commerce with infinite regulations, impossible to be remembered and observed; ordain seizures of their property for every failure; take away the trial of such property by jury, and give it to arbitrary judges of your own appointing, and of the lowest characters in the country, whose salaries and emoluments are to arise out of the duties or condemnations, and whose appointments are during pleasure. Then let there be a formal declaration of both Houses, that opposition to your edicts is treason, and that persons suspected of treason in the provinces may, according to some obsolete law, be seized and sent to the metropolis of the empire for trial; and pass an act, that those there charged with certain other offenses, shall be sent away in chains from their friends and country to be tried in the same manner for felony. Then erect a new Court of Inquisition among them, accompanied by an armed force, with instructions to transport all such suspected persons; to be ruined by the expense, if they bring over evidences to prove their innocence, or be found guilty and hanged, if they cannot afford it. And, lest the people should think you cannot possibly go any farther, pass another solemn declaratory act, "that King, Lords, Commons had, have, and of right ought to have, full power and authority to make statutes of sufficient force and validity to bind the unrepresented provinces in all cases whatsoever." This will include spiritual with temporal, and, taken together, must operate wonderfully to your purpose; by convincing them, that they are at present under a power something like that spoken of in the Scriptures, which can not only kill their bodies, but damn their souls to all eternity, by compelling them, if it pleases, to worship the Devil.

XI. To make your taxes more odious, and more likely to procure resistance, send from the capital a board of officers to superintend the collection, composed of the most indiscreet, ill-bred, and insolent you can find. . . .

XII. Another way to make your tax odious, is to misapply the produce of it. If it was originally appropriated for the defense of the provinces, the better support of government, and the administration of justice, where it may be necessary, then apply none of it to that defense, but bestow it where it is not necessary, in augmenting salaries or pensions to every governor, who had distinguished himself by his enmity to the people, and by calumniating them to their sovereign. This will make them pay it more unwillingly, and be more apt to quarrel with those that collect it and those that imposed it, who will quarrel again with them, and all shall contribute to your main purpose, of making them weary of your government.

XIII. If the people of any province have been accustomed to support their own governors and judges . . . , you are to apprehend that such governors and judges may be thereby influenced to treat the people kindly, and to do them justice. This is another reason for applying part of that revenue in larger salaries to such governors and judges, given, as their commissions are, during your pleasure only; forbidding them to take any salaries from their provinces; that thus the people may no longer hope any kindness from their governors, or (in crown cases) any justice from their judges. . . .

XIV. If the parliaments of your provinces should dare to claim rights, or complain of your administration, order them to be harassed with repeated dissolutions. . . .

XV. Convert the brave, honest officers of your navy into pimping tide-waiters and colony officers of the customs. . . . Then let these boats' crews land upon every farm in their way, rob the orchards, steal the pigs and the poultry, and insult the inhabitants. If the injured and exasperated farmers, unable to procure other justice, should attack the aggressors, drub them, and burn their boats; you are to call this high treason and rebellion, order fleets and armies into their country, and threaten to carry all the offenders three thousand miles to be hanged, drawn and quartered. O! this will work admirably!

XVI. If you are told of discontents in your colonies, never believe that they are general, or that you have given occasion for them; therefore do not think of applying any remedy, or of changing any offensive measure. . . .

XVII. If you see rival nations rejoicing at the prospect of your disunion with your provinces, and endeavoring to promote it; . . . let not that offend you. Why should it, since you all mean the same thing? . . .

XIX. Send armies into their country under pretense of protecting the inhabitants; but, instead of garrisoning the forts on their frontiers with those troops, to prevent incursions, demolish those forts, and order the troops into the heart of the country, that the savages may be encouraged to attack the frontiers, and that the troops may be protected by the inhabitants. This will seem to proceed from your ill will or your ignorance, and contribute farther to produce and strengthen an opinion among them, that you are no longer fit to govern them.

XX. Lastly, invest the general of your army in the provinces, with great and unconstitutional powers, and free him from the control of even your own civil governors. Let him have troops enough under his command . . . and who knows but . . . he may take it into his head to set up for himself? If he should, and you have carefully practised these few excellent rules of mine, take my word for it, all the provinces will immediately join him; and you will that day (if you have not done it sooner) get rid of the trouble of governing them, and all the plagues attending their commerce and connection from thenceforth and forever.

X *The Impulse Toward Nationalism*

THE INTENSE emotion with which Americans responded to the grievances of the 1760's and 1770's was an indication that they already considered themselves a country apart from Great Britain. Even earlier the colonists had developed the habit of referring to themselves as "Americans." In the decade of the 1760's they were increasingly conscious that they were a distinctive people, sharing a common culture. This consciousness remained unshaken in the years that followed.

The revolutionary crisis sharpened the necessity for thinking critically about the nature of the Americans' identity and about the quality of their loyalty to the Crown. The moderate author of the "Letters of a Pennsylvania Farmer" was still loyal to the Crown and sensitive to the advantages of maintaining the British imperial connections; yet he too was conscious that America was his country (No. 73). After 1770 the awareness of difference was stronger still; the American seemed a completely new type of man (No. 74). The ties of the old allegiance became less binding as the grievances became more intense and as the conflict sharpened into war. By 1776 *Common Sense* was pointing to the conclusion that the logical outcome of American nationality was total separation from Britain (No. 75); and that led shortly to the Declaration of Independence (*see below*, No. 82).

Victory in the war and the attainment of independence were, at the same time, sources of confidence and challenges to future action. On the one hand, the ability to beat back the British was providential and a token of almost unlimited progress yet to come (No. 76). On the other hand, the necessity for justifying the revolution was a stimulus driving the Americans forward in many fields of activity (*see below*, Nos. 92, 134). Meanwhile there were already strong efforts to find appropriately distinctive forms that would express the identity of the Americans as a nation. It seemed foolish thus that Americans should allow themselves still to be restricted by the archaic structure of the English language (No. 77). By the same token it was undignified that they should as yet fail to have fixed upon a distinctive national designation (No. 78). The strong sense of nationality expressed in these attitudes would continue to grow after the turn of the century. Stimulated by a second war against Britain, national sentiments then affected every feature of American life (No. 79).

73. *Letters from a Farmer in Pennsylvania,* 1767

Letter No. III, in John Dickinson, *Political Writings* (Wilmington, 1801), I, 167–73.

THE MEANING of . . . [these letters] is, to convince the people of these colonies that they are at this moment exposed to the most imminent dangers; and to persuade them immediately, vigorously, and unanimously, to exert themselves, in the most firm, and most peaceable manner, for obtaining relief.

The cause of liberty is a cause of too much dignity, to be sullied by turbulence and tumults. It ought to be maintained in a manner suitable to her nature. Those who engage in it, should breathe a sedate, yet fervent spirit, animating them to actions of prudence, justice, modesty, bravery, humanity and magnanimity. . . .

Every government at some time or other falls into wrong measures. This may proceed from mistake or passion. But every such measure does not dissolve the obligation between the governors and the governed. The mistake may be corrected; the passion may subside. It is the duty of the governed, to endeavor to rectify the mistake, and to appease the passion. They have not at first any other right, than to represent their grievances, and to pray for redress. . . . If their applications are disregarded, *then* that kind of opposition becomes justifiable, which can be made without breaking the laws, or disturbing the public peace. This consists in the prevention of the oppressors reaping advantage from their oppressions, and not in their punishment. For experience may teach them what reason did not; and

harsh methods cannot be proper till milder ones have failed.

If at length it becomes undoubted, that an inveterate resolution is formed to annihilate the liberties of the governed, the English history affords frequent examples of resistance by force. What particular circumstances will in any future case justify such resistance, can never be ascertained till they happen. Perhaps it may be allowable to say generally, that it never can be justifiable, until the people are fully convinced, that any further submission will be destructive to their happiness. . . .

Resistance, in the case of colonies against their mother country, is extremely different from the resistance of a people against their prince. A nation may change their king, or race of kings, and retaining their ancient form of government, be gainers by changing. . . . But if once we are separated from our mother country, what new form of government shall we adopt, or where shall we find another Britain, to supply our loss? Torn from the body to which we are united by religion, liberty, laws, affections, relation, language and commerce, we must bleed at every vein.

In truth, the prosperity of these provinces is founded on their dependence on Great Britain; and when she returns to "her old good humor, and her old good nature". . . I hope they will always think it their duty and interest, as it most certainly will be, to promote her welfare by all the means in their power....

If, however, it shall happen by an unfortunate course of affairs, that our applications to His Majesty and the Parliament for redress prove ineffectual, let us then take another step, by withholding from Great Britain, all the advantages she has been used to receive from us. Then let us try, if our ingenuity, industry, and fru-

gality, will not give weight to our remonstrances. Let us all be united with one spirit in one cause. Let us invent—let us work—let us save—let us, continually, keep up our claim, and incessantly repeat our complaints. But, above all, let us implore the protection of that infinitely good and gracious Being, "by whom kings reign, and princes decree justice."

74. *The American, a New Man, 1770–95*

Michel Guillaume St. Jean de Crèvecoeur, *Letters from an American Farmer* (London, 1782), 45–59, 62–6, 69–80, 121–5, 130–1, 146–8, 150–8, 162–7, 170–1, 176–8, 182–98, 201–3.

I WISH I could be acquainted with the feelings and thoughts which must agitate the heart and present themselves to the mind of an enlightened Englishman, when he first lands on this continent.... He is arrived on a new continent; a modern society offers itself to his contemplation, different from what he had hitherto seen. It is not composed, as in Europe, of great lords who possess everything, and of a herd of people who have nothing. Here are no aristocratical families, no courts, no kings, no bishops, no ecclesiastical dominion, no invisible power giving to a few a very visible one, no great manufacturers employing thousands, no great refinements of luxury. The rich and the poor are not so far removed from each other as they are in Europe.... We are a people of cultivators, scattered over an immense territory, communicating with each other by means of good roads and navigable rivers, united by the silken bands of mild government, all respecting the laws, without dreading their power, because they are equitable. We are all animated with the spirit of an industry which is unfettered and unrestrained, because each person works for himself.

If he travels through our rural districts, ...[the stranger] views not the hostile castle and the haughty mansion con-

trasted with the clay-built hut and miserable cabin.... A pleasing uniformity of decent competence appears throughout our habitations. The meanest of our log-houses is a dry and comfortable habitation. Lawyer or merchant are the fairest titles our towns afford; that of a farmer is the only appellation of the rural inhabitants of our country.... There, on a Sunday, he sees a congregation of respectable farmers and their wives, all clad in neat homespun, well-mounted, or riding in their own humble wagons. There is not among them an esquire, saving the unlettered magistrate. There he sees a parson as simple as his flock, a farmer who does not riot on the labor of others. We have no princes, for whom we toil, starve, and bleed. We are the most perfect society now existing in the world. Here man is free as he ought to be.

The next wish of this traveler will be, to know whence came all these people? They are a mixture of English, Scotch, Irish, French, Dutch, Germans, and Swedes. From this promiscuous breed, that race, now called Americans, have arisen. In this great American asylum, the poor of Europe have by some means met together.... To what purpose should they ask one another what countrymen they are? Alas, two-thirds of them had no country. Can a wretch, who wanders about, who works and starves, whose life is a continual scene of sore affliction or pinching penury; can that man call England or any other kingdon his country, a country that had no bread for him, whose fields produced him no harvest; who met with nothing but the frowns of the rich, the severity of the laws, with jails and punishments; who owned not a single foot of the extensive surface of this planet? No! Urged by a variety of motives, here they came. Everything has tended to regenerate them: new laws, a new mode of living, a new social system. Here they are become men. In Europe they were so many useless plants, wanting vegetative mold and refreshing showers. They withered, and were mowed down by want, hunger, and war. But now, by the power of transplantation, like all other plants, they have taken root and flourished! Formerly they were not numbered in any civil lists of their country, except in those of the poor; here they rank as citizens.

By what invisible power has this surprising metamorphosis been performed? By that of the laws and that of . . . [the people's] industry. The laws, the indulgent laws, protect them as they arrive, stamping on them the symbol of adoption. They receive ample rewards for their labors; these accumulated rewards procure them lands; those lands confer on them the title of freemen; and to that title every benefit is affixed which men can possibly require. This is the great operation daily performed by our laws. Whence proceed these laws? From our government. Whence that government? It is derived from the original genius and the strong desire of the people ratified and confirmed by the Crown.

What attachment can a poor European emigrant have for a country where he had nothing? The knowledge of the language, the love of a few kindred as poor as himself, were the only cords that tied him. His country is now that which gives him land, bread, protection, and consequence. . . . He is either a European, or the descendant of a European; hence, that strange mixture of blood, which you will find in no other country. . . . *He* is an American, who, leaving behind him all his ancient prejudices and manners, receives new ones from the new mode of life he has embraced, the new government he obeys, and the new rank he holds. . . . Here individuals of all nations are melted into a new race of men, whose labors and posterity will one day cause great changes in the world. Americans are the western pilgrims, who are carrying along with them that great mass of arts, sciences, vigor, and industry, which began long since in the east. They will finish the great circle.

The Americans were once scattered all over Europe. Here they are incorporated into one of the finest systems of population which has ever appeared, and which will hereafter become distinct by the power of the different climates they inhabit. The American is a new man, who acts upon new principles; he must therefore entertain new ideas and form new opinions. From involuntary idleness, servile dependence, penury, and useless labor, he has passed to toils of a very different nature, rewarded by ample subsistence.—This is an American. . . .

There is no wonder that this country has so many charms, and presents to Europeans so many temptations to remain in it. A traveler in Europe becomes a stranger as soon as he quits his own kingdom; but it is otherwise here. We know, properly speaking, no strangers. This is every person's country; the variety of our soils, situations, climates, governments, and produce, hath something which must please everybody. No sooner does an European arrive, . . . than his eyes are opened upon the fair prospect. When in England, he was a mere Englishman; here he stands on a larger portion of the globe. He does not find, as in Europe, a crowded society, where every place is over-stocked; he does not feel that perpetual collision of parties, that difficulty of beginning, that contention which oversets so many. There is room for everybody in America. Has he any particular talent or industry, he exerts it in order to procure a livelihood, and it succeeds. . . .

A European, when he first arrives seems limited in his intentions as well as in his views; but he very suddenly alters his scale; . . . he no sooner breathes our air than he forms schemes, and embarks in designs he never would have thought of in his own country. . . . Thus Europeans become Americans.

But how is this accomplished in that crowd of low indigent people, who flock here every year from all parts of Europe? . . . Let me select one as an epitome of the rest; he is hired, he goes to work, and works moderately; instead of being employed by a haughty person, he finds himself with his equal, placed at the substantial table of the farmer, or else at an inferior one as good; his wages are high, his bed is not like that bed of sorrow on which he used to lie. . . . He begins to feel the effects of a sort of resurrection; . . . he now feels himself a man, because he is treated as such. Judge what an alteration there must arise in the mind and the thoughts of this man; he begins to forget his former servitude and dependence. His heart involuntarily swells and glows; this first swell inspires him with those new thoughts which constitute an American.

75. *Common Sense, 1776*

Thomas Paine, *Common Sense* (London, 1791), 4, 30–3.

THE CAUSE of America is in a great measure the cause of all mankind. Many circumstances hath, and will arise, which are not local, but universal, and through which the principles of all lovers of mankind are affected, and in the event of which their affections are interested. The laying a country desolate with fire and sword, declaring war against the natural rights of mankind, and extirpating the defenders thereof from the face of the earth, is the concern of every man to whom nature hath given the power of feeling; of which class, regardless of party censure, is the AUTHOR. . . .

It has lately been asserted in Parliament, that the colonies have no relation to each other but through the parent country, i.e., that Pennsylvania and the Jerseys, and so on for the rest, are sister colonies by the way of England; this is certainly a very round-about way of proving relationship, but it is the nearest and only true way of proving enemyship, if I may so call it. France and Spain never were, nor perhaps ever will be, our enemies as Americans, but as our being the subjects of Great Britain.

But Britain is the parent country, say some. Then the more shame upon her conduct. Even brutes do not devour their young, nor savages make war upon their families: wherefore the assertion, if true, turns to her reproach; but it happens not to be true. . . . Europe and not England, is the parent country of America. This new world hath been the asylum for the persecuted lovers of civil and religious liberty from every part of Europe. Hither have they fled, not from the tender embraces of the mother, but from the cruelty of the monster; and it is so far true of England, that the same tyranny which drove the first emigrants from home, pursues their descendants still.

In this extensive quarter of the globe, we forget the narrow limits of three hundred and sixty miles (the extent of England) and carry our friendship on a larger scale; we claim brotherhood with every European Christian, and triumph in the generosity of the sentiment.

It is pleasant to observe by what regular gradations we surmount the force of local prejudice, as we enlarge our acquaintance with the world. A man born in any town in England divided into parishes, will naturally associate most with his fellow-parishioners, because their interests in many cases will be common, and distinguish him by the name of neighbor; if he meet him but a few miles from home, he drops the narrow idea of a street, and salutes him by the name of townsman; ... but if in their foreign excursions they should associate in France, or any other part of Europe, their local remembrance would be enlarged into that of Englishman. And by a just parity of reasoning, all Europeans meeting in America ... are countrymen; for England, Holland, Germany, or Sweden, when compared with the whole, stand in the same places on the larger scale, which the divisions of street, town, and country do on the smaller ones; distinction too limited for continental minds. Not one third of the inhabitants even of this province, are of English descent. Wherefore I reprobate the phrase of parent or mother country applied to England only, as being false, selfish, narrow, and ungenerous.

But admitting that we were all of Eng-lish descent, what does it amount to? Nothing. Britain being now an open enemy, extinguishes every other name and title. And to say that reconciliation is our duty, is truly farcical. The first King of England, of the present line (William the Conqueror) was a Frenchman, and half the peers of England are descendants from the same country; wherefore by the same method of reasoning, England ought to be governed by France.

Much has been said of the united strength of Britain and the colonies; that in conjunction they might bid defiance to the world. But this is mere presumption; the fate of war is uncertain: neither do the expressions mean anything; for this continent would never suffer itself to be drained of inhabitants, to support the British arms in either Asia, Africa, or Europe.

Besides, what have we to do with setting the world at defiance? Our plan is commerce, and that, well attended to, will secure us the peace and friendship of all Europe; because it is the interest of all Europe to have America a free port. Her trade will always be a protection, and her barrenness of gold and silver secure her from invaders.

76. *The Greatness of America*, 1782

Philip Freneau, "Philosopher of the Forest, X" in *Miscellaneous Works* (Philadelphia, 1788), 364–7.

It is not easy to conceive what will be the greatness and importance of North America in a century or two ... if the present fabric of Nature is upheld, and the people retain those bold and manly sentiments of freedom, which actuate them at this day. Agriculture, the basis of a nation's greatness, will here, most probably, be advanced to its summit of perfection; and its attendant, commerce, will so agreeably and usefully employ mankind, that wars will be forgotten; nations, by a free intercourse with this vast and fertile continent, ... will again become brothers ... and no longer treat each other as savages and monsters. The iron generation will verge to decay, and those days of felicity advance which have been so often wished for by all good men, and which are so beautifully described by the prophetic sages of ancient times. ...

It is a standing rule in philosophy, that Nature does nothing in vain. A potent nation, now at war with these republics, has proclaimed her resolution to lay waste what she cannot reclaim by conquest, and schemes are projected to oblige such to re-emigrate to Europe as shall escape the fury of the destroyers. But if this new world was not to become at some time or another the receptacle of numerous civilized nations, from one extremity to the other, for what visible purpose could Nature have formed these vast lakes in the bosom of her infant empire . . . ? These lakes having, severally, a communication with each other, and lastly with the Atlantic Ocean, towards the northeast; approaching also very near, by the west, to several of the navigable branches of the Mississippi, from an easy communication through a long tract of country, the intercourse between the various parts of which would, in future times, at least for the purposes of commerce, be extremely difficult and laborious, were it not for this continuation of waters, that for ages have been waiting to receive the barque of traffic, urged forward by the sail or the stroke of the springy oar; as the soil bordering thereon has no less impatiently expected the operations of the industrious plough.

During a very considerable part of the year, the southwest wind blows unremittedly on the face of this serpentine river, the Ohio; and even at other times, the current of air is more prevalent in that direction than in any other, which

being directly opposed to the course of the stream, moving at the rate of one mile hourly, is it not evident that Providence, Nature, or Fate, has so ordered this matter, that the commercial vessels hereafter sailing northward thereon may have favorable gales to make an answerable progress against a current that is still contrary and the same, and that those bound to the south may have the assistance of the ebbing stream to combat the adverse winds with more advantage.—It would carry me far beyond the bounds of a short essay, to point out every particular, indicating the future importance of this newly discovered country; and it is really astonishing, as I intimated before, that a nation endued with the divine gift of reason, if they would exercise that gift, should at this day entertain a serious thought of reducing, by force of arms, this immense continent to their absolute sway; a continent beholding two hemispheres, abounding with a hardy and active race of inhabitants, producing everything within itself proper for its own maintenance and defense; a continent extending through such a number of degrees of latitude and longitude, from the limits of the torrid zone, the circle of the northern tropic, to those frozen streams and icy mountains, where, chilled with the extreme rigors of perpetual winter, Nature seems to have lost her vegetative powers.

77. *An American Language, 1789*

Noah Webster, "Essay on the Necessity, Advantages and Practicability of Reforming the Mode of Spelling" in *Dissertations on the English Language* (Boston, 1789), 391, 393–8, 405–6.

IT HAS been observed by all writers on the English language, that the orthography or spelling of words is very irregular; the same letters often representing different sounds, and the same sounds often expressed by different letters. For this ir-

regularity, two principal causes may be assigned.

1. The changes to which the pronunciation of a language is liable, from the progress of science and civilization.

2. The mixture of different languages,

occasioned by revolutions in England, or by a predilection of the learned, for words of foreign growth and ancient origin. . . .

But such is the state of our language. The pronunciation of the words which are strictly English, has been gradually changing for ages, and since the revival of science in Europe, the language has received a vast accession of words from other languages, many of which retain an orthography very ill-suited to exhibit the true pronunciation.

The question now occurs: ought the Americans to retain these faults which produce innumerable inconveniencies in the acquisition and use of the language, or ought they at once to reform these abuses, and introduce order and regularity into the orthography of the AMERICAN TONGUE?

Let us consider this subject with some attention. . . . The principal alterations necessary to render our orthography sufficiently regular and easy, are these:

1. The omission of all superfluous or silent letters; as *a* in *bread*. Thus *bread, head, give, breast, built, meant, realm, friend*, would be spelt *bred, hed, giv, brest, bilt, ment, relm, frend*. Would this alteration produce any inconvenience, any embarrassment or expense? By no means. On the other hand, it would lessen the trouble of writing, and much more, of learning the language; it would reduce the true pronunciation to a certainty; and while it would assist foreigners and our own children in acquiring the language, it would render the pronunciation uniform, in different parts of the country, and almost prevent the possibility of changes.

2. A substitution of a character that has a certain definite sound, for one that is more vague and indeterminate. Thus by putting *ee* instead of *ea* or *ie*, the words *mean, near, speak, grieve, zeal*, would become *meen, neer, speek, greev, zeel*. This alteration would not occasion a moment's trouble; at the same time it would prevent a doubt respecting the pronunciation; whereas the *ea* and *ie* having different

sounds, may give a learner much difficulty. Thus *greef* should be substituted for *grief; kee* for *key; beleev* for *believe; laf* for *laugh; dawter* for *daughter; plow* for *plough; tuf* for *tough; proov* for *prove; blud* for *blood;* and *draft* for *draught.* In this manner *ch* in Greek derivatives should be changed into *k;* for the English *ch* has a soft sound, as in *cherish;* but *k* always has a hard sound. Therefore *character, chorus, cholic, architecture,* should be written *karacter, korus, kolic, arkitecture;* and were they thus written, no person could mistake their true pronunciation.

Thus *ch* in French derivatives should be changed into *sh; machine, chaise, chevalier,* should be written *masheen, shaze, shevaleer;* and *pique, tour, oblique,* should be written *peek, toor, obleek.*

3. A trifling alteration in a character or the addition of a point would distinguish different sounds, without the substitution of a new character. Thus a very small stroke across *th* would distinguish its two sounds. A point over a vowel, in this manner, *à,* or *ò,* or *ī,* might answer all the purposes of different letters. And for the dipthong *ow,* let the two letters be united by a small stroke, or both engraven on the same piece of metal, with the left hand line of the *w* united to the *o*.

These, with a few other inconsiderable alterations, would answer every purpose, and render the orthography sufficiently correct and regular.

The advantages to be derived from these alterations are numerous, great and permanent.

1. The simplicity of the orthography would facilitate the learning of the language. It is now the work of years for children to learn to spell; and after all, the business is rarely accomplished. A few men, who are bred to some business that requires constant exercise in writing, finally learn to spell most words without hesitation; but most people remain, all their lives, imperfect masters of spelling, and liable to make mistakes, whenever they take up a pen to write a short note.

Nay, many people, even of education and fashion, never attempt to write a letter, without frequently consulting a dictionary.

But with the proposed orthography, a child would learn to spell, without trouble, in a very short time, and the orthography being very regular, he would ever afterwards find it difficult to make a mistake. It would, in that case, be as difficult to spell *wrong* as it is now to spell *right*. . . .

2. A correct orthography would render the pronunciation of the language as uniform as the spelling in books. A general uniformity thro the United States, would be the event of such a reformation as I am here recommending. All persons, of every rank, would speak with some degree of precision and uniformity. Such a uniformity in these states is very desirable; it would remove prejudice, and conciliate mutual affection and respect.

3. Such a reform would diminish the number of letters about one sixteenth or eighteenth. This would save a page in eighteen; and a saving of an eighteenth in the expense of books, is an advantage that should not be overlooked.

4. But a capital advantage of this reform in these states would be, that it would make a difference between the English orthography and the American. This will startle those who have not attended to the subject; but I am confident that such an event is an object of vast political consequence. For,

The alteration, however small, would encourage the publication of books in our own country. It would render it, in some measure, necessary that all books should be printed in America. The English would never copy our orthography for their own use; and consequently the same impressions of books would not answer for both countries. The inhabitants of the present generation would read the English impressions; but posterity, being taught a different spelling, would prefer the American orthography.

Besides this, a national language is a band of national union. Every engine should be employed to render the people of this country national; to call their attachments home to their own country; and to inspire them with the pride of national character. However they may boast of Independence, and the freedom of their government, yet their opinions are not sufficiently independent; an astonishing respect for the arts and literature of their parent country, and a blind imitation of its manners, are still prevalent among the Americans. Thus an habitual respect for another country, deserved indeed and once laudable, turns their attention from their own interests, and prevents their respecting themselves. . . .

Sensible I am how much easier it is to propose improvements, than to introduce them. . . . But America is in a situation the most favorable for great reformations; and the present time is, in a singular degree, auspicious. The minds of men in this country have been awakened. New scenes have been, for many years, presenting new occasions for exertion; unexpected distresses have called forth the powers of invention; and the application of new expedients has demanded every possible exercise of wisdom and talents. Attention is roused; the mind expanded; and the intellectual faculties invigorated. Here men are prepared to receive improvements, which would be rejected by nations whose habits have not been shaken by similar events.

Now is the time, and this the country, in which we may expect success, in attempting changes favorable to language, science and government. Delay, in the plan here proposed, may be fatal; under a tranquil general government, the minds of men may again sink into indolence; a national acquiescence in error will follow; and posterity be doomed to struggle with difficulties, which time and accident will perpetually multiply.

Let us then seize the present moment, and establish a national language, as well as a national government. Let us remember that there is a certain respect due to the opinions of other nations. As an independent people, our reputation abroad demands that, in all things, we should be federal; be national; for if we do not respect ourselves, we may be assured that other nations will not respect us. In short, let it be impressed upon the mind of every American, that to neglect the means of commanding respect abroad, is treason against the character and dignity of a brave independent people.

78. *A National Name, 1799*

"A Letter from [William Tudor] the Treasurer of the Massachusetts Historical Society to [James Sullivan] the President, on the Propriety and Expediency of an Appropriate National Name" (December 12, 1799), Massachusetts Historical Society, *Collections* (1798), V–VI, 149–55.

A PERIOD of twenty-three years has elapsed since the people of these United States seized upon the right; and after an eventful and glorious, belligerent contest established their claim to the sovereignty of an independent nation. But they have never yet assumed an appropriate name to designate them as such, when singly, and personally applied. In this respect our country exhibits a singular exception to that of all others, who are in possession of supreme political power.

The appellation of *United States* is merely descriptive of our national confederacy, and cannot attach to the individual citizens, who are the subjects of this federal government. Therefore, if an inhabitant of New York was asked by a foreigner, to what country he belonged, his reply would be, that he was an American, and not, that he was a free denizen of the United States; because, that he might be, and yet be a Swede or a Scotchman. Besides, the term *American* is of indefinite extent, and indiscriminately includes all the native inhabitants of this immense continent, from Patagonia to Baffin's Bay; and from the Caribbean Archipelago in the Atlantic, to the shores of California, on the North Pacific Ocean. The Mustee and Creole of Cuba or Barbados; the tawny savage of the Oronque, as well as his fiercer brother of Lake Superior, are all *Americans,* as truly, as the wealthy native of Maryland, or the sober citizen of Philadelphia. At least, so are they considered on the continent of Europe.

And hence it was, that in the years 1775 and 1776, the French, for want of a national, discriminate mark, called all the inhabitants belonging to the then thirteen revolted colonies, by the general name of *Bostonians.* They could not designate them as English, Scotch or Irishmen, for we were at open, determined war with Great Britain; and with her government, had indignantly shaken off the name of Britons; and they were aware of the impropriety, if not absurdity, of calling them Americans, because that was confounding a brave, intelligent, and free people, occupying a distinct territory, with every species of inhabitants which the new world had bred. Little acquainted as they then were with this country, and finding that the most firm, systematic hostility to all the plans of the British cabinet originated in, and were strenuously and steadily pursued by the inhabitants of Boston, . . . perhaps the adoption and appropriation of that term, for a short period, was not amiss. But it ought to have taught us, that with our change of civil dominion, it had become necessary and proper to vary our national name, or rather to adopt a distinct and definite one.

To denominate ourselves Americans instead of Englishmen, was as incorrect as it would be for the individuals who now compose the French Republic, to relinquish the name of Frenchmen, and call themselves Europeans. The latter marks them as inhabitants of a principal section of the globe, but certainly involves in it nothing descriptive of the nation they compose.

To illustrate this position a little farther, permit me to detail a short conversation. I was once asked by a gentleman at Paris, what countryman I was. I answered, that I was an American. "Born in Mexico, perhaps, Sir?" No; I am not a Mexican. "You are, perhaps, from Canada?" No; for then I should have declared myself a Canadian. "But suppose you had been born in the island of St. Croix, or Trinidad, what would you have called yourself then?" In the first case a Dane, in the other a Spaniard. "And why do you call yourself now an American?" Because my countrymen, who are the citizens of the United States, have chosen to be so designated. "Well, my good friend, I had the fortune to be born on the banks of the Gambia, where my father was then settled as a factor, with his family, and yet I should scarcely thank any person, who should think proper, on that account, to represent me as an African."

Should it be alleged, that when we adopted the term AMERICANS, it was intended as an emphatic, and exclusive appropriation, specially applicable to the citizens and people of the United States; the answer is, that such a gentilitious assumption is too general; and to render it sufficiently discriminate, it would be indispensably necessary for the rest of the world to agree in naming anew, the heterogeneous millions who inhabit the two vast peninsulas of North and South America, together with all the numerous islands which are appendant to them.

In our intercourse with foreign countries, it is not barely a cause of inconvenience and confusion; but in some parts of Europe, even a stigma is affixed, to our strangely merging our specific, national character in a name designatory of all

the natives of the most extended quarter of the earth; or more properly, being destitute of any name. And does not sound policy dictate the prudence of a measure which should unite all the provincial distinctions of Vermontese and Georgians, Carolinians and New-Englandmen, Virginians and Pennsylvanians, in one general, aggregate, national title: to be adopted by the legislature of the United States, and formally declared as the name and peculiar description of all the free citizens of our national confederacy.

It has been a prevailing sentiment for ages, that great injustice was done to the intrepid talents of that immortal navigator, Columbus, in permitting an inferior adventurer to deprive him of the honor of giving name, as he had birth, to half the globe. But the Florentine explorer of the southern continent, Americus Vesputius, with all his address, might not have succeeded, had not his Christian name easily admitted a termination similar to that of two other quarters of the earth, and furnished a corresponding sound with that of the opposite continent of Africa.

With a view of rendering a partial retribution to the memory of the illustrious discoverer of the western world; in some degree to vindicate public gratitude, as well as to assign a new name to the new nation, which our revolutionary war had created, reiterated, private attempts were made to denominate the extensive country which composes the dominions of the United States, COLUMBIA; but hitherto without success. And the term *Columbians* seems confined to orators and poets, who retain it for the purpose of aiding a sonorous sentence, or rounding a musical period. So difficult is it to produce an alteration in any popular usage, which has obtained the sanction of time; unless the amendment is justified by public authority, and becomes the language of the laws.

The philosophic historian of the two Indies, puzzled for a more suitable distinction, denotes Anglo-Americans. An amphibolous compound, in the assumption of which, the Abbé Raynal has been followed by most of the foreign geographers. And it is not uncommon to find the inhabitants of the United States styled by British writers, *the ci-devant colonists;* and sometimes the *people of the revolted colonies.* Nor ought we to complain as being subjected to such a mongrel description, so long as we continue unclassed among other nations, by the public neglect of granting to the people of the United States the right of assuming a specific name.

There is a pride of country inherent to the human character. A Swiss would resent being called a Neapolitan; and so would a Creek Indian, if mistaken for a Tuscarora. A national diversity marks the physical, as well as geographical and political boundaries of different regions, in a barbarous, equally with a cultivated state of society. Hence a natural, if not strong reason, given by Negroes for their dislike of mulattoes: because, say the blacks, *Mulatto he no gotee no country.*

Aware how much easier it is to subvert than to supply, I would not wish to escape from the task of furnishing a name in some measure appropriate, if I dared to hazard the ridicule that must attach to so presumptuous an attempt by an obscure individual. Permit me then, sir, only to suggest, that the vast territory included within the limits of the United States, exhibits a scale of production on which nature has stamped her boldest features. Her lakes and mountains, forests and rivers, astonish, while they distinguish this from all other countries, and might justify a title of the proudest import. But the obstacles which present themselves against affixing an appellation, thus geographically descriptive, and at the same time applicable to the inhabitants, are various, if not insuperable; whereas the recollection that the national district of COLUMBIA will very soon contain the capital of the empire, irresistibly forces upon the mind a term which supersedes the difficulty; has

long been familiar to our ears, and would therefore, most probably, be cheerfully acquiesced in by a majority of the citizens of the United States; and its adoption be speedily, and effectually, communicated to all foreign countries through the medium of the custom-house, by an insertion in the register of every vessel, and other official fiscal certificates. Why *Columbian* is not equal, in sound and meaning, to that of *Hibernian,* or *Caledonian,* is left to the discovery of those who prefer the terms *Scotch* and *Irish* only because they contain fewer syllables, and are best understood in vulgar parlance.

The ancient and modern history, both of civilized, and barbarous nations, afford many examples of a whole people deriving a name from the metropolis of their respective countries; and a few, adopting that of their particular founders, or primary legislators; but in neither do we find any nation, the citizens of the United States excepted, who were not distinguished by a peculiar appellation, differing from that of their government.

Although there may not at present be any grounds for apprehension that our inhabitants, like those of one of the states of Greece, may be subjected to a nickname; under which history has preserved their records, and which, even at this distant period, continues proverbial; yet it is not impossible, without some public provision against it, that they may be saddled with one, founded on accident, whim, caprice, resentment or ridicule, and which may obtain a foreign currency, from a concurrence of circumstances, in despite of every effort to control it.

The youth and fair fame of our nation, the comparative paucity of our population, the innovations, and reforms, which mark the present eventful era, all conspire to facilitate the adoption of a name suited to our circumstances as an independent people; and which, there can be little doubt, that the rest of the world would acquiesce in, after the same shall have received a governmental sanction, and have been declared by the supreme authority of our country, as the name and designation, by which the free citizens of these United States, shall, forever thereafter be known and called.

79. *Binding the Republic Together, 1817*

J. C. Calhoun, "Speech on the Bill to set aside the Bank dividends and bonus as a permanent fund for the construction of roads and canals, delivered in the House of Representatives, February 4th, 1817," in *Works,* R. K. Crallé, ed. (New York, 1883), II, 189–91.

BUT THERE are higher and more powerful considerations why Congress ought to take charge of this subject. If we were only to consider the pecuniary advantages of a good system of roads and canals, it might, indeed, admit of some doubt whether they ought not to be left wholly to individual exertions; but, when we come to consider how intimately the strength and political prosperity of the republic are connected with this subject, we find the most urgent reasons why we should apply our resources to them. In many respects, no country, of equal population and wealth, possesses equal materials of power with ours. . . .

In one respect, and, in my opinion, in one only, are we materially weak. We occupy a surface prodigiously great in proportion to our numbers. The common strength is brought to bear with great difficulty on the point that may be menaced by an enemy. It is our duty, then, as far as in the nature of things it can be effected, to counteract this weakness. Good roads and canals, judiciously laid out, are the proper remedy. In the recent war, how much did we suffer for the want of them! Besides the tardiness and the consequential inefficacy of our military movements, to what an increased expense was the country put for the article of transportation alone! In the event of another war, the saving, in this particular, would go far towards indemnifying us for the expense of constructing the means of transportation. . . .

But, on this subject of national power,

what can be more important than a perfect unity in every part, in feelings and sentiments? And what can tend more powerfully to produce it than overcoming the effects of distance? No state, enjoying freedom, ever occupied anything like as great an extent of country as this republic. One hundred years ago, the most profound philosophers did not believe it to be even possible. They did not suppose it possible that a pure republic could exist on as great a scale even as the island of Great Britain. What then was considered as chimerical, we now have the felicity to enjoy; and, what is more remarkable, such is the happy mold of our government—so wisely are the state and general powers arranged—that much of our political happiness derives its origin from the extent of our republic. It has exempted us from most of the causes which distracted the small republics of antiquity.

Let it not, however, be forgotten; let it be for ever kept in mind, that it exposes us to the greatest of all calamities—next to the loss of liberty—and even to that in its consequence—disunion. We are great, and rapidly . . . growing. This is our pride and our danger; our weakness and our strength. . . . We are under the most imperious obligation to counteract every tendency to disunion. The strongest of all cements is, undoubtedly, the wisdom, justice, and above all, the moderation of this House; yet the great subject on which we are now deliberating, in this respect deserves the most serious consideration. Whatever impedes the intercourse of the extremes with this, the center of the republic, weakens the union. The more enlarged the sphere of commerical circulation—the more extended that of social intercourse—the more strongly are we bound together—the more inseparable are our destinies. Those who understand the human heart best know how powerfully distance tends to break the sympathies of our nature. Nothing—not even dissimilarity of language—tends more to estrange man from man.

Let us, then, bind the republic together with a perfect system of roads and canals. Let us conquer space. It is thus the most distant parts of the republic will be brought within a few days' travel of the center; it is thus that a citizen of the West will read the news of Boston still moist from the press. The mail and the press are the nerves of the body politic. By them, the slightest impression made on the most remote parts, is communicated to the whole system; and the more perfect the means of transportation, the more rapid and true the vibration. To aid us in this great work—to maintain the integrity of this republic, we inhabit a country presenting the most admirable advantages. Belted around, as it is, by lakes and oceans —intersected in every direction by bays and rivers, the hand of industry and art is tempted to improvement. So situated, blessed with a form of government at once combining liberty and strength, we may reasonably raise our eyes to a most splendid future, if we only act in a manner worthy of our advantages. If, however, neglecting them, we permit a low, sordid, selfish and sectional spirit to take possession of this House, this happy scene will vanish. We will divide;—and in its consequences will follow, misery and despotism.

XI ✦ *The War for Independence*

THE DIFFERENCES between the mother country and the colonies were resolved by force of arms. A mounting list of grievances led the colonists to resist what they conceived to be oppressive laws. The desire for imperial order blinded British statesmen to the necessities of the situation and tempted them to the use of force. A clash followed. The first outbreak occurred at Boston, the American center most affected by radicalism; but soon the whole nation was involved.

In the spring of 1775 the patience of the rebel leaders was exhausted; moderates found it difficult to exercise a restraining influence. Americans like Patrick Henry were already convinced that the acts of government ought to be violently resisted, no matter what the cost (No. 80). Given that temper, the insistence of the English upon the use of troops to restore order resulted in the open clash at Concord and Lexington (No. 81). The shots fired there echoed through the continent and the possibility of repairing the break became ever dimmer thereafter. By the spring of 1776 the logic of independence was inescapable; and the Declaration set into memorable words both the specific grievances and the general principles for which the revolutionaries were to fight (82).

Success, however, came only after a long, difficult struggle. In the early years of war the fighting men had ample cause to be discouraged (No. 83). Hopes remained high; but only after the battle of Saratoga in 1777 revealed the ability of the American militia (No. 84) was there a solid foundation for those hopes. A year later the conclusion of the treaty of alliance with France (No. 85) made possible the foreign aid that supplied the weapons of victory.

Meanwhile serious internal crises plagued the new government. The disaffected loyalists remained an internal danger until they were compelled to migrate or to acquiesce in the revolution (No. 86). The problems of controlling prices and production threatened the stability of the new government and even the flow of supplies to its armies (No. 87). And all the while the founders of the nation were compelled to give thought also to the future organization of its economy and its polity (*see below*, Sections XII–XIV).

It was with great relief that they greeted the final treaty of peace signed in 1783 (No. 88), a settlement on highly favorable terms and one that left both Britain and France competing for the future friendship of the United States.

80. *There Is No Peace, 1775*

Patrick Henry, *Life, Correspondence and Speeches.* W. W. Henry, ed. (New York, 1891), I, 263–6.

I ASK gentlemen, sir, what means this martial array, if its purpose be not to force us to submission? Can gentlemen assign any other possible motive for it? Has Great Britain any enemy in this quarter of the world, to call for all this accumulation of navies and armies? No, sir, she has none. They are meant for us: they can be meant for no other. They are sent over to bind and rivet upon us those chains, which the British ministry have been so long forging. . . .

Let us not, I beseech you, sir, deceive ourselves longer. Sir, we have done everything that could be done, to avert the storm which is now coming on. We have petitioned, we have remonstrated, we have supplicated, we have prostrated ourselves before the throne, and have implored its interposition to arrest the tyrannical hands of the ministry and parliament. Our petitions have been slighted; our remonstrances have produced additional violence and insult; our supplications have been disregarded; and we have been spurned, with contempt, from the foot of the throne. In vain, after these things, may we indulge the fond hope of peace and reconciliation. There is no

longer any room for hope. If we wish to be free, if we mean to preserve inviolate those inestimable privileges for which we have been so long contending, if we mean not basely to abandon the noble struggle in which we have been so long engaged, and which we have pledged ourselves never to abandon until the glorious object of our contest shall be obtained, we must fight!—I repeat it, sir, we must fight!! An appeal to arms and to the God of Hosts is all that is left us!

They tell us, sir, that we are weak—unable to cope with so formidable an adversary. . . . We shall not fight our battles alone. There is a just God who presides over the destinies of nations; and who will raise up friends to fight our battles for us. The battle, sir, is not to the strong alone; it is to the vigilant, the active, the brave. Besides, sir, we have no election. If we were base enough to desire it, it is now too late to retire from the contest. There is no retreat, but in submission and slavery! Our chains are forged. Their clanking may be heard on the plains of Boston! The war is inevitable—and let it come! I repeat it, sir, let it come!

It is in vain, sir, to extenuate the matter.

Gentlemen may cry, peace, peace—but there is no peace. The war is actually begun! The next gale that sweeps from the north will bring to our ears the clash of resounding arms! Our brethren are already in the field! Why stand we here idle? What is it that gentlemen wish?

What would they have? Is life so dear, or peace so sweet, as to be purchased at the price of chains and slavery? Forbid it, Almighty God! I know not what course others may take; but as for me, give me liberty, or give me death!

81. *A Roar of Musketry, 1775*

"A Letter from Col. Paul Revere to the Corresponding Secretary," Massachusetts Historical Society, *Collections,* V, (1798), 106–10.

IN THE fall of 1774 and winter of 1775, I was one of upwards of thirty, chiefly mechanics, who formed ourselves into a committee for the purpose of watching the movements of the British soldiers, and gaining every intelligence of the movements of the tories. We held our meetings at the Green Dragon tavern. We were so careful that our meetings should be kept secret, that every time we met, every person swore upon the Bible, that they would not discover any of our transactions, but to Messrs. Hancock, Adams, Doctors Warren, Church, and one or two more.... In the Winter, towards the Spring, we frequently took turns, two and two, to watch the soldiers, by patrolling the streets all night. The Saturday night preceding the 19th of April, about 12 o'clock at night, the boats belonging to the transports were all launched, and carried under the sterns of the men of war. (They had been previously hauled up and repaired.) We likewise found that the grenadiers and light infantry were all taken off duty.

From these movements, we expected something serious was to be transacted. On Tuesday evening, the 18th, it was observed that a number of soldiers were marching towards the bottom of the Common. About 10 o'clock, Dr. Warren sent in great haste for me, and begged that I would immediately set off for Lexington, where Messrs. Hancock and Adams were, and acquaint them of the movement, and

that it was thought they were the objects. When I got to Dr. Warren's house, I found he had sent an express by land to Lexington—a Mr. William Dawes.

The Sunday before, ... I had been to Lexington. ... I returned at night through Charlestown; there I agreed with a Colonel Conant and some other gentlemen, that if the British went out by water, we would show two lanterns in the North Church steeple; and if by land, one, as a signal; for we were apprehensive it would be difficult to cross the Charles River, or get over Boston neck. I left Dr. Warren, called upon a friend, and desired him to make the signals. I then went home, took my boots and surtout, went to the north part of the town, where I had kept a boat; two friends rowed me across Charles River. ... They landed me on the Charlestown side. When I got into town, I met Colonel Conant, and several others; they said they had seen our signals. I told them what was acting, and went to get me a horse. ... Richard Devens, Esq., who was one of the Committee of Safety, came to me and told me that he came down the road from Lexington after sundown that evening; that he met ten British officers, all well mounted, and armed, going up the road.

I set off upon a very good horse; it was then about eleven o'clock, and very pleasant. After I had passed Charlestown Neck, ... I saw two men on horseback, under a tree. When I got near them, I discovered they were British officers. One tried to get ahead of me, and the other to take me. I turned my horse very quick, and galloped towards Charlestown Neck, and then pushed for the Medford road. The one who chased me, endeavoring to cut me off, got into a clay pond. . . . I got clear of him, and went through Medford, over the bridge, and up to Menotomy. In Medford, I awaked the captain of the minute men; and after that, I alarmed almost every house, till I got to Lexington.

I found the Messrs. Hancock and Adams at the Rev. Mr. Clark's; I told them my errand. . . . After I had been there about half an hour, Mr. Dawes came; we refreshed ourselves, and set off for Concord, to secure the stores, etc. there. We were overtaken by a young Dr. Prescot, whom we found to be a high son of liberty. I told them of the ten officers that Mr. Devens met, and that it was probable we might be stopped before we got to Concord. . . . I likewise mentioned, that we had better alarm all the inhabitants till we got to Concord. The young doctor much approved of it, and said, he would stop with either of us, for the people between that and Concord knew him, and would give the more credit to what we said.

We had got nearly half way [when] Mr. Dawes and the doctor stopped to alarm the people of a house. I was about one hundred rods ahead, when I saw two men, in nearly the same situation as those officers were near Charlestown. I called for the doctor and Mr. Dawes to come up; in an instant I was surrounded by four. . . . The doctor . . . came up; and we tried to get past them. But they, being armed with pistols and swords, . . . forced us into the pasture. The doctor jumped his horse over a low stone wall, and got to Concord. I observed a wood at a small distance, and made for that. When I got there, out started six officers, on horseback, and ordered me to dismount. One of them, who appeared to have the com-

mand, examined me, where I came from, and what my name was? I told him. . . . He demanded what time I left Boston? I told him; and added, that their troops had catched aground in passing the river, and that there would be five hundred Americans there in a short time, for I had alarmed the country all the way up. He immediately rode towards those who stopped us, when all five of them came down upon a full gallop; one of them, whom I afterwards found to be a Major Mitchel, of the 5th Regiment, clapped his pistol to my head, called me by name, and told me he was going to ask me some questions, and if I did not give him true answers, he would blow my brains out. He then asked me similar questions to those above. He then ordered me to mount my horse, after searching me for arms. He then ordered them to advance, and to lead me in front. When we got to the road, they turned down towards Lexington. . . .

We rode till we got near Lexington meetinghouse, when the militia fired a volley of guns, which appeared to alarm them very much. The major inquired of me how far it was to Cambridge, and if there were any other road? After some consultation, the major rode up to the sergeant, and asked if his horse was tired? He answered him, he was—(he was a sergeant of Grenadiers, and had a small horse)—then, said he, take that man's horse. I dismounted, and the sergeant mounted my horse, when they all rode towards Lexington meetinghouse. I went across the burying-ground, and some pastures, and came to the Rev. Mr. Clark's house, where I found Messrs. Hancock and Adams. I told them of my treatment, and they concluded to go from that house towards Woburn. . . .

An elderly man came in; he said he had just come from the tavern, that a man had come from Boston, who said there were no British troops coming. Mr. Lowell and myself went towards the tavern, when we met a man on a full gallop, who told us the troops were coming up the rocks. . . . Mr. Lowell asked me to go the the tavern with him, to get a trunk of papers belonging to Mr. Hancock. We went up chamber; and while we were getting the trunk, we saw the British very near, upon a full march. We hurried towards Mr. Clark's house. In our way, we passed through the militia. There were about fifty. When we had got about one hundred yards from the meetinghouse, the British troops appeared on both sides of the meetinghouse. In their front was an officer on horseback. They made a short halt; *when I saw, and heard, a gun fired,* which appeared to be a pistol. Then I could distinguish two guns, and then a continual roar of musketry; when we made off with the trunk.

82. *Declaration of Independence, 1776*

F. N. Thorpe, ed., *Federal and State Constitutions* (Washington, 1909), I, 3–6.

WHEN in the course of human events, it becomes necessary for one people to dissolve the political bands which have connected them with another, and to assume among the powers of the earth, the separate and equal station to which the laws of Nature and of Nature's God entitle them, a decent respect to the opinions of mankind requires that they should declare the causes which impel them to the separation.

We hold these truths to be self-evident, that all men are created equal, that they are endowed by their Creator with certain unalienable rights, that among these are life, liberty and the pursuit of happiness. That to secure these rights, governments are instituted among men, deriving their just powers from the consent of the governed, That whenever any form of government becomes destructive of these ends, it is the right of the people to alter or to abolish it, and to institute new government, laying its foundation on such principles and organizing its powers in such form, as to them shall seem most likely to effect their safety and happiness. Prudence, indeed, will dictate that governments long established should not be changed for light and transient causes; and accordingly all experience hath shown, that mankind are more disposed to suffer, while evils are sufferable, than to right themselves by abolishing the forms to which they are accustomed. But when a long train of abuses and usurpations, pursuing invariably the same object evinces a design to reduce them under absolute despotism, it is their right, it is their duty, to throw off such government, and to provide new guards for their future security. —Such has been the patient sufferance of these colonies; and such is now the necessity which constrains them to alter their former systems of government. The history of the present King of Great Britain is a history of repeated injuries and usurpations, all having in direct object the establishment of an absolute tyranny over these states. To prove this, let facts be submitted to a candid world.

He has refused his assent to laws, the most wholesome and necessary for the public good.

He has forbidden his governors to pass laws of immediate and pressing importance, unless suspended in their operation till his assent should be obtained; and when so suspended, he has utterly neglected to attend to them.

He has refused to pass other laws for the accommodation of large districts of people, unless those people would relinquish the right of representation in the legislature, a right inestimable to them and formidable to tyrants only.

He has called together legislative bodies at places unusual, uncomfortable, and distant from the depository of their public records, for the sole purpose of fatiguing them into compliance with his measures.

He has dissolved representative houses repeatedly, for opposing with manly firmness his invasions on the rights of the people.

He has refused for a long time, after such dissolutions, to cause others to be elected; whereby the legislative powers, incapable of annihilation, have returned to the people at large for their exercise; the state remaining in the mean time exposed to all the dangers of invasion from without, and convulsions within.

He has endeavored to prevent the population of these states; for that purpose obstructing the laws for naturalization of foreigners; refusing to pass others to encourage their migration hither, and raising the conditions of new appropriations of lands.

He has obstructed the administration of justice, by refusing his assent to laws for establishing judiciary powers.

He has made judges dependent on his will alone, for the tenure of their offices, and the amount and payment of their salaries.

He has erected a multitude of new offices, and sent hither swarms of officers to harass our people, and eat out their substance.

He has kept among us, in times of peace, standing armies without the consent of our legislature.

He has affected to render the military independent of and superior to the civil power.

He has combined with others to subject us to a jurisdiction foreign to our constitution, and unacknowledged by our laws; giving his assent to their acts of pretended legislation:

For quartering large bodies of armed troops among us:

For protecting them, by a mock trial, from punishment for any murders which they should commit on the inhabitants of these states:

For cutting off our trade with all parts of the world:

For imposing taxes on us without our consent:

For depriving us in many cases, of the benefits of trial by jury:

For transporting us beyond seas to be tried for pretended offenses:

For abolishing the free system of English laws in a neighboring province, establishing therein an arbitrary government, and enlarging its boundaries so as to render it at once an example and fit instrument for introducing the same absolute rule into these colonies:

For taking away our charters, abolishing our most valuable laws; and altering fundamentally the forms of our governments:

For suspending our own legislatures, and declaring themselves invested with power to legislate for us in all cases whatsoever.

He has abdicated government here, by declaring us out of his protection and waging war against us.

He has plundered our seas, ravaged our coasts, burnt our towns, and destroyed the lives of our people.

He is at this time transporting large armies of foreign mercenaries to complete the works of death, desolation and tyranny, already begun with circumstances of cruelty and perfidy scarcely paralleled in the most barbarous ages, and totally unworthy the head of a civilized nation.

He has constrained our fellow citizens taken captive on the high seas to bear arms against their country, to become the executioners of their friends and brethren, or to fall themselves by their hands.

He has excited domestic insurrections amongst us, and has endeavored to bring on the inhabitants of our frontiers, the merciless Indian savages, whose known rule of warfare, is an undistinguished destruction of all ages, sexes and conditions.

In every stage of these oppressions we have petitioned for redress in the most humble terms. Our repeated petitions have been answered only by repeated injury. A prince, whose character is thus marked by every act which may define a tyrant, is unfit to be the ruler of a free people.

Nor have we been wanting in attention to our British brethren. We have warned them from time to time of attempts by their legislature to extend an unwarrantable jurisdiction over us. We have reminded them of the circumstances of our emigration and settlement here. We have appealed to their native justice and magnanimity, and we have conjured them by the ties of our common kindred to disavow these usurpations, which would inevitably interrupt our connections and correspondence. They too have been deaf to the voice of justice and of consanguinity. We must, therefore, acquiesce in the necessity, which denounces our separation, and hold them, as we hold the rest of mankind, enemies in war, in peace friends.

We, therefore, the representatives of the united states of America, in General Congress, assembled, appealing to the Supreme Judge of the world for the rectitude of our intentions, do, in the name, and by authority of the good people of these colonies, solemnly publish and declare, that these united colonies are, and of right ought to be free and independent states; that they are absolved from all allegiance to the British Crown, and that all political connection between them and the state of Great Britain, is and ought to be totally dissolved; and that as free and independent states, they have full power to levy war, conclude peace, contract alliances, establish commerce, and to do all other acts and things which independent states may of right do. And for the support of this Declaration, with a firm reliance on the protection of Divine Providence, we mutually pledge to each other our lives, our fortunes and our sacred honor.

83. *At Valley Forge, 1777*

Albigence Waldo, "Diary," *Pennsylvania Magazine of History and Biography*, XXI (1897), 306–7.

DECEMBER 14. Prisoners and deserters are continually coming in. The army, which has been surprisingly healthy hitherto, now begins to grow sickly from the continued fatigues they have suffered this campaign. Yet they still show a spirit of alacrity and contentment not to be expected from so young troops. I am sick—discontented—and out of humor. Poor food—hard lodging—cold weather—fatigue—nasty clothes—nasty cookery—vomit half my time—smoked out of my senses—the Devil's in't—I can't endure it —why are we sent here to starve and freeze—what sweet felicities have I left at home! A charming wife—pretty children—good beds—good food—good cookery—all agreeable—all harmonious. Here all confusion—smoke and cold—hunger and filthiness—a pox on my bad luck. There comes a bowl of beef soup

—full of burnt leaves and dirt, sickish enough such to make a Hector spew—away with it, boys—I'll live like the chameleon upon air.

"Poh! Poh!" cries Patience within me, "you talk like a fool. Your being sick covers your mind with a melancholic gloom, which makes everything about you appear gloomy. See the poor soldier: when in health, with what cheerfulness he meets his foes and encounters every hardship; if barefoot, he labors through the mud and cold with a song in his mouth extolling War and Washington; if his food be bad, he eats it notwithstanding with seeming content—blesses God for a good stomach and whistles it into digestion."

But harkee, Patience, a moment. There comes a soldier, his bare feet are seen through his worn-out shoes, his legs nearly naked from the tattered remains of an only pair of stockings, his breeches not sufficient to cover his nakedness, his shirt hanging in strings, his hair disheveled, his face meager; his whole appearance pictures a person forsaken and discouraged. He comes, and cries with an air of wretchedness and despair, I am sick, my feet lame, my legs are sore, my body covered with this tormenting itch—my clothes are worn out, my constitution is broken, my former activity is exhausted by fatigue, hunger, and cold, I fail fast, I shall soon be no more!

And all the reward I shall get will be: "Poor Will is dead!"

People who live at home in luxury and ease, quietly possessing their habitations, enjoying their wives and families in peace, have but a very faint idea of the unpleasing sensations and continual anxiety the man endures who is in a camp, and is the husband and parent of an agreeable family. These same people are willing we should suffer everything for their benefit and advantage, and yet are the first to condemn us for not doing more!

84. *Domestic Arrangements at Saratoga, 1777*

Baroness von Riedesel, *Letters and Journals* (Albany, 1867), 115–34.

As WE were to march farther, I had a large calash made for me, in which I, my children, and both my women servants had seats; and in this manner I followed the army, in the midst of the soldiers, who were merry, singing songs, and burning with a desire for victory. We passed through boundless forests and magnificent tracts of country, which, however, were abandoned by all the inhabitants, who fled before us and reinforced the army of the American general, Gates. In the sequel this cost us dearly, for every one of them was a soldier by nature, and could shoot very well; besides, the thought of fighting for their fatherland and their freedom inspired them with still greater courage....

On the seventh of October, my husband, with the whole General Staff, decamped. Our misfortunes may be said to date from this moment.... I observed considerable movement among the troops. My husband thereupon informed me that there was to be a reconnaissance, which, however, did not surprise me, as this often happened. On my way homeward I met many savages in their war-dress, armed with guns. To my question where they were going, they cried out to me, "War! war!" which meant that they were going to fight. This com-

pletely overwhelmed me, and I had scarcely got back to my quarters when I heard skirmishing and firing, which by degrees became constantly heavier, until finally the noises became frightful. It was a terrible cannonade, and I was more dead than alive....

On the ninth, we spent the whole day in a pouring rain, ready to march at a moment's warning. The savages had lost their courage, and they were seen in all directions going home. The slightest reverse of fortune discouraged them, especially if there was nothing to plunder. My chambermaid did nothing, cursed her situation, and tore out her hair. I entreated her to compose herself, or else she would be taken for a savage. Upon this she became still more frantic and asked "whether that would trouble me." And when I answered "Yes," she tore her bonnet off her head, letting her hair hang down over her face, and said, "You talk well! You have your husband! But we have nothing to look forward to, except dying miserably on the one hand, or losing all we possess on the other!"...

Toward evening we at last came to Saratoga.... I was wet through and through by the frequent rains, and was obliged to remain in this condition the entire night, as I had no place whatever where I could change my linen. I therefore seated myself before a good fire and undressed my children, after which we laid ourselves down together upon some straw. I asked General Phillips, who came up to where we were, why we did not continue our retreat while there was yet time, as my husband had pledged himself to cover it and bring the army through?

"Poor woman," answered he, "I am amazed at you! Completely wet through, have you still the courage to wish to go further in this weather! Would that you were only our commanding general! He halts because he is tired, and intends to spend the night here and give us a supper."

In this latter achievement especially, General Burgoyne was very fond of indulging. He spent half the nights in singing and drinking and amusing himself with the wife of a commissary, who was his mistress, and who, as well as he, loved champagne.

On the tenth, at seven o'clock in the morning, I drank some tea by way of refreshment; and we now hoped from one moment to another that at last we would again get under way. General Burgoyne, in order to cover our retreat, caused the beautiful houses and mills at Saratoga, belonging to General Schuyler, to be burned. An English officer brought some excellent broth, which he shared with me, as I was not able to refuse his urgent entreaties. Thereupon we set out upon our march, but only as far as another place not far from where we had started. The greatest misery and the utmost disorder prevailed in the army. The commissaries had forgotten to distribute provisions among the troops. There were cattle enough, but not one had been killed. More than thirty officers came to me who could endure hunger no longer. I had coffee and tea made for them, and divided among them all the provisions with which

my carriage was constantly filled; for we had a cook who, although an arrant knave, was fruitful in all expedients, and often in the night crossed small rivers in order to steal from the country people, sheep, poultry and pigs. He would then charge us a high price for them—a circumstance, however, that we only learned a long time afterward.

At last my provisions were exhausted, and in despair at not being able to be of any further help, I called to me Adjutant General Patterson, who happened at that moment to be passing by, and said to him passionately: "Come and see for yourself these officers, who have been wounded in the common cause, and who now are in want of everything, because they do not receive that which is due them. It is, therefore, your duty to make a representation of this to the General." At this he was deeply moved, and the result was that a quarter of an hour afterward, General Burgoyne came to me himself and thanked me very pathetically for having reminded him of his duty. He added, moreover, that a general was much to be pitied when he was not properly served nor his commands obeyed.... He then gave the most express orders that the provisions should be properly distributed. This only hindered us anew, besides not in the least bettering our situation. The General seated himself at table, and the horses were harnessed to our calashes ready for departure.

The whole army clamored for a retreat, and my husband promised to make it possible, provided only that no time was lost. But General Burgoyne, to whom an order had been promised if he brought about a junction with the army of General Howe, could not determine upon this course, and lost everything by his loitering.

About two o'clock in the afternoon, the firing of cannon and small arms was again heard, and all was alarm and confusion. My husband sent me a message telling me to betake myself forthwith into a house which was not far from there. I seated myself in the calash with my children, and had scarcely driven up to the house when I saw, on the opposite side of the Hudson River, five or six men with guns aimed at us. Almost involuntarily I threw the children on the bottom of the calash and myself over them. At the same instant the churls fired, and shattered the arm of a poor English soldier behind us, who was already wounded, and was also on the point of retreating into the house. Immediately after our arrival a frightful cannonade began, principally directed against the house in which we had sought shelter, probably because the enemy believed, from seeing so many people flocking around it, that all the generals made it their headquarters. Alas! It harbored none but wounded soldiers or women! We were finally obliged to take refuge in a cellar, in which I laid myself down in a corner not far from the door. . . .

One of our greatest annoyances was the stench of the wounds when they began to suppurate. One day I undertook the care of Major Plumpfield, adjutant of General Phillips, through both of whose cheeks a small musket ball had passed, shattering his teeth and grazing his tongue. He could hold nothing whatever in his mouth. . . . We had some Rhine wine. I gave him a bottle of it, in hopes that the acidity of the wine would cleanse his wound. He kept some continually in his mouth, and that alone acted so beneficially that he became cured, and I again acquired one more friend. . . .

In this horrible situation we remained six days. Finally, they spoke of capitulating, as by temporizing for so long a time our retreat had been cut off. A cessation of hostilities took place, and my husband, who was thoroughly worn out, was able, for the first time in a long while, to lie down upon a bed. . . . But about one o'clock in the night, someone came and asked to speak to him. It was with the greatest reluctance that I found myself obliged to awaken him. I observed that the message did not please him, as he immediately sent the man back to headquarters. . . . Soon after this, General Burgoyne requested the presence of all the generals and staff-officers at a council-of-war, which was to be held early the next morning, in which he proposed to break the capitulation, already made with the enemy, in consequence of some false information just received. It was, however, finally decided that this was neither practicable nor advisable; and this was fortunate for us, as the Americans said to us afterwards, that had the capitulation been broken we all would have been massacred, which they could have done the more easily as we were not over four or five thousand men strong, and had given them time to bring together more than twenty thousand. . . .

On the seventeenth of October the capitulation was consummated. The generals waited upon the American General-in-Chief, Gates, and the troops laid down their arms and surrendered themselves prisoners of war.

85. *An Appeal for French Aid, 1777*

Letter from Benjamin Franklin, Silas Deane, and Arthur Lee to Vergennes, January 5, 1777, in Francis Wharton, *Revolutionary Diplomatic Correspondence of the United States* (Washington, 1889), II, 245–6.

SIR: The Congress, the better to defend their coasts, protect their trade, and drive off the enemy, have instructed us to apply to France for eight ships of the line, completely manned, the expense of which they will undertake to pay. As other princes of Europe are lending or hiring their troops to Britain against America, it is apprehended that France may, if she thinks fit, afford our independent states the same kind of aid, without giving England any first cause of complaint. But if England should on that account declare war, we conceive that by the united force of France, Spain, and America, she will lose all her possessions in the West Indies, much the greatest part of that commerce which has rendered her so opulent, and be reduced to that state of weakness and humiliation which she has, by her perfidy, her insolence, and her cruelty, both in the east and the west, so justly merited.

We are also instructed to solicit the court of France for an immediate supply of twenty or thirty thousand muskets and bayonets, and a large quantity of ammunition and brass field pieces, to be sent under convoy. The United States engage for the payment of the arms, artillery, and ammunition, and to defray the expense of the convoy. This application has now become the more necessary, as the private purchase made by Mr. Deane of those articles is rendered ineffectual by an order forbidding their exportation.

We also beg it may be particularly considered, that while the English are masters of the American seas, and can, without fear of interruption, transport with such ease their army from one part of our extensive coast to another, and we can only meet them by land marches, we may possibly, unless some powerful aid is given us or some strong diversion be made in our favor, be so harassed and be put to such immense distress, as that finally our people will find themselves reduced to the necessity of ending the war by an accommodation.

The courts of France and Spain may rely with the fullest confidence that whatever stipulations are made by us in case of granting such aid, will be ratified and punctually fulfilled by the Congress, who are determined to found their future character, with regard to justice and fidelity, on a full and perfect performance of all their present engagements.

North America now offers to France and Spain her amity and commerce. She is also ready to guarantee in the firmest manner to those nations all ... [their] present possessions in the West Indies, as well as those they shall acquire from the enemy in a war that may be consequential of such assistance as she requests. The interests of the three nations are the same. The opportunity of cementing them and of securing all the advantages of that commerce, which in time will be immense, now presents itself. If neglected, it may never again return; and we cannot help suggesting that a considerable delay may be attended with fatal consequences.

86. *Dealing with the Tories, 1779*

"A Whig," in the *Pennsylvania Packet*, August 5, 1779, reprinted in Frank Moore, *Diary of the American Revolution* (New York, 1860), 166–8.

AMONG the many errors America has been guilty of during her contest with Great Britain, few have been greater, or attended with more fatal consequences to these states, than her lenity to the Tories. At first it might have been right, or perhaps political; but is it not surprising that, after repeated proofs of the same evils resulting therefrom, it should still be continued? We are all crying out against the depreciation of our money, and entering into measures to restore it to its value; while the Tories, who are one principal cause of the depreciation, are taken no notice of, but suffered to live quietly among us. We can no longer be silent on this subject, and see the independence of the country, after standing every shock from without, endangered by internal enemies. Rouse, America! your danger is great—great from a quarter where you least expect it. The Tories, the Tories will yet be the ruin of you! 'Tis high time they were separated from among you. They are now busy engaged in undermining your liberties. They have a thousand ways of doing it, and they make use of them all.

Who were the occasion of this war? The Tories! Who persuaded the tyrant of Britain to prosecute it in a manner before unknown to civilized nations, and shocking even to barbarians? The Tories! Who prevailed on the savages of the wilderness to join the standard of the enemy? The Tories! Who have assisted the Indians in taking the scalp from the aged matron, the blooming fair one, the helpless infant, and the dying hero? The Tories! Who advised and who assisted in burning your towns, ravaging your country, and violating the chastity of your women? The Tories! Who are the occasion that thousands of you now mourn the loss of your dearest connections? The Tories! Who have always counteracted the endeavors of Congress to secure the liberties of this country? The Tories! Who refused their money when as good as specie, though stamped with the image of his most sacred Majesty? The Tories! Who continue to refuse it? The Tories! Who do all in their power to depreciate it? The Tories! Who propagate lies among us to discourage the Whigs? The Tories! Who corrupt the minds of the good people of these States by every species of insidious counsel? The Tories! Who hold a traitorous correspondence with the enemy? The Tories! Who daily sends them intelligence? The Tories! Who take the oaths of allegiance to the states one day, and break them the next? The Tories! Who prevent your battalions from being filled? The Tories! Who dissuade men from entering the army? The Tories! Who persuade those who have enlisted to desert? The Tories! Who harbor those who do desert?

The Tories! In short, who wish to see us conquered, to see us slaves, to see us hewers of wood and drawers of water? The Tories!

And is it possible that we should suffer men, who have been guilty of all these and a thousand other calamities which this country has experienced, to live among us! To live among us, did I say? Nay, do they not move in our assemblies? Do they not insult us with their impudence? Do they not hold traitorous assemblies of their own? . . . In short, do they not enjoy every privilege of the brave soldier who has spilt his blood, or the honest patriot who has sacrificed his all in our righteous cause? Yes—to our eternal shame be it spoken—they do. Those very men who wish to entail slavery on our country, are caressed and harbored among us. . . .

'Tis time to rid ourselves of these bosom vipers. An immediate separation is necessary. I dread to think of the evils every moment is big with, while a single Tory remains among us. May we not soon expect to hear of plots, assassinations, and every species of wickedness their malice and rancor can suggest? . . . Did not that villain Matthews, when permitted to live among us at New York, plot the assassination of General Washington? He did; he was detected, and had he received his deserts, he would now have been in gibbets, instead of torturing our unfortunate friends, prisoners in New York, with every species of barbarity. Can we hear this, and still harbor a Tory among us?

For my own part, whenever I meet one in the street, or at the coffee house, my blood boils within me. Their guilt is equalled only by their impudence. They strut, and seem to bid defiance to every one. In every place, and in every company, they spread their damnable doctrines, and then laugh at the pusillanimity of those who let them go unpunished. I flatter myself, however, with the hopes of soon seeing a period to their reign, and a total end to their existence in America. Awake, Americans, to a sense of your danger. No time to be lost. Instantly banish every Tory from among you. Let America be sacred only to freemen.

Drive far from you every baneful wretch who wishes to see you fettered with the chains of tyranny. Send them where they may enjoy their beloved slavery to perfection—send them to the island of Britain; there let them drink the cup of slavery and eat the bread of bitterness all the days of their existence—there let them drag out a painful life, despised and accursed by those very men whose cause they have had the wickedness to espouse. Never let them return to this happy land—never let them taste the sweets of that independence which they strove to prevent. Banishment, perpetual banishment, should be their lot.

87. *Supplies,* 1777

"Patrick Henry to R. H. Lee, March 28, 1777," in Henry, *Life,* I, 515.

DEAR SIR: The practise of engrossing all foreign goods and country produce has gotten to an enormity here, particularly in the latter articles. Corn flour and meat are bought up . . . in so much that it is almost impossible to furnish the public demands, in such time as the necessities of the army require. A gentleman here in partnership with Mr. Morris, has speculated very largely in such articles as the army wants. The public agent complains he is anticipated. I hope the practise will be effectually stopped, or fatal consequences must ensue. I write to the General that our enlistments go on badly. Indeed, they are almost stopped. The Georgia service has hurt it much. The terrors of the smallpox, added to the lies of deserters and the want of necessaries, are fatal objections to the continental service. Perhaps two-thirds of the six new battalions are enlisted, but in broken quotas scattered far and wide, they move slowly. . . .

Your affectionate friend, P. HENRY Jr.

Can you tell us nothing from France?

88. *Treaty of Paris,* 1783

Definitive Treaty, September 3, 1783, ratified January 14, 1784. W. M. Malloy, compiler, *Treaties, Conventions, International Acts, Protocols and Agreements between the United States of America and Other Powers, 1776–1909* (Washington, 1910), I, 586–90.

IN THE name of the Most Holy and Undivided Trinity.

It having pleased the Divine Providence to dispose the hearts of the most serene and most potent Prince George the Third, by the grace of God King of Great Britain, France, and Ireland, Defender of the Faith, Duke of Brunswick and Luneburg, Arch-Treasurer and Prince Elector of the Holy Roman Empire, etc., and of the United States of America, to forget all past misunderstandings and differences that have unhappily interrupted the good correspondence and friendship which they mutually wish to restore; and to establish such a beneficial and satisfactory intercourse between the two countries, upon the ground of reciprocal advantages and mutual convenience, as may promote and secure to both perpetual peace and harmony . . . [they] have constituted and appointed . . . plenipotentiaries for the concluding and signing the present definitive treaty; who, after having reciprocally communicated their respective full powers, have agreed upon and confirmed the following articles:

ARTICLE I. His Britannic Majesty acknowledges the said United States, viz. New Hampshire, Massachusetts Bay, Rhode Island, and Providence Plantations, Connecticut, New York, New Jersey, Pennsylvania, Delaware, Maryland, Virginia, North Carolina, South Carolina, and Georgia, to be free, sovereign and independent states; that he treats with them as such, and for himself, his heirs and successors, relinquishes all claims to the government, propriety and territorial rights of the same, and every part thereof.

ARTICLE II. [Boundaries established].

ARTICLE III. It is agreed that the people of the United States shall continue to enjoy unmolested the right to take fish of every kind on the Grand Bank, and on all the other banks of Newfoundland; also in the Gulf of Saint Lawrence, and at all other places in the sea where the inhabitants of both countries used at any time heretofore to fish. And also that the inhabitants of the United States shall have liberty to take fish of every kind on such part of the coast of Newfoundland as British fishermen shall use (but not to dry or cure the same on that island) and also on the coasts, bays and creeks of all other of His Britannic Majesty's dominions in America; and that the American fishermen shall have liberty to dry and cure fish in any of the unsettled bays, harbors and creeks of Nova Scotia, Magdalen Islands, and Labrador, so long as the same shall remain unsettled; but so soon as the same or either of them shall be settled, it shall not be lawful for the said fishermen to dry or cure fish at such settlements, without a previous agreement for that purpose with the inhabitants, proprietors or possessors of the ground.

ARTICLE IV. It is agreed that creditors on either side shall meet with no lawful impediment to the recovery of the full value in sterling money, of all bona fide debts heretofore contracted.

ARTICLE V. It is agreed that the Congress shall earnestly recommend it to the legislatures of the respective states, to provide for the restitution of all estates, rights and properties which have been confiscated, belonging to real British subjects, and also of the estates, rights and properties of persons resident in districts in the possession of His Majesty's arms, and who have not borne arms against the said United States. And that persons of any other description shall have free liberty to go to any part or parts of any of the thirteen United States, and therein to remain twelve months, unmolested in their endeavors to obtain the restitution of such of their estates, rights and properties as may have been confiscated; and that Congress shall also earnestly recommend to the several states a reconsideration and revision of all acts or laws regarding the premises, so as to render the said laws or acts perfectly consistent, not only with justice and equity, but with that spirit of conciliation which, on the return of the blessings of peace, should universally prevail. And that Congress shall also earnestly recommend to the several states, that the estates, rights and properties of such last mentioned persons, shall be restored to them, they refunding to any persons who may be now in possession, the *bona fide* price (where any has been given) which such persons may have paid on purchasing any of the said lands, rights or properties, since the confiscation. And it is agreed, that all persons who have any interest in confiscated lands, either by debts, marrriage settlements or otherwise, shall meet with no lawful impediment in the prosecution of their just rights.

ARTICLE VI. That there shall be no future confiscations made, nor any prosecutions commenced against any person or persons for, or by reason of, the part which he or they may have taken in the present war; and that no person shall, on that account, suffer any future loss or damage, either in his person, liberty or property; and that those who may be in confinement on such charges, at the time of the ratification of the treaty in America, shall be immediately set at liberty, and the prosecutions so commenced be discontinued.

ARTICLE VII. There shall be a firm and perpetual peace between His Britannic Majesty and the said states, and between the subjects of the one and the citizens of the other, wherefore all hostilities, both by sea and land, shall from henceforth cease: All prisoners on both sides shall be set at liberty, and His Britannic Majesty shall, with all convenient speed, and without causing any destruction, or carrying away any Negroes or other property of the American inhabitants, withdraw all his armies, garrisons and fleets from the said United States, and from every post, place and harbor within the same; leaving in all fortifications the American artillery that may be therein: And shall also order and cause all archives, records, deeds and papers, belonging to any of the said states, or their citizens, which, in the course of the war, may have fallen into the hands of his officers, to be forthwith restored and delivered to the proper states and persons to whom they belong.

ARTICLE VIII. The navigation of the river Mississippi, from its source to the ocean, shall for ever remain free and open to the subjects of Great Britain, and the citizens of the United States.

ARTICLE IX. In case it should so happen that any place or territory belonging to Great Britain or to the United States, should have been conquered by the arms of either from the other, before the arrival of the said provisional articles in America, it is agreed, that the same shall be restored without difficulty, and without requiring any compensation.

XII ❧ *The Economy of a New Nation*

INDEPENDENCE clarified, if it did not at once solve, some of the problems that had plagued Americans through the middle decades of the eighteenth century. It now became apparent that it had not simply been political dependence that had bound the colonies in economic subjection to the mother country. Even freed, the United States was still an underdeveloped country that required connections with the more advanced productive systems of Europe. At the same time, independence had deprived it of some of the advantages of a position in the British Empire; and the disorders of the revolutionary period complicated the adjustment to the new economic order (No. 89).

But the Revolution also produced its compensating advantages. It evoked a spirit of determination and a resolution to make continuing growth the evidence of the success of the nation (*see above*, No. 76). The war had also taught the Americans the utility of co-operation and had begun the development of financial institutions immensely useful in the future. The problems of finance thus gave them their first banking experience, in the Bank of North America, created under national auspices (No. 90). So too, the revolutionaries were willing to use the government they created to support the economy. A lecture on law in the 1790's, for instance, reflected a view of the corporation as a governmental body, that would later have enormous economic significance (No. 91).

The most pressing problems were those of commerce; the American merchants suffered from losses of shipping during the war and from the loss of the English connection thereafter. Lord Sheffield, indeed, had boasted that Great Britain would be the gainer by the independence of the colonies. That argument, indignantly rejected by the Americans (No. 92), nevertheless had an element of truth; and it took ingenuity and enterprise to develop new channels of trade.

Such considerations led many to hope that the development of manufacturing would not only give employment to a large part of the population, but would also supply the merchants with the essential commodities of trade. Hamilton's report on manufactures contained an analysis of the potential strength of the nation (No. 93), as well as an ambitious scheme for furthering industrial development. The actual slowness of this development was reflected in the primitive level of manufacturing at the opening of the nineteenth century (Nos. 94, 95).

The foundation of the economy remained agricultural. The older parts of the country followed the lines of development marked out earlier. But there was an enormous increase in output as settlement spread deep into the West. The national land system that developed from the ordinance of 1785 (No. 96) provided a basis for a liberal policy that encouraged grants for settlement over those for speculation. Although the difficulties of migration were still great (No. 97) and communications were still poor, the number of settlers rose rapidly and with it total productivity.

89. *The Aftermath of the Revolution, 1785–86*

James Madison to Thomas Jefferson, August 20, 1785, and August 12, 1786; Madison, *Letters and Other Writings* (Philadelphia, 1865), I, 173–4, 242–6.

I HAD the additional pleasure ... [at Harpers Ferry] of seeing the progress of the works on the Potomac. About fifty hands were employed at these falls ..., who seemed to have overcome the greatest difficulties. Their plan is to slope the fall by opening the bed of the river, in such a manner as to render a lock unnecessary, and, by means of ropes fastened to the rocks, to pull up and ease down the boats where the current is most rapid. At the principal falls 150 hands I was told were at work, and that the length of the canal will be reduced to less than a mile, and carried through a vale which does not require it to be deep. Locks will here be unavoidable. The undertakers are very sanguine. Some of them who are most so talk of having the entire work finished in three years. ...

A negotiation is set on foot between Pennsylvania, Maryland, and Delaware, for a canal from the head of Chesapeake to the Delaware. Maryland as I understand heretofore opposed the undertaking, and Pennsylvania means now to make her consent to it a condition on which the opening of the Susquehannah within the limits of Pennsylvania will depend. Unless this is permitted the opening undertaken within the limits of Maryland will be of little account. It is lucky that both parties are so dependent on each other as to be thus mutually forced into measures of general utility. I am told that Pennsylvania has complied with the joint request of Virginia and Maryland for a road between the head of Potomac and the waters of the Ohio and the secure and free use of the latter through her jurisdiction. These fruits of the Revolution do great honor to it. I wish all our proceedings merited the same character.

Unhappily there are but too many belonging to the opposite side of the account. At the head of these is to be put the general rage for paper money. Pennsylvania and North Carolina took the lead in this folly. In the former the sum emitted was not considerable, the funds for sinking it were good, and it was not made a legal tender. It issued into circulation partly by way of loan to individuals on landed security, partly by way of payment to the public creditors. Its present depreciation is about 10 or 12 per cent. In North Carolina the sums issued at different times has been of greater amount, and it has constantly been a tender. It issued partly in payments to military creditors and latterly, in purchases of tobacco on public account. The agent I am informed was authorized to give nearly the double of the current price, and as the paper was a tender, debtors ran to him with their tobacco and the creditors paid the expense of the farce. The depreciation is said to be 25 or 30 per cent in that state.

South Carolina was the next in order. Her emission was in the way of loans to individuals, and is not a legal tender. But land is there made a tender in case of suits which shuts the Courts of Justice, and is perhaps as great an evil. . . .

In Rhode Island, £100,000 (dollar at 6s.) has lately been issued in loans to individuals. It is not only made a tender, but severe penalties annexed to the least attempt direct or indirect to give a preference to specie. Precautions dictated by distrust in the rulers soon produced it in the people. Supplies were withheld from the market, the shops were shut, popular meetings ensued, and the State remains in a sort of convulsion.

The legislature of Massachusetts at their last session rejected a paper emission by a large majority. Connecticut and New Hampshire also have as yet foreborne. . . . The Senate of Maryland has hitherto been a bar to paper in that state. The clamor for it is now universal, and as the periodical election of the Senate happens at this crisis, and the whole body is unluckily by their Constitution to be chosen at once, it is probable that a paper emission will be the result. . . .

That these [experiments] must fail is morally certain; for . . . this fictitious money will rather feed than cure the spirit of extravagance which sends away the coin to pay the unfavorable balance, and will therefore soon be carried to market to buy up coin for that purpose. From that moment depreciation is inevitable. . . .

Among the numerous ills with which this practice is pregnant, one I find is that it is producing the same warfare and retaliation among the states as were produced by the state regulations of commerce. Massachusetts and Connecticut have passed laws enabling their citizens who are debtors to citizens of states having paper money, to pay their debts in the same manner as their citizens who are creditors to citizens of the latter states are liable to be paid their debts.

The states which have appointed deputies to [the] Annapolis [Convention] are New Hampshire, Massachusetts, Rhode Island, New York, New Jersey, Pennsylvania, Delaware, and Virginia. . . . Many gentlemen, both within and without Congress, wish to make this meeting subservient to a plenipotentiary convention for amending the Confederation. Though my wishes are in favor of such an event, yet I despair so much of its accomplishment at the present crisis that I do not extend my views beyond a commercial reform. . . .

The machinations of Great Britain with regard to commerce have produced much stress and noise in the northern states, particularly in Boston. . . . The sufferers are everywhere calling for such augmentation of the power of Congress as may effect relief. How far the southern states and Virginia in particular will join in this proposition cannot be foreseen. . . . If anything should reconcile Virginia to the idea of giving Congress a power over her trade, it will be that this power is likely to annoy Great Britain against whom the animosities of our citizens are still strong. . . . Should . . . other causes prevail in frustrating the scheme of the eastern and middle states of a general retaliation on Great Britain, I tremble for the event. A majority of the states deprived of a regular remedy for their distresses by the want of a federal spirit in the minority must feel the strongest motives to some irregular experiments.

The danger of such a crisis makes me surmise that the policy of Great Britain results as much from the hope of effecting a breach in our confederacy as of monopolizing our trade.

Our internal trade is taking an arrangement from which I hope good consequences. Retail stores are spreading all over the country, many of them carried on by native adventurers, some of them branched out from the principal stores at the heads of navigation.

90. *A Bank, 1782*

Robert Morris, January 8, 1782, in Jared Sparks, ed., *The Diplomatic Correspondence of the American Revolution* (Boston, 1830), XII, 76–7.

I HAVE the honor to transmit herewith an ordinance passed by the United States in Congress assembled the 31st day of December, 1781, incorporating the subscribers of the Bank of North America, together with sundry resolutions recommending to the several states to pass such laws as they may judge necessary for giving the said ordinance its full operation. The resolutions of the 26th of May last speak so clearly to the points necessary to be established by those laws, that I need not enlarge on them. Should anything more be found necessary upon experience, the President and Directors will no doubt make suitable applications to Congress, or to the states respectively, as the case may require.

It affords me great satisfaction to inform you that this Bank commenced its operations yesterday, and I am confident that with proper management, it will answer the most sanguine expectations of those

who befriend the institution. It will facilitate the management of the finances of the United States. The several states may, when their respective necessities require, and the abilities of the bank will permit, derive occasional advantages and accommodations from it. It will afford to the individuals of all the states a medium for their intercourse with each other, and for the payment of taxes more convenient than the precious metals, and equally safe. It will have a tendency to increase both the internal and external commerce of North America, and undoubtedly will be infinitely useful to all the traders of every state in the Union, provided, as I have already said, it is conducted on principles of equity, justice, prudence, and economy. The present directors bear characters, which cannot fail to inspire confidence, and as the corporation is amenable to the laws, power can neither sanctify any improper conduct, nor protect the guilty.

91. *Smaller Societies Within the State, 1790*

James Wilson, "Lectures on Law," *Works.* Bird Wilson, ed. (Philadelphia, 1804), II, 425–8.

IN A state, smaller societies may be formed by a part of its members. . . . These smaller societies, like states, are deemed to be

moral persons, but not in a state of natural liberty; because their actions are cognizable by the superior power of the state, and are regulated by its laws. . . . To these societies, the name of corporations is generally appropriated, though somewhat improperly; for that the term is strictly applicable to supreme as well as to inferior bodies politic. In obedience, however, to the arbitress of language, I shall designate those smaller societies by the name of corporations; and to the consideration of them I now proceed.

A corporation is described to be a person in a political capacity created by the law, to endure in perpetual succession. Of these artificial persons a great variety is known to the law. They have been formed to promote and to perpetuate the interests of commerce, of learning, and of religion. It must be admitted, however, that, in too many instances, those bodies politic have, in their progress, counteracted the design of their original formation. Monopoly, superstition, and ignorance, have been the unnatural offspring of literary, religious, and commercial corporations. This is not mentioned with a view to insinuate, that such establishments ought to be prevented or destroyed: I mean only to intimate, that

they should be erected with caution, and inspected with care. . . .

When a corporation is duly established, there are many powers, rights, and capacities, which are annexed to it tacitly and of course.

It has perpetual succession, unless a period of limitation be expressed in the instrument of its establishment. This succession is, indeed, the great end of an incorporation; and, for this reason, there is, in all aggregate bodies politic, a power necessarily implied of filling vacancies by the election of new members. . . .

Another and a most important power, tacitly annexed to corporations by the very act of their establishment, is the power of making by-laws. This, indeed, is the principal reason for erecting many of the bodies corporate. Their nature or their circumstances are peculiar; and provisions peculiarly adapted to them cannot be expected from the general law of the land. For this reason, they are invested with authority to make regulations for the management of their own interests and affairs. These regulations, however, must not be contrary to the overruling laws of the state.

92. *A Favorable Prospect for American Trade,* 1794

Tench Coxe, *A View of the United States of America* (Philadelphia, 1794), 149–53.

IT WILL . . . be very easy to show, that the private shipping of the United States does not depend upon British laws. The tables, which accompany the report on the American fisheries, from the Department of State, clearly prove, that we are not dependent on Great Britain for that branch of commerce. In the regulation of our coasting trade, which employs above 100,-000 tons of shipping, and which will constantly increase with our population, manufactures, and use of coal, British laws can have no operation. In our commerce with the Baltic, and the North, with all the Netherlands, the Hanse towns, France,

Spain, Portugal, through the Straits, with most parts of Africa and India, and the colonies of the European nations, except the British, their navigation act cannot affect us. It appears moreover, that our ships are so "many," as to have amounted to 360,000 tons of vessels laden in our ports, by a return which is incomplete, while those of Great Britain and her dominions were 225,000 tons. But it is possible, that considerable deductions from the British tonnage may happen. There is little doubt, that the diminutions of our importations from their dominions . . . by reason of our intercourse with other nations, and the great improvement of our own resources and manufactures, will be followed by further commercial acquisitions from liberal nations, by the constant introduction of new foreign manufactures, and the discovery and attainment of new internal resources. If, for example, cotton be raised and imported, and spinning mills be erected, Manchester importations will decrease. . . . If by these and other means, our imports from Great Britain should be finally reduced to such a sum, as will purchase only so much rice, tobacco, and other articles, as its people consume, those articles will not be shipped indirectly to foreign countries, through British ports, as is now the case. These indirect shipments afford British vessels more than an equal chance in the competition with ours from America to England; because the property is generally on English account, and it gives them so far the command of the carriage from England to other parts of Europe. From these circumstances, it will be perceived, that it is interesting to our private shipping, and consequently to our success in the establishment of a navy, that we continue, by prudent and salutary means, to decrease our importations from each foreign country, so as in a greater degree to equalize them with the consumption, which that country actually makes of our productions. This, however, it is conceived, ought not to be attempted, by any precipitate or coercive means; but by the establishment of our mercantile credit in other countries, by commercial enterprise, capital, and manufacturing industry.

A second cause, which renders the intercourse in the shape of exportation to Great Britain inordinately great, is to be found in the old private debts due to that country from this. These, so far as they will be paid by money or goods, are considerably diminished. . . . Part of the old debts . . . must be received in the soil and buildings of this country. When these shall be accepted by the creditor, they will still remain immovable; and he will find himself, or his child, transformed into an American freeholder, to his profit and that of the United States. . . .

A third cause, which has produced an extraordinary intercourse in the shape of importations from Great Britain, has been the want of credit from other nations. We now annually import from that kingdom about $900,000, in articles not of its growth, produce, or manufacture; and though we have reduced this from about $2,200,000 since the separation of the two countries, there is yet that great value expensively, because circuitously, imported. The pursuit of this accustomed track, established in the time of the old British monopoly, has been one cause of these unnatural importations. But the chief cause was *the credit* we found from England. The British merchants will probably continue to afford the greatest accommodations of this kind; but it is evident that the citizens of other countries will furnish us with credit, and sometimes in more eligible shapes. They will give us their cash articles and their coin, to be employed in ready-money trades at home and abroad, in manufactures and foreign commerce. In proof of this may be adduced the respondentia credits in India and China, the purchases into our several bank stocks, the investment of monies in our lands, and in our navigation, trade, and manufactures.

93. *Report on Manufactures, 1791*

Alexander Hamilton, "Report Communicated to the House of Representatives, Dec. 5, 1791," *Works.* H. C. Lodge, ed. (New York, 1904), IV, 70, 87, 98–9, 107–9, 110, 111, 113–15, 117–18.

THE EXPEDIENCY of encouraging manufactures in the United States ... appears at this time to be pretty generally admitted. The embarrassments which have obstructed the progress of our external trade, have led to serious reflections on the necessity of enlarging the sphere of our domestic commerce. The restrictive regulations, which, in foreign markets, abridge the vent of the increasing surplus of our agricultural produce ... beget an earnest desire that a more extensive demand for that surplus may be created at home. ...

Manufacturing establishments not only occasion a positive augmentation of the produce and revenue of the society, but ... they [also] contribute essentially to rendering them greater than they could possibly be without such establishments. These circumstances are:

1. The division of labor.

2. An extension of the use of machinery.

3. Additional employment to classes of the community not ordinarily engaged in the business.

4. The promoting of emigration from foreign countries.

5. The furnishing greater scope for the diversity of talents and dispositions, which discriminate men from each other.

6. The affording a more ample and various field for enterprise.

7. The creating, in some instances, a new, and securing, in all, a more certain and steady demand for the surplus produce of the soil.

Each of these circumstances has a considerable influence upon the total mass of industrious effort in a community; together, they add to it a degree of energy and effect which is not easily conceived. ...

This idea of an extensive domestic market for the surplus produce of the soil, is of the first consequence. It is, of all things, that which most effectually conduces to a flourishing state of agriculture. ... Manufactories ... by their tendency to procure a more certain demand for the surplus produce of the soil, ... cause the lands ... in cultivation to be better improved and more productive. And while, by their influence, the condition of each individual farmer would be meliorated, the total mass of agricultural production would probably be increased. For this must evidently depend as much upon the degree of improvement, if not more, than upon the number of acres under culture.

It merits particular observation, that the multiplication of manufactories not only furnishes a market for those articles which have been accustomed to be produced in abundance in a country, but it likewise creates a demand for such as were either unknown or produced in inconsiderable quantities. ...

The foregoing considerations seem sufficient to establish, as general propositions, that it is the interest of nations to diversify the industrious pursuits of the individuals who compose them; that the establishment of manufactures is calculated not only to increase the general stock of useful and productive labor, but even to improve the state of agriculture in particular,—certainly to advance the interests of those who are engaged in it. ...

The objections to the pursuit of manufactures in the United States which next present themselves to discussion, represent an impracticability of success, arising from three causes: scarcity of hands, dearness of labor, want of capital.

The two first circumstances are, to a certain extent, real. . . . But . . . various considerations . . . lessen their force, and tend to afford an assurance that they are not sufficient to prevent the advantageous prosecution of many very useful and extensive manufactories.

With regard to scarcity of hands, the fact itself must be applied with no small qualification to certain parts of the United States. . . . But there are circumstances . . . that materially diminish, everywhere, the effect. . . . These circumstances are: the great use which can be made of women and children . . . ; the employment of persons ordinarily engaged in other occupations, during the seasons or hours of leisure . . . ; [and] lastly, the attraction of foreign emigrants. . . .

As to the dearness of labor (another of the obstacles alleged), this has relation principally to two circumstances: one, . . . the scarcity of hands; the other, the greatness of profits. . . . The scarcity of hands . . . is mitigated by all the considerations which have been adduced as lessening that deficiency.

So far as the dearness of labor may be a consequence of the greatness of profits in any branch of business, it is no obstacle to its success. The undertaker can afford to pay the price. There are grounds to conclude, that undertakers of manufactures in this country can, at this time, afford to pay higher wages to the workmen they may employ, than are paid to similar workmen in Europe. . . .

The supposed want of capital for the prosecution of manufactures in the United States, is the most indefinite of the objections which are usually opposed to it. . . . The following considerations are of a nature to remove all inquietude on the score of the want of capital:

The introduction of banks . . . has a powerful tendency to extend the active capital of a country. Experience of the utility of these institutions is multiplying them in the United States. It is probable that they will be established wherever they can exist with advantage; and wherever they can be supported, if administered with prudence, they will add new energies to all pecuniary operations.

The aid of foreign capital may safely, and with considerable latitude, be taken into calculation. Its instrumentality has been long experienced in our external commerce; and it has begun to be felt in various other modes. Not only our funds, but our agriculture, and other internal improvements, have been animated by it. It has already, in a few instances, extended even to our manufactures. . . .

But . . . it is satisfactory to have good grounds of assurance, that there are domestic resources, of themselves adequate to it. It happens that there is a species of capital, actually existing with the United States, which relieves from all inquietude on the score of want of capital. This is the funded debt. . . .

Public funds answer the purpose of capital, from the estimation in which they are usually held by moneyed men; and, consequently, from the ease and dispatch with which they can be turned into money. This capacity of prompt convertibility into money causes a transfer of stock to be, in a great number of cases, equivalent to a payment in coin. And where it does not happen to suit the party who is to receive, to accept a transfer of stock, the party who is to pay is never at a loss to find, elsewhere, a purchaser of his stock, who will furnish him, in lieu of it, with the coin of which he stands in need.

Hence, in a sound and settled state of the public funds, a man possessed of a sum in them, can embrace any scheme of business which offers, with as much confidence as if he were possessed of an equal sum in coin.

94. *Philadelphia Industry, 1805*

C. W. Janson, *Stranger in America* (London, 1807), 195–6.

IN PHILADELPHIA and the adjacent towns a considerable quantity of stockings are made, and other small manufactures carried on. But for want of a regular demand, the manufacturers are obliged to attend the market twice a week. Thus they lose one third of their time in endeavoring to sell what they make in the other two thirds. This is not the greatest hardship under which they labor. The contempt shown to domestic manufacture . . . obliges him to make great sacrifices. Thus this industrious part of the community too often comes to poverty and distress.

A few patriotic individuals have lately associated themselves for the purpose of assisting these unfortunate people. They propose an application to the legislature for a charter to incorporate a company for encouraging the sale of American manufactures, of woolen, cotton, and linen. The funds of the proposed company are to arise from a subscription of one hundred dollars each. . . . A warehouse is to be opened for the reception of finished and marketable goods of the above-mentioned fabrics, where the articles shall be deposited at the makers' prices. They are then to be inspected by competent judges of the commodities, who shall say how much, in their judgment, they ought to sell for. The company are then to advance one half in cash on the amount of the price fixed, and the other half when the goods are sold, subject to a very small deduction, to form a fund, from which, after subtracting the expenses of the establishment, the profits or interest on the capital will arise. . . . The owners of goods left for sale at the warehouse may at any time withdraw them, on repaying the money advanced and the expenses incurred; and all goods that may remain unsold, and which the owner will not redeem, shall be sold by auction at stated periods, and if more shall be received for them than the money advanced, and the charges, the surplus shall be paid to the owner of the goods.

95. *American Manufactures, 1813*

Niles Weekly Register, Vol. III (January 23, 1813), 328.

IT IS cause of rejoicing that many . . . millions of dollars have latterly been invested in domestic manufacturing establishments. . . . Hence a powerful home influence is spreading itself through society, and the people are becoming more abstracted from foreign considerations. In the city of Baltimore are now sold various kinds of goods to the value of at least half a million of dollars per annum, all of which species, five years ago, were received from abroad; . . . and many very valuable establishments for the chief sale of domestic goods have sprung up in different parts of the city; while every day brings to market some new commodity.

It is true that the manufactures of the United States are not yet adequate to the consumption of the country; but hundreds of thousands are clothed entirely with home-made apparel; while many of our most important branches of mechanical industry are completely supplied with all their tools and apparatus from other workshops among us. Our bountiful country pours forth its resources; and genius applies its productions to the wants and conveniences of life. Our progress in improvement has no parallel; nor is the increase of our population more surprising than the proceeds of our manufactures, rising in all their varied form in every direction, and pursued with an eye to profit in almost every farm house in the United States. The merino breed of sheep is spreading with astonishing rapidity. . . . The manufacture of all the coarser kinds of cotton goods, with some of the most delicate fabrics, may be considered as fully established. The western states will supply us with an abundance of hemp and hempen manufactures. The chief part of the heavy metallic articles are now made amongst us, while many of the lighter kinds are extensively and profitably furnished. The woolen manufacture keeps pace with the rest. . . . Ancient prejudices have yielded to the impulses of patriotism or the dictates of prudence, and it has become fashionable to use home manufactures. . . . Six years ago our whole export of flour, beef, pork and provisions, generally, did no more than pay for the foreign liquors we consumed: the case is materially altered—the long despised whiskey, rectified and improved, has driven from the side-board English rum and French brandy, or suffers them to remain as mere monuments of former favor. Our most dashing bucks are proud to boast a homespun coat; and the prudent housewife, delighted, exhibits her newly made table linen, sheeting, carpets, etc. This is that pride that destroys a foreign influence—it is an honest pride, and should be encouraged, and so indeed it is—for no man is ashamed for his apparel, though it be coarse, if it is clean and decent, and HOME-SPUN.

Seeing the importance of domestic manufactures in lessening our connection with the old world, corrupted and corrupting, the patriot heart leaps with joy at the speedy prospect of "reversing the tables" upon it, in making it the necessity of foreign nations to depend on us for those raw materials and articles of food which it was our object to exchange for their productions. . . . Then will our country stand on high ground; and wealth flow gradually in from all quarters, without subjecting us to foreign partialities or the gamblings of commerce. . . .

This time is not far distant. . . . The righteous war for our seamen and our rights, grossly violated, is one of the grand means by which a good Providence will bring about a blessed union of the people, in directing them to look AT HOME for all they desire. Let the real American be of good cheer—we shall triumph by land as well as by sea; but more than all in establishing a HOME INFLUENCE that will guard and defend happy Columbia amidst the "throes and convulsions of the old world," when "infuriated man, through blood and slaughter, shall seek his liberty," with horrors unprecedented.

96. Land Ordinance, 1785

J. C. Fitzpatrick, ed., *Journals of the Continental Congress* (Washington, 1933), XXVIII, 375–81.

BE IT ordained by the United States in Congress assembled, that the territory ceded by individual states to the United States, which has been purchased of the Indian inhabitants, shall be disposed of in the following manner:

A surveyor from each state shall be appointed by Congress, or a committee of the States. . . . The geographer, under whose direction the surveyors shall act, shall occasionally form such regulations for their conduct, as he shall deem necessary. . . .

The surveyors, as they are respectively

qualified, shall proceed to divide the said territory into townships of six miles square, by lines running due north and south, and others crossing these at right angles, as near as may be . . . ; and each surveyor shall be allowed and paid at the rate of two dollars for every mile, in length, he shall run, including the wages of chain carriers, markers, and every other expense attending the same.

The first line, running north and south as aforesaid, shall begin on the river Ohio, at a point that shall be found to be due north from the western termination of a line, which has been run as the southern boundary of the state of Pennsylvania; and the first line, running east and west, shall begin at the same point, and shall extend throughout the whole territory. . . . The geographer shall designate the townships, or fractional parts of townships, by numbers progressively from south to north; always beginning each range with number one; and the ranges shall be distinguished by their progressive numbers to the westward. The first range, extending from the Ohio to the lake Erie, being marked number one. The geographer shall personally attend to the running of the first east and west line; and shall take the latitude of the extremes of the first north and south line, and of the mouths of the principal rivers.

The lines shall be measured with a chain; shall be plainly marked by chaps on the trees, and exactly described on a plat; whereon shall be noted by the surveyor, at their proper distances, all mines, salt springs, salt licks and mill seats, that shall come to his knowledge, and all water courses, mountains and other remarkable and permanent things, over and near which such lines shall pass, and also the quality of the lands.

The plats of the townships respectively, shall be marked by subdivisions into lots of one mile square, or 640 acres, in the same direction as the external lines, and numbered from 1 to 36; always beginning the succeeding range of the lots with the number next to that with which the preceding one concluded. . . .

As soon as seven ranges of townships, and fractional parts of townships, in the direction from south to north, shall have been surveyed, the geographer shall transmit plats thereof to the board of treasury, who shall record the same, with the report, in well-bound books to be kept for that purpose. And the geographer shall make similar returns, from time to time, of every seven ranges as they may be surveyed. The Secretary at War shall have recourse thereto, and shall take by lot therefrom, a number of townships . . . as will be equal to one-seventh part of the whole of such seven ranges, as nearly as may be, for the use of the late continental army; and he shall make a similar draught, from time to time, until a sufficient quantity is drawn to satisfy the same, to be applied in manner hereinafter directed. The board of treasury shall, from time to time, cause the remaining numbers . . . to be drawn for, in the name of the thirteen states respectively, according to the quotas in the last preceding requisition on all the states. . . .

The board of treasury shall transmit a copy of the original plats, previously noting thereon, the townships, and fractional parts of townships, which shall have fallen to the several states, by the distribution aforesaid, to the commissioners of the loan office of the several states, who, after giving notice of not less than two nor more than six months, by causing advertisements to be posted up at the court houses, or other noted places in every county, and to be inserted in one newspaper, published in the states of their residence respectively, shall proceed to sell the townships . . . at public vendue, in the following manner, viz: The township . . . No. 1, in the first range, shall be sold entire; and No. 2, in the same range, by lots; and thus in alternate order through the whole of the first range. The township . . . No. 1, in the second range, shall be sold by lots; and No. 2, in the same range, entire; and so in alternate order through the whole of the second range; and the third range shall be sold in the same manner as the first, and the fourth in the same manner as the second, and thus alternately throughout all the ranges; provided, that none of the lands ... be sold under the price of one dollar the acre ... besides the expense of the survey and other charges thereon, which are hereby rated at thirty-six dollars the township ... to be paid at the time of sales; on failure of which payment, the said lands shall again be offered for sale.

There shall be reserved for the United States out of every township, the four lots, being numbered 8, 11, 26, 29. ... There shall be reserved the lot No. 16, of every township, for the maintenance of public schools, within the said township; also one-third part of all gold, silver, lead and copper mines, to be sold, or otherwise disposed of as Congress shall hereafter direct.

When any township ... shall have been sold as aforesaid, and the money or certificates received therefor, the loan officer shall deliver a deed ... which deeds shall be recorded in proper books, by the commissioner of the loan office, and shall be certified to have been recorded, previous to their being delivered to the purchaser, and shall be good and valid to convey the lands in the same described.

The commissioners of the loan offices respectively, shall transmit to the board of treasury every three months, an account of the townships, fractional parts of townships, and lots committed to their charge; specifying therein the names of the persons to whom sold, and the sums of money or certificates received for the same; and shall cause all certificates by them received, to be struck through with a circular punch; and they shall be duly charged in the books of the treasury, with the amount of the moneys or certificates, distinguishing the same, by them received as aforesaid.

If any township, or fractional part of a township or lot, remains unsold for eighteen months after the plat shall have been received, by the commissioners of the loan office, the same shall be returned to the board of treasury, and shall be sold in such manner as Congress may hereafter direct.

And whereas Congress ... stipulated grants of land to certain officers and soldiers of the late continental army, ... be it ordained, that the Secretary at War ... determine who are the objects of the above resolutions and engagements, and the quantity of land to which such persons or their representatives are respectively entitled, and cause the townships, or fractional parts of townships, hereinbefore reserved for the use of the late continental army, to be drawn for in such manner as he shall deem expedient, to answer the purpose of an impartial distribution. ...

The board of treasury, and the commissioners of the loan offices in the states, shall, within eighteen months, return receipts to the Secretary at War, for all deeds which have been delivered, as also all the original deeds which remain in their hands for want of applicants, having been first recorded; which deeds so returned, shall be preserved in the office, until the parties or their representatives require the same.

And be it further ordained, that three townships adjacent to lake Erie be reserved ... for the use of the officers, men, and others, refugees from Canada, and the refugees from Nova Scotia, who are or may be entitled to grants of land under resolutions of Congress. ...

And be it further ordained, that the towns of Gnadenhutten, Schoenbrun and Salem, on the Muskingum, and so much of the lands adjoining to the said towns, with the buildings and improvements thereon, shall be reserved for the sole use of the Christian Indians, who were formerly settled there, or the remains of that society, as may, in the judgment of the geographer, be sufficient for them to cultivate.

Saving and reserving always, to all officers and soldiers entitled to lands on the northwest side of the Ohio, by donation or bounty from the Commonwealth of Virginia ... all rights to which they are so entitled. ... And to the end, that the said rights may be fully and effectually

secured ... be it ordained, that no part of the land included between the rivers called Little Miami and Sciota, on the northwest side of the river Ohio, be sold, or in any manner alienated, until there shall first have been laid off and appropriated for the said officers and soldiers ... the lands they are entitled to.

97. *The Journey Westward*, 1792

Gilbert Imlay, A *Topographical Description of the Western Territory* (London, 1792), 142–8.

TRAVELERS or emigrants take different methods of transporting their baggage, goods, or furniture, from the places they may be at to the Ohio, according to circumstances, or their object in coming to the country. For instance, if a man is traveling only for curiosity, or has no family or goods to remove, his best way would be to purchase horses, and take his route through the wilderness. But provided he has a family or goods of any sort to remove, his best way, then, would be to purchase a wagon and team of horses to carry his property to Redstone Old Fort, or to Pittsburgh, according as he may come from the northern or southern states.

A good wagon will cost at Philadelphia about £ 10 ... and the horses about £ 12 each. ... The wagon may be covered with canvas, and, if it is the choice of the people, they may sleep in it at nights with the greatest safety. But if they should dislike that, there are inns of accommodation the whole distance on the different roads. To allow the horses a plenty of hay and corn would cost about 1s. *per diem,* each horse; supposing you purchase your forage in the most economical manner, i.e. of the farmers, as you pass along, from time to time as you may want it, and carry it in your wagon; and not of innkeepers, who must have their profits. The provisions for the family I would purchase in the same manner; and by having two

or three camp kettles, and stopping every evening when the weather is fine upon the brink of some rivulet, and by kindling a fire they may soon dress their food. ...

The distance which one of those wagons may travel one day with another is little short of twenty miles. So that it will be a journey from Alexandria to Redstone Old Fort of eleven or twelve days, from Baltimore a day or two longer, and from Philadelphia to Pittsburgh I should suppose it would require nearly twenty days; as the roads are not so good as from the two former places.

From these prices the expense of removing a family, from either of the seaports I have mentioned to the Ohio, may be computed with tolerable exactitude.

The best time for setting out for this country from any of the Atlantic ports, is the latter end of either September or April. The autumn is perhaps the most eligible of the two; as it is most likely that the roads across the mountain will be drier, and provisions and forage are then both more plentiful and cheap than in the spring.

If this mode should not suit the convenience of the party, by reason of their not wanting a wagon or horses when they arrive in this country, they may have their goods brought out to Redstone Old Fort from Alexandria for 15s. per cwt. and in like proportion from Baltimore and Philadelphia.

At Redstone Old Fort, or Pittsburgh, they can either buy a boat, which will cost them about 5s. per ton, or freight their goods to Kentucky for about 1s. per cwt. There is no regular business of this sort; but as there are always boats coming down the river, 1s. per cwt. is the common charge for freight. But more frequently when there is boat room to spare, it is given to such as are not able to purchase a boat, or have not a knowledge of the navigation. However, that is a business which requires no skill, and there are always numbers of people coming down, who will readily conduct a boat for the sake of a passage.

The distance from Philadelphia by land to Kentucky is between seven and eight hundred miles; from Baltimore nearly seven hundred; nearly six hundred from Alexandria; and upwards of five hundred from Richmond. The roads and accommodations are tolerably good to the borders of the wilderness; through which it is hardly possible for a carriage to pass, great part of the way being over high and steep hills, upon the banks of the rivers and along defiles, which in some places seem to threaten you at every step with danger. This is the only route the people coming from the upper parts of Virginia and North Carolina can take at present to get into the country; the gap of Cumberland Mountain being the only place it can be passed without the greatest difficulty. The opening the Tennessee will afford a convenient communication with the Mississippi. The wilderness, which was formerly two hundred miles through, without a single habitation, is reduced from the settlement of Powel's Valley, to nearly one half of that distance; and it is to be expected that in a few years more that the remainder of the distance will afford settlements for the accommodation of people traveling that route; when a good road may be made quite to Kentucky. The canals ... which are cutting on the Potomac, and the removal of the obstructions in Cheat River, will render the passage from Alexandria, or the federal city to the Ohio, both cheap and easy.

XIII Order in Society

Almost from the start American life had disturbed the traditional European order of society which the colonists had brought with them to America. The Revolution therefore produced a social as well as a political crisis. Independence cut Americans off from the familiar sources of authority; and the emigration of the Tories deprived the new society of a substantial part of its old leadership.

New political leaders had appeared. But it was difficult to know in what light to regard them, for all social relationships were unclear. The problems erupted in a debate, at the very first organization of the new federal government, over the question of which titles should be used to designate the new officials. Senator William Maclay, a forthright democrat contemptuous of all titles, described his argument with Vice President John Adams (No. 98), touching upon implications very wide in significance.

Many men, then, hoped that development of a stable agricultural life would restore the social order. In that context a natural aristocracy could safely begin to assert itself, so Thomas Jefferson, for one, imagined (No. 99; *see also below,* No. 111). Descriptions of the rural countryside, by those who grew up there (No. 100) and by those who traveled through it (No. 101), revealed areas in which such hopes seemed capable of realization (No. 102).

The nation was not simply rural; cities played an important part in its life. The old city of Boston enjoyed relative stability and order (No. 103). But the raw capital on the Potomac was still backward in all the graces of living (No. 104). Whether old or new, all the cities were exposed to the onslaught of disasters such as that which struck Philadelphia and New York in the 1790's (No. 105).

Furthermore, in the background loomed two immensely complicated problems American democracy did not yet wish to confront. Two groups were not regarded as integrally a part of the nation. The Indians, unassimilated, remained apart and seemed to some actually to have deteriorated as a result of contact with the whites (No. 106); and although slavery had begun to disappear in the North and was declining in the South, this had not clarified the status of the Negro (No. 107). These were somber problems for the future.

98. *On Titles and Ceremonies, 1789*

William Maclay, *Journal.* First published 1890. These extracts are given as edited by Charles A. Beard (New York, 1927), 6–11, 22–3, 24–5, 26–7.

30TH APRIL, Thursday.—This is a great, important day. Goddess of etiquette, assist me while I describe it. . . . The Senate met. The Vice President rose in the most solemn manner. . . . He often, in the midst of his important airs—I believe when he is at loss for expressions . . . suffers an unmeaning kind of vacant laugh to escape him. This was the case today, and really to me bore the air of ridiculing the farce he was acting. "Gentlemen, I wish for the direction of the Senate. The President will, I suppose, address the Congress. How shall I behave? How shall we receive it? Shall it be standing or sitting?"

Here followed a considerable deal of talk. . . . Mr. Lee began with the House of Commons (as is usual with him), then the House of Lords, then the King, and then back again. The result of his information was, that the Lords sat and the Commons stood on the delivery of the King's speech. Mr. Izard got up and told how often he had been in the Houses of Parliament. He said a great deal of what he had seen there. [He] made, however, this sagacious discovery, that the Commons stood because they had no seats to sit on, being arrived at the bar of the House of Lords. It was discovered after some time that the King sat, too, and had his robes and crown on.

Mr. Adams got up again and said he had been very often indeed at the Parliament on those occasions, but there always was such a crowd, and ladies along, that for his part he could not say how it was. Mr. Carrol got up to declare that he thought it of no consequence how it was in Great Britain; they were no rule to us, etc. But all at once the Secretary, who had been out, whispered to the Chair that the Clerk from the Representatives was at the door with a communication. Gentlemen of the Senate, how shall he be received? A silly kind of resolution of the committee on that business had been laid on the table some days ago. The amount

of it was that each House should communicate to the other what and how they
chose; it concluded, however, something
in this way: That everything should be
done with all the propriety that was
proper. . . . Mr. Lee . . . reprobated the
rule; declared that the Clerk should not
come within the bar of the House; that
the proper mode was for the Sergeant-
at-Arms, with the mace on his shoulder,
to meet the Clerk at the door and receive his communication; we are not, however, provided for this ceremonious way
of doing business, having neither mace nor
sergeant nor Masters in Chancery, who
carry down bills from the English
Lords. . . .

May 1st.—Attended at the Hall at
eleven. The prayers were over and the
minutes reading. When we came to the
minute of the [President's] speech it stood,
His most gracious speech. I looked all
around the Senate. Every countenance
seemed to wear a blank. The Secretary
was going on. I must speak or nobody
would. "Mr. President, we have lately had
a hard struggle for our liberty against
kingly authority. The minds of men are
still heated: everything related to that
species of government is odious to the
people. The words prefixed to the President's speech are the same that are usually
placed before the speech of his Britannic
Majesty. I know they will give offense.
I consider them as improper. I therefore
move that they be struck out, and that
it stand simply address or speech, as may
be judged most suitable." . . . The question
was put and carried for erasing the words
without a division. . . .

May 8th. . . . Senate formed. The Secretary, as usual, had made some mistakes,
which were rectified, and now Mr. Els-
worth moved for the report of the Joint
Committee to be taken up on the subject
of titles. It was accordingly done. Mr. Lee
led the business. He took his old ground
—all the world, civilized and savage,
called for titles; that there must be something in human nature that occasioned this

general consent; that, therefore, he conceived it was right. . . .

At last I got up and first answered Lee
as well as I could with nearly the same
arguments, drawn from the Constitution,
as I had used on the 23rd ult. I mentioned that within the space of twenty
years back more light had been thrown
on the subject of governments and on
human affairs in general than for several
generations before; that this light of
knowledge had diminished the veneration
for titles, and that mankind now considered themselves as little bound to imitate the follies of civilized nations as the
brutalities of savages; that . . . the impression now on the minds of the citizens of
these states was that of horror for kingly
authority. . . .

But I will minute no more. The debate
lasted till half after three o'clock, and it
ended in appointing a committee to consider of a title to be given to the President. This whole silly business is the work
of Mr. Adams and Mr. Lee. . . . I had,
to be sure, the greatest share in this debate, and must now have completely sold
. . . every particle of court favor, for a
court our House seems determined on,
and to run into all the fooleries, fopperies,
fineries, and pomp of royal etiquette; and
all this for Mr. Adams.

May 9th. . . . Senate formed. It took a
long time to correct the minutes. Otis keeps
them miserably. At length the committee
came in and reported a title—*His Highness
the President of the United States of
America and Protector of the Rights of the
Same.* . . .

Up now got the Vice President, and for
forty minutes did he harangue us from
the chair. . . .

"Gentlemen, I must tell you that it is
you and the President that have the making of titles. Suppose the President to have
the appointment of Mr. Jefferson at the
court of France. Mr. Jefferson is, in virtue
of that appointment, the most illustrious,
the most powerful, and what not. But the
President must be himself something that

includes all the dignities of the diplomatic corps and something greater still. What will the common people of foreign countries, what will the sailors and the soldiers say, 'George Washington, President of the United States'? They will despise him *to all eternity....*"

He said fifty more things, equally injudicious, which I do not think worth minuting. It is evident that he begins to despair of getting the article of titles through the House of Representatives, and has turned his eye to get it done solely by the Senate....

His new leaf appeared so absurd I could not help some animadversions on it. I rose. Mr. President, the Constitution of the United States has designated our Chief Magistrate by the appellation of the *President of the United States of America.* This is his title of office, nor can we alter, add to, or diminish it without infringing the Constitution....

Can, then, the President and Senate do that which is prohibited to the United States at large? Certainly not. Let us read the Constitution: *No title of nobility shall be granted by the United States.* The Constitution goes further. The servants of the public are prohibited from accepting them from any foreign state, king, or prince.

So that the appellations and terms given to nobility in the Old World are contraband language in the United States, nor can we apply them to our citizens consistent with the Constitution. As to what the common people, soldiers, and sailors of foreign countries may think of us, I do not think it imports us much. Perhaps the less they think, or have occasion to think of us, the better.

99. *Agrarian Society,* 1787

Thomas Jefferson, *Notes on Virginia* (Philadelphia, 1801), 323–6.

THE POLITICAL economists of Europe have established it as a principle that every state should endeavor to manufacture for itself; and this principle, like many others, we transfer to America, without calculating the difference of circumstance which should often produce a difference of result. In Europe the lands are either cultivated, or locked up against the cultivator. Manufacture must therefore be resorted to of necessity, not of choice, to support the surplus of their people. But we have an immensity of land courting the industry of the husbandman. Is it best then that all our citizens should be employed in its improvement, or that one half should be called off from that to exercise manufactures and handicraft arts for the other?

Those who labor in the earth are the chosen people of God, if ever he had a chosen people, whose breasts he has made his peculiar deposit for substantial and genuine virtue. It is the focus in which he keeps alive that sacred fire, which otherwise might escape from the face of the earth. Corruption of morals in the mass of cultivators is a phenomenon of which no age nor nation has furnished an example. It is the mark set on those who, not looking up to heaven, to their own soil and industry, as does the husbandman, for their subsistence, depend for it on the casualties and caprice of customers. Dependence begets subservience and venality, suffocates the germ of virtue, and prepares fit tools for the designs of ambition. This, the natural progress and consequence of the arts, has sometimes perhaps been retarded by accidental circumstances; but, generally speaking, the proportion which the aggregate of the other classes of citizens bears in any state to that of its husbandmen is the proportion of its unsound to its healthy parts, and is a good enough barometer whereby to measure its degree of corruption.

While we have land to labor then, let us never wish to see our citizens occupied at a workbench, or twirling a distaff. Carpenters, masons, smiths, are wanting in husbandry; but for the general operations of manufacture, let our workshops remain in Europe. It is better to carry provisions and materials to workmen there than bring them to the provisions and materials, and with them their manners and principles. The loss by the transportation of commodities across the Atlantic will be made up in happiness and permanence of government. The mobs of great cities add just so much to the support of pure government, as sores do to the strength of the human body. It is the manners and spirit of a people which preserve a republic in vigor.

100. *New England Country Life, 1800*

S. G. Goodrich, *Recollections of a Lifetime* (New York, 1856), I, 59–61, 77–81, 83–4.

THE TOWN was originally settled by a sturdy race of men, mostly the immediate descendants of English emigrants, some from Norwalk and some from Milford. Their migration over an intervening space of savage hills, rocks, and ravines, into a territory so forbidding, and their speedy conversion of this into a thriving and smiling village, are witnesses to their courage and energy. . . .

Nearly all the inhabitants of Ridgefield were farmers, with the few mechanics that were necessary to carry on society in a somewhat primeval state. Even the persons not professionally devoted to agriculture, had each his farm, or at least his garden and home lot, with his pigs, poultry, and cattle. The population might have been 1200, comprising two hundred families. All could read and write, but in point of fact, beyond the Almanac and Watts' Psalms and Hymns, their literary acquirements had little scope. There were, I think, four newspapers, all weekly, published in the state: one at Hartford, one at New London, one at New Haven, and one at Litchfield. There were, however, not more than three subscribers to all these in our village. We had, however, a public library of some two hundred volumes, and what was of equal consequence—the town was on the road which was then the great thoroughfare, connecting Boston with New York, and hence it had means of intelligence from travelers constantly passing through the place, which kept it up with the march of events. . . .

Our neighbor . . . had been a tailor, but having thriven in his affairs, and now advanced to the age of some fifty years, had become a farmer—such a career, by the way, being common at the time; for the prudent mechanic, adding to his house and his lands, as his necessities and his thrift dictated, usually ended as the proprietor of an ample house, fifty to a hundred acres of land, and an ample barn, stocked with half a dozen cows, one or two horses, a flock of sheep, and a general assortment of poultry.

The home of this . . . neighbor . . . was situated on the road leading to Salem, there being a wide space in front occupied by the wood-pile, which in these days was not only a matter of great importance, but of formidable bulk. The size of the wood-pile was indeed in some sort an index to the rank and condition of the proprietor. The house itself was a low edifice, forty feet long, and of two stories in front; the rear being what was called a *breakback*, that is, sloping down to a height of ten feet; this low part furnishing a shelter for garden tools, and various household instruments. The whole was constructed of wood; the outside being of the dun complexion assumed by unpainted wood, exposed to the weather for twenty or thirty years, save only that the roof was tinged of a reddish-brown by a fine moss that found sustenance in the chestnut shingles.

To the left was the garden, which in the productive season was a wilderness of onions, squashes, cucumbers, beets, parsnips, and currants, with the never-failing tansey for bitters, horseradish for seasoning, and fennel for keeping old women awake in church time. . . .

The interior of the house presented a parlor with plain, whitewashed walls, a home-made carpet upon the floor, calico curtains at the window, and a mirror three feet by two against the side, with a mahogany frame. To these must be added eight chairs and a cherry table, of the manufacture of Deacon Hawley. The keeping or sitting room had also a carpet, a dozen rushbottom chairs, a table, etc. The kitchen was large—fully twenty feet square, with a fireplace six feet wide and four feet deep. On one side, it looked out upon the garden, the squashes and cucumbers climbing up and forming festoons over the door; on the other a view was presented of the orchard, embracing first a circle of peaches, pears, and plums, and beyond, a widespread clover field, embowered with apple-trees. Just by, was the well, with its tall sweep, the old oaken bucket dangling from the pole. The kitchen was in fact the most comfortable room in the house; cool in summer, and perfumed with the breath of the garden and the orchard; in winter, with its roaring blaze of hickory, it was a cosy resort, defying the bitterest blasts of the season. Here the whole family assembled at meals, save only when the presence of company made it proper to serve tea in the parlor. . . .

The cellar, extending under the whole house, was a vast receptacle, and by no means the least important part of the establishment. In the autumn, it was supplied with three barrels of beef and as many of pork, twenty barrels of cider, with numerous bins of potatoes, turnips, beets, carrots, and cabbages. The garret, which was of huge dimensions, at the same time displayed a labyrinth of dried pumpkins, peaches, and apples—hung in festoons upon the rafters, amid bunches of summer savory, boneset, fennel, and other herbs—the floor being occupied by heaps of wool, flax, tow, and the like.

The barn corresponded to the house. It was a low brown structure, having abundance of sheds built on to it, without the least regard to symmetry. I need not say it was well stocked with hay, oats, rye, and buckwheat. Six cows, one or two horses, three dozen sheep, and an ample supply of poultry, including two or three broods of turkeys, constituted its living tenants. . . .

In most families, the first exercise of the morning was reading the Bible, followed by a prayer, at which all were assembled, including the servants and helpers of the kitchen and the farm. Then came the breakfast, which was a substantial meal, always including hot viands, with vegetables, applesauce, pickles, mustard, horseradish, and various other condiments. Cider was the common drink for laboring people; even children drank it at will. Tea was common, . . . coffee was almost unknown. Dinner was a still more hearty and varied repast—characterized by abundance of garden vegetables; tea was a light supper.

The day began early: breakfast was had at six in summer and seven in winter; dinner at noon—the work people in the fields being called to their meals by a conchshell. . . . Tea—the evening meal, usually took place about sundown. In families where all were laborers, all sat at table, servants as well as masters—the food being served before sitting down. In families where the masters and mistresses did not share the labors of the household or the farm, the meals of the domestics were had separate. There was, however, in those days a perfectly good understanding and good feeling between the masters and servants.... Our servants, during all my early life, were of the neighborhood, generally the daughters of respectable farmers and mechanics, and respecting others, were themselves respected and cherished.

101. *Virginia Society, 1788*

J. P. Brissot de Warville, *Nouveau voyage dans les États-Unis d'Amérique* (Paris, 1791). Taken from the text in Oscar Handlin, *This Was America* (Cambridge, 1949), 68–87. Reprinted by permission of the publisher. Copyright by the President and Fellows of Harvard College.

GENERAL [WASHINGTON] came home in the evening fatigued from a journey to lay out a new road in some part of his plantations. He has often been compared to Cincinnatus; the comparison is doubtless just. This celebrated general is nothing more at present than a good farmer, constantly occupied in the care of his estate and the improvement of cultivation....

Everything has an air of simplicity in his house. His table is good, but not ostentatious; and no deviation is seen from regularity and domestic economy. Mrs. Washington superintends the whole, and adds to the qualities of an excellent housewife that simple dignity which ought to characterize a woman whose husband has acted the greatest part on the theater of human affairs. She also possesses that amenity, and manifests that attention to strangers, which render hospitality so charming....

The practice of racing, borrowed from the English by the Virginians, is falling into disuse. The places well known for this business are all abandoned, and it is not a misfortune; they are centers of gambling, drunkenness, and quarrels.

The General informed me that he could perceive a great reformation in his countrymen in this respect, that they are less given to intoxication. It is no longer fashionable for a man to force his guests to drink and to make it an honor to send them home drunk. You no longer hear the taverns resounding with the noisy parties once so common. The sessions of the courts of justice are no longer the theaters of gambling, inebriation, and bloodshed.

102. *Republican Manners, 1806*

Janson, *Stranger in America*, 85–8.

ARRIVED at your inn, let me suppose, like myself, you had fallen in with a landlord, who at the moment would condescend to take the trouble to procure you refreshment after the family hour.... He will sit by your side, and enter in the most familiar manner into conversation; which is prefaced, of course, with a demand of your business, and so forth. He will then start a political question (for here every individual is a politician), force your answer, contradict, deny, and, finally, be ripe for a quarrel, should you not acquiesce in all his opinions.

When the homely meal is served up, he will often place himself opposite to you at the table, at the same time declaring, that "though he thought he had eaten a hearty dinner, yet he will pick a bit with you." Thus will he sit, drinking out of your glass, and of the liquor you are to pay for, belching in your face, and committing other excesses still more indelicate and disgusting. Perfectly inattentive to your accommodation, and regardless of your appetite, he will dart his fork into the best of the dish, and leave you to take the next cut. If you arrive at the dinner-hour, you are seated with "mine hostess" and her dirty children, with whom you have often to scramble for a plate, and even the servants of the inn; for liberty and equality level all ranks upon the road, from the host to the hostler. The children, imitative of their free and polite papa, will also seize your drink, slobber in it, and often snatch a dainty bit from your plate. This is esteemed wit, and consequently provokes a laugh, at the expense of those who are paying for the board. . . .

The arrogance of domestics in this land of republican liberty and equality, is particularly calculated to excite the astonishment of strangers. To call persons of this description *servants,* or to speak of their *master* or *mistress,* is a grievous affront. Having called one day at the house of a gentleman of my acquaintance, on knocking at the door, it was opened by a servant-maid, whom I had never before seen, as she had not been long in his family. The following is the dialogue, word for word, which took place on this occasion:—"Is your master at home?"—"I have no master."—"Don't you live here?"—"I *stay* here."—"And who are you then?"—"Why, I am Mr. ———'s *help.* I'd have you to know, *man,* that I am no *sarvant;* none but *negers* are *sarvants.*"

103. *The Bostonians, 1788*

Brissot, *Nouveau voyage, loc. cit,* No. 101.

THE BOSTONIAN mothers are reserved; their air is however frank, good and communicative. Entirely devoted to their families, they are occupied in rendering their husbands happy, and in training their children. The law which imposes heavy penalties, such as the pillory and imprisonment for adultery has scarcely ever been called into execution, because families are happy; and they are pure, because they are happy.

Neatness without luxury is a characteristic feature of this purity of manners; and this neatness is seen everywhere in Boston, in dress, in houses, and churches. Nothing is more charming than a church on Sunday. The good cloth coat covers the men, while calicoes and chintzes serve the women and children, unspoiled by those gewgaws which whim and caprice have added among our women. Powder and pomade never sully the heads of infants and children. I see them with

pain, however, on the heads of men who invoke the art of the hairdresser; for, unhappily, this art has already crossed the seas. . . .

There are many clubs in Boston. I went several times to a private club that convened once a week, and was much pleased with their politeness to strangers and the knowledge displayed in their conversation. There is no true cafe in Boston, New York, or Philadelphia. One house in each town, that they call a coffee house, serves as a merchants' exchange. . . .

The Bostonians . . . think of the useful before the beautiful. They have no brilliant monuments, but they have neat and commodious churches, they have good houses, they have superb bridges, and excellent ships. Their streets are well illuminated at night, while many ancient cities of Europe containing proud monuments of art have never yet thought of preventing the fatal effects of nocturnal darkness.

104. *The National Capital, 1806*

Janson, *Stranger in America,* 202–6.

THE ... AVENUES, as they are pompously called, which lead to the American seat of government, are the worst roads I passed in the country. ... In the winter season, during the sitting of Congress, every turn of your wagon wheel ... is for many miles attended with danger. The roads are never repaired; deep ruts, rocks, and stumps of trees, every minute impede your progress, and often threaten your limbs with dislocation.

Arrived at the city, you are struck with its grotesque appearance. In one view from the capitol hill, the eye fixes upon a row of uniform houses, ten or twelve in number, while it faintly discovers the adjacent tenements to be miserable wooden structures, consisting, when you approach them, of two or three rooms one above another. ... The hotel, ... like every other private adventure, failed: the walls and the roof remain, but not a window! and, instead of accommodating the members of Congress, and travelers of distinction, as proposed, a number of the lowest order of Irish have long held the title of *naked possession.* ... Turning the eye, a well-finished edifice presents itself, surrounded by lofty trees, which never felt the stroke of the axe. The President's house, the offices of state, and a little theater, where an itinerant company repeated, during a part of the last year, the lines of Shakespeare, Otway, and Dryden, to empty benches, terminate the view of the Pennsylvania, or Grand Avenue.

Speculation, the life of the American, embraced the design of the new city. Several companies of speculators purchased lots, and began to build handsome streets, with an ardor that soon promised a large and populous city. Before they arrived at the attic story, the failure was manifest; and in that state at this moment

are the walls of many scores of houses begun on a plan of elegance. In some parts, purchasers have cleared the wood from their grounds, and erected temporary wooden buildings. Others have fenced in their lots, and attempted to cultivate them; but the sterility of the land ... is such, that this plan has also failed. The country adjoining consists of woods in a state of nature, and in some places of mere swamps, which give the scene a curious patchwork appearance. ... The city ... never can become a place of commerce, while Baltimore lies on one side, and Alexandria on the other. ... Nor can the wild and uneven spot laid out into streets be cleared and leveled for building upon, for many years, even with the most indefatigable exertions.

The Capitol, of which two wings are now finished, is of hewn stone, and will be a superb edifice, worthy of its name. ...

The President's house, of which a correct view is given in the frontispiece to this volume, is situated one mile from the Capitol, at the extremity of Pennsylvania Avenue. The contemplated streets of this embryo city are called avenues, and every state gives name to one. That of Pennsylvania is the largest; in fact I never heard of more than that and the New Jersey Avenue. Except some houses uniformly built, in one of which lives Mr. Jefferson's printer, John Harrison Smith, a few more of inferior note, with some public-houses, and here and there a little grog-shop, this boasted avenue is as much a wilderness as Kentucky, with this disadvantage, that the soil is good for nothing. Some half-starved cattle browsing among the bushes, present a melancholy spectacle to a stranger, whose expectation has been wound up by the illusive description of speculative writers. So very thinly is the city peopled, and so little is it frequented, that quails and other birds are constantly shot within a hundred yards of the Capitol, and even during the sitting of the houses of Congress. . . .

Neither park, nor mall, neither churches, theaters, nor colleges, could I discover so lately as the summer of 1806. A small place has indeed been erected . . . in the Pennsylvania Avenue, called a theater, in which Mr. Green and the Virginia company of comedians were nearly starved the only season it was occupied, and were obliged to go off to Richmond during the very height of the sitting of Congress. . . .

The President's house is certainly a neat but plain piece of architecture, built of hewn stone, said to be of a better quality than Portland stone, as it will cut like marble, and resist the change of the seasons in a superior degree. Only part of it is furnished; the whole salary of the President would be inadequate to the expense of completing it in a style of suitable elegance. Rooms are fitted up for himself, an audience chamber, and apartments for Mr. Thomas Man Randolph, and Mr. Epps, and their respective families, who married two of his daughters, and are members of the House of Representatives.

The ground around it, instead of being laid out in a suitable style, remains in its ancient rude state, so that, in a dark night, instead of finding your way to the house, you may, perchance, fall into a pit, or stumble over a heap of rubbish.

105. *Yellow Fever in Philadelphia, 1793*

Samuel Breck, *Recollections.* H. E. Scudder, ed. (Philadelphia, 1877), 193–6.

IN JULY, 1793, the yellow fever broke out, and, spreading rapidly in August, obliged all the citizens who could remove to seek safety in the country. . . . I was compelled to return to the city on the 8th of September, and spend the 9th there. My business took me down to the Swedes' church and up Front Street to Walnut Street wharf, where I had my counting-house. Everything looked gloomy, and forty-five deaths were reported for the 9th. In the afternoon, when I was about returning to the country, I passed by the lodgings of the Vicomte de Noailles, who had fled from the revolutionists of France. He was standing at the door, and calling to me, asked me what I was doing in town. "Fly," said he, "as soon as you can, for pestilence is all around us." And yet it was nothing then to what it became three or four weeks later, when from the first to the twelfth of October one thousand persons died. On the twelfth a smart frost came and checked its ravages.

The horrors of this memorable affliction were extensive and heart-rending. Nor were they softened by professional skill. The disorder was in a great measure a stranger to our climate, and was awkwardly treated. Its rapid march, being from ten victims a day in August to one hundred a day in October, terrified the physicians, and led them into contradictory modes of treatment. They, as well as the guardians of the city, were taken by surprise. No hospitals or hospital stores were in readiness to alleviate the sufferings of the poor. For a long time nothing could be done other than to furnish coffins for the dead and men to bury them. At length a large house in the neighborhood was appropriately fitted up for the reception of patients, and a few pre-eminent philanthropists volunteered to superintend it. . . .

In private families the parents, the children, the domestics lingered and died, frequently without assistance. The wealthy soon fled; the fearless or indifferent remained from choice, the poor from necessity. The inhabitants were reduced thus to one-half their number, yet the malignant action of the disease increased, so that those who were in health one day were buried the next. The burning fever occasioned paroxysms of rage which drove the patient naked from his bed to the street, and in some instances to the river, where he was drowned. Insanity was often the last stage of its horrors.

In November, when I returned to the city and found it repeopled, the common topic of conversation could be no other than this unhappy occurrence; the public journals were engrossed by it, and related many examples of calamitous suffering. One of these took place on the property adjacent to my father's. The respectable owner . . . ventured to brave the disorder, and fortunately escaped its attack. . . . In the height of the sickness, when death was sweeping away its hundreds a week, a man applied to him for leave to sleep one night on the stable floor. The gentleman, like every one else, inspired with fear and caution, hesitated. The stranger pressed his request, assuring him that he had avoided the infected parts of the city, that his health was very good, and promised to go away at sunrise the next day. Under these circumstances he admitted him into his stable for that night. At peep of day the gentleman went to see if the man was gone. On opening the door he found him lying on the floor delirious

and in a burning fever. Fearful of alarming his family, he kept it a secret from them, and went to the committee of health to ask to have the man removed.

The committee was in session day and night at the City Hall in Chestnut Street . . . . The attendants on the dead stood on the pavement in considerable numbers soliciting jobs, and until employed they were occupied in feeding their horses out of the coffins which they had provided in anticipation of the daily wants. These speculators were useful, and, albeit with little show of feeling, contributed greatly to lessen, by competition, the charges of interment. The gentleman . . . reached the room in which the committee was assembled, and . . . obtained the services of a quack doctor, none other being in attendance. They went together to the stable, where the doctor examined the man, and then told the gentleman that at ten o'clock he would send the cart with a suitable coffin, into which he requested to have the dying stranger placed. The poor man was then alive and begging for a drink of water. His fit of delirium had subsided, his reason had returned, yet the experience of the *soi-disant* doctor enabled him to foretell that his death would take place in a few hours. It did so, and in time for his corpse to be conveyed away by the cart at the hour appointed. This sudden exit was of common occurrence. The whole number of deaths in 1793 by yellow fever was more than four thousand. Again it took place in 1797, '98 and '99, when the loss was six thousand, making a total in these four years of ten thousand.

106. *Indian Adjustment, 1795*

"Observations on the Indians . . . in a letter from General Lincoln, October 29, 1795," Massachusetts Historical Society, *Collections*, V (1798; reprinted 1835), 10–12.

FOR people . . . to quit the ideas they imbibed in youth, and to forsake the long-trodden path made conspicuous by the

footsteps of their fathers . . . requires a degree of fortitude and a spirit of enterprise, which doth not fall to the share of every man. . . . If this is true of us, with all the light which has been scattered in our paths, and with the peculiar advantages we are under of judging for ourselves what is right, we must not be surprised at the obstinacy of those who have had infinitely less advantages, and whose prejudices, in favor of ancient customs, are proportionately strong to their want of light, and of the means of judging rightly. . . .

I have always discovered, when among the Indian nations, that there existed the greatest difficulty in conveying any new ideas to their mind from the barrenness of their language, and in many instances it has been impossible to convey to them the sentiments attempted. This inconvenience may always remain; for a copious language is not to be acquired in a savage life. Their distance, by their habits, from the enlightened world, gives them few opportunities of extending their ideas; consequently their language will not expand; and without ideas, they cannot have language. On the whole, I am fully in opinion . . . that the Indian nations will never be civilized. . . .

Should the Indian nations in general never become civilized, we may, I think, point to the consequences. Nature forbids civilized and uncivilized people possessing the same territory; for the means pursued by the civilized, to obtain a support, counteracts the wishes and designs of the savage. While the former are busily employed in removing from the earth its natural growth, as necessary to their establishing themselves as husbandmen, the latter are wishing to increase that natural shelter, and hiding place, for the beasts of the forest; for without a covering they cannot be retained, but will seek new feeding grounds. Consequently the savage must retire to those lands where they can with more ease obtain a supply. Their new position cannot, however, long avail them; for civilization and cultivation will make rapid strides, and progress fast towards them; and they must necessarily make way for such approaches, by following the game, (which takes the first alarm), or leave their present pursuits and modes of living, and oppose the cultivator by cultivation. The savage arm is too feeble, in any other way, to counteract the progress of their civilized neighbors. But it is hardly to be expected, that they will, in time, see the importance of this measure, considering their prejudices and attachments; but will continue retiring before the enlightened husbandman, until they shall meet those regions of the north, into which he cannot pursue them. There, in my opinion, they will be set down, and left, in the undisturbed possession of a country, unenvied by any; as the last resort of a people, who, having sacrificed every consideration to their love of ease, were now compelled, by the effects of their obstinacy and disobedience, to give up all hope of ever regaining those hospitable tracts from which they had retired, and which they had surrendered to others. . . . Being now in the possession of a country fitted, by nature, to the life of a sportsman, they will probably continue as a people until time shall be no more.

107. *Forebodings on Slavery, 1803*

St. George Tucker, *Blackstone's Commentaries* (Philadelphia, 1803), I, Pt. 2, Appendix, Note H, 31–2, 58, 63–4, 68–70, 73–5.

WHILST America hath been the land of promise to Europeans and their descendants, it hath been the vale of death to millions of the wretched sons of Africa. The genial light of liberty, which hath here shone with unrivaled luster on the former, hath yielded no comfort to the latter, but to them hath proved a pillar of darkness. . . . Whilst we were offering up vows at the shrine of liberty . . . we were imposing upon our fellow men, who differ in complexion from us, a slavery, ten thousand times more cruel than the utmost extremity of those grievances and oppressions, of which we complained. . . .

Not only the right of property, and the right of personal liberty, but even the right of personal security, has been, at times either wholly annihilated, or reduced to a shadow. . . . Many actions, indifferent in themselves, being permitted by the law of nature to all mankind, and by the laws of society to all free persons, are either rendered highly criminal in a slave, or subject him to some kind of punishment or restraint. . . .

Frequently the laws of nature have been set aside in favor of institutions, the pure result of prejudice, unsurpation, and tyranny. We have found actions, innocent or indifferent, punishable with a rigor scarcely due to any, but the most atrocious, offenses against civil society; justice distributed by an unequal measure to the master and the slave; and even the hand of mercy arrested, where mercy might have been extended to the wretched culprit, had his complexion been the same with that of his judges. . . .

It is . . . I trust, unjust to censure the present generation for the existence of slavery in Virginia; for I think it unquestionably true, that a very large proportion of our fellow-citizens lament that as a misfortune, which is imputed to them as a reproach. . . . Considerations of policy, as well as justice and humanity, must evince the necessity of eradicating the evil, before it becomes impossible to do it without tearing up the roots of civil society with it. . . .

The extirpation of slavery from the United States, is a task equally arduous and momentous. To restore the blessings of liberty to near a million of oppressed individuals, who have groaned under the yoke of bondage, and to their descendants, is an object, which those who trust in Providence, will be convinced would not be unaided by the Divine Author of our being, should we invoke his blessing upon our endeavors. Yet human prudence forbids that we should precipitately engage in a work of such hazard as a general and simultaneous emancipation. The mind of a man must in some measure be formed for his future condition. The early impressions of obedience and submission, which slaves have received among us, and the no less habitual arrogance and assumption of superiority, among the whites, contribute, equally, to unfit the former for freedom, and the latter for equality. To expel them all at once from the United States, would . . . be to devote them only to a lingering death by famine, by disease, and other accumulated miseries. . . . To establish such a colony in the territory of the United States, would probably lay the foundation of intestine wars, which would terminate only in their extirpation, or final expulsion. To attempt it in any other quarter of the globe would be attended with the utmost cruelty to the colonists, themselves, and the destruction of their whole race. . . .

"But why not retain and incorporate the blacks into the state?" This question has been well answered by Mr. Jefferson, and who is there so free from prejudices among us, as candidly to declare that he has none against such a measure? The recent scenes transacted in the French colonies in the West Indies are enough to make one shudder with the apprehension of realizing similar calamities in this country. Such probably would be the event of an attempt to smother those prejudices which have been cherished for a period of almost two centuries.

XIV *The State Polities*

THE REVOLUTION was not negative only. Although touched off by concrete grievances, it embodied also the determination to create a nation. Those who fought for independence were destroying an old government and also bringing a new one into existence.

The people of the colonies had no sooner severed their connections with the Crown than they set themselves the task of devising the polities appropriate to a free society. Since government depended upon the consent of the governed, it was widely recognized that the first step was to frame constitutions which would state the social compact between the rulers and the ruled. The necessity for such a step was forcefully set forth in the memorandum of the town of Pittsfield in Massachusetts (No. 108). It was also widely recognized that the constitutions ought explicitly to proclaim the rights the people reserved to themselves; the Virginia Bill of Rights (No. 109) eloquently did so and became the model for similar statements in other states.

The constitutions drew upon colonial experience, upon English and French political theories, and, most of all, upon the logic of the revolutionary ideas with which the colonists had resisted imperial oppression. The constitution of Massachusetts (No. 110) was typical and in the future often imitated.

It early became clear that new states would soon join the original ones. The nation had no desire to keep any of its possessions as colonies. Rather, they were to be treated as territories, endowed with limited powers of government in preparation for the eventual date at which they would become partners equal in rights with the original states. The Northwest Ordinance (No. 111) set forth the terms of government for the existing territories.

After the first decade of experimentation, state government was gratifyingly stable. Political contests were largely within the framework of the existing constitutions. Later changes included some extensions of the principles in the Bill of Rights, as in the Virginia Act establishing religious freedom (No. 112).

The more important contests were over the control rather than the form of state governments. The central issue was the role of an aristocracy. All Americans recognized that a European ruling class had no place in a democratic republic. But some insisted that natural aristocracy would inevitably emerge and should either be controlled or be used in the interests of the whole society (No. 113). On the other hand, there were fears that the American group that aspired to rule would be based upon finance rather than on land or birth, and that such an aristocracy would be far more difficult to limit (No. 114).

108. *Pittsfield Memorial, 1776*

J. E. A. Smith, *History of Pittsfield* (Boston, 1869), 351–4.

TO THE HONORABLE COUNCIL AND THE HON-
ORABLE HOUSE OF REPRESENTATIVES OF
THE COLONY OF MASSACHUSETTS BAY IN
GENERAL ASSEMBLY MET AT WATERTOWN,
MAY 29, 1776

THE PETITION and memorial of the town of Pittsfield in said colony humbly showeth,—

That they have the highest sense of the importance of civil and religious liberty, the destructive nature of tyranny and lawless power, and the absolute necessity of legal government to prevent anarchy and confusion.

That they, with their brethren in the other towns in this county, were early and vigorous in opposing the destructive measures of British administration against these colonies; that they early signed the non-importation league and covenant, raised minute-men, agreed to pay them, ordered their public moneys to be paid to Henry Gardner, Esq., receiver-general, cast in their mite for the relief of Boston, and conformed in all things to the doings of the honorable Continental and Provincial Congresses. . . .

We further beg leave to represent that we are deeply affected at the misrepresentations that have been made of us and the county in the General Court as men deeply in debt, dishonest, ungovernable, heady, intractable, without principle and good conduct, and ever ready to oppose lawful authority, as mobbers, disturbers of peace, order, and union, unwilling to submit to any government, or even to pay our debts; so that, we have been told, a former House of Representatives had it actually in contemplation to send an armed force, to effect that by violence which reason only ought to effect at the present day. We beg leave, therefore, to lay before your Honors our principles, real views, and designs in what we have hitherto done, and what object we are reaching after; with this assurance, that, if we have erred, it is through ignorance, and not bad intention.

We beg leave, therefore, to represent that we have always been persuaded that the people are the fountain of power; that, since the dissolution of the power of Great Britain over these colonies, they have fallen into a state of nature.

That the first step to be taken by a people in such a state for the enjoyment or restoration of civil government among them is the formation of a fundamental constitution as the basis and ground-work of legislation; that the approbation, by the majority of the people, of this fundamental constitution is absolutely necessary to give life and being to it; that then, and not till then, is the foundation laid for legislation. . . .

A representative body may form, but cannot impose said fundamental constitution upon a people, as they, being but servants of the people, cannot be greater than their masters, and must be responsible to them; that, if this fundamental constitution is above the whole legislature, the legislature certainly cannot make it; it must be the approbation of the majority which gives life and being to it; that said fundamental constitution has not been formed for this Province; the corner-stone is not yet laid, and whatever building is reared without a foundation must fall to ruins. . . .

These are some of the truths we firmly believe, and are countenanced in believing them by the most respectable political writers of the last and present century, especially by Mr. Burgh in his political disquisitions, for the publication of which one-half of the Continental Congress were subscribers.

We beg leave further to represent, that we by no means object to the most speedy institution of legal government through this Province, and that we are as earnestly desirous as any others of this great blessing.

That, knowing the strong bias of human nature to tyranny and despotism, we have nothing else in view but to provide for posterity against the wanton exercise of power, which cannot otherwise be done than by the formation of a fundamental constitution.

What is the fundamental constitution of this Province? What are the inalienable rights of the people? the power of the rulers? how often to be elected by the people, etc.? Have any of these things been as yet ascertained? Let it not be said by future posterity, that, in this great, this noble, this glorious contest, we made no provision against tyranny among ourselves. . . .

We beg leave further to represent these as the sentiments of by far the majority of the people of this county, as far as we can judge; and being so agreeable to rea-

son, scripture, and common sense, as soon as the attention of the people of this Province is awakened we doubt not the majority will be with us.

We beg leave further to observe, that, if this honorable body shall find that we have embraced errors dangerous to the safety of these colonies, it is our petition that our errors may be detected, and you shall be put to no further trouble from us. But, without an alteration in our judgment, the terrors of this world will not daunt us. We are determined to resist Great Britain to the last extremity, and all others who may claim a similar power over us. Yet we hold not to an *imperium imperio;* we will be determined by the majority.

Your petitioners, therefore, beg leave to request that this honorable body would form a fundamental constitution for this Province, after leave is asked and obtained from the honorable Continental Congress, and that said constitution be sent abroad for the approbation of the majority of the people of this colony; that, in this way, we may emerge from a state of nature, and enjoy again the blessings of civil government.

109. *Virginia Bill of Rights, 1776*

Poore, *Federal and State Constitutions,* Part II, 1908–9.

SECTION 1. That all men are by nature equally free and independent, and have certain inherent rights, of which, when they enter into a state of society, they cannot, by any compact, deprive or divest their posterity; namely, the enjoyment of life and liberty, with the means of acquiring and possessing property, and pursuing and obtaining happiness and safety.

SEC. 2. That all power is vested in, and consequently derived from, the people; that magistrates are their trustees and servants, and at all times amenable to them.

SEC. 3. That government is, or ought to be, instituted for the common benefit,

protection, and security of the people, nation, or community; of all the various modes and forms of government, that is best which is capable of producing the greatest degree of happiness and safety, and is most effectually secured against the danger of maladministration; and that, when any government shall be found inadequate or contrary to these purposes, a majority of the community hath an indubitable, inalienable, and indefeasible right to reform, alter, or abolish it, in such manner as shall be judged most conducive to the public weal.

SEC. 4. That no man, or set of men,

are entitled to exclusive or separate emoluments or privileges from the community, but in consideration of public services; which, not being descendible, neither ought the offices of magistrate, legislator, or judge to be hereditary.

SEC. 5. That the legislative and executive powers of the State should be separate and distinct from the judiciary; and that the members of the two first may be restrained from oppression, by feeling and participating the burdens of the people, they should, at fixed periods, be reduced to a private station ... and the vacancies be supplied by frequent, certain, and regular elections. ...

SEC. 6. That elections of members to serve as representatives of the people, in assembly, ought to be free; and that all men, having sufficient evidence of permanent common interest with, and attachment to, the community, have the right of suffrage. ...

SEC. 7. That all power of suspending laws, or the execution of laws, by any authority, without consent of the representatives of the people, is injurious to their rights, and ought not to be exercised.

SEC. 8. That in all capital or criminal prosecutions a man hath a right to demand the cause and nature of his accusation, to be confronted with the accusers and witnesses, to call for evidence in his favor, and to a speedy trial by an impartial jury ... ; nor can he be compelled to give evidence against himself; that no man be deprived of his liberty, except by the law of the land or the judgment of his peers.

SEC. 9. That excessive bail ought not to be required, nor excessive fines imposed, nor cruel and unusual punishments inflicted.

SEC. 10. That general warrants, whereby an officer or messenger may be commanded to search suspected places without evidence of a fact committed, or to seize any person or persons not named, or whose offense is not particularly described and supported by evidence, are grievous and oppressive, and ought not to be granted.

SEC. 11. That in controversies respecting property, and in suits between man and man, the ancient trial by jury is preferable to any other. ...

SEC. 12. That the freedom of the press is one of the great bulwarks of liberty, and can never be restrained but by despotic governments.

SEC. 13. That a well-regulated militia ... is the proper ... defense of a free state; that standing armies, in time of peace, should be avoided, as dangerous to liberty; and that in all cases the military should be under strict subordination to, and governed by, the civil power. ...

SEC. 16. That religion, or the duty which we owe to our Creator, and the manner of discharging it, can be directed only by reason and conviction, not by force or violence; and therefore all men are equally entitled to the free exercise of religion, according to the dictates of conscience; and that it is the mutual duty of all to practice Christian forbearance, love, and charity towards each other.

110. *Constitution of Massachusetts, 1780*

F. N. Thorpe, ed., *Federal and State Constitutions* (Washington, 1909), III, 1888–94, 1899–1900, 1905.

Preamble

THE END of the institution, maintenance, and administration of government is to secure the existence of the body politic, to protect it, and to furnish the individuals who compose it with the power of enjoying, in safety and tranquillity, their natural rights and the blessings of life; and whenever these great objects are not obtained the people have a right to alter the government, and to take measures necessary for their safety, prosperity, and happiness.

The body politic is formed by a voluntary association of individuals; it is a social compact by which the whole people covenants with each citizen, and each citizen with the whole people, that all shall be governed by certain laws for the common good. . . .

We, therefore, the people of Massachusetts, acknowledging, with grateful hearts, the goodness of the great Legislator of the universe, in affording us, in the course of His providence, an opportunity, deliberately and peaceably, without fraud, violence, or surprise, of entering into an original, explicit and solemn compact with each other, and of forming a new constitution of civil government for ourselves and posterity; . . . do agree upon, ordain, and establish the following declaration of rights and frame of government as the constitution of the Commonwealth of Massachusetts.

Part the First

A DECLARATION OF THE RIGHTS OF THE INHABITANTS OF THE COMMONWEALTH OF MASSACHUSETTS

ARTICLE I. All men are born free and equal, and have certain natural, essential, and unalienable rights; among which may be reckoned the right of enjoying and defending their lives and liberties; that of acquiring, possessing, and protecting property; in fine, that of seeking and obtaining their safety and happiness.

ART. II. It is the right as well as the duty of all men in society, publicly and at stated seasons, to worship the Supreme Being. . . . And no subject shall be hurt, molested, or restrained . . . for worshipping God in the manner . . . most agreeable to the dictates of his own conscience, . . . provided he doth not disturb the public peace or obstruct others in their religious worship.

ART. III. As the happiness of a people and the . . . preservation of civil government . . . depend upon piety, religion, and morality, . . . the people . . . have a right to invest their legislature with power to authorize and require . . . the several towns, parishes, precincts, and other bodies politic or religious societies to make suitable provision, at their own expense, for the institution of the public worship of God and for the support and maintenance of public Protestant teachers of piety, religion, and morality in all cases where such provision shall not be made voluntarily.

And the people . . . have also a right to, and do, invest their legislature with authority to enjoin upon all the subjects an attendance upon the instructions of the public teachers aforesaid, at stated times and seasons. . . .

And all moneys paid by the subject to the support of public worship and of the public teachers aforesaid shall, if he require it, be uniformly applied to the support of the public teacher or teachers of his own religious sect or denomination, provided there be any on whose instructions he attends. . . .

And every denomination of Christians, demeaning themselves peaceably and as good subjects of the commonwealth, shall be equally under the protection of the law; and no subordination of any one sect or denomination to another shall ever be established by law.

ART. IV. The people of this commonwealth have the sole and exclusive right of governing themselves as a free, sovereign, and independent state; and do, and forever hereafter shall, exercise and enjoy every power, jurisdiction, and right which is not, or may not hereafter be, by them expressly delegated to the United States of America in Congress assembled.

ART. V. All power residing originally

in the people, and being derived from them, the several magistrates and officers of government . . . are at all times accountable to them.

ART. VI. No man nor corporation or association of men have any other title to obtain advantages, or particular and exclusive privileges distinct from those of the community, than what arises from the consideration of services rendered to the public; and this title being in nature neither hereditary nor transmissible . . . ; the idea of a man born a magistrate, lawgiver, or judge is absurd and unnatural.

ART. VII. Government is instituted for the common good . . . and not for the profit, honor, or private interest of any one man, family, or class of men. . . .

ART. VIII. In order to prevent those who are vested with authority from becoming oppressors, the people have a right at such periods and in such manner as they shall establish by their frame of government, to cause their public officers to return to private life; and to fill up vacant places by certain and regular elections and appointments.

ART. IX. All elections ought to be free; and all the inhabitants of this commonwealth, having such qualifications as they shall establish by their frame of government, have an equal right to elect officers, and to be elected, for public employments.

ART. X. Each individual of the society has a right to be protected by it in the enjoyment of his life, liberty, and property, according to standing laws. He is obliged, consequently, to contribute his share to the expense of this protection; to give his personal service, or an equivalent, when necessary; but no part of the property of any individual can, with justice, be taken from him, or applied to public uses, without his own consent, or that of the representative body of the people. . . .

ART. XI. Every subject of the commonwealth ought to find a certain remedy, by having recourse to the laws, for all injuries or wrongs which he may receive in his person, property, or character. . . .

ART. XII. No subject shall be held to answer for any crimes or offense, until the same is fully and plainly, substantially, and formally, described to him; or be compelled to accuse, or furnish evidence against himself. And every subject shall have a right to produce all proofs that may be favorable to him; to meet the witnesses against him face to face, and to be fully heard in his defense by himself, or his counsel. . . . And no subject shall be arrested, imprisoned, despoiled, or deprived of his property, immunities, or privileges, put out of the protection of the law, exiled or deprived of his life, liberty, or estate, but by the judgment of his peers, or the law of the land. . . .

ART. XXIII. No subsidy, charge, tax, impost, or duties, ought to be established, fixed, laid, or levied, under any pretext whatsoever, without the consent of the people, or their representatives in the legislature.

ART. XXIX. It is essential to the rights of every individual, his life, liberty, property, and character, that there be an impartial interpretation of the laws, and administration of justice. It is the right of every citizen to be tried by judges as free, impartial, and independent as the lot of humanity will admit. . . . Therefore . . . the judges of the supreme judicial court should hold their offices as long as they behave themselves well; and . . . they should have honorable salaries ascertained and established by standing laws.

ART. XXX. In the government of this commonwealth, the legislative department shall never exercise the executive and judicial powers, or either of them; the executive shall never exercise the legislative and judicial powers, or either of them; the judicial shall never exercise the legislative and executive powers, or either of them; to the end it may be a government of laws, and not of men.

Part the Second

THE FRAME OF GOVERNMENT

The people inhabiting the territory formerly called the Province of Massachusetts Bay do hereby solemnly and mutually agree with each other to form themselves into a free, sovereign, and independent body politic or state, by the name of the Commonwealth of Massachusetts.

Chapter I. The Legislative Power

ARTICLE I. The department of legislation shall be formed by two branches, a Senate and House of Representatives; each of which shall have a negative on the other.

The legislative body shall assemble every year on the last Wednesday in May, and at such other times as they shall judge necessary; and shall dissolve and be dissolved on the day next preceding the said last Wednesday in May; and shall be styled the *General Court of Massachusetts.*

ART. II. No bill or resolve of the senate or house of representatives shall become a law, and have force as such, until it shall have been laid before the governor for his revisal; and if he, upon such revision, approve thereof, he shall signify his approbation by signing the same. But if he have any objection to the passing of such bill or resolve, he shall return the same, together with his objections thereto, in writing, to the Senate or House of Representatives, in whichsoever the same shall have originated, who shall enter the objections sent down by the governor, at large, on their records, and proceed to reconsider the said bill or resolve. But if after such reconsideration, two-thirds of the said Senate or House of Representatives shall, notwithstanding the said objections, agree to pass the same, it shall, together with the objections, be sent to the other branch of the legislature, where it shall also be reconsidered, and if approved by two-thirds of the members present, shall have the force of law; but in all such cases, the vote of both houses shall be determined by yeas and nays. . . .

And in order to prevent unnecessary delays, if any bill or resolve shall not be returned by the governor within five days after it shall have been presented, the same shall have the force of a law.

ART. III. The General Court shall forever have full power and authority to erect and constitute judicatories and . . . courts. . . .

ART. IV. And further, full power and authority are hereby given and granted to the said General Court from time to time, to make, ordain, and establish all manner of wholesome and reasonable orders, laws, statutes, and ordinances, directions and instructions . . . so as the same be not repugnant or contrary to this Constitution, as they shall judge to be for the good and welfare of this Commonwealth . . . ; and to impose and levy proportional and reasonable assessments, rates, and taxes, upon all the inhabitants of, and persons resident, and estates lying, within the said Commonwealth. . . .

Chapter II. Executive Power

ARTICLE I. There shall be a supreme executive magistrate, who shall be styled "The governor of the commonwealth of Massachusetts;" and whose title shall be "His excellency."

ART. II. The governor shall be chosen annually; and no person shall be eligible to this office, unless, at the time of his election, he shall have been an inhabitant of this commonwealth for seven years next preceding; and unless he shall, at the same time, be seized, in his own right, of a freehold, within the commonwealth, of the value of one thousand pounds; and unless he shall declare himself to be of the Christian religion. . . .

Chapter III. Judiciary Power

ARTICLE I. . . . All judicial officers, duly appointed, commissioned, and sworn, shall hold their offices during good behavior, excepting such concerning whom there is different provision made in this constitution: provided, nevertheless, the governor, with consent of the council, may remove them upon the address of both houses of the legislature.

ART. II. Each branch of the legislature, as well as the governor and council, shall have authority to require the opinions of the justices of the supreme judicial court upon important questions of law, and upon solemn occasions.

111. *Northwest Ordinance, 1787*

C. C. Tansill, ed., *Documents Illustrative of the Formation of the Union of the American States* (69 Congress, 1 Session, House Document, No. 398) (Washington, 1927), 47–54.

[Sections 1 and 2 omitted.]

SEC. 3. . . . There shall be appointed, from time to time, by Congress, a governor, whose commission shall continue in force for the term of three years, unless sooner revoked by Congress; he shall reside in the district, and have a freehold estate therein, in one thousand acres of land, while in the exercise of his office.

Sec. 4. There shall be appointed from time to time, by Congress, a secretary, whose commission shall continue in force for four years, unless sooner revoked; he shall reside in the district, and have a freehold estate therein, in five hundred acres of land, while in the exercise of his office. It shall be his duty to keep and preserve the acts and laws passed by the legislature, and the public records of the district, and the proceedings of the governor in his executive department, and transmit authentic copies of such acts and proceedings every six months to the Secretary of Congress. There shall also be appointed a court, to consist of three judges, any two of whom to form a court, who shall have a common-law jurisdiction and reside in the district, and have each therein a freehold estate, in five hundred acres of land, while in the exercise of their offices; and their commissions shall continue in force during good behavior.

Sec. 5. The governor and judges, or a majority of them, shall adopt and publish in the district such laws of the original states, criminal and civil, as may be necessary, and best suited to the circumstances of the district, and report them to Congress from time to time, which laws shall be in force in the district until the organization of the general assembly therein, unless disapproved of by Congress; but afterwards the legislature shall have authority to alter them as they shall think fit.

Sec. 6. The governor, for the time being, shall be commander-in-chief of the militia, appoint and commission all officers in the same below the rank of general officers; all general officers shall be appointed and commissioned by Congress.

Sec. 7. Previous to the organization of the general assembly the governor shall appoint such magistrates, and other civil officers, in each county or township, as he shall find necessary for the preservation of the peace and good order in the same. After the general assembly shall be organized, the powers and duties of magistrates and other civil officers shall be regulated and defined by the said assembly; but all magistrates and other civil officers, not herein otherwise directed, shall, during the continuance of this temporary government, be appointed by the governor.

Sec. 8. . . . For the execution of process, criminal and civil, the governor shall . . . proceed, from time to time . . . to lay out the parts of the district in which the Indian titles shall have been extinguished, into counties and townships, subject, however, to such alterations as may thereafter be made by the legislature.

Sec. 9. So soon as there shall be five thousand free male inhabitants, of full age, in the district, upon giving proof thereof to the governor, they shall receive authority ... to elect representatives from their counties or townships, to represent them in the general assembly. Provided, that for every five hundred free male inhabitants there shall be one representative, and so on, progressively ... until the number of representatives shall amount to twenty-five; after which the number and proportion of representatives shall be regulated by the legislature. Provided, that no person be eligible or qualified to act as a representative unless he shall have been a citizen of one of the United States three years, and be a resident in the district, or unless he shall have resided in the district three years; and, in either case, shall likewise hold in his own right, in fee-simple, two hundred acres of land within the same. Provided also, that a freehold in fifty acres of land in the district, having been a citizen of one of the states, and being resident in the district, or the like freehold and two years' residence in the district, shall be necessary to qualify a man as an elector of a representative.

Sec. 10. The representatives thus elected shall serve for the term of two years. ...

Sec. 11. The general assembly, or legislature, shall consist of the governor, legislative council, and a house of representatives. The legislative council shall consist of five members, to continue in office five years, unless sooner removed by Congress; any three of them to be a quorum; and the members of the council shall be nominated and appointed in the following manner, to wit: As soon as representatives shall be elected the governor shall appoint a time and place for them to meet together, and when met they shall nominate ten persons, resident in the district, and each possessed of a freehold in five hundred acres of land, and return their names to Congress, five of whom Congress shall ap-

point and commission to serve as aforesaid; ... And the governor, legislative council, and house of representatives shall have authority to make laws in all cases for the good government of the district, not repugnant to the principles and articles in this ordinance established and declared. And all bills, having passed by a majority in the house, and by a majority in the council, shall be referred to the governor for his assent; but no bill, or legislative act whatever, shall be of any force without his assent. The governor shall have power to convene, prorogue, and dissolve the general assembly when, in his opinion, it shall be expedient.

Sec. 12. ... As soon as a legislature shall be formed in the district, the council and house assembled, in one room, shall have authority, by joint ballot, to elect a delegate to Congress, who shall have a seat in Congress, with a right of debating, but not of voting, during this temporary government.

Sec. 13. And for extending the fundamental principles of civil and religious liberty, which form the basis whereon these republics, their laws, and constitutions are erected; to fix and establish those principles as the basis of all laws, constitutions, and governments, which forever hereafter shall be formed in the said territory; to provide, also, for the establishment of states, and permanent government therein, and for their admission to a share in the federal councils on an equal footing with the original states, at as early periods as may be consistent with the general interest:

Sec. 14. It is hereby ordained and declared, by the authority aforesaid, that the following articles shall be considered as articles of compact between the original states and the people and states in the said territory, and forever remain unalterable, unless by common consent, to wit:

Article I

No person, demeaning himself in a peaceable and orderly manner, shall ever be molested on account of his mode of worship, or religious sentiments, in the said territory.

Article II

The inhabitants of the said territory shall always be entitled to the benefits of the writs of habeas corpus and of the trial by jury, of a proportionate representation of the people in the legislature, and of judicial proceedings according to the course of the common law. All persons shall be bailable, unless for capital offenses, where the proof shall be evident, or the presumption great. All fines shall be moderate; and no cruel or unusual punishment shall be inflicted. No man shall be deprived of his liberty or property, but by the judgment of his peers, or the law of the land, and, should the public exigencies make it necessary, for the common preservation, to take any person's property, or to demand his particular services, full compensation shall be made for the same. And, in the just preservation of rights and property, it is understood and declared that no law ought ever to be made or have force in the said territory that shall, in any manner whatever, interfere with or affect private contracts, or engagements, bona fide, and without fraud previously formed.

Article III

Religion, morality, and knowledge being necessary to good government and the happiness of mankind, schools and the means of education shall forever be encouraged. The utmost good faith shall always be observed toward the Indians; their lands and property shall never be taken from them without their consent; and in their property, rights, and liberty they never shall be invaded or disturbed unless in just and lawful wars authorized by Congress; but laws founded in justice and humanity shall, from time to time, be made, for preventing wrongs being done to them and for preserving peace and friendship with them.

Article IV

The said territory, and the states which may be formed therein, shall forever remain a part of this confederacy of the United States of America. . . . The inhabitants and settlers in the said territory shall be subject to pay a part of the federal debts contracted, or to be contracted, and a proportional part of the expenses of government to be apportioned on them by Congress, according to the same common rule and measure by which apportionments thereof shall be made on the other states; and the taxes for paying their proportion shall be laid and levied by the authority and direction of the legislatures of the district, or districts, or new states, as in the original states. . . . The legislatures of those districts, or new states, shall never interfere with the primary disposal of the soil by the United States in Congress assembled. . . .

Article V

There shall be formed in the said territory not less than three or more than five states. . . . And whenever any of the said states shall have sixty thousand free inhabitants therein, such state shall be admitted by its delegates into the Congress of the United States, on an equal footing with the original states, in all respects whatever; and shall be at liberty to form a permanent constitution and state government. Provided, the constitution and government, so to be formed, shall be republican, and in conformity to the principles contained in these articles. And, so far as it can be consistent with the general interest of the confederacy, such admission shall be allowed at an earlier period, and when there may be a less number of free inhabitants in the state than sixty thousand.

Article VI

There shall be neither slavery nor involuntary servitude in the said territory, otherwise than in the punishment of crimes, whereof the party shall have been duly convicted: Provided always, that any person escaping into the same, from whom labor and service is lawfully claimed in any one of the original states, such fugitive may be lawfully reclaimed, and conveyed to the person claiming his or her labor or service as aforesaid.

112. *Virginia Act for Establishing Religious Freedom, 1786*

Hening, *Statutes at Large*, XII, 84–6.

WHEREAS Almighty God hath created the mind free; that all attempts to influence it by temporal punishments or burthens, or by civil incapacitations, tend only to beget habits of hypocrisy and meanness, and are a departure from the plan of the Holy Author of our religion, Who . . . chose not to propagate it by coercions . . . ; that the impious presumption of legislators and rulers, . . . who being themselves but fallible and uninspired men, have assumed dominion over the faith of others, setting up their own opinions and modes of thinking as the only true and infallible, and as such endeavoring to impose them on others, hath established and maintained false religions over the greatest part of the world, and through all time; that to compel a man to furnish contributions of money for ' the propagation of opinions which he disbelieves, is sinful and tyrannical; that even the forcing him to support this or that teacher of his own religious persuasion, is depriving him of the comfortable liberty of giving his contributions to the particular pastor, whose morals he would make his pattern, and whose powers he feels most persuasive to righteousness, and is withdrawing from the ministry those temporary rewards, which proceeding from an approbation of their personal conduct, are an additional incitement to earnest and unremitting labors for the instruction of mankind; that our civil rights have no dependence on our religious opinions . . . ; that therefore the proscribing any citizen as unworthy the public confidence by laying upon him an incapacity of being called to offices of trust and emolument, unless he profess or renounce this or that religious opinion, is depriving him injuriously of those privileges and advantages to which in common with his fellow-citizens he has a natural right; that it tends only to corrupt the principles of that religion it is meant to encourage, by bribing with a monopoly of worldly honors and emoluments, those who will externally profess and conform to it; . . . that to suffer the civil magistrate to intrude his powers into the field of opinion, and to restrain the profession or propagation of principles . . . is a dangerous fallacy, which at once destroys all religious liberty, because he . . . will make his opinions the rule of judgment, and approve or condemn the sentiments of others only as they shall square with or differ from his own; that it is time enough for the rightful purposes of civil government, for its officers to interfere when principles break out into overt acts against peace and good order; and finally that truth is great and will prevail if left to herself, that she is the proper and sufficient antagonist to error, and has nothing to fear from the conflict, unless by human interposition disarmed of her natural weapons, free argument and debate. . . .

Be it enacted by the General Assembly. That no man shall be compelled to frequent or support any religious worship, place, or ministry whatsoever, nor shall be enforced, restrained, molested, or burthened in his body or goods, nor shall otherwise suffer on account of his religious opinions or belief; but that all men shall be free to profess, and by argument to maintain, their opinion in matters of religion, and that the same shall in no wise diminish, enlarge, or affect their civil capacities.

And though we well know that this assembly elected by the people for the ordinary purposes of legislation only, have no power to restrain the acts of succeeding assemblies, constituted with powers equal to our own, and that therefore to declare this act to be irrevocable would be of no effect in law; yet we are free to declare, and do declare, that the rights hereby asserted are of the natural rights of mankind, and that if any act shall be hereafter passed to repeal the present, or to narrow its operation, such act will be an infringement of natural right.

113. *A Natural Aristocracy, 1813*

Thomas Jefferson to John Adams, October 28, 1813. Printed in Thomas Jefferson, *Writings*, A. A. Lipscomb and A. E. Bergh, eds. (Washington, 1903), XIII, 396–97; and *Works*, P. L. Ford, ed. (New York, 1905), XI, 343–5.

I AGREE with you that there is a natural aristocracy among men. The grounds of this are virtue and talents. Formerly, bodily powers gave place among the aristoi. But since the invention of gunpowder has armed the weak as well as the strong with missile death, bodily strength, like beauty, good humor, politeness, and other accomplishments, has become but an auxiliary ground of distinction.

There is also an artificial aristocracy, founded on wealth and birth, without either virtue or talents; for with these it would belong to the first class. The natural aristocracy I consider as the most precious gift of nature, for the instruction, the trusts, and government of society. And, indeed, it would have been inconsistent in creation to have formed man for the social state and not to have provided virtue and wisdom enough to manage the concerns of the society. May we not even say that that form of government is the best which provides the most effectually for a pure selection of these natural aristoi into the offices of government?

The artificial aristocracy is a mischievous ingredient in government, and provision should be made to prevent its ascendancy. On the question, what is the best provision, you and I differ; but we differ as rational friends, using the free exercise of our own reason and mutually indulging its errors. You think it best to put the pseudo-aristoi into a separate chamber of legislation, where they may be hindered from doing mischief by their co-ordinate branches, and where also they may be a protection to wealth against the agrarian and plundering enterprises of the majority of the people. I think that to give them power in order to prevent them from doing mischief is arming them for it and increasing instead of remedying the evil. For if the co-ordinate branches can arrest their action, so may they that of the co-ordinates. Mischief may be done negatively as well as positively. . . .

Nor do I believe them necessary to protect the wealthy; because enough of these will find their way into every branch of the legislation to protect themselves. From fifteen to twenty legislatures of our own, in action for thirty years past, have proved that no fears of an equalization of property are to be apprenhended from them. I think the best remedy is exactly that provided by all our constitutions: to leave to the citizens the free election and separation of the aristoi from the pseudo-aristoi, of the wheat from the chaff. In general they will elect the real good and wise. In some instances, wealth may corrupt and birth blind them, but not in sufficient degree to endanger the society.

114. *Financial Aristocracy, 1814*

John Taylor, *An Inquiry into the Principles and Policy of the Government of the United States.* R. F. Nichols, ed. (New Haven, 1950), 42, 46–7, 57, 59, 65–6, 71, 93.

MR. ADAMS has omitted a cause of aristocracy . . . namely, exclusive wealth. This, by much the most formidable with which mankind have to contend, is necessarily omitted, whilst he is ascribing aristocracy to nature; and being both artificial and efficacious, it contributes to sustain the opinion, "that as aristocracy is thus artificially created, it may also be artificially destroyed.". . .

As the aristocracies of priestcraft and conquest decayed, that of patronage and paper stock grew; not the rival, but the instrument of a king; without rank or title; regardless of honor; of insatiable avarice; and neither conspicuous for virtue and knowledge, or capable of being collected into a legislative chamber. Differing in all its qualities from Mr. Adams's natural aristocracy, and defying his remedy, it is condensed and combined by an interest, exclusive, and inimical to public good.

Why has Mr. Adams written volumes to instruct us how to manage an order of nobles, sons of the Gods, of exclusive virtue, talents, and wealth, and attended by the pomp and fraud of superstition; or one of feudal barons, holding great districts of unalienable country, warlike, high spirited, turbulent and dangerous; now that these orders are no more: whilst he passes over in silence the aristocracy of paper and patronage, more numerous, more burdensome, unexposed to public jealousy by the badge of title, and not too honorable or high spirited to use and serve executive power, for the sake of pillaging the people? Are these odious vices, to be concealed under apprehensions of ancient aristocracies, which, however natural, are supplanted by this modern one? . . .

Talents and virtue are now so widely distributed, as to have rendered a monopoly of either, equivalent to that of antiquity, impracticable; and if an aristocracy ought to have existed, whilst it possessed such a monopoly, it ought not also to exist, because this monopoly is irretrievably lost. The distribution of wealth produced by commerce and alienation, is equal to that of knowledge and virtue, produced by printing; but as the first distribution might be artificially counteracted, with a better prospect of success than the latter, aristocracy has abandoned a reliance on a monopoly of virtue, renown and abilities, and resorted wholly to a monopoly of wealth, by the system of paper and patronage. Modern taxes and frauds to collect money, and not ancient authors, will therefore afford the best evidence of its present character. . . .

Let us moderns cease to boast of our victory over superstition and the feudal system, and our advancement in knowledge. Let us neither pity, ridicule or despise the ancients, as dupes of frauds and tricks, which we can so easily discern; lest some ancient sage should rise from his grave, and answer, "You moderns are duped by arts more obviously fraudulent, than those which deceived us. The agency of the Gods was less discernible, than the effects of paper and patronage. . . ."

Whatever destroys an unity of interest between a government and a nation, infallibly produces oppression and hatred. Human conception is unable to invent a scheme, more capable of afflicting mankind with these evils, than that of paper and patronage. It divides a nation into two groups, creditors and debtors; the first supplying its want of physical strength, by alliances with fleets and armies, and practising the most unblushing corruption. A consciousness of inflicting or suffering injuries, fills each with malignity towards the other. This malignity first begets a multitude of penalties, punishments and executions, and then vengeance.

A legislature, in a nation where the system of paper and patronage prevails, will be governed by that interest, and legislate in its favor. It is impossible to do this, without legislating to the injury of of the other interest, that is, the great mass of the nation. Such a legislature . . . will lavish the revenue, to enrich themselves. They will borrow for the nation, that they may lend. They will offer lenders great profits, that they may share in them. . . . And they will finally avow and maintain their corruption, by establishing an irresistible standing army, not to defend the nation, but to defend a system for plundering the nation. . . .

It is said that paper systems being open to all, are not monopolies. He who has money, may buy stock. All then is fair, as every man (meaning however only every monied man) may share in the plunder.

Every man may enlist in an army, yet an army may enslave a nation. A monopoly may be open to a great number, yet those who do engage in it, may imbibe the spirit of faction; but it cannot be open to all, because no interest, which must subsist upon a nation, can consist of that nation; as I cannot fatten myself by eating myself. If every citizen should go into an army, it would transform that army into the nation itself, and its pay and subsistence would cease. In like manner the profits of paper, were they generally or universally distributed, would cease; because each citizen would be his own paymaster. Had the objection been as true in practice as it is plausible in theory, these answers suffice to prove, that it would have converted paper aristocracies into paper democracies. . . .

Few would deny these premises or the inference, if it was proposed to revive oracles or feudal services. These causes of aristocracy are distinctly seen, because they do not exist. They have no counsel in court. They are, therefore, better understood than when they flourished. But both the premises and the inference are denied, when they implicate the aristocracy of paper and patronage. This cause of aristocracy is not seen, because it does exist; and the more oppressive it shall become, the greater will be the difficulty of discovering its existence. The two first are exposed naked to our view; and the third, disguised in the garb of republicanism, and uttering patriotic words, joins the mob in kicking them about, by way of diverting the public attention from itself.

XV ✽ *The Federal Government*

THE NATURE of the struggle for independence, the necessities of war, and the awareness of their own nationality, early induced the Americans to give thought to the form of confederation under which they would govern themselves. The Continental Congress, to begin with, was simply the consultative body of a group of independent states. A more stable and more durable relationship was clearly necessary.

Yet it was difficult to find an instructive precedent. The history of past federations was not encouraging and the sense of local particularism was strong. Although the Albany Plan (*see above*, No. 59) offered a model, the first frame of government, the Articles of Confederation (No. 115), was not ratified until 1778. The Articles sufficed to bring the country successfully through the war. But within a few years its inadequacies were intolerable. It was replaced, in 1788, by the Constitution which thereafter remained the fundamental charter of the United States (No. 116).

The process of devising the Constitution evoked a good deal of thought about the nature of federal government. The supporters of the new government vigorously proclaimed its advantages, and particularly the greater strength it gave the central government. Madison explained the problems the Constitutional Convention considered, and also argued that the Constitution was more appropriate to a republic than the Articles (No. 117). The new Constitution, it was hoped, would also provide a means by which the government could rise above the contending interests of factions and pursue the common welfare (No. 118).

The new government in itself was not less democratic than the governments created by the state constitutions. The debate on suffrage in the Constitutional Convention revealed an unwillingness to restrict the right to vote (No. 119). Essentially, those who had promoted the Constitution labored for a government strong enough to realize the national aspirations of the people, as Franklin pointed out at the close of the convention (No. 120).

The Constitution endured, but it did not endure unchanged. Within two decades twelve amendments had been incorporated in it, the first ten ratified at once on December 15, 1791, the eleventh on January 8, 1798, and the twelfth on September 25, 1804 (No. 121; *see also below*, No. 232). Furthermore, judicial interpretation expanded and altered the intent of the written document, as did the case of Marbury *v.* Madison, which established the doctrine of judicial review (No. 122).

115. *Articles of Confederation, 1777*

J. D. Richardson, compiler, *Messages and Papers of the Presidents* (Washington, 1896), I, 9–17.

ARTICLE I. The style of this confederacy shall be "The United States of America."

ARTICLE II. Each state retains its sovereignty, freedom and independence, and every power, jurisdiction and right, which is not by this confederation expressly delegated to the United States, in Congress assembled.

ARTICLE III. The said states hereby severally enter into a firm league of friendship with each other, for their common defense, the security of their liberties, and their mutual and general welfare, binding themselves to assist each other, against all ... attacks made upon them. . . .

ARTICLE IV. The better to secure and perpetuate mutual friendship and intercourse among the people of the different states in this union, the free inhabitants of each of these states, paupers, vagabonds and fugitives from justice excepted, shall be entitled to all privileges and immunities of free citizens in the several states; and the people of each state shall have free ingress and regress to and from any other state, and shall enjoy therein all the privileges of trade and commerce, subject to the same duties, impositions and restrictions as the inhabitants thereof respectively, provided . . . that no imposition, duties or restriction shall be laid by any state, on the property of the United States, or either of them.

If any person guilty of, or charged with treason, felony, or other high misdemeanor in any state, shall flee from justice, and be found in any of the United States, he shall upon demand of the governor or executive power . . . be delivered up and removed to the state having jurisdiction of his offense.

Full faith and credit shall be given in each of these states to the records, acts and judicial proceedings of the courts and magistrates of every other state.

ARTICLE V. For the more convenient management of the general interests of the United States, delegates shall be annually appointed in such manner as the legislature of each state shall direct, to meet in Congress on the first Monday in November, in every year, with a power reserved to each state, to recall its delegates, or any of them, at any time within the year, and to send others in their stead. . . .

No state shall be represented in Congress by less than two, nor by more than seven members; and no person shall be capable of being a delegate for more than three years in any term of six years; nor shall any person, being a delegate, be capable of holding any office under the United States, for which he, or another for his benefit receives any salary, fees or emolument of any kind. . . .

In determining questions in the United States, in Congress assembled, each state shall have one vote.

Freedom of speech and debate in Congress shall not be impeached or questioned in any court, or place out of Congress, and the members of Congress shall be protected in their persons from arrests and imprisonments, during the time of their going to and from, and attendance on Congress, except for treason, felony, or breach of the peace.

ARTICLE VI. No state without the consent of the United States in Congress assembled, shall send any embassy to, or receive any embassy from, or enter into any conference, agreement, alliance or treaty with any king prince or state; nor shall any person holding any office of profit or trust under the United States, or any of them, accept of any present, emolument, office or title of any kind whatever from any king, prince or foreign state; nor shall the United States in Congress assembled, or any of them, grant any title of nobility.

No two or more states shall enter into any treaty, confederation or alliance whatever between them, without the consent of the United States in Congress assembled, specifying accurately the purposes for which the same is to be entered into, and how long it shall continue.

No state shall lay any imposts or duties, which may interfere with any stipulations in treaties, entered into by the United States in Congress assembled, with any king, prince or state, in pursuance of any treaties already proposed by Congress, to the courts of France and Spain. . . .

No state shall engage in any war without the consent of the United States in Congress assembled, unless such state be actually invaded by enemies . . . : nor shall any state grant commissions to any ships . . . nor letters of marque or reprisal, except it be after a declaration of war by the United States in Congress assembled, . . . unless such state be infested by pirates, in which case vessels of war may be fitted out for that occasion, and kept so long as the danger shall continue, or until the United States in Congress assembled shall determine otherwise.

ARTICLE VII. When land forces are raised by any state for the common defense, all officers of or under the rank of colonel, shall be appointed by the legislature of each state. . . .

ARTICLE VIII. All charges of war, and all

other expenses that shall be incurred for the common defense or general welfare, and allowed by the United States in Congress assembled, shall be defrayed out of a common treasury, which shall be supplied by the several states, in proportion to the value of all land within each state, granted to or surveyed for any person, as such land and the buildings and improvements thereon shall be estimated according to such mode as the United States in Congress assembled, shall from time to time direct and appoint. The taxes for paying that proportion shall be laid and levied by the authority and direction of the legislatures of the several states within the time agreed upon by the United States in Congress assembled.

ARTICLE IX. The United States in Congress assembled, shall have the sole and exclusive right and power of determining on peace and war, . . . of sending and receiving ambassadors, entering into treaties and alliances, . . . of granting letters of marque and reprisal in times of peace, appointing courts for the trial of piracies and felonies committed on the high seas and establishing courts for receiving and determining finally appeals in all cases of captures. . . .

The United States in Congress assembled shall also be the last resort on appeal in all disputes and differences now subsisting or that hereafter may arise between two or more states concerning boundary, jurisdiction or any other cause whatever. . . .

The United States in Congress assembled shall also have the sole and exclusive right and power of regulating the alloy and value of coin struck by their own authority, or by that of the respective states —fixing the standard of weights and measures throughout the United States—regulating the trade and managing all affairs with the Indians, not members of any of the states, provided that the legislative right of any state within its own limits be not infringed or violated—establishing and regulating post-offices . . . throughout all the United States, and exacting such postage on the papers passing through the same as may be requisite to defray the expenses of the said office—appointing all officers of the land forces, in the service of the United States, excepting regimental officers—appointing all the officers of the naval forces, and commissioning all officers whatever in the service of the United States—making rules for the government and regulation of the said land and naval forces, and directing their operations.

The United States in Congress assembled shall have authority to appoint a committee, to sit in the recess of Congress, to be denominated "A Committee of the States," and to consist of one delegate from each state; and to appoint such other committees and civil officers as may be necessary . . . —to appoint one of their number to preside, provided that no person be allowed to serve in the office of president more than one year in any term of three years; to ascertain the necessary sums of money to be raised . . . , and to appropriate and apply the same for defraying the public expenses—to borrow money, or emit bills on the credit of the United States . . . —to build and equip a navy—to agree upon the number of land forces, and to make requisitions from each state for its quota. . . .

The United States in Congress assembled shall never engage in a war, nor grant letters of marque and reprisal in time of peace, nor enter into any treaties or alliances, nor coin money, nor regulate the value thereof, nor ascertain the sums . . . necessary for the defense and welfare of the United States . . . nor emit bills, nor borrow money . . . nor appropriate money, nor agree upon the number of vessels of war to be built or purchased, or the number of land or sea forces to be raised, nor appoint a commander in chief of the army or navy, unless nine states assent to the same. Nor shall a question on any other point, except for adjourning from day to day be determined, unless by the votes of a majority of the United States in Congress assembled. . . .

ARTICLE X. The Committee of the States, or any nine of them, shall be authorised to execute, in the recess of Congress, such of the powers of Congress as the United States in Congress assembled, by the consent of nine states, shall from time to time think expedient to vest them with; provided that no power be delegated to the said Committee, for the exercise of which, by the Articles of Confederation, the voice of nine states in the Congress of the United States assembled is requisite.

ARTICLE XI. Canada acceding to this confederation, . . . shall be admitted into, and entitled to all the advantages of this union. But no other colony shall be admitted into the same, unless such admission be agreed to by nine states.

ARTICLE XII. All bills of credit emitted, monies borrowed and debts contracted by, or under the authority of Congress, before the assembling of the United States, in pursuance of the present Confederation, shall be deemed and considered as a charge against the United States, for payment and satisfaction whereof the said United States, and the public faith are hereby solemnly pledged.

ARTICLE XIII. Every state shall abide by the determinations of the United States in Congress assembled, on all questions which by this confederation are submitted to them. And the Articles of this Confederation shall be inviolably observed by every state, and the union shall be perpetual; nor shall any alteration at any time hereafter be made in any of them; unless such alteration be agreed to in a Congress of the United States, and be afterwards confirmed by the legislatures of every state.

And whereas it hath pleased the Great Governor of the World to incline the hearts of the legislatures we respectively represent in Congress, to approve of, and to authorize us to ratify the said Articles of Confederation and perpetual union. Know ye that we . . . do by these presents . . . fully and entirely ratify and confirm . . . the said Articles of Confederation. . . . And we do further solemnly plight and engage the faith of our respective constituents, that they shall abide by the determinations of the United States in Congress assembled, on all questions, which by the said Confederation are submitted to them. And that the Articles thereof shall be inviolably observed by the states we respectively represent, and that the union shall be perpetual.

116. *The Constitution of the United States of America, 1787*

Richardson, *Messages and Papers,* I, 21–38.

WE THE people of the United States, in order to form a more perfect union, establish justice, insure domestic tranquility, provide for the common defense, promote the general welfare, and secure the blessings of liberty to ourselves and our posterity, do ordain and establish this Constitution for the United States of America.

Article I

SECTION 1. All legislative powers herein granted shall be vested in a Congress of the United States, which shall consist of a Senate and House of Representatives.

SECTION 2. 1. The House of Representatives shall be composed of members chosen every second year by the people of the several States, and the electors in each State shall have the qualifications requisite for electors of the most numerous branch of the State legislature.

2. No person shall be a representative who shall not have attained to the age of twenty-five years, and been seven years a citizen of the United States, and who shall not, when elected, be an inhabitant of

that State in which he shall be chosen.

3. Representatives and direct taxes shall be apportioned among the several States which may be included within this Union, according to their respective numbers, which shall be determined by adding to the whole number of free persons, including those bound to service for a term of years, and excluding Indians not taxed, three-fifths of all other persons. The actual enumeration shall be made within three years after the first meeting of the Congress of the United States, and within every subsequent term of ten years, in such manner as they shall by law direct. The number of representatives shall not exceed one for every thirty thousand, but each State shall have at least one representative; and until such enumeration shall be made, the State of New Hampshire shall be entitled to choose three, Massachusetts eight, Rhode Island and Providence Plantations one, Connecticut five, New York six, New Jersey four, Pennsylvania eight, Delaware one, Maryland six, Virginia ten, North Carolina five, South Carolina five, and Georgia three.

4. When vacancies happen in the representation from any State, the executive authority thereof shall issue writs of election to fill such vacancies.

5. The House of Representatives shall choose their speaker and other officers; and shall have the sole power of impeachment.

SECTION 3. 1. The Senate of the United States shall be composed of two senators from each State, chosen by the legislature thereof, for six years; and each senator shall have one vote.

2. Immediately after they shall be assembled in consequence of the first election, they shall be divided as equally as may be into three classes. The seats of the senators of the first class shall be vacated at the expiration of the second year, of the second class at the expiration of the fourth year, and of the third class at the expiration of the sixth year, so that one third may be chosen every second year;

and if vacancies happen by resignation, or otherwise, during the recess of the legislature of any State, the executive thereof may make temporary appointments until the next meeting of the legislature, which shall then fill such vacancies.

3. No person shall be a senator who shall not have attained to the age of thirty years, and been nine years a citizen of the United States, and who shall not, when elected, be an inhabitant of that State for which he shall be chosen.

4. The Vice President of the United States shall be President of the Senate, but shall have no vote, unless they be equally divided.

5. The Senate shall choose their other officers, and also a president *pro tempore*, in the absence of the Vice President, or when he shall exercise the office of President of the United States.

6. The Senate shall have the sole power to try all impeachments. When sitting for that purpose, they shall be on oath or affirmation. When the President of the United States is tried, the chief justice shall preside: and no person shall be convicted without the concurrence of two thirds of the members present.

7. Judgment in cases of impeachment shall not extend further than to removal from office, and disqualification to hold and enjoy any office of honor, trust or profit under the United States: but the party convicted shall nevertheless be liable and subject to indictment, trial, judgment and punishment, according to law.

SECTION 4. 1. The times, places, and manner of holding elections for senators and representatives, shall be prescribed in each State by the legislature thereof; but the Congress may at any time by law make or alter such regulations, except as to the places of choosing senators.

2. The Congress shall assemble at least once in every year, and such meeting shall be on the first Monday in December, unless they shall by law appoint a different day.

SECTION 5. 1. Each House shall be the

judge of the elections, returns and qualifications of its own members, and a majority of each shall constitute a quorum to do business; but a smaller number may adjourn from day to day, and may be authorized to compel the attendance of absent members, in such manner, and under such penalties as each House may provide.

2. Each House may determine the rules of its proceedings, punish its members for disorderly behavior, and, with the concurrence of two thirds, expel a member.

3. Each House shall keep a journal of its proceedings, and from time to time publish the same, excepting such parts as may in their judgment require secrecy; and the yeas and nays of the members of either House on any question shall, at the desire of one fifth of those present, be entered on the journal.

4. Neither House, during the session of Congress, shall, without the consent of the other, adjourn for more than three days, nor to any other place than that in which the two Houses shall be sitting.

SECTION 6. 1. The Senators and Representatives shall receive a compensation for their services, to be ascertained by law, and paid out of the Treasury of the United States. They shall in all cases, except treason, felony, and breach of the peace, be privileged from arrest during their attendance at the session of their respective Houses, and in going to and returning from the same; and for any speech or debate in either House, they shall not be questioned in any other place.

2. No Senator or Representative shall, during the time for which he was elected, be appointed to any civil office under the authority of the United States, which shall have been created, or the emoluments whereof shall have been increased, during such time; and no person holding any office under the United States shall be a member of either house during his continuance in office.

SECTION 7. 1. All bills for raising revenue shall originate in the House of Representatives; but the Senate may propose or concur with amendments as on other bills.

2. Every bill which shall have passed the House of Representatives and the Senate, shall, before it become a law, be presented to the President of the United States; If he approve he shall sign it, but if not he shall return it, with his objections, to that House in which it shall have originated, who shall enter the objections at large on their Journal, and proceed to reconsider it. If after such reconsideration two thirds of that House shall agree to pass the bill, it shall be sent, together with the objections, to the other House, by which it shall likewise be reconsidered, and if approved by two thirds of that House, it shall become a law. But in all such cases the votes of both houses shall be determined by yeas and nays, and the names of the persons voting for and against the bill shall be entered on the Journal of each House respectively. If any bill shall not be returned by the President within ten days (Sundays excepted) after it shall have been presented to him, the same shall be a law, in like manner as if he had signed it, unless the Congress by their adjournment prevent its return, in which case it shall not be a law.

3. Every order, resolution, or vote to which the concurrence of the Senate and House of Representatives may be necessary (except on a question of adjournment) shall be presented to the President of the United States; and before the same shall take effect, shall be approved by him, or being disapproved by him, shall be repassed by two thirds of the Senate and House of Representatives, according to the rules and limitations prescribed in the case of a bill.

SECTION 8. The Congress shall have power

1. To lay and collect taxes, duties, imposts, and excises, to pay the debts and provide for the common defense and general welfare of the United States; but all duties, imposts, and excises shall be uniform throughout the United States;

2. To borrow money on the credit of the United States;

3. To regulate commerce with foreign nations, and among the several States, and with the Indian tribes;

4. To establish a uniform rule of naturalization, and uniform laws on the subject of bankruptcies throughout the United States;

5. To coin money, regulate the value thereof, and of foreign coin, and fix the standard of weights and measures;

6. To provide for the punishment of counterfeiting the securities and current coin of the United States;

7. To establish post offices and post roads;

8. To promote the progress of science and useful arts, by securing for limited times to authors and inventors the exclusive right to their respective writings and discoveries;

9. To constitute tribunals inferior to the Supreme Court;

10. To define and punish piracies and felonies committed on the high seas, and offenses against the law of nations;

11. To declare war, grant letters of marque and reprisal, and make rules concerning captures on land and water;

12. To raise and support armies, but no appropriation of money to that use shall be for a longer term than two years;

13. To provide and maintain a navy;

14. To make rules for the government and regulation of the land and naval forces;

15. To provide for calling forth the militia to execute the laws of the Union, suppress insurrections and repel invasions;

16. To provide for organizing, arming, and disciplining the militia, and for governing such part of them as may be employed in the service of the United States, reserving to the States respectively, the appointment of the officers, and the authority of training the militia according to the discipline prescribed by Congress; .

17. To exercise exclusive legislation in all cases whatsoever, over such district (not exceeding ten miles square) as may, by cession of particular States, and the acceptance of Congress, become the seat of the government of the United States, and to exercise like authority over all places purchased by the consent of the legislature of the State in which the same shall be, for the erection of forts, magazines, arsenals, dockyards, and other needful buildings; and

18. To make all laws which shall be necessary and proper for carrying into execution the foregoing powers, and all other powers vested by this Constitution in the government of the United States, or in any department or officer thereof.

SECTION 9. 1. The migration or importation of such persons as any of the States now existing shall think proper to admit, shall not be prohibited by the Congress prior to the year one thousand eight hundred and eight, but a tax or duty may be imposed on such importation, not exceeding ten dollars for each person.

2. The privilege of the writ of habeas corpus shall not be suspended, unless when in cases of rebellion or invasion the public safety may require it.

3. No bill of attainder or ex post facto law shall be passed.

4. No capitation, or other direct, tax shall be laid, unless in proportion to the census or enumeration hereinbefore directed to be taken.

5. No tax or duty shall be laid on articles exported from any State.

6. No preference shall be given by any regulation of commerce or revenue to the ports of one State over those of another: nor shall vessels bound to, or from, one State be obliged to enter, clear, or pay duties in another.

7. No money shall be drawn from the Treasury, but in consequence of appropriations made by law; and a regular statement and account of the receipts and expenditures of all public money shall be published from time to time.

8. No title of nobility shall be granted

by the United States: and no person holding any office of profit or trust under them, shall, without the consent of the Congress, accept of any present, emolument, office, or title, of any kind whatever, from any king, prince, or foreign state.

SECTION 10. 1. No State shall enter into any treaty, alliance, or confederation; grant letters of marque and reprisal; coin money; emit bills of credit; make anything but gold and silver coin a tender in payment of debts; pass any bill of attainder, ex post facto law, or law impairing the obligation of contracts, or grant any title of nobility.

2. No State shall, without the consent of the Congress, lay any imposts or duties on imports or exports, except what may be absolutely necessary for executing its inspection laws: and the net produce of all duties and imposts laid by any State on imports or exports, shall be for the use of the Treasury of the United States; and all such laws shall be subject to the revision and control of the Congress.

3. No State shall, without the consent of Congress, lay any duty of tonnage, keep troops, or ships of war in time of peace, enter into any agreement or compact with another State, or with a foreign power, or engage in war, unless actually invaded, or in such imminent danger as will not admit of delay.

Article II

SECTION 1. 1. The executive power shall be vested in a President of the United States of America. He shall hold his office during the term of four years, and, together with the Vice President, chosen for the same term, be elected as follows:

2. Each State shall appoint, in such manner as the legislature thereof may direct, a number of electors, equal to the whole number of senators and representatives to which the State may be entitled in the Congress: but no senator or representative, or person holding an office of trust or profit under the United States, shall be appointed an elector.

The electors shall meet in their respective States, and vote by ballot for two persons, of whom one at least shall not be an inhabitant of the same State with themselves. And they shall make a list of all the persons voted for, and of the number of votes for each; which list they shall sign and certify, and transmit sealed to the seat of the government of the United States, directed to the president of the Senate. The president of the Senate shall, in the presence of the Senate and House of Representatives, open all the certificates, and the votes shall then be counted. The person having the greatest number of votes shall be the President, if such number be a majority of the whole number of electors appointed; and if there be more than one who have such majority, and have an equal number of votes, then the House of Representatives shall immediately choose by ballot one of them for President; and if no person have a majority, then from the five highest on the list the said House shall in like manner choose the President. But in choosing the President, the votes shall be taken by States, the representation from each State having one vote; a quorum for this purpose shall consist of a member or members from two thirds of the States, and a majority of all the States shall be necessary to a choice. In every case, after the choice of the President, the person having the greatest number of votes of the electors shall be the Vice President. But if there should remain two or more who have equal votes, the Senate shall choose from them by ballot the Vice President.

3. The Congress may determine the time of choosing the electors, and the day on which they shall give their votes; which day shall be the same throughout the United States.

4. No person except a natural born citizen, or a citizen of the United States, at

the time of the adoption of this Constitution, shall be eligible to the office of President; neither shall any person be eligible to that office who shall not have attained to the age of thirty-five years, and been fourteen years a resident within the United States.

5. In case of the removal of the President from office, or of his death, resignation, or inability to discharge the powers and duties of the said office, the same shall devolve on the Vice President, and the Congress may by law provide for the case of removal, death, resignation, or inability, both of the President and Vice President, declaring what officer shall then act as President, and such officer shall act accordingly, until the disability be removed, or a President shall be elected.

6. The President shall, at stated times, receive for his services a compensation, which shall neither be increased nor diminished during the period for which he shall have been elected, and he shall not receive within that period any other emolument from the United States, or any of them.

7. Before he enter on the execution of his office, he shall take the following oath or affirmation:—"I do solemnly swear (or affirm) that I will faithfully execute the office of President of the United States, and will to the best of my ability, preserve, protect and defend the Constitution of the United States."

SECTION 2. 1. The President shall be commander in chief of the army and navy of the United States, and of the militia of the several States, when called into the actual service of the United States; he may require the opinion, in writing, of the principal officer in each of the executive departments, upon any subject relating to the duties of their respective offices, and he shall have power to grant reprieves and pardons for offenses against the United States, except in cases of impeachment.

2. He shall have power, by and with the advice and consent of the Senate, to make treaties, provided two thirds of the senators present concur; and he shall nominate, and by and with the advice and consent of the Senate, shall appoint ambassadors, other public ministers and consuls, judges of the Supreme Court, and all other officers of the United States, whose appointments are not herein otherwise provided for, and which shall be established by law: but the Congress may by law vest the appointment of such inferior officers, as they think proper, in the President alone, in the courts of law, or in the heads of departments.

3. The President shall have power to fill up all vacancies that may happen during the recess of the Senate, by granting commissions which shall expire at the end of their next session.

SECTION 3. He shall from time to time give to the Congress information of the state of the Union, and recommend to their consideration such measures as he shall judge necessary and expedient; he may, on extraordinary occasions, convene both Houses, or either of them, and in case of disagreement between them with respect to the time of adjournment, he may adjourn them to such time as he shall think proper; he shall receive ambassadors and other public ministers; he shall take care that the laws be faithfully executed, and shall commission all the officers of the United States.

SECTION 4. The President, Vice President, and all civil officers of the United States, shall be removed from office on impeachment for, and conviction of, treason, bribery, or other high crimes and misdemeanors.

Article III

SECTION 1. The judicial power of the United States shall be vested in one Supreme Court, and in such inferior courts as the Congress may from time to time ordain and establish. The judges, both of the Supreme and inferior courts, shall hold their offices during good behavior, and shall, at stated times, receive for their services, a compensation, which shall not be diminished during their continuance in office.

SECTION 2. 1. The judicial power shall extend to all cases, in law and equity, arising under this Constitution, the laws of the United States, and treaties made, or which shall be made, under their authority;—to all cases affecting ambassadors, other public ministers and consuls;—to all cases of admiralty and maritime jurisdiction;—to controversies to which the United States shall be a party;—to controversies between two or more States;—between a State and citizens of another State;—between citizens of different States;—between citizens of the same State claiming lands under grants of different States, and between a State, or the citizens thereof, and foreign States, citizens or subjects.

2. In all cases affecting ambassadors, other public ministers and consuls, and those in which a State shall be party, the Supreme Court shall have original jurisdiction. In all the other cases before mentioned, the Supreme Court shall have appellate jurisdiction, both as to law and fact, with such exceptions, and under such regulations as the Congress shall make.

3. The trial of all crimes, except in cases of impeachment, shall be by jury; and such trial shall be held in the State where the said crimes shall have been committed; but when not committed within any State, the trial shall be at such place or places as the Congress may by law have directed.

SECTION 3. 1. Treason against the United States shall consist only in levying war against them, or in adhering to their enemies, giving them aid and comfort. No person shall be convicted of treason unless on the testimony of two witnesses to the same overt act, or on confession in open court.

2. The Congress shall have power to declare the punishment of treason, but no attainder of treason shall work corruption of blood, or forfeiture except during the life of the person attained.

Article IV

SECTION 1. Full faith and credit shall be given in each State to the public acts, records, and judicial proceedings of every other State. And the Congress may by general laws prescribe the manner in which such acts, records and proceedings shall be proved, and the effect thereof.

SECTION 2. 1. The citizens of each State shall be entitled to all privileges and immunities of citizens in the several States.

2. A person charged in any State with treason, felony, or other crime, who shall flee from justice, and be found in another State, shall on demand of the executive authority of the State from which he fled, be delivered up to be removed to the State having jurisdiction of the crime.

3. No person held to service or labor in one State under the laws thereof, escaping into another, shall, in consequence of any law or regulation therein, be discharged from such service or labor, but shall be delivered up on claim of the party to whom such service or labor may be due.

SECTION 3. 1. New States may be admitted by the Congress into this Union; but no new State shall be formed or erected within the jurisdiction of any other State; nor any State be formed by the junction of two or more States, or parts of States, without the consent of the legislatures of the States concerned as well as of the Congress.

2. The Congress shall have power to dispose of and make all needful rules and regulations respecting the territory or other property belonging to the United States; and nothing in this Constitution shall be so construed as to prejudice any claims of the United States, or of any particular State.

SECTION 4. The United States shall guarantee to every State in this Union a republican form of government, and shall protect each of them against invasion; and on application of the legislature, or of the executive (when the legislature cannot be convened) against domestic violence.

Article V

The Congress, whenever two thirds of both Houses shall deem it necessary, shall propose amendments to this Constitution, or, on the application of the legislatures of two thirds of the several States, shall call a convention for proposing amendments, which in either case, shall be valid to all intents and purposes, as part of this Constitution when ratified by the legislatures of three fourths of the several States, or by conventions in three fourths thereof, as the one or the other mode of ratification may be proposed by the Congress; Provided that no amendment which may be made prior to the year one thousand eight hundred and eight shall in any manner affect the first and fourth clauses in the ninth section of the first article; and that no State, without its consent, shall be deprived of its equal suffrage in the Senate.

Article VI

1. All debts contracted and engagements entered into, before the adoption of this Constitution, shall be as valid against the United States under this Constitution, as under the Confederation.

2. This Constitution, and the laws of the United States which shall be made in pursuance thereof; and all treaties made, or which shall be made, under the authority of the United States, shall be the supreme law of the land; and the judges in every State shall be bound thereby, anything in the Constitution or laws of any State to the contrary notwithstanding.

3. The senators and representatives before mentioned, and the members of the several State legislatures, and all executive and judicial officers, both of the United States and of the several States, shall be bound by oath or affirmation to support this Constitution; but no religious test shall ever be required as a qualification to any office or public trust under the United States.

Article VII

The ratification of the conventions of nine States shall be sufficient for the establishment of this Constitution between the States so ratifying the same.

117. *Report on the Constitution, 1787*

James Madison to Thomas Jefferson, October 24, 1787, Madison, *Writings*, I, 344, 352–3.

IT APPEARED to be the sincere and unanimous wish of the Convention to cherish and preserve the Union of the States. No proposition was made, no suggestion was thrown out, in favor of a partition of the Empire into two or more confederacies.

It was generally agreed that the objects of the Union could not be secured by any system founded on the principle of a confederation of sovereign states. A *voluntary* observance of the federal law by all the members could never be hoped for. A *compulsive* one could evidently never be reduced to practice, and if it could, involved equal calamities to the innocent and the guilty. . . .

Hence was embraced the alternative of a government which, instead of operating on the states, should operate without their intervention on the individuals composing them; and hence the change in the principle and proportion of representation.

This ground-work being laid, the great objects which presented themselves were:

1. to unite a proper energy in the executive, and a proper stability in the legislative departments, with the essential characters of republican government. 2. to draw a line of demarkation which would give to the general government every power requisite for general purposes, and leave to the states every power which might be most beneficially administered by them. 3. to provide for the different interests of different parts of the Union. 4. to adjust the clashing pretensions of the large and small states. . . .

If then there must be different interests and parties in society; and a majority when united by a common interest or passion cannot be restrained from oppressing the minority, what remedy can be found in a republican government, where the majority must ultimately decide, but that of giving such an extent to its sphere, that no common interest or passion will be likely to unite a majority of the whole number in an unjust pursuit? In a large society, the people are broken into so many interests and parties, that a common sentiment is less likely to be felt, and the requisite concert less likely to be formed, by a majority of the whole. . . .

The great desideratum in government is, so to modify the sovereignty as that it may be sufficiently neutral between different parts of the society to control one part from invading the rights of another, and at the same time sufficiently controlled itself, from setting up an interest adverse to that of the entire society. . . . In the extended republic of the United States, the general government would hold a pretty even balance between the parties of particular states, and be at the same time sufficiently restrained by its dependence on the community, from betraying its general interests.

118. *The Union a Check on Faction, 1787*

Federalist Papers, No. 10.

AMONG the numerous advantages promised by a well-constructed union, none deserves to be more accurately developed than its tendency to break and control the violence of faction. The friend of popular governments never finds himself so much alarmed for their character and fate as when he contemplates their propensity to this dangerous vice. He will not fail, therefore, to set a due value on any plan which, without violating the principles to which he is attached, provides a proper cure for it. . . . Complaints are everywhere heard from our most considerate and virtuous citizens, equally the friends of public and private faith and of public and personal liberty, that our governments are too unstable; that the public good is disregarded in the conflicts of rival parties; and that measures are too often decided, not according to the rules of justice and the rights of the minor party, but by the superior force of an interested and overbearing majority. . . . That prevailing and increasing distrust of public engagements, and alarm for private rights . . . must be chiefly, if not wholly, effects of the unsteadiness and injustice with which a factious spirit has tainted our public administrations.

By a faction, I understand a number of citizens, whether amounting to a majority or minority of the whole, who are united and actuated by some common impulse of passion, or of interest, adverse to the rights of other citizens or to the permanent and aggregate interests of the community.

There are two methods of curing the mischiefs of faction: the one, by removing its causes; the other, by controlling its effects.

There are again two methods of removing the causes of faction: the one, by destroying the liberty which is essential to its existence; the other, by giving to every citizen the same opinions, the same passions, and the same interests.

It could never be more truly said than of the first remedy, that it was worse than the disease. . . .

The second expedient is as impracticable as the first would be unwise. As long as the reason of man continues fallible, and he is at liberty to exercise it, different opinions will be formed. As long as the connection subsists between his reason and his self-love, his opinions and his passions will have a reciprocal influence on each other; and the former will be objects to which the latter will attach themselves. The diversity in the faculties of men, from which the rights of property originate, is not less an insuperable obstacle to a uniformity of interests. . . .

The latent causes of faction are thus sown in the nature of man; and we see them everywhere brought into different degrees of activity, according to the different circumstances of civil society. . . . But the most common and durable source of factions has been the various and unequal distribution of property. Those who hold and those who are without property have ever formed distinct interests in society. Those who are creditors and those who are debtors fall under a like discrimination. A landed interest, a manufacturing interest, a mercantile interest, a moneyed interest, with many lesser interests, grow up of necessity in civilized nations, and divide them into different classes, actuated by different sentiments and views. The regulation of these various and interfering interests forms the principal task of modern legislation, and involves the spirit of party and faction in the necessary and ordinary operations of the government.

No man is allowed to be a judge in his own cause; because his interest would certainly bias his judgment and, not improbably, corrupt his integrity. With equal, nay, with greater reason, a body of men are unfit to be both judges and

parties at the same time; yet what are many of the most important acts of legislation, but so many judicial determinations, not indeed concerning the rights of single persons, but concerning the rights of large bodies of citizens? And what are the different classes of legislators, but advocates and parties to the causes which they determine? . . .

It is in vain to say that enlightened statesmen will be able to adjust these clashing interests and render them all subservient to the public good. Enlightened statesmen will not always be at the helm. Nor, in many cases, can such an adjustment be made at all, without taking into view indirect and remote considerations, which will rarely prevail over the immediate interest which one party may find in disregarding the rights of another or the good of the whole.

The inference to which we are brought is that the causes of faction cannot be removed, and that relief is only to be sought in the means of controlling its effects.

If a faction consists of less than a majority, relief is supplied by the republican principle, which enables the majority to defeat its sinister views by regular vote. It may clog the administration, it may convulse the society; but it will be unable to execute and mask its violence under the forms of the Constitution. When a majority is included in a faction, the form of popular government, on the other hand, enables it to sacrifice to its ruling passion or interest both the public good and the rights of other citizens. To secure the public good and private rights against the danger of such a faction, and at the same time to preserve the spirit and the form of popular government, is then the great object to which our inquiries are directed. . . .

By what means is this object attainable? Evidently by one of two only. Either the existence of the same passion or interest in a majority, at the same time, must be prevented; or the majority, having such coexistent passion or interest, must be rendered, by their number and local situation, unable to concert and carry into effect schemes of oppression. If the impulse and the opportunity be suffered to coincide, we well know that neither moral nor religious motives can be relied on as an adequate control. They are not found to be such on the injustice and violence of individuals, and lose their efficacy in proportion to the number combined together; that is, in proportion as their efficacy becomes needful. . . .

A republic, by which I mean a government in which the scheme of representation takes place, opens a different prospect, and promises the cure for which we are seeking. Let us examine the points in which it varies from pure democracy, and we shall comprehend both the nature of the cure and the efficacy which it must derive from the union.

The two great points of difference between a democracy and a republic are: first, the delegation of the government, in the latter, to a small number of citizens elected by the rest; secondly, the greater number of citizens, and greater sphere of country, over which the latter may be extended.

The effect of the first difference is, on the one hand, to refine and enlarge the public views, by passing them through the medium of a chosen body of citizens, whose wisdom may best discern the true interest of their country, and whose patriotism and love of justice will be least likely to sacrifice it to temporary or partial considerations. Under such a regulation, it may well happen that the public voice, pronounced by the representatives of the people, will be more consonant to

the public good than if pronounced by the people themselves, convened for the purpose. . . .

The other point of difference is, the greater number of citizens and extent of territory which may be brought within the compass of republican than of democratic government; and it is this circumstance principally which renders factious combinations less to be dreaded in the former, than in the latter. The smaller the society, the fewer probably will be the distinct parties and interests composing it; the fewer the distinct parties and interests, the more frequently will a majority be found of the same party; and the smaller the number of individuals composing a majority, and the smaller the compass within which they are placed, the more easily will they concert and execute their plans of oppression. Extend the sphere, and you take in a greater variety of parties and interests; you make it less probable that a majority of the whole will have a common motive to invade the rights of other citizens; or if such a common motive exists, it will be more difficult for all who feel it to discover their own strength, and to act in unison with each other. Besides other impediments, it may be remarked that where there is a consciousness of unjust or dishonorable purposes, communication is always checked by distrust, in proportion to the number whose concurrence is necessary.

Hence it clearly appears that the same advantage which a republic has over a democracy, in controlling the effects of faction, is enjoyed by a large over a small republic—is enjoyed by the Union over the States composing it.

119. *The Convention Debate on Suffrage, 1787*

James Madison, *Debates in the Federal Convention of 1787.* Gaillard Hunt and J. B. Scott, eds. (New York, 1920), 352–5.

MR. GOUVERNEUR MORRIS [arguing in favor of a suffrage limited to freeholders] did not conceive the difficulty of defining

"freeholders" to be insuperable. Still less, that the restriction could be unpopular. Nine-tenths of the people are at present freeholders, and these will certainly be pleased with it. As to merchants, etc., if they have wealth and value the right, they can acquire it. If not, they don't deserve it.

Col. MASON. We all feel too strongly the remains of ancient prejudices, and view things too much through a British medium. A freehold is the qualification in England, and hence it is imagined to be the only proper one. The true idea . . . was that every man having evidence of attachment to and permanent common interest with the society ought to share in all its rights and privileges. Was this qualification restrained to freeholders? . . . Does nothing besides property mark a permanent attachment? Ought the merchant, the moneyed man, the parent of a number of children whose fortunes are to be pursued in his own country, to be viewed as suspicious characters, and unworthy to be trusted with the common rights of their fellow citizens?

Mr. MADISON. The right of suffrage is certainly one of the fundamental articles of republican government, and ought not to be left to be regulated by the legislature. A gradual abridgment of this right has been the mode in which aristocracies have been built on the ruins of popular forms. Whether the Constitutional qualification ought to be a freehold, would with him depend much on the probable reception such a change would meet with in States where the right was now exercised by every description of people. In several of the States a freehold was now the qualification. Viewing the subject in its merits alone, the freeholders of the country would be the safest depositories of Republican liberty. In future times a

great majority of the people will not only be without landed, but any other sort of, property. These will either combine under the influence of their common situation; in which case, the rights of property and the public liberty will not be secure in their hands: or which is more probable, they will become the tools of opulence and ambition, in which case there will be equal danger on another side. . . .

Dr. FRANKLIN. It is of great consequence that we should not depress the virtue and public spirit of our common people; of which they displayed a great deal during the war, and which contributed principally to the favorable issue of it. . . . This proceeded he said from the different manner in which the common people were treated in America and Great Britain. He did not think that the elected had any right in any case to narrow the privileges of the electors. . . . He was persuaded also that such a restriction as was proposed would give great uneasiness in the populous States. The sons of a substantial farmer, not being themselves freeholders, would not be pleased at being disfranchised, and there are a great many persons of that description. . . .

Mr. RUTLEDGE thought the idea of restraining the right of suffrage to the freeholders a very unadvised one. It would create division among the people and make enemies of all those who should be excluded.

On the question for striking out as moved by Mr. Gouverneur Morris, from the word 'qualifications' to the end of the III article,

N.H. no. Mass. no. Conn. no. Pa. no. Del. ay. Md. divided. Va. no. N.C. no. S.C. no. Geo. not present.

120. *The Constitution Necessary, 1787*

Benjamin Franklin at the Constitutional Convention, September 17, 1787, Madison, *Debates*, 577–9.

MR. PRESIDENT: I confess that there are several parts of this Constitution which I do not at present approve, but I am not sure I shall never approve them. For, having lived long, I have experienced many instances of being obliged, by better information or fuller consideration, to change my opinions even on important subjects, which I once thought right, but found to be otherwise. It is therefore that, the older I grow, the more apt I am to doubt my own judgment. . . .

In these sentiments, sir, I agree to this Constitution, with all its faults—if they are such; because I think a general government necessary for us, and there is no form of government but what may be a blessing to the people, if well administered; and I believe, farther, that this is likely to be well administered for a course of years, and can only end in despotism, as other forms have done before it, when the people shall become so corrupted as to need despotic government, being incapable of any other. I doubt, too, whether any other convention we can obtain, may be able to make a better Constitution. For, when you assemble a number of men, to have the advantage of their joint wisdom, you inevitably assemble with those men all their prejudices, their passions, their errors of opinion, their local interests, and their selfish views. From such an assembly can a perfect production be expected? It therefore astonishes me, sir, to find this system approaching so near to perfection as it does; and I think it will astonish our enemies, who are waiting with confidence to hear that our councils are confounded like those of the builders of Babel, and that our States are on the point of separation, only to meet hereafter for the purpose of cutting one another's throats.

Thus I consent, sir, to this Constitution, because I expect no better, and because I am not sure that it is not the best. The opinions I have had of its errors I sacrifice to the public good. I have never whispered a syllable of them abroad. Within these walls they were born, and here they shall die. . . . Much of the strength and efficiency of any government in procuring and securing happiness to the people, depends on opinion, on the general opinion of the goodness of the government, as well as of the wisdom and integrity of its governors. I hope, therefore, that for our own sakes, as a part of the people, and for the sake of posterity, we shall act heartily and unanimously in recommending this Constitution . . . wherever our influence may extend, and turn our future thoughts and endeavors to the means of having it well administered.

121. *Amendments, 1791–1804*

First Ten Amendments, passed by Congress, September 25, 1789; ratified by three-fourths of the states, December 15, 1794. Eleventh amendment passed by Congress, March 5, 1794; ratified January 8, 1798. Twelfth amendment passed December 12, 1803; ratified September 25, 1804.

Article I

CONGRESS shall make no law respecting an establishment of religion, or prohibiting the free exercise thereof; or abridging the freedom of speech, or of the press; or the right of the people peaceably to assemble, and to petition the government for a redress of grievances.

Article II

A well regulated militia, being necessary to the security of a free State, the right of the people to keep and bear arms, shall not be infringed.

Article III

No soldier shall, in time of peace, be quartered in any house, without the consent of the owner, nor in time of war, but in a manner to be prescribed by law.

Article IV

The right of the people to be secure in their persons, houses, papers, and effects, against unreasonable searches and seizures, shall not be violated, and no warrants shall issue, but upon probable cause, supported by oath or affirmation, and particularly describing the place to be searched, and the persons or things to be seized.

Article V

No person shall be held to answer for a capital, or otherwise infamous crime, unless on a presentment or indictment of a grand jury, except in cases arising in the land or naval forces, or in the militia, when in actual service in time of war or public danger; nor shall any person be subject for the same offense to be twice put in jeopardy of life or limb; nor shall be compelled in any criminal case to be a witness against himself, nor be deprived of life, liberty, or property, without due process of law; nor shall private property be taken for public use without just compensation.

Article VI

In all criminal prosecutions, the accused shall enjoy the right to a speedy and public trial, by an impartial jury of the State and district wherein the crime shall have been committed,which district shall have been previously ascertained by law, and to be informed of the nature and cause of the accusation; to be confronted with the witnesses against him; to have compulsory process for obtaining witnesses in his favor, and to have the assistance of counsel for his defense.

Article VII

In suits at common law, where the value in controversy shall exceed twenty dollars, the right of trial by jury shall be preserved, and no fact tried by a jury shall be otherwise reëxamined in any court of the United States, than according to the rules of the common law.

Article VIII

Excessive bail shall not be required,

nor excessive fines imposed, nor cruel and unusual punishments inflicted.

Article IX

The enumeration in the Constitution of certain rights shall not be construed to deny or disparage others retained by the people.

Article X

The powers not delegated to the United States by the Constitution, nor prohibited by it to the States, are reserved to the States respectively, or to the people.

Article XI

The judicial power of the United States shall not be construed to extend to any suit in law or equity, commenced or prosecuted against one of the United States by citizens of another State, or by citizens or subjects of any foreign State.

Article XII

The electors shall meet in their respective States, and vote by ballot for President and Vice President, one of whom, at least, shall not be an inhabitant of the same State with themselves; they shall name in their ballots the person voted for as President, and in distinct ballots, the person voted for as Vice President, and they shall make distinct lists of all persons voted for as President and of all persons voted for as Vice President, and of the number of votes for each, which lists they shall sign and certify, and transmit sealed to the seat of the government of the United States, directed to the President of the Senate;—The President of the Senate shall, in the presence of the Senate and House of Representatives, open all the certificates and the votes shall then be counted;—The person having the greatest number of votes for President, shall be the President, if such number be a majority of the whole number of electors appointed; and if no person have such majority, then from the persons having the highest numbers not exceeding three on the list of those voted for as President, the House of Representatives shall choose immediately, by ballot, the President. But in choosing the President, the votes shall be taken by States, the representation from each State having one vote; a quorum for this purpose shall consist of a member or members from two-thirds of the States, and a majority of all the States shall be necessary to a choice. And if the House of Representatives shall not choose a President whenever the right of choice shall devolve upon them, before the fourth day of March next following, then the Vice President shall act as President, as in the case of the death or other constitutional disability of the President. The person having the greatest number of votes as Vice President shall be the Vice President, if such number be a majority of the whole number of electors appointed, and if no person have a majority, then from the two highest numbers on the list, the Senate shall choose the Vice President; a quorum for the purpose shall consist of two-thirds of the whole number of Senators, and a majority of the whole number shall be necessary to a choice. But no person constitutionally ineligible to the office of President shall be eligible to that of Vice President of the United States.

122. *Marbury* v. *Madison, 1803*

Opinion of Chief Justice John Marshall, 1 Cranch, 173–80.

THE ACT to establish the judicial courts of the United States authorizes the Supreme Court "to issue writs of mandamus, in cases warranted by the principles and usages of law, to any courts appointed, or persons holding office, under the authority of the United States."

The Secretary of State, being a person holding an office under the authority of the United States is precisely within the letter of the description; and if this court is not authorized to issue a writ of mandamus to such an officer, it must be because the law is unconstitutional, and therefore absolutely incapable of conferring the authority and assigning the duties which its words purport to confer and assign.

The Constitution vests the whole judicial power of the United States in one Supreme Court, and such inferior courts as Congress shall, from time to time, ordain and establish. This power is expressly extended to all cases arising under the laws of the United States; and consequently, in some form, may be exercised over the present case; because the right claimed is given by a law of the United States.

In the distribution of this power it is declared, that "the Supreme Court shall have original jurisdiction in all cases affecting ambassadors, other public ministers and consuls, and those in which a state shall be a party. In all other cases, the Supreme Court shall have appellate jurisdiction.". . .

The authority, therefore, given to the Supreme Court, by the act establishing the judicial courts of the United States, to issue writs of mandamus to public officers, appears not to be warranted by the Constitution; and it becomes necessary to inquire whether a jurisdiction so conferred can be exercised.

The question whether an act repugnant to the Constitution can become the law of the land, is a question deeply interesting to the United States; but, happily not of an intricacy proportioned to its interest. It seems only necessary to recognize certain principles supposed to have been long and well established, to decide it.

That the people have an original right

to establish for their future government such principles as, in their opinion, shall most conduce to their own happiness, is the basis on which the whole American fabric has been erected. The exercise of this original right is a very great exertion, nor can it nor ought it to be frequently repeated. The principles therefore so established are deemed fundamental. And as the authority from which they proceed is supreme and can seldom act, they are designed to be permanent.

This original and supreme will organizes the government, and assigns to different departments their respective powers. It may either stop here or establish certain limits not to be transcended by those departments.

The government of the United States is of the latter description. The powers of the legislature are defined and limited; and that those limits may not be mistaken or forgotten, the Constitution is written. To what purpose are powers limited, and to what purpose is that limitation committed to writing, if these limits may, at any time, be passed by those intended to be restrained? The distinction between a government with limited and unlimited powers is abolished if those limits do not confine the persons on whom they are imposed and if acts prohibited and acts allowed are of equal obligation. It is a proposition too plain to be contested, that the Constitution controls any legislative act repugnant to it; or, that the legislature may alter the Constitution by an ordinary act.

Between these alternatives there is no middle ground. The Constitution is either a superior paramount law, unchangeable by ordinary means, or it is on a level with ordinary legislative acts, and, like other acts, is alterable when the legislature shall please to alter it.

If the former part of the alternative be true, then a legislative act contrary to the Constitution is not law; if the latter part be true, then written constitutions are absurd attempts, on the part of the people, to limit a power in its own nature illimitable.

Certainly all those who have framed written constitutions contemplate them as forming the fundamental and paramount law of the nation, and consequently the theory of every such government must be that an act of the legislature repugnant to the constitution is void.

This theory is essentially attached to a written constitution, and is consequently to be considered, by this court, as one of the fundamental principles of our society. It is not, therefore, to be lost sight of in the further consideration of this subject.

If an act of the legislature repugnant to the constitution is void, does it, notwithstanding its invalidity, bind the courts and oblige them to give it effect? Or, in other words, though it be not law, does it constitute a rule as operative as if it was a law? This would be to overthrow in fact what was established in theory, and would seem, at first view, an absurdity too gross to be insisted on. It shall, however, receive a more attentive consideration.

It is emphatically the province and duty of the judicial department to say what the law is. Those who apply the rule to particular cases must of necessity expound and interpret that rule. If two laws conflict with each other, the courts must decide on the operation of each.

So if a law be in opposition to the Constitution; if both the law and the Constitution apply to a particular case, so that the court must either decide that case conformably to the law, disregarding the Constitution, or conformably to the Constitution, disregarding the law, the court must determine which of these conflicting rules governs the case. This is of the very essence of judicial duty.

If, then, the courts are to regard the Constitution, and the Constitution is superior to any ordinary act of the legislature, the Constitution, and not such ordinary act, must govern the case to which they both apply. . . .

The judicial power of the United States is extended to all cases arising under the Constitution. Could it be the intention of those who gave this power to say that in using it the Constitution should not be looked into? That a case arising under the Constitution should be decided without examining the instrument under which it arises? This is too extravagant to be maintained.

In some cases, then, the Constitution must be looked into by the judges. And if they can open it at all, what part of it are they forbidden to read or to obey?

There are many other parts of the Constitution which serve to illustrate this subject.

It is declared that "no tax or duty shall be laid on articles exported from any state." Suppose a duty on the export of cotton, of tobacco, or of flour, and a suit instituted to recover it, ought judgment to be rendered in such a case? Ought the judges to close their eyes on the Constitution, and only see the law?

The Constitution declares "that no bill of attainder or *ex post facto* law shall be passed." If, however, such a bill should be passed, and a person should be prosecuted under it, must the court condemn to death those victims whom the Constitution endeavors to preserve?

"No person," says the Constitution, "shall be convicted of treason unless on the testimony of two witnesses to the same overt act, or on confession in open court." Here the language of the Constitution is addressed especially to the courts. It prescribes, directly for them, a rule of evidence not to be departed from. If the legislature should change that rule, and declare one witness, or a confession out of court, sufficient for conviction, must the constitutional principle yield to the legislative act?

From these, and many other selections which might be made, it is apparent that the framers of the Constitution contemplated that instrument as a rule for the government of courts, as well as of the legislature. Why otherwise does it direct the judges to take an oath to support it? This oath certainly applies in an especial manner to their conduct in their official character. . . .

The oath of office, too, imposed by the legislature, is completely demonstrative of the legislative opinion on this subject. It is in these words: "I do solemnly swear that I will administer justice without respect to persons, and do equal right to the poor and to the rich; and that I will faithfully and impartially discharge all the duties incumbent on me as————, according to the best of my abilities and understanding, agreeably to the Constitution and laws of the United States." Why does a judge swear to discharge his duties agreeably to the Constitution of the United States, if that Constitution forms no rule for his government?—if it is closed upon him, and cannot be inspected by him? . . .

It is also not entirely unworthy of observation, that in declaring what shall be the supreme law of the land, the Constitution itself is first mentioned, and not the laws of the United States generally, but those only which shall be made in pursuance of the Constitution, have that rank.

Thus, the particular phraseology of the Constitution of the United States confirms and strengthens the principle, supposed to be essential to all written constitutions, that a law repugnant to the Constitution is void, and that courts, as well as other departments, are bound by that instrument. [Mandamus denied.]

XVI 🦋 *The United States and Europe's Wars*

INDEPENDENCE compelled the United States to establish diplomatic relations with the nations of Europe and Africa. This problem was difficult enough in itself, given the youth of the country and the inexperience of its statesmen. But it was enormously complicated by the fact that for almost a quarter of a century after 1790 Europe was involved in a great series of wars, with France and England the chief antagonists.

With the coming of peace in 1783 the United States hoped to establish friendly relations and favorable commercial agreements with the leading nations of Europe (No. 123). The Anglo-French war destroyed that hope; for it seemed to put upon the Americans the burden of a choice between the former mother country and the former ally. President Washington's initial response was a proclamation of neutrality (No. 124); and he attempted, throughout his administration, to hold to that policy (No. 125).

But potent forces pulled the government in opposing directions. Some Americans viewed the French Revolution as a further stage in a process that carried the ideals of the American Revolution to the Old World; and they conceived it their duty to assist (No. 126). Other groups were antagonized by the radical character of the French Revolution and desired to re-establish commercial connections with England. Jay's Treaty which envisaged the restoration of close ties with Great Britain evoked a storm of controversy and divided the nation into opposing parties (No. 127). A well-known editor, himself a partisan of the English connection, expressed the attitude that made this a party question (No. 128).

There were also problems in the West. Spain controlled the mouth of the Mississippi at New Orleans, a port of vital interest to all shippers in the Valley. Pinckney's treaty put off the necessity for immediate action (No. 129). But the acquisition of Louisiana by France again threatened American interests and led to the purchase of the whole territory by the United States (No. 130).

The Anglo-French war had no such happy outcome for the United States. Neutral trading was profitable, but it embroiled the nation in conflicts with both England and France (No. 131). An embargo attempted to remove the complaints by eliminating their causes (No. 132). But these issues soon became enmeshed with those of expansive settlement; the sentiment for war mounted not only in order to protect American neutral rights, but also in order to gain territory. An opponent of the war, in 1812, set forth the motives thus involved (No. 133). The war brought no significant gains to the United States, but it embodied and stimulated nationalistic sentiments.

123. *Treaties of Commerce, 1784*

Instructions to the American Ministers Appointed to Negotiate Treaties of Commerce, May 7, 1784. From the secret journals of Congress, quoted in Francis Wharton, *Revolutionary Diplomatic Correspondence of the United States* (Washington, 1889), VI, 802–4.

RESOLVED, That in the formation of these treaties the following points be carefully stipulated:

1. That each party shall have a right to carry their own produce, manufactures, and merchandise, in their own bottoms to the ports of the other, and thence the produce and merchandise of the other, paying, in both cases, such duties only as are paid by the most favored nation. . . .

2. That with the nations holding territorial possessions in America, a direct and similar intercourse be admitted between the United States and such possessions; or if this cannot be obtained, then a direct and similar intercourse between the United States and certain free ports within such possessions; that if this neither can be obtained, permission be stipulated to bring from such possessions, in their own bottoms, the produce and merchandise thereof to their states directly; and for these states to carry in their own bottoms their produce and merchandise to such possessions directly.

3. That these United States be considered in all such treaties, and in every case arising under them, as one nation, upon the principles of the federal constitution.

124. *Neutrality Proclamation, 1793*

By President George Washington, April 22, 1793, Richardson, *Messages and Papers*, I, 156.

WHEREAS it appears that a state of war exists between Austria, Prussia, Sardinia, Great Britain, and the United Netherlands on the one part and France on the other, and the duty and interest of the United States require that they should with sincerity and good faith adopt and pursue a conduct friendly and impartial toward the belligerent powers:

I have therefore thought fit . . . to declare the disposition of the United States to observe the conduct aforesaid toward those powers respectively, and to exhort and warn the citizens of the United States carefully to avoid all acts and proceedings whatsoever which may in any manner tend to contravene such disposition.

And I do hereby also make known that whatsoever of the citizens of the United States shall render himself liable to punishment or forfeiture under the law of nations by committing, aiding, or abetting hostilities against any of the said powers, or by carrying to any of them those articles which are deemed contraband by the modern usage of nations, will not receive the protection of the United States against such punishment or forfeiture; and further, that I have given instructions to those officers to whom it belongs to cause prosecutions to be instituted against all persons who shall, within the cognizance of the courts of the United States, violate the law of nations with respect to the powers at war, or any of them.

125. *Washington's Farewell Address, 1796*

Richardson, *Messages and Papers*, I, 221–3.

OBSERVE good faith and justice toward all nations. Cultivate peace and harmony with all. Religion and morality enjoin this conduct. And can it be that good policy does not equally enjoin it? It will be worthy of a free, enlightened, and at no distant period a great nation to give to mankind the magnanimous and too novel example of a people always guided by an exalted justice and benevolence. Who can doubt that in the course of time and things the fruits of such a plan would richly repay any temporary advantages which might be lost by a steady adherence to it? . . .

In the execution of such a plan nothing is more essential than that permanent, inveterate antipathies against particular nations and passionate attachments for others should be excluded, and that in place of them just and amicable feelings toward all should be cultivated. The nation which indulges toward another an habitual hatred or an habitual fondness is in some degree a slave. It is a slave to its animosity or to its affection, either of which is sufficient to lead it astray from its duty and its interest. Antipathy in one nation against another disposes each more readily to offer insult and injury, to lay hold of slight causes of umbrage, and to be haughty and intractable when accidental or trifling occasions of dispute occur.

Hence frequent collisions, obstinate, envenomed, and bloody contests. The nation prompted by ill will and resentment sometimes impels to war the government contrary to the best calculations of policy. The government sometimes participates in the national propensity, and adopts through passion what reason would reject. At other times it makes the animosity of the nation subservient to projects of hostility, instigated by pride, ambition, and other sinister and pernicious motives. The peace often, sometimes perhaps the liberty, of nations has been the victim.

So, likewise, a passionate attachment of one nation for another produces a variety of evils. Sympathy for the favorite nation, facilitating the illusion of an imaginary common interest in cases where no real common interest exists, and infusing into one the enmities of the other, betrays the former into a participation in the quarrels and wars of the latter without adequate inducement or justification. It leads also to concessions to the favorite nation of privileges denied to others, which is apt doubly to injure the nation making the concessions by unnecessarily parting with what ought to have been retained, and by exciting jealousy, ill will, and a disposition to retaliate in the parties from whom equal privileges are withheld; and it gives to ambitious, corrupted, or deluded citizens (who devote themselves to the favorite nation) facility to betray or sacrifice the interests of their own country without odium, sometimes even with popularity. . . .

As avenues to foreign influence in innumerable ways, such attachments are particularly alarming to the truly enlightened and independent patriot. How many opportunities do they afford to tamper with domestic factions, to practice the arts of seduction, to mislead public opinion, to influence or awe the public councils! Such an attachment of a small or weak toward a great and powerful nation dooms the former to be the satellite of the latter. Against the insidious wiles of foreign influence (I conjure you to believe me, fellow-citizens) the jealousy of a free people ought to be constantly awake, since history and experience prove that foreign influence is one of the most baneful foes of republican government. But that jealousy, to be useful, must be impartial, else it becomes the instrument of the very influence to be avoided, instead of a defense against it. . . .

The great rule of conduct for us in regard to foreign nations is, in extending our commercial relations to have with them as little political connection as possible. So far as we have already formed engagements let them be fulfilled with perfect good faith. Here let us stop.

Europe has a set of primary interests which to us have none or a very remote relation. Hence she must be engaged in frequent controversies, the causes of which are essentially foreign to our concerns. Hence, therefore, it must be unwise in us to implicate ourselves by artificial ties in the ordinary vicissitudes of her politics or the ordinary combinations and collisions of her friendships or enmities.

Our detached and distant situation invites and enables us to pursue a different course. If we remain one people, under an efficient government, the period is not far off when we may defy material injury from external annoyance; when we may take such an attitude as will cause the neutrality we may at any time resolve upon to be scrupulously respected; when belligerent nations, under the impossibility of making acquisitions upon us, will not lightly hazard the giving us provocation; when we may choose peace or war, as our interest, guided by justice, shall counsel.

Why forego the advantages of so peculiar a situation? Why quit our own to stand upon foreign ground? Why, by interweaving our destiny with that of any part of Europe, entangle our peace and prosperity in the toils of European ambition, rivalship, interest, humor, or caprice?

It is our true policy to steer clear of permanent alliances with any portion of the foreign world, so far, I mean, as we are now at liberty to do it; for let me not be understood as capable of patronizing infidelity to existing engagements. I hold the maxim no less applicable to public than to private affairs that honesty is always the best policy. I repeat, therefore, let those engagements be observed in their genuine sense. But in my opinion it is unnecessary and would be unwise to extend them.

126. *Ode to the Rights of Man, 1793*

Philip Freneau, "Ode," at the feast in honor of Citizen Genêt, June 1, 1793, *Poems* (F. L. Pattee, ed., Princeton, 1902–07), III, 91–101.

GOD save the Rights of man!
Give us a heart to scan
Blessings so dear:
Let them be spread around
Wherever man is found,
And with the welcome sound
Ravish his ear.

Let us with France agree,
And bid the world be free,
While tyrants fall!
Let the rude savage host
Of their vast numbers boast—
Freedom's almighty trust
Laughs at them all! . . .

No more is valour's flame
Devoted to a name,
Taught to adore—
Soldiers of Liberty
Disdain to bow the knee,
But teach Equality
To every shore.

The world at last will join
To aid thy grand design,
Dear Liberty!
To Russia's frozen lands
The generous flame expands:
On Afric's burning sands
Shall man be free!

127. Jay's Treaty, 1794

Concluded November 19, 1794; proclaimed February 29, 1796. Text from Malloy, *Treaties*, I, 590–605.

I. THERE shall be a firm, inviolable and universal peace, and a true and sincere friendship between His Britannic Majesty ... and the United States of America. ...

II. His Majesty will withdraw all his troops and garrisons from all posts and places within the boundary lines assigned by the treaty of peace to the United States. This evacuation shall take place on or before [June 1, 1796]. ... All settlers and traders, within the precincts or jurisdiction of the said posts, shall continue to enjoy, unmolested, all their property of every kind, and shall be protected therein. They shall be at full liberty to remain there, or to remove with all or any part of their effects; and it shall also be free to them to sell their lands, houses, or effects, or to retain the property thereof, at their discretion; such of them as shall continue to reside within the said boundary lines, shall not be compelled to become citizens of the United States, or to take any oath of allegiance to the government thereof. ...

III. It is agreed that it shall at all times be free to His Majesty's subjects, and to the citizens of the United States, and also to the Indians dwelling on either side of the said boundary line, freely to pass and repass by land or inland navigation, into the respective territories and countries of the two parties, on the continent of America (the country within the limits of the Hudson's Bay Company only excepted) and to navigate all the lakes, rivers and waters thereof, and freely to carry on trade and commerce with each other. ... The river Mississippi shall, however, according to the treaty of peace, be entirely open to both parties. ...

VI. Whereas it is alleged by divers British merchants and others His Majesty's subjects, that debts, to a considerable amount, which were bona fide contracted before the peace, still remain owing to them by citizens or inhabitants of the United States, and that by the operation of various lawful impediments since the peace, not only the full recovery of the said debts has been delayed, but also the value and security thereof have been, in several instances, impaired and lessened, so that by the ordinary course of judicial proceedings, the British creditors cannot now obtain ... adequate compensation for the losses and damages which they have thereby sustained. It is agreed, that in all such cases, where full compensation for such losses and damages cannot, for whatever reason, be actually obtained ... by the said creditors in the ordinary course of justice, the United States will make full and complete compensation for the same to the said creditors. ...

VII. Whereas complaints have been made by divers merchants and others, citizens of the United States, that during the course of the war in which His Majesty is now engaged, they have sustained considerable losses and damage, by reason of irregular or illegal captures or condemnations of their vessels and other property, under color of authority or commissions from His Majesty, and that from various circumstances belonging to the said cases, adequate compensation for the losses and damages so sustained cannot now be actually obtained ... by the ordinary course of judicial proceedings; it is agreed, that in all such cases, ... full and complete compensation for the same will be made by the British government to the said complainants. ...

X. Neither the debts due from individuals of the one nation to individuals of the other, nor shares, nor monies which they may have in the public funds, or in the public or private banks, shall ever in any event of war or national differences be sequestered or confiscated. . . .

XI. It is agreed between His Majesty and the United States of America, that there shall be a reciprocal and entirely perfect liberty of navigation and commerce between their respective people, in the manner, under the limitations and on the conditions specified in the following articles.

XII. His Majesty consents that it shall and may be lawful, during the time hereinafter limited, for the citizens of the United States to carry to any of His Majesty's islands . . . in the West Indies from the United States, in their own vessels, not being above the burthen of seventy tons, any goods or merchandises, being of the growth, manufacture or produce of the said States, which it is . . . lawful to carry to the said islands . . . from the said States in British vessels. . . .

And His Majesty also consents that it shall be lawful for the said American citizens to purchase, load and carry away . . . from the said islands . . . all such articles . . . as may now by law be carried from thence to the said States in British vessels. . . .

Provided always, that the said American vessels do carry and land their cargoes in the United States only, it being expressly agreed . . . that . . . the United States will prohibit . . . the carrying any molasses, sugar, coffee, cocoa, or cotton in American vessels, either from His Majesty's islands or from the United States to any part of the world except the United States. . . . Provided also, that it shall . . . be lawful, during the same period, for British vessels to import from the said islands into the United States, and to export from the United States to the said islands all articles whatever, being of the growth . . . of the said islands or of the United States respectively. . . . [This article sus-

pended as a result of amendment in the Senate.]

XIII. His Majesty consents that the vessels belonging to the citizens of the United States of America, shall be admitted and hospitably received, in all the seaports and harbors of the British territories in the East Indies. And that the citizens of the said United States, may freely carry on a trade between the said territories and the said United States, in all articles of which the importation or exportation . . . shall not be entirely prohibited. . . .

XIV. There shall be between all the dominions of His Majesty in Europe and the territories of the United States, a reciprocal and perfect liberty of commerce and navigation. The people and inhabitants of the two countries respectively, shall have liberty freely and securely, and without hindrance and molestation, to come with their ships and cargoes to the lands, countries, cities, ports, places and rivers, within the dominions and territories aforesaid, to enter into the same, to resort there, and to remain and reside there, without any limitation of time. Also to hire and possess houses and warehouses for the purposes of their commerce, and generally the merchants and traders on each side, shall enjoy the most complete protection and security for their commerce; but subject always as to what respects this article to the laws and statutes of the two countries respectively. . . .

XVII. It is agreed, that in all cases where vessels shall be captured or detained on just suspicion of having on board enemy's property, or of carrying to the enemy any of the articles which are contraband of war; the said vessel shall be brought to the nearest or most convenient port; and if any property of an enemy should be found on board such vessel, that part only which belongs to the enemy shall be made prize, and the vessel shall be at liberty to proceed with the remainder without any impediment. . . .

XXII. It is expressly stipulated, that neither of the said contracting parties will order or authorize any acts of reprisal against the other, on complaints of injuries or damages, until the said party shall first have presented to the other a statement thereof, verified by competent proof and evidence, and demanded justice and satisfaction, and the same shall either have been refused or unreasonably delayed. . . .

XXVI. If at any time a rupture should take place, (which God forbid) between His Majesty and the United States, [the] merchants and others of each of the two nations, residing in the dominions of the other, shall have the privilege of remaining and continuing their trade, so long as they behave peaceably, and commit no offense against the laws; and in case their conduct should render them suspected, and the respective governments should think proper to order them to remove, the term of twelve months from the publication of the order shall be allowed them for that purpose, to remove with their families, effects and property; but this favor shall not be extended to those who shall act contrary to the established laws; . . .

XXVIII. It is agreed, that the first ten articles of this treaty shall be permanent, and that the subsequent articles, except the twelfth, shall be limited in their duration to twelve years.

128. *Foreign Affairs and Politics, 1795–97*

Noah Webster to Oliver Woolcott, July 30, 1795; to "the Public," March 4, 1797; and to Rufus King, June 1, 1797, in Noah Webster, *Letters*. H. R. Warfel, ed. (New York, 1953), 129–30, 145–6, 156–9.

I AM of the opinion that the [Jay] Treaty, as modified by the Senate, makes no sacrifices which are dishonorable to us as a nation and none which are very prejudicial to the United States. The objections raised against it are, many of them at least, totally unfounded. I believe, in the present state of America, it would be good policy to carry it into effect as a temporary agreement. . . .

The Northern states will, if left to themselves, acquiesce in the ratification of the Treaty, if that should be or is the determination of the President. The clubs are not yet strong enough to even threaten any general disorder. At the same time, these societies are secretly extending their force, and in my apprehension some decisive legislative remedy must be speedily applied to extirpate the evil, or we must ultimately be governed by irregular town meetings. In this thing much, however, depends on the war in Europe.

But in the Southern states the danger appears to be more real. The circumstances which led and still lead the people of those states to a close connection with French politics, you very well know. . . . The opposition to our government, then, is general; and to me it bodes an ultimate separation between us and them.

The peace of our country stands almost committed in either event. A rejection of the Treaty leaves all the causes of hostility unadjusted, with the addition of double exasperation of temper. A ratification threatens evil commotions, at least in the Southern states. A rejection sacrifices Mr. [John] Jay and perhaps many of his friends, and ratification threatens the popularity of the President, whose personal influence is now more essential than ever to our Union. . . .

When the States General first assembled in France, for the dignified and glorious object of reforming the abuses in the French government and raising the people from their degraded state of vassalage to the rank of freemen, I exulted in the joyful event. . . . My faith in the goodness of the cause and the purity of the intentions of the reformers continued unabated, till . . . the impious project of attacking the independence of other nations began to unfold itself in France. The declaration of the Convention in 1791, annexing Avignon to France without the consent of the Pope, and the conquest of Savoy and attack upon Geneva and the Netherlands in 1792, left no room to doubt the ambitious views of the republicans. But the decree of November 19, 1792, was a formal and solemn avowal of the most daring projects of throwing the world into confusion that have been exhibited since the incursions of the Goths and Vandals.

Still, my belief in the utility of the revolution furnished apologies for the violent measures of the French; nor could I consent to believe the revolutionists would carry into effect their unjustifiable views, especially towards their allies and free countries. But the mission of Mr. Genêt to the United States compelled me to abandon my faith. The bold and insulting attacks of that minister on the independence and government of the United States left no room to question that the insidious views of the French republicans extended to gain a controlling influence over all nations and countries. . . . The most effectual means of carrying their point in this country was the establishment of popular clubs, which were gradually and secretly to acquire numbers and strength till they were able to bid defiance to the constitutional authorities. . . .

I saw in these clubs . . . a league of societies, disciplined to the orders of chiefs, whose views were concealed, even from the members themselves, and which must be crushed in its infancy or it would certainly crush the government. Fortunately, the dispersed situation of the American people and their good sense defeated this vast and profound plan of the enemy. . . . An explosion in the western country alarmed our unsuspecting yeomanry, unfolded to them the insidious wiles of our

secret foes, and the societies, to use the energetic language of an eloquent statesman, have been "frowned" into public contempt. . . .

If we look to the projects of the French, we shall see not only the policy but the necessity of an union between Great Britain and the United States for the protection of trade. The present war . . . is now prolonged by the French on the maxim . . . *English commerce must be annihilated.* If France should persist in this project, her extent, population, and means may, under the operation of her military republic, enable her at some future time to go far in accomplishing her object. . . .

Great Britain must seek some powerful aid. Where is it to be found? . . . There is . . . no choice for Great Britain. The United States form the only commercial power on earth capable of effectually seconding the naval force of Great Britain, and of protecting the trade of the Atlantic.

It is remarkable that the Americans, next to the British, make the best seamen in the world; and with the same system of naval tactics, whenever they become necessary for our defense, the Americans will be second to no people in their skill and bravery. . . . In this respect, Great Britain, as a naval power, will find the United States her most safe and useful ally. . . .

France hereafter may become formidable to all the commercial nations of Europe. . . . To oppose this formidable nation and her gigantic strength, a new and formidable power must be created, or Europe and the trade of the Atlantic will be at her mercy. Where shall this power arise? . . .

The United States, in the course of things, will be able to resist all the schemes of France. But time is requisite. At present we want the aid of the British navy; and I am firmly persuaded that the ultimate existence of Great Britain as a commanding power in Europe depends on the commercial and finally on the naval aid of the United States. . . .

The first, and perhaps the only, step at present necessary is for Great Britain to relax her rules in regard to neutral vessels and give American bottoms all the freedom and privileges which are guaranteed by what is called the modern law of nations. In short, to let American vessels go freely and unmolested to her enemies without seizing, searching, and confiscation. The advantages derived to nations at war from the license of taking a little property at sea out of neutral vessels are so trivial that I could never see the policy of it. The practice neither adds to their own strength nor weakens that of the enemy. . . . At the same time it never fails to irritate neutrals and multiply the enemies of the powers at war. The friendship of commercial nations is of infinitely more consequence to nations at war than the pittance of property taken by individuals from neutral vessels. . . .

In short, while the United States remain neutral, all that Great Britain has to do to reap the utmost advantage from us is to desist from vexing our trade and to protect our vessels and seamen on the high seas as she does her own. By such protection, Great Britain immediately derives a benefit to herself by saving the property of her best customers and thus enriching herself, and she will ultimately reap a still richer harvest from this protection in the attachment and the protection of the Americans, whose aid will, in all human probability, be highly useful to her, if not essential to her existence.

129. *Pinckney's Treaty, 1795*

Concluded, November 27, 1795; proclaimed, August 2, 1796. Text from Malloy, *Treaties*, II, 1640–9.

His Catholic Majesty and the United States of America, desiring to consolidate, on a permanent basis, the friendship . . . between the two parties, have determined to establish, by a convention, several points, the settlement whereof will be . . . of general advantage . . . to both nations. . . .

To prevent all disputes on the subject of the boundaries . . . it is hereby declared and agreed as follows . . . : The southern boundary of the United States . . . shall be designated by a line beginning on the River Mississippi, at the . . . thirty-first degree of latitude north . . . which from thence shall be drawn due east to the middle of the River Apalachicola . . . , thence along the middle thereof to its junction with the Flint; thence straight to the head of St. Mary's River, and thence down the middle thereof to the Atlantic Ocean. . . .

The two high contracting parties shall . . . maintain peace and harmony among the several Indian nations who inhabit the country adjacent to the . . . boundaries of the two Floridas. . . .

It shall be lawful for . . . the subjects of His Catholic Majesty, and the . . . inhabitants of the said United States, to sail with their ships . . . from any port to the places of those who now are . . . at enmity with His Catholic Majesty or the United States. . . . And it is hereby stipulated that free ships shall also give freedom to goods, and that everything shall be deemed free . . . on board the ships belonging to the subjects of either of the contracting parties, although the whole lading, or any part thereof, should appertain to the enemies of either; contraband goods being always excepted. . . .

The two high contracting parties, hoping that the . . . friendship which happily reigns between them will be further increased by this treaty . . . will in future give to their mutual commerce all the . . . favor which the advantage of both countries may require. . . . His Catholic Majesty will permit the citizens of the United States, for the space of three years from this time, to deposit their merchandise and effects in the port of New Orleans, and to export them from thence without paying any other duty than a fair price for the hire of the stores; and His Majesty promises either to continue this permission, if he finds during that time that it is not prejudicial to the interests of Spain, or if he should not agree to continue it there, he will assign to them on another part of the banks of the Mississippi an equivalent establishment.

130. *Louisiana Purchase, 1803*

President Thomas Jefferson to Congress, October 17, 1803, in Richardson, *Messages and Papers,* I, 358, 360–2.

CONGRESS witnessed, at their late session, the extraordinary agitation produced in the public mind by the suspension of our right of deposit at the port of New Orleans, no assignment of another place having been made according to treaty. They were sensible that the continuance of that privation would be more injurious to our nation than any consequences which could flow from any mode of redress, but reposing just confidence in the good faith of the government whose officer had committed the wrong, friendly and reasonable representations were resorted to, and the right of deposit was restored.

Previous, however, to this period, we had not been unaware of the danger to which our peace would be perpetually exposed whilst so important a key to the commerce of the western country remained under foreign power. . . . Propositions had, therefore, been authorized for obtaining, on fair conditions, the sovereignty of New Orleans, and of other possessions in that quarter interesting to our quiet, to such extent as was deemed practicable. . . . The enlightened government of France saw, with just discernment, the importance to both nations of such liberal arrangements as might best and permanently promote the peace, friendship, and interests of both; and the property and sovereignty of all Louisiana, which had been restored to them, have on certain conditions been transferred to the United States by instruments bearing date the 30th of April last. When these shall have received the con-

stitutional sanction of the Senate, they will without delay be communicated to the representatives also, for the exercise of their functions, as to those conditions which are within the powers vested by the Constitution in Congress. Whilst the property and sovereignty of the Mississippi and its waters secure an independent outlet for the produce of the Western states, and an uncontrolled navigation through their whole course, free from collision with other powers and the dangers to our peace from that source, the fertility of the country, its climate and extent, promise in due season important aids to our treasury, an ample provision for our posterity, and a widespread [field] for the blessings of freedom and equal laws. . . .

Should the acquisition of Louisiana be constitutionally confirmed and carried into effect, a sum of nearly thirteen millions of dollars will then be added to our public debt, most of which is payable after fifteen years; before which term the present existing debts will all be discharged by the established operation of the sinking fund. When we contemplate the ordinary annual augmentation of imposts from increasing population and wealth, the augmentation of the same revenue by its extension to the new acquisition, and the economies which may still be introduced into our public expenditures, I cannot but hope that Congress in reviewing their resources will find means to meet the intermediate interest of this additional debt without recurring to new taxes, and applying to this object only the ordinary progression of our revenue....

We have seen with sincere concern the flames of war lighted up again in Europe, and nations with which we have the most friendly and useful relations engaged in mutual destruction. While we regret the miseries in which we see others involved let us bow with gratitude to that kind Providence which, inspiring with wisdom and moderation our late legislative councils while placed under the urgency of the greatest wrongs, guarded us from hastily entering into the sanguinary contest, and left us only to look on and to pity its ravages.... Separated by a wide ocean from the nations of Europe, and from the political interests which entangle them together, with productions and wants which render our commerce and friendship useful to them and theirs to us, it cannot be the interest of any to assail us, nor ours to disturb them. We should be most unwise, indeed, were we to cast away the singular blessings of the position in which nature has placed us, the opportunity she has endowed us with of pursuing, at a distance from foreign contentions, the paths of industry, peace, and happiness; of cultivating general friendship, and of bringing collisions of interest to the umpirage of reason rather than of force.

131. *A Review of Impediments to Neutral Trade,* 1808

Report of a Senate Committee, April 16, 1808, *American State Papers. Foreign Relations* (Washington, 1832), III, 220.

ON A review of the several orders, decrees, and decisions of Great Britain and France, within the period of the existing war, it appears that ... various and heavy injuries have been committed against the neutral commerce and navigation of the United States under the following heads:

1st. The British order of June, 1803, unlawfully restricting the trade of the United States with a certain portion of the unblockaded ports of her enemies, and condemning vessels with innocent cargoes, on a return from ports where they had deposited contraband articles.

2d. The capture and condemnation, in the British courts of admiralty, of American property, on a pretended principle, debarring neutral nations from a trade with the enemies of Great Britain interdicted in time of peace. The injuries suffered by the citizens of the United States, on this head, arose, not from any public order of the British council, but from a variation in the principle upon which the courts of admiralty pronounced their decisions....

3d. Blockades notified to the minister of the United States at London, and thence made a ground of capture against the trade of the United States, in entire disregard of the law of nations, and even of the definition of legal blockades, laid down by the British Government itself....

4th. To these injuries, immediately authorized by the British Government, might be added other spurious blockades by British naval commanders, particularly that of the Island of Curaçao, which, for a very considerable period, was made a pretext for very extensive spoliations on the commerce of the United States.

5th. The British proclamation of October last, which makes it the duty of the British officers to impress from American merchant vessels all such of their crews as might be taken or mistaken for British subjects; those officers being the sole and absolute judges in the case.

For the decrees and acts of the French Government violating the maritime law of nations, in respect to the United States, the committee refers to the instances contained in the report of the Secretary of

State, January 25, 1806, to the Senate, in one of which, viz: a decree of the French General Ferrand, at St. Domingo, are regulations sensibly affecting the neutral and commercial rights of the United States.

The French act, next in order of time, is the decree of November 21, 1806, declaring the British isles in a state of blockade, and professing to be a retaliation on antecedent proceedings of Great Britain, violating the law of nations.

This decree was followed, first, by the British order of January, 1807, professing to be a retaliation on that decree, and subjecting to capture the trade of the United States, from the port of one belligerent to a port of another; and secondly, by the orders of November last, professing to be a further retaliation on the same decree, and prohibiting the commerce of neutrals with the enemies of Great Britain, as explained in the aforesaid letter of Mr. Erskine.

These last British orders again have been followed by the French decree of December 17, purporting to be a retaliation on the said orders, and to be put in force against the commerce of the United States. . . .

The committee forbear to enter into a comparative view of these proceedings of the different belligerent powers, deeming it sufficient to present the materials from which it may be formed. They think it their duty, nevertheless, to offer the following remarks, suggested by a collective view of the whole:

The injury and dangers resulting to the commerce of the United States from the course and increase of these belligerent measures, and from similar ones adopted by other nations, were such as first to induce the more circumspect of our merchants and ship-owners no longer to commit their property to the high seas, and at length to impose on Congress the indispensable duty of interposing some legislative provision for such an unexampled state of things.

Among other expedients, out of which a choice was to be made, may be reckoned: 1st. a protection of commerce by ships of war; 2d. a protection of it by self-armed vessels; 3d. a war of offense as well as of defense; 4th. a general suspension of foreign commerce; 5th. an embargo on our vessels, mariners, and merchandise.

132. *The Embargo, 1807*

Act of December 22, 1807, 10 Congress, 1 Session. Text in *Annals of Congress Debates and Proceedings in the Congress of the United States* (Washington, 1852), XVIII, appendix, 2814–15.

BE IT enacted . . . that an embargo be, and hereby is, laid on all ships and vessels in the ports and places within the limits or jurisdiction of the United States, cleared or not cleared, bound to any foreign port or place; and that no clearance be furnished to any ship or vessel bound to such foreign port or place, except vessels under the immediate direction of the President of the United States; and that the President be authorized to give such instructions to the officers of the revenue, and of the Navy and revenue cutters of the

United States, as shall appear best adapted for carrying the same into full effect. . . .

And be it further enacted, that, during the continuance of this act, no registered, or sea-letter vessel, having on board goods, wares, and merchandise, shall be allowed to depart from one port of the United States to any other within the same, unless the master, owner, consignee, or factor of such vessel shall first give bond, with one or more sureties, to the collector of the district from which she is bound to depart, in a sum of double the value of the vessel and cargo, that the said goods, wares, or merchandise, shall be relanded in some port of the United States, dangers of the sea excepted; which bond, and also a certificate from the collector where the same may be relanded, shall by the collector, respectively, be transmitted to the Secretary of the Treasury. All armed vessels possessing public commissions from any foreign power, are not to be considered as liable to the embargo laid by this act.

133. *The War Hawks Attacked, 1811*

Speech of John Randolph in the House of Representatives, December 10, 1811, 12 Congress, 1 Session, *Annals*, XXIII, 446–7.

HE COULD but smile at the liberality of the gentleman, in giving Canada to New York, in order to strengthen the Northern balance of power, while at the same time he forewarned her that the Western scale must preponderate.... He could almost fancy that he saw the Capitol in motion towards the falls of [the] Ohio—after a short sojourn taking its flight to the Mississippi, and finally alighting on Darien; which, when the gentleman's dreams are realized, will be a most eligible seat of government for the new republic (or empire) of the two Americas! ...

This war of conquest, a war for the acquisition of territory and subjects, is to be a new commentary on the doctrine that republics are destitute of ambition—that they are addicted to peace, wedded to the happiness and safety of the great body of their people. But it seems this is to be a holiday campaign—there is to be no expense of blood, or treasure, on our part— Canada is to conquer herself—she is to be subdued by the principles of fraternity. The people of that country are first to be seduced from their allegiance, and converted into traitors, as preparatory to the making them good citizens. Although he must acknowledge that some of our flaming patriots were thus manufactured, he did not think the process would hold good with a whole community. It was a dangerous experiment. We were to succeed in the French mode by the system of fraternization—all is French! ...

He was not surprised at the war spirit which was manifesting itself in gentlemen from the South. In the year 1805–06, in a struggle for the carrying trade of belligerent colonial produce, this country had been most unwisely brought into collision with the great powers of Europe. By a series of most impolitic and ruinous measures, utterly incomprehensible to every rational, sober-minded man, the Southern planters, by their own votes, had succeeded in knocking down the price of cotton to seven cents, and of tobacco (a few choice crops excepted) to nothing—and in raising the price of blankets (of which a few would not be amiss in a Canadian campaign), coarse woolens, and every article of first necessity, 300 or 400 per cent. And now that, by our own acts, we have brought ourselves into this unprecedented condition, we must get out of it in any way, but by an acknowledgment of our own want of wisdom and forecast. But is war the true remedy? Who will profit by it? Speculators—a few lucky merchants, who draw prizes in the lottery—commissaries and contractors. Who must suffer by it? The people. It is their blood, their taxes, that must flow to support it....

He was gratified to find gentlemen acknowledging the demoralizing and destructive consequences of the non-importation law—confessing the truth of all that its opponents foretold when it was enacted. And will you plunge yourselves in war, because you have passed a foolish and ruinous law, and are ashamed to repeal it? "But our good friend the French Emperor stands in the way of its repeal," and as we cannot go too far in making sacrifices to him, who has given such demonstration of his love for the Americans, we must, in point of fact, become parties to his war. "Who can be so cruel as to refuse him this favor?" His imagination shrunk from the miseries of such a connection. He called upon the House to reflect whether they were not about to abandon all reclamation for the unparalleled outrages, "insults and injuries" of the French government, to give up our claim for plundered millions; and asked what reparation or atonement they could expect to obtain in hours of future dalliance, after they should have made a tender of their person to this great deflowerer of the virginity of republics. We had by our own wise (he

would not say *wise-acre*) measures, so increased the trade and wealth of Montreal and Quebec, that at last we began to cast a wistful eye at Canada. Having done so much towards its improvement by the exercise of "our restrictive energies" we began to think the laborer worthy of his hire, and to put in claim for our portion. Suppose it ours, are we any nearer to our point? As his minister said to the King of Epirus, "may we not as well take our bottle of wine before as after this exploit?" Go! march to Canada! leave the broad bosom of the Chesapeake and her hundred tributary rivers—the whole line of sea-coast from Machias to St. Mary's, unprotected! You have taken Quebec—have you conquered England? Will you seek for the deep foundations of her power in the frozen deserts of Labrador?

XVII Cultural Independence

PRIDE in the achievement of independence and the necessity for justifying the Revolution convinced Americans that they would be able to create a new culture that would express the newness of their nationality. Cultural independence was to match the political separateness of the United States.

At first, the Revolution was enormously stimulating (No. 134). Confident of their own originality, the Americans made determined efforts to assure cultural independence of Europe (No. 135). But resources were simply not adequate. The effort to create a national university, for instance, was dear to the heart of Washington, but came to nothing (No. 136).

Indeed, the country for a time slipped into a disappointingly dull and arid period. Religion had largely lost its force as an organizing element in culture, and ministers were no longer the intellectual or cultural leaders of their communities (No. 137). Furthermore, many men were suspicious that culture was but a tool of the aristocracy designed to degrade the ordinary folk, and they were therefore hostile to any public expenditures on this account (No. 138). Even those who did not see a conspiracy in culture nevertheless tended to regard literature as worthy of serious patronage only if it was edifying and helped advance an individual toward the goals of his life (No. 139).

A few young men who grew up after the turn of the century felt the stirrings of a desire to create a great literature and a great drama; and their enthusiasm somewhat compensated for the want of technical skill (No. 140). But the predominant cultural preoccupations of the times were of another order, as the diary of a minister in a small city shows (No. 141). Little progress had yet been made in fulfilling the excessive hopes of the revolutionary period.

134. *The Revolution and Culture, 1789*

David Ramsay, *History of the American Revolution*
(Philadelphia, 1789), II, 315-24.

THE American Revolution ... gave occasion for the display of abilities which, but for that event, would have been lost to the world. When the war began, the Americans were a mass of husbandmen, merchants, mechanics and fishermen; but the necessities of the country gave a spring to the active powers of the inhabitants, and set them on thinking, speaking and acting, in a line far beyond that to which they had been accustomed. ... While the Americans were guided by the leading strings of the mother country, they had no scope nor encouragement for exertion. All the departments of government were established and executed for them, but not by them. In the years 1775 and 1776 the country, being suddenly thrown into a situation that needed the abilities of all its sons, these generally took their places, each according to the bent of his inclination. As they severally pursued their objects with ardor, a vast expansion of the human mind speedily followed.

This displayed itself in a variety of ways. It was found that the talents for great stations did not differ in kind, but only in degree, from those which were necessary for the proper discharge of the ordinary business of civil society. ... The great bulk of those, who were the active instruments of carrying on the revolution, were self-made, industrious men. These who by their own exertions, had established or laid a foundation for establishing personal independence, were most generally trusted, and most successfully employed in establishing that of their country. In these times of action, classical education was found of less service than good natural parts, guided by common sense and sound judgment. ...

The Americans knew but little of one another, previous to the revolution. Trade and business had brought the inhabitants of their seaports acquainted with each other, but the bulk of the people in the interior country were unacquainted with their fellow citizens. A continental army, and Congress composed of men from all the states, by freely mixing together, were assimilated into one mass. Individuals of both, mingling with the citizens, disseminated principles of union among them. Local prejudices abated. By frequent collision asperities were worn off, and a foundation was laid for the establishment of a nation, out of discordant materials. Intermarriages between men and women of different states were much more common than before the war, and became an additional cement to the union. Unreasonable jealousies had existed between the inhabitants of the eastern and of the southern states; but on becoming better acquainted with each other, these in a great measure subsided. A wiser policy prevailed. Men of liberal minds led the way in discouraging local distinctions, and the great body of the people, as soon as reason got the better of prejudice, found that their best interests would be most effectually promoted by such practices and sentiments as were favorable to union.

Religious bigotry had broken in upon the peace of various sects, before the American war. This was kept up by partial establishments, and by a dread that the Church of England through the power of the mother country, would be made to triumph over all other denominations. These apprehensions were done away by the Revolution. The different sects, having nothing to fear from each other, dismissed all religious controversy. A proposal for introducing bishops into America before the war, had kindled a flame among the dissenters; but the Revolution was no sooner accomplished, than a scheme for that purpose was perfected, with the consent and approbation of all those sects who had previously opposed it. . . . The world will soon see the result of an experiment in politics, and be able to determine whether the happiness of society is increased by religious establishments, or diminished by the want of them.

Though schools and colleges were generally shut up during the war, yet many of the arts and sciences were promoted by it. The geography of the United States before the Revolution was but little known; but the marches of armies, and the operations of war, gave birth to many geographical enquiries and discoveries, which otherwise would not have been made. A passionate fondness for studies of this kind, and the growing importance of the country, excited one of its sons, the Reverend Mr. Morse, to travel through every state of the Union, and amass a fund of topographical knowledge, far exceeding anything heretofore communicated to the public. The necessities of the states led to the study of tactics, fortification, gunnery, and a variety of other arts connected with war, and diffused a knowledge of them among a peaceable people, who would otherwise have had no inducement to study them. . . .

Surgery was one of the arts which was promoted by the war. From the want of hospitals and other aids, the medical men of America, had few opportunities of perfecting themselves in this art. . . . The melancholy events of battles, gave the American students an opportunity of seeing, and learning more in one day, than they could have acquired in years of peace. It was in the hospitals of the United States, that Dr. Rush first discovered the method of curing the lockjaw by bark and wine, added to other invigorating remedies, which has since been adopted with success in Europe, as well as in the United States. . . .

In establishing American independence, the pen and the press had merit equal to that of the sword. As the war was the people's war, and was carried on without funds, the exertions of the army would have been insufficient to effect the revolution, unless the great body of the people had been prepared for it, and also kept in a constant disposition to oppose Great Britain. To rouse and unite the inhabitants, and to persuade them to patience for several years, under present sufferings, with the hope of obtaining remote advantages for their posterity, was a work of difficulty. This was effected in a great measure by the tongues and pens of the well informed citizens, and on it depended the success of military operations. . . .

The early attention which had been paid to literature in New England, was also eminently conducive to the success of the Americans in resisting Great Britain. . . . In the year the Boston port act was passed, there were in the four eastern colonies, upwards of two thousand graduates of . . . colleges . . . who by their knowledge and abilities, were able to influence and direct the great body of the people to a proper line of conduct, for opposing the encroachments of Great Britain on their liberties. . . . From the influence which knowledge had in securing and preserving the liberties of America, the present generation may trace the wise policy of their fathers, in erecting schools and colleges. They may also learn that it is their duty to found more, and support all such institutions. Without the advantages derived from these lights of this new world, the United States would probably have fallen in their unequal contest with Great Britain. Union which was essential to the success of their resistance, could scarcely have taken place, in the measures adopted by an ignorant multitude. . . .

As literature had in the first instance favored the Revolution, so in its turn, the Revolution promoted literature. The study of eloquence and of the belles lettres, was more successfully prosecuted in America, after the disputes between Great Britain and her colonies began to be serious, than it ever had been before. The various orations, addresses, letters, dissertations and other literary performances which the war made necessary, called forth abilities where they were, and excited the rising generation to study arts, which brought with them their own reward. Many incidents afforded materials for the favorites of the muses, to display their talents. . . . Francis Hopkinson rendered essential service to his country by turning the artillery of wit and ridicule on the enemy. Philip Freneau labored successfully in the same way. Royal proclamations and other productions which issued from royal printing presses were by the help of a warm imagination, arrayed in such dresses as rendered them truly ridiculous. Trumbull with a vein of original Hudibrastic humor, diverted his countrymen so much with the follies of their enemies, that for a time they forgot the calamities of war. . . . Barlow increased the fame of his country and of the distinguished actors in the Revolution, by the bold design of an epic poem ably executed, on the idea that Columbus foresaw in vision, the great scenes that were to be transacted on the theater of that New World, which he had discovered. . . . The principles of their mother tongue, were first unfolded to the Americans since the Revolution, by their countryman Webster. Pursuing an unbeaten track, he has made discoveries in the genius and construction of the English language, which had escaped the researches of preceding philolo-

gists. These and a group of other literary characters have been brought into view by the Revolution. . . .

From the later periods of the Revolution till the present time, schools, colleges, societies and institutions for promoting literature, arts, manufactures, agriculture, and for extending human happiness, have been increased far beyond anything that ever took place before the Declaration of Independence. Every state in the union, has done more or less in this way, but Pennsylvania has done the most. The following institutions have been very lately founded in that state, and most of them in the time of the war or since the peace. A university in the city of Philadelphia; a college of physicians in the same place; Dickinson College at Carlisle; Franklin College at Lancaster; the Protestant Episcopal academy in Philadelphia; academies at York, at Germantown, at Pittsburgh and Washington; and an academy in Philadelphia for young ladies; societies for promoting political enquiries; for the medical relief of the poor, under the title of the Philadelphia Dispensary; for promoting the abolition of slavery, and the relief of free Negroes unlawfully held in bondage; for propagating the gospel among the Indians, under the direction of the United Brethren; for the encouragement of manufactures and the useful arts; for alleviating the miseries of prisons. Such have been some of the beneficial effects, which have resulted from that expansion of the human mind, which has been produced by the Revolution, but these have not been without alloy. . . .

In consequence of the war, the institutions of religion have been deranged, the public worship of the Deity suspended, and a great number of the inhabitants deprived of the ordinary means of obtaining that religious knowledge, which tames the fierceness, and softens the rudeness of human passions and manners. Many of the temples dedicated to the service of the most High were destroyed, and these from a deficiency of ability and inclination, are not yet rebuilt. The clergy were left to suffer, without proper support. The depreciation of the paper currency was particularly injurious to them. It reduced their salaries to a pittance, so insufficient for their maintenance, that several of them were obliged to lay down their profession, and engage in other pursuits. . . . No class of citizens have contributed more to the Revolution than the clergy, and none have hitherto suffered more in consequence of it. From the diminution of their number, and the penury to which they have been subjected, civil government has lost many of the advantages it formerly derived from the public instructions of that useful order of men.

135. *The Penalties for Education Abroad, 1785*

Act of February 7, 1785, A. D. Candler, ed., *Colonial Records of the State of Georgia* (Atlanta, 1904–16), XIX, Part 2, 378.

AND be it enacted, by the authority aforesaid that if any person or persons under the age of sixteen years shall after the passing of this act be sent abroad without the limits of the United States and reside there three years for the purpose of receiving an education under a foreign power, such person or persons after their return to this state shall for three years be considered and treated as aliens in so far as not to be eligible to a seat in the legislature or executive authority or to hold any office civil or military in the state for that term and so in proportion for any greater number of years as he or they shall be absent as aforesaid, but shall not be injured or disqualified in any other respect.

136. *A National University, 1796*

President George Washington's Address to Congress, December 7, 1796, Richardson, *Messages and Papers*, I, 202.

THE ASSEMBLY to which I address myself, is too enlightened not to be fully sensible how much a flourishing state of the arts and sciences contributes to national prosperity and reputation. True it is, that our country, much to its honor, contains many seminaries of learning highly respectable and useful; but the funds upon which they rest are too narrow to command the ablest professors, in the different departments of liberal knowledge, for the institution contemplated, though they would be excellent auxiliaries.

Amongst the motives to such an institution, the assimilation of the principles, opinions, and manners of our countrymen, by the common education of a portion of our youth from every quarter, well deserves attention. The more homogeneous our citizens can be made in these particulars, the greater will be our prospect of permanent union; and a primary object of such a national institution should be, the education of our youth in the science of government. In a republic, what species of knowledge can be equally important, and what duty more pressing on its legislature, than to patronize a plan for communicating it to those who are to be the future guardians of the liberties of the country?

137. *Old-Time Preaching, 1819*

Charles G. Finney, *Memoirs*. (New York, 1876), 6.

THE PREACHING was by an aged clergyman, an excellent man, and greatly beloved and venerated by his people; but he read his sermons in a manner that left no impression whatever on my mind. He had a monotonous, humdrum way of reading what he had probably written many years before.

To give some idea of his preaching, let me say that his manuscript sermons were just large enough to put into a small Bible. I sat in the gallery, and observed that he placed his manuscript in the middle of his Bible, and inserted his fingers at the places where were to be found the passages of Scripture to be quoted in the reading of his sermon. This made it necessary to hold his Bible in both hands, and rendered all gesticulation with his hands impossible. As he proceeded he would read the passages of Scripture where his fingers were inserted, and thus liberate one finger after another until the fingers of both hands were read out of their places. When his fingers were all read out, he was near the close of the sermon. His reading was altogether unimpassioned and monotonous; and although the people attended very closely and reverentially to his reading; yet, I must confess, it was to me not much like preaching.

When we retired from meeting, I often heard the people speak well of his sermons; and sometimes they would wonder whether he had intended any allusion, in what he said, to what was occurring among them. It seemed to be always a matter of curiosity to know what he was aiming at, especially if there was anything more in his sermon than a dry discussion of doctrine. And this was really quite as good preaching as I had ever listened to in any place.

138. *Culture and Liberty, 1798*

William Manning, *Key of Libberty Shewing the Causes Why a Free Government Has Always Failed*. Samuel Eliot Morison, ed. (Billerica, 1922), 18–21, 26, 28–9, 35–7.

THE REASONS why a free government has always failed is from the unreasonable demands and desires of the few. They can't bear to be on a level with their fellow creatures, or submit to the determinations of a legislature where (as they call it) the swinish multitude are fairly represented, but sicken at the idea, and are ever hankering and striving after monarchy or aristocracy where the people have nothing to do in matters of government but to support the few in luxury and idleness.

For these and many other reasons a large majority of those that live without labor are ever opposed to the principles and operation of a free government, and though the whole of them do not amount to one eighth part of the people, yet by their combinations, arts and schemes have always made out to destroy it sooner or later. . . .

Solomon said, train up a child in the way he should go, and when he is old he will not depart from it. And it is as true that if a child is trained up in the way he should not go, when he is old he will keep to it. It is the universal custom and practice of monarchical and despotic government to train up their subjects as much in ignorance as they can in matters of government, and to teach them to reverence and worship great men in office, and to take for truth whatever they say without examining for themselves.

Consequently, whenever revolutions are brought about and free governments established it is by the influence of a few leading men, who, after they have obtained their object (like other men), can never receive compensation and honors enough from the people for their services; and the people being brought up from their youths to reverence and respect such men, they go on old ways and neglect to search and see for themselves and take care of their own interests. Also being naturally very fond of being flattered, they readily hear to measures proposed by great men who, they are convinced, have done them good services. This is the principal ground on which the few work to destroy a free government....

In a free government the few, finding their schemes and views of interest borne down by the many, to gain the power they can't constitutionally obtain, always endeavor to get it by cunning and corruption, conscious at the same time that usurpation, when once begun, the safety of the usurper consists only in grasping the whole. To effect this ..., they ... unite their plans and schemes by associations, conventions and correspondences with each other. The merchants associate by themselves, the physicians by themselves, the ministers by themselves, the judicial and executive officers are by their professions often called together and know each other's minds, and all literary men and the overgrown rich, that can live without laboring, can spare time for consultation. All being bound together by common interest, which is the strongest bond of union, join in their secret correspondence to counteract the interests of the many and pick their pockets, which is effected only for want of the means of knowledge among them....

Learning is of the greatest importance to the support of a free government, and to prevent this the few are always crying up the advantages of costly colleges, national academies and grammar schools, in order to make places for men to live without work, and so strengthen their party; but are always opposed to cheap schools and women's schools, the only or principal means by which learning is spread among the many....

The doctors have established their medical societies and have both their state and county meetings, by which they have so nearly annihilated quackery of all kinds, that a poor man can't get so great cures of them now for a guinea, as he could fifty years ago of an old squaw for half a pint of rum. The business of a midwife could be performed fifty years ago for half a dollar, and now it costs a poor man five whole ones....

The ministers of the Congregational order and others, for aught I know, have formed themselves into societies and many of them are incorporated and have their state and county meetings which may be of great service or absolutely necessary in their sacred functions. But it is no breach of charity to suppose that they have some political purposes in them; nor do I deny their right to meddle in politics. But ... instead of preaching about and praying for officers of government as infallible beings, or so perfect that we ought to submit to and praise them for all they do (when in fact they are all our servants and at all times accountable to the people), they ought to teach their hearers to be watchful of men in power, and to guard their own rights and privileges with a jealous eye, and teach them how to do it in a constitutional way.

If their principles forbid this they had better let politics entirely alone, for if they use their great influence to mislead and prejudice their hearers against the true principles of a free government (as many of them have done of late) by praising our executive for making the British treaty, and in short by praising monarchical and despotic government, and running down and blackguarding republican principles and the French nation, they are in fact acting a treasonable and rebellious part and doing all in their power to destroy the government; and their hearers ought not to attend on such teachings. . . . It has been the general practice of all arbitrary governments to prostitute religion to political purposes, and make a handle of this order of men to mislead, flatter, and drive the people by the terrors of the other world into submission to their political schemes and interests. Consequently they ought to be watched and guarded against above all other orders, especially when they preach politics. . . .

No person who is a friend to liberty will be against a large expense in learning, but it ought to be promoted in the cheapest and best manner possible, which in my opinion would be:—For every state to maintain as many colleges in convenient parts thereof as would be attended upon to give the highest degrees of learning, and for every county to keep as many grammar schools or academies in convenient parts thereof as would be attended to by both sexes summer and winter, and no student or scholar to pay anything for tuition, and for the county schools to pay a particular attention to teaching the English language and qualifying its scholars to teach and govern common schools for little children.

And for every town to be obliged to keep as much as six weeks of writing school in the winter and twelve weeks of a woman school in the summer in every part of the town, so that none should be thronged with too many scholars, nor none have too far to travel, and every person be obliged to send his children to school, for the public are as much interested in the learning of one child as another.

If this method of learning was established we should soon have a plenty of school masters and mistresses as cheap as we could hire other labor, and labor and learning would be connected together and lessen the number of those that live without work. Also we should have a plenty of men to fill the highest offices of state for less than half we now give. But instead of this mode of learning the few are always striving to oblige us to maintain great men with great salaries and to maintain grammar schools in every town to teach our children *a b c* all which is only to give employ to gentlemen's sons and make places for men to live without work. For there is no more need of a man's having a knowledge of all the languages to teach a child to read, write and cipher, than there is for a farmer to have the mariner's art to hold plow. . . .

The principal knowledge necessary for a free man to have is obtained by the liberty of the press or public newspapers. But this kind of knowledge is almost ruined of late by the doings of the few. But a few years ago we could have the whole news by one paper in a week, and could put some dependence on what was printed. But the few, being closely combined and determined to destroy our government, find it necessary to destroy the liberty of the press first. To effect this they employ no printers but those that will adhere strictly to their views and interests, and use all the arts and rhetoric hell can invent to blackguard the republican printers and all they print, and strive to make the people believe falsehood for truths and truths for falsehood. And as they have money and leisure they have their papers every day in the week. Consequently the republican printers double their papers, so that a laboring man must now be at the expense of three or four dollars annually and read and study half his time, and then be at a loss to know what is true and what not— thus the few have almost ruined the liberty of the press.

139. *Literature and the Goals of Life, 1786*

Patrick Henry to his daughter, c.1786, in Henry, *Life*, II, 308–9.

CULTIVATE your mind by the perusal of those books which instruct while they amuse. Do not devote much of your time to novels; there are a few which may be useful and improving in giving a higher tone to our moral sensibility; but they tend to vitiate the taste, and to produce a disrelish for substantial intellectual food. Most plays are of the same cast, they are not friendly to the delicacy which is one of the ornaments of the female character. History, geography, poetry, moral essays, biography, travels, sermons, and other well-written religious productions, will not fail to enlarge your understanding, to render you a more agreeable companion, and to exalt your virtue. A woman devoid of rational ideas of religion, has no security for her virtues; it is sacrificed to her passions, whose voice, not that of God, is her only governing principle. Besides, in those hours of calamity to which families must be exposed, where will she find support, if it be not in the just reflections upon that all-ruling Providence which governs the universe, whether inanimate or animate?

140. *A Playwright's Youth, 1808–19*

M. M. Noah to William Dunlap, July 11, 1832, in William Dunlap, *A History of the American Theatre* (New York, 1832), 380–4.

I HAD an early hankering for the national drama, a kind of juvenile patriotism, which burst forth, for the first time, in a few sorry doggerels in the form of a prologue to a play, which a Thespian company, of which I was a member, produced in the South Street Theatre, the old American Theatre in Philadelphia. The idea was probably suggested by the sign of the Federal Convention at the tavern opposite the theater. You, no doubt, remember the picture and the motto: an excellent piece of painting of the kind, representing a group of venerable personages engaged in public discussions, with the following distich:
These thirty-eight great men have signed a powerful deed,
That better times, to us, shall very soon succeed.
The sign must have been painted soon after the adoption of the federal constitution, and I remember to have stood "many a time and oft," gazing, when a boy, at the assembled patriots, particularly the venerable head and spectacles of Dr. [Benjamin] Franklin, always in conspicuous relief. In our Thespian corps, the honor of cutting the plays, substituting new passages, casting parts, and writing couplets at the exits, was divided between myself and a fellow of infinite wit and humor by the name of [George] Helmbold, who subsequently became the editor of a scandalous little paper called the *Tickler*. He was a rare rascal, perpetrated all kind of calumnies, was constantly mulcted in fines, sometimes imprisoned, was full of faults which were forgotten in his conversational qualities and dry sallies of genuine wit, particularly in his Dutch stories. After years of singular vicissitudes, Helmbold joined the army as a common soldier, fought bravely during the late war, obtained a commission, and died.

Our little company soon dwindled away. The expenses were too heavy for our pockets. Our writings and performances were sufficiently wretched, but as the audience was admitted without cost, they were too polite to express any disapprobation. We recorded all our doings in a little weekly paper, published, I believe, by Jemmy Riddle, at the corner of Chestnut and Third Street, opposite the tavern kept by that sturdy old democrat, Israel Israel.

From a boy, I was a regular attendant at the Chestnut Street Theater, during the management of Wignell and Reinagle, and made great efforts to compass the purchase of a season ticket, which I obtained generally of the treasurer, George Davis, for $18. Our habits through life are frequently governed and directed by our early steps. I seldom missed a night, and always retired to bed after witnessing a good play, gratified and improved, and thus, probably, escaped the haunts of taverns and the pursuits of depraved pleasures, which too frequently allure and destroy our young men. Hence I was always the firm friend of the drama, and had an undoubted right to oppose my example through life to the horror and hostility expressed by sectarians to plays and playhouses generally.

Independent of several of your plays which had obtained possession of the stage, and were duly incorporated in the legitimate drama, the first call to support the productions of a fellow townsman was, I think, [James Nelson] Barker's opera of the *Indian Princess*. Charles Ingersoll had previously written a tragedy, a very able production for a very young man, which was supported by all the "good society." But Barker, who was "one of us," an amiable and intelligent young fellow, who owed nothing to hereditary rank, though his father was a Whig and a soldier of the Revolution, was in reality a fine-spirited poet, a patriotic ode writer, and, finally, a gallant soldier of the late war. The managers gave Barker an excellent chance with all his plays, and he had merit and popularity to give them in return full houses.

About this time [1808], I ventured to attempt a little melodrama, under the title of *The Fortress of Sorrento*, which, not having money enough to pay for printing, nor sufficient influence to have acted, I thrust the manuscript in my pocket, and having occasion to visit New York, I called in at David Longworth's Dramatic Repository one day, spoke of the little piece, and struck a bargain with him by giving him the manuscript in return for a copy of every play he had published, which at once furnished me with a tolerably large dramatic collection. I believe the play never was performed, and I was almost ashamed to own it, but it was my first regular attempt at dramatic composition.

In the year 1812, while in Charleston, S.C., Mr. [Charles] Young requested me to write a piece for his wife's benefit. You remember her, no doubt, remarkable as she was for her personal beauty and amiable deportment. It would have been very ungallant to have refused, particularly as he requested that it should be a "breeches part," to use a green-room term, though she was equally attractive in every character. . . .

I soon produced the little piece, which was called *Paul and Alexis, or the Orphans of the Rhine*. I was, at that period, a very active politician, and my political opponents did me the honor to go to the theater the night it was performed for the purpose of hissing it, which was not attempted until the curtain fell and the piece was successful. After three years' absence in Europe and Africa, I saw the same piece performed at the Park [Theater] under the title of *The Wandering Boys*, which even now holds possession of the stage. It seems Mr. Young sent the manuscript to London, where the title was changed, and the bantling cut up, altered and considerably improved.

About this time, John Miller, the American bookseller in London, paid us a visit. Among the passengers in the same ship was a fine English girl of great talent and promise, Miss Lee Sugg, afterwards Mrs. Hackett. She was engaged at the Park as a singer, and Phillips, who was here about the same period fulfilling a most successful engagement, was decided and unqualified in his admiration of her talent. Everyone took an interest in her success. She was gay, kind-hearted and popular, always in excellent spirits, and always perfect. Anxious for her success I ventured to write a play for her benefit, and, in three days finished the patriotic piece of *She Would Be a Soldier, or the Battle of Chippewa,* which, I was happy to find, produced her an excellent house. . . .

After this play, I became in a manner domiciliated in the green-room. My friends, [Stephen] Price and [Edmund Shaw] Simpson, who had always been exceedingly kind and liberal, allowed me to stray about the premises like one of the family, and, always anxious for their success, I ventured upon another attempt for a holiday occasion, and produced *Marion, or the Hero of Lake George.* It was played on the twenty-fifth of November [1821], Evacuation Day, and I bustled about among my military friends to raise a party in support of a military play, and what with generals, staff officers, rank and file, the Park Theater was so crammed that not a word of the play was heard, which was a very fortunate affair for the author. The managers presented me with a pair of handsome silver pitchers, which I still retain as a memento of their good will and friendly consideration. You must bear in mind that while I was thus employed in occasional attempts at playwriting, I was engaged in editing a daily journal, and in all the fierce contests of political strife. I had, therefore, but little time to devote to all that study and reflection so essential to the success of dramatic composition.

My next piece, I believe, was written for the benefit of a relative and friend who wanted something to bring a house, and as the struggle for liberty in Greece was at that period the prevailing excitement, I finished the melodrama of *The Grecian Captive,* which was brought out with all the advantages of good scenery and music. As a good house was of more consequence to the actor than fame to the author, it was resolved that the hero of the piece should make his appearance on an elephant, and the heroine on a camel, which were procured from a neighboring menagerie, and the *tout ensemble* was sufficiently imposing. Only it happened that the huge elephant, in shaking his skin, so rocked the castle on his back, that the Grecian general nearly lost his balance and was in imminent danger of coming down from his high estate, to the infinite merriment of the audience.

On this occasion, to use another significant phrase, a "gag" was hit upon of a new character altogether. The play was printed, and each auditor was presented with a copy gratis, as he entered the house. Figure to yourself a thousand people in a theater, each with a book of the play in hand. Imagine the turning over a thousand leaves simultaneously, the buzz and fluttering it produced, and you will readily believe that the actors entirely forgot their parts, and even the equanimity of the elephant and camel were essentially disturbed.

My last appearance as a dramatic writer was in another national piece called *The Siege of Tripoli* which the managers persuaded me to bring out for my own benefit, being my first attempt to derive any profit from dramatic efforts. The piece was elegantly got up, the house crowded with beauty and fashion, everything went off in the happiest manner, when, a short time after the audience had retired, the Park Theater was discovered to be on fire and in a short time was a heap of ruins.

141. *New England Pastimes, 1791–97*

William Bentley, *Diary* (Salem, 1905–07), I, 253–5, 379–80, 381, 392; II, 127, 235.

[APRIL 28, 1791] Puerile sports usual in these parts of New England. To begin with the calendar month of January. The youth of the male sex are busy on their skates. They commonly learn upon their trunks, which are pieces of wood, of the length of the foot, turning up at the heel and about one inch square, holes made at the heel, and bridle with the same straps as the skate, and is properly the wooden skate. The skate is of three kinds: the common skate, which is a plain iron without ornament; the Holland skate, which swells upon its center, and descends into parallel lines on the surface with the edge of the skate, and is nearly a right line; and the curve skate, which in an erect posture is in contact with the ice only at the heel. The straps are fixed differently, but commonly two straps, one at the heel, and the other at the head, are drawn through the wood, and secured so that the ends on each side hang out two inches, and through these the lines pass at discretion. The trunks are going out of use, as the skate becomes more cheap. The wood is shaped much like the violin, only smaller in proportion at the head, and the female screws which fasten the heel of the iron to the wood, plays on top, with points to fix the heel of the shoes. The sled, sufficient for one or two boys is supplied with skates on each side of the whole length. When these are not to be had, iron hoops are used, worn bright, and nailed on. The single sleds are used to descend upon the snow and ice by laying upon the sled, and guiding it by the feet behind. The double sleds are guided by the person who sets before.

After pottering time is over, which is running upon the broken ice without falling into the water and requires great ac-tivity, comes on marble time. These are imported from Europe, are perfectly round, and commonly of a clay color. The other colors, especially black and white, are called men, and are of double value; the spotted are called gaydoes. In April the top comes into play, commonly in ring top. They are smaller than these imported, being higher, but not of so great a diameter. They are a perfect cone on the lower part and are covered with a spiral groove for the cord. The core, or iron inserted in the bottom upon which the top moves is often half an inch in length. Then comes the shuttlecock and lasts through May. The action required in this diversion is continued but easy, and the females in proper apartments enjoy it as well as the males.

Afterwards the bat and ball and the game at rickets. The ball is made of rags covered with leather in quarters and covered with double twine, sewed in knots over the whole. The bat is from two to three feet long, round on the back side but flattened considerably on the face, and round at the end, for a better stroke. The ricket is played double, and is full of violent exercise of running. In the autumn comes the kite, of all sizes, which is round at top. At one third of the length it descends for the two-thirds in right lines to a point. The cords which fasten it to the line are fixed at the wings which are commonly ornamented, and the whole is balanced by a tail, or string with rows of rags or paper at proper distances.

Before winter comes on the football, which is differently pursued in different places. In Marblehead, even heads of families engage in it, and all the fisher-men while at home in this season. The bruising of shins has rendered it rather disgraceful to those of better education, who use a hand ball, thrown up against a house or fence instead of the football, which is unfriendly to clothes, as well as safety.

Such is the usual succession of puerile diversions. They do not last for the same exact periods. The snow and ice determine the use of skates and sleds. The contractions in the postures of playing at marbles renders this uncomfortable in hot and dusty seasons. The top has no convenience in dry weather. The exercise of the shuttlecock comes on, while the bathing time lasts. The bat and ball as the weather begins to be cool, and the kite in the fine weather of our autumn afternoons before sundown, and while time enough remains after school exercises.

Bathing is as little used as in any part of the world perhaps. The children after May are tolerated by their parents by the old rule of once a day. But it is rare to see any person in the morning, or in the waters which flow immediately from the sea. They enter at the nearest place however great its inconveniences. The children follow their wishes, and bathe at high noon, and the men bathe in the evening. The women are very private, and late at night if they ever venture, and house baths are very few indeed. A few years ago such things were only in the physician's hands. . . .

[July 6, 1792] We had the first special Lodge this evening, and a charge was read from the "Freemason's Pocket Companion," of which two copies were at the Lodge, of different editions. I saw also Head's answer, etc. to *Masonry the way to Hell*, an abusive publication in the form of a sermon. On this occasion the following form of prayer was used.

O universal Creator, on the pillars of w.s. & b. thy works stand fast. In feeble imitation we raise a temple to thy praise. It is formed of those rich materials with which heaven is built and upon which it must stand forever. It is of the same proportions upon which thy world was fashioned, and they are inspired by thee the master builder. Of its pillars pure self love is the base, w.s. & b. are the columns. But social happiness are its capitals. It rests on the foundation of thy throne, and stands conspicuous to thy honor. In triumph we welcome thy children to its glory. With the right hand of honor we accept this Brother. If he be firm we will build upon him a palace. If he be faithful we will make him a door of cedar. We will spread a pavement under his feet, and the canopy of heaven shall cover him. We shall prepare him a plain path. Divine wisdom shall instruct him, his actions shall all be right, and truth shall encircle him. The sun shall give him light by day, and the moon by night, and the eye of the master shall be upon him for council, and for hope. His life shall be in pledge for his friend, and when he shall stretch out his hand, it shall never return empty. On his right hand and left he shall find friends to take him by the hand, and his feet shall never slide. His eyes shall be closed when he dies, and the arm of friendship shall raise him to the helping hand of his God from heaven. . . .

[July 7, 1792] Yesterday the strolling actors in town to act comic, sing sailor's songs and dance jigs for the amusement of all who will give three shillings. There were above one hundred at the exhibition and generally well pleased. This is intended as the entering wedge of theatrical exhibitions, in favor of which Gardiner has published, and against which the clergy of Boston in general have protested. . . .

[July 12, 1792] The theatrical mimics have exhibited a second time on Tuesday evening, and had their company increased from 120 to 150. They have ordered the town crier to give notice that they have (perhaps a mistake) assigned this evening, and as the court of pleas is in the town they may add to their number. The crier in the street at sundown is not a good sign. The best people have attended on these occasions. . . .

[September 12, 1792] The singers at my house this evening, a very large company to which I added the French gentlemen in the neighborhood....

[September 13, 1792] For the first time I was present with the fire club, called Union. The principal members were present. The evening passed in agreeable conversation, and on subjects adapted to the meeting....

[Feb. 16, 1795]. Mr. Freeman accompanied me to several new buildings. Over the arch of the Tontine Segment, I was led to the room now fitting for the town library. It is to be finished in a circular form, and has a very promising appearance in the present progress of the work. Over this room the Historical Society have their apartment, which is to be finished in a square. Several natural curiosities are already collected, and a foundation is laid for a good library upon the plan of their institution. The principal books respecting America have been already collected but their number is small. Piles of gazettes afford the eye little entertainment. Their table is of an oval form and suits the general appearance of the room.

We passed from the Tontine buildings to the theater, into which we were admitted by Colonel Tyler. We visited the gallery, the slips, the boxes, and from the boxes had a view of the assembly room which we did not enter. The theater is handsomely finished, but as it was the first building of the kind which I had ever seen, I was pleased, rather than disposed to judge. I found the friends of the theater were not a little solicitous to induce the clergy to attend the exhibitions, and they invited us to the theater as they would have invited us to a lecture from some favorite preacher....

[August 30, 1797]. Went to the market house to see the elephant. The crowd of spectators forbade me any but a general and superficial view of him. He was six feet four inches high. Of large volume, his skin black, as though lately oiled. A short hair was on every part, but not sufficient for a covering. His tail hung one third of his height, but without any long hairs at the end of it. His legs were still at command at the joints, but he could not be persuaded to lie down. The keeper repeatedly mounted him but he persisted in shaking him off. Bread and hay were given him and he took bread out of the pockets of the spectators. He also drank porter and drew the cork, conveying the liquor from his trunk into his throat. His tusks were just to be seen beyond the flesh, and it was said had been broken. We say *his* because the common language. It is a female and teats appeared just behind the fore-legs.

PART FOUR

Young America, 1820-70

IN THE half century after 1820 the expansion of American society shifted to continental dimensions. The rapidity of growth dominated every aspect of the culture of the United States and reshaped its political and social institutions.

For two hundred years, settlement had spread westward from the Atlantic Coast to just beyond the Alleghenies. Now, in fifty years, it reached toward the Mississippi and beyond, pushed deep into Texas in the Southwest and into Minnesota in the Northwest, and, overtopping the mountains, attained the Pacific in Oregon and California. A population that grew both by natural increase and by immigration supplied the human resources for this conquest of space; and phenomenal economic development supplied the productive instruments for it. Conversely, the spread of settlement encouraged immigration and stimulated the birth rate; and it significantly influenced the system of production as a whole.

The great strength of the American economy was still its agriculture. The states of the Old Northwest were now beyond the frontier stage, and the products of their farms increased steadily in volume. To them were added the newer prairie lands. While the South concentrated now on its great staple, cotton, the North produced an abundance of grains and meats, for which there were ample markets in the new cities of the East and of Europe. Meanwhile, commerce thrived, as it had earlier; and the long-anticipated development of manufacturing added new strength to the nation. A network of canals and railroads had emerged and an integrated transportation system was beginning to tie together the various sectors of the economy and regions of the nation.

These developments imposed a heavy burden upon the whole society. The human beings involved could not immediately adjust to the necessities of an ever-changing situation. In the new circumstances, for instance, old religious forms failed adequately to serve men's needs; there ensued a period of much experimentation. At the same time the material conditions of life were difficult on the frontier and in the factories; and that took a heavy toll in energy.

Nonetheless, there was still an insistence that the Republic ought to produce a culture worthy of its ideals. The task was difficult, for poverty of skills and techniques continued to hamper serious growth. Yet, the basic cultural institutions did develop: schools, libraries, museums, theaters, and a newspaper and periodical press. What was more, in literature there were substantial achievements of which the "flowering of New England" was but one aspect.

Out of the disparity between the cultural aims of the society and its material needs, arose the impulse toward improvement. Man was innately good and progress toward indefinite perfectibility was his destiny. If, in fact, he was still retarded, that was due to no deficiencies inherent in him, but rather to evils in the social institutions that surrounded him. Could these but be rectified or reformed by the action of men, then the liberated individual would be able to fulfill himself. Such was the creed with which Americans now approached the problems of their times, confident that organized reform movements could solve all problems.

Reform operated both through voluntary means and through the agency of the State. The reformers were willing enough to use the methods of persuasion and exhortation. But the results were slow in coming by these means. They were willing also to call upon the power of the government to assist them. At this point their interests touched upon the political organization of the states and of the Federal Government.

Politically, the most striking characteristic of this period was the gradual emergence of a shifting and fluctuating two-party system. At first the parties held together as groups of the friends and enemies of Andrew Jackson. But they also acquired economic and political programs that attracted the support of a variety of sectional and group interests. So the tariff, internal improvements, monetary policy and expansion came to divide men into political parties. But, as expansion reached into the interior of the continent, all other issues became subsidiary to that of slavery.

For the status of slavery had been thoroughly transformed in this period. The invention of the cotton gin earlier and the expansion of cotton manufacturing after 1820 created a growing demand for that staple and gave slavery a new lease on life. It was no longer regarded as a dying institution, but as a permanent part of the life of the South and one that was to be defended as a positive good. Slavery expanded into the rich Southwest, into regions laid open to settlement after the removal of the Indians from Georgia, and its defenders sought to extend it even farther through the whole West. Here they collided head-on with the free Northern farmers who believed the destiny of the West was theirs.

In the very decades when the slaveholders came to believe the institution would endure, many other Americans were becoming convinced it must disappear. The bondage of the Negro challenged the faith in the reform impulse and produced the abolition movement. Sectional divisions after 1850 became ever more serious.

The critical point came after the victory of the Republican Party in 1860. Lincoln's election seemed an imminent threat to the security of many Southerners. Their response was secession and the creation of a separate confederacy.

If the crisis was a shock to Northern opinion, there was relatively little dissension as to the appropriate response to it. The great objective was Union, which embodied all the democratic hopes of the Americans; and for that they were willing to embark upon the Civil War. Pockets of copperhead resistance to the War were effective only in limited areas.

The war was disastrous, in terms of its cost in lives and resources, But, in its course, the issues were more clearly defined in terms of slavery or freedom. From the sufferings of the conflict came at last peace and the end of slavery. But the old problems were not thereby altogether liquidated; the newer era which then began inherited many of the difficulties of the past.

Meanwhile, the expansive process had had serious international consequences. At the beginning of the period Americans had already come to think the whole hemisphere predestined for their use; and some such conviction had been implicit in the Monroe Doctrine. But the consciousness of a manifest destiny for American expansion had not been static. It had led to the aggressive thrusts outward in the North and in the South. The Oregon question had been peaceably resolved. But the American occupation of Texas had led to the Mexican War and ultimately to the acquisition of the great southwest territories which reached to the Pacific in California. Yet that had not seemed to satiate the appetite of the Americans. In the 1850's they had already been casting designing glances at Cuba and at the Caribbean area in general.

XVIII ❦ *Conquering a Continent*

THE RATE of continental expansion accelerated steadily through the influence of the growing ease of acquiring land (No. 142). Low prices, encouraging legislation —particularly the Preëmption Act of 1841 and the Homestead Act of 1863—and an efficient system of sales and distribution stimulated the flow of settlers to every part of the frontier (No. 143).

In the Southwest the spread of slavery accompanied westward migration. The internal trade in Negroes gave the institution a particularly harsh quality in the new regions (No. 144; *see also below*, Section XXV). On the other hand, Northern settlement was entirely by families seeking moderate-sized farms. The migrants came mostly from New England and the middle states, with some additions from Europe. They aspired for the opportunity to work hard and to make something of themselves, as one of them explained to his family (No. 145). Yet the rewards of the West were sometimes so abundant as to outdistance modest expectations. By the 1860's the great wheat farms of Minnesota were operating on a scale inconceivable a few years earlier (No. 146).

Looking back at this period from later, it seemed almost idyllic in the clearness of its limited goals and the excitement of its occasional glimpses of the wider world. Mark Twain, who was born and grew up in these years, recalled with nostalgia the attractiveness of the ambitions of life on the Mississippi (No. 147).

Expansion had also quite another character. The farm products moving east and the finished goods moving west passed through an ever greater number of growing cities (No. 148). Internal commerce supported a variety of types, from the romantic Santa Fé trader (*see below*, No. 153) to the cautious shopkeeper of Cincinnati. Immigrants made up a substantial proportion of the population of these towns. Those with capital and skill thrived and counted themselves fortunate when they considered the improvement in their status (No. 149). But the newcomers without skills or capital suffered the hardships of severe and unrewarded labor (No. 150). And for all, successful and unsuccessful alike, migration took a toll in personal tensions that significantly affected American social development (*see below*, Section XX).

142. *The Ease of Acquiring Land, 1832*

American Quarterly Review [Philadelphia], XXII [1832], 280.

LAND is now sold in tracts of eighty acres, at $1.25 an acre. For $100, an unimproved tract of eighty acres may be purchased. In any of the states west of the Ohio River, a laborer can earn 75 cents per day, and if his living . . . cost 25 cents a day . . . he can, by the labor of two hundred days, or about eight months, purchase a farm. But as the working days in a year, excluding bad weather, would not amount to more than two hundred, it may be safely asserted, that a laborer can purchase a tract of eighty acres, by one year's steady labor. Again, a laborer can get his boarding and $10 per month, the year round, which would amount to $120, and if $20 be deducted for clothing, he will in this way have earned the purchase money of a farm, in one year.

All kinds of stock can be raised in that country with facility, and at little cost. A good horse is worth fifty dollars, a cow from five to eight dollars, a fat steer from ten to fifteen, and hogs two dollars per hundred pounds. A man then can purchase eighty acres of land, by the sale of two horses, or from eight to twelve head of cattle, or twenty to twenty-five hogs; and as individuals are not prevented from settling on the public land, but rather encouraged, the means are thus afforded to farmers of acquiring this property, previous to the purchase of land. Mechanics' wages are much higher; and those who work in the most useful arts, such as carpenters, blacksmiths, shoemakers, etc., are greatly needed. An individual of this class, may earn enough money to buy eighty acres, in six months. A person who teaches a common English school, receives three dollars per quarter for each pupil, and such persons are in great demand. A school of thirty scholars will yield ninety dollars per quarter, or $360 per year. . . . Such an individual may in one year buy a tract of land.

143. *Methods of Land Sales, 1836*

Harriet Martineau, *Society in America* (London, 1837), II, 91–3.

THE METHODS according to which the sales of the public lands in the United States are conducted are excellent. The lots are so divided as to preclude all doubt and litigation about boundaries. There is a general land office at Washington, and a subordinate one in each district, where all business can be transacted with readiness and exactitude. Periodical sales are made of lands which it is desirable to bring into the market. These are disposed of to the highest bidder. The advance of the population into the wilderness is thus made more regular than it would be if there were not a rendezvous in each district . . . ; titles are made more secure; and less impunity is allowed to fraud.

The preemption laws, originally designed for the benefit of poor settlers, have been the greatest provocatives to fraud. It seemed hard that a squatter, who had settled himself on unoccupied land, and done it nothing but good, should be turned off without remuneration, or compelled to purchase his own improvements; and in 1830, a bill was therefore passed, granting a preemption right to squatters who had taken such possession of unsold lands. It provided that when two individuals had cultivated a quarter section of land (one hundred and sixty acres), each should have a preemption right with regard to half the cultivated portion; and each also to a preemption of eighty acres anywhere else in the same land district. Of course, abundance of persons took advantage of this law to get the best land very cheap. Two men, by merely cutting down, or blazing a few trees, or "camping out" for a night or two, on a good quarter-section, have secured it at the minimum price. A report to Congress states that there is reason to believe that "large companies have been founded, who procure affidavits of improvements to be made, get the warrants issued upon them, and whenever a good tract of land is ready for sale, cover it over with their *floats* (warrants of the required habitation), and thus put down competition. The frauds upon the public, within the past year (1835), from this single source, have arisen to many millions of dollars." Such errors in matters of detail are sure to be corrected soon after being discovered. The means will speedily be found of showing a due regard to the claims of squatters, without precipitating the settlement of land by unfairly reducing its price in the market. Whatever methods may tend to lessen rather than to increase the facilities for occupying new land, must, on the whole, be an advantage, while the disproportion between land and labor is so great as it is now in the western regions of the United States.

144. *Migration to the Southwest, 1836*

Tyrone Power, *Impressions of America* (Philadelphia, 1836), II, 80–2.

WE PASSED in the course of this night several camps of emigrants, on the move from the Carolinas and Georgia; they managed to keep their fires blazing in the forest, in spite of the falling shower; occasionally might be seen a huge pine crackling and burning throughout as it lay on the ground, whilst, ranged to windward, stood the wagons and huts of the campers.

The rich alluvial lands of Alabama, recently belonging to the Indian reserves, and now on sale by government or through land-speculators, are attracting thousands of families from the washed-out and impoverished soil of the older Southern states; and during this and the preceding season, the numbers moving along this and the other great lines towards the Southwest are incredible. . . .

At a season like the present, the sufferings of these families must be considerable. The caravan usually consists of from two to four tilt wagons, long and low-roofed; each laden, first with the needful provisions and such household gear as may be considered indispensable; next, over this portion of the freight is stowed the family of the emigrant planter, his wife, and commonly a round squad of white-haired children, with their attendants. On the march these vehicles are preceded and surrounded by the field slaves, varying in numbers from half a dozen to fifty or sixty, according to the wealth of the proprietor. A couple of mounted travelers commonly complete the cavalcade, which moves over these roads at the rate of twelve or fifteen miles a day. At night, or when the team gives out, or the wagons are fairly stalled, or set fast, the party prepares to camp. The men cut down a tree for fire, and with its branches make such rude huts as their time and ingenuity may best contrive; the females prepare the evening meal, and perform such domestic duties as may be needful. On these occasions I have frequently passed amongst or halted by them, and have been surprised at the air of content and good humor commonly prevailing in their rude camps, despite the apparent discomfort and privation to which they were exposed.

Many of the Negroes, however, I am informed, are exceedingly averse to a removal from the sites on which they have been bred, and where their connections are formed. In these cases, planters who are uncertain of the personal attachment of their slaves, generally dispose of them amongst their neighbors. When they are really attached to their owners, however, there is little difficulty experienced in their removal.

In most of the parties I encountered, I should say, judging fairly by their deportment and loud merriment, despite the great fatigue and constant exposure, the affair was taken in a sort of holiday spirit, no way warranted by their half-naked miserable appearance.

Thus they crawl onward from day to day, for weeks or months, until they have reached that portion of the forest, or canebrake, fixed upon for the plantation; and here the enterprising settler has to encounter new toil, and a long series of privations, cheered however by the hope, seldom a delusive one, of ultimate wealth accumulating to the survivors of the party; for, unhappily, health is the sacrifice, I believe, generally paid for the possession of the fat soil lying along these sluggish rivers.

Along the whole line of our route from Augusta in Georgia to the banks of the Alabama, we found the road covered by parties of this description; and, according to the opinions of well-informed residents, with whom I conversed on this subject, not fewer than ten thousand families have quitted the two Carolinas and Georgia during the course of this season.

145. *On Free Settlement, 1851*

Dr. Kaspar Koepfli's Address to His Family on the Founding of a Settlement in the State of Illinois. September, 1851. From Solomon Koepfli, *Geschichte der Ansiedlung von Highland* (Highland, 1859), 39–43, as translated by Guy S. Métraux, "Social and Cultural Aspects of Swiss Immigration" (Yale University dissertation, 1949).

AT LAST, my dears, we believe that we have found what we have sought for such a long time: a new home which suits our needs and plans. Thirty miles east of here lies a lovely region, richly endowed by nature, where a world of activity awaits all of you. There you shall find, above all, a good and fertile soil from which it is possible to reap with profit most of the products of the temperate zone; you will also find limitless pastures for cattle-raising where herds of thousands of heads may find the richest food from the deeply-rooted grasses. There is also sufficient forest land to set up a great number of farms, yet not enough to have the whole prairie built upon. Thus there shall be still for at least half a century, free pastures for great herds of cattle. The district is sufficiently supplied with good water; in the forests there are frequent water sources and also limestone deposits. . . . The proximity of the Mississippi and of St. Louis, will afford at little cost an outlet for agricultural products. So you see, the district that we saw has all the qualities that a new settlement requires for prosperity. However, I would not want any one of you to hold illusions about your future life there. What awaits you in this region, which, as of now, is not much better than a wilderness, is a life full of hardships, want and toil. By this choice we shall close ourselves off from the rest of the world for many years. There, we shall be entirely thrown on our own resources and each one must renounce the pleasure of society outside those that we can organize among ourselves.

What must give us, there, pleasure and inner peace, is the satisfaction that we shall find in the accomplished tasks; the fruits of our labor must give us joy and that shall be enough. I am sure, for my part, of having found there what I sought for such a long time. There awaits us a world of activity. Upon your decision depends, perhaps, not only your happiness, but that of many families who will, I do not doubt one instant, follow our steps.

Once more consider everything. If you fear that you are not equal to the task which awaits you there, give it up; do not go there and seek a comfortable and, to some extent, profitable life in the immediate proximity of an already settled town. Once the land . . . has been purchased, no one can think of going back. Then one must consistently and untiringly keep on working. . . . If your forces are sufficient, . . . I am sure that you shall have laid the foundations of your happiness.

146. *The Wheat Fields, 1868*

G. W. Schatzel, "Among the Wheatfields of Minnesota," *Harper's New Monthly Magazine*, January, 1868, 193–4, 197, 198, 199.

WHEAT is planted in Minnesota as early as the weather and ground will permit. In April the plow is put to the soil and the seed sown, or earlier if possible; they plow deep, and allow one and a half to two bushels of seed to the acre. . . .

As one goes over the country in the fall of the year he sees vast tracts of "new breaking," where the virgin soil, black as ink, and rich almost to glutinousness, has been broken by the plow, and the soil turned bottom upward in long, dark bands or layers as far as the eye can reach. Here it is exposed for months to the wind and weather till it decomposes and becomes fit for agricultural purposes. Every year vast tracts of prairie are thus turned over, or "broken," and with the next the loam is leveled and the seed is cast in; and thus large additions are annually made to the aggregate amount of acres of wheat.

Take your stand on one of these "new breaking-pieces," and look perhaps in any direction, and you will find yourself inclosed by its dreary strips of black loam; not a blade of grass nor a single leaf will appear. It is a picture of desolation and vacancy; nature and life are in their embryo; not a glimpse can be seen of their future creations. Nothing can exceed the contrast between this and what these same fields will present a year or two afterward, when they stand yellow with the harvest, an emblem of cheerfulness and prosperity.

Farms are generally 160 acres in extent—a "quarter section" being usually the quantity bought and worked. Under the Homestead Law lands are constantly taken up, the cost being a mere trifle for fees, etc. The settler is required to locate on it, put up a small house, do some fencing and "breaking," and pass a night on it at least once every six months. . . .

These wild lands thus entered are worth about $5 per acre, and when "improved" rise to $15 or $25 according to circumstances. At the end of five years' residence, government gives a clean deed of the property. Many, however, having the means, prefer to buy the land outright at the start, paying the government price, $1.25 per acre.

Wheat matures from about the beginning to the middle of August. The whole country then awakens from its long slothfulness. Business revives. Interest, energy, and happiness everywhere appear. No one who has never witnessed the dullness pervading all departments of business during the winter and spring can comprehend the great and sudden transformation which the incoming crop produces. Mechanics, tradesmen, wheat-buyers, railroads, steamboats—all seem to be indued with new life and vigor; everywhere is activity, bustle and confusion. . . .

A rough-looking set of fellows [appeared], each armed with a bundle or valise. They were laborers come from Iowa and Missouri to work in the harvest. Able-bodied, hardy, of all shapes and sizes, they looked like a detachment of Goths and Vandals on a marauding expedition to our peaceful hills and vales. They were the first installment of "field-hands" from below, come to assist our farmers to gather in their crops. Starting from the vicinity of St. Louis, they had worked in field after field. When one section of country was harvested migrating farther north, till they had gradually toiled their way through to Minnesota. . . .

It was now the second week in August. Wheat was fast ripening; some was ready for the reaper, and an immense quantity had been cultivated, which would all in a few days have to be gathered in. . . .

A large amount of land had been sown and labor was scarce. . . . Hundreds of farms, all over the state, still lay untouched by the scythe. And now the husbandmen grew really frightened. In their eager, almost frenzied efforts to secure hands and save their crops (for now it had come to this), they went excitedly into the towns to buy up work at any price. . . .

The standing grain is cut by the reaper, and is raked off the machine by the machine itself, or else by the farmer, armed with a rake, in swaths every four or five feet apart. These are immediately seized upon by the "binders," and made into "bundles." Stooping over each swath, the binder draws from it a handful of long even grain, of which he forms a band, and encompasses with it the swath, tying the ends together, and making the bundle compact and tight. It is then thrown to one side, and the binder, without a moment's loss of time, proceeds to do the same with another. The making of the "bands" requires skill and dexterity, which only practice can give. First, the handful of even-cut grain is drawn from the swath, as just noticed; the top ends, containing the berries of the wheat, are firmly grasped by one hand, while with the other the straw is separated, and by a rapid and peculiar overhand movement and management of the fingers a sort of knot is formed in the berry end; and then the binder, still keeping his finger firmly fixed on the knot, stoops on the swath, grasps it up all clean in his arms, surrounds it with the band, squeezes it tightly together till it forms the smallest possible compass, and then joins the two detached ends of his band in a knot by a quick circular movement and the insertion of his thumb.

"Shocking" comes next in order. After all the wheat is "bound" you see the field strewn with an infinity of bundles. These must all be set up into "shocks." Ordinarily a dozen go to one shock. The "shocker" glances at a spot as nearly in the center of the twelve nearest bundles as he can find, and fixes upon it as the site for his building—for it is customary to talk of "building" these shocks. Then he starts out to gather in his materials; here he seizes one bundle, there he grasps another, two more are rolled up under his arms, and perhaps two more are tugged along, half dragged on the ground, and all are thus borne to the place designated. Here, dropping all save two, he plants these latter firmly on the ground, with the ends containing the ears of wheat uppermost, and at the same time presses them firmly against each other, so that they will stand secure, and mutually support each other. Two more such couples as these are set up, forming a row two

deep and three long. Against this row, on opposite sides, four other bundles find their places, all firmly planted and pressed together, and all having the wheat ends upward. Ten bundles have thus been made to do service. And now the shock is capped by putting on the two final bundles, called "caps" in the vernacular of the field. They are laid crosswise on top, having both their ends flattened out and bent downward, so as more fully to cover the bundles underneath and protect them from the rain should a shower arise. By being spread out and flattened in this manner they lie more securely on the pile, and are less liable to be whisked off by a sudden gust of wind. You can shock more rapidly, of course, than you can bind. Harvest-hands bind about two and a half—sometimes three—acres a day each, and "set up" or shock eight or ten acres in the same time. Generally four or five binders "follow" a reaper, and bind as fast as it can cut. An intense rivalry exists between the various reapers, and agents are in the field constantly during the season, advocating the merits of their different machines. . . .

When the wheat is all shocked the next thing is to stack it. A wagon goes around from shock to shock, with men armed with pitchforks following it, and the grain is all taken in and carried to the stackers. These arrange the bundles on the ground in an immense circle, filling in with others. Some of these stacks are quite large, reaching twenty or thirty feet from the ground. Here it is that the wheat is finally threshed out. Those farmers who have threshing-machines set about immediately to thresh. Others have to wait till those in the business come around to do it for them. The machine is moved by horsepower; eight or ten of these animals going round a circle, and turning a central axis, which imparts its motion to the machinery. A couple of men constantly feed it with bundles of wheat, which it soon digests into pure wheat and separated straw. Those who make it a business to go over the country from farm to farm with their threshing-machines, charge for their work a regulated price, say about six or seven cents per bushel. One of these machines costs about $700 to $800; a year or two's work will pay for its cost; and as they are expected to last several years they leave a good margin of profit. From three to four hundred bushels are threshed out in a day. After this the wheat is bagged in sacks of two bushels each; each sack being marked with its owner's name; and then it is put into wagons and hauled to the nearest market.

147. *Ambition, 1850's*

Mark Twain (Samuel L. Clemens), *Life on the Mississippi* (1874), Chapter iv. From the Hartford edition of 1901.

WHEN I was a boy, there was but one permanent ambition among my comrades in our village on the west bank of the Mississippi River. That was, to be a steamboatman. We had transient ambitions of other sorts, but they were only transient. When a circus came and went, it left us all burning to become clowns; the first Negro minstrel show that ever came to our section left us all suffering to try that kind of life; now and then we had a hope that, if we lived and were good, God would permit us to be pirates. These ambitions faded out, each in its turn; but the ambition to be a steamboatman always remained.

One day a cheap, gaudy packet arrived upward from St. Louis, and another downward from Keokuk. Before these events, the day was glorious with expectancy; after they had transpired, the day was a dead and empty thing. Not only the boys, but the whole village, felt this. After all these years I can picture that old time to myself now, just as it was then: the white town drowsing in the sunshine of a summer's morning; the streets empty, or pretty nearly so; one or two clerks sitting in front of the Water Street stores, with their splint-bottomed chairs tilted back against the walls, chins on breasts, hats slouched over their faces, asleep—with shingle-shavings enough around to show what broke them down; a sow and a litter of pigs loafing along the sidewalk, doing a good business in watermelon rinds and seeds; two or three lonely little freight piles scattered about the "levee"; a pile of "skids" on the slope of the stone-paved wharf, and the fragrant town drunkard asleep in the shadow of them; two or three wood flats at the head of the wharf, but nobody to listen to the peaceful lapping of the wavelets against them; the great Mississippi, the majestic, the magnificent Mississippi, rolling its mile-wide tide along, shining in the sun; the dense forest away on the other side; the "point" above the town, and the "point" below, bounding the river-glimpse and turning it into a sort of sea, and withal a very still and brilliant and lonely one. Presently a film of dark smoke appears above one of those remote "points"; instantly a Negro drayman, famous for his quick eye and prodigious voice, lifts up the cry, "S-t-e-a-m-boat a-comin'!" and the scene changes! The town drunkard stirs, the clerks wake up, a furious clatter of drays follows, every house and store pours out a human contribution, and all in a twinkling the dead town is alive and moving. Drays, carts, men, boys, all go hurrying from many quarters to a common center, the wharf. Assembled there, the people fasten their eyes upon the coming boat as upon a wonder they are seeing for the first time. And the boat *is* rather a handsome sight, too. She is long and sharp and trim and pretty; she has two tall, fancy-topped chimneys, with a gilded device of some kind swung between them;

a fanciful pilot-house, all glass and "gingerbread," perched on top of the "texas" deck behind them; the paddle-boxes are gorgeous with a picture or with gilded rays above the boat's name; the boiler-deck, the hurricane-deck, and the texas deck are fenced and ornamented with clean white railings; there is a flag gallantly flying from the jackstaff; the furnace doors are open and the fires glaring bravely; the upper decks are black with passengers; the captain stands by the big bell, calm, imposing, the envy of all; great volumes of the blackest smoke are rolling and tumbling out of the chimneys—a husbanded grandeur created with a bit of pitch-pine just before arriving at a town; the crew are grouped on the forecastle; the broad stage is run far out over the port bow, and an envied deck-hand stands picturesquely on the end of it with a coil of rope in his hand; the pent steam is screaming through the gauge-cocks; the captain lifts his hand, a bell rings, the wheels stop; then they turn back, churning the water to foam, and the steamer is at rest. Then such a scramble as there is to get aboard, and to get ashore, and to take in freight and to discharge freight, all at one and the same time; and such a yelling and cursing as the mates facilitate it all with! Ten minutes later the steamer is under way again, with no flag on the jackstaff and no black smoke issuing from the chimneys. After ten more minutes the town is dead again, and the town drunkard asleep by the skids once more.

My father was a justice of the peace, and I supposed he possessed the power of life and death over all men, and could hang anybody that offended him. This was distinction enough for me as a general thing; but the desire to be a steamboatman kept intruding, nevertheless. I first wanted to be a cabin-boy, so that I could come out with a white apron on and shake a table-cloth over the side, where all my old comrades could see me; later I thought I would rather be the deck-hand who stood on the end of the stage-plank with

the coil of rope in his hand, because he was particularly conspicuous. But these were only day-dreams—they were too heavenly to be contemplated as real possibilities. By and by one of our boys went away. He was not heard of for a long time. At last he turned up as apprentice engineer or "striker" on a steamboat. This thing shook the bottom out of all my Sunday-school teachings. That boy had been notoriously worldly, and I just the reverse; yet he was exalted to this eminence, and I left in obscurity and misery. There was nothing generous about this fellow in his greatness. He would always manage to have a rusty bolt to scrub while his boat tarried at our town, and he would sit on the inside guard and scrub it, where we all could see him and envy him and loathe him. And whenever his boat was laid up he would come home and swell around the town in his blackest and greasiest clothes, so that nobody could help remembering that he was a steamboatman; and he used all sorts of steamboat technicalities in his talk, as if he were so used to them that he forgot common people could not understand them. He would speak of the "labboard" side of a horse in an easy, natural way that would make one wish he was dead. And he was always talking about "St. Looy" like an old citizen; he would refer casually to occasions when he was "coming down Fourth Street," or when he was "passing by the Planter's House," or when there was a fire and he took a turn on the brakes of "the old Big Missouri"; and then he would go on and lie about how many towns the size of ours were burned down there that day. Two or three of the boys had long been persons of consideration among us because they had been to St. Louis once and had a vague general knowledge of its wonders, but the day of their glory was over now. They lapsed into humble silence, and learned to disappear when the ruthless "cub"-engineer approached. This fellow had money, too, and hair oil. Also an ignorant silver watch and a shiny brass watch chain. He wore a leather belt and used no suspenders. If ever a youth was cordially admired and hated by his comrades, this one was. No girl could withstand his charms. He "cut out" every boy in the village. When his boat blew up at last, it diffused a tranquil contentment among us such as we had not known for months. But when he came home the next week, alive, renowned, and appeared in church all battered up and bandaged, a shining hero, stared at and wondered over by everybody, it seemed to us that the partiality of Providence for an undeserving reptile had reached a point where it was open to criticism.

148. *Midwestern Town, 1836*

Martineau, *Society in America*, I, 349–52.

CHICAGO looks raw and bare, standing on the high prairie above the lake-shore. The houses appeared all insignificant, and run up in various directions, without any principle at all. A friend of mine who resides there had told me that we should find the inns intolerable, at the period of the great land sales, which bring a concourse of speculators to the place. It was even so. The very sight of them was intolerable; and there was not room for our party among them all. I do not know what we should have done (unless to betake ourselves to the vessels in the harbor), if our coming had not been foreknown, and most kindly provided for. We were divided between three families, who had the art of removing all our scruples about intruding on perfect strangers. None of us will lose the lively and pleasant associations with the place, which were caused by the hospitalities of its inhabitants.

I never saw a busier place than Chicago was at the time of our arrival. The streets were crowded with land speculators, hurrying from one sale to another. A Negro, dressed up in scarlet, bearing a scarlet flag, and riding a white horse with housings of scarlet, announced the times of sale. At every street-corner where he stopped, the crowd flocked round him; and it seemed as if some prevalent mania infected the whole people. The rage for speculation might fairly be so regarded. As the gentlemen of our party walked the streets, store-keepers hailed them from their doors, with offers of farms, and all manner of land-lots, advising them to speculate before the price of land rose higher. A young lawyer, of my acquaintance there, had realized five hundred dollars per day, the five preceding days, by merely making out titles to land. Another friend had realized, in two years, ten times as much money as he had before fixed upon as a competence for life. Of course, this rapid money-making is a merely temporary evil. A bursting of the bubble must come soon. The absurdity of the speculation is so striking, that the wonder is that the fever should have attained such a height as I witnessed. The immediate occasion of the bustle which prevailed, the week we were at Chicago, was the sale of lots, to the value of two millions of dollars, along the course of a projected canal; and of another set, immediately behind these. Persons not intending to game, and not infected with mania, would endeavor to form some reasonable conjecture as to the ultimate value of the lots, by calculating the cost of the canal, the risks from accident, from the possible competition from other places, etc., and, finally, the possible profits, under the most favorable circumstances, within so many years' purchase. Such a calculation would serve as some sort of guide as to the amount of purchase money to be risked. Whereas, wild land on the banks of a canal, not yet even marked out, was selling at Chicago for more than rich land, well improved, in the finest part of the valley of the Mohawk, on the banks of a canal which is already the medium of an almost inestimable amount of traffic. If sharpers and gamblers were to be the sufferers by the impending crash at Chicago, no one would feel much concerned; but they, unfortunately, are the people who encourage the delusion, in order to profit by it. Many a high-spirited, but inexperienced, young man;

many a simple settler, will be ruined for the advantage of knaves.

Others, besides lawyers and speculators by trade, make a fortune in such extraordinary times. A poor man at Chicago had a preëmption right to some land, for which he paid in the morning one hundred and fifty dollars. In the afternoon, he sold it to a friend of mine for five thousand dollars.

149. *A Shopkeeper's Life, 1836–39*

Gustavus Wulfing, *Letters*. J. M. Wulfing, ed. (Fulton, 1941), 39, 43, 45–6, 118–19.

I soon realized that farming was not the right thing for us. I did not get a chance to learn the language and customs; I had to work and sweat all day ... to raise enough for our needs. We decided to return to Cincinnati, and I started a small jewelry business by myself. With the aid of our Lord I hope to earn enough to make a living for us and to be able to put a few dollars aside. I intend to import jewelry from Germany and am convinced that I can make money. Christiane is happy that we gave up the much-praised country life. She was always by herself. Here she can visit the Backhaus family ... with whom we are well acquainted. We were fortunate to find a nice and comfortable home, and I have learned English so well that I am able to transact business. ...

We have three German churches here —a Catholic, an Evangelical, and a Lutheran, and each church has a school of its own. We joined the Lutheran church, as we liked the pastor best. The Evangelical minister operates a flour mill, and also a blacksmith shop.... All churches —German or English—are heated. Our pastor gets a salary of about six hundred dollars per year, and three hundred dollars will cover his living expenses if managed wisely. There are several print-

ing establishments and two German-language newspapers; also two companies of German militiamen to protect the city in case of need....

We live about the same way as in Germany. In the morning we have coffee, wheat bread, and butter; at noon a piece of meat, which is better and cheaper than in Germany, with potatoes and cabbage— on Sundays soup, and in the evening coffee or tea. Christiane takes care of the household and of the children, who often play ..."grandmother and aunt"—and I attend to my business. In the evening, when the children are in bed, I read to Christy from the Bible, or *Hasenkamp's Letters*, or something else. Sunday mornings Christy and I alternate in going to church. There is no church in the afternoon, and we spend our time visiting the Backhaus or the Pauck family, or they call on us, and we serve coffee, bread, and butter.

When the weather is bad we stay at home and pass the time by talking about our beloved ones who stayed in Germany, about this country, or our dangerous and troublesome trip, or our experiences on the farm, etc.; and our conversation will always wind up with: "Our Lord guided us well, He protected and shielded us from danger and injury, and He showed us immeasurable kindness which far exceeded our comprehension." The many fine German books which we brought with us give us much pleasure, and we realize now what a great treasure they represent. . . .

Generally speaking, a merchant must have capital to be successful in Germany. In this country the lack of money can be overcome by a spirit of enterprise and by diligence; and respectable conduct is frequently all that is needed to get credit. Fritz, as well as I, could buy a stock worth a thousand dollars on credit terms. I do not like to make use of this, as I prefer to do business in a small way; I pay cash for all purchases and this will give me a good credit-rating. German penny-pinchers are not known; Americans do not worry much about the future. If a fellow has only one dollar left, he does not mind spending it, as most people feel that tomorrow will take care of itself; they can work a day and this will give them money to cover their needs.

To do business is not very difficult when you know the American ways. I earned six dollars yesterday. A few days ago I happened to be in a coffee house and heard that the owner wanted to buy goods for which he was willing to pay twelve dollars. I knew where to get these for seven dollars on the same street. I bought the goods for him, took a roundabout way, delivered the same and made five dollars profit in about fifteen minutes. Of course this does not happen every day, but there are similar chances every hour of the day; more than once I could not find time to eat lunch. . . .

I am pleased that Julius wants to come to America. I assure you that it is my honest opinion that he will do better in this country than he would in Germany, even if someone should give him a thousand *Taler* on the condition that he stay. If he becomes a teacher he would be lucky to earn after many years as much as three hundred *Taler* per annum, and if he were fortunate enough to earn more,

the entire country would talk about such unheard of luck; if he is not inclined to become a teacher, even a still higher salary would not make him happy.

If he wishes to become a merchant, he would have to go into a hardware store, or some other store, and he would have to pass through an apprenticeship of four to six years, and then serve as a soldier; or, if he is not subject to army service, he would be a humble traveling salesman or an office attendant until he succeeds enough, by exercising the greatest thrift, to start a small store, etc. He would not be able to help his brother, no matter how hard he tried; and Friedrich would have to go through the same struggle to be able to earn a living. If the two boys wish, or are compelled, to stay in Germany, I would advise them to learn a good old-fashioned trade, simply because I know from my own experience what opportunities a merchant without capital has in Germany. Think this over most carefully and tell it to all concerned.

If Julius comes to America this summer, I shall give him room and board besides fifty dollars or more the first year, and we shall treat him as our own child. As soon as I get his answer and the consent of his guardian, I shall send $100.00 and letters of recommendation, and I shall give him complete instructions about the best way to make the trip. If he makes up his mind to come, he should make every effort to learn English. By the time Friedrich is confirmed, Julius will have saved enough to loan him $100.00, so that he can come to this country too, and in this way he would be a great help to his younger brother. I do not wish to promise too much, and for that reason I promise to pay only fifty dollars for the first year; however, I intend to pay him more, and I feel certain that it will be more, if I am satisfied with him. I hope he is good, industrious, loyal, and orderly, and I ask you to give me as much information about him as you can.

150. *The Irish Laborer, 1836*

Power, *Impressions of America*, II, 149-52.

I ONLY wish that the wise men at home who coolly charge the present condition of Ireland upon the inherent laziness of her population, could be transported to this spot, to look upon the hundreds of fine fellows laboring here beneath a sun that at this winter season was at times insufferably fierce, and amidst a pestilential swamp whose exhalations were fetid to a degree scarcely endurable even for a few moments; wading amongst stumps of trees, mid-deep in black mud, clearing the spaces pumped out by powerful steam engines; wheeling, digging, hewing, or bearing burdens it made one's shoulders ache to look upon; exposed meantime to every change of temperature, in log huts, laid down in the very swamp, on a foundation of newly-felled trees, having the water lying stagnant between the floor logs, whose interstices, together with those of the sidewalls, are open, pervious alike to sun, or wind, or snow. Here they subsist on the coarsest fare, holding life on a tenure as uncertain as does the leader of a forlorn hope; excluded from all the advantages of civilization; often at the mercy of a hard contractor, who wrings his profits from their blood; and all this for a pittance that merely enables them to exist, with little power to save, or a hope beyond the continuance of the like exertion.

Such are the laborers I have seen here, and have still found them civil and courteous, with a ready greeting for the stranger inquiring into their condition, and a quick jest on their own equipment, which is frequently, it must be admitted, of a whimsical kind.

Here too were many poor women with their husbands; and when I contemplated their wasted forms and haggard sickly looks, together with the close swamp whose stagnant air they were doomed to breathe, whose aspect changeless and deathlike alone met their eyes, and fancied them, in some hour of leisure, calling to memory the green valley and the pure river, or the rocky glen and sparkling brook of their distant home, with all the warmth of coloring the imaginative spirit of the Irish peasant can so well supply, my heart has swelled and my eyes have filled with tears.

I cannot hope to inspire the reader with my feelings upon a mere sketch like this; but if I could set the scene of these poor laborers' exile fairly forth, with all the sad accompaniments detailed; could I show the course of the hardy, healthy pair, just landed, to seek fortune on these long-sighed-for shores, with spirits newly lifted by hope and brighter prospects from the apathy into which compulsory idleness and consequent recklessness had reduced them at home; and then paint the spirit-sinking felt on a first view of the scene of their future labor,—paint the wild revel designed to drown remembrance, and give heart to the newcomers; describe the nature of the toil where exertion is taxed to the uttermost, and the weary frame stimulated by the worst alcohol, supplied by the contractor, at a cheap rate for the purpose of exciting a rivalry of exertion amongst these simple men.

Next comes disease, either a sweeping pestilence that deals wholesale on its victims, or else a gradual sinking of mind and body; finally, the abode in the hospital, if any comrade is interested enough for the sufferer to bear him to it; else, the solitary log hut and quicker death. Could these things, with their true colors, be set forth in detail before the veriest grinder of the poor that ever drove the peasant to curse and quit the soil of his birth, he would cover his eyes from the light of heaven, and feel that he yet possessed a heart and human sympathy.

At such works all over this continent the Irish are the laborers chiefly employed, and the mortality amongst them is enormous,—a mortality I feel certain might be vastly lessened by a little consideration being given to their condition by those who employ them. At present they are, where I have seen them working here, worse lodged than the cattle of the field; in fact, the only thought bestowed upon them appears to be, by what expedient the greatest quantity of labor may be extracted from them at the cheapest rate to the contractor. I think, however, that a better spirit is in progress amongst the companies requiring this class of laborers; in fact, it becomes necessary this should be so, since, prolific as is the country from whence they are drawn, the supply would in a little time cease to keep pace with the demand, and slave labor cannot be substituted to any extent, being much too expensive; a good slave costs at this time two hundred pounds sterling, and to have a thousand such swept off a line of canal in one season, would call for prompt consideration.

XIX ※ *The Development of a National Economy*

TERRITORIAL expansion most directly affected agriculture; but it ultimately recast also every other branch of the economy. Commerce, transportation, finance, and industry all advanced under the stimulus of the growth of population and resources.

In some regions of the country commerce was still the measure of national wealth. And indeed, trade of every sort flourished to mid-century; it reached deep into the rural interior (No. 151); and it found new outlets, in California (No. 152), in the Mexican provinces (No. 153), and overseas. Until the Civil War dealt shipping a staggering blow, commerce thrived.

Its prosperity was bound in with a revolution that expanded and reorganized the communications system of the nation. The older turnpikes and river waterways were now supplemented by novel means of transportation. The Erie Canal (No. 154) was the most important; but others appeared in every part of the country. Yet the canals were hardly complete before the railroads spread across the nation and created a vast home market for industry and agriculture (No. 155). Political decisions prevented the Federal Government from assisting in these internal improvements (*see below*, Section XXIV). On the other hand, the states were active; and legal interpretation tended to encourage rapid new developments (No. 156).

The financial requirements of expansion put a heavy strain on the rudimentary banking system of the nation. The efforts to control credit and currency through the Bank of the United States were only moderately successful; and they collapsed altogether after the Bank became embroiled in a political war with Andrew Jackson (*see below*, Section XXIV). Restraints on speculative inflation were thereafter effective in only a few localities. Elsewhere, the banks expanded almost without limit, on the assumption that they created wealth (No. 157; *see also above*, No. 148). Expansion was halted temporarily by the Specie Circular (No. 158), which led to panic and a collapse of speculative values (Nos. 159, 160). Recovery permitted further expansion, but led to a renewed panic in 1857.

Meanwhile, manufacturing had entered upon a development that would grow in significance through the nineteenth century. The New England textile factories were still rural, paternalistic enterprises (No. 161); but they were an omen of what was yet to come.

151. *Going to Store, 1852*

Robert Carlton [pseud. of B. R. Hall], *The New Purchase* (New York, 1843), I, 253.

IN A New Purchase country, "going to store" is as much for recreation as business, and preparation is made as for any other treat or amusement. The store is, too, the place for news, recent and stale—for gymnastics, wrestling, pitching quoits, running—for rifle shooting—for story-telling, etc.—and hence, a purchaser's stay is not in direct ratio to his intended bargains, but rather in the inverse; a fellow having only six cents to spend, will sometimes lounge in and around a store for six hours! Nor must even that be wholly imputed to the fellow's idleness. It is in part, owing to his unwillingness to part with—cash; and when it is considered how very difficult it was then, and maybe now, in the New Purchase to get hold of "silver," then it will appear that to lay out even a fipenny-bit must have become a matter for very solemn reflection, and very lengthy chaf-

fering. In my time, rarely indeed, could two cash dollars be seen circulating together; and having then no banks, and being suspicious of all foreign paper, we carried on our operations almost exclusively by trade. For goods, store-keepers received the vast bulk of their pay in produce, which was converted into cash at Louisville, Cincinnati, or more frequently at New Orleans. The great house of Glenville and Carlton paid for all things in —leather. Hence, occasionally when a wood-chopper must have shoes and yet had no produce, but offered to pay in "chopping," we, not needing that article, and being indebted to several neighbors who did, used to send the man and his axe as the circulating medium in demand among our own creditors, to chop out the bills against us.

152. *The California Trade, 1840*

R. H. Dana, Jr., *Two Years Before the Mast* (Published 1840; this extract is from the edition, New York, 1921), 83–4.

THE NEXT day, the cargo having been entered in due form, we began trading. The trade-room was fitted up in the steerage, and furnished out with the lighter goods, and with specimens of the rest of the cargo; and . . . a young man who came out from Boston with us, before the mast, was taken out of the forecastle, and made supercargo's clerk. He was well qualified for the business, having been

clerk in a counting-house in Boston. . . .

For a week or ten days all was life on board. The people came off to look and to buy—men, women, and children; and we were continually going in the boats, carrying goods and passengers,—for they have no boats of their own. Everything must dress itself and come aboard and see the new vessel, if it were only to buy a paper of pins. The agent and his clerk managed the sales, while we were busy in the hold or in the boats. Our cargo was an assorted one; that is, it consisted of everything under the sun. We had spirits of all kinds (sold by the cask), teas, coffee, sugars, spices, raisins, molasses, hardware, crockery ware, tinware, cutlery, clothing of all kinds, boots and shoes from Lynn, calicoes and cottons from Lowell, crepes, silks; also, shawls, scarfs, neck-laces, jewelry, and combs for the ladies; furniture; and in fact, everything that can be imagined, from Chinese fire-works to English cart-wheels—of which we had a dozen pairs with their iron rims on.

The Californians are an idle, thriftless people, and can make nothing for them-selves. The country abounds in grapes, yet they buy bad wine made in Boston and brought round by us, at an immense price, and retail it among themselves at a *real* (12½ cents) by the small wineglass. Their hides too, which they value at two dollars in money, they give for something which costs seventy-five cents in Boston; and buy shoes (as like as not, made of their own hides, which have been carried twice round Cape Horn) at three and four dollars, and "chicken-skin" boots at fifteen dollars apiece. Things sell, on an average, at an advance of nearly three hundred per cent upon the Boston prices. This is partly owing to the heavy duties which the government, in their wisdom, with the intent, no doubt, of keeping the silver in the country, has laid upon im-ports. These duties, and the enormous expenses of so long a voyage, keep all the merchants, but those of heavy capital, from engaging in the trade. Nearly two-thirds of all the articles imported into the country from round Cape Horn, for the last six years, have been by the single house of Bryant, Sturgis and Co., to whom our vessel belonged and who have a permanent agent on the coast.

153. *The Santa Fé Trade, 1830's*

Josiah Gregg, *Commerce of the Prairies* (1845). Reprinted in R. G. Thwaites, *Early Western Travels.* (Cleveland, 1904–07), XIX, 188–93, 229, 256–7.

As THE navigation of the Missouri River had considerably advanced towards the year 1831, and the advantages of some point of debarkation nearer the western frontier were very evident . . . , the new town of Independence . . . soon began to take the lead as a place of debarkation, outfit and departure. . . . It is to this beau-tiful spot, already grown up to be a thriv-ing town, that the prairie adventurer . . . is latterly in the habit of repairing, about the first of May, as the caravans usually set out some time during that month. Here they purchase their provisions for the road, and many of their mules, oxen, and even some of their wagons—in short, load all their vehicles, and make their final preparations for a long journey across the prairie wilderness. . . .

Independence . . . has become the gen-eral "port of embarkation" for every part of the great western and northern "prairie ocean." Besides the Santa Fé caravans, most of the Rocky Mountain traders and trappers, as well as emigrants to Oregon, take this town in their route. During the season of departure, therefore, it is a place of much bustle and active business. . . .

The ordinary supplies for each man's consumption during the journey [to Santa Fé] are about fifty pounds of flour, as many more of bacon, ten of coffee and twenty of sugar, and a little salt. Beans, crackers, and trifles of that description . . . are seldom to be found in any of the stores on the road. The buffalo is chiefly de-pended upon for fresh meat, and great is the joy of the traveler when that noble animal first appears in sight.

The wagons now most in use upon the

prairies are manufactured in Pittsburgh; and are usually drawn by eight mules or the same number of oxen. Of late years, however, I have seen much larger vehicles employed, with ten or twelve mules harnessed to each, and a cargo of goods of about five thousand pounds in weight. . . .

The supplies being at length procured, and all necessary preliminaries systematically gone through, the trader begins the difficult task of loading his wagons. Those who understand their business, take every precaution so to stow away their packages that no jolting on the road can afterwards disturb the order in which they had been disposed. . . .

At last all are fairly launched upon the broad prairie—the miseries of preparation are over—the thousand anxieties occasioned by wearisome consultations and delays are felt no more. The charioteer, as he smacks his whip, feels a bounding elasticity of soul within him, which he finds it impossible to restrain;—even the mules prick up their ears with a peculiarly conceited air, as if in anticipation of that change of scene which will presently follow. Harmony and good feeling prevail everywhere. The hilarious song, the *bon mot* and the witty repartee, go round in quick succession; and before people have had leisure to take cognizance of the fact, the lovely village of Independence, with its multitude of associations, is already lost to the eye. . . .

The rank of captain is, of course, but little more than nominal. Every proprietor of a two-horse wagon is apt to assume as much authority as the commander himself, and to issue his orders without the least consultation at headquarters. It is easy then to conceive that the captain has anything but an enviable berth. He is expected to keep order while few are disposed to obey—loaded with execrations for every mishap, whether accidental or otherwise; and when he attempts to remonstrate he only renders himself ridiculous, being entirely without power to enforce his commands. It is to be regretted

that some system of "maritime law" has not been introduced among these traders to secure subordination, which can never be attained while the commander is invested with no legal authority. . . .

The arrival of a caravan at Santa Fé changes the aspect of the place at once. Instead of the idleness and stagnation which its streets exhibited before, one now sees everywhere the bustle, noise and activity of a lively market town. As the Mexicans very rarely speak English, the negotiations are mostly conducted in Spanish.

Taking the circuit of the stores, I found they usually contained general assortments, much like those to be met with in the retail variety stores of the west. The stocks of the inexperienced merchants are apt to abound in unsalable goods—*mulas*, as the Mexicans figuratively term them.

Although a fair variety of dry goods, silks, hardware, etc., is to be found in this market, domestic cottons, both bleached and brown, constitute the great staple, of which nearly equal quantities ought to enter into a "Santa Fé assortment." The demand for these goods is such that at least one half of our stocks of merchandise is made up of them. However, although they afford a greater nominal per centum than many other articles, the profits are reduced by their freight and heavy duty. In all the southern markets, where they enter into competition, there is a decided preference given to the American manufactures over the British, as the former are more heavy and durable. The demand for calicoes is also considerable, but this kind of goods affords much less profit. The quantity in an assortment should be about equal to half that of domestics. Cotton velvets, and drillings (whether bleached, brown or blue, and especially the latter), have also been in much request. But all the coarser cotton goods, whether shirtings, calicoes or drillings, &c., were prohibited by the *Arancel* of 1837; and still continue to be, with some modifications.

154. *The Canals, 1833*

James Stuart, *Three Years in North America* (Edinburgh, 1833), I, 54–6, 58–9.

THE CANALS are works of which the State of New York has great reason to be proud. . . . Their whole course is within the State of New York, that of the Erie Canal, westward by the valley of the Mohawk, and of the Champlain Canal, northward by that of the Hudson. . . . They were commenced in July 1817, and completed in October 1825. . . . The object of the Erie Canal is to form a communication between New York and the internal . . . seas of North America, and through them to the great western country of the United States, and the rivers Ohio, Mississippi, and Missouri. The object of the Champlain Canal is to form a communication through Lake Champlain, and the river Richelieu or Chambly, with the St. Lawrence and Canada.

The Erie Canal includes 83 locks 90 feet long, and 18 aqueducts, one of which is about 1200, and two about 800, feet in length. The canal is 40 feet wide at the top, and four feet deep. . . . The whole expense amounted to about nine millions of dollars, and the revenue for the year 1827 was 859,000 dollars. . . .

The work was not long successfully carried on, before the State of Ohio . . . followed the example of the State of New York, and began to consider how Governor Clinton's great project of completing the communication to the western rivers of America, by a canal from Lake Erie to the Ohio, was to be effected.

They obtained plans and estimates, which, before proceeding, they transmitted to Governor Clinton for his opinion and advice. The governor's reply . . . was most satisfactory. . . . Accordingly, the legislature of Ohio, in February 1825, authorized the construction of their great canal, 320 miles long, from Lake Erie by Chillicothe, and passing near Columbus, the seat of legislature of the state, to the river Ohio.

Much of it is now finished. When completed, three years hence, the market of New Orleans will not be more open to the western states,—to the people of Missouri, Indiana, and Ohio,—than that of New York or of Montreal, and the greater part of the United States,—all of it, in fact, except what is situated to the westward of the Mississippi, will, as stated in one of Clinton's admirable addresses, "form one vast island, susceptible of circumnavigation, to the extent of many thousand miles. The most distant parts of the confederacy will then be in a state of approximation, and the distinctions of eastern and western, of southern and northern interests, will be entirely prostrated."

155. *The Influence of Railroads, 1852*

I. D. Andrews, *Report on the Trade and Commerce of the British North American Colonies* (Washington, 1853), 380–7. Appears in 32 Congress, 1 Session, *Senate Executive Documents*, No. 112 and *House Executive Documents*, No. 136.

THE WIDE space that separates the producing and consuming classes . . . necessarily implies the exportation of the surplus products of each. The western farmer has no . . . [local] demand for the wheat he raises, as the surplus of all his neighbors is the same in kind. The aggregate surplus of the district in which he resides has to be exported to find a consumer; and the producer for a similar reason is obliged to import all the various articles that enter into consumption which his own industry does not immediately supply; and farther, as the markets for our agricultural products lie either upon the extreme verge of the country, or in Europe, the greater part of our domestic commerce involves a through movement of nearly all the articles of which it is composed. . . .

Railroads in the United States exert a much greater influence upon the value of property, than in other countries. . . . The actual increase in the value of lands, due to the construction of railroads . . . can only be approximated, and must in most cases fall far short of the fact. Not only are cultivated lands, and city and village lots, lying immediately upon the route affected, but the real estate in cities, hundreds and thousands of miles distant. The railroads of Ohio exert as much influence in advancing the prices of real property in the city of New York, as do the roads lying within that state. . . . But taking only the farming lands of the particular district traversed by a railroad, where the influence of such a work can be more directly seen, there is no doubt that in such case the increased value is many times greater than the cost of the road. . . . It is believed that the construction of the three thousand miles of railroad of Ohio will add to the value of the landed property in the state at least five times the cost of the roads, assuming this to be $60,000,000. In addition to the very rapid advance in the price of farming lands, the roads of Ohio are stimulating the growth of her cities with extraordinary rapidity, so that there is much greater probability that the above estimate will be exceeded, than not reached, by the actual fact. We are not left to estimate in this matter. In the case of the State of Massachusetts, what is conjecture in regard to the new states has with her become a matter of history. The valuation

of that state went up, from 1840 to 1850, from $290,000,000 to $580,000,000—an immense increase, and by far the greater part of it due to the numerous railroads she has constructed. . . .

But such results do not by any means give the most forcible illustration of their use. . . . Deposits [of iron or coal] may be entirely valueless without a railroad. With one, every ton of ore they contain is worth one, two, three, or four dollars, as the case may be. . . . Without coal it is impossible to conceive the spectacle that we should have presented as a people, so entirely different would it have been from our present condition. Neither our commerical nor our manufacturing, nor, consequently, our agricultural interests, could have borne any relation whatever to their present enormous magnitude. Yet all this result has been achieved by a few railroads and canals in Pennsylvania, which have not cost over $50,000,000. With these works, coal can be brought into the New York market for about $3.50 per ton; without them, it could not have been made available either for ordinary fuel or as a motive power. . . .

There is no other country in the world where an equal amount of labor produces an equal bulk of freight for railroad transportation. One reason is, that the great mass of our products is of a coarse, bulky character, of very low comparative value, and consisting chiefly of the products of the soil and forest. We manufacture very few high-priced goods, labor being more profitably employed upon what are at present more appropriate objects of industry. The great bulk of the articles carried upon railroads is grains, cotton, sugar, coal, iron, livestock, and articles of a similar character. The difference between the value of a pound of raw and manufactured cotton is measured frequently by dollars, yet both may pay the same amount of freight. Wheat, corn, cattle, and lumber, all pay a very large sum for transportation in proportion to their values. Again . . . the transportation of many of our important products involves a through transportation. Take, for instance, a cotton-producing state like Mississippi. Nearly the whole industry of this state is engaged in the cultivation of this article. Of the immense amount produced no part is consumed or used within the state. The entire staple goes abroad; but as the aggregate industry of the people is confined to the production of one staple, it follows that all articles entering into consumption must be imported; so that, over the channels through which the cotton of this state is sent to market, an equal value or tonnage must be imported.... This necessity, both of an inward and outward movement, equal to the whole bulk of the surplus agricultural product, is peculiar to the United States, and is one of the reasons of the large receipts of our roads....

The general views above stated, in reference to the earnings of the railroads in the United States, are fully borne out by the result. Investments in these works have probably yielded a better return ... than the ordinary rates of interest prevailing throughout the country. Such is the case with the roads of Massachusetts, the state in which these works have been carried to the greatest extent, and have cost the most per mile, and amongst which are embraced a number of expensive and unproductive lines....

By far the greater number of our roads in progress are in the interior of the country—in our agricultural districts, that do not possess an amount of accumulated capital equal to their cost. A business adequate to the support of a railroad may exist without the means to construct one. The construction of a railroad, too, creates opportunities for investment which promise a much greater return than the stock in such a work. While, therefore, our people are disposed to make every reasonable sacrifice to secure a railroad, they prefer, and in fact they find it more for their interest, to borrow a portion of the amount required, than to invest the whole

means directly in the project. They can better afford to secure the cooperation of foreign capital, by offering high premiums for its use, than to embarrass themselves by making a permanent investment of too large a proportion of their own immediate means. These facts sufficiently explain the reasons why the borrowing of a considerable portion of the cost of our roads has become so universal a rule....

In the outset, money was furnished slowly and cautiously, and then only upon the most unquestioned security. As the result began to demonstrate the safety and productiveness of these investments, capital was more freely afforded, and became less exacting in its conditions. The result has been, that a confidence in the safety of our railroads, as investments of capital, has become general, not only in this country, but in Europe; and companies whose means and prospective advantages entitle them to credit, find no difficulty in borrowing a reasonable sum upon the security of their roads, with which to complete them. The amount usually borrowed for our roads in progress averages from $5,000 to $10,000 per mile. The general custom requires that a sum equal to the one sought to be borrowed shall be first paid in, or secured for construction. A road that will cost $20,000 per mile is considered a sufficient security for a loan of $10,000 per mile....

This rule, which establishes the proportions to be supplied by those engaged in the construction, and capitalists, is well calculated to promote the best advantage of both parties. The fact that the people on the line of the contemplated road are willing to furnish one-half of the means requisite for construction ... is sufficient evidence that in the opinion of such people, the construction of such work is justified by a prospective business. The interest they have in it also is a sufficient guarantee that its affairs will be carefully and prudently managed. The large amount paid in and at stake divests the project of all speculative features.

156. *Charles River Bridge* v. *Warren Bridge*, 1837

11 Peters, 420, 508–12.

THIS act of incorporation . . . confers . . . the ordinary faculties of a corporation, for the purpose of building the bridge; and establishes certain rates of toll, which the company are authorized to take. This is the whole grant. There is no exclusive privilege given to them over the waters of Charles River, above or below their bridge; no right to erect another bridge themselves, nor to prevent other persons from erecting one, no engagement from the State, that another shall not be erected; and no undertaking not to sanction competition, nor to make improvements that may diminish the amount of its income. . . . If the plaintiff is entitled to them, it must be implied, simply from the nature of the grant, and cannot be inferred from the words by which the grant is made. . . .

The inquiry then is, does the charter contain such a contract on the part of the State? Is there any such stipulation to be found in that instrument? It must be admitted on all hands, that there is none— no words that even relate to another bridge, or to the diminution of their tolls, or to the line of travel. If a contract on that subject can be gathered from the charter, it must be by implication, and cannot be found in the words used. Can such an agreement be implied?

The rule of construction before stated is an answer to the question. In charters of this description, no rights are taken from the public, or given to the corporation, beyond those which the words of the charter, by their natural and proper construction, purport to convey. There are no words which import such a contract . . . and none can be implied. . . . The whole community are interested in this inquiry, and they have a right to require that the power of promoting their comfort and convenience, and of advancing the public prosperity, by providing safe, convenient, and cheap ways for the transportation of produce and the purposes of travel, shall not be construed to have been surrendered or diminished by the State, unless it shall appear by plain words that it was intended to be done. . . .

Indeed, the practice and usage of almost every State in the Union old enough to have commenced the work of internal improvement, is opposed to the doctrine contended for. . . . Turnpike roads have been made in succession, on the same line of travel; the later ones interfering materially with the profits of the first. These corporations have, in some instances, been utterly ruined by the introduction of newer and better modes of transportation and traveling. In some cases, railroads have rendered the turnpike roads on the same line of travel so entirely useless, that the franchise of the turnpike corporation is not worth preserving. Yet in none of these cases have the corporations supposed that their privileges were invaded, or any contract violated on the part of the State. . . .

And what would be the fruits of this doctrine of implied contracts on the part of the States, and of property in a line of travel by a corporation, if it should now be sanctioned by this court? . . . If it is to be found in the charter to this bridge, the same process of reasoning must discover it, in the various acts which have been passed, within the last forty years, for turnpike companies. . . . If this court should establish the principles now contended for, what is to become of the numerous railroads established on the same line of travel with turnpike companies, and which have rendered the franchises of the turnpike corporations of no value? . . . You will soon find the old turnpike corporations awakening from their sleep and calling upon this court to put down the improvements which have taken their place. The millions of property which have been invested in railroads and canals upon lines of travel which had been before occupied by turnpike corporations will be put in jeopardy. We shall be thrown back to the improvements of the last century, and obliged to stand still until the claims of the old turnpike corporations shall be sat-isfied, and they shall consent to permit these States to avail themselves of the lights of modern science, and to partake of the benefit of those improvements which are now adding to the wealth and prosperity, and the convenience and comfort, of every other part of the civilized world.

157. *Country Banks, 1839*

Condy Raguet, *Treatise on Currency and Banking* (Philadelphia, 1839), 131–5.

IT IS an opinion very frequently expressed, that the establishment of banks in the western and southwestern country, has been a great source of prosperity to the cities and towns where they have been located. . . . Cincinnati, Louisville, Nashville, Natchez, Vicksburg, and numerous other places, it is said, owe a large share of their prosperity to the establishment of banks; and as these have all been banks of circulation, it is concluded that therefore banks of circulation must have powers to create national wealth. . . .

Nothing but capital, that is something possessing an intrinsic value, can possibly be the means of setting industry in motion, and . . . banks have not the power of creating such capital by a mere issue of promissory notes. It may, then, fairly be concluded, that as far as any real prosperity has been ascribed to the circulating principle, . . . the position is fallacious. . . . But, at the same time, I am prepared to admit, that as far as the capitals of the banks referred to have been subscribed by capitalists residing in the Atlantic cities, those cities and towns have reaped all the benefits resulting from the borrowing of a foreign capital. . . . That capital . . . was . . . but a fund in the Atlantic cities, drawn upon and sold to the western merchants as a remittance to pay up their existing debts, or to purchase new supplies of goods. It was thus a capital . . . really paid up in dry-goods, hardware, and groceries; and the effect, therefore, upon the pros-perity of the western towns, was precisely the same as that of obtaining from individual merchants, or in any other way upon credit, an equal amount of merchandise, with this difference, that the credit might not cost as much through the process of a bank, as if obtained through a purchase of goods in the ordinary way.

This difference in the cost of the credit, however, is all the benefit that the western cities and towns can have reaped from borrowing foreign capital through bank charters. . . . As a set off to it, it may very fairly be assumed, that in the scramble for discounts made on the first opening of the banks, the loans of capital and credit were not as judiciously made for the general interests of the country, as sales of merchandise would have been by the eastern merchants, as is shown by the fact that immense sums were loaned to planters who embarked in speculations in lands and slaves, and to merchants who embarked in shipments of cotton, and who ultimately became embarrassed or ruined by these operations. . . . All the benefit which the western and southwestern states have derived from the establishment amongst them of banks constructed upon foreign capital over and above the benefits which those states would have derived from their merchants buying and selling an equal amount of foreign goods on credit, has been more than counterbalanced by the evils resulting from incautious loans of capital and credit.

158. *The Specie Circular, 1836*

July 11, 1836, communicated to the Senate, December 14, 1836. From *American State Papers, Public Lands* (Washington, 1861), VIII, 910.

THE PRESIDENT of the United States has given directions, and you are hereby instructed, after the 15th day of August next, to receive in payment of the public lands nothing except what is directed by the existing laws, viz.: gold and silver. . . .

The principal objects of the President, in adopting this measure, being to repress alleged frauds, and to withhold any countenance or facilities in the power of the government from the monopoly of the public lands in the hands of speculators and capitalists, to the injury of the actual settlers in the new States, and of emigrants in search of new homes, as well as to discourage the ruinous extension of bank issues and bank credits, by which those results are generally supposed to be promoted, your utmost vigilance is required, and relied on, to carry this order into complete execution.

159. *The Panic of 1837*

Nicholas Biddle, *Two Letters Addressed to the Hon. J. Quincy Adams, Embracing a History of the Re-Charter of the Bank of the United States* (London, 1837), 16–18.

ON A sudden, without any intimation of the coming shock, an order was issued by the Secretary, declaring that [bank] . . . notes were no longer receivable, and of course inviting all who held the notes, and had deposits in these banks, to convert them into specie. It in fact made at once the whole amount of their circulation and private deposits a specie demand upon them.—The first consequence was, that the banks nearest the land offices ceased making loans. The next was, that they strove to fortify themselves by accumulating specie. . . .

The commercial community were thus taken by surprise. The interior banks making no loans, and converting their Atlantic funds into specie, the debtors in the interior could make no remittances to the merchants in the Atlantic cities, who are thus thrown for support on the banks of those cities at a moment when they are unable to afford relief on account of the very abstraction of their specie to the West. . . .

By this unnatural process the specie of New York and the other commercial cities is piled up in the western states, not circulated, not used, but held as a defense against the Treasury—and while the West cannot use it—the East is suffering for the want of it. The result is, that the commercial intercourse between the West and the Atlantic is almost wholly suspended, and the few operations which are made are burthened with the most extravagant expense. In November, 1836, the interest of money has risen to 24 per cent—merchants are struggling to preserve their credit by ruinous sacrifices—and it costs five or six times as much to transmit funds from the west and southwest, as it did in November, 1835. . . . Thus while the exchanges with all the world are in our favor—while Europe is alarmed, and the Bank of England itself uneasy at the quantity of specie we possess—we are suffering, because, from mere mismanagement, the whole ballast of the currency is shifted from one side of the vessel to the other.

In the absence of good reasons for these measures, and as a pretext for them, it is said that the country has over-traded—that the banks have over-issued, and that the purchasers of public lands have been very extravagant. I am not struck by the truth or the propriety of these complaints. The phrase of overtrading is very convenient but not very intelligible. If it means anything, it means that our dealings with other countries have brought us in debt to those countries. In that case the exchange turns against our country, and is rectified by an exportation of specie or stocks in the first instance—and then by reducing the imports to the exports.—Now the fact is, that at this moment, the exchanges are all in favor of this country. . . . Accordingly, much specie has come in—none goes out. . . . How then has the country over-traded? Exchange with all the world is in favor of New York. . . . Her merchants have sold goods to the merchants of the interior, who are willing to pay, and under ordinary circumstances able to pay—but by the mere fault of the government, . . . their debtors are disabled from making immediate payment. It is not that the Atlantic merchants have sold too many goods, but that the government prevents their receiving payment for any. . . .

Then as to the banks. It is quite probable that many of the banks have extended their issues—but whose fault is it? Who called these banks into existence? The Executive. Who tempted and goaded them to these issues? Undoubtedly the Executive. The country five years ago was in possession of the most beautiful machinery of currency and exchanges the world ever saw. It consisted of a number of state banks protected, and, at the same time, restrained by the Bank of the United States.

The people of the United States through their representatives rechartered that institution. But the Executive, discontented with its independence, rejected the act of Congress—and the favorite topic of declamation was that the states would make banks, and that these banks could create a better system of currency and exchanges. The states accordingly made banks—and then followed idle parades about the loans of these banks, and their enlarged dealings in exchange. And what is the consequence? The Bank of the United States has not ceased to exist more than seven months, and already the whole currency and exchanges are running into inextricable confusion, and the industry of the country is burthened with extravagant charges on all the commercial intercourse of the Union. And now, when these banks have been created by the Executive, and urged into these excesses, instead of gentle and gradual remedies, a fierce crusade is raised against them—the funds are harshly and suddenly taken from them, and they are forced to extraordinary means of defense against the very power which brought them into being. They received, and were expected to receive, in payment for the Government, the notes of each other, and the notes of other banks, and the facility with which they did so, was a ground of special commendation by the Government. And now that Government has let loose upon them a demand for specie, to the whole amount of these notes.

160. *Flush Times and Their Result, 1837*

J. G. Baldwin, *The Flush Times of Alabama and Mississippi* (New York, 1854), 81–4, 89–90.

IN THE fullness of time the new era had set in—the era of the second great experiment of independence: the experiment, namely, of credit without capital, and enterprise without honesty. The Age of Brass had succeeded the Arcadian period when men got rich by saving a part of their earnings. . . . A new theory, not found in the works on political economy, was broached. It was found out that the prejudice in favor of the metals (brass excluded) was an absurd superstition; and that, in reality, anything else, which the parties interested in giving it currency chose, might serve as a representative of value and medium for exchange of property; and as gold and silver had served for a great number of years as representatives, the republican doctrine of rotation in office required they should give way. Accordingly it was decided that Rags, a very familiar character, and very popular and easy of access, should take their place.

Rags belonged to the school of progress. . . . The leading fiscal idea of his system was to democratize capital, and to make, for all purposes of trade, credit and enjoyment of wealth, the man that had no money a little richer, if anything, than the man that had a million. The principle of success and basis of operation, though inexplicable in the hurry of the time, is plain enough now: it was faith. Let the public believe that a smutted rag is money, it is money. . . .

This country was just settling up. Marvelous accounts had gone forth of the fertility of its virgin lands; and the productions of the soil were commanding a high price remunerating to slave labor as it had never been remunerated before. Emigrants came flocking in from all corners of the Union, especially from the slaveholding states. The new country seemed to be a reservoir, and every road leading to it a vagrant stream of enterprise and adventure. Money, or what passed for money, was the only cheap thing to be had. Every crossroad and every avocation presented an opening,—through which a fortune was seen by the adventurer in near perspective. Credit was a thing of course. To refuse it —if the thing was ever done—were an insult for which a bowie-knife were not a too summary or exemplary a means of redress. The state banks were issuing their bills by the sheet, like a patent steam printing-press its issues; and no other showing was asked of the applicant for the loan than an authentication of his great distress for money. Finance, even in its most exclusive quarter, had thus already got, in this wonderful revolution, to work upon the principles of the charity hospital. If an overseer grew tired of supervising a plantation and felt a call to the mercantile life, even if he omitted the compendious method of buying out a merchant wholesale, stock, house and good will, and laying down, at once, his bull-whip for the yard-stick—all he had to do was to go on to New York, and present himself in Pearl Street with a letter avouching his citizenship, and a clean shirt, and he was regularly given a through ticket to speedy bankruptcy.

Under this stimulating process prices rose like smoke. Lots in obscure villages were held at city prices; lands, bought at the minimum cost of government, were sold at from thirty to forty dollars per acre, and considered dirt cheap at that. . . .

But this state of things could not last forever: society cannot always stand on its head with its heels in the air. . . .

The Specie Circular was issued without warning, and the splendid lie of a false credit burst into fragments. It came in the midst of the dance and the frolic. . . . Its effect was like that of a general creditor's bill in the chancery court, and a marshalling of all the assets of the tradespeople. General Jackson was no fairy; but he did some very pretty fairy work, in converting the bank bills back again into rags and oak-leaves. Men worth a million were insolvent for two millions: promising young cities marched back again into the wilderness. The ambitious town plat was reannexed to the plantation, like a country girl taken home from the city. The frolic was ended, and what headaches, and feverish limbs the next morning!

161. *The New England Mills, 1836*

Martineau, *Society in America*, II, 247–50.

I VISITED the corporate factory establishment at Waltham, within a few miles of Boston. The Waltham Mills were at work before those of Lowell were set up. The establishment is for the spinning and weaving of cotton alone, and the construction of the requisite machinery. Five hundred persons were employed at the time of my visit. The girls earn two, and some three, dollars a week, besides their board. The little children earn one dollar a week. Most of the girls live in the houses provided by the corporation, which accommodate from six to eight each. When sisters come to the mill, it is a common practice for them to bring their mother to keep house for them and some of their companions, in a dwelling built by their own earnings. In this case, they save enough out of their own board to clothe themselves, and have their two or three dollars a week to spare. Some have thus cleared off mortgages from their fathers' farms; others have educated the hope of the family at college; and many are rapidly accumulating an independence. I saw a whole street of houses built with the earnings of the girls; some with piazzas, and green venetian blinds; and all neat and sufficiently spacious.

The factory people built the church, which stands conspicuous on the green in the midst of the place. The minister's salary (eight hundred dollars last year) is raised by a tax on the pews. The corporation gave them a building for a lyceum, which they have furnished with a good library, and where they have lectures every winter. . . .

The managers of the various factory establishments keep the wages as nearly equal as possible, and then let the girls freely shift about from one to another. When a girl comes to the overseer to inform him of her intention of working at the mill, he welcomes her, and asks how long she means to stay. It may be six months, or a year, or five years, or for life. She declares what she considers herself fit for, and sets to work accordingly. If she finds that she cannot work so as to keep up with the companion appointed to her, or to please her employer or herself, she comes to the overseer, and volunteers to pick cotton, or sweep the rooms, or undertake some other service that she can perform.

The people work about seventy hours per week, on the average. The time of work varies with the length of the days, the wages continuing the same. All look like well-dressed young ladies. The health is good; or rather (as this is too much to be said about health anywhere in the United States), it is no worse than it is elsewhere. . . .

The shoemaking at Lynn is carried on almost entirely in private dwellings, from the circumstance that the people who do it are almost all farmers or fishermen likewise. A stranger who has not been enlightened upon the ways of the place would be astonished at the number of small square erections, like miniature schoolhouses, standing each as an appendage to a dwelling-house. These are the "shoe shops," where the father of the family and his boys work, while the women within are employed in binding and trimming. Thirty or more of these shoe shops may be counted in a walk of half-a-mile. When a Lynn shoe manufacturer receives an order, he issues the tidings. The leather is cut out by men on his premises; and then the work is given to those who apply for it; if possible, in small quantities, for the sake of dispatch. The shoes are brought home on Friday night, packed off on Saturday, and in a fortnight or three weeks are on the feet of dwellers in all parts of the Union. The whole family works upon shoes during the winter; and in the summer, the father and sons turn out into the fields, or go fishing. I knew of an instance where a little boy and girl maintained the whole family, while the earnings of the rest went to build a house. I saw very few shabby houses.... The place is unboundedly prosperous, through the temperance and industry of the people.

The deposits in the Lynn Savings' Bank in 1834, were about $34,000, the population of the town being then four thousand. Since that time, both the population and the prosperity have much increased. It must be remembered, too, that the mechanics of America have more uses for their money than are open to the operatives of England. They build houses, buy land, and educate their sons and daughters.

XX 🐾 *The International Consequences of Expansion*

THE OUTWARD thrust along the edge of settlement brought the United States into continuing contact with its neighbors on the North American continent, and particularly with Great Britain, Mexico, and Russia. The American statesmen approached the problems of diplomacy with a confidence nurtured by the certainty of their own power and strength and of their potential for growth. It was the manifest destiny of the United States to extend the influence of its free institutions throughout the New World. And, while the precise nature of that extension might be unclear, the superior virtues of American political and social institutions left no doubt but that they would ultimately exclude the great powers of Europe from the Western Hemisphere.

Something of that certainty spoke through the Monroe Doctrine (No. 162), initially directed at Russia and supported by Britain, but ultimately to become the symbol of American hegemony on the North American continent.

Meanwhile, American settlers were proceeding in their own fashion to the farther West, in the south across the border to Texas and in the north toward the disputed Oregon Territory. The Texans made good their own independence, but they thought of themselves as Americans (No. 163) and only political factors delayed their incorporation in the Union (*see below*, No. 220). As for Oregon, it took long years of negotiation before an acceptable compromise with the British was arrived at (No. 164).

Ties with Texas had embroiled the United States in difficulties with Mexico. Some Americans counted this fortunate, for they were ambitious to annex substantial areas of Mexican land. The developing war, which resulted in great accessions of territory, was not evaded by the United States once the Oregon question was settled, as President Polk's diary indicates (No. 165).

The gains of 1848 did not satiate the expansionists, who already looked to other fields for conquest in Cuba and in the Caribbean. Interest in a Central-

American canal led to difficulties with England, which were postponed for a half century by the Clayton-Bulwer Treaty (No. 166). But the Ostend Manifesto indicated that southern expansionists intended to acquire Cuba, by whatever means were necessary (No. 167).

The Civil War was a setback. But the distractions of internal conflict did not prevent the United States from pursuing its long-term interests. The possibilities of foreign intervention were decisively rejected (Nos. 168, 169); and the effort by France to extend its influence in Mexico met a stern and effective rebuff (No. 170).

162. *The Monroe Doctrine, 1823*

President James Monroe's Message to Congress, December 2, 1823, Richardson, *Messages and Papers*, II, 209, 217–19.

AT THE proposal of the Russian imperial government, made through the minister of the Emperor residing here, a full power and instructions have been transmitted to the Minister of the United States at St. Petersburg, to arrange, by amicable negotiation, the respective rights and interests of the two nations on the northwest coast of this continent. A similar proposal had been made by his Imperial Majesty to the government of Great Britain, which has likewise been acceded to. The government of the United States has been desirous, by this friendly proceeding, of manifesting the great value which they have invariably attached to the friendship of the Emperor, and their solicitude to cultivate the best understanding with his government. In the discussions to which this interest has given rise, and in the arrangements by which they may terminate, the occasion has been judged proper for asserting, as a principle in which the rights and interests of the United States are involved, that the American continents, by the free and independent condition which they have assumed and maintain, are henceforth not to be considered as subjects for future colonization by any European powers. . . .

It was stated at the commencement of the last session, that a great effort was then making in Spain and Portugal, to im-

prove the condition of the people of those countries, and that it appeared to be conducted with extraordinary moderation. It need scarcely be remarked, that the result has been, so far, very different from what was then anticipated. Of events in that quarter of the globe, with which we have so much intercourse, and from which we derive our origin, we have always been anxious and interested spectators. The citizens of the United States cherish sentiments the most friendly, in favor of the liberty and happiness of their fellow men on that side of the Atlantic. In the wars of the European powers in matters relating to themselves, we have never taken any part, nor does it comport with our policy so to do. It is only when our rights are invaded, or seriously menaced, that we resent injuries, or make preparation for our defense. With the movements in this hemisphere, we are, of necessity, more immediately connected, and by causes which must be obvious to all enlightened and impartial observers. The political system of the allied powers is essentially different, in this respect, from that of America. This difference proceeds from that which exists in their respective governments. And to the defense of our own . . . under which we have enjoyed unexampled felicity, this whole nation is devoted. We owe it, therefore, to candor, and to the amicable relations existing between the United States and those powers, to declare, that we should consider any attempt on their part to extend their system to any portion of this hemisphere, as dangerous to our peace and safety.

With the existing colonies or dependencies of any European power, we have not interfered, and shall not interfere. But with the governments who have declared their independence, and maintained it, and whose independence we have, on great consideration, and on just principles, acknowledged, we could not view any interposition for the purpose of oppressing them, or controlling, in any other manner, their destiny, by any European power, in any other light than as the manifestation of an unfriendly disposition towards the United States. In the war between those new governments and Spain, we declared our neutrality at the time of their recognition, and to this we . . . shall continue to adhere, provided no change shall occur, which . . . shall make a corresponding change, on the part of the United States, indispensable to their security.

The late events in Spain and Portugal show that Europe is still unsettled. Of this important fact, no stronger proof can be adduced than that the allied powers should have thought it proper . . . to have interposed, by force, in the internal concerns of Spain. To what extent such interposition may be carried, on the same principle, is a question in which all independent powers, whose governments differ from theirs, are interested; even those most remote, and surely none more so than the United States. Our policy, in regard to Europe, which was adopted at an early stage of the wars which have so long agitated that quarter of the globe, nevertheless remains the same, which is, not to interfere in the internal concerns of any of its powers; to consider the government de facto as the legitimate government for us; to cultivate friendly relations with it, and to preserve those relations by a frank, firm, and manly policy; meeting, in all instances, the just claims of every power; submitting to injuries from none.

But, in regard to those continents, circumstances are eminently and conspicuously different. It is impossible that the allied powers should extend their political system to any portion of either continent, without endangering our peace and happiness. Nor can anyone believe that our Southern brethren, if left to themselves, would adopt it of their own accord. It is equally impossible, therefore, that we should behold such interposition, in any form, with indifference. If we look to the comparative strength and resources of Spain and those new governments, and their distance from each other, it must be obvious that she can never subdue them. It is still the true policy of the United States to leave the parties to themselves, in the hope that other powers will pursue the same course.

163. *From the Alamo, 1836*

Letter of February 24, 1836. Quoted in H. Yoakum, *History of Texas* (New York, 1856), II, 76–7.

To the People of Texas and all Americans in the world—

FELLOW Citizens and Compatriots: I am besieged, by a thousand or more of the Mexicans under Santa Anna—I have sustained a continual bombardment for twenty-four hours and have not lost a man. The enemy have demanded a surrender at discretion, otherwise the garrison are to be put to the sword, if the place is taken—I have answered the summons with a cannon shot, and our flag still waves proudly from the walls. I shall never surrender or retreat. Then, I call on you in the name of liberty, of patriotism and of everything dear to the American character, to come to our aid, with all dispatch. The enemy are receiving reinforcements daily and will no doubt increase to three or four thousand in four or five days. Though this call may be neglected, I am determined to sustain myself as long as possible and die like a soldier who never forgets

what is due to his own honor and that of his country.

> *Victory or death!*
> W[ILLIAM] BARRET TRAVIS.
> *Lieutenant Colonel. commanding.*

P.S. The Lord is on our side. When the enemy appeared in sight we had not three bushels of corn. We have since found in deserted houses eighty or ninety bushels and got into the walls twenty or thirty head of beeves.—

> T[RAVIS]

164. *The Oregon Treaty, 1846*

Concluded June 15, 1846; proclaimed August 5, 1846. Malloy, *Treaties,* I, 656–8.

THE United States of America and Her Majesty the Queen of the United Kingdom of Great Britain and Ireland, deeming it to be desirable for the future welfare of both countries that the state of doubt and uncertainty which has hitherto prevailed respecting the sovereignty and government of the territory on the northwest coast of America, lying westward of the Rocky or Stony Mountains, should be finally terminated by an amicable compromise of the rights mutually asserted by the two parties over the said territory, have respectively named plenipotentiaries. . . .

Who, after having communicated to each other their respective full powers, found in good and due form, have agreed upon and concluded the following articles:

Article I. From the point on the forty-ninth parallel of north latitude, where the boundary laid down in existing treaties and conventions between the United States and Great Britain terminates, the line of boundary between the territories of the United States and those of Her Britannic Majesty shall be continued westward along the said forty-ninth parallel of north latitude to the middle of the channel which

separates the continent from Vancouver's Island, and thence southerly through the middle of the said channel, and of Fuca's Straits, to the Pacific Ocean: Provided, however, that the navigation of the whole of the said channel and straits, south of the forty-ninth parallel of north latitude, remain free and open to both parties.

Article II. From the point at which the forty-ninth parallel of north latitude shall be found to intersect the great northern branch of the Columbia River, the navigation of the said branch shall be free and open to the Hudson's Bay Company, and to all British subjects trading with the same, to the point where the said branch meets the main stream of the Columbia, and thence down the said main stream to the ocean, with free access into and through the said river or rivers, it being understood that all the usual portages along the line thus described shall, in like manner, be free and open. In navigating the said river or rivers, British subjects, with their goods and produce, shall be treated on the same footing as citizens of the United States. . . .

Article IV. The farms, lands, and other property of every description belonging to the Puget's Sound Agricultural Company, on the north side of the Columbia River, shall be confirmed to the said company. In case, however, the situation of those farms and lands should be considered by the United States to be of public and political importance, and the United States government should signify a desire to obtain possession of the whole, or of any part thereof, the property so required shall be transferred to the said government, at a proper valuation, to be agreed upon between the parties.

165. *Through War and Peace, 1845–48*

J. K. Polk, *Diary of a President.* Allan Nevins, ed. (New York, 1929), 2–4, 81–3, 117–18, 214–16, 306, 326.

[AUGUST 26, 1845]. The President again called up the Oregon question. He remarked that he had at different times communicated to the several members of the Cabinet the settled decision to which his mind had come. He proceeded briefly to repeat his decision, in substance as follows, viz., that Mr. Buchanan's note in reply to Mr. Pakenham should assert and enforce our right to the whole Oregon territory from 42° to 54° 40′ north latitude; that he should distinctly state that the proposition which had been made to compromise on the 49th parallel of north latitude had been made, first in deference to what had been done by our predecessors, and second, with an anxious desire to preserve peace between the two countries. That this proposition, made as it was for the reasons stated and in a liberal spirit of compromise, had been rejected by the British Minister in language, to say the least of it, scarcely courteous or respectful, and that, too, without submitting any counter proposition on his part, was now withdrawn by the United States, and should no longer be considered as pending for the consideration of the British Government. The President said, in summing the reasons which he assigned for this decision, let the argument of our title to the whole country be full, let the proposition to compromise at latitude 49° be withdrawn, and then let the matter rest, unless the British Minister chose to continue the negotiation.

Mr. Buchanan said that he assented to the views of the President as the argument of title and withdrawal of our proposition to compromise at 49° were concerned, but that he thought a paragraph should be inserted to the effect that any further proposition which the British Minister might submit would be deliberately considered by the United States. To this the President objected upon the ground that our proposition for 49° had been rejected flatly, without even a reference by the British Minister to his Government. . . . Any proposition less favorable than 49° the President said he would promptly reject. Why then invite a proposition which cannot for a moment be entertained? Let our proposition be absolutely withdrawn and then let the British Minister take his own course. If he chooses to close the negotiation he can do so. If he chooses to make a proposition he can as well do it without our invitation as with it. Let him take the one course or the other, the United States will stand in the right in the eyes of the whole civilized world, and if war was the consequence England would be in the wrong. The President further remarked that he had reflected much on this subject; that it had occupied his thoughts more than any and all others during his Administration, and that though he had given his assent to the proposition to compromise at 49°, he must say he did not regret that it had been rejected by the British Minister. We had shown by it our anxious desire to do

full justice to Great Britain and to preserve peace, but it having been rejected
he felt no longer bound by it, and would
not be now willing to compromise on that
boundary.

Mr. Buchanan then intimated that if the
President's views were carried out, we
would have war. To which the President
replied, if we do have war it will not be
our fault. Mr. Buchanan said that war
would probably be the result ultimately,
but he expressed the opinion that the people of the United States would not be
willing to sustain a war for the country
north of 49°, and that if we were to have
war he would like it to be for some better
cause, for some of our rights of person or
property or of national honor violated. The
President differed with Mr. Buchanan as
to the popular sentiment, and he thought
we had the strongest evidence that was to
be anywhere seen that the people would
be prompt and ready to sustain the government in the course which he proposed
to pursue.

Mr. Buchanan then had allusion to our
difficulties with Mexico, and thought his
reply to Mr. Pakenham ought to be postponed until we could know whether we
would have actual war with that country
or not. The President said he saw no necessary connection between the two questions; that the settlement of the one was
not dependent on the other; that we
should do our duty towards both Mexico
and Great Britain and firmly maintain our
rights, and leave the rest to God and the
country. Mr. Buchanan said he thought
God would not have much to do in justifying us in a war for the country north of
49°. Mr. Buchanan then suggested that his
reply should be postponed until late in
September. The President objected to this.
He said that a postponement would carry
the idea to Great Britain, as well as to
our own people, of hesitancy and indecision on our part, which so far as his
opinions were concerned would be an erroneous inference. . . .

May 9th, 1846.—The Cabinet held a
regular meeting today; all the members
present. I brought up the Mexican question, and the question of what was the
duty of the administration in the present
state of our relations with that country.
The subject was very fully discussed. All
agreed that if the Mexican forces at
Matamoras committed any act of hostility
on General Taylor's forces I should immediately send a message to Congress recommending an immediate declaration of
war. I stated to the Cabinet that up to
this time, as we knew, we had heard of no
open act of aggression by the Mexican
army, but that the danger was imminent
that such acts would be committed. I said
that in my opinion we had ample cause
of war, and that it was impossible that
we could stand in *statu quo,* or that I
could remain silent much longer; that I
thought it was my duty to send a message
to Congress very soon and recommend
definite measures. I told them that I
thought I ought to make such a message
by Tuesday next, that the country was
excited and impatient on the subject, and
if I failed to do so I would not be doing
my duty. I then propounded the distinct
question to the Cabinet, and took their
opinions individually, whether I should
make a message to Congress on Tuesday,
and whether in that message I should recommend a declaration of war against
Mexico. All except the Secretary of the
Navy gave their advice in the affirmative.
Mr. Bancroft dissented but said if any act
of hostility should be committed by the
Mexican forces he was then in favor of
immediate war. Mr. Buchanan said he
would feel better satisfied in his course if
the Mexican forces had or should commit
any act of hostility, but that as matters
stood we had ample cause of war against
Mexico, and he gave his assent to the
measure. It was agreed that the message
should be prepared and submitted to the
Cabinet in their meeting on Tuesday. A
history of our causes of complaint against
Mexico had been at my request previously
drawn up by Mr. Buchanan. I stated that

what was said in my annual message in December gave that history as succinctly and satisfactorily as Mr. Buchanan's statement, that in truth it was the same history in both, expressed in different language, and that if I repeated that history in a message to Congress now I had better employ the precise language used in my message of December last. Without deciding this point the Cabinet passed to the consideration of some other subjects of minor importance. . . .

About six o'clock P.M. General R. Jones, the Adjutant-General of the army, called and handed to me dispatches received from General Taylor by the southern mail which had just arrived, giving information that a part of the Mexican army had crossed the Del Norte and attacked and killed and captured two companies of dragoons of General Taylor's army consisting of sixty-three officers and men. The dispatch also stated that he had on that day (26th April) made a requisition on the governors of Texas and Louisiana for four regiments each, to be sent to his relief at the earliest practicable period. Before I had finished reading the dispatch, the Secretary of War called. I immediately summoned the Cabinet to meet at half past seven o'clock this evening. The Cabinet accordingly assembled at that hour; all the members present. The subject of the dispatch received this evening from General Taylor, as well as the state of our relations with Mexico, were fully considered. The Cabinet were unanimously of opinion, and it was so agreed, that a message should be sent to Congress on Monday laying all the information in my possession before them and recommending vigorous and prompt measures to enable the executive to prosecute the war. The Secretary of War and the Secretary of State agreed to put their clerks to work to copy the correspondence between Mr. Slidell and the Mexican Government and Secretary of State and the correspondence between the War Department and General Taylor, to the end that these docu-

ments should be transmitted to Congress with my message on Monday. . . .

June 30th, 1846.—This was the regular day of meeting of the Cabinet. . . . A discussion arose between Mr. Buchanan and Mr. Walker in regard to the objects of the war against Mexico, in the course of which Mr. Buchanan expressed himself in favor of acquiring the Rio Grande as our western boundary as high up as the Passo in about latitude 32° of north latitude and thence west to the Pacific. He expressed himself as being opposed to acquiring any territory by treaty with Mexico south of 32° of north latitude. He spoke of the unwillingness of the North to acquire so large a country that would probably become a slaveholding country if attached to the United States. Mr. Walker warmly resisted Mr. Buchanan's views, and insisted that we should if practicable acquire by treaty all the country north of a line drawn from the mouth of the Rio Grande in latitude about 26° west to the Pacific. Mr. Buchanan said . . . that if we attempted to acquire all this territory the opinion of the world would be against us, and especially as it would become a slaveholding country, whereas while it was in possession of Mexico slavery did not exist in it. Mr. Walker remarked that he would be willing to fight the whole world sooner than suffer other powers to interfere in the matter.

I remained silent until the discussion had proceeded to a considerable length, when I spoke and said in substance that the causes and objects of the war were as I supposed well understood, and that when we came to make peace the terms of the peace would be a subject for consideration. As to the boundary which we should establish by a treaty of peace, I remarked that I preferred the 26° to any boundary north of it, but that if it was found that that boundary could not be obtained I was willing to take 32°, but that in any event we must obtain Upper California and New Mexico in any treaty of peace we should make. The other members of the Cabinet expressed no opinions, not being called upon to do so. The discussion between Mr. Buchanan and Mr. Walker was an animated one. . . .

April 13th, 1847.—At the request of Mr. Buchanan I summoned the Cabinet to meet at ten o'clock this morning. All the members attended shortly after that hour. Mr. Buchanan submitted for consideration the project of a treaty with Mexico, which he had prepared in pursuance of the decision of the Cabinet on Saturday last, to be borne by Mr. Trist to the headquarters of the army in Mexico and to be concluded and signed by him if the Mexican government acceded to it. The boundary proposed in the project was the Rio Grande from its mouth to the point where it intersects the southern boundary of New Mexico, the whole of the provinces of New Mexico and Upper and Lower California to be ceded to the United States. There was a stipulation in a separate article securing to the United States the right of passage and transit from the Gulf of Mexico and the Pacific Ocean across the Isthmus of Tehuantepec. The consideration which Mr. Buchanan in his draft of a treaty proposed to pay, in addition to the assumption of the claims of our citizens against Mexico, was $15,-000,000, in installments of $3,000,000 per annum. I expressed the hope that this boundary and concession might be obtained for this or even a less sum, but that I was willing to pay a larger sum for it if it could not be had for that sum, and that I thought Mr. Trist should be authorized to give more, if he found that to be the only obstacle in concluding a treaty. I was willing to make the consideration double that sum ($30,000,000) if the cession could not be obtained for a less sum, rather than fail to make a treaty. Mr. Buchanan earnestly resisted this and was in favor of restricting the offer to the $15,000,000. This point gave rise to much conversation and discussion. I stated my reasons at some length for being willing to enlarge the sum to $30,-000,000, if the treaty could not be had

for that sum. Among these reasons were, first, that the continuance of the war for less than twelve months would cost more than that sum; and secondly, that the country ceded to the United States would be worth, in the public lands acquired and commercial advantages, more than fourfold the $30,000,000. The members of the Cabinet expressed their opinions freely. Mr. Walker attached greater importance to the free passage across the Isthmus of Tehuantepec than to the cession of New Mexico and the Californias, and if that object could be obtained he was willing to pay $30,000,000, but without it he was not. Mr. Buchanan still opposed the enlargement of the consideration. Finally all the Cabinet except Mr. Buchanan yielded to my views, and it was agreed that Mr. Trist should be furnished with confidential instructions authorizing him in his discretion, if the treaty could not be obtained for a less sum, to stipulate to pay $30,000,000. It was further agreed that if the passage across the Isthmus of Tehuantepec could not be obtained, the maximum sum to be paid for the other cessions of the proposed treaty should not exceed $25,000,000. It was agreed, also, that if Lower California could not be obtained, that then the maximum sum to be paid for the Rio Grande as a boundary and the cession of New Mexico and Upper California should not exceed $20,000,000. To these several propositions all the Cabinet except Mr. Buchanan agreed, and he being overruled yielded and said he would modify the project of the treaty and prepare the instructions accordingly. I stated, and it was understood by all, that the several sums mentioned were maximums to which Mr. Trist might go in the last resort, but that he would procure the treaty for as much less sum as possible. In the course of the discussion Mr. Walker insisted that the free passage across the Isthmus of Tehuantepec should be a *sine qua non* to the making of any treaty. To this I objected and stated that it constituted no part of the object for which we had engaged in the war. The balance of the Cabinet, though agreeing that it was important, yet concurred with me in opinion that it should not be a *sine qua non* in the making of a treaty. . . .

February 21st, 1848.—At twelve o'clock the Cabinet met; all the members present. I made known my decision upon the Mexican Treaty, which was that under all the circumstances of the case, I would submit it to the Senate for ratification, with a recommendation to strike out the tenth article. I assigned my reasons for my decision. They were, briefly, that the treaty conformed on the main question of limits and boundary to the instructions given to Mr. Trist in April last; and that though, if the treaty was now to be made, I should demand more territory, perhaps to make the Sierra Madre the line, yet it was doubtful whether this could ever be obtained by the consent of Mexico. I looked, too, to the consequences of its rejection. A majority of one branch of Congress is opposed to my administration; they have falsely charged that the war was brought on and is continued by me with a view to the conquest of Mexico; and if I were now to reject a treaty made upon my own terms, as authorized in April last, with the unanimous approbation of the Cabinet, the probability is that Congress would not grant either men or money to prosecute the war. . . .

May 30th, 1848.—I informed the Cabinet today that I desired to invite their attention, not for the purpose of immediate decision, but for consideration, to the important question whether a proposition should not be made to Spain to purchase the island of Cuba. The subject was freely discussed. The great importance of the island to the United States, and the danger, if we did not acquire it, that it might fall into the hands of Great Britain, were considered. Mr. Walker, the Secretary of the Treasury, was earnestly in favor of making the attempt to purchase it, and was willing to pay one hundred millions of dollars for it. Mr. Mason, the Secretary of the Navy, concurred in opinion with Mr. Walker. Mr. Johnson, the Postmaster-General, had objections to incorporating the Spanish population of Cuba into our Union, and did not seem to favor the idea of purchasing it. Mr. Buchanan, the Secretary of State, expressed a general wish to acquire Cuba, but thought there were objections to making the attempt at this time. He feared that if it became known that such a step was contemplated, that it might act prejudicially to the Democratic party in the next Presidential election. He said he would reflect on the subject and be prepared to give me his advice upon the subject hereafter. I intimated my strong conviction that the effort should be made without delay to purchase the island.

166. *The Clayton-Bulwer Treaty, 1850*

Concluded April 19, 1850; proclaimed, July 5, 1850, Malloy, *Treaties*, I, 659–63.

I. THE GOVERNMENTS of the United States and Great Britain hereby declare that neither the one nor the other will ever obtain or maintain for itself any exclusive control over the [Isthmian] . . . ship canal; agreeing that neither will ever erect or maintain any fortifications commanding the same, or . . . exercise any dominion over Nicaragua, Costa Rica, the Mosquito Coast, or any part of Central America; nor will either make use of any protection which either affords . . . or of any intimacy, . . . alliance, connection or influence that either may possess with any state or government through whose territory the said canal may pass, for the purpose of acquiring or holding, directly or indirectly, for the citizens or subjects of the one, any rights or advantages in regard to commerce or navigation through the said canal which shall not be offered on the same terms to the citizens or subjects of the other.

II. Vessels of the United States or Great Britain traversing the said canal shall, in case of war between the contracting parties, be exempted from blockade, detention or capture by either of the belligerents; and this provision shall extend to such a distance from the two ends of the said canal as may hereafter be found expedient to establish.

III. In order to secure the construction of the said canal, the contracting parties engage that if any such canal shall be undertaken upon fair and equitable terms by any parties having the authority of the local government or governments through whose territory the same may pass, then the persons employed in making the said canal, and their property used, or to be used, for that object, shall be protected, from the commencement of the said canal to its completion, by the Governments of the United States and Great Britain, from unjust detention, confiscation, seizure or any violence whatsoever. . . .

V. The contracting parties further engage, that when the said canal shall have been completed, they will protect it from interruption, seizure or unjust confiscation, and that they will guarantee the neutrality thereof, so that the said canal may forever be open and free, and the capital invested therein secure. . . .

VI. The contracting parties in this convention engage to invite every state with which both or either have friendly intercourse to enter into stipulations with them similar to those which they have entered into with each other, to the end that all other states may share in the honor and advantage of having contributed to a work of such general interest and importance as the canal herein contemplated. And the contracting parties likewise agree that each shall enter into treaty stipulations with such of the Central American states as they may deem advisable, for the purpose of more effectually . . . constructing and maintaining the said canal . . . ; and they also agree that . . . should any differences . . . obstruct the execution of the said canal, the Governments of the United States and Great Britain will use their good offices to settle such differences in the manner best suited to promote the interests of the said canal, and to strengthen the bonds of friendship and alliance which exist between the contracting parties. . . .

VIII. The Governments of the United States and Great Britain . . . hereby agree to extend their protection, by treaty stipulations, to any other practicable communications, whether by canal or railway, across the isthmus which connects North and South America, and especially to the interoceanic communications, should the same prove to be practicable, whether by canal or railway, which are now proposed to be established by the way of Tehuantepec or Panama. In granting, however, their joint protection to any such canals or railways as are by this article specified, it is always understood by the United States and Great Britain that the parties constructing or owning the same shall impose no other charges or conditions of traffic thereupon than the aforesaid Governments shall approve of as just and equitable; and that the same canals or railways, being open to the citizens and subjects of the United States and Great Britain on equal terms, shall also be open on like terms to the citizens and subjects of every other state which is willing to grant thereto such protection as the United States and Great Britain engage to afford.

167. *The Ostend Manifesto, 1854*

James Buchanan, John Y. Mason, and Pierre Soulé, United States ambassadors, to William L. Marcy, Secretary of State, October 18, 1854, 33 Congress, 2 Session (1855), *House Executive Documents*, No. 93, pp. 127–32.

WE HAVE arrived at the conclusion, and are thoroughly convinced, that an immediate and earnest effort ought to be made by the government of the United States to purchase Cuba from Spain....

It can scarcely be apprehended that foreign powers, in violation of international law, would interpose their influence with Spain to prevent our acquisition of the island. Its inhabitants are now suffering under the worst of all possible governments, that of absolute despotism, delegated by a distant power to irresponsible agents, who are changed at short intervals, and who are tempted to improve the brief opportunity thus afforded to accumulate fortunes by the basest means.

As long as this system shall endure, humanity may in vain demand the suppression of the African slave trade in the island. This is rendered impossible whilst that infamous traffic remains an irresistible temptation and a source of immense profit to needy and avaricious officials, who, to attain their ends, scruple not to trample the most sacred principles under foot....

Under no probable circumstances can Cuba ever yield to Spain one per cent on the large amount [$120,000,000] which the United States are willing to pay for its acquisition. But Spain is in imminent danger of losing Cuba, without remuneration.

Extreme oppression, it is now universally admitted, justifies any people in endeavoring to relieve themselves from the yoke of their oppressors. The sufferings which the corrupt, arbitrary, and unrelenting local administration necessarily entails upon the inhabitants of Cuba, cannot fail to stimulate and keep alive that spirit of resistance and revolution against Spain, which has, of late years, been so often manifested. In this condition of affairs it is vain to expect that the sympathies of the people of the United States will not be warmly enlisted in favor of their oppressed neighbors....

But if Spain, dead to the voice of her own interest, and actuated by stubborn pride and a false sense of honor, should refuse to sell Cuba to the United States, then the question will arise, What ought to be the course of the American government under such circumstances?...

After we shall have offered Spain a price for Cuba far beyond its present value, and this shall have been refused, it will then be time to consider the question, does Cuba, in the possession of Spain, seriously endanger our internal peace and the existence of our cherished Union?

Should this question be answered in the affirmative, then, by every law, human and divine, we shall be justified in wresting it from Spain if we possess the power; and this upon the very same principle that would justify an individual in tearing down the burning house of his neighbor if there were no other means of preventing the flames from destroying his own home.

Under such circumstances we ought neither to count the cost nor regard the odds which Spain might enlist against us. We forbear to enter into the question, whether the present condition of the island would justify such a measure. We should, however, be recreant to our duty, be unworthy of our gallant forefathers, and commit base treason against our posterity, should we permit Cuba to be

Africanized and become a second St. Domingo, with all its attendant horrors to the white race, and suffer the flames to extend to our own neighboring shores, seriously to endanger or actually to consume the fair fabric of our Union.

168. *An English Liberal on the* Trent *Case, 1861*

John Bright to Senator Charles Sumner, December 7, 1861, quoted in Massachusetts Historical Society, *Proceedings,* XLV (1911), 152-3.

THERE is more calmness here in the public mind, which is natural after last week's explosion; but I fear the military and naval demonstrations of our Government point to trouble, and I am not sure that it would grieve certain parties here if any decent excuse could be found for a quarrel with you. You know the instinct of aristocracy and of powerful military services, and an ignorant people is easily led astray on questions foreign to their usual modes of thought. I have no doubt you will be able to produce strong cases from English practice in support of the present case, but I doubt if any number of these will change opinion here. It will be said, and is said already, that if we did wrong fifty years ago, it is no reason why you should do wrong now. The law is the law and it shall not be broken, and we take our law officers' law for our law.

Now what is to be done? You must put the matter in such a shape as to save your honor (The retention of the Commissioners cannot be worth a farthing to you in comparison to the desperate evil of war with England—as the result of any arbitration you may give up anything without any wound to your honor.), and to put our Government in the wrong if they refuse your proposition. I see no way but to state your case in all its completeness, and then to offer to leave the question to the decision of some tribunal—say the French Emperor, or the King of Holland, or the King of Prussia, or the Emperor of Russia, or any two of them—and at the same time to restate your willingness so to amend and define international law as to make such cases of difficulty impossible hereafter. Such a fair, and I will say, Christian course will disarm multitudes of our people, and whatever may be the secret wishes of our Government, it will, I cannot but believe, be compelled to yield; and you may rest assured, that such a course on your part will do much to create a more generous feeling here with respect to your main question.

At all hazards you must not let this matter grow to a war with England, even if you are right and we are wrong. War will be fatal to your idea of restoring the Union and we know not what may survive its evil influences. I am not now considering its effects here—they may be serious enough, but I am looking alone to your great country, the hope of freedom and humanity, and I implore you not on any feeling that nothing can be conceded, and that England is arrogant and seeking a quarrel, to play the game of every enemy of your country. Nations in great crises and difficulties, have often done that which in their prosperous and powerful hour they would not have done, and they have done it without humiliation or disgrace. You may disappoint your enemies by the moderation and reasonableness of your conduct, and every honest and good man in England will applaud your wisdom. Put all the fire-eaters in the wrong, and Europe will admire the sagacity of your Government.

169. *Congress on Foreign Mediation, 1863*

Senate resolutions against foreign mediation, March 3, 1863, Edward McPherson, *Political History of the United States of America during the Great Rebellion* (Washington, 1865), 346.

RESOLVED (the House of Representatives concurring), That . . . Congress cannot hesitate to regard every proposition of foreign interference in the present contest as so far unreasonable and inadmissible that its only explanation will be found in a misunderstanding of the true state of the question, and of the real character of the war in which the Republic is engaged.

That the United States are now grappling with an unprovoked and wicked rebellion, which is seeking the destruction of the Republic that it may build a new power, whose cornerstone, according to the confession of its chief, shall be slavery; that for the suppression of this rebellion, and thus to save the Republic and to prevent the establishment of such a power, the national government is now employing armies and fleets, in full faith that through these efforts all the purposes of conspirators and rebels will be crushed; that while engaged in this struggle, on which so much depends, any proposition from a foreign power, whatever form it may take, having for its object the arrest of these efforts, is, just in proportion to its influence, an encouragement to the rebellion, and to its declared pretensions, and, on this account, is calculated to prolong and embitter the conflict, to cause increased expenditure of blood and treasure, and to postpone the much-desired day of peace; that, with these convictions, and not doubting that every such proposition, although made with good intent, is injurious to the national interests, Congress will be obliged to look upon any further attempt in the same direction as an unfriendly act which it earnestly deprecates, to the end that nothing may occur abroad to strengthen the rebellion or to weaken those relations of good will with foreign powers which the United States are happy to cultivate.

That the rebellion from its beginning, and far back even in the conspiracy which preceded its outbreak, was encouraged by the hope of support from foreign powers; that its chiefs frequently boasted that the people of Europe were so far dependent upon regular supplies of the great southern staples that, sooner or later, their governments would be constrained to take side with the rebellion in some effective form, even to the extent of forcible intervention, if the milder form did not prevail; that the rebellion is now sustained by this hope, which every proposition of foreign interference quickens anew, and that, without this life-giving support, it must soon yield to the just and paternal authority of the national government; that, considering these things, which are aggravated by the motive of the resistance thus encouraged, the United States regret that foreign powers have not frankly told the chiefs of the rebellion that the work in which they are engaged is hateful, and that a new government, such as they seek to found, with slavery as its acknowledged cornerstone, and with no other declared object of separate existence, is so far shocking to civilization and the moral sense of mankind that it must not expect welcome or recognition in the commonwealth of nations.

That the United States, confident in the justice of their cause, which is the cause, also, of good government and of human rights everywhere among men; anxious for the speedy restoration of peace, which shall secure tranquillity at home and remove all occasion of complaint abroad;

and awaiting with well-assured trust the final suppression of the rebellion, through which all these things, rescued from present danger, will be secured forever, and the Republic, one and indivisible, triumphant over its enemies, will continue to stand an example to mankind, hereby announce, as their unalterable purpose, that the war will be vigorously prosecuted, according to the humane principles of Christian states, until the rebellion shall be overcome; and they reverently invoke upon their cause the blessings of Almighty God.

170. *The French in Mexico, 1866*

Secretary of State William H. Seward to the Marquis de Montholon, February 12, 1866, 39 Congress, 1 Session (1866), *House Executive Documents*, No. 93, 29–30.

IT IS my duty to insist that, whatever were the intentions, purposes, and objects of France, the proceedings which were adopted by a class of Mexicans for subverting the republican government there, and for availing themselves of French intervention to establish on its ruins an imperial monarchy, are regarded by the United States as having been taken without the authority, and prosecuted against the will and opinions, of the Mexican people. . . . The United States have not seen any satisfactory evidence that the people of Mexico have spoken, and have called into being or accepted the so-called empire which it is insisted has been set up in their capital. The United States, as I have remarked on other occasions, are of opinion that such an acceptance could not have been freely procured or lawfully taken at any time in the presence of the French army of invasion. The withdrawal of the French forces is deemed necessary to allow such a proceeding to be taken by Mexico. . . .

This position is held, I believe, without one dissenting voice by our countrymen. I do not presume to say that this opinion of the American people is accepted or will be adopted generally by other foreign powers, or by the public opinion of mankind. The Emperor is quite competent to form a judgment upon this important point for himself. I cannot, however, properly exclude the observation that, while this question affects by its bearings, incidentally, every republican state in the American hemisphere, every one of those states has adopted the judgment which, on the behalf of the United States, is herein expressed. Under these circumstances it has happened, either rightfully or wrongfully, that the presence of European armies in Mexico, maintaining a European prince with imperial attributes, without her consent and against her will, is deemed a source of apprehension and danger, not alone to the United States, but also to all the independent and sovereign republican states founded on the American continent and its adjacent islands. France is acquainted with the relations of the United States towards the other American states to which I have referred, and is aware of the sense that the American people entertain in regard to the obligations and duties due from them to those other states.

XXI ❧ *Social Aspects of Expansion*

EXPANSION yielded abundant material results; but it was expensive in terms of human energy. The incessant mobility of a constantly shifting population, even more than earlier, imposed a severe strain upon all personal and social relationships.

American life, for instance, exerted a disorganizing effect upon religion. All denominations suffered. In the frontier regions the absence of settled forms left the field almost entirely to the ministrations of occasional revivalists. Even in the towns this provoked emotional disorder (No. 171); in the countryside the difficulties were still more pronounced. The connection between poverty, insecurity, and religion emerged in the early life of the prophet of Mormonism (No. 172). But the ancient sects suffered also. Despite its rigid discipline and hierarchical organization, the Catholic Church was confused by immigration (No. 173). Nor could the Jews carry the tradition of orthodoxy intact across to the New World (No. 174).

Life on the frontier, as always, imparted a harshness to the behavior of those who lived cut off from the influence of more stable civilization. Violence was common (No. 175). Ignorance of manners verged on brutality (No. 176). Yet the crudeness of manners reflected not the absence of standards of morality but the needs of a new situation (No. 177).

The growing city faced problems of expansion. The lack of sanitary facilities and the rapid rise of population was conducive to disease. The mass of incoming immigrants were compelled to accept work on terms that permitted them only the poorest accommodations (No. 178; *see also above*, No. 150). It was difficult to enforce the law anywhere, and this often left a gap filled by individual violence, as in San Francisco (No. 179); but even old, established Eastern cities were periodically troubled by riots. Meanwhile, the growing burden of poverty produced also a variety of other social ills (No. 180).

171. *A Revival in Cincinnati, 1827*

F. M. Trollope, *Domestic Manners of the Americans* (London, 1832). From the New York edition of 1901, pp. 108–13.

IT WAS in the middle of summer, but the service ... did not begin till it was dark. The church was well lighted, and crowded almost to suffocation. On entering, we found three priests standing side by side. ... We took our places in a pew close to the rail which surrounded it.

The priest who stood in the middle was praying; the prayer was extravagantly vehement, and offensively familiar in expression. When this ended, a hymn was sung, and then another priest took the center place, and preached. The sermon had considerable eloquence, but of a frightful kind. The preacher described, with ghastly minuteness, the last feeble fainting moments of human life, and then the gradual progress of decay after death, which he followed through every process up to the last loathsome stage of decomposition. Suddenly changing his tone, which had been that of sober accurate description, into the shrill voice of horror, he bent forward his head, as if to gaze on some object beneath the pulpit. And . . . the preacher made known to us what he saw in the pit that seemed to open before him. . . . No image that fire, flame, brimstone, molten lead, or red-hot pincers could supply, with flesh, nerves, and sinews quivering under them, was omitted. The perspiration ran in streams from the face of the preacher; his eyes rolled, his lips were covered with foam, and every feature had the deep expression of horror it would have borne had he, in truth, been gazing at the scene he described. The acting was excellent. At length he gave a languishing look to his supporters on each side, as if to express his feeble state, and then sat down, and wiped the drops of agony from his brow.

The other two priests arose, and began to sing a hymn. It was some seconds before the congregation could join as usual; every upturned face looked pale and horror-struck. When the singing ended another took the center place, and began in a sort of coaxing affectionate tone, to ask the congregation if what their dear brother had spoken had reached their hearts? Whether they would avoid the hell he had made them see? "Come, then!" he continued, stretching out his arms towards them, "come to us and tell us so, and we will make you see Jesus, the dear gentle Jesus, who shall save you from it. But you must come to him! You must not be ashamed to come to him! . . . Come, then! come to the anxious bench, and we will show you Jesus! Come! Come! Come!"

Again a hymn was sung, and while it continued, one of the three was employed in clearing one or two long benches that went across the rail, sending the people back to the lower part of the church. The singing ceased, and again the people were invited, and exhorted not to be ashamed of Jesus, but to put themselves upon "the anxious benches," and lay their heads on his bosom. . . .

And now in every part of the church a movement was perceptible, slight at first, but by degrees becoming more decided. Young girls arose, and sat down, and rose again; and then the pews opened, and several came tottering out, their hands clasped, their heads hanging on their bosoms, and every limb trembling, and still the hymn went on; but as the poor creatures approached the rail their sobs and groans became audible. They seated themselves on the "anxious benches"; the hymn ceased, and two of the three priests walked down from the tribune, and going, one to the right, and the other to the left, began whispering to the poor tremblers seated there. These whispers were inaudible to us, but the sobs and groans increased to a frightful excess. Young creatures, with features pale and distorted, fell on their knees on the pavement, and soon sunk forward on their faces; the most violent cries and shrieks followed, while from time to time a voice was heard in convulsive accents, exclaiming, "Oh Lord!" "Oh Lord Jesus!" "Help me, Jesus!" and the like.

Meanwhile the two priests continued to walk among them; they repeatedly mounted on the benches, and trumpet-mouthed proclaimed to the whole congregation "the tidings of salvation," and then from every corner of the building arose in reply, short sharp cries of "Amen!" "Glory!" "Amen!" while the prostrate penitents continued to receive whispered comfortings, and from time to time a mystic caress. More than once I saw a young neck encircled by a reverend arm. Violent hysterics and convulsions seized many of them, and when the tumult was at the highest, the priest who remained above again gave out a hymn as if to drown it.

It was a frightful sight to behold innocent young creatures, in the gay morning of existence, thus seized upon, horror-struck, and rendered feeble and enervated for ever. One young girl, apparently not more than fourteen, was supported in the arms of another some years older; her face was pale as death; her eyes wide open, and perfectly devoid of meaning; her chin and bosom wet with slaver; she had every appearance of idiotism. I saw a priest approach her, he took her delicate hand, "Jesus is with her! Bless the Lord!" he said, and passed on. . . .

It is hardly necessary to say, that all who obeyed the call to place themselves on the "anxious benches" were women, and by far the greater number, very young women. The congregation was, in general, extremely well-dressed, and the smartest and most fashionable ladies of the town were there; during the whole revival, the churches and meeting-houses were every day crowded with well-dressed people.

172. *The Preparation of Joseph Smith, 1830*

Lucy Smith, *Biographical Sketches of Joseph Smith the Prophet* [by his mother] (London, 1853), 90–9.

SHORTLY after the death of Alvin, a man commenced laboring in the neighborhood, to effect a union of the different churches, in order that all might be agreed, and thus worship God with one heart and with one mind.

This seemed about right to me, and I felt much inclined to join in with them; in fact, the most of the family appeared quite disposed to unite with their numbers; but Joseph, from the first, utterly refused even to attend their meetings, saying . . . "I can take my Bible, and go into the woods, and learn more in two hours, than you can learn at meeting in two years. . . ."

The shock occasioned by Alvin's death, in a short time passed off, and we resumed our usual avocations. . . . A short time before the house was completed, a man, by the name of Josiah Stoal, came from Chenango county, New York, with the view of getting Joseph to assist him in digging for a silver mine. He came for Joseph on account of having heard that he possessed certain keys, by which he could discern things invisible to the natural eye.

Joseph endeavored to divert him from his vain pursuit, but he was inflexible in his purpose, and offered high wages to those who would dig for him, in search of said mine, and still insisted upon having Joseph to work for him. Accordingly, Joseph and several others, returned with him and commenced digging. After laboring for the old gentleman about a month, without success, Joseph prevailed upon him to cease his operations; and it was from this circumstance of having worked by the month, at digging for a silver mine, that the very prevalent story arose of Joseph's having been a money digger. . . .

Soon after his return, we received intelligence of the arrival of a new agent for the Everson land, of which our farm was a portion. This reminded us of the last payment, which was still due, and which must be made before we could obtain a deed of the place.

Shortly after this, a couple of gentlemen, one of whom was the before-named Stoal, the other a Mr. Knight, came into the neighborhood for the purpose of procuring a quantity of either wheat or flour; and we, having sown considerable wheat, made a contract with them, in which we agreed to deliver a certain quantity of flour to them the ensuing fall, for which we were to receive a sufficient amount of money to make the final payment on our farm. This being done, my husband sent Hyrum to Canandaigua to inform the new agent of the fact, namely, that the money should be forthcoming as soon as the twenty-fifth of December 1825. This, the agent said, would answer the purpose, and he agreed to retain the land until that time. . . .

When the time had nearly arrived for the last payment to be made, and when my husband was about starting for Mr. Stoal's and Mr. Knight's, in order to get the money to make the same, Joseph called my husband and myself aside, and said, "I have been very lonely ever since Alvin died, and I have concluded to get married; and if you have no objections to my uniting myself in marriage with Miss Emma Hale, she would be my choice in preference to any other woman I have ever seen." We were pleased with his choice, and . . . requested him to bring her home with him, and live with us. Accordingly he set out with his father for Pennsylvania. . . .

One afternoon my attention was suddenly arrested by a trio of strangers who were just entering. Upon their near approach I found one of these gentlemen to be Mr. Stoddard, the principal carpenter in building the house in which we then lived. . . .

They proceeded to inform my son [Hyrum], that he need put himself to no further trouble with regard to the farm; "for," said they, "we have bought the place, and paid for it, and we now forbid your touching anything on the farm; and we also warn you to leave forthwith, and give possession to the lawful owners."

This conversation passed within my hearing. . . . I was overcome, and fell back into my chair almost deprived of sensibility. When I recovered, we (Hyrum and myself) talked to them some time, endeavoring to persuade them to change their vile course; but the only answer we could get from them was, "Well, we've got the place, and d——n you, help yourselves if you can."

Hyrum, in a short time, went to an old friend, Dr. Robinson, and related to him the grievous story. Whereupon, the old gentleman sat down, and wrote at some considerable length the character of the family—our industry, and faithful exertions to secure a home, with many commendations calculated to beget confidence in us with respect to business transactions. And, keeping this writing in his own hands, he went through the village, and in an hour procured sixty subscribers. He then sent the same, by the hand of Hyrum, to the land agent, who lived in Canandaigua.

On receiving this, the agent was highly enraged. He said the men had told him that Mr. Smith and his son Joseph had run away, and that Hyrum was cutting down the sugar orchard, hauling off the rails, burning them, and doing all manner of mischief to the farm. That, believing this statement, he was induced to sell the place, for which he had given a deed, and received the money.

Hyrum told him the circumstances under which his father and brother had left home; also the probability of their being detained on the road, to attend to some business. Upon this, the agent directed him to address a number of letters to my husband, and have them sent and deposited in public-houses on the road which he traveled, that, perchance some of them might meet his eye, and thus cause him to return more speedily than he would otherwise. He then despatched a messenger to those individuals to whom he had given a deed of the farm in question, with the view of making a compromise with them. . . .

The agent strove to . . . persuade them to retract, and let the land go back into Mr. Smith's hands again. . . . Finally, they agreed; if Hyrum could raise them one thousand dollars, by Saturday at ten o'clock in the evening, they would give up the deed.

It was now Thursday about noon, and Hyrum was at Canandaigua, which was nine miles distant from home, and hither he must ride before he could make the first move towards raising the required amount. He came home with a heavy heart. When he arrived, he found his father, who had returned a short time before him. His father had fortunately found, within fifty miles of home, one of those letters which Hyrum had written. . . .

The anxiety of mind that I suffered that day can more easily be imagined than described. I now looked upon the proceeds of our industry, which smiled around us on every hand, with a kind of yearning attachment that I never before had experienced; and our early losses I did not feel so keenly, for I then realized that we were young, and by making some exertions we might improve our circumstances; besides, I had not felt the inconveniences of poverty as I had since. . . .

[The business of the farm was finally adjusted with the Smiths remaining as tenants. Joseph had come back] and remained with us, until the difficulty about the farm came to an issue; he then took leave for Pennsylvania, on the same business as before mentioned, and the next January returned with his wife, in good health and fine spirits.

Not long subsequent to his return, my husband had occasion to send him to Manchester, on business. As he set off early in the day, we expected him home

at most by six o'clock in the evening, but . . . he did not get home till the night was far spent. On coming in, he threw himself into a chair, apparently much exhausted. . . .

Presently he smiled, and said in a calm tone, "I have taken the severest chastisement that I have ever had in my life."

My husband, supposing that it was from some of the neighbors, was quite angry, and observed, "I would like to know what business anybody has to find fault with you!"

"Stop, father, stop," said Joseph, "it was the angel of the Lord; as I passed by the hill of Cumorah, where the plates are, the angel met me, and said that I had not been engaged enough in the work of the Lord; that the time had come for the Record to be brought forth; and that I must be up and doing, and set myself about the things which God had commanded me to do. But, father, give yourself no uneasiness concerning the reprimand which I have received, for I now know the course that I am to pursue, so all will be well."

It was also made known to him at this interview, that he should make another effort to obtain the plates, on the twenty-second of the following Sept., but this he did not mention to us at that time.

173. *The Difficulties of Catholic Immigrants, 1850*

Archbishop John Hughes, "Archiepiscopal Reminiscences of the Diocese of New York," 1838–1858 (H. J. Browne, ed.), United States Catholic Historical Society, *Historical Records and Studies*, XXXIX–XL (1952), 164–8.

SERIOUS evils have resulted to religion especially in this city, as immediate and remote consequences of the "Irish Famine," in 1847 and 1848. . . . The outlet of escape from Ireland, for those who survived, was America;—which, in other words, means

the port of New York. During those years, the arrivals of this class were oftentimes at the rate of 1000 and 2000 per day. The utter destitution in which they reached these shores, is almost inconceivable. But besides this, they had imbibed, and brought with them the seeds of disease and pestilence. . . . The municipal authorities and the laws of the state, which amply provide that no human being shall be allowed to die of starvation or exposure, provided, indeed, for the physical wants of this unhappy class. But in the meantime, for all that related to their moral and religious welfare, they may be said to have passed away from the faith of their ancestors. . . .

They were protected in the different public institutions, which the authorities had provided for that purpose. But as soon as their increasing years, or recovered health permitted it, they were indentured as servants in the city, or as servants among the farmers and mechanics in the country, who were willing to receive them. Thus they have been, and continue to be, scattered over the surface of the land, and estranged in too many instances from even the opportunities of learning their religion, or of practicing its duties. . . .

For these evils it is not in our power to provide a remedy; we have done all that it has been possible for us, to gather up and restore the scattered débris of the Irish nation, as the same have been cast into our community, already overburdened with its own local wants, and, own moral afflictions. . . .

From these remarks, you will infer enough to form some idea of the condition of the state of religion in New York as resulting from the immediate and remote evils entailed upon us, in consequence mainly of the Irish Famine. . . .

The emigration for the last twenty years has been excessive; and whilst it has done much to build up Catholic churches, and form congregations, throughout the interior, and especially in the West, it has afflicted this city in a remarkable degree. The explanation of this observation will occur to you in considering an obvious fact,—which is, that the better class of emigrants, those who have some means, those who have industrious habits,—robust health,—superior intelligence, naturally pass through this city, and push onwards in search of localities in which the resources of industrial life are less developed than here. On the other hand, the destitute, the disabled, the broken down, the very aged, and the very young, and I had almost added, the depraved, of all nations, having reached New York, usually settle down here—for want of means, or through want of inclination to go farther.

174. *Learning Among the Jews, 1846–48*

I. M. Wise, *Reminiscences.* David Philipson, ed. (Cincinnati, 1901). From the New York reprinting of 1945, pp. 23, 71–2, 79–80.

SUCH was the status of the synagogues of New York in 1846. Outside of Lilienthal and Merzbacher, there was not one leader who could read unpunctuated Hebrew, or, with the exception of a few private individuals. . . , had the least knowledge of Judaism, its history and literature. . . . I found at that time in New York but three men in private life who possessed any Jewish or Talmudic learning. . . .

Two-thirds of all the Israelites of Albany and of America before 1848 were uneducated and uncultured. Their Judaism consisted in a number of inherited customs and observances. The less these were understood, the holier were they considered. Every one made things as easy and as convenient as possible in practice. People did not observe the Sabbath . . . but at home and in the synagogue everything had to be conducted in the most orthodox fashion, i.e., in the manner in which every one had seen it in his early home. However, the people came from all lands. Every one had his own customs, and every one wanted to have these ... observed generally. Hence arose a Babel-like confusion. ... Rudeness goes hand in hand with ignorance. A fight at the congregational meeting, the escape of the president by a window in order to avoid threatened danger, lengthy and unprofitable altercations in place of debates—such things were not rare. ...

The German Jews of America read little or no English at that time. The *Occident* was published for native-born, English, some Polish, and Dutch Jews. The latter were Talmudically orthodox; the native Jews were, if I may say so, tinged with Christian thought. They read only Christian religious literature, because there was no Jewish literature of this kind. They substituted God for Jesus, unity for trinity, the future Messiah for the Messiah who had already appeared, etc. There were Episcopalian Jews in New York, Quaker Jews in Philadelphia, Huguenot Jews in Charleston, and so on, everywhere according to the prevailing sect. Cabalistic mysticism underlay everything. ... It was but a step from Judaism to Christianity, and vice versa.

175. *Violence in Georgia, 1834*

Martineau, *Society in America*, I, 285–6.

WHEN we drew near to Columbus, Georgia, we were struck with amazement at the stories that were told ... in the stage, about recent attempts on human life in the neighborhood; and at the number of incidents of the same kind which were the news of the day along the road. Our driver from Macon had been shot at, in attempting to carry off a young lady. A gentleman, boarding in the hotel at Columbus, was shot in the back, in the street, and laid by for months. No inquiry was made, or nothing came of it. The then present governor of the State of Mississippi had recently stood over two combatants, pistol in hand, to see fair play. ... The landlord of the house where we stopped to breakfast on the day we were to reach Columbus, April 9th, 1835, was, besides keeping a house of entertainment, a captain of militia, and a member of the legislature of Georgia. He was talking over with his guests a late case of homicide in a feud between the Myers and Macklimore families. He declared that he would have laws like those of the Medes and Persians against homicide; and, in the same breath, said that if he were a Myers, he would shoot Mr. Macklimore and all his sons.

176. *Manners in Pioneer Illinois, 1822*

C. H. Tillson, A *Woman's Story of Pioneer Illinois.*
M. M. Quaife, ed. (Chicago, 1919), 57–64.

WHEN we arrived at his house ... [Brice Hanna] came up to the carriage, and told us there was another house on the other side of the swamp where we could stay; that he had been from home all the week; that his wife was sick, and that we could not be accommodated anyhow. Your father told him that it was nearly sunset, and that he should not attempt to go through a five-mile swamp until he could do it by daylight, so we unpacked ourselves and moved towards the house. ...

There was but one room in the main cabin, which I at once perceived was unusually clean for an establishment of that kind. There were two beds nicely made, with clean pillows and handsome bed-quilts, the floor clean, and the coarse chairs looking as if they had just been scrubbed. In a large, open fireplace was a cheerful fire of oak logs, which were supported by one old iron andiron and a stone on the other side. But what most puzzled me was a pretty woman—who did not seem to be more than twenty— sitting with her feet on a chair, and with pillows around her, and holding her infant in her lap. . . . She looked a little annoyed when we first went in, but politely asked us to be seated, and by her manner we concluded that she was mistress of the mansion.

Brice . . . finally came in bringing a stone, which he threw down with an oath, saying he had had his eye on that rock for some time, and thought it would be a match for the one in the fireplace. He commenced pulling out the andiron, swearing at the fire for being too hot. His wife looked on tremblingly, and asked why he was not willing to have the andiron remain, as it was "a heap handier than the stone." With another string of oaths he jerked out the poor andiron, and taking it to the door he threw it as far as he could into the yard. Such things might do for the broadcloth gentry, but he did not belong to the gentry; at the same time giving one of his menacing glances at us. . . .

The poor wife would shrink down when the blast was heaviest, but after he had gone would brighten up again. When one of the storms had subsided and he had gone out . . . I ventured to ask her how long she had been a cripple. She said only a few months; that just before her baby was born she fell into the well and broke some of her bones, and was so hurt all over that she had not been able to walk since, and if it had been God's will she should have wished never to have come out alive. . . .

After awhile the fiend again made his appearance. . . . All at once a happy thought seemed to occur to him, and looking at us with malicious satisfaction he commenced a furious rubbing and scratching, pushing up his sleeves and looking at his wrists. He turned suddenly around and asked us if we had any beds of our own to stretch on for the night. He had seen all we took from the carriage, and knew that we had no beds along, and looked satanically happy when he announced that we would all get the itch, as all in the house had it. . . . Such startling information would have been fearful had I not looked at the honest face of the poor wife, who, without uttering a word, showed plainly that it was news to her, and I felt sure it was only a scheme of his own to make us uncomfortable. He seemed disappointed that he had not made a greater sensation, and as no one replied to his last effort he settled himself to think of something else disagreeable.

At last, with a more extended swear than before, he said he was tired, and was going to bed; it would do for gentry, who could stay in bed as long as they pleased, to sit up late, "but I'm no gentry, and I'm going to bed." There were two beds in the room, standing foot to foot, on the side opposite the fire-place. One was for us, the other for Brice, wife and baby. . . . Although I did not believe there was any danger, I took the precaution to spread some pocket-handkerchiefs over the pillows, and by only removing my outside garments and putting on gloves, . . . felt pretty secure as to infection, but not quite comfortable as respected the mood of mine host. Being very tired I thought I would lie down, but not allow myself to sleep. Our trunks were deposited in the same room where we were, and I imagined that there had been a suspicious eyeing throughout the evening, and that the inside as well as the out might prove attractive. . . . I was very tired, and Morpheus finally overcame all my resolutions and made me forgetful of danger.

I do not know how long I had slept, when aroused by the crying of the baby and the coarse swearing of the father. He scolded his wife for letting it cry, and then cursed the "little imp; imp of the devil." The wife said the child needed caring for, and would not go to sleep without it; that it must be taken to the fire and made dry and comfortable, but he swore he would gag the squalling brat. After a while he sprang out of bed and pulling the child from under the bed clothes, declared he would roast it. There was in the fireplace a large fire, made of oak logs, which were all aglow and gave light to the whole room. He took the baby under one arm, and with two or three bounds was at the fireplace. He commenced raking open the coals, still holding baby under his arm, swearing he would make a back-log; "yes, I'll brile ye." I kept both eyes open and trembled for the fate of the baby, when, to my surprise, he seated himself, carefully warmed the dry linen that was hanging by the fire, and in the most handy manner performed all that a good nurse or mother could have done. And now that baby was dry and there was no good reason for crying, and swearing did not soothe, he pressed "the brat, imp of the devil," to his breast, and commenced singing a good Methodist hymn in a soft, subdued voice, and had it been my first impression I should have supposed him a most devout Christian. A more sudden change from the profane to the devotional could not be imagined. . . .

As soon as it was light we were up and ready for a leave-taking. At the five-mile house on the other side of the swamp we found a plain, decent family, who gave us a breakfast of "common doings," corn bread and bacon, without any attempt at "wheat bread and chicken fixings," and from them we heard more of Brice Hanna. The man told us that Brice had a good farm and in his way kept his family comfortable, took pride in having the best wagon and horses in the county. He had always been proud of his wives, the one we saw being his third, but his greatest pride was in his peculiar capacity for swearing.

177. *The Standards of the Frontier, 1826*

Timothy Flint, *Recollections of the Last Ten Years* (Boston, 1826), 173, 175–8.

I HAVE traveled in these regions thousands of miles under all circumstances of exposure and danger, . . . alone, or in company only with such as needed protection, instead of being able to impart it; and this too, in many instances, where I was not known as a minister, or where such knowledge would have had no influence in protecting me. I have never carried the slightest weapon of defense. I scarcely remember to have experienced anything that resembled insult, or to have felt myself in danger from the people. I have often seen men that had lost an eye. Instances of murder, numerous and horrible in their circumstances, have occurred in my vicinity. But they were such lawless rencounters, as terminate in murders everywhere, and in which the drunkenness, brutality, and violence were mutual. . . .

When we look around these immense regions, and consider that I have been in settlements three hundred miles from any court of justice, when we look at the position of the men, and the state of things, the wonder is that so few outrages and murders occur. . . . The backwoodsman of the West, as I have seen him, is generally an amiable and virtuous man. His general motive for coming here is to be a freeholder, to have plenty of rich land, and to be able to settle his children about him. It is a most virtuous motive. . . . You find, in truth, that he has vices and barbarisms, peculiar to his situation. His manners are rough. He wears, it may be, a long beard. He has a great quantity of bear or deer skins wrought into his household establishment, his furniture and dress. He carries a knife, or a dirk in his bosom, and when in the woods has a rifle on his back, and a pack of dogs at his heels. . . . But remember, that his rifle and his dogs are among his chief means of support and profit. Remember, that all his first days here were passed in dread of the savages. Remember, that he still encounters them, still meets bears and panthers.

Enter his door, and tell him you are benighted, and wish the shelter of his cabin for the night. The welcome is indeed seemingly ungracious: "I reckon you can stay," or "I suppose we must let you stay." But this apparent ungraciousness is the harbinger of every kindness that he can bestow, and every comfort that his cabin can afford. . . . His wife, timid, silent, reserved, but constantly attentive to your comfort, does not sit at the table with you, but like the wives of the patriarchs, stands and attends on you. You are shown to the best bed which the house can offer. When this kind of hospitality has been afforded you as long as you choose to stay, and when you depart, and speak about your bill, you are most commonly told with some slight mark of resentment, that they do not keep tavern. Even the flaxen-headed urchins will turn away from your money. . . .

If we were to try them by the standard of New England customs and opinions, that is to say, the customs of a people under entirely different circumstances, there would be many things in the picture, that would strike us offensively. They care little about ministers, and think less about paying them. They are averse to all, even the most necessary restraints. They are destitute of the forms and observances of society and religion; but they are sincere and kind without professions, and have a coarse, but substantial morality.

178. *The Occupations of the Poor, 1852*

New York Association for Improving the Condition of the Poor, *Ninth Annual Report, 1852,* 25–7.

IN ALL our Atlantic cities, more than half the needy are Irish and German; but whether foreigners or natives, the men requiring aid are generally without mechanical skill, mostly mere day laborers, who have become accustomed only to the rudest and humblest employments. The women of the same class are like the men in these respects, with the additional disadvantage of finding less demand for their services, and less wages. . . . Little evidently can be done to increase the productiveness of this class of laborers; yet some have vainly imagined in respect to the women, that they could be so improved in the art of sewing and other appropriate female occupations, as to command for them employment and good wages. But were this practicable, as experience has proved it not to be, yet the promised result cannot be realized while there is so large a surplus of such labor in the market. . . .

The result of special inquiries directed to the occupations of the poor, show that of the foreigners relieved, more than three-fourths are common laborers, among the men, and washers, housecleaners, sewers, etc., among the women, there being about an equal proportion of each. In other words, they are mostly persons who have been trained to no trade or regular employment, and having little skill in any, are forced to accept of such as is offered.

Hence, during the busy season, the men work about the wharves, or as diggers, hodmen, etc., and the women as rough washers, housecleaners, coarse sewers, or in any other rude work they can find to do. Such occupations being, at best, irregular and precarious; and the women especially, being poorly qualified even for these, it is not surprising that they have but little work and small wages, or that they often need extraneous aid. . . .

But in this city, where there is so large a redundance of labor, even the possession of industrial skill affords no guaranty either for employment or good wages. Here are probably more than twelve thousand seamstresses, whose dependence for a livelihood is on the needle in its various applications for the clothing trade; about two thousand cap-sewers, and several thousand shoe-binders, exclusive of numerous other thousands, who in different ways "ply the polished shaft" for support. Take the case of one of these females for an illustration. The prices paid usually range so low, that with steady work and long hours, the most expert sewer can make but a scanty living. This . . . is in consequence of the rivalry of the employed among themselves, and not the fault of the employer. . . . The difficulty exists in the fact, that there are more laborers of this class pressing on the market than the market can absorb.

179. *The Vigilantes, 1851*

M. F. Williams, *History of the San Francisco Committee of Vigilance of 1851* (Berkeley, 1921), 456–8, 460, 464–5.

California Courier, June 10, 1851

It is clear to every man that San Francisco is partially in the hands of criminals, and that crime has reached a crisis where the fate of life and property are in imminent jeopardy. There is no alternative now left us but to lay aside business and direct our whole energies as a people to seek out the abodes of these villains and execute summary vengeance upon them. . . . What now shall be done? Are we to continue to threaten, and nothing more? . . . Why stop, under the present unsafe and uncertain state of affairs, to have a thief, or one who attempts to fire the city, placed in the hands of law officers, from whose clutches they can, with ease, be relieved by false swearing, and the ingenuity of lawyers? or what is equally as certain, their escape from prison? Where the guilt of the criminal is clear and unquestionable, the first law of nature demands that they be instantly shot, hung, or burned alive. . . . We must strike terror into their hearts. . . .

No man, since we became a city, has been hung in San Francisco. Some fifty murders have been committed, but no murderer has suffered death for his crimes.

We ask again, what shall be done? We are in the midst of a revolution, and we should meet the emergencies of our condition with firm hearts and well-braced nerves. We have no time to talk about the defects of the laws—of the dangers which beset us; but we must act, and act at once—act as men do in revolutionary times. . . .

Statement of James Neall, Jr.

On Sunday [June 8] . . . George [Oakes] . . . in conversation with me, upon the perilous condition of society at that time, said we ought to take some steps to see if we could not change these things, and suggested that we should go up and have a talk with Sam Brannan, and we went up to Brannan's office. . . . We there found Mr. Brannan and his clerk, and sat down and talked the matter [over]. . . . We . . . concluded that something must be done, and it was suggested that each one of us should give Mr. Brannan's clerk, Mr. Wardwell, the names of such men as we could mention, whom we knew to be reliable, to invite them to meet us at 12 o'clock noon the next day, at the California Engine House . . . to devise some means of protecting ourselves from the depredations of this hoard of ruffians, who seemed to have possession of the city. There was no such thing as doing anything with them before the courts; that had been tried in vain. Notices were sent out to parties to the effect that they were nominated, each as chairman of a committee for his neighborhood, to invite their fellow citizens, good reliable men, to meet . . . as above indicated. . . .

Statement of William T. Coleman

I was early at the building, and found a number of gentlemen there, probably thirty or forty already. An organization was formed, and the objects of the meeting stated, with a brief discussion. Articles had been already prepared for the mode of organization, and some thirty or forty names were enrolled, and it was styled the *Committee of Vigilance of San Francisco*, the avowed objects of the Committee being to vigilantly watch and pursue the outlaws and criminals who were infesting the city, and bring them to justice, through the regularly constituted courts, if that could be, through more summary and direct process, if must be. Each member pledged his word of honor, his life and fortune if need be, for the protection of his fellow members, for the protection of life and property of the citizens and of the community, and for purging the city of the bad characters who were making themselves odious in it. After arranging for a concert of action, watchwords, and a signal to be used to call the members to the rendezvous . . . and detailing officers for immediate duty, enrolling a number of members, all among the most re-

spectable, substantial and well-known citizens of the place, and the disposition of some needed business,—the Committee adjourned for the evening. . . .

Statement of G. W. Ryckman

When any men were arrested and turned over to the Committee, they were tried by the Executive and such trials were as honest and impartial as ever a man had, and no man was convicted without an abundance of testimony, such as would convict any human being in any court of justice; only we could not allow any alibis to come in to screen these fellows. After the trial and conviction of the prisoner, the case was referred to the General Committee for its action, and the testimony was sent to them. They invariably confirmed the decisions of the Executive Committee, and it was impossible for them to do otherwise, in the face of such proofs as were offered.

The Committee was composed mostly of our best men; the salt of San Francisco joined us. Everything was organized in a proper and unmistakable shape, so that every man had his duty to perform, and he had to report daily to the Committee, and if anything had transpired it was properly noted. Every man had his place, and there was a place for every man; there were no drones there. . . .

Charge of Judge Alexander Campbell to the Grand Jury After the Execution of James Stuart

The question has now arisen, whether the laws made by the constitutional authorities of the State are to be obeyed and executed, or whether secret societies are to frame and execute laws for the government of this county, and to exercise supreme power over the lives, liberty and property of our citizens. . . . Are the people willing to throw away the safeguards which the experience of ages has proved necessary . . . and to place life, liberty, property and reputation at the mercy of a secret society? If such be the disposition of the people . . . it is time for every man who values his life, safety and honor, to shake the dust from his feet and seek out some new home, where he may hope to enjoy the blessings of liberty under the law. But if, on the other hand, we have not quite forgotten the principles upon which our government is formed— . . . if we believe that persons accused of crime should have an open, public and impartial trial by a fair jury of unprejudiced citizens, and should have a reasonable opportunity of making their defense, of employing counsel and summoning witnesses; if we believe that the good name and reputation of our citizens is to be protected from a secret scrutiny, where accusations are made under the influence of fear, by persons of questionable character;—if we believe that our houses are to be protected from unreasonable searches without color of authority, it is our solemn and bounden duty to take immediate and energetic measures for the suppression of the spirit of reckless violence which overrules the laws and sets the Constitution at defiance.

When you first assembled, the Court called your attention to the unlawful execution of a man named Jenkins by an association of citizens. We considered that act was greatly palliated by the circumstances . . . that the laws had been defective, and that perhaps there had been some laxity in their administration; that the county had no sufficient jail for the detention of prisoners; that crime had increased to a fearful extent, and that a portion of our citizens, deeming that the law afforded them no protection, had in that instance undertaken to execute what they conceived to be summary justice, in violation of the law, but with a sincere desire to advance the public interest. We further stated that the law had been amended in many respects, so as to secure the speedy trial and conviction of offenders . . . that the county jail had been put in a proper condition for the safe keeping of prisoners, and we expressed the hope that no further attempt would be made

to interfere with the legally organized tribunals of justice. . . . From the time of your assembling, the Court, the Grand Jury, and all the officers have been actively and constantly engaged in the performance of their duties. At the time when they were making every possible effort to dispose of the criminal business of the county, and when the Court was in actual session and in the performance of its duties; and association of persons, of armed and organized men, have undertaken to trample on the Constitution, defy the laws, and assume unlimited power over the lives of the community. There is no excuse or palliation for the deed. . . . Every person who in any manner acted, aided, abetted or assisted in taking Stuart's life, or counseled or encouraged his death, is undoubtedly GUILTY OF MURDER. It is your sworn and solemn duty, which you cannot evade without perjuring yourselves, carefully and fully to investigate this matter, and to do your share towards bringing the guilty to punishment. Upon your fearless and faithful discharge of the trust confided to you, depends, in a great measure, the future peace, order and tranquility of the community.

California Courier, July 14, 1851

No such committee could exist in any form in this city, if the whole body of the community did not consider that necessity and policy demanded it. The committee is composed of peace loving and orderly citizens—many of them are elders, deacons and conspicuous members of the church. They are not composed of rowdies or blood thirsty men. . . . We are not going to complain of Judge Campbell's charge —but we can tell him that the men who hung Stuart cannot be indicted, convicted and executed in California, while the records of the Courts show that some of our best citizens have been shot down in cold blood, and that the murderers have been permitted entirely to run at large or to slip through their hands, unwhipped and unavenged of justice.

180. *Poverty and Social Disorder, 1833*

McDowall's   Journal   (New   York),   I   (January, 1833),   3.

I WAS invited to go to the Five Points and aid a few Sabbath School teachers in opening and establishing a school on the Sabbath for the benefit of the children in that place. . . . Being assured that a more poor and dissipated group of human beings could not be found elsewhere, my mind was decided, and I soon found myself in the midst of a scene of wickedness, such as I had never before witnessed, and had supposed not to exist in Christendom. I will not alarm your fears by a description of the licentiousness, intemperance, thieving, rioting, blasphemy, bitterness, fighting, and murder then or now practised there, but will barely remark, that although the school was opened, and the children were received in it, no abiding impression was made on their infant minds.

That fact led me to investigate the cause. I found that the children lived in brothels, or mingled daily in intercourse with children in such houses, and that, as soon as the school was out, the children returned to their residence, and saw, and conversed, and ate, and drank, and slept, with the offcast of both sexes. The cause of failing to produce an abiding influence over the children's minds . . . I attempted to remove. . . .

We went from house to house, reading the scriptures, praying and exhorting all men and women to be reconciled to God through our Lord Jesus Christ. With tears and much entreaty we warned them to flee from the wrath to come. This course we pursued for several weeks, commencing in the morning at nine o'clock and continuing until one—returning after dinner and continuing till tea time. In the evening, accompanied by different gentlemen, we went out at eight o'clock, and usually returned at ten or eleven. . . . As you may well suppose, a powerful impression was made on that population. More than twenty public riots were suppressed by mild measures, and hundreds of vile fellows, from the country and different parts of the city, were shamed away and afraid to return. Many of the brothel keepers complained that our praying and preaching had driven off and kept away so many men that the girls they kept could not pay their board; and the girls themselves began to reflect seriously upon their future prospects. Some were convinced of the evil of their way; and when we urged them to reform, they replied that they could not—that if they ceased to do evil, they would starve. We believe they lied, and that they loved vice too well to abandon it, as thousands of them evidently do.

But one day we were sorely tried. We had a prayer meeting, and several of them were present. It was one of the most solemn meetings I ever witnessed. All were in tears. The women had attended several previous meetings, and on this occasion one of the girls present had privately stolen away from her keeper. . . . This woman entreated us to take her away from that place, and so did all the others save one. But what could we do? We told them to go away home, or to service. . . . Each told her doleful tale. We knew that they were egregious liars, and that but little confidence could be reposed in their representations; yet the circumstances attending these histories of themselves, given unasked, and with tears flowing from their eyes, induced us to pause and reflect. Are these things so? was the question my mind labored to answer.

The next day we pursued the same course. On leaving one of those craters of hell, a young, but intelligent female, stood at the door on the sidewalk. Mr. Cunningham, whose silver locks, wrinkled face, and meek demeanor, make him venerable, said to her, "My child, O why will you live so?" "Sir," replied the girl, "I can live no other way." "Madam," said I to her, "...you have youth and health on your side, you can support yourself by the labor of your hands." "I can," said she, "and I will work for you, and go now." "But I cannot employ you. Go seek a service place." "I have no character, and can procure no place. I did procure a service place, but some gentleman visiting at the house knew me, and informed the mistress of my character, and she dismissed me immediately.... And if I get another service place, the gentlemen will detect my character in that, and I shall be dismissed from that also." She ceased speaking and sobbed aloud. My heart ached. What,

said I to myself, is it true that no virtuous family will knowingly have one of the wretched women in their house?...

My tongue was tied. I felt the force of that apostolical censure on those who said, "Be ye warmed, and clothed, and fed," but gave them neither fuel nor raiment nor bread. Still skeptical, I resolved to know the truth of her story. I went through the prisons and hospitals, the almshouse and the brothels, and made extensive inquiries of the imprisoned, the sick, the paupers and the lewd running at large, and then conversed with gentlemen and ladies acquainted with the state of city manners and habits, and found that all testified to the same thing that this young woman said. Here then was an end to my missionary labors.

XXII ꙮ *Cultural Nationalism*

As THE NATION grew in strength after 1820, many Americans hoped that it would at last be capable of fulfilling its cultural promise. As its wealth and power increased, it was plausible to expect that achievements in the arts and sciences would more adequately express the spirit of its free institutions. To that end, President John Quincy Adams spoke to Congress of the means by which the government might further knowledge (No. 181). In more general terms a philosopher summoned his fellow citizens to devote their own efforts to the task of creating a culture worthy of their distinctiveness and individuality (No. 182).

Yet the task proved difficult. True, a renaissance in literature—particularly in New England—produced a number of distinguished writers. But the orbit of their contemporary influence was narrow. There were limits to the capacity of this society to develop a stable culture. Even at the end of the period, these limitations were a drag upon literary American taste (No. 183). Unfortunately, the backwardness of higher education impeded progress in this regard. Men like Ticknor had early exposed the need for reforms (No. 184); but the only notable progress in education in these years came at the elementary level (*see below*, Section XXIII).

Generally, the cultural tastes of the times remained simple, attracted by the curious, the gigantic, and the unusual. A museum was still primarily an assemblage of curiosities (No. 185). The greatest American showman exploited this interest in a variety of forms (No. 186). The developing theater occasionally brought classical drama to American audiences; but the masses in the audience had simpler tastes (No. 187). A well-known actor of the day found his most popular role in a part that permitted him to combine a simple story with extravagant pantomime (No. 188).

There were, however, some developments encouraging for the future. The public library got its start in this period (No. 189). The lecture platform began to bring men of a high level of intelligence to the simplest audiences (No. 190). Finally, practical means were being explored, by which government support of higher education would one day lead to the further growth of American universities (No. 191).

181. *Government and Knowledge, 1825*

President John Quincy Adams, Message to Congress, December 6, 1825, Richardson, *Messages and Papers*, II, 311–14.

THE GREAT object of the institution of civil government is the improvement of the condition of those who are parties to the social compact, and no government... can accomplish the lawful ends of its institution but in proportion as it improves the condition of those over whom it is established. Roads and canals, by multiplying and facilitating the communications and intercourse between distant regions and multitudes of men, are among the most important means of improvement. But moral, political, intellectual improvement are duties assigned by the Author of our Existence to social no less than to individual man. For the fulfillment of those duties governments are invested with power, and to the attainment of the end— the progressive improvement of the condition of the governed—the exercise of delegated powers is a duty as sacred and indispensable as the usurpation of powers not granted is criminal and odious.

Among the first, perhaps the very first, instrument for the improvement of the condition of men is knowledge, and to the acquisition of much of the knowledge adapted to the wants, the comforts, and enjoyments of human life public institutions and seminaries of learning are essential....

In assuming her station among the civilized nations of the earth it would seem that our country had contracted the engagement to contribute her share of mind, of labor, and of expense to the improvement of those parts of knowledge which lie beyond the reach of individual acquisition, and particularly to geographical and astronomical science.... Of the cost of these undertakings, ... it would be unworthy of a great and generous nation to take a second thought. One hundred expeditions of circumnavigation like those of Cook and La Pérouse would not burden the exchequer of the nation fitting them out so much as the ways and means of defraying a single campaign in war. But if we take into account the lives of those benefactors of mankind of which their services in the cause of their species were the purchase, how shall the cost of those heroic enterprises be estimated, and what compensation can be made to them or to their countries for them? Is it not by bearing them in affectionate remembrance? Is it not still more by imitating their example—by enabling countrymen of our own to pursue the same career and to hazard their lives in the same cause? ...

It is not my design to recommend the equipment of an expedition for circumnavigating the globe for purposes of scientific research and inquiry. We have objects of useful investigation nearer home, and to which our cares may be more beneficially applied. The interior of our own territories has yet been very imperfectly explored. Our coasts along many degrees of latitude upon the shores of the Pacific Ocean, though much frequented by our spirited commercial navigators, have been barely visited by our public ships. The River of the West, first fully discovered and navigated by a countryman of our own, still bears the name of the ship in which he ascended its waters, and claims the protection of our armed national flag at its mouth. With the establishment of a military post there or at some other point of that coast, recommended by my predecessor and already matured in the deliberations of the last Congress, I would suggest the expediency of connecting the equipment of a public ship for the exploration of the whole northwest coast of this continent.

The establishment of an uniform standard of weights and measures was one of the specific objects contemplated in the formation of our Constitution, and to fix that standard was one of the powers delegated by express terms in that instrument to Congress. The governments of Great Britain and France have scarcely ceased to be occupied with inquiries and speculations on the same subject since the existence of our Constitution, and with them it has expanded into profound, laborious, and expensive researches into the figure of the earth and the comparative length of the pendulum vibrating seconds in various latitudes from the equator to the pole. These researches have resulted in the composition and publication of several works

highly interesting to the cause of science. The experiments are yet in the process of performance. Some of them have recently been made on our own shores, within the walls of one of our own colleges, and partly by one of our own fellow-citizens. It would be honorable to our country if the sequel of the same experiments should be countenanced by the patronage of our Government, as they have hitherto been by those of France and Britain.

Connected with the establishment of an university, or separate from it, might be undertaken the erection of an astronomical observatory, with provision for the support of an astronomer, to be in constant attendance of observation upon the phenomena of the heavens, and for the periodical publication of his observations. . . . On the comparatively small territorial surface of Europe there are . . . upward of 130 of these light-houses of the skies, while throughout the whole American hemisphere there is not one. If we reflect a moment upon the discoveries which in the last four centuries have been made in the physical constitution of the universe by the means of these buildings and of observers stationed in them, shall we doubt of their usefulness to every nation? And while scarcely a year passes over our heads without bringing some new astronomical discovery to light, which we must fain receive at second hand from Europe, are we not cutting ourselves off from the means of returning light for light while we have neither observatory nor observer upon our half of the globe and the earth revolves in perpetual darkness to our unsearching eyes?

182. *The American Scholar*, 1837

Ralph Waldo Emerson, "American Scholar," Oration at Cambridge, August 31, 1837, *Nature. Addresses and Lectures* (Boston, 1850), 105–11.

I READ with joy some of the auspicious signs of the coming days, as they glimmer already through poetry and art, through

philosophy and science, through church and state.

One of these signs is the fact that the

same movement which effected the elevation of what was called the lowest class in the state, assumed in literature a very marked and as benign an aspect. Instead of the sublime and beautiful, the near, the low, the common, was explored and poetized. That which had been negligently trodden under foot by those who were harnessing and provisioning themselves for long journeys into far countries, is suddenly found to be richer than all foreign parts. The literature of the poor, the feelings of the child, the philosophy of the street, the meaning of household life, are the topics of the time. It is a great stride. It is a sign—is it not?—of new vigor when the extremities are made active, when currents of warm life run into the hands and the feet. I ask not for the great, the remote, the romantic; what is doing in Italy or Arabia; what is Greek art, or Provençal minstrelsy; I embrace the common, I explore and sit at the feet of the familiar, the low. Give me insight into today, and you may have the antique and future worlds. What would we really know the meaning of? The meal in the firkin; the milk in the pan; the ballad in the street; the news of the boat; the glance of the eye; the form and the gait of the body;—show me the ultimate reason of these matters; show me the sublime presence of the highest spiritual cause lurking, as always it does lurk, in these suburbs and extremities of nature; let me see every trifle bristling with the polarity that ranges it instantly on an eternal law; and the shop, the plough, and the ledger referred to the like cause by which light undulates and poets sing;—and the world lies no longer a dull miscellany and lumber-room, but has form and order. There is no trifle; there is no puzzle; but one design unites and animates the farthest pinnacle and the lowest trench. . . .

Another sign of our times, also marked by an analogous political movement, is the new importance given to the single person. Every thing that tends to insulate the individual,—to surround him with barriers of natural respect, so that each man shall feel the world is his, and man shall treat with man as a sovereign state with a sovereign state,—tends to true union as well as greatness. "I learned," said the melancholy Pestalozzi, "that no man in God's wide earth is either willing or able to help any other man." Help must come from the bosom alone. The scholar is that man who must take up into himself all the ability of the time, all the contributions of the past, all the hopes of the future. He must be an university of knowledges. If there be one lesson more than another which should pierce his ear, it is: The world is nothing, the man is all; in yourself is the law of all nature, and you know not yet how a globule of sap ascends; in yourself slumbers the whole of Reason; it is for you to know all; it is for you to dare all.

Mr. President and Gentlemen, this confidence in the unsearched might of man belongs, by all motives, by all prophecy, by all preparation, to the American Scholar. We have listened too long to the courtly muses of Europe. The spirit of the American freeman is already suspected to be timid, imitative, tame. Public and private avarice make the air we breathe thick and fat. The scholar is decent, indolent, complaisant. See already the tragic consequence. The mind of this country, taught to aim at low objects, eats upon itself. There is no work for any but the decorous and the complaisant. Young men of the fairest promise, who begin life upon our shores, inflated by the mountain winds, shined upon by all the stars of God, find the earth below not in unison with these, but are hindered from action by the disgust which the principles on which business is managed inspire, and turn drudges, or die of disgust, some of them suicides. What is the remedy? They did not yet see, and thousands of young men as hopeful now crowding to the barriers for the career do not yet see, that if the single man plant himself indomitably on his instincts, and there abide, the huge world will come round to him. Patience,—patience; with the shades of all the good and great for company; and for solace the perspective of your own infinite life; and for work the study and the communication of principles, the making those instincts prevalent, the conversion of the world. Is it not the chief disgrace in the world, not to be an unit;—not to be reckoned one character;—not to yield that peculiar fruit which each man was created to bear, but to be reckoned in the gross, in the hundred, or the thousand, of the party, the section, to which we belong; and our opinion predicted geographically, as the north, or the south? Not so, brothers and friends,—please God, ours shall not be so. We will walk on our own feet; we will work with our own hands; we will speak our own minds. The study of letters shall be no longer a name for pity, for doubt, and for sensual indulgence. The dread of man and the love of man shall be a wall of defense and a wreath of joy around all. A nation of men will for the first time exist, because each believes himself inspired by the Divine Soul which also inspires all men.

183. *American Literary Taste, 1857*

Oliver Wendell Holmes, *Autocrat of the Breakfast-Table* (Boston, 1859), 305–6.

THESE United States furnish the greatest market for intellectual green fruit of all the places in the world. I think so, at any rate. The demand for intellectual labor is so enormous and the market so far from nice, that young talent is apt to fare like unripe gooseberries,—get plucked to make a fool of. Think of a country which buys eighty thousand copies of the *Proverbial Philosophy,* while the author's admiring [English] countrymen have been buying twelve thousand! How can one let his fruit hang in the sun until it gets fully ripe, while there are eighty thousand such hungry mouths ready to swallow it and proclaim its praises?

Consequently, there never was such a collection of crude pippins and half-grown windfalls as our native literature displays among its fruits. There are literary green-groceries at every corner, which will buy anything, from a button-pear to a pineapple. It takes a long apprenticeship to train a whole people to reading and writing. The temptation of money and fame is too great for young people. Do I not remember that glorious moment when the late Mr.—we won't say who,—editor of the—we won't say what, offered me the sum of fifty cents per double-columned quarto page for shaking my young boughs over his foolscap apron? Was it not an intoxicating vision of gold and glory? I should doubtless have reveled in its wealth and splendor, but for learning that the fifty cents was to be considered a rhetorical embellishment, and by no means a literal expression of past fact or present intention.

184. *American Colleges, 1825*

George Ticknor, *Life, Letters and Journals* (Boston, 1876–77), I, 356–9.

IT IS, I think, an unfortunate circumstance, that all our colleges have been so long considered merely places for obtaining a degree of Bachelor of Arts, to serve as a means and certificate whereon to build the future plans and purposes of life. Such a state of things was, indeed, unavoidable at the earlier period of [Harvard] College, when there was only a President, who sometimes lived permanently in Boston, and a few tutors, who kept a school in Newton; for the number of scholars was so small that it was possible to teach only by classes, and each student, the number being also small, could pass through the hands of every one of them, and receive from every one all the instruction he could give.

But now the state of the case is reversed. There are twenty or more teachers, and three hundred students, and yet the division into classes remains exactly the same, and every student is obliged to pass through the hands of nearly or quite every instructor. Of course, the recitations become mere examinations, and it cannot be attempted to give more than the most superficial view of very important subjects, even to those who would gladly investigate them thoroughly, because they must keep with the class to which they are bound, and hurry on from a teacher and a subject to which they have, perhaps, important reasons for being attached, to another teacher and another subject, wherein their present dispositions and final pursuits in life make it impossible for them to feel any interest. But at the same time that we at once perceive this system . . .

has been carried too far, . . . we must still feel that it has in some respects its peculiar advantages. The majority of the young men who come to Cambridge should not be left entirely to themselves to choose what they will study, because they are not competent to judge what will be most important for them; and yet no parent would wish to have his child pursue branches of knowledge which he is sure can never be of use to him in future life. . . .

Now if this be the condition of the College, which I do not doubt, or if anything like it exist there, which nobody will deny, it is perfectly apparent that a great and thorough change must take place in its discipline and instruction; not to bring it up to the increasing demands of the community, but to make it fulfil the purposes of a respectable high school, to which young men may be safely sent to be prepared for the study of a profession. . . .

A change must take place. The discipline of college must be made more exact, and the instruction more thorough. All now is too much in the nature of a show, and abounds too much in false pretences. . . . It is seen that we are neither an university—which we call ourselves— nor a respectable high school,—which we ought to be.

185. *Peale's Museum, 1826*

Anne Royall, *Sketches of History, Life, and Manners, in the United States* (New Haven, 1826), 211, 212, 217, 218.

IT MAY readily be supposed, that the idea of seeing a place so celebrated as the museum of Philadelphia, inspired me with no common curiosity. . . . The museum is in Chestnut Street. . . . I soon discovered it by a sign, and after crossing a gallery, came to a stair-case, wide enough to admit a wagon and team. I made but a few steps, before one of them springing

under my feet, rung a bell, to my great surprise, and upon gaining the stairs, I was met by a man whose business it is to receive the money paid, which is twenty-five cents. The first object of my inquiry, was the mammoth skeleton, but I was greatly disappointed in its appearance. The skeleton is indeed as large as is represented, but it had not that formidable, dread-inspiring aspect which my romantic turn led me to expect, and with which I expected to be overwhelmed. I beheld it without surprise or emotion. It is standing upon its feet in a small room, which is lighted by a large window, enclosed with a rail as high as one's breast, and presenting its side foremost. . . . The whole has a very dark appearance, and in many parts it is quite black. In some instances the bone is as hard as iron, while other parts seem to be in a moldering condition. . . .

This skeleton was found by accident, in Ulster county . . . on a farm. . . . In 1801, Mr. C. W. Peale, of Philadelphia, purchased the right of digging for the skeleton, and after six weeks of intense labor, his efforts were crowned with success. He obtained the skeleton perfect, except [two ribs]. . . .

Although I was not thrown into hysterics at the sight of the mammoth skeleton, I found enough of the marvelous in the museum to remunerate for the disappointment. Amongst these were the sea-lion, the skeleton of a horse, which,

when living, measured twenty hands in height, with a human figure on its back! a sheep weighing 214 pounds . . . , the devil-fish—in short, ten thousand things wonderful and pleasing . . . [including] two hundred portraits of our most distinguished men. . . .

The museum was founded by Mr. Peale, in 1784; this indefatigable man has done more since that time, than one would suppose could be done by a whole nation —the collection is endless. . . . I had not the pleasure of seeing Mr. Peale, but was much gratified in the acquaintance of his son, and by seeing a full length portrait of the old gentleman, painted by himself—it stands in the museum. The young Mr. Peale is a small man, upon whom, however, nature and art have lavished their favors; I met with him in the museum, and received from him those marks of politeness and attention, which none but the learned and the refined know how to bestow. . . . After paying once, you have free liberty of the museum as often as you choose to call.

186. *Tom Thumb and Jenny Lind, 1842–50*

P. T. Barnum, *Life* (New York, 1855), 243–4, 296, 307, 312–16.

I HAD heard of a remarkably small child in Bridgeport; and by my request my brother brought him to the hotel. He was the smallest child I ever saw that could walk alone. He was not two feet in height, and weighed less than sixteen pounds. He was a bright-eyed little fellow, with light hair and ruddy cheeks, was perfectly healthy, and as symmetrical as an Apollo. He was exceedingly bashful, but after some coaxing he was induced to converse with me. . . .

He was only five years old, and to exhibit a dwarf of that age might provoke the question, How do you know that he *is* a dwarf? Some license might indeed

be taken with the facts, but even with this advantage I really felt that the adventure was nothing more than an experiment, and I engaged him for the short term of *four weeks at three dollars per week*—all charges, including traveling and boarding of himself and mother, being at my expense.

They arrived in New York on Thanksgiving Day, December 8, 1842, and Mrs. Stratton was greatly astonished to find her son heralded in my Museum bills as General TOM THUMB, a dwarf of eleven years of age, just arrived from England!

This announcement contained two deceptions. I shall not attempt to justify them, but may be allowed to plead the circumstances in extenuation. The boy was undoubtedly a dwarf, and I had the most reliable evidence that he had grown little, if any, since he was six months old; but had I announced him as only five years of age, it would have been impossible to excite the interest or awaken the curiosity of the public. The thing I aimed at was, to assure them that he was *really a dwarf* —and in *this,* at least, they were not deceived.

It was of no consequence, in reality, where he was born or where he came from, and if the announcement that he was a *foreigner* answered my purpose, the people had only themselves to blame if they did not get their money's worth when they visited the exhibition. I had observed . . . the American fancy for European exotics; and if the deception . . . has done anything toward checking our disgraceful preference for foreigners, I may readily be pardoned for the offense I here acknowledge. . . .

In October, 1849, I first conceived the idea of bringing Jenny Lind to this country. I had never heard her sing. . . . Her reputation, however, was sufficient for me. I usually jump at conclusions, and almost invariably find that my first impressions are the most correct. It struck me, when I first thought of this speculation, that if properly managed it must prove immensely profitable, provided I could engage the "Swedish Nightingale" on any terms with the range of reason. As it was a great undertaking, I considered the matter seriously for several days, and all my "cipherings" and calculations gave but one result—immense success. . . .

I may as well here state, that although I relied prominently upon Jenny Lind's reputation as a great musical *artiste,* I also took largely into my estimate of her success with all classes of the American public, her character for extraordinary benevolence and generosity. Without this peculiarity in her disposition, I never would have dared make the engagement

which I did, as I felt sure that there were multitudes of individuals in America who would be prompted to attend her concerts by this feeling alone.

Thousands of persons covered the shipping and piers, and other thousands had congregated on the wharf at Canal street, to see her. The wildest enthusiasm prevailed as the noble steamer approached the dock. . . . A superb bower of green trees, decorated with beautiful flags, was discovered upon the wharf, together with two triumphal arches, on one of which was inscribed, "Welcome, Jenny Lind!" The second was surmounted by the American eagle, and bore the inscription, "Welcome to America!" These decorations were probably not produced by magic, and I do not know that I can reasonably find fault with some persons who suspected that I had a hand in their erection. . . .

Jenny Lind's first concert was fixed to come off at Castle Garden on Wednesday evening, September 11, and most of the tickets were sold at auction on the Saturday and Monday previous to the concert. Genin the hatter laid the foundation of his fortune by purchasing the first ticket at $225.

The proprietors of the Garden saw fit to make the usual charge of one shilling to all persons who entered the premises, yet three thousand persons were present at the auction. One thousand tickets were sold on the first day for an aggregate sum of $10,141. . . .

The reception of Jenny Lind on her first appearance, in point of enthusiasm, was probably never before equaled in the world. As Mr. Benedict led her towards the foot-lights, the entire audience rose to their feet and welcomed her with three cheers, accompanied by the waving of thousands of hats and handkerchiefs. This was by far the largest audience that Jenny had ever sung before. She was evidently much agitated, but the orchestra commenced, and before she had sung a dozen notes of "Casta Diva," she began to recover her self-possession, and long before the *scena* was concluded, she was as calm as if sitting in her own drawing-room. Towards the last portion of the *cavatina,* the audience were so completely carried away by their feelings, that the remainder of the air was drowned in a perfect tempest of acclamation. Enthusiasm had been wrought to its highest pitch, but the musical powers of Jenny Lind exceeded all the brilliant anticipations which had been formed, and her triumph was complete. . . .

It would seem as if the Jenny Lind mania had reached its culminating point before hearing her, and I confess that I feared the anticipations of the public were too high to be realized, and hence that there would be a reaction after the first concert, but I was happily disappointed. The transcendent musical genius of the Swedish Nightingale was superior to all the pictures which fancy could paint, and the *furore* did not attain its highest point until she had been heard. The people

were in ecstasies; the powers of editorial acumen, types and ink, were inadequate to sound her praises. The Rubicon was passed. . . .

The great assembly at Castle Garden was not gathered by Jenny Lind's great musical genius and powers alone. She was effectually brought before the public before they had seen or heard her. She appeared in the presence of a jury already excited to enthusiasm in her behalf. She more than met their expectations, and all the means I had adopted to prepare the way were thus abundantly justified.

As a manager, I worked by setting others to work. Biographies of the Swedish Nightingale were largely circulated; "Foreign Correspondence" glorified her talents and triumphs by narratives of her benevolence; and "printer's ink" was employed, in every possible form, to put and keep Jenny Lind before the people.

187. *The Boys in the Bowery Pit, 1840*

Elton's Songs and Melodies (New York, 1840), 72.

I'm sitting in the Bowery pit, amongst
  the "gallus boys,"
A seeing of the play go on, and listening
  to the noise,
The hi-hies and the whistling, an earthquake's nothing to it,
For kicking up a thund'ring din, oh,
  they're the boys to do it.

When Cony, with his dog, comes on, you
  ought to hear the cry,
And when the dog gets wounded and
  makes believe to die,
When Blanchard comes, with sword in
  hand, and he and Cony fight,
The hearts of all the "gallus boys" are
  brimfull of delight.

But presently the actors are seen looking
  at the wings,

As if they were a watching for somebody
  or some things;
The "gallus boys" are wide awake, they
  know what's coming now,
For J. R. Scott is coming on, and then
  there's such a row.

Just at this time a little boy climbs up
  upon his seat,
And one behind, who cannot see, soon
  knocks him off his feet;
A cry of "pass him round," then is echoed
  through the pit,
And ground and lofty tumbling is no circumstance to it.

And when the play is over, and we are
  going out,
Some boy from home puts out the gas,
  and then sets up a shout;

Another one grabs at your cap, or, if you
    wear a plug,
'Tis jammed down, by no gentle hand,
    on your unresisting mug.

Oh, if you want to see some fun, go to the
    Bowery pit,

Especially upon some night when there's
    a benefit,
And I'll be bound that you will think, amid
    the din and noise,
That they are "gallus" bloods indeed, and
    nothing but the "boys."

188. *Rip Van Winkle, 1859*

Joseph Jefferson, *Autobiography* (New York, [1897]), 222–8.

For myself, like some of those already mentioned, I had always been, more or less, a legitimate actor, and the hope of entering the race for dramatic fame as an individual and single attraction never came into my head until, in 1858, I acted *Asa Trenchard* in "Our American Cousin"; but as the curtain descended the first night on that remarkably successful play, visions of large type, foreign countries, and increased remuneration floated before me, and I resolved to be a star if I could. A resolution to this effect is easily made; its accomplishment is quite another matter. . . .

During these delightful reveries it came up before me that in acting *Asa Trenchard* I had, for the first time in my life on the stage, spoken a pathetic speech; and though I did not look at the audience during the time I was acting,—for that is dreadful,—I felt that they both laughed and cried. I had before this often made my audience smile, but never until now had I moved them to tears. This to me novel accomplishment was delightful, and in casting about for a new character my mind was ever dwelling on reproducing an effect where humor would be so closely allied to pathos that smiles and tears should mingle with each other. Where could I get one? There had been many written, and as I looked back into the dramatic history of the past a long line of lovely ghosts loomed up before me, . . . charming fellows all, but not for me. I felt I could not do them justice.

Besides, they were too human. I was looking for a myth—something intangible and impossible. But he would not come. Time went on, and still with no result.

During the summer of 1859 . . . I thought to myself, "Washington Irving, the author of *The Sketch-Book*, in which is the quaint story of Rip Van Winkle." Rip Van Winkle! There was to me magic in the sound of the name as I repeated it. Why, was not this the very character I wanted? An American story by an American author was surely just the theme suited to an American actor.

In ten minutes I had gone to the house and returned to the barn with *The Sketch-Book*. I had not read the story since I was a boy. I was disappointed with it; not as a story, of course, but the tale was purely a narrative. The theme was interesting, but not dramatic. The silver Hudson stretches out before you as you read, the quaint red roofs and queer gables of the old Dutch cottages stand out against the mist upon the mountains; but all this is descriptive. The character of *Rip* does not speak ten lines. What could be done dramatically with so simple a sketch? How could it be turned into an effective play? . . .

Still I was so bent upon acting the part that I started for the city, and in less than a week, by industriously ransacking the theatrical wardrobe establishments for old leather and mildewed cloth, and by personally superintending the making of wigs, each article of my costume was completed; and all this too before I had written a line of the play or studied a word of the part.

This is working in an opposite direction from all the conventional methods in the study and elaboration of a dramatic character.... I can only account for my getting the dress ready before I studied the part to the vain desire I had of witnessing myself in the glass, decked out and equipped as the hero of the Catskills.

I got together the three old printed versions of the drama and the story itself. The plays were all in two acts. I thought it would be an improvement in the drama to arrange it in three, making the scene with the specter crew an act by itself. This would separate the poetical from the domestic side of the story. But by far the most important alteration was in the interview with the spirits. In the old versions they spoke and sang. I remembered that the effect of this ghostly dialogue was dreadfully human, so I arranged that no voice but *Rip's* should be heard. This is the only act on the stage in which but one person speaks while all the others merely gesticulate, and I was quite sure that the silence of the crew would give a lonely and desolate character to the scene and add to its supernatural weirdness. By this means, too, a strong contrast with the single voice of *Rip* was obtained by the deathlike stillness of the "demons" as they glided about the stage in solemn silence. It required some thought to hit upon just the best questions that could be answered by a nod and shake of the head, and to arrange that at times even *Rip* should propound a query to himself and answer

it; but I had availed myself of so much of the old material that in a few days after I had begun my work it was finished.

In the seclusion of the barn I studied and rehearsed the part, and by the end of the summer I was prepared to transplant it from the rustic realms of an old farmhouse to a cosmopolitan audience in the city of Washington, where I opened at Carusi's Hall under the management of John T. Raymond.... I had by repeated experiments so saturated myself with the action of the play that a few days served to perfect the rehearsals. I acted on these occasions with all the point and feeling that I could muster. This answered the double purpose of giving me freedom and of observing the effect of what I was doing on the actors. They seemed to be watching me closely, and I could tell by little nods of approval where and when the points hit.

I became each day more and more interested in the work; there was in the subject and the part much scope for novel and fanciful treatment. If the sleep of twenty years was merely incongruous, there would be room for argument pro and con; but as it is an impossibility, I felt that the audience would accept it at once, not because it was an impossibility, but from a desire to know in what condition a man's mind would be if such an event could happen. Would he be thus changed? His identity being denied both by strangers, friends, and family, would he at last almost accept the verdict and exclaim, "Then I am dead, and that is a fact"? This was the strange and original attitude of the character that attracted me.

189. *A Public Library, 1851*

George Ticknor to Edward Everett, July 14, 1851, Ticknor, *Life*, II, 300–2.

I HAVE seen with much gratification ... that you interest yourself in the establishment of a public library in Boston;—I mean a library open to all the citizens, and from which all, under proper restrictions, can take out books....

Such a free public library, if adapted to the wants of our people, would be the crowning glory of our public schools. But I think it important that it should be adapted to our peculiar character; that is, that it should come in at the end of our system of free instruction, and be fitted to continue and increase the effects of that system by the self-culture that results from reading.

The great obstacle to this with us is not—as it is in Prussia and elsewhere—a low condition of the mass of the people, condemning them, as soon as they escape from school, and often before it, to such severe labor . . . that they have no leisure for intellectual culture, and soon lose all taste for it. Our difficulty is, to furnish means specially fitted to encourage a love for reading, to create an appetite for it, which the schools often fail to do, and then to adapt these means to its gratification. That an appetite for reading can be very widely excited is plain, from what the cheap publications of the last twenty years have accomplished, gradually raising the taste from such poor trash as the novels with which they began, up to the excellent and valuable works of all sorts which now flood the country, and are read by the middling classes everywhere, and in New England, I think, even by a majority of the people.

Now what seems to me to be wanted in Boston is, an apparatus that shall carry this taste for reading as deep as possible into society. . . . To do this I would establish a library . . . in which any popular books, tending to moral and intellectual improvement, should be furnished in such numbers of copies that many persons, if they desired it, could be reading the same work at the same time; in short, that not only the best books of all sorts, but the pleasant literature of the day, should be made accessible to the whole people at the only time when they care for it, i.e. when it is fresh and new. I would, therefore, continue to buy additional copies of any book of this class, almost as long as they should continue to be asked for, and thus, by following the popular taste,—unless it should demand something injurious,—create a real appetite for healthy general reading. This appetite, once formed, will take care of itself. It will, in the great majority of cases, demand better and better books; and can, I believe, by a little judicious help, rather than by any direct control or restraint, be carried much higher than is generally thought possible.

190. *Lyceums and Their Wants,* 1869

The Lyceum (Boston), August, 1869, No. 1.

THE NEED of an intermediate agency between lyceums and lecturers has been felt for a long time in New England and elsewhere. Committees find constant difficulty in reaching lecturers; and lecturers in putting themselves in communication with committees.

The Boston Lyceum Bureau supplies this want of a common center of communication. It is already the agent of more than two hundred lecturers, readers, and musicians, and its list is not yet completed. It is prepared to supply any demand that may be made on it for Lyceum lectures, commencement orations, occasional speeches, vocal or instrumental musicians, elocutionary readers or dramatic personators.

Any committee that has already engaged its full list of lecturers, in case of a failure on their part during the course of the coming season, can be supplied with a substitute at the shortest notice, by telegraphing or addressing the Boston Lyceum Bureau.

For nearly all the lecturers and readers

on this list, no engagement can be made, either by themselves or others, excepting through the agency of this Bureau.

Although $50 is the lowest sum named on the list, Lyceums that are struggling under difficulties, or Lyceums that are willing to take "off nights," can be supplied at even lower rates.

"*Modifications*," as used in the list, means both more and less—in a city, "$50 with modifications," may mean $60 or $75, and in a village $30 or $40. But the rates will always be stated in advance.

The Bureau will furnish several different lists, of ten lectures and entertainments each, for the aggregate sums of $350, $400, $450, $500, $600, $700, and upwards, on receipt of a fee of five dollars; which, if any course shall be engaged through the Bureau, will be refunded to the Lyceum.

Committees, in applying for any lecturer, should name several dates that will suit them, and we will then fix the first day of the number that is left at our disposal, or that can be arranged into a convenient route for the lecturer.

The list herewith submitted is the best and most varied, both as regards names and subjects, that has ever been offered in this country for the consideration of committees. We guarantee that every engagement made by us shall be promptly met, or that the name of the lecturer who fails, unless a satisfactory explanation is made to the committee, shall be promptly erased from our list.

No charge whatever will be made to Lyceums for any engagements that we may make for them.

Address: JAMES REDPATH
Boston Lyceum Bureau . . .

AMES, MRS. NELLIE
Subject—"Working Women of New York." Mrs. Ames is the author of the serial, "Up Broadway," published in the "Revolution." Recommended by a distinguished N.Y. author, as "a lady of great talent, a fine speaker,

and has the magnetism necessary to enchain an audience."
Terms—$100.

BARNARD, CHARLES, 2D.
Subjects—"My Jack-knife, and how to use it." A lecture on the theory and practice of pruning, illustrated on the blackboard. "Glass-farming." A lecture on the forcing of plants.
Terms—$50 with modifications.
(Mr. Barnard is better known by his newspaper name of Jane Kingsford, and his recent books, "Farming by Inches," and "My Ten Rod Farm."\
. . .

BILLINGS, JOSH
Subjects—"Milk." "A Plaintive Discourse on Natral Hist'ry." The last lecture is "warranted for 60 days." Terms—Outside of New England, Mr. Billings' average terms are $90.40, "with the privilege of throwing off the $90 if I was a mind to, but never to discount the 40 cents." In New England, his terms range from $75.40 to $100.40. Time.—All December. Lyceums who desire to secure him should apply soon. . . .

GUNNING, W. D.
Subjects—Eight lectures on Geology, to be delivered either as a course, or separately. A syllabus of these lectures will be sent on application.
Terms—$50 and expenses, and upwards, for one lecture, or $250 for the course—one lecture weekly, for eight successive weeks—with modifications.
Mr. Gunning is recommended by Profs. Agassiz, Wood, Harley and others. . . .

HIGGINSON, COL. T. W.
Subjects—"Democracy and Literature." "The Aristocracy of the Dollar."
Terms—$75, with modifications. . . .

JAMES, HENRY
Subject—"Carlyle."
Terms—$50, and upwards. . . .

SIKES, WIRT
Subjects—"After Dark in New York."
"Assassins."
Terms—$75 to $100. . . .

SUMNER, HON. CHARLES
(Senator Sumner, if his other engagements permit, will lecture during October and November. All applications must be made to this Bureau, and a route will be arranged as early as possible. Lyceums that desire to secure Senator Sumner should name a series of dates from which a selection can be made. It is hardly necessary to add that early applications will be necessary.) . . .

TWAIN, MARK
Subject—"Curiosities of California."
Terms—$100, with modifications.
(This celebrated humorist has been a very successful lecturer in the West. This is his first season in New England. Lyceums must apply for him at an early date, unless they can secure their hall for any evening.)

191. *Agricultural Colleges, 1858*

Greensboro, North Carolina, *Times*, April 17, 1858, as quoted in E. W. Knight, ed., *Documentary History of Education in the South* (Chapel Hill, 1952), III, 445–6.

IT MAY be that some of our readers have seen notice of a bill introduced into Congress, providing for the establishment of agricultural colleges in the several states of the Union, from a percent of the proceeds of the public lands. We say it *may be* that such a notice has been seen, because we think it exceedingly doubtful, from the fact that it has met with little attention from Congress and still less from the public press. . . .

In a government of popular sentiment like ours, the press is the main moving power. It both furnishes the material and leads the direction of public thought.— Hence it is important, it is indispensable, to gain the coöperation of the press in prosecuting with success any work of great importance. And in what direction shall we look for a more important work, than the enriching of our farming interest. If he is called a benefactor who, where one blade of grass grew before, can make two, what a grand field is opening for the exercise of beneficence by the general government.

For example, in some of our wheat growing states, fourteen bushels per acre is an average crop; while in some of the scientific farming countries of Europe the average crop is forty bushels per acre.— According to the last census report, the annual product of wheat is not less than 110,000,000 bushels. By the increased fertility of the land, it would be from the above estimate 300,000,000, being an increase of 190,000,000, which, at 50 cents per bushel, would be equivalent to a donation of $90,000,000 to the farmers of the country; more by $20,000,000 than is required to carry on the entire machinery of our Federal Government. Is there nothing to be gained in the difference between fourteen and forty bushels of wheat to the acre?

And further, the exhaustion and deterioration of the soil by the modes of farming in the United States, has been estimated at ten cents per acre annually. There are about 130,000,000 acres of arable land in the United States. There must be, therefore, a loss of $13,000,000 annually, and mostly for want of practical skill in resuscitation of the land.

From these two items, by no means the most important, some idea may be gained of the good to result from the establishment of these colleges.

XXIII 🌿 *The Reform Impulse*

THERE WAS an unpleasant contrast by mid-century between the problems created by expansion, and American social and cultural ideals. This challenge to the assumption that American conditions encouraged constant improvement and the indefinite progress of mankind evoked a determined response.

In part, that response was eleemosynary and sprang from religious sources that enjoined upon the wealthy aid to the humble and acquiescent (No. 192). But the response also took the form of dynamic, aggressive, reform movements. Since man was innately good, it was assumed that only the impediment of outworn institutions held him back from the indefinite perfectibility that was his destiny. It was therefore the duty and the obligation of man to reform those ancient institutions and thus to permit the individual to realize his highest potentialities. This conviction was behind the intense frenzy of the multitudinous reform movements (No. 193).

The outlets of these energies were as numerous as the problems of the society. It was distressing, at the beginning of the period, for instance, to observe the retarded state of education (No. 194).

In this area, reform called not merely for a reorganization of the school system, but for an entirely new approach to the process of education, one that would treat the child in accord with his highest capacities as a human being (No. 195). Nor was education to be restricted as it had been in the past. It was to extend to women as well as to men (No. 196), for women were now claiming liberation and equality of status (No. 197).

Indeed, reform was the means for ameliorating the condition of all underprivileged groups. Thus, the deterioration of the position of the artisans and the persistence of economic injustice called for a total reconstruction of the productive system (No. 198).

Since man was perfectible, even the least well-endowed were capable of improvement. None were so low as to be beyond redemption, living evidence of the essential goodness of man. The insane, for instance, were not to linger in darkness; they could be healed (No. 199). Even those totally deprived of the use of their senses were somehow to be brought to a consciousness of their humanity, as Samuel Gridley Howe succeeded in doing for Laura Bridgman (No. 200).

This confidence would come into conflict with the persistence of the institution of slavery. Was the Negro, too, not a man, capable of perfectibility? This question would animate the abolition movement for decades. (*See below,* Section XXV.) And already it provoked conflicts as to the meaning of freedom, that would remain troubling until the Civil War (No. 201).

192. *Contentment, 1837*

C. M. Sedgwick, *Poor Rich Man and Rich Poor Man* (New York, 1837), 38–40.

"I DECLARE," said Uncle Phil, after the first salutations were passed, surveying the table with ineffable satisfaction, "you've set out what I call a tea, Susy. You beat 'em all in York—they live dreadful poor down there. To be sure, your Aunt Betsey lives in a brick house, and has a sight of furniture, and a gimcrack of a timepiece on her mantelpiece (it don't go half so true as our old wooden one), and high plated candlesticks, and such knick-knacks; yet she has all her bread to buy by the loaf, and the milk is sky-blue; as to cream, I don't believe they ever heard on't. Cakes and pies are scarce, I tell you. I don't believe peppergrass has come there yet, for I never saw a spear of it on the table, nor a speck of cheese. But the worst of all is the water. Poor Jock would have choked before he would have drank a drop of it; and they live in such a dust and hurra, I tho't when we drove in it was gineral training; but they carried on so every day;—and then there is such a stifled-up feeling—I did pity 'em."

Persons capable of more accurate comparison than Uncle Phil, may well pity those who, when summer is in its beauty, are shut up within the walls of a city, deprived of the greatest of all luxuries, which even the poorest country people enjoy—sweet air, ample space, pure water, and quiet only broken by pleasant sounds. . . .

"Ah, father," replied Susan, "you must remember we don't set out such a table very often here. I am sure I never could if we had not such kind neighbors; but, when they are kind, it don't seem to me to make much difference whether you are rich or poor."

Susan's simple remark had an important bearing on that great subject of inequality of condition, which puzzles the philosopher, and sometimes disturbs the Christian. But did not our happy little friend suggest a solution to the riddle? Has not Providence made this inequality the necessary result of the human condition, and is not the true agrarian principle to be found in the voluntary exercise of those virtues that produce an interchange of benevolent offices? If there were a perfect community of goods, where would be the opportunity for the exercise of the virtues, of justice, and mercy, humility, fidelity, and gratitude? If the rights of the poor of all classes were universally acknowledged, if intellectual and moral education were what they should be, the deaf would hear, and the blind would see; and the rich man would no longer look with fear upon the poor man, nor the poor man with envy on the rich. This true millennium is on its way. "Blessed are those who wait!"

193. *The Reformer, 1840's*

Ralph Waldo Emerson, "Man the Reformer" (lecture before the Mechanics' Apprentices' Library Association, Boston, January 25, 1841), *Nature*, 239–45.

THE IDEA which now begins to agitate society has a wider scope than our daily employments, our households, and the institutions of property. We are to revise the whole of our social structure, the state, the school, religion, marriage, trade, science, and explore their foundations in our own nature; we are to see that the world not only fitted the former men but fits us, and to clear ourselves of every usage which has not its roots in our own mind. What is a man born for but to be a reformer, a remaker of what man has made; a renouncer of lies; a restorer of truth and good, imitating that great Nature which embosoms us all, and which sleeps no moment on an old past, but every hour repairs herself, yielding us every morning a new day, and with every pulsation a new life? Let him renounce everything which is not true to him, and put all his practices back on their first thoughts, and do nothing for which he has not the whole world for his reason. If there are inconveniences and what is called ruin in the way, because we have so enervated and maimed ourselves, yet it would be like dying of perfumes to sink in the effort to reattach the deeds of every day to the holy and mysterious recesses of life.

The power, which is at once spring and regulator in all efforts of reform, is the conviction that there is an infinite worthiness in man, which will appear at the call of worth, and that all particular reforms are the removing of some impediment. Is it not the highest duty that man should be honored in us? I ought not to allow any man, because he has broad lands, to feel that he is rich in my presence. I ought to make him feel that I can do without his riches, that I cannot be bought—neither by comfort, neither by pride—and though I be utterly penniless, and receiving bread from him, that he is the poor man beside me. And if, at the same time, a woman or a child discovers a sentiment of piety, or a juster way of thinking than mine, I ought to confess it by my respect and obedience, though it go to alter my whole way of life. . . .

Every great and commanding moment in the annals of the world is the triumph of some enthusiasm. . . . There will dawn ere long on our politics, on our modes of living, a nobler morning . . . in the sentiment of love. This is the one remedy for all ills, the panacea of nature. We must be lovers, and at once the impossible becomes possible. Our age and history, for these thousand years, has not been the history of kindness, but of selfishness. Our distrust is very expensive. The money we spend for courts and prisons is very ill laid out. We make, by distrust, the thief, and burglar, and incendiary, and by our court and jail we keep him so. An acceptance of the sentiment of love throughout Christendom for a season would bring the felon and the outcast to our side in tears, with the devotion of his faculties to our service. See this wide society of laboring men and women. We allow ourselves to be served by them, we live apart from them, and meet them without a salute in the streets. We do not greet their talents, nor rejoice in their good fortune, nor foster their hopes, nor in the assembly of the people vote for what is dear to them. . . . We complain that the politics of masses of the people are controlled by designing men, and let in opposition to manifest justice and the common weal, and to their own interest. But the people do not wish to be represented or ruled by the ignorant and base. They only vote for these, because they were asked with the voice and semblance of kindness. They will not vote for them long. They inevitably prefer wit and probity. . . . Let our affection flow out to our fellows; it would operate in a day the greatest of all revolutions. It is better to work on institutions by the sun than by the wind. The state must consider the poor man, and all voices must speak for him. Every child that is born must have a just chance for his bread. Let the amelioration in our laws of property proceed from the concession of the rich, not from the grasping of the poor. Let us begin by habitual imparting. Let us understand that the equitable rule is that no one should take more than his share, let him be ever so rich.

194. *Pennsylvania Education, 1822*

William Duane, response to a questionnaire from the Kentucky Assembly, July 12, 1822 (Lowell H. Harrison, ed.), *Pennsylvania Magazine of History*, LXXIII (1949), 316–22.

HAS ANY system of common schools been established by law in your state?

Answer: There is in Pennsylvania, a general, but very imperfectly executed system for the instruction of the children of poor persons, and there is a particular law which embraces the children of the District of Philadelphia, county and city. The former . . . is not effective, owing in a principal measure to its want of vigorous and systematic prosecution, the insufficiency of the means, . . . to reward competent teachers and thereby secure their zeal, and the accordant want of any definite method by which the progress or the elementary instruction could be suitably inculcated. Another circumstance which probably might be overcome if there was any effective or coherent system, is the reaction of two kinds of pride; that of the opulent who are repugnant to the idea of . . . education in anything like a school, that has the denomination or attribute of being for the poor, or as their ideas associate it, with charity. This unfortunate pride extends to the actually poor themselves; by which I mean that class of men, who acquire their subsistence by useful labors in all the arts, agricultural, mechanical and liberal. . . . I know of no college or other institution, that is not conducted upon a system that appears to me barbarous and adverse to the development of the intellect of the species. I know of no female school but one, and that is confined to a few pupils. It is conducted by a Madame Fitegeot of this city, who is a disciple of Pestalozzi of Switzerland, and teaches in his method, somewhat modified to the prejudices of society. . . .

Are your counties or townships divided into school districts, with one school in each, or otherwise?

Answer: The schools of a public foundation are in townships, but they are not general, and I believe very few. The schools in this district, have, within three years, been assimilated to the forms of mutual instruction of the celebrated English teacher, Lancaster; a system that has the common defect of all modern systems, that of a method of *rote,* communicated and confirmed *orally;* but which confines its impressions to the mere accumulation of words, and appears to leave out of view the only important part of education, that of acquiring and comprehending ideas, or facts. This system . . . is connected with the most unfortunate of all prejudices—that is *cheapness.* The mercenary spirit is one of the most fatal of all the causes that injure morals, knowledge and education. . . . This poverty-stricken system . . . is not adapted to unfold human faculties, nor to form or to confirm sound minds. As far as it can render services, probably it does so here; but it is a lamentable evidence of the imperfection or the perversion of the most generous intentions. . . .

Is any particular qualification required in teachers?

Answer: Qualifications are not duly attended to, and it would be preposterous to expect adequate talents for the stipends allowed. At a private school in one of the townships adjacent to this city, a very excellent classical scholar and able mathematician, who had been a captain in our army, attempted to become a teacher. When he enquired what his allowance was to be, the answer was, what is the lowest sum you can possibly subsist on? The pursuit was necessarily abandoned....

Of what improvement does your system seem to be susceptible?

Answer: The existing system (if no system can be so called), admits of a total abrogation, and requires it. The subject of education is treated of in many excellent works, but there appears to be no regard paid to them in practice, though in discourse they are themes of admiration by the very persons who utterly disregard them.

Do the people of your state appear to be satisfied with the present plan?

Answer: This question involves a remarkable dilemma. If passiveness were to be the rule of judgment, as to the satisfaction of the people, I believe there is not in the universe a people who (by that criterion), are better satisfied with the present plan, or absence of all plan. But

if individuals are asked, the measure of intelligence of the individual will regulate the answer. No intelligent and upright man can approve of the present state of education; a great proportion of the population appear to be insensible or indifferent; and among the opulent, the improvement of the understanding and the heart, enters very little into the consideration. *"My son, make money,"* is the order of the day. But this is only a necessary effect of the social state, in which money is the substitute and the criterion of every virtue, to which human rights, human liberty, social virtue and public character are all sacrificed. There is nothing sacred or revered which is not sacrificed to money. When the government and the laws, and the habits of thinking, are thus radically vitiated, it is not to be expected that any other effect can be produced.

195. *Education and the Child,* 1844

Horace Mann, *Reply to the "Remarks"* of 31 Boston Schoolmasters (Boston, 1844), 130–1, 135–6.

HERE, then, is the philosophy of *School Discipline*. Authority, Force, Fear, Pain! The ideas of Childhood and Punishment indissolubly associated together....

Authority, Force, Fear, Pain! These motives, taken from the nethermost part of the nethermost end of the scale of influences, are to be inscribed on the lintels and door-posts of our schoolhouses.... These are the motives, by which the children of Boston,—and if this doctrine prevails, the children of the State also,—are to be so trained, that when they are emancipated from the parental hand, and are endowed with the privileges and ennobled by the enfranchisement of free citizens, they shall think rather of duty than of the policeman, and dwell in that moral freedom wherewith God makes all good men free, rather than abstain from infrac-

tions either of the human or the divine law, through dread of the dungeon or the gallows-tree.

Throughout this whole section, *conscience* is nowhere referred to, as one of the motive-powers in the conduct of children. The *idea* seems not to have entered into the mind of the writer, that any such agency could be employed in establishing the earliest, as well as the latest relations, between teacher and pupil. That powerful class of motives which consists of affection for parents, love for brothers and sisters, whether older or younger than themselves, justice and the social sentiment towards schoolmates, respect for elders, the pleasures of acquiring knowledge, the duty of doing as we would be done by, the connection between present conduct, and success, estimation, eminence, in future life, the presence of an unseen eye,—not a syllable of all these is set forth with any earnestness, or insisted upon, as the true source and spring of human actions. . . .

The "Remarks" say,—where "the spirit of opposition is too strong to be overruled by those higher and more refined motives upon which we should always rely when they are active, we are left without resource unless we appeal to fear." I deny that any Christian man, or any enlightened heathen man, is left without resource, under such circumstances, "unless he appeals to fear." He has the resource of conscience, which is no more extinguished in the child's soul, by the clamorous passions that, for a time, may have silenced its voice, than the stars of heaven are annihilated by the cloud which for a moment obscures them from our vision. He has the resource of social and filial affections. He has the love of knowledge and of truth, which never, in all its forms, is, or can be, eradicated from a sane mind. If the teacher is what he ought to be, he has the resource of a pure and lofty example, in his own character; and he moves before the eyes of his pupils as a personification of dignity and learning and benevolence. What a damning sentence does a teacher pronounce upon himself, when he affirms that he has no resources in his own attainments, his own deportment, his own skill, his own character; but only in the cowhide and birch, and in the strong arm that wields them!

There are always recuperative energies in a child. The last elements of faith and hope and duty, are never trodden wholly out of his soul. God has inwrought these elements into the nature of every child. . . . The existence of this substance is safe in any hands, for it is immortal. . . .

Was it not, and is it not, one of the grand objects in the institution and support of common schools, to bring those children who are cursed by a vicious parentage, who were not only "conceived and brought forth," but have been nurtured in "sin;" who have never known the voice of love and kindness; who have daily fallen beneath the iron blows of those parental hands that should have been outstretched for their protection;—was it not, and is it not, I say, one of the grand objects of our schools to bring this class of children under humanizing and refining influences; to show them that there is something besides wrath and stripes and suffering, in God's world; to lift these outcast and forlorn beings from their degradation, by gentle hands, and to fold them to warm and cherishing bosoms?

196. *Maternal Instruction, 1845*

Godey's Lady's Book, March, 1845, p. 108.

MEN have been busying themselves these six thousand years nearly to improve society. They have framed systems of philosophy and government, and conferred on their own sex all the advantages which power, wealth and knowledge could bestow. They have founded colleges and institutions of learning without number, and provided themselves teachers of every art and science; and, after all, the mass of mankind are very ignorant and very wicked. Wherefore is this? Because the *mother*, whom God constituted the first teacher of every human being, has been degraded by men from her high office; or, what is the same thing, been denied those privileges of education which only can enable her to discharge her duty to her children with discretion and effect. God created the woman as a *help-meet* for man in every situation; and while he, in his pride, rejects her assistance in his intellectual and moral career, he never will succeed to improve in his nature and reach that perfection in knowledge, virtue and happiness, which his faculties are constituted to attain.

If half the effort and expense had been directed to enlighten and improve the minds of females which have been lavished on the other sex, we should now have a very different state of society. Wherever a woman is found excelling in judgment and knowledge, either by natural genius or from better opportunities, do we not see her children also excel? Search the records of history, and see if it can be found that a great and wise man ever descended from a weak and foolish mother. . . . Yet, strange to say, the inference which ought to follow, namely, that in attempting to improve society, the first, most careful and continued efforts should be to raise the standard of female education, and qualify woman to become the educator of her children, has never yet been acted upon. . . .

What is true of the maternal influence respecting sons is, perhaps, more important in the training of daughters. The fashionable schools are a poor substitute for such example and instruction as a thoroughly educated and right principled mother would bestow on her daughters. . . . The tone of family education and of society needs to be raised. This can never be done till greater value is set on the cultivated female intellect. Young ladies must be inspired with high moral principles, noble aims, and a spirit of self-improvement to become what they ought to be. Maternal instruction is the purest and safest means of opening the fountain of knowledge to the young mind.

197. *Declaration of Female Independence, 1848*

"Declaration of Sentiments of the Seneca Falls Convention" (July 19–20, 1848). Quoted in E. C. Stanton, S. B. Anthony, and M. J. Gage, *History of Woman Suffrage* (Rochester, 1887), I, 70–1.

WHEN, in the course of human events, it becomes necessary for one portion of the family of man to assume among the people of the earth a position different from that which they have hitherto occupied, but one to which the laws of nature and of nature's God entitle them, a decent respect to the opinions of mankind requires that they should declare the causes that impel them to such a course. . . .

The history of mankind is a history of repeated injuries and usurpations on the part of man toward woman, having in direct object the establishment of an absolute tyranny over her. To prove this, let facts be submitted to a candid world.

He has never permitted her to exercise her inalienable right to the elective franchise.

He has compelled her to submit to laws, in the formation of which she had no voice.

He has withheld from her rights which are given to the most ignorant and degraded men—both natives and foreigners.

Having deprived her of this first right of a citizen, the elective franchise, thereby leaving her without representation in the halls of legislation, he has oppressed her on all sides.

He has made her, if married, in the eye of the law, civilly dead.

He has taken from her all right in property, even to the wages she earns.

He has made her, morally, an irresponsible being, as she can commit many crimes with impunity, provided they be done in the presence of her husband. In the covenant of marriage, she is compelled to promise obedience to her husband, he becoming, to all intents and purposes, her master—the law giving him power to deprive her of her liberty, and to administer chastisement.

He has so framed the laws of divorce, as to what shall be the proper causes, and in case of separation, to whom the guardianship of the children shall be given, as to be wholly regardless of the happiness of women—the law, in all cases, going upon a false supposition of the supremacy of man, and giving all power into his hands.

After depriving her of all rights as a married woman, if single, and the owner of property, he has taxed her to support a government which recognizes her only when her property can be made profitable to it.

He has monopolized nearly all the profitable employments, and from those she is permitted to follow, she receives but a scanty remuneration. He closes against her all the avenues to wealth and distinction which he considers most honorable to himself. As a teacher of theology, medicine or law, she is not known.

He has denied her the facilities for obtaining a thorough education, all colleges being closed against her.

He allows her in church, as well as state, but a subordinate position, claiming apostolic authority for her exclusion from the ministry, and, with some exceptions, from any public participation in the affairs of the church.

He has created a false public sentiment by giving to the world a different code of morals for men and women, by which moral delinquencies which exclude women from society, are not only tolerated, but deemed of little account in man. . . .

He has endeavored, in every way that he could, to destroy her confidence in her own powers, to lessen her self-respect, and to make her willing to lead a dependent and abject life.

Now, in view of this entire disfranchisement of one-half the people of this country, their social and religious degradation—in view of the unjust laws above mentioned, and because women do feel themselves aggrieved, oppressed and fraudulently deprived of their most sacred rights, we insist that they have immediate admission to all the rights and privileges which belong to them as citizens of the United States.

In entering upon the great work before us, we anticipate no small amount of misconception, misrepresentation and ridicule; but we shall use every instrumentality within our power to effect our object. We shall employ agents, circulate tracts, petition the state and national legislatures, and endeavor to enlist the pulpit and the press in our behalf.

198. *Social Destiny of Man, 1840*

Albert Brisbane, *Social Destiny of Man* (Philadelphia, 1840), 103–5, 111–12.

SLAVERY is not an isolated fact, a single blot upon our social order; it is a symptom, a part of a vast social malady, which is much deeper than is supposed; and which must be cured to eradicate the numberless evils, (one of which slavery is), which are the disgrace and scourge of human societies. That malady is repugnant industry. If labor be repulsive, degrading and but poorly rewarded how are the mass to be forced to it otherwise than by constraint? Constraint is the hideous means which society has made use of to insure production, and the creation of riches; it acts with a two-fold power, one of which is the whip and punishments, the other want and privations. . . .

If labor be repulsive, repugnant, man

will not undergo it, unless he be forced to it; society, therefore, to guarantee the persistence of the mass in labor, must reduce them to want, force them to it by their own necessities, and by those of their families. Thus, the very foundation of our societies is injustice and oppression; and if we disguise this false basis with a little political liberty, social evils and social servitude are not the less its results. The changes which have taken place in the condition of the laboring classes since the commencement of societies, have only been so many varieties of one general tyranny; at one epoch we see them Pariahs, at another slaves, at another serfs, and now they are the working classes. Individual slavery, as it universally existed in antiquity, has been changed and replaced by the collective servitude of the mass in modern times. . . .

This system of industrial servitude is the lot of the laboring classes of the fourth society, called civilization. But its falseness does not end here; to it is added the violation of the fundamental right of man, the right to labor. . . . If man were created to go through a course of existence, which is dependent on labor, if its right be not guaranteed him, his right to existence even is not acknowledged.

If we look at the cities of civilized Europe—and sometimes at our own—we see the laboring classes wandering from manufactory to manufactory, or shop to shop, inquiring for work and refused it. Without any means of existence while out of employ, pressed by want, often by starvation, they reduce the price of their day's labor, selling fourteen and more hours of monotonous drudgery out of each twenty-four for a miserable pittance. If they manage to avoid actual famine, slow starvation, unhealthy and excessive labor and anxiety, sow the seeds of disease, undermine the constitution, and counteract the healthy influence, which labor should have on the human frame.

To creatures thus situated, what mockery to offer them the right to vote, or the guarantee of not being thrown into prison without a writ of habeas corpus! Are they free, because they possess these illusory guarantees, when they are at the same time the slaves of labor, the serfs of capitalists? It is true, the whip does not force them to labor, like the real slave; but does not the alternative of want or famine do it as effectually? If their bodies cannot be sold, they have to bargain their liberty and their time, without being able to dispose scarcely of an hour. No: civil liberty is perfectly illusory without industrial liberty; it is a step-stone, a mere means of enabling man to attain to his destiny.

199. *Memorial on the Insane, 1843*

Dorothea L. Dix, *Memorial to the Massachusetts Legislature* (Boston, 1843), 3–5, 24–5, 32.

ABOUT two years since leisure afforded opportunity, and duty prompted me to visit several prisons and almshouses in the vicinity of this metropolis. I found, near Boston, in the jails and asylums for the poor, a numerous class brought into unsuitable connection with criminals and the general mass of paupers. I refer to idiots and insane persons, dwelling in circumstances not only adverse to their own physical and moral improvement, but productive of extreme disadvantages to all other persons brought into association with them.

I applied myself diligently to trace the causes of these evils, and sought to supply remedies. As one obstacle was surmounted, fresh difficulties appeared. Every new investigation has given depth to the conviction that it is only by decided, prompt, and vigorous legislation the evils to which I refer, and which I shall proceed more fully to illustrate, can be remedied.

I shall be obliged to speak with great plainness, and to reveal many things revolting to the taste, and from which my woman's nature shrinks with peculiar sensitiveness. But truth is the highest consideration. *I tell what I have seen*—painful and shocking as the details often are— that from them you may feel more deeply the imperative obligation which lies upon you to prevent the possibility of a repetition or continuance of such outrages upon humanity. If I inflict pain upon you, and move you to horror, it is to acquaint you with sufferings which you have the power to alleviate, and make you hasten to the relief of the victims of legalized barbarity. . . .

I proceed, gentlemen, briefly to call your attention to the present state of insane persons confined within this Commonwealth, in *cages, closets, cellars, stalls, pens! Chained, naked, beaten with rods,* and *lashed* into obedience!

As I state cold, severe facts, I feel obliged to refer to persons, and definitely to indicate localities. But it is upon my subject, not upon localities or individuals, I desire to fix attention; and I would speak as kindly as possible of all wardens, keepers, and other responsible officers, believing that most of these have erred not through hardness of heart and willful cruelty, so much as want of skill and

knowledge, and want of consideration. Familiarity with suffering, it is said, blunts the sensibilities, and where neglect once finds a footing other injuries are multiplied. This is not all, for it may justly and strongly be added that, from the deficiency of adequate means to meet the wants of these cases, it has been an absolute impossibility to do justice in this matter. Prisons are not constructed in view of being converted into county hospitals, and almshouses are not founded as receptacles for the insane. And yet, in the face of justice and common sense, wardens are by law compelled to receive, and the masters of almshouses not to refuse, insane and idiotic subjects in all stages of mental disease and privation.

It is the Commonwealth, not its integral parts, that is accountable for most of the abuses which have lately, and do still exist. I repeat it, it is defective legislation which perpetuates and multiplies these abuses. . . .

It is not few but many, it is not a part but the whole, who bear unqualified testimony to this evil. A voice strong and deep comes up from every almshouse and prison in Massachusetts where the insane are or have been, protesting against such evils. . . .

Gentlemen, I commit to you this sacred cause. Your action upon this subject will affect the present and future condition of hundreds and of thousands.

200. *Laura Bridgman, 1842*

Charles Dickens, *American Notes* (London, 1893), 26–34, 38.

I SAT down in another room, before a girl, blind, deaf, and dumb; destitute of smell; and nearly so, of taste: before a fair young creature with every human faculty, and hope, and power of goodness and affection, inclosed within her delicate frame, and but one outward sense—the

sense of touch. There she was, before me; built up, as it were, in a marble cell, impervious to any ray of light, or particle of sound; with her poor white hand peeping through a chink in the wall, beckoning to some good man for help, that an immortal soul might be awakened,

Long before I looked upon her, the help had come. Her face was radiant with intelligence and pleasure. Her hair, braided by her own hands, was bound about a head, whose intellectual capacity and development were beautifully expressed in its graceful outline, and its broad open brow; her dress, arranged by herself, was a pattern of neatness and simplicity; the work she had knitted, lay beside her; her writing-book was on the desk she leaned upon.—From the mournful ruin of such bereavement, there had slowly risen up this gentle, tender, guileless, grateful-hearted being. . . .

I have extracted a few disjointed fragments of her history, from an account, written by that one man who has made her what she is. It is a very beautiful and touching narrative; and I wish I could present it entire.

Her name is Laura Bridgman. "She was born in Hanover, New Hampshire, on the twenty-first day of December, 1829. She is described as having been a very sprightly and pretty infant, with bright blue eyes. She was, however, so puny and feeble until she was a year and a half old, that her parents hardly hoped to rear her. She was subject to severe fits, which seemed to rack her frame almost beyond her power of endurance: and life was held by the feeblest tenure: but when a year and a half old, she seemed to rally; the dangerous symptoms subsided; and at twenty months old, she was perfectly well. . . .

"But suddenly she sickened again; her disease raged with great violence during five weeks, when her eyes and ears were inflamed, suppurated, and their contents were discharged. But though sight and hearing were gone forever, the poor child's sufferings were not ended. The fever raged during seven weeks; for five months she was kept in bed in a darkened room; it was a year before she could walk unsupported, and two years before she could sit up all day. It was now observed that her sense of smell was almost entirely destroyed; and, consequently, that her taste was much blunted.

"It was not until four years of age that the poor child's bodily health seemed restored, and she was able to enter upon her apprenticeship of life and the world.

"But what a situation was hers! The darkness and the silence of the tomb were around her: no mother's smile called forth her answering smile, no father's voice taught her to imitate his sounds:—they, brothers and sisters, were but forms of matter which resisted her touch, but which differed not from the furniture of the house, save in warmth, and in the power power of locomotion; and not even in these respects from the dog and the cat.

"But the immortal spirit which had been implanted within her could not die, nor be maimed nor mutilated; and though most of its avenues of communication with the world were cut off, it began to manifest itself through the others. As soon as she could walk, she began to explore the room, and then the house; she became familiar with the form, density, weight, and heat, of every article she could lay her hands upon. She followed her mother, and felt her hands and arms, as she was occupied about the house; and her disposition to imitate, led her to repeat everything herself. She even learned to sew a little, and to knit."

The reader will scarcely need to be told, however, that the opportunities of communicating with her, were very, very limited; and that the moral effects of her wretched state soon began to appear. Those who cannot be enlightened by reason, can only be controlled by force; and this, coupled with her great privations, must soon have reduced her to a worse condition than that of the beasts that perish, but for timely and unhoped-for aid.

"At this time, I was so fortunate as to hear of the child, and immediately hastened to Hanover to see her. I found her with a well-formed figure; a strongly-marked, nervous-sanguine temperament; a large and beautifully-shaped head; and the whole system in healthy action. The parents were easily induced to consent to her coming to Boston, and on the 4th of October, 1837, they brought her to the Institution.

"For a while, she was much bewildered; and after waiting about two weeks, until she became acquainted with her new locality, and somewhat familiar with the inmates, the attempt was made to give her knowledge of arbitrary signs, by which she could interchange thoughts with others. . . .

"The first experiments were made by taking articles in common use, such as knives, forks, spoons, keys, etc., and pasting upon them labels with their names printed in raised letters. These she felt very carefully, and soon, of course, distinguished that the crooked lines '*s p o o n*,' differed as much from the crooked lines '*k e y*,' as the spoon differed from the key in form.

"Then small detached labels, with the same words printed upon them, were put into her hands; and she soon observed that they were similar to the ones pasted on the articles. She showed her perception of this similarity by laying the label '*k e y*' upon the key, and the label '*s p o o n*' upon the spoon. She was encouraged here by the natural sign of approbation, patting on the head.

"The same process was then repeated with all the articles which she could handle; and she very easily learned to place the proper labels upon them. It was evident, however, that the only intellectual exercise was that of imitation and memory. She recollected that the label '*b o o k*' was placed upon a book, and she repeated the process first from imitation, next from memory, with only the motive of love of approbation, but apparently without the intellectual perception of any relation between the things.

"After a while, instead of labels, the individual letters were given to her on detached bits of paper: they were arranged side by side so as to spell '*b o o k*,'

'*k e y*,' etc.; then they were mixed up in a heap and a sign was made for her to arrange them herself, so as to express the words '*b o o k*,' '*k e y*,' etc.; and she did so.

"Hitherto, the process had been mechanical, and the success about as great as teaching a very knowing dog a variety of tricks. The poor child had sat in mute amazement, and patiently imitated everything her teacher did; but now the truth began to flash upon her: her intellect began to work: she perceived that here was a way by which she could herself make up a sign of anything that was in her own mind, and show it to another mind; and at once her countenance lighted up with a human expression: it was no longer a dog, or parrot: it was an immortal spirit, eagerly seizing upon a new link of union with other spirits! I could almost fix upon the moment when this truth dawned upon her mind, and spread its light to her countenance; I saw that the great obstacle was overcome; and that henceforward nothing but patient and persevering, but plain and straightforward, efforts were to be used.

"The result thus far, is quickly related, and easily conceived; but not so was the process; for many weeks of apparently unprofitable labor were passed before it was effected. . . .

"The whole of the succeeding year was passed in gratifying her eager inquiries for the names of every object which she could possibly handle; in exercising her in the use of the manual alphabet; in extending in every possible way her knowledge of the physical relations of things; and in proper care of her health.

"At the end of the year a report of her case was made, from which the following is an extract.

" 'It has been ascertained beyond the possibility of doubt, that she cannot see a ray of light, cannot hear the least sound, and never exercises her sense of smell, if she have any. Thus her mind dwells in darkness and stillness, as profound as that of a closed tomb at midnight. Of beautiful sights, and sweet sounds, and pleasant odors, she has no conception; nevertheless, she seems as happy and playful as a bird or a lamb; and the employment of her intellectual faculties, or the acquirement of a new idea, gives her a vivid pleasure, which is plainly marked in her expressive features. . . .

" 'During the year she has attained great dexterity in the use of the manual alphabet of the deaf mutes; and she spells out the words and sentences which she knows, so fast and so deftly, that only those accustomed to this language can follow with the eye the rapid motions of her fingers.

" 'But wonderful as is the rapidity with which she writes her thoughts upon the air, still more so is the ease and accuracy with which she reads the words thus written by another; grasping their hands in hers, and following every movement of their fingers, as letter after letter conveys their meaning to her mind. It is in this way that she converses with her blind playmates, and nothing can more forcibly show the power of mind in forcing matter to its purpose, than a meeting between them. For if great talent and skill are necessary for two pantomimes to paint their thoughts and feelings by the movements of the body, and the expression of the countenance, how much greater the difficulty when darkness shrouds them both, and the one can hear no sound!' . . ."

Such are a few fragments from the simple but most interesting and instructive history of Laura Bridgman. The name of her great benefactor and friend, who writes it, is Doctor Howe. There are not many persons, I hope and believe, who, after reading these passages, can ever hear that name with indifference. . . .

Ye who have eyes and see not, and have ears and hear not; ye who are as the hypocrites of sad countenances, and disfigure your faces that ye may seem unto men to fast; learn healthy cheerfulness, and mild contentment, from the deaf, and dumb, and blind! Self-elected saints with gloomy brows, this sightless, earless, voiceless child may teach you lessons you will do well to follow. Let that poor hand of hers lie gently on your hearts; for there may be something in its healing touch akin to that of the Great Master whose precepts you misconstrue, whose lessons you pervert, of whose charity and sympathy with all the world, not one among you in his daily practice knows as much as many of the worst among those fallen sinners, to whom you are liberal in nothing but the preachment of perdition!

201. *Liberty to Reform, 1835*

Reverend Elijah P. Lovejoy, "To My Fellow-Citizens," November 5, 1835, in J. C. Lovejoy and Owen Lovejoy, *Memoir of the Rev. Elijah P. Lovejoy* (New York, 1838), 144, 153–4.

SEE the danger, and the natural and inevitable result to which the first step here will lead. Today a public meeting declares that you shall not discuss the subject of slavery, in any of its bearings, civil or religious. Right or wrong, the press must be silent. Tomorrow, another meeting decides that it is against the peace of society, that the principles of Popery shall be discussed, and the edict goes forth to muzzle the press. The next day, it is in a similar manner, declared that not a word must be said against distilleries, dram shops, or drunkenness. And so on to the end of the chapter. The truth is, my fellow-citizens, if you give ground a single inch, there is no stopping place. I deem it, therefore, my duty to take my stand upon the Constitution. Here is firm ground —I feel it to be such. And I do most respectfully, yet decidedly, declare to you my fixed determination to maintain this ground. We have slaves, it is true, but *I* am not one. I am a citizen of these United States, a citizen of Missouri, free-born; and having never forfeited the inestimable privileges attached to such a condition, I cannot consent to surrender them. But while I maintain them, I hope to do it with all that meekness and humility that become a Christian, and especially a Christian minister. I am ready, not to fight, but to suffer, and if need be, to die for them. . . .

I *do,* therefore, as an American citizen, and Christian patriot, and in the name of liberty, and law, and religion, solemnly protest against all these attempts, howsoever or by whomsoever made, to frown down the liberty of the press, and forbid the free expression of opinion. Under a deep sense of my obligations to my country, the church, and my God, I declare it to be my fixed purpose to submit to no such dictation. And I am prepared to abide the consequences. I have appealed to the Constitution and laws of my country; if they fail to protect me, I appeal to God, and with Him I cheerfully rest my cause.

Fellow-citizens, they told me that if I returned to the city, from my late absence, you would surely lay violent hands upon me, and many of my friends besought me not to come. I disregarded their advice, because I plainly saw, or thought I saw, that the Lord would have me come. And up to this moment that conviction of duty has continued to strengthen, until now I have not a shadow of doubt that I did right. I have appeared openly among you, in your streets and market-places, and now I openly and publicly throw myself into your hands. I can die at my post, but I cannot desert it.

XXIV ⚜ *The Party System and Politics*

AT THE OPENING of the period some men, still preoccupied with the issues of an older age, feared universal manhood suffrage as a threat to the established order (No. 202). Yet, although constitutional changes in the next two decades abolished the surviving property qualifications in almost all the states, the defenders of property nevertheless remained secure in their faith in the protective power of the American Constitution (No. 203). The old question had lost its importance.

Instead, the years between 1820 and 1850 were largely given over to political debates of national economic issues, on which men were divided according to their personal, sectional, and factional interests. The hopes for industrial development thus produced a movement in favor of a protective tariff contrary to the desires of the southern planters. The old arguments in favor of the tariff were still advanced (*see above,* No. 93); and they gained effectiveness from association with the "American System" (No. 204). The effort of South Carolina to nullify the tariff provoked an angry response from President Jackson (No. 205), but the level of the duties thereafter was rather low. The protectionists found it difficult to counter the view that these measures were simply a means of taking money from one group in the population and transferring it to another (No. 206).

Clay and his followers associated the tariff with internal improvements in the American System (No. 207). Yet, while the states actively furthered projects for transportation development, President Jackson's veto of the Maysville Road bill inhibited federal action for several decades (No. 208).

The relationship of the federal government to the monetary system also had political implications. Jackson's veto of the bill to recharter the Bank of the United States touched off a long controversy. His argument that the Bank constituted a monopoly (No. 209) was countered by the argument that only a sound central bank could preserve the financial stability of the nation (*see above*, No. 159).

As the decade of the 1830's drew to a close, there was a general tendency for two parties to take opposing sides on these issues. The Whigs tended to favor the Bank, internal improvements, and the tariff; the Democrats to oppose them. But these were not hard and fast divisions. A personal and factional element still infused politics and sometimes outweighed economic considerations. In the election of 1840 the Whig appeal for popular support rested upon the attractiveness of a hero and upon a flamboyant election campaign (No. 210). The election of 1844 confirmed the Whig views of the utility of such tactics (No. 211); and in the election of 1848 they made a determined effort to avoid the consideration of large issues (No. 212). Only toward the end of the 1850's did the intrusion of new and more pressing issues cause a realignment in politics (No. 213). And that in turn was due to the growing prominence of the inescapable problem of slavery (*see below*, Section XXV).

202. *On Universal Suffrage, 1821*

Chancellor James Kent, "Remarks to the New York Constitutional Convention, 1821," *Report of the Proceedings . . . of the Convention of 1821* (Albany, 1821), 220–1.

THE SENATE has hitherto been elected by the farmers of the state—by the free and independent lords of the soil, worth at least $250 in freehold estate, over and above all debts charged thereon. The Governor has been chosen by the same electors, and we have hitherto elected citizens of elevated rank and character. Our Assembly has been chosen by freeholders, possessing a freehold of the value of $50, or by persons renting a tenement of the yearly value of $5, and who have been rated and actually paid taxes to the state. By the report before us, we propose to annihilate, at one stroke, all those property distinctions and to bow before the idol of universal suffrage. That extreme democratic principle, when applied to the legislative and executive departments of the government, has been regarded with terror, by the wise men of every age, because in every European republic, ancient and modern, in which it has been tried, it has terminated disastrously, and been productive of corruption, injustice, violence, and tyranny. And dare we flatter ourselves that we are a peculiar people, who can run the career of history, exempted from the passions which have disturbed and corrupted the rest of mankind? . . .

Now, sir, I wish to preserve our Senate as the representative of the landed interest. I wish those who have an interest in the soil, to retain the exclusive possession of a branch in the legislature, as a stronghold in which they may find safety through all the vicissitudes which the State may be destined, in the course of Providence, to experience. I wish them to be always enabled to say that their freeholds cannot be taxed without their consent. The men of no property, together with the crowds of dependents connected with great manufacturing and commercial establishments, and the motley and undefinable population of crowded ports, may, perhaps, at some future day, under skillful management predominate in the Assembly, and yet we should be perfectly safe if no laws could pass without the free consent of the owners of the soil. That security we at present enjoy; and it is that security which I wish to retain.

The apprehended danger from the experiment of universal suffrage applied to the whole legislative department, is no dream of the imagination. It is too mighty an excitement for the moral constitution of men to endure. The tendency of universal suffrage, is to jeopardize the rights of property, and the principles of liberty. There is a constant tendency . . . in the poor to covet a share in the plunder of the rich; in the debtor to relax or avoid the obligation of contracts; in the majority to tyrannize over the minority, and trample down their rights; in the indolent and profligate, to cast the whole burthens of society upon the industrious and the virtuous; and *there is a tendency in ambitious and wicked men to inflame these combustible materials*. It requires a vigilant government, and a firm administration of justice, to counteract that tendency. . . .

Who can undertake to calculate with any precision, how many millions of people this great state will contain in the course of this and the next century? . . . We are no longer to remain plain and simple republics of farmers, like the New England colonists, or the Dutch settlements on the Hudson. We are fast becoming a great nation, with great commerce, manufactures, population, wealth, luxuries, and with the vices and miseries that they engender.

203. *Liberty and Knowledge, 1831*

Daniel Webster in *Speeches of Chancellor Kent and Daniel Webster at a Public Dinner . . . March 25, 1831* (Boston, 1831), 16, 23.

AND who will venture to say, that in any government, now existing in the world, there is greater security for persons or property than in the United States? We have tried these popular institutions in times of great excitement and commotion; they have stood substantially firm and steady, while . . . thrones, resting on ages of proscription, have tottered and fallen; and while, in other countries, the earthquake of unrestrained popular commotion has swallowed up all law, and all liberty, and all right together. Our government has been tried in peace, and it has been tried in war; and has proved itself fit for both. . . . It can stand . . . everything, but the marring of its own beauty, and the weakening of its own strength. . . . It can stand everything, but disorganization, disunion, and nullification. . . .

Among all the principal civilized states of the world, that government is most secure against the danger of popular commotion, which is itself entirely popular. It seems, indeed, that the submission of everything to the public will, under Constitutional restraints, imposed by the people themselves, furnishes, itself, security that that will desire nothing wrong.

Certain it is, that popular constitutional

liberty, as we enjoy it, appears, in the present state of the world, as sure and stable a basis for government to rest upon, as any government of enlightened states can find, or does find. Certain it is, that in these times of so much popular knowledge, and so much popular activity, those governments which do not admit the people to partake in their administration, but keep the people under and beneath, sit on materials for an explosion, which may take place at any moment, and blow them into a thousand atoms. . . .

Gentlemen, our country stands, at the present time, on commanding ground. . . . There are two principles, gentlemen, strictly and purely American, which are now likely to overrun the civilized world.

Indeed they seem the necessary result of the progress of civilization and knowledge. These are, first, popular governments, restrained by written constitutions; and, secondly, universal education. Popular governments and general education, acting and reacting, mutually producing and reproducing each other, are the mighty agencies which, in our days, appear to be exciting, stimulating, and changing civilized societies. Man everywhere is now found demanding a participation in government; and he will not be refused; and he demands knowledge as necessary to self-government. On the basis of these two principles, liberty and knowledge, our own American System rests.

204. *The American System, 1824*

Henry Clay, Speech in Congress, March 31, 1824, on the "American System," in *Annals of Congress, 18 Congress, 1 Session, 1823–24* (Washington, 1856), 1971–2.

THE CREATION of a home market is not only necessary to procure for our agriculture a just reward of its labors, but it is indispensable to obtain a supply of our necessary wants. If we cannot sell, we cannot buy. That portion of our population . . . which makes comparatively nothing that foreigners will buy, has nothing to make purchases with from foreigners. . . . Our exports, supplied by the planting interest . . . may enable the planting interest to supply all its wants; but they bring no ability to the interests not planting. . . . It is in vain to tantalize us with the greater cheapness of foreign fabrics. There must be an ability to purchase, . . . and a cheap article is as much beyond the grasp of him who has no means to buy, as a high one. . . .

But this home market, highly desirable as it is, can only be created and cherished by the protection of our own legislation against the inevitable prostration of our industry, which must ensue from the ac-

tion of foreign policy and legislation. The effect and the value of this domestic care of our own interests will be obvious from a few facts and considerations. Let us suppose that half a million of persons are now employed abroad, in fabricating for our consumption those articles of which, by the operation of this bill, a supply is intended to be provided within ourselves. That half a million of persons are, in effect, subsisted by us; but their actual means of subsistence are drawn from foreign agriculture. If we could transport them to this country, and incorporate them in the mass of our own population, there would instantly arise a demand for an amount of provisions equal to that which would be requisite for their subsistence throughout the whole year. That demand, in the article of flour alone, would not be less than the quantity of about 900,000 barrels. . . . But 900,000 barrels of flour exceeded the entire quantity exported last year, by nearly 150,000 barrels. What activity would not this give?...But if, instead of these five hundred thousand artisans emigrating from abroad, we give, by this bill, employment to an equal number of our own citizens now engaged in unprofitable agriculture,...the beneficial effect upon...our farming labor would be nearly doubled. The quantity would be diminished...and the value of the residue would be enhanced.

205. *Proclamation on Nullification, 1832*

President Andrew Jackson, "Proclamation on Nullification," December 10, 1832, Richardson, *Messages and Papers*, II, 640–4, 648–9, 652, 654.

WHEREAS a convention assembled in the State of South Carolina have passed an ordinance by which they declare "that the several acts and parts of acts of the Congress of the United States purporting to be laws for the imposing of duties and imposts on the importation of foreign commodities...are null and void and no law";...

[And] whereas the said ordinance prescribes to the people of South Carolina a course of conduct in direct violation of their duty as citizens...and having for its object the destruction of the Union.... To preserve this bond of our political existence from destruction,...I, Andrew Jackson, President of the United States, have thought proper to issue this my proclamation,...declaring the course which duty will require me to pursue, and, appealing to the understanding and patriotism of the people, warn them of the consequences that must inevitably result from an observance of the dictates of the convention....

The ordinance is founded...on the strange position that any one state may not only declare an act of Congress void, but prohibit its execution.... There is no appeal from the state decision.... But reasoning on this subject is superfluous, when our social compact, in express terms, declares that the laws of the United States, its Constitution, and treaties made under it are the supreme law of the land; and, for greater caution, adds "that the judges in every state shall be bound thereby, anything in the constitution or laws of any state to the contrary notwithstanding."....No federative government could exist without a similar provision....

I consider, then, the power to annul a law of the United States, assumed by one state, incompatible with the existence of the Union, contradicted expressly by the letter of the Constitution, unauthorized by its spirit, inconsistent with every principle on which it was founded, and destructive of the great object for which it was formed....

The Constitution of the United States...forms a government, not a league; and whether it be formed by compact between the states or in any other manner, its character is the same. It is a government in which all the people are represented, which operates directly on the people individually, not upon the states....Each state...cannot...possess any right to secede, because such secession does not break a league, but destroys the unity of a nation; and any injury to that unity is...an offense against the whole Union.... Secession, like any other revolutionary act, may be morally justified by the extremity of oppression; but to call it a constitutional right is confounding the meaning of terms....

Because the Union was formed by a compact, it is said the parties to that compact may, when they feel themselves aggrieved, depart from it; but it is precisely because it is a compact that they cannot. A compact is an agreement or binding obligation. It may by its terms have a sanction or penalty for its breach, or it may not. . . . A government . . . always has a sanction, express or implied; and in our case it is both necessarily implied and expressly given. An attempt, by force of arms, to destroy a government is an offense . . . and such government has the right by the law of self-defense to pass acts for punishing the offender. . . .

This, then, is the position in which we stand. A small majority of the citizens of one state in the Union have elected delegates to a state convention; that convention has ordained that all the revenue laws of the United States must be repealed, or that they are no longer a member of the Union. . . . It is the intent of this instrument to *proclaim*, not only that the duty imposed on me by the Constitution "to take care that the laws be faithfully executed" shall be performed to the extent of the powers already vested in me by law, . . . but to warn the citizens of South Carolina . . . of the danger they will incur by obedience to the illegal and disorganizing ordinance of the convention.

206. *Friar Tuck Legislation, 1844*

W. C. Bryant, in *Evening Post* (New York), April 26, 1844. Quoted in W. C. Bryant, *Life and Works* (Parke Godwin, ed., New York, 1884), VI, 397–9.

A SPEAKER, Mr. Thomas Gisborne, at one of the recent meetings of the Anti-Corn Law League, made a happy allusion to what he called Friar Tuck legislation. He had in his mind the story which is told in some of the old chronicles of Robin Hood and his merry foresters, when they were once assembled in Congress to deliberate upon the proper distribution of a pretty large amount of spoils. These legislators, persuaded by the soft and honeyed words of Friar Tuck, left it to him to frame a law for the proper adjustment of their claims. When the law was reported, by the able committee which had it in charge, it became instantly evident that Friar Tuck himself would get much the largest share. Public opinion, continues the history, thereupon went against the holy man, and a league was formed to resist the iniquity of his decision.

Now, what did the good friar in the emergency? Why, he met the people boldly and openly, and said, "For whose benefit are laws made, I should like to know?" And then immediately answering his own question, lest some silly objector might give it another turn, he went on, "First, for the benefit of those who make them, and afterward as it may happen."

Nor did the disinterested judge stop there, but he proceeded, "Am I not the lawmaker, and shall I not profit by my own law?" The story runs, we believe, that the good man next quietly pocketed his share of the booty and left his unreasonable companions to make the best of what remained.

Friar Tuck represents a class; he is a type and pattern of a large circle of imitators; his peculiar method of legislation is not obsolete. There are many persons at this day whose morality seems to be framed according to the same standard. Members of the United States Congress, for instance, who pass tariff laws to put money into their own pockets, are the legitimate descendants of Friar Tuck.

It is quite remarkable how many are the points of resemblance between this legislation of Sherwood Forest and that of the manufacturers at Washington. In the first place, the plunder to be distributed is raised from the people, in either case, without their being formally consulted; in the one by high duties, in the other by the strong arm. Then the persons who take upon themselves to decide how this plunder is to be divided, like Friar Tuck, have a deep interest in the result, and generally manage to appropriate to themselves the largest share. They are the owners of manufacturing capital, and they contrive to make this capital return an enormous interest. "For what benefit," they gravely ask, "are laws made?" and then answer, "First for the benefit of those who make them, and afterward as it may happen." Let us impose high duties; let us fill our pockets; let us who make the laws take all that we can get—and as to the people, the mass of laborers and consumers, why that's as it may happen! ...

But there is one point in which the resemblance does not hold. Friar Tuck was a bold, straightforward, open-mouthed statesman, willing to proclaim his principles and justify the consequences to which they led. His followers in Congress act upon precisely the same principles, but assign another reason. He avowed that he wished to cram his pocket; they hold up some mock pretense of public good. "Shall I not benefit by my own law?" he said, and gathered up his gains; but they gather the gain and leave the reason unsaid, or rather hypocritically resort to some more palatable reason. The advantage of consistency is on the side of Robin Hood's priest. There is a frankness in his philosophy which throws the sneaking duplicity of the legislators of the cotton mills quite into the shade.

207. *Internal Improvements, 1824*

Henry Clay, Speech on Internal Improvements, January 14, 1824, *Annals of Congress, 1823–24,* 1035, 1040–1.

THE POWER to regulate commerce among the several states, if it has any meaning, implies authority to foster it, to promote it, to bestow on it facilities similar to those which have been conceded to our foreign trade. It cannot mean only an empty authority to adopt regulations, without the capacity to give practical effect to them. All the powers of this government should be interpreted in reference to its first, its best, its greatest object, the union of these states. And is not that union best invigorated by an intimate, social, and commercial connection between all the parts of the confederacy? Can that be accomplished, that is, can the federative objects of this government be attained, but by the application of federative resources? ...

The bill ... is no western bill. It is emphatically a national bill, comprehending all, looking to the interests of the whole. The people of the West never thought of, never desired, never asked, for a system exclusively for their benefit. The system contemplated by this bill looks to great national objects, and proposes the ultimate application to their accomplishment of the only means by which they can be effected, the means of the nation.

208. *Taxes and Improvements, 1829–30*

Andrew Jackson, Maysville Road Veto, to the House of Representatives, May 27, 1830, Richardson, *Messages and Papers,* II, 489–93.

THE DESIRE to enlist the aid of the general government in the construction of such [works] as from their nature ought to devolve upon it, and to which the means of the individual States are inadequate, is both rational and patriotic.... At the proper time this policy will ... prevail under circumstances more auspicious to its successful prosecution than those which now exist.

But great as this object undoubtedly is, it is not the only one which demands the fostering care of the government. The preservation and success of the republican principle rest with us. To elevate its character and extend its influence rank among our most important duties; and the best means to accomplish this desirable end are those which will rivet the attachment of our citizens to the government of their choice by the comparative lightness of their public burthens and by the attraction which the superior success of its operations will present to the admiration and respect of the world. Through the favor of an overruling and indulgent Providence our country is blessed with general prosperity, and our citizens exempted from the pressure of taxation . . . ; yet . . . many of the taxes collected from our citizens through the medium of imposts have for a considerable period been onerous. In many particulars, these taxes have borne severely upon the laboring and less prosperous classes of the community, being imposed on the necessaries of life. . . . They have been cheerfully borne because they were thought to be necessary to the support of government and the payment of the debts unavoidably incurred in the acquisition and maintenance of our national rights and liberties. But have we a right to calculate on the same cheerful acquiescence, when it is known that the necessity for their continuance would cease were it not for irregular, improvident, and unequal appropriations of the public funds? Will not the people demand, as they have a right to do, such a prudent system of expenditure as will pay the debts of the Union and authorize the reduction of every tax to as low a point as the wise observance of the necessity to protect that portion of our manufactures and labor whose prosperity is essential to our national safety and independence will allow? When the national debt is paid, the duties upon those articles which we do not raise may be repealed with safety, and still leave, I trust, without oppression

to any section of the country, an accumulating surplus fund, which may be beneficially applied to some well-digested system of improvement. . . .

How gratifying the effect of presenting to the world the sublime spectacle of a Republic of more than twelve million happy people, in the fifty-fourth year of her existence—after having passed through two protracted wars . . . free from debt and with all her immense resources unfettered! What a salutary influence would not such an exhibition exercise upon the cause of liberal principles and free government throughout the world! . . . A course of policy destined to witness events like these cannot be benefited by a legislation which tolerates a scramble for appropriations that have no relation to any general system of improvement. . . .

If it be the wish of the people that the construction of roads and canals should be conducted by the Federal Government, it is . . . indispensably necessary, that a previous amendment of the Constitution, delegating the necessary power and defining and restricting its exercise with reference to the sovereignty of the States, should be made. Without it nothing extensively useful can be effected. The right to exercise as much jurisdiction as is necessary to preserve the works and to raise funds by the collection of tolls to keep them in repair cannot be dispensed with. The Cumberland Road should be an instructive admonition of the consequences of acting without this right. Year after year contests are witnessed, growing out of efforts to obtain the necessary appropriations for completing and repairing this useful work. Whilst one Congress may claim and exercise the power, a succeeding one may deny it; and this fluctuation of opinion must be unavoidably fatal to any scheme which from its extent would promote the interests and elevate the character of the country. . . .

As long as the encouragement of domestic manufactures is directed to national ends it shall receive from me a temperate but steady support. There is no necessary connection between it and the system of appropriations. On the contrary, it appears to me that the supposition of their dependence upon each other is calculated to excite the prejudices of the public against both. . . . This policy, like every other, must abide the will of the people, who will not be likely to allow any device, however specious, to conceal its character and tendency.

209. *The Bank a Monopoly, 1832*

President Andrew Jackson, Bank of the United States Veto, July 10, 1832, Richardson, *Messages and Papers*, II, 576–8.

A BANK of the United States is in many respects convenient for the government and useful to the people. Entertaining this opinion, and deeply impressed with the belief that some of the powers and privileges possessed by the existing bank are unauthorized by the Constitution, subversive of the rights of the States, and dangerous to the liberties of the people, I felt it my duty at an early period of my administration to call the attention of Congress to the practicability of organizing an institution combining all its advantages and obviating these objections. I sincerely regret that in the act before me I can perceive none of those modifications of the bank charter which are necessary, in my opinion, to make it compatible with justice, with sound policy, or with the Constitution of our country.

The present corporate body . . . will have existed at the time this act is intended to take effect twenty years. It enjoys an exclusive privilege of banking under the authority of the general government, a monopoly of its favor and support, and, as a necessary consequence, almost a monopoly of the foreign and domestic exchange. The powers, privileges, and favors bestowed upon it in the original charter, by increasing the value of the stock far above its par value, operated as a gratuity of many millions to the stockholders. . . .

The act before me proposes another gratuity to the holders of the same stock, and in many cases to the same men, of at least seven millions more. This donation finds no apology in any uncertainty as to the effect of the act. On all hands it is conceded that its passage will increase at least 20 or 30 per cent more the market price of the stock, subject to the payment of the annuity of $200,000 per year secured by the act, thus adding in a moment one-fourth to its par value. It is not our own citizens only who are to receive the bounty of our government. More than eight millions of the stock of this bank are held by foreigners. By this act the American Republic proposes virtually to make them a present of some millions of dollars. For these gratuities to foreigners and to some of our own opulent citizens the act secures no equivalent whatever. . . .

Every monopoly and all exclusive privileges are granted at the expense of the public, which ought to receive a fair equivalent. The many millions which this act proposes to bestow on the stockholders of the existing bank must come directly or indirectly out of the earnings of the American people. . . . They should at least exact for them as much as they are worth in open market. The value of the monopoly in this case may be correctly ascertained. The twenty-eight millions of stock would probably be at an advance of 50 per cent, and command in market at least $42,000,-000, subject to the payment of the present bonus. The present value of the monopoly, therefore, is $17,000,000, and this the act proposes to sell for three millions, payable in fifteen annual installments of $200,000 each.

It is not conceivable how the present stockholders can have any claim to the special favor of the government. The present corporation has enjoyed its monopoly during the period stipulated in the original contract. If we must have such a corporation, why should not the government sell out the whole stock and thus secure to the people the full market value of the privileges granted? Why should not Congress create and sell twenty-eight millions of stock, incorporating the purchasers with all the powers and privileges secured in this act and putting the premium upon the sales into the treasury?

But this act does not permit competition in the purchase of this monopoly. It seems to be predicated on the erroneous idea that the present stockholders have a prescriptive right not only to the favor but to the bounty of Government. It appears that more than a fourth part of the stock is held by foreigners and the residue is held by a few hundred of our own citizens, chiefly of the richest class. For their benefit does this act exclude the whole American people from competition in the purchase of this monopoly and dispose of it for many millions less than it is worth. . . .

I cannot perceive the justice or policy of this course. If our Government must sell monopolies, it would seem to be its duty to take nothing less than their full value, and if gratuities must be made once in fifteen or twenty years let them not be bestowed on the subjects of a foreign government nor upon a designated and favored class of men in our own country. It is but justice and good policy, as far as the nature of the case will admit, to confine our favors to our own fellow citizens, and let each in his turn enjoy an opportunity to profit by our bounty.

210. *And Tyler Too, 1840*

T. H. Benton, *Thirty Years' View* (New York, 1856), II, 203–7.

Mr. Van Buren was the Democratic candidate. His administration had been so acceptable to his party, that his nomination in a convention was a matter of form, gone through according to custom. . . .

On the part of the Whigs . . . the leading statesmen of the . . . party were again passed by to make room for a candidate more sure of being elected. The success of General Jackson had turned the attention of those who managed the presidential nominations to military men, and an "odor of gunpowder" was considered a sufficient attraction to rally the masses. . . . Availability, to use their own jargon, was the only ability which these managers asked— that is, available for the purposes of the election, and for their own advancement, relying on themselves to administer the government. Mr. Clay, the prominent man, and the undisputed head of the party, was not deemed available; and it was determined to set him aside.

How to do it was the question. He was a man of too much power and spirit to be rudely thrust aside. Gentle, and respectful means were necessary to get him out of the way; and for that purpose he was concertedly importuned to withdraw from the canvass. He would not do so, but wrote a letter submitting himself to the will of the convention. When he did so he certainly expected an open decision—a vote in open convention—every delegate acting responsibly, and according to the will of his constituents.

Not so the fact. He submitted himself to the convention: the convention delivered him to a committee: the committee disposed of him in a back chamber. It devised a process for getting at a result, which is a curiosity in the chapter of ingenious inventions . . . —a secure way to produce an intended result without showing the design, and without leaving a trace behind to show what was done: and of which none but itself can be its own delineator: and, therefore, here it is:

"Ordered, That the delegates from each state be requested to assemble as a delegation, and appoint a committee, not exceeding three in number, to receive the views and opinions of such delegation, and communicate the same to the assembled committees of all the delegations, to be by them respectively reported to their principals; and that thereupon the delegates from each state be requested to assemble as a delegation, and ballot for candidates for the offices of President and Vice President, and having done so, to commit the ballot designating the votes of each candidate, and by whom given, to its committee; and thereupon all the committees shall assemble and compare the several ballots, and report the result of the same to their several delegations, together with such facts as may bear upon the nomination; and said delegation shall forthwith reassemble and ballot again for candidates for the above offices, and again commit the result to the above committees, and if it shall appear that a majority of the ballots are for any one man for candidate for President, said committee shall report the result to the convention for its consideration; but if there shall be no such majority, then the delegations shall repeat the balloting until such a majority shall be obtained, and then report the same to the convention for its consideration. That the vote of a majority of each delegation shall be reported as the vote of that state; and each state represented here shall vote its full electoral vote by such delegation in the committee.". . .

The device of this resolution becomes historical, and commends itself to the commentators upon our Constitution. The people are to elect the President. Here is a process through multiplied filtrations by which the popular sentiment is to be deduced from the masses, collected in little streams, then united in one swelling current, and poured into the hall of the convention—no one seeing the source, or course of any one of the streams. . . . But it was done. Those who set the sum could work it: and the quotient was political death to Mr. Clay. The result produced was—for General Scott, 16 votes: for Mr. Clay, 90 votes: for General Harrison, 148 votes. And as the law of these conventions swallows up all minorities in an ascertained majority, so the majority for General Harrison swallowed up the 106 votes given to Mr. Clay and General Scott, made them count for the victor, presenting him as the unanimity candidate of the convention, and the defeated candidates and all their friends bound to join in his support. And in this way the election of 1840 was effected! . . .

From the beginning it had been foreseen that there was to be an embittered contest—the severest ever known in our country. Two powers were in the field against Mr. Van Buren, each strong within itself, and truly formidable when united —the whole Whig party, and the large league of suspended banks, headed by the Bank of the United States—now criminal as well as bankrupt, and making its last struggle for a new national charter in the effort to elect a President friendly to it. In elections as in war money is the sinew of the contest, and the broken and suspended banks were in a condition, and a temper, to furnish that sinew without stint. By mutual support they were able to make their notes pass as money; and, not being subject to redemption, it could be furnished without restraint, and with all the good will of a self-interest in putting down the Democratic party, whose hard-money policy, and independent treasury scheme, presented it as an enemy to paper money and delinquent banks. The influence of this moneyed power over its debtors, over presses, over traveling agents, was enormous, and exerted to the uttermost, and in amounts of money almost fabulous; and in ways not dreamed of.

The mode of operating divided itself into two general classes, one coercive—addressed to the business pursuits and personal interests of the community: the other seductive, and addressed to its passions. The phrases given out in Congress against the financial policy of the administration became texts to speak upon, and hints to act upon. Carrying out the idea that the reelection of Mr. Van Buren would be the signal for the downfall of all prices, the ruin of all industry, and the destruction of all labor, the newspapers in all the trading districts began to abound with such advertisements as these: "The subscriber will pay six dollars a barrel for flour if Harrison is elected, and three dollars if Van Buren is." "The subscriber will pay five dollars a hundred for pork if Harrison is elected, and two and a half if Van Buren is." And so on through the whole catalogue of marketable articles, and through the different kinds of labor: and these advertisements were signed by respectable men, large dealers in the articles mentioned, and well able to fix the market price for them. . . .

The class of inducements addressed to the passions and imaginations of the people were such as history blushes to record. Log-cabins, coonskins, and hard cider were taken as symbols of the party, and to show its identification with the poorest and humblest of the people: and these cabins were actually raised in the most public parts of the richest cities, ornamented with coonskins after the fashion of frontier huts, and cider drank in them out of gourds in the public meetings which gathered about them: and the virtues of these cabins, these skins, and this cider were celebrated by traveling and stationary orators. The whole country was put into commotion by traveling parties and public gatherings. Steamboats and all public conveyances were crowded with parties singing doggerel ballads made for the occasion, accompanied with the music of drums, fifes, and fiddles; and incited by incessant speaking. A system of public gatherings was got up which pervaded every state, county and town—which took place by day and by night, accompanied by every preparation to excite; and many of which gatherings were truly enormous in their numbers. . . .

By arts like these the community was worked up into a delirium, and the election was carried by storm. Out of 294 electoral votes Mr. Van Buren received but 60: out of twenty-six states he received the votes of only seven. He seemed to have been abandoned by the people! On the contrary he had been unprecedently supported by them—had received a larger popular vote than ever had been given to any President before! and three hundred and sixty-four thousand votes more than he himself had received at the previous presidential election when he beat the same General Harrison fourteen thousand votes. Here was a startling fact, and one to excite inquiry in the public mind. How could there be such overwhelming defeat with such an enormous increase of strength on the defeated side? This question pressed itself upon every thinking mind; and it was impossible to give it a solution consistent with the honor and purity of the elective franchise. For, after making all allowance for the greater number of voters brought out on this occasion than at the previous election by the extraordinary exertions now made to bring them out, yet there would still be required a great number to make up the five hundred and sixty thousand votes which General Harrison received over and above his vote of four years before. The belief of false and fraudulent votes was deep-seated. . . . Many thought it right, for the sake of vindicating the purity of elections, to institute a scrutiny into the votes; but nothing of the kind was attempted, and on the second Wednesday in February, 1841, all the electoral votes were counted without objection.

211. *What the Politicians Want, 1844*

Philip Hone to Henry Clay, November 28, 1844,
Henry Clay, *Works* (Calvin Colton, ed., New York,
1863), IV, 120.

THE RESULT of this election has satisfied me that no such man as Henry Clay can ever be President of the United States. The party leaders, the men who make Presidents, will never consent to elevate one greatly their superior; they suffer too much by the contrast, their aspirations are checked, their power is circumscribed, the clay cannot be molded into an idol suited to their worship. Moreover, a statesman, prominent as you have been for so long a time, must have been identified with all the leading measures affecting the interests of the people, and those interests are frequently different in the several parts of our widely extended country. What is meat in one section is poison in another. Give me, therefore, a candidate of an inferior grade, one whose talents, patriotism and public services have never been so conspicuous as to force him into the first ranks. He will get all the votes which the best and wisest man could secure, and some, which for the reasons I have stated, he could not.

212. *A Hero Again, 1848*

B. P. Poore, *Perley's Reminiscenses* (Philadelphia,
1886), I, 345–7.

WHEN the Whig National Convention met at Philadelphia, on the 7th of June, there was a bitter feeling between the respective friends of Webster and Clay, but they were all doomed to disappointment. The Northern delegates to the Whig National Convention might have nominated either Webster, Clay, Scott, or Corwin, as they had a majority of fifty-six over the delegates from the Southern states, and cast twenty-nine votes more than was necessary to choose a candidate. But they refused to unite on any one, and on the fourth ballot sixty-nine of them voted with the Southern Whigs and secured the nomination of Zachary Taylor. . . .

As the Whig National Convention had adjourned without passing a single declaration of the party's principles, General Taylor's letter of acceptance was awaited with intense interest. It was believed that he would outline some policy which would be accepted and which would unite the Whig party. A month elapsed, and no letter of acceptance was received by Governor Morehead, who had presided over the Convention, but the Postmaster at Baton Rouge, where General Taylor lived, addressed the Postmaster-General a letter, saying that with the report for the current quarter from that office, two bundles of letters were forwarded for the Dead-Letter Office, they having been declined on account of the non-payment of the postage by the senders. It was in the ten-cent and non-prepayment time. Of the forty-eight letters thus forwarded to the Dead-Letter Office, the Baton Rouge Postmaster said a majority were addressed to General Taylor, who had declined to pay the postage on them and take them out of the office, because his mail expenses had become burdensome. The General had since become aware that some of the letters were of importance, and asked for their return. In due course, the letters were sent back to Baton Rouge, and among them was Governor Morehead's letter notifying the General of the action of the Philadelphia Convention.

General Taylor's letter of acceptance was thus dated a month and five days after the letter of notification had been written. It was "short and sweet." He expressed his thanks for the nomination, said he did not seek it, and that if he were elected President, for which position he did not think he possessed the requisite qualifications, he would do his best. He discussed nothing, laid down no principles, and gave no indications of the course he would pursue. Thurlow Weed, who had assumed the direction of the Whig campaign, was not satisfied with this letter, and sent the draft of another one, more explicit, and indorsed by Mr. Fillmore. This General Taylor had copied, and signed it as a letter addressed to his kinsman, Captain Allison. In it he pledged himself fully to Whig principles, and it was made the basis of an effective campaign.

Mr. Webster, who at first denounced the nomination as one "not fit to be made," was induced, by the payment of a considerable sum of money, to make a speech in favor of the ticket. Nathaniel P. Willis wrote a stirring campaign song, and at the request of Thurlow Weed, the writer of these reminiscences wrote a campaign life of the General, large editions of which were published at Boston and Albany for gratuitous distribution. It ignored the General's views on the anti-slavery question. Meanwhile, the Massachusetts Abolitionists and ultra-Webster men, with the Barnburner wing of the Democratic party in New York, and several other disaffected factions, met in convention at Buffalo. They there nominated Martin Van Buren for President and Mr. Charles Francis Adams for Vice-President, and adopted as a motto, "Free Speech, Free Soil, Free Labor, and Free Men." This party attracted enough votes from the Democratic ticket in the State of New York to secure the triumph of the Whigs, and Martin Van Buren, who had been defeated by the Southern Democrats, had in return the satisfaction of effecting their defeat.

213. *Political Realignment, 1856*

William H. Seward, "Political Parties of the Day" (Speech at Auburn, New York, October 21, 1856), *Works* (G. E. Baker, ed., Boston, 1884), IV, 277–81.

SOCIETY is now in a transition state or stage so far as political parties are concerned. Two or three years ago, the American people were divided into two well-defined, distinct and organized parties, the Whigs and the Democrats. Today, instead of these two parties, we see three masses uncertainly defined, and apparently at least quite unorganized, namely, Americans, Democrats, and Republicans; and we see portions of each of these easily detached and passing over to the others, while a very considerable number of citizens stand hesitating whether to join one or the other, or to stand aloof still longer from all.

Such a transition stage, although unusual, is not unnatural. Established parties are built on certain policies and principles, and they will stand and remain so long as those policies and principles are of paramount importance and no longer. . . .

What has produced the disorganization and confusion which we have all seen and wondered at, the dissolution of the Whig party, and the disorganization of the Democratic party, and given room and verge for the American or Know-Nothing party? You all answer, the agitation of slavery. And you answer truly. Answer again. What shall I discourse upon? The contest of the American colonies with Great Britain, and the characters of the Whigs and Tories? No, that is a subject for the Fourth of July. The adoption of the Constitution, and the disputes between Federalists and Republicans? No, let them sleep. The tariff, National Bank and internal improvements, and the controversies of the Whigs and Democrats? No, they are past and gone. What then, of Kansas, . . . the extension of slavery in the territories of the United States? Ah yes, that is the theme . . . and nothing else. Now of what is it that the Americans in the North and in the South are debating in their councils, so far as their debates are suffered to transpire? The abrogation and restoration of the Missouri Compromise and nothing else. The Democrats also in the North and South, they speak of nothing else but saving the Union from destruction, by means of suppressing this very debate about the extension of slavery.

Is this question about the extension of slavery new, unreal, and imaginary, the mere illusion of an hour? . . . No, it is an ancient and eternal conflict between two entirely antagonistic systems of human labor existing in American society, not unequal in their forces; a conflict for not merely toleration, but for absolute political sway in the Republic, between the system of free labor with equal and universal suffrage, free speech, free thought, and free action, and the system of slave labor with unequal franchises secured by arbitrary, oppressive and tyrannical laws. . . .

It is a question between a small minority which cannot even maintain itself, except by means of continually increasing concessions and new and more liberal guarantees, and a majority that could never have been induced to grant even any guarantees except by threats of disunion and that can expect no return for new and further concessions and guaranties, but increasing exactions and ultimate aggressions or secessions. The slaveholders can never be content without dominion which abridges personal freedom as well as circumscribes the domain of the non-slaveholding freemen. Non-slaveholding freemen can never permanently submit to such dominion. Nor can the competition or contention cease, for the reason that the general conscience of mankind throws its weight on the side of freedom and presses onward the resistants to oppose the solicitations and aggressions of the slaveholding class. Heretofore opposing political combinations long established, and firmly entrenched in traditions and popular affections, have concurred in the policy of suppressing this great and important question, but they have broken under its pressure at last. Henceforth, the antagonistical elements will be left to clash without hindrance. Heretofore the broad field of the national territories allowed each of the contending interests ample room without coming into direct conflict with the other. Henceforth, the two interests will be found contending for common ground claimed by both, and which can be occupied only by one of them.

XXV *Slavery and Abolition*

THE DEVELOPMENT of cotton culture reversed the expectation of many Southerners that slavery was doomed to die of itself. The institution became bound in with an important sector of the economy; and plantation life fell increasingly into durable patterns (No. 214). Slavery was less often regarded as an evil—necessary or not—and was more often justified and defended. A distinguished Southern statesman explained to the world that this institution was a positive good, more advantageous to humanity than the system of free labor (No. 215).

The new view had serious consequences. Within the South it called for an adjustment in the fundamental conceptions of law and social order, in the interests of maintaining the slave as a chattel (No. 216). Moreover, the non-slave-holding whites, disgruntled by the necessity of competing with unfree labor, regarded slavery as the source of the South's difficulties; and they resented the planters who profited by it (No. 217).

The South, now committed to slavery, found its relationships with the North poisoned by the developing abolition movement. The notion that part of the country would be forever slave was intolerable to men who accepted the premises of reform. Those who struggled to improve the condition of the dependent classes felt a special obligation toward the most dependent of all classes, the slaves. Garrison expressed the moral indignation the institution aroused (No. 218). Although the movement was internally divided, its growth was stimulated by the activities of free Negroes and fugitives (No. 219); and its influence widened steadily.

The irrepressible conflict of views came to focus on the question as to whether slavery ought to extend into the new territories or not. Efforts at compromise succeeded up to 1850; Northerners acquiesced on the assumption that peace could thus be earned and that the forces of nature would themselves set limits to slavery (No. 220). But after 1850 compromise was no longer effective. The Kansas-Nebraska Act seemed to show that there were no limits to the ambitions of the slaveholders; and the Dred Scott decision denied that Congress could exclude slavery from the territories (No. 221). John Brown's violence (No. 222) was, a poet saw, a portent for the future (No. 223). And the tragic figure who would bear the greatest burden of the future of the war began to understand what he had meant when he observed that a house divided against itself could not stand (No. 224).

214. *A Georgia Rice Plantation, 1854–59*

Extracts from the Plantation Records of Louis Manigault, Argyle Island, Georgia, in Commons, *Documentary History*, I, 141–7. Reprinted by permission of the publishers, The Arthur H. Clark Company.

CONSIDERING the immense losses we have experienced during the past three years, the cholera having swept off in 1852 and 1854 many of our very best hands, a destructive freshet visiting us in August, 1852, just in the midst of harvest, [and a] ... hurricane ... [in] 1854, ... I do not complain of our present crop. Rice this year, caused as is supposed by the now pending Crimean War, has been very high, and our entire crop has sold well. I lost my overseer, Mr. S. F. Clark, of consumption in December, 1855, but since the last cholera (December, 1854) we have lost no one of any consequence, and perfect health has prevailed on the plantation.

My thresher was much out of order, but the boiler has been added to, and power increased, etc., all being in good order for the next crop. Besides the above quantity of rice sent to market in Charleston, I have kept back fifteen hundred bushels for seed. . . .

Upon the death of my overseer (December 10, 1855) I was left alone on the plantation. We soon finished threshing the crop and I went to work preparing the lands for the next year. . . . The latter part of February was now approaching; still we had no overseer. At last we were recommended . . . a young man who had acted as sub-overseer for two or three years . . . on Black River, . . . Mr. Leonard Venters, twenty-four years of age. . . . He struck me as being very young; I explained, however, all concerning our mode of "water culture" and how our crops were treated on Savannah River. . . . We commenced planting on the 15th of March, and finished the entire tract of 638 acres . . . on the third of May, when we began to hoe rice and I left the plantation for the summer. Venters made two great and fatal mistakes. He drew off his "sprout water" too rapidly, prostrating his rice to the ground; and again he kept his fields dry too long, before he could get at them to give first hoeing. His rice was all stunted, sickly, and grass took him. We have made one half a crop. He says "he will do better another year, that now he sees into it," and as is well known, "never change an overseer if you can help it." We try him once (but only once) more. We have purchased nineteen Negroes, among them thirteen prime hands costing in all $11,850. Also 771 acres high land on Georgia Main, for cholera camps, children's summer residence, etc., costing $2,195. . . .

My expectations with regard to the overseer's improving upon his past year's sad experience were vain. Mr. Venters did do a little better than before, as far as an increase in the crop was concerned, but very little. Moreover, elated by a strong and very false religious feeling he began to injure the plantation a vast deal, placing himself on a par with the Negroes, by even joining in with them at their prayer meetings, breaking down long established discipline, which in every case is so difficult to preserve, favoring and siding in any difficulty with the people, against the drivers, besides causing numerous grievances which I now have every reason to suppose my neighbors knew; and perhaps I was laughed at and ridiculed for keeping in my employ such a man. I discharged Mr. Venters, and on January 8th, 1858, engaged Mr. William H. Bryan, . . . aged thirty-one years, with a wife and two children. . . . I now leave the plantation (April, 1858) with Mrs. Manigault for Europe until December next. . . .

The crop of 1858, W. H. Bryan overseer, has turned out wretchedly. From what I can learn since my return from Europe . . . there has been gross neglect and great want of attention on the part of the overseer. For the first time we allowed the overseer's family to reside, during the summer, at our pineland tract called "Camp," leaving it to Mr. Bryan when, and how often, he should visit them. He took advantage of this, and for days did not visit the plantation, neglecting all things.

215. *The Permanence of Slavery, 1844*

Secretary of State J. C. Calhoun to Pakenham, April 18, 1844, Calhoun, *Works*, V, 333–4, 336–9.

THE UNDERSIGNED . . . regards with deep concern the avowal, for the first time made to this Government, "that Great Britain desires and is constantly exerting herself to procure the general abolition of slavery throughout the world.". . .

[The United States] remained passive so long as the policy on the part of Great Britain, which has led to its adoption, had no immediate bearing on their peace and safety. While they conceded to Great Britain the right of adopting whatever policy she might deem best, in reference to the African race, within her own possessions, they on their part claim the same right for themselves. The policy she has adopted in reference to the portion of that race in her dominions may be humane and wise; but it does not follow, if it prove so with her, that it would be so in reference to the United States and other countries, whose situation differs from hers. But, whether it would be or not, it belongs to each to judge and determine for itself. With us it is a question to be decided, not by the Federal Government, but by each member of this Union, for itself, according to its own views of its domestic policy, and without any right on the part of the Federal Government to interfere in any manner whatever. . . . A large number of the states has decided, that it is neither wise nor humane to change the relation which has existed, from their first settlement, between the two races; while others, where the African is less numerous, have adopted the opposite policy.

It belongs not to the Government to question whether the former have decided wisely or not; and if it did, the undersigned would not regard this as the proper occasion to discuss the subject. He does not, however, deem it irrelevant to state that, if the experience of more than half a century is to decide, it would be neither humane nor wise in them to change their policy. The census and other authentic documents show that, in all instances in which the states have changed the former relation between the two races, the condition of the African, instead of being improved, has become worse. They have been invariably sunk into vice and pauperism, accompanied by the bodily and mental inflictions incident thereto—deafness, blindness, insanity, and idiocy—to a degree without example; while, in all other states which have retained the ancient relation between them, they have improved greatly in every respect—in number, comfort, intelligence, and morals—as the following facts, taken from such sources, will serve to illustrate:

The number of deaf and dumb, blind, idiots, and insane, of the Negroes in the states that have changed the ancient relation between the races, is one out of every ninety-six; while in the states adhering to it, it is one out of every six hundred and seventy-two—that is, seven to one in favor of the latter, as compared with the former.

The number of whites, deaf and dumb, blind, idiots, and insane, in the states that have changed the relation, is one in every five hundred and sixty-one; being nearly six to one against the free Blacks in the same states.

The number of Negroes who are deaf and dumb, blind, idiots, and insane, paupers, and in prison in the states that have changed, is one out of every six; and in the states that have not, one out of every one hundred and fifty-four; or twenty-two to one against the former, as compared with the latter. . . .

In Massachusetts, where the change in the ancient relation of the two races was first made (now more than sixty years since), where the greatest zeal has been exhibited in their behalf, and where their number is comparatively few (but little more than 8,000 in a population of upwards of 730,000), the condition of the African is amongst the most wretched. By the latest authentic accounts, there was one out of every twenty-one of the Black population in jails or houses of correction; and one out of every thirteen was either deaf and dumb, blind, idiot, insane, or in prison. On the other hand, the census and other authentic sources of information establish the fact that the condition of the African race throughout all the states, where the ancient relation between the two has been retained, enjoys a degree of health and comfort which may well compare with that of the laboring population of any country in Christendom; and it may be added, that in no other condition, or in any other age or country, has the Negro race ever attained so high an elevation in morals, intelligence, or civilization.

If such be the wretched condition of the race in their changed relation, where their number is comparatively few, and where so much interest is manifested for their improvement, what would it be in those states where the two races are nearly equal in numbers, and where, in consequence, would necessarily spring up mutual fear, jealousy, and hatred, between them? It may, in truth, be assumed as a maxim, that two races differing so greatly and in so many respects, cannot possibly exist together in the same country, where their numbers are nearly equal, without the one being subjected to the other. Experience has proved that the existing relation, in which the one is subjected to the other, in the slaveholding states, is consistent with the peace and safety of both, with great improvement to the inferior; while the same experience proves that the relation which it is the desire and object of Great Britain to substitute in its stead in this and all other countries, under the plausible name of the abolition of slavery, would (if it did not destroy the inferior by conflicts, to which it would lead) reduce it to the extremes of vice and wretchedness. In this view of the subject it may be asserted, that what is called slavery is in reality a political institution, essential to the peace, safety, and prosperity of those states of the Union in which it exists. . . . Could [Great Britain] succeed in accomplishing, in the United States, what she avows to be her desire and the object of her constant exertions to effect throughout the world, so far from being wise or humane, she would involve in the greatest calamity the whole country, and especially the race which it is the avowed object of her exertions to benefit.

216. *Cases from Slave Law, 1824–28*

Quoted in Helen T. Catterall, *Judicial Cases Concerning American Slavery and the Negro* (Washington, 1926), I, 140–1, 156.

ALDRIDGE *v. the Commonwealth* . . . [Virginia, 1824]. The petitioner was "indicted as 'a free man of color,' for the larceny of banknotes of the value of one hundred and fifty dollars. . . . He was convicted of the crime charged, and the jury ascertained the number of stripes to be inflicted on him, to be thirty-nine." The Supreme Court pronounced judgment that "he receive thirty-nine stripes on his bare back on the 26th of June next, and that after that day, he be sold as a slave, and transported and banished beyond the limit of the United States, in the manner prescribed by law, etc."

Held: the act of February 21, 1823, is not contrary to the Constitution of the State. The Bill of Rights . . . never was contemplated . . . to extend to the whole population of the State. Can it be doubted, that it not only was not intended to apply to our slave population, but that the free Blacks and mulattoes were also not comprehended in it? The leading and most prominent feature in that paper, is the equality of civil rights and liberty. And yet, nobody has ever questioned the power of the Legislature, to deny to free Blacks and mulattoes, one of the first privileges of a citizen, that of voting at elections, although they might in every particular, except color, be in precisely the same condition as those qualified to vote. The numerous restrictions imposed on this class of people in our statute book, many of which are inconsistent with the letter and spirit of the Constitution, both of this State and of the United States, as respects the free whites, demonstrate, that, here, those instruments have not been considered to extend equally to both classes of our population. We will only instance the restriction upon the migration of free Blacks into this State, and upon their right to bear arms.

As to the ninth section of the Bill of Rights, denouncing cruel and unusual punishments, we have no notion that it has any bearing on this case.

217. *The Retarded South, 1858*

H. R. Helper, *Impending Crisis of the South* (New York, 1860), 21–3, 25, 59, 120–1.

IT IS a fact well known to every intelligent Southerner that we are compelled to go to the North for almost every article of utility and adornment, from matches, shoe-pegs and paintings up to cotton mills, steamships and statuary; that we have no foreign trade, no princely merchants, nor respectable artists; that, in comparison with the free states, we contribute nothing to the literature, polite arts and inventions of the age; that, for want of profitable employment at home, large numbers of our native population find themselves necessitated to emigrate to the West, whilst the free states retain not only the larger proportion of those born within their own limits, but induce, annually, hundreds of thousands of foreigners to settle and remain amongst them; that almost everything produced at the North meets with ready sale, while, at the same time, there is no demand, even among our own citizens, for the productions of Southern industry; that, owing to the absence of a proper system of business amongst us, the North becomes, in one way or another, the proprietor and dispenser of all our floating wealth, and that we are dependent on Northern capitalists for the means necessary to build our railroads, canals and other public improvements; that if we want to visit a foreign country, even though it may lie directly south of us, we find no convenient way of getting there except by taking passage through a Northern port; and that nearly all the profits arising from the exchange of commodities, from insurance and shipping offices, and from the thousand and one industrial pursuits of the country, accrue to the North, and are there invested in the erection of those magnificent cities and stupendous works of art which dazzle the eyes of the South, and attest the superiority of free institutions!

The North is the Mecca of our merchants, and to it they must and do make two pilgrimages per annum—one in the spring and one in the fall. All our commercial, mechanical, manufactural, and literary supplies come from there. We want Bibles, brooms, buckets and books, and we go to the North; . . . we want furniture, crockery, glassware and pianos, and we go to the North; we want toys, primers, school books, fashionable apparel, machinery, medicines, tombstones, and a thousand other things, and we go to the North for them all. Instead of keeping our money in circulation at home, by patronizing our own mechanics, manufacturers, and laborers, we send it all away to the North, and there it remains; it never falls into our hands again.

In one way or another we are more or less subservient to the North every day of our lives. In infancy we are swaddled in Northern muslin; in childhood we are humored with Northern gewgaws; in youth we are instructed out of Northern books; at the age of maturity we sow our "wild oats" on Northern soil; in middle-life we exhaust our wealth . . . in giving aid and succor to every department of Northern power; in the decline of life we remedy our eye-sight with Northern spectacles, and support our infirmities with Northern canes; in old age we are drugged with Northern physic; and, finally, when we die, our inanimate bodies, shrouded in Northern cambric, are stretched upon the bier, borne to the grave in a Northern carriage, entombed with a Northern spade, and memorized with a Northern slab! . . .

The causes which have impeded the progress and prosperity of the South, which have dwindled our commerce, and other similar pursuits, into the most contemptible insignificance; sunk a large majority of our people in galling poverty and ignorance, rendered a small minority conceited and tyrannical, and driven the rest away from their homes; entailed upon us a humiliating dependence on the Free States; disgraced us in the recesses of our own souls, and brought us under reproach in the eyes of all civilized and enlightened nations—may all be traced to one common source, and there find solution in the most hateful and horrible word, that was ever incorporated into the vocabulary of human economy—*Slavery!* . . .

In wilfully traducing and decrying everything north of Mason and Dixon's line, and in excessively magnifying the importance of everything south of it, the oligarchy have, in the eyes of all liberal and intelligent men, only made an exhibition of their uncommon folly and dishonesty. For a long time, it is true, they have succeeded in deceiving the people, in keeping them humbled in the murky sloughs of poverty and ignorance, and in instilling into their untutored minds passions and prejudices expressly calculated to strengthen and protect the accursed institution of slavery; . . .

Non-slaveholders of the South! farmers, mechanics and workingmen, we take this occasion to assure you that the slaveholders, the arrogant demagogues whom you have elected to offices of power and profit, have hoodwinked you, trifled with you, and used you as mere tools for the consummation of their wicked designs. They have purposely kept you in ignorance, and have, by molding your passions and prejudices to suit themselves, induced you to act in direct opposition to your dearest rights and interests. . . . They have taught you to hate the abolitionists, who are your best and only true friends. Now, as one of your own number, we appeal to you to join us in our patriotic endeavors to rescue the generous soil of the South from the usurped and desolating control of these political vampires. Once and forever, at least so far as this country is concerned, the infernal question of slavery must be disposed of; a speedy and perfect abolishment of the whole institution is the true policy of the South—and this is the policy which we propose to pursue.

218. *The Abolition Principle, 1831*

W. L. Garrison, "Statement of Principles," *Liberator* (Boston), January 1, 1831.

DURING my recent tour for the purpose of exciting the minds of the people by a series of discourses on the subject of slavery, every place that I visited gave fresh evidence of the fact, that a greater revolution in public sentiment was to be effected in the free states—and particularly in New England—than at the South. I found contempt more bitter, opposition more active, detraction more relentless, prejudice more stubborn, and apathy more frozen, than among slave owners themselves. Of course, there were individual exceptions to the contrary. This state of things afflicted, but did not dishearten me. I determined, at every hazard, to lift up the standard of emancipation in the eyes of the nation, within sight of Bunker Hill and in the birthplace of liberty. That standard is now unfurled; and long may it float, unhurt by the spoliations of time or the missiles of a desperate foe—yea, till every chain be broken, and every bondman set free! Let southern oppressors tremble—let their secret abettors tremble—let their northern apologists tremble—let all the enemies of the persecuted Blacks tremble. . . .

In defending the great cause of human rights, I wish to derive the assistance of all religions and of all parties. Assenting to the "self-evident truth" maintained in the American Declaration of Independence, "that all men are created equal, and endowed by their Creator with certain inalienable rights—among which are life, liberty and the pursuit of happiness," I shall strenuously contend for the immediate enfranchisement of our slave population. In Park Street Church, on the Fourth of July, 1829, in an address on slavery, I unreflectingly assented to the popular but pernicious doctrine of gradual abolition. I

seize this opportunity to make a full and unequivocal recantation, and thus publicly to ask pardon of my God, of my country, and of my brethren the poor slaves, for having uttered a sentiment so full of timidity, injustice and absurdity. A similar recantation, from my pen, was published in the *Genius of Universal Emancipation* at Baltimore, in September, 1829. My conscience is now satisfied.

I am aware, that many object to the severity of my language; but is there not cause for severity? I will be as harsh as truth, and as uncompromising as justice. On this subject, I do not wish to think, or speak, or write, with moderation. No! No! Tell a man whose house is on fire, to give a moderate alarm; tell him to moderately rescue his wife from the hands of the ravisher; tell the mother to gradually extricate her babe from the fire into which it has fallen;—but urge me not to use moderation in a cause like the present. I am in earnest—I will not equivocate—I will not excuse—I will not retreat a single inch —AND I WILL BE HEARD.

219. *A Fugitive Speaks, 1850*

Frederick Douglass, *Lectures on American Slavery* [December 1, 1850] (Buffalo, 1851), 7–11.

MORE than twenty years of my life were consumed in a state of slavery. My childhood was environed by the baneful peculiarities of the slave system. I grew up to manhood in the presence of this hydra-headed monster—not as a master—not as an idle spectator—not as the guest of the slaveholder; but as A SLAVE, eating the bread and drinking the cup of slavery with the most degraded of my brother bondmen, and sharing with them all the painful conditions of their wretched lot. In consideration of these facts, I feel that I have a right to speak, and to speak *strongly*. Yet, my friends, I feel bound to speak truly. . . .

First of all, I will state, as well as I can,

the legal and social relation of master and slave. A master is one (to speak in the vocabulary of the Southern states) who claims and exercises a right of property in the person of a fellow man. This he does with the force of the law and the sanction of Southern religion. The law gives the master absolute power over the slave. He may work him, flog him, hire him out, sell him, and in certain contingencies, *kill* him, with perfect impunity. The slave is a human being, divested of all rights—reduced to the level of a brute—a mere "chattel" in the eye of the law—placed beyond the circle of human brotherhood—cut off from his kind—his name, which the "recording angel" may have enrolled in heaven, among the blessed, is impiously inserted in a *master's ledger,* with horses, sheep and swine. In law, the slave has no wife, no children, no country, and no home. He can own nothing, possess nothing, acquire nothing, but what must belong to another. To eat the fruit of his own toil, to clothe his person with the work of his own hands, is considered stealing. He toils that another may reap the fruit; he is industrious that another may live in idleness; he eats unbolted meal, that another may eat the bread of fine flour; he labors in chains at home, under a burning sun and biting lash, that another may ride in ease and splendor abroad; . . . he is sheltered only by the wretched hovel, that a master may dwell in a magnificent mansion; and to this condition he is bound down as by an arm of iron.

From this monstrous relation, there springs an unceasing stream of most revolting cruelties. The very accompaniments of the slave system, stamp it as the offspring of hell itself. To ensure good behavior, the slaveholder relies on *the whip;* to induce proper humility, he relies on *the whip;* to rebuke what he is pleased to term insolence, he relies on *the whip;* to supply the place of wages, as an incentive to toil, he relies on *the whip;* to bind down the spirit of the slave, to imbrute and destroy his manhood, he relies on *the whip,* the chain, the gag, the thumbscrew, the pillory, the bowie-knife, the pistol, and the blood-hound. . . . It makes no difference whether the slaveholder worships the God of the Christians or is a follower of Mahomet, he is the minister of the same cruelty, and the author of the same misery. *Slavery* is always *slavery;* always the same foul, haggard and damning scourge, whether found in the Eastern or the Western Hemisphere.

There is a still deeper shade to be given to this picture. The physical cruelties are indeed sufficiently harassing and revolting; but they are as a few grains of sand on the seashore, or a few drops of water in the great ocean, compared with the stupendous wrongs which it inflicts on the mental, moral and religious nature of its hapless victims. It is only when we contemplate the slave as a moral and intellectual being, that we can adequately comprehend the unparalleled enormity of slavery, and the intense criminality of the slaveholder. I have said that the slave was a man. "What a piece of work is man? How noble in reason! How infinite in faculties! In form and moving, how express and admirable! In action, how like an angel! In apprehension how like a God! the beauty of the world! the paragon of animals!" . . .

It is *such* a being that is smitten and blasted. The first work of slavery is to mar and deface those characteristics of its victims which distinguish *men* from *things,* and *persons* from *property.* Its first aim is to destroy all sense of high moral and religious responsibility. It reduces man to a mere machine. It cuts him off from his maker, it hides from him the laws of God, and leaves him to grope his way from time to eternity in the dark, under the arbitrary and despotic control of a frail, depraved and sinful fellow-man. . . .

The great mass of slaveholders look upon education among the slaves as utterly subversive of the slave system. I *well* remember when my mistress first announced to my master that she had discovered that I could read. His face colored at once, with surprise and chagrin. He said that "I was ruined, and my value as a slave destroyed; that a slave should know nothing but to obey his master; that to give a Negro an inch would lead him to take an ell; that having learned how to read, I would soon want to know how to write; and that, by and by, I would be running away." I think my audience will bear witness to the correctness of this philosophy, and to the literal fulfillment of this prophecy.

220. *Slavery in the Territories, 1850*

Daniel Webster, Speech in the Senate, March 7, 1850. Quoted in Daniel Webster, *Works* (Boston, 1851), V, 350–3.

Now, as to California and New Mexico, I hold slavery to be excluded from those territories by a law even superior to that which admits and sanctions it in Texas. I mean the law of nature, of physical geography, the law of the formation of the earth. That law settles for ever, with a strength beyond all terms of human enactment, that slavery cannot exist in California or New Mexico. Understand me, Sir; I mean slavery as we regard it; the slavery of the colored race as it exists in the Southern States. . . . It is as impossible that African slavery, as we see it among us, should find its way, or be introduced, into California and New Mexico, as any other natural impossibility. California and New Mexico are Asiatic in their formation and scenery. They are composed of vast ridges of mountains, of great height, with broken ridges and deep valleys. The sides of these mountains are entirely barren; their tops capped by perennial snow. There may be in California, now made free by its constitution, and no doubt there are, some tracts of valuable land. But it is not so in New Mexico. . . . What is there in New Mexico that could, by any possibility, induce any body to go there with slaves? There are some narrow strips of tillable land on the borders of the rivers; but the rivers themselves dry up before midsummer is gone. All that the people can do in that region is to raise some little articles, some little wheat for their tortillas, and that by irrigation. And who expects to see a hundred black men cultivating tobacco, corn, cotton, rice, or anything else, on lands in New Mexico, made fertile only by irrigation?

I look upon it, therefore, as a fixed fact, to use the current expression of the day, that both California and New Mexico are destined to be free, . . . free by the arrangement of things ordained by the Power above us. I have therefore to say, in this respect also, that this country is fixed for freedom, to as many persons as shall ever live in it, by a less repealable law than that which attaches to the right of holding slaves in Texas; and I will say further, that, if a resolution or a bill were now before us, to provide a territorial government for New Mexico, I would not vote to put any prohibition into it whatever. Such a prohibition would be idle, as it respects any effect it would have upon the territory; and I would not take pains uselessly to reaffirm an ordinance of nature, nor to reenact the will of God. . . .

Sir, wherever there is a substantive good to be done, wherever there is a foot of land to be prevented from becoming slave territory, I am ready to assert the principle of the exclusion of slavery. I am pledged to it from the year 1837; I have been pledged to it again and again; and I will perform those pledges; but I will not do a thing unnecessarily that wounds the feelings of others, or that does discredit to my own understanding.

221. *The Dred Scott Decision, 1857*

19 Howard, 393.

THE QUESTION is simply this: can a Negro, whose ancestors were imported into this country and sold as slaves, become a member of the political community formed and brought into existence by the Constitution of the United States, and as such become entitled to all the rights, and privileges, and immunities, guaranteed by that instrument to the citizen? One of which rights is the privilege of suing in a court of the United States in the cases specified in the Constitution. . . . The court must be understood as speaking in this opinion . . . of those persons [only] who are the descendants of Africans who were imported into this country and sold as slaves. . . .

The question before us is, whether the class of persons described in the plea in abatement compose a portion of this people, and are constituent members of this sovereignty? We think they are not, and that they are not included, and were not intended to be included, under the word "citizens" in the Constitution, and can, therefore, claim none of the rights and privileges which that instrument provides for and secures to citizens of the United States. On the contrary, they were at that time considered as a subordinate and inferior class of beings, who had been subjugated by the dominant race, and whether emancipated or not, yet remained subject to their authority, and had no rights or privileges but such as those who held the power and the government might choose to grant them. . . .

It is very clear, therefore, that no state can, by any act or law of its own, passed since the adoption of the Constitution, introduce a new member into the political community created by the Constitution of the United States. It cannot make him a member of this community by making him a member of its own. And for the same reason it cannot introduce any person, or description of persons, who were not intended to be embraced in this new political family, which the Constitution brought into existence, but were intended to be excluded from it.

The question then arises, whether the provisions of the Constitution, in relation to the personal rights and privileges to which the citizen of a state should be entitled, embraced the Negro African race, at that time in this country, or who might afterwards be imported, who had then or should afterwards be made free in any state; and to put it in the power of a single state to make him a citizen of the United States, and endue him with the full rights of citizenship in every other state without their consent. Does the Constitution of the United States act upon him whenever he shall be made free under the laws of a state, and raised there to the rank of a citizen, and immediately clothe him with all the privileges of a citizen in every other state, and in its own courts?

The court think the affirmative of these propositions cannot be maintained. And if it cannot, the plaintiff in error could not be a citizen of the State of Missouri, within the meaning of the Constitution of the United States, and, consequently, was not entitled to sue in its courts.

It is true, every person, and every class and description of persons, who were at the time of the adoption of the Constitution recognized as citizens in the several states, became also citizens of this new political body; but none other; it was formed by them, and for them and their posterity, but for no one else. . . .

The Act of Congress, upon which the plaintiff relies, declares that slavery and involuntary servitude, except as a punishment for crime, shall be forever prohibited in all that part of the territory ceded by France, under the name of Louisiana, which lies north of thirty-six degrees thirty minutes north latitude, and not included within the limits of Missouri. And the difficulty which meets us at the threshold of this part of the inquiry is, whether Congress was authorized to pass this law under any of the powers granted to it by the Constitution. . . .

The counsel for the plaintiff has laid much stress upon that article in the Constitution which confers on Congress the power "to dispose of and make all needful rules and regulations respecting the territory or other property belonging to the United States;" but, in the judgment of the court, that provision has no bearing on the present controversy, and the power there given, whatever it may be, is confined, and was intended to be confined, to the territory which at that time belonged to, or was claimed by, the United States, and was within their boundaries as settled by the Treaty with Great Britain, and can have no influence upon a territory afterwards acquired from a foreign government. . . .

At the time when the territory in question was obtained by cession from France, it contained no population fit to be associated together and admitted as a state; and it therefore was absolutely necessary to hold possession of it as a territory belonging to the United States until it was settled and inhabited by a civilized community capable of self-government, and in a condition to be admitted on equal terms with the other states as a member of the Union. But, as we have before said, it was acquired by the general government as the representative and trustee of the people of the United States, and it must, therefore, be held in that character for their common and equal benefit. . . .

But until that time arrives, it is undoubtedly necessary that some government should be established, in order to organize society, and to protect the inhabitants in their persons and property; and as the people of the United States could act in this matter only through the government which represented them, and through which they spoke and acted when the territory was obtained, it was not only within the scope of its powers, but it was its duty to pass such laws and establish such a government as would enable those by whose authority they acted to reap the advantages anticipated from its acquisition, and to gather there a population which would enable it to assume the position to which it was destined among the states of the Union. . . .

It seems, however, to be supposed, that there is a difference between property in a slave and other property, and that different rules may be applied to it in expounding the Constitution of the United States. . . .

Now, as we have already said in an earlier part of this opinion, upon a different point, the right of property in a slave is distinctly and expressly affirmed in the Constitution. The right to traffic in it, like an ordinary article of merchandise and property, was guaranteed to the citizens of the United States, in every state that might desire it, for twenty years. And the government in express terms is pledged to protect it in all future time, if the slave escapes from his owner. . . .

Upon these considerations, it is the opinion of the court that the Act of Congress which prohibited a citizen from holding and owning property of this kind in the territory of the United States north of the line therein mentioned, is not warranted by the Constitution, and is therefore void; and that neither Dred Scott himself, nor any of his family, were made free by being carried into this territory; even if they had been carried there by the owner, with the intention of becoming a permanent resident.

222. *Last Speech to the Court, 1859*

John Brown, Last Speech to the Court, November 2, 1859, in John Brown, *Life and Letters* (F. B. Sanborn, ed., Boston, 1885), 584–5.

I HAVE, may it please the Court, a few words to say.

In the first place, I deny everything but what I have all along admitted,—the design on my part to free the slaves. I intended certainly to have made a clean thing of that matter, as I did last winter, when I went into Missouri and there took slaves without the snapping of a gun on either side, moved them through the country, and finally left them in Canada. I designed to have done the same thing again, on a larger scale. That was all I intended. I never did intend murder, or treason, or the destruction of property, or to excite or incite slaves to rebellion, or to make insurrection.

I have another objection; and that is, it is unjust that I should suffer such a penalty. Had I interfered in the manner which I admit, and which I admit has been fairly proved . . . had I so interfered in behalf of the rich, the powerful, the intelligent, the so-called great, or in behalf of any of their friends, . . . and suffered and sacrificed what I have in this interference, it would have been all right; and every man in this court would have deemed it an act worthy of reward rather than punishment.

This court acknowledges, as I suppose, the validity of the law of God. I see a book kissed here which I suppose to be the Bible, or at least the New Testament. That teaches me that all things whatsoever I would that men should do to me, I should do even so to them. It teaches me, further, to "remember them that are in bonds, as bound with them." I endeavored to act up to that instruction. I say, I am yet too young to understand that God is any respecter of persons. I believe that to have interfered as I have done—as I have always freely admitted I have done—in behalf of His despised poor, was not wrong, but right. Now, if it is deemed necessary that I should forfeit my life for the furtherance of the ends of justice, and mingle my blood further with the blood of my children and with the blood of millions in this slave country whose rights are disregarded by wicked, cruel and unjust enactments,—I submit; so let it be done!

Let me say one word further.

I feel entirely satisfied with the treatment I have received on my trial. Considering all the circumstances, it has been more generous than I expected. But I feel no consciousness of guilt. I have stated from the first what was my intention, and what was not. I never had any design against the life of any person, nor any disposition to commit treason, or excite slaves to rebel, or make any general insurrection. I never encouraged any man to do so, but always discouraged any idea of that kind.

Let me say, also, a word in regard to the statements made by some of those connected with me. I hear it has been stated by some of them that I have induced them to join me. But the contrary is true. I do not say this to injure them, but as regretting their weakness. There is not one of them but joined me of his own accord, and the greater part of them at their own expense. A number of them I never saw, and never had a word of conversation with, till the day they came to me; and that was for the purpose I have stated.

Now I have done.

223. *The Portent, 1859*

Herman Melville, "The Portent," in *Selected Poems* (F. O. Matthiessen, ed.; Norfolk, Connecticut, 1947), 9.

HANGING from the beam,
Slowly swaying (such the law),
Gaunt the shadow on your green,
Shenandoah!
The cut is on the crown
(Lo, John Brown),
And the stabs shall heal no more.

Hidden in the cap
Is the anguish none can draw;
So your future veils its face,
Shenandoah!
But the streaming beard is shown
(Weird John Brown),
The meteor of the war.

224. *A House Divided, 1858*

Abraham Lincoln, Speech at Chicago, July 10, 1858, in *Speeches and Writings* (R. P. Basler, ed.; Cleveland, 1946), 392–3. Reprinted by permission of the World Publishing Company.

AT SPRINGFIELD . . . I said . . . that "we are now far into the fifth year since a policy was instituted for the avowed object and with the confident promise of putting an end to slavery agitation; under the operation of that policy, that agitation has [not] only not ceased, but has constantly augmented. I believe it will not cease until a crisis shall have been reached and passed. A house divided against itself cannot stand. I believe this government cannot endure permanently half slave and half free. I do not expect the Union to be dissolved. . . . I do not expect the house to fall, but I do expect it will cease to be divided. It will become all one thing or all the other. Either the opponents of slavery will arrest the spread of it, and place it where the public mind shall rest in the belief that it is in the course of ultimate extinction, or its advocates will push it forward until it shall become alike lawful in all the States North as well as South."

What is the paragraph? . . . Now, . . . if you will carefully read that passage over, . . . I did not say that I was in favor of anything in it. I only said what I expected would take place. I made a prediction only—it may have been a foolish one perhaps. I did not even say that I desired that slavery should be put in course of ultimate extinction. I do say so now, however, so there need be no longer any difficulty about that. . . . I know what I meant, and I will not leave this crowd in doubt, if I can explain it to them, what I really meant in the use of that paragraph.

I am not, in the first place, unaware that this Government has endured eighty-two years, half slave and half free. I know that. I am tolerably well acquainted with the history of the country, and I know that it has endured eighty-two years, half slave and half free. I believe—and that is what I meant to allude to there—I believe it has endured because, during all that time, until the introduction of the Nebraska Bill, the public mind did rest, all the time, in the belief that slavery was in course of ultimate extinction.

XXVI 🌿 *The War and Its Aftermath*

AT THE ELECTION of 1860 all the old fears came to the surface. A panicky mood spread through the Union as the separation, long dreaded, seemed now unavoidable. Almost every social institution had already divided over the slavery issue. Was now the nation also to be split?

Despite efforts at moderation and compromise, the Southern radicals would not yield to a government of which Lincoln was President. South Carolina led the way toward secession and was followed in time by the other Southern states (No. 225), which drew together in the Confederacy.

Lincoln faced the problem with resolution. His inaugural address expressed his own view that the critical problem was preservation of the Union, in which he saw involved the fate of free government everywhere. To that course he consistently held. He was anxious to avoid a war, but on the central question of Union he would not compromise (No. 226).

Nor would the Southerners. They took the initiative in firing on Fort Sumter; and that precipitated the war (No. 227). There followed four years of bitter fighting. This struggle reached from the Atlantic deep into the trans-Mississippi West and showed vast alternations of fortune. Bitterly contested, the war was enormously expensive in men and wealth (No. 228). Southern hopes for success depended to a considerable degree upon securing foreign aid. The certainty that cotton was king supported those hopes. But Northern protests put off recognition of the Confederacy (*see above,* Nos. 168, 169); and the Emancipation Proclamation injected a moral element into the struggle that made European intervention still more difficult (No. 229). After Gettysburg, the South struggled desperately on. But defeat was only a matter of time.

Standing at the battlefield of Gettysburg before the war ended, Lincoln had set into very general terms the objectives of the war (No. 230). But to reduce those aims to the concrete was far more difficult. Having suffered through a bitter war, men were not disposed to compromise on programs for reconstruction. In the contrast over reconstruction, both sides were defeated. The radicals, who looked forward to a total remodeling of the South, in which the Negro would be completely equal with the whites (No. 231), managed to secure the enactment of the Thirteenth, Fourteenth, and Fifteenth Amendments, 1865–70 (No. 232). But they failed to make those amendments effective. Given the practical conditions of Southern life, control of the freedmen often brought them back to the verge of bondage (No. 233). The Negro soon learned, therefore, that his emancipation was effective within limited terms only (No. 234).

225. *South Carolina Secedes, 1860*

Declaration of Causes Which Induced the Secession of South Carolina, in Frank Moore, ed., *The Rebellion Record* (New York, 1861), I, Documents and Narratives, 3–4.

By ... [the] Constitution, certain duties were imposed upon the several states, and the exercise of certain of their powers were restrained, which necessarily implied their continued existence as sovereign states. But, to remove all doubt, an amendment was added, which declared that the powers not delegated to the United States by the Constitution, nor prohibited by it to the states, are reserved to the states, respectively, or to the people. On the 23rd May, 1788, South Carolina, by a convention of her people, passed an ordinance assenting to this Constitution, and afterwards altered her own Constitution to conform herself to the obligations she had undertaken.

Thus was established, by compact between the states, a government with defined objects and powers, limited to the express words of the grant. This limitation left the whole remaining mass of power subject to the clause reserving it to the states or the people, and rendered unnecessary any specification of reserved rights.

We hold that the government thus established is subject to the two great principles asserted in the Declaration of Independence; and we hold further, that the mode of its formation subjects it to a third fundamental principle, namely, the law of compact. We maintain that in every compact between two or more parties, the obligation is mutual; that the failure of one of the contracting parties to perform a material part of the agreement, entirely releases the obligation of the other; and that, where no arbiter is provided, each party is remitted to his own judgment to determine the fact of failure, with all its consequences.

In the present case, that fact is established with certainty. We assert that fourteen of the states have deliberately refused for years to fulfill their constitutional obligations, and we refer to their own statutes for the proof.

The Constitution of the United States, in its fourth Article, provides as follows:

"No person held to service or labor in one state under the laws thereof, escaping into another, shall, in consequence of any law or regulation therein, be discharged from such service or labor, but shall be delivered up, on claim of the party to whom such service or labor may be due." ...

In many of ... [the non-slaveholding] states the fugitive is discharged from the service of labor claimed, and in none of them has the state government complied with the stipulation made in the Constitution. ... Thus the constitutional compact has been deliberately broken and disregarded by the non-slaveholding states; and the consequence follows that South Carolina is released from her obligation.

The ends for which this Constitution was framed are declared by itself to be "to form a more perfect union, to establish justice, insure domestic tranquillity, provide for the common defense, promote the general welfare, and secure the blessings of liberty to ourselves and our posterity."

These ends it endeavored to accomplish by a federal government, in which each state was recognized as an equal, and had separate control over its own institutions. The right of property in slaves was recognized by giving to free persons distinct political rights; by giving them the right to represent, and burdening them with direct taxes for, three-fifths of their slaves; by authorizing the importation of slaves for twenty years; and by stipulating for the rendition of fugitives from labor.

We affirm that these ends for which this government was instituted have been defeated, and the government itself has been destructive of them by the action of the non-slaveholding states. Those states have assumed the right of deciding upon the propriety of our domestic institutions; and have denied the rights of property established in fifteen of the states and recognized by the Constitution; they have denounced as sinful the institution of slavery; they have permitted the open establishment among them of societies, whose avowed object is to disturb the peace of and eloin the property of the citizens of other states. They have encouraged and assisted thousands of our slaves to leave their homes; and those who remain, have been incited by emissaries, books, and pictures, to servile insurrection.

For twenty-five years this agitation has been steadily increasing, until it has now secured to its aid the power of the common government. Observing the *forms* of the Constitution, a sectional party has found within that article establishing the executive department, the means of subverting the Constitution itself. A geographical line has been drawn across the Union, and all the states north of that line have united in the election of a man to the high office of President of the United States whose opinions and purposes are hostile to slavery. He is to be intrusted with the administration of the common government, because he has declared that that "government cannot endure permanently half slave, half free," and that the public mind must rest in the belief that slavery is in the course of ultimate extinction.

This sectional combination for the subversion of the Constitution has been aided, in some of the states, by elevating to citizenship persons who, by the supreme law of the land, are incabable of becoming citizens; and their votes have been used to inaugurate a new policy, hostile to the South, and destructive of its peace and safety.

On the 4th of March next this party will take possession of the government. It has announced that the South shall be excluded from the common territory, that the judicial tribunal shall be made sectional, and that a war must be waged against slavery until it shall cease throughout the United States.

The guarantees of the Constitution will then no longer exist; the equal rights of the states will be lost. The slaveholding states will no longer have the power of self-government, or self-protection, and the federal government will have become their enemy.

Sectional interest and animosity will deepen the irritation; and all hope of remedy is rendered vain, by the fact that the public opinion at the North has invested a great political error with the sanctions of a more erroneous religious belief.

We, therefore, the people of South Carolina, by our delegates in convention assembled, appealing to the Supreme Judge of the world for the rectitude of our intentions, have solemnly declared that the Union heretofore existing between this state and the other states of North America is dissolved, and that the State of South Carolina has resumed her position among the nations of the world, as separate and independent state, with full power to levy war, conclude peace, contract alliances, establish commerce, and to do all other acts and things which independent states may of right do.

226. *Lincoln's Inaugural Address, 1861*

Delivered, March 4, 1861; in Richardson, *Messages and Papers*, VI, 5–12.

APPREHENSION seems to exist among the people of the Southern States, that by the accession of a Republican administration their property, and their peace, and personal security, are to be endangered. There has never been any reasonable cause for such apprehension. Indeed, the most ample evidence to the contrary has all the while existed . . . in nearly all the published speeches of him who now addresses you. I do but quote from one of those speeches when I declare that "I have no purpose, directly or indirectly, to interfere with the institution of slavery in the states where it exists. I believe I have no lawful right to do so, and I have no inclination to do so." Those who nominated and elected me did so with full knowledge that I had made this, and many similar declarations and had never recanted them. And more than this, they placed in the platform, for my acceptance, and as a law to themselves, and to me, the clear and emphatic resolution . . . "that the maintenance inviolate of the rights of the states, and especially the right of each state to order and control its own domestic institutions according to its own judgment exclusively, is essential to that balance of power on which the perfection and endurance of our political fabric depend." . . .

I now reiterate these sentiments, and in doing so I only press upon the public attention the most conclusive evidence of which the case is susceptible, that the property, peace and security of no section are to be in any wise endangered by the now incoming administration. I add too, that all the protection which, consistently with the Constitution and the laws, can be given, will be cheerfully given to all the states when lawfully demanded, for whatever cause—as cheerfully to one section as to another.

There is much controversy about the delivering up of fugitives from service or labor. The clause . . . plainly written in the Constitution . . . was intended by those who made it, for the reclaiming of . . . fugitive slaves; and the intention of the lawgiver is the law. All members of Congress swear their support to the whole Constitution—to this provision as much as to any other. . . . Now, if they would make the effort in good temper, could they not, with nearly equal unanimity, frame and pass a law, by means of which to keep good that unanimous oath?

There is some difference of opinion whether this clause should be enforced by national or by state authority, but surely that difference is not a very material one. If the slave is to be surrendered, it can be of but little consequence to him, or to others, by which authority it is done. And should any one, in any case, be content that his oath shall go unkept, on a merely unsubstantial controversy as to *how* it shall be kept?

Again: In any law upon this subject, ought not all the safeguards of liberty known in civilized and humane jurisprudence to be introduced, so that a free man be not, in any case, surrendered as a slave? And might it not be well, at the same time to provide by law for the enforcement of that clause in the Constitution which guarantees that "citizens of each state shall be entitled to all privileges and immunities of citizens in the several states?"

I take the official oath today with no mental reservations and with no purpose to construe the Constitution or laws by any hypercritical rules. And while I do not choose now to specify particular acts of Congress as proper to be enforced, I do suggest that it will be much safer for all, both in official and private stations, to conform to, and abide by, all those acts which stand unrepealed, than to violate any of them, trusting to find impunity in having them held to be unconstitutional.

It is seventy-two years since the first inauguration of a President under our national Constitution. During that period fifteen different and greatly distinguished citizens have, in succession, administered the executive branch of the government. They have conducted it through many perils; and, generally, with great success. Yet, with all this scope of precedent, I now enter upon the same task for the brief constitutional term of four years, under great and peculiar difficulty. A disruption of the Federal Union, heretofore only menaced, is now formidably attempted.

I hold, that in contemplation of universal law, and of the Constitution, the union of these states is perpetual. Perpetuity is implied, if not expressed, in the fundamental law of all national governments. . . . Continue to execute all the express provisions of our national Constitution, and the Union will endure forever—it being impossible to destroy it, except by some action not provided for in the instrument itself. . . .

The proposition that . . . the Union is perpetual, [is] confirmed by the history of the Union itself. The Union is much older than the Constitution. It was formed in fact, by the Articles of Association in 1774. It was matured and continued by the Declaration of Independence in 1776. It was further matured and the faith of all the then thirteen states expressly plighted and engaged that it should be perpetual, by the Articles of Confederation in 1778. And finally, in 1787, one of the declared objects for ordaining and establishing the Constitution, was *"to form a more perfect Union."*

But if [the] destruction of the Union, by one, or by a part only, of the states be lawfully possible, the Union is *less* perfect than before the Constitution, having lost the vital element of perpetuity.

It follows from these views that no state, upon its own mere motion, can lawfully get out of the Union; that *resolves* and *ordinances* to that effect are legally void, and that acts of violence, within any state or states, against the authority of the United States, are insurrectionary or revolutionary, according to circumstances.

I therefore consider that in view of the Constitution and the laws, the Union is unbroken; and to the extent of my ability I shall take care, as the Constitution itself expressly enjoins upon me, that the laws of the Union be faithfully executed in all the states. Doing this I deem to be only a simple duty on my part, and I shall perform it, so far as practicable, unless my rightful masters, the American people, shall withhold the requisite means, or, in some authoritative manner, direct the contrary. I trust this will not be regarded as a menace, but only as the declared purpose of the Union that it *will* constitutionally defend and maintain itself.

In doing this there needs to be no bloodshed or violence; and there shall be none, unless it be forced upon the national authority. The power confided to me will be used to hold, occupy, and possess the property and places belonging to the government, and to collect the duties and imposts; but beyond what may be necessary for these objects, there will be no invasion, no using of force against or among the people anywhere. Where hostility to the United States in any interior locality shall be so great and universal as to prevent competent resident citizens from holding the Federal offices, there will be no attempt to force obnoxious strangers among the people for that object. While the strict legal right may exist in the government to enforce the exercise of these offices, the attempt to do so would be so irritating and so nearly impracticable withal, that I deem it better to forego, for the time, the uses of such offices. . . .

That there are persons in one section or another who seek to destroy the Union at all events, and are glad of any pretext to do it, I will neither affirm nor deny; but if there be such, I need address no word to them. To those, however, who really love the Union, may I not speak?

Before entering upon so grave a matter as the destruction of our national fabric, with all its benefits, its memories and its hopes, would it not be wise to ascertain precisely why we do it? Will you hazard so desperate a step, while there is any possibility that any portion of the ills you fly from have no real existence? Will you, while the certain ills you fly to are greater than all the real ones you fly from? Will you risk the commission of so fearful a mistake?

All profess to be content in the Union, if all constitutional rights can be maintained. Is it true, then, that any right, plainly written in the Constitution, has been denied? I think not. . . . Think, if you can, of a single instance in which a plainly written provision of the Constitution has ever been denied. If, by the mere force of numbers a majority should deprive a minority of any clearly written constitutional right, it might, in a moral point of view, justify revolution—certainly would, if such a right were a vital one. But such is not our case. All the vital rights of minorities and of individuals are so plainly assured to them by affirmations and negations, guarantees and prohibitions in the Constitution, that controversies never arise concerning them. But no organic law can ever be framed with a provision specifically applicable to every question which may occur in practical administration. No foresight can anticipate, nor any document of reasonable length contain express provisions for all possible questions. Shall fugitives from labor be surrendered by national or by state authority? The Constitution does not ex-

pressly say. *May* Congress prohibit slavery in the territories? The Constitution does not expressly say. *Must* Congress protect slavery in the territories? The Constitution does not expressly say.

From questions of this class spring all our constitutional controversies, and we divide upon them into majorities and minorities. If the minority will not acquiesce, the majority must, or the government must cease. There is no other alternative, for continuing the government is acquiescence on one side or the other. If a minority, in such case, will secede rather than acquiesce, they make a precedent which, in turn, will divide and ruin them; for a minority of their own will secede from them whenever a majority refuses to be controlled by such a minority. For instance, why may not any portion of a new confederacy, a year or two hence, arbitrarily secede again, precisely as portions of the present Union now claim to secede from it? All who cherish disunion sentiments are now being educated to the exact temper of doing this. . . .

Plainly, the central idea of secession is the essence of anarchy. A majority, held in restraint by constitutional checks and limitations, and always changing easily with deliberate changes of popular opinions and sentiments is the only true sovereign of a free people. Whoever rejects it, does of necessity fly to anarchy or to despotism. Unanimity is impossible. The rule of a minority, as a permanent arrangement, is wholly inadmissible; so that, rejecting the majority principle, anarchy or despotism in some form is all that is left.

I do not forget the position assumed by some, that constitutional questions are to be decided by the Supreme Court; nor do I deny that such decisions must be binding in any case, upon the parties to a suit, as to the object of that suit, while they are also entitled to very high respect and consideration in all parallel cases by all other departments of the government. And while it is obviously possible that such decision may be erroneous in any given case, still the evil effect following it, being limited to that particular case, with the chance that it may be overruled and never become a precedent for other cases, can better be borne than could the evils of a different practice. At the same time, the candid citizen must confess that if the policy of the government upon vital questions affecting the whole people is to be irrevocably fixed by decisions of the Supreme Court, the instant they are made in ordinary litigation between parties, in personal actions, the people will have ceased to be their own rulers, having to that extent practically resigned their government into the hands of that eminent tribunal. Nor is there in this view any assault upon the court or the judges. It is a duty from which they may not shrink, to decide cases properly brought before them; and it is no fault of theirs if others seek to turn their decisions to political purposes.

One section of our country believes slavery is *right* and ought to be extended, while the other believes it is *wrong* and ought not to be extended. This is the only substantial dispute. The fugitive-slave clause of the Constitution, and the law for the suppression of the foreign slave trade, are each as well enforced, perhaps, as any law can ever be in a community where the moral sense of the people imperfectly supports the law itself. The great body of the people abide by the dry legal obligation in both cases, and a few break over in each. This, I think, cannot be perfectly cured; and it would be worse in both cases *after* the separation of the sections, than before. The foreign slave trade, now imperfectly suppressed, would be ultimately revived without restriction in one section; while fugitive slaves, now only partially surrendered, would not be surrendered at all by the other.

Physically speaking, we cannot separate. We cannot remove our respective sections from each other, nor build an impassable wall between them. A husband and wife may be divorced, and go out of the presence, and beyond the reach of each other; but the different parts of our country cannot do this. They cannot but remain face to face; and intercourse, either amicable or hostile, must continue between them. Is it possible, then, to make that intercourse more advantageous or more satisfactory, *after* separation than *before?* Can aliens make treaties easier than friends can make laws? Can treaties be more faithfully enforced between aliens than laws can among friends? . . .

This country, with its institutions, belongs to the people who inhabit it. Whenever they shall grow weary of the existing government, they can exercise their *constitutional* right of amending it, or their *revolutionary* right to dismember or overthrow it. . . .

Why should there not be a patient confidence in the ultimate justice of the people? Is there any better or equal hope in the world? In our present differences, is either party without faith of being in the right? If the Almighty Ruler of Nations, with His eternal truth and justice, be on your side of the North or on yours of the South, that truth and that justice will surely prevail by the judgment of this great tribunal of the American people. . . .

My countrymen, one and all, think calmly and *well* upon this whole subject. Nothing valuable can be lost by taking time. . . . Intelligence, patriotism, Christianity, and a firm reliance on Him, who has never yet forsaken this favored land, are still competent to adjust, in the best way, all our present difficulty.

In *your* hands, my dissatisfied fellow-countrymen, and not in *mine,* is the momentous issue of civil war. The government will not assail *you.* You can have no conflict without being yourselves the aggressors. *You* have no oath registered in Heaven to destroy the government, while *I* shall have the most solemn one to "preserve, protect, and defend" it.

I am loath to close. We are not enemies, but friends. We must not be enemies. Though passion may have strained, it must not break our bonds of affection. The mystic chords of memory, stretching from every battlefield and patriot grave to every living heart and hearthstone, all over this broad land, will yet swell the chorus of the Union, when again touched, as surely they will be, by the better angels of our nature.

227. *The Firing on Sumter, 1861*

M. B. Chesnut, *Diary from Dixie* (I. D. Martin and M. L. Avary, eds.; New York, 1905), 35-6, 37-40. Copyright 1905 by D. Appleton Company. Reprinted by permission of the publishers Appleton-Century-Crofts, Inc.

[APRIL] 12th.—Anderson will not capitulate. Yesterday's was the merriest, maddest dinner we have had yet. Men were audaciously wise and witty. We had an unspoken foreboding that it was to be our last pleasant meeting. . . .

I do not pretend to go to sleep. How can I? If Anderson does not accept terms at four, the orders are he shall be fired upon. I count four, St. Michael's bells chime out, and I begin to hope. At half-past four the heavy booming of a cannon. I sprang out of bed, and on my knees prostrate I prayed as I never prayed before.

There was a sound of stir all over the house, pattering of feet in the corridors. All seemed hurrying one way. I put on my double gown and a shawl and went too. It was to the housetop. The shells were bursting. In the dark I heard a man say, "Waste of ammunition." I knew my husband was rowing about in a boat somewhere in that dark bay, and that the shells were roofing it over, bursting toward the Fort. If Anderson was obstinate, Colonel Chesnut was to order the fort on one side to open fire. Certainly fire had begun. The regular roar of the cannon, there it was. And who could tell what each volley accomplished of death and destruction?

The women were wild there on the housetop. Prayers came from the women and imprecations from the men. And then a shell would light up the scene. Tonight they say the forces are to attempt to land.

We watched up there, and everybody wondered that Fort Sumter did not fire a shot. . . .

We hear nothing, can listen to nothing; boom, boom, goes the cannon all the time. The nervous strain is awful, alone in this darkened room. "Richmond and Washington ablaze," say the papers—blazing with excitement. Why not? To us these last days' events seem frightfully great. We were all women on that iron balcony. Men are only seen at a distance now. . . .

April 13th.—Nobody has been hurt after all. How gay we were last night! Reaction after the dread of all the slaughter we thought those dreadful cannon were making. Not even a battery the worse for wear. Fort Sumter has been on fire. Anderson has not yet silenced any of our guns. So the aides, still with swords and red sashes by way of uniform, tell us. But the sound of those guns makes regular meals impossible. None of us go to table. Tea-trays pervade the corridors, going everywhere. Some of the anxious hearts lie on their beds and moan in solitary misery. Mrs. Wigfall and I solace ourselves with tea in my room. These women have all a satisfying faith. "God is on our side," they say. When we are shut in Mrs. Wigfall and I ask, "Why?" "Of course, He hates the Yankees," we are told, "You'll think that well of Him."

Not by one word or look can we detect any change in the demeanor of these Negro servants. Lawrence sits at our door, sleepy and respectful, and profoundly indifferent. So are they all, but they carry it too far. You could not tell that they even heard the awful roar going on in the bay, though it had been dinning in their ears night and day. People talk before them as if they were chairs and tables. They make no sign. Are they stolidly stupid? or wiser than we are; silent and strong, biding their time? . . .

April 15th.—I did not know that one could live such days of excitement. Some one called: "Come out! There is a crowd coming." A mob it was, indeed, but it was headed by Colonels Chesnut and Manning. The crowd was shouting and showing these two as messengers of good news. They were escorted to Beauregard's headquarters. Fort Sumter had surrendered! Those upon the housetops shouted to us, "The fort is on fire." That had been the story once or twice before.

228. *Observations at Gettysburg, 1863*

A. J. L. Fremantle, *Three Months in the Southern States* (Edinburgh, 1863), 258–60, 261, 262–3, 265–7, 268, 269–73, 274, 275, 276–7.

[July 1] At 3 P.M. we began to meet wounded men coming to the rear, and the number of these soon increased most rapidly, some hobbling alone, others on stretchers carried by the ambulance corps, and others in the ambulance wagons. Many of the latter were stripped nearly naked, and displayed very bad wounds. This spectacle, so revolting to a person unaccustomed to such sights, produced no impression whatever upon the advancing troops, who certainly go under fire with the most perfect nonchalance. They show no enthusiasm or excitement, but the most complete indifference. This is the effect of two years' almost uninterrupted fighting.

We now began to meet Yankee prisoners coming to the rear in considerable numbers. Many of them were wounded, but they seemed already to be on excellent terms with their captors, with whom they had commenced swapping canteens, tobacco, etc. Among them was a Pennsylvanian colonel, a miserable object from a wound in his face. In answer to a question, I heard one of them remark, with a laugh, "We're pretty nigh whipped already." We next came to a Confederate soldier carrying a Yankee color, belonging, I think, to a Pennsylvania regiment, which he told us he had just captured. . . .

3d July (Friday)—At 6 A.M. I rode to the field with Colonel Manning, and went over that portion of the ground which, after a fierce contest, had been won from the enemy yesterday evening. The dead were being buried, but great numbers were still lying about; also many mortally wounded, for whom nothing could be done. Amongst the latter were a number of Yankees dressed in bad imitations of the Zouave costume. They opened their glazed eyes, as I rode past, in a painfully imploring manner.

We joined Generals Lee and Longstreet's staff. They were reconnoitering and making preparations for renewing the attack. . . . The distance between the Confederate guns and the Yankee position— *i.e.,* between the woods crowning the opposite ridges—was at least a mile—quite open, gently undulating, and exposed to artillery the whole distance. This was the ground which had to be crossed in to-day's attack. Pickett's division, which had just come up, was to bear the brunt in Longstreet's attack, together with Heth and Pettigrew in Hill's corps. Pickett's division was a weak one (under 5,000), owing to the absence of two brigades.

At noon all Longstreet's dispositions were made. His troops for attack were deployed into line, and lying down in the woods; his batteries were ready to open. The General then dismounted and went to sleep for a short time. . . .

The road at Gettysburg was lined with Yankee dead, and as they had been killed on the 1st, the poor fellows had already begun to be very offensive. . . . I soon began to meet many wounded men returning from the front. Many of them asked in piteous tones the way to a doctor or an ambulance. The further I got, the greater became the number of the wounded. At last I came to a perfect stream of them flocking through the woods in numbers as great as the crowd in Oxford Street in the middle of the day. Some were walking alone on crutches composed of two rifles, others were supported by men less badly wounded than themselves, and others were carried on stretchers by the ambulance corps; but in no case did I see a sound man helping the wounded to the rear, unless he carried the red badge of the ambulance corps. They were still under a heavy fire; the shells were continually bringing down great limbs of trees, and carrying further destruction amongst this melancholy procession.

I saw all this in much less time than it takes to write it, and although astonished to meet such vast numbers of wounded, I had not seen enough to give me any idea of the real extent of the mischief.

When I got close up to General Longstreet, I saw one of his regiments advancing through the woods in good order; so, thinking I was just in time to see the attack, I remarked to the General that "I wouldn't have missed this for anything." Longstreet was seated at the top of a snake fence at the edge of the wood, and looking perfectly calm and imperturbed. He replied, laughing, "The devil you wouldn't! I would like to have missed it very much; we've attacked and been repulsed: look there!"

For the first time I then had a view of the open space between the two positions, and saw it covered with Confederates slowly and sulkily returning towards

us in small broken parties, under a heavy fire of artillery. But the fire where we were was not so bad as further to the rear: for although the air seemed alive with shell, yet the greater number burst behind us.

The General told me that Pickett's division had succeeded in carrying the enemy's position and capturing his guns, but after remaining there twenty minutes, it had been forced to retire, on the retreat of Heth and Pettigrew on its left. No person could have been more calm or self-possessed than General Longstreet under these trying circumstances, aggravated as they now were by the movements of the enemy, who began to show a strong disposition to advance. I could now thoroughly appreciate the term bulldog, which I had heard applied to him by the soldiers. Difficulties seem to make no other impression upon him than to make him a little more savage. . . .

If Longstreet's conduct was admirable, that of General Lee was perfectly sublime. He was engaged in rallying and in encouraging the broken troops, and was riding about a little in front of the wood, quite alone—the whole of his staff being engaged in a similar manner further to the rear. His face, which is always placid and cheerful, did not show signs of the slightest disappointment, care, or annoyance; and he was addressing to every soldier he met a few words of encouragement, such as, "All this will come right in the end; we'll talk it over afterwards; but, in the meantime, all good men must rally. We want all good and true men just now," etc. . . .

I saw General Willcox (an officer who wears a short round jacket and a battered straw hat) come up to him, and explain, almost crying, the state of his brigade. General Lee immediately shook hands with him and said cheerfully, "Never mind, General, *all this has been MY fault*—it is *I* that have lost this fight, and you must help me out of it in the best way you can." . . .

Soon afterwards I rode to the extreme front. . . . I was immediately surrounded by a sergeant and about half-a-dozen gunners, who seemed in excellent spirits and full of confidence, in spite of their exposed situation. The sergeant expressed his ardent hope that the Yankees might have spirit enough to advance and receive the dose he had in readiness for them.

They spoke in admiration of the advance of Pickett's division, and of the manner in which Pickett himself had led it. When they observed General Lee they said, "We've not lost confidence in the old man: this day's work won't do him no harm. 'Uncle Robert' will get us into Washington yet; you bet he will!" etc.

229. *The Emancipation Proclamation, 1863*

United States Statutes at Large, XII (1859–63), 1268–9.

WHEREAS on the twenty-second day of September, in the year of our Lord 1862, a proclamation was issued by the President of the United States, containing, among other things, the following, to wit:

"That on the first day of January, . . . 1863, all persons held as slaves within any state or designated part of a state, the people whereof shall then be in rebellion against the United States, shall be then, thenceforward, and forever, free; and the Executive Government of the United States, including the military and naval authority thereof, will recognize and maintain the freedom of such persons, and will do no act or acts to repress such persons, or any of them, in any efforts they may make for their actual freedom.

"That the Executive will on the first day of January aforesaid, by proclamation, designate the states and parts of states, if any, in which the people thereof, respectively, shall then be in rebellion against the United States; and the fact that any state or the people thereof, shall on that day be in good faith represented in the Congress of the United States, by members chosen thereto at elections wherein a majority of the qualified voters of such states shall have participated, shall, in the absence of strong countervailing testimony, be deemed conclusive evidence that such state, and the people thereof,

are not then in rebellion against the United States."

Now, therefore, I, Abraham Lincoln, President of the United States, by virtue of the power in me vested as Commander-in-Chief of the Army and Navy of the United States, in time of actual armed rebellion against the authority and government of the United States, and as a fit and necessary war measure for suppressing said rebellion, do, on this first day of January . . . 1863, and in accordance with my purpose so to do, publicly proclaimed for the full period of one hundred days from the day first above mentioned, order and designate as the states and parts of states wherein the people thereof, respectively, are this day in rebellion against the United States the following, to wit:

Arkansas, Texas, Louisiana (except the parishes of St. Bernard, Plaquemines, Jefferson, St. John, St. Charles, St. James, Ascension, Assumption, Terre Bonne, Lafourche, St. Mary, St. Martin, and Orleans, including the city of New Orleans), Mississippi, Alabama, Florida, Georgia, South Carolina, North Carolina, and Virginia (except the forty-eight counties designated as West Virginia, and also the counties of Berkeley, Accomac, Northhampton, Elizabeth City, York, Princess Anne, and Norfolk, including the cities of Norfolk and Portsmouth), and which excepted parts are for the present left precisely as if this proclamation were not issued.

And by virtue of the power and for the purpose aforesaid, I do order and declare that all persons held as slaves within said designated states and parts of states are, and henceforward shall be, free; and that the Executive Government of the United States, including the military and naval authorities thereof, will recognize and maintain the freedom of said persons.

And I hereby enjoin upon the people so declared to be free to abstain from all violence, unless in necessary self-defense; and I recommend to them that, in all cases when allowed, they labor faithfully for reasonable wages.

And I further declare and make known that such persons of suitable condition, will be received into the armed service of the United States to garrison forts, positions, stations, and other places, and to man vessels of all sorts in said service.

And upon this act, sincerely believed to be an act of justice, warranted by the Constitution upon military necessity, I invoke the considerate judgment of mankind and the gracious favor of Almighty God.

230. *The Gettysburg Address,* 1863

"Address at the Dedication of the Gettysburg Cemetery, November 19, 1863," in Abraham Lincoln, *Complete Works* (J. G. Nicolay and John Hay, eds.; New York, 1905), IX, 209–10.

FOURSCORE and seven years ago our fathers brought forth on this continent a new nation, conceived in liberty, and dedicated to the proposition that all men are created equal.

Now we are engaged in a great civil war, testing whether that nation or any nation so conceived and so dedicated, can long endure. We are met on a great battlefield of that war. We have come to dedicate a portion of that field as a final resting-place for those who here gave their lives that that nation might live. It is altogether fitting and proper that we should do this.

But, in a larger sense, we cannot dedicate—we cannot consecrate—we cannot hallow—this ground. The brave men, living and dead, who struggled here, have consecrated it far above our poor power to add or detract. The world will little note nor long remember what we say here, but it can never forget what they did here. It is for us, the living, rather, to be dedicated here to the unfinished work which they who fought here have thus far so nobly advanced. It is rather for us to be here dedicated to the great task remaining before us—that from these honored dead we take increased devotion to that cause for which they gave the last full measure of devotion; that we here highly resolve that these dead shall not have died in vain—that this nation, under God, shall have a new birth of freedom; and that government of the people, by the people, for the people, shall not perish from the earth.

231. *The South a Conquered Province,* 1865

Speech of Representative Thaddeus Stevens, December 18, 1865, *Congressional Globe* (1865), 73.

THE LATE war between two acknowledged belligerents severed their original compacts and broke all the ties that bound them together. The future condition of the conquered power depends on the will of the conqueror. They must come in as new states or remain as conquered provinces. Congress . . . is the only power that can act in the matter. . . .

Congress alone can do it. . . . Congress must create states and declare when they are entitled to be represented. Then each House must judge whether the members presenting themselves from a recognized state possess the requisite qualifications of age, residence, and citizenship; and whether the election and returns are according to law. . . .

It is obvious from all this that the first duty of Congress is to pass a law declaring the condition of these outside or defunct states, and providing proper civil governments for them. Since the conquest they have been governed by martial law. Military rule is necessarily despotic, and ought not to exist longer than is absolutely necessary. As there are no symptoms that the people of these provinces will be prepared to participate in constitutional government for some years, I know of no arrangement so proper for them as territorial governments. There they can learn the principles of freedom and eat the fruit of foul rebellion. Under such governments, while electing members to the territorial legislatures, they will necessarily mingle with those to whom Congress shall extend the right of suffrage. In territories Congress fixes the qualifications of electors; and I know of no better place nor better occasion for the conquered rebels and the conqueror to practice justice to

all men, and accustom themselves to make and obey equal laws. . . .

They ought never to be recognized as capable of acting in the Union, or of being counted as valid states, until the Constitution shall have been so amended as to make it what its framers intended; and so as to secure perpetual ascendancy to the party of the Union; and so as to render our republican government firm and stable forever. The first of those amendments is to change the basis of representation among the states from federal numbers to actual voters. . . . With the basis unchanged the 83 Southern members, with the Democrats that will in the best times be elected from the North, will always give them a majority in Congress and in the Electoral College. . . . I need not depict the ruin that would follow. . . .

But this is not all that we ought to do before these inveterate rebels are invited to participate in our legislation. We have turned, or are about to turn, loose four million slaves without a hut to shelter them or a cent in their pockets. The infernal laws of slavery have prevented them from acquiring an education, understanding the commonest laws of contract, or of managing the ordinary business of life. This Congress is bound to provide for them until they can take care of themselves. If we do not furnish them with homesteads, and hedge them around with protective laws; if we leave them to the legislation of their late masters, we had better have left them in bondage.

232. *The Reconstruction Amendments, 1865–70*

Thirteenth Amendment, passed by Congress, February 1, 1865; ratified December 18, 1865. Fourteenth Amendment passed by Congress June 16, 1866; ratified July 23, 1868. Fifteenth Amendment, passed by Congress, February 27, 1869; ratified March 30, 1870.

Article XIII

SECTION 1. Neither slavery nor involuntary servitude, except as punishment for crime whereof the party shall have been

duly convicted, shall exist within the United States, or any place subject to their jurisdiction.

SECTION 2. Congress shall have power

to enforce this article by appropriate legislation.

Article XIV

SECTION 1. All persons born or naturalized in the United States, and subject to the jurisdiction thereof, are citizens of the United States and of the state wherein they reside. No state shall make or enforce any law which shall abridge the privileges or immunities of citizens of the United States; nor shall any state deprive any person of life, liberty, or property, without due process of law; nor deny to any person within its jurisdiction the equal protection of the laws.

SECTION 2. Representatives shall be apportioned among the several states according to their respective numbers, counting the whole number of persons in each state, excluding Indians not taxed. But when the right to vote at any election for the choice of electors for President and Vice President of the United States, representatives in Congress, the executive and judicial officers of a state, or the members of the legislature thereof, is denied to any of the male inhabitants of such state, being twenty-one years of age, and citizens of the United States, or in any way abridged, except for participation in rebellion, or other crime, the basis of representation therein shall be reduced in the proportion which the number of such male citizens shall bear to the whole number of male citizens twenty-one years of age in such state.

SECTION 3. No person shall be a Senator or Representative in Congress, or elector of President and Vice President, or hold any office, civil or military, under the United States, or under any state, who having previously taken an oath, as a member of Congress, or as an officer of the United States, or as a member of any state legislature, or as an executive or judicial officer of any state, to support the Constitution of the United States, shall have engaged in insurrection or rebellion against the same, or given aid or comfort to the enemies thereof. But Congress may by a vote of two thirds of each House, remove such disability.

SECTION 4. The validity of the public debt of the United States, authorized by law, including debts incurred for payment of pensions and bounties for services in suppressing insurrection or rebellion, shall not be questioned. But neither the United States nor any state shall assume or pay any debt or obligation incurred in aid of insurrection or rebellion against the United States, or any claim for the loss or emancipation of any slave; but all such debts, obligations, and claims shall be held illegal and void.

SECTION 5. The Congress shall have power to enforce, by appropriate legislation, the provisions of this article.

Article XV

SECTION 1. The right of citizens of the United States to vote shall not be denied or abridged by the United States or by any state on account of race, color, or previous condition of servitude.

SECTION 2. The Congress shall have power to enforce this article by appropriate legislation.

233. *A Black Code, 1865*

Laws of Mississippi, 1865 (Jackson, 1866), 91–3.

ALL freedmen, free Negroes and mulattoes in this State, over the age of eighteen years, found on the second Monday in January, 1866, or thereafter, with no lawful employment or business, or found unlawfully assembling themselves together, either in the day or night time, and all white persons so assembling with freedmen, free Negroes or mulattoes, or usually associating with freedmen, free Negroes or mulattoes, on terms of equality, or living in adultery or fornication with a freedwoman, free Negro, or mulatto, shall be deemed vagrants, and on conviction thereof shall be fined in the sum of not exceeding, in the case of a freedman, free Negro or mulatto, fifty dollars, and a white man two hundred dollars, and imprisoned at the discretion of the court, the free Negro not exceeding ten days, and the white man not exceeding six months. . . .

And in case any freedman, free Negro or mulatto shall fail for five days after the imposition of any fine or forfeiture upon him or her for violation of any of the provisions of this act to pay the same, that it shall be . . . the duty of the sheriff of the proper county to hire out said freedman, free Negro or mulatto, to any person who will, for the shortest period of service, pay said fine and forfeiture and all costs: *Provided*, a preference shall be given to the employer, if there be one, in which case the employer shall be entitled to deduct and retain the amount so paid from the wages of such freedman, free Negro or mulatto, then due or to become due; and in case said freedman, free Negro, or mulatto cannot be hired out, he or she

may be dealt with as a pauper. . . .

The same duties and liabilities existing among white persons of this State shall attach to freedmen, free Negroes and mulattoes, to support their indigent families and all colored paupers; and that in order to secure a support for such indigent freedmen, free Negroes, and mulattoes, it shall be lawful and is hereby made the duty of the county police of each county in this State, to levy a poll or capitation tax on each and every freedman, free Negro, or mulatto, between the ages of eighteen and sixty years, not to exceed the sum of one dollar annually to each person so taxed, which tax . . . shall . . . constitute a fund to be called the Freedmen's Pauper Fund, which shall be applied by the commissioners of the poor for the maintenance of the poor of the freedmen, free Negroes, and mulattoes. . . .

If any freedman, free Negro, or mulatto shall fail or refuse to pay any tax levied according to the provisions of . . . this act, it shall be *prima facie* evidence of vagrancy, and it shall be the duty of the sheriff to arrest such freedman, free Negro, or mulatto or such person refusing or neglecting to pay such tax, and proceed at once to hire for the shortest time such delinquent taxpayer to any one who will pay the said tax, with accruing costs, giving preference to the employer, if there be one.

234. *After the War, 1870*

Recollections of Katie Rowe of Arkansas, in B. A. Botkin, *Lay My Burden Down* (Chicago, 1945), 116–17. Reprinted by permission of the University of Chicago Press. Copyright, 1945.

WHEN we git back to Monroe to the old place, us niggers git a big surprise. We didn't hear about it, but some Old Master's kinfolks back in Virginia done come out there and fix the place up and kept it for him while we in Colorado, and it

look 'bout as good as when we left it.

He cut it up in chunks and put us niggers out on it on the halves, but he had to sell part of it to git the money to git us mules and tools and food to run on. Then after while he had to sell some more, and he seem like he git old mighty fast.

Young Master been in the big battles in Virginia, and he git hit, and then he git sick, and when he come home he just like a old man he was so feeble.

About that time they was a lot of people coming into that country from the North, and they kept telling the niggers that the thing for them to do was to be free, and come and go where they please.

They try to git the darkies to go and vote, but none of us folks took much stock by what they say. Old Master tell us plenty time to mix in the politics when the young-uns git educated and know what to do.

Just the same he never mind iffen we go to the dances and the singing and such. He always lent us a wagon iffen we want to borry one to go in, too.

Some the niggers what work for the white folks from the North act pretty uppity and big, and come pestering round the dance places and try to talk up ructions amongst us, but it don't last long.

The Ku Kluckers start riding round at night, and they pass the word that the darkies got to have a pass to go and come and to stay at the dances. They have to git the pass from the white folks they work for, and passes writ from the Northern people wouldn't do no good. That the way the Kluckers keep the darkies in line.

The Kluckers just ride up to the dance ground and look at everybody's passes, and iffen some darky there without a pass or got a pass from the wrong man, they run him home, and iffen he talk big and won't go home they whup him and make him go.

Any nigger out on the road after dark liable to run across the Kluckers, and he better have a good pass! All the dances got to bust up at about 'leven o'clock, too.

One time I seen three-four Kluckers on hosses, all wrapped up in white, and they was making a black boy git home. They was riding hosses, and he was trotting down the road ahead of 'em. Ever' time he stop and start talking, they pop the whip at his heels, and he start trotting on. He was so mad he was crying, but he was gitting on down the road just the same.

I seen 'em coming, and I gits out my pass Young Master writ so I could show it, but when they ride by one in front just turns in his saddle and look back at t'other men and nod his head, and they just ride on by without stopping to see my pass. That man knowed me, I reckon. I looks to see iffen I knowed the hoss, but the Kluckers sometime swapped they hosses round amongst 'em, so the hoss maybe wasn't hisn.

They wasn't very bad 'cause the niggers round there wasn't bad, but I hear plenty of darkies git whupped in other places 'cause they act up and say they don't have to take off they hats in the white stores and such.

Any nigger that behave hisself and don't go running round late at night and drinking never had no trouble with the Kluckers.

PART FIVE

The Impact of Industrialization, 1870-1914

For a decade after Appomattox, the issues of the War continued to absorb the attention of Americans. How the seceded states were to be reconstructed, what the Negroes' status was to be, these were the questions that occupied men's attentions. Yet, already other events were overshadowing these problems.

In the next half century the energies of the United States were devoted to sustaining the transformation induced by the rapid industrialization of the nation's productive system and to adjusting its way of life to the new situation thus created.

Radical changes in manufacturing almost immediately revolutionized American industry. The primitive factories of an earlier era had little in common with the great establishments that now pre-empted the American scene. Everything, it seemed, combined to yield a favorable result. Immense natural resources of coal and iron, of copper and oil, were discovered and exploited. Railroads supplied an efficient transportation system. New machines turned by steam and electric power were more productive than ever before. An immense home market, protected by a tariff, absorbed the products of the new plants. Immigration supplied an inexhaustible source of labor, willing to work at almost any rate. And aggres-

sive entrepreneurs with abundant capital pushed their enterprises toward operations on an ever-expanding scale. Here, for the future, was the source of America's power.

This was also the source of immediate problems. The new concerns were
of a size never previously approached; and they raised crucial questions with regard to their relationship to government. In the struggle for advantage under a
ruthlessly competitive system, few men were scrupulous as to the means they used
to secure favorable rates of transportation or to establish advantageous positions
in the national market. The largest producers were capable of coercing their lesser
competitors through trusts and similar arrangements in order to regulate and control the conditions of production. As the scope of the industrial operations became
broader, such practices became more common and the position of the great corporations more threatening.

The defenders of the corporations justified them on the grounds of their
socially useful efficiency. But many Americans feared the effects of monopolies
upon their democracy and worried about the influence upon free government of
gigantic enterprises devoted to increasing the fortunes of a few rather than to
serving the many. Such fears created the antitrust movement, that culminated in
the series of efforts to subject corporations to the control of the state.

The rise of modern industry also created massive discontent within the
labor force. The old artisan groups were being pressed toward extinction under
the new conditions of production; and they united with similarly disaffected
groups in a national association, the Knights of Labor. Meanwhile, the craft
unions drew together in another form of organization from which the American
Federation of Labor developed. Both groups attracted skilled workers. The unskilled were left largely unorganized and susceptible to the leadership of various
radicals who from time to time attempted to mobilize their support. Desperation
frequently drove large groups of laborers to strikes and often to violence.

Part of that desperation came from the fact that the grievances of the
workingmen were social as well as economic. Relatively low incomes were the
more oppressive because the laborers were compelled to use them under the painful conditions of life created by the growing American cities. A rapid rise in numbers made it difficult to supply housing accommodations of any sort; large masses
of men were driven into the overcrowded slums. Under these conditions misery
thrived, and also disease, vice, and crime. Only the efforts of a handful of dedicated social workers did anything to assist those who suffered under such circumstances.

Industrialization affected also the farm. New mechanized techniques and
the further extension of settlement across the Great Plains transformed agricultural production and yielded an ever larger volume of commodities. To some extent, the growth of urban markets absorbed the rising stocks of farm products.
But prices fell steadily throughout these years, creating an angry wave of agricultural discontent. Discontent led the farmer on in the quest for the economic
panaceas of cheap money or government regulation. Sometimes it led him into
new political movements. And often it was accompanied by a kind of nostalgic
wish for the return of a simpler era.

The tendency to look backward was characteristic of many phases of American culture in these years. In the face of the growing complexity and ugliness of American life many men were disposed to idealize the purer, olden times. Their own culture seemed to suffer by contrast with that of earlier ages; and the effort to catch up, to accomplish too much at once, led to uncertainty and poverty of taste. Yet in some areas, as in architecture, the creative spirits of these years groped toward an authentic style that would adequately express the civilization within which they were located.

Most important, the problems of the period roused the social consciousness of many Americans. Some were disposed to acquiesce and to accept uncritically the standards of their society. But more characteristic was the recognition of the moral necessity for making choices among the diversified values of the national culture.

By the end of the century that consciousness was drawing men toward the progressive movement. This was by no means a consistent and coördinated party with a definable program of reforms. More properly, progressivism was a diffuse sentiment based on the belief that some profound change in attitudes was essential if society were to cope successfully with the problems of the new order. There was a growing certainty that great wealth was socially irresponsible and that the productive system, unsuperintended, failed to distribute an equitable share of the products of industry to everyone. Steadily, this sentiment built up toward a program for the reform of abuses and the regulation of the economy in the social interest.

This sentiment culminated in the election of 1912, when, to some degree, every candidate ran on what he claimed to be a progressive platform. The first years of Woodrow Wilson's administration were occupied with a program of reform, enunciated under the slogans of the "New Freedom." But the hopes embodied in these developments were cut short by the intrusion of the World War.

All this while, the United States had been involved in wider new areas of concern. Occasional efforts between the Civil War and the last decade of the century to extend American interests in the Caribbean had borne no fruit. But expansive ambitions were more effective when supported by the humanitarian impulses set in motion by the Cuban revolution. The Spanish-American War, begun to secure independence for Cuba, ended with the acquisition of a colonial empire.

Imperialism, thus thrust unexpectedly upon the United States, presented many challenging problems; and the decade after 1900 found Americans often perplexed by their new obligations. Yet the growing power of the nation had convinced many that it was now time to play a more vigorous and more positive role in world affairs. Events after 1914 would provide them with the opportunity.

XXVII 🦢 *The Rise of Modern Industry*

BY THE END of the nineteenth century even the old industries had been transformed by the necessities of large-scale production. The textile factories were now far removed from the simple plants of earlier days in Lowell (No. 235). The change was more dramatic still in the new industries such as steel or automobiles; large labor forces worked at complex machines to transform raw materials, drawn from every part of the country, into finished goods that would be sold in many parts of the world. The dramatic symbol of these changes was the technology which made them possible (No. 236).

The men most closely involved with the new industries regarded them as solely the product of their own ingenuity and enterprise. Adherence to the traditional virtues and a willingness to work hard led to success (No. 237). Or, it was explained, fortune came as the reward for labor, innovation, and technical improvement (No. 238). These personal qualities were certainly consequential, although the vehemence with which they were defended reflected also the desire to justify the incredible fortunes some men amassed.

But factors of another order were also involved. The plant which prospered was the one which had favorable connections with the railroads; in these years control of the railroad network was more than ever critical in the fate of each enterprise (No. 239). Few industries, moreover, escaped involvement in speculation, despite the warnings of Carnegie and Ford. The feverish hope for quick gains and the dangerous thrill of possible losses led many businessmen to the stock exchange (No. 240). And speculation made room for the figure of the promoter, whose activities acquired a far-reaching importance (No. 241). Many industries, sucked into the process of concentration through which the trusts gained power, became entangled in disturbing relationships with the government (*see below,* Section XXVIII).

235. *The Textile Company,* 1897

P. G. Hubert, Jr., "The Business of a Factory,"
Scribner's Magazine, XXI (1897), 307–30.

MOST of our cotton-mills and paper-mills are stock corporations, largely because of the vast capital needed. The larger the plant the cheaper the product, is an axiom in the cotton business, especially when staple goods, such as sheetings, are to be made. . . .

In the cotton industry it is fair to assume that in a mill making medium goods, $1,000 are invested in building, machinery, and stock for every workman employed, and that the yearly product will be worth $1,000. Of this $1,000 about $600 go for other purposes than labor, leaving $400 for labor and profits. At present any business attracts capital that offers six per cent net profit, with four per cent for a sinking fund or reserve for the maintenance of plant. Taking, therefore, $100 as the capitalist's share, there remains about $300 for labor, which is about the wages of a good female weaver. . . .

In the past good water-power has been of the chief importance in the selection of a mill site. . . . Steam, however, is rapidly replacing water-power, notwithstanding the improvements made in turbine wheels. In most of the older mills of New England steam now shares about equally the work with water, while in the new mills it takes almost the whole burden. . . .

Within the last few years . . . much has been said and written about the rise of the Southern cotton-mill depending wholly upon steam-power. The mill at last, it is said, has gone to the cotton, and the fall of the New England mills is only a question of time. Experts differ as to this. Some men with whom I have talked hold that the cotton manufacturing, and, in fact, all other kinds of manufacture, is only a temporary affair at the South, and this wholly for climatic reasons. Just now the poor whites, from which class the mill-hands of the Southern States are recruited, enjoy the novelty of steady work after generations of idleness, and are dazzled with the gew-gaws and finery they can purchase with the money earned. They work—and this is the sole real advantage enjoyed by Southern mills over their Northern competitors—for about one-third less wages than the same class of labor at the North, and submit to even longer hours. It is also common for two shifts, one for day and one for night, to be employed in Southern mills, thus getting double duty from the plant. . . .

In some parts of the country, natural gas has proved as much of an inducement as water-power, and in many western communities manufacturers are offered land, water-power, gas, exemption from taxes, etc., as inducements to come and establish plants.

When the margin of profit is so close as in any of the industries I have had occasion to mention—cotton, paper, shoes—apparently trifling things may mean success or failure. For instance, a girl who uses the left hand in adjusting a certain movement of the spindle instead of the right, does it, taking a thousand repetitions of the operation to make an average, about one-fifth of a second faster than the girl who uses the right hand. This seems an insignificant trifle, but multiply its effects by the million, in this particular trifle as well as others, and the mill in which the faster method is enforced will forge ahead of the one in which it is not. . . .

The business organization of most big factories is simple enough. Almost all cotton-mill properties are managed by a board of directors elected by the stockholders. These directors appoint officers, among whom the treasurer and the agent are the important personages, the first having charge of the finances, the buying of supplies, payment of expenses, and selling of goods; the second having the actual manufacture of the goods under his control. . . . The treasurer of most New England manufacturing corporations lives in Boston, where the goods are sold, and the agent lives near the mills. . . . The agent employs a head or superintendent for each of the important departments, such as the carding, roving, spinning, weaving, bleaching, printing, and packing. Under these superintendents there may be many or few foremen, according to the character of the work. In some departments where the work is all of the same character, each girl of the three hundred in a room doing precisely what her neighbor does, year in and year out, a few foremen suffice. In one room . . . eight hundred feet long by seventy feet wide, the girls who tend the spindles need small advice, and being paid by the product turned out from their machines, they need small supervision. In other departments, the print works, for instance, there are a variety of operations requiring comparatively few men, but a high grade of intelligence and constant supervision by expert foremen. . . .

At half-past six in the morning the bell rings for work to begin; there is an hour's intermission at noon, and then from one to six it goes on again. On Saturdays all work in most cotton-mills stops for the day at noon. The law limits factory work in Massachusetts to fifty-eight hours a week. In New York State there is no such limit. . . .

Next in importance, or perhaps even of more importance than the character of the hands, comes the character of the machinery in use. The entire machinery of a mill may be said to change every twenty years. . . . Nine-tenths of the machinery used in cotton and woolen manufacture, ninety-nine hundredths of that used in shoe making, and all of that used in paper-mills is made in this country. In cotton-mills we still use English carders, as the machines for cleaning the cotton from small imperfections are called. In return for their carders we have given the English the most important improvement made in cotton manufacture during this generation— the Rabbeth spindle, which makes ten thousand revolutions a minute, as against half that speed with the old-fashioned spindle. . . .

That the purchase of raw material for a big factory requires the services of a dozen experts may well be imagined, when the vast sums of money involved are considered. In one cotton-mill of New England there was used last year 25,000 bales of cotton, worth about $1,000,000, 8,000,-000 pounds of wool, 50,000 tons of coal, and $100,000 worth of coloring matter and dyes. It is hardly necessary to say that an expert at a liberal salary the year round is essential for each of these purchases. The cotton buyer spends his whole time in the South watching the growing crops, purchasing sometimes a year before the crop is grown, keeping an eye on the stock on hand in different parts of the country and calculating to a nicety exactly

what will be needed and when. . . . The same is true of the wool, and the coal buyer lives in the mining regions of Pennsylvania. The coloring matter used in printing a yard of calico that sells for ten cents costs less than the twentieth part of a cent, yet fortunes have been spent in recent years in efforts to reduce this cost. It is said that one mill-owner of Rhode Island spent $70,000 inside of three years in experiments to replace madder dyes, the experiments, by the way, leading to nothing valuable in the end. The chemist at one cotton-mill I have in mind, a modest man, who spends his time mixing colors and testing dyes in his laboratory, receives a salary of $5,000 a year. He has to know not only how to prepare the colors for the printers, but how to insure their permanency. "Will it wash?" is about the first question asked by every woman who examines a piece of calico on the dry-goods counter. The chemist is responsible for that. . . .

A factory having been put up in a suitable spot, equipped with proper machinery, and a force of competent hands engaged, the important question arises: What kind of goods shall be made? This is a question to be decided by the persons who sell the product of the mill—the selling agents. . . . The corporation seeks high and low for designs. . . . We can surpass the world at machinery, but as yet we have to go to Paris for our designs. Each of the big mills where printed goods are made keeps its man in Paris watching the new designs and buying the best he can from the professional designers, of which there are a hundred in Paris, some of them earning as high as $20,000 a year. . . .

The question is often asked: How do the men who make designs know what kind of goods the public is going to demand? The designs for next winter's goods are already finished. How does the artist know that the fickle public is not going to discard all that it has admired this year, and go wild over what it now ignores? . . . Well, the truth seems to be that sudden or violent as these fluctuations appear, there is really an evolutionary process involved. Each style or fashion has in it the germs of what is to follow, perhaps visible only to experts, but to be discerned. The designer accents the peculiar attributes of a pattern that has found favor one year in order to create his design for the next season. The short life of a design is somewhat surprising. Out of the six or eight hundred patterns made during this last year by the largest calico-mill in the country it is not likely that ten will be called for two years hence. The designs . . . for every class of goods have to be virtually new every year. . . . When times are hard and business dull the public, or the great caterers for the public, the retail shops, are more exacting than ever in demanding novelties. . . .

The element of chance thus enters more or less into any manufacture dependent upon changes of fashion. As the styles for summer have to be made in winter, and those for winter in summer, a manufacturer cannot wait to see what the public wants; he has to take his chances. . . . What he has made may or may not meet with favor. Fortunes are often made when fashion veers in favor of a particular style of goods. At one time a few years ago all the women suddenly wanted dresses made of bunting, which material, before that, had been used chiefly for flags; the mills equipped with machinery for making bunting were driven night and day, for the stock was soon exhausted, while manufacturers of ordinary dress goods looked on with envy. The demand for bunting ceased as suddenly as it arose. . . .

The demand for novelties, always novelties, imposes a constant expense and drain upon all manufacturing corporations, and yet it is the novelties that offer the greatest field for profit. Staple goods not affected by fashion must be sold almost at cost because every mill can make them, and the stocks of such goods on hand are always enormous. When orders are scarce and a mill agent hesitates about letting his hands go for fear that he may not be able to get the best of them back in time of need, the force may be used in turning out coarse staple goods, sure to find a market some day. But such work offers only a minimum margin of profit. One case of fancy goods that sell well brings in a larger profit than one hundred cases of some staple article that every mill in the country, North and South, can turn out. . . . Every year the mills of this country turn out from three to five thousand new designs, of which perhaps one thousand find a profitable sale.

A factory having produced a stock of goods from the best designs to be obtained by its agents here and abroad, the next step is to sell at a profit. Twenty-five years ago the mill or factory sold all its goods to the jobbers, who in turn distributed them to the retailers throughout the country. . . . Within the last ten or fifteen years the small jobber has been eliminated. In 1850 there were half a hundred dry-goods jobbers in New York City and as many in Boston, all doing a good business. Today the number has dwindled to half a dozen in each city. . . . The selling agents of the mills now go direct to the retailer, because the retailers have in many instances become buyers upon a much larger scale than the small jobber of former days. At certain seasons Boston and New York, twenty-five or thirty years ago, were overrun with the buyers of dry-goods houses from all parts of the country. There were hotels and even newspapers devoted to these buyers and their doings. Much of this business has passed away. Today the traveling men, "drummers," of the mills and the few large jobbing houses that have survived, scour the country, taking their samples to the retailer. . . . Some of the big department stores now obtain a monopoly of certain patterns or designs by taking the whole output of the mill, thus doing what was formerly in the power of only the greatest of jobbers. . . .

The search for a foreign outlet for American manufactures began more than half a century ago and still goes on. Every year some new market is discovered. Our old competitor, England, fights hard, but we can often beat her on her own ground. Everyone may know that we send our New England cotton cloth to the British colonies by the thousand cases, but it may be news to many that 25,000 American ploughs went to the Argentine Republic last year, and that the thousands of watches distributed to the Japanese army as rewards of bravery were made in this country. American trade-marks have always been and now are of exceptional value the world over.

236. *Recent Economic Changes, 1889*

D. A. Wells, *Recent Economic Changes* (New York, 1889), 27, 63–7.

MAN in general has attained to such a greater control over the forces of Nature, and has so compassed their use, that he has been able to do far more work in a given time, produce far more product, measured by quantity in ratio to a given amount of labor, and reduce the effort necessary to insure a comfortable subsistence in a far greater measure than it was possible for him to accomplish twenty or thirty years anterior to the time of the present writing (1889)....

Although the great natural labor-saving agencies had been recognized and brought into use many years prior to 1870, their powers were long kept ... in abeyance; because it required time for the ... methods, by which the world's work of production and distribution was carried on, to adjust themselves to new conditions; and until this was accomplished, an almost infinite number and variety of inventions ... were matters of promise rather than of consummation. But, with the extension of popular education and the rapid diffusion of intelligence, all new achievements in science and art have been brought in recent years so much more rapidly "within the sphere of the every-day activity of the people" ... "that stages of development which ages ago required centuries for their consummation, ... now complete themselves in years.". . .

Fifty years ago the "sciences" were little more than a mass of ill-digested facts or "unassorted laws," and ... in ... physics and chemistry comparatively little had been accomplished in the way of industrial application and direction. To say, indeed, what the world did not have half a century ago is almost equivalent to enumerating all those things which in their understanding, possession, and common use the world now regards as constituting the dividing lines between civilization and barbarism. Thus, fifty years ago the railroad and the locomotive were practically unknown. The ocean steam marine dates from 1838, when the *Sirius* and *Great Western* —the two pioneer vessels—crossed the Atlantic to New York. Electricity had then hardly got "beyond the stage of an elegant amusement," and the telegraph was not really brought into practical use before 1844. The following is a further partial list of the inventions, discoveries, and applications whose initial point of "being" is not only more recent than the half-century, but whose fuller or larger development in a majority of instances is also referable to a much more recent date: The mechanical reapers, mowing and seeding machines, the steam-plow and most other eminently labor-saving agricultural devices; the Bessemer process and the steel rail (1857); the submarine and transoceanic telegraph cables (1866); photography and all its adjuncts; electro-plating and the electro-type; the steam-hammer, repeating and breech-loading fire-arms, and rifled and steel cannon; gun-cotton and dynamite; the industrial use of India-rubber and gutta-percha; the steam-excavator and steam-drill; the sewing-machine; the practical use of the electric light; the application of dynamic electricity as a motor for machinery; the steam fire-engine; the telephone, microphone, spectroscope, and the process of spectral analysis; the polariscope; the compound steam-engine; the centrifugal process of refining sugar; the rotary printing-press; hydraulic lifts, cranes, and elevators; the "regenerative" furnace, iron and steel ships, pressed glass, wire rope, petroleum and its derivatives, and analine dyes; the industrial use of the metal nickel, cotton-seed oil, artificial butter, stearine-candles, natural gas, cheap postage, and the postage-stamp. Electricity, which a very few years ago was regraded as something wholly immaterial, has now acquired a sufficiently objective existence to admit of being manufactured and sold the same as pig-iron or leather....

It will be interesting also here to call attention to some of the agencies productive of further extensive economic changes which are now in the process of development, or which are confidently predicted as certain to occur in the not very remote future.

Thus ... the steam-engine ... as a machine ... is most imperfect, inasmuch as the very best steam-engines only utilize about one sixth of the power (work) which resides in the fuel ... consumed in the generation of steam. The entire displacement of the steam-engine as it now exists is, therefore, not only essential to

further great material progress, but is confidently expected to happen at no very distant period by those eminently qualified to express an opinion on this subject. ...

The rapidity with which electric motors for stationary power are supplanting the steam-engine should not be overlooked. Thus, in the United States alone it is estimated that between seven thousand and eight thousand such motors for driving machinery were in operation at the close of the year 1888. Notwithstanding, furthermore, the present wide utilization of telegraphy and the telephone as a means of annihilating time and space, ... both of these instrumentalities are really in their infancy, and ... before the commencement of the twentieth century ... the business and social correspondence of the people of every highly civilized country will be mainly transacted upon an electric basis. ...

Speaking generally, moreover, there is no reason for doubting that the wonderful material evolution of recent years will be continued, unless man himself interposes obstacles, although the goal to which this evolution tends can not be predicted or possibly imagined. "The deeper the insight we obtain into the mysterious workings of Nature's forces," says Werner Siemens, ... "the more we are convinced that we are still standing only in the vestibule of science, that an immeasurable field still lies before us, and that it is very questionable whether mankind will ever arrive at a full knowledge of nature."

237. *How to Succeed, 1880's*

Andrew Carnegie, *Autobiography* (New York, 1924), 122–3, 131–2, 152–4.

THE Keystone Bridge Works have always been a source of satisfaction to me. Almost every concern that had undertaken to erect iron bridges in America had failed. Many of the structures themselves had fallen and

some of the worst railway disasters in America had been caused in that way. ... But nothing has ever happened to a Keystone Bridge. ... There has been no luck about it. We used only the best material and enough of it, making our own iron and later our own steel. We were our own severest inspectors, and would build a safe structure or none at all. . . . Any piece of work bearing the stamp of the Keystone Bridge Works (and there are few states in the Union where such are not to be found) we were prepared to underwrite. . . .

This policy is the true secret of success. Uphill work it will be for a few years until your work is proven, but after that it is smooth sailing. Instead of objecting to inspectors they should be welcomed by all manufacturing establishments. A high standard of excellence is easily maintained, and men are educated in the effort to reach excellence. I have never known a concern to make a decided success that did not do good, honest work, and even in these days of the fiercest competition, when everything would seem to be matter of price, there lies still at the root of great business success the very much more important factor of quality. The effect of attention to quality, upon every man in the service, from the president of the concern down to the humblest laborer, cannot be overestimated. And bearing on the same question, clean, fine workshops and tools, well-kept yards and surroundings are of much greater importance than is usually supposed. . . .

One day [Henry Phipps] . . . asked his brother John to lend him a quarter of a dollar. John saw that he had important use for it and handed him the shining quarter without inquiry. Next morning an advertisement appeared in the "Pittsburgh Dispatch":

"A willing boy wishes work."

This was the use the energetic and willing Harry had made of his quarter, probably the first quarter he had ever spent at one time in his life. A response came from the well-known firm of Dilworth and Bidwell. They asked the "willing boy" to call. Harry went and obtained a position as errand boy, and as was then the custom, his first duty every morning was to sweep the office. He went to his parents and obtained their consent, and in this way the young lad launched himself upon the sea of business. There was no holding back a boy like that. It was the old story. He soon became indispensable to his employers, obtained a small interest in a collateral branch of their business; and then, ever on the alert, it was not many years before he attracted the attention of Mr. Miller, who made a small investment for him with Andrew Kloman. That finally resulted in the building of the iron mill in Twenty-ninth Street. . . . The errand boy is now one of the richest men in the United States. . . .

I have never bought or sold a share of stock speculatively in my life, except one small lot of Pennsylvania Railroad shares that I bought early in life for investment and for which I did not pay at the time because bankers offered to carry it for me at a low rate. I have adhered to the rule never to purchase what I did not pay for, and never to sell what I did not own. In those early days, however, I had several interests that were taken over in the course of business. They included some stocks and securities that were quoted on the New York Stock Exchange, and I found that when I opened my paper in the morning I was tempted to look first at the quotations of the stock market. As I had determined to sell all my interests in every outside concern and concentrate my attention upon our manufacturing concerns in Pittsburgh, I further resolved not even to own any stock that was bought and sold upon any stock exchange. With the exception of trifling amounts which came to me in various ways I have adhered strictly to this rule.

Such a course should commend itself to every man in the manufacturing business and to all professional men. For the manufacturing man especially the rule would seem all-important. His mind must be kept calm and free if he is to decide wisely the problems which are continually coming before him. Nothing tells in the long run like good judgment, and no sound judgment can remain with the man whose mind is disturbed by the mercurial changes of the Stock Exchange. . . . Speculation is a parasite feeding upon values, creating none.

238. *Technological Innovation, 1908*

Henry Ford, *My Life and Work* (New York, 1922), 16–17, 71–5, 79–81. Copyright 1922 Doubleday & Company, renewed 1949 by Mary Owens Crowther, reprinted by permission of Doubleday & Company, Inc.

An "improved" product is one that has been changed. That is not my idea. I do not believe in starting to make until I have discovered the best possible thing. This, of course, does not mean that a product should never be changed, but I think that it will be found more economical in the end not even to try to produce an article until you have fully satisfied yourself that utility, design, and material are the best. . . . The place to start manufacturing is with the article. The factory, the organization, the selling, and the financial plans will shape themselves to the article. . . . Rushing into manufacturing without being certain of the product is the unrecognized cause of many business failures. People seem to think that the big thing is the factory or the store or the financial backing or the management. The big thing is the product, and any hurry in getting into fabrication before designs are completed is just so much waste time. I spent twelve years before I had a Model T—which is what is known today as the Ford car— that suited me. We did not attempt to go into real production until we had a real product. That product has not been essentially changed. . . .

Our big changes have been in methods of manufacturing. They never stand still. I believe that there is hardly a single operation in the making of our car that is the same as when we made our first car of the present model. That is why we make them so cheaply. . . .

During the season 1908–1909 we continued to make Models "R" and "S", four-cylinder runabouts and roadsters, the models that had previously been so successful, and which sold at $700 and $750. But "Model T" swept them right out. We sold 10,607 cars—a larger number than any manufacturer had ever sold. The price for the touring car was $850. On the same chassis we mounted a town car at $1,000, a roadster at $825, a coupé at $950, and a landaulet at $950.

This season demonstrated conclusively to me that it was time to put the new policy in force. . . . Therefore in 1909 I announced one morning, without any previous warning, that in the future we were going to build only one model, that the model was going to be "Model T," and that the chassis would be exactly the same for all cars, and I remarked:

"Any customer can have a car painted any color that he wants so long as it is black."

I cannot say that any one agreed with me. The selling people could not of course see the advantages that a single model would bring about in production. More than that, they did not particularly care. They thought that our production was good enough as it was and there was a very decided opinion that lowering the sales price would hurt sales, that the people who wanted quality would be driven away and that there would be none to replace them. There was very little conception of the motor industry. A motor car was still regarded as something in the way of a luxury. The manufacturers did a good deal to spread this idea. Some clever persons invented the name "pleasure car" and the advertising emphasized the pleasure features. The sales people had ground for their objections and particularly when I made the following announcement:

> I will build a motor car for the great multitude. It will be large enough for the family but small enough for the individual to run and care for. It will be constructed of the best materials, by the best men to be hired, after the simplest designs that modern engineering can devise. But it will be so low in price that no man making a good salary will be unable to own one—and enjoy with his family the blessing of hours of pleasure in God's great open spaces.

This announcement was received not without pleasure. The general comment was: "If Ford does that he will be out of business in six months."

The impression was that a good car could not be built at a low price, and that, anyhow, there was no use in building a low-priced car because only wealthy people were in the market for cars. The 1908–1909 sales of more than ten thousand cars had convinced me that we needed a new factory. We already had a big modern factory—the Piquette Street plant. It was as good as, perhaps a little better than, any automobile factory in the country. But I did not see how it was going to care for the sales and production that were inevitable. So I bought sixty acres at Highland Park, which was then considered away out in the country from Detroit. The amount of ground bought and the plans for a bigger factory than the world has ever seen were opposed. The question was already being asked: "How soon will Ford blow up?"

Nobody knows how many thousand times it has been asked since. It is asked only because of the failure to grasp that a principle rather than an individual is at work, and the principle is so simple that it seems mysterious. . . .

We were, almost overnight it seems, in great production. How did all this come about?

Simply through the application of an inevitable principle. By the application of intelligently directed power and machinery. In a little dark shop on a side street an old man had labored for years making axe handles. Out of seasoned hickory he fashioned them, with the help of a draw shave, a chisel, and a supply of sandpaper. Carefully was each handle weighed and balanced. No two of them were alike. The curve must exactly fit the hand and must conform to the grain of the wood. From dawn until dark the old man labored. His average product was eight handles a week, for which he received a dollar and a half each. And often some of these were unsaleable—because the balance was not true.

Today you can buy a better axe handle, made by machinery, for a few cents. And you need not worry about the balance. They are all alike—and every one is perfect. Modern methods applied in a big way have not only brought the cost of axe handles down to a fraction of their former cost—but they have immensely improved the product.

It was the application of these same methods to the making of the Ford car that at the very start lowered the price and heightened the quality. We just developed an idea. The nucleus of a business may be an idea. That is, an inventor or a thoughtful workman works out a new and better way to serve some established human need; the idea commends itself, and people want to avail themselves of it. In this way a single individual may prove, through his idea or discovery, the nucleus of a business. But the creation of the body and bulk of that business is shared by everyone who has anything to do with it. No manufacturer can say: "I built this business"—if he has required the help of thousands of men in building it. It is a joint production. Everyone employed in it has contributed something to it. By working and producing they make it possible for the purchasing world to keep coming to that business for the type of service it provides, and thus they help establish a custom, a trade, a habit which supplies them with a livelihood. That is the way our company grew. . . .

A Ford car contains about five thousand parts—that is counting screws, nuts, and all. Some of the parts are fairly bulky and others are almost the size of watch parts. In our first assembling we simply started to put a car together at a spot on the floor and workmen brought to it the parts as they were needed in exactly the same way that one builds a house. When we started to make parts it was natural to create a single department of the factory to make that part, but usually one workman performed all of the operations necessary on a small part. The rapid press of production made it necessary to devise plans of production that would avoid having the workers falling over one another. . . .

The first step forward in assembly came when we began taking the work to the men instead of the men to the work. We now have two general principles in all operations—that a man shall never have to take more than one step, if possibly it can be avoided, and that no man need ever stoop over.

The principles of assembly are these:

(1) Place the tools and the men in the sequence of the operation so that each component part shall travel the least possible distance while in the process of finishing.

(2) Use work slides or some other form of carrier so that when a workman completes his operation, he drops the part always in the same place—which place must always be the most convenient place to his hand—and if possible have gravity carry the part to the next workman for his operation.

(3) Use sliding assembling lines by which the parts to be assembled are delivered at convenient distances.

The net result of the application of these principles is the reduction of the necessity for thought on the part of the worker and the reduction of his movements to a minimum. He does as nearly as possible only one thing with only one movement. . . .

Along about April 1, 1913, we first tried the experiment of an assembly line. We tried it on assembling the fly-wheel magneto. We try everything in a little way first—we will rip out anything once we discover a better way, but we have to know absolutely that the new way is going to be better than the old before we do anything drastic.

I believe that this was the first moving line ever installed. The idea came in a general way from the overhead trolley that the Chicago packers use in dressing beef. We had previously assembled the fly-wheel magneto in the usual method. With one workman doing a complete job he could turn out from thirty-five to forty pieces in a nine-hour day, or about twenty minutes to an assembly. What he did alone was then spread into twenty-nine operations; that cut down the assembly time to thirteen minutes, ten seconds. Then we raised the height of the line eight inches—this was in 1914—and cut the time to seven minutes. Further experimenting with the speed that the work should move at cut the time down to five minutes. In short, the result in this: by the aid of scientific study one man is now able to do somewhat more than four did only a comparatively few years ago. That line established the efficiency of the method and we now use it everywhere. The assembling of the motor, formerly done by one man, is now divided into eighty-four operations—those men do the work that three times their number formerly did.

239. *Railroad Rates, 1905*

R. S. Baker, "The Railroad Rate," *McClure's Magazine*, XXVI (1905), 59.

THE RAILROAD is, indeed, the essential tool of industry throughout the world. It is the regulator of business. It holds the scales of destiny. It decides where cities shall be located, and how fast they shall grow, it marks out in no small degree the wheat and corn areas, it sets boundaries for the business of the coal miners of Illinois as against those of Pennsylvania, it marks definitely how far the lumber of Washington shall go, it decides whether flour shall be manufactured in Minneapolis or Buffalo, and whether the chief export business in grain shall be done at the port of New York or the port of New Orleans.

And the great fact arising out of these conditions . . . is that . . . the control of the very instrument of business destiny is in the hands of a comparatively few private citizens who are handling the tool not to build up the nation properly, not to do real justice as between Chicago and New York, or between Rockefeller and the independent refiner, or between wheat and flour, not to make the rate-system simple and time-saving, but to fill their own pockets in as short a time as possible. Hill says that the State of Washington shall grow, Tuttle says that Pittsburgh shall not grow, the Western railroads say that Chicago and Kansas City shall butcher the beef, the Eastern roads allow Rockefeller to dominate the oil industry and become dangerously rich. It is terrible power to place in the hands of a few men—fewer every year—about ten men, now, sitting in Wall Street. . . .

When a shipper or a citizen who thinks he is wronged attempts to get relief, he must submit his case, not to an impartial tribunal, but to his adversary in the case. What justice can be hoped for? He is poor, he does not understand railroad condi-

tions, he does not dare, single-handed, to make a fight for the whole community and take the chance of earning the further enmity of the railroad; his adversary is rich, employs the best legal talent, is entrenched in power. Out of hopelessness of justice has arisen the present widespread demand, voiced by President Roosevelt, for some tribunal which is at once impartial and powerful enough to do justice as between the railroad and the citizen. The people have asked that the government, through the Interstate Commerce Commission, be made such a tribunal, in other words, that in case of dispute over a rate, the government of the United States shall say, once for all, what is right and reasonable. They believe that such great power is better in the hands of the government than in the hands of individuals. This demand the railroad owners are opposing with all the ability, legal acumen, money power, and political influence that they can command.

The plea of the men who control the railroads is that everything now is as good as it can possibly be, that there are no rules governing rate-making, and that there cannot be; that the present laws are amply sufficient. But I take it as fundamental in rate-making as in every other human activity, that there are orderly principles to be discovered and justice-making laws to be laid down. No sensible person, surely, who beholds the utter chaos, the injustice and immorality of the present system, will assert that this is the best we can do for ourselves! And the magnitude of the task . . . should pique our enthusiasm and inspire our energy, rather than crush us to weak submission. No greater, no more fundamental work than this now lies ready to our hands. It is not only weak but absurd to assert that the American cannot rise to it. And in solving his own problems, he will establish new principles for the world.

240. *The Wheat Pit,* 1900

Frank Norris, *A Deal in Wheat* (New York, 1903). As reprinted in *Works* (Will Irwin, ed.; New York, 1928), IV, 176–8. Copyright 1903 by Doubleday & Company, Inc.

JUST as Going mounted the steps on the edge of the pit the great gong struck, a roar of a hundred voices developed with the swiftness of successive explosions, the rush of a hundred men surging downward to the center of the pit filled the air with the stamp and grind of feet, a hundred hands in eager strenuous gestures tossed upward from out the brown of the crowd, the official reporter in his cage on the margin of the pit leaned far forward with straining ear to catch the opening bid, and another day of battle was begun.

Since the sale of the hundred thousand bushels of wheat to Truslow the "Hornung crowd" had steadily shouldered the price higher until on this particular morning it stood at one dollar and a half. That was Hornung's price. No one else had any grain to sell.

But not ten minutes after the opening, Going was surprised out of all countenance to hear shouted from the other side of the pit these words:

"Sell May at one-fifty."

Going was for the moment touching elbows with Kimbark on one side and with Merriam on the other, all three belonging to the "Hornung crowd." Their answering challenge of "*Sold*" was as the voice of one man. They did not pause to reflect upon the strangeness of the circumstance. (That was for afterward.) Their response to the offer was as unconscious as reflex action and almost as rapid, and before the pit was well aware of what had happened the transaction of one thousand bushels was down upon Going's trading-card and fifteen hundred dollars had changed hands. But here was a marvel—the whole available supply of wheat cornered, Hornung master of the situation, invincible, unassailable; yet behold a man willing to sell, a Bear bold enough to raise his head.

"That was Kennedy, wasn't it, who made that offer?" asked Kimbark, as Going noted down the trade—"Kennedy, that new man?"

"Yes; who do you suppose he's selling for; who's willing to go short at this stage of the game?"

"Maybe he ain't short."

"Short! Great heavens, man; where'd he get the stuff?"

"Blamed if I know. We can account for every handful of May! Steady! Oh, there he goes again."

"Sell a thousand May at one-fifty," vociferated the bear-broker, throwing out his hand, one finger raised to indicate the number of "contracts" offered. This time it was evident that he was attacking the Hornung crowd deliberately, for, ignoring the jam of traders that swept toward him, he looked across the pit to where Going and Kimbark were shouting "*Sold! Sold!*" and nodded his head.

A second time Going made memoranda of the trade, and either the Hornung holdings were increased by two thousand bushels of May wheat or the Hornung bank account swelled by at least three thousand dollars of some unknown short's money.

Of late—so sure was the bull crowd of its position—no one had even thought of glancing at the inspection sheet on the bulletin board. But now one of Going's messengers hurried up to him with the announcement that this sheet showed receipts at Chicago for that morning of twenty-five thousand bushels, and not credited to Hornung. Someone had got hold of a line of wheat overlooked by the "clique" and was dumping it upon them.

"Wire the Chief," said Going over his shoulder to Merriam. This one struggled out of the crowd, and on a telegraph blank scribbled:

"Strong bear movement—New man— Kennedy—Selling in lots of five contracts —Chicago receipts twenty-five thousand."

The message was dispatched, and in a few moments the answer came back, laconic, of military terseness.

"Support the market."

And Going obeyed, Merriam and Kimbark following, the new broker fairly throwing the wheat at them in thousand-bushel lots.

"Sell May at 'fifty; sell May; sell May." A moment's indecision, an instant's hesitation, the first faint suggestion of weakness, and the market would have broken under

them. But for the better part of four hours they stood their ground, taking all that was offered, in constant communication with the Chief, and from time to time stimulated and steadied by his brief, unvarying command:

"Support the market."

At the close of the session they had bought in the twenty-five thousand bushels of May. Hornung's position was as stable as a rock, and the price closed even with the opening figure—one dollar and a half.

But the morning's work was the talk of all La Salle Street. Who was back of that raid? What was the meaning of this unexpected selling? For weeks the pit trading had been merely nominal. Truslow, the Great Bear, from whom the most serious attack might have been expected, had gone to his country seat at Geneva Lake, in Wisconsin, declaring himself to be out of the market entirely. He went bass-fishing every day.

241. *The Promoter,* 1900

A. D. Noyes, *Forty Years of American Finance* (New York, 1909), 286–90, 294–6.

THE PROSPEROUS trade, abundant capital, and overflowing confidence which prevailed in 1899 had created a new situation. The promoter—a name which now grew suddenly familiar on all American markets—asked the owners of a dozen or more competing plants, in a given industry, to name a selling price. Naturally, as their own retirement from business was involved, the price the owners fixed was high. A banking syndicate would be formed, however, to provide the money requisite for the purchase, and for a handsome payment to the middleman. Thus acquired, the manufacturing plants would be combined and incorporated under the name American Milling Company or United States Spinning Company or In-

ternational Weaving Company, and the stock would be offered to the public.

As it turned out and as the bankers had expected, the public was in exactly the mood to respond to the invitation. The shares were readily absorbed; other combinations followed. Still, the investment fund showed no symptom of exhaustion. Presently the more venturesome spirits among promoters began to combine these already large industrial combinations into a single company, and to sell the stock of that, at inflated valuations, to the public. This would have been a step too far, but for the fact that profits of manufacture, notably in the steel and iron trade, went on increasing faster than promoters could turn their expectations into stock.

One conspicuous expert in this business, who rose from the sphere of traveling salesman of a wire-making firm to the leadership of a great combination in the steel trade, was asked on the witness-stand, in March, 1902, to describe the history of his amalgamations. They began, he said, by the combination of seven wire factories in Illinois into one corporation, which was called the Consolidated Steel and Wire Company. Two months later this company was bought up, along with seven more mills, by the American Steel and Wire Company of Illinois, which issued $24,000,000 stock. This was in 1898. Early in 1899 he organized the American Steel and Wire Company of New Jersey, which paid $33,600,000 for the Illinois Company's $24,000,000 stock, added eleven other wire plants, and issued its own stock in the comfortable sum of $90,000,000. The witness was asked what had become of $26,000,000 stock whose destination was not accounted for, and said he did not know. One might possibly imagine that this wholesale "watering" of capital would at least have led the investing public to bid a low price for the inflated stock; but it did not. Of the $90,-000,000 stock thus issued in the above-described "watering" process, $40,000,000 was preferred as to dividend. It started out on the Stock Exchange at $94 per share, rose in two months to $106, and sold at $112 a year or two afterwards. The $50,000,000 common stock, all of which was virtually given away as a bonus in the "deal," started at $45 per share, and in two months actually rose to $92. . . .

The climax of this great speculation came from a peculiar cause. . . .

What actually was happening was this. People connected with one corporation would borrow large sums of money, and use that money to buy up shares of another subsidiary or competing corporation. They were buying, however, not for themselves, but for the company with which they were identified; and their purpose was, as soon as the property had been obtained, to hand it over, issue new stock or bonds of their own corporation, sell such securities to the public, and use the proceeds to reimburse themselves, with a handsome bonus. There was the famous case, for instance, of the Chicago, Burlington & Quincy Railway. This company's stock, amounting to $110,000,000, sold at the end of 1900 for $144 per share, which was considered by most people rather high. People identified with the Northern Pacific Railway bought up the stock at a seemingly reckless rate, pushed its price above $180, and then announced that a bond would be issued by the Northern Pacific and Great Northern Companies to pay $200 a share for the whole of the Burlington stock. These bonds were later sold on the open market, the result, of course, being that the supply of securities on the market was increased by some $50,000,000.

XXVIII ✎ *The Trusts and Their Critics*

A TRUST was a legal device for unifying the operations of a number of separate and competing companies. The classic example had been formed by John D. Rockefeller to eliminate competition among the refiners of oil. But the term was also more generally used to describe a complex of practices by which large corporations established sufficient control over the market to eliminate or minimize competition. In that more general sense the trust became a political and social issue; for it raised the question of what attitude the government should take in the face of the accumulation of enormous power in the hands of private individuals and organizations.

The defenders of the trusts argued that the device was socially desirable since it eliminated inefficient practices (No. 242). Some critics, on the other hand, insisted that the trusts' power was illegally derived; and that even if they were more efficient than small enterprise, they ought to be strictly controlled by the state (No. 243). Others pointed to serious abuses that grew out of the concentration of wealth and corporate control in relatively few hands (No. 244). Still others denied altogether that the trusts were really more efficient than small-scale enterprise (No. 245). Meanwhile, the trusts had become political scapegoats, to which was attached the blame for financial stringency and indeed for all the ills of the economy (No. 246).

The debate stimulated the demand for the control of corporate enterprise. The earliest agitation was for state regulation of railroad rates. The laws to that effect were upheld in a decision of the federal Supreme Court which recognized the general power of government to act in this sphere (No. 247). The federal government assumed a primary role in this regard as the interstate character of American business became more pronounced. Demand for action on the trusts finally led to the enactment of the Sherman Act, which defined any conspiracy to effect a monopoly in restraint of trade as a crime (No. 248). Prosecutions under the act were lax for some years, but ultimately the best known of the trusts, Standard Oil of New Jersey, was brought to trial. The decision in its case established an influential distinction between reasonable and unreasonable combinations (No. 249). Nevertheless, three years later a variety of new abuses provoked further regulation in the Clayton Act (No. 250).

242. *The Efficiency of Concentration,* 1899

J. D. Rockefeller, testimony, December 30, 1899, *Report of the United States Industrial Commission,* I, 796–7.

Q. To what advantages, or favors, or methods of management do you ascribe chiefly the success of the Standard Oil Company?—A. I ascribe the success of the Standard to its consistent policy to make the volume of its business large through the merits and cheapness of its products. It has spared no expense in finding, securing, and utilizing the best and cheapest methods of manufacture. It has sought for the best superintendents and workmen and paid the best wages. It has not hesitated to sacrifice old ma-chinery and old plants for new and better ones. It has placed its manufactories at the points where they could supply markets at the least expense. It has not only sought markets for its principal products, but for all possible by-products, sparing no expense in introducing them to the public. It has not hesitated to invest millions of dollars in methods of cheapening the gathering and distribution of oils by pipe lines, special cars, tank steamers, and tank wagons. It has erected tank stations at every important railroad station to cheapen the storage and delivery of its products. It has spared no expense in forcing its products into the markets of the world among people civilized and uncivilized. It has had faith in American oil, and has brought together millions of money for the purpose of making it what it is, and holding its markets against the competition of Russia and all the many countries which are producers of oil. . . .

Q. What are, in your judgment, the chief advantages from industrial combinations —(a) financially to stockholders; (b) to the public?—A. All the advantages which can be derived from a cooperation of persons and aggregation of capital. Much that one man cannot do alone two can do together, and once admit the fact that cooperation, or, what is the same thing, combination, is necessary on a small scale, the limit depends solely upon the necessities of business. Two persons in partnership may be a sufficiently large combination for a small business, but if the business grows or can be made to grow, more persons and more capital must be taken in. The business may grow so large that a partnership ceases to be a proper instrumentality for its purposes, and then a corporation becomes a necessity. . . . Our Federal form of government, making every corporation created by a state foreign to every other state, renders it necessary for persons doing business through corporate agency to organize corporations in some or many of the different states in which their business is located. Instead of doing business through the agency of one corporation they must do business through the agencies of several corporations. If the business is extended to foreign countries, and Americans are not today satisfied with home markets alone, it will be found helpful and possibly necessary to organize corporations in such countries, for Europeans are prejudiced against foreign corporations as are the people of many of our states. These different corporations thus become cooperating agencies in the same business and are held together by common ownership of their stocks.

It is too late to argue about advantages of industrial combinations. They are a necessity. And if Americans are to have the privilege of extending their business in all the states of the Union, and into foreign countries as well, they are a necessity on a large scale, and require the agency of more than one corporation. Their chief advantages are:

(1) Command of necessary capital.
(2) Extension of limits of business.
(3) Increase of number of persons interested in the business.
(4) Economy in the business.
(5) Improvements and economies which are derived from knowledge of many interested persons of wide experience.
(6) Power to give the public improved products at less prices and still make a profit for stockholders.
(7) Permanent work and good wages for laborers.

I speak from my experience in the business with which I have been intimately connected for about forty years. Our first combination was a partnership and afterward a corporation in Ohio. That was sufficient for a local refining business. But dependent solely upon local business we should have failed years ago. We were forced to extend our markets and to seek for export trade. This latter made the seaboard cities a necessary place of business, and we soon discovered that manufacturing for export could be more economically carried on at the seaboard, hence refineries at Brooklyn, at Bayonne, at Philadelphia, and necessary corporations in New York, New Jersey, and Pennsylvania.

We soon discovered as the business grew that the primary method of transporting oil in barrels could not last. The package often cost more than the contents, and the forests of the country were not sufficient to supply the necessary material for an extended length of time. Hence we . . . adopted the pipe-line system, and found capital for pipe-line construction equal to the necessities of the business.

To operate pipe-lines required franchises from the states in which they were located, and consequently corporations in those states, just as railroads running through different states are forced to operate under separate state charters. To perfect the pipe-line system of transportation required in the neighborhood of $50,000,000 of capital. This could not be obtained or maintained without industrial combination. The entire oil business is dependent upon its pipe-line system. Without it every well would shut down and every foreign market would be closed to us.

The pipe-line system required other improvements, such as tank cars upon railways, and finally the tank steamer. Capital had to be furnished for them and corporations created to own and operate them.

Every step taken was necessary in the business if it was to be properly developed, and only through such successive steps and by such an industrial combination is America today enabled to utilize the bounty which its land pours forth, and to furnish the world with the best and cheapest light ever known, receiving in return therefor from foreign lands nearly $50,000,000 per year, most of which is distributed in payment of American labor.

I have given a picture rather than a detail of the growth of one industrial combination. It is a pioneer, and its work has been of incalculable value. There are other American products besides oil for which the markets of the world can be opened, and legislators will be blind to our best industrial interests if they unduly hinder by legislation the combination of persons and capital requisite for the attainment of so desirable an end.

243. *Lords of Industry, 1884*

H. D. Lloyd, "Lords of Industry," *North American Review*, CXXXVIII (June, 1884), 550–3.

ON THE theory of "too much of everything" our industries, from railroads to workingmen, are being organized to prevent milk, nails, lumber, freights, labor, soothing syrup, and all these other things, from becoming too cheap. The majority have never yet been able to buy enough of anything. The minority have too much of everything to sell. Seeds of social trouble germinate fast in such conditions. Society is letting these combinations become institutions without compelling them to adjust their charges to the cost of production, which used to be the universal rule of price. Our laws and commissions to regulate the railroads are but toddling steps in a path in which we need to walk like men. The change from competition to combination is nothing less than one of those revolutions which march through

history with giant strides. It is not likely that this revolution will go backward. . . .

Man, the only animal which forgets, has already in a century or two forgotten that the freedom, the independence of his group, of the state and even of the family, which he has enjoyed for a brief interval, have been unknown in most of the history of our race, and in all the history of most races. The livery companies of London, with their gloomy guildhalls, their wealth, their gluttony and wine-bibbing, their wretched Irish estates, exist today vain reminders to us of a time when the entire industry of Europe was regimented into organizations, voluntary at first, afterward adopted by the law, which did what our pools of railroads, laborers, manufacturers, and others are trying to do. . . .

Those were not exceptional times. Our

day of free competition and free contract has been the exceptional era in history. Explorer, pioneer, protestant, reformer, captain of industry could not move in the harness of the guild brother, the vassal, the monk, and were allowed to throw away mediaeval uniforms. But now "the individual withers; the world is more and more." Society having let the individual overrun the new worlds to be conquered, is reestablishing its lines of communication with him. Literary theorists still repeat the cant of individualism in law, politics, and morals; but the world of affairs is gladly accepting, in lieu of the liberty of each to do as he will with his own, all it can get of the liberty given by laws that let no one do as he might with his own. . . . A rope cannot be made of sand; a society cannot be made of competitive units.

We have given competition its own way, and have found that we are not good enough or wise enough to be trusted with this power of ruining ourselves in the attempt to ruin others. Free competition could be let run only in a community where everyone had learned to say and act "I am the state." We have had an era of material inventions. We now need a renaissance of moral inventions, contrivances to tap the vast currents of moral magnetism flowing uncaught over the face of society. Morals and values rise and fall together. If our combinations have no morals, they can have no values. If the tendency to combination is irresistible, control of it is imperative. Monopoly and anti-monopoly, odious as these words have become to the literary ear, represent the two great tendencies of our time: monopoly, the tendency to combination; anti-monopoly, the demand for social control of it. As the man is bent toward business or patriotism, he will negotiate combinations or agitate for laws to regulate them. The first is capitalistic, the second is social. The first, industrial; the second, moral. The first promotes wealth; the second, citizenship. These combinations are not to be waved away as fresh pictures of folly or total depravity. There is something in them deeper than that. . . .

Our young men can no longer go west; they must go up or down. Not new land, but new virtue must be the outlet for the future. Our halt at the shores of the Pacific is a much more serious affair than that which brought our ancestors to a pause before the barriers of the Atlantic, and compelled them to practice living together for a few hundred years. We cannot hereafter, as in the past, recover freedom by going to the prairies; we must find it in the society of the good. In the presence of great combinations, in all departments of life, the moralist and patriot have work to do of a significance never before approached during the itinerant phases of our civilization. It may be that the coming age of combination will issue in a nobler and fuller liberty for the individual than has yet been seen, but that consummation will be possible, not in a day of competitive trade, but in one of competitive morals.

244. *Concentration of Capital, 1913*

"Report of the Committee Appointed Pursuant to House Resolutions 429 and 504 to Investigate the Concentration of Control of Money and Credit," 62 Congress, 3 Session (1913), *House Report No. 1593* (Washington, 1913), 56, 86–7, 89–90.

THIS increased concentration of control of money and credit has been effected principally as follows:

First, through consolidations of competitive or potentially competitive banks and trust companies. . . .

Second, through the same powerful interests becoming large stockholders in potentially competitive banks and trust companies. This is the simplest way of acquiring control, but since it requires the largest investment of capital, it is the least used. . . .

Third, through the confederation of potentially competitive banks and trust companies by means of the system of interlocking directorates.

Fourth, through the influence which the more powerful banking houses, banks, and trust companies have secured in the management of insurance companies, railroads, producing and trading corporations, and public utility corporations, by means of stockholdings, voting trusts, fiscal agency contracts, or representation upon their boards of directors, or through supplying the money requirements of railway, industrial, and public utilities corporations and thereby being enabled to participate in the determination of their financial and business policies.

Fifth, through partnership or joint account arrangements between a few of the leading banking houses, banks, and trust companies in the purchase of security issues of the great interstate corporations, accompanied by understandings of recent growth—sometimes called "banking ethics"—which have had the effect of effectually destroying competition between such banking houses, banks, and trust companies in the struggle for business or in the purchase and sale of large issues of such securities. . . .

It is a fair deduction from the testimony that the most active agents in forwarding and bringing about the concentration of control of money and credit through one or another of the processes above described have been and are: J. P. Morgan & Co.; First National Bank of New York; National City Bank of New York; Lee, Higginson & Co., of Boston and New York; Kidder, Peabody & Co., of Boston and New York; Kuhn, Loeb & Co. . . .

The resources of Morgan & Co. are un-known; its deposits are $163,000,000. The resources of the First National Bank are $150,000,000 and those of its appendage, the First Security Co., at a very low estimate, $35,000,000. The resources of the National City Bank are $274,000,-000; those of its appendage, the National City Co., are unknown, though the capital of the latter is alone $10,000,000. Thus, leaving out of account the very considerable part which is unknown, the institutions composing this group have resources of upward of $632,000,000, aside from the vast individual resources of Messrs. Morgan, Baker, and Stillman.

Further . . . the members of this group, through stock holdings, voting trusts, interlocking directorates, and other relations, have become in some cases the absolutely dominant factor, in others the most important single factor, in the control of the following banks and trust companies in the city of New York: . . . in all, 7, with total resources of $968,000,000 which, added to the known resources of members of the group themselves, makes $1,600,000,000 as the aggregate of known banking resources in the city of New York under their control or influence.

If there be added also the resources of the Equitable Life Assurance Society controlled through stock ownership of J. P. Morgan, $504,000,000, the amount becomes $2,104,000,000. . . .

Summary of directorships held by these members of the group.—Exhibit 134-B . . . shows the combined directorships in the more important enterprises held by Morgan & Co., the First National Bank, the National City Bank, and the Bankers and Guaranty Trust Cos., which latter two, as previously shown, are absolutely controlled by Morgan & Co. through voting trusts. It appears there that firm members or directors of these institutions together hold:

One hundred and eighteen directorships in 34 banks and trust companies having total resources of $2,679,000,000 and total deposits of $1,983,000,000.

Thirty directorships in 10 insurance companies having total assets of $2,293,-000,000.

One hundred and five directorships in 32 transportation systems having a total capitalization of $11,784,000,000 and a total mileage (excluding express companies and steamship lines) of 150,200.

Sixty-three directorships in 24 produc-ing and trading corporations having a total capitalization of $3,339,000,000.

Twenty-five directorships in 12 public utility corporations having a total capitalization of $2,150,000,000.

In all, 341 directorships in 112 corporations having aggregate resources or capitalization of $22,245,000,000.

245. *The Inefficiency of Banker Control, 1913*

L. D. Brandeis, *Other People's Money* (1913; reprinted in New York, 1932), 203–6.

BANKER-MANAGEMENT fails, partly because the private interest destroys soundness of judgment and undermines loyalty. It fails partly, also, because banker directors are led by their occupation (and often even by the mere fact of their location remote from the operated properties) to apply a false test in making their decisions. Prominent in the banker-director mind is always this thought: "What will be the probable effect of our action upon the market value of the company's stock and bonds, or, indeed, generally upon stock exchange values?" The stock market is so much a part of the investment-banker's life, that he cannot help being affected by this consideration, however disinterested he may be. . . . And with the best of intentions, directors susceptible to such influences are led to unwise decisions. . . .

Thus, expenditures necessary for maintenance, or for the ultimate good of a property are often deferred by banker-directors, because of the belief that the making of them *now*, would (by showing smaller net earnings), create a bad, and even false, impression on the market. Dividends are paid which should not be, because of the effect which it is believed reduction or suspension would have upon the market value of the company's securities. To exercise a sound judgment in the difficult affairs of business is, at best, a delicate operation. And no man can suc-cessfully perform that function whose mind is diverted, however innocently, from the study of, "what is best in the long run for the company of which I am director?" The banker-director is peculiarly liable to such distortion of judgment by reason of his occupation and his environment. But there is a further reason why, ordinarily, banker-management must fail.

The banker, with his multiplicity of interests, cannot ordinarily give the time essential to proper supervision and to acquiring that knowledge of the facts necessary to the exercise of sound judgment. . . . Real efficiency in any business in which conditions are ever changing must ultimately depend, in large measure, upon the correctness of the judgment exercised, almost from day to day, on the important problems as they arise. And how can the leading bankers, necessarily engrossed in the problems of their own vast private businesses, get time to know and to correlate the facts concerning so many other complex businesses? Besides, they start usually with ignorance of the particular business which they are supposed to direct. When the last paper was signed which created the Steel Trust, one of the lawyers (as Mr. Perkins frankly tells us) said: "That signature is the last one necessary to put the steel industry, on a large scale, into the hands of men who do **not** know anything about it."

The New Haven System is not a railroad, but an agglomeration of a railroad plus 121 separate corporations, control of which was acquired by the New Haven after that railroad attained its full growth of about 2000 miles of line. In administering the railroad and each of the properties formerly managed through these 122 separate companies, there must arise from time to time difficult questions on which the directors should pass judgment. The real managing directors of the New Haven system during the decade of its decline were: J. Pierpont Morgan, George F. Baker, and William Rockefeller. Mr. Morgan was, until his death in 1913, the head of perhaps the largest banking house in the world. Mr. Baker was, until 1909, President and then Chairman of the Board of Directors of one of America's leading banks (the First National of New York), and Mr. Rockefeller was, until 1911, President of the Standard Oil Company. Each was well advanced in years. Yet each of these men, besides the duties of his own vast business, and important private interests, undertook to "guide, superintend, govern and manage," not only the New Haven but also ... other corporations, some of which were similarly complex.

246. *The Conspiracy of Business, 1895*

W. H. Harvey, *Up to Date, Coin's Financial School Continued* (Chicago, 1895), 36–42.

"WE ARE approaching a crisis in the history of the world! 'Conservative business interests' appeal for quietude. It is not because they prefer slavery for humanity to temporary withdrawal of the minds of the people from business; nor because the roar of the Stock Exchange is more pleasant to them than the contemplation of a grander civilization; but because the necessities of life hold them to business, and under stress of mind make them irritable and unconscious of any other relief except that provided for them by the civilization in which they live. They cry 'confidence'! It is a natural cry. The law of self-defense prompts it. Two per cent of the people in this country own over fifty per cent of its wealth! Fifty million of souls in this republic own in their own right no place they can call home.

"And yet it is unpopular to utter these truths. The fact that it is unpopular assists in perpetuating the quality of civilization that produces it. Until that prejudice is broken, and the sunlight of impartial reason illumines the human intellect and permits an analysis of the situation, there will be no hope for a better and purer civilization.

"Your property has been confiscated by law! A law as cunning as the hand of the forger that raises a check! Amid this wreck of prosperity and human happiness a mailed hand with half-drawn sword is about to strike to still the voice that utters a protest. Your constitution has been violated! Unless the business men of America examine this trouble from a patriotic standpoint, that great chart of constitutional liberty will be torn to shreds! ... A despotic government is the only protection to tyrants! Selfishness accumulates the wealth of the nation; its votaries and defenders seize the reins of government, brow-beat and malign the people they have impoverished, and drive them to resistance—and then comes coercion—despair. Such is Monarchy! Such is Despotism!

"When 'Liberty Bell' pealed forth the alarm in 1776 it was treason to King George. The 'conservative business interests' of the colonies tried to hush the rising spirit of freedom and justice. These same 'conservative business interests' are now trying to hush the protest against the crime that has pillaged this land—a crime that has transformed the honest, industrious farmers into tenants—a crime that has transferred forty thousand million dollars of property from the many to the few—a crime that has placed 97 per cent of the people under a debt to the remaining three per cent. . . . It is a crime that has Europeanized America. A crime that is left as a heritage to your children and your children's children!" . . .

"This crime . . . brought a falling market, so the manufacturer found that the time intervening between the purchase of his raw material, and the sale of the finished article months after on the market, had consumed the profits. Long time payments on contracts made, and debts contracted, required more and more property to be sacrificed to purchase ever appreciating dollars, to make the payments when due; until this silent influence had drawn within its reach all the industries of the country and placed all property under tribute to it. For twenty-one years this silent influence has been at work! It has withered hope and fostered misery!" . . .

"This wound inflicted upon the republic is deep. . . . It was inflicted by 'honorable' men! They say it is an 'honest dollar'!

Those who would forge deeds to your property will not hesitate to forge words!" . . .

"It is a *dear* dollar, so dear that a farmer must give up two bushels of wheat to buy one of them, where before he purchased one dollar with one bushel of wheat. The cotton planter must give up twenty pounds of cotton to buy one of these dear dollars, where before he purchased one of them with seven pounds of cotton. A debt for $1,000 that 1,000 bushels of wheat would have paid ten years ago, now requires 2,000 bushels of wheat. The men who committed this crime, and all accessories to the crime after the fact, who have attempted to profit by it, own your debts to the amount of 40,000 million of dollars payable in these 'honest' dollars, and have the courts and machinery of law to enforce their payment, payment in a dollar of their own making, to get which you must sacrifice your all! The enforcement of an unjust law, that deprives you of your property, and brings to you and your family hunger and want, is despotism. It means strife. It means bloodshed. It means a military government. It means an autocracy!"

247. *Munn v. Illinois*, 1877

94 U.S., 124–6.

WHEN one becomes a member of society, he necessarily parts with some rights or privileges which, as an individual not affected by his relations to others, he might retain. "A body politic," as aptly defined in the preamble of the Constitution of Massachusetts, "is a social compact by which the whole people covenants with each citizen, and each citizen with the whole people, that all shall be governed by certain laws for the common good." This does not confer power upon the whole people to control rights which are purely and exclusively private. . . ; but it does authorize the establishment of laws requiring each citizen to so conduct himself, and so use his own property, as not unnecessarily to injure another. . . . From this source come the police powers, which, as was said by Mr. Chief Justice Taney in the *License Cases*, . . . "are nothing more or less than the powers of government inherent in every sovereignty, . . . that is to say, . . . the power to govern men and things." Under these powers the government regulates the conduct of its citizens one towards another, and the manner in which each shall use his own property, when such regulation becomes necessary for the public good. In their exercise it has been customary in England from time immemorial, and in this country from its first colonization, to regulate ferries, common carriers, hackmen, bakers, millers, wharfingers, innkeepers, etc., and in so doing to fix a maximum of charge to be made for services rendered, accommodations furnished, and articles sold. To this day, statutes are to be found in many of the states upon some or all these subjects; and we think it has never yet been successfully contended that such legislation came within any of the constitutional prohibitions against interference with private property....

From this it is apparent that, down to the time of the adoption of the Fourteenth Amendment, it was not supposed that statutes regulating the use, or even the price of the use, of private property necessarily deprived an owner of his property without due process of law. Under some circumstances they may, but not under all. The amendment does not change the law in this particular; it simply prevents the states from doing that which will operate as such a deprivation.

This brings us to inquire as to the principles upon which this power of regulation rests, in order that we may determine what is within and what without its operative effect. Looking, then, to the common law, from whence came the right which the Constitution protects, we find that when private property is "affected with a public interest, it ceases to be *juris privati* only." This was said by Lord Chief Justice Hale more than two hundred years ago.... Property does become clothed with a public interest when used in a manner to make it of public consequence, and affect the community at large. When, therefore, one devotes his property to a use in which the public has an interest, he, in effect, grants to the public an interest in that use, and must submit to be controlled by the public for the common good, to the extent of the interest he has thus created. He may withdraw his grant by discontinuing the use; but, so long as he maintains the use, he must submit to the control.

248. *The Sherman Antitrust Act, 1890*

An Act to Protect Trade and Commerce against Unlawful Restraints and Monopolies. *United States Statutes at Large*, Vol. XXVI (1889–91), 209–10.

EVERY contract, combination in the form of trust or otherwise, or conspiracy, in restraint of trade or commerce among the several states, or with foreign nations, is hereby declared to be illegal. Every person who shall make any such contract or engage in any such combination or conspiracy, shall be deemed guilty of a misdemeanor, and, on conviction thereof, shall be punished by fine not exceeding five thousand dollars, or by imprisonment not exceeding one year, or by both said punishments, in the discretion of the court.

Every person who shall monopolize, or attempt to monopolize, or combine or conspire with any other person or persons, to monopolize any part of the trade or commerce among the several states, or with foreign nations, shall be deemed guilty of a misdemeanor, and, on conviction thereof, shall be punished by fine not exceeding five thousand dollars, or by imprisonment not exceeding one year, or by both said punishments....

Every contract, combination in form of trust or otherwise, or conspiracy, in restraint of trade or commerce in any territory of the United States or of the District of Columbia, or in restraint of trade or commerce between any such territory and another, or between any such territory or territories and any state or states or the District of Columbia, or with foreign nations, or between the District of Columbia and any state or states or foreign nations, is hereby declared illegal. Every person who shall make any such contract or engage in any such combination or conspiracy, shall be deemed guilty of a misdemeanor, and, on conviction thereof, shall be punished by fine not exceeding five thousand dollars, or by imprisonment not exceeding one year, or by both said punishments. . . .

The several circuit courts of the United States are hereby invested with jurisdiction to prevent and restrain violations of this act; and it shall be the duty of the several district attorneys of the United States, in their respective districts, under the direction of the Attorney-General, to institute proceedings in equity to prevent and restrain such violations. . . .

Whenever it shall appear to the court before which any proceeding under section four of this act may be pending, that the ends of justice require that other parties should be brought before the court, the court may cause them to be summoned, whether they reside in the district in which the court is held or not;

and subpoenas to that end may be served in any district by the marshal thereof.

Any property owned under any contract or by any combination, or pursuant to any conspiracy (and being the subject thereof) mentioned in section one of this act, and being in the course of transportation from one state to another, or to a foreign country, shall be forfeited to the United States, and may be seized and condemned by like proceedings as those provided by law for the forfeiture, seizure and condemnation of property imported into the United States contrary to law.

Any person who shall be injured in his business or property by any other person or corporation by reason of anything forbidden or declared to be unlawful by this act, may sue therefor in any circuit court of the United States in the district in which the defendant resides or is found, without respect to the amount in controversy, and shall recover threefold the damages by him sustained, and the costs of suit, including a reasonable attorney's fee.

That the word "person," or "persons," wherever used in this act shall be deemed to include corporations and associations existing under or authorized by the laws of either the United States, the laws of any of the territories, the laws of any state, or the laws of any foreign country.

249. *A Rule of Reason, 1911*

Standard Oil Company of New Jersey, *et al., v.* The United States, 221 U.S., 59–60, 61–2.

In view of the many new forms of contracts and combinations which were being evolved from existing economic conditions, it was deemed essential by an all-embracing enumeration to make sure that no form of contract or combination by which an undue restraint of interstate or foreign commerce was brought about could save such restraint from condemnation. The

statute under this view evidenced the intent not to restrain the right to make and enforce contracts, whether resulting from combinations or otherwise, which did not unduly restrain interstate or foreign commerce, but to protect that commerce from being restrained by methods, whether old or new, which would constitute an interference that is an undue restraint.

And as the contracts or acts embraced in the provision were not expressly defined, since the enumeration addressed itself simply to classes of acts, those classes being broad enough to embrace every conceivable contract or combination which could be made concerning trade or commerce or the subjects of such commerce, and thus caused any act done by any of the enumerated methods anywhere in the whole field of human activity to be illegal if in restraint of trade, it inevitably follows that the provision necessarily called for the exercise of judgment which required that some standard should be resorted to for the purpose of determining whether the prohibitions contained in the statute had or had not in any given case been violated. Thus not specifying but indubitably contemplating and requiring a standard, it follows that it was intended that the standard of reason which had been applied at the common law and in this country in dealing with subjects of the character embraced by the statute, was intended to be the measure used for the purpose of determining whether in a given case a particular act had or had not brought about the wrong against which the statute provided. . . .

In other words, having by the first section forbidden all means of monopolizing trade . . . the second section seeks, if possible, to make the prohibitions of the act all the more complete and perfect by embracing all attempts to reach the end prohibited by the first section, that is, restraints of trade, by any attempt to monopolize, or monopolization thereof, even although the acts by which such re-

sults are attempted to be brought about or are brought about are not embraced within the general enumeration of the first section. And, of course, when the second section is thus harmonized with and made as it was intended to be the complement of the first, it becomes obvious that the criteria to be resorted to in any given case for the purpose of ascertaining whether violations of the section have been committed, is the rule of reason guided by the established law and by the plain duty to enforce the prohibitions of the act and thus the public policy which its restrictions were obviously enacted to subserve. And it is worthy of observation . . . that although the statute by the comprehensiveness of the enumerations embodied in both the first and second sections makes it certain that its purpose was to prevent undue restraints of every kind and nature, nevertheless by the omission of any direct prohibition against monopoly in the concrete it indicates a consciousness that the freedom of the individual right to contract when not unduly or improperly exercised was the most efficient means for the prevention of monopoly, since the operation of the centrifugal and centripetal forces resulting from the right to freely contract was the means by which monopoly would be inevitably prevented if no extraneous or sovereign power imposed it and no right to make unflawful contracts having a monopolistic tendency were permitted. In other words that freedom to contract was the essence of freedom from undue restraint on the right to contract.

250. *The Clayton Act, 1914*

An Act to supplement existing laws against unlawful restraints and monopolies, and for other purposes (1914). *United States Statutes at Large,* Vol. XXXVIII, Part I (1913–15), 730–3, 734, 738. Amended May 15, 1916, and May 26, 1920, *Federal Anti-Trust Laws with Amendments* (Washington, 1922), 18.

IT SHALL be unlawful for any person engaged in commerce ... to discriminate in price between different purchasers of commodities ... where the effect of such discrimination may be to substantially lessen competition or tend to create a monopoly in any line of commerce: *Provided,* That nothing herein contained shall prevent discrimination in price between purchasers of commodities on account of differences in the grade, quality, or quantity of the commodity sold, or that makes only due allowance for difference in the cost of selling or transportation, or discrimination in price in the same or different communities made in good faith to meet competition: *And provided further,* That nothing herein contained shall prevent persons engaged in selling goods, wares, or merchandise in commerce from selecting their own customers in bona fide transactions and not in restraint of trade.

It shall be unlawful for any person engaged in commerce ... to lease or make a sale or contract for sale of goods ... or other commodities, whether patented or unpatented, for use, consumption or resale ... or fix a price charged therefor, or discount from, or rebate upon, such price, on the condition, agreement or understanding that the lessee or purchaser thereof shall not use or deal in the goods ... or other commodities of a competitor or competitors of the lessor or seller, where the effect of such lease, sale, or contract for sale or such condition, agreement or understanding may be to substantially lessen competition or tend to create a monopoly in any line of commerce. ...

The labor of a human being is not a commodity or article of commerce. Nothing contained in the antitrust laws shall be construed to forbid the existence and operation of labor, agricultural, or horticultural organizations, instituted for the purposes of mutual help ... or to forbid or restrain individual members of such organizations from lawfully carrying out the legitimate objects thereof; nor shall such organizations, or the members thereof, be held or construed to be illegal combinations or conspiracies in restraint of trade, under the antitrust laws. ...

No corporation engaged in commerce shall acquire, directly or indirectly, the whole or any part of the stock or other share capital of another corporation engaged also in commerce, where the effect of such acquisition may be to substantially lessen competition between the corporation whose stock is so acquired and the corporation making the acquisition, or to restrain such commerce in any section or community, or tend to create a monopoly of any line of commerce.

No corporation shall acquire, directly or indirectly, the whole or any part of the stock or other share capital of two or more corporations engaged in commerce where the effect of such acquisition, or the use of such stock by the voting or granting of proxies or otherwise, may be to substantially lessen competition between such corporations, or any of them ... or to restrain such commerce in any section or community, or tend to create a monopoly of any line of commerce.

This section shall not apply to corporations purchasing such stock solely for investment and not using the same by voting or otherwise to bring about, or in attempting to bring about, the substantial lessening of competition. Nor shall anything contained in this section prevent a corporation engaged in commerce from causing the formation of subsidiary corporations for the actual carrying on of their immediate lawful business, or the natural and legitimate branches or extensions thereof, or from owning and holding all or a part of the stock of such subsidiary corporations, when the effect of such formation is not to substantially lessen competition.

Nor shall anything herein contained be construed to prohibit any common carrier . . . from aiding in the construction of branches or short lines so located as to become feeders to the main line of the company so aiding in such construction or from acquiring or owning all or any part of the stock of such branch lines, nor to prevent any such common carrier from acquiring and owning all or any part of the stock of a branch or short line constructed by an independent company where there is no substantial competition between the company owning the branch line so constructed and the company owning the main line acquiring the property or an interest therein, nor to prevent such common carrier from extending any of its lines through the medium of the acquisition of stock or otherwise of any other such common carrier where there is no substantial competition between the company extending its lines and the company whose stock, property, or any interest therein is so acquired. . . .

After two years from the date of the approval of this act no person shall at the same time be a director or other officer or employee of more than one bank, banking association or trust company . . . either of which has deposits, capital, surplus, and undivided profits aggregating more than $5,000,000. . . .

No bank, banking association or trust company, organized or operating under the laws of the United States, in any city or incorporated town or village of more than two hundred thousand inhabitants, as shown by the last preceding decennial census of the United States, shall have as a director or other officer or employee any private banker or any director or other officer or employee of any other bank, banking association or trust company located in the same place: *Provided,* That nothing in this section shall apply to mutual savings banks not having a capital stock represented by shares: *Provided further,* That a director or other officer or employee of such bank, banking association, or trust company may be a director or other officer or employee of not more than one other bank or trust company organized under the laws of the United States or any state where the entire capital stock of one is owned by stockholders in the other: *And provided further,* That nothing contained in this section shall forbid a director of class A of a Federal reserve bank, as defined in the Federal Reserve Act, from being an officer or director or both an officer and director in one member bank. *And provided further,* That nothing in this Act shall prohibit any private banker or other officer, director, or employee of any member bank or class A director of a Federal reserve bank, who shall first procure the consent of the Federal Reserve Board, which board is hereby authorized at its discretion, to grant, withhold, or revoke such consent, from being an officer, director, or employee of not more than two other banks, banking associations, or trust companies, whether organized under the laws of the United States or any state, if such other bank, banking association, or trust company is not in substantial competition with such bank or member bank. . . .

After two years from the date of the approval of this Act no person at the same time shall be a director in any two or more corporations, any one of which has capital, surplus, and undivided profits aggregating more than $1,000,000, engaged in whole or in part in commerce, other than banks, banking associations, trust companies and common carriers . . . if such corporations are or shall have been theretofore . . . competitors, so that the elimination of competition by agreement between them would constitute a violation of any of the provisions of any of the antitrust laws. . . .

After two years from the approval of this Act no common carrier engaged in commerce shall have any dealings in securities, supplies or other articles of commerce, or shall make or have any contracts for construction or maintenance of any kind, to the amount of more than $50,000, in the aggregate, in any one year, with another corporation, firm, partnership or association when the said common carrier shall have upon its board of directors or as its president, manager, or as its purchasing or selling officer, or agent in the particular transaction, any person who is at the same time a director, manager, or purchasing or selling officer of, or who has any substantial interest in, such other corporation, firm, partnership, or association, unless and except such purchases shall be made from, or such dealings shall be with, the bidder whose bid is the most favorable to such common carrier, to be ascertained by competitive bidding under regulations to be prescribed by rule or otherwise by the Interstate Commerce Commission. . . .

No restraining order or injunction shall be granted by any court of the United States, or a judge or the judges thereof, in any case between an employer and employees or between employers and employees . . . growing out of, a dispute concerning terms or conditions of employment, unless necessary to prevent irreparable injury to property. . . .

And no such restraining order or injunction shall prohibit any person or persons, whether singly or in concert, from terminating any relation of employment, or from ceasing to perform and work or labor, or from recommending, advising, or persuading others by peaceful means to do so; or from attending at any place where any such person or persons may lawfully be, for the purpose of peacefully obtaining or communicating information, or from peacefully persuading any person to work or to abstain from working; or from ceasing to patronize or to employ any party to such dispute, or from recommending, advising, or persuading others by peaceful and lawful means so to do; from paying or giving to, or withholding from, any person engaged in such dispute, any strike benefits or other moneys or things of value; or from peaceably assembling in a lawful manner, and for lawful purposes; or from doing any act or thing which might lawfully be done in the absence of such dispute by any party thereto.

XXIX *The Birth of the Labor Movement*

UNDER THE NEW conditions laborers no longer were able as isolated individuals to negotiate directly and freely with their employers. Rather, they sought the aid of unions to act for them; and such intermediary organizations were widely advocated (No. 251).

The Knights of Labor was the first to organize a substantial number of members. This association was not confined to industrial laborers; it sprang from an old artisan union and drew together a miscellaneous group of working people, professional men and reformers (No. 252). Its largest gains in membership came almost accidentally, as the result of strikes during which desperate laborers drifted to it for want of any other leadership (No. 253). It was, however, unable to assimilate and retain these new members in its ranks (No. 254).

Meanwhile, the craft organizations of skilled workers had drawn together in the American Federation of Labor. The Federation concentrated on simple unionism, bargaining for the improvement of the conditions of its own members. The strike was its last resort (No. 255). Attracted at first by the possibility of improving conditions through legislation, it quickly shifted to a program of more limited objectives (No. 256).

The American Federation of Labor left the mass of unskilled workers largely unorganized; and when they struck, it was through desperation. Only the radical anarchists or socialists were willing to lead them. Employers, in these years, were not prepared to negotiate with such groups. All too often violence was used to suppress strikes; and this brought on equally violent retaliation. The Haymarket Riot (No. 257) was used as the pretext for convicting a number of anarchist leaders (No. 258). The task of union organizers was often impeded by lawless brutality (No. 259).

Violence was not always effective, however, as the successful Lawrence strike demonstrated (No. 260). And violence generated the atmosphere within which the I.W.W., the Industrial Workers of the World, grew in strength and in influence down until the outbreak of the World War (No. 261).

251. *The Labor Question, 1911*

Washington Gladden, *The Labor Question* (New York, 1911), 80–4, 86–8.

THERE is one department of our life, and this the largest interest of all, which has not been democratized. Our industries are still largely on an autocratic or feudalistic basis. We have been trying to correlate a political democracy with an industrial feudalism. They do not work well together. I do not think that they will endure together.... The working men will lose their political liberty, or they will gain their industrial liberty. I do not think that they will lose their votes; I think that they will gain their right to have a voice in determining what wages they shall receive and under what conditions they shall work....

I am speaking, of course, of the large system of industry under which the world's work is now mainly done.... Under this system the capitalist manager assumes the exclusive right to fix the rate of wages, the hours of labor, the conditions under which the work is done. He cannot, of course, discuss these matters with each of his one thousand or ten thousand workmen; there can, therefore, be no semblance of a bargain in the case; it is an ultimatum; the employer presents it, the working man can take it or leave it. It would be absurd for a single laborer to propose to chaffer about wages or hours of labor with the American Steel Corporation or the Pennsylvania Railroad Company. Out of these circumstances very naturally grows the assumption, on the part of the employer, that the right as well as the power to fix the laborer's wages belongs exclusively to him. When, therefore, any man or any body of men proposes to have something to say about it, he indignantly resents the proposal; he calls it interfering with his business. What he says to them is precisely this: "It is none of your business what wages you shall receive; it is my business to tell you how much you can have, and I cannot permit any one to dictate to me about my business." ...

The working men found out, a good while ago, that the only possible way of preserving and enforcing their right of contract in the sale of their labor was by uniting together and insisting on collective bargaining with their employers. If the capitalist manager's one thousand or ten thousand employees unite in presenting their demands, they may succeed in getting some attention to them. By union and organization they may keep themselves from being reduced to a position of dependence and servitude, and may establish their right to a share in the wealth created by their labor and a voice in the distribution of the product of industry. ...

There is no other way, I repeat, under the pressure of the stupendous combinations of capital, to rescue labor from degradation except by the firm organization of labor. There is no salvation for our democracy under the wage system but in this concerted resistance of the wage-workers. That they are prone to abuse their power has been fully admitted, and we all know how impossible are some of their methods, and how needful it sometimes is to resist and defeat their aggressions. The acquisition of power by those who have long been deprived of it, is apt to be attended by outbreaks of willfulness and arrogance. ... I do not expect to see lawlessness disappear from trade-unionism so long as there is so strong a disposition among employers to insist on making trade-unions outlaws. When workmen's right to combine for the protection of their interests is fully and frankly conceded, we shall, I believe, soon see a great diminution of violence.

252. *The Knights of Labor*, 1869

T. V. Powderly, *Thirty Years of Labor* (Columbus, 1889), 131–3, 135, 136–7, 138, 243–5.

DURING the Civil War ... the great demand for clothing ... created a corresponding demand for tailors, and drew the attention of men to that trade who had never sewed a stitch, or even pricked the finger end with the needle as apprentices. ...

When the skilled workmen, those who had spent long years at low wages, and had served years as apprentices, saw the inroads that were being made upon the tailoring trade by the introduction of so many incompetent workmen to the bench, they began to question whether it was not time to ... stem the tide of ruin that was setting in against their trade. No action was taken until the employers ... in the hope of realizing still greater gains, inaugurated a scheme to reduce the wages of the tailors. ...

The garment cutters of Philadelphia ... called a meeting in the autumn of 1862, and ... from this meeting grew the organization afterwards known as the "Garment Cutters' Association of Philadelphia." It grew in strength and influence. ...

In ... 1869, a lack of interest having manifested itself among the members, it was deemed advisable by some to introduce new features, and make some changes which innovations in work-shop regulation seemed to demand. ... Eight or nine of the older and more reliable of the Garment Cutters' Association ...

agreed to draw up plans for the organization of a new order. . . . On December 9, 1869, a resolution was offered at a meeting of the . . . Association: "To dissolve and divide the funds among the members in good standing." The motion met with but little opposition, and its passage was practically unanimous.

Immediately after the dissolution of the Garment Cutters' Association, several members . . . met . . . and proceeded to organize by electing James L. Wright as temporary chairman, and Robert McCauley as temporary secretary. After a free and deliberate discussion of the subject of organization, the question was put to each person present: "Have you any objections to connect yourself with a secret organization?" The following answered in the negative by stating that they had no objections to offer: James L. Wright, Wm. H. Phillips, U. S. Stephens, Robert McCauley, William Cook, James M. Hilsea, Joseph S. Kennedy, Robert W. Keen, and David Westcott.

Mr. Keen was then placed in charge of the door, a pledge of secrecy was administered to all present, and a password was given out to be used on subsequent occasions. Various plans were considered, and . . . referred to a committee . . . with instructions to . . . prepare . . . a secret work, such as would be suitable for the government of such a body. . . . On December 28, 1869, . . . the name of the new association was made a subject for discussion, and it was decided to call it the Knights of Labor, and the local name of the body was to be Garment Cutters' Assembly.

[AIMS OF THE KNIGHTS OF LABOR]

Preamble
THE RECENT alarming development and aggression of aggregated wealth, which, unless checked, will invariably lead to the pauperization and hopeless degradation of the toiling masses, render it imperative, if we desire to enjoy the blessings of life, that a check should be placed upon its power and upon unjust accumulation, and a system adopted which will secure to the laborer the fruits of his toil; and as this much-desired object can only be accomplished by the thorough unification of labor, . . . we have formed the ***** with a view of securing the organization and direction, by cooperative effort, of the power of the industrial classes; and we submit to the world the objects sought to be accomplished by our organization, calling upon all who believe in securing "the greatest good to the greatest number" to aid and assist us:—

I. To bring within the folds of organization every department of productive industry, making knowledge a standpoint for action, and industrial and moral worth, not wealth, the true standard of individual and national greatness.

II. To secure to the toilers a proper share of the wealth that they create. . . .

III. To . . . [demand] . . . from the various governments the establishment of bureaus of labor statistics.

IV. The establishment of cooperative institutions, productive and distributive.

V. The reserving of the public lands . . . for the actual settler. . . .

VI. The abrogation of all laws that do not bear equally upon capital and labor, the removal of unjust technicalities, delays, and discriminations in the administration of justice, and the adopting of measures providing for the health and safety of those engaged in mining, manufacturing, or building pursuits.

VII. The enactment of laws to compel chartered corporations to pay their employees weekly. . . .

VIII. The enactment of laws giving mechanics and laborers a first lien on their work for their full wages.

IX. The abolishment of the contract system on national, state, and municipal work.

X. The substitution of arbitration for strikes. . . .

XI. The prohibition of the employment of children in workshops, mines, and factories before attaining their fourteenth year.

XII. To abolish the system of letting out by contract the labor of convicts....

XIII. To secure for both sexes equal pay for equal work.

XIV. The reduction of the hours of labor to eight per day....

XV. To prevail upon governments to establish a purely national circulating medium, based upon the faith and resources of the nation, and issued directly to the people, without the intervention of any system of banking corporations.

253. *The Union Pacific Strike, 1884*

J. R. Buchanan, *Story of a Labor Agitator* (New York: Outlook Company, 1903), 75–8.

THERE is no record of another such strike in the whole history of the labor movement in this country. Not a shop on the system was organized when the notice of reduction was posted, and yet, inside of thirty-six hours, every shop from Omaha to Ogden and upon all the branch lines was on strike. The peculiarity of this strike is further emphasized by the knowledge that before the cut the Union Pacific was paying higher wages to its shopmen than was paid by any other railroad west of the Missouri River. The company counted upon this latter fact to help make the reduction successful, evidently not realizing that by paying the best wages it had secured the best mechanics and, as a consequence, the most independent men in the trades concerned.

There was another illustration of spontaneous unanimity in that strike. On Friday telegrams came from the officials of the temporary organizations of the men at all points on the system requesting the committee appointed at our Denver meeting to act for the whole system in dealing with the company. Ellis, Kansas, started that movement; and the others followed in quick order. The Denver committee accepted the responsibility, and at once notified the general manager of the road, at Omaha, to that effect, at the same time wiring him a copy of the resolution adopted at Denver, the substance of which was approved by the men at all other points.

Saturday afternoon the company recalled the order reducing wages, and announced that on Monday work would be resumed at the old scale of prices,—a complete victory for the men in four days.

As soon as the order was recalled, some of the men were for abandoning further steps in the line of organization. They said they had gotten along all right without organization before the cut, and had shown that it was a simple matter to secure united action when necessary. They were told by myself and others that they were sadly mistaken if they believed that the company had abandoned its purpose of reducing wages; that it would try again when the outlook was favorable, and that never again would a wholesale cut be undertaken.... We predicted that in future the company would select one department or one shop at a time, and would give no intimation that the intention was eventually to reduce all. Therefore the men should perfect their organizations and form a federation that would put them in a position to act all together at the first sign of danger, no matter which branch was threatened or attacked. We urged upon them the adoption of the motto of the Knights of Labor, "An injury to one is the concern of all."

When the situation was fully explained, the advice given by the union men who were taking an active interest in the matter was acted upon, and several organizers were put upon the road within a week from the close of the strike. The Knights of Labor was the organization chosen, and within thirty days we had a healthy assembly at each important point on the system. I organized assemblies in all the shop towns on the line from Omaha to Cheyenne, inclusive.

254. Reasons for the Decline of the Knights, 1900

Testimony of J. C. Schonfarber, *Report of the Industrial Commission on the Relations and Conditions of Capital and Labor* (Washington, 1901), VII, 423–5.

[WITH] the great influx of membership in 1886, the organization became so large that it became very unwieldy.... The general officers of the order did not measure up to the capacity of handling such a large body of men successfully and conservatively. Many of those who came in had never been in any kind of an organization; many of them had been in trade unions of various kinds or trade bodies, but had fallen out because they did not receive immediate benefits; and they saw in our platform a way, they thought, out of the wilderness; and they were not patient enough to acquire that result by study, slow growth and slow work; and they sought to secure the remedies in a rush. The result of that was numerous strikes [which] ... had the effect in our case of losing numerous members to the organization and a vast expenditure of money.

The session of the General Assembly in 1886, in Richmond, Virginia, was probably the largest convention of labor organizations ever held in this country that I know of, and some of its actions were precipitate and, I think, hastily carried out afterwards. For instance, there were some resolutions passed there in reference to tradesmen, mechanics, which had a direct effect on the cigar makers. Mr. Powderly, who was then the General Master Workman of the order, of course, proceeded to carry out the results of that convention. It resulted very disastrously to the organization. The question, if I remember rightly, came up in that convention as to whether a man could be affiliated with two labor organizations at the same time; and the General Assembly decided that he could not safely do so; ... with the result that a radical resolution was passed there, ... and the general officers of the order ... proceeded to carry that law out to the best of their ability, with the result that a large number, if not the majority of the cigar makers went out in a body from the Knights of Labor, and with them probably went numerous other men. That was one of the troubles, one of the causes of the decimation of membership.

The next result was politics, of course—going into party politics. We said in our platform that most of the relief to come to us must come through legislation, and there came the question whether the organization should go into politics as a body or not.... In some localities there were independent movements of the laboring people, and in other localities there was an indication that the men were in favor of the General Assembly or the general officers lining up into a national labor party, and attempting to elect their own candidates to Congress and to office. I think those political questions coming up drove men out of the organization.... New York was one of the centers in which organized labor received its most severe blow in 1886 and 1887. In 1886 Mr. George ran for mayor and polled some

68,000 votes, and a large number of the labor people of New York thought that Mr. George was honestly elected mayor of New York City; and when he did not come up, when he did not take his seat, that disheartened a number of men, and they dropped out of the organization and segregated themselves into strict trades unions, almost hopeless in their despair. . . .

Q. Is it not the trend now to take the craft into the craft rights and craft privileges and craft lines of organization, and to keep it within itself, and settle with the parties in interest, the employers or capitalists?—A. Yes; and there is a reason for that. . . . I believe that the employers are more favorable to settling with the craft than they are with the mixed bodies, because when they come to deal with the mixed body on a strike or lockout they find that the number of men interested besides the one trade is so wide and far reaching that if they do not make the concessions asked, the strike is accentuated rather than settled . . . ; whereas, if they can keep the printers in the contest separate from the machinists and the miners and the shoemakers, and only deal with them, one by one, they can kill those crafts. . . . The organized industries of the country would sooner deal with a particular craft than they would with the general working people, because they can compel submission from the isolated craft a great deal quicker than they can from the general body of working people.

255. *Union Tactics, 1883*

Testimony of Samuel Gompers, August, 1883. *Report of the Committee of the Senate upon the Relations between Labor and Capital* (Washington, 1885), I, 367–8.

STRIKES ought to be . . . the last means which workingmen resort to to protect themselves against the almost never satisfied greed of the employers. . . . From the year 1873 to 1878 the cigarmakers of this country were reduced in wages systematically every spring and every fall. . . . At that time the cigarmakers' organization was in a very weak and puerile condition. Further, the manufacturers of cigars throughout that period managed to introduce a system of truck or "pluck-me" payments, by which the workingmen were paid in kind, cigars, and were required to go out and sell them to any grogshop or other place of any description where they could sell them; or they would receive store orders, or, in the case of single men, they would be required to board at certain hotels or boarding houses. . . .

When our organizations commenced to emerge and reorganize throughout the country, the first year there were seventeen strikes in our trade, of which twelve or thirteen were successful. The rest were either lost or compromised. In the year following we had forty-six strikes, of which thirty-seven, I think, were successful, three lost, and six compromised. In these last two years, . . . I am convinced that we have had over one hundred and sixty or one hundred and seventy strikes, and the strikes have been successful except in, perhaps, twenty instances, where they may have been lost or compromised. The truck system of which I spoke exists no longer in our trade. . . .

Formerly, before the organization, men would probably strike for an advance of wages in the dull season, and be content that they were not reduced in the busy season. Our experience has taught us to adopt a different mode of action. . . . When we obtain an increase of wages when times are fair, our object is to endeavor to obtain fair wages during the dull season also, and, while we have made provision not to strike for an increase of wages during those periods, we are always in a position to strike against a reduction of wages or the introduction of the truck system, or other obnoxious rules. . . . For the purpose of accomplishing this object, it is entirely valueless to organize a union during a strike, and . . . it is little better than valueless to organize just immediately before a strike. . . . If we are desirous of gaining anything in a strike, we must prepare in peace for the turbulent time which may come. And the Cigar-Makers' International Union, of which I now speak especially, is an organization that has in its treasury between $130,000 and $150,000 ready to be concentrated within five days at any time at any given point.

256. *American Federation of Labor, 1886*

Samuel Gompers, *Seventy Years of Life and Labor* (New York, 1925), 215–17, 219, 225–8, 264–5, 268, 270–1, 284. Copyright, 1925, by Samuel Gompers. Renewal, 1952, by Mrs. Gertrude G. Gompers. Published by E. P. Dutton & Co., Inc.

THE CONCEPTION of a national federation of trade unions was then clear to no one. Its development, together with policies and methods, was the natural evolution of the principles we cigarmakers worked out first in No. 144 and later in the C.I.U. and applied to widely varying problems and situations. Economic need and betterment could best be served by mobilizing and controlling economic power. This was the simple basis upon which all policies were squared. . . .

The congress met November 15, 1881, in Pittsburgh. It was the first national meeting of labor men from all the trades that I attended. I was thirty-one at that time and was looked upon as one of the youngsters. Many of the delegates were familiar, for New York was then, as now, the center of national industrial life. . . .

The Committee on Platform proposed legislation needed to protect wage-earners. That report shows so concretely what was in the minds of labor men of that day, that I wish to enumerate the subjects:

Compulsory education laws.
Prohibition of labor of children under fourteen years.
Licensing of stationary engineers.
Sanitation and safety provisions for factories.
Uniform apprentice laws.
National eight-hour law.
Prohibition of contract convict labor.
Law prohibiting the order or truck system of wage payment.
Law making wages a first lien upon the product of labor.
Repeal of all conspiracy law.
National Bureau of Labor Statistics.
Protection of American industry against cheap foreign labor.
Laws prohibiting importation of foreign workers under contract.
Chinese exclusion.

The mere enumeration of these objectives indicates the scope of the work awaiting a national organization in that pioneer period of industrialism which brought new problems in human relations in industry and therefore in society. . . .

Our committee issued a call to national and international trade unions to send delegates to a conference to be held in Columbus, Ohio, December 8, 1886. . . . We needed a consolidated organization for the promotion of trade unionism under which work could go forward daily for the organization of all workers of America, skilled as well as unskilled. We needed a central office and officers who could give all their time to the Federation work. The old

Federation was committed to relief by legislation. As year by year we learned the inadequacy of our program, we tried to revise our constitution to authorize action in the economic field. Now the time had come to stop patchwork, and rebuild. We had learned the need of an alliance for defense and mutual help. . . .

During the first day's session of the Federation, a telegram was received from Mr. Powderly giving the names of five Knights of Labor appointed to discuss trade union differences. Our Trade Union Committee met with them and found that they had not even the power of recommendation and that they declared the "treaty" had been rejected at Cleveland. The K. of L. committee suggested nothing but absorption by the K. of L. and loss of trade autonomy. The Order had reached a stage of intoxication with power that prevented clear thinking and wise action. . . .

The Columbus meetings unanimously decided that a Federation should be formed and that all trade union organizations should be eligible, whether affiliated or unaffiliated to the Federation of Trades and Labor Unions and the conference appointed a committee of five to confer with a committee from the Federation of Trades and Labor Unions. Acting under instructions from the Federation, I met this committee and stated the Federation had resolved to turn over all moneys, papers, and effects to the new American Federation of Labor requesting only the publication of our Legislative Committee's report. Then the officers and delegates of the old Federation disbanded or merged in with the new Federation which was organized under the title of the American Federation of Labor. . . .

I was president of a Federation that had been created but yet had to be given vitality. I felt that the trade union movement stood or fell with the success of the Federation and gave everything within me to the work. The new movement had to establish itself as a working agency. This could be done only by rendering service and establishing a reputation for ability to do things. To accomplish these ends I had to be active in labor matters, not only in New York, but in as wide a field as I could reach. What I could do was so terribly restricted by finances that I was constantly chafing. . . . Early officers of trade union organizations had no such office rooms, equipment, and staff assistants as are now the rule with every . . . organization. In the pioneer days many carried their offices in their coat pockets during the day while they earned a living at their trades and gave such time as they could in the evenings to official business.

The new idea of united action by all the trades, which the Federation represented, had to make its way slowly by earning a place for itself in the minds and experiences of all workers. It got such scanty support as could be drawn from meager funds after they had served the urgent and manifold needs of the trade. The central trade office had only such equipment as was indispensable, and the Federation had less. . . .

After struggling with the Knights of Labor situation for months, I wrote to P. J. McGuire:

Talk of harmony with the Knights of Labor is bosh. They are just as great enemies of trade unions as any employer can be, only more vindictive. I tell you they will give us no quarter and I would give them their own medicine. It is no use trying to placate them or even to be friendly. They will not coöperate with a mere trades union as they call our organization. The time will come, however, when the workingmen of the country will see and distinguish between a natural and an artificial organization.

Nor was that day very slow in coming. The Knights of Labor rapidly lost in prestige and numbers.

After careful consideration of the conference and subsequent events, we delegates ended our report to the Denver convention of the A.F. of L. with the following conclusions:

We are convinced that evolutionary trade unionism contains within itself the germs of growth and expansion to the loftiest heights of human aspiration, and that the temporary annoyance of obstructionists is preferable to the surrender of any jot or tittle of

those principles of economic truth upon which our organizations are based.

We believe in that harmony; but that harmony, in our judgment, can only be brought about by a firm insistence that the trade union shall be permitted to occupy unmolested its natural and historic field of labor for the benefit and advancement of the wage-earning classes.

257. *Haymarket, 1886*

Buchanan, *Story of a Labor Agitator*, 294–7.

[IN] May, 1886 . . . the first extensive effort was made to inaugurate the eight-hour workday in the United States. A great many employers opposed the demand for the shorter day, and strikes followed. There were serious conflicts between the strikers and their sympathizers on the one hand and the authorities on the other hand in several industrial centers, the disturbances at Chicago and Milwaukee being especially noteworthy.

On the night of the 4th of May the tragedy of the Chicago Haymarket occurred. . . . In consequence of an eight-hour strike at the McCormick Reaper Works, in Chicago, there was a clash between the police and a crowd of workingmen—some of them being strikers—and several persons were seriously injured by the bullets and clubs of the policemen. A meeting was called for the following night, in the Haymarket Square, to "protest against the brutality of the police." The speakers at the meeting were all members of the Anarchist groups, though some of them were also identified with the more conservative branches of the labor movement. The speeches at this meeting were not nearly so violent in tone as had been numerous previous speeches, made by the same men, on the Lake Front and in other

parts of Chicago. Carter Harrison the First was mayor of the city at the time. He was present at the meeting for nearly an hour—leaving for home a short time before the hour at which it was intended to close the meeting; and he declared, on the witness stand, that he heard nothing that presaged lawless acts. But within a few minutes after he had taken his departure several hundred policemen marched out of the Desplaines Street Station, half a block away, and headed for the crowd assembled around the truck, from which Sam Fielden was then making an address. The captain of the police ordered the meeting to disperse. Fielden said, "Captain, this is an orderly assemblage." The captain repeated his order, and some person—neither court proceedings nor any other record tells us who—threw a bomb into the midst of the policemen. Sixty-six policemen were prostrated by the explosion, seven never to rise again and an eighth to die soon after. . . . Many arrests were made of men charged with complicity in the bomb-throwing; eight were indicted. After a long trial, seven were found guilty of murder in the first degree and sentenced to be hanged, and one was sentenced to fifteen years in the state penitentiary for distributing the handbills announcing the Haymarket meeting.

258. *Speech to the Court, 1886*

Albert Parsons, *Life of Albert R. Parsons* (Chicago, 1889), 160–1, 165, 168–9, 183–4.

THE PROSECUTION in this case throughout has been a capitalistic prosecution, inspired by ... that class of persons who think that working people have but one right and one duty to perform, viz.: Obedience. ... We were prosecuted ostensibly for murder until near the end of the trial, when all at once the jury is commanded— yea, commanded—to render a verdict against us as Anarchists. ...

Now, the money-makers, the business men, those people who deal in stocks and bonds, the speculators and employers ... have no conception of this labor question. ... They don't want to know anything about it, and they won't hear anything about it, and they propose to club, lock up, and, if necessary, strangle those who insist on their hearing this question. Can it be any longer denied that there is such a thing as the labor question in this country? ...

I am a Socialist. I am one of those, although myself a wage slave, who holds that it is wrong ... for me to undertake to make my escape from wage slavery by becoming a master and an owner of another's labor. I refuse to do it. Had I chosen another path in life, I might be living upon an avenue of the city of Chicago today, surrounded in my beautiful home with luxury and ease, and servants to do my bidding. But I chose the other road, and instead I stand here today upon the scaffold, as it were. This is my crime. Before high heaven this and this alone is my crime. I have been false, I have been untrue, and I am a traitor to the infamies that exist today in capitalistic society. ...

We were told by the prosecution that law is on trial; that Government is on trial. That is what the gentlemen on the other side stated to the jury. ... Well, up to near the conclusion of this trial we, the defendants, supposed that we were indicted and being tried for murder. Now, if the law is on trial and if the Government is on trial, who has placed it upon trial? And I leave it to the people of America whether the prosecution in this case have made out a case; ... I charge upon them a willful, a malicious, a purposed violation of every law which guarantees every right to every American citizen. They have violated free speech. In the prosecution of this case they have violated a free press. They have violated the right of public assembly. Yea, they have even violated and denounced the right of self-defense. I charge the crime home to them. ...

I have violated no law of this country. Neither I nor my colleagues here have violated any legal right of American citizens ... and we defy the prosecution to rob the people of America of these dearly bought rights.

259. *Mother Jones at Work, 1900(?)*

M. H. Jones, *Autobiography* (Chicago, 1925), 41–4.

TOM HAGGERTY was in charge of the Fairmont field. One Sunday morning, the striking miners of Clarksburg started on a march to Monongha to get out the miners in the camps along the line. We camped in the open fields and held meetings on the road sides and in barns, preaching the gospel of unionism.

The Consolidated Coal Company that owns the little town of New England forbade the distribution of the notices of our meeting and arrested anyone found with a notice. But we got the news around. Several of our men went into the camp. They went in twos. One pretended he was deaf and the other kept hollering in his ear as they walked around, "Mother Jones is going to have a meeting Sunday afternoon outside the town on the sawdust pile." Then the deaf fellow would ask him what he said and he would holler to him again. So the word got around the entire camp and we had a big crowd.

When the meeting adjourned, three miners and myself set out for Fairmont City. The miners, Jo Battley, Charlie Blakelet and Barney Rice walked but they got a little boy with a horse and buggy to drive me over. I was to wait for the boys just outside the town, across the bridge, just where the interurban car comes along.

The little lad and I drove along. It was dark when we came in sight of the bridge which I had to cross. A dark building stood beside the bridge. It was the Coal Company's store. It was guarded by gunmen. There was no light on the bridge and there was none in the store. . . .

I got out of the buggy where the road joins the interurban tracks, just across the bridge. I sent the lad home.

"When you pass my boys on the road tell them to hurry up. Tell them I'm waiting just across the bridge."

There wasn't a house in sight. The only people near were the gunmen whose dark figures I could now and then see moving on the bridge. It grew very dark. I sat on the ground, waiting. I took out my watch, lighted a match and saw that it was about time for the interurban.

Suddenly the sound of "Murder! Murder! Police! Help!" rang out through the darkness. Then the sound of running and

Barney Rice came screaming across the bridge toward me. [Blakelet] followed, running so fast his heels hit the back of his head. "Murder! Murder!" he was yelling.

I rushed toward them. "Where's Jo?" I asked.

"They're killing Jo—on the bridge—the gunmen."

At that moment the interurban car came in sight. It would stop at the bridge. I thought of a scheme.

I ran onto the bridge, shouting, "Jo! Jo! The boys are coming. They're coming! The whole bunch's coming. The car's most here!"

Those bloodhounds for the coal company thought an army of miners was in the interurban car. They ran for cover, barricading themselves in the company's store. They left Jo on the bridge, his head broken and the blood pouring from him. I tore my petticoat into strips, bandaged his head, helped the boys to get him on to the interurban car, and hurried the car into Fairmont City.

We took him to the hotel and sent for a doctor who sewed up the great, open cuts in his head. I sat up all night and nursed the poor fellow. He was out of his head and thought I was his mother.

The next night Tom Haggerty and I addressed the union meeting, telling them just what had happened. The men wanted to go clean up the gunmen but I told them that would only make more trouble. The meeting adjourned in a body to go see Jo. They went up to his room, six or eight of them at a time, until they had all seen him.

We tried to get a warrant out for the arrest of the gunmen but we couldn't because the coal company controlled the judges and the courts.

Jo was not the only man who was beaten up by the gunmen. There were many and the brutalities of these bloodhounds would fill volumes.

260. *The Strike at Lawrence, 1912*

"Report on Strike of Textile Workers in Lawrence, Massachusetts, in 1912," 62 Congress, 2 Session, *Senate Document*, No. 870 (Washington, 1912), 9, 11, 13–15.

THE STRIKE involved all of the textile mills in Lawrence and occurred in the early part of 1912. . . . During the first few days of the strike approximately 14,000 employees withdrew from their work, later accessions increased the number on strike to approximately 23,000, and at the time of the settlement of the strike there were still about 17,000 employees out.

The immediate cause of the strike was a reduction in earnings, growing out of the state law which became effective January 1, 1912, and which reduced the hours of employment for women and for children under 18 years of age from 56 to 54 hours per week. In January, 1910, through an enactment of the legislature, the hours of this class of employees had been reduced from 58 to 56 hours a week, and at that time the rates of pay for both time workers and pieceworkers were readjusted so that the earnings under the 56-hour week remained the same as under the 58-hour week.

The law provided that notice should be posted in all mills showing the exact number of hours and fractions of an hour that were to be worked each day after January 1, in order to bring about the 54-hour week. The necessary notices concerning hours required by law were posted in all the mills, but no notices were posted concerning any change in the rates for time- or pieceworkers. In the minds of the employees there was unquestionably much uncertainty as to what their earnings were to be under the new schedule of hours. . . .

Although dissatisfaction over the possibility of a reduction in earnings on account of the shortened hours had really begun before the 1st of January, it is evident that the mill officials did not appreciate the extent of this dissatisfaction or the possibilities latent in it. . . .

After the 1st of January the feeling on the part of the employees that they were to suffer a reduction of earnings grew steadily, and with it a correspondingly increasing feeling of unrest and a determination to resist any such reduction.

Up to the beginning of the strike there was little or no effective organization among the employees, taken as a whole. A few of the skilled crafts, composed principally of English-speaking workers, had their own separate organizations, but the ten crafts thus organized had at the time of the strike only approximately 2,500 members. The Industrial Workers of the World had also some years before this, established an organization in Lawrence. At the beginning of the strike they claimed a membership of approximately 1,000. . . . But it is estimated by active members of the organization that at the beginning of January, 1912, there were not more than 300 paid-up members on the rolls of the Industrial Workers. . . .

The increasing dissatisfaction over the prospect of reduced earnings began to make itself more manifest among the low-paid non-English-speaking employees. In the absence of any effective form of organization among this class of employees, it was difficult to formulate an articulate expression of opposition to the reduction in earnings or to bring it properly before the mill officials; but as the first pay day for time worked in 1912 approached, meetings began to be held which indicated clearly the possibilities of trouble that lay in the situation. . . .

Shortly after the strike began a "strike

committee," representing a large majority of the strikers and presided over by a member of the general executive board of the Industrial Workers of the World, formulated demands which included: fifteen per cent increase in wages on the 54-hour basis; double time for overtime work; ... abolition of all bonus and premium systems; no discrimination against the strikers for activity during the strike.

The "strike committee" did not change its demands throughout the strike except that after the arrest of Ettor and Giovannitti the demand for their release from jail on bail was added. The demands of the organizations affiliated with the Central Labor Union, made just before the middle of February, differed from the demands made by the "strike committee" in that advances were demanded for specific occupations or crafts; the increase demanded for most of the occupations was 15 per cent, although in a few occupations 20 per cent increase was asked, and in the case of some of the more skilled crafts as low as 4 per cent was asked.

On January 11, the date of the beginning of the strike, there was no violence, but on the next day, when several thousand employees quit work, they marched in a body and forced their way into two of the mills. Property was destroyed in the mills, mill windows were broken by pieces of ice thrown by the strikers, and also there was a collision between the strikers and police. On the following Monday morning there was more marching; also, property was destroyed in other mills, and again there was a collision between the strikers and the police. ...

To assist in maintaining order in Lawrence during the strike the regular police force was augmented by the appointment of special police and by the addition of metropolitan park police from other sections of the state and also through the calling out of a number of companies of militia. The militia remained on duty in Lawrence throughout the strike. Two deaths resulted from collisions between strikers and the authorities; one, a young Syrian, was stabbed with a bayonet, and the other, an Italian woman, was shot and killed during a riot. ...

The employees who were members of the Industrial Workers of the World, practically all of the unskilled workers, and some of the skilled crafts united for the purpose of the strike and selected a "strike committee," and this committee handled the strike. The "strike committee" was not a committee of the Industrial Workers of the World and a number of its members were not, to the close of the strike, affiliated with that organization. The chairman of the "strike committee," however, and several of the dominant figures in the conduct of the strike were members of the Industrial Workers at the time the strike began.

From the beginning of the strike there was no cooperation between the crafts organized on trade-union lines and represented by the Central Labor Union and the "strike committee," but there was, on the contrary, considerable hostility, which continued with increasing bitterness up to the conclusion of the strike. The strikers represented by the "strike committee" had, as already indicated, formulated their demands and made them public within a few days after the beginning of the strike.

It had been believed by the mill representatives during the early part of the strike that the skilled operatives affiliated with the Central Labor Union were not on strike, but had left the mill either on account of lack of work or through fear of violence. In the early part of February, however, these organizations definitely joined the strike and, in a series of meetings, they drew up a list of grievances to be submitted to the mills.

Thus what, in the beginning, had been a disorganized and more or less inarticulate protest against a reduction equivalent to two hours' earnings per week, and which had been started by a comparatively few unskilled, non-English-speaking employees, developed into an organized strike of over 20,000 employees, who demanded a considerable increase in wages and radical changes in working conditions affecting more than 30,000 textile workers in Lawrence....

As a result of the strike some 30,000 textile-mill employees secured an increase in wages of from 5 to 20 per cent; increased compensation for overtime; and the reduction of the premium period in certain occupations from four weeks to two weeks. Also, as an indirect result of the Lawrence strike, material increases in wages were granted to thousands of employees in other textile mills throughout New England.

261. *Wobbly Principles*, 1905

W. D. Haywood, *Bill Haywood's Book* (New York, 1929), 177.

UNIVERSAL economic evils afflicting the working class can be eradicated only by a universal working-class movement. Such a movement of the working class is impossible while separate craft and wage agreements are made favoring the employer against other crafts in the same industry, and while energies are wasted in fruitless jurisdiction struggles which serve only to further the personal aggrandizement of union officials.

A movement to fulfill these conditions must consist of one great industrial union embracing all industries,—providing for craft autonomy locally, industrial autonomy internationally, and working-class unity generally.

It must be founded on the class struggle, and its general administration must be conducted in harmony with the recognition of the irrepressible conflict between the capitalist class and the working class.

It should be established as the economic organization of the working class, without affiliation to any political party.

All power should rest in a collective membership.

Local, national and general administration, including union labels, buttons, badges, transfer cards, initiation fees, and per capita tax, should be uniform throughout....

Workingmen bringing union cards from industrial unions in foreign countries should be freely admitted into the organization.

XXX ✣ *Problems of Urban Life*

THE EFFECTS of industrial expansion touched every feature of American life after 1870—and most of all the cities. The factory was no longer situated in the small towns; it had become thoroughly urban. The metropolitan centers grew in number and in size, and they accommodated both industrial and commercial enterprises. All observers were astounded by the rapidity of growth in the new, as well as in the old, cities (No. 262). But the pace generated a host of very troublesome problems.

The men of the time defined the problems of city life in a variety of ways. For some people of wealth the core of the question was how to create the orderly and graceful social forms appropriate to their fortunes (No. 263). For other well-to-do folk the problem resolved itself into consideration of the means by which best to protect themselves against the lower elements, huddled in the dangerous slums in the very heart of the city and given over to vice, crime, and gambling (No. 264).

More perspicacious Americans, however, realized that gambling and crime grew out of a more complex pattern of life. A large part of the urban population was made up of immigrants, thrust out of Europe by economic disaster and attracted by the promise of the New World's opportunities (No. 265); millions landed in the United States and became a part of the labor force that made industrialization possible. The cost of transition was a long period of maladjustment. The cities grew too fast to house adequately these newcomers whose earning power was insufficient to supply them with decent accommodations. The strain on housing produced conditions in which cleanliness and order were well-nigh impossible (No. 266). Great metropolitan regions were reduced to slums in which life imposed intolerable burdens upon the human beings confined there (No. 267). The gallant efforts of social workers hardly touched the central problems of poverty.

Few could escape from those problems. Those who left the city to seek labor in construction work often met calamitous disasters (No. 268). Only on the farms was there hope; and the American farmers in these years faced imposing difficulties of their own (*see below*, Section XXXI).

262. *The Wonder of Chicago, 1882*

G. A. Sala, *America Revisited* (London, 1883), II, 125–9.

Forty years ago this city which now contains five hundred thousand inhabitants, and in another fifteen will probably contain a million, was a petty Indian trading post. The business portion of the city is now fourteen feet above the level of Lake Michigan. It was formerly much lower, but in 1856 the entire district was raised bodily to a height of nine feet by means of jack-screws inserted beneath the houses and worked night and day by half-turns and with an imperceptible motion. The city stands on the ridge dividing the basin of the Mississippi from that of the St. Lawrence, and is surrounded by a prairie extending several hundreds of miles south and west. In 1870 the population was about three hundred thousand.

Now ponder yet again. In October, 1871, Chicago was "burnt up." The fire originated on a Sunday evening in a small barn in DeHoven Street, in the south part of the western division of the city, the proximate cause of the conflagration being the upsetting of a kerosene lamp, by the light of which a cow was being milked. . . . The houses in the first division were mostly of wood, and there were several large timber-yards along the bank of the adjacent Chicago River. Then and there the flames swept with irresistible fury, and were carried by a strong westerly wind into the south division, a district thickly covered with stores, warehouses, and public buildings of stone or brick, many of which were erroneously supposed to be fireproof. The fire raged during the whole of Monday, crossing the main channel of the Chicago River, and carrying all before it in the northern district, chiefly occupied by dwelling houses. The last house which caught fire was destroyed on Sunday morning; but the ruins smoldered for months afterwards.

The total area burned up was close on three and a half square miles. Nearly 18,000 houses were destroyed, 200 persons lost their lives, and fully 200,000 more were rendered destitute. Not including depreciation of real estate and loss of business, the total loss occasioned by the fire was set down at 190 millions of dollars, out of which tremendous aggregate some thirty millions were covered by insurance; although one of the first results of the fire was to "bankrupt" half of the fire offices throughout the Union. Policies to a heavy amount were, however, held in English offices, which paid promptly. ... The consequence is that English fire insurance companies have been doing an immense business in Chicago ever since: the Western business men having shown signs of a pardonable partiality to ensure their property in offices which do not "bust" when fire risks fall in. Thus, on that fatal morrow of the fire, might the people of Chicago say, with Seneca, "One day betwixt a great city and none.". ...

But the Prairie City saw not the end of her miseries in the giant blaze of 1871. In July, 1874, another great fire swept over Chicago, destroying eighteen blocks, or sixty acres of buildings, in the heart of the city, and destroying over four million dollars' worth of property. On the Saturday night preceding my arrival here a vast range of bonded warehouses went up. ...

But Chicago has proved herself equal to the occasion; whether the city was to be screwed up or burned down she has preserved her high spirits and her untiring enterprise and go-aheadedness. On the day after the first fire there appeared in the midst of a mass of smoldering ruins, a pole surmounted by a board on which these words were writ large: "All lost except wife, children, and energy. Real estate agency, carried on as usual in the next shanty." And the undismayed real estate agent is alive to tell the tale, a prosperous gentleman, who proudly exhibits the "wife, children, and energy" placard in his handsome office. He has reason to be proud.

The wonderful Prairie City now ranks next in commercial importance to New York. Chicago is the largest grain market and emporium in the world. ... Her lumber trade is tremendous. She employs seventy thousand pairs of hands in her iron and steel works, her flour mills, her cotton factories, her boot and shoe manufactories, and her tanneries. And, in the year ending March, 1879, she slaughtered and packed 5,000,000 hogs and 65,000 head of cattle, in addition to curing innumerable hams.

263. *Making Society, 1890*

Ward McAllister, *Society as I Have Found It* (New York, 1890), 157–62, 212–13, 216–17.

AT THIS time there were not more than one or two men in New York who spent, in living and entertaining, over sixty thousand dollars a year. There were not half a dozen chefs in private families in this city. Compare those days to these, and see how easily one or two men of fortune could then control, lead, and carry on society, receive or shut out people at their pleasure. ... All this many of us saw, and saw how it worked, and we resolved to band together the respectable element of the city, and by this union make such strength that no individual could withstand us. . . . We . . . have found that the good and wise men of this community could always control society. This they have done and are still doing. Our first step then in carrying out these views was to arrange for a series of "cotillion dinners."

I must here explain, that behind what I call the "smart set" in society, there always stood the old, solid, substantial, and respected people. Families who held great social power as far back as the birth of this country, who were looked up to by society, and who always could, when they so wished, come forward and exercise their power, when, for one reason or another, they would take no active part, joining in it quietly, but not conspicuously. Ordinarily, they preferred, like the gods, to sit upon Olympus. . . . What I intend to convey is that the heads of these families, feeling secure in their position, knowing that they had great power when they chose to exercise it, took no leading part in society's daily routine. They gave handsome dinners, and perhaps, once a year, a fine ball. . . . To this day, if one of these old families, even one of its remotest branches, gives a day reception, you will find the street in which they live blockaded with equipages. . . .

The mistake made by the world at large is that fashionable people are selfish, frivolous, and indifferent to the welfare of their fellow-creatures; all of which is a popular error, arising simply from a want of knowledge of the true state of things. The elegancies of fashionable life nourish and benefit art and artists; they cause the expenditure of money and its distribution; and they really prevent our people and country from settling down into a humdrum rut and becoming merely a money-making and money-saving people, with nothing to brighten up and enliven life; they foster all the fine arts; but for

fashion what would become of them? They . . . adorn their houses with works of art, and themselves with all the taste and novelty they can find in any quarter of the globe, calling forth talent and ingenuity. Fashionable people cultivate and refine themselves, for fashion demands this of them. . . . I have found as warm, sympathetic, loving hearts in the garb of fashion as out of it. A thorough acquaintance with the world enables them to distinguish the wheat from the chaff, so that all the good work they do is done with knowledge and effect. The world could not dispense with it. . . .

I resolved in 1872 to establish in New York an American Almack's, taking men instead of women, being careful to select only the leading representative men of the city, who had the right to create and lead society. I knew all would depend upon our making a proper selection.

There is one rule in life I invariably carry out—never to rely wholly on my own judgment, but to get the advice of others, weigh it well and satisfy myself of its correctness, and then act on it. I went in this city to those who could make the best analysis of men; who knew their past as well as their present, and could foresee their future. In this way, I made up an Executive Committee of three gentlemen, who daily met at my house, and we went to work in earnest to make a list of those we should ask to join in the undertaking. One of this committee, a very bright, clever man, hit upon the name of Patriarchs for the Association, which was at once adopted, and then, after some discussion, we limited the number of Patriarchs to twenty-five, and that each Patriarch, for his subscription, should have the right of inviting to each ball four ladies and five gentlemen, including himself and family; that all distinguished strangers, up to fifty, should be asked; and then established the rules governing the giving of these balls—all of which, with some slight modifications, have been carried out to the letter to this day. . . .

The social life of a great part of our community, in my opinion, hinges on this and similar organizations, for it and they are organized social power, capable of giving a passport to society to all worthy of it. We thought it would not be wise to allow a handful of men having royal fortunes to have a sovereign's prerogative, i.e., to say whom society shall receive, and whom society shall shut out. We thought it better to try and place such power in the hands of representative men, the choice falling on them solely because of their worth, respectability, and responsibility.

264. *Playing Policy, 1892*

Helen Campbell, *Darkness and Daylight; or, Lights and Shadows of New York Life* (Hartford, 1892), 639–40.

"PLAYING policy" is a cheap way of gambling, but one on which hundreds if not thousands of dollars are risked every day in New York. Sums as low as three cents can be risked upon it, and there are policy-shops where bets of one cent are taken.

The play is upon numbers which are drawn daily, usually in Kentucky or Louisiana, and sent by telegraph. The numbers are from 1 to 78; the room where the game is played is, like those of other cheap gambling-dens, usually at the rear of a cigar-store, barroom, or other place where it does not rouse suspicion if many persons are seen entering. A long counter extends the entire length of the room, and behind this counter, near its center, sits the man who keeps the game and is called the "writer." He is not the proprietor, but simply a clerk on a salary, and his duties are to copy the slips handed up by the players, mark them with the amount of money paid, and watch to see that no fraud is practiced.

There are twenty-five plays every morning and the same number in the evening at the regular shops, and they all got their winning numbers from a central office in Broad Street. Near the "writer" is an iron spike or hook on which are the policy slips; each slip contains the winning numbers and is placed faced downwards so that nobody can see what it is. Let us now see how the scheme is worked.

I am about to try my luck at policy, and for this purpose enter a shop and pass through to the rear. If there are ten people in the room it is an even chance that three or four of them will be Negroes, as the colored brethren are very fond of this game of chance. The assemblage is promiscuous and not at all select.

Along the counter are numerous slips of paper for general use. I take one of the slips and write upon it five pairs of numbers, using any numbers from 1 to 78. I give this slip to the "writer," with fifteen cents, and say,

"Put me in for five gigs at three cents."

Two numbers are called a "saddle" and three numbers a "gig." There are numerous combinations in the game, but "gigs" and "saddles" are the most popular. I wait until the other players have put in their bets, which the "writer" copies and records and then hands back to the players, just as he copies and returns mine. When all the bets are in he takes the first policy slip from the spike or hook aforesaid, writes upon a slate the numbers he finds on the slip and then hangs it up where everybody can see it. He writes them in two columns of twelve numbers each, and if I have guessed two of the numbers in either column in one of my gigs, I walk up to the counter and present my ticket for payment, receiving ten times the amount of my wager.

But a man stands as good a chance of

being struck by lightning as he does of winning at this rate. Nevertheless the game is full of seductiveness on account of its possibilities and also on account of its cheapness. Some of the shops have telephone connections, and a customer who is known to the establishment can play policy without leaving his office, by simply telephoning his guesses. That a large amount of money may be lost at policy is shown by the circumstance that quite recently the cashier of an important law firm in New York City embezzled $125,000 of the money of his employers. When the defalcation was discovered and investigated it was found that this enormous sum had been spent in playing policy in a notorious shop on Broadway.

265. *The New Colossus, 1883*

Emma Lazarus, "The New Colossus," in *Poems* (Boston, 1889), I, 202–3.

Not like the brazen giant of Greek fame,
With conquering limbs astride from land to land;
Here at our sea-washed, sunset gates shall stand
A mighty woman with a torch, whose flame
Is the imprisoned lightning, and her name
Mother of Exiles. From her beacon-hand
Glows world-wide welcome; her mild eyes command
The air-bridged harbor that twin cities frame.
"Keep, ancient lands, your storied pomp!" cries she
With silent lips. "Give me your tired, your poor,
Your huddled masses yearning to breathe free,
The wretched refuse of your teeming shore.
Send these, the homeless, tempest-tost to me,
I lift my lamp beside the golden door!"

266. *How the Other Half Lived, 1890*

J. A. Riis, *How the Other Half Lives* (New York, 1890), 43–6, 74–6, 229–32, 235–6, 237–9.

Suppose we look into . . . No.—Cherry Street. Be a little careful, please! The hall is dark and you might stumble over the children pitching pennies back there. Not that it would hurt them; kicks and cuffs are their daily diet. They have little else. Here where the hall turns and dives into utter darkness is a step, and another, another. A flight of stairs. You can feel your way, if you cannot see it. Close? Yes! What would you have? All the fresh air that ever enters these stairs comes from the hall-door that is forever slamming, and from the windows of dark bedrooms that in turn receive from the stairs their sole supply of the elements God meant to be free, but man deals out with such niggardly hand. That was a woman filling her pail by the hydrant you just bumped against. The sinks are in the hallway, that all the tenants may have access—and all be poisoned alike by their summer stenches. Hear the pump squeak! It is the lullaby of tenement-house babes. In summer, when a thousand thirsty throats pant for a cooling drink in this block, it is worked in vain. But the saloon, whose open door you passed in the hall, is always there. The smell of it has followed you up. Here is a door. Listen! That short hacking cough, that tiny, helpless wail—what do they mean? They mean that the soiled bow of white you saw on the door downstairs will have another story to tell—Oh! a sadly familiar story—before the day is at an end. The child is dying with measles. With half a chance it might have lived; but it had none. That dark bedroom killed it.

"It was took all of a suddint," says the mother, smoothing the throbbing little body with trembling hands. There is no unkindness in the rough voice of the man in the jumper, who sits by the window grimly smoking a clay pipe, with the little life ebbing out in his sight, bitter as his words sound; "Hush, Mary! If we cannot keep the child, need we complain—such as we?"

Such as we! What if the words ring in your ears as we grope our way up the stairs and down from floor to floor, listening to the sounds behind the closed doors —some of quarreling, some of coarse songs, more of profanity. They are true. When the summer heats come with their suffering they have meaning more terrible than words can tell. Come over here. Step carefully over this baby—it is a baby, spite of its rags and dirt—under these iron bridges called fire-escapes, but loaded down, despite the incessant watchfulness of the firemen, with broken household goods, with wash-tubs and barrels, over which no man could climb from a fire.

This gap between dingy brick-walls is the yard. That strip of smoke-colored sky up there is the heaven of these people. Do you wonder the name does not attract them to the churches? That baby's parents live in the rear tenement here. She is at least as clean as the steps we are now climbing. There are plenty of houses with half a hundred such in them. The tenement is much like the one in front we just left, only fouler, closer, darker.... A hundred thousand people lived in rear tenements in New York last year....

The stale-beer dive, is known about "the Bend" by the more dignified name of the two-cent restaurant. Usually, as in this in-stance, it is in some cellar giving on a back alley. Doctored, unlicensed beer is its chief ware. Sometimes a cup of "coffee" and a stale roll may be had for two cents. The men pay the score. To the women ... the place is free. The beer is collected from the kegs put on the sidewalk by the saloon-keeper to await the brewer's cart, and is touched up with drugs to put a froth on it. The privilege to sit all night on a chair, or sleep on a table, or in a barrel, goes with each round of drinks. Generally an Italian, sometimes a Negro, occasionally a woman, "runs" the dive. Their customers, alike homeless and hopeless in their utter wretchedness, are the professional tramps. ... The meanest thief is infinitely above the stale-beer level. Once upon that plane there is no escape....

The exploits of the Paradise Park Gang in the way of highway robbery showed last summer that the embers of the scat-tered Whyo Gang, upon the wreck of which it grew, were smoldering still. The hanging of Driscoll broke up the Whyos because they were a comparatively small band, and, with the incomparable master-spirit gone, were unable to resist the angry rush of public indignation that followed the crowning outrage. This is the history of the passing away of famous gangs from time to time. The passing is more apparent than real, however. Some other daring leader gathers the scattered elements about him soon, and the war on society is re-sumed. ... By day they loaf in the corner groggeries on their beat, at night they plunder the stores along the avenues, or lie in wait at the river for unsteady feet straying their way. The man who is sober and minds his business they seldom molest, unless he be a stranger inquiring his way, or a policeman and the gang twenty against the one. The tipsy wayfarer is their chosen victim, and they seldom have to look for him long. One has not far to go to the river from any point in New York. The man who does not know where he is going is sure to reach it sooner or later. Should he foolishly resist or make an outcry—dead men tell no tales. "Floaters" come ashore every now and then with pockets turned inside out, not always evidence of a post-mortem inspection by dock-rats. Police patrol the rivers as well as the shore on constant look-out for these, but seldom catch up with them. If overtaken after a race during which shots are often exchanged from the boats, the thieves have an easy way of escaping and at the same time destroying the evidence against them; they simply upset the boat. They swim, one and all, like real rats; the lost plunder can be recovered at leisure the next day by diving or grappling. The loss of the boat counts for little. Another is stolen, and the gang is ready for business again.

The fiction of a social "club," which most of the gangs keep up, helps them to a pretext for blackmailing the politicians and the storekeepers in their bailiwick at the annual seasons of their picnic, or ball. The "thieves' ball" is as well known and recognized an institution on the East Side as the Charity Ball in a different social stratum, although it does not go by that name, in print at least. Indeed, the last thing a New York tough will admit is that he is a thief. He dignifies his calling with the pretense of gambling. He does not steal: he "wins" your money or your watch, and on the police returns he is a "speculator." If, when he passes around the hat for "voluntary" contributions, any storekeeper should have the temerity to refuse to chip in, he may look for a visit from the gang on the first dark night, and account himself lucky if his place escapes being altogether wrecked. The Hell's Kitchen Gang and the Rag Gang both have distinguished themselves within recent times by blowing up objectionable stores with stolen gunpowder. . . .

At least one hundred and fifty thousand women and girls earn their own living in New York, [apart from] . . . the large number who are not wholly dependent upon their own labor, while contributing by it to the family's earnings. These alone constitute a large class of the women wage-earners, and it is characteristic of the situation that the very fact that some need not starve on their wages condemns the rest to that fate. The pay they are willing to accept all have to take. What the "everlasting law of supply and demand," that serves as such a convenient gag for public indignation, has to do with it, one learns from observation all along the road of inquiry into these real woman's wrongs. To take the case of the saleswomen for illustration: . . . investigation . . . disclosed . . . that wages averaging from $2 to $4.50 a week were reduced by excessive fines, "the employers placing a value upon time lost that is not given to services rendered." A little girl, who received two dollars a week, made cash sales amounting to $167 in a single day, while the receipts of a fifteen-dollar male clerk in the same department footed up only $125; yet for some trivial mistake the girl was fined sixty cents out of her two dollars. The practice prevailed in some stores of dividing the fines between the superintendent and the timekeeper at the end of the year. In one instance they amounted to $3,000. . . . One of the causes for fine in a certain large store was sitting down. The law requiring seats for saleswomen, generally ignored, was obeyed faithfully in this establishment. The seats were there, but the girls were fined when found using them. . . .

Here is the case of a woman employed in the manufacturing department of a Broadway house. . . . She averages three dollars a week. Pays $1.50 for her room; for breakfast she has a cup of coffee; lunch she cannot afford. One meal a day is her allowance. This woman is young, she is pretty. She has "the world before her." Is it anything less than a miracle if she is guilty of nothing worse than the "early and improvident marriage," against which moralists exclaim as one of the prolific causes of the distress of the poor? Almost any door might seem to offer welcome escape from such slavery as this. "I feel so much healthier since I got three square meals a day," said a lodger in one of the Girls' Homes. Two young sewing-girls came in seeking domestic service, so that they might get enough to eat. They had been only half-fed for some time, and starvation had driven them to the one door at which the pride of the American-born girl will not permit her to knock, though poverty be the price of her independence.

267. *Life on Halsted Street, 1910*

Jane Addams, *Twenty Years at Hull-House* (New York, 1911), 97–100, 173–4. Copyright 1911 and used with permission of The Macmillan Company.

HALSTED STREET is thirty-two miles long, and one of the great thoroughfares of Chicago; Polk Street crosses it midway between the stockyards to the south and the shipbuilding yards on the north branch of the Chicago River. For the six miles between these two industries the street is lined with shops of butchers and grocers, with dingy and gorgeous saloons, and pretentious establishments for the sale of ready-made clothing. Polk Street, running west from Halsted Street, grows rapidly more prosperous; running a mile east to State Street, it grows steadily worse, and crosses a network of vice on the corners of Clark Street and Fifth Avenue.

Hull-House once stood in the suburbs, but the city has steadily grown up around it and its site now has corners on three or four foreign colonies. Between Halsted Street and the river live about ten thousand Italians—Neapolitans, Sicilians, and Calabrians, with an occasional Lombard or Venetian. To the south on Twelfth Street are many Germans, and side streets are given over almost entirely to Polish and Russian Jews. Still farther south, these Jewish colonies merge into a huge Bohemian colony, so vast that Chicago ranks as the third Bohemian city in the world. To the northwest are many Canadian-French, clannish in spite of their long residence in America, and to the north are Irish and first-generation Americans. On the streets directly west and farther north are well-to-do English-speaking families, many of whom own their houses and have lived in the neighborhood for years; one man is still living in his old farmhouse. . . .

Self-government breaks down in such a ward. The streets are inexpressibly dirty, the number of schools inadequate, sanitary legislation unenforced, the street lighting bad, the paving miserable and altogether lacking in the alleys and smaller streets, and the stables foul beyond description. Hundreds of houses are unconnected with the street sewer. The older and richer inhabitants seem anxious to move away as rapidly as they can afford it. They make room for newly arrived immigrants who are densely ignorant of civic duties.

This substitution of the older inhabitants is accomplished industrially also, in the south and east quarters of the ward. The Jews and Italians do the finishing for the great clothing manufacturers, formerly done by Americans, Irish and Germans, who refused to submit to the extremely low prices to which the sweating system has reduced their successors. As the design of the sweating system is the elimination of rent from the manufacture of clothing, the "outside work" is begun after the clothing leaves the cutter. An unscrupulous contractor regards no basement as too dark, no stable loft too foul, no rear shanty too provisional, no tenement room too small for his work-room, as these conditions imply low rental. Hence these shops abound in the worst of the foreign districts where the sweater easily finds his cheap basement and his home finishers.

The houses of the ward, for the most part wooden, were originally built for one family and are now occupied by several. They are after the type of the inconvenient frame cottages found in the poorer suburbs twenty years ago. Many of them were built where they now stand; others were brought thither on rollers, because their previous sites had been taken for factories. The fewer brick tenement buildings which are three or four stories high are comparatively new, and there are few large tenements. The little wooden houses have a temporary aspect, and for this reason, perhaps, the tenement-house legislation in Chicago is totally inadequate. Rear tenements flourish; many houses have no water supply save the faucet in the back yard, there are no fire escapes, the garbage and ashes are placed in wooden boxes which are fastened to the street pavements. . . .

"Goosie," as the children for years called a little boy . . . was brought to the nursery wrapped up in his mother's shawl, [and] always had his hair filled with the down and small feathers from the feather brush factory where she worked. One March morning, Goosie's mother was hanging out the washing on a shed roof at six o'clock, doing it thus early before she left for the factory. Five-year-old Goosie was trotting at her heels handing her clothespins, when he was suddenly blown off the roof by the high wind into the alley below. His neck was broken by the fall and as he lay piteous and limp on a pile of frozen refuse, his mother cheerily called him to "climb up again," so confident do overworked mothers become that their children cannot get hurt. After the funeral, as the poor mother sat in the nursery postponing the moment when she must go back to her empty rooms, I asked her, in a futile effort to be of comfort, if there was anything more we could do for her. The overworked, sorrow-stricken woman looked up and replied, "If you could give me my wages for tomorrow, I would not go to work in the factory at all. I would like to stay at home all day and hold the baby. Goosie was always asking me to take him and I never had any time." This statement revealed the condition of many nursery mothers who are obliged to forego the joys and solaces which belong to even the most poverty-stricken. The long hours of factory labor necessary for earning the support of a child leave no time for the tender care and caressing which may enrich the life of the most piteous baby.

268. *Working on the Railroad, 1910*

Pascal d'Angelo, *Son of Italy* (New York: The Macmillan Co., 1924), 99–114.

As soon as the office door was flung open we timidly approached it and entered. A young man was putting out some glaring signs in Italian calling for "braccianti" or laborers. Inside, a pompous gentleman loomed in back of a wooden counter. . . . Majestically, the man put on a pair of eyeglasses and scanned us. Other laborers, strangers to us, were crowding into the place.

Giorgio asked him how long we had to wait for a job, and how much it would cost to get to the place.

"It is like this," uttered the almost obese-looking man in a sonorous Neapolitan dialect, "you can start tomorrow if you want. The place is in West Virginia, which you may know, though I doubt it. I'll give you a letter of recommendation, and it will cost you five dollars for the fare—that is, if you all go together on one ticket, or else it will cost you eight dollars.". . .

High railroad fares are usually what keep laborers near this hell-hole metropolis. Going to a distant job is a gamble. A man may pay a large part of his scanty savings for fare. And when he gets there he may find living conditions impossible and the foreman too overbearing. Perhaps he will be fired at the end of [the] week. Where will he be then?

The obese gentleman mumbled almost to himself, "This is on the Cumberland Railroad."...

Each one of us gave the pompous gentleman five dollars for the fare, and handing us the ticket and letter he announced that at three o'clock the same day we could leave New York for our destined labors in West Virginia. And we could arrive there in time to go to work the following day.

We had about two hours to get ready. We all went to get our bundles and our one valise in which we had our common possessions. These consisted of pots, four old tin plates, rather yellow-looking, some spoons and forks for use in case we should ever dare to cook macaroni.... The rest of our armaments were a needle, thread, an old pair of pants from which we used to strip pieces of cloth for patching our clothes, remnants of a linen shirt and numerous buttons taken from shirts and drawers which we had thrown away when they reached the unpatchable stage. We got our personal bundles ready, Andrea swung the heavy valise on his broad shoulder, and we set out toward the distant dock of the Pennsylvania Railroad. And there on our presenting the ticket we would be led, transported, and conveyed to the land of sunshine and warmth....

Finally we were in the train speeding through dull winter landscapes toward our new job.

It was during the night hours that we got off a local train and stood shivering and confused on a dark platform.

"Can this be the place?" we thought.

An icy sword-like wind assailed us. We shivered. It was bitter cold, worse than New York. And where were the oranges? And where the flowers?

The region was indistinct around us, its hilly distances glimmering faintly with long stretches of wet snow. Inside the small wooden station was a dimly lit room. In a body, we entered and presented our checks to the baggage master.

He shook his head. There was no baggage for us. Perhaps it would arrive the following day. We were angered at the delay, for in our baggage were our warm quilts and mattress covers that we used to fill with straw or dried leaves on reaching a new place. We would have been considerably more angered at the time had we known where our poor baggage had gone. For there is another town in Pennsylvania also called Williamsport; and the carelessness of the baggage agent in New York had caused our belongings to be sent there.

Out we went, like a flock of sheep in the darkness where our feet sank at every step into wet sticky snow. It was beginning to rain as we started on our tramp toward the job which was about four miles away on the other side of the Potomac River....

On reaching the West Virginia side we again plunged into the hilly darkness.... On we went. Miles appeared very long that night. And finally, after a seemingly endless walk we reached the camp. Shining with the rain that had frozen to their black walls, five long shanties appeared in the dark. At one side was the camp store, a small shack where the commissary man sold bread, clothes, liquors and other necessities at the most exorbitant prices.

We knocked at the door of the first shanty. A man peeked out. At our request he slipped a jacket over his shoulders and came out to guide us toward the shanty where Mike the commissary man was.

On our entrance Mike was just opening a bottle of beer. He peered curiously at us. Four other men were playing cards around an empty beer keg which they used for a table.

Looking us over with fishy gray eyes Mike stepped out toward our party. Georgio Vanno explained who we were and Mike grunted for answer.

We announced our predicament, that

we had no blankets or mattress covers and were wet to the skin.

He shrugged his shoulders, mumbling "Too bad. But I can't help you. You may sleep in the next shanty where there is room for you." Saying which, he turned toward his beer bottle and smacked his lips.

We went out and hurried into the next shanty where only four other men were living at the time. Along the walls were broad shelves of pine boards on which we could sleep.

The driving wind shook the thin walls of the shanty which were merely composed of boards with tar paper nailed on the outside. Undecided, shivering, we all stood there. They had a stove in the place, but no coal; nor was there a stove pipe through which the smoke could pass out.

One of the four who was lying on the shelf turned about under his warm blanket and grumbled that we could get some soft coal at the boiler house. When we finally succeeded in starting a fire, however, it was impossible to stand the gas given off by the soft coal.

Without any appreciable success we tried to dry our clothes. It was getting very late. And gradually tiredness and sleep won us. Drearily we threw ourselves on the boards over which we had strewn some dirty straw.

When we arose early next morning our muscles were all stiffened and ached terribly. In order to limber ourselves a little we moved up and down the shanty.

A frost had succeeded the icy rain and we felt the wet of our clothes piercing our bodies like sharp needles.

The commissary man came in and said that we had better hurry out to work or we would get no food whatever from his store. And standing he glared about to see if anyone was sick or unable to rise. Seeing us all up, he went rumbling on, and returned after a while with the foreman who was to boss us.

The creaking and cracked floor was strewn with straw which had fallen from the shelves or "beds." Straw covered our clothes and hair. The whole inside of the shanty with its forlorn occupants gave a picture of moral wreck and bitterness. We were pigs in our sty.

This commissary man, Mike, though violent and ferocious, was really not so bad at heart. Once or twice he would, when drunk, threaten a few of the men with a rifle. But outside of that he was rather better than many others I have had the misfortune to know.

The commissary system prevails throughout this country. In its most extreme workings it results in perpetual peonage of the unlucky laborers who get caught. Usually the lure is high wages and free transportation to some distant locality. My own uncle, Giuseppe d'Angelo, was attracted to a place in Florida where he was held eight months before he was able to effect an escape. The food they gave him was vile and the living conditions were unspeakable. The laborers—white men—were guarded by ferocious Negroes with guns which they used at the least excuse. And this in free America. No wages are paid, and the men are told that instead of expecting any they themselves are in debt to the company.

A commissary man contracts to furnish the company with laborers. In return he is given the privilege of running the camp store—an absolute monopoly most of whose profits go to men higher up. He also has a free hand over the men, firing, hiring, robbing and even preventing poor unfortunates from leaving.

The commissary man always tries to get acquainted with men who have a large number of friends among the workers and who can persuade them to go where he wants. This sort of man get perhaps 15 or 20 cents more per day—which is considered an envied privilege, besides the fact that his board bill is always lower than anyone else's.

Each man has a small book in which are marked the prices of the objects he buys. The commissary man also keeps a book. And it is his book that counts, not the laborer's. If you try to save money and spend very little you will find when pay day comes that you are charged with as much debt as someone else who ate his fill. In the more decent places, where men are not slaves, the man who does not spend enough usually gets fired after a few warnings. A laborer is compelled to buy from the camp store at prices which would make a New York profiteer green with envy. And what they do receive after the commissary bill is deducted amounts to very little.

The foremen are helpless and subordinate to the commissary man. When work is scarce it is the married men who are the first to be fired, for the single as a rule spend more. And a man who drinks every cent he earns is considered a "good" man. The most welcome person is an organizer —not of unions—but of games. For during games the beer flows freely, for whoever loses must buy drinks. . . .

We followed our new foreman down the road. We were by now auguring ourselves bad luck.

"Who knows how it will end?" muttered Antonio.

We thought of our lost baggage and our vanished dreams of a sunny climate. Sheeplike we followed our foreman to where a large gang was already working. There were little engines called "donkey" puffing back and forth. A steam shovel was lifting a big rock caught in its iron teeth. Steam drillers were battering the stony bank alongside the railroad. Derricks were swinging the heaviest boulders about 20 feet above the ground with amazing ease.

Now and then a Cumberland Valley Railroad freight train would pass by; then a coal train; then a passenger train. . . .

Several weeks passed. We were dissatisfied with the place. Some talked of leaving. Some talked of staying a little while more. Rumors were reaching us of good jobs in other parts.

One day we were working on an embankment. A derrick was perched above us. We used it to lift big boulders into the cars that were pulled on the improvised tracks by the donkey engines. There was a snap, a yell. One of the guys or cables that held the derrick broke. Down crashed the enormous structure. Shouting together we leaped away. There was a howl of pain, blood-curdling and piercing. We turned our startled eyes. Two men were pinned under the derrick. One of them was Teofilo, the other our huge Andrea.

It seemed almost the work of an instant that snapped the life of the smaller man. Andrea was still alive, though, his face twisted by agony. Teofilo stared off into infinity.

Quickly we all rushed together to lift the derrick. But we were too excited; and as we raised a ponderous weight, in spite of our taut muscles, it slid down the embankment. With a horrible grinding sound of flesh and bones it crushed the last life out of Andrea Lenta. We covered our eyes with our arms and groaned.

Within a few days after this fatal accident the gang broke up. We had lost all heart; work in that place was oppressive; we felt enslaved. And finally, discouraged and saddened by our loss, we decided to quit. Sadly we returned to New York.

XXXI ⁂ *The Farmers' Dilemmas*

For American farmers the period after 1870 opened in a blaze of enthusiasm. Memories of the high prices of Civil War times nurtured unlimited optimism, and the immense areas still available for settlement west of the Mississippi promised ever greater abundance. The poet's vision was inflamed by the very prospect of the prairies (No. 269); and the scientist, surveying the region, saw hopes for the redemption even of very arid lands (No. 270). When men thought of the possibility of using the new machines of agriculture on these virgin lands, they could see no bounds to future progress. Providence seemed to have arranged these new areas for a prosperity greater than husbandmen had ever experienced before (No. 271).

Indeed, the output of agriculture rose steadily. But the farmer discovered often that he nonetheless suffered from falling prices, which threatened to push him to the wall. At first, and particularly in the Old Northwest, the difficulties seemed to arise from the avarice of selfish transportation monopolies; and the farmers then sought relief in government control of railroads (No. 272; *see also above*, No. 247).

Experience showed, however, that the problem was more complex; for the American farmer was attempting to adapt traditional family enterprise to the conditions of a modern world market in which prices were set by larger forces than he could control (No. 273). There was no disposition, yet, to lose faith in the accepted organization of agriculture; indeed men looked back to an earlier period with nostalgia (*see above*, No. 147). Rather, the blame for the disorder was located in the operations of an international financial conspiracy which controlled markets and made the farmers its victims (No. 274). Such grievances were most bitter in regions of farm debt and of tenancy, and particularly in the South (No. 275).

These difficulties cast a somber shadow over the life of the American agriculturist. Defeat was too familiar (No. 276); and the narrow life of the country and of the rural township had a constricting effect upon the human beings confined there (No. 277). Hence, a tone of bitterness crept into the political movements that voiced the farmers' protests (*see below*, No. 295).

269. *Poem of the Prairies, 1882*

Walt Whitman, "The Prairies and Great Plains in Poetry"; and "America's Characteristic Landscape," in *Complete Prose Works* (New York, 1902), I, 270–1, 272–3.

MY DAYS and nights, as I travel here— what an exhilaration!—not the air alone, and the sense of vastness, but every local sight and feature. Everywhere something characteristic—the cactuses, pinks, buffalo grass, wild sage—the receding perspective, and the far circle-line of the horizon all times of day, especially forenoon—the clear, pure, cool, rarefied nutriment for the lungs, previously quite unknown—the black patches and streaks left by surface-conflagrations—the deep-plough'd furrow of the "fire-guard"—the slanting snow-racks built all along to shield the railroad from winter drifts—the prairie-dogs and the herds of antelope—the curious "dry rivers"—occasionally a "dug-out" or corral—Fort Riley and Fort Wallace— those towns of the northern plains (like ships on the sea), Eagle-Tail, Coyote, Cheyenne, Agate, Monotony, Kit Carson —with ever the ant-hill and the buffalo-wallow—ever the herds of cattle and the cow-boys ("cow-punchers"), to me a strangely interesting class, bright-eyed as hawks, with their swarthy complexions and their broad-brimm'd hats—apparently always on horseback, with loose arms slightly raised and swinging as they ride....

Speaking generally as to the capacity and sure future destiny of that plain and prairie area (larger than any European kingdom) it is the inexhaustible land of wheat, maize, wool, flax, coal, iron, beef and pork, butter and cheese, apples and grapes—land of ten million virgin farms—to the eye at present wild and unproductive—yet experts say that upon it when irrigated may easily be grown enough wheat to feed the world.

Then as to scenery (giving my own thought and feeling), while I know the standard claim is that Yosemite, Niagara Falls, the upper Yellowstone and the like, afford the greatest natural shows, I am not so sure but the Prairies and the Plains, while less stunning at first sight, last longer, fill the esthetic sense fuller, precede all the rest, and make North America's characteristic landscape.

Indeed through the whole of this journey, with all its shows and varieties, what most impress'd me, and will longest remain with me, are these same prairies. Day after day, and night after night, to my eyes, to all my senses—the esthetic one most of all—they silently and broadly unfolded. Even their simplest statistics are sublime.

270. *The Arid Region, 1879*

J. W. Powell, *Report on the Lands of the Arid Region of the United States* (Washington, 1879), 6, 7–10, 23–4.

IN ORDER to set forth the characteristics of these lands and the conditions under which they can be most profitably utilized, it is deemed best to discuss first a somewhat limited region in detail as a fair type of the whole.... It is proposed to take up for this discussion only the area embraced in Utah Territory....

Having determined from the operations of irrigation that one cubic foot per second of water will irrigate from 80 to 100 acres of land when the greatest economy is used, and having determined the volume of water or number of cubic feet per second flowing in the several streams of Utah by the most thorough methods available under the circumstances, it appears that within the territory, excluding a small portion in the southeastern corner where the survey has not yet been completed, the amount of land which it is possible to redeem by this method is about 2,262

square miles, or 1,447,920 acres. Of course this amount does not lie in a continuous body, but is scattered in small tracts along the water courses. . . . That is, 2.8 per cent of the lands under consideration can be cultivated by utilizing all the available streams during the irrigating season. . . .

This statement of the facts relating to the irrigable lands of Utah will serve to give a clearer conception of the extent and condition of the irrigable lands throughout the Arid Region. Such as can be redeemed are scattered along the water courses, and are in general the lowest lands of the several districts to which they belong. . . .

The Arid Region is somewhat more than four-tenths of the total area of the United States, and as the agricultural interests of so great an area are dependent upon irrigation it will be interesting to consider certain questions relating to the economy and practicability of distributing the waters over the lands to be redeemed.

There are two considerations that make irrigation attractive to the agriculturist. Crops thus cultivated are not subject to the vicissitudes of rainfall; the farmer fears no droughts; his labors are seldom interrupted and his crops rarely injured by storms. This immunity from drought and storm renders agricultural operations much more certain than in regions of greater humidity. Again, the water comes down from the mountains and plateaus freighted with fertilizing materials derived from the decaying vegetation and soils of the upper regions, which are spread by the flowing water over the cultivated lands. It is probable that the benefits derived from this source alone will be full compensation for the cost of the process.

271. *The New West, 1887*

W. M. Thayer, *Marvels of the New West* (Norwich, 1887), 628, 630, 637–8, 640–5, 710–11.

WHO has not heard of the cornfields of Kansas and the wheatfields of Dakota? Not that all the mammoth fields of corn and wheat are found in these localities; for the New West, clear to the Pacific coast, challenges the world to survey its empire of golden grain. . . .

The wildest dream has become reality. . . . Nothing is too large for belief. Twenty and even thirty thousand acre farms, and a hundred bushels to the acre, is not an extravagant story now. Corn eighteen feet high, with ears long and heavy enough for a policeman's club, is not questioned now even by the uninitiated. Harvests like an army with banners, waving their golden plumes above the house which the farmer occupies, require no stretch of the imagination to realize.

We have seen Kansas corn several feet higher than the dwelling which the owner occupied. The stocks were marvelously stout as compared with Eastern corn, and seemed to defy ordinary methods of harvesting. An axe appeared as necessary to lay that field of corn flat as in gathering a crop of hoop-poles. . . .

A farm of twenty or thirty thousand acres . . . is divided into sections, with superintendent and army of employees for each section, who go to work with military precision and order. The . . . workers . . . [move] forward like a column of cavalry, turning over a hundred acres of soil in an incredibly brief period of time. . . . Under this arrangement the earth is easily conquered by this mighty army of ploughers, who move forward to the music of rattling machines and the tramp of horses. It is an inspiring spectacle,—the almost boundless prairie farm and the cohorts of hopeful tillers marching over it in triumph. Steam also reinforces the battalions of workers on many bonanza farms, largely multiplying the amount of labor performed. . . .

"Necessity is the mother of invention"; and so the wheat-raisers found a way of harvesting their enormous crops. Our forefathers used the sickle, a very slow and unsatisfactory method of gathering grain. Less than a hundred years ago the "cradle" . . . created a revolution in harvesting. . . . But even the "cradle" could not avail much on the vast wheatfields of the New West. . . . One hundred men could cradle but three hundred acres per day at the most; and one hundred days, at this rate, would be required for harvesting. This would "cost more than it comes to." Western farmers could not afford the expense. It was absolutely necessary that some other method of harvesting grain should be discovered, and it was. A machine for cutting, binding, and placing the bundles in an upright position met the needs of the hour. The problem of harvesting the largest fields of grain was solved by this invention. . . .

"The wheat that is standing in the field in the morning is found in sacks, and frequently at the shipping depot, ready to be put on the steamer or cars for market before night. We have known it to be carried to mill and returned to the farm in the form of flour, and cooked, so that the hands who cut it in the morning ate it at supper in the form of warm biscuit. We have in the San Joaquin valley, working successfully, combined headers and threshers. These machines move before the horses,—from twenty to twenty-four horses or mules to each machine,—cut and thresh and sack the grain, and leave the sacks in piles. Four men work them, and cut and thresh from twenty-five to forty acres a day. . . ."

Eastern farmers cannot understand how it is that North Dakota, with its cold, piercing winters and terrible blizzards, and summers swept by cyclones, can produce more wheat per acre than even California. A scientist explains the matter as follows: "The qualities of climate which bear on wheat-raising in North Dakota, and contribute more regularly, uniformly, and efficiently to the growth of the crop than any found in more southerly climes, are, more daily sunshine,—the days, by reason of the higher altitude, being longer,—cool nights which always favor the cereal crops, deep frosts which gradually melt and supply moisture to the growing plant, less intense heat during the maturing months, fewer injurious caprices of weather at the critical period of growth, and natural climatic conditions which render possible the production of hard spring wheat,—a cheap crop, by reason of its being a quick crop of only about one hundred days from seeding to maturity.". . .

The New West . . . is a veritable "Wonderland," as crowded with OPPORTUNITIES as it is with marvels. Men live rapidly here—a whole month in one day, a whole year in a month. Some have lived a hundred years in the twenty-five or thirty they have spent here. They have seen an empire rise and grow rich and powerful in that time. The changes wrought under their own eyes have been almost as startling as transformations under the wand of a magician,—such strides of progress as usually exist only in dreams. It seems as if God had concentrated His wisdom and power upon this part of our country, to make it His crowning work of modern civilization on this Western Continent. For its history is Providence illustrated,—God in the affairs of men to exhibit the grandeur of human enterprise and the glory of human achievement. . . .

Why did the settlement of our country begin in the East instead of in the West? Why did the "Pilgrim Fathers" land on the coast of New England instead of the coast of California? . . . The same hand that guided them to the "rock-bound shores" of the Atlantic might have led them to the "gold-fretted shores" of the Pacific. There is no solution to the problem except in the wonder-working Providence of God. On this continent was to be built up the largest, richest, most intelligent, and powerful Christian nation on earth. A fearless, self-sacrificing, intelligent, hardy Christian race, disciplined by perils and hardships indescribable, could alone lay the foundations and work out the grand problem. Hence, rocks were better for them than nuggets of gold. . . .

All the conditions indicate that in the Divine Plan it was absolutely necessary to lay the foundations in granite that the superstructure might be finished in gold. Neither science, art, learning, or religion was competent to handle such marvelous wealth as lay concealed within the domain of the New West. When "the fullness of time" came, religion and learning, science and art, commerce and enterprise, had multiplied their institutions and power so wonderfully, that they could employ the millions and billions of wealth marvelously evolved to lift up humanity, and contribute to the more rapid growth of a model Christian civilization.

272. *The Farmers' Demands, 1873–74*

Resolutions of the Springfield Convention, April 2, 1873; and Declaration of Purpose of the National Grange, 1874. Quoted in Jonathan Periam, *The Groundswell* (Cincinnati, 1874), 286–9; *Proceedings of the Seventh Session of the National Grange of the Patrons of Husbandry* [St. Louis, February 11, 1874] (New York, 1874), 56–60.

A Farmers' Convention, 1873

RESOLVED, by the farmers of Illinois, in mass meeting assembled, that all chartered monopolies, not regulated and controlled by law, have proved in that respect detrimental to the public prosperity, corrupting in their management, and dangerous to republican institutions.

Resolved, that the railways ... have proved themselves arbitrary, extortionate, and ... opposed to free institutions and free commerce between states. ...

Resolved, that we regard it as the undoubted power, and the imperative duty of the legislature, to pass laws fixing reasonable maximum rates for freight and passengers, without classification of roads, and that we urge upon our General Assembly the passage of such laws. ...

Resolved, that we urge the passage of a bill enforcing the principle that railroads are public highways, and requiring railroads to make connections with all roads whose tracks meet or cross their own, and to receive and transmit cars and trains offered over their roads at reasonable maximum rates, ... and empowering the making of connections by municipal corporations for that purpose, and for the public use. ...

Whereas, the constitution of 1870, Article XI, Section 13, prohibits any railroad company from issuing watered stock ... and, whereas, this article of the constitution has probably been violated by nearly all the railroad companies in the state; therefore, Resolved, that it is the duty of the railroad commissioners to look carefully into this matter, and to commence proceedings in all clear cases by *quo war-*

ranto, or otherwise, against all railroad companies which have disregarded this important provision of the organic law of the state. ...

Resolved, that we are in favor of the immediate repeal of the protective duties on iron, steel, lumber, and all materials which enter into the construction of railroad cars, steamships, sailing vessels, agricultural implements, etc., and that we urge upon Congress immediate action for this purpose, that cheap railroads and cheap ships are necessary to cheap freights; and that we invite the railroad companies to cooperate with us to that end.

Declaration of Purpose of the National Grange, 1874

GENERAL OBJECTS. ... United by the strong and faithful tie of agriculture, we mutually resolve to labor for the good of our Order, our country, and mankind. ...

SPECIFIC OBJECTS. ... We shall endeavor to advance our cause by laboring to accomplish the following objects:

To develop a better and higher manhood and womanhood among ourselves. To enhance the comforts and attractions of our homes, and strengthen our attachments to our pursuits. To foster mutual understanding and cooperation. To maintain inviolate our laws, and to emulate each other in labor to hasten the good time coming. To reduce our expenses, both individual and corporate. To buy less and produce more, in order to make our farms self-sustaining. To diversify our crops, and crop no more than we can cultivate. ... To systematize our work, and calculate intelligently on probabilities. To discountenance the credit system, the mortgage system, the fashion system, and every other system tending to prodigality and bankruptcy.

We propose meeting together, talking together, working together, buying together, selling together, and in general acting together for our mutual protection and advancement, as occasion may require. We shall avoid litigation as much as possible by arbitration in the Grange. . . .

BUSINESS RELATIONS. . . . For our business interests, we desire to bring producers and consumers, farmers and manufacturers into the most direct and friendly relations possible. Hence we must dispense with a surplus of middlemen, not that we are unfriendly to them, but we do not need them. Their surplus and their exactions diminish our profits. . . .

Transportation companies of every kind are necessary to our success, . . . their interests are intimately connected with our interests, and harmonious action is mutually advantageous. . . . We shall, therefore, advocate for every state the increase in every practicable way, of all facilities for transporting cheaply to the seaboard, or between home producers and consumers, all the productions of our country. We adopt it as our fixed purpose to "open out the channels in nature's great arteries that the life-blood of commerce may flow freely.". . .

We are opposed to such spirit and man-agement of any corporation or enterprise as tends to oppress the people and rob them of their just profits. We are not enemies to capital, but we oppose the tyranny of monopolies. We long to see the antagonism between capital and labor removed by common consent, and by an enlightened statesmanship worthy of the nineteenth century. We are opposed to excessive salaries, high rates of interest, and exorbitant per cent profits in trade. They greatly increase our burdens, and do not bear a proper proportion to the profits of producers. We desire only self-protection and the protection of every true interest of our land by legitimate transactions, legitimate trade, and legitimate profits. . . .

OUTSIDE COOPERATION. . . . Ours being peculiarly a farmers' institution, we cannot admit all to our ranks. Many are excluded by the nature of our organization, not because they are professional men, or artisans, or laborers, but because they have not a sufficient direct interest in tilling the soil, or may have some interest in conflict with our purposes. But we appeal to all good citizens for their cordial cooperation to assist in our efforts toward reform, that we may eventually remove from our midst the last vestige of tyranny and corruption. We hail the general desire for fraternal harmony, equitable compromises, and earnest cooperation, as an omen of our future success.

273. *An Iowa Farm, 1870's*

Herbert Quick, *One Man's Life* (Indianapolis, 1925), 207–9, 212–17.

WE GREW wonderful wheat at first; the only problem was to get it to market and to live on the proceeds when it was sold. My father hauled his wheat from the Iowa River to Waterloo, and even to Iowa City, when it was the railhead for our part of the country; hauled it slowly over mere trails across the prairie. It took him three days to market a load of wheat in Waterloo. . . .

But the worst, however, was yet to come. A harvest came when we found that something was wrong with the wheat. No longer did the stalks stand clean and green as of old until they went golden in the sun. The broad green blades were spotted red and black with rust. Still it grew tall and rank; but as it matured it showed signs of disease. The heads did not fill well. Some blight was at work on it. However, we thought next year all would be well again. And when it grew worse year by year, it became a blight not only on the life of the grain but on human life as well. Wheat was almost our sole cash crop. If it failed, what should we do? And it was failing!

We were incurring, of course, the penalty for a one-crop system. We ought to have known that it was inevitable. . . .

This . . . gave me my first contact with the phenomenon which puzzles so many city people. If the farmers are losing money on a certain crop, why in the world don't they change to something else? It is not so easy to change as the city man may think. The wheat growers of the Central States at the time of this writing have been losing money on their wheat for years; but if they endeavor to change, they are confronted by a great problem. Such a change means the adoption of an entirely new rotation of crops. They have for years used a three- or four-year rotation—wheat, then corn, then clover. The sowing of the wheat gives them the chance to put in their fertilizer. They are used to this system. Any change from it involves the risking of a new crop on which losses are also probable. . . .

The fields of grain had always been a delight to me. . . . But now all the poetry went out of it. There was no joy for the soul of the boy who was steeped in such poetry as he could stumble upon, in these grain-fields threatened by grasshoppers, eaten by chinchbugs, blackened with molds and rusts, their blades specked as with the shed blood of the husbandman, their gold dulled by disease, their straw crinkling down in dead brittleness instead of rising and falling and swaying with the beautiful resiliency of health and abundance. . . .

All this time, while we were playing the role of the tortured victims in the tragedy of the wheat, we were feeling our way toward some way out. We knew that our fields would grow great crops of maize— it was a good corn country. But if there was more than one person who grew and fed cattle for the market there, I did not know of it. The average small farmer grew into the combination of hogs and corn. Gradually we changed over from wheat farming to big cornfields and populous hog lots. And then the price of both corn and pork went down, down, down, until corn sold for less than ten cents a bushel in our depreciated money and hogs for even less than three cents a pound. We had not found out about the balanced ration and the hog's need of pasture; and after a few generations of a diet of corn, the swine lost vitality and the crop of young pigs failed save where there was milk for them. The villain of misfortune still pursued us. . . .

Gradually we worked out a better *modus vivendi*—worked it out in a welter of debt and a depression which has characterized the rural mind to this day. Corn and hogs came to pay us as little as had wheat; yet for a while they were our only recourse, for the soil refused to grow wheat. For a long time there was plenty of open prairie on which cattle could be grazed freely. . . . Then the expanding acres of wheat land cut us off from any extended range of free grass. We had no fencing until barbed wire came in. So our cows were picketed on the prairie, led to water and cared for much as the Danes handle their cows now.

In spite of these difficulties, however, it gradually dawned upon us that by the sale of butter we were getting a little money from time to time. And though eggs were sometimes as low as eight cents a dozen, they brought in some funds. The skim milk restored our hogs to health. Without conscious planning, we were entering the business of mixed farming. My mother's butter was famed in all the nearby villages. In view of all the pains she took with it, it should have been; for she met the hot weather of our Iowa summers by hanging both cream and butter down the well where it was cool. Finally a creamery was started in Holland, a small town near us; and by this time we had a nice little herd of cows. A tank was made where water could be pumped through it and in this we set our cans of milk; and the cream hauler of the creamery came, skimmed off the cream, gave us tickets for it and hauled it away, thus giving us the cash when we went to town and saving the women the work of making the butter. It was the first contact of the factory system with the Iowa farm.

All this made life easier both as to labor and money. But it was not our only amelioration. We began to have a better food supply ... [as] our strawberries, raspberries, grapes, gooseberries, currants and cherries yielded abundantly. I had a patch of raspberries which I pruned and tended on a system of my own which gave us all we could consume and furnished dividends for our friends. In place of the old regimen of dried fruits and just dry groceries, we were surfeited on jams, jellies, preserves and other delicious viands; and with our supply of milk and cream, found the pioneer epoch definitely past so far as the larder was concerned. The prairie had been tamed. Iowa had been civilized. Our eighty-acre farm was furnishing us a real living for the first time....

The farmer is often accused by the city dweller of being a confirmed calamity howler. He is. He is such because almost every calamity which comes on the land hits him sooner or later. Whenever any other industry shifts from under an economic change it shifts it in part upon the farmer, and the farmer is unable to shift it in his turn; while most other shiftees can, by adding to prices or wages, get from under the load. The farmer is so placed that there is nothing beyond him but the wall. He is crushed against it. There is nothing under him but the earth. He is pressed into it. He is the end of the line in the economic game of crack the whip, and he is cracked off.

274. *Wall Street and the Farmer,* 1891

W. A. Peffer, *The Farmer's Side* (New York, 1891), 42, 56, 58–63, 121–3.

FARMERS are passing through the "valley and shadow of death"; farming as a business is profitless; values of farm products have fallen 50 per cent since the great war, and farm values have depreciated 25 to 50 per cent during the last ten years; farmers are overwhelmed with debts secured by mortgages on their homes, unable in many instances to pay even the interest as it falls due, and unable to renew the loans because securities are weakening by reason of the general depression; many farmers are losing their homes under this dreadful blight, and the mortgage mill still grinds. We are in the hands of a merciless power; the people's homes are at stake....

The American farmer of today is altogether a different sort of a man from his ancestor of fifty or a hundred years ago. ...All over the West, ... the farmer thrashes his wheat all at one time, he disposes of it all at one time, and in a great many instances the straw is wasted. He sells his hogs, and buys bacon and pork; he sells his cattle, and buys fresh beef and canned beef or corned beef, as the case may be; he sells his fruit, and buys it back in cans. ... Not more than one farmer in fifty now keeps sheep at all; he relies upon the large sheep farmer for the wool, which is put into cloth or clothing ready for his use. Instead of having clothing made up on the farm in his own house or by a neighbor woman or country tailor a mile away, he either purchases his clothing ready made at the nearest town, or he buys the cloth and has a city tailor make it up for him. Instead of making implements which he uses about the farm—forks, rakes, etc., he goes to town to purchase even a handle for his axe or his mallet; ... indeed, he buys nearly everything now that he produced at one time himself, and these things all cost money.

Besides all this, and what seems stranger than anything else, whereas in the earlier time the American home was a free home, unencumbered, ... and whereas but a small amount of money was then needed for actual use in conducting the business of farming, there was always enough of it among the farmers to supply the demand, now, when at least ten times as much is needed, there is little or none to be obtained. ...

The railroad builder, the banker, the money changer, and the manufacturer undermined the farmer. ... The manufacturer came with his woolen mill, his carding mill, his broom factory, his rope factory, his wooden-ware factory, his cotton factory, his pork-packing establishment, his canning factory and fruit-preserving houses; the little shop on the farm has given place to the large shop in town; the wagon-maker's shop in the neighborhood has given way to the large establishment in the city where men by the thousand work and where a hundred or two hundred wagons are made in a week; the shoemaker's shop has given way to large establishments in the cities where most of the work is done by machines; the old smoke house has given way to the packing house, and the fruit cellars have been displaced by preserving factories. The farmer now is compelled to go to town for nearly everything that he wants. ... And what is worse than all, if he needs a little more money than he has about him, he is compelled to go to town to borrow it. But he does not find the money there; in place of it he finds an agent who will "negotiate"

a loan for him. The money is in the East ... five thousand miles away. He pays the agent his commission, pays all the expenses of looking through the records and furnishing abstracts, pays for every postage stamp used in the transaction, and finally receives a draft for the amount of money required, minus these expenses. In this way the farmers of the country today are maintaining an army of middlemen, loan agents, bankers, and others, who are absolutely worthless for all good purposes in the community. ...

These things, however, are on only the mechanical side of the farmer. His domain has been invaded by men of his own calling, who have taken up large tracts of land and farmed upon the plan of the manufacturers who employ a great many persons to perform the work under one management. This is "bonanza" farming. ... The aim of some of the great "bonanza farms" of Dakota has been to apply machinery so effectually that the cultivation of one full section, or six hundred and forty acres, shall represent one year's work of only one man. This has not yet been reached, but so far as the production of the grain of wheat is concerned, one man's work will now give to each of one thousand persons enough for a barrel of flour a year, which is the average ration. ...

The manufacture of oleomargarine came into active competition with farm butter. And about the same time a process was discovered by which a substitute for lard was produced—an article so very like the genuine lard taken from the fat of swine that the farmer himself was deceived by it. ...

From this array of testimony the reader need have no difficulty in determining for himself "how we got here." The hand of the money changer is upon us. Money dictates our financial policy; money controls the business of the country; money is despoiling the people. ... These men of Wall Street ... hold the bonds of nearly every state, county, city and township in the Union; every railroad owes them more than it is worth. Corners in grain and other products of toil are the legitimate fruits of Wall Street methods. Every trust and combine made to rob the people had its origin in the example of Wall Street dealers.... This dangerous power which money gives is fast undermining the liberties of the people. It now has control of nearly half their homes, and is reaching out its clutching hands for the rest. This is the power we have to deal with.

275. *Debt and Tenancy, 1902*

Final Report of the Industrial Commission, 1902 (Washington, 1902), XIX, 97, 98–9.

IN THE cotton counties around Dallas, Waco, and the bottoms of the Brazos River, Texas, 75 per cent of the best cotton land is owned by men who live in large towns, and is farmed by a poor and shiftless class of whites and Negroes who, under the strict and unceasing supervision of the owner, or his agent, generally make for the owner a handsome profit upon the present valuation. The cotton planter with, say, 2,000 acres of fertile land divides it into tracts varying from 50 to 100 acres each. Each tract is fenced and improved to the extent of a house, barn, and corncrib. This tract is leased for a year, beginning with January 1. Although the planters prefer that the tenants should furnish their own stock, implements, and seed, it is difficult to find renters who are sufficiently well equipped or have enough capital to take the land on such terms. In nearly every case the landlord is expected to furnish everything, including food and clothing for the family, until such time as the crop is harvested and sold....

When the planter, in many parts of the Southern states, leases his ground and furnishes nothing to make a crop, he receives one-third or one-fourth of the crop. Cash rental is the exception rather than the rule. Where the planter furnishes the livestock, implements, and supplies, he gets one-half of the cotton and one-half of the corn, and deducts from the renter's share of the crop money an amount sufficient to pay liberal prices for all supplies furnished and liberal interest on the money. The result of this system is that the renters rarely ever succeed in laying by a surplus. On the contrary, their experiences are so discouraging that they seldom remain on the same farm for more than a year. They are not only unable to lay by any money, but their children remain uneducated and half clothed. The system is apparently one of the most undesirable, so far as its effect on the community is concerned....

The tenant system or crop-sharing system, which seems to be the prevailing feature of land tenure throughout the cotton belt, is not regarded as an advantageous arrangement between the tenants and landlords, but, on the contrary, would be gladly gotten rid of for a better system if the conditions permitted it.... Under this system the crop, to a great extent, and the land, generally, are apt to be neglected. The tenant is desirous of expending as little labor as possible and the landlord of getting the largest crop return. The permanent value of the land is apt to be sacrificed for lack of competent supervision, and deterioration of the property in general is quite certain to grow at a more rapid rate than under a different system of occupancy. The renter has little or no interest in the maintenance of permanent improvements. This is especially true where the contract is made for a year at a time, admitting of frequent changes of tenants and enabling them to evade the responsibilities of careful management and methods of cultivation. Consequently both the permanent improvements and the quality of the soil deteriorate under this system. The tenant is, furthermore, at a disadvantage in exchanging his crop for family supplies. He sells his corn at the lowest price to the country merchant from whom he gets his provisions in exchange, paying the highest price the country merchant sees fit to demand. This same corn which is sold early in the fall may have to be bought back from the country merchant by the tenant late in the winter at from 50 to 100 per cent advance.

276. *Defeat, 1880's*

Hamlin Garland, *Main-Traveled Roads* (New York, 1922; first published 1891), 75–6, 79–82.

"THE WORST of it is," said Grant, without seeing Howard, "a man can't get out of it during his lifetime, and I don't know that he'll have any chance in the next—the speculator'll be there ahead of us."

The rest laughed, but Grant went on grimly:

"Ten years ago Wess, here, could have got land in Dakota pretty easy, but now it's about all a feller's life's worth to try it. I tell you things seem shuttin' down on us fellers."

"Plenty o' land to rent," suggested some one.

"Yes, in terms that skin a man alive. More than that, farmin' ain't so free a life as it used to be. This cattle-raisin' and butter-makin' makes a nigger of a man. Binds him right down to the grindstone and he gets nothin' out of it—that's what rubs it in. He simply wallers around in the manure for somebody else. I'd like to know what a man's life is worth who lives as we do? How much higher is it than the lives the niggers used to live?"...

"A man like me is helpless," Grant was saying. "Just like a fly in a pan of molasses. There's no escape for him. The more he tears around the more liable he is to rip his legs off."...

She sat down opposite him, with her elbows on the table, her chin in her palm, her eyes full of shadows.

"I'd like to go to a city once. I never saw a town bigger'n La Crosse. I've never seen a play, but I've read of 'em in the maga-zines. It must be wonderful; they say they have wharves and real ships coming up to the wharf, and people getting off and on....

"I hate farm-life," she went on with a bitter inflection. "It's nothing but fret, fret, and work the whole time, never going any place, never seeing anybody but a lot of neighbors just as big fools as you are. I spend my time fighting flies and washing dishes and churning. I'm sick of it all."

Howard was silent. What could he say to such an indictment? The ceiling swarmed with flies which the cold rain had driven to seek the warmth of the kitchen. The gray rain was falling with a dreary sound outside, and down the kitchen stove pipe an occasional drop fell on the stove with a hissing, angry sound.

The young wife went on with a deeper note:

"I lived in La Crosse two years, going to school, and I know a little something of what city life is. If I was a man, I bet I wouldn't wear my life out on a farm, as Grant does. I'd get away and I'd do something. I wouldn't care what, but I'd get away."

There was a certain volcanic energy back of all the woman said, that made Howard feel she would make the attempt. She did not know that the struggle for a place to stand on this planet was eating the heart and soul out of men and women in the city, just as in the country. But he could say nothing. If he had said in conventional phrase, sitting there in his soft clothing, "We must make the best of it all," the woman could justly have thrown the dish-cloth in his face. He could say nothing.

"I was a fool for ever marrying," she went on, while the baby pushed a chair across the room. "I made a decent living teaching, I was free to come and go, my money was my own. Now I'm tied right down to a churn or a dish-pan, I never have a cent of my own. *He's* growlin' 'round half the time, and there's no chance of his ever being different."

She stopped with a bitter sob in her throat. She forgot she was talking to her husband's brother. She was conscious only of his sympathy.

As if a great black cloud had settled down upon him, Howard felt it all—the horror, hopelessness, imminent tragedy of it all. The glory of nature, the bounty and splendor of the sky, only made it the more benumbing....

In the sitting room where his mother sat sewing there was not an ornament, save the etching he had brought. The clock stood on a small shelf, its dial so much defaced that one could not tell the time of day; and when it struck, it was with noticeably disproportionate deliberation, as if it wished to correct any mistake into which the family might have fallen by reason of its illegible dial.

The paper on the walls showed the first concession of the Puritans to the Spirit of Beauty, and was made up of a heterogeneous mixture of flowers of unheard-of-shapes and colors, arranged in four different ways along the wall. There were no books, no music, and only a few newspapers in sight—a bare, blank, cold, drab-colored shelter from the rain, not a home. Nothing cozy, nothing heart-warming; a grim and horrible shed.

"What are they doing? It can't be they're at work such a day as this," Howard said, standing at the window.

"They find plenty to do, even on rainy days," answered his mother. "Grant always has some job to set the men at. It's the only way to live."

"I'll go out and see them." He turned suddenly. "Mother, why should Grant treat me so? Have I deserved it?"

Mrs. McLane sighed in pathetic hopelessness. "I don't know, Howard. I'm worried about Grant. He gets more an' more downhearted an' gloomy every day. Seems if he'd go crazy. He don't care how he looks any more, won't dress up on Sunday. Days an' days he'll go aroun' not sayin' a word."

277. A Country Town, 1882

E. W. Howe, *Story of a Country Town* (New York, 1917; first published 1882), 228–32, 237, 239–43.

THERE was one thing I noticed of Twin Mounds which is probably true of every other country town—it was constantly threatened either with great prosperity or great danger, but whether the event threatening the prosperity or the danger came to pass, the town progressed about the same. There was no perceptible effect from any of the events the people were certain would prove either very disastrous or of great benefit....

I never formed a good opinion of a man there that I was not finally told something to his discredit by another citizen, causing me to regard him with great suspicion, and if I said a good word for any of them, it was proved beyond question immediately that he was a very unscrupulous, a very ridiculous, a very weak, and a very worthless man. There were no friendships among them, and they all hated each other in secret, there being much quiet satisfaction when one of them failed. There seemed to be no regular aristocracy, either, for I heard so frequently how ignorant and awkward the prominent citizens were when they first came, that I finally found them all out. . . .

Very few of the Twin Mounds men had positive opinions of their own, as they seemed to have got them second-handed from some source, and none of them was original or natural in his methods of conducting business, or in his habits. Two or three times a year most of them visited a city a good many miles away, where they spent a great deal of money they could not afford, to create an impression that they were accustomed to what they supposed was good society, and where they met men who filled their ideas of greatness. These they mimicked, each one choosing a different example; so it happened that the men of Twin Mounds were very ridiculous. There was a lawyer, I remember, who had met somewhere a distinguished member of his profession, who shook hands (Ho! ho!) with everybody, and (Ha! ha!) patronizingly wanted to know how they were getting along. It was not his natural way, and as he only adopted it because he believed it would make him popular, it became him very poorly. . . .

As I grew older, and began to notice more, I thought that every man in Twin Mounds had reason to feel humiliated that he had not accomplished more, but most of them were as conceited as though there was nothing left in the world worthy of their attention. Their small business affairs, their quarrels over the Bible, and an occasional term in the town council, or a mention for the legislature or a county office, satisfied them, and they were as content as men who really amounted to something.

Although I believe there never was a more virtuous community, the men pretended to believe that their associates were great libertines, and many of the women were scandalized in an unjust and cruel manner. The men rather took a pride in reputations of this sort, for they never had any other, and, although pretending to deny it, they really hoped the people would continue to accuse them. I have known citizens of this description to stay out late at night, and take aimless rides into the country, to create the impression that they were having clandestine meetings with the first ladies of the town. The people watched each other so closely that there was no opportunity to be other than honest and circumspect in this particular, even if they had been differently inclined, and since the men were always looking for amours, but never found them, and believed that others were notoriously successful, they must have had a very contemptible opinion of themselves when they thought about the matter candidly. . . .

Lytle Biggs, being a professional politician, was often in town, and . . . he was of the opinion that while I was a little delicate in asking him for the favor, I was burning with impatience to hear more of his philosophy. I had enjoyed it very much at first, and laughed a great deal at his oddities, and though it finally grew tiresome, I could not very well flatly tell him so. Hence he came in frequently when I was very busy, and when I knew he was not in a philosophical humor, but reasoning that I had grown to expect it, and had little other amusement, he consented to favor me with a few of his thoughts. . . .

"The farmer follows the furrow because he can make more at that than at anything else; he is no more oppressed than other men, except as his ignorance makes it possible, for there never was an age when it was not profitable to be sensible (the world being full of unscrupulous men), therefore the pretense that a man cannot be honest except he plough or sow for a living is not warranted by the facts. Getting up very early in the morning, and going about agricultural work all day in rough clothes, does not particularly tend to clear the conscience, but because politicians who occasionally have use for them have said these things, the farmers go on accepting them, stubbornly refusing to be undeceived, because it is unpleasant to acknowledge ignorance after you have once thought yourself very cunning. In my time, I have harangued a meeting of well-to-do farmers over the wrongs they were suffering at the hands of miserable tradesmen, —they call them middlemen,—who did not know one day whether they would be able to open their doors the next, and received earnest applause, after which I got ten dollars for a charter for an Alliance (which cost me at the rate of two dollars a thousand) without difficulty....

"I see occasional notices in your publication to the effect that Chugg, the groceryman, or whatever the name or the business may be, has just returned from the East, which is extremely dull, and that he is extremely glad to get back to the enterprising, the pushing, the promising, the noble, and the beautiful West. That is YOUR way of being a humbug, for in reality Chugg is glad to get back to the West because he is of some importance here, and none there. The East is full of hungry and ragged men who are superior in every way to the prominent citizen of the name of Chugg, and Chugg knows it, therefore he is glad to get back where he is looked upon as a superior creature. I

have no hesitancy in saying privately that the people in this direction are not warranted in the belief that all the capable and energetic men have left the East, though it would be disastrous to say as much publicly. When I am in the East it occurs to me with great force that the miles of splendid business buildings I see on every hand must be occupied by talented and energetic men, and as we have no such buildings in the West, it follows that we have no such men. When I see towering manufactories—swarming with operatives who would be ornaments to the best society out here—I think that at least a few men of energy and capacity have been left to operate them, for ordinary men could not do it. I ride down the long avenues of private palaces, each one of them worth a township in the Smoky Hill country, and I am convinced that we are mistaken in the opinion that a man must live on the frontier in order to be energetic....

"Men who are prosperous, or men who live in elegant houses, do not come West, but it is the unfortunate, the poor, the indigent, the sick—the lower classes, in short—who came here to grow up with the country, having failed to grow up with the country where they came from."

XXXII ✥ *Culture in the Gilded Age*

FEW OBSERVERS of American life failed to be impressed by the richness of its material achievements; few also failed to comment on the paucity of qualities that make a civilization interesting (No. 278). To some extent, the appearance of emptiness in American culture was the product of a false comparison with Europe. But it was also the result of the difficulty of establishing the arts under the conditions set by American society.

For some sensitive Americans, the difficulties of a creative response to their times seemed to rise out of an inability to use their own cultural past (No. 279).

But, more important, was the narrowness of viewpoint of men too much occupied with the immediate challenges of earning a livelihood or fortune to be able to recognize the authentic values of art or literature (No. 280). For such people, culture was a mild form of recreation, equally indulged in at the opera, at the theater, in light reading, or in sports (No. 281). In this atmosphere of genial eclecticism there was little to encourage the development of taste. Artists and architects indulged the whims of their clients in a variety of styles, all equally irrelevant because all equally lacked inner meaning for those who used them (No. 282).

There were elements of hope. The architect who savagely criticized the monstrous buildings of New York and Chicago himself led a revolution in skyscraper design. Some elements of folk art had already attained wide recognition (No. 283). And American philosophy moved into an exciting and creative period, because it had a recognized role in the maturing universities and in society (No. 284); and because its eloquent statements offered meaningful answers to the questions Americans then were asking (No. 285; *see also below*, Section XXXIII).

278. *Distinction and Beauty, 1888*

Matthew Arnold, *Civilization in the United States* (Boston, 1888), 169–81.

BUT we must get nearer still to the heart of the question raised as to the character and worth of American civilization. I have said how much the word civilization really means—the humanization of man in society; his making progress there towards his true and full humanity.... What human nature, I say, demands in civilization, if it is to stand as a high and satisfying civilization, is best described by the word *interesting*....

Now, the great sources of the *interesting* are distinction and beauty: that which is elevated, and that which is beautiful. Let us take the beautiful first, and consider how far it is present in American civilization. Evidently, this is that civilization's weak side. There is little to nourish and delight the sense of beauty there....

The charm of beauty which comes from ancientness and permanence of rural life the country would not yet have in a high degree, but it has it in an even less degree than might be expected.

Then the Americans come originally, for the most part, from that great class in English society amongst whom the sense for conduct and business is much more strongly developed than the sense for beauty. If we in England were without the cathedrals, parish churches, and castles of the Catholic and feudal age, and without the houses of the Elizabethan age, but had only the towns and buildings which the rise of our middle class has created in the modern age, we should be in much the same case as the Americans. We should be living with much the same absence of training, for the sense of beauty through the eye, from the aspect of outward things. The American cities have hardly anything to please a trained or a natural sense for beauty.... One architect of genius they had—Richardson.... Much of his work was injured by the conditions under which he was obliged to execute it; I can recall but one building, and that of no great importance, where he seems to have had his own way, to be fully himself; but that is indeed excellent. In general, where the Americans succeed best in their architecture—in that art so indicative and educative of a people's sense for beauty—is in the fashion of their villa-cottages in wood. These are often original and at the same time very pleasing, but they are pretty and coquettish, not beautiful.

Of the really beautiful in the other arts, and in literature, very little has been produced there as yet. . . . The American artists live chiefly in Europe; all Americans of cultivation and wealth visit Europe more and more constantly. The mere nomenclature of the country acts upon a cultivated person like the incessant pricking of pins. What people in whom the sense for beauty and fitness was quick could have invented, or could tolerate, the hideous names ending in *ville*, the Briggsvilles, Higginsvilles, Jacksonvilles, rife from Maine to Florida; the jumble of unnatural and inappropriate names everywhere? On the line from Albany to Buffalo you have, in one part, half the names in the classical dictionary to designate the stations. . . .

So much as to beauty, and as to the provision, in the United States, for the sense of beauty. As to distinction, and the interest which human nature seeks from enjoying the effect made upon it by what is elevated, the case is much the same. There is very little to create such an effect, very much to thwart it. . . . An austere and intense religion imposed on their Puritan founders the discipline of respect, and so provided for them the thrill of awe; but this religion is dying out. The Americans have produced plenty of men strong, shrewd, upright, able, effective; very few who are highly distinguished. . . .

In truth, everything is against distinction in America, and against the sense of elevation to be gained through admiring and respecting it. The glorification of "the average man," who is quite a religion with statesmen and publicists there, is against it. The addiction to "the funny

man," who is a national misfortune there, is against it. Above all, the newspapers are against it.

It is often said that every nation has the government it deserves. What is much more certain is that every nation has the newspapers it deserves. The newspaper is the direct product of the want felt; the supply answers closely and inevitably to the demand. . . . If one were searching for the best means to efface and kill in a whole nation the discipline of respect, the feeling for what is elevated, one could not do better than take the American newspapers. The absence of truth and soberness in them, the poverty in serious interest, the personality and sensation-mongering are beyond belief. There are a few newspapers which are in whole, or in part, exceptions. The *New York Nation,* a weekly paper, may be paralleled with the *Saturday Review* as it was in its old and good days; but the *New York Nation* is conducted by a foreigner, and has an extremely small sale. . . .

The Americans used to say to me that what they valued was news, and that this their newspapers gave them. I at last made the reply: "Yes, news for the servants' hall!" I remember that a New York newspaper, one of the first I saw after landing in the country, had a long account . . . of a young woman who had married a man who was a bag of bones, as we say, and who used to exhibit himself as a skeleton; of her growing horror in living with this man, and finally of her death. All this in the most minute detail, and described with all the writer's powers of rhetoric. This has always remained by me as a specimen of what the Americans call news.

I once declared that in England the born lover of ideas and of light could not but feel that the sky over his head is of brass and iron. And so I say that, in America, he who craves for the *interesting* in civilization, he who requires from what surrounds him satisfaction for his sense of beauty, his sense for elevation, will feel the sky over his head to be of brass and iron. The human problem, then, is as yet solved in the United States most imper- fectly; a great void exists in the civiliza- tion over there; a want of what is elevated and beautiful, of what is interesting.

279. *Improvised Europeans, 1903–05*

Henry Adams to Henry James, November 18, 1903, to Brooks Adams, June 5, 1905, and to William James, December 9, 1907. Henry Adams, *Letters* (Boston, 1938), 414, 453, 485.

THE PAINFUL truth is that all of my New England generation, counting the half-century, 1820–1870, were in actual fact only one mind and nature; the individual was a facet of Boston. We knew each other to the last nervous center, and feared each other's knowledge. We looked through each other like micro-scopes. There was absolutely nothing in us that we did not understand merely by looking in the eye. There was hardly a difference even in depth, for Harvard College and Unitarianism kept us all shal-low. We knew nothing—no! but really nothing! of the world. One cannot exag-gerate the profundity of ignorance of Story in becoming a sculptor, or Sumner in becoming a statesman, or Emerson in becoming a philosopher. Story and Sum-ner, Emerson and Alcott, Lowell and Longfellow, Hillard, Winthrop, Motley, Prescott, and all the rest, were the same mind,—and so, poor worm!—was I! . . .

God knows that we knew our want of knowledge! the self-distrust became intro-spection—nervous self-consciousness—ir-ritable dislike of America, and antipathy to Boston. . . . Improvised Europeans, we were, and—Lord God!—how thin! No, but it is too cruel! Long ago,—at least thirty years ago,—I discovered it, and have painfully held my tongue about it. . . .

If you asked me to find out five hun-dred persons in the world to whom you would like to give the volume [*Mont-Saint-Michel and Chartres*], I could say only that, as far as you and I know, five hundred do not exist,—nor half that num-ber—nor a quarter of it.

"As far as you and I know," and I sus-pect we know of everybody worth know-ing. Thousands of people exist who think they want to read. Barring a few Jews, they are incapable of reading fifty consec-utive pages, or of following the thought if they did. I never yet heard of ten men who had ever read my history and never one who had read Hay's *Lincoln*.

Therefore I am inclined to think that I have got to be satisfied anyway with you for an audience, and it is more appre-ciative in me to say at once that you are audience enough. . . . There are already some fifty copies afloat, and I'll bet ten to one that half of them have not been once read. Yet they've been given only to the most appreciative and cultivated personal friends.

Of course there are several hundred thousand persons in Boston and out of it, who are lecture-goers and frequent librar-ies; and there are one or two million young women who read poetry in Browning Clubs, and mostly come to Paris to study art when they can. I imagine that neither you nor I care much to be admired by these, but in any case they will admire us the more at second hand. We need not lift a finger to reach that class, who are quite passive, and mere reed-ponds of receptiv-ity. . . .

Weary of my own imbecility, I tried to clean off a bit of the surface of my mind, in 1904, by printing a volume on the twelfth century, where I could hide, in the last hundred pages, a sort of anchor in history. I knew that not a hundred people in America would understand what I meant, and these were all taught in Jesuit schools, where I should be a hell-born scorpion. I need not publish when no one would read or understand.

Then I undertook,—always to clean my own mind,—a companion study of the twentieth century, where I could hide—in a stack of rubbish meant only to feed the foolish—a hundred more pages meant to complete the first hundred of 1904. No one would take the smallest interest in these. I knew they were safe. So was I.

280. *Stage Indecency, 1905*

The New York Herald, October 31, 1905. Reprinted in M. J. Moses and J. M. Brown, eds., *The American Theatre as Seen by Its Critics 1752–1934* (New York, 1934), 163–6.

"The Lid" was lifted by Mr. Arnold Daly and "the limit" of stage indecency reached last night in the Garrick Theater in the performance of one of Mr. George Bernard Shaw's "unpleasant comedies" called *Mrs. Warren's Profession.*

"The limit of indecency" may seem pretty strong words, but they are justified by the fact that the play is morally rotten. It makes no difference that some of the lines may have been omitted and others toned down; there was superabundance of foulness left. The whole story of the play, the atmosphere surrounding it, the incidents, the personalities of the characters are wholly immoral and degenerate. The only way successfully to expurgate *Mrs. Warren's Profession* is to cut the whole play out. You cannot have a clean pig sty. The play is an insult to decency because—

It defends immorality.

It glorifies debauchery.

It besmirches the sacredness of a clergyman's calling.

It pictures children and parents living in calm observance of most unholy relations.

And, worst of all, it countenances the most revolting form of degeneracy by flippantly discussing the marriage of brother and sister, father and daughter, and makes the one supposedly moral character of the play, a young girl, declare that choice of shame, instead of poverty is eminently right. . . .

Mrs. Warren tells her daughter all the revolting details of her life of shame, and glories in it, as it saved her and "Liz," her sister, the drudgery of menial labor. You may think that the pure and clever daughter is shocked, but forgives and tries to reclaim her mother. Not a bit of it. Her views coincide with those of her shameless parent, and Vivian admits that in the circumstances she herself would have considered licentiousness and sin quite the better choice. She almost envies the career of her aunt, who became rich through the ill-gotten gains of the "profession" of shame and is posing now as the social leader in a cathedral town and the chaperon of young girls.

The clergyman, who, mind you, is not made by Mr. Shaw a deposed or unfrocked clergyman, but the spiritual and religious head of a large and prominent church, confesses himself to be a debauchee and a rake—a subject which father and son familiarly discuss and laugh over. The clergyman sits up all night with Crofts and becomes bestially intoxicated; then he starts in to write his sermon for the following day. . . .

There was not one redeeming feature about it last night, not one ray of sunshine, of cleanliness, to lighten up the moral darkness of situation and dialogue; not the semblance of a moral lesson pointed.

281. *Recreation in the 1890's*

A. D. Noyes, *The Market Place* (Boston, 1938),
83–4, 85–8.

OUT-OF-DOOR sports, popular amusements, literature, the drama, the opera, all entered a new and interesting phase. Even American architecture began to take on new life. Whether because the habit was shaken of clinging to established (and often meretricious) traditions, or because more frequent contact with the best European art had changed the viewpoint, or because, as in those days used to be believed, imagination had been stimulated in thousands of Americans by the grace and beauty of Chicago's White City of 1893—whatever the cause, houses with individuality of their own were replacing the obnoxious structures of the preceding quarter century. . . .

The great vogue of the bicycle, due to replacement of the precarious high wheel with what was long known as the "safety bicycle," enlarged both the area of nearby travel and the vogue of out-of-door exercise. All of us rode. . . . It is not easy to recall as a reminiscent picture the Saturday afternoon "bicycle procession" on Riverside Drive, in which some of the best-known citizens and stage celebrities would participate. Traces of the "cinder track" laid down for bicyclers along the Drive may still be discovered, but they resemble the geological relics of a former civilization; the path is patronized nowadays only by pedestrians or nurses with baby carriages. Along with use of the bicycle, open-air sports were coming everywhere into vogue; women for the first time participated in more strenuous activities than the orthodox croquet and archery of older decades. The nineties saw the sudden rise of the "Gibson girl" as a recognized feminine type; also the entry of women into the field of practical employment. It was not long before the nineties

that the appearance of well-dressed young women in the stream of humanity moving up or down Wall Street and lower Broadway would occasion curious glances from male pedestrians, who considered that part of the city as their own preserve. In the nineties, woman's participation in active downtown life began to be taken as a matter of course. . . .

Playhouses of the nineties did not present the popular drama with supporting casts as thoroughly trained and with stage mounting as picturesque as those of a later period, and the "problem play" was then only doubtful experiment. Augustus Thomas, himself a prolific playwright of the character drama, recalled in after life that his own successes of that period were achieved while Rosina Vokes was drawing crowded audiences to *My Milliner's Bill;* while Maude Adams, still in her teens, was charming her audiences in *The Midnight Bell;* while Belasco was training Mrs. Leslie Carter for *The Heart of Maryland,* and when long runs at Broadway theaters were assured for Sothern in *Lord Chumley* and Denman Thompson in *The Old Homestead.* . . .

Judged by the present conception of the drama, those were days of simple things. Yet there are few survivors of that period who do not look back a bit wistfully at the popular drama of the nineties. The decade was, indeed . . . an era in which home and foreign stars, high in the theatrical firmament, illuminated the New York stage. Edwin Booth had gone, but Joseph Jefferson still drew the public with his *Rip Van Winkle* or *Cricket on the Hearth,* and the famous "all-star *Hamlet*" at the Lester Wallack benefit in 1888, when Booth played the Danish prince, Modjeska "Ophelia," and Jefferson the first grave-digger, was only a few years back. Augustin Daly's company was at the zenith of its popularity; its revivals of Shakespearian comedy, interspersed with lighter contemporary plays, presented by such experienced actors as John Drew, Ada Rehan, and James Lewis, were performances with which the participant in everyday conversation had to be acquainted. The season of Henry Irving and Ellen Terry was a regular event. We went again and again to enjoy the commanding charm of Terry's "Portia," "Beatrice," and "Olivia"—they have never since been done as that tall and graceful actress of the nineties performed them. . . .

As to the opera, it doubtless lacked those brilliant stage settings to which the Metropolitan has accustomed its patrons in these later days; but it may well be doubted if the foreign singers who were presented in the nineties can nowadays be matched, in New York or elsewhere. The battle for ascendancy between Italian and Wagnerian opera had ended in a victory for the German school, so apparently complete that old-timers like George William Curtis, in *Harper's* "Editor's Easy Chair," wrote all but apologetically of their own past delight in listening to Verdi and Donizetti. Nevertheless, the De Reszkes, Alvary, Van Rooy, Sembrich, Nordica, Calvé, and Lilli Lehmann, a galaxy of operatic stars never matched in any music center before or since, are among the particular memories of the nineties. It was in those days that music

lovers installed Anton Seidl and his orchestra in an open summer pavilion at Brighton, Coney Island, while Payne (often to Seidl's visible disgust) was displaying his elaborate fireworks at Manhattan Beach, and New Yorkers who could break away for the afternoon and evening crowded down by the Rapid Transit to that nowadays very proletarianized resort.

In one respect the social amenities of the period presented a characteristic picture which is today among the legends of New York's past. In the middle nineties the art of after-dinner speaking reached its prime; it is nowadays hardly more than a tradition. The joyous expectancy with which, when chairs had been pushed back, napkins tossed beside the coffee cups, and cigars lighted up to introduce the real business of the evening, the assemblage awaited the exchange of humorous epigram and persiflage from well-known wits at the speakers' table reflected one of the bright spots in New York life. Yale and Harvard dinners were events of a season. The next morning's newspapers, the next day's talk in clubs and business offices, would pass along wider circulation rejoinders like Horace Porter's acknowledgment to the Clover Club, after being introduced as a New Yorker from whom, if you dropped a twenty-dollar dinner in the slot, up comes the speech. Porter replied that, if one of the chairman's speeches is dropped into the slot, up comes the dinner.

282. *The Architecture of Illusion, 1890*

L. H. Sullivan, *Kindergarten Chats* (New York, 1947), 107–10, 115, 138, 139, 140–1.

HERE indeed is an architecture to be studied! For the roar of the streets is not louder than the roar of what lines the streets—a quarreling herd, ranged mile after mile, pressing hard, shoulder to shoulder, tied hands, tied feet, leering

and howling at the passer, or smirking and winking and giggling—an uncanny lot, the most extraordinary aggregation in the world's vast menagerie. Oh, this hocus-pocus, does it not sicken one in his heart! Does one not blush to the roots that he, too, must go by the name. Oh, the sadness of it! The wearisome pessimism!

Think of the generations to come, when once they shall realize to the full the nature of the blight that has thus been laid upon them by a generation which says: After us the deluge! It will surely be a deluge of tears and bitterness, and a contempt toward this generation of Manhattanites. They will curse the eminent and the shyster alike, for they will find no rational pretext to discriminate between their works. Oh, the pity of it! the pity of it! When a noble art is so near to the hand! Oh, the pity of it! . . .

Must I then specify? Must I show you this French château, this Château de Blois on this street corner, here, in New York, and still you do not laugh! Must you wait until you see a modern man come out of its door, before you laugh? Have you no sense of humor, no sense of pathos? Must I then explain to you that while the man may live in the house physically, he cannot live in it morally, mentally or spiritually, that he and his house are a paradox? That he himself is an illusion when he believes his château to be real. Must we go again to our ABC? Is it not self-evident to all but the man and his kind that the "château" is a *humoresque*—and he another? That château and their kind were in place and time only in France?

Must I show you other and similar curios of this period, and that period, and that period, and this and that "style"! Faugh! The word makes me sick! Will not the one suffice? Are you not a bright youngster? Can you not translate? Can you not generalize? To satisfy you must I take you to see another maudlin riot, called office-building, with one barbarism heaped upon another until the incongruous mass reaches the limit of its idiocy in height, and culminates, perchance, in a Greek temple?—a solecism more extravagant, if possible, than the château?

Must I show you another library, or it may be a court-house, or a bank: with its piddling classic, its awful niceties, its refinements, its everlasting misconceptions, its kickshaws of culture, its jejune woolgathering? . . .

So is this populous island, with its huge, ostentatious spread of material wealth, a thing of poverty and rags to him who can weigh values in the balance of sanity. It stands for the stertorous negation of democracy; the cancellation of that which is best, noblest and enduring in the heart, in the mind, in the spirit; and for the asseveration of that which is paltry and transitory in life's values. So stands this island. Let not its contagion spread! . . .

And what, doctor mine, shall we say of [Chicago] this flat smear, this endless drawl of streets and shanties, large and small, this ocean of smoke? It is a thousand miles away from New York. Is it then an epitome of American civilization, an index of our art? Is this a true exponent of democracy? You have told me of thought—is thought here? You have talked to me of imagination—is imagination here? Are filth in the air, and slime under foot, or dust in the nostrils, indices of enlightenment; or is Chicago a *sui generis* in turn? New York may be revolting to you, but this Chicago thing is infinitely repulsive to me. There at least was a physical if not a moral cleanliness, an outward if not an inward cheerfulness. But this foul spot on the smiling prairie, this blotch on the fair face of Nature! . . .

Chicago is indeed a *sui generis*. Seventy years ago it was a mudhole—today it is a human swamp.

It is the *City of Indifference*. Nobody cares. Its nominal shibboleth, "I will"—its actuality, "I won't"; with the subscription: "Not how good but how cheap"! Impoverishment of heart and mind are here conjoined. They seem to glory in conjunction. . . .

Accepting, therefore, New York and Chicago as representing certain miscarriages of democracy, each group so distinctive in its way, that I have called them the opposite poles or nodes, expressible of certain phases of degeneracy afflicting our land and people, we have but to turn, to regain our balance of view, to the country at large and the people at large. In passing, let me say that I am not disposed to ignore or minimize the sane moral and mental and emotional forces, within those cities, which make for righteousness. Far from it, I gladly recognize them and hope that some day they may prevail. But I do say that they are not characteristic of those cities, and the balance of forces at present is heavily against them. . . .

The architect is a product of the body social, a product of our civilization. This you have shown me clearly. My simile breaks down here in a measure, but let it go—I'm through with it. So we approach him from two sides—as a product and as an agency; so of course I come at once to his true function, namely the double one: to interpret and to initiate! . . .

Of course, I assume that other men than architects may be and are products and agencies, and interpret and initiate. The dramatist may be such, the merchant such and many others: in fact, in the broadest sense, all are such, in larger or lesser degree, under the terms and conditions of modern civilization. But not one of these is expected to interpret the wants of the people with a view to initiate buildings. Hence the true function of the architect is to initiate such buildings as shall correspond to the real needs of the people. . . .

To my own statement that the true function of the architect is to initiate such buildings as shall correspond to the real needs of the people, I now add your statement, that he must cause a building to grow naturally, logically and poetically out of its conditions. Now all of this means . . . that the real architect is first, last and all the time, not a merchant, broker, manufacturer, business man, or anything of that sort, but a poet who uses not words but building materials as a medium of expression. Just in the same sense that a great painter uses pigments as his medium of expression; a musician, tones; a sculptor, the marble block; a literatus, the written word; and an orator, the spoken word—and, like them, to be truly great, really useful, he must impart to the passive materials a subjective or spiritual human quality which shall make them live for other humans—otherwise he fails utterly and is, in a high sense, a public nuisance instead of a public benefactor. . . .

If it is true that this is the core of the matter, what's the use of talking about the so-called practicabilities. It can go without the saying, can't it, that a knowledge of administration, construction, equipment, materials, methods, processes and workmanship are part of his technical equipment whereby he has the efficiency and power to express the poetic thought—just as language and a knowledge of words are the technical equipment of the literatus. It is not, I take it, the words that make the poem, it is the manner in which the words are marshaled, organized and vitalized, that makes a poem a poem. And just so with building materials; they must be organized and vitalized in order that a real building may exist. Therefore to vitalize building materials, to animate them collectively with a thought, a state of feeling, to charge them with a subjective significance and value, to make them a visible part of the genuine social fabric, to infuse into them the true life of the poeple, to impart to them the best that is in the people, as the eye of the poet, looking below the surface of life, sees the best that is in the people—such is the real function of the architect; for, understood in these terms, the architect is one kind of poet, and his work one form of poetry—using the word in its broad, inclusive, actual sense. And if this view of the function of the architect be the true one, the real one, I can now understand . . . your contempt for what is currently called scholarship and culture. Truly it is inspiring, when one begins to acquire the faculty of looking at things with the inner or spiritual eye! Truly such an eye illuminates that which it sees, and opens to the inner view, and to the grasp of understanding, the great world of realities.

283. *Spirituals*, 1903

W. E. B. DuBois, *Souls of Black Folks* (first published, 1903; reprinted New York, 1953), 251–3, 257–9, 261–4.

LITTLE of beauty has America given the world save the rude grandeur God himself stamped on her bosom; the human spirit in this new world has expressed itself in vigor and ingenuity rather than in beauty. And so by fateful chance the Negro folk-song—the rhythmic cry of the slave—stands today not simply as the sole American music, but as the most beautiful expression of human experience born this side the seas. . . .

Away back in the thirties the melody of these slave songs stirred the nation, but the songs were soon half forgotten. Some, like "Near the lake where drooped the willow," passed into current airs and their source was forgotten; others were caricatured on the "minstrel" stage and their memory died away. Then in wartime came the singular Port Royal experiment after the capture of Hilton Head, and perhaps for the first time the North met the Southern slave face to face and heart to heart with no third witness. The Sea Islands of the Carolinas, where they met, were filled with a Black folk of primitive type, touched and molded less by the world about them than any others outside the Black Belt. Their appearance was uncouth, their language funny, but their hearts were human and their singing stirred men with a mighty power. Thomas Wentworth Higginson hastened to tell of these songs, and Miss McKim and others urged upon the world their rare beauty. But the world listened only half credulously until the Fisk Jubilee Singers sang the slave songs so deeply into the world's heart that it can never wholly forget them again. . . .

These songs are the articulate message of the slave to the world. They tell us in these eager days that life was joyous to the black slave, careless and happy. I can easily believe this of some, of many. But not all the past South, though it rose from the dead, can gainsay the heart-touching witness of these songs. They are the music of an unhappy people, of the children of disappointment; they tell of death and suffering and unvoiced longing toward a truer world, of misty wanderings and hidden ways. . . .

The words that are left to us are not without interest, and, cleared of evident dross, they conceal much of real poetry and meaning beneath conventional theology and unmeaning rhapsody. Like all primitive folk, the slave stood near to Nature's heart. Life was a "rough and rolling sea" like the brown Atlantic of the Sea Islands; the "Wilderness" was the home of God, and the "lonesome valley" led to the way of life. "Winter'll soon be over," was the picture of life and death to a tropical imagination. The sudden wild thunder-storms of the South awed and impressed the Negroes,—at times the rumbling seemed to them "mournful," at times imperious:

> "My Lord calls me,
> He calls me by the thunder,
> The trumpet sounds it in my soul."

The monotonous toil and exposure is painted in many words. One sees the ploughmen in the hot, moist furrow, singing:

"Dere's no rain to wet you,
Dere's no sun to burn you,
Oh, push along, believer,
I want to go home."

The bowed and bent old man cries, with thrice-repeated wail:

"O Lord, keep me from sinking down,"

and he rebukes the devil of doubt who can whisper:

"Jesus is dead and God's gone away."

Yet the soul-hunger is there, the restlessness of the savage, the wail of the wanderer. . . .

Over the inner thoughts of the slaves and their relations one with another the shadow of fear ever hung, so that we get but glimpses here and there, and also with them, eloquent omissions and silences. Mother and child are sung, but seldom father; fugitive and weary wanderer call for pity and affection, but there is little of wooing and wedding; the rocks and the mountains are well known, but home is unknown. Strange blending of love and helplessness sings through the refrain:

"Yonder's my ole mudder,
Been waggin' at de hill so long;
'Bout time she cross over,
Git home bime-by."

Elsewhere comes the cry of the "motherless" and the "Farewell, farewell, my only child.". . .

Through all the sorrow of the Sorrow Songs there breathes a hope—a faith in the ultimate justice of things. The minor cadences of despair change often to triumph and calm confidence. Sometimes it is faith in life, sometimes a faith in death, sometimes assurance of boundless justice in some fair world beyond. But whichever it is, the meaning is always clear: that sometime, somewhere, men will judge men by their souls and not by their skins. . . .

If somewhere in this whirl and chaos of things, there dwells Eternal Good, pitiful yet masterful, then anon in His good time America shall rend the Veil and the prisoned shall go free. Free, free as the sunshine trickling down the morning into these high windows of mine, free as yonder fresh young voices welling up to me from the caverns of brick and mortar below—swelling with song, instinct with life, tremulous treble and darkening bass. My children, my little children, are singing to the sunshine, and thus they sing:

"Let us cheer the weary traveler,
Cheer the weary traveler,
Let us cheer the weary traveler
Along the heavenly way."

And the traveler girds himself, and sets his face toward the Morning, and goes his way.

284. *Clergymen Without a Church, 1900*

George Santayana, *Character and Opinion in the United States* (New York: W. W. Norton & Company, Inc., 1934), 43–6, 49–51, 55, 57–9, 163.

THE STATE of Harvard College, and of American education generally, . . . had this remarkable effect on the philosophers there: it made their sense of social responsibility acute, because they were consciously teaching and guiding the community, as if they had been clergymen; and it made no less acute their moral loneliness, isolation, and forced self-reliance, because they were like clergymen without a church, and not only had no common philosophic doctrine to transmit, but were expected not to have one. They were invited to be at once genuine philosophers and popular professors; and the degree to which some of them managed to unite these contraries is remarkable, especially if we consider the character of the academic public they had to serve and to please.

While the sentiments of most Americans in politics and morals, if a little vague, are very conservative, their democratic instincts, and the force of circumstances, have produced a system of education which anticipates all that the most extreme revolution could bring about; and while no one dreams of forcibly suppressing private property, religion, or the family, American education ignores these things, and proceeds as much as possible as if they did not exist. The child passes very young into a free school, established and managed by the municipal authorities; the teachers, even for the older boys, are chiefly unmarried women, sensitive, faithful, and feeble; their influence helps to establish that separation which is so characterisitc of America between things intellectual, which remain wrapped in a feminine veil and, as it were, under glass, and the rough business and passions of life. The lessons are ambitious in range, but are made as easy, as interesting, and as optional as possible; the stress is divided between what the child likes now and what he is going to need in his trade or profession. The young people are sympathetically encouraged to instruct themselves and to educate one another. They romp and make fun like young monkeys, they flirt and have their private "brainstorms" like little supermen and superwomen. They are tremendously in earnest about their college intrigues and intercollegiate athletic wars. They are fond, often compassionately fond, of their parents, and home is all the more sacred to them in that they are seldom there. They enjoy a surprising independence in habits, friendships, and opinions. Brothers and sisters often choose different religions.

The street, the school, the young people's club, the magazine, the popular novel, furnish their mental pabulum.

The force of example and of passing custom is all the more irresistible in this absence of authority and tradition; for this sort of independence rather diminishes the power of being original, by supplying a slenderer basis and a thinner soil from which originality might spring. Uniformity is established spontaneously without discipline, as in the popular speech and ethics of every nation. Against this tendency to uniformity the efforts of a cultivated minority to maintain a certain distinction and infuse it into their lives and minds are not very successful. . . .

Such was the education and such the atmosphere of intellectual innocence which prevailed in the public—mostly undergraduates—to which the Harvard philosophers adapted their teaching and to some extent their philosophy. The students were intelligent, ambitious, remarkably able to "do things"; they were keen about the matters that had already entered into their lives, and invincibly happy in their ignorance of everything else. A gentle contempt for the past permeated their judgments. They were not accustomed to the notion of authority, nor aware that it might have legitimate grounds; they instinctively disbelieved in the superiority of what was out of reach. About high questions of politics and religion their minds were open but vague; they seemed not to think them of practical importance. . . . Instead they had absorbing local traditions of their own, athletic and social, and their college life was their true education, an education in friendship, cooperation, and freedom. . . .

Life, for the undergraduates, was full of droll incidents and broad farce; it drifted good-naturedly from one commonplace thing to another. Standing packed in the tinkling horse-car, their coat-collars above their ears and their feet deep in the winter straw, they jogged in a long half-hour to Boston, there to enjoy the delights of female society, the theater, or a good dinner. And in the summer days, for Class Day and Commencement, feminine and elderly Boston would return the visit, led by the governor of Massachusetts in his hired carriage-and-four, and by the local orators and poets, brimming with jokes and conventional sentiments, and eager not so much to speed the youngsters on their career, as to air their own wit, and warm their hearts with punch and with collective memories of youth. It was an idyllic, haphazard, humoristic existence, without fine imagination, without any familiar infusion of scholarship, without articulate religion: a flutter of intelligence in a void, flying into trivial play, in order to drop back, as soon as college days were over, into the drudgery of affairs. There was the love of beauty, but without the sight of it; for the bits of pleasant landscape or the works of art which might break the ugliness of the foreground were a sort of aesthetic miscellany, enjoyed as one enjoys a museum; there was nothing in which the spirit of beauty was deeply interfused, charged with passion and discipline and intricate familiar associations with delicate and noble things. . . .

When Harvard was reformed, . . . the immediate object was not to refine college life or render it more scholarly. . . . The object was rather to extend the scope of instruction, and make it more advanced. It is natural that every great city, the capital of any nation or region, should wish to possess a university in the literal sense of the word—an encyclopædic institute, or group of institutes, to teach and foster all the professions, all the arts, and all the sciences. Such a university need have nothing to do with education, with the transmission of a particular moral and intellectual tradition. Education might be courteously presupposed. The teacher . . . would be an expert in some science, delivering lectures for public instruction, while perhaps privately carrying on investigations with the aid of a few disciples

whom he would be training in his specialty. . . .

The browsing undergraduate could simply range with a looser tether, and he was reenforced by a fringe of graduates who had not yet had enough, or who were attracted from other colleges. These graduates came to form a sort of normal school for future professors, stamped as in Germany with a Ph. D.; and the teachers in each subject became a committee charged with something of the functions of a registry office, to find places for their nurslings. The university could thus acquire a national and even an international function, drawing in distinguished talent and youthful ambition from everywhere, and sending forth in various directions its apostles of light and learning.

I think it is intelligible that in such a place and at such a crisis philosophy should have played a conspicuous part, and also that it should have had an ambiguous character. There had to be, explicit or implicit, a philosophy for the college. . . . A chief part of that traditional faith was the faith in freedom, in inquiry; and it was necessary, in the very interests of the traditional philosophy, to take account of all that was being said in the world, and to incorporate the spirit of the times in the spirit of the fathers. Accordingly, no single abstract opinion was particularly tabooed at Harvard; granted industry, sobriety, and some semblance of theism, no professor was expected to agree with any other. I believe the authorities would have been well pleased, for the sake of completeness, to have added a Buddhist, a Moslem, and a Catholic scholastic to the philosophical faculty, if only suitable sages could have been found, house-trained, as it were, and able to keep pace with the academic machine and to attract a sufficient number of pupils. . . .

It seems, then, that the atmosphere of the new world has already affected philosophy in two ways. In the first place, it has accelerated and rendered fearless the disintegration of conventional categories; a disintegration on which modern philosophy has always been at work, and which has precipitated its successive phases. In the second place, the younger cosmopolitan America has favored the impartial assemblage and mutual confrontation of all sorts of ideas. It has produced, in intellectual matters, a sort of happy watchfulness and insecurity. Never was the human mind master of so many facts and sure of so few principles.

285. *Logic and Will, 1897*

William James, *The Will to Believe* (New York, 1897), 22–3, 28–30.

ARE there not somewhere forced opinions in our speculative questions, and can we (as men who may be interested at least as much in positively gaining truth as in merely escaping dupery) always wait with impunity till the coercive evidence shall have arrived? It seems *a priori* improbable that the truth should be so nicely adjusted to our needs and powers as that. In the great boarding-house of nature, the cakes and the butter and the syrup seldom come out so even and leave the plates so clean. Indeed, we should view them with scientific suspicion if they did.

Moral questions immediately present themselves as questions whose solution cannot wait for sensible proof. A moral question is a question not of what sensibly exists, but of what is good, or would be good if it did exist. Science can tell us what exists; but to compare the *worths,* both of what exists and of what does not exist, we must consult not science, but what Pascal calls our heart. . . . The question of having moral beliefs at all or not having them is decided by our will. . . .

I, . . . for one, cannot see my way to accepting the agnostic rules for truth-seeking, or wilfully agree to keep my willing nature out of the game. I cannot do so for this plain reason, that *a rule of thinking which would absolutely prevent* *me from acknowledging certain kinds of truth if those kinds of truth were really there, would be an irrational rule.* That for me is the long and short of the formal logic of the situation, no matter what the kinds of truth might materially be. . . .

When I look at the religious question as it really puts itself to concrete men, and when I think of all the possibilities which both practically and theoretically it involves, then this command that we shall put a stopper on our heart, instincts, and courage, and *wait*—acting of course meanwhile more or less as if religion were *not* true—till doomsday, or till such time as our intellect and senses working together may have raked in evidence enough,—this command, I say, seems to me the queerest idol ever manufactured in the philosophic cave. . . . No one of us ought to issue vetoes to the other, nor should we bandy words of abuse. We ought, on the contrary, delicately and profoundly to respect one another's mental freedom: then only shall we bring about the intellectual republic; then only shall we have that spirit of inner tolerance without which all our outer tolerance is soulless, and which is empiricism's glory; then only shall we live and let live, in speculative as well as in practical things.

XXXIII 🦋 *Spirit in the Service of the Age*

BOTH THE ACHIEVEMENTS and the problems of American society were reflected in the ideas of themselves and of their role in society that men now formulated. The contrast between what had been accomplished and what yet remained to be done troubled the men of these times.

Certainly there were grounds for arguing, as a preacher did in a sermon delivered more than five thousand times, that wealth and success were accessible to every man (No. 286). Since that was so, no radical changes were necessary in a social order that assured the prosperity of the fittest. Tampering with the natural processes that governed society would only impede progress (No. 287; *see also below*, Nos. 362, 369).

Yet the existence of poverty posed a problem for the conscience of Americans. A best-selling novel confronted the realities of the times with the ideals of Christianity (No. 288). And, within the churches, in all the sects, there was continuing agitation about the relationship of the gospel to society (*see above*, No. 251).

There was also a secular basis for the same concern. Science seemed to point to the necessity for social action. An anthropologist raised penetrating questions on the connection between equality and progress (No. 289); and the economists, organizing, felt it necessary to plot a chart for social reform (No. 290). A program for social reconstruction could therefore be phrased in terms of the laws of scientific development (No. 291). In a more sophisticated fashion a philosopher formulated the contemporary relationship of morality to democracy and thereby posed an imperative toward action (No. 292).

Beyond this difference in views between the advocates and the opponents of change was the deeper American conflict between the spirit of self-confident individualism and the necessity for communal action. Almost at the start of the period, a poet had phrased the terms of this conflict (No. 293). And an episode in Mark Twain's story graphically portrays some dilemmas of conscience for the Americans of his time (No. 294).

286. *Acres of Diamonds, 1890's*

R. H. Conwell, *Acres of Diamonds* (New York, 1915), 17–21.

I SAY again that the opportunity to get rich, to attain unto great wealth, is ... within the reach of almost every man and woman who hears me speak tonight, and I mean just what I say. ... I have come to tell you ... that the men and women sitting here, who found it difficult perhaps to buy a ticket to this lecture or gathering tonight, have within their reach "acres of diamonds," opportunities to get largely wealthy. There never was a place on earth more adapted than the city of Philadelphia today, and never in the history of the world did a poor man without capital have such an opportunity to get rich quickly and honestly as he has now in our city. . . . Unless some of you get richer for what I am saying tonight my time is wasted.

I say that you ought to get rich, and it is your duty to get rich. How many of my pious brethren say to me, "Do you, a Christian minister, spend your time going up and down the country advising young people to get rich, to get money?" "Yes, of course I do." They say, "Isn't that awful! Why don't you preach the gospel instead of preaching about man's making money?" "Because to make money honestly is to preach the gospel." That is the reason. The men who get rich may be the most honest men you find in the community.

"Oh," but says some young man here tonight, "I have been told all my life that if a person has money he is very dishonest and dishonorable and mean and contemptible." My friend, that is the reason why you have none, because you have that idea of people. The foundation of your faith is altogether false. Let me say here clearly, and say it briefly . . . ninety-eight out of one hundred of the rich men of America are honest. That is why they are rich. That is why they are trusted with

money. That is why they carry on great enterprises and find plenty of people to work with them. . . .

Money is power, and you ought to be reasonably ambitious to have it. You ought because you could do more good with it than you could without it. Money printed your Bible, money builds your churches, money sends your missionaries, and money pays your preachers. . . .

I say, then, you ought to have money. If you can honestly attain unto riches in Philadelphia, it is your Christian and godly duty to do so. It is an awful mistake of these pious people to think you must be awfully poor in order to be pious.

Some men say, "Don't you sympathize with the poor people?" Of course I do, or else I would not have been lecturing these years. I won't give in but what I sympathize with the poor, but the number of poor who are to be sympathized with is very small. To sympathize with a man whom God has punished for his sins, thus to help him when God would still continue a just punishment, is to do wrong, no doubt about it, and we do that more than we help those who are deserving. While we should sympathize with God's poor—that is, those who cannot help themselves—let us remember there is not a poor person in the United States who was not made poor by his own shortcomings, or by the shortcomings of someone else. It is all wrong to be poor, anyhow.

287. *The Fallacy of Reform,* 1894

W. G. Sumner, "The Absurd Effort to Make the World Over," *Forum,* XVII (1894), 98–9, 100, 101–2.

DEMOCRACY never has done anything, either in politics, social affairs, or industry, to prove its power to bless mankind. If we confine our attention to the United States, there are three difficulties with regard to its alleged achievements, and they all have the most serious bear-

ing on the proposed democratization of industry.

1. The time during which democracy has been tried in the United States is too short to warrant any inferences. . . .

2. American democracy . . . is a consequence. There are economic and sociologi-

cal causes for our political vitality and vigor, for the ease and elasticity of our social relations, and for our industrial power and success. Those causes have also produced democracy, given it success, and have made its faults and errors innocuous. Indeed . . . in the economic forces which control the material prosperity of a population lie the real causes of its political institutions, its social class-adjustments, its industrial prosperity, its moral code, and its world-philosophy. If democracy and the industrial system are both products of the economic conditions which exist, it is plainly absurd to set democracy to defeat those conditions in the control of industry. . . .

3. Democracy in the United States has . . . been living on a capital inherited from aristocracy and industrialism. . . . Our democracy is limited at every turn by institutions which were developed in England in connection with industrialism and aristocracy, and these institutions are of the essence of our system. While our people are passionately democratic in temper and will not tolerate a doctrine that one man is not as good as another, they have common sense enough to know that he is not; and it seems that they love and cling to the conservative institutions quite as strongly as they do to the democratic philosophy. They are, therefore, ruled by men who talk philosophy and govern by the institutions. . . .

The question, therefore, arises, if it is proposed to reorganize the social system on the principles of American democracy, whether the institutions of industrialism are to be retained. If so, all the virus of capitalism will be retained. . . . We may find that instead of democratizing capitalism we have capitalized democracy. . . . Can anyone imagine that the masterfulness, the overbearing disposition, the greed of gain, and the ruthlessness in methods, which are the faults of the master of industry at his worst, would cease when he was a functionary of the State, which had relieved him of risk and endowed him with authority? . . .

If this poor old world is as bad as they say, one more reflection may check the zeal of the headlong reformer. It is at any rate a tough old world. It has taken its trend and curvature and all its twists and tangles from a long course of formation. . . . If we puny men by our arts can do anything at all to straighten them, it will only be by modifying the tendencies of some of the forces at work, so that, after a sufficient time, their action may be changed a little and slowly the lines of movement may be modified. This effort, however, can at most be only slight, and it will take a long time. In the meantime spontaneous forces will be at work, compared with which our efforts are like those of a man trying to deflect a river, and these forces will have changed the whole problem before our interferences have time to make themselves felt. . . .

Everyone of us is a child of his age and cannot get out of it. He is in the stream and is swept along with it. All his sciences and philosophy come to him out of it. Therefore the tide will not be changed by us. It will swallow up both us and our experiments. It will absorb the efforts at change and take them into itself as new but trivial components, and the great movement of tradition and work will go on unchanged by our fads and schemes. The things which will change it are the great discoveries and inventions, the new reactions inside the social organism, and the changes in the earth itself on account of changes in the cosmical forces. These causes will make of it just what, in fidelity to them, it ought to be. The men will be carried along with it and be made by it. The utmost they can do by their cleverness will be to note and record their course as they are carried along, which is what we do now, and is that which leads us to the vain fancy that we can make or guide the movement. That is why it is the greatest folly of which a man can be capable, to sit down with a slate and pencil to plan out a new social world.

288. *In His Steps*, 1889

C. M. Sheldon, *In His Steps* (New York, 1889), 7–8, 9–12.

THE ENTIRE congregation was startled by the sound of a man's voice. It came from the rear of the church, from one of the seats under the gallery. The next moment the figure of a man came out of the shadow there and walked down the middle aisle. Before the startled congregation fairly realized what was going on the man had reached the open space in front of the pulpit and had turned about facing the people.

"I've been wondering since I came in here . . . if it would be just the thing to say a word at the close of the service. I'm not drunk and I'm not crazy, and I'm perfectly harmless; but if I die, as there is every likelihood I shall in a few days, I want the satisfaction of thinking that I said my say in a place like this, and before this sort of a crowd.". . .

"I lost my job ten months ago. I am a printer by trade. The new linotype machines are beautiful specimens of invention, but I know six men who have killed themselves inside of the year just on account of those machines. Of course I don't blame the newspapers for getting the machines. Meanwhile, what can a man do? I know I never learned but the one trade, and that's all I can do. I've tramped all over the country trying to find something. There are a good many others like me. I'm not complaining, am I? Just stating facts. But I was wondering as I sat there under the gallery, if what you call following Jesus is the same thing as what He taught. What did He mean when He said, 'Follow me'? The minister said,"— here the man turned about and looked up at the pulpit—"that it is necessary for the disciple of Jesus to follow His steps, and he said the steps are obedience, faith, love, and imitation. But I did not hear him tell you just what he meant that to mean, especially the last step. What do you Christians mean by following the steps of Jesus?

"I've tramped through this city for three days trying to find a job; and in all that time I've not had a word of sympathy or comfort except from your minister here, who said he was sorry for me and hoped I would find a job somewhere. I suppose it is because you get so imposed on by the professional tramp that you have lost your interest in the other sort. I'm not blaming anybody, am I? Just stating facts. Of course I understand you can't go out of your way to hunt up jobs for people like me. I'm not asking you to; but what I feel puzzled about is, what is meant by following Jesus? What do you mean when you sing, 'I'll go with Him, with Him all the way?' Do you mean that you are suffering and denying yourselves and trying to save lost, suffering humanity just as I understand Jesus did? . . . I understand there are more than five hundred men in this city in my case. Most of them have families. My wife died four months ago. I'm glad she is out of trouble. My little girl is staying with a printer's family until I find a job. Somehow I get puzzled when I see so many Christians living in luxury and singing 'Jesus, I my cross have taken, all to leave and follow Thee,' and remember how my wife died in a tenement in New York City, gasping for air and asking God to take the little girl too. Of course I don't expect you people can prevent every one from dying of starvation, lack of proper nourishment and tenement air, but what does following Jesus mean? I understand that Christian people own a good many of the tenements. . . . I heard some people singing at a church prayer meeting the other night,

"All for Jesus, all for Jesus,
All my being's ransomed powers,
All my thoughts, and all my doings,
All my days and, all my hours,"

and I kept wondering as I sat on the steps outside just what they meant by it. It seems to me there's an awful lot of trouble in the world that somehow wouldn't exist if all the people who sing such songs went and lived them out. I suppose I don't understand. But what would Jesus do?"

289. *Ancient Society, 1877*

L. H. Morgan, *Ancient Society* (New York, 1877), v–vii, 84–5, 551–2.

IT CAN now be asserted upon convincing evidence that savagery preceded barbarism in all the tribes of mankind, as barbarism is known to have preceded civilization. The history of the human race is one in source, one in experience, and one in progress. . . .

Throughout the latter part of the period of savagery, and the entire period of barbarism, mankind in general were organized in gentes, phratries and tribes. These organizations prevailed throughout the entire ancient world upon all the continents, and were the instrumentalities by means of which ancient society was organized and held together. . . . The principal institutions of mankind originated in savagery, were developed in barbarism, and are maturing in civilization. . . .

The council was the great feature of ancient society, Asiatic, European and American, from the institution of the gens in savagery to civilization. It was the instrument of government as well as the supreme authority over the gens, the tribe, and the confederacy. . . .

The simplest and lowest form of the council was that of the gens. It was a democratic assembly because every adult male and female member had a voice upon all questions brought before it. It elected and deposed its sachem and chiefs, it elected Keepers of the Faith, it condoned or avenged the murder of a gentilis, and it adopted persons into the gens. It

was the germ of the higher council of the tribe, and of that still higher of the confederacy, each of which was composed exclusively of chiefs as representatives of the gentes.

Such were the rights, privileges and obligations of the members of an Iroquois gens; and such were those of the members of the gentes of the Indian tribes generally, as far as the investigation has been carried. When the gentes of the Grecian and Latin tribes are considered, the same rights, privileges and obligations will be found to exist. . . .

All the members of an Iroquois gens were personally free, and they were bound to defend each other's freedom; they were equal in privileges and in personal rights, the sachem and chiefs claiming no superiority; and they were a brotherhood bound together by the ties of kin. Liberty, equality, and fraternity, though never formulated, were cardinal principles of the gens. These facts are material, because the gens was the unit of a social and governmental system, the foundation upon which Indian society was organized. A structure composed of such units would of necessity bear the impress of their character, for as the unit so the compound. It serves to explain that sense of independence and personal dignity universally an attribute of Indian character. . . .

During the Later Period of barbarism a new element, that of aristocracy, had a marked development. The individuality of persons, and the increase of wealth now possessed by individuals in masses, were laying the foundation of personal influence. Slavery, also, by permanently degrading a portion of the people, tended to establish contrasts of condition unknown in the previous ethnical periods. This, with property and official position, gradually developed the sentiment of aristocracy, which has so deeply penetrated modern society, and antagonized the democratical principles created and fostered by the gentes. It soon disturbed the balance of society by introducing unequal privileges, and degrees of respect for individuals among people of the same nationality, and thus became the source of discord and strife.... Property and office were the foundations upon which aristocracy planted itself.

Whether this principle shall live or die has been one of the great problems with which modern society has been engaged through the intervening periods. As a question between equal rights and unequal rights, between equal laws and unequal laws, between the rights of wealth, of rank and of official position, and the power of justice and intelligence, there can be little doubt of the ultimate result. Although several thousand years have passed away without the overthrow of privileged classes, excepting in the United States, their burdensome character upon society has been demonstrated.

Since the advent of civilization, the outgrowth of property has been so immense, its forms so diversified, its uses so expanding and its management so intelligent in the interests of its owners, that it has become, on the part of the people, an unmanageable power. The human mind stands bewildered in the presence of its own creation. The time will come, nevertheless, when human intelligence will rise to the mastery over property, and define the relations of the state to the property it protects, as well as the obligations and the limits of the rights of its owners. The interests of society are paramount to individual interests, and the two must be brought into just and harmonious relations. A mere property career is not the final destiny of mankind, if progress is to be the law of the future as it has been of the past.... The dissolution of society bids fair to become the termination of a career of which property is the end and aim; because such a career contains the elements of self-destruction. Democracy in government, brotherhood in society, equality in rights and privileges, and universal education, foreshadow the next higher plane of society to which experience, intelligence and knowledge are steadily tending. It will be a revival, in a higher form, of the liberty, equality and fraternity of the ancient gentes.

290. *American Economic Association, 1886*

R. T. Ely, "Report of the Organization of the American Economic Association," *Publications of the American Economic Association,* I (1886), 15–17.

No ONE invited to join this association, certainly no one who has been active in calling this meeting, contemplates a form of pure socialism. "We recognize the necessity of individual initiative." We would do nothing to weaken individual activity, but we hold that there are certain spheres of activity which do not belong to the individual, certain functions which the great cooperative society, called the state, must perform to keep the avenues open for those who would gain a livelihood by their own exertions. The avenues to wealth and preferment are continually blocked by the greed of combinations of men and by monopolists, and individual effort and initiative are thus discouraged. Two examples will suffice—You know that in the Western grazing regions water is often scarce, and those who control the streams virtually own the country. Now it is a notorious fact that unlawful combinations seize upon these streams and, keeping others from them, retain exclusive privileges which shut off effectually individual exertions on the part of those not in the ring. A second example is found in unjust discriminations in freight charges which have built up the fortunes of the favored, and ruined competitors. In looking over the field of economic life, it is evident that there is a wide feeling of discouragement, repressing the activities of the individual, because the avenues to material well-being are so often blocked. Then there are things which individuals ought not to perform because the functions concerned are public; and in certain places the wastes of private competition are too enormous. There are, likewise, important things which individual effort is powerless to effect, e.g., the education of the masses.

We hold that the doctrine of *laissez-faire* is unsafe in politics and unsound in morals, and that it suggests an inadequate explanation of the relations between the state and the citizens. In other words we believe in the existence of a system of social ethics; we do not believe that any man lives for himself alone, nor yet do we believe social classes are devoid of mutual obligations corresponding to their infinitely varied interrelations. All have duties as well as rights, and, as Emerson said several years ago, it is time we heard more about duties and less about rights. We who have resolved to form an American Economic Association hope to do something towards the development of a system of social ethics. . . .

Laissez-faire . . . stands for a well-known, though rather vague set of ideas, to which appeal is made every day in the year by the bench, the bar, the newspapers and our legislative bodies. It means that government, the state, the people in their collective capacity, ought not to interfere in industrial life; that, on the contrary, free contract should regulate all the economic relations of life and public authority should simply enforce this, punish crime and preserve peace. It means that the laws of economic life are natural laws like those of physics and chemistry, and that this life must be left to the free play of natural forces. One adherent uses these words: "This industrial world is governed by natural laws. . . . These laws are superior to man. Respect this providential order—let alone the work of God."

The platform then emphasizes the mission of the State and the mission of the individual in that State. To distinguish between the proper functions of the two must be one of the purposes of our association.

291. *The Laws of Progress, 1881*

Henry George, *Progress and Poverty* (New York, 1881), 455–7, 465, 466, 467, 475, 477–8, 479, 483, 486–7.

THE INCENTIVES to progress are the desires inherent in human nature—the desire to gratify the wants of the animal nature, and the wants of the sympathetic nature; the desire to be, to know, and to do—desires that short of infinity can never be satisfied, as they grow by what they feed on.

Mind is the instrument by which man advances, and by which each advance is secured and made the vantage ground for new advances. Though he may not by taking thought add a cubit to his stature, man may by taking thought extend his knowledge of the universe and his power over it, in what, so far as we can see, is an infinite degree. . . .

Mental power is, therefore, the motor of progress, and men tend to advance in proportion to the mental power . . . which is devoted to the extension of knowledge, the improvement of methods, and the betterment of social conditions.

Now mental power is a fixed quantity —that is to say, there is a limit to the work a man can do with his mind, as there is to the work he can do with his body; therefore, the mental power which can be devoted to progress is only what is left after what is required for non-progressive purposes.

These non-progressive purposes in which mental power is consumed may be classified as maintenance and conflict. . . . In a separated state the whole powers of man are required to maintain existence, and mental power is only set free for higher uses by the association of men in communities, which permits the division of labor and all the economies which come with the coöperation of increased numbers. . . . Improvement becomes possible as men come together in peaceful association, and the wider and closer the association, the greater the possibilities of improvement. And as the wasteful expenditure of mental power in conflict becomes greater or less as the moral law which accords to each an equality of rights is ignored or is recognized, equality (or justice) is the second essential of progress.

Thus association in equality is the law of progress. Association frees mental power for expenditure in improvement, and equality (or justice, or freedom—for the terms here signify the same thing, the recognition of the moral law) prevents the dissipation of this power in fruitless struggles.

Here is the law of progress, which will explain all diversities, all advances, all halts, and retrogressions. Men tend to progress just as they come closer together, and by coöperation with each other increase the mental power that may be devoted to improvement, but just as conflict is provoked, or association develops inequality of condition and power, this tendency to progression is lessened, checked, and finally reversed. . . .

But the great cause of inequality is in the natural monopoly which is given by the possession of land. . . . And inequality once established, the ownership of land tends to concentrate as development goes on. . . .

The unequal distribution of the power and wealth gained by the integration of men in society tends to check, and finally to counterbalance, the force by which improvements are made and society advances. On the one side, the masses of the community are compelled to expend their mental powers in merely maintaining existence. On the other side, mental power is expended in keeping up and intensifying the system of inequality in ostentation, luxury, and warfare. . . . Invention may for awhile to some degree go on; but it will be the invention of refinements in luxury, not the inventions that relieve toil and increase power. . . . For as it tends to lessen the mental power devoted to improvement, so does inequality tend to render men adverse to improvement. . . .

What has destroyed every previous civilization has been the tendency to the unequal distribution of wealth and power. This same tendency, operating with increasing force, is observable in our civilization today, showing itself in every progressive community, and with greater intensity the more progressive the community. Wages and interest tend constantly to fall, rent to rise, the rich to become very much richer, the poor to become more helpless and hopeless, and the middle class to be swept away. . . .

And when the disparity of condition increases, so does universal suffrage make it easy to seize the source of power, for the greater is the proportion of power in the hands of those who feel no direct interest in the conduct of government; who, tortured by want and embruted by poverty, are ready to sell their votes to the highest bidder or follow the lead of the most blatant demagogue. . . .

Now this transformation of popular government into despotism of the vilest and most degrading kind, which must inevitably result from the unequal distribution of wealth, is not a thing of the far future. It has already begun in the United States, and is rapidly going on under our eyes. . . .

Where that course leads is clear to whoever will think. As corruption becomes chronic; as public spirit is lost; as traditions of honor, virtue, and patriotism are weakened; as law is brought into contempt and reforms become hopeless; then in the festering mass will be generated volcanic forces, which shatter and rend when seeming accident gives them vent. Strong, unscrupulous men, rising up upon occasion, will become the exponents of blind popular desires or fierce popular passions, and dash aside forms that have lost their vitality. The sword will again be mightier than the pen, and in carnivals of destruction brute force and wild frenzy will alternate with the lethargy of a declining civilization. . . .

These industrial depressions, which cause as much waste and suffering as famines or wars, are like the twinges and shocks which precede paralysis. Everywhere is it evident that the tendency to inequality, which is the necessary result of material progress where land is monopolized, cannot go much further without carrying our civilization into that downward path which is so easy to enter and so hard to abandon. Everywhere the increasing intensity of the struggle to live, the increasing necessity for straining every nerve to prevent being thrown down and trodden under foot in the scramble for wealth, is draining the forces which gain and maintain improvements.

292. *Intelligence, 1910*

John Dewey, *Influence of Darwin on Philosophy* (New York, 1910), 59–60, 67–9, 72, 73, 74. By permission of Henry Holt and Company, Inc. Copyright 1910.

DEMOCRACY, the crucial expression of modern life, is not so much an addition to the scientific and industrial tendencies as it is the perception of their social or spiritual meaning. Democracy is an absurdity where faith in the individual as individual is impossible; and this faith is impossible when intelligence is regarded as a cosmic power, not an adjustment and application of individual tendencies. It is also impossible when appetites and desires are conceived to be the dominant factor in the constitution of most men's characters, and when appetite and desire are conceived to be manifestations of the disorderly and unruly principle of nature. . . .

Democracy is estimable only through the changed conception of intelligence, that forms modern science, and of want, that forms modern industry. . . . The substitution, for *a priori* truth and deduction, of fluent doubt and inquiry meant trust in human nature in the concrete; in individual honesty, curiosity, and sympathy. The substitution of moving commerce for fixed custom meant a view of wants as the dynamics of social progress, not as the pathology of private greed. . . .

The transformation in attitude, to which I referred, is the growing belief that the proper business of intelligence is discrimination of multiple and present goods and of the varied immediate means of their realization; not search for the one remote aim. The progress of biology has accustomed our minds to the notion that intelligence is not an outside power presiding supremely but statically over the desires and efforts of man, but is a method of adjustment of capacities and conditions within specific situations. History . . . has discovered itself in the idea of process. The genetic standpoint makes us aware that the systems of the past are neither fraudulent impostures nor absolute revelations; but are the products of political, economic, and scientific conditions whose change carries with it change of theoretical formulations. The recognition that intelligence is properly an organ of adjustment in difficult situations makes us aware that past theories were of value so far as they helped carry to an issue the social perplexities from which they emerged. But the chief impact of the evolutionary method is upon the present. Theory having learned what it cannot do, is made responsible for the better performance of what needs to be done, and what only a broadly equipped intelligence can undertake: study of the conditions out of which come the obstacles and the resources of adequate life, and developing and testing the ideas that, as working hypotheses, may be used to diminish the causes of evil and to buttress and expand the sources of good. . . .

From this point of view there is no separate body of moral rules. . . . The business of morals . . . is to utilize physiology, anthropology, and psychology to discover all that can be discovered of man, his organic powers and propensities. . . . Its business is . . . to converge all the instrumentalities of the social arts, of law, edu-

cation, economics, and political science upon the construction of intelligent methods of improving the common lot. . . .

No, nature is not an unchangeable order, unwinding itself majestically from the reel of law under the control of deified forces. It is an indefinite congeries of changes. Laws are . . . convenient formulations of selected portions of change followed through a longer or shorter period of time. . . . Knowledge of nature does not mean subjection to predestination, but insight into courses of change; an insight which is formulated in "laws," that is, methods of subsequent procedure.

Knowledge of the process and conditions of physical and social change through experimental science and genetic history has one result with a double name: increase of control, and increase of responsibility; increase of power to direct natural change, and increase of responsibility for its equitable direction toward fuller good. Theory . . . means practice itself made responsible to intelligence; to intelligence which relentlessly scrutinizes the consequences of every practice. . . .

In the end, men do what they can do. They refrain from doing what they cannot do. They do what their own specific powers in conjunction with the limitations and resources of the environment permit. The effective control of their powers is not through precepts, but through the regulation of their conditions. If this regulation is to be not merely physical or coercive, but moral, it must consist of the intelligent selection and determination of the environments in which we act; and in an intelligent exaction of responsibility for the use of men's powers.

293. *Democratic Vistas,* 1880's

Walt Whitman, "Democratic Vistas," in *Complete Prose Works*, II, 50, 51–3, 61–2, 143–5.

AMERICA . . . counts, as I reckon, for her justification and success . . . almost entirely on the future. Nor is that hope unwar-

ranted. Today, ahead, though dimly yet, we see, in vistas, a copious, sane, gigantic offspring. For our New World I consider far less important for what it has done, or what it is, than for results to come. Sole among nationalities, these States have assumed the task to put in forms of lasting power and practicality . . . the moral political speculations of ages, long, long deferr'd, the democratic republican principle, and the theory of development and perfection by voluntary standards, and self-reliance. . . .

The United States are destined either to surmount the gorgeous history of feudalism, or else prove the most tremendous failure of time. Not the least doubtful am I on any prospects of their material success. The triumphant future of their business, geographic and productive departments, on larger scales and in more varieties than ever, is certain. In those respects the republic must soon (if she does not already) outstrip all examples hitherto afforded, and dominate the world.

Admitting all this, . . . I say that, far deeper than these, what finally and only is to make of our western world a nationality superior to any hither known, and out-topping the past, must be vigorous, yet unsuspected Literatures, perfect personalities and sociologies, original, transcendental, and expressing (what, in highest sense, are not yet express'd at all) democracy and the modern. . . .

I say we had best look our times and lands searchingly in the face, like a physician diagnosing some deep disease. Never was there, perhaps, more hollowness at heart than at present, and here in the United States. Genuine belief seems to have left us. The underlying principles of the States are not honestly believ'd in (for all this hectic glow, and these melodramatic screamings), nor is humanity itself believ'd in. What penetrating eye does not everywhere see through the mask? The spectacle is appalling. . . . The future of America is in certain respects as dark as it is vast. Pride, competition, segregation, vicious willfulness, and license beyond example, brood already upon us. . . Athwart and over the roads of our

progress loom huge uncertainity, and dreadful, threatening gloom. . . .

Short as the span of our national life has been, already have death and downfall crowded close upon us—and will again crowd close, no doubt, even if warded off. Ages to come may never know, but I know, how narrowly during the late secession war . . . our nationality (wherein bound up, as in a ship in a storm, depended, and yet depend, all our best life, all hope, all value), just grazed, just by a hair escaped destruction. Alas! to think of them! the agony and bloody sweat of certain of those hours! those cruel, sharp, suspended crises!

Even today, amid these whirls, incredible flippancy, and blind fury of parties, infidelity, entire lack of first-class captains and leaders, added to the plentiful meanness and vulgarity of the ostensible masses —that problem, the labor question, beginning to open like a yawning gulf, rapidly widening every year—what prospect have we? . . . It seems as if the Almighty had spread before this nation charts of imperial destinies, dazzling as the sun, yet with many a deep intestine difficulty, and human aggregate of cankerous imperfection,—saying, lo! the roads, the only plans of development, long and varied with all terrible balks and ebullitions. You said in your soul, I will be empire of empires, overshadowing all else, past and present. . . . If these, O lands of America, are indeed the prizes, the determinations of your soul, be it so. But behold the cost, and already specimens of the cost. Thought you greatness was to ripen for you like a pear? If you would have greatness, know that you must . . . pay for it with a proportionate price. For you too, as for all lands, the struggle, the traitor, the wily person in office, scrofulous wealth, the surfeit of prosperity, the demonism of greed, the hell of passion, the decay of faith, the long postponement, the fossil-like lethargy, the ceaseless need of revolutions, prophets, thunderstorms, deaths, births, new projections and invigorations of ideas and men.

294. *Conscience, 1884*

Mark Twain, *Adventures of Huckleberry Finn* (first printed, 1884; New York, 1912), 125–30.

JIM said it made him all over trembly and feverish to be so close to freedom. Well, I can tell you it made me all over trembly and feverish, too, to hear him, because I begun to get it through my head that he *was* most free—and who was to blame for it? Why, *me*. I couldn't get that out of my conscience, no how nor no way. It got to troubling me so I couldn't rest; I couldn't stay still in one place. It hadn't ever come home to me before, what this thing was that I was doing. But now it did; and it stayed with me, and scorched me more and more. I tried to make out to myself that *I* warn't to blame, because *I* didn't run Jim off from his rightful owner; but it warn't no use, conscience up and says, every time, "But you knowed he was running for his freedom, and you could 'a' paddled ashore and told somebody." That was so—I couldn't get around that no way. That was where it pinched. Conscience say to me, "What had poor Miss Watson done to you that you could see her nigger go off right under your eyes and never say one single word? What did that poor old woman do to you that you could treat her so mean? Why, she tried to learn you your book, she tried to learn you your manners, she tried to be good to you every way she knowed how. *That's* what she done."

I got to feeling so mean and so miserable I most wished I was dead. I fidgeted up and down the raft, abusing myself to myself, and Jim was fidgeting up and down past me. We neither of us could keep still. Every time he danced around and says, "Dah's Cairo!" it went through me like a shot, and I thought if it *was* Cairo I reckoned I would die of miserableness.

Jim talked out loud all the time while I was talking to myself. He was saying how the first thing he would do when he got to a free state he would go to saving up money and never spend a single cent, and when he got enough he would buy his wife, which was owned on a farm close to where Miss Watson lived; and then they would both work to buy the two children, and if their master wouldn't sell them, they'd get an Ab'litionist to go and steal them.

It most froze me to hear such talk. He wouldn't ever dared to talk such talk in his life before. Just see what a difference it made in him the minute he judged he was about free. It was according to the old saying, "Give a nigger an inch and he'll take an ell." Thinks I, this is what comes of my not thinking. Here was this nigger, which I had as good as helped to run away, coming right out flat-footed and saying he would steal his children—children that belonged to a man I didn't even know; a man that hadn't ever done me no harm.

I was sorry to hear Jim say that, it was such a lowering of him. My conscience got to stirring me up hotter than ever, until at last I says to it, "Let up on me—it ain't too late yet—I'll paddle ashore at the first light and tell." I felt easy and happy and light as a feather right off. All my troubles was gone. I went to looking out sharp for a light, and sort of singing to myself. By and by one showed. Jim sings out: "We's safe, Huck, we's safe! Jump up and crack yo' heels! Dat's de good ole Cairo at las', I jis knows it!"

I says:

"I'll take the canoe and go and see, Jim. It mightn't be, you know."

He jumped and got the canoe ready, and put his old coat in the bottom for me to set on, and give me the paddle; and as I shoved off, he says:

"Pooty soon I'll be a-shout'n' for joy, en I'll say, it's all on accounts o' Huck; I's a free man, en I couldn't ever ben free ef it hadn't ben for Huck; Huck done it. Jim won't ever forgit you, Huck; you's de bes' fren' Jim's ever had, en you's de *only* fren' ole Jim's got now."

I was paddling off, all in a sweat to tell on him; but when he says this, it seemed to kind of take the tuck all out of me. I went along slow then, and I warn't right down certain whether I was glad I started or whether I warn't. When I was fifty yards off, Jim says:

"Dah you goes, de ole true Huck; de on'y white genlman dat ever kep' his promise to ole Jim."

Well, I just felt sick. But I says, I *got* to do it—I can't get *out* of it. Right then along comes a skiff with two men in it with guns, and they stopped and I stopped. One of them says:

"What's that yonder?"

"A piece of raft," I says.

"Do you belong on it?"

"Yes, sir."

"Any men on it?"

"Only one, sir."

"Well, there's five niggers run off tonight up yonder, above the head of the bend. Is your man white or black?"

I didn't answer up prompt. I tried to, but the words wouldn't come. I tried for a second or two to brace up and out with it, but I warn't man enough—hadn't the spunk of a rabbit. I see I was weakening; so I just give up trying, and up and says:

"He's white."

"I reckon we'll go and see for ourselves."

"I wish you would," says I, "because it's pap that's there, and maybe you'd help me tow the raft ashore where the light is. He's sick—and so is mam and Mary Ann."

"Oh, the devil! we're in a hurry, boy. But I s'pose we've got to. Come, buckle to your paddle, and let's get along."

I buckled to my paddle and they laid to their oars. When we had made a stroke or two, I says:

"Pap'll be mighty much obleeged to you, I can tell you. Everybody goes away when I want them to help me tow the raft ashore, and I can't do it by myself."

"Well, that's infernal mean. Odd, too. Say, boy, what's the matter with your father?"

"It's the—a—the—well, it ain't anything much."

They stopped pulling. It warn't but a mighty little ways to the raft now. One says:

"Boy, that's a lie. What *is* the matter with your pap? Answer up square now, and it'll be the better for you."

"I will, sir, I will, honest—but don't leave us, please. It's the—the—Gentlemen, if you'll only pull ahead, and let me heave you the headline, you won't have to come a-near the raft—please do."

"Set her back, John, set her back!" says one. They backed water. "Keep away boy—keep to looard. Confound it, I just expect the wind has blowed it to us. Your pap's got the smallpox, and you know it precious well. Why didn't you come out and say so? Do you want to spread it all over?"

"Well," says I, a-blubbering, "I've told everybody before, and they just went away and left us."

"Poor devil, there's something in that. We are right down sorry for you, but we—well, hang it, we don't want the smallpox, you see. Look here, I'll tell you what to do. Don't you try to land by yourself, or you'll smash everything to pieces. You float along down about twenty miles, and you'll come to a town on the left-hand side of the river. It will be long after sun-up then, and when you ask for help you tell them your folks are all down with chills and fever. Don't be a fool again, and let people guess what is the matter. Now we're trying to do you a kindness; so you just put twenty miles between us, that's a good boy. It wouldn't do any good to land yonder where the light is—it's only a wood-yard. Say, I reckon your father's poor, and I'm bound to say he's in pretty hard luck. Here, I'll put a twenty dollar gold piece on this board, and you get it when it floats by. I feel mighty mean to leave you; but my kingdom! it won't do to fool with smallpox, don't you see?"

"Hold on, Parker," says the man, "here's a twenty to put on the board for me. Good-by, boy; you do as Mr. Parker told you, and you'll be all right.". . .

They went off and I got aboard the raft, feeling bad and low, because I knowed very well I had done wrong, and I see it warn't no use for me to try to learn to do right; a body that don't get *started* right when he's little ain't got no show—when the pinch comes there ain't

nothing to back him up and keep him to his work, and so he gets beat. Then I thought a minute, and says to myself, hold on; s'pose you'd a done right and give Jim up, would you felt better than what you do now? No, says I, I'd feel bad —I'd feel just the same way I do now. Well, then, says I, what's the use you learning to do right when it's troublesome to do right and ain't no trouble to do wrong, and the wages is just the same? I was stuck. I couldn't answer that. So I reckoned I wouldn't bother no more about it, but after this always do whichever come handiest at the time.

XXXIV ❧ *The Progressive Movement*

IN THE LAST decade of the nineteenth century, farmers—and, to a lesser extent, laborers—with grievances turned to politics for redress as a matter of course. The Populist platform of 1892 expressed the program of these discontented groups (No. 295). But they were not capable of gaining national control, even after they joined forces with the Democratic party in 1896 (No. 296). Ultimately they lost strength, were often swayed by demagogues, and expressed themselves largely in the kind of muckraking accusations criticized by Theodore Roosevelt (No. 297).

The Progressive movement ultimately gained the support of these groups. But it sprang from another source, from the conviction that a moral tone could be imparted to society through its scientific reorganization. Lester Ward, for instance, explained how planning could render the institutions of society more efficient (No. 298); and Herbert Croly set forth the arguments for national action toward that end (No. 299). Application of the idea that the expert through government could order society came readily on the municipal (No. 300) and state levels (No. 301). But, as Lord Bryce had already pointed out, all the tendencies in American life operated to centralize power in the federal government (No. 302); and the test of the Progressive movement was its ability to gain control of the national government. That was the task the new party set for itself in 1912 (No. 303). In that test, it failed. Yet the Progressive principles had by then become widely current; and many of them were translated into action under the administration of Woodrow Wilson. The Constitutional amendments which provided for the income tax and the direct election of senators had already been passed by Congress before the election, and they were ratified shortly thereafter (No. 304; *see also below*, No. 378).

295. *The Populist Platform, 1892*

People's Platform of 1892, in K. H. Porter, *National Party Platforms* (New York, 1924), 167–9.

WE HAVE witnessed for more than a quarter of a century the struggles of the two great political parties for power and plunder, while grievous wrongs have been inflicted upon the suffering people. We charge that the controlling influence[s] dominating both these parties have permitted the existing dreadful conditions to develop without serious effort to prevent or restrain them. Neither do they now promise us any substantial reform. . . .

We believe that the power of government—in other words, of the people—should be expanded (as in the case of the postal service) as rapidly and as far as the good sense of an intelligent people and the teachings of experience shall justify, to the end that oppression, injustice and poverty, shall eventually cease in the land. . . .

We declare, therefore,

First—That the union of the labor forces of the United States this day consummated shall be permanent and perpetual; may its spirit enter into all hearts for the salvation of the Republic and the uplifting of mankind.

Second—Wealth belongs to him who creates it, and every dollar taken from industry without an equivalent is robbery. "If any will not work, neither shall he eat." The interests of rural and civic labor are the same; their enemies are identical.

Third—We believe that the time has come when the railroad corporations will either own the people or the people must own the railroads, and should the government enter upon the work of owning and managing all railroads, we should favor an amendment to the Constitution by which all persons engaged in the government service shall be placed under a civil service regulation of the most rigid character, so as to prevent the increase of the power of the national administration by the use of such additional government employees.

Finance—We demand a national currency, safe, sound, and flexible, issued by the general government only, a full legal tender for all debts, public and private, and that without the use of banking corporations. . . .

1. We demand free and unlimited coinage of silver and gold at the present legal ratio of 16 to 1.

2. We demand that the amount of circulating medium be speedily increased to not less than $50 per capita.

3. We demand a graduated income tax.

4. We believe that the money of the country should be kept as much as possible in the hands of the people, and hence we demand that all state and national revenues shall be limited to the necessary expenses of the government, economically and honestly administered.

5. We demand that postal savings banks be established by the government for the safe deposit of the earnings of the people and to facilitate exchange.

Transportation—Transportation being a means of exchange and a public necessity, the government should own and operate the railroads in the interest of the people. The telegraph and telephone, like the post office system, being a necessity for the transmission of news, should be owned and operated by the government in the interest of the people.

Land—The land, including all the natural sources of wealth, is the heritage of the people, and should not be monopolized for speculative purposes, and alien ownership of land should be prohibited. All land now held by railroads and other corporations in excess of their actual needs, and all lands now owned by aliens, should be reclaimed by the government and held for actual settlers only.

296. *The Cross of Gold, 1896*

W. J. Bryan, Speech in the Chicago Convention, July 8, 1896, in W. J. Bryan, *Speeches* (New York, 1909), I, 248–9.

You come to us and tell us that the great cities are in favor of the gold standard; we reply that the great cities rest upon our broad and fertile prairies. Burn down your cities and leave our farms, and your cities will spring up again as if by magic; but destroy our farms and the grass will grow in the streets of every city in the country.

My friends, we declare that this nation is able to legislate for its own people upon every question, without waiting for the aid or consent of any other nation on earth; and upon that issue we expect to carry every state in the Union. I shall not slander the inhabitants of the fair State of Massachusetts nor the inhabitants of the State of New York by saying that, when they are confronted with the proposition, they will declare that this nation is not able to attend to its own business. It is the issue of 1776 over again. Our ancestors, when but three millions in number, had the courage to declare their political independence of every other nation; shall we, their descendants, when we have grown to seventy millions, declare that we are less independent than our forefathers? No, my friends, that will never be the verdict of our people. Therefore, we care not upon what lines the battle is fought. If they say bimetallism is good, but that we cannot have it until other nations help us, we reply that, instead of having a gold standard because England has, we will restore bimetallism, and then let England have bimetallism because the United States has it. If they dare to come out in the open field and defend the gold standard as a good thing, we will fight them to the uttermost. Having behind us the producing masses of this nation and the world, supported by the commercial interests, the laboring interests, and the toilers everywhere, we will answer their demand for a gold standard by saying to them: You shall not press down upon the brow of labor this crown of thorns, you shall not crucify mankind upon a cross of gold.

297. *The Muckraker, 1906*

Theodore Roosevelt to George H. Lorimer, May 12, 1906, in *Letters* (E. E. Morison, ed., Cambridge, 1952), V, 263, 264–5, 266, 267, 268, 269. Reprinted by permission of the publishers. Copyright 1952 by the President and Fellows of Harvard College.

Now the very fact that I wish to see unceasing and merciless warfare waged upon corruption, cruelty and treachery and all kindred forms of evil in public life, makes me resent the overstatement which must surely defeat its own ends. It is just this overstatement of which, in my judgment, Phillips is guilty in *The Plum Tree*. . . .

Now, I feel that almost each individual fact brought forward by Phillips is true by itself, and yet that these facts are so grouped as to produce a totally false impression. Of course there are some things that he alleges that I never have seen or heard of. I do not believe that ever, under any circumstances, the "Wall Street crowd" made to any man any advance even remotely resembling that he describes as made to Scarborough. I do not for a moment believe that there is or has been any powerful senatorial boss who in our time had been influential in handling at the same moment the nominations of the two parties. In fact, I do not for a moment believe that in our time any boss in one party has had any effect upon the presidential nomination of the other. I know that there are many wealthy men who have changed parties at different elections, and supported, for instance, Cleveland first and then McKinley. To my somewhat grim amusement, the chief representatives of this class, or at least the majority, went into a futile conspiracy against me of which they sought to make Mr. Hanna the head; and at that time they expected that if they could not nominate Mr. Hanna or someone who would be agreeable to Mr. Hanna, they would nominate Mr. Parker on the Democratic ticket and turn in and elect him. But their plan miscarried at every point, and it was merely a purely rich men's conspiracy, not a politicians' at all. . . .

Again, Mr. Phillips errs in making his big politicians think only of that which is directly to their own pecuniary interests. For example, Hale and Foraker both violently opposed me this year on the rate matter no less than on other matters. They have stood for the forces that I am combating. But to me the most exasperating fact has been that I do not question their entire sincerity in standing against me. How Hale, having no earthly interest at stake, can nevertheless be so rabid against the upbuilding of the navy, and the Philippine tariff, I do not know. But I do know that he is entirely disinterested, and that the rich men have no control over him. Foraker, again, while violently against me on corporation matters, is as enthusiastic

for the Philippine tariff bill and for the navy and for Panama and a proper foreign policy generally as any human being can be, and this without the slightest personal interest in any of the matters. . . .

But to my mind the worst mistake that Phillips fell into—a mistake which has naturally resulted in his since enlisting under the banner of Hearst—was the mistake of painting all evil as due to corrupt commercialism, and all rich men as influenced only by what was base. There are plenty of rich men exactly such as he describes, just as there are Senators and Congressmen such as he describes, and bosses, state and city, such as he describes. But so there are plenty of labor leaders, plenty of men engaged in the effort to persuade poor people to organize for their own betterment, who are murderers, incendiaries, corruptionists, blackmailers, bribe takers and brutal scoundrels generally. . . . In the Senate the chief opponents of what is decent and right during the last few years have been men like Tillman. I have had to ride roughshod now and then over the men who accept Mr. Aldrich as their leader, but it has not been anything like as often as I have found it necessary in the interest of the country, in the interest of justice and decency, to ride roughshod over the men like Tillman. Tillman has sometimes been right; but not nearly as often as Aldrich.

It is with these rich men as with the bosses and corrupt politicians. In New York State and New York City I have seen at times things as bad done by the machines and the bosses, and the people they represent, as Mr. Phillips describes; and I have no question that the same is true of other states with which I am less familiar. But there are lights in the pictures as well as shadows! No other Governor of New York ever handled the big men of Wall Street as I did; as see my Franchise Tax bill; it cost me violent enmity; but plenty of rich men stood by me!

As for these rich men, I can speak quite disinterestedly. They are not my friends and never have been. My tastes, unfortunately, were wholly alien from those which I hope my sons will possess in sufficient quantity to make them able to do their part in the industrial world. . . .

I have never had these rich men ask favors from me save as I have had the leaders of labor organizations ask favors, or as I have had representatives of almost any body of citizens ask me.

298. *Sociocracy, 1893*

Lester Ward, *Psychic Factors in Civilization* (Boston, 1897), 323–4, 325–9.

SOCIETY . . . has overthrown the rule of brute force by the establishment of government. It has supplanted autocracy by aristocracy and this by democracy, and now it finds itself in the coils of plutocracy. . . . Shall it then let itself be crushed? It need not. There is one power and only one that is greater than that which now chiefly rules society. That power is society itself. There is one form of government that is stronger than autocracy or aristocracy or democracy, or even plutocracy, and that is *sociocracy.*

The individual has reigned long enough. The day has come for society to take its affairs into its own hands and shape its own destinies. The individual has acted . . . in the only way he could. With a consciousness, will, and intellect of his own he could do nothing else than pursue his natural ends. He should not be denounced nor called any names. . . . Society should learn its great lesson from him. . . . It should imagine itself an individual, with all the interests of an individual, and becoming fully conscious of these interests it should pursue them with the same indomitable will with which the individual pursues his interests. Not only this, it must be guided, as he is guided, by the social intellect, armed with all the knowledge that all individuals combined, with so great labor, zeal, and talent have placed in its possession, constituting the social intelligence. . . .

How then, it may be asked, do democracy and sociocracy differ? . . . A majority acting for society is a different thing from society acting for itself, even though, as must always be the case, it acts through an agency chosen by its members. All democratic governments are largely party governments. The electors range themselves on one side or the other of some party line, the winning side considers itself the state as much as Louis the Fourteenth did. The losing party usually then regards the government as something alien to it and hostile, like an invader, and thinks of nothing but to gain strength enough to overthrow it at the next opportunity. . . .

From the standpoint of society this is child's play. . . . Once get rid of this puerile gaming spirit and have attention drawn to the real interests of society, and it will be seen that upon nearly all important questions all parties and all citizens are agreed, and that there is no need of this partisan strain upon the public energies. This is clearly shown at every change in the party complexion of the government. The victorious party . . . finds that it has little to do but carry out the laws in the same way that its predecessors had been doing. . . . But in the factitious excitement of partisan struggles where professional politicians and demagogues on the one hand, and the agents of plutocracy on the other, are shouting discordantly in the ears of the people, the real interests of society are, temporarily at least, lost sight of, clouded and obscured, and men lose their grasp on the real issues, forget even their own best interests, which, however selfish, would be a far safer guide, and the general result usually is that these are neglected and nations continue in the hands of mere politicians who are easily managed by the shrewd representatives of wealth.

Sociocracy will change all this. Irrelevant issues will be laid aside. The important objects upon which all but an interested few are agreed will receive their proper degree of attention, and measures will be considered in a non-partisan spirit with the sole purpose of securing these objects.

Take as an illustration the postal telegraph question. . . . What society wants is the cheapest possible system. It wants to know with certainty whether a national postal telegraph system would secure this universally desired object. It is to be expected that the agents of the present telegraph companies would try to show that it would not succeed. . . . But why be influenced by the interests of such a small number of persons, however worthy, when all the rest of mankind are interested in the opposite solution? The investigation should be a disinterested and strictly scientific one, and should actually settle the question in one way or the other. If it was found to be a real benefit, the system should be adopted. There are today a great number of these strictly social questions before the American people, questions which concern every citizen in the country, and whose solution would doubtless profoundly affect the state of civilization attainable on this continent. Not only is it impossible to secure this, but it is impossible to secure an investigation of them on their real merits. . . .

And so it would be throughout. Society would inquire in a business way without fear, favor, or bias, into everything that concerned its welfare, and if it found obstacles it would remove them, and if it found opportunities it would improve them. In a word, society would do under the same circumstances just what an intelligent individual would do. It would further, in all possible ways, its own interests.

299. *The Promise of American Life,* 1909

Herbert Croly, *The Promise of American Life* (New York, 1909), 149–50, 176, 179, 180, 181, 189–90, 191–3, 213–14. Copyright 1909 by The Macmillan Company and used with permission.

How utterly confusing it is, consequently, to consider reform as equivalent merely to the restoration of the American democracy to a former condition of purity and excellence! . . . It cannot be restored, even if we would; and the public interest has nothing to gain by its restoration. The usurpation of power by "trusts" and "Bosses" is more than anything else an expression of a desirable individual initiative and organizing ability—which have been allowed to become dangerous and partly corrupt, because of the incoherence and the lack of purpose and responsibility in the traditional American political and economic system. A "purification" might well destroy the good with the evil; and even if it were successful in eradicating certain abuses, would only prepare the way for the outbreak in another form of the tendency towards individual aggrandizement and social classification. No amount of moral energy, directed merely towards the enforcement of the laws, can possibly avail to accomplish any genuine or lasting reform. It is the laws themselves which are partly at fault, and still more at fault is the group of ideas and traditional practices behind the laws. . . .

The best method of approaching a critical reconstruction of American political ideas will be by means of an analysis of the meaning of democracy. . . . The assertion of the doctrine of popular sovereignty is . . . rather the beginning than the end of democracy. There can be no democracy where the people do not rule; but government by the people is not necessarily democratic. The popular will must in a democratic state be expressed somehow in the interest of democracy itself; and we have not traveled very far towards a satisfactory conception of democracy until this democratic purpose has received some definition. . . .

Society is organized politically for the benefit of all the people. Such an organization may permit radical differences among individuals in the opportunities and possessions they actually enjoy; but no man would be able to impute his own success or failure to the legal framework of society. Every citizen would be getting a "Square Deal."

Such is the idea of the democratic state, which the majority of good Americans believe to be entirely satisfactory. It should endure indefinitely, because it seeks to satisfy every interest essential to associated life. The interest of the individual is protected, because of the liberties he securely enjoys. The general social interest is equally well protected, because the liberties enjoyed by one or by a few are enjoyed by all. Thus the individual and the social interests are automatically harmonized. The virile democrat in pursuing his own interest "under the law" is contributing effectively to the interest of society, while the social interest consists precisely in the promotion of these individual interests, in so far as they can be equally exercised. The divergent demands of the individual and the social interest can be reconciled by grafting the principle of equality on the thrifty tree of individual rights, and the ripe fruit thereof can be gathered merely by shaking the tree. . . .

But the principle of equal rights, like the principle of ultimate popular political responsibility, is not sufficient; and because of its insufficiency results in certain dangerous ambiguities and self-contradictions. American political thinkers have always repudiated the idea that by equality of rights they meant anything like equality of performance or power. The utmost varieties of individual power and ability are bound to exist and are bound to bring about many different levels of individual achievement. Democracy both recognizes the right of the individual to use his powers to the utmost, and encourages him to do so by offering a fair field and, in case of success, an abundant reward. The democratic principle requires an equal start in the race, while expecting at the same time an unequal finish. But Americans who talk in this way seem wholly blind to the fact that under a legal system which holds private property sacred there may be equal rights, but there cannot possibly be any equal opportunities for exercising such rights. The chance which the individual has to compete with his fellows and take a prize in the race is vitally affected by material conditions over which he has no control. It is as if the competitor in a Marathon cross country run were denied proper nourishment or proper training, and was obliged to toe the mark against rivals who had every benefit of food and discipline. Under such conditions he is not as badly off as if he were entirely excluded from the race. . . . But it would be absurd to claim that, because all the rivals toed the same mark, a man's victory or defeat depended exclusively on his own efforts. Those who have enjoyed the benefits of wealth and thorough education start with an advantage which can be overcome only by very exceptional men,—men so exceptional, in fact, that the average competitor without such benefits feels himself disqualified for the contest. . . .

The net result has been that . . . the strong and capable men not only conquer, but they seek to perpetuate their conquests by occupying all the strategic points in the economic and political battlefield— whereby they obtain certain more or less permanent advantages over their fellow-democrats. Thus in so far as the equal rights are freely exercised, they are bound to result in inequalities; and these inequalities are bound to make for their own perpetuation, and so to provoke still further discrimination. . . .

The only way in which the thoroughgoing adherent of the principle of equal rights can treat these tendencies to discrimination, when they develop, is rigidly to repress them; and this tendency to repression is now beginning to take possession of those Americans who represent the pure Democratic tradition. They propose to crush out the chief examples of effective individual and associated action, which their system of democracy has encouraged to develop. They propose frankly to destroy, so far as possible, the economic organization which has been built up under stress of competitive conditions; and by assuming such an attitude they have fallen away even from the pretense of impartiality, and have come out as frankly representative of a class interest. But even to assert this class interest efficiently they have been obliged to abandon, in fact if not in word, their correlative principle of national irresponsibility. Whatever the national interest may be, it is not to be asserted by the political practice of non-interference. The hope of automatic democratic fulfillment must be abandoned. The national government must step in and discriminate; but it must discriminate, not on behalf of liberty and the special individual, but on behalf of equality and the average man. . . .

The situation which these laws are supposed to meet is always the same. A certain number of individuals enjoy, in the beginning, equal opportunities to perform certain acts; and in the competition resulting therefrom some of these individuals or associations obtain advantages over their competitors, or over their fellow-citizens whom they employ or serve. Sometimes these advantages and the practices whereby they are obtained are profitable to a larger number of people than they

injure. Sometimes the reverse is true. In either event the state is usually asked to interfere by the class whose economic position has been compromised. It by no means follows that the state should acquiesce in this demand. In many cases interference may be more costly than beneficial. Each case must be considered on its merits. But whether in any particular case the state takes sides or remains impartial, it most assuredly has a positive function to perform on the premises. If it remains impartial, it simply agrees to abide by the results of natural selection. If it interferes, it seeks to replace natural with artificial discrimination. In both cases it authorizes discriminations which in their effect violate the doctrine of "equal rights." Of course, a reformer can always claim that any particular measure of reform proposes merely to restore to the people a "Square Deal"; but that is simply an easy and thoughtless way of concealing novel purposes under familiar formulas. Any genuine measure of economic or political reform will, of course, give certain individuals better opportunities than those they have been recently enjoying, but it will reach this result only by depriving other individuals of advantages which they have earned.

Impartiality is the duty of the judge rather than the statesman, of the courts rather than the government. The state which proposes to draw a ring around the conflicting interests of its citizens and interfere only on behalf of a fair fight will be obliged to interfere constantly and will never accomplish its purpose. In economic warfare, the fighting can never be fair for long, and it is the business of the state to see that its own friends are victorious. . . . While preserving at times an appearance of impartiality so that its citizens may enjoy for a while a sense of the reality of their private game, it must on the whole make the rules in its own interest. It must help those men to win who are most capable of using their winnings for the benefit of society. . . .

Americans have always been both patriotic and democratic, just as they have always been friendly both to liberty and equality, but in neither case have they brought the two ideas or aspirations into mutually helpful relations. As democrats they have often regarded nationalism with distrust, and have consequently deprived their patriotism of any sufficient substance and organization. As nationalists they have frequently regarded essential aspects of democracy with a wholly unnecessary and embarrassing suspicion. They have been after a fashion Hamiltonian, and Jeffersonian after more of a fashion; but they have never recovered from the initial disagreement between Hamilton and Jefferson. If there is any truth in the idea of a constructive relation between democracy and nationality this disagreement must be healed. They must accept both principles loyally and unreservedly; and by such acceptance their "noble national theory" will obtain a wholly unaccustomed energy and integrity. The alliance between the two principles will not leave either of them intact; but it will necessarily do more harm to the Jeffersonian group of political ideas than it will to the Hamiltonian. The latter's nationalism can be adapted to democracy without an essential injury to itself, but the former's democracy cannot be nationalized without being transformed. . . . It must cease to be a democracy of indiscriminate individualism, and become one of selected individuals who are obliged constantly to justify their selection; and its members must be united not by a sense of joint irresponsibility, but by a sense of joint responsibility for the success of their political and social ideal. They must become, that is, a democracy devoted to the welfare of the whole people by means of a conscious labor of individual and social improvement; and that is precisely the sort of democracy which demands for its realization the aid of the Hamiltonian nationalistic organization and principle.

300. *The Expert, 1912*

R. H. Dana, *Antitoxin for Municipal Waste and Corruption* (Baltimore, 1912), 38–9. Reprinted from *National Municipal Review*.

WE SHOULD secure for the permanent heads of departments experienced men of high character and training and tenure based on merit and fitness, persons who believe in the merit system and wish to see its principle enforced even in the excepted places, and municipal contracts honestly and efficiently made and strictly carried out; clean streets and better security for the public health; a day's work for a day's pay; engineers and other scientific men encouraged to accept municipal work as a career; more independent supervision and investigation because the experts are not personal appointees of the politicians; better methods of accounting; continuity of public policies carried out on broad plans for the future; more definite fixing of responsibility between the political executives and the expert administrators; and finally, the removal of all political plunder from politics. . . .

Such a system . . . could be most easily applied in the commission form of city government, which provides that those in charge of each department shall be immediately under the authority of the supervisors. It could also be applied where the heads of departments are under the control of political boards. In cities, and especially in large cities, where a mayor is the chief executive he needs some cabinet officers to aid him in determining executive policies and in supervising the departments. In a small city not carrying on much public business, the mayor might be the sole political head of all the departments. In larger cities we should doubtless need a thorough revision of the charter with reference to what positions should be purely political, and what should be expert; but in general it is believed that we should need not more than from four to eight political chiefs, helping to determine the policies of and supervising an equal number of large departments, each department having its expert chief with his expert assistants under him. In all kinds of municipal government we should need charter provisions giving to the experts the proper powers and independence of tenure. . . . In regard to law enforcement, I may say that twenty cities in Massachusetts have this year put their chiefs of police under civil service rules with the unanimous approval of the state association of chiefs of police.

Much has been said about "heads" of departments. This has caused confusion, because one person has in mind a political head, and another has in mind an expert head. There should be both a political head and an expert head, each a different person and each with clearly defined powers.

301. *The Wisconsin Idea,* 1912

F. C. Howe, *Wisconsin: An Experiment in Democracy* (New York, 1912), 39–40, 46, 50, 184–5, 190–1.

WE HAVE assumed that our evils are personal, ethical, in some way traceable to the political incapacity of our people. I do not believe this is true. I know of no country where politics occupies so absorbing a place in the press, in the public mind, or in the discussions of so many people as it does in America. I doubt if voters are any more partisan than they are in Germany or England, or that business interests are any more influential in determining our political affiliations than in foreign countries. . . .

The explanation of our cities and states is not personal or ethical at all. It is institutional and economic. We have made representative government almost impossible by the complicated machinery of nominations and elections, by the distribution of powers and responsibility among so many officials, by the rigidity of our written constitutions. In addition, we have lured business into politics by privileges of colossal value. We have minimized the sovereignty of the community and exalted the sovereignty of private property. So many public functions have been entrusted to private hands that we have aligned the wealth, the power, and the talent of the community against the government. . . .

The university is the fourth department of the state, along with the judicial, executive, and legislative branches. There is no provision for this in the constitution, no reference to it in the laws. But whether you sit in the office of the governor or of President Van Hise, you see evidences of the most intimate relationship between the two. The university is the nerve center of the commonwealth, impelling it to action in almost every field of activity. It has been the direct inspiration of many of the progressive laws of the past decade. It has adjusted its teachings to state problems. It loans its equipment and encourages its professors to enter the state service. . . .

The close union of the university with politics prevented any serious reaction during the years which followed the election of La Follette to the Senate. University graduates occupied many of the important state offices, whether elective or appointive. In 1910 there were thirty-five professors and instructors giving part of their time to the public service. . . .

A large number of the graduates from the schools of economics and politics enter the public service in Wisconsin, at Washington, and in other states and cities. Requests come to Madison from all over the country for men to fill positions in civil and social work. And apparently graduates prefer public to private work, administrative posts rather than academic ones. Wisconsin has created a new profession, the profession of public service. . . .

I know of no place in America where officials work with more devotion than they do in Wisconsin. There is an enthusiasm in the public service that is unique. It is not confined to men from the university, it seems to animate almost all officials. Politics is a profession to which men give the best that is in them. Members of the appointive commissions, which occupy such a prominent place in the administration of the state, many members of the legislature as well as officials in the subordinate posts, are animated by a love of public service that is very different from the motives which lead men to seek public place in other states. . . .

Democracy not only produced the expert, it elevated him to office. It recognized the necessity of research, of training, of science, in the highly complex business of government. One of the first acts of the Socialist administration in Milwaukee was the organization of a bureau of economy and efficiency to aid its officials in their work. It sent to the university for an instructor to train its aldermen in problems of city administration. The legislative reference bureau, the railroad commission, the board of public affairs, the industrial commission, are all filled with experts or professors from the university. Forestry, agriculture, and road building have been recognized as requiring the aid of the scientist.

Democracy, too, began to use its powers to serve, to serve people as well as business, to serve humanity as well as property. Democracy has begun a war on poverty, on ignorance, on disease, on human waste. The state is using its collective will to promote a program of human welfare.

Wisconsin is dispelling the fears of those who distrusted democracy. It is demonstrating the possibility of using the state as an instrument for the well-being of all people. It is laying the foundations for a commonwealth whose ideal it is to serve.

302. *Centralizing Tendencies, 1894*

James Bryce, *American Commonwealth* (New York, 1894). From the edition of 1910, II, 904–5. Copyright 1894, 1910 by The Macmillan Company and used with permission. First edition 1888.

AT THIS moment state rights are in question only so far as certain economic benefits might be obtained by a further extension of federal authority, nor has either party an interest in advocating the supersession of state action in any department of government. The conservatism of habit and well-settled legal doctrine which would resist any such proposal is very strong. State autonomy, as well as local government within each state, is prized by every class in the community. . . .

It is nevertheless impossible to ignore the growing strength of the centripetal and unifying forces. I have already referred to the influence of easier and cheaper communications, of commerce and finance, of the telegraph, of the filling up of the intermediate vacant spaces in the West. There is an increasing tendency to invoke congressional legislation to deal with matters, such as railroads, which cannot be adequately handled by state laws, or to remove divergencies, such as those in the law of marriage and divorce, which give rise to practical inconveniences. So the various parties which profess to champion the interests of the farmers or of workingmen recur to the federal government as the only agency strong enough and wide-reaching enough to give effect to their proposals, most of which indeed would obviously be impracticable if tried in the narrow area of one or a few states. State patriotism, state rivalry, state vanity, are no doubt still conspicuous, yet the political interest felt in state governments is slighter than it was before the Civil War, while national patriotism has become warmer and more pervasive. The role of the state is socially and morally, if not legally, smaller now than it then was, and ambitious men look on a state legislature as little more than a stepping-stone to Congress. Moreover, the interference of the federal executive to suppress by military power disorders which state authorities have seemed unable or unwilling to deal with has shown how great a reserve of force lies in its hands, and has led peace-loving citizens to look to it as their ultimate resort in troublous times.

303. *Armageddon, 1912*

Theodore Roosevelt's Confession of Faith Before the Progressive National Convention, August 6, 1912 (pamphlet). Full text in Works *(New York, 1926), XVII.*

THE OLD parties are husks, with no real soul within either, divided on artificial lines, boss-ridden and privilege-controlled, each a jumble of incongruous elements, and neither daring to speak out wisely and fearlessly what should be said on the vital issues of the day. This new movement is a movement of truth, sincerity, and wisdom, a movement which proposes to put at the service of all our people the collective power of the people, through their governmental agencies.... We propose boldly to face the real and great questions of the day, and not skilfully to evade them as do the old parties....

The prime need today is to face the fact that we are now in the midst of a great economic revolution. There is urgent necessity of applying both common sense and the highest ethical standard to this movement for better economic conditions among the mass of our people if we are to make it one of healthy evolution and not one of revolution....

The first essential in the Progressive program is the right of the people to rule. ...We should provide by national law for presidential primaries. We should provide for the election of United States Senators by popular vote. We should provide for a short ballot; nothing makes it harder for the people to control their public servants than to force them to vote for so many officials that they cannot really keep track of any one of them, so that each becomes indistinguishable in the crowd around him. There must be stringent and efficient corrupt-practices acts, applying to the primaries as well as the elections; and there should be publicity of campaign contributions during the campaign....

The American people, and not the courts, are to determine their own fundamental policies. The people should have power to deal with the effect of the acts of all their governmental agencies. This must be extended to include the effects of judicial acts as well as the acts of the executive and legislative representatives of the people. Where the judge merely does justice as between man and man, not dealing with constitutional questions, then the interest of the public is only to see that he is a wise and upright judge. Means should be devised for making it easier than at present to get rid of an incompetent judge; means should be devised by the bar and the bench acting in conjunction with the various legislative bodies to make justice far more expeditious and more certain than at present. . . . Our prime concern is that in dealing with the fundamental law of the land, in assuming finally to interpret it, and therefore finally to make it, the acts of the courts should be subject to and not above the final control of the people as a whole. . . .

Our purpose is not to impugn the courts, but to emancipate them from a position where they stand in the way of social justice; and to emancipate the people, in an orderly way, from the iniquity of enforced submission to a doctrine which would turn constitutional provisions which were intended to favor social justice and advancement into prohibitions against such justice and advancement. . . .

I especially challenge the attention of the people to the need of dealing in far-reaching fashion with our human resources, and therefore our labor power. . . . In the last twenty years an increasing percentage of our people have come to depend on industry for their livelihood, so that today the wage-workers in industry rank in importance side by side with the tillers of the soil. As a people we cannot afford to let any group of citizens or any individual citizen live or labor under conditions which are injurious to the common welfare. Industry, therefore, must submit to such public regulation as will make it a means of life and health, not of death or inefficiency. We must protect the crushable elements at the base of our present industrial structure. . . .

We hold that under no industrial order, in no commonwealth, in no trade, and in no establishment should industry be carried on under conditions inimical to the social welfare. The abnormal, ruthless, spendthrift industry of establishment tends to drag down all to the level of the least considerate. . . .

We stand for a living wage. Wages are subnormal if they fail to provide a living for those who devote their time and energy to industrial occupations. The monetary equivalent of a living wage varies according to local conditions, but must include enough to secure the elements of a normal standard of living—a standard high enough to make morality possible, to provide for education and recreation, to care for immature members of the family, to maintain the family during periods of sickness, and to permit of reasonable saving for old age.

Hours are excessive if they fail to afford the worker sufficient time to recuperate and return to his work thoroughly refreshed. We hold that the night labor of women and children is abnormal and should be prohibited. We hold that the seven-day working week is abnormal, and we hold that one day of rest in seven should be provided by law. We hold that the continuous industries, operating twenty-four hours out of twenty-four, are abnormal, and where, because of public necessity or of technical reasons (such as molten metal), the twenty-four hours must be divided into two shifts of twelve hours or three shifts of eight, they should by law be divided into three of eight. . . .

It is abnormal for any industry to throw back upon the community the human wreckage due to its wear and tear, and the hazards of sickness, accident, invalidism, involuntary unemployment, and old age should be provided for through insurance. This should be made a charge in whole or in part upon the industries, the employer, the employee, and perhaps the people at large to contribute severally in some degree. Wherever such standards are not met by given establishments, by given industries, are unprovided for by a legislature, or are balked by unenlightened courts, the workers are in jeopardy, the progressive employer is penalized, and the community pays a heavy cost in lessened efficiency and in misery. What Germany has done in the way of old-age pensions or insurance should be studied by us, and the system adapted to our uses, with whatever modifications are rendered necessary by our different ways of life and habits of thought.

Working women have the same need to combine for protection that working men have; the ballot is as necessary for one class as for the other; we do not believe that with the two sexes there is identity of function; but we do believe that there should be equality of right; and therefore we favor woman suffrage. Surely, if women could vote, they would strengthen the hands of those who are endeavoring to deal in efficient fashion with evils such as the white-slave traffic; evils which can in part be dealt with nationally, but which in large part can be reached only by determined local action, such as insisting on the widespread publication of the names of the owners, the landlords, of houses used for immoral purposes....

The present conditions of business cannot be accepted as satisfactory.... Our aim is to promote prosperity, and then see to its proper division. We do not believe that any good comes to any one by a policy which means destruction of prosperity; for in such cases it is not possible to divide it because of the very obvious fact that there is nothing to divide. We wish to control big business so as to secure among other things good wages for the wage-workers and reasonable prices for the consumers. Wherever in any business the prosperity of the business man is obtained by lowering the wages of his workmen and charging an excessive price to the consumers, we wish to interfere and stop such practices....

It is utterly hopeless to attempt to control the trusts merely by the antitrust law. ... What is needed is the application to all industrial concerns and all cooperating interests engaged in interstate commerce in which there is either monopoly or control of the market of the principles on which we have gone in regulating transportation concerns engaged in such commerce. The antitrust law should be kept on the statute books and strengthened so as to make it genuinely and thoroughly effective against every big concern tending to monopoly or guilty of antisocial practices. At the same time, a national industrial commission should be created which should have complete power to regulate and control all the great industrial concerns engaged in interstate business—which practically means all of them in this country. This commission should exercise over these industrial concerns like powers to those exercised over the railways by the Interstate Commerce Commission, and over the national banks by the comptroller of the currency, and additional powers if found necessary....

I believe in a protective tariff, but I believe in it as a principle, approached from the standpoint of the interests of the whole people, and not as a bundle of preferences to be given to favored individuals. In my opinion, the American people favor the principle of a protective tariff, but they desire such a tariff to be established primarily in the interests of the wage-worker and the consumer....

We believe that there exists an imperative need for prompt legislation for the improvement of our national currency system. The experience of repeated financial crises in the last forty years has proved that the present method of issuing, through private agencies, notes secured by government bonds is both harmful and unscientific.... The issue of currency is fundamentally a governmental function. The system to be adopted should have as its basic principles soundness and elasticity....

There can be no greater issue than that of conservation in this country. Just as we must conserve our men, women and children, so we must conserve the resources of the land on which they live. We must conserve the soil so that our children shall have a land that is more and not less fertile than that our fathers dwelt in. We must conserve the forests, not by disuse but by use, making them more valuable at the same time that we use them. We must conserve the mines. Moreover, we must insure so far as possible the use of certain types of great natural resources for the benefit of the people as a whole. . . .

Surely there never was a fight better worth making than the one in which we are engaged. It little matters what befalls any one of us who for the time being stands in the forefront of the battle. I hope we shall win, and I believe that if we can wake the people to what the fight really means we shall win. But, win or lose, we shall not falter. . . . Our cause is based on the eternal principle of righteousness; and even though we who now lead may for the time fail, in the end the cause itself shall triumph. Six weeks ago, here in Chicago, I spoke to the honest representatives of a convention which was not dominated by honest men; a convention wherein sat, alas! a majority of men who, with sneering indifference to every principle of right, so acted as to bring to a shameful end a party which had been founded over a half-century ago by men in whose souls burned the fire of lofty endeavor. Now to you men who, in your turn, have come together to spend and be spent in the endless crusade against wrong, to you who face the future resolute and confident, to you who strive in a spirit of brotherhood for the betterment of our nation, to you who gird yourselves for this great new fight in the never-ending warfare for the good of mankind, I say in closing: We stand at Armageddon, and we battle for the Lord.

304. *The Progressive Amendments, 1909–13*

Sixteenth Amendment, passed by Congress, July 12, 1909; ratified, February 25, 1913. Seventeenth Amendment passed, May 16, 1912; ratified, May 31, 1913.

Article XVI

THE CONGRESS shall have power to lay and collect taxes on incomes, from whatever source derived, without apportionment among the several states, and without regard to any census or enumeration.

Article XVII

The Senate of the United States shall be composed of two senators from each state, elected by the people thereof, for six years; and each senator shall have one vote. The electors in each state shall have the qualifications requisite for electors of the most numerous branch of the state legislature.

When vacancies happen in the representation of any state in the Senate, the executive authority of such state shall issue writs of election to fill such vacancies: *Provided,* That the legislature of any state may empower the executive thereof to make temporary appointments until the people fill the vacancies by election as the legislature may direct.

This amendment shall not be so construed as to affect the election or term of any senator chosen before it becomes valid as part of the Constitution.

XXXV 🎴 *The United States and a Wider World*

AT THE OPENING of this period the United States reached from ocean to ocean, and seemed to some to have attained its continental limits. But that by no means satisfied the expansive urges of all Americans. The decades that followed saw frequent projects to extend American sovereignty beyond the oceans' edges. The old justification, that an American mission had predestined the nation to expand, was still being expounded in vigorous and forceful terms (No. 305).

These traditional ideas gained force from the support of newer imperialist arguments. The crucial importance of sea power in world history, it was said, demanded that the United States strengthen its navy and acquire a chain of bases in critical parts of the world (No. 306). The necessity for civilizing and making customers of the backward peoples of the earth added still another reason for expansion (No. 307). The new expansionist conceptions differed from the old; they did not anticipate that the territories thereafter to be acquired would become integral parts of the Union, but rather that they were to be colonies governed by he United States.

These ideas did not altogether conquer public opinion. Mr. Dooley mocked the pretentiousness of the imperialists' ideas (Nos. 308, 309); and a more penetrating critique showed the subversion of American ideals implicit in imperialism (No. 310).

Nevertheless, fateful decisions extended American rule outside its continental limits. The area of longest concern was Latin America. In 1895, a conflict between Great Britain and Venezuela gave the United States a pretext for intervention (No. 311). And the long conflict between Spain and its Cuban colony led in 1898 to a war from which America emerged with an extensive overseas empire. This empire riased more problems than it solved. Interest in the Caribbean involved the United States in the construction of an isthmian canal and in the revolution which made Panama independent (No. 312; *see also above,* No. 166). More generally, it led President Theodore Roosevelt to take an extended view of the meaning of the Monroe Doctrine and of the position of the United States in Latin America (No. 313).

The acquisition of the Philippines also gave the United States extensive interests in the Orient. In the struggle among the great powers for control of the collapsing Chinese Empire it was difficult to work out a consistent American policy. On the one hand, the United States tended to favor the "open door" with equality of economic opportunities for the citizens of all nations (No. 314). On the other, it was inclined, for strategic reasons, to seek some kind of accommodation with the expanding power of Japan (No. 315). Already these questions were casting portentous shadows into the future (*see below,* No. 343).

305. *Our Country, 1885*

Josiah Strong, *Our Country* (New York, 1885), 171–8.

THERE is abundant reason to believe that the Anglo-Saxon race is to be, is, indeed, already becoming, more effective here than in the mother country. The marked superiority of this race is due, in large measure, to its highly mixed origin. . . . There is here a new commingling of races; and, while the largest injections of foreign blood are substantially the same elements that constituted the original Anglo-Saxon admixture, so that we may infer the general type will be preserved, there are strains of other bloods being added, which, if Mr. Emerson's remark is true, that "the best nations are those most widely related," may be expected to improve the stock, and aid it to a higher destiny. . . .

Again, another marked characteristic of the Anglo-Saxon is what may be called an instinct or genius for colonizing. His unequaled energy, his indomitable perseverance, and his personal independence, made him a pioneer. He excels all others in pushing his way into new countries. It was those in whom this tendency was strongest that came to America, and this inherited tendency has been further developed by the westward sweep of successive generations across the continent. . . .

Again, nothing more manifestly distinguishes the Anglo-Saxon than his intense and persistent energy; and he is developing in the United States an energy which, in eager activity and effectiveness, is peculiarly American. This is due partly to the fact that Americans are much better fed than Europeans, and partly to the undeveloped resources of a new country, but more largely to our climate, which acts as a constant stimulus. . . . Moreover, our social institutions are stimulating. In Europe the various ranks of society are, like the strata of the earth, fixed and fossilized. There can be no great change without a terrible upheaval, a social earthquake. Here society is like the waters of the sea, mobile. . . . Everyone is free to become whatever he can make of himself; free to transform himself from a rail-splitter or a tanner or a canal-boy, into the nation's President. Our aristocracy, unlike that of Europe, is open to all comers. Wealth, position, influence, are prizes offered for energy; and every farmer's boy, every apprentice and clerk, every friendless and penniless immigrant, is free to enter the lists. Thus many causes cooperate to produce here the most forceful and tremendous energy in the world.

What is the significance of such facts? These tendencies infold the future; they are the mighty alphabet with which God writes His prophecies. May we not, by a careful laying together of the letters, spell out something of His meaning? It seems to me that God, with infinite wisdom and skill, is training the Anglo-Saxon race for an hour sure to come in the world's future. Heretofore there has always been in the history of the world a comparatively unoccupied land westward, into which the crowded countries of the East have poured their surplus populations. But the widening waves of migration, which millenniums ago rolled east and west from the valley of the Euphrates, meet today on our Pacific coast. There are no more new worlds. The unoccupied arable lands of the earth are limited, and will soon be taken. The time is coming when the pressure of population on the means of subsistence will be felt here as it is now felt in Europe and Asia. Then will the world enter upon a new stage of its history—

the final competition of races, for which the Anglo-Saxon is being schooled. . . .

Then this race of unequaled energy, with all the majesty of numbers and the might of wealth behind it—the representative, let us hope, of the largest liberty, the purest Christianity, the highest civilization—having developed peculiarly aggressive traits calculated to impress its institutions upon mankind, will spread itself over the earth. If I read not amiss, this powerful race will move down upon Mexico, down upon Central and South America, out upon the islands of the sea, over upon Africa and beyond. And can any one doubt that the result of this competition of races will be the "survival of the fittest"? . . . To this result no war of extermination is needful; the contest is not one of arms, but of vitality and of civilization. . . . It would seem as if these inferior tribes were only precursors of a superior race, voices in the wilderness crying: "Prepare ye the way of the Lord!"

The savage is a hunter; by the incoming of civilization the game is driven away and disappears. . . . The savage is ignorant of many diseases of civilization which, when he is exposed to them, attack him before he learns how to treat them. Civilization also has its vices, of which the uninitiated savage is innocent. . . . Bring savages into contact with our civilization, and its destructive forces become operative at once, while years are necessary to render effective the saving influences of Christian instruction. Moreover, the pioneer wave of our civilization carries with it more scum than salt. Where there is one missionary, there are hundreds of miners or traders or adventurers ready to debauch the native. Whether the extinction of inferior races before the advancing Agnlo-Saxon seems to the reader sad or otherwise, it certainly appears probable. . . .

Is there room for reasonable doubt that this race, unless devitalized by alcohol and tobacco, is destined to dispossess many weaker races, assimilate others, and mold the remainder, until, in a very true and important sense, it has Anglo-Saxonized mankind?

306. *Sea Power, 1897*

A. T. Mahan, *The Interests of America in Sea Power* (Boston, 1897), 6, 8–9, 12–15, 18–22.

To AFFIRM the importance of distant markets, and the relation to them of our own immense powers of production, implies logically the recognition of the link that joins the products and the markets, —that is, the carrying trade. . . . Further, . . . the acknowledgment . . . carries with it a view of the relations of the United States to the world radically distinct from the simple idea of self-sufficingness. We shall not follow far this line of thought before there will dawn the realization of America's unique position, facing the older worlds of the East and West. . . .

The opening of a canal through the Central American Isthmus, . . . by modifying the direction of trade routes, will induce a great increase of commercial activity and carrying trade throughout the Caribbean Sea. . . . This now comparatively deserted nook of the ocean will become, like the Red Sea, a great thoroughfare of shipping, and will attract, as never before in our day, the interest and ambition of maritime nations. Every position in that sea will have enhanced commercial and military value, and the canal itself will have become a strategic center of the most vital importance. . . . It will be a link between the two oceans; but . . . the use, unless most carefully guarded by treaties, will belong wholly to the belligerent which controls the sea by its naval power. In case of war, the United States will ... be impotent, as against any of the great maritime powers, to control the Central American canal. Militarily speaking, and having reference to European complications only, the piercing of the Isthmus is nothing but a disaster to the United States, in the present state of her military and naval preparation. It is especially dangerous to the Pacific coast; but the increased exposure of one part of our seaboard reacts unfavorably upon the whole military situation. . . .

The United States is woefully unready, not only in fact but in purpose to assert in the Caribbean and Central America a weight of influence proportioned to the extent of her interests. We have not the navy, and, what is worse, we are not willing to have the navy, that will weigh seriously in any disputes with those nations whose interests will conflict there with our own. We have not, and we are not anxious to provide, the defense of the seaboard which will leave the navy free for its work at sea. We have not, but many other powers have, positions, either within or on the borders of the Caribbean, which not only possess great natural advantages for the control of that sea, but have received and are receiving that artificial strength of fortification and armament which will make them practically inexpugnable. . . . That which I deplore . . . is that the nation neither has nor cares to have its sea frontier so defended, and its navy of such power, as shall suffice, with the advantages of our position, to weigh seriously when inevitable discussions arise . . . about the Caribbean Sea or the canal. Is the United States, for instance, prepared to allow Germany to acquire the Dutch stronghold of Curaçao, fronting the Atlantic outlet of both the proposed canals of Panama and Nicaragua? Is she prepared to acquiesce in any foreign power purchasing from Haiti a naval station on the Windward Passage, through which pass our steamer routes to

the Isthmus? Would she acquiesce in a foreign protectorate over the Sandwich Islands, that great central station ... on our lines of communication with both Australia and China? . . .

Yet, were our sea frontier as strong as it now is weak, passive self-defense, whether in trade or war, would be but a poor policy, so long as this world continues to be one of struggle and vicissitude. All around us now is strife; "the struggle of life," "the race of life," are phrases so familiar that we do not feel their significance till we stop to think about them. . . . Are our people, however, so unaggressive that they are likely not to want their own way in matters where their interests turn on points of disputed right, or so little sensitive as to submit quietly to encroachment by others, in quarters where they long have considered their own influence should prevail?

Our self-imposed isolation in the matter of markets, and the decline of our shipping interest in the last thirty years, have coincided singularly with an actual remoteness of this continent from the life of the rest of the world. The writer has before him a map of the North and South Atlantic oceans, showing the direction of the principal trade routes and the proportion of tonnage passing over each; and it is curious to note what deserted regions, comparatively, are the Gulf of Mexico, the Caribbean Sea, and the adjoining countries and islands. . . . The significance is unmistakable; Europe has now little mercantile interest in the Caribbean Sea.

When the Isthmus is pierced, this isolation will pass away, and with it the indifference of foreign nations. From wheresoever they come and whithersoever they afterward go, all ships that use the canal will pass through the Caribbean. Whatever the effect produced upon the prosperity of the adjacent continent and islands by the thousand wants attendant upon maritime activity, around such a focus of trade will center large commercial and political interests. To protect and develop its own, each nation will seek points of support and means of influence in a quarter where the United States always has been jealously sensitive to the intrusion of European powers. The precise value of the Monroe Doctrine is understood very loosely by most Americans, but the effect of the familiar phrase has been to develop a national sensitiveness, which is a more frequent cause of war than material interests; and over disputes caused by such feelings there will preside none of the calming influence due to the moral authority of international law, with its recognized principles. . . .

Whether they will or no, Americans must now begin to look outward. The growing production of the country demands it. An increasing volume of public sentiment demands it. The position of the United States, between the two Old Worlds and the two great oceans, makes the same claim, which will soon be strengthened by the creation of the new link joining the Atlantic and Pacific. The tendency will be maintained and increased by the growth of the European colonies in the Pacific, by the advancing civilization of Japan, and by the rapid peopling of our Pacific states with men who have all the aggressive spirit of the advanced line of national progress.

307. *The Regeneration of the World, 1900*

Speech by Senator A. J. Beveridge, January 9, 1900, *Congressional Record,* 56 Congress, 1 Session, XXXIII, pt. 1, pp. 711–12.

MR. PRESIDENT, this question is deeper than any question of party politics; deeper than any question of the isolated policy of our country even; deeper even than any question of constitutional power. It is elemental. It is racial. God has not been preparing the English-speaking and Teutonic peoples for a thousand years for nothing but vain and idle self-contemplation and self-admiration. No! He has made us the master organizers of the world to establish system where chaos reigns. He has given us the spirit of progress to overwhelm the forces of reaction throughout the earth. He has made us adepts in government that we may administer government among savage and senile peoples. Were it not for such a force as this the world would relapse into barbarism and night. And of all our race He has marked the American people as His chosen nation to finally lead in the regeneration of the world. This is the divine mission of America, and it holds for us all the profit, all the glory, all the happiness possible to man. We are trustees of the world's progress, guardians of its righteous peace. The judgment of the Master is upon us: "Ye have been faithful over a few things; I will make you ruler over many things."

What shall history say of us? Shall it say that we renounced that holy trust, left the savage to his base condition, the wilderness to the reign of waste, deserted duty, abandoned glory, forget our sordid profit even, because we feared our strength and read the charter of our powers with the doubter's eye and the quibbler's mind? Shall it say that, called by events to captain and command the proudest, ablest, purest race of history in history's noblest work, we declined that great commission? . . .

Mr. President and Senators, adopt the resolution offered, that peace may quickly come and that we may begin our saving, regenerating, and uplifting work. . . . Reject it, and the world, history, and the American people will know where to forever fix the awful responsibility for the consequences that will surely follow such failure to do our manifest duty. How dare

we delay when our soldiers' blood is flowing?

308. *Senator Beveridge Speaks, 1900*

F. P. Dunne, *Mr. Dooley's Philosophy* (New York, 1900), 130, 131.

"His subject was th' Ph'lippeens, an' he said he'd just come fr'm there. 'I have cruised,' he says, 'f'r two thousan' miles through th' Ar-rchey Pelago—that's a funny name—ivry minyit a surprise an' delight to those that see me,' he says. 'I see corn growin' on banana threes; I see th' gloryous heights iv Ding Dong that ar-re irradyatin' civilization like quills upon th' fretful porcypine,' he says. 'I see rice, coffee, rolls, cocoanuts, choice seegars, oats, hay, hard and soft coal, an' Gen'ral Otis—an' there's a man that I rayspict,' he says. 'I see flowers bloomin' that was superyor to anny conservatory in Poolasky county,' he says. 'I see th' low and vicious inhabitants iv th' counthry soon, I thrust, to be me fellow-citizens, an' as I set there an' watched th' sea rollin' up its uncounted millyons iv feet

iv blue wather, an' th' stars sparklin' like lamp-posts we pass in th' night, as I see th' mountains raisin' their snow-capped heads f'r to salute th' sun, while their feet extinded almost to th' place where I shtud; whin I see all th' glories iv that almost, I may say, thropical clime, an' thought what a good place this wud be f'r to ship base-burnin' parlor stoves, an' men's shirtings to th' accursed natives iv neighborin' Chiny, I says to mesilf, 'This is no mere man's wurruk. A Higher Power even than Mack, much as I rayspict him, is in this here job. We cannot pause, we cannot hesitate, we cannot delay, we cannot even stop! We must, in other wurruds, go on with a holy purpose in our hearts, th' flag over our heads an' th' inspired wurruds iv A. Jeremiah Beveridge in our ears,' he says. An' he set down.

309. *The China Situation, 1900*

Dunne, *Mr. Dooley's Philosophy*, 78–82.

"Th' LORD f'rgive f'r sayin' it, Hinnissy, but if I was a Chinyman, which I will fight anny man f'r sayin', an' was livin' at home, I'd tuck me shirt into me pants, put me braid up in a net, an' go out an' take a fall out iv th' in-vader if it cost me me life. Here am I, Hop Lung Dooley, r-runnin' me little liquor store an' p'rhaps raisin' a family in th' town iv Koochoo. I don't like foreigners there anny more thin I do here. Along comes a bald-headed man with chin whiskers from Baraboo, Wisconsin, an' says he: 'Benighted an' haythen Dooley,' says he, 'ye have no

God,' he says. 'I have,' says I. 'I have a lot iv thim,' says I. 'Ye ar-re an oncultivated an' foul crather,' he says. 'I have come six thousan' miles f'r to hist ye fr'm th' mire iv ignorance an' irrellijon in which ye live to th' lofty plane iv Baraboo,' he says. An' he sets down on an aisy chair, an' his wife an' her friends come in an' they inthrojooce Mrs. Dooley to th' modhren improvements iv th' corset an' th' hat with th' blue bur-rd onto it, an' put shame into her because she hasn't let her feet grow, while th' head mission'ry reads me a pome out iv th' *Northwesthren Christ-*

yan Advocate. 'Well,' says I, 'look here, me good fellow,' I says. 'Me an' me people has occupied these here primises f'r manny years,' I says, 'an' here we mean to stay,' I says. 'We're doin' th' best we can in th' matther iv gods,' says I. 'We have thim cast at a first-rate foundhry,' I says, 'an' we sandpa-aper thim ivry week,' says I. 'As f'r knowin' things,' I says, 'me people wrote pomes with a markin' brush whin th' likes iv ye was r-runnin' ar-round wearin' a short pelisse iv sheepskins an' batin' each other to death with stone hammers,' says I. An' I'm f'r firin' him out, but bein' a quite man I lave him stay.

"Th' nex' day in comes a man with a suit iv clothes that looks like a tablecloth in a section house, an' says he: 'Poor ignorant haythen,' he says, 'what manner iv food d'ye ate?' he says. 'Rice,' says I, 'an' rats is me fav'rite dish,' I says. 'Deluded wretch,' says he. 'I riprisint Armour an' Company, an' I'm here to make ye change ye'er dite,' he says. 'Hinceforth ye'll ate th' canned roast beef iv merry ol' stock yards or I'll have a file iv sojers into fill ye full iv ondygistible lead,' he says. An' afther him comes th' man with Aunt Miranda's Pan Cakes an' Flaked Bran an' Ye'll-perish-if-ye-don't-eat-a-biscuit an' other riprisintatives iv Westhern Civilization, an' I'm to be shot if I don't take thim all.

"Thin a la-ad runs down with a chain an' a small glass on three sticks an' a gang iv section men that answers to th' name iv Casey, an' pro-ceeds f'r to put down a railroad. 'What's this f'r?' says I. 'We ar-re th' advance guard iv Westhren Civilization,' he says, 'an we're goin' to give ye a railroad so ye can go swiftly to places that ye don't want to see,' he says. 'A counthry that has no railroads is beneath contimpt,' he says. 'Casey,' he says, 'sthretch th' chain acrost yon graveyard,' he says. 'I aim f'r to put th' thrack just befure that large tombstone marked Riquiescat in Pace, James H. Chung-a-lung,' he says. 'But,' says I, 'ye will disturb pah's

bones,' says I, 'if ye go to layin' ties,' I says. 'Ye'll be mixin' up me ol' man with th' Cassidy's in th' nex' lot that,' I says, 'he niver spoke to save in anger in his life,' I says. 'Ye're an ancestor worshiper, heathen,' says the la-ad, an' he goes on to tamp th' mounds in th' cimitry an ballast th' thrack with th' remains iv th' deceased. An' afther he's got through along comes a Fr-rinchman, an' an Englishman, an' a Rooshan, an' a Dutchman, an' says wan iv them: 'This is a comfortable lookin' saloon,' he says. 'I'll take th' bar, ye take th' ice-box an' th' r-rest iv th' fixtures.' 'What f'r?' says I. 'I've paid th' rent an' th' license,' says I. 'Niver mind,' says he. 'We're th' riprisintatives iv Westhren Civilization,' he says, 'an' 'tis th' business iv Westhren Civilization to cut up th' belongings iv Easthren Civilization,' he says. 'Be off,' he says, 'or I'll pull ye'er hair,' he says. 'Well,' says I, 'this thing has gone far enough,' I says. 'I've heerd me good ol' cast-iron gods or josses abused,' I says, 'an' I've been packed full iv canned goods, an' th' Peking Lightnin' Express is r-runnin' sthraight through th' lot where th' bones iv me ancesthors lies,' I says. "I've shtud it all,' I says, 'but whin ye come here to bounce me off iv me own primises,' I says, 'I'll have to take th' leg iv th' chair to ye,' I says. An' we're to th' flure.

"That's th' way it stands in Chiny, Hinnissy, an' it looks to me as though Westhren Civilization was in f'r a bump. I mind wanst whin a dhrunk prize fighter come up th' r-road and wint to sleep on Slavin's steps. Some iv th' good sthrong la-ads happened along an' they were near bein' at blows over who shud have his watch an' who shud take his hat. While they were debatin' he woke up an' begin cuttin' lose with hands an' feet, an' whin he got through he made a collection iv th' things they dhropped in escapin' an' marched ca'mly down th' sthreet. Mebbe 'twill tur-rn out so in Chiny, Hinnissy. I see be th' pa-apers that they'se four hundherd millyons iv thim boys an' be hivins!

'twuddent surprise me if whin they got through batin' us at home, they might say to thimselves: 'Well, here goes f'r a jaunt ar-roun' the wurruld.' Th' time may come, Hinnissy, whin ye'll be squirtin' wather over Hop Lee's shirt while a man named Chow Fung kicks down ye'er sign an' heaves rocks through ye'er windy. The time may come, Hinnissy. Who knows? . . . Annyhow, 'tis a good thing f'r us they ain't Christyans an' haven't larned properly to sight a gun."

310. *Liberty or Dominion*

W. G. Sumner, "Conquest of the United States by Spain," (1898), *War and Other Essays* (New Haven, 1911), 303–5.

THERE is not a civilized nation which does not talk about its civilizing mission just as grandly as we do.

Now each nation laughs at all the others when it observes these manifestations of national vanity. You may rely upon it that they are all ridiculous by virtue of these pretensions, including ourselves. The point is that each of them repudiates the standards of the others, and the outlying nations, which are to be civilized, hate all the standards of civilized men. We assume that what we like and practice, and what we think better, must come as a welcome blessing to Spanish-Americans and Filipinos. This is grossly and obviously untrue. They hate our ways. They are hostile to our ideas. Our religion, language, institutions and manners offend them. They like their own ways, and if we appear amongst them as rulers, there will be social discord in all the great departments of social interest. The most important thing which we shall inherit from the Spaniards will be the task of suppressing rebellions. If the United States takes out of the hands of Spain her mission, on the ground that Spain is not executing it well, and if this nation in turn attempts to be school-mistress to others, it will shrivel up into the same vanity and self-conceit of which Spain now presents an example. To read our current literature one would think that we were already well on the way to it.

Now, the great reason why all these enterprises which begin by saying to somebody else, We know what is good for you better than you know yourself and we are going to make you do it, are false and wrong is that they violate liberty; or, to turn the same statement into other words, the reason why liberty, of which we Americans talk so much, is a good thing is that it means leaving people to live out their own lives in their own way, while we do the same. If we believe in liberty, as an American principle, why do we not stand by it? Why are we going to throw it away to enter upon a Spanish policy of dominion and regulation?

311. *The Olney Doctrine, 1895*

Secretary of State Richard Olney, Letter of Instruction to American Ambassador T. F. Bayard in London, July 20, 1895. In U.S. Document 3368, 54 Congress, 1 Session, *House Documents* (1896), I, No. 1, pp. 552–3, 554–5, 557–8, 559, 560.

THOSE charged with the interests of the United States are now forced to . . . decide to what extent . . . the United States may and should intervene in a controversy between and primarily concerning only Great Britain and Venezuela and to decide how far it is bound to see that the integrity of Venezuelan territory is not impaired by the pretensions of its powerful antagonist. . . . If any such right and duty exist, their due exercise and discharge will not permit of any action that shall not be efficient and . . . shall not result in the accomplishment of the end in view. . . .

That there are circumstances under which a nation may justly interpose in a controversy to which two or more other nations are the direct and immediate parties is an admitted canon of international law. . . . We are concerned at this time, however, not so much with the general rule as with a form of it which is peculiarly and distinctively American. Washington, in the solemn admonitions of the Farewell Address, explicitly warned his countrymen against entanglements with the politics or the controversies of European powers. . . . The Monroe administration . . . did not hesitate to accept and apply the logic of the Farewell Address by declaring in effect that American non-intervention in European affairs necessarily implied and meant European non-intervention in American affairs. . . .

It was realized that it was futile to lay down such a rule unless its observance could be enforced. It was manifest that the United States was the only power in this hemisphere capable of enforcing it. It was therefore courageously declared not merely that Europe ought not to interfere in American affairs, but that any European power doing so would be regarded as antagonizing the interests and inviting the opposition of the United States. . . .

The precise scope and limitations of this rule cannot be too clearly apprehended. . . . The rule in question has but a single purpose and object. It is that no European power or combination of European powers shall forcibly deprive an American state of the right and power of self-government and of shaping for itself its own political fortunes and destinies. . . . Whether moral or material interests be considered, it can not but be universally conceded that those of Europe are irreconcilably diverse from those of America, and

that any European control of the latter is necessarily both incongruous and injurious. . . .

The safety and welfare of the United States are so concerned with the maintenance of the independence of every American state as against any European power as to justify and require the interposition of the United States whenever that independence is endangered. . . . The states of America, South as well as North, by geographical proximity, by natural sympathy, by similarity of governmental constitutions, are friends and allies, commercially and politically, of the United States. To allow the subjugation of any of them by an European power is, of course, to completely reverse that situation. . . . But that is not all. The people of the United States have a vital interest in the cause of popular self-government. . . . But . . . they are content with such assertion and defense of the right of popular self-government as their own security and welfare demand. It is in that view more than in any other that they believe it not to be tolerated that the political control of an American state shall be forcibly assumed by an European power. . . .

Today the United States is practically sovereign on this continent, and its fiat is law upon the subjects to which it confines its interposition. Why? . . . It is because, in addition to all other grounds, its infinite resources combined with its isolated position render it master of the situation and practically invulnerable as against any or all other powers. . . .

The application of the doctrine to the boundary dispute between Great Britain and Venezuela remains to be made and presents no real difficulty. Though the dispute relates to a boundary line, yet, as it is between states, it necessarily imports political control to be lost by one party and gained by the other. . . .

Great Britain cannot be deemed a South American state within the purview of the Monroe Doctrine, nor, if she is appropriating Venezuelan territory, is it material that she does so by advancing the frontier of an old colony instead of by the planting of a new colony. . . . It is not admitted, however, and therefore cannot be assumed, that Great Britain is in fact usurping dominion over Venezuelan territory. While Venezuela charges such usurpation, Great Britain denies it, and the United States, until the merits are authoritatively ascertained, can take sides with neither. But while this is so—while the United States may not, under existing circumstances at least, take upon itself to say which of the two parties is right and which wrong— it is certainly within its right to demand that the truth shall be ascertained. . . .

It being clear, therefore, that the United States may legitimately insist upon the merits of the boundary question being determined, it is equally clear that there is but one feasible mode of determining them, viz., peaceful arbitration.

312. *Canal Diplomacy, 1904*

John Hay to Rafael Reyes, January 5, 1904. *Senate Executive Documents* (U.S. Document 6582), 63 Congress, 2 Session, Document No. 474, pp. 494, 495, 497, 500, 503–4.

ON JUNE 28, 1902, the President of the United States gave his approval to the act now commonly referred to as the Spooner Act, to provide for the construction of the interoceanic canal. Following the report of the Isthmian Canal Commission, which confirmed the opinion expressed by the Colombian Government, it embodied the formal decision of the United States in favor of the Panama route. It accordingly authorized the President to acquire, at a cost not exceeding $40,000,000, "the rights, privileges, franchises, concessions," and other property of the New Panama Canal Company, . . . and to obtain from Colombia on such terms as he might deem reasonable perpetual control for the purposes of the canal of a strip of land not less than six miles wide. . . .

After the Spooner Act was approved, negotiations were duly initiated by Colombia. They resulted on January 22, 1903, in the conclusion of the Hay-Herran Convention. By this convention every reasonable desire of the Colombian Government was believed to be gratified. . . .

Some time after the convention was signed the Government of the United States learned, to its utter surprise, that the Government of Colombia was taking with the canal company the position that a further permission, in addition to that contained in the convention, was necessary to the transfer of its concessions . . . to the United States, and that, as a preliminary to this permission, the companies must enter into agreements with Colombia for the cancellation of all her obligations . . . under the concession. This proceeding seemed all the more singular in the light of the negotiations between the two Governments. The terms in which the convention authorized the New Panama Canal Company to sell and transfer its "rights, privileges, properties, and concessions" to the United States were the same as those embodied in the original draft of a treaty presented to this Government by the Colombian minister on March 31, 1902.

No change in this particular was ever suggested by Colombia, in all the discussions that followed, until November 11, 1902. On that day the Colombian minister presented a memorandum in which it was proposed that the authorization should be so modified that "the permission accorded by Colombia to the canal and the railroad companies to transfer their rights to the United States" should "be regulated by a previous special arrangement entered into by Colombia." To this proposal this department answered that "the United

States considers this suggestion wholly inadmissible." The proposition was then abandoned by Colombia, and the convention was nearly three months later signed without any modification of the absolute authorization to sell. . . .

The explanations put forward in Colombia's "statement of grievances" merely repeat the pleas devised at the Colombian capital. The sudden discovery that the terms of the convention, as proposed and signed by the Colombian Government, involved a violation of the Colombian constitution, because it required a cession to the United States of the "sovereignty" which is expressly recognized and confirmed, could be received by this Government only with the utmost surprise. Nevertheless, the Colombian Senate unanimously rejected the convention. . . .

Advices came to this Government, not only through the press but also through its own officials, of the existence of dangerous conditions on the Isthmus, as well as in the adjacent states whose interests were menaced. Disorders in that quarter were not new. In the summer of 1902, as well as in that of 1901, this Government had been obliged by its forces to maintain order on the transit route, and it took steps, as it had done on previous occasions, to perform a similar duty should the necessity arise. . . .

The reasonableness of these precautions soon became evident. The people of Panama rose against an act of the Government at Bogotá that threatened their most vital interests with destruction and the interests of the whole world with grave injury. The movement assumed the form of a declaration of independence. The avowed object of this momentous step was to secure the construction of the interoceanic canal. It was inspired by the desire of the people at once to safeguard their own interests and at the same time to assure the dedication of the Isthmus to the use for which Providence seemed to have designed it. . . .

By the declaration of independence of the Republic of Panama a new situation was created. On the one hand stood the Government of Colombia invoking in the name of the treaty of 1846 the aid of this Government in its efforts to suppress the revolution; on the other hand stood the Republic of Panama that had come into being in order that the great design of that treaty might not be forever frustrated, but might be fulfilled. The Isthmus was threatened with desolation by another civil war, nor were the rights and interests of the United States alone at stake, the interests of the whole civilized world were involved. The Republic of Panama stood for those interests; the Government of Colombia opposed them. Compelled to choose between these two alternatives, the Government of the United States . . . did not hesitate. It recognized the independence of the Republic of Panama, and upon its judgment and action in the emergency the powers of the world have set the seal of their approval.

In recognizing the independence of the Republic of Panama, the United States necessarily assumed toward that Republic the obligations of the treaty of 1846. Intended, as the treaty was, to assure the protection of the sovereign of the Isthmus, whether the government of that sovereign ruled from Bogotá or from Panama, the Republic of Panama, as the successor in sovereignty of Colombia, became entitled to the rights and subject to the obligations of the treaty. . . .

Under all the circumstances the department is unable to regard the complaints of Colombia . . . as having any valid foundation. The responsibility lies at Colombia's own door rather than at that of the United States. This Government, however, recognizes the fact that Colombia has, as she affirms, suffered an appreciable loss. This Government has no desire to increase or accentuate her misfortunes, but is willing to do all that lies in its power to ameliorate her lot. The Government of the United States, in common with the whole civilized world, shares in a sentiment of sorrow over the unfortunate conditions which have long existed in the Republic of Colombia by reason of the factional and fratricidal wars which have desolated her fields, ruined her industries, and impoverished her people.

Entertaining these feelings, the Government of the United States would gladly exercise its good offices with the Republic of Panama, with a view to bring about some arrangement on a fair and equitable basis. For the acceptance of your proposal of a resort to the Hague Tribunal, this Government perceives no occasion.

313. *The Roosevelt Doctrine,* 1904

President Theodore Roosevelt, Annual Message to Congress, December 6, 1904, *Congressional Record,* 58 Congress, 3 Session, XXIX, 19.

ANY country whose people conduct themselves well can count upon our hearty friendship. If a nation shows that it knows how to act with reasonable efficiency and decency in social and political matters, if it keeps order and pays its obligations, it need fear no interference from the United States. Chronic wrongdoing, or an impotence which results in a general loosening of the ties of civilized society, may in America, as elsewhere, ultimately require intervention by some civilized nation, and in the Western Hemisphere the adherence of the United States to the Monroe Doctrine may force the United States, however reluctantly, in flagrant cases of such wrongdoing or impotence, to the exercise of an international police power. If every country washed by the Carribean Sea would show the progress in stable and just civilization which, with the aid of the Platt Amendment, Cuba has shown since our troops left the island, and which so many of the republics in both Americas are constantly and brilliantly showing, all questions of interference by this nation with their affairs would be at an end.

Our interests and those of our southern neighbors are in reality identical. They have great natural riches, and if within their borders the reign of law and justice obtains, prosperity is sure to come to them. While they thus obey the primary laws of civilized society they may rest assured that they will be treated by us in a spirit of cordial and helpful sympathy. We would interfere with them only in the last resort, and then only if it became evident that their inability or unwillingness to do justice at home and abroad had violated the rights of the United States or had invited foreign aggression to the detriment of the entire body of American nations.

314. *Spheres of Influence,* 1899

Secretary of State John Hay to A. D. White, September 6, 1899, Malloy, *Treaties,* I, 246–7.

SIR: At the time when the Government of the United States was informed by that of Germany that it had leased from His Majesty the Emperor of China the port of Kiao-chao and the adjacent territory in the province of Shantung, assurances were given to the ambassador of the United States at Berlin by the Imperial German minister for foreign affairs that the rights and privileges insured by treaties with China to citizens of the United States would not thereby suffer or be in anywise impaired within the area over which Germany had thus obtained control.

More recently, however, the British Government recognized by a formal agreement with Germany the exclusive right of the latter country to enjoy in said leased area and the contiguous "sphere of influence or interest" certain privileges, more especially those relating to railroads and mining enterprises; but, as the exact nature and extent of the rights thus recognized have not been clearly defined, it is possible that serious conflicts of interest may at any time arise, not only between British and German subjects within said area, but that the interests of our citizens may also be jeopardized thereby.

Earnestly desirous to remove any cause of irritation and to insure at the same time to the commerce of all nations in China the undoubted benefits which should accrue from a formal recognition by the various powers claiming "spheres of interest" that they shall enjoy perfect equality of treatment for their commerce and navigation within such "spheres," the Government of the United States would be pleased to see His German Majesty's Government give formal assurances and lend its cooperation in securing like assurances from the other interested powers that each within its respective sphere of whatever influence—

First. Will in no way interfere with any treaty port or any vested interest within any so-called "sphere of interest" or leased territory it may have in China.

Second. That the Chinese treaty tariff of the time being shall apply to all merchandise landed or shipped to all such ports as are within said "sphere of interest" (unless they be "free ports"), no matter to what nationality it may belong, and that duties so leviable shall be collected by the Chinese Government.

Third. That it will levy no higher harbor dues on vessels of another nationality frequenting any port in such "sphere" than shall be levied on vessels of its own na-

tionality, and no higher railroad charges over lines built, controlled, or operated within its "sphere" on merchandise belonging to citizens or subjects of other nationalities transported through such "sphere" than shall be levied on similar merchandise belonging to its own nationals transported over equal distances.

The liberal policy pursued by His Imperial German Majesty in declaring Kiaochao a free port and in aiding the Chinese Government in the establishment there of a customhouse are so clearly in line with the proposition which this Government is anxious to see recognized that it entertains the strongest hope that Germany will give its acceptance and hearty support.

The recent ukase of His Majesty the Emperor of Russia declaring the port of Ta-lien-wan open during the whole of the lease under which it is held from China, to the merchant ships of all nations, coupled with the categorical assurances made to this Government by His Imperial Majesty's representative at this capital at the time, and since repeated to me by the present Russian ambassador, seem to insure the support of the Emperor to the proposed measure. Our ambassador at the Court of St. Petersburg has, in consequence, been instructed to submit it to the Russian Government and to request their early consideration of it. A copy of my instruction on the subject to Mr. Tower is herewith inclosed for your confidential information.

The commercial interests of Great Britain and Japan will be so clearly served by the desired declaration of intentions, and the views of the governments of these countries as to the desirability of the adoption of measures insuring the benefits of equality of treatment of all foreign trade throughout China are so similar to those entertained by the United States, that their acceptance of the propositions herein outlined and their cooperation in advocating their adoption by the other powers can be confidently expected.

315. *Root-Takahira Agreement, 1908*

K. Takahira to Elihu Root, November 30, 1908, *Papers Relating to the Foreign Relations of the United States, 1908* (Washington, 1912), 510–11.

THE EXCHANGE of views between us, which has taken place at the several interviews which I have recently had the honor of holding with you, has shown that Japan and the United States holding important outlying insular possessions in the region of the Pacific Ocean, the governments of the two countries are animated by a common aim, policy, and intention in that region.

Believing that a frank avowal of that aim, policy, and intention would not only tend to strengthen the relations of friendship and good neighborhood, which have immemorially existed between Japan and the United States, but would materially contribute to the preservation of the general peace, the Imperial Government have authorized me to present to you an outline of their understanding of that common aim, policy, and intention:

1. It is the wish of the two governments to encourage the free and peaceful development of their commerce on the Pacific Ocean.

2. The policy of both governments, uninfluenced by any aggressive tendencies, is directed to the maintenance of the existing status quo in the region above mentioned and to the defense of the principle of equal opportunity for commerce and industry in China.

3. They are accordingly firmly resolved reciprocally to respect the territorial possessions belonging to each other in said region.

4. They are also determined to preserve the common interest of all powers in China by supporting by all pacific means at their disposal the independence and integrity of China and the principle of equal opportunity for commerce and industry of all nations in that Empire.

5. Should any event occur threatening the status quo as above described or the principle of equal opportunity as above defined, it remains for the two governments to communicate with each other in order to arrive at an understanding as to what measures they may consider it useful to take.

If the foregoing outline accords with the view of the government of the United States, I shall be gratified to receive your confirmation.

PART SIX

America in a Disordered World, 1914-39

IN THE summer of 1914 war swept across Europe. The Western world never recovered from that disaster.

The relevance to their own lives of these distant battles was not at first clear to Americans. The ocean's expanse seemed adequate guarantee against involvement. Yet, as the months went by, it was ever more difficult to isolate the United States from the bitter contest in the Old World. Ties of sentiment and economic interest joined with a concern over the disregard of international morality to draw the United States into a position in which it had no alternative but to take part in the war. By the spring of 1917 it seemed to most Americans that only an Allied victory could guarantee the perpetuation of the values they most cherished.

Although the United States was late in entering the war, it devoted enormous energy to winning it. Unbelievably, an army was raised, trained, and transported across the ocean. Even more important, American industry began to turn out in mass the weapons that drove the Germans to surrender.

Peace was more difficult to attain than victory. Europe was exhausted; revolutions raged through the eastern and central sections of the continent and all established governments were insecure and hesitant. The world looked to the United States for leadership, and more particularly to President Wilson, who had summed up eloquently the moral purpose of the war. Yet, in the drawn-out and exhausting peace negotiations, the President found himself entangled in a web of conflicting interests and previous agreements that hampered his freedom of action. On point after point compromise was inevitable. But on one redeeming feature Wilson was inflexible. He insisted upon inclusion in the treaty terms of the provision for a League of Nations, counting on a body that would represent world opinion to rectify in time any injustices that the settlement itself might have caused.

But when he returned home, Wilson found his own people unenthusiastic about his cherished project. Political errors made the task of securing ratification of the treaty difficult. But more important, significant bodies of opinion turned away from the ideals for which the war had been fought. Some saw in the League simply a device to perpetuate an unjust peace. Others, moved by nationalism, were not willing to have the United States involved in any supra-national organization. The combination prevented the treaty from securing the majority in the Senate necessary for ratification.

The failure was characteristic, for it affected domestic attitudes as well. It set loose a wave of xenophobia that expressed hostility to everything with foreign and international connections, and that insisted upon conformity to a narrow conception of 100 per cent Americanism. The intolerant demand for uniformity did not pass away for more than a decade.

Even in the years after World War I, the United States was not capable of separating itself from the affairs of the wider world. The complex problems of international debts, reparations, and disarmament involved it in the affairs of Europe. The United States retained significant interests in Latin America and was compelled to adjust its attitudes toward its hemispheric neighbors in the face of unstable conditions throughout the world. And, in the Far East, a long series of disturbances in China led the United States to ponder seriously its attitude toward that part of the world. After 1930, all these concerns were rendered more difficult by the rise of aggressive fascist powers in Japan and Germany. In both of these countries the practice of ruthless expansion was already under way, and at point after point it touched on the vital interests of the United States. These problems were still unresolved when a new war brought them to a new crisis in 1939.

For most of the intervening period Americans had given more attention to domestic than to foreign affairs, and the character of the internal development long gave primacy to economic questions. In these years the capacity to produce was as impressive as ever in both agriculture and industry. Yet there seemed some fundamental disorder in the functioning of the economic system. A brief depression after the war had been troubling, and the farmers never fully recovered from that setback. Industry did enjoy seven years of prosperity, in a boom that sent values to unprecedented highs and let loose a gigantic wave of speculation. But the boom led to the panic of 1929 and to the depression that lasted a decade thereafter. For some ten years, a substantial part of the labor force remained unemployed, and that was a token of deep disturbance in the functioning of the whole American economy.

It was impossible then to evade the challenge of profound changes in economic policy. The confidence in the natural operation of economic forces, vigorously asserted in the 1920's, could not be so confidently reiterated after 1929. Moreover, it was now recognized that the Federal Government had an obligation to take a hand, not only in the relief of the unemployed and in the regulation of some branches of the economy, but also in supplying long-term direction toward broadly desirable economic objectives. The New Deal set the goals for reform, recovery, and planning; and the change took such a deep hold it would not thereafter be easily reversed.

Debate over these issues and policies often revealed a new attitude toward reform. The government was becoming particularly sensitive to the needs of the underprivileged. It gave the labor movement active protection, and this was responsible for the widespread growth of labor organizations after 1932. The conception of social security involved the obligation of government to support dependents and revolutionized their whole relationship to American life. And out of the action of the New Deal in the TVA campaign came a fruitful conception of regional planning.

Many of these changes set off intense political struggles. The cataclysmic defeat of the Democratic party in the 1920's had threatened to destroy it as an effective national political instrument. The Republican party was confidently in control—stable, conservative, and capable of surviving even the shock of occasional scandals. But the responsibility for the depression shattered its power and prestige. The events of 1932 drew into politics millions of voters who had theretofore been apathetic, but who were now excitedly mobilized by the New Deal program. A strong labor vote, active support by the minority groups, as well as the necessities of the farmers, shaped a coalition around the New Deal and gave it effective political strength through the rest of the decade.

All these changes produced serious social tensions. At the start of the period there was still an effort to maintain the traditional system of morality and beliefs, although these were being rudely shattered by the generation of the 1920's. The depression completed the unsettling effects of the war. Family ties seemed less binding, the rate of divorce grew rapidly, and a multitude of tensions displayed themselves.

Nevertheless, these tensions offered a kind of relief from some of the nation's earlier cultural inhibitions. The 1920's began a long period of cultural experimentation, with the arts more highly developed than ever before. Indeed, the challenge of the depression seemed to evoke a new, creative response from Americans, as if, the god of the market place having failed, there was an incentive to thinking of the spirit. Under the pressure of these changes men began to examine the older bases of their beliefs.

XXXVI 🎋 *The World War*

AT THE outbreak of the war in Europe there was general agreement in the United States that the country ought to remain neutral. President Wilson expressed the will of the nation when he called upon his fellow citizens to refrain from involvement in thought or action (No. 316).

It was difficult, however, to hold to this policy. Command of the sea and long-standing commercial connections enabled the Allies to turn to the United States for supplies. Shortly after the war began, the American government was asked to judge whether loans to these belligerents were a species of contraband (No. 317). At that time, in response to the reservations of Secretary of State Bryan, the government frowned upon a general bond issue but decided to permit commercial credits to encourage exports. This action built up a significant interest in the United States in favor of an Allied victory, as the new Secretary of State Lansing soon realized (No. 318). As the issue of neutral rights arose, it became more awkward to press American grievances as vigorously against the Allies as against the Germans (No. 319).

This difficulty was the more significant because the German offenses were of a type that particularly outraged American conceptions of international morality. Undoubtedly other factors also contributed to the turn toward the English and French; ties of sentiment, of economic interest, and the influence of propaganda built up favorable attitudes toward the Allies. But in the mind of the President and of many of his fellow citizens, the decisive consideration was the disregard of the Germans for human lives and for the principles of neutrality. The long negotiations that followed the sinking of the *Lusitania* stated the issue (No. 320); and when the Germans resumed submarine warfare in 1917, the United States seemed to have no alternative but war. In April, President Wilson came before the Congress to ask for a declaration of war (No. 321). By then, all were with the President except a few doubters like Senator Norris (No. 322). Yet, significantly, the President himself was fully conscious of the risks to the values he and all Americans cherished (No. 323).

The war itself demanded decisive action in the mobilization of men, materials (No. 324), and morale (No. 325). Yet unity of action permitted the country to solve its problems with relative ease and to meet the costs of the war without undue strain.

316. *The True Spirit of Neutrality, 1914*

Woodrow Wilson, Message to Congress, August 19, 1914, 63 Congress, 2 Session, *Senate Documents*, No. 566, pp. 3–4.

THE EFFECT of the war upon the United States will depend upon what American citizens say and do. Every man who really loves America will act and speak in the true spirit of neutrality, which is the spirit of impartiality and fairness and friendliness to all concerned. The spirit of the nation in this critical matter will be determined largely by what individuals and society and those gathered in public meetings do and say, upon what newspapers and magazines contain, upon what ministers utter in their pulpits, and men proclaim as their opinions upon the street.

The people of the United States are drawn from many nations, and chiefly from the nations now at war. It is natural and inevitable that there should be the utmost variety of sympathy and desire among them with regard to the issues and circumstances of the conflict. Some will wish one nation, others another, to succeed in the momentous struggle. It will be easy to excite passion and difficult to allay it. Those responsible for exciting it will assume a heavy responsibility, responsibility for no less a thing than that the people of the United States, whose love of their country and whose loyalty to its government should unite them as Americans all, bound in honor and affection to think first of her and her interests, may be divided in camps of hostile opinion, hot against each other, involved in the war itself in impulse and opinion if not in action.

Such divisions amongst us would be fatal to our peace of mind and might seriously stand in the way of the proper performance of our duty as the one great nation at peace, the one people holding itself ready to play a part of impartial mediation and speak the counsels of peace and accommodation, not as a partisan, but as a friend.

I venture, therefore, my fellow countrymen, to speak a solemn word of warning to you against that deepest, most subtle, most essential breach of neutrality which may spring out of partisanship, out of passionately taking sides. The United States must be neutral in fact as well as in name during these days that are to try men's souls. We must be impartial in thought as well as in action, must put a curb upon our sentiments as well as upon every transaction that might be construed as a preference of one party to the struggle before another.

317. *The Worst of Contrabands, 1914*

"Munitions Industry Hearings," 74 Congress, 2 Session, *Senate Hearings*, Part 25, January 7, 8, 1936 (Washington, 1937), 7665–6.

SECRETARY OF STATE W. J. BRYAN TO PRESIDENT WOODROW WILSON, AUGUST 10, 1914:
I BEG to communicate to you an important matter which has come before the Department. Morgan Company of New York have asked whether there would be any objection to their making a loan to the French Government and also the Rothschilds—I suppose that is intended for the French Government. I have conferred with Mr. Lansing and he knows of no legal objection to financing this loan, but I have suggested to him the advisability of presenting to you an aspect of the case which is not legal but I believe to be consistent with our attitude in international matters. It is whether it would be advisable for this Government to take the position that it will not approve of any loan to a belligerent nation. The reasons that I would give in support of this proposition are:

First: Money is the worst of all contrabands because it commands everything else. The question of making loans contraband by international agreement has been discussed, but no action has been taken. I know of nothing that would do more to prevent war than an international agreement that neutral nations would not loan to belligerents. While such an agreement would be of great advantage, could we not by our example hasten the reaching of such an agreement? We are the one great nation which is not involved and our refusal to loan to any belligerent would naturally tend to hasten a conclusion of the war. We are responsible for the use of our influence through example and as we cannot tell what we can do until we try, the only way of testing our influence is to set the example and observe its effect. This is the fundamental reason in support of the suggestion submitted.

Second: There is a special and local reason, it seems to me, why this course would be advisable. Mr. Lansing observed in the discussion of the subject that a loan would be taken by those in sympathy with the country in whose behalf the loan was negotiated. If we approved of a loan to France we could not, of course, object to a loan to Great Britain, Germany, Russia, Austria or to any other country, and if loans were made to these countries our citizens would be divided into groups, each group loaning money to the country which it favors and this money could not be furnished without expressions of sympathy. These expressions of sympathy are disturbing enough when they do not rest upon pecuniary interests—they would be still more disturbing if each group was pecuniarily interested in the success of the nation to whom its members had loaned money.

Third: The powerful financial interests which would be connected with these loans would be tempted to use their influence through the newspapers to support the interests of the Government to which they had loaned because the value of the security would be directly affected by the result of the war. We would thus find our newspapers violently arrayed on one side or the other, each paper supporting a financial group and pecuniary interest. All of this influence would make it all the more difficult for us to maintain neutrality as our action on various questions that would

arise would affect one side or the other and powerful financial interests would be thrown into the balance. . . .

P.S.—Mr. Lansing calls attention to the fact that an American citizen who goes abroad and voluntarily enlists in the army of a belligerent nation loses the protection of his citizenship while so engaged, and asks why dollars, going abroad and enlisting in war, should be more protected. As we cannot prevent American citizens going abroad at their own risk, so we cannot prevent dollars going abroad at the risk of the owners, but the influence of the Government is used to prevent American citizens from doing this. Would the Government not be justified in using its influence against the enlistment of the nation's dollars in a foreign war?

ROBERT LANSING, MEMORANDUM OF A CONVERSATION WITH THE PRESIDENT RELATIVE TO LOANS AND BANK CREDITS TO BELLIGERENT GOVERNMENTS, OCTOBER 23, 1914

From my conversation with the President I gathered the following impressions as to his views concerning bank credits of belligerent governments in contradistinction to a public loan floated in this country.

There is a decided difference between an issue of government bonds, which are sold in open market to investors, and an arrangement for easy exchange in meeting debts incurred in trade between a government and American merchants.

The sale of bonds draws gold from the American people. The purchasers of bonds are loaning their savings to the belligerent government, and are, in fact, financing the war.

The acceptance of Treasury notes or other evidences of debt in payment for articles purchased in this country is merely a means of facilitating trade by a system of credits which will avoid the clumsy and impractical method of cash payments. As trade with belligerents is legitimate and proper it is desirable that obstacles, such as interference with an arrangement of credits or easy method of exchange, should be removed.

The question of an arrangement of this sort ought not to be submitted to this Government for its opinion, since it has given its views on loans in general, although an arrangement as to credits has to do with a commercial debt rather than with a loan of money.

The above are my individual impressions of the conversation with the President who authorized me to give them to such persons as were entitled to hear them, upon the express understanding that they were my own impressions and that I had no authority to speak for the President or the Government.

318. *Loans for Our Own Good, 1915*

Secretary of State Robert Lansing to President Wilson, September 6, 1915, "Lansing Papers, 1914–1920," *Papers Relating to the Foreign Relations of the United States* (Washington, 1939), I, 144–7.

MY DEAR MR. PRESIDENT: Doubtless secretary McAdoo has discussed with you the necessity of floating government loans for the belligerent nations, which are purchasing such great quantities of goods in this country, in order to avoid a serious financial situation which will not only affect them but this country as well.

Briefly the situation, as I understand it, is this: Since December 1st, 1914, to June 30, 1915, our exports have exceeded our imports by nearly a billion dollars, and it is estimated that the excess will be from July 1st to December 31, 1915, a billion and three quarters. Thus for the year 1915 the excess will be approximately two and [a] half billions of dollars.

It is estimated that the European banks have about three and [a] half billions of dollars in gold in their vaults. To withdraw any considerable amount would disastrously affect the credit of the European nations, and the consequence would be a general state of bankruptcy.

If the European countries cannot find means to pay for the excess of goods sold to them over those purchased from them, they will have to stop buying and our present export trade will shrink proportionately. The result would be restriction of outputs, industrial depression, idle capital and idle labor, numerous failures, financial demoralization, and general unrest and suffering among the laboring classes.

Probably a billion and three quarters of the excess of European purchases can be taken care of by the sale of American securities held in Europe and by the transfer of trade balances of Oriental countries, but that will leave three quarters of a billion to be met in some other way. Furthermore, even if that is arranged, we will have to face a more serious situation in January, 1916, as the American securities held abroad will have been exhausted.

I believe that Secretary McAdoo is convinced and I agree with him that there is only one means of avoiding this situation which would so seriously affect economic conditions in this country, and that is the flotation of large bond issues by the belligerent governments. Our financial institutions have the money to loan and wish to do so. On account of the great balance of trade in our favor the proceeds of these loans would be expended here. The result would be a maintenance of the credit of the borrowing nations based on their gold reserve, a continuance of our commerce at its present volume and industrial activity with the consequent employment of capital and labor and national prosperity.

The difficulty is—and this is what secretary McAdoo came to see me about—

that the Government early in the war announced that it considered "war loans" to be contrary to "the true spirit of neutrality." A declaration to this effect was given to the press about August 15, 1914, by Secretary Bryan. . . . In October, 1914, after a conference with you, I gave my "impressions" to certain New York bankers in reference to "credit loans," but the general statement remained unaffected. . . .

Manifestly the Government has committed itself to the policy of discouraging general loans to belligerent governments. The practical reasons for the policy at the time we adopted it were sound, but basing it on the ground that loans are "inconsistent with the true spirit of neutrality" is now a source of embarrassment. . . . We are face to face with what appears to be a critical economic situation, which can only be relieved apparently by the investment of American capital in foreign loans to be used in liquidating the enormous balance of trade in favor of the United States.

Can we afford to let a declaration as to our conception of "the true spirit of neutrality" made in the first days of the war stand in the way of our national interests which seem to be seriously threatened?

If we cannot afford to do this, how are we to explain away the declaration and maintain a semblance of consistency?

My opinion is that we ought to allow the loans to be made for our own good, and I have been seeking some means of harmonizing our policy, so unconditionally announced, with the flotation of general loans. As yet I have found no solution to the problem.

Secretary McAdoo considers that the situation is becoming acute and that something should be done at once to avoid the disastrous results which will follow a continuance of the present policy.

319. *Neutral Rights, 1915*

O. G. Villard, *Fighting Years* (New York, 1939), 261–3, 266–7.

I CALLED upon Robert Lansing at his residence on Sunday evening, May 16. At that time counselor of the State Department, he received me in the most friendly manner. . . . I said I felt that excellent as the *Lusitania* note was it would not bring the German Government to terms as effectively as we all wished if there were not correspondingly strong action against Great Britain. While it was true that the British had not taken American lives in violation of international law and in a particularly brutal and cowardly fashion, as had the Germans, they had none the less sinned gravely. . . . I asked him if the time had not come to show that our government was determined to hold the scales even by sending the sharpest kind of a note to London.

To my surprise he replied that . . . the conduct of Great Britain was unbearable. It had promised in writing not to put cotton on the contraband list and now had done so. He was entirely of my opinion that this was the moment to act and in no uncertain manner "In fact," he said, "I have drafted just such a note in as strong language as I could write. . . . A messenger . . . has gone . . . to put the note into Mr. Wilson's hands in New York tomorrow morning. I hope it will be dispatched at once." I could not begin to express my gratification for the more I thought about the situation the more convinced I was of the profound effect that such a note would have in Berlin, as well as in London. I then took my courage in both hands and asked him if he did not think the time had come to make some publication about this note and whether

I might do so in *The Evening Post* the next day, protecting, of course, the source of my information. To my joy he said: "Yes, I think it should be done. You may go ahead, with discretion." . . .

The next day I carefully wrote the story, notified John Gavit that it was coming, and directed him to hold it until the last edition and then play it up as much as possible. It carried the head, "England's Turn Next to Receive a Reminder." The dispatch began: "Unless all signs fail, it it to be England's turn next. There is at this writing an excellent prospect that shortly—very shortly—perhaps within seventy-two hours, she will be haled before the Presidential bar of justice to receive from Mr. Wilson information as to just how this Government feels in regard to her violations of international law and practice. It goes without saying that when this is done the information will be imparted in a note that will not fall behind that to Germany in vigor and skill. The friendly tone will be there, too. . . ." I added that : "It is felt in unofficial circles here that the Government, to maintain its self-respect, must act as vigorously in this matter as it did in the *Lusitania* affair. It has right and justice on its side. . . ."

The dispatch made a sensation. Every managing editor in New York called his Washington office to inquire why I had been allowed to scoop the town in that way. A horde of correspondents rushed to the State Department, to Mr. Bryan, and Mr. Lansing. Mr. Bryan denied all knowledge of it. Mr. Lansing looked the reporters straight in the face and without blinking told them that he could not imagine how Mr. Villard had conceived such an idea! . . .

The effect in England of my "beat" was immediate. On the following Friday the New York papers carried a long statement issued by the London Foreign Office "to correct what the Government believes to be a misunderstanding of Great Britain's attitude toward American ships and American cargoes in other neutral bottoms." . . .

To return to Mr. Lansing's note, Mr. Bryan was strongly in favor of its being sent and, when the President did not act upon the note, on the ground that it might complicate our relations with Germany or even seem to weaken our attitude toward that country, since the sending of it might be interpreted as a yielding to Germany, everybody in the State Department was profoundly concerned, as the German newspapers were daily demanding that we should hold the scales even. . . .

Nothing moved the President. The Lansing note, despite accumulating proof of further British aggressions, lay upon Mr. Wilson's desk from May until the following October. When it was sent it was weak and emasculated.

320. *The* Lusitania *Negotiations, 1915*

Robert Lansing, *War Memoirs* (Indianapolis, 1935), 28–30, 31–2.

PRIOR to the destruction of the *Lusitania* on that fateful seventh of May, the British passenger steamer *Falaba* with American citizens on board had been torpedoed on March twenty-eighth, and on May first the American vessel *Gulflight* had been attacked. In the first case an American citizen had been drowned, and in the second case two or more Americans had lost their lives. These cases, while arousing less excitement because so few were killed, involved the same principle, the same disregard of rights, and were, therefore, joined with the *Lusitania* sinking in the representations and the protest made to the German Government against the use of submarines as commerce-destroyers. These representations were embodied in an instruction sent to Ambassador Gerard at Berlin on May thirteenth, in which appears the following significant phrase: "that it [the Government of the United States] must hold the Imperial German Government to a strict accountability for any infringement of those rights [of American citizens], intentional or incidental."

The instruction in substance called upon the German Government to cease submarine attacks against merchant ships since they could not be made according to the accepted rules of humane naval warfare.

On May twenty-eighth the German Minister of Foreign Affairs made a long and detailed reply to the American note, which he supplemented with another on June first concerning the case of the American vessel *Gulflight*. These notes contained excuses for the method employed by German submarine commanders and sought to cast the blame upon the British and American shipowners in subjecting their vessels to the risk of being attacked by passing through the sea war-zone, which had been proclaimed by Germany without color of legal right and which covered a great ocean area embracing the waters about the British Isles. There was, however, in the German reply no intimation that the existing practice would cease.

It was the note in answer to these two unsatisfactory German communications to which Mr. Bryan objected. Rather than sign it he resigned from the Cabinet, believing that, if the American note as drafted were delivered to the German Government, it would result in war, and Mr. Bryan was unalterably opposed to the United States becoming a participant in the conflict whatever the provocation might be. With his conscientiousness in dealing with all questions, with his belief that war was always avoidable and, therefore, unjustifiable, and with his firm

conviction that the reply of the United States, which the President had approved, would in the end bring about war between the United States and Germany, Mr. Bryan's withdrawal from the Cabinet was consistent wtih his avowed principles and with his conception of right and duty.

On the day that he resigned Mr. Bryan issued a public statement giving the reasons for his action. In that statement he said:

"Two of the points on which we (the President and I) differ, each conscientious in his conviction, are:

"First, as to the suggestion of investigation by an international commission, and,

"Second, as to warning Americans against traveling on belligerent vessels or with cargoes of ammunition."

He argued on the first point that the principle of the "Bryan Peace Treaties," as to an investigation before going to war, should be applied to the *Lusitania* case, although he had failed prior to the war in an attempt to negotiate such a treaty with the German Empire. Furthermore, the first draft of the note to Germany, which Mr. Bryan approved, included this principle, and the President agreed to it. Later, however, Mr. Wilson struck out the provision when some of his advisers strongly objected to it. As to the second point, Mr. Bryan declared that no American citizen should do anything which might involve his country in war even though he were compelled to surrender a strict legal right in order to avoid becoming the cause of such a disaster. . . .

To the American note, which caused Mr. Bryan's resignation and to which, after Mr. Bryan read it, no additions or amendments were made, . . . the German Government sent a reply dated July 8, 1915. It contained the assurance "that American ships will not be hindered in the prosecution of *legitimate* shipping and the lives of American citizens on *neutral* vessels shall not be placed in jeopardy." The italics are mine, and indicate the two words which made the assurance worthless. The word "legitimate" was open to various interpretations and would unavoidably introduce discussion and controversy in every case that might arise. The word "neutral" was intended to limit the rights of American citizens by forcing them to take passage on vessels belonging to nations which were not at war, and practically denied to them the protection to which they were entitled under international law, when traveling on inoffensive merchant ships of belligerent nationality.

The assurance in no way met the demands of the United States or insured against a repetition of the *Lusitania* horror. The United States had insisted that the international rules requiring a belligerent to "visit and search" a merchant ship should be complied with. As to that, the German Government replied that to have done so in the case of the *Lusitania* would have been to expose the submarine to almost certain destruction by being rammed by the great liner, an act for which, the Germans asserted, the British Government had offered a substantial pecuniary reward.

321. *The War Message, 1917*

President Wilson, Message to Congress, *Congressional Record*, 65 Congress, 1 Session, LV, Part 1, 102–4.

ON THE third of February last I officially laid before you the extraordinary announcement of the Imperial German Government that on and after the first day of February it was its purpose to put aside all restraints of law or of humanity and use its submarines to sink every vessel that sought to approach either the ports of Great Britain and Ireland or the western coasts of Europe or any of the ports controlled by the enemies of Germany within the Mediterranean. That had seemed to be the object of the German submarine warfare earlier in the war, but since April of last year the Imperial Government had somewhat restrained the commanders of its undersea craft in conformity with its promise then given to us that passenger boats should not be sunk and that due warning would be given to all other vessels which its submarines might seek to destroy, when no resistance was offered or escape attempted, and care taken that their crews were given at least a fair chance to save their lives in their open boats. The precautions taken were meager and haphazard enough, as was proved in distress instance after instance in the progress of the cruel and unmanly business, but a certain degree of restraint was observed. The new policy has swept every restriction aside. Vessels of every kind, whatever their flag, their character, their cargo, their destination, their errand, have been ruthlessly sent to the bottom without warning and without thought of help or mercy for those on board, the vessels of friendly neutrals along with those of belligerents. Even hospital ships and ships carrying relief to the sorely bereaved and stricken people of Belgium, though the latter were provided with safe conduct through the proscribed areas by the German Government itself and were distinguished by unmistakable marks of identity, have been sunk with the same reckless lack of compassion or of principle. . . .

I am not now thinking of the loss of property involved, immense and serious as that is, but only of the wanton and wholesale destruction of the lives of noncombatants, men, women, and children, engaged in pursuits which have always, even in the darkest periods of modern history, been deemed innocent and legitimate. Property can be paid for; the lives of peaceful and innocent people cannot be. The present German submarine warfare against commerce is a warfare against mankind.

It is a war against all nations. American ships have been sunk, American lives taken, in ways which it has stirred us very deeply to learn of, but the ships and people of other neutral and friendly nations have been sunk and overwhelmed in the waters in the same way. There has been no discrimination. The challenge is to all mankind. Each nation must decide for itself how it will meet it. The choice we make for ourselves must be made with a moderation of counsel and a temperateness of judgment befitting our character and our motives as a nation. We must put excited feeling away. Our motive will not be revenge or the victorious assertion of the physical might of the nation, but only the vindication of right, of human right, of which we are only a single champion. . . .

There is one choice we cannot make, we are incapable of making; we will not choose the path of submission and suffer the most sacred rights of our nation and our people to be ignored or violated. The wrongs against which we now array ourselves are no common wrongs; they cut to the very roots of human life.

With a profound sense of the solemn and even tragical character of the step I am taking and of the grave responsibilities which it involves, but in unhesitating obedience to what I deem my constitutional duty, I advise that the Congress declare the recent course of the Imperial German Government to be in fact nothing less than war against the government and people of the United States; that it formally accept the status of belligerent which has thus been thrust upon it; and that it take immediate steps not only to put the country in a more thorough state of defense but also to exert all its power and employ all its resources to bring the Government of the German Empire to terms and end the war. . . .

While we do these things, these deeply momentous things, let us be very clear, and make very clear to all the world what our motives and our objects are. . . . Our object . . . is to vindicate the principles of peace and justice in the life of the world as against selfish and autocratic power and to set up amongst the really free and self-governed peoples of the world such a concert of purpose and of action as will henceforth insure the observance of those principles. . . .

We have no quarrel with the German people. We have no feeling towards them but one of sympathy and friendship. It was not upon their impulse that their government acted in entering this war. It was not with their previous knowledge or approval. It was a war determined upon as wars used to be determined upon in the old, unhappy days when peoples were nowhere consulted by their rulers and wars were provoked and waged in the interest of dynasties or of little groups of ambitious men who were accustomed to use their fellow men as pawns and tools. . . .

It is a distressing and oppressive duty, Gentlemen of the Congress, which I have performed in thus addressing you. There are, it may be, many months of fiery trial and sacrifice ahead of us. It is a fearful thing to lead this great peaceful people into war, into the most terrible and disastrous of all wars, civilization itself seeming to be in the balance. But the right is more precious than peace, and we shall fight for the things which we have always carried nearest our hearts,—for democracy, for the right of those who submit to authority to have a voice in their own governments, for the rights and liberties of small nations, for a universal dominion of right by such a concert of free peoples as shall bring peace and safety to all nations and make the world itself at last free.

322. *Opposition to War, 1917*

Speech of Senator George Norris, April 4, 1917, *Congressional Record*, 65 Congress, 1 Session, LV, Part 1, 213.

WE HAVE loaned many hundreds of millions of dollars to the allies in this controversy. While such action was legal and countenanced by international law, there is no doubt in my mind but the enormous amount of money loaned to the allies in this country has been instrumental in bringing about a public sentiment in favor of our country taking a course that would make every bond worth a hundred cents on the dollar and making the payment of every debt certain and sure. Through this instrumentality and also through the instrumentality of others who have not only made millions out of the war in the manufacture of munitions, etc., and who would expect to make millions more if our country can be drawn into the catastrophe, a large number of the great newspapers and news agencies of the country have been controlled and enlisted in the greatest propaganda that the world has ever known, to manufacture sentiment in favor of war. It is now demanded that the American citizens shall be used as insurance policies to guarantee the safe delivery of munitions of war to belligerent nations. The enormous profits of munition manufacturers, stockbrokers, and bond dealers must be still further increased by our entrance into the war. This has brought us to the present moment, when Congress, urged by the President and backed by the artificial sentiment, is about to declare war and engulf our country in the greatest holocaust that the world has ever known.

323. *The Meaning of War, 1917*

Report of a conversation with the President, J. L. Heaton, *Cobb of "The World"* (New York, 1924), 268–70. Copyright, 1924, by E. P. Dutton & Co., Inc.

THE NIGHT before he asked Congress for a declaration of war against Germany he sent for me. I was late getting the message somehow and didn't reach the White House till 1 o'clock in the morning. "The old man" was waiting for me, sitting in his study with the typewriter on his table, where he used to type his own messages.

I'd never seen him so worn down. He looked as if he hadn't slept, and he said he hadn't. He said he was probably going before Congress the next day to ask a declaration of war, and he'd never been so uncertain about anything in his life as about that decision. For nights, he said, he'd been lying awake going over the whole situation; over the provocation given by Germany, over the probable feeling in the United States, over the consequences to the settlement and to the world at large if we entered the melee.

He tapped some sheets before him and said that he had written a message and expected to go before Congress with it as it stood. He said he couldn't see any alternative, that he had tried every way he knew to avoid war. "I think I know what war means," he said, and he added that if there were any possibility of avoiding war he wanted to try it. "What else can I do?" he asked. "Is there anything else I can do?"

I told him his hand had been forced by Germany, that so far as I could see we couldn't keep out.

"Yes," he said, "but do you know what that means?" He said war would overturn the world we had known; that so long as we remained out there was a preponderance of neutrality, but that if we joined with the Allies the world would be off the peace basis and onto a war basis.

It would mean that we should lose our heads along with the rest and stop weighing right and wrong. It would mean that a majority of people in this hemisphere would go war-mad, quit thinking and devote their energies to destruction. The President said a declaration of war would mean that Germany would be beaten and so badly beaten that there would be a dictated peace, a victorious peace.

"It means," he said, "an attempt to reconstruct a peacetime civilization with war standards, and at the end of the war there will be no bystanders with sufficient power to influence the terms. There won't be any peace standards left to work with. There will be only war standards."

The President said that such a basis was what the Allies thought they wanted, and that they would have their way in the very thing that America had hoped against and struggled against. W. W. was uncanny that night. He had the whole panorama in his mind. He went on to say that so far as he knew he had considered every loophole of escape and as fast as they were discovered Germany deliberately blocked them with some new outrage.

Then he began to talk about the consequences to the United States. He had no illusions about the fashion in which we were likely to fight the war.

He said when a war got going it was just war and there weren't two kinds of it. It required illiberalism at home to reinforce the men at the front. We couldn't fight Germany and maintain the ideals of government that all thinking men shared. He said we would try it but it would be too much for us.

"Once lead this people into war," he said, "and they'll forget there ever was such a thing as tolerance. To fight you must be brutal and ruthless, and the spirit of ruthless brutality will enter into the very fiber of our national life, infecting Congress, the courts, the policeman on the beat, the man in the street." Conformity would be the only virtue, said the President, and every man who refused to conform would have to pay the penalty.

He thought the Constitution would not survive it; that free speech and the right of assembly would go. He said a nation couldn't put its strength into a war and keep its head level; it had never been done.

"If there is any alternative, for God's sake, let's take it," he exclaimed. Well I couldn't see any, and told him so.

The President didn't have illusions about how he was going to come out of it, either. He'd rather have done anything else than head a military machine. All his instincts were against it. He foresaw too clearly the probable influence of a declaration of war on his own fortunes; the adulation certain to follow the certain victory, the derision and attack which would come with the deflation of excessive hopes and in the presence of world responsibility. But if he had it to do over again he would take the same course. It was just a choice of evils.

324. *Mobilizing Economic Resources, 1917–18*

War Industries Board, "An Outline of the Board's Origins, Functions and Organization, November 10, 1918." Reprinted also in B. M. Baruch, *American Industry in the War* (New York, 1941), 4–6.

IT IS not enough to mobilize the nation's military strength. There must be a mobilization of her full economic resources—industrial, agricultural and financial. These must be organized, coordinated, and directed with the same strategy that governs the operations of the purely military arms of service.

The prodigious strain upon the world's productive capacity must be met and balanced to provide the means of warfare and to maintain the civilian population as well as to preserve the economic fabric.

America today is the chief source of strength to the forces engaged in the conflict against German world domination. That strength is expressed in terms of man power and material—the one military, and the second industrial.

To control and regulate industry in all its direct and indirect relations to the war and to the nation, the President has created the War Industries Board and placed the responsibility for its operation in the hands of the chairman. . . .

The War Industries Board is charged with the duty of procuring an adequate flow of materials for the great war-making agencies of the Government—the War and Navy Departments—and for the two agencies in immediate affiliation with these military arms—the Emergency Fleet Corporation and the Railroad Administration.

Also, the Board provides supplies necessary to the military needs of our associates in the war, and those commodities required by neutrals in exchange for materials essential to us.

Finally, and of paramount importance, the Board, in alliance with the Food, Fuel, and Labor Administrations, provides for the country's civilian needs, the protection of which is a particular duty of the organization.

It is not only the duty of the War Industries Board to stimulate and expand production in those industries making war essentials, it is equally the Board's duty to protect, as far as may be, those industries not immediately essential to the war program. It is the policy of the Board, where retrenchment and curtailment are necessary, to keep alive, even though it be necessary to skeletonize, the enterprises in this group, and not to destroy them. Whenever possible, conversion of industries from a nonwar production to an essential output is effected.

The War Industries Board is a method of control devised by the President to equalize the strain placed upon the American industrial structure by the war. It stimulates and expands the production of those materials essential to the war program and at the same time it depresses and curtails the production of those things not of a necessitous nature. This is done by regulation, in consonance with other executive branches, of the basic economic elements: (a) facilities, (b) materials, (c) fuel, (d) transportation, (e) labor, and (f) capital.

The method of control is through a preference list, on which are placed those industries whose output is essential to the war's progress. The priority indicated by the preference list is the master key to the six elements named.

Further, the Board regulates all and controls certain other industries of first-rate war importance, it fixes prices through the price-fixing committee, it creates new and converts old facilities, it clears the national business requirements, and it leads to conservation, which is needed to bridge the gap between the extraordinary demand and the available supply—a gap which exists in almost all the great commercial staples.

325. *Mobilizing Opinion, 1917–18*

George Creel, *Rebel at Large* (New York, 1947), 194–9.

NOT the least of the fears that agitated the country in the first days of war was with respect to the attitude of our foreign born. From every section came gloomy predictions of wholesale disloyalty that would manifest itself in armed uprisings, sabotage, incendiarism, and domestic riot, making monster internment camps a stern necessity. Even actual revolutions were predicted in such German centers as Milwaukee, St. Louis, and Cincinnati. . . .

To meet this troubling situation, I called in Josephine Roche, . . . and established a Division of Work among the Foreign Born. Getting under way with her usual certainty, she established close relations with some twenty racial groups, utilizing existing organizations wherever possible, and began a drive that carried down from cities to remote hamlets. It was not only that their own speakers, their own writers, and their own newspapers were used to make for full understanding, but through volunteer helpers Miss Roche went into homes and aided bewildered thousands to solve the problems presented by draft regulations, income-tax provisions, and other laws that confused them. . . .

From the start Miss Roche met with the ugly antagonism of the countless "patriotic" bodies that sprang up all over the land. It was not that these groups were blood-thirsty, or that they did not want to be helpful, but simply that chauvinism was forced upon them by the necessities of their organization. As they were dependent for existence upon cash donations, it was essential that they "make a showing" in order that contributions might continue to be attracted. As they were outside the regular war machinery, and especially as they were not organized for fixed service, it was inevitable that these "societies" and "leagues" should turn to the emotions as a field of activity, and try to create an effect by noise, attack, and hysteria. . . .

Not the least of their complaints was our refusal to preach a gospel of hate. From the first we held that undocumented "atrocity stories" were bound to have bad reactions, for if the Germans could manage to refute one single charge, they would use it to discredit our entire indictment. This view was shared by the President and the War Department, and once on the authority of General Pershing, and again by direction of General March, we issued denials of "horror stuff" unsupported by date and place. The chauvinists, however, managed to figure largely in the Liberty Loan drives, over which the Committee had no control, and flooded the country with posters showing "bloody boots," trampled children, and mutilated women. . . .

The National Security League and the American Defense Society, officered by prominent citizens, were easily the most active and obnoxious. At all times their patriotism was a thing of screams, violence, and extremes, and their savage intolerances had the burn of acid. From the first they leveled attacks against the foreign-language groups, and were chiefly responsible for the development of a mob spirit in many sections. . . .

A principal demand of the chauvinists was for a prohibition against every other language but English. No effort at distinction was made, for along with their attacks on German they also clamored for a ban against Italian, French, Czech, Spanish, Russian, Danish, Norse, and Swedish, the languages of our allies and the neutrals. Several states yielded to this vicious pressure, an example being this proclamation by the governor of Iowa:

First, English should and must be the only medium of instruction in public, private, denominational or other similar schools;

Second, conversation in public places, on trains or over the telephone must be in the English language;

Third, all public addresses should be in the English language; and

Fourth, let those who cannot speak or understand English conduct their religious worship in their homes. . . .

The sweep of mean intolerance, of course, developed a mob spirit, and in some states loyalty meetings of the foreign groups were actually stoned. In one Texas town, virtually all of the young men of the Czechoslovak colony volunteered, and their departure was made the occasion of a great demonstration. Many old people were there, and the speeches were made in Czech. Without any attempt to inquire into the nature of the meeting, "native patriots" smashed the windows with rocks, attacked the audience, and drove them from the building as though they had been Huns caught in some atrocity.

In the Northwest, where Germans and Scandinavians figured largely, there was not only a pro-German sentiment in the beginning, but people had been fed the lie that it was a "rich man's war," without other purpose than to protect the loans of Wall Street bankers. What more important than to preach the gospel of Americanism? Yet when the Committee

tried to send its speakers in, the chauvinists barred them. Even when we persisted, and arranged Liberty Loan rallies and patriotic meetings, they had to be held in the fields or in barns. Parades were stopped by home guards, automobiles were overturned, and on one wretched occasion a baby of six months was torn from its mother's arms by the powerful stream from a fire hose. "Tar and feather parties" were common, and even deportations took place. . . .

The press, from which we had the right to expect help, failed us miserably. One alien speaking dirrespectfully of the flag could be sure of front-page notice, but ten thousand aliens could gather in a great patriotic demonstration without earning an agate line. Paderewski told me that nothing depressed his people more than the manner in which the newspapers ignored Polish loyalty meetings, and Dr. Masaryk had the same story to tell about the Czechoslovaks. Hungarian-Americans, Yugoslavs, the National Croatian Society, Scandinavian organizations, and Dutch groups staged spectacular parades and voted thousands for Liberty bonds, all without getting more than a line or two.

As a consequence, the chauvinists had the field to themselves, singing their hymns of hate and damning officials for inefficiency and spinelessness when they failed to produce traitors to be put before a firing squad. Not until the Praeger lynching did the madness show signs of abatement. This poor devil, absolutely innocent as proved afterward, was lynched by a mob that refused to grant his pleas for an interpreter. I went to President Wilson at once, and his public denunciation of the mob spirit sobered the people as a whole, if not the super-patriots.

XXXVII ※ *Failure of the Peace*

BEFORE the armistice, the objectives of the war had seemed clear and luminous in outline. President Wilson had been able to give them eloquent expression in the Fourteen Points, a program for peace that appealed to the imagination of the whole world (No. 326).

But it was another matter to reduce these objectives to the specific terms of a treaty of peace. When the statesmen gathered, they found it necessary to take account of a number of considerations other than the popular ideals. A series of secret treaties among the Allies had committed the great powers other than the United States to settlements that were not always in accord with Wilson's ideals (No. 327). Famine was sweeping across devastated Central Europe (No. 328); and the seizure of power by the Bolsheviks in Russia, together with revolutions in other parts of the continent, complicated all the problems of making peace (No. 329). Tragically, also, the bitterness of the war had begun to overshadow the idealism in terms of which Americans had entered it. The desire for revenge made it more difficult to secure an equable peace treaty (No. 330).

No doubt Wilson recognized the shortcomings of the Treaty of Versailles, as did his intimate friend Colonel House (No. 331). The establishment of the League of Nations, the President hoped, would compensate for all the compromises to which he had been compelled to agree; and on the League he fixed all his hopes for the future peace of the world (No. 332). But a substantial opposition developed toward the League in the Senate. This opposition united the President's political antagonists with some Senators opposed to any further involvement in European affairs, and with others who considered the League merely a device for enforcing an unjust peace (No. 333). Their combined power led to rejection of the whole treaty.

In the years that followed, the war as well as the peace came to seem a great betrayal. Distrust of everything foreign and international welled up in many areas of American opinion. This suspicion was supported by the development of racist ideas (No. 334) that found expression in the powerful new Ku Klux Klan, directed against Catholics, Negroes, and Jews (No. 335). Ultimately it also endowed with success the movement to restrict immigration. The literacy test, vetoed by President Wilson in 1915, had been passed over opposition in 1917 (No. 336); and now a series of laws sharply limited the number of immigrants to be admitted in the future and did so in accord with a quota system based on racist assumptions.

Xenophobia also contributed to the Red scare. The fear that radicals were undermining American society took unreasoning hold of the minds of many men (No. 337). The concept of freedom of speech was narrowed (No. 338); and waves of violence suppressed radical and labor agitators. In a case that disturbed the country for many years, two innocent men were tried and convicted of murder because they were both foreign and radical. The eloquent words of one of them expressed the will to resist the spirit of these years (No. 339).

326. *The Fourteen Points, 1918*

Woodrow Wilson, *The Fourteen Points*, 65 Congress, 2 Session, *House Document No. 765*, Serial No. 7443 (Washington, 1918), 3–7.

THERE is no confusion of counsel among the adversaries of the Central Powers, no uncertainty of principle, no vagueness of detail. The only secrecy of counsel, the only lack of fearless frankness, the only failure to make definite statement of the objects of the war, lies with Germany and her allies. The issues of life and death hang upon these definitions. No statesman who has the least conception of his responsibility ought for a moment to permit himself to continue this tragical and appalling outpouring of blood and treasure unless he is sure beyond a peradventure that the objects of the vital sacrifice are part and parcel of the very life of society and that the people for whom he speaks think them right and imperative as he does. . . .

It will be our wish and purpose that the processes of peace, when they are begun, shall be absolutely open and that they shall involve and permit henceforth no secret understandings of any kind. The day of conquest and aggrandizement is gone by; so is also the day of secret covenants entered into in the interest of particular governments and likely at some unlooked-for moment to upset the peace of the world. . . . This happy fact . . . makes it possible for every nation whose purposes are consistent with justice and the peace of the world to avow now or at any other time the objects it has in view. . . .

We demand in this war . . . nothing peculiar to ourselves. It is that the world be made fit and safe to live in; and particularly that it be made safe for every peace-loving nation which, like our own, wishes to live its own life, determine its own institutions, be assured of justice and fair dealing by the other peoples of the world as against force and selfish aggression. All the peoples of the world are in effect partners in this interest, and for our own part we see very clearly that unless justice be done to others it will not be done to us. The program of the world's peace, therefore, is our program; and that program, the only possible program, as we see it, is this:

I. Open covenants of peace, openly arrived at, after which there shall be no private international understandings of any kind but diplomacy shall proceed always frankly and in the public view.

II. Absolute freedom of navigation upon the seas, outside territorial waters, alike in peace and in war, except as the seas may be closed in whole or in part by international action for the enforcement of international covenants.

III. The removal, so far as possible, of all economic barriers and the establishment of an equality of trade conditions among all the nations consenting to the peace and associating themselves for its maintenance.

IV. Adequate guarantees given and taken that national armaments will be reduced to the lowest point consistent with domestic safety.

V. A free, open-minded, and absolutely impartial adjustment of all colonial claims, based upon a strict observance of the principle that in determining all such questions of sovereignty the interests of the populations concerned must have equal weight with the equitable claims of the government whose title is to be determined.

VI. The evacuation of all Russian territory and such a settlement of all questions affecting Russia as will secure the best and freest cooperation of the other nations of the world in obtaining for her an unhampered and unembarrassed opportunity for the independent determination of her own political development and national policy and assure her of a sincere welcome into the society of free nations under institutions of her own choosing; and, more than a welcome, assistance also of every kind that she may need and may herself desire. . . .

VII. Belgium, the whole world will agree, must be evacuated and restored, without any attempt to limit the sovereignty which she enjoys in common with all other free nations. No other single act will serve as this will serve to restore confidence among the nations in the laws which they have themselves set and determined for the government of their relations with one another. Without this healing act the whole structure and validity of international law is forever impaired.

VIII. All French territory should be freed and the invaded portions restored, and the wrong done to France by Prussia in 1871 in the matter of Alsace-Lorraine, which has unsettled the peace of the world for nearly fifty years, should be righted, in order that peace may once more be made secure in the interest of all.

IX. A readjustment of the frontiers of Italy should be effected along clearly recognizable lines of nationality.

X. The peoples of Austria-Hungary, whose place among the nations we wish to see safeguarded and assured, should be accorded the freest opportunity of autonomous development.

XI. Rumania, Serbia, and Montenegro should be evacuated; occupied territories restored; Serbia accorded free and secure access to the sea; and the relations of the several Balkan states to one another determined by friendly counsel along historically established lines of allegiance and nationality; and international guarantees of the political and economic independence and territorial integrity of the several Balkan states should be entered into.

XII. The Turkish portions of the present Ottoman Empire should be assured a secure sovereignty, but the other nationalities which are now under Turkish rule should be assured an undoubted security of life and an absolutely unmolested opportunity of autonomous development, and the Dardanelles should be permanently opened as a free passage to the ships and commerce of all nations under international guarantees.

XIII. An independent Polish state should be erected which should include the territories inhabited by indisputably Polish populations, which should be assured a free and secure access to the sea, and whose political and economic independence and territorial integrity should be guaranteed by international covenant.

XIV. A general association of nations must be formed under specific covenants for the purpose of affording mutual guarantees of political independence and territorial integrity to great and small states alike.

In regard to these essential rectifications of wrong and assertions of right we feel ourselves to be intimate partners of all the governments and peoples associated together against the Imperialists. We cannot be separated in interest or divided in purpose. We stand together until the end.

For such arrangements and covenants we are willing to fight and to continue to fight until they are achieved; but only because we wish the right to prevail and desire a just and stable peace such as can be secured only by removing the chief provocations to war, which this program does remove. We have no jealousy of German greatness, and there is nothing in this program that impairs it. We grudge her no achievement or distinction of learning or of pacific enterprise such as have made her record very bright and very enviable. We do not wish to injure her or to block in any way her legitimate influence or power. We do not wish to fight her either with arms or with hostile arrangements of trade if she is willing to associate herself with us and the other peace-loving nations of the world in covenants of justice and law and fair dealing. We wish her only to accept a place of equality among the peoples of the world—

the new world in which we now live— instead of a place of mastery.

Neither do we presume to suggest to her any alteration or modification of her institutions. But it is necessary, we must frankly say, and necessary as a preliminary to any intelligent dealings with her on our part, that we should know whom her spokesmen speak for when they speak to us, whether for the Reichstag majority or for the military party and the men whose creed is imperial domination.

327. *The Secret Treaties, 1918*

Villard, *Fighting Years*, 340–1.

ON JANUARY 25, 26, 28, 1918, I published in *The Evening Post* the famous secret treaties. . . . These vitally important documents were found in the Russian archives when the Bolsheviki took over the government and were promptly published in full in all of the then existing Russian dailies. Every effort was made by the Allies to keep them out of the United States and to prevent our officials from reading and understanding them. Our great press associations were either too ignorant to appreciate their value, were unaware of the opportunity for one of the greatest scoops on record, or were too subservient to our government to undertake the publication; not even when I published them were they carried by the Associated Press. One day a man walked into my office with a note from Amos Pinchot saying that the bearer had a matter of the utmost importance to discuss with me. He was a Russian, apparently a sailor or stoker. He produced far from fresh copies of a Vladivostok newspaper containing the secret treaties in full; from their appearance the papers looked as if he had worn them ashore between his skin and his undershirt. He asked a moderate price, received it, and departed, leaving upon my desk the means for me

to render what would have been the greatest public service of my journalistic career had the officials in Washington been aware of their duty to their country and if the editors of the United States had had sufficient intelligence and knowledge of what the war was all about to appreciate the tremendous significance of these documents, revealing as they did the hidden policies and the sordid bargains of our hypocritical Allies.

I had the treaties translated and the accuracy of the translation was never questioned. Then, in order to obtain the widest possible circulation for them, I offered them at low rates to the leading newspapers of the country. Only nine took them. . . . If there were others which recognized the sensational character of what I offered them, their editors probably felt that there was too much dynamite in the publication or that they might get into trouble with the government, and they also failed to understand what a service to their countrymen they could render by the publication. As it turned out, nobody in Washington asked us any questions about the publication or how we got the documents. . . . The censorship officials were certainly not clever when they failed to understand the importance of these documents and the light in which they placed the Allies. No one who understood them could thereafter claim that the Allies had clean hands or that they had played fair.

At the Peace Conference the whole fight centered on how far Mr. Wilson could set aside the underhand bargains contained in those documents.

328. *Famine, 1918*

Villard, *Fighting Years*, 445–7.

MR. LLOYD GEORGE may have been impressed by my report but it was not until a month later that he rose in Parliament and informed the members that a new and more terrible enemy than the Germans had appeared in Europe—hunger. But he did not tell the members that he, Wilson, Clemenceau, and Orlando were responsible because of those months lost between November and April when they delayed and wrangled, during which food should have been allowed into all the war-wrecked countries. . . . The sudden surrender of Hungary to Bela Kun and the Communists severely jolted the higher circles but brought about no noteworthy change. Count Karolyi had for weeks in vain been foretelling just what had happened and begging for food to prevent it. Some of the American delegation merely blamed Senator Lodge and the Senate for having amended the Hoover Food Bill so as to prevent the delivery of food to any of the former enemies. Still the Allies would take no warning and let Bavaria finally go Communist.

On March 26 Hugh Gibson and I lunched with Herbert Hoover in his rooms at the Crillon. Hoover came half an hour late and, without apology, dropped into a chair exhausted. "What day is today?" he asked. "March 26." "Well," said he, "ever since December 4 I have tried to get permission for the little German fishing fleet to go to sea. It took me until Christmas to get English consent and now at last I have the French permission after fighting them again all morning." Thereupon he began to curse with the ease and skill of a coal miner and called the French every kind of a name.

This humane and courageous fight of Hoover's for a sensible policy toward the defeated country and Russia stands out as his finest achievement. Indeed, it seems to me that he was at his best all through the Peace Conference, nearly always standing on the side of justice and decency and speaking right out for his beliefs. That his dreadful fear of Bolshevism was one of his most compelling motives is true; that does not detract from the great effort he made to stop the continuance of loss of life in Germany because of semi-starvation. . . . But even Hoover's splendid example did not convince the higher-ups, nor did the sensational refusal of the British soldiers of General Plumer's army in Germany to stand guard over starving women and children without at least sharing their food with them. . . .

The ability men had to deceive themselves at that time was beyond belief. The Big Four apparently thought that they could delay the making of the peace and not invite disaster. They really believed that their military success gave them the right to deprive Germany of millions of her people, much of her soil, half of her coal supply, and three-fourths of her iron ore, all of her colonies, all her great steamships, the free use of her railways, and free disposal of her industrial products, and get away with it without paying a dreadful price. In the United States the failure to understand the situation was beyond belief. . . . How, we asked, was it possible for the Secretary of the Navy, Josephus Daniels, to exclaim exultantly that Germany had been rendered impotent for all time to come?

329. *The Bolsheviks, 1918*

Washington Post, February 26, 1918, in I. E. Bennett, ed., *Editorials from the Washington Post* (Washington, 1921), 177.

GERMANY accepts the abject proposal of the Bolsheviki, which is that the representatives of the Russian "government" will go to Brest-Litovsk to sign a peace treaty on the terms laid down by Germany. Thus, so far as the German masters and the Russian marplots can arrange it, there will be no further fighting. The Bolsheviki are to withdraw from western Russia and turn the country over to the conqueror. The army is to be demobilized, the fleet interned, and Petrograd is to be delivered over as a hostage to the Germans.

The world will never believe that this surrender of Russian territory and honor was made by honest men. The belief is firmly fixed that the leaders of the Bolsheviki, the men who really contrived Russia's downfall, are traitors, in the pay of Germany.

The betrayal is of stupendous consequence to the world. It changes the course of history in every nation. It realigns the forces of this war and tends to prolong the struggle beyond the ken of statesmanship. It aggrandizes Germany enormously, and injects into the famished and exhausted German spirit a fresh exultation and a hope of eventual victory over the great Western Allies.

330. *A Dictated Peace, 1918*

Washington Post, August 8, 1918, *ibid.*, 281–2.

BEFORE the echo of the Allies' victorious guns has died away along the Marne there is heard an insistent note, demanding that the allied powers shall not "crush Germany." The demand comes from Germany in the form of propaganda, and from allied countries it issues from that assortment of pacifists, sentimentalists, traitors, defeatists, and nondescript scoundrels who have done so much to cripple the arm of efficiency. Doubtless, as Germany's inevitable defeat becomes more apparent, . . . the enemy will strain every nerve to snatch by peace what he is unable to grasp by war.

For this reason, as well as because of the serious conditions in all countries which demand an end of war, it is most welcome news that the United States Government intends to increase its avail-able man power to hasten complete victory. . . .

The prime consideration now is energy in the field and firmness in policy. "Unconditional surrender" are the words that should be inscribed on every bullet and bomb that goes to Germany. The world will be defeated if it suspends hostilities to discuss Germany's ideas of a proper peace. There will be no secure freedom of nations if the Allies do not impose their will on Germany. They must dictate the terms of peace, and Germany must accept what they dictate. If Germany should be treated with the magnanimity that is due to a chivalrous enemy, the savages in control of that empire would twist the concession into a dagger with which to stab their benefactors.

331. *Reflections on the Treaty, 1919*

Charles Seymour, ed., *Intimate Papers of Colonel House* (Boston, 1926–28), IV, 487–9.

I AM leaving Paris, after eight fateful months, with conflicting emotions. Looking at the Conference in retrospect, there is much to approve and much to regret. It is easy to say what should have been done, but more difficult to have found a way of doing it.

The bitterness engendered by the war, the hopes raised high in many quarters because of the victory, the character of the men having the dominant voice in the making of the Treaty, all had their influence for good or for evil.... There seemed to be no full realization of the conditions which had to be met. An effort was made to enact a peace upon the usual lines. This should never have been attempted. The greater part of civilization had been shattered and history could guide us but little in the making of this peace.

How splendid it would have been had we blazed a new and better trail. However it is to be doubted whether this could have been done, even if those in authority had so decreed, for the peoples back of them had to be reckoned with. ...Wilson might have had the power and influence if he had remained in Washington and kept clear of the Conference. When he stepped from his lofty pedestal and wrangled with the representatives of

other states upon equal terms, he became as common clay....

To those who are saying that the Treaty is bad and should never have been made and that it will involve Europe in infinite difficulties in its enforcement, I feel like admitting it. But I would also say in reply that empires cannot be shattered and new states raised upon their ruins without disturbance. To create new boundaries is always to create new troubles....

While I should have preferred a different peace, I doubt whether it could have been made, for the ingredients for such a peace as I would have had were lacking at Paris. And even if those of us like Smuts, Botha, and Cecil could have had our will, as much trouble might have followed a peace of our making as seems certain to follow this.

The same forces that have been at work in the making of this peace would be at work to hinder the enforcement of a different kind of peace, and no one can say with certitude that anything better than had been done could be done at this time. We have had to deal with a situation pregnant with difficulties and one which could be met only by an unselfish and idealistic spirit, which was almost wholly absent and which was too much to expect of men come together at such a time and for such a purpose.

332. *Wilson's Speech at Pueblo, 1919*

Woodrow Wilson, "Speech at Pueblo, Colorado, September 25, 1919," *Congressional Record*, LVIII, Part 7 (October 6, 1919), 6425, 6426.

WHEN you come to the heart of the covenant, my fellow citizens, you will find it in article 10.... There is nothing in the

other contentions with regard to the League of Nations, but there is something in article 10 that you ought to realize and ought to accept or reject. . . . What is article 10? . . . Article 10 provides that every member of the League covenants to respect and preserve the territorial integrity and existing political independence of every other member of the League as against external aggression. Not against internal disturbance. There was not a man at that table who did not admit the sacredness of the right of self-determination, the sacredness of the right of any body of people to say that they would not continue to live under the government they were then living under, and under article 11 of the covenant they are given a place to say whether they will live under it or not. For . . . article 11 . . . makes it the right of any member of the League at any time to call attention to anything, anywhere, that is likely to disturb the peace of the world or the good understanding between nations upon which the peace of the world depends. . . .

Yet article 10 strikes at the taproot of war. Article 10 is a statement that the very things that have always been sought in imperialistic wars are henceforth foregone by every ambitious nation in the world. I would have felt very lonely, my fellow countrymen, and I would have felt very much disturbed if, sitting at the peace table in Paris, I had supposed that

I was expounding my own ideas. . . . I proposed nothing whatever at the peace table at Paris that I had not sufficiently certain knowledge embodied the moral judgment of the citizens of the United States. I had gone over there with, so to say, explicit instructions. Don't you remember that we laid down fourteen points which should contain the principles of the settlement? They were not my points. In every one of them I was conscientiously trying to read the thought of the people of the United States, and after I uttered those points I had every assurance given me that could be given me that they did speak the moral judgment of the United States and not my single judgment. Then when it came to that critical period just a little less than a year ago, when it was evident that the war was coming to its critical end, all the nations engaged in the war accepted those fourteen principles explicitly as the basis of the armistice and the basis of the peace. In those circumstances I crossed the ocean under bond to my own people and to the other governments with which I was dealing. The whole specification of the method of settlement was written down and accepted beforehand, and we were architects building on those specifications.

333. *The League Means War, 1919*

Senator William E. Borah, Speech of November 19, 1919, *Congressional Record,* LVIII, Part 9 (November 19, 1919), 8783–4.

Sɪʀ, we are told that this treaty means peace. Even so, I would not pay the price. Would you purchase peace at the cost of any part of our independence? We could have had peace in 1776—the price was high, but we could have had it. . . . All through that long and trying struggle, particularly when the clouds of adversity lowered upon the cause, there was a cry of peace—let us have peace. We could have had peace in 1860; Lincoln was

counseled by men of great influence and accredited wisdom to let our brothers— and, thank Heaven, they are brothers— depart in peace. But the tender, loving Lincoln, bending under the fearful weight of impending civil war, an apostle of peace, refused to pay the price, and a reunited country will praise his name forevermore—bless it because he refused peace at the price of national honor and national integrity. Peace upon any other basis than national independence, peace purchased at the cost of any part of our national integrity, is fit only for slaves, and even when purchased at such a price it is a delusion, for it cannot last.

But your treaty does not mean peace— far, very far, from it. If we are to judge the future by the past it means war. Is there any guaranty of peace other than the guaranty which comes of the control of the war-making power by the people? Yet what great rule of democracy does the treaty leave unassailed? The people in whose keeping alone you can safely lodge the power of peace or war nowhere, at no time and in no place, have any voice in this scheme for world peace. Autocracy which has bathed the world in blood for centuries reigns supreme. Democracy is everywhere excluded. This, you say, means peace.

Can you hope for peace when love of country is disregarded in your scheme, when the spirit of nationality is rejected, even scoffed at? Yet what law of that moving and mysterious force does your treaty not deny? With a ruthlessness unparalleled your treaty in a dozen instances runs counter to the divine law of nationality. Peoples who speak the same language, kneel at the same ancestral tombs, moved by the same traditions, animated by a common hope, are torn asunder, broken in pieces, divided, and parceled out to antagonistic nations. And this you call justice. This, you cry, means peace. Peoples who have dreamed of independence, struggled and been patient, sacrificed and been hopeful, peoples who were told that through this peace conference they should realize the aspirations of centuries, have again had their hopes dashed to earth. . . . No; your treaty means injustice. It means slavery. It means war. And to all this you ask this Republic to become a party.

334. *The Great Race, 1916*

Madison Grant, *The Passing of the Great Race* (revised edition, New York, 1918), 86, 88, 89–90, 91, 92. Copyright 1918 by Charles Scribner's Sons, 1946 by De Forest Grant. Reprinted with the permission of Charles Scribner's Sons.

RACE consciousness . . . in the United States, down to and including the Mexican War, seems to have been very strongly developed among native Americans and it still remains in full vigor today in the South, where the presence of a large Negro population forces this question upon the daily attention of the whites.

In New England, however, whether through the decline of Calvinism or the growth of altruism, there appeared early in the last century a wave of sentimentalism, which at that time took up the cause of the Negro and in so doing apparently destroyed, to a large extent, pride and consciousness of race in the North. The agitation over slavery was inimical to the Nordic race, because it thrust aside all national opposition to the intrusion of hordes of immigrants of inferior racial value and prevented the fixing of a definite American type. . . .

The native American by the middle of the nineteenth century was rapidly acquiring distinct characteristics. . . . The Civil War, however, put a severe, perhaps fatal, check to the development and expansion of this splendid type by destroying great numbers of the best breeding stock on both sides and by breaking up the home ties of many more. If the war had not occurred these same men with their descendants would have populated the Western states instead of the racial nondescripts who are now flocking there. . . .

These new immigrants were no longer exclusively members of the Nordic race as were the earlier ones who came of their own impulse to improve their social conditions. The transportation lines advertised America as a land flowing with milk and honey and the European governments took the opportunity to unload upon careless, wealthy and hospitable America the sweepings of their jails and asylums. The result was that the new immigration . . . contained a large and increasing number of the weak, the broken and the mentally crippled of all races drawn from the lowest stratum of the Mediterranean basin and the Balkans, together with hordes of the wretched, submerged populations of the Polish ghettos. Our jails, insane asylums and almshouses are filled with their human flotsam and the whole tone of American life, social, moral and political has been lowered and vulgarized by them.

With a pathetic and fatuous belief in the efficacy of American institutions and environment to reverse or obliterate immemorial hereditary tendencies, these newcomers were welcomed and given a share in our land and prosperity. The American taxed himself to sanitate and educate these poor helots and as soon as they could speak English, encouraged them to enter into the political life, first of municipalities and then of the nation. . . .

These immigrants adopt the language of the native American, they wear his clothes, they steal his name and they are beginning to take his women, but they seldom adopt his religion or understand his ideals and while he is being elbowed out of his own home the American looks calmly abroad and urges on others the suicidal ethics which are exterminating his own race. . . .

It is evident that in large sections of the country the native American will entirely disappear. He will not intermarry with inferior races and he cannot compete in the sweat shop and in the street trench with the newcomers. Large cities from the days of Rome, Alexandria, and Byzantium have always been gathering points of diverse races, but New York . . . will produce many amazing racial hybrids and some ethnic horrors that will be beyond the powers of future anthropologists to unravel.

One thing is certain; in any such mixture, the surviving traits will be determined by competition between the lowest and most primitive elements and the specialized traits of Nordic man; his stature, his light colored eyes, his fair skin and light colored hair, his straight nose and his splendid fighting and moral qualities, will have little part in the resultant mixture.

335. *The Fiery Cross, 1924*

The Fiery Cross (weekly newspaper published by the Klan in Indianapolis, Indiana), February 8, 1924, cited in Michael Williams, *Shadow of the Pope* (New York, 1932), 313–14. Copyright 1932, by Michael Williams.

THE GROWTH of the Klan . . . is a symptom of certain forces that are at work—a movement to counteract un-American ideas and standards that are in evidence. . . . Old stock Americans have become restless, . . . they are dissatisfied with the denationalizing forces at work in the country. . . . The

American people know there is something wrong, and they are talking among themselves as to where the trouble is. They know the arrogant claims of the Papacy to temporal power and that the Romish church is not in sympathy with American ideals and institutions. They know that

Rome is in politics, and that she often drives the thin edge of her wedge with a muffled hammer; they have seen the results of her activities in other lands. They know the facts as to Rome's opposition to the Bible in our public schools and to our public school system itself. They know she is opposed to a free press, free speech, and to other democratic principles.

These old stock Americans are coming to believe that the Jews dominate the economic life of the nation, while the Catholics are determined to dominate the political and religious life. And they have apprehensions that the vast alien immigration is at the root an attack upon Protestant religion with its freedom of conscience, and is therefore a menace to American liberties.

They have seen Roman canon law come into conflict with American law, and they are not willing to have a foreign power dictate to them, or pursue a policy destructive to true Americanism. Many of these American patriots have heard about a great building now being erected in Washington in preparation as the residence of the Pope transferred from the Vatican to the national capital. And whether this is true or false, it is believed by a large number of citizens. At any rate, the American people know there is something wrong. They are afraid of the race groups that adhere to their own language and race prejudice and religious superstitions, and have no sympathy with out Americanism. They have their forebodings as to the union of Jews and Catholics in their opposition to the Bible in our public schools. And they are determined that Romanism with its political ambitions and with whatever allies it may have, shall not carry out any plot against our free institutions and against the very government itself.

336. *The Literacy Test,* 1915

President Wilson's Veto Message of January 28, 1915, in Albert Shaw, ed., *President Wilson's State Papers and Addresses* (New York, 1918), 95–6.

IN TWO particulars of vital consequence this bill embodies a radical departure from the traditional and long-established policy of this country, a policy in which our people have conceived the very character of their Government to be expressed, the very mission and spirit of the nation in respect of its relations to the peoples of the world outside their borders. It seeks to all but close entirely the gates of asylum which have always been open to those who could find nowhere else the right and opportunity of constitutional agitation for what they conceived to be the natural and inalienable rights of men; and it excludes those to whom the opportunities of elementary education have been denied, without regard to their character, their purposes, or their natural capacity.

Restrictions like these, adopted earlier in our history as a nation, would very materially have altered the course and cooled the humane ardors of our politics. The right of political asylum has brought to this country many a man of noble character and elevated purpose who was marked as an outlaw in his own less fortunate land, and who has yet become an ornament to our citizenship and to our public councils. The children and the compatriots of these illustrious Americans must stand amazed to see the representatives of their nation now resolved, in the fullness of our national strength and at the maturity of our great institutions, to risk turning such men back from our shores without test of quality or purpose. It is difficult for me to believe that the full effect of this feature of the bill was realized when it was framed and adopted, and it is impossible for me to assent to it in the form in which it is here cast.

The literacy test and the tests and restrictions which accompany it constitute an even more radical change in the policy of the nation. Hitherto we have generously kept our doors open to all who were not unfitted by reason of disease or incapacity for self-support or such personal records and antecedents as were likely to make them a menace to our peace and order or to the wholesome and essential relationships of life. In this bill it is proposed to turn away from tests of character and of quality and impose tests which exclude and restrict; for the new tests here embodied are not tests of quality or of character or of personal fitness, but tests of opportunity. Those who come seeking opportunity are not to be admitted unless they have already had one of the chief of the opportunities they seek, the opportunity of education. The object of such provisions is restriction, not selection.

If the people of this country have made up their minds to limit the number of immigrants by arbitrary tests and so reverse the policy of all the generations of Americans that have gone before them, it is their right to do so. I am their servant and have no license to stand in their way. But I do not believe that they have. I respectfully submit that no one can quote their mandate to that effect. Has any political party ever avowed a policy of restriction in this fundamental matter, gone to the country on it, and been commissioned to control its legislation? Does this bill rest upon the conscious and universal assent and desire of the American people? I doubt it. It is because I doubt it that I make bold to dissent from it.

337. *Alien and Domestic Reds, 1919*

Washington Post, December 24, 1919, in Bennett, *Editorials from Washington Post*, 479–80.

A FEW anarchists have been deported on a ship bound for Russia, and red Russia at that, while thousands of American citizens remain to spread treasonable doctrines, without any attempt by Congress to single out and punish domestic enemies.

The Department of Labor is under criticism on the allegation that it harbors officials who are pro-Bolshevik, and at heart enemies of the American Government. In these circumstances it seems strange that the department should have sent the Russian reds to a place where they will be free to mingle and conspire with the Lenin-Trotsky murderers. Why were the reds sent to soviet Russia, instead of to that part of Russia under control of loyal Russians? The action of this government will be construed as unfriendly by the Russians who are fighting against the Bolsheviki. . . .

In the meantime the enactment of legislation defining a domestic enemy, and imposing appropriate penalties upon American citizens convicted of crimes against their government, should engage the attention of Congress. The anarchists who have just been deported and the larger number of alien anarchists who remain are aided and encouraged by many well-known Americans who are becoming bolder and bolder in their advocacy of violence. . . .

The American citizen, native or naturalized, who willfully spreads the spirit of destruction and violence is a traitor. He deserves death. He lifts his hand against the government and the flag as truly as any traitor who gives aid and comfort to the enemy. If by speaking or writing he inculcates the doctrine of violence as a means of reform he is a willful, voluntary, dastardly coward and traitor, incurably vile, and an insufferable pollution of the air of true liberty. In strict justice he should suffer death, but as governments are more than tolerant, and as the United States has not the slightest conception of the damage that is wrought by these traitors, it is not to be expected that they will be given their dues.

The best that can be expected—the least that should be accepted by the people—is a law that will enable the courts to distinguish a criminal outrage of the rights of free speech and free assembly, and thereupon to deprive of the voting privilege and send to prison any citizen convicted of preaching, teaching or inculcating the doctrine of violence as a means of reform. . . . The man who scatters the firebrands of anarchy in his speech, and then, when called to account, takes refuge in the "right of free speech," is no better than the murderer who disguises himself in his victim's clothing in order to escape.

The strong hand of the United States must take hold of these native and naturalized criminals. The enemy is not without the gate, but within.

338. *A Clear and Present Danger*, 1919

Opinion of Mr. Justice Holmes, Schenck v. United States (1919), 249 U.S., 50–2.

THE DOCUMENT in question, upon its first printed side, recited the first section of the Thirteenth Amendment, said that the idea embodied in it was violated by the Conscription Act, and that a conscript is little better than a convict. . . . The other and later printed side of the sheet was headed "Assert Your Rights." It stated reasons for alleging that anyone violated the Constitution when he refused to recognize "your right to assert your opposition to the draft," and went on "If you do not assert and support your rights, you are helping to deny or disparage rights which it is the solemn duty of all citizens and residents of the United States to retain." It described the arguments on the other side as coming from cunning politicians and a mercenary capitalist press, and even silent consent to the conscription law as helping to support an infamous conspiracy. It denied the power to send our citizens away to foreign shores to shoot up the people of other lands, . . . winding up "You must do your share to maintain, support, and uphold the rights of the people of this country." Of course the document would not have been sent unless it had been intended to have some effect, and we do not see what effect it could be expected to have upon persons subject to the draft except to influence them to obstruct the carrying of it out. The defendants do not deny that the jury might find against them on this point.

But it is said, suppose that that was the tendency of this circular, it is protected by the First Amendment to the Constitution. . . .

We admit that in many places and in ordinary times the defendants in saying all that was said in the circular would have been within their constitutional rights. But the character of every act depends upon the circumstances in which it is done. . . . The most stringent protection of free speech would not protect a man in falsely shouting fire in a theater and causing a panic. It does not even protect a man from an injunction against uttering words that may have all the effect of force. . . . The question in every case is whether the words used are used in such circumstances and are of such a nature as to create a clear and present danger that they will bring about the substantive evils that Congress has a right to prevent. It is a question of proximity and degree. When a nation is at war many things that might be said in time of peace are such a hindrance to its effort that their utterance will not be endured so long as men fight and that no court could regard them as protected by any constitutional right.

339. *Sacco-Vanzetti, 1927*

Bartolomeo Vanzetti, Statement after sentencing, April 9, 1927, and letter to Dante Sacco, in M. D. Frankfurter and Gardner Jackson, *Letters of Sacco and Vanzetti* (New York, 1928), v, 321–3. Copyright 1928 by The Viking Press, Inc.

Statement After Sentencing

IF IT had not been for these thing, I might have to live out my life talking at street corners to scorning men. I might have die, unmarked, unknown, a failure. Now we are not a failure. This is our career and our triumph. Never in our full live could we hope to do such work for tolerance, for joostice, for man's onderstanding of man as now we do by accident. Our words—our lives—our pains—nothing! The taking of our lives—lives of a good shoemaker and a poor fish-peddler—all! That last moment belongs to us—that agony is our triumph.

Letter to Sacco's Son

My Dear Dante: I still hope, and we will fight until the last moment, to re-vindicate our right to live and to be free, but all the forces of the State and of the money and reaction are deadly against us because we are libertarians or anarchists.

I write little of this because you are now and yet too young to understand these things and other things of which I would like to reason with you.

But, if you do well, you will grow and understand your father's and my case and your father's and my principles, for which we will soon be put to death.

I tell you now that all I know of your father, he is not a criminal, but one of the bravest men I ever knew. Some day you will understand what I am about to tell you. That your father has sacrificed everything dear and sacred to the human heart and soul for his fate in liberty and justice for all. That day you will be proud of your father, and if you come brave enough, you will take his place in the struggle between tyranny and liberty and you will vindicate ... [our] names and our blood.

If we have to die now, you shall know, when you will be able to understand this tragedy in its fullest, how good and brave your father has been ... during these eight years of struggle, sorrow, passion, anguish and agony.... I would like you to also remember me as a comrade and friend to your father, your mother and Ines, Susie and you, and I assure you that neither have I been a criminal, that I have committed no robbery and no murder, but only fought modestily to abolish crimes from among mankind and for the liberty of all.

Remember Dante, each one who will say otherwise of your father and I, is a liar, insulting innocent dead men who have been brave in their life. Remember and know also, Dante, that if your father and I would have been cowards and hypocrits and rinnegetors of our faith, we would not have been put to death. They would not even have convicted a lebbrous dog; not even executed a deadly poisoned scorpion on such evidence as that they framed against us. They would have given a new trial to a matricide and abitual felon on the evidence we presented for a new trial.

Remember, Dante, remember always these things; we are not criminals; they convicted us on a frame-up; they denied us a new trial; and if we will be executed after seven years, four months and seventeen days of unspeakable tortures and wrong, it is for what I have already told you; because we were for the poor and against the exploitation and oppression of the man by the man.

The documents of our case, which you and other ones will collect and preserve, will prove to you that your father, your mother, Ines, my family and I have sacri-ficed by and to a State Reason of the American Plutocratic reaction.

The day will come when you will understand the atrocious cause of the above written words, in all its fullness. Then you will honor us.

Now Dante, be brave and good always. I embrace you.

P.S. I left the copy of *An American Bible* to your mother now, for she will like to read it, and she will give it to you when you will be bigger and able to understand it. Keep it for remembrance. It will also testify to you how good and generous Mrs. Gertrude Winslow has been with us all. Good-bye Dante.

XXXVIII ⁂ *Continuing Problems of International Peace*

THE WAR and the unsuccessful peace spread among Americans a deep suspicion with regard to the great powers of Europe (No. 340). In the next two decades this suspicion convinced many that isolation and neutrality were the only safe policies in the troubled era through which the Old World was passing (*see below*, No. 406). But from the start, other Americans recognized that the United States could not detach itself from the effects of events outside its borders; such men were determined to do what they could to restore international stability and prosperity by peaceful means. The United States was active in efforts toward disarmament and toward settlement of the financial problems of the 1920's. It was one of the prime movers of the Kellogg-Briand Pact renouncing the use of war (No. 341); and the program of reciprocal trade agreements stimulated steps toward the recovery of the world economy (No. 342).

Furthermore, long-standing American concern in the Orient could not be stifled. Although the United States, in the Lansing-Ishii agreements, had seemed to recognize the special interests of Japan in the Far East (No. 343), it returned to the traditional policy of respect for the open door and for the territorial integrity of China in the Nine-Power Treaty signed during the Washington Conference (No. 344). Meanwhile, unwillingness to grant the Philippines their independence made it clear that American interest in the Far East would persist (No. 345).

Japanese expansion in the 1930's, therefore, raised serious problems. Protests against her movement into Manchuria took the form of non-recognition (No. 346). There were also complaints about the violation of American rights after the China incident (No. 347). Disregard of these protests and the activities of the Italian and German aggressors in other parts of the world had already led the President to express the desire for a quarantine against aggressors (No. 348). But that desire was stated in vague and uncertain terms. What it meant was not yet apparent.

Given the situation in Europe and Asia, stability in American relations with Latin-America was evidently desirable. A significant effort was made to ease the bitter resentments left by earlier conflicts. The Coolidge administration took the first steps. But the new attitude was most clearly formulated in Franklin D. Roosevelt's policy of the "good neighbor" (No. 349). It involved the progressive modification of the conceptions of the Monroe Doctrine and the sharing of mutual responsibilities for the defense of the Western Hemisphere (No. 350). These intentions were made specific in a series of agreements from 1936 onward which proclaimed the solidarity of the American republics, established modes for co-ordinate efforts to prevent a war (No. 351), and, in the Declaration of Lima, set up the means of mutual defense (No. 352).

Meanwhile, the United States, in 1933, had also established diplomatic relations with the Soviet Union (No. 353).

340. *Unregenerate Europe, 1921*

Chicago Tribune, November 13, 1921, in *A Century of Tribune Editorials* (Chicago, 1947), 91–2.

IT IS natural that pacifists and excited humanitarians should stress the evil consequences of the World War at this time. It is equally natural that foreign statesmen and public agencies should join them in keeping this phase of the European situation before us. It gives a tremendous momentum to the pacifist propaganda, and it relieves the governments and peoples of Europe of a large part of their responsibility for the present condition of their affairs.

But the American mind should clear itself on this point. No one will deny that the war is responsible directly for a vast wastage of life and property. But what needs recognition and emphasis at this moment . . . is that had common sense and self-control governed the policies of the governments and the sentiments of the peoples of Europe their affairs would not be tottering now on the rim of chaos. . . .

It is chiefly the folly which has been persistently demonstrated by governments and people since the war that is responsible for Europe's condition today. It is because the moment hostilities ceased and the enemy was disarmed, victors and vanquished turned their backs on the healing and constructive principles they had solemnly asserted from time to time when matters were going against them at the battle front, that the European nations almost without exception have been going downhill. . . .

If we wish to know why Europe is in the present state, we cannot do better than to draw a parallel between the assertions of purpose and principle of the allies and "associated" powers in 1916, 1917, and 1918, and what has actually happened since November 11, 1918.

The war was a gigantic folly and waste. No one will deny that. But it was not so foolish nor so wasteful as the peace which has followed it. The European governments, . . . would have us believe they are mere victims of the war. They say nothing of what the war did for them. We might remind them that they profited as well as lost by the war. Many of them were freed from agelong tyranny. They got rid of kaisers and saber clattering aristocracies. They were given freedom, and their present state shows how little they have known how to profit by it. They have been given new territories and new resources, and they have shown how little

they deserve their good fortune. The last three years in Europe . . . have been marked by new wars and destruction, by new animosities and rivalries, by a refusal to face facts, make necessary sacrifices and compromises for financial and economic recovery, by greedy grabbing of territory and new adventures in the very imperialism which brought about the war.

It is well for Americans and their representatives to keep this in mind. . . . America would be foolish to contribute to the support of present methods or give any encouragement to the spirit which now prevails in the old world.

341. *Kellogg-Briand Pact,* 1929

Treaty for the Renunciation of War. Signed in Paris, August 27, 1928; proclaimed January 24, 1929. Department of State, *Publication,* No. 468 (Washington, 1933), 4–5.

ART. 1. The high contracting parties solemnly declare in the names of their respective peoples that they condemn recourse to war for the solution of international controversies, and renounce it as an instrument of national policy in their relations with one another.

Art. 2. The high contracting parties agree that the settlement or solution of all disputes or conflicts of whatever nature or of whatever origin they may be, which may arise among them, shall never be sought except by pacific means.

Art. 3. The present treaty shall be ratified by the high contracting parties named in the preamble in accordance with their respective constitutional requirements, and shall take effect as between them as soon as all their several instruments of ratification shall have been deposited at Washington.

This treaty shall, when it has come into effect as prescribed in the preceding paragraph, remain open as long as may be necessary for adherence by all the other powers of the world.

342. *Reciprocal Trade,* 1936

Cordell Hull, "Address Before the Chamber of Commerce of the United States, April 30, 1936," Department of State, *Commercial Policy Series,* No. 24 (Washington, 1936), 3–4, 6, 7–9.

A RAPID and drastic contraction of international trade of the kind that the world has witnessed during the past few years constitutes a double attack upon the economic well-being of each nation's population. The necessary materials habitually obtained in other parts of the globe be-

came more difficult to secure. The surplus national production habitually shipped to other countries becomes more difficult to sell. . . . The whole economic structure becomes disrupted. Vast unemployment ensues. . . . Financial investment and other forms of savings become impaired or are wholly destroyed. Distress spreads throughout the nation in ever-widening circles.

Economic distress quickly translates itself into social instability and political unrest. It opens the way for the demagogue and the agitator, foments international strife, and frequently leads to the supplanting of orderly democratic government by tyrannical dictatorships. It breeds international friction, fear, envy, and resentment, and destroys the very foundations of world peace. Nations are tempted to seek escape from distress at home in military adventures beyond their frontiers. And as fear of armed conflict spreads, even peace-loving nations are forced to divert their national effort from the creation of wealth and from peaceful well-being to the construction of armaments. Each step in the armament race bristles with new menace of economic disorganization and destruction, multiplies fear for the future, dislocates normal constructive processes of economic life, and leads to greater impoverishment of the world's population. . . .

The foreign-trade program of this Government is based fundamentally upon what to us is an indisputable assumption—namely, that our domestic recovery can be neither complete nor durable unless our surplus-creating branches of production succeed in regaining at least a substantial portion of their lost foreign markets. Our production of cotton, lard, tobacco, fruits, copper, petroleum products, automobiles, machinery, electrical and office appliances, and a host of other specialties is geared to a scale of operation the output of which exceeds domestic consumption by 10 to 50 per cent. In his message to Congress recommending the passage of the Trade Agreements Act, the President urged the need of restoring foreign markets in order that our surplus-producing industries may be "spared in part, at least, the heartbreaking readjustments that must be necessary if the shrink-

age of American foreign commerce remains permanent. . . ."

Since the end of the World War, we have revised our general tariff structure upward on three different occasions. The third and most drastic of these revisions, embodied in the Smoot-Hawley Tariff Act, occurred at the very outset of the depression, from the devastating effects of which the world is just beginning to recover. Through that ill-starred action, we helped to set into motion a vicious spiral of retaliation and counter-retaliation, and to start a race for a forcible contraction of international trade on a stupendous scale. In this race some nations have far outstripped us in the scope and effectiveness of restrictive action. Our export trade has become the victim of the formidable array of economic armament created by other nations, just as the export trade of other nations has likewise become the victim of our thrust into the heights of super-protectionism.

If international trade is to function again on an adequate scale, and if we are to regain our fair share of that trade, the nations of the world must retrace their steps from this supreme folly. . . . The nations, in the matter of tariffs, must embark upon a sound middle course between extreme economic internationalism and extreme economic nationalism. All excesses in the matter of trade barriers should be removed, and all unfair trade methods and practices should be abandoned.

When we were formulating our basic policy, there were two ways open to us to make our vital contribution to the process of economic demobilization. We could undertake a downward revision of our tariff by unilateral and autonomous action, in the hope that other nations would, as a result, also begin to move away from their present suicidal policies in the field of foreign trade. Or else we could, by the negotiation of bilateral trade agreements, attempt a mitigation of trade barriers on a reciprocal basis.

We chose the second course as offering

by far the better promise of trade improvement. . . . The bilateral method, combined with the principle of equality of treatment . . . contemplates simultaneous action by many countries and, in its effects, operates to drive down excessive trade barriers throughout the world. Moreover, it affords us an opportunity to secure in each country the relaxation of restrictions with respect to those of our export commodities the sale of which in that country's markets is either of special importance to us or else has been particularly hard-hit by recently established restrictions. It was in order to make possible the securing of such concessions for our export trade by negotiation with other countries that Congress empowered the President, for a three-year period, to conclude reciprocal trade agreements and, in connection with such agreements, to modify, within strictly defined limits, customs duties and other import restrictions operative in the United States.

343. *Lansing-Ishii Agreement, 1917*

Robert Lansing to Kikujiro Ishii, Japanese Ambassador on Special Mission, November 2, 1917, in *Papers Relating to the Foreign Relations of the United States, 1917* (Washington, 1926), 264.

THE GOVERNMENTS of the United States and Japan recognize that territorial propinquity creates special relations between countries, and consequently the Government of the United States recognizes that Japan has special interests in China, particularly in that part to which her possessions are contiguous.

The territorial sovereignty of China, nevertheless, remains unimpaired, and the Government of the United States has every confidence in the repeated assurances of the Imperial Japanese Government that while geographical position gives Japan such special interests, they have no desire to discriminate against the trade of other nations or to disregard the commercial rights heretofore granted by China in treaties with other powers.

The Governments of the United States and Japan deny that they have any purpose to infringe in any way the independence or territorial integrity of China, and they declare, furthermore, that they always adhere to the principle of the so-called Open Door or equal opportunity for commerce and industry in China.

Moreover, they mutually declare that they are opposed to the acquisiton by any government of any special rights or privileges that would affect the independence or territorial integrity of China, or that would deny to the subjects or citizens of any country the full enjoyment of equal opportunity in the commerce and industry of China.

344. *The Nine-Power Treaty, 1922*

Signed February 6, 1922. 67 Congress, 2 Session, *Senate Documents* (1921–22) Vol. X, Document 126, pp. 895–6.

ARTICLE I. The Contracting Powers, other than China, agree:

(1) To respect the sovereignty, the independence, and the territorial and administrative integrity of China;

(2) To provide the fullest and most unembarrassed opportunity to China to develop and maintain for herself an effective and stable government;

(3) To use their influence for the purpose of effactually establishing and maintaining the principle of equal opportunity

for the commerce and industry of all nations throughout the territory of China;

(4) To refrain from taking advantage of conditions in China in order to seek special rights or privileges which would abridge the rights of subjects or citizens of friendly States, and from countenancing action inimical to the security of such States....

ARTICLE III. With a view to applying more effectually the principles of the Open Door or equality of opportunity in China for the trade and industry of all nations, the Contracting Powers, other than China, agree that they will not seek, nor support their respective nationals in seeking:

(a) any arrangement which might purport to establish in favor of their interests any general superiority of rights with respect to commercial or economic development in any designated region of China;

(b) any such monopoly or preference as would deprive the nationals of any other Power of the right of undertaking any legitimate trade or industry in China, or of participating with the Chinese Government, or with any local authority, in any category of public enterprise, or which by reason of its scope, duration or geographical extent is calculated to frustrate

the practical application of the principle of equal opportunity....

China undertakes to be guided by the principles stated in the foregoing stipulations of this Article in dealing with applications for economic rights and privileges from governments and nationals of all foreign countries, whether parties to the present Treaty or not.

ARTICLE IV. The Contracting Powers agree not to support any agreements by their respective nationals with each other designed to create Spheres of Influence or to provide for the enjoyment of mutually exclusive opportunities in designated parts of Chinese territory....

ARTICLE VI. The Contracting Powers, other than China, agree fully to respect China's rights as a neutral in time of war to which China is not a party; and China declares that when she is a neutral she will observe the obligations of neutrality.

ARTICLE VII. The Contracting Powers agree that, whenever a situation arises which in the opinion of any one of them involves the application of the stipulations of the present Treaty, and renders desirable discussion of such application, there shall be full and frank communication between the Contracting Powers concerned.

345. *Philippine Independence, 1927*

President Coolidge's Veto Message, 1927, *The New York Times*, April 7, 1927, pp. 1, 4.

THE PROBLEMS which would arise from a status of independence ... should be seriously considered by the people of the Philippines. In noting the constructive advance which they have made on the road of progress under the American flag, the blessings of peace, security, hospitality, liberty and opportunity that they have enjoyed, they should not lose sight of the fact that without the material aid extended to them and which they still need these conditions could not have existed.

With a condition of peace, progress and prosperity hitherto unknown in their history, with self-government largely attained, with advantages enjoyed in many cases greater than those of American citizens, the people of the Philippines may well reflect seriously before wishing to embark on the unchartered stormy sea of independence, surrounded by unknown dangers, in a craft ill fitted for the difficulties to be met. Independence is an intangible ideal which has often brought disillusionment and disaster in its train. Peace, progress, prosperity, security, liberty and freedom are tangible benefits not lightly to be cast aside. The foundation of our policy has ever been the welfare of the people of the Philippines. That is today our constant goal.

The United States assumed its burden of responsibilities in the Philippine Islands, not in a spirit of aggression, of avarice, of exploitation, but with a sincere desire to promote the best interests of the people of the Islands. In that spirit it has guided them on the road of progress. It cannot, if it would, avoid the obligation of deciding the degree of self-government which the people of the Philippine Islands are capable of sustaining at any given time. The responsibility, both to the Philippine people and to civilization, is there. It cannot be shifted.

The ability of a people to govern themselves is not easily attained. History is filled with failures of popular government. It cannot be learned from books; it is not a matter of eloquent phrases. Liberty, freedom, independence, are not mere words the repetition of which brings fulfillment. They demand long, arduous, self-sacrificing preparation. Education, knowledge, experience, sound public opinion, intelligent participation by the great body of the people, high ideals—these things are essential. The degree in which they are possessed determines the capability of a people to govern themselves. In frankness and with the utmost friendliness, I must state my sincere conviction that the people of the Philippine Islands have not yet attained the capability of full self-government.

How can this ultimate goal best be attained? Certainly not by constant agitation and opposition. That policy but stands in the way of progress. In government, as in social relationships "liberty exists in proportion to wholesome self-restraint." Demonstration of the ability to carry on successfully the large powers of government already possessed would be far more convincing than continued agitation for complete independence.

Power brings responsibility to the people of the Philippines as well as to the people of the United States. Friendly cooperation in promoting the welfare of the Philippine Islands should be our constant aim. Along that road alone lies progress.

346. *The Issue in Manchuria,* 1932

Secretary of State Stimson to Senator Borah, February 23, 1932, Department of State, *Press Releases,* Publ. No. 295, pp. 204–5.

THE RECENT events . . . in China, especially the hostilities which having been begun in Manchuria and have latterly been extended to Shanghai, . . . have tended to bring home the vital importance of the faithful observance of the covenants therein to all of the nations interested in the Far East. . . . Regardless of cause or responsibility, it is clear beyond peradventure that a situation has developed which cannot, under any circumstances, be reconciled with the obligations of the covenants of these two treaties, and that if the treaties had been faithfully observed such a situation could not have arisen. The signatories of the Nine-Power Treaty and of the Kellogg-Briand Pact who are not parties to that conflict are not likely to see any reason for modifying the terms of those treaties. To them the real value of the faithful performance of the treaties has been brought sharply home by the perils and losses to which their nationals have been subjected in Shanghai.

That is the view of this Government. We see no reason for abandoning the enlightened principles which are embodied in these treaties. We believe that this situation would have been avoided had these covenants been faithfully observed, and no evidence has come to us to indicate that a due compliance with them would have interfered with the adequate protection of the legitimate rights in China of the signatories of those treaties and their nationals.

On January 7th last, upon the instruction of the President, this Government formally notified Japan and China that it would not recognize any situation, treaty, or agreement entered into by those Governments in violation of the covenants of these treaties, which affected the rights of our Government or its citizens in China. If a similar decision should be reached and a similar position taken by the other governments of the world, a caveat will be placed upon such action which, we believe, will effectively bar the legality hereafter of any title or right sought to be obtained by pressure or treaty violation, and which, as has been shown by history in the past, will eventually lead to the restoration to China of rights and titles of which she may have been deprived.

In the past our Government, as one of the leading powers on the Pacific Ocean, has rested its policy upon an abiding faith in the future of the people of China and upon the ultimate success in dealing with them on the principles of fair play, patience, and mutual good will. We appreciate the immensity of the task which lies before her statesmen in the development of her country and its Government. The delays in her progress, the instability of her attempts to secure a responsible government, were foreseen by Messrs. Hay and Hughes and their contemporaries and were the very obstacles which the policy of the Open Door was designed to meet. We concur with those statesmen, representing all the nations, in the Washington Conference who decided that China was entitled to the time necessary to accomplish her development. We are prepared to make that our policy for the future.

347. *American Rights in China, 1938*

United States Note to Japan Regarding Violation of American Rights in China, December 31, 1938. Department of State, *Press Releases* (1938), XIX, No. 483, pp. 491–2.

TREATIES which bear upon the situation in the Far East ... have constituted collectively an arrangement for safeguarding ... the correlated principles ... of national integrity and ... of equality of economic opportunity. Experience has shown that impairment of the former of these principles is followed almost invariably by disregard of the latter. Whenever any government begins to exercise political authority in areas beyond the limits of its lawful jurisdiction there develops inevitably a situation in which the nationals of that government demand and are accorded, at the hands of their government, preferred treatment, whereupon equality of opportunity ceases to exist and discriminatory practices, productive of friction, prevail.

The admonition that enjoyment by the nationals of the United States of nondiscriminatory treatment in China—a general and well-established right—is henceforth to be contingent upon an admission by the Government of the United States of the validity of the conception of Japanese authorities of a "new situation" and a "new order" in East Asia, is, in the opinion of this Government, highly paradoxical.

This country's adherence to and its advocacy of the principle of equality of opportunity do not flow solely from a desire to obtain ... commercial benefits. ... They flow from a firm conviction that observance of that principle leads to economic and political stability. . . . The principle of equality of economic opportunity is, moreover, one to which over a long period and on many occasions the Japanese Government has given definite approval. . . .

The people and the Government of the United States could not assent to the establishment, at the instance of and for the special purposes of any third country, of a regime which would arbitrarily deprive them of the long-established rights of equal opportunity and fair treatment which are legally and justly theirs along with those of other nations. . . .

With regard to the implication in the Japanese Government's note that the "conditions of today and tomorrow" in the Far East call for a revision of the ideas and principles of the past, this Government desires to recall to the Japanese Government its position on the subject of revision of agreements.

This Government had occasion in the course of a communication delivered to the Japanese Government on April 29, 1934, to express its opinion that "treaties can lawfully be modified or be terminated, but only by processes prescribed or recognized or agreed upon by the parties to them."

In the same communication this Government also said, "In the opinion of the American people and the American Government no nation can, without the assent of the other nations concerned, rightfully endeavor to make conclusive its will in situations where there are involved the rights, the obligations and the legitimate interests of other sovereign states.". . .

In the light of these facts, and with reference especially to the purpose and the character of the treaty provisions from time to time solemnly agreed upon for the very definite purposes indicated, the Government of the United States deprecates the fact that one of the parties to these agreements has chosen to embark . . . upon a course directed toward the arbitrary creation . . . regardless of treaty pledges . . . of a "new order" in the Far East. Whatever may be the changes which have taken place in the situation in the Far East and whatever may be the situation now, these matters are of no less interest and concern to the American Government than have been the situations which have prevailed there in the past, and such changes as may henceforth take place there, changes which may enter into the producing of a "new situation" and a "new order," are and will be of like concern to this Government. This Government is also well aware that the situation has changed. . . . This Government does not admit, however, that there is need or warrant for any one power to take upon itself to prescribe what shall be the terms and conditions of a "new order" in areas not under its sovereignty and to constitute itself the repository of authority and the agent of destiny in regard thereto.

348. A *Quarantine of Aggressors*, 1937

F. D. Roosevelt, Address at Chicago, Illinois, October 5, 1937, in "Development of United States Foreign Policy," 77 Congress, 2 Session, *Senate Documents*, No. 188, pp. 21–4.

THE HIGH aspirations expressed in the Briand-Kellogg Peace Pact . . . have of late given way to a haunting fear of calamity. The present reign of terror and international lawlessness began a few years ago . . . through unjustified interference in the internal affairs of other nations or the invasion of alien territory in violation of treaties; . . . now . . . the very foundations of civilization are seriously threatened. The landmarks and traditions which have marked the progress of civilization toward a condition of law, order and justice are being wiped away.

Without a declaration of war and without warning or justification of any kind, civilians, including vast numbers of women and children, are being ruthlessly murdered with bombs from the air. In times of so-called peace, ships are being attacked and sunk by submarines without cause or notice. Nations are fomenting and taking sides in civil warfare in nations that have never done them any harm. Nations claiming freedom for themselves deny it to others. . . .

If those things come to pass in other parts of the world, let no one imagine that America will escape, that America may expect mercy, that this Western Hemisphere will not be attacked and that it will continue tranquilly and peacefully to carry on the ethics and the arts of civilization.

If those days come, "there will be no safety by arms, no help from authority, no answer in science. The storm will rage till every flower of culture is trampled and all human beings are leveled in a vast chaos."

If those days are not to come to pass— if we are to have a world in which we can breathe freely and live in amity without fear—the peace-loving nations must make a concerted effort to uphold laws and principles on which alone peace can rest secure.

The peace-loving nations must make a concerted effort in opposition to those violations of treaties and those ignorings of humane instincts which today are creating a state of international anarchy and instability from which there is no escape through mere isolation or neutrality.

Those who cherish their freedom and recognize and respect the equal right of their neighbors to be free and live in peace must work together for the triumph of law and moral principles in order that peace, justice and confidence may prevail

in the world. There must be a return to a belief in the pledged word, in the value of a signed treaty. There must be recognition of the fact that national morality is as vital as private morality. . . .

There is a solidarity and interdependence about the modern world, both technically and morally, which makes it impossible for any nation completely to isolate itself from economic and political upheavals in the rest of the world. . . . There can be no stability or peace either within nations or between nations except under laws and moral standards adhered to by all. International anarchy destroys every foundation for peace. It jeopardizes either the immediate or the future security of every nation, large or small. It is, therefore, a matter of vital interest and concern to the people of the United States that the sanctity of international treaties and the maintenance of international morality be restored.

The overwhelming majority of the peoples and nations of the world today want to live in peace. . . . The peace, the freedom and the security of ninety percent of the population of the world is being jeopardized by the remaining ten percent. . . . Surely the ninety percent . . . can and must find some way to make their will prevail.

The situation is definitely of universal concern. The questions involved relate not merely to violations of specific provisions of particular treaties; they are questions of war and of peace, of international law and especially of principles of humanity. It is true that they involve definite violations of agreements, and especially of the Covenant of the League of Nations, the Briand-Kellogg Pact and the Nine-Power Treaty. But they also involve problems of world economy, world security and world humanity.

It is true that the moral consciousness of the world must recognize the importance of removing injustices and well-founded grievances; but at the same time it must be aroused to the cardinal necessity of honoring sanctity of treaties, of respecting the rights and liberties of others and of putting an end to acts of international aggression.

It seems to be unfortunately true that the epidemic of world lawlessness is spreading. When an epidemic of physical disease starts to spread, the community approves and joins in a quarantine of the patients in order to protect the health of the community against the spread of the disease.

It is my determination to pursue a policy of peace. It is my determination to adopt every practicable measure to avoid involvement in war. It ought to be inconceivable that in this modern era, and in the face of experience, any nation could be so foolish and ruthless as to run the risk of plunging the whole world into war by invading and violating, in contravention of solemn treaties, the territory of other nations that have done them no real harm and are too weak to protect themselves adequately. Yet the peace of the world and the welfare and security of every nation, including our own, is today being threatened by that very thing. . . .

War is a contagion, whether it be declared or undeclared. It can engulf states and peoples remote from the original scene of hostilities. We are determined to keep out of war, yet we cannot insure ourselves against the disastrous effects of war and the dangers of involvement. We are adopting such measures as will minimize our risk of involvement, but we cannot have complete protection in a world of disorder in which confidence and security have broken down. . . .

Most important of all, the will for peace on the part of peace-loving nations must express itself to the end that nations that may be tempted to violate their agreements and the rights of others will desist from such a course. There must be positive endeavors to preserve peace.

America hates war. America hopes for peace. Therefore, America actively engages in the search for peace.

349. *The Good Neighbor, 1936*

F. D. Roosevelt, Speech at Chautauqua, New York, August 14, 1936. In *Peace and War. United States Foreign Policy 1931–1941* (Washington, 1943), 323–5.

LONG before I returned to Washington as President of the United States I had made up my mind that, pending what might be called a more opportune moment on other continents, the United States could best serve the cause of peaceful humanity by setting an example. That was why on the 4th of March, 1933, I made the following declaration:

In the field of world policy I would dedicate this nation to the policy of the good neighbor—the neighbor who resolutely respects himself and, because he does so, respects the rights of others—the neighbor who respects his obligations and respects the sanctity of his agreements in and with a world of neighbors.

This declaration represents my purpose; but it represents more than a purpose, for it stands for a practice. To a measurable degree it has succeeded; the whole world now knows that the United States cherishes no predatory ambitions. We are strong; but less powerful nations know that they need not fear our strength. We seek no conquest: we stand for peace.

In the whole of the Western Hemisphere our good-neighbor policy has produced results that are especially heartening.

The noblest monument to peace and to neighborly economic and social friendship in all the world is not a monument in bronze or stone, but the boundary which unites the United States and Canada—3,000 miles of friendship with no barbed wire, no gun or soldier, and no passport on the whole frontier.

Mutual trust made that frontier—to extend the same sort of mutual trust throughout the Americas was our aim.

The American republics to the south of us have been ready always to cooperate with the United States on a basis of equality and mutual respect, but before we inaugurated the good-neighbor policy there was among them resentment and fear, because certain administrations in Washington had slighted their national pride and their sovereign rights.

In pursuance of the good-neighbor policy, and because in my younger days I had learned many lessons in the hard school of experience, I stated that the United States was opposed definitely to armed intervention.

We have negotiated a Pan American convention embodying the principle of non-intervention. We have abandoned the Platt Amendment which gave us the right to intervene in the internal affairs of the Republic of Cuba. We have withdrawn American marines from Haiti. We have signed a new treaty which places our relations with Panama on a mutually satisfactory basis. We have undertaken a series of trade agreements with other American countries to our mutual commercial profit. At the request of two neighboring republics, I hope to give assistance in the final settlement of the last serious boundary dispute between any of the American nations.

350. *Fair Dealing Among Nations, 1936*

Secretary of State Cordell Hull, "Opening Address to the Inter-American Conference for the Maintenance of Peace," Buenos Aires, December 5, 1936, Department of State, *Conference Series*, No. 25, pp. 12–14.

INTERNATIONAL agreements have lost their force and reliability as a basis of relations between nations. This extremely ominous and fateful development constitutes the most dangerous single phenomenon in the world of today; not international law merely, but that which is higher—moral law—and the whole integrity and honor of governments are in danger of being ruthlessly trampled upon. There has been a failure of the spirit. There is no task more urgent than that of remaking the basis of trusted agreement between nations. They must ardently seek the terms of new agreements and stand behind them with unfailing will. The vitality of international agreements must be restored.

If the solemn rights and obligations between nations are to be treated lightly or brushed aside, the nations of the world will head straight toward international anarchy and chaos. . . . Trust in each nation's honor and faith in its given word must be restored by the concerted resolve of all governments.

It is to the interest of everyone that there be an end of treaties broken by arbitrary unilateral action. Peaceful procedure, agreements between the signatories, and mutual understanding must be restored as the means of modifying or ending international agreements.

In the accomplishment of the high aims and purposes of this eightfold program, the people of every nation have an equal interest. We of this hemisphere have reason to hope that these great objectives may receive the support of all peoples. If peace and progress are to be either maintained or advanced, the time is overripe for renewed effort on each nation's part. There can be no delay. Through past centuries, the human race fought its way up from the low level of barbarism and war to that of civilization and peace. This accomplishment has only been partial, and it may well be but temporary. . . .

The nations of this continent should omit no word or act in their attempt to meet the dangerous conditions which endanger peace. Let our actions here at Buenos Aires constitute the most potent possible appeal to peacemakers and warmakers throughout the world.

So only does civilization become real.

So only can we rightly ask that universal support which entitles governments to speak for their peoples to the world not with the voice of propaganda but with that of truth. Having affirmed our faith, we should be remiss if we were to leave anything undone which will tend to assure our peace here and make us powerful for peace elsewhere. In a very real sense, let this continent set the high example of championing the forces of peace, democracy, and civilization.

351. *To Prevent War, 1937*

"Maintenance, Preservation and Reestablishment of Peace. Convention between the United States of America and Other American Republics," Department of State, *Treaty Series,* No. 922 (Washington, 1937), 1–5.

THE GOVERNMENTS represented at the Inter-American Conference for the Maintenance of Peace,

Considering:

That according to the statement of Franklin D. Roosevelt, the President of the United States, to whose lofty ideals the meeting of this Conference is due, the measures to be adopted by it "would advance the cause of world peace, inasmuch as the agreements which might be reached would supplement and reinforce the efforts of the League of Nations and of all other existing or future peace agencies in seeking to prevent war";

That every war or threat of war affects directly or indirectly all civilized peoples and endangers the great principles of liberty and justice which constitute the American ideal and the standard of American international policy;

That the Treaty of Paris of 1928 (Kellogg-Briand Pact) has been accepted by almost all the civilized states, whether or not members of other peace organizations, and that the Treaty of Non-Aggression and Conciliation of 1933 (Saavedra Lamas Pact signed at Rio de Janeiro) has the ap-

proval of the twenty-one American Republics represented in this Conference,

Have resolved to give contractual form to these purposes by concluding the present Convention.

ARTICLE 1. In the event that the peace of the American Republics is menaced, and in order to coordinate efforts to prevent war, any of the Governments of the American Republics signatory to the Treaty of Paris of 1928 or to the Treaty of Non-Aggression and Conciliation of 1933, or to both, whether or not a member of other peace organizations, shall consult with the other governments of the American Republics, which, in such event, shall consult together for the purpose of finding and adopting methods of peaceful cooperation.

ARTICLE 2. In the event of war, or a virtual state of war between American States, the governments of the American Republics represented at this Conference shall undertake without delay the necessary mutual consultations, in order to exchange views and to seek, within the obligations resulting from the pacts above-mentioned and from the standards of international morality, a method of peaceful collaboration; and, in the event of an international war outside America which might menace the peace of the American Republics, such consultation shall also take place to determine the proper time and manner in which the signatory states, if they so desire, may eventually cooperate in some action tending to preserve the peace of the American continent.

ARTICLE 3. It is agreed that any question regarding the interpretation of the present Convention, which it has not been possible to settle through diplomatic channels, shall be submitted to the procedure of conciliation provided by existing agreements, or to arbitration or to judicial settlement. . . .

ARTICLE 5. The present Convention shall remain in effect indefinitely but may be denounced by means of one year's notice, after the expiration of which period the Convention shall cease in its effects as regards the party which denounces it but shall remain in effect for the remaining signatory States. Denunciations shall be addressed to the Government of the Argentine Republic, which shall transmit them to the other contracting States.

352. *Declaration of Lima, 1938*

"Declaration of the Solidarity of America, December 24, 1938, Eighth International Conference of American States," Department of State, *Press Releases* (1938), XIX, No. 482, pp. 474–5.

THE Eighth International Conference of American States

Considering:

That the peoples of America have achieved spiritual unity through the similarity of their republican institutions, their unshakable will for peace, their profound sentiment of humanity and tolerance, and through their absolute adherence to the principles of international law, of the equal sovereignty of states and of individual liberty without religious or racial prejudices;

That on the basis of such principles and will, they seek and defend the peace of the continent and work together in the cause of universal concord;

That respect for the personality, sovereignty, and independence of each American state constitutes the essence of international order sustained by continental solidarity, which historically has found expression in declarations of various states, or in agreements which were applied, and sustained by new declarations and by treaties in force;

That the Inter-American Conference for the Maintenance of Peace, held at Buenos Aires, approved on December 21, 1936,

the declaration of the principles of inter-American solidarity and cooperation, and approved, on December 23, 1936, the protocol of nonintervention; the Governments of the American States

Declare:

First. That they reaffirm their continental solidarity and their purpose to collaborate in the maintenance of the principles upon which the said solidarity is based;

Second. That faithful to the above-mentioned principles and to their absolute sovereignty, they reaffirm their decision to maintain them and to defend them against all foreign intervention or activity that may threaten them;

Third. And in case the peace, security or territorial integrity of any American republic is thus threatened by acts of any nature that may impair them, they proclaim their common concern and their determination to make effective their solidarity, coordinating their respective sovereign wills by means of the procedure of consultation, established by conventions in force and by declarations of the inter-American conferences, using the measures which in each case the circumstances may make advisable. It is understood that the Governments of the American Republics will act independently in their individual capacity, recognizing fully their juridical equality as sovereign states;

Fourth. That in order to facilitate the consultations established in this and other American peace instruments, the Ministers for Foreign Affairs of the American Repub-lics, when deemed desirable and at the initiative of any one of them, will meet in their several capitals by rotation and without protocolary character. Each government may, under special circumstances or for special reasons, designate a representative as a substitute for its Minister of Foreign Affairs;

Fifth. This Declaration shall be known as the "Declaration of Lima."

353. *Relations with the Soviet Union, 1933*

F. D. Roosevelt to Maxim Litvinov, November 16, 1933, in F. D. Roosevelt, *Public Papers and Addresses* (New York, 1938–50), II, 474–5.

I AM glad to have received the assurance expressed in your note to me of this date that it will be the fixed policy of the Government of the Union of Soviet Socialist Republics:

1. To respect scrupulously the indisputable right of the United States to order its own life within its own jurisdiction in its own way and to refrain from interfering in any manner in the internal affairs of the United States, its territories or possessions.

2. To refrain, and to restrain all persons in government service and all organizations of the government or under its direct or indirect control, including organizations in receipt of any financial assistance from it, from any act overt or covert liable in any way whatsoever to injure the tranquillity, prosperity, order, or security of the whole or any part of the United States, its territories or possessions, and, in particular, from any act tending to incite or encourage armed intervention, or any agitation or propaganda having as an aim, the violation of the territorial integrity of the United States, its territories or possessions, or the bringing about by force of a change in the political or social order of the whole or any part of the United States, its territories or possessions.

3. Not to permit the formation or residence on its territory of any organization or group—and to prevent the activity on its territory of any organization or group, or of representatives or officials of any organization or group—which makes claim to be the Government of, or makes attempt upon the territorial integrity of, the United States, its territories or possessions; not to form, subsidize, support or permit on its territory military organizations or groups having the aim of armed struggle against the United States, its territories or possessions, and to prevent any recruiting on behalf of such organizations and groups.

4. Not to permit the formation or residence on its territory of any organization or group—and to prevent the activity on its territory of any organization or group, or of representatives or officials of any organization or group—which has as an aim the overthrow or the preparation for the overthrow of, or the bringing about by force of a change in, the political or social order of the whole or any part of the United States, its territories or possessions.

It will be the fixed policy of the Executive of the United States within the limits of the powers conferred by the Constitution and the laws of the United States to adhere reciprocally to the engagements above expressed.

XXXIX 𑁋 *The Economy in Prosperity and Depression*

THE POST-WAR boom blinded many Americans to the dangers that lay concealed in their economic system. Yet even before 1929, serious observers saw signs of weakness there (No. 354). Prices and values, spiraling upward, rested on a very flimsy base. When the base began to teeter, the whole structure disintegrated. The financial panic of 1929 led to a complete collapse of the speculative boom in securities. But the long depression that ensued revealed still deeper weaknesses in the whole American economy.

The farm problem remained as burdensome as ever. Even the well-to-do agriculturalists suffered; and the marginal farmers plunged over the brink of disaster (No. 355). Industrial labor also entered upon a trying period. Unemployment mounted rapidly, and remained high through the decade of the 1930's (No. 356). Some of the more severe hardships of the first years of depression (No. 357) were alleviated by relief measures. But it did not prove possible to put all those who wished to work back on their jobs.

The depression called renewed attention to certain long-standing problems glossed over in more prosperous years. Continued concentration of control evoked charges of monopoly when numerous small businesses went to the wall, incapable of holding out against their larger competitors (No. 358). Yet the essential strength of the American capacity to produce still surprised foreign observers, even those from the Soviet Union (No. 359). The problem that confronted the country was how in the future to use the elements of strength and how to eliminate the sources of weakness.

354. *Economic Trends of the 1920's*

National Bureau of Economic Research, *Recent Economic Changes in the United States* (New York, 1929), II, 862–8, 873–7, 909–10. Copyright 1928 by The McGraw-Hill Book Company and used with permission.

How the United States managed to attain a higher per capita income in 1922–1927 than ever before, though conditions in most other countries were not favorable, and though its basic industry, agriculture, was depressed, is the outstanding problem of the cycles of 1921–1924, 1924–1927 and 1927 to date.... Many partial answers to this question ... may be condensed into one: since 1921, Americans have applied intelligence to the day's work more effectively than ever before.... The old process of putting science into industry has been followed more intensively than before; it has been supplemented by tentative efforts to put science into business management, trade-union policy, and government administration.

Concrete instances of technical improvements in many mining, metallurgical, and fabricating processes are given in the chapters on industry. The remarkable results achieved are demonstrated statistically from census data showing output per worker. Similar, though less striking, instances appear in ... construction. Without help from any extraordinary invention, the railroads also have attained a higher level of operating efficiency. In farming there is an intriguing report of new machines and new methods coming into use. Here too, the record of average output per worker shows considerable gains.

All this means that since 1921 Americans have found ways of producing more physical goods per hour of labor than before. They have received larger average incomes because they have produced more commodities and services. That is true in the aggregate, although not all who have contributed to the increase in physical production have shared in the increase of real income....

While the details of the latest technical advances always possess thrilling interest, perhaps there is more of promise for the future in ... recent changes in economic policy. The efforts to apply scientific methods to such matters are in an early stage of development. The sciences which underlie these efforts—psychology, sociology, economics—are far less advanced than physics and chemistry. The experts who are making the applications—personnel managers, advertising specialists, sales directors, business economists and statisticians—are less rigorously trained than engineers. It is even harder to measure the results they achieve than to determine what difference a new machine makes in unit costs. Nor are business executives so generally convinced of the practical value of the rather intangible services which the new professions can render as they are of the indispensability of engineering advice. Yet it is conceivable that applications of the social sciences, now in their tentative stage, will grow into contributions of great moment to economic welfare. Certainly ... many enterprising business concerns and some enterprising trade unions are trying new policies, and often getting results which they deem good.

Perhaps none of the changes reported here will prove more important in the long run than the change in the economic theories on which the American Federation of Labor and certain outside unions are acting. That organizations of wage earners should grasp the relations between productivity and wages, and that they should take the initiative in pressing constructive plans for increasing efficiency upon employers, is not wholly without precedent; but the spread of such ideas and the vigor with which they are acted on by large organizations must startle those who have believed that trade unions are brakes upon economic progress.

Scarcely less significant is the report from the employing side.... The art of business management turned a corner in 1921, cultivating since then more skillful understanding of the whole situation and nicer adjustment of means to the immediate environment. Numerous corporations and some trade associations are maintaining research bureaus of their own. Among the managerial devices experimented with, are coordinated staffs in place of one "big boss," bonus payments to executives and "incentive wages" for the rank and file, operating budgets, forecasts of business conditions, close inventory control, personnel management and employee representation. Most of these devices are attempts to understand and to utilize the psychological forces which control human behavior, or the economic forces which control business activity. "There is today not only more production per man, more wages per man and more horsepower per man; there is also more management per man.". . . Even marketing is being permeated by applied psychology. Costly investigations of "consumer appeal," of advertising "pull," of "sales resistance". . . show that sales managers are trying to base their planning upon factual studies of human behavior. And the rapid spread of chain stores and of installment selling show that marketing methods are no more standing still than is industrial technique. . . .

Among the consequences which improvements in industrial technique or in business methods produce in an individualistic state, are hardships of various kinds. The victims are partly business competitors who are a bit slow in adopting new methods; partly industries or geographic regions affected indirectly; partly individuals who find their services no longer needed. To follow all the complicated difficulties produced by recent economic advances in the United States is out of the question; but a few chains of cause and effect may be traced link by link. . . .

The technical advances of recent years in the United States have been largely advances in the direction of more economical production. A greater volume of goods has been turned out at lower costs per unit. Now larger supplies sent to market tend to depress prices. . . . The remarkable fact is that prices sagged through the prosperous year 1926. Taking the whole period from 1922 to 1927, the trend has been a gently declining one. Prices at wholesale have fallen at the rate of 0.1 per cent per annum. . . .

Sagging prices make it harder to conduct business with profit because many of the expenses of an enterprise are fixed by long contracts or by understandings hard to alter, and cannot be cut to offset a reduction in selling rates. . . . Concerns in the van of technical progress have done handsomely. But the prices at which they could market their large outputs with profit to themselves have meant loss and even failure to less aggressive rivals. . . . The average number of failures in 1922–1927 has actually exceeded the number in 1921, but the total and the average liabilities have grown smaller. . . .

Scarcely less characteristic of our period than unit-cost reductions is the rapid expansion in the production and sale of products little used or wholly unknown a generation or even a decade ago. Among consumers' goods, the conspicuous instances are automobiles, radios and rayon. But the list includes also oil-burning furnaces, gas stoves, household electrical appliances in great variety, automobile accessories, antifreezing mixtures, cigarette lighters, propeller pencils, wrist watches, airplanes, and what not. Among producers' goods we have the truck and the tractor competing with the horse and the mule, reinforced concrete competing with brick and lumber, the high-tension line competing with the steam engine, fuel oil competing with coal, not to mention excavating machines, belt conveyors, paint sprayers, and "automatics" of many sorts competing with manual labor.

Changes in taste are in large part merely the consumers' response to the solicitation of novel products, effectively presented by advertising. But that is not all of the story; the consumer is free to choose what he likes among the vociferous offerings, and sometimes reveals traces of initiative. . . . Americans are consuming fewer calories per capita; they are eating less wheat and corn but more dairy products, vegetable oils, sugar, fresh vegetables and fruit. More families than ever before are sending their sons and daughters to college—surely that is not a triumph of "high-powered" salesmanship. Young children, girls and women, are wearing lighter and fewer clothes. The short skirt, the low shoe, the silk or rayon stocking, "athletic" underwear, the soft collar, sporting suits and sporting goods, have an appeal which makers of rival articles have not been able to overcome. And, in a sense, every consumers' good, from college to candy, is a rival of every other consumers' good, besides being a rival of the savings bank.

"When the makers of one product get a larger slice of the consumer's dollar, the slices left for the makers of other products get smaller." This way of accounting for the hardships met by certain long-established industries in 1922–1927, such, for example, as the leather and woolen trades, is popular and sound, so far as it goes. But it does not take account of the fact that desire for new goods, or the pressure of installment purchases once made, may lead people to work harder or more steadily, and so get more dollars to spend. Presumably the enticements of automobiles and radios, of wrist watches and electric refrigerators, of correspondence courses and college, have steadied many youths, set many girls hunting for jobs and kept many fathers of families to the mark. Also a considerable part of the country's former bill for intoxicants has been available to spend in other ways. . . . Consumption per capita has increased in volume to match the increased per capita output of consumers' goods taken altogether. Yet the increase in consumption has not been rapid enough to prevent shifts in the kind of goods bought from pressing hard upon the makers of articles waning in popular favor. . . .

Among all the hardships imposed by increasing efficiency, most publicity has been given to the decline in the number of wage earners employed by factories. That is a matter of the gravest concern in view of the millions of families affected or threatened by the change, and in view of their slender resources. To it special attention has been paid in this investigation.

The new phrase coined to describe what is happening, "technological unemployment," designates nothing new in the facts, though the numbers affected may be large beyond precedent. . . .

To recall these familiar facts should not diminish by one jot our rating of the hardships suffered by men who are thrown out of jobs. They and their families often undergo severe privation before new employment can be found; the new jobs may pay less than the old or be less suitable; too often the displaced man never finds a new opening. Technical progress is continually made at cost to individuals who have committed no fault and committed no avoidable error of judgment. No organized plan has been evolved for preventing such hardships, aside from the schemes devised by some trade unions for tiding their members over mechanical revolutions in their crafts. . . .

Forecasting the future is no part of the present task. But we should not close the record without noting that recent developments may appear less satisfactory in retrospect than they appear at present.

Even on the face of affairs, all is not well. . . . The condition of agriculture, the volume of unemployment, the textile trades, coal mining, the leather industries, present grave problems not only to the people immediately concerned, but also to their fellow citizens. How rapidly these conditions will mend, we do not know. Some may grow worse.

Nor can we be sure that the industries now prosperous will prolong indefinitely their recent record of stability. . . . If we are to maintain business prosperity, we must continue to earn it month after month and year after year by intelligent effort. The incomes disbursed to consumers, and to wage earners in particular, must be increased on a scale sufficient to pay for the swelling volume of consumers' goods sent to market. The credit structure must be kept in due adjustment to the earnings of business enterprises. Security prices must not outrun prospective profits capitalized at the going rate of interest. Commodity stocks must be held in line with current sales. Over-commitments of all sorts must be avoided. The building of new industrial equipment must be not overrapid. These and the similar matters which might be mentioned present delicate problems of management which will find their practical solutions in the daily decisions of business executives.

355. *Disadvantaged Farmers, 1938*

C. C. Taylor, H. W. Wheeler, and E. L. Kirkpatrick, *Disadvantaged Classes in American Agriculture* (Washington, 1938), 9, 18, 19, 20, 22, 27–38, 39, 48.

APPROXIMATELY 7,700,000 persons lived in farm-operator households whose income was below $600 in 1929. To these should be added an estimated 6,000,000 members of married farm laborers' families, the great majority of which have incomes below this level. Thus probably more than 13,000,000 farm persons are living in what might be called slum homes. Even more forbidding is the fact that of the 1,700,000 farm-operator families with incomes below $600, approximately 900,000 had incomes of less than $400 in 1929, and approximately 400,000 had incomes of less than $250. . . .

Farm families with gross farm income of $600 or less per year are scattered widely throughout the nation and can be found in all states and in almost all counties. They are much more prevalent, however, in some areas than in others, and in many counties they constitute more than 50 per cent of all farm families. . . . They tend to concentrate in well-marked areas —the Appalachian-Ozark Highlands, the Cotton Belt, the Lake States Cut-Over, and northern New Mexico and Arizona. . . .

Low income is prevalent in all of the bad-land areas; it pretty well blankets the Southern tenancy area, but does not prevail in the Northern tenant belt. . . . There is very little relationship between low income areas and heavy farm-labor areas, because the more prosperous farms in the nation are the ones that employ the great mass of farm laborers, and because sharecropping is substituted for wage labor to a great extent throughout the Cotton Belt. . . .

The systematic, gradual path to land ownership, which has been virtually synonymous with success in agriculture, is allegedly accomplished by way of the so-called "agricultural ladder." The assumption is that the ambitious beginner starts his climb as a hired hand, serves an indeterminate apprenticeship in this capacity, then steps rung by rung from wage-worker to sharecropper, tenant, and eventual owner. Whether this process works or not, the farm laborer occupies the lowest rung on this agricultural ladder and is today finding it increasingly difficult to move up even to the next higher rung as sharecropper or tenant; the prospect of eventual land ownership is scarcely within the realm of possibility for the great majority. . . .

The agricultural labor class included almost one out of every five workers gainfully employed in agriculture in 1930. During the peak season in that year, there were over 2,700,000 paid farm laborers in the United States. If this number were swelled by those counted as croppers in the 1930 Census, the number would have been almost 3½ millions. If, in addition, these included the 1,600,000 unpaid family workers reported in the 1930 Census, the number would have been over 5,000,000, exclusive of those migratory workers of whom there is no accurate count. . . .

Not all farm laborers are definitely disadvantaged or handicapped in the opportunity to advance to farm management or ownership. Some are young persons who are serving an apprenticeship in agriculture, so to speak, and will sooner or later find themselves renters or owners of farms. In the meantime, they are accumulating capital and experience, in keeping with the theory by which the agricultural ladder is presumed to work. However, with the ascent growing steadily slower and more difficult, many of them will never move above their present status. Many farm laborers are no longer young men, and even if they manage to climb to that next higher step, and into tenancy, they will be poor prospects for farm ownership. . . .

The farm laborers stand at the bottom of the social as well as the economic ladder. During periods of low farm-commodity prices they, together with other farm people, suffer a decline in annual income. During periods of pronounced depression, they must meet the competition of urban migrants seeking farm employment as well as other farm people who are seeking to supplement their depleted resources. During periods of high prices, the farm laborer's wages and perquisites increase, but he is not in a position to gain by rising land values, nor, because of competition for farms, does he find it easier to become a renter or owner. . . .

The farm laborer at best is a young man who is working as a hired laborer only temporarily, while he is accumulating enough capital to buy a team of horses and some farm machinery in order to start farming as a renter. He is perhaps one of the neighbor boys who is working for a man whom he has known all his life. He probably lives as a part of that man's family and is definitely starting the climb up the agricultural ladder.

At worst, these laborers are part of that great mass of migratory farm workers whose paths weave a network over three-fourths of the states in this country. . . . The living conditions of this latter group are admittedly deplorable and shocking.

. . . Their unfortunate situation is accentuated by the prejudice of local communities against absorbing migrant workers, both because of their undesirability and because it will probably increase their relief burden and other community expenses. They lack health protection and school opportunities, and have difficulty in getting public relief because they have no legal residence. Frequent campaigns to enforce local vagrancy ordinances, and the exercise of border controls against their interstate migration add to their difficulties. There is no opportunity for community participation of any kind. . . .

The existence of almost 3,000,000 tenant families, the members of whose households constitute approximately 13,000,000 farm people, sets a social problem of the first magnitude with which the nation must wrestle in an intelligent and constructive way, for farm tenancy in many of its aspects is a disadvantaging condition in the lives of those who live and work in that status. The fact that the rate of tenancy has moved up from 25.6 per cent in 1880 to 42.1 per cent in 1935, and the fact that the number of farm tenant families has almost trebled between 1880 and 1935 clearly indicate that this condition is being aggravated rather than alleviated as time goes on.

Not every farm tenant family is living in poverty nor under economic and social conditions from which it cannot extricate itself. Thousands are tenants by choice. They prefer to invest their capital in operating equipment and handle relatively large acreages, rather than invest in land and handle relatively small acreages. More than 500,000 farm tenants in 1930 were relatives of their landlords, many of them with some expectation of at least partially inheriting the farms they operated, and thousands of others through successful farming will gradually climb the ladder to the status of ownership. . . .

At its best, tenant status is a normal rung on the ladder from farm labor toward farm ownership. . . . At its worst, tenancy forces family living standards below levels of decency; develops rural slums; and breeds poverty, illiteracy, and disease. In such circumstances, tenant families live in houses of poor construction, almost universally in need of repair, often without doors and windows, with leaky roofs and sometimes even without floors. Seldom are these houses equipped with running water, electricity, bathrooms or indoor toilets. The surroundings are usually unsightly and devoid of beauty. The poorer tenant family's food is simple, lacks in variety, and often lacks some of the essentials of good nutrition. Their clothing, in a great many cases, is inadequate for the mere protection of the body, much less to provide any sense of satisfaction. The incessant movement from farm to farm and from community to community of families living under such conditions constitutes a disintegrating influence upon all social institutions and all forms and types of social participation. Systematic church attendance is impossible, neighborhood relations are constantly disrupted, and the children of tenant parents find their school attendance periodically interrupted. . . .

Other less tangible effects of tenant and sharecropper status are persistent and disadvantaging. Those who know their lives intimately feel strongly that a sense of fear pervades their thoughts and actions, engendered unquestionably by their uncertainty and insecurity, their utter lack of opportunity to depend on any definite source of income even in their immediate future. It is probably this sense of fear and uncertainty that leads them to grasp rather desperately at will-o'-the-wisp, get-rich-quick, money-making schemes—enterprises about which they know little and for which they are almost totally unfitted. Their hope for improved income and living conditions, which often is the impelling force behind their ceaseless moving, causes them to shift from one landowner to another. The frequent intermingling of former renters and owners or sons of owners, lowered to cropper status, on the same land with so-called "poor white trash," and colored families breeds serious ill feeling. Contact with landowners who are sometimes hard taskmasters nurtures a potential sense of distrust and may fan it into open hostility and sometimes violence. Those who have dropped back to cropper status, and conversely those who have risen above it, are frankly resented and misunderstood if they attempt to gain the confidence and cooperation of croppers who need their assistance. The unfortunate plight of the croppers inherently leads to misunderstanding, unhappiness, and discontent.

356. *Unemployment in the 1930's*

Paul Webbink, "Unemployment in the United States, 1930–40," *American Economic Review*, XXX, Part 2 (1940), 250–1

WITHIN a few months after the stock market collapse of October, 1929, unemployment had been catapulted from its status of a vague worry to be considered some future day into the position of one of the country's foremost preoccupations. Unemployment increased steadily, with only a few temporary setbacks, from the fall of 1929 to the spring of 1933. Even a cursory reference to the several existing estimates of unemployment will amply show the rapidity with which unemployment established itself as an economic factor of the first order of importance.

For March, 1930, the estimates range from nearly 3,250,000 to more than 4,-000,000. A year later these had doubled to between 7,500,000 and almost 8,000-000. By March, 1932, a further increase of roughly 50 per cent had occurred, bringing the estimates to between 11,250,-000 and nearly 12,500,000. Then came the peak early in 1933. By March, 1933, according to the independent estimates of Dr. Woytinsky, nonagricultural employment had fallen more than 8,050,000 over the spring of 1930, while the supply of persons who might normally be considered to be seekers of gainful work had during the same time increased by 1,200,000. Adding to these an estimated 1,850,000 "additional" workers brought on the labor market through the unemployment of usual breadwinners, and the approximately 3,-200,000 persons . . . already unemployed in April, 1930, a total of 14,300,000 is reached. Other estimates for March, 1933, range from Robert Nathan's 13,577,000 to the National Industrial Conference Board's 14,586,000, the American Federation of Labor's 15,389,000, and more than 16,000,000 on the part of the Congress of Industrial Organizations.

The spring and summer months of 1933 brought the "NRA boom" and a sudden fall of 3,000,000 or 4,000,000 in the number of unemployed. This still left unemployment at a level of 10,000,000 or 11,-000,000 but a gradual diminution occurred during the next four years, and by September, 1936, the volume of unemployment was set by various estimators at between 5,378,000 and 8,145,000. A sharp increase resulted from the renewed depression of the winter 1937–38, reaching, according to Woytinsky, a total somewhat over 9,000,000, in March, 1938, or according to others, a level of 10,000,000 or 11,000,000. That a decided drop in unemployment has taken place during the subsequent two and a half years is recognized by all of the estimates; the magnitude of the drop . . . is still a controversial issue.

It would require an immoderate rashness to try at this point to identify the specific factors which resulted in the fact that unemployment was throughout the decade a problem of major importance. In a broad sense the factors responsible for the tremendous volume of unemployment were the factors responsible for the depression as a whole. It is hardly feasible, however—either now or in the future—to obtain agreement upon the proper weights to each of the forces which contributed to the sum-total, including the condition of the world markets, the influence of internal financial and industrial policies, the role of governmental measures, technological changes, shifts in the composition of the population, and changes in standards of consumption and in the desire of individuals to enter the labor market or to increase their participation in it.

357. *No One Has Starved, 1932*

"No One Has Starved," *Fortune*, September, 1932, pp. 21, 22–8. Reprinted by special permission. Copyright 1932 by Time Inc.

FEW if any of the industrial areas have been able to maintain a minimum decency level of life for their unemployed. Budgetary standards as set up by welfare organizations, public and private, after years of experiment have been discarded. Food only, in most cases, is provided and little enough of that. Rents are seldom paid. Shoes and clothing are given in rare instances only. Money for doctors and dentists is not to be had. And free clinics are filled to overflowing. Weekly allowances per family have fallen as low as $2.39 in New York with $3 and $4 the rule in most cities and $5 a high figure. And even on these terms funds budgeted for a twelve-month period have been exhausted in three or four. . . .

About 1,000,000 out of ... [New York City's] 3,200,000 working population are unemployed. Last April 410,000 were estimated to be in dire want. Seven hundred and fifty thousand in 150,000 families were receiving emergency aid while 160,000 more in 32,000 families were waiting to receive aid not then available. Of these latter families—families which normally earn an average of $141.50 a month—the average income from all sources was $8.20. Of families receiving relief, the allowance has been anything from a box of groceries up to $60 a month. In general, New York relief, in the phrase of Mr. William Hodson, executive director of the New York Welfare Council, has been on "a disaster basis." And the effects have been disaster effects. It is impossible to estimate the number of deaths in the last year in which starvation was a contributing cause. But ninety-five persons suffering directly from starvation were admitted to the city hospitals in 1931, of whom twenty died; and 143 suffering from malnutrition, of whom twenty-five died. . . .

The situation in Philadelphia was described by its Community Council in July, 1932, as one of "slow starvation and progressive disintegration of family life." . . . Of the city's 445,000 families with employable workers 210,000 had workers unemployed or on part time, about one in four had no worker employed on full time, and 12 per cent had no worker employed. Even the average person unemployed had been out of work for thirty-seven weeks and had had only a little over one week of casual or relief work during the period. . . . The Governor of the state estimated that 250,000 persons in Philadelphia "faced actual starvation." Over the state at large the same conditions held. In June, 1931, 919,000 or 25 per cent of the normally employed in the state were unemployed, according to the "secret" report then submitted to the Governor, and the number had risen to 1,000,-000 by December and to 1,250,000 in August, 1932. One hundred and fifty thousand children were in need of charity. Malnutrition had increased in forty-eight counties—27 per cent of school children being undernourished. . . . New patients in the tuberculosis clinics had doubled. And the general death rate and disease rate had risen. . . .

Unemployed in Chicago number . . . 40 per cent of its employable workers while the number for the state at large is about one in three of the gainfully employed. . . . The minimum relief budget has been $2.40 per week for an adult and $1.50 per week for a child for food, with $22 to $23 per month to a family. But these figures have since been cut to $2.15 weekly for a man, $1.10 for a child. And persons demanding relief must be completely destitute to receive it. Rents are not paid by the relief agencies and housing is, in certain sections, unspeakably bad. . . .

In Youngstown, due to the local optimism, no united relief was undertaken until January, 1931. Meantime homeless men slept in the garbage in the municipal incinerator to keep warm. In January an abandoned police station was made into a flophouse. Attempts of Communists to organize the flophouseholders failed and a bond issue was eventually floated. Men in desperate need get two days work a week. . . .

Obviously, however, urban figures give an incomplete picture of the whole industrial situation, for they do not include such areas as the industrial area of New Jersey. In Passaic County, for example, 23,749 persons, heads of families, representing 90,699 of the county's 300,000 population, have applied for relief. The authorities have been forced to pick 12,171 families, about half, and give them relief amounting to about $9 a month per family. And in Paterson 8,500 of the registered 12,000 unemployed are without relief of any kind. Moreover, the situation in the textile areas of the state is complicated by the fact that certain employers have taken advantage of the necessity of their employees to reestablish sweatshop conditions. Under such circumstances the employed as well as the unemployed become a burden upon the community. But elsewhere in the textile mill towns even the pretense of a living wage has been dropped. North Carolina has 100,000 unemployed textile workers with another 100,000 on the payrolls of closed plants, most of whom are begging on the roads, having long ago exhausted their savings from the low wage paid them before the depression. And those employed on part time are hardly better off since the full-time wage now averages about $6.50. In Georgia, in the Piedmont Mill Village of Egan Park, fifteen families have banded together to keep alive on a total weekly income of $10. And similar stories come from other towns in the region. . . . It is hardly necessary to add that malnutrition, undernourishment, rickets, tuberculosis, and other diseases increase under such conditions. And that relief in these areas is badly organized or nonexistent.

The story of factory unemployment is, however, only part of the story. In agriculture and in mining, particularly soft-coal mining, the depression is not in its fourth year but in its eighth or tenth or twelfth. It is estimated that there is a destitute coal-mining population of 1,-200,000 souls dependent upon some 240,-000 unemployed and distressed bituminous miners, most of whom live in six states in regions where coal mining is the only important enterprise, where merchants are bankrupt, banks closed, schools without funds, and once wealthy residents in actual want. And this situation is of many years' standing for even in the boom years of 1928 and 1929 the industry as a whole lost a total of $41,000,000. The American Friends Service Committee, which has worked with children in Kentucky, West Virginia, and Williamson and Franklin counties, Illinois, estimates that of the 500,000 soft-coal workers making a living in 1928 only 300,000 are now

employed and on wages often as low as $8 a week. Over the entire area from 20 per cent to 99 per cent of the children are found to be underweight and the probability is that 20,000 children and 20,000 adults will shortly be in actual and pressing want.

Kentucky conditions have been well aired as a result of the fascist policy pursued by the local authorities, particularly in Harlan County. Miners in that county who work at all work one to one and a half days a week with payment in scrip from which the company deducts an average of $11.80 monthly for rent, medical attention, powder and caps, and insurance. To pay this deduction, a man must mine forty-five tons a month, which means he must work nine days. Most of them work a total of six days and the result is a load of debt with no balance for food. As a consequence, pellagra—a deficiency disease of the nerve centers finally causing insanity—is common. In Pineville, Kentucky, 157 children are fed one meal a day at a soup kitchen—the meal consisting of boiled potatoes, boiled beans, and cornbread, an ideal pellagra-breeding diet. Most of the miners attempt to farm but the land is poor and jars for canning are too expensive for a community in which cash is practically nonexistent. Moreover, there was last year a severe drought in this district, and a great many miners' crops were destroyed by sun and pests—a fact which must be compared with the September, 1931, statement of Executive-Director Croxton of the President's Organization on Unemployment Relief to the effect that the unemployment situation in West Virginia and Kentucky would be alleviated by the "bountiful crops.". . .

So it goes from one city to another and out into the mill towns and the mine villages and on beyond into the farms where the hides of a carload of cattle will hardly buy a pair of shoes and alfalfa costing $12 a ton to raise sells at $2.50 and the tractors rust in the fields.

The difficulty with such facts is that in mass they cease to have meaning. And the reiteration of the statement that hundreds of thousands of people have faced or are facing starvation with inadequate doles to support them merely produces skepticism. "They haven't starved yet," remarks the reader. "They get along somehow."

It is true they get along somehow. But just how they get along is another matter. There were eleven days in Philadelphia last April when private funds had run out and public funds were not yet available. During that period, the relief organizations studied ninety-one families to see just how people get along under those circumstances. They found out. One woman borrowed fifty cents, bought stale bread at three and one half cents a loaf, and the family lived on it for eleven days. Another put the last food order into soup stock and vegetables, and made a soup. When a member of the family was hungry, he ate as little as he could. Another picked up spoiled vegetables along the docks and except for three foodless days, the family ate them. Another made a stew with her last food order, which she cooked over and over daily to keep it from spoiling. Another family lived on dandelions. Another on potatoes. Another had no food for two and one-half days. And one

in ten of the women were pregnant and one in three of the children of nursing age. And they "got along.". . .

The depression, along with its misery, has produced its social curiosities, not the least of which is the wandering population it has spilled upon the roads. Means of locomotion vary but the objective is always the same—somewhere else. No one has yet undertaken to estimate the number of hitchhikers whose thumbs jerk onward along the American pike, nor the number of spavined Fords dragging destitute families from town to town in search of a solvent relative or a generous friend. But the total migratory population of the country has been put at 600,000 to 1,000,-000. . . .

The presence of these wandering groups is curious and significant. . . . When millions of people have no relation to the land and are able at the same time to find cheap transportation, the effect of an economic crisis is not to fix them in one place but to drive them elsewhere. And the consequence, as regards these groups, is a complete failure of local relief. The destitute families of the Fords and the homeless men of the flat cars are entitled to relief in no city. As the history of the Bonus Expeditionary Force after its ouster from Washington makes clear.

358. *Degrees of Concentration, 1941*

Temporary National Economic Committee, *Final Report of the Executive Secretary . . . on the Concentration of Economic Power* (Washington, 1941), 7–9.

THESE early trusts and their successor companies no longer enjoy exclusive occupancy of their respective fields. But the almost complete monopolization of a market by a single firm is by no means a thing of the past. Today one company in each field controls all, or nearly all, of the nation's supply of aluminum, nickel, molybdenum, magnesium, shoe machinery, glass container machinery, and scien-

tific precision glass, provides nearly all of the domestic telephone service and all of the trans-oceanic service, and operates all of the sleeping and parlor cars. Other concerns stand in a similar position with respect to important segments of the markets for international cable and radio communication, oil pipe-line, and railway freight transportation and trans-oceanic aviation. There are, in addition, numerous public utility corporations and innumerable small-town enterprises which enjoy complete monopolies in the local markets which they serve. . . .

In some fields two establishments together control the supply. Two companies provide all of the domestic telegraph service; two control all of the submarine cables between the United States and several foreign countries; two offer the only radio-telegraph service to many points abroad. Two companies, in each field, account for all, or nearly all, of the nation's supply of bananas, of plate glass and safety glass, of bulbs, tubing and rod, and bases for electric lamps, of electric accounting machines, of railroad air brakes, of oxyacetylene, of sulphur, and certain chemicals. In many local markets, on a smaller scale, two petty enterprises share a trade. Under circumstances such as these, formal or informal understandings governing price and production are readily attained. Each firm of a pair controlling the whole supply is likely to act as if it were a monopolist. In their effect upon the market, duopoly and monopoly tend to be substantially the same. . . .

There are still other markets in which one or two concerns turn out all or almost all of the supply. Ninety-five percent of the heat-resisting glassware produced in the United States is manufactured and distributed by the Corning Glass Works. Natural gas is delivered to many consuming areas by a single pipe-line system. The rates and services of pipe-lines in intrastate commerce have long been regulated by state utilities commissions, but those of lines in interstate commerce were not subject to effective control until they were brought within the jurisdiction of the Federal Power Commission by the Federal Natural Gas Act of 1938. About 50 percent of the American supply of borates, used in the production of borax and boric acid, has been provided since 1921 by the Pacific Coast Borax Co., an American affiliate of Borax Consolidated, Ltd., of Great Britain, another 40 percent by the American Potash & Chemical Corporation. All of the sodium nitrate sold in the United States in recent years has been supplied by the Chilean Nitrate Sales Corporation and the Barrett Co., a subsidiary of the Allied Chemical & Dye Corporation. The United States Tariff Commission, in a report covering some 2,250 synthetic organic chemicals in 1938, listed only one producer for nearly 1,200 of these items and only two for more than 350.

359. *Ford and the Russians, 1937*

Ilya Ilf and Eugene Petrov, *Little Golden America.* Charles Malamuth, translator (New York, 1937), 115–20, 129–30. Copyright 1937 by Rinehart & Company, Inc. Reprinted by permission.

ALONG a glass-covered gallery which connected two buildings, in the yellowish light of day, slowly floated automobile parts hung on conveyor chains. This slow, stubborn, irrevocable movement could be seen everywhere. Everywhere, overhead, on the level of the shoulder or almost at the level of the floor rode automobile parts —stamped sides of hoods, radiators, wheels, motor blocks; sand forms in which the liquid metal still shone; brass horns, lights, fenders, steering wheels, gears. They either went up or came down or turned the corner. At times they came out into the fresh air and moved under a little wall, swaying on their hooks like the bodies of sheep. Millions of objects floated simultaneously. It took one's breath away to behold this spectacle.

This was no factory; this was a river, sure of itself, a trifle deliberate, which increases the rate of its flow as it reaches its mouth. It flowed day and night, in inclement weather and on sunny days. Millions of parts were carried by this river to one point, where the miracle happened —the hatching of an automobile.

On the chief Ford conveyor the work proceeds with feverish speed. We were amazed by the gloomy and worried appearance of people busy at a conveyor. Their work absorbed them completely. There was not even time enough to raise their heads. But it was not only a matter of physical fatigue. These people seemed to be depressed in spirit, seemed to be overcome at the conveyor with a state of daily madness that lasts for six hours, after which, upon returning home they must rest for a long time, get well, recuperate, in order on the next day again to grow mad for a while.

The work is so divided here that the men on the conveyors don't know how to do anything, have no professions, no trades. Workers here do not manage the machines; they merely tend them. Therefore, one does not see here that sense of self-esteem which is found among trained American workers with a trade. The Ford employee receives a good wage. He himself represents no technical value. Any minute he can be dismissed, replaced by somebody else. In twenty-two minutes his successor will learn to manufacture automobiles. Working for Ford gives a man a livelihood, but does not raise his qualifications and does not assure his future. That is why Americans try not to work for Ford; and when they do, they go as mechanics or as clerks. The men who work for Ford are Mexicans, Poles, Czechs, Italians, Negroes.

The conveyor moves. One after the other excellent cheap machines roll off. They drive through the wide gates into the world, into the prairie, into freedom. The people who have made them remain behind, in confinement. Here is an astounding picture of the triumph of technique and the misfortune of man. . . .

A bell rang out. The conveyor stopped.

Little automobile trains with lunch for the workers drove into the building. Without washing their hands, the workers walked up to the little wagons, bought their sandwiches, tomato juice, oranges, and sat down on the floor. . . .

The automobile made before our eyes by people who have no trade exhibited remarkable qualities. It made sharp turns at a speed of fifty-five miles an hour, was very steady, in third gear went as slow as five miles an hour, and took the dip as gently as if there were no dip at all.

"Yes, yes!" Mr. Adams said exultantly. "Mr. Ford knows how to make automobiles. You do not even begin to appreciate progress made in this business. A 1935 Ford is better than a 1928 Cadillac. In seven years the machine of the cheap class has become better than the machine of the best class. . . ."

Here not only flowed parts combining into automobiles, and not only automobiles flowed out of the factory gates in an uninterrupted line, but the factory itself changed constantly, improved upon itself, and augmented its equipment. . . .

In the morning we called on Mr. Sorensen, manager of all the Ford plants scattered throughout the world.

We passed through a hall, on the clean hardwood floor of which were spread out the parts of a standard automobile. Just as we were, in our hats and coats, we were led into the glass-enclosed office of the manager. Here stood a large desk. There was not a single piece of paper upon it— only one telephone and a calendar. We wanted to find out as soon as possible what occupies the time of a manager who does not sign any papers, who does not ply the telephone morning, noon, and night, a manager in whose anteroom, instead of even a single visitor, lie oiled machine parts.

A tall thin man in a gray suit entered the office. His head was gray, his face was ruddy, and his walk was that of an athlete. In his hand was a small black object made of some plastic. This was Mr.

Sorensen, a Dane by descent, the son of a stovesetter, himself at one time a stovesetter but later a patternmaker. . . .

He at once began to talk about the machine part he held in his hand. At one time it used to be made of steel; now it is made out of plastic and tested at once.

"We are constantly on the move," said Mr. Sorensen. "Therein lies the essence of the automobile industry. We cannot stop for a minute. Otherwise we shall be left behind. We must think now of what we shall be doing in 1940.". . .

We . . . began to talk about Ford. . . . "Oh," said Mr. Sorensen, "thirty-five years ago Mr. Ford built his automobile in some barn and came to me in the small foundry where I was working. At that time he was an ordinary mechanic, while I was a patternmaker. He brought me his blueprint and asked me to make a model. And nothing has changed since that day. To this day Mr. Ford brings me his ideas and I put them into practice.". . .

Ford looked younger than his seventy-three years, and only his old brown hands with their swollen knuckles betrayed his age. We were told that occasionally in the evenings he goes out dancing.

We began at once to talk about the midget factories.

"Yes," said Mr. Ford, "I see the possibility of creating small factories, even steel foundries. But so far I am not yet opposed to large factories."

He said that he sees the future country covered with small factories, sees the workers liberated from the oppression of traders and financiers.

"The farmer," continued Ford, "makes bread. We make automobiles. But between us stands Wall Street, the banks, which want to have a share of our work without doing anything themselves.". . .

Ford detests Wall Street. He knows full well that if Morgan is given even one share of stock, all the other shares will soon likewise be his. The Ford enterprise is the only one in the United States not dependent on the banks. . . .

The Ford method of work long ago exceeded the limits of mere manufacture of automobiles or other objects. Yet, although all his activities and the activities of other industrialists have transformed America into a country where no one knows any longer what will happen tomorrow, he continues to tell himself and the people around him:

"That is no concern of mine. I have my task. I make automobiles."

In farewell, Henry Ford, who is interested in the Soviet Union and is quite sympathetic to it, asked us:

"What is the financial situation of your country now?"

The day previous we happened to have read in *Pravda* the famous article by Grinko, and were, therefore, able to give him the very latest information.

"That's very good," said the amazing mechanic, smiling suddenly the wrinkled smile of a grandfather. "Don't ever get into debt, and help one another."

We said that that is how we usually do things, but nevertheless promised to transmit his words verbatim to Michael Ivanovich Kalinin.

XL 🌺 Problems of Economic Policy

THE FLAMBOYANT prosperity of the 1920's encouraged some men to believe that the remaining economic problems would disappear almost of themselves. It was true that labor still had grievances and that the farmer could hardly be said to enjoy his share of the national well-being. But no doubt these residual difficulties would be resolved by the automatic operations of the market place, and without the intervention of the government. A distinguished economist then hopefully sketched the operations of a balance that would of itself rectify disorders as they appeared; in the case of labor, for instance, if each individual were free to bargain for himself competitively there would be no need for unions or for social legislation (No. 360). This would obviate the danger that was pointed out by a lawyer; namely, that to permit government functionaries to intrude in such matters would threaten the principle of a fixed constitution (No. 361).

Consequently, the political leaders through the decade resisted efforts to draw the government into actions that interfered with immutable economic laws. President Coolidge was not swayed by the plight of the farmer (No. 362). Nor did the depression shake President Hoover's convictions; for emergency measures, he felt, tended to perpetuate themselves and were a menace to liberty (No. 363).

The New Deal broke almost at once with this whole line of thought. The crisis was too deep to admit of equivocation. Franklin D. Roosevelt, as a candidate, pointed out that the situation in the United States called for more than palliative reforms (No. 364). Unclear as to means at first (No. 365), he gradually developed a program. Drawing upon earlier progressive ideas, an economist close to the administration pointed to the inescapable necessity for planning in a democracy (No. 366). And a new government agency assumed that task as an unavoidable function of the Federal Government (No. 367).

360. *A Balanced Economy, 1925*

T. N. Carver, *The Present Economic Revolution in the United States* (Boston, 1925), 236–9, 241–4.

THERE is said to be an equilibrium of supply and demand when the quantity of a given commodity for sale at a given price is exactly equal to the amount that would be bought at that price, so that there are no sellers with unsold supplies or buyers willing to pay the price but unable to get any of the commodity. The price that will bring about such an equilibrium is said to be an equilibrium price. On the labor market, for example, there may be said to be an equilibrium of the demand for and the supply of a given kind of labor when every laborer of that class can get work, and every employer who wants help can get it. The wage that would attract exactly the number of laborers that employers were willing to hire would be the equilibrium wage. There would be no labor-

ers willing to work for that wage and unable to get work, and no employers willing to pay it and unable to get help. . . .

There must be an equilibrium wage. To decree otherwise would create worse evils than it would cure. To decree higher wages for all comers would encourage still earlier marriages and larger families, or it would stimulate still greater immigration, or in some other way induce larger numbers to offer themselves for hire in the industries in question. At the same time it would not induce employers to hire so many as at the lower wages. The result would be wholesale unemployment. . . .

If, however, the supply of labor of the grade in question could be materially reduced, or the opportunities for employment increased, the situation would automatically cure itself. The supply of labor could be decreased, either by raising the standard of living..., by the restriction of the immigration of that grade of labor, or by an improved system of popular education.... The demand for labor could be increased by encouraging the expansion of industry, by encouraging as many talented men as possible to go into business,... or by encouraging the accumulation of capital.... It would then take a higher wage to induce as many men to offer themselves for hire as employers would be willing to hire. We should still have an equilibrium wage, and at the same time a wage that would be more satisfactory from every social point of view. In short, we should then be applying our remedy to the cause rather than to the symptom of the disease....

A by-product of this balanced condition is that laborers need none of those special aids or helps in bargaining that most of us have tolerated, and some have advocated in the past. With bargaining power equalized, as it would be under a properly balanced industrial system, the individual of whatever class, trade, or occupation can be his own master and make his own arrangements, bargains, or voluntary agreements with other individuals, retaining his freedom and prospering under it....

Another result would be to make most of our social legislation unnecessary. Neither the laborer nor anybody else would need the state or any paternalistic organization to safeguard his interest beyond protecting him against violence and fraud. When every man can take his pick among several jobs, the job that provides the best working conditions would attract him, and the competition of employers for men would compel them to offer satisfactory conditions in order to get and hold an adequate number of laborers.

361. *A Fixed Constitution, 1924*

James M. Beck, *Constitution of the United States* (New York, 1924), vii, viii, ix, xi. Copyright 1924 by Doubleday & Company, Inc.

SOCIETY is a continuing and very sacred compact between the dead, the living, and the unborn. The living owe a solemn debt to the dead to transmit the heritage of the past to the unborn.... While the living are the masters of their own destiny, yet a wise and just people will be influenced, without being too rigidly restrained, by those principles and traditions which have the sanction of the past....

What is a constitution? In the American sense, it is primarily a form of government, which seeks to distribute governmental power in a manner that is most conducive to the public security and the common weal.... It not only creates the mechanics of government, but establishes as a great ideal a system of fundamental principles, which have been so tested by long experience as to have a peculiar sanction. The dead of a single generation may have had no greater wisdom than the living; but the dead of many generations have had at least a greater collective experience....

The great purpose of the Constitution is to assert those eternal verities of liberty and justice, and the living generation may as well pay heed in this respect to the tested wisdom of a mighty past as to the noble beauty of a Gothic cathedral, which is not less inspiring because its builders are dead.

A constitution, therefore, is something more than a scheme of government; it is the definite expression of the higher law. It need not be in writing; for it can be based upon prescriptive usage, as well as upon formal written statement. Its essential spirit is that of a higher law. . . .

The American Constitution is the most conspicuous and effective manifestation of a higher law. That such a subjection of the living to the higher law, as evolved by the dead, should in this feverish age create antagonism, is natural.

362. *Tampering with Economic Law,* 1924

President Calvin Coolidge's veto of the McNary-Haugen Bill, May 23, 1928. 70 Congress, 1 Session, *Senate Miscellaneous Documents* (1928), II, No. 141, pp. 1–7, 9–10.

SENATE bill 3555, called the Surplus Control Act . . . contains not only the so-called equalization fee and other features . . . prejudicial, in my opinion, to sound public policy and to agriculture, but also new and highly objectionable provisions. . . . The bill . . . is unconstitutional. . . .

In its essentials the objectionable plan proposed here is the stimulation of the price of agricultural commodities and products thereof by artificially controlling the surpluses so that there will be an apparent scarcity on the market. This is to be done by means of a board having supposedly adequate powers and adequate funds to accomplish such purpose through various agencies, governmental and private. The surpluses of the different selected commodities so accumulated by the board are then to be sold by export and otherwise directly or through such agencies at whatever loss is necessary in making the disposition. The fund to pay the losses and other costs while at first furnished by the Government is ultimately to be replaced and thereafter replenished from time to time by means of a tax or fee charged against the product. The theory is that the enhanced price of the commodity would enable the producer to pay the equalization fee and still reap a profit. . . .

A detailed analysis of all of the objections to the measure would involve a document of truly formidable proportions. However, its major weaknesses and perils may be summarized under six headings. . . .

I. *Price fixing.*—This measure is as cruelly deceptive in its disguise as governmental price-fixing legislation and involves . . . the impossible scheme of attempted governmental control of buying and selling . . . through political agencies. . . . The bill carefully avoids any direct allusion to such price-fixing functions, but there can be no doubt about its intentions . . . to impose upon the farmer and upon the consumers of farm produce a regime of futile, delusive experiments with price fixing, with indirect governmental buying and selling, and with a nationwide system of regulatory policing, intolerable espionage, and tax collection on a vast scale.

These provisions would disappoint the farmer by naively implying that the law of supply and demand can thus be legislatively distorted in his favor. Economic history is filled with the evidences of the ghastly futility of such attempts. Fiat prices match the folly of fiat money. . . .

II. *The equalization fee,* which is the kernal of this legislation, is a sales tax upon the entire community. . . . Furthermore, such a procedure would certainly involve an extraordinary relinquishment of the taxing power on the part of Congress, because the tax would not only be levied without recourse to legislative authority but its proceeds would be expended entirely without the usual safeguards of congressional control of appropriations. This would be a most dangerous nullification of one of the essential checks and balances which lie at the very foundation of our Government. . . .

III. *Widespread bureaucracy.*—A bureaucratic tyranny of unprecedented proportions would be let down upon the backs of the farm industry and its distributors throughout the nation. . . . Thousands of contracts involving scores of different grades, quantities, and varieties of products would have to be signed by the board with the 4,400 millers, the 1,200 meat-packing plants, the 3,000 or more cotton and woolen mills, and the 2,700 canners. If this bill had been in operation in 1925 it would have involved collections upon an aggregate of over 16,000,000,000 units of wheat, corn, and cotton.

The bill undertakes to provide insurance against loss, but presumably only against reasonable and unavoidable loss. Just what this might be would involve judgment on the part of Government employees upon tens of thousands of transactions running into billions of dollars. This is bureaucracy gone mad. . . .We cannot maintain a bureaucracy of such vast proportions engaged in buying and selling without constant danger of corruption, mismanagement, and prodigious tax burdens. No private agency of so gigantic and complex a character attempting to juggle with profound economic principles in such fashion could survive under such circumstances, and the chances for a governmental trading organization would be even less. . . .

IV. *Encouragement to profiteering and wasteful distribution by middlemen.* . . . It seems almost incredible that the farmers in this country are being offered this scheme of legislative relief in which the only persons who are guaranteed to benefit are the exporters, packers, millers, canners, spinners, and other processors. Their profits are definitely assured. They have, in other words, no particular incentive toward careful operation, since each

of them holding a contract, no matter how unscrupulous, wasteful, or inefficient his operations may have been, would be fully reimbursed for all of his losses. . . .

Surely there could be no more direct means of destroying the very germ of American commercial genius which is so frankly envied by our foreign rivals—the tireless search for better and more efficient business methods, the competitive zeal for superior service and for adequate returns through large sales of better merchandise at lower prices. . . .

V. *Stimulation of overproduction.*—The bill runs counter to an economic law as well settled as the law of gravitation. Increased prices decrease consumption; they also increase production. These two conditions are the very ones that spell disaster to the whole program. . . .

VI. *Aid to our foreign agricultural competitors.*—This measure continues . . . to give substantial aid to the foreign competitors of American agriculture and industry. It continues the amazing proposal to supply foreign workers with cheaper food than those of the United States, and this at the expense of the American farm industry, thereby encouraging both the foreign peasant, whose produce is not burdened with the costs of any equalization fees, and also affording through reduced food prices the means of cutting the wage rates paid by foreign manufacturers. . . .

All of this assumes that the foreign countries will permit the carrying out of the plan, but many of those countries are interested in the production of their own agricultural industries and will not hesitate to impose higher tariff duties or anti-dumping laws to prevent such undue depression of their own markets. Furthermore, they would be inclined to institute discriminatory measures in favor of our competitors by way of retaliation. The markets for our surpluses would thus be limited if not fatally obstructed. To stake the future prosperity of American agriculture upon the course of action to be taken by foreign governments acting under such hostile impulses is altogether too hazardous. . . . The real objective of the plan in this bill is to raise domestic prices to artificially high levels by governmental price fixing and to dump the surplus abroad. . . .

We should avoid the error of seeking in laws the cause of the ills of agriculture. This mistake leads away from a permanent solution, and serves only to make political issues out of fundamental economic problems that cannot be solved by political action. . . . I have believed at all times that the only sound basis for further Federal Government action in behalf of agriculture would be to encourage its adequate organization to assist in building up marketing agencies and facilities in the control of the farmers themselves. I want to see them undertake, under their own management, the marketing of their products under such conditions as will enable them to bring about greater stability in prices and less waste in marketing, but entirely within unalterable economic laws. Such a program, supported by a strong protective tariff on farm products, is the best method of effecting a permanent cure of existing agricultural ills. Such a program is in accordance with the American tradition and the American ideal of reliance on and maintenance of private initiative and individual responsibility, and the duty of the Government is discharged when it has provided conditions under which the individual can achieve success.

363. *The Challenge to Liberty, 1934*

Herbert Hoover, *The Challenge to Liberty* (New York, 1934), 192–7, 198–9, 203–14. Copyright 1934 by the Curtis Publishing Co. & Charles Scribner's Sons. Reprinted with the permission of Charles Scribner's Sons.

ONE may disagree and keep silent as to the justification of some of these measures if they are to be limited to an "emergency," for in the march of a great people that is relatively unimportant if that is all of it. Then these dangers and stresses will disappear as an eddy in the stream of national life. The important thing is whether this drift from essential liberties is to be permanent. If not permanent, these emergency measures will have served the purpose of having exhausted the pent-up panaceas of a generation and broken them on the wheel of resistant human behavior and the spirit of a people with a heritage of liberty.

The threat of the continuance of these "emergency" acts is a threat to join the Continental retreat of human progress backward through the long corridor of time. In the demands for continuance there lies a mixture of desperate seeking for justification of their adoption and subtle ambitions of those advocating other philosophies. Whatever the motive, the promise of permanence now stares the American people starkly in the face. It is not the mere evolution of an economic procedure that this regimentation implies— it steps off the solid highways of true American liberty into the dangerous quicksands of governmental dictation. . . .

The unit of American life is the family and the home. Through it vibrates every hope of the future. It is the economic unit as well as the moral and spiritual unit. But it is more than this. It is the beginning of self-government. . . . The purpose of American life is the constant betterment of all these homes. If we sustain that purpose every individual may have the vision of decent and improving life. That vision is the urge of America. It creates the buoyant spirit of our country. The inspiring hope of every real American is for an enlarged opportunity for his children.

The obligation of our generation to them is to pass on the heritage of liberty which was entrusted to us. To secure the blessings of liberty to ourselves and to our posterity was the purpose in sacrifice of our fathers. We have no right to load upon our children unnecessary debts from our follies or to force them to meet life in regimented forms which limit their self-expression, their opportunities, their achievements. . . .

Our American system and its great purpose are builded upon by the positive conception that "men are endowed by their Creator with certain unalienable Rights, that among these are Life, Liberty, and the pursuit of Happiness"; that the purpose and structure of government is to protect these rights; that upon them the government itself shall not encroach. From these liberties has come that unloosing of creative instincts and aspirations which have builded this, the greatest nation of all time. . . .

Yet today forces have come into action from ignorance, panic, or design which, either by subtle encroachment or by the breaking down of their safeguards, do endanger their primary purpose. These liberties are of urgent practical importance. The very employment upon which millions depend for their bread is today delayed because of the disturbance of confidence in their security.

There are those who assert that revolution has swept the United States. That is not true. But there are some who are trying to bring it about. At least they are following the vocal technique which has led elsewhere to the tragedy of liberty. Their slogans; their promise of Utopia; their denunciation of individual wickedness as if these were the wards of liberty; their misrepresentation of deep-seated causes; their will to destruction of confidence and consequent disorganization in order to justify action; their stirring of class feeling and hatred; their will to clip and atrophy the legislative arm; their resentment of criticism; their chatter of boycott, of threat and of force—all are typical enough of the methods of more violent action. . . .

Even partial regimentation cannot be made to work and still maintain live democratic institutions. Representative government will sooner or later be at conflict with it along the whole front, both in the incidentals of daily working and in the whole field of free choice by the people. If it be continued the Congress must further surrender its checks and balances on administration and its free criticism since these, with intensified duties to its constituents, create interferences that will make efficient administration of this regimented machine impossible.

For any plan of regimentation to succeed it must have not only powers of rigid discipline but adamant continuity. Does anyone believe that with the interferences of the Congress and the storms of a free press any government can impose discipline and follow a consistent and undeviating course in directing the activities of 125,000,000 highly diversified people? Because such a course is impossible Fascism and Sovietism have suppressed both free speech and representative government. . . .

We cannot extend the mastery of government over the daily life of a people without somewhere making it master of people's souls and thoughts. That is going on today. It is part of all regimentation.

Even if the government conduct of business could give us the maximum of efficiency instead of least efficiency, it would be purchased at the cost of freedom. It would increase rather than decrease abuse and corruption, stifle initiative and invention, undermine the development of leadership, cripple the mental and spiritual energies of our people, extinguish equality of opportunity, and dry up the spirit of liberty and the forces which make progress.

It is a false liberalism that interprets itself into government dictation, or operation of commerce, industry and agriculture. Every move in that direction poisons the very springs of true liberalism. It poisons political equality, free thought, free press, and equality of opportunity. It is the road not to liberty but to less liberty. True liberalism is found not in striving to spread bureaucracy, but in striving to set bounds to it. Liberalism is a force proceeding from the deep realization that economic freedom cannot be sacrificed if political freedom is to be preserved. True liberalism seeks all legitimate freedom first in the confident belief that without such freedom the pursuit of other blessings is in vain.

The nation seeks for solution of its many difficulties. These solutions can come alone through the constructive forces from the system built upon liberty. They cannot be achieved by the destructive forces of regimentation. The purification of liberty from abuses, the restoration of confidence in the rights of men, the release of the dynamic forces of initiative and enterprise are alone the methods by which these solutions can be found and the purpose of American life assured.

364. *Government Must Serve, 1932*

Franklin D. Roosevelt, "Commonwealth Club Address," *Public Papers*, I, 743–4, 746–8, 749, 750–3, 754–5.

THE ISSUE of government has always been whether individual men and women will have to serve some system of government or economics, or whether a system of government and economics exists to serve individual men and women. This question has persistently dominated the discussion of government for many generations. On questions relating to these things men have differed, and for time immemorial it is probable that honest men will continue to differ. . . .

Hamilton, and his friends, building toward a dominant centralized power were . . . defeated in the great election of 1800, by Mr. Jefferson's party. Out of that duel came the two parties, Republican and Democratic, as we know them today. So began, in American political life, the new day, the day of the individual against the system, the day in which individualism was made the great watchword of American life. The happiest of economic conditions made that day long and splendid. On the Western frontier, land was substantially free. No one, who did not shirk the task of earning a living, was without opportunity to do so. Depressions could, and did, come and go; but they could not alter the fundamental fact that most of the people lived partly by selling their labor and partly by extracting their livelihood from the soil, so that starvation and dislocation were practically impossible. At the very worst there was always the possibility of climbing into a covered wagon and moving west where the untilled prairies afforded a haven for men to whom the East did not provide a place. So great were our natural resources that we could offer this relief not only to our own people, but to the distressed of all the world; we could invite immigration from Europe, and welcome it with open arms. Traditionally, when a depression came a new section of land was opened in the West; and even our temporary misfortune served our manifest destiny.

It was in the middle of the nineteenth century that a new force was released and a new dream created. The force was what is called the industrial revolution, the advance of steam and machinery and the rise of the forerunners of the modern industrial plant. The dream was the dream of an economic machine, able to raise the standard of living for everyone; to bring luxury within the reach of the humblest; to annihilate distance by steam power and later by electricity, and to release everyone from the drudgery of the heaviest manual toil. It was to be expected that this would necessarily affect government. Heretofore, government had merely been called upon to produce conditions within which people could live happily, labor peacefully, and rest secure. Now it was called upon to aid in the consummation of this new dream. There was, however, a shadow over the dream. To be made real, it required use of the talents of men of tremendous will and tremendous ambition, since by no other force could the problems of financing and engineering and new developments be brought to a consummation.

So manifest were the advantages of the machine age, however, that the United States fearlessly, cheerfully, and, I think, rightly, accepted the bitter with the sweet. . . . No price was too high to pay for the advantages which we could draw from a finished industrial system. The history of the last half century is accordingly in large measure a history of a group of financial Titans, whose methods were not scrutinized with too much care, and who were honored in proportion as they produced the results, irrespective of the means they used. . . . As long as we had free land; as long as population was growing by leaps and bounds; as long as our industrial plants were insufficient to supply our own needs, society chose to give the ambitious man free play and unlimited reward provided only that he produced the economic plant so much desired.

During this period of expansion, there was equal opportunity for all and the business of government was not to interfere but to assist in the development of industry. . . .

In retrospect we can now see that the turn of the tide came with the turn of the century. We were reaching our last frontier; there was no more free land and our industrial combinations had become great uncontrolled and irresponsible units of power within the state. Clear-sighted men saw with fear the danger that opportunity would no longer be equal; that the growing corporation, like the feudal baron of old, might threaten the economic freedom of individuals to earn a living. In that hour, our anti-trust laws were born. . . .

A glance at the situation today only too clearly indicates that equality of opportunity as we have known it no longer exists. Our industrial plant is built; the problem just now is whether under existing conditions it is not overbuilt. Our last frontier has long since been reached, and there is practically no more free land. More than half of our people do not live on the farms or on lands and cannot derive a living by cultivating their own property. There is no safety valve in the form of a Western prairie to which those thrown out of work by the Eastern economic machines can go for a new start. We are not able to invite the immigration from Europe to share our endless plenty. We are now providing a drab living for our own people.

Our system of constantly rising tariffs has at last reacted against us to the point of closing our Canadian frontier on the north, our European markets on the east, many of our Latin-American markets to the south, and a goodly proportion of our Pacific markets on the west, through the retaliatory tariffs of those countries. It has forced many of our great industrial institutions which exported their surplus production to such countries, to establish plants in such countries, within the tariff walls. This has resulted in the reduction of the operation of their American plants, and opportunity for employment.

Just as freedom to farm has ceased, so also the opportunity in business has narrowed. It still is true that men can start small enterprises, trusting to native shrewdness and ability to keep abreast of competitors; but area after area has been preempted altogether by the great corporations, and even in the fields which still have no great concerns, the small man starts under a handicap. The unfeeling statistics of the past three decades show that the independent business man is running a losing race.... Recently a careful study was made of the concentration of business in the United States. It showed that our economic life was dominated by some six hundred odd corporations who controlled two-thirds of American industry. Ten million small business men divided the other third. More striking still, it appeared that if the process of concentration goes on at the same rate, at the end of another century we shall have all American industry controlled by a dozen corporations, and run by perhaps a hundred men. Put plainly, we are steering a steady course toward economic oligarchy, if we are not there already.

Clearly, all this calls for a reappraisal of values. A mere builder of more industrial plants, a creator of more railroad systems, an organizer of more corporations, is as likely to be a danger as a help. The day of the great promoter or the financial Titan, to whom we granted anything if only he would build, or develop, is over. Our task now is not discovery or exploitation of natural resources, or necessarily producing more goods. It is the soberer, less dramatic business of administering resources and plants already in hand, of seeking to reestablish foreign markets for our surplus production, of meeting the problem of underconsumption, of adjusting production to consumption, of distributing wealth and products more equitably, of adapting existing economic organizations to the service of the people. The day of enlightened administration has come.

Just as in older times the central government was first a haven of refuge, and then a threat, so now in a closer economic system the central and ambitious financial unit is no longer a servant of national desire, but a danger. I would draw the parallel one step farther. We did not think because national government had become a threat in the eighteenth century that therefore we should abandon the principle of national government. Nor today should we abandon the principle of strong economic units called corporations, merely because their power is susceptible of easy abuse. In other times we dealt with the problem of an unduly ambitious central government by modifying it gradually into a constitutional democratic government. So today we are modifying and controlling our economic units.

As I see it, the task of government in its relation to business is to assist the development of an economic declaration of rights, an economic constitutional order. This is the common task of statesman and business man. It is the minimum requirement of a more permanently safe order of things.

Happily, the times indicate that to create such an order not only is the proper policy of government, but it is the only line of safety for our economic structures as well. We know, now, that these economic units cannot exist unless prosperity is uniform, that is, unless purchasing power is well distributed throughout every group in the nation. That is why even the most selfish of corporations for its own interest would be glad to see wages restored and unemployment ended and to bring the Western farmer back to his accustomed level of prosperity and to assure a permanent safety to both groups. That is why some enlightened industries themselves endeavor to limit the freedom of action of each man and business group within the industry in the common interest of all; why business men everywhere are asking a form of organization which will bring the scheme of things into balance, even though it may in some measure qualify the freedom of action of individual units within the business....

Every man has a right to life; and this means that he has also a right to make a comfortable living. He may by sloth or crime decline to exercise that right; but it may not be denied him. We have no actual famine or dearth; our industrial and agricultural mechanism can produce enough and to spare. Our government formal and informal, political and economic, owes to everyone an avenue to possess himself of a portion of that plenty sufficient for his needs, through his own work.

Every man has a right to his own property; which means a right to be assured, to the fullest extent attainable, in the safety of his savings. By no other means can men carry the burdens of those parts of life which, in the nature of things, afford no chance of labor; childhood, sickness, old age. In all thought of property, this right is paramount; all other property rights must yield to it. If, in accord with this principle, we must restrict the operations of the speculator, the manipulator, even the financier, I believe we must accept the restriction as needful, not to hamper individualism but to protect it. . . .

This implication is, briefly, that the responsible heads of finance and industry instead of acting each for himself, must work together to achieve the common end. They must, where necessary, sacrifice this or that private advantage; and in reciprocal self-denial must seek a general advantage. It is here that formal government—political government, if you choose —comes in. Whenever in the pursuit of this objective the lone wolf, the unethical competitor, the reckless promoter, the Ishmael or Insull whose hand is against every man's, declines to join in achieving an end recognized as being for the public welfare, and threatens to drag the industry back to a state of anarchy, the government may properly be asked to apply restraint. Likewise, should the group ever use its collective power contrary to the public welfare, the government must be swift to enter and protect the public interest.

The government should assume the function of economic regulation only as a last resort, to be tried only when private initiative, inspired by high responsibility, with such assistance and balance as government can give, has finally failed. As yet there has been no final failure, because there has been no attempt; and I decline to assume that this nation is unable to meet the situation.

365. *Action Now, 1933*

F. D. Roosevelt, Inaugural Address, March 4, 1933, *Public Papers*, II, 11–13.

THIS is preeminently the time to speak the truth, the whole truth, frankly and boldly. Nor need we shrink from honestly facing conditions in our country today. This great nation will endure as it has endured, will revive and will prosper. So, first of all, let me assert my firm belief that the only thing we have to fear is fear itself—nameless, unreasoning, unjustified terror which paralyzes needed efforts to convert retreat into advance. In every dark hour of our national life a leadership of frankness and vigor has met with that understanding and support of the people themselves which is essential to victory. I am convinced that you will again give that support to leadership in these critical days.

In such a spirit on my part and on yours we face our common difficulties. They concern, thank God, only material things. Values have shrunken to fantastic levels; taxes have risen; our ability to pay has fallen; government of all kinds is faced by serious curtailment of income; the means of exchange are frozen in the currents of trade; the withered leaves of industrial enterprise lie on every side; farmers find no markets for their produce; the savings of many years in thousands of families are gone.

More important, a host of unemployed citizens face the grim problem of existence, and an equally great number toil with little return. Only a foolish optimist can deny the dark realities of the moment. . . .

Plenty is at our doorstep, but a generous use of it languishes in the very sight of the supply. . . .

Recognition of the falsity of material wealth as the standard of success goes hand in hand with the abandonment of the false belief that public office and high political position are to be valued only by the standards of pride of place and personal profit; and there must be an end to a conduct in banking and in business which too often has given to a sacred trust the likeness of callous and selfish wrongdoing. Small wonder that confidence languishes, for it thrives only on honesty, on honor, on the sacredness of obligations, on faithful protection, on unselfish performance; without them it cannot live.

Restoration calls, however, not for changes in ethics alone. This nation asks for action, and action now.

Our greatest primary task is to put people to work. This is no unsolvable problem if we face it wisely and courageously. It can be accomplished in part by direct recruiting by the government itself, treating the task as we would treat the emergency of a war, but at the same time, through this employment, accomplishing greatly needed projects to stimulate and reorganize the use of our natural resources.

Hand in hand with this we must frankly recognize the over-balance of population in our industrial centers and, by engaging on a national scale in a redistribution, endeavor to provide a better use of the land for those best fitted for the land. The task can be helped by definite efforts to raise the values of agricultural products and with this the power to purchase the output of our cities. . . .

Finally, in our progress toward a resumption of work we require two safeguards against a return of the evils of the old order: there must be a strict supervision of all banking and credits and investments, so that there will be an end to speculation with other people's money; and there must be provision for an adequate but sound currency.

366. *Social Management, 1934*

R. G. Tugwell, "The Responsibilities of Partnership," Address before the Iowa State Bankers Association, at Des Moines, Iowa, June 27, [1934], 1–4, 13, 23–4.

THERE is another kind of planning, however, to which liberals and experimentalists can consent. It involves looking forward; and it involves a purposeful evolution of society. But it does not involve rigid theoretical commitment to a finished system. It recognizes the fluidity and the complexity of human events; and it asks for instead of rejecting creativeness.

I prefer to call this "social management" rather than planning, simply because of confusion over that word. And I think of it as a democratic rather than an auto-

cratic process—a living and changing thing, built up out of our own characteristic materials, not borrowed, not preconceived, highly practical and constantly revised. It is my conception of history that we move into a future which is partly unknown and incalculable, partly clear and foreseeable. That future will be different because we have lived and affected it. We ought to use all the foresight we have; we ought to guide our course in the direction which seems clearly—at the moment—desirable. But we ought not to shut out later generations from management in their time. And, for this reason, we ought to be careful about influencing their thought. A whole theory of education is obviously involved in this, as well as a definition of what we mean by "management."

The program we must adopt for the immediate future is compounded of a natively American mixture, some of the elements of which are: mass production, machine processes, scientific management, constant invention, scope for initiative, democratic methods, decentralized administration and judgment by results. These methods, forces and materials exist. They are here among us now. The question is whether we shall recognize it and work with them or attempt to ignore them and work against them. I am all for working with them and for shaping them into instruments for the common good.

In saying this last, I have, as I realize, made a commitment, rendered a prejudgment. It is, however, only a very general one and is, again, something which is acceptable to the American spirit. . . . I might start by saying that it is absurd that any American who is willing to live by our going rules—working for a living, accepting family responsibilities and the like—should be denied the goods which make up a relatively high standard of living. The social management I have in mind—or "planning" if you insist on preferring it—might be directed toward that immediate achievement without doing violence to any of our notions of what is American or what is common to our generally accepted objectives. . . . As I see it, all the quarrels about planning are not differences about what we want, but rather differences about ways of getting it. . . . Social management, democratically conceived, would therefore involve the social organization of the processes of production and distribution, taking advantage of ordinary and useful motives (with reduced stress on the monetary one, which seems to me to have been overempha-

sized), and existing machinery and methods, to achieve first a wider distribution and use of goods, and later (for this is likely to occupy our generation) whatever further aims seem desirable.

Two devices now being used seem to me cases exactly in point: A.A.A. and N.R.A. Neither involves planning in the forced sense. Both provide opportunity for it in the democratic sense. Both are voluntary; but both provide certain compulsions for minorities when cooperation is withheld. Both take advantage of our own institutions; and both compel recognition of the need for widely social as against individual and group action. Both will result in considerable change; and both ought to raise the levels of ordinary living. They represent, therefore, social management. They are, in that sense, "planning." Everyone is interested in how far they may go in these ways; and how his own interests may be affected. And this is why, I take it, they are considered to be admissible if those who are administering them will say that they do not represent planning. For planning is a label which scares business men. They see in it all sorts of horrid connotations. Suppose, then, we say that they represent an effort in social management which will not work unless farmers in the one case, and industrialists in the other, make them work. The government cannot do it; that is obvious; indeed it can do little more than provide a legal structure which will give the opportunity for cooperation. Outside of this, it can provide compulsion on a defined minority, whatever Congress decides that minority ought to be; and it can guard the public interest in whatever respect it may be threatened. . . .

If this is true, but only if it is true, we can look with confidence to a future in which industry and government are to be partners, and agriculture and government are to be part of the same firm. It is my idea, as I have tried to say, that the world we live in has got itself so tied together that none can suffer alone or enjoy prosperity alone. If this is true, again we are at the beginning of a time when we shall realize and put into practice a new rule which is also an old one. Hanging together or hanging separately is not a hard choice to make once the issue is presented clearly. It is my belief that we are forced to make it by the sheer hard facts of modern technique, and that having made it we shall gradually lose the fear of government interference. . . .

The partnership with government cannot be conceived of as merely an alliance between business rulers only and the government, to be directed as they see fit. For years, sometimes in indefensible ways, they have succeeded in obtaining from the government privileges which they desired and which often they abused. The essence of the New Deal is the determination that the government shall become an active and intelligent partner, using its position to help, not only big business men, but also others interested in the enterprise,—the farmers, the workers, the investors and the consumers.

These matters, serious as they seem to those of us who have immediate responsibility for administration because they force us to work in an atmosphere of suspicion and distrust, are of no more than passing interest. They represent nothing significant for the future, but are rather the survival of the old in the new. We must distinguish clearly what is living and growing from what is dead or dying. It is always this way. Those who have been favored under existing arrangements resent any change. And those who seem to be responsible for change, even though they are only agents of forces which are too strong for any ultimate resistance, are made the targets for that resentment.

We are moving now, after a period of reaction, into a new cooperative age in which the measures of justice will be more accurate in economic terms. Resistance may be strong enough to bring on another period of reaction; but it cannot ultimately prevail. Our appeal is to the forces which are strongest in the human heart, the desire to obtain security and the opportunity to work effectively; the need for assurance of equal opportunity and the knowledge that in working for ourselves and those we love we are working also for the good of mankind. I have said before that in this I am conservative; that I am willing to work for the conserving of all those things in America which I grew up to love and respect. This, I take it, does not preclude a willingness to treat radically those forces which are enemies of the common good. There cannot be a retreat in this battle because if we retreat again and precipitate the kind of disaster from which we are just emerging, there will be nothing left to conserve. The lines, therefore, are laid; we are all of us enlisted for the duration of this war; if we win, there still may not be much credit in it, but we shall all be able to lay down our emergency tasks with the personal knowledge that we have fought a good fight.

367. *National Planning, 1934*

National Planning Board, *Final Report—1933–34* (Washington, 1934), 33–4.

PLANNING is not mechanical and organizational alone, but must rest within a set of general understandings, on values to which the nation is devoted, and for which it is willing to sacrifice lesser values. The general understanding on which our democratic system rests is that the happiness and interests of the people are paramount and that special privilege and personal ambition are subordinate to the larger national and popular purpose.

Democracy assumes that the gains of

civilization are essentially mass gains, and should be enjoyed by the whole people who created them, rather than by special classes or persons.

Our government was set up for this purpose, and national planning should be directed toward this end. Ways and means of attaining these ends vary from time to time, but the general aim and purpose of our national endeavor is plain. Plans directed toward this end fall within the scope and spirit of the Constitution and of our American national goals. . . .

The increasing yield of our soil and the expanding productivity of our industry make it possible to reach higher standards of living than ever before, provided we are able to develop the necessary social attitudes and arrangements to insure the just participation in the gifts of nature, science, and technology, by the whole people. The justice which looms so large in the preamble to the Constitution does not consist in production alone, but in a way of life in which the masses of the community enjoy their share in the gains of our civilization. Liberty in any social system must be read in its necessary relation to the common welfare; for liberty which does not bring common welfare and social justice loses its very soul.

That statesmanlike national planning will bring us nearer the American goal our experience clearly shows in every range of our life, local, national, public, and private. Statesmanlike planning might prevent the vast losses caused by inattention, as in the case of soil erosion and flood and misuse of national resources. It might prevent the wastes arising from conflicting and clashing policies, as in the case of land reclamation and land retirement, the industrial wastes arising from lack of reasonable coordination, the still more tragic wastage of human material through inattention to the protection and security of productive labor. It might make possible the invention of new technological and managerial devices for increasing the productivity of mankind and social devices for insuring the just participation of our people in their products.

In moments of industrial insecurity and wide-spread and bitter distress, the possibility of a far finer and richer life for the mass of mankind than ever before may seem a mocking unreality. But the sober fact is that in America, with its abundance of natural resources, with its technological and managerial ability, with its energetic and capable blend of peoples, a new world is within our reach if we can organize and act to take possession of it. What stands between us and the realization of the hopes that gleamed before the eyes of our people from the earliest days are only our own attitudes and our social and political management.

There is every reason to believe that the stream of scientific invention will roll on still faster in the next generation, and if statesmanship and science can keep even pace, the new world may become a marvel of human achievement. It is not our capacity to produce that fails us, but our capacity to plan the wisest use of our wealth of resources in materials and men. The gray, sober facts of science and technology, the cold engineering figures expressing our production possibilities, show what might be done if skepticism, confusion, and timidity do not paralyze us in the presence of the incredible richness of American opportunity.

XLI ❧ *New Dimensions of Reform*

THE NEW TEMPER of the times after 1933 made its effects felt in widening circles. The objectives of reform that transcended the questions of economic policy were not modified but discarded; a new view of the obligations of the state to its citizens took their place.

The magnitude of the change can be measured by using child labor as an example. In the 1920's there was widespread recognition of the necessity for some action to end the intolerable abuses (No. 368). Yet the Supreme Court had proceeded to declare unconstitutional a federal law discouraging the use of child labor (No. 369). True, the children affected suffered (No. 370). But action in this matter seemed beyond the competence of government.

After 1933 this and similar problems became almost irrelevant. At first it seemed as if economic recovery and planning through the N.R.A. would be enough (No. 371). But almost at once the government began to set itself much wider goals (No. 372). It aimed at no less than the provision of a minimal level of social security for all its citizens (No. 373). The concern of government was not to be limited to dependent groups. A variety of other reforms showed the will to act wherever action might be useful. The dignity of all labor was to be recognized and the right of collective bargaining assured (No. 374). There followed a rapid and dramatic expansion in the ranks of union organizations. Or again, the government now showed a particular concern for the needs of youth (No. 375). And, finally, the conception of planning became the basis for a program of regional development in the widest social terms, as the experience of the TVA pointed out (No. 376).

368. *Children's Work, 1922*

"Child Labor and the Welfare of Children in an Anthracite Coal-Mining District," U.S. Children's Bureau, *Publication No. 106* (Washington, 1922), 15–16, 18–20.

THE LIFE of the district revolves around the mines and for the boys more than for their fathers their place of employment was the mines. The canvass made by the Children's Bureau showed that for the district as a whole 90.4 per cent of the boys doing full-time work were in mining as compared with 78 per cent of their fathers.... The fact that the breakers offered opportunities for profitable employment of young boys is the explanation of the large number of boys employed in connection with the mining of anthracite coal....

These breakers which tower above the town ... are great barn-like structures filled with chutes, sliding belts, and great crushing and sorting machines. Around these machines a scaffolding was built on which the workers stand or sit. The coal is raised from the mine to the top of the breaker and dumped down the chute into a crushing machine, which breaks it into somewhat smaller lumps. These are carried along a moving belt or gravity incline on each side of which men and boys stand or sit picking out pieces of slate and any coal which has slate mixed with it. . . .

Whatever the hazards and dangers of the breakers are, underground work is much more undesirable for young boys. . . . Young boys were working daily underground at the time this investigation was made. . . . Of the trapper boys, seventeen were only thirteen and three were only twelve years old when they began to do regular full-day duty at this work. . . .

The boys who turned by hand the ventilating fans frequently worked on the dangerous robbing sections where the last remaining coal is being cut away from pillars and walls and where, in consequence, the roof sometimes falls in or the section is filled with a waste material known as slush. The men interviewed told of the nervous strain they experienced when they worked at robbing. Turning the fans for these workers was the first underground work for twelve boys. . . . A few other boys were employed underground, as oilers and laborers doing a variety of work.

It is unnecessary to point out the dangers of underground work. Where electric cars are operated, where dynamiting is done, where supports give way and cave-ins and squeezes occur, and rock and coal fall, serious accidents and sudden death, more terrible to endure because of the victim's isolation and consequent

distance from relief of any kind, are incidents of the occupation. . . .

Accidents . . . occurred to boys in the breakers as well as underground. . . . One boy told of a friend who had dropped a new cap in the rollers and how in trying to pull it out his arm was caught, crushed, and twisted. . . . One boy told of the death of another while watching the dam beneath the breaker. He and some of the other breaker boys had helped to extricate the mutilated body from the wheels in which their companion was caught; he himself had held the bag into which the recovered parts of the dead body were put. . . .

No compensation was paid forty-four boys who were incapacitated for a period of two weeks or more as the result of injuries recieved while they were employed in the mines, although the Pennsylvania compensation law entitled them to receive it. Of those who received compensation, eleven boys reported that they were paid in all less than $5; nine that they received from $5 to $10; twenty-three from $10 to $25; twelve received between $25 and $50; four between $50 and $75; five between $75 and $100; while three reported that they received $100 or more. . . .

Public opinion had already prohibited underground work in Pennsylvania and in most other states, and the Federal Government had imposed a penalty in the form of a tax if children under sixteen were employed in or about a mine. The real problem here, as in many other parts of the country, was how to secure the enforcement of the child-labor laws that had been enacted.

369. *Hammer* v. *Dagenhart, 1918*

Opinion of the Court by Mr. Justice Day (June 3, 1918), 247 U.S. Reports, 269–70, 271–2, 273–4, 275–7.

THE CONTROLLING question for decision is: Is it within the authority of Congress in regulating commerce among the states

to prohibit the transportation in interstate commerce of manufactured goods, the product of a factory in which, within thirty days prior to their removal therefrom, children under the age of fourteen have been employed or permitted to work, or children between the ages of fourteen and sixteen years have been employed or permitted to work more than eight hours in any day, or more than six days in any week, or after the hour of seven o'clock P.M. or before the hour of six o'clock A.M.?

The power essential to the passage of this act, the Government contends, is found in the commerce clause of the Constitution which authorizes Congress to regulate commerce with foreign nations and among the states.

In *Gibbons* v. *Ogden,* . . . Chief Justice Marshall, speaking for this court, and defining the extent and nature of the commerce power, said, "It is the power to regulate; that is, to prescribe the rule by which commerce is to be governed." In other words, the power is one to control the means by which commerce is carried on, which is directly the contrary of the assumed right to forbid commerce from moving and thus destroy it as to particular commodities. But it is insisted that adjudged cases in this court establish the doctrine that the power to regulate given to Congress incidentally includes the authority to prohibit the movement of ordinary commodities and therefore that the subject is not open for discussion. The cases demonstrate the contrary. . . .

In each of these instances the use of interstate transportation was necessary to the accomplishment of harmful results. In other words, although the power over interstate transportation was to regulate, that could only be accomplished by prohibiting the use of the facilities of interstate commerce to effect the evil intended.

This element is wanting in the present case. The thing intended to be accomplished by this statute is the denial of the facilities of interstate commerce to those manufacturers in the states who employ children within the prohibited ages. The act in its effect does not regulate transportation among the states, but aims to standardize the ages at which children may be employed in mining and manufacturing within the states. The goods shipped are of themselves harmless. The act permits them to be freely shipped after thirty days from the time of their removal from the factory. When offered for shipment, and before transportation begins, the labor of their production is over, and the mere fact that they were intended for interstate commerce transportation does not make their production subject to federal control under the commerce power. . . .

It is further contended that the authority of Congress may be exerted to control interstate commerce in the shipment of child-made goods because of the effect of the circulation of such goods in other states where the evil of this class of labor has been recognized by local legislation, and the right to thus employ child labor has been more rigorously restrained than in the state of production. In other words, that the unfair competition, thus engendered, may be controlled by closing the channels of interstate commerce to manufacturers in those states where the local laws do not meet what Congress deems to be the more just standard of other states.

There is no power vested in Congress to require the states to exercise their police power so as to prevent possible unfair competition. . . .

The grant of power to Congress over the subject of interstate commerce was to enable it to regulate such commerce, and not to give it authority to control the states in their exercise of the police power over local trade and manufacture. . . .

A statute must be judged by its natural and reasonable effect. . . . The control by Congress over interstate commerce cannot authorize the exercise of authority not entrusted to it by the Constitution. . . . The maintenance of the authority of the states over matters purely local is as essential to the preservation of our institutions as is the conservation of the supremacy of the federal power in all matters entrusted to the nation by the Federal Constitution. . . .

The power of the states to regulate their purely internal affairs by such laws as seem wise to the local authority is inherent and has never been surrendered to the general government. . . . To sustain this statute would not be in our judgment a recognition of the lawful exertion of congressional authority over interstate commerce, but would sanction an invasion by the federal power of the control of a matter purely local in its character, and over which no authority has been delegated to Congress in conferring the power to regulate commerce among the states. . . .

In our view the necessary effect of this act is, by means of a prohibition against the movement in interstate commerce of ordinary commercial commodities, to regulate the hours of labor of children in factories and mines within the states, a purely state authority. Thus the act in a twofold sense is repugnant to the Constitution. It not only transcends the authority delegated to Congress over commerce but also exerts a power as to a purely local matter to which the federal authority does not extend. The far reaching result of upholding the act cannot be more plainly indicated than by pointing out that if Congress can thus regulate matters entrusted to local authority by prohibition of the movement of commodities in interstate commerce, all freedom of commerce will be at an end, and the power of the states over local matters may be eliminated, and thus our system of government be practically destroyed.

For these reasons we hold that this law exceeds the constitutional authority of Congress.

370. *A Thankless Child,* 1923

Lowell Mellett, "How Sharper than a Serpent's Tooth to Have a Thankless Child," *Labor,* November 17, 1923, pp. 1, 3. Reprinted in Grace Abbott, ed., *The Child and the State* (Chicago, 1938), I, 515–17.

THIS is the story of an ungrateful child. The story of a lad for whom all the machinery of the American judiciary was turned to preserve his constitutional rights and who, after six years, has not yet brought himself to give thanks. The boy is Reuben Dagenhart, of Charlotte, North Carolina.

Six years ago, Federal Judge James E. Boyd, of the western North Carolina district, interposed the majesty of the law in Reuben's behalf. Some months later Chief Justice White and Justices Day, Van Devanter, McReynolds, and Pitney did the same. They declared . . . that the Congress of the United States could not take away from young Reuben Dagenhart his "constitutional" right to work more hours every day than a boy of fourteen ought to work. . . .

And should not the Dagenhart boys be grateful for that? Well, Reuben isn't.

I found him at his home in Charlotte. He is about the size of the office boy— weighs a hundred and five pounds, he told me. But he is a married man with a child. He is twenty years old.

"What benefit," I asked him, "did you get out of the suit which you won in the United States Supreme Court?" . . .

"I don't see that I got any benefit. I guess I'd been a lot better off if they hadn't won it. Look at me! A hundred and five pounds, a grown man and no education. I may be mistaken, but I think the years I've put in in the cotton mills have stunted my growth. They kept me from getting any schooling. I had to stop school after the third grade and now I need the education I didn't get. . . . From twelve years old on, I was working twelve hours a day—from six in the morning till seven at night, with time out for meals. And sometimes I worked nights besides. Lifting a hundred pounds and I only weighed sixty-five pounds myself." . . .

"Just what did you and John get out of that suit, then?" was asked.

"Why, we got some automobile rides when them big lawyers from the North was down here. Oh, yes, and they bought both of us a coca-cola! That's all we got out of it."

"What did you tell the judge when you were in court?"

"Oh, John and me never was in court!

Just Paw was there. John and me was just little kids in short pants. I guess we wouldn't have looked like much in court. We were working in the mill while the case was going on. But Paw went up to Washington." . . .

"It would have been a good thing for all the kids in this state if that law they passed had been kept. Of course, they do better now than they used to. You don't see so many babies working in the factories, but you see a lot of them that ought to be going to school."

371. *National Industrial Recovery Act, 1933*

F. D. Roosevelt, Statement on N.I.R.A.—"To Put People Back to Work," June 16, 1933, *Public Papers*, II, 251–2, 254–5.

THE LAW I have just signed was passed to put people back to work, to let them buy more of the products of farms and factories and start our business at a living rate again. This task is in two stages; first, to get many hundreds of thousands of the unemployed back on the payroll by snowfall and, second, to plan for a better future for the longer pull. While we shall not neglect the second, the first stage is an emergency job. It has the right of way.

The second part of the Act gives employment through a vast program of public works. Our studies show that we should be able to hire many men at once and to step up to about a million new jobs by October 1st, and a much greater number later. We must put at the head of our list those works which are fully ready to start now. Our first purpose is to create employment as fast as we can, but we should not pour money into unproved projects.

We have worked out our plans for action. Some of the work will start tomorrow. I am making available $400,000,000 for state roads under regulations which I have just signed, and I am told that the states will get this work under way at once. I

have also just released over $200,000,000 for the Navy to start building ships under the London Treaty.

In my Inaugural I laid down the simple proposition that nobody is going to starve in this country. It seems to me to be equally plain that no business which depends for existence on paying less than living wages to its workers has any right to continue in this country. By "business" I mean the whole of commerce as well as the whole of industry; by workers I mean all workers, the white collar class as well as the men in overalls; and by living wages I mean more than a bare subsistence level—I mean the wages of decent living.

Throughout industry, the change from starvation wages and starvation employment to living wages and sustained employment can, in large part, be made by an industrial covenant to which all employers shall subscribe. It is greatly to their interest to do this because decent living, widely spread among our 125,000,000 people, eventually means the opening up to industry of the richest market which the world has known. It is the only way to utilize the so-called excess capacity of our industrial plants. This is the principle that makes this one of the most important laws that ever has come from Congress because, before the passage of this Act, no such industrial covenant was possible.

On this idea, the first part of the Act proposes to our industry a great spontaneous cooperation to put millions of men back in their regular jobs this summer. The idea is simply for employers to hire more men to do the existing work by reducing the work-hours of each man's week and at the same time paying a living wage for the shorter week.

No employer and no group of less than all employers in a single trade could do this alone and continue to live in business competition. But if all employers in each trade now band themselves faithfully in these modern guilds—without exception— and agree to act together and at once, none will be hurt and millions of workers, so long deprived of the right to earn their bread in the sweat of their labor, can raise their heads again. The challenge of this law is whether we can sink selfish interest and present a solid front against a common peril. . . .

As to the machinery, we shall use the practical way of accomplishing what we are setting out to do. When a trade association has a code ready to submit and the association has qualified as truly representative, and after reasonable notice has been issued to all concerned, a public hearing will be held by the Administrator or a deputy. A Labor Advisory Board appointed by the Secretary of Labor will be responsible that every affected labor group, whether organized or unorganized, is fully and adequately represented in an advisory capacity and any interested labor group will be entitled to be heard through representatives of its own choosing. An Industrial Advisory Board appointed by the Secretary of Commerce will be responsible that every affected industrial group is fully and adequately represented in an advisory capacity and any interested industrial group will be entitled to be heard through representatives of its own choos-

ing. A Consumers Advisory Board will be responsible that the interests of the consuming public will be represented and every reasonable opportunity will be given to any group or class who may be affected directly or indirectly to present their views.

At the conclusion of these hearings and after the most careful scrutiny by a competent economic staff the Administrator will present the subject to me for my action under the law.

I am fully aware that wage increases will eventually raise costs, but I ask that managements give first consideration to the improvement of operating figures by greatly increased sales to be expected from the rising purchasing power of the public. That is good economics and good business. The aim of this whole effort is to restore our rich domestic market by raising its vast consuming capacity. If we now inflate prices as fast and as far as we increase wages, the whole project will be set at naught. We cannot hope for the full effect of this plan unless, in these first critical months, and, even at the expense of full initial profits, we defer price increases as long as possible. If we can thus start a strong, sound, upward spiral of business activity, our industries will have little doubt of black-ink operations in the last quarter of this year. The pent-up demand of this people is very great and if we can release it on so broad a front, we need not fear a lagging recovery. There is greater danger of too much feverish speed.

In a few industries, there has been some forward buying at unduly depressed prices in recent weeks. Increased costs resulting from this government-inspired movement may make it very hard for some manufacturers and jobbers to fulfill some of their present contracts without loss. It will be a part of this wide industrial cooperation for those having the benefit of these forward bargains (contracted before the law was passed) to take the initiative in revising them to absorb some share of the increase in their suppliers' costs, thus raised in the public interest. It is only in such a willing and considerate spirit, throughout the whole of industry, that we can hope to succeed.

372. *The Task of Reconstruction, 1934*

F. D. Roosevelt, Message to Congress, June 8, 1934, *Public Papers*, III, 288–9, 291–2.

OUR task of reconstruction does not require the creation of new and strange values. It is rather the finding of the way once more to known, but to some degree forgotten, ideals and values. If the means and details are in some instances new, the objectives are as permanent as human nature.

Among our objectives I place the security of the men, women and children of the nation first. This security for the individual and for the family concerns itself primarily with three factors. People want decent homes to live in; they want to locate them where they can engage in productive work; and they want some safeguard against misfortunes which cannot be wholly eliminated in this manmade world of ours.

In a simple and primitive civilization homes were to be had for the building. The bounties of nature in a new land provided crude but adequate food and shelter. When land failed, our ancestors moved on to better land. It was always possible to push back the frontier, but the frontier has now disappeared. Our task involves making a better living out of the lands that we have.

So, also, security was attained in the earlier days through the interdependence of members of families upon each other and of the families within a small community upon each other. The complexities of great communities and of organized industry make less real these simple means of security. Therefore, we are compelled to employ the active interest of the nation as a whole through government in order to encourage a greater security for each individual who composes it.

With the full cooperation of the Congress we have already made a serious attack upon the problem of housing in our great cities. Millions of dollars have been appropriated for housing projects by Federal and local authorities, often with the generous assistance of private owners. The task thus begun must be pursued for many years to come. . . .

In regard to the second factor, economic circumstances and the forces of nature themselves dictate the need of constant thought as to the means by which a wise government may help the necessary readjustment of the population. We cannot fail to act when hundreds of thousands of families live where there is no reasonable prospect of a living in the years to come. This is especially a national problem. Unlike most of the leading nations of the world, we have so far failed to create a national policy for the development of our land and water resources and for their better use by those people who cannot make a living in their present positions. Only thus can we permanently eliminate many millions of people from the relief rolls on which their names are now found. . . .

The third factor relates to security against the hazards and vicissitudes of life. Fear and worry based on unknown danger contribute to social unrest and economic demoralization. If, as our Constitution tells us, our Federal Government was established among other things "to promote the general welfare," it is our plain duty to provide for that security upon which welfare depends. Next winter we may well undertake the great task of furthering the security of the citizen and his family through social insurance. . . .

I am convinced that social insurance

should be national in scope, although the several states should meet at least a large portion of the cost of management, leaving to the Federal Government the responsibility of investing, maintaining and safeguarding the funds constituting the necessary insurance reserves. . . .

These three great objectives—the security of the home, the security of livelihood, and the security of social insurance—are, it seems to me, a minimum of the promise that we can offer to the American people. They constitute a right which belongs to every individual and every family willing to work. They are the essential fulfillment of measures already taken toward relief, recovery and reconstruction.

373. *Social Security, 1935*

Frances Perkins, "The Social Security Act" (September 2, 1935), *Vital Speeches*, I (1934–35), 792–4.

PEOPLE who work for a living . . . can join with all other good citizens . . . in satisfaction that the Congress has passed the Social Security Act. This act establishes unemployment insurance as a substitute for haphazard methods of assistance in periods when men and women willing and able to work are without jobs. It provides for old age pensions which mark great progress over the measures upon which we have hitherto depended in caring for those who have been unable to provide for the years when they no longer can work. It also provides security for dependent and crippled children, mothers, the indigent disabled, and the blind.

Old people who are in need, unemployables, children, mothers and the sightless, will find systematic regular provisions for needs. The Act limits the Federal aid to not more that $15 per month for the individual, provided the state in which he resides appropriates a like amount. There is nothing to prevent a state from contributing more than $15 per month in special cases and there is no requirement to allow as much as $15 from either state or Federal funds when a particular case has some personal provision and needs less than the total allowed.

Following essentially the same procedure, the Act as passed provides for Federal assistance to the states in caring for the blind, a contribution by the state of up to $15 a month to be matched in turn by a like contribution by the Federal Government. The Act also contains provision for assistance to the states in providing payments to dependent children under sixteen years of age. There also is provision in the Act for cooperation with medical and health organizations charged with rehabilitation of physically handicapped children. The necessity for adequate service in the fields of public and maternal health and child welfare calls for the extension of these services to meet individual community needs. Consider for a moment those portions of the Act which, while they will not be effective this present year, yet will exert a profound and far-reaching effect upon millions of citizens. I refer to the provision for a system of old-age benefits supported by the contributions of employer and employees, and to the section which sets up the initial machinery for unemployment insurance.

Old-age benefits in the form of monthly payments are to be paid to individuals who have worked and contributed to the insurance fund in direct proportion to the total wages earned by such individuals in the course of their employment subsequent to 1936. The minimum monthly payment is to be $10, the maximum $85.

These payments will begin in the year 1942 and will be to those who have worked and contributed. . . .

In conjunction with the system of old-age benefits, the Act recognizes that unemployment insurance is an integral part of any plan for the economic security of millions of gainfully employed workers. It provides for a plan of cooperative Federal-state action by which a state may enact an insurance system, compatible with Federal requirements and best suited to its individual needs. . . .

Federal legislation was framed in the thought that the attack upon the problems of insecurity should be a cooperative venture participated in by both the Federal and state Governments, preserving the benefits of local administration and national leadership. It was thought unwise to have the Federal Government decide all questions of policy and dictate completely what the states should do. Only very necessary minimum standards are included in the Federal measure leaving wide latitude to the states. . . .

This is truly legislation in the interest of national welfare. We must recognize that if we are to maintain a healthy economy and thriving production, we need to maintain the standard of living of the lower income groups of our population who constitute 90 per cent of our purchasing power. The President's Committee on Economic Security, of which I had the honor to be chairman, in drawing up the plan, was convinced that its enactment into law would not only carry us a long way toward the goal of economic security for the individual, but also a long way toward the promotion and stabilization of mass purchasing power without which the present economic system cannot endure. . . .

Our social security program will be a vital force working against the recurrence of severe depressions in the future. We can, as the principle of sustained purchasing power in hard times makes itself felt in every shop, store, and mill, grow old without being haunted by the specter of a poverty ridden old age or of being a burden on our children.

The cost of unemployment compensation and old-age insurance are not actually additional costs. In some degree they have long been borne by the people, but irregularly, the burden falling much more heavily on some than on others, and none of such provisions offering an orderly or systematic assurance to those in need. The years of depression have brought home to all of us that unemployment entails huge costs to government, industry and the public alike.

Unemployment insurance will within a short time considerably lighten the public burden of caring for those unemployed. It will materially reduce relief costs in future years. In essence, it is a method by which reserves are built up during periods of employment from which compensation is paid to the unemployed in periods when work is lacking.

The passage of this act with so few dissenting votes and with so much intelligent public support is deeply significant of the progress which the American people have made in thought in the social field and awareness of methods of using cooperation through government to overcome social hazards against which the individual alone is inadequate.

374. *National Labor Relations Act, 1935*

United States Statutes at Large, XLIX, Part I, pp. 449–53.

SECTION 1. The denial by employers of the right of employees to organize and the refusal by employers to accept the procedure of collective bargaining lead to strikes and other forms of industrial strife or unrest, which have the intent or the necessary effect of burdening or obstructing commerce. . . . The inequality of bargaining power between employees who do not possess full freedom of association or actual liberty of contract, and employers who are organized in the corporate or other forms of ownership association substantially burdens and affects the flow of commerce, and tends to aggravate recurrent business depressions, by depressing wage rates and the purchasing power of wage earners in industry and by preventing the stabilization of competitive wage rates and working conditions within and between industries.

Experience has proved that protection by law of the right of employees to organize and bargain collectively safeguards commerce from injury, impairment, or interruption, and promotes the flow of commerce by removing certain recognized sources of industrial strife and unrest, by encouraging practices fundamental to the friendly adjustment of industrial disputes arising out of differences as to wages, hours, or other working conditions, and by restoring equality of bargaining power between employers and employees.

It is hereby declared to be the policy of the United States to eliminate the causes of certain substantial obstructions to the free flow of commerce . . . by encouraging the practice and procedure of collective bargaining and by protecting the exercise by workers of full freedom of association, self-organization, and designation of representatives of their own choosing, for the purpose of negotiating the terms and conditions of their employment or other mutual aid or protection. . . .

Section 3. There is hereby created a board, to be known as the "National Labor Relations Board" . . . which shall be composed of three members, who shall be appointed by the President, by and with the advice and consent of the Senate. . . .

Section 5 . . . . The Board may, by one or more of its members or by such agents . . . as it may designate, prosecute any inquiry necessary to its functions. . . .

Section 6. The Board shall have authority . . . to make, amend, and rescind such rules and regulations as may be necessary to carry out the provisions of this Act. . . .

Section 7. Employees shall have the right to self-organization, to form, join, or assist labor organizations, to bargain collectively through representatives of their own choosing, and to engage in concerted activities, for the purpose of collective bargaining or other mutual aid or protection.

Section 8. It shall be an unfair labor practice for an employer—

(1) To interfere with, restrain, or coerce employees in the exercise of the rights guaranteed in section 7.

(2) To dominate or interfere with the formation or administration of any labor organization or contribute financial or other support to it: *Provided,* That subject to rules and regulations made and published by the Board pursuant to section 6 (a), an employer shall not be prohibited from permitting employees to confer with him during working hours without loss of time or pay.

(3) By discrimination in regard to hire or tenure of employment or any term or condition of employment to encourage or discourage membership in any labor organization: *Provided,* That nothing in this Act, . . . or in any other statute of the United States, shall preclude an employer from making an agreement with a labor organization (not established, maintained, or assisted by any action defined in this Act as an unfair labor practice) to require as a condition of employment membership therein, if such labor organization is the representative of the employees as provided in section 9(a), in the appropriate collective bargaining unit covered by such agreement when made.

(4) To discharge or otherwise discriminate against an employee because he has

filed charges or given testimony under this Act.

(5) To refuse to bargain collectively

with the representatives of his employees, subject to the provisions of section 9.

375. *National Youth Administration, 1935*

A. W. Williams, *Work, Wages and Education* (Cambridge, 1940), 40–7. Reprinted by permission. Copyright 1940 by the President and Fellows of Harvard College.

It has remained for the Federal Government, through the National Youth Administration, to put into actual practice the dream that progressive-minded school people have long cherished. The National Youth Administration has provided through its student-work program part-time paid employment in the schools for young people who need financial assistance in order to remain in shcool. We have purposely left the actual direction of the program in the hands of the school people themselves in order to achieve several objectives.

First, the contribution of their labor as supervisors and administrators has made it possible to put all the Federal funds available for this program into actual wages to the young people themselves. Second, it has eliminated any possibility of an effort, or even the appearance of effort, on the part of a Federal agency to interfere with that sacred area of educational policy traditionally reserved to state and local authorities. But most important of all is the third reason, the fact that in the student-work program we have placed in the hands of the educators of America a new educational medium and tool. The fact that in virtually every high school and college of this country the Federal Government has put into the hands of the principal, president, or dean a certain number of paid, part-time jobs has a revolutionary significance in the educational world with which most of the theoretical pedagogues have not yet fully caught up. But school people generally are beginning more and more to explore, develop, and realize the educational benefits of this program in a way that should influence profoundly the future direction of education. . . .

Because the National Youth Administration is a new agency, and perhaps in part because we are not essentially an educational agency, I think it has been possible for us to experiment with certain techniques which may have value for educators. First of all we have proceeded on the assumption that youth is a time of experimentation, of groping for the right career, for the right direction, of self-searching. We have tried, therefore, to give young people on our projects a chance to try their hands at a variety of kinds of work in order to learn a little of what different jobs really mean and which ones might be actually suited to the particular aptitudes of the individual. We have accompanied this by individual and group occupational counseling and by the development of simple but comprehensive occupational studies, analyzing the conditions, requirements, and opportunities of different types of work. Furthermore, we have organized a kind of instruction, both on and off the job, related to the work the young person is doing. We have tried, in short, to break down the arbitrary division between work and study in order to give a comprehensive understanding and sense of direction to young people in the difficult period of their transition from childhood to productive independence.

Even though we in the National Youth Administration think we have learned some interesting things about the educational needs of young people who leave school long before their educational potential is exhausted, we are not anxious to take over the work of the schools. In fact, we think that there is no inherent reason to make an arbitrary dividing line between the program of National Youth Administration projects for young people in school and young people out of school. We should like to see many of the boys and girls on our out-of-school work projects who thought they had left the classroom behind them forever go back to school on a part-time basis, and we are working with the Office of Education and school authorities in several cities on an experimental basis to that very end.

The educators have been quick to recognize that if the schools are to reclaim for the classroom this group that have deliberately left school behind them once, it must be on a new and experimental basis specifically designed to meet their needs. Neither the traditional academic course designed to prepare students for the equally traditional classical college education nor vocational training directed toward the development of a single skill will fill the need of these young people. A new type of education, experimental and realistic in the best sense of those words, is needed to give them an understanding of the world which they have already entered. This is the world of work in which man uses the techniques and machines made possible by science to adapt the wealth of nature to his needs. It is the world of economic organization whereby the processes of production and distribution are made to work with a present degree of efficiency which is marvelous in terms of the overwhelming complexity of relationships, but appalling in the discrepancy between potential abundance and actual poverty. It is the world of social organization whereby citizens living in a high degree of mutual interdependence solve their common problems and provide for their common welfare. It is the world of medical science bringing nearer the dream of health and vigor for all, the world of new media of communication making possible but somehow failing to produce the understanding of all people of the world of each other, the world of new media for the entertainment and expression of the genius and aspiration of a people. These are a few of the things which education should help young people growing up in a new kind of world to understand.

376. TVA, 1939

D. E. Lilienthal, *TVA—Democracy on the March* (New York, 1944), 5–6, 218–22. Copyright 1944 by David E. Lilienthal.

THE SPIRIT in which the task is undertaken; its purpose, whether for the welfare of the many or the few; the methods chosen—these will determine whether men will live in freedom and peace, whether their resources will be speedily exhausted or will be sustained, nourished, made solid beneath their feet not only for themselves but for the generations to come.

The physical achievements that science and technology now make possible may bring no benefits, may indeed be evil, unless they have a moral purpose, unless they are conceived and carried out for the benefit of the people themselves. Without such a purpose, advances in technology may be disastrous to the human spirit; the industrialization of a raw material area may bring to the average man only a new kind of slavery and the destruction of democratic institutions.

But such a moral purpose alone is not enough to insure that resource development will be a blessing and not a curse.

Out of TVA experience in this valley I am persuaded that to make such a purpose effective two other principles are essential. First, that resource development must be governed by the unity of nature herself. Second, that the people must participate actively in that development.

The physical job is going to be done; of that I think we can be sure. But if, in the doing, the unity of nature's resources is disregarded, the price will be paid in exhausted land, butchered forests, polluted streams, and industrial ugliness. And, if the people are denied an active part in this great task, then they may be poor or they may be prosperous but they will not be free. . . .

The whole point of the TVA experience . . . is that the best way, perhaps the only way the job can be done effectively is by observing the unity of nature, by following democratic methods, by the active daily participation of the people themselves. . . .

We have a choice. There is the important fact. Men are not powerless; they have it in their hands to use the machine to augment the dignity of human existence. True, they may have so long denied themselves the use of that power to decide, which is theirs, may so long have meekly accepted the dictation of bosses of one stripe or another or the ministrations of benevolent nursemaids, that the muscles of democratic choice have atrophied. But that strength is always latent; history has shown how quickly it revives. How we shall use physical betterment—that decision is ours to make. We are not carried irresistibly by forces beyond our control, whether they are given some mystic term or described as the "laws of economics." We are not inert objects on a wave of the future.

Except for saints and great ascetics, I suppose most people would agree that poverty and physical wretchedness are evils, in and of themselves. But because extreme poverty is an evil it does not follow that a comfortable or a high material standard of living is good. A Tennessee Valley farm wife who now has an electric pump that brings water into her kitchen may or may not be more generous of spirit, less selfish, than when she was forced to carry her water from the spring day after day. A once destitute sharecropper who now has an interesting factory job at good wages and lives in a comfortable house in town may or may not be more tolerant, more rational, more thoughtful of others, more active in community concerns. We all know that some of the least admirable men are found among those who have come up from poverty to a "high standard of living."

Whether happiness or unhappiness, freedom or slavery, in short whether good or evil results from an improved environment depends largely upon how the change has been brought about, upon the methods by which the physical results have been reached, and in what spirit and for what purpose the fruits of that change are used. Because a higher standard of living, a greater productiveness and a command over nature are not good in and of themselves does not mean that we cannot make good of them, that they cannot be a source of inner strength. . . .

Democracy is a literal impossibility without faith that on balance the good in man far outweighs the evil. Every effort to cherish the overtones of human imagination in music, painting, or poetry rests upon that same faith, makes that same assumption. And so it is with what we have been seeking to do in this valley. To call it "materialistic" answers nothing. The rock upon which all these efforts rest is a faith in human beings. . . .

There is a . . . widely held objection to such an enterprise as we have seen in this valley. The hideous belief has been spread over the earth that the price of material progress and freedom from want must be the complete surrender of individual freedom. The acceptance of this doctrine has been indeed the principal event of our lifetime. And it remains the faith of the people of Germany and Japan, the most advanced technical nations of the continent of Europe and in all the Orient. . . .

The technical results in the Tennessee Valley, the achievements of many kinds of experts, are of course matters of no little importance. But, speaking as an administrator and a citizen, unless these technical products strengthen the conviction that machines and science can be used by men for their greater individual and spiritual growth, then so far as I am concerned the physical accomplishments and the material benefits would be of dubious value indeed.

There are few who fail to see that modern applied science and the machine are threats to the development of the individual personality, the very purpose of democratic institutions. It is for this reason that the experience of the last ten years in the valley of the Tennessee is heartening. In this one valley (in some ways the world in microcosm) it has been demonstrated that methods can be developed—methods I have described as grassroots democracy—which do create an opportunity for greater happiness and deeper experience, for freedom, in the very course of technical progress. Indeed this valley, even in the brief span of a decade, supports a conviction that when the use of technology has a moral purpose and when its methods are thoroughly democratic, far from forcing the surrender of individual freedom and the things of the spirit to the machine, the machine can be made to promote those very ends.

XLII Political Developments

THE END of the World War found the country in a conservative political mood. The Progressive party had collapsed in 1916 (No. 377); and there seemed no prospect that it would early come to life again. The constitutional amendments had no significant effect upon political life (No. 378); and even the oil-lease scandals of the Harding administration seemed no cause for political upheaval. In 1928, Alfred E. Smith, whom most liberals supported, went down to a crashing defeat, for which pervasive prosperity and religious bigotry were together responsible (No. 379).

President Hoover, approaching the election of 1932, was not confident, but nevertheless saw no reason for shifting his political position. But now, masterly political tactics had given Franklin Delano Roosevelt the Democratic nomination (No. 380). Capitalizing upon the depression, the Democrats swept all before them in a vigorous, fresh campaign that Hoover never understood (No. 381).

In the years that followed, the capacity of the New Deal to act gave Roosevelt an unshakable hold on popular opinion and support. Under new leadership the Democratic party survived both splinter movements on the left, as in the EPIC movement in California (No. 382), and attacks from the right as by the Liberty League in 1936 (No. 383). In the campaign of 1936 Alfred Landon was hopelessly outdistanced (Nos. 384, 385). The only serious split in the New Deal political coalition came as a result of the effort to reform the Supreme Court. The President's resentment of those who had deserted his leadership on this and other issues led him on in the unsuccessful attempt to "purge" those on whose backing he could not count (No. 386). Yet, the mounting support of organized labor more than compensated for the losses he suffered on this occasion (No. 387).

377. *The Progressive Convention, 1916*

W. A. White, *Autobiography* (New York, 1946), 524–7. Copyright 1946 by The Macmillan Company and used with permission.

A MESSENGER from Perkins' room in the Blackstone told me that Colonel Roosevelt was on the wire, and I hurried to the telephone. . . . Among other things that I tried to convey to the Colonel was that our convention was a gathering of rather highly placed people. This amazed him, and he came right back with the statement that I was the only one who had told him so, and he understood it was a mob of irresponsibles. It was upon the basis of the information that came from Perkins' room, from a group of bankers, brokers, a few industrialists, newspaper proprietors like Munsey and Stoddard, that the Colonel had formed his judgment, and written the letter which was in Perkins' hand two days before the nomination of Hughes. Sometime during those two days I heard of the letter, and the Colonel may have told me of it over the phone. . . . The convention was not in session when we talked to him, and did not convene until Saturday morning. In the meantime, we gathered the conspirators, a score or two of us, and made our Saturday plans.

When the convention opened Saturday morning, our plans were laid. Bainbridge Colby was to nominate Roosevelt as quickly as possible after the convention preliminaries were finished. . . . We knew that once the name came before the convention on any kind of motion, it would prevail. The nomination would be made. When Robins recognized Colby, Perkins, sitting on the platform back of the chair, instinctively knew what was up. He literally leaped to the speaker's stand and began crying out in a distrait and almost

hysterical voice. Harold Ickes recalls that no one knew exactly what he was trying to say. Robins shoved Perkins back into his chair, and Colby in less than a hundred words put Roosevelt's name before the convention. Such a burst of cheering, so full of joy, so charged with exultation, I never had heard. . . . Governor Hiram Johnson seconded the Colby resolution. By ayes and nays on the spot the nomination was made. In a few moments the nomination of John M. Parker, former governor of Louisiana, for Vice President followed.

The nomination of Roosevelt was made at noon—nearly exactly noon. I am satisfied that what Perkins was trying to say before the convention was that he had a letter from Colonel Roosevelt declaring that he could not accept the nomination of the convention. I understood before the convention assembled that morning that Perkins had such a letter. He may have told me. But we, the conspirators, carried out our plot. The job was done.

Then a most amazing thing happened. Hughes had not been nominated by the Republicans. Perkins could not be sure that he would be nominated, though it was strongly presumed that he would be. But after the nomination of Roosevelt and after our noon adjournment, during which time Hughes was nominated by the Republicans, Perkins still withheld the letter from Roosevelt. We gathered there that afternoon and started a money-raising campaign. Still Perkins withheld the letter. We were going on into the campaign. Every hour that we sat there raising money—

and we raised something over a hundred thousand dollars and were pledging strongly—I watched the proceedings from a box where I sat with Ida Tarbell and some friends from the *American Magazine* (probably Steffens and Ray Stannard Baker). I was glowing with a kind of terror such as a train dispatcher might feel who had two engines approaching on the same track. I knew of the letter. From hour to hour I wondered if it had been withdrawn, and tried to think what could have happened that caused its withdrawal. The Republicans completed their ticket and adjourned. We remained in session until late afternoon, raising money, making plans, rejoicing.

At last the collision came. The letter was presented. In amazement that great throng heard it. The last words, "But your candidate I cannot be," fell upon them like a curse. For a moment there was silence. Then there was a roar of rage. It was the cry of a broken heart such as no convention ever had uttered in this land before. Standing there in the box I had tears in my eyes, I am told. I saw hun-

dreds of men tear the Roosevelt picture or the Roosevelt badge from their coats, and throw it on the floor. They stalked out buzzing like angry bees and I followed them. . . .

It was the end of a great adventure, politically and emotionally probably the greatest adventure of my life.

My despair came because I did not realize what had happened. It was merely ebb tide. Since the Civil War had destroyed slavery in this country and the tide went out with Reconstruction and the corruption of Grant's day, a new tide had been flowing in, and for fifteen years since the century's turn had been pounding upon the rocks of privilege, and of social and economic injustice, crumbling them here and there, and making inroads upon bastions and ramparts. This Progressive movement was a part of a revolution. And as I stood there heartbroken upon the shore at ebb tide, I did not realize how soon and how strong the tide would come flowing in, and what rocks and docks and earthworks would meet in that flowing current.

378. *The Post-War Amendments, 1917–33*

Eighteenth Amendment, passed December 17, 1917, ratified January 29, 1918; Nineteenth Amendment, passed June 5, 1919, ratified August 26, 1920; Twentieth Amendment, passed March 3, 1932, ratified January 23, 1933; Twenty-first Amendment, passed February 20, 1933, ratified December 5, 1933. *See also below, No. 439.*

Article XVIII

AFTER one year from the ratification of this article, the manufacture, sale, or transportation of intoxicating liquors within, the importation thereof into, or the exportation thereof from the United States and all territory subject to the jurisdiction thereof for beverage purposes is hereby prohibited.

The Congress and the several states shall have concurrent power to enforce this article by appropriate legislation.

This article shall be inoperative unless

it shall have been ratified as an amendment to the Constitution by the legislatures of the several states, as provided in the Constitution, within seven years from the date of submission hereof to the states by Congress.

Article XIX

The right of citizens of the United States to vote shall not be denied or abridged by the United States or by any state on account of sex.

The Congress shall have power by appropriate legislation to enforce the provisions of this article.

Article XX

SECTION 1. The terms of the President and Vice President shall end at noon on the 20th day of January, and the terms of Senators and Representatives at noon on the 3d day of January, of the years in which such terms would have ended if this article had not been ratified; and the terms of their successors shall then begin.

SECTION 2. The Congress shall assemble at least once in every year, and such meeting shall begin at noon on the 3d day of January, unless they shall by law appoint a different day.

SECTION 3. If, at the time fixed for the beginning of the term of the President, the President-elect shall have died, the Vice President-elect shall become President. If a President shall not have been chosen before the time fixed for the beginning of his term, or if the President-elect shall have failed to qualify, then the Vice President-elect shall act as President until a President shall have qualified; and the Congress may by law provide for the case wherein neither a President-elect nor a Vice President-elect shall have qualified, declaring who shall then act as President, or the manner in which one who is to act shall be selected, and such person shall act accordingly until a President or Vice President shall have qualified.

SECTION 4. The Congress may by law provide for the case of the death of any of the persons from whom the House of Representatives may choose a President whenever the right of choice shall have devolved upon them, and for the case of the death of any of the persons from whom the Senate may choose a Vice President whenever the right of choice shall have devolved upon them.

SECTION 5. Sections 1 and 2 shall take effect on the 15th day of October following the ratification of this article.

SECTION 6. This article shall be inoperative unless it shall have been ratified as an amendment to the Constitution by the legislatures of three-fourths of the several states within seven years from the date of its submission.

Article XXI

SECTION 1. The Eighteenth Article of amendment to the Constitution of the United States is hereby repealed.

SECTION 2. The transportation or importation into any state, territory, or possession of the United States for delivery or use therein of intoxicating liquors in violation of the laws thereof, is hereby prohibited.

SECTION 3. This article shall be inoperative unless it shall have been ratified as an amendment to the Constitution by conventions in the several states, as provided in the Constitution, within seven years from the date of submission thereof to the states by the Congress.

379. *The Election of 1928*

A. E. Smith, *Up to Now* (New York, 1929), 407–8, 410–11, 412–14. Copyright 1929 by Alfred E. Smith. Reprinted by permission of The Viking Press, Inc.

THE REPUBLICAN party, for thirty-five years, in each succeeding Presidential year has resorted to the false and misleading issue of prosperity.... The Republican party resorted to its old tactics and once more brought down from the garret the old full dinner pail, polished it up and pressed it into service. No sensible person believes that the success of the Democratic ticket in the last presidential election would have had any effect upon the prosperity of the country. I do not personally believe that the leaders of the Republican party believe their own issues or have faith in them as far as prosperity goes. But it is a good catchword. It appeals to millions of unthinking people. . . .

Of course the hypocritical attitude of the Republican party on the question of prohibition is known to every man, woman and child in the country. In control of the government for eight solid years during which prohibition is supposed to have been effective, they were themselves compelled to deplore the conditions incident to an attempt at its enforcement. The Republican party has used the prohibition issue to soft-soap the drys and to exercise a kind of political blackmail against the wets. . . .

I was probably the outstanding victim of the last half century of a whispering campaign. Suddenly, as though by a preconcerted arrangement a story started to circulate about me, and came from various parts of the country with the same general purport. A woman in Syracuse wrote to a woman in West Virginia that I was intoxicated at the New York State Fair on Governor's Day and to such a degree that it required two men to hold me up while I was delivering an address from the grandstand. A Republican state senator who acted as escort to me that day by appointment from the State Department of Agriculture, flatly denied that any such thing happened. Photographs and motion pictures had been taken of me from the minute I entered the fair grounds until I stepped aboard the New York Central train to go home. These showed plainly that the story had absolutely no foundation in fact. . . .

The most un-American and undemocratic issue that could be raised against any man was raised with startling effect against me in the last campaign and that was the question of my religion. . . .

The woman chairman of the Democratic county committee of North Carolina told me that the state was flooded from one end to another with all kinds of anti-Catholic literature and anti-Catholic propaganda containing lying and scurrilous statements about the Catholic church and about me. She ventured the suggestion, borne of her experience in campaigning, that it could not have been sent through the state to such an extent as it was, for less than half a million dollars.

The distressing thing about any degree of success in a campaign of that kind is the exhibition of so much ignorance in a country which has expended so many billions of dollars in the cost of public education. The very people who are asking us to adhere to our constitution on the liquor question seem to be the first to disagree publicly with that part of the constitution which says: "No religious test shall ever be required as a qualification to any office or public trust under the United States."

It is amazing in this day and age that such countless thousands of people are so stupid as to believe the absolutely false and senseless propaganda that was whispered around during the last campaign. It has its humorous side. I was talking to a prominent citizen of Georgia who told me that in certain churches in that state they had pictures of me attending ceremonies incident to the opening of the Holland Tunnel under the Hudson River between New York and New Jersey, and he expressed himself as surprised to think that opponents of mine were able to convince large numbers of people that that tunnel was actually to be constructed not to New Jersey but into the basement of the Vatican in Rome in the event of my election. . . .

In the city of Savannah two Democratic women, one a supporter of mine and the other an opponent, were arguing about my election. The woman who opposed me stated that she had done so because of my religion. When her friend reminded her that she had supported a Catholic for Mayor of Savannah she replied, "That's different. He is an Irish Catholic. Smith is a Roman Catholic."

380. *Nominating F.D.R., 1932*

J. A. Farley, *Jim Farley's Story* (New York, 1948), 21–4.

[IN THE Convention of 1932, at the first ballot,] the vote was announced as 666 and one-fourth for Roosevelt, which was 450 votes ahead of his nearest rival, but a good way short of the 770 needed to nominate. I leaned back and looked over the hall to see where the break for the bandwagon would begin. I was so sure that the opposition lines would break that the disappointment was almost more than I could bear. Nothing happened. Not a single delegate shifted. Two years of tireless work seemed headed for political oblivion. I closed my mind to such gloomy thoughts and charged into action.

On the floor I pleaded with Mayor A. J. Cermak to switch Illinois, knowing full well Indiana would follow his lead. Cermak was sympathetic, but regretful his delegation could not switch without a caucus. I knew better, but could do nothing. He had everything in his hands at that moment—national prominence, possibly the Senate which he had his eyes on, and life itself,—but he postponed the decision and political opportunity passed him by. Had he jumped to our bandwagon then, he would not have been in Miami a few months later seeking political favors only to stop an assassin's wild bullet aimed at Roosevelt. . . .

Our situation was desperate. There were indications that we could not hold our delegates through the fourth ballot. Up and down hotel corridors, the convention wise men were pronouncing Roosevelt out of the picture.

The crisis was at hand.

Ed Flynn, Frank Walker, Joe Guffey, Vincent Dailey, and a few other trusted men went to Louie Howe's suite in the Congress Hotel. He was lying on the floor in his shirt sleeves between two blowing electric fans. He had sat through the night beside the radio. Never physically strong, he was racked by strangling asthma during the Chicago stay. He had been unable to visit the convention hall. He looked as though he couldn't last through the day. But his mind was plotting the coralling of votes for "Franklin," as he always called Roosevelt. I flung myself on the floor beside him, and, while the others stood back, whispered to him, "Texas is our only chance." Louie agreed.

Pat Harrison called Rayburn at my request. The conference lasted only a few minutes. Like many another event in history, it was casual and without any heroic statements. I said we needed the Lone Star State to win; that the alternative was a victory-sapping deadlock, and that we could swing the vice-presidential nomination to Garner. Neither Sam nor Silliman Evans, who accompanied him, made any promise. Sam merely said, "We'll see what can be done." That was good enough for me, and I raced back to Howe's room.

When I poured my story into the ear of the man who had worked for years for such a moment, he blinked and said, "That's fine." Roosevelt was far more effusive when I broke the news to him over our private line. . . .

Rayburn was rounding the Texans up for a caucus. Jack Garner had called from Washington with the curt instruction, "I think it is time to break that thing up," referring to the impending deadlock. The California delegation met to caucus in an adjoining hotel room. Rayburn informed McAdoo that he was about to telephone Garner and advised McAdoo to release the California delegation. The conversation between Garner and Rayburn is a model of brevity.

"Do you authorize me to release the Texas delegation from voting for you for the presidential nomination?" Rayburn asked.

"Yes."

"Do you release the Texas delegation from voting for you for the presidential nomination?"

"Yes.". . .

When news of the shifts were brought to me, I knew all was over and that the nomination lay ahead. I wasted no time in gloating, but went around to urge various delegations to join the band wagon procession. I was particularly interested in securing the New York delegation in the interests of party harmony, aware that Smith had an idolizing personal following. I saw John F. Curry, Tammany leader, and John H. McCooey, Brooklyn leader. Curry was adamant, so I abandoned the effort, aware that politicians often believe what they want to believe.

Neither the California nor the Texas delegation could have been released without Garner's direct authorization. The California delegation was under constant pressure from various quarters as its forty-four votes were a great prize. Publisher William Randolph Hearst had been largely responsible for securing the delegation for Garner. Various of his associates, who were attending the convention, were doubtful of the wisdom of opposition to Roosevelt. Hearst had long been a political foe of Smith, and he loathed Baker, who had been an ardent advocate of American entry into the League of Nations. Several Hearst men were worried over the Baker threat. Joseph P. Kennedy, who was closely associated with Hearst, called the publisher to warn him of the blossoming Baker movement and to urge him to use his influence to get the California delegation to switch to Roosevelt.

Damon Runyon, the noted Hearst writer, brought the publisher's secretary, Joseph Willicombe, to see me. They suggested a phone call to Hearst at his San Simeon, California, ranch. The publisher listened courteously as I emphasized the menace of the Baker movement, which he deplored, but he did not commit himself. A number of others made similar calls. I am sure Hearst threw his weight to Roosevelt because he decided Baker must be stopped.

381. *The Election of 1932*

Herbert Hoover, *Memoirs* (New York, 1952), III, 234, 329, 335–6, 340, 343. Copyright 1952 by The Macmillan Company and used with permission.

ROOSEVELT's campaign has historical importance, because the new techniques which he introduced have affected all campaigns since. They mostly revolved around personal attacks. He delivered a multitude of ghost-written speeches, some written by irresponsible or ignorant men.

His friend, Judge Samuel I. Rosenman, organized early in the campaign what became widely known as the Brain Trust. The working force appeared to be Felix Frankfurter, professor of law at Harvard; Raymond Moley, professor of public law at Columbia; Adolf A. Berle, Jr., asso-ciate professor of corporation law at Columbia; Joseph D. McGoldrick, assistant professor of government at Columbia; Rexford Guy Tugwell, professor of economics at Columbia; and Thomas Corcoran, a sometime instructor at Harvard. Most significant of the group were Frankfurter and Tugwell, both devoted to "planned economy," the latter being the intellectual heir of Thorstein Veblen. One or two other professors, who were originally drawn into the Brain Trust, subsequently withdrew.

Nonacademic contributors to the Brain

Trust included Louis Howe, Roosevelt's secretary; Hugh S. Johnson, an able but vituperative former army officer; Basil O'Connor, Roosevelt's law partner; Donald A. Richberg, a railroad labor lawyer; Harry Hopkins, a professional social worker; Charles W. Taussig, a molasses millionaire; and Senators T. J. Walsh, Elmer Thomas, and George Norris, three great masters of demagoguery....

All through the 1932 campaign, something was in the air far more sinister than even the miasmic climate of depression or a political campaign. I was convinced that Roosevelt and some members of his Brain Trust were proposing to introduce parts of the collectivism of Europe into the United States under their oft-repeated phrase "planned economy." That was an expression common to all collectivist systems. Paraded as liberalism, it had all the tactics and strategies of its European counterparts.

Their "economic planning" was not the long-established American process of revising our government problems by prior study of their solution. Their purposes were stated in various disguises of new meanings, hidden in old and well understood words and in terms of glorious objectives. They involved the pouring of a mixture of socialism and fascism into the American system....

I resolved finally to deal with the whole collectivist color of the New Deal in an address at Madison Square Garden in New York on October 31st. My colleagues thought the subject too academic to impress a people who were largely unaccustomed to ideological discussion and would see little danger in Roosevelt's statements. But I felt that I must state my position and warn the people that the dangers from the New Dealers were more

dangerous to free men than the depression itself....

I then reviewed the evidences of collectivist intentions ... and continued: ...

In my acceptance speech four years ago at Palo Alto I stated that—

"One of the oldest aspirations of the human race was the abolition of poverty. By poverty I mean the grinding by undernourishment, cold, ignorance, fear of old age of those who have the will to work."

I stated that—

"In America today we are nearer a final triumph over poverty than in any land. The poorhouse has vanished from among us; we have not reached that goal, but, given a chance to go forward, we shall, with the help of God, be in sight of the day when poverty will be banished from this nation."

Our Democratic friends have quoted this passage many times in this campaign. I do not withdraw a word of it. When I look about the world even in these times of trouble and distress I find it more true in this land than anywhere else under the traveling sun. I am not ashamed of it, because I am not ashamed of holding ideals and purposes for the progress of the American people....

My countrymen, the proposals of our opponents represent a profound change in American life—less in concrete proposal, bad as that may be, than by implication and by evasion. Dominantly in their spirit they represent a radical departure from the foundations of 150 years which have made this the greatest nation in the world. This election is not a mere shift from the ins to the outs. It means deciding the direction our nation will take over a century to come."

As we expected, we were defeated in the election.

382. *Epic, 1934*

Upton Sinclair, *EPIC Answers* (Los Angeles, [1934]), 1–4.

EPIC proposes to End Poverty in California; the name being derived from the first letters of these four words. The people of our State find themselves in the fifth year of a depression; and if our analysis is correct, this is a permanent crisis. . . . We in the United States have to deal with a permanently unemployed group of not less than twelve million. Including dependents, this means one-fourth of our population. If three-fourths have to carry one-fourth upon their backs, it means bankruptcy for cities, counties, states and nation. . . .

In our State of California we have now more than a million persons dependent upon public charity for their existence. Many of our counties are already bankrupt. Our State will be more than a hundred million dollars "in the hole" by the end of 1934, and bankruptcy has only been averted by the Federal Government stepping in to take the burden of feeding the hungry. The Federal Government is now supporting the banks, the insurance companies, the railroads, the great industrial corporations; the home-owners, the farmers, the veterans, the unemployed. Bankruptcy for the Federal Government is only a question of months.

To this problem there can be but one solution. It is necessary to put the unemployed at productive labor. A million people in California must be made self-sustaining. They must have access to the land to grow their own food; they must have access to the factories to produce their own clothing and building materials, out of which to make their own homes. We must take them off the backs of the little tax-payers, and stop forcing the latter out of their homes and off their ranches. There must be prompt action, for the crisis is desperate and the next breakdown may lead to attempts at revolt and civil war. . . .

The EPIC plan proposes that the State of California shall set up land colonies in which the unemployed farm workers shall live and produce the food required by the million destitute persons in our State. Operating thus upon a large scale, the farm workers can live in what will amount to new villages, with all the advantages of modern civilization: kitchens and cafeterias operated by the community, a social hall with opportunities for recreation, a church, a schoolhouse, a store, a library, a motion-picture theater, etc. Living thus, the people will have the benefits of mass production by machinery; they will have the advantages of country life without its loneliness and backwardness.

The factories will be great productive units owned and managed by the State. There also will be social buildings with kitchens, cafeterias, lecture halls, libraries, etc. The State will maintain a system of distribution, whereby the food is brought into the cities and the manufactured products are taken out to the land colonies, and all the products of the system are made available at cost. Those who produce will receive the full social value of their product, so they will be able to buy what they have produced, and for the first time consumption will balance production. There can be no overproduction in such a system; when the system produces a surplus, the people will be on a vacation instead of out of a job. They will own the surplus.

383. *The Liberty League, 1936*

Jouett Shouse, *Why? the American Liberty League* (Washington, [1935]).

THE CONSTITUTION of the United States amounts to a contract between the people and the officers of government; executive, legislative, and judicial. That contract delegates to officials the power to do certain things and it forbids them to do certain other things.

Contracts may be modified or cancelled, but only by mutual consent or by methods specified in the contracts. The Federal Constitution contains adequate provisions for its own modification through the orderly processes of amendment. If the American people wish to change the form of their government from a federal republic with limited powers to an absolute dictatorship or to state socialism, they can do so by appropriate amendments to the Constitution. However, so far, they have done nothing of the kind, and the existing contract is still binding, whether it is observed or not.

One basic purpose of the American Liberty League is to see to it that this contract is complied with—faithfully, honestly, completely, and without evasion under the camouflage of giving new names to unconstitutional proposals. . . .

The League's aims are very definite. They are as public as it has been possible to make them. They are embodied in its articles of incorporation as follows:

The particular business and objects of the Society shall be to defend and uphold the Constitution of the United States and to gather and disseminate information that (1) will teach the necessity of respect for the rights of persons and property as fundamental to every successful form of government and (2) will teach the duty of government to encourage and protect individual and group initiative and

enterprise, to foster the right to work, earn, save and acquire property, and to preserve the ownership and lawful use of property when acquired.

It will be noted that the statement of principles links the "rights of persons and property." There is a very good reason for that conjunction. In the view of those who comprise the membership of the League the superficially drawn distinction between "human rights" and "property rights" is a catch-phrase and nothing more. The two so-called categories of rights are inseparable in any society short of Utopia or absolute communism. To protect a man's so-called human rights and strip him of his property rights would be to issue him a fishing license and then prohibit him from baiting his hook.

Furthermore there is one very clear lesson to be learned from history—namely, that governmental disregard for property rights soon leads to disregard for other rights. A bureaucracy or despotism that robs citizens of their property does not like to be haunted by its victims.

The prevention of governmental encroachments upon the rights of citizens was one of the principal reasons for the division of the Federal Government into the legislative, judicial and executive branches. Where one man, or one bureau, is lawmaker, prosecuting attorney, judge, jury, and sheriff, there is no protection for the citizen.

There is no justification, under the traditional American system of government, for permitting an executive bureau to issue orders having the force of laws and subjecting citizens to criminal or civil penalties; there is no justification for permitting an executive official to take over the legislative prerogative of levying taxes and specifying the purposes and manner of disbursement of taxes.

The need for rigid observance of constitutional restrictions is always greater in emergencies than in more normal times because the emergencies produce constant pressure for disregard or evasion of limitations. . . .

The American Liberty League believes that Congress, having been elected to represent the people, should not shirk its task by delegating authority to bureaus to promulgate arbitrary regulations having the force of laws. Likewise, the League

believes that Congress should not attempt to delegate judicial power to executive bureaus. The courts of the nation and not government bureaus should pass upon questions of civil justice.

It is also the belief of the League that the right to authorize the spending of public funds and to raise revenue is solely the function of the legislative branch of the government and that balanced budgets and sound fiscal policies are possible only while Congress retains its full responsibility for the nature and manner of spending public money.

384. *Freedom with Security, 1936*

A. M. Landon, *America at the Crossroads* (New York, 1936), 32–4.

FREEDOM from the coercive hand of government has always been a distinctive feature of American life. Even before the recent revival of dictatorships, the citizens of foreign countries were subject to restrictions unknown in America. Their goings and comings were closely watched and regulated. They could not open new businesses without the consent of a bureaucratic government. Their established businesses were subject to incessant bureaucratic meddling. Economic and social development was bound to be slow under these conditions.

In contrast, the American way of life has left men and women free from these restrictions. Our people have been free to develop their own lives as they saw fit and to cooperate with one another on a voluntary basis. They have been encouraged to start any honest enterprise that would enable them to support their families, give the public the goods and services it wanted, and make jobs for themselves and others. Under this encouragement, business has expanded here faster than elsewhere, the public has had more goods; workers have had higher wages and shorter hours; children have had bet-

ter school facilities; all have had higher standards of living. There has been more leisure for spiritual and cultural things.

This freedom of enterprise which has distinguished the American way of life exists not for the few, but for all. It has benefited every American whether he worked for himself or for someone else. Under freedom, more enterprises are started than under government control of production. Let us not forget, however, that a fair distribution of economic and social benefits is yet to be brought about.

Now I take it that we Americans lived under a system of freedom because we wanted to live that way. We still like it better than any other way. We know there are many wrongs to right. Only the misguided will claim that this system is perfect or that all its results are desirable. We do not contend that individual effort can of itself overcome many of the handicaps placed on great numbers of individuals by the workings of our industrial civilization. The record proves, however, that our system gives the most personal liberty to human beings and offers on the whole the highest possible standard of life to the greatest numbers. It is a system which permits the driving force of free initiative to produce more of the good things of life and thus promote a more rapid improvement of human welfare than can be found anywhere outside of America.

We have found by experience that American institutions serve our purpose better than those of any other country. We not only want to safeguard our freedom, but we also want security and abundance of the good things of life. We are told, however, by defeatists that we cannot have both. We must, they say, choose between freedom and security. They insist we must give up one in order to gain the other. Let us not surrender to any such counsel of despair. Let us not abandon our determination to win security and abundance without sacrificing any of our precious heritage of freedom.

I believe the greatest need of the American people today is a revival of confidence, confidence in themselves and in their ability to work out their own problems. We find in almost every depression that there is a certain percentage of people who lose confidence in themselves. They begin to doubt whether they are really capable of getting out of the difficulties. And it is usually at this point that someone comes along with the idea of finding a superman and turning it all over to him.

385. *Strange Bedfellows in 1936*

Westbrook Pegler, *Dissenting Opinions of Mr. Westbrook Pegler* (New York, 1938), 312–15.

THIS has been a pretty grim campaign, but it can't be said that Henry Mencken has failed us in a dark hour. For years we looked to Mr. Mencken for our laughs and, though there was a savage quality to his humor, he lightened the curse of prohibition and even found nonsense in the solemn brutality of the Borgias of the Methodist Board of Prohibition and Public Morals.

Now we discover Mr. Mencken staggering down the street under the unwieldy weight of an enormous Landon banner, a sunflower in his lapel as big as a four-passenger omelette, a white ribbon on his sleeve and Mabel Walker Willebrandt on his arm. Mr. Mencken has come out for Mr. Landon and, though he attempts to make certain reservations, there is no such thing as a little bit of Landon. . . . When Mr. Mencken takes the gentleman from Kansas he must also take prohibition and even Herbert Hoover whom he once denounced as a fat Coolidge. It would be hard for any humorist to conceive a more hilarious scene, but then, Mr. Mencken is a master and when he sets out to be funny

we don't expect any one to top his gags. . . .

Father Coughlin, born of that stock which long cried persecution and fought for religious freedom, cooperating with the remnants of the Ku Klux Klan and talking anti-Semitism, is a weird figure in the parade of nightmare creatures of the current fight. But we had no background on Coughlin and as far as the man himself is concerned, his present is not inconsistent with his past, for he didn't have any previous political existence.

Mr. Mencken, however, was committed against everything that Mr. Landon represents from the bumbling pomposity and dumb arrogance of the Old Deal to honorary college degrees and lodge buttons. He was not so much a crusader as the mischievous brat of the whole American neighborhood. A crusader does his enemies the honor of taking them seriously and fighting them with earnest mirthlessness, but Henry Mencken's method was to kick them in the pants when they were bent over tying their shoe and they were always tying their shoe.

Nobody ever got so much fun out of

ridiculing the very people and principles whom he has now joined like a convert twitching down the sawdust aisle of one of Billy Sunday's old revivals and though he claims to retain certain of his old heresies it is plain that a good man has weakened at last, and for no specified cause. It could hardly be a fear for his possessions because Henry is a fellow who never did crowd himself to make all the money he could and even today if he would play that typewriter instead of sitting around discussing liver trouble with a lot of doctors from Johns Hopkins he could make more money than even Mr. Roosevelt's bailiffs could snatch away.

Maybe, as one who contributed more than any other individual to the deflation of public authority and American institutions, Mr. Mencken now looks on his work, observes that the rabble has taken literally his contempt for human and divine discipline and is afraid the mob will come marching up his street, busting windows indiscriminately and slugging everybody with a well-fed appearance such as his.

I expect to read soon that Mr. Mencken has joined the Shriners and the Elks and I hope to be present to cover the story when he joins the Tennessee fundamentalists and is totally immersed in Goose Crick wearing a white night shirt and blubbering "Hallelujah, Brother" between plunges in the cleansing flood.

386. *The Purge of 1938*

S. I. Rosenman, *Working with Roosevelt* (New York, 1952), I, 176–7, 179–80. Copyright 1952 by Harper & Brothers.

"PURGE" was the name given by Roosevelt's opponents to his efforts to let people know what representatives were supporting his program and what representatives were not. It was certainly a loaded word. The President did not desire to prevent any community from choosing its own representatives; but he did desire that the people should make an informed choice, that they should not necessarily assume that all Democratic representatives —just because they were called Democrats—were supporting the Democratic administration or the Democratic platform. He hoped that, having the facts, the people would not return these men to office.

The purge had its birth in Roosevelt's personal resentment at the two major legislative defeats dealt him by members of his own party—the defeat of the Supreme Court plan in the spring and summer of 1937; and the defeat of two other pieces of legislation in the Extraordinary Session in the fall of 1937: the wages and hours bill and the administrative reorganization bill. There was no doubt of his animosity toward those who were willing to run on a liberal party platform with him and then vote against the very platform pledges on which they had been elected. I often heard him express himself about such "shenanigans" in a way that left no doubt about how he felt. But even deeper was his feeling—and I believe this was the fundamental reason for the purge—that the reactionary Democrats were doing a distinct and permanent injury to the nation. They were blocking the steps that he thought were essential to raise the American standard of living and make the nation strong enough to meet the growing menace from abroad.

The first factor—the personal one—was so strong that, in my opinion, it blinded the President to the great dangers to his own standing and prestige that were inherent in his entry into purely local primary party contests. His disregard of these dangers was also due to his confidence in himself and in the public support that he thought he could muster. Some of the people then very close to him whose judgment he trusted—notably Corcoran, Ickes and Hopkins—had been strongly urging this course. They had been active in trying to get the President's program through the Congress and had failed. Now they felt that the quickest way to remedy this failure was to prevent the re-election of some of those who had blocked him—with the idea that the other opponents would then capitulate. I heard the President express the same thought when it was suggested to him that a purge might be the wrong approach. . . .

On the other hand, Farley and those most active in the Democratic National Committee did not want to pick and choose among Democrats as pro-New Deal or anti-New Deal. Indeed, I think Farley thought it was definitely no part of his function as chairman to interfere in these local fights. That is why Corcoran was in the purge fight and Farley out.

I am sure that by the end of the unsuccessful Extraordinary Session of 1937 the idea of the purge was rapidly forming in Roosevelt's mind, and that during the 1938 session it became fixed. For the first public announcement of it, he chose a fireside chat on June 24, 1938. The talk was ostensibly to discuss the accomplishments and failures of the Seventy-fifth Congress which had just adjourned. . . .

In this fireside chat—delivered on one of the hottest of Washington nights—the President did three things: first, he listed the accomplishments of the session of the Congress just ended; second, he pointed out the acts of obstruction by the Congress; third, he stated what he intended to do about the Congressmen who were repudiating the platform on which they had been elected. . . .

With these considerations and motives in mind, Roosevelt went out into the primary campaigns of 1938 in the home states of several Senators and Congressmen. It was a difficult, if not impossible, job that he had assumed. The men whom he tried to defeat were all popular in their own home states; they had all served for many years and had become firmly entrenched in their local political organizations. He was asking enrolled Democrats to reject these old officeholders; most of the voters to whom he was talking had voted for these same Congressmen time and again. Strong as the President's personal appeal and logic were, they were outweighed by the long personal relationships that these Congressmen had developed over the years with their constituents; by the entrenched political machinery which operated in favor of the Congressman in office; by the fact that generally the candidates Roosevelt backed did not have sufficient political following or standing to produce the votes. Besides, there was present the resentment which is nearly always aroused to some degree when a national figure interferes in a local political situation in a state where he does not live and vote. . . .

The only contest the President won was in New York, in the defeat of Congressman O'Connor.

He never forgot the lesson of 1938—and never tried again.

387. *Labor and Roosevelt, 1936*

Louis Waldman, *Labor Lawyer* (New York, 1944), 284–7.

IN JUNE, 1936, the second annual labor conference . . . was devoted to a discussion of practical methods by which a labor party could be brought into existence in New York State. Present at these discussions were representatives of the Building

Service Employees International Union, the International Ladies Garment Workers Union, the Amalgamated Clothing Workers, and officials of the Millinery Workers Union.

The first meeting of the labor leaders was not wholly satisfactory. But before the conference had concluded its sessions, . . . we had worked out a tentative plan for the creation of the American Labor Party. During these talks I had pointed out to the representatives of the needle trades unions that an ideal political situation existed in New York in so far as labor and the right-wing Socialists were concerned. On the one hand, there were several thousand politically experienced Socialists who had been thrust out of the Socialist party by the militants. On the other hand, there were the tens of thousands of members of progressive trade unions who felt that they could not support the visionary policies of the militants. Jokingly I referred to myself during the conferences as something of a political matchmaker and predicted that the political marriage between the right-wing Socialists and the New York unions would be an amicable and successful one.

After convincing the doubting Thomases in the labor movement of the advisability of entering into this arrangement, my task was also to convince my right-wing associates, the Social Democrats. It was no easy job. . . . They felt that the endorsement of Roosevelt would be "jumping into the lap of James A. Farley." "Farley is the boss of the Democratic Party; if Roosevelt wins, Farley wins," they reasoned. And as to Governor Lehman, many right-wing Socialists dismissed him with the characterization that he was just another "conservative banker.". . .

After weeks of work on my part, . . . the People's Party endorsed Roosevelt and Lehman, elected me state chairman and designated a committee to deal with the representatives of the proposed labor party. . . . Shortly after, an agreement between us and the labor leaders having been reached, the People's Party abandoned its own name and its independent political existence, resumed the name of Social Democratic Federation, and merged with the newly formed American Labor Party. Under the merger agreement, the American Labor Party was to become the political expression of the progressive, labor and Social Democratic elements of the state, functioning on a broad democratic basis. It was to exclude Communists seeking affiliation through unions, through groups with disguised names, or as individuals. And until such time as the voters could enroll and in the primaries elect their own committees and officers, the Social Democratic Federation was to name three members to the Party's State Committee and State Executive Committee. And so, Algernon Lee, Dr. Louis Hendin, a labor journalist, and I were designated to what soon turned out to be one of the toughest and most unpleasant jobs in my entire political experience.

XLIII ☙ *Signs of Social Strain*

IN THE 1920's the traditional virtues still received respectful recognition. The accepted ideas of right and wrong, of morality, and of religious faith were cautiously reiterated through the established cultural institutions of the nation. So a widely read columnist could seriously warn his readers against the evil consequences of poker-playing (No. 388); and William Jennings Bryan gave his life to maintain the fundamentalist conception of the literal truth of the Biblical story of the creation (No. 389).

Yet the underlying tensions in this society could not be concealed by clutching at the pretense that the traditional conceptions were still whole and unmarred. The reading of religious literature noticeably declined (No. 390). The war and the disillusion of peace, the rapid pace of urban living and the impact of science, all called for adjustments that most men found difficult to make. The youth of the period were particularly unsettled and, in the midst of Prohibition, sometimes sought release in intoxication (No. 391). Crime assumed the dimensions of big business (No. 392). Indeed, the growing preoccupation with sports reflected some of the same uneasiness and tension (No. 393).

The hardships of the depression, and the growing threat of war in the 1930's, combined with older sources of uneasiness to produce violent strains in many aspects of social organization. Two incidents are illustrative. A long-drawn-out case, that resulted in the conviction of a group of Negro boys on trumped-up charges of rape, displayed the ugly antagonisms based upon fear of race differences and of radicals (No. 394). And the panic spread through the nation by a misunderstood radio broadcast in October, 1938, revealed the extent to which other hidden fears then disturbed Americans (No. 395).

388. *Poker and Success, 1920*

Arthur Brisbane, *Book of Today* (New York: The International Magazine Company, 1924), 127–9.

IF THE recording angel could look down ... on all the "friendly" poker games in America, he would be able to make a very good and accurate list of the future failures of the United States.

A man who, after early youth, continues to waste his time with cards amounts to little ordinarily. But even the card players, the poor, silly geese of the friendly poker games, could succeed.

If the men who play poker or gamble on the races, with waste of time in studying horses, could put into their work the real energy that they waste in gambling, these men would be successful. . . .

It is not stupendous genius that makes the ordinary successful man. The men of millions are not men with brains constructed in some unusual way. And the more worthy and decent successful men— those who work unselfishly for others with good results—are not really different from their fellow human beings.

Each of us contains in himself enough force and energy to make him succeed. But the difficulty for each of us is to use his power in the right way.

There is enough energy wasted in poker to make a hundred thousand successful men every year. The ingenuity foolish young men display in trying to get money to bet on races would make them really successful in starting a business of their own, if they could use that energy in the right way. There is plenty of energy, plenty of desire to succeed, in this world.

But there are . . . too many who put the crumbs of their real vitality into their work, and put the whole loaf into their dissipations.

They play cards, they make one day and lose the next. They spend in proportion to their exceptional winnings which keeps them poor. They stint, and often lie and cheat and steal, in proportion to what they lose, which makes them worthless. And in the end the "friendly game" in which they think that they neither win nor lose means that they lose absolutely their chance in life, and cannot possibly win anything.

Keep away from friendly games, and all gambling games. Don't try to get something without effort, or without giving something in return. Remember that the force you throw away in dissipation will make you successful in real work if you will only compel yourself to be a worker.

389. *The Dayton Case,* 1925

Clarence Darrow, *Story of My Life* (New York, 1932), 244–5, 248–9, 256, 258–65, 267–8. Copyright 1932 by Charles Scribner's Sons and reprinted with their permission.

FOR years I had been interested in the campaign that culminated in "the Dayton Case." ... Men and women calling themselves "fundamentalists" had been very actively seeking to control the schools and universities of America. The members of this body claimed to believe that the various books that are bound together and are called "the Bible" are inspired in their every statement; that the whole of these books was virtually written by the Almighty and is in every part literally true. ...

Between the periods of many presidential campaigns, and during the dearth of real issues, Mr. William Jennings Bryan placed himself at the head of this movement. ... I had been a close observer of Mr. Bryan's campaigns against knowledge, and I was somewhat acquainted with history and felt that I knew what it meant. I knew how the bill that Mr. Bryan and his organization sponsored was put through, and they had already announced that they would carry the campaign to every state in the Union. ...

I was in New York not long after the arrest of Mr. Scopes, and saw that Mr. Bryan had volunteered to go to Dayton to assist in the prosecution. At once I wanted to go. My object, and my only object, was to focus the attention of the country on the program of Mr. Bryan and the other fundamentalists in America. I

knew that education was in danger from the source that has always hampered it— religious fanaticism. To me it was perfectly clear that the proceedings bore little semblance to a court case, but I realized that there was no limit to the mischief that might be accomplished unless the country was roused to the evil at hand. ...

The bailiff was calling the court to order, "Tennessee versus Scopes." The judge was sinking into his seat beneath a monster sign, saying, "*Read your Bible daily.*" He had a palmleaf fan in one hand, and in the other the Bible and the statutes. As he laid these down on his desk I wondered why he thought he would need the statutes. To the end of the trial I did not know. ...

Down below, at a long table, near the judge's bench, sat William Jennings Bryan, wearing as few clothes as possible. So few, indeed, that had he seen some girl so arrayed he would have considered her a bad sort, and straightway turned his head the other way. His shirt sleeves were rolled up as high as they would go, and his soft collar and shirt front were turned away from his neck and breast about as far as any one less modest would venture; not for the fray, but because of the weather. In his hand was the largest palmleaf fan that could be found, apparently, with which he fought off the heat waves—and flies. ...

The courtroom was packed, and still the people crowded together in the hallways, on the staircases; and the yard, too, was filling up. Spectators had come from near and far. "Hot dog" booths and fruit peddlers and ice-cream venders and sandwich sellers had sprung into existence like mushrooms on every corner and everywhere between, mingling with the rest, ready to feed the throng. Evangelist tents were propped up at vantage points around the town square, where every night one not knowing what was going on would have thought hordes of howling dervishes were holding forth. . . .

When the courtroom was packed just short of bursting apart, it seemed, the judge ordered the doors closed over the sweltering audience, and with great solemnity and all the dignity possible announced that Brother Twitchell would invoke the Divine blessing. This was new to me. I had practiced law for more than forty years, and had never before heard God called in to referee a court trial. . . .

Before the opening of the next session I arose and stated what had happened in the matter, pointed out the character of the case, and made my objection to the court opening the proceedings with prayer. The judge overruled the motion, of course. The people assembled looked as though a thunderbolt had stunned them, and the wrath of the Almighty might be hurled down upon the heads of the defense. . . .

I made a complete and aggressive opening of the case. I did this for the reason that we never at any stage intended to make any arguments in the case. We knew that Mr. Bryan was there to make a closing speech about "The Prince of Peace" and the importance of "The Rock of Ages" above the "age of rocks" and that the closing address he meant should thrill the world was doubtless prepared for the press in manifold copies before he left Florida, and that it would be for the consumption and instruction of those who knew nothing about either "The Rock of Ages" or "the age of rocks." We knew that such of the assembled multitudes as had the capacity to understand would refuse to learn. By not making a closing argument on our side we could cut him out.

We realized that a jury drawn from Dayton, Tenn., would not permit a man to commit such a heinous crime as Scopes had been guilty of and allow him to go scot-free. However, there were questions to be argued concerning the meaning of the statute, and what power the legislature had to make the teaching of science a criminal offense. . . .

The State brought in a number of bright little boys who were pupils of the school taught by Mr. John T. Scopes. They told how Mr. Scopes had tried to poison their young minds and imperil their souls by telling them that life began in the sea from a single cell that gradually developed into the different structures that are now scattered over the earth. The boys said, on cross-examination, that they did not see how this had done them any harm, but Mr. Bryan and the judge knew better. . . .

But the days of the trial were no more interesting than the night life of Dayton. Pop-corn merchants and sleight-of-hand artists vied with evangelists for the favor and custom of the swarms that surged back and forth along the few squares that were the center of the community; speeches were bawled at street corners under the glare of trying artificial-lighting arrangements; the venders raised their voices to drown the evangelists who were the old-time sort who seemed to believe every word they said and were really interested in saving souls; and each worked his own side of the street, up and down. . . .

The judge was much impressed with Mr. Bryan as a leader of the faith, and when some question would be raised and argued he would adjourn court for a day or two to consider it and then come in and automatically decide in favor of the mouthpiece of the fundamentalists. Only a small percentage of the people could crowd into the courthouse at any session. The congestion added to the suffocating temperature, and the two policemen were kept busy offsetting the tropical atmosphere around the judge's sanctified spot. One policeman solaced his own stifled feelings with a wad of tobacco that swiftly melted away into a cuspidor at his feet, and the other worked off his pent-up patience on a gob of gum that had the advantage of being of an indestructible brand, so far as could be guessed. Whether he chewed the same flavor as the judge fished out of his mouth and pasted on the underside of his desk every noon after lunch I had no way of knowing. The judge was always a little late coming in, partly because newspaper photographers waylaid him as well as others, and His Honor was a particularly obliging subject. . . .

Rumors began to go the round to the effect that there was danger of the floor in the courtroom giving way. The exact origin of this report was never quite made known, but together with that came another pretty generally credited to the judge, suggesting that a platform should be built down on the ground and the case continued outdoors. The crowd readily seconded the motion, and no one blamed the judge, for it was his first, and, as it turned out, his last real appearance, excepting for a few vagrant lectures that he attempted on or against "EEvolution" after the trial was over. So we moved down to the courthouse lawn. . . .

The jury was given front seats, and right before them was a great sign flaunting letters two feet high, where every one could see the magic words: "READ YOUR BIBLE DAILY." As for the improved accommodations for the audience—well, there were now acres of audience, branching off into the surrounding streets, waiting for the curtain to rise.

I began the proceedings by calling attention to the flaming instructions to the populace and the jury to *"Read your Bible daily"* and made a motion, for the sake of getting it into the record, pointing out the very evident purpose of influencing the jury, and asked to have the banner removed. Every one paused in awe at the audacity, but it was not a rainy day so that I was taking no chance with lightning. The judge and all the rest of the prosecution expressed great astonishment at any such motion; Mr. Bryan's voice rose above all the others. However, we stood our ground until the attorneys for the prosecution . . . consented to the removal of the blessed banner.

The judge had admitted one of our witnesses to give testimony as to the meaning of the word "evolution" and to describe the process of it as taught. . . . Then I called Mr. W. J. Bryan as an expert on the meaning of the word "religion." At once every lawyer for the prosecution was on his feet objecting to the proceeding. The judge asked me if I considered it important. I reminded him that the statute was based on a conflict between evolution and religion, and that we were entitled to prove the meaning of the words so that the jury could determine whether there was any conflict. Mr. Bryan relieved the situation by saying that he was perfectly willing to take the stand, that he was ready to defend religion anywhere against any infidel. . . . And of course this left the judge with nothing to decide. . . .

Bryan twisted and dodged and floundered, to the disgust of the thinking element, and even his own people. That night an amount of copy was sent out that the reporters claimed was unprecedented in court trials. My questions and Bryan's answers were printed in full, and the story seems to have reached the whole world.

When court adjourned it became evident that the audience had been thinking, and perhaps felt that they had heard something worth while. Much to my surprise, the great gathering began to surge toward me. They seemed to have changed sides in a single afternoon. A friendly crowd followed me toward my home. Mr. Bryan left the grounds practically alone. The people seemed to feel that he had failed and deserted his cause and his followers when he admitted that the first six days might have been periods of millions of ages long. Mr. Bryan had made himself ridiculous and had contradicted his own faith. I was truly sorry for Mr. Bryan. But I consoled myself by thinking of the years through which he had busied himself tormenting intelligent professors with impudent questions about their faith, and seeking to arouse the ignoramuses and bigots to drive them out of their positions. It is a terrible transgression to intimidate and awe teachers with fear of want.

The next morning I reached court prepared to continue the examination all that day. The judge convened court down in the yard, and another preacher asked the blessing and guidance of the Almighty. After allowing time for taking pictures, the judge arose, rested one hand on the statutes and the other on the Oxford Bible, and said that he had been thinking over the proceedings of the day before AND —in spite of Mr. Bryan's willingness again to take the stand—he believed that the testimony was not relevant, and he had

decided to refuse to permit any further examination of Mr. Bryan and should strike the whole of his testimony from the record. Mr. Bryan and his associates forgot to look surprised. It needed no lawyer to grasp that the attorneys for the prosecution could see the effect Mr. Bryan's answers were having on their case and the public in general, and had concluded that something must be done; so it was arranged that the judge should be there in the morning to relieve them of their distress in court. The ruling of the court was by that time extended to forbid the testimony of our scientists as to the meaning of evolution.

The court held that the jury had the statute before them and had heard the testimony of the witnesses proving that Scopes had told his pupils that life began in the sea and had gradually evolved to the various forms of life, including man, that now live upon the earth. The State had offered in evidence the first and second chapters of Genesis, and the jury could judge whether these were in conflict with the teaching of Scopes.

390. *Religious Reading, 1933*

Hornell Hart, "Changing Attitudes and Interests," *Recent Social Trends in the United States. Report of the President's Research Committee* (New York, 1933), I, 401–2, 410–11. By permission. Copyright 1933 by McGraw-Hill Book Company, Inc.

AMONG readers of periodicals and books the relative attention given the Bible has fallen notably during the past quarter century. . . . Of all the books classified by subject in the *United States Catalog* in 1903–1905, 19.7 per thousand were about the Bible; in 1931 only 10.9 per thousand were on that subject. Among articles indexed by subject in the *Reader's Guide* 1.9 per thousand were about the Bible in 1905–1909, while only 0.5 per thousand were on that subject in 1929–1930 and only 0.4 in 1930–1931. . . .

Not only have the proportions of books

and of articles shown declines between 1905–1909 and 1930–1932 of 44 to 80 per cent in the relative attention given the Bible, but both books and articles showed marked recoveries in 1923 to 1926 with subsequent drops which established new low points in 1930. These humps on the curves are easily understood when the proportions of books and articles on Fundamentalism, Modernism, creeds, dogmas, sacraments and theology are examined. Both for books and for articles these subjects reached their highest proportion of attention in the period including 1925—

the year in which John Scopes was tried at Dayton, Tennessee, on the charge of having taught evolution in violation of the state law on the subject. The trial was, of course, merely one climactic episode in a protracted controversy. Revivals of discussion, both of Fundamentalism and the Bible, came earlier in the magazine than in the book data. It seems probable, then, that the temporary revival of interest in the Bible was related to the Fundamentalist controversy, though presumably other elements entered in.

When the unweighted data are compared with the indexes weighted according to circulation it is found that the bulge of interest in the Bible during and immediately after the Fundamentalist controversy was largely a popular phenomenon, probably due to the advertising value of a spectacle. Serious scholarly interest declined more sharply and showed less recovery and more relapse. . . .

The change from traditional Christianity to open-minded religion is evident also from a statistical analysis of the attitude indicators recorded in the representative articles analyzed. The most important statistical changes have involved four outstanding tendencies:

1. The 1930 and 1931 articles tend to accept science as a chief ally in the religious quest instead of regarding it as an antagonist to be fought against or as a disturbing foreign element to be reconciled or adjusted to. In the 1905 articles, 151 references to science were found, of which 40 percent were antagonistic; in the 1930 articles, 352 references to science were found, of which only 18 percent were antagonistic.

2. The recent articles emphasize progress and openmindedness. It used to be widely implied that religious truth had been revealed perfectly, once for all, nineteen centuries ago. This idea has disappeared from recent religious articles in the periodicals analyzed. Creeds, dogmas, authority, the divinity of Jesus and the like, which received 114 favorable references and only 36 unfavorable in 1905, had 116 unfavorable and only ten favorable references in 1930.

3. References to God increased from 108 in 1905 to 221 in 1930 but more skepticism has recently been expressed on the subject. The doubts raised have related chiefly to the question of whether God is personal. The approving references relate neither to the ancient Hebrew Jehovah, nor to the omniscient, omnipotent Deity of medieval metaphysics, but rather to the conceptions which well known scientists and philosophers have recently been discussing under such terms as Creative Coordination, Holism, Creative Synthesis or the Integrating Process at work in the universe.

4. Interest and belief in a life beyond death have dropped to a fraction of the level which they held a quarter-century ago in these periodicals. Articles on these topics numbered 0.57 per thousand in 1910–1914 and only 0.15 per thousand in 1930–1931. In the articles analyzed intensively for 1905, 99 references to a future life were noted, of which 78 per cent were favorable; in 1930 only thirteen such references were found, of which twelve were antagonistic. The goals avowed in these recent articles on religion are fulfillment of personality, the attainment of rich experience and the achievement of basic values here on earth.

391. *The Lost Generation, 1936*

Maxine Davis, *The Lost Generation, A Portrait of American Youth Today* (New York, 1936), 148–9, 152, 153–5. Copyright 1936 by The Macmillan Company and used with permission.

WE SEE this generation drinking, and drinking heavily.... We go to a picnic of high-school boys and girls near Wichita, in "Dry" Kansas, and see bootleg gin disappear in such quantities as to startle a Broadway bartender.

We're invited to a party one Sunday afternoon in Knoxville, in "Dry" Tennessee. "Corn" is not only the refreshment offered in unlimited quantity, but it is also the only subject of conversation.

We never count sexes, but we are sure we see girls drinking more heavily than boys. We're amused one day in New York when we see a young couple in a Park Avenue cocktail room. The girl is drinking a Scotch and soda. Her escort is imbibing milk.

In most of the hotels where there is dancing, we observe young people coming into the bars for drinks between dances.

In San Francisco, in both the fashionable St. Francis Hotel and the Palace Hotel are rooms marked "Ladies' Bar—Gentlemen admitted when accompanying ladies." This perhaps shows a more liberal spirit than in New York dispensaries, which are marked "Ladies' Bar," and nothing is said about gentlemen accompanying them!

We are not happy at the sight of drinking at sporting events. That is a development since our schooldays too. We never had any rules about it. It wasn't usual; it wasn't done....

That there is a great deal of drinking generally isn't only our own observation. The Federal Treasury announces that we're spending about seven cents out of every dollar of our income for alcohol. That's three and a half billions a year! Brewers and distillers announce happily that their business still tends to increase.

The Drys of course blame this on repeal. We doubt this, because we see just as much drinking in the still dry states as in the wide-open ones.

The answer to this is in part, no doubt, buried deep in psychology; in the spirits of men and women, and boys and girls so accustomed to meager lives that they must drink for merriment—for hope—for release....

We find other phenomena, well known to psychologists but never realities to us until we see them ourselves. Escape from their daily lives whether via the movies, or romantic reading, or by dangerous indulgence in drinking, becomes as vital a factor in these young lives as bread or breathing.

These youngsters daydream to throw off reality. One pretty girl in Little Rock tells us a story we hear, with slight variations, all too often. "Jerry—the man I'm engaged to—runs a filling station. He wants to be a doctor. So he's working till he can save enough money. He's twenty-five now. Isn't that pretty late to start being a doctor? Of course, we enjoy planning on it. He's a grand person. He's real highbrow. We read good books together, and we have a good time laughing at the filling station. But I'm worried—"

We burn out an electric fuse, doing some thrifty pressing in a hotel in Salt Lake City, and are pleased when a youth in striped denim overalls and a charmingly cultivated manner comes to repair the damage.

"I do all sorts of odd jobs around," he informs us. "It's a funny way for a fellow who got halfway through dentistry at the University of Michigan to end up, isn't it? No money to finish, you see, and no ability to do anything but excavate your molars and vacuum-clean the hall carpets.". . .

Inability to find work develops all sorts of persecution complexes. Here's a lad in St. Louis who blames the business men. Says he, "The majority of these men have not been satisfied with robbing our parents of their life savings which they had earned through years of hard work. No ma'am. Their minds are so small and busy trying to build a kingdom or a monument for themselves that they are completely ignoring the American youth and are depriving us of our chance. Some of us have parents who have lost everything. So it's up to us to shoulder responsibility and provide for our homes. We go out and seek employment with greatest of earnestness, and what do we run into? So-called business leaders of this country who refuse to give us work, fearing that if they do we would stoop to their level and rob them as they robbed our parents. That's what has happened to several friends of mine just recently, and to me."

This boy is no less uncommon than the lad who thinks some of his teachers are "against him" and prevent him from getting a job.

Nor is it unusual to find young men and women escaping the implications of the fact that they have no job, or cannot afford to marry on what they are earning, by blaming their parents. Often they hold their families responsible for their inability to secure adequate employment, and it's not rare for them to develop an actual hatred of their families. . . .

Overcrowding is a constant cause of family friction, which adds to the sense of frustration of the unemployed, or unhappily occupied young person. The depression years have seen families doubled up—girls sleeping on the davenport in an aunt's home; boys sharing their rooms with a couple of unwelcome small cousins, and

so on. All this domestic discomfort increases these youngsters' natural discontent and despair, and it is not surprising to find that they hold their mothers and fathers guilty.

Inability to marry, we observe, causes untold misery, for, as we've seen, satisfaction of a biological urge isn't enough for our youth, even when they do indulge it. They want a home of their own, children, a place in the community. Thus when they can't marry the girls they love, they develop a sense of inferiority, inadequacy, which we often fear may leave them with an unbalanced viewpoint all their lives.

Yet, in spite of all this, this generation is, on the whole, rather remarkable. Those who are not destroyed by circumstance have quality.

The term "flaming youth" so popular in our day is a phrase they scarcely know. They don't believe, with us of our time, that "youth must be served."

They aren't afraid of hard work. As we've seen, they'll do anything.

There is little snobbery among them. With the exception of boys and girls in some sections of the South, they have little sense of social place. In the South, they make up for this inherited snobbery because they are taught that "Good citizenship should be the first avocation of a gentleman." And if, as its corollary, they unconsciously hold that only a "gentleman" has a right to be a citizen in the full sense, why, they're not aggressive about it. Not within the limits of the white race.

Neither the rich nor the poor are particularly money-conscious. They're not cocky as we were, nor do they show any indications of that cynicism which characterized us in our youth. They have the most serious situation, psychologically and economically, that has ever faced a generation of American boys and girls.

392. *Gang Origins in the 1920's*

"Report of the Special Senate Committee to Investigate Organized Crime in Interstate Commerce," 82 Congress, 1 Session, *Senate Report*, No. 307 (1951), 50–1, 150, 151.

CHICAGO, by virtue of its size and its location as a center of communications, transportation, and distribution of goods, has been and remains a focal point for the activities of organized criminals in the United States. This does not mean that the law-enforcement officials of the city have been uniformly lax in the performance of their duties, although the committee has found evidence of deplorable laxity on the part of individual officials. It does mean that because of the history of the city, its physical location and its great size, the job of law enforcement in Chicago remains a tremendous responsibility and challenge to the law-enforcement agencies and to the citizens of Chicago and its surrounding areas. . . .

The roots of the criminal group operating in Chicago today go back to the operations of the Torrio-Capone gang which terrorized Chicago in the 1920's. Records seized by the police during that period indicated that John Torrio, Al Capone, Jacob Guzik, Tony Accardo, Joseph Fusco, Frank Nitti, John Patton, Murray Humphries, Paul (Ricca) DeLucia, Alexander Greenberg, and others had built up an illegal empire netting millions of dollars a year. In the late 1920's, Torrio abdicated his leadership and Al Capone took over. The activities of the Capone gang at this time consisted largely of illegal liquor rackets, prostitution, gambling, and the control of horse-racing and dog-racing tracks. During this period the gang was particularly powerful in Burnham, Illinois, a suburb of Chicago, whose mayor, John Patton, was closely associated with Torrio and Capone.

In 1924, the Torrio-Capone gang manned the polls during the mayoralty election in Cicero, another Chicago suburb, as part of a plan to take over the local government in Cicero. Following the 1924 election, Cicero became the headquarters for gang operations, and gang influence is still strong there today. In 1931, Al Capone was brought to trial and sentenced for Federal income-tax evasion after all attempts to establish his bootlegging operations had failed to put him in prison. Capone's place as leader of the gang was then taken by Frank Nitti, who, like Capone, was believed to have an interest in the Manhattan Brewery Co., and was an old-time member of the Torrio-Capone gang. At the time of Capone's conviction, the men who were believed to be important members of his underworld empire were, among others, Nitti, Louis Campagna, Paul Ricca, Jacob Guzik, Tony Accardo, Charles Fischetti, Edward Vogel, Hymie Levin, and Ralph Capone. . . .

Until the repeal of the eighteenth amendment in 1933, the manufacture and distribution of bootleg liquor constituted an important source of revenue for the Capone syndicate. After repeal, the Chicago underworld, like racketeers all over the country, concentrated its attention on the revenue possibilities of illegal gambling, extortion rackets, and infiltration of legitimate enterprises.

In Chicago, in many of the service industries, in the liquor industry, and in the unions, there has been a long history of activity by former Capone mobsters. Violence and bombings still occur. There is little doubt that members of the Capone syndicate use proceeds from their illegitimate activities to buy their way into hotels, restaurants, laundry services, dry-cleaning establishments, breweries, and wholesale and retail liquor businesses. In all such businesses their "contacts" give them a substantial advantage. . . .

The race wire service . . . makes it possible for organized criminal syndicates to gain a foothold in every community in the country. Bookmaking provides the richest source of revenue from gambling operations and the wire service, which transmits up-to-minute information about racing news, is essential to big-time bookmakers. A bookmaker who does not have the wire service cannot compete with one who has. . . . The organization which controls the wire service can, in effect, control bookmaking operations. . . .

The racing wire news service first assumed importance under the ownership of M. L. Annenberg, some 30 years ago. Annenberg had been circulation manager for several large metropolitan newspapers and had likewise interested himself in the distribution of racing news publications known as scratch sheets. These scratch sheets contained information with respect to various aspects of horse racing which was intended to guide prospective bettors.

He conceived the idea of establishing a telegraphic news service which would carry over the wires fast and accurate information on racing for bookmakers and, with the big daily news distribution loops as his model, set up his own method of racing news coverage.

In the days when Annenberg, now deceased, was building newspaper circulations, competition between daily papers in metropolitan areas was intense. . . . The fight for circulation was a rough-and-tumble affair. Often violence was resorted to in order to cut down the circulation of a rival journal. Obviously many of those who participated in the circulation wars were strong-arm individuals to whom street brawls for control of newsstands and distribution outlets were everyday affairs.

To obtain the news from race tracks was the first problem of the new wire service. Some track owners were willing to sell the exclusive privilege of reporting from their enclosures to the news service which Annenberg named Nationwide News Service. However, some tracks were unwilling to cooperate and here it was necessary for the news to be purloined. For this purpose it was only natural for Annenberg to employ some of the individuals who had been associated with him in the newspaper-circulation wars. Crews were formed to telegraph racing information from some point near the track, if not inside it, to a central location in Chicago, whence it was relayed to other distribution points in the various states. From these latter subcenters of distribution local distributors furnished it to bookmakers.

393. *Athletics, 1933*

Recent Social Trends, II, 927–33. By permission. Copyright 1933 by McGraw-Hill Book Company, Inc.

A STRIKING feature of the expansion of golf is the rapidity with which the game has swept over the country. . . . Playing facilities are now sufficiently widespread to be accessible to millions of people, and many new courses are being constructed every year.

It is significant that golf makes such heavy demands upon space that conveniently located golf courses cannot be provided in sufficient numbers without prohibitive expense. Moreover, golf, as it has been developed, is an expensive game requiring a large outlay of capital for playing facilities, as well as a considerable expenditure of both time and money on the part of individual players. Its period of most rapid growth coincided with the rise of a business cycle when plenty of money was available for recreational pursuits. . . .

The trend toward greater participation in outdoor sports can also be seen in the growing popularity of tennis. . . . The number of public tennis courts in the various cities of the United States in 1930, reported in the *Yearbook* of the National Recreation Association, was 8,167. . . . Through this remarkable growth of public tennis courts the game has become national in scope and is played by all classes of people. Public tennis courts are now as crowded as public golf courses, the number of players increasing as rapidly as playing facilities multiply. . . . The present popularity of tennis and golf seems to give some indication of a trend away from bodily contact games toward those sports which allow an equal and companionable participation of the sexes. . . .

Evidence of the popularity of games, played by both professional and amateur teams, can be found in the increasing size of grandstands and stadia, the large amount of space given to sports by newspapers, and the broadcasting of games play by play over nationwide networks of radio stations. Every city has its athletes whose prowess is a matter of local pride and concern. Following the fortunes of favorite teams and players is an important leisure time pursuit for large numbers of people.

Among athletic sports which are popular public spectacles, college football has outstanding public support. The whole nation demands information concerning victories and defeats of better known teams, and the accomplishments of the more successful players also receive wide publicity. During the past few years, in spite of record breaking crowds at some of the games, considerable discussion has arisen concerning the future of college football and its possible decline in public favor. Critics are pointing to the fact that students in general seem less excited than formerly over the outcome of games, and that the public quickly loses interest in

teams which fall below championship caliber. . . .

[Nevertheless,] attendance more than doubled between 1921 and 1930. . . . Available evidence, therefore, seems to indicate that college football is not on the wane. . . .

The spectacular increase in attendance at football games during the past decade has been accompanied by a wave of grandstand and stadium building far surpassing any previous development of this kind. According to reports from 135 institutions, the seating facilities for football spectators increased from 929,523 in 1920 to 2,307,-850 in 1930, a gain of 148 per cent. These institutions reported 74 concrete stadia, 55 of which had been built since 1920. Only one of these college stadia in 1920 had a seating capacity of more than 70,-000, while there were seven in this class in 1930.

In so far as present evidence indicates, therefore, football can hardly be regarded as a passing fad which will soon give way to something else. The huge investments in stadia, which must be paid off in future years, make almost inevitable the continued approval of the game by college administrative authorities. Its capacity to produce gate receipts and its value as an advertising medium are assets that cannot be ignored. Moreover, the game itself has those combat elements which make it a thrilling spectacle, entirely apart from the colorful features provided by rival student bodies. . . .

Professional baseball, which has for many years provided public spectacles of great interest to thousands of people, is already showing the effect of growing competition with other sports and amusements. More than ten million people attended the games of the two major leagues during the season of 1930, approximately a million more than in 1920, but this increase has not kept pace with the growth of population in the 11 cities in which these leagues operate. While the population increased 20.5 per cent in these cities between 1920 and 1930, the attendance at games made a gain of only 11.5 per cent. The curve of attendance is still mounting upward but has made no spectacular rise within recent years, as has been the case with college football. The minor leagues of professional baseball, operating in cities of smaller size in all sections of the country, are facing a much more serious situation as far as public support is concerned. The three leagues belonging to Class AA, the highest ranking division among the minors, have had a marked decline since 1928, and the attendance in 1930 was considerably less than in 1923. Four of the smaller leagues suspended operations during 1930; three others experienced a 21 per cent decline in attendance between 1927 and 1930.

While the throngs attending athletic games and sports leave an impression of a widespread mania to be amused by others, it is in fact becoming difficult to maintain public interest in games where

championships are not at stake or where widely known and popular players do not participate. . . . When due consideration is given to the available evidence, there is no reason to believe that Americans are becoming a nation of spectators who prefer to watch rather than to play games. On the contrary, interest in sports as public spectacles has already been equalled, if not surpassed, by the demand for more adequate playing facilities and their extensive use by the public. Moreover, in the rise of American athletic sports, the roles of participant and observer have been combined to their mutual advantage. Attendance at professional games and contests has stimulated interest in athletics and aided in developing a public opinion strong enough to secure municipal appropriations for athletic fields, playgrounds and golf courses. The profits from college football are often the funds which make possible comprehensive programs of intramural athletics for the student bodies.

394. *The Scottsboro Boys, 1931*

Walter White, *A Man Called White* (New York, 1948), 127, 128, 130–1, 133. Copyright 1948 by Walter White. Reprinted by permission of The Viking Press, Inc.

A FEW days after the arrest the defendants were returned to Scottsboro, indicted on charges of rape, and in the minimum time allowed under the law were placed on trial. National Guardsmen with drawn bayonets, tear-gas bombs, and machine guns made the antiquated Jackson County courthouse appear like a fortified position in an advanced battle zone. More than ten thousand whites, many of them making no effort to conceal weapons, jammed the courthouse grounds and the streets of the sleepy little town of fifteen hundred population. . . .

Victoria Price was put on the stand. Jauntily she told in great detail, obviously loving every minute of the rapt attention accorded her, of the six mythical criminal

assaults she had undergone. Ruby Bates followed her on the stand. Less of an extrovert and obviously more reluctant to tell the lies she had been coached to tell, she however corroborated sufficiently the lurid recital of the flamboyant Victoria Price to insure the sentencing to death of eight of the defendants and to life imprisonment of the ninth. The prosecutor asked only for life imprisonment for him because he had "celebrated" his fourteenth birthday in jail as he awaited trial.

It is certain that convictions were inevitable in that atmosphere. But if there had been any slightest chance of a fair trial, that chance went glimmering when Judge Hawkins revealed that he had received a telegram from a Communist organization in New York City, the International Labor Defense, asserting that he as presiding judge would be held personally responsible unless the nine defendants were immediately released. . . .

The defendants and their parents and guardians together presented one of the most damning indications of Southern race prejudice I have ever seen—all of them had been given little education and had been ground by poverty and bigotry all their lives. It was an exciting new experience for them to be addressed as "Mister" or "Missus" and to be treated by white people as human beings on a plane of equality which they had never known before from the "good, white, hundred per cent Americans" of their native South.

When, by various means, the defendants and their parents and guardians became convinced that the ILD was the organization which they wished to defend them, there was no alternative left except for the NAACP to withdraw from the case, making public its reasons for so doing, with an itemized accounting of moneys raised and expended in the case.

In control of the case, the Communists proceeded to publicize and agitate it in every part of the world. Public meetings of the NAACP were particularly the target of the campaign. A favorite device was to announce in such a meeting that one of the Scottsboro mothers was present and demanded the right to speak. If permission was granted, a Communist would make a lengthy introduction expounding the merits of Communism. If permission were denied, at a prearranged signal Communists in the audience or their sympathizers would join in a shout demanding that the mother be heard. There were only five living "mothers" of the nine defendants, but many more than five "mothers" were produced in various parts of the country at public gatherings. In one instance a colored woman presented as a Scottsboro mother had lived for more than twenty years in the Northern city in which she spoke. All this apparently was based upon strategy at that time being followed by Communists throughout the world, namely, to attempt to organize with greatest vigor among the most exploited and oppressed group in each "capitalist" country as the most fertile soil for revolutionary propaganda. It will be remembered that the Scottsboro case came two years after the stock market collapse of 1929 and as America moved into the most serious economic depression it had ever known.

395. *Invasion from Mars, 1938*

Hadley Cantril (with Hazel Gandet and Herta Herzog), *Invasion from Mars. A Study in the Psychology of Panic* (Princeton, 1947), 47, 49, 53–4.

LONG before the broadcast had ended, people all over the United States were praying, crying, fleeing frantically to escape death from the Martians. Some ran to rescue loved ones. Others telephoned farewells or warnings, hurried to inform neighbors, sought information from newspapers or radio stations, summoned ambulances and police cars. At least six million people heard the broadcast. At least a million of them were frightened or disturbed. . . .

Mrs. Joslin, who lives in a poor section of a large eastern city and whose husband is a day laborer, said, "I was terribly frightened. I wanted to pack and take my child in my arms, gather up my friends and get in the car and just go north as far as we could. But what I did was just set by one window, prayin', listenin', and scared stiff and my husband by the other sniffin' and lookin' out to see if people were runnin'. Then when the announcer said 'evacuate the city,' I ran and called my boarder and started with my child to rush down the stairs, not waitin' to ketch my hat or anything. When I got to the foot of the stairs I just couldn't get out, I don't know why. Meantime my husband he tried other stations and found them still runnin'. He couldn't smell any gas or see people runnin', so he called me back and told me it was just a play. So I set down, still ready to go at any minute till I heard Orson Welles say, 'Folks, I hope we ain't alarmed you. This is just a play!' Then, I just set!" . . .

Sylvia Holmes, a panic-stricken Negro housewife who lived in Newark, thinking the end of the world was near, in her excitement overstepped the bounds of her usual frugality. "We listened getting more and more excited. We all felt the world was coming to an end. Then we heard 'Get gas masks!' That was the part that got me. I thought I was going crazy. It's a wonder my heart didn't fail me because I'm nervous anyway. I felt if the gas was on, I wanted to be together with my husband and nephew so we could all die together. So I ran out of the house. I guess I didn't know what I was doing. I stood on the corner waiting for a bus and I thought every car that came along was a bus and I ran out to get it. People saw how excited I was and tried to quiet me, but I kept saying over and over again to everybody I met: 'Don't you know New

Jersey is destroyed by the Germans—it's on the radio.' I was all excited and I knew that Hitler didn't appreciate President Roosevelt's telegram a couple of weeks ago. While the U.S. thought everything was settled, they came down unexpected. The Germans are so wise they were in something like a balloon and when the balloon landed—that's when they announced the explosion—the Germans landed. When I got home my husband wasn't there so I rushed in next door and warned the neighbors that the world was coming to an end. My aunt was there and she tried to quiet me and said, 'If God is coming that way, we just have to wait—go home and be quiet—don't be excited.' I went home. My knees were shaking so, I could hardly walk up the stairs. I found my nephew had come home and gone to bed. I woke him up. I looked in the ice-box and saw some chicken left from Sunday dinner that I was saving for Monday night dinner. I said to my nephew, 'We may as well eat this chicken—we won't be here in the morning.' Then my husband came in. When I told him about it, he wasn't as excited as I was, but he thought it was the end of the world coming, too. He turned on our radio to WOR. It was eleven o'clock and we heard it announced that it was only a play. It sure felt good—just like a burden was lifted off me."

XLIV ⁓ *Cultural Maturity*

AMERICAN CULTURE, now as earlier, reflected the social difficulties of the society within which it was located. At the opening of the period newspapers were still the primary means of communication, but as time went on, they more often shared the field with the slick magazines, the movies, and the radio. All these mass media, although confused as to their objectives, were prosperous and high in technical competence (No. 396). The tastes and standards of the mass of the people were predominantly shaped by the vague and uncertain interests of the middle class for whom George Babbitt spoke (No. 397). Their ideals were perhaps most strikingly embodied in the Radio City Music Hall, New York City, a vast cathedral, destined to be the setting for motion pictures produced to cater to the tastes of Main Street (No. 398). Under such circumstances, many of the more sensitive artists were alienated, and either withdrew from the country entirely by emigration, or did so spiritually within the closed circles of the "avant-garde" media (No. 399). On the other hand, science which could be pragmatically tested in terms of immediate results, remained high in social esteem. The foundations supplied an institutional base and the resources for impressive development (No. 400).

The depression cut across the whole cultural life of the nation. It was at once a shock and a stimulus. The activities of the government injected quite a new factor into the situation. Artists and writers now found access to fresh audiences and to public support (No. 401). In the new trends there were dangers of conformity and regimentation, but also exciting creative possibilities (No. 402). Meanwhile, the social problems of the decade, as well as the political innovations that challenged tradition, presented writers with provocative subject matter (No. 403).

While the means of expression were often inadequate, the creative mind in America could yet present a social ideal, inchoate and insecure now, but still tenaciously held in a world of rapid change. A novelist thus set down his vision of the meaning of the American dream (No. 404); and a dramatist fittingly defined the defiant individualism of the man who continued to stand up against injustice, even in defeat (No. 405).

396. *The American Press, 1920's*

Sudhindra Bose, *Fifteen Years in America* (Calcutta, 1920), 122–5, 127–9, 135–8, 142–4.

"NEWSPAPERS can get along," said an editor of my acquaintance, "much better without editorials than without news. Our papers want news—news with snap and sparkle." Truly, American newspapers are at their best in news service. But what is news? According to some it is anything that has happened or is likely to happen, but "nothing is news that happened farther back than yesterday." . . . There are many journalists, however, who define news as anything which is out of the ordinary, the bizarre, the dramatic, or the unexpected. "If you see a dog biting a man," remarked an editor, "it is no news. . . . But if you see a man biting a dog wire us instantly." . . .

Good journalism, according to a suc-cessful newspaper publisher, meant the art of knowing when "hell was going to break loose," and having a reporter there to write it out. The reporter is the most indispensable member of a newspaper staff. . . . He has a marvelous "nose for news," a heaven-born instinct for news-getting. He is alert, keen, resourceful, and always ready on call. . . . The reporter, however, is not always above faking and romancing. . . .

Reporters in this mile-a-minute age have to work under tremendous pressure. They have no time for leisurely composition and careful revision. The reporter writes out his article on the typewriter as fast as his nimble fingers can pound away on the keyboard, while the waiting printer snatches it away sheet by sheet. There is absolutely no opportunity for remodeling, for finishing touches. . . .

It is no idle fancy to say that American newspaper style—in the best papers at any rate—is terse, clear-cut, and forceful. It has the precision, the directness of a Springfield rifle bullet. Concreteness is one of the most noticeable features of American journalism. . . . Moreover, the news is presented in very popular language. Remembering that the average newspaper reader does not care to hunt through dictionaries and cyclopedias, the reporter translates terms, scientific and legal phraseology, into everyday English. . . .

Great significance is attached to headlines. They tell the essential facts of a story in such a way that a busy reader should be able to get the main news by a hasty look. Sensational newspapers use scare heads in immense type. It is to be noted that headlines are sometimes used to mislead the unwary. . . . The Hearst papers have frequently headlines consisting of only two or three smashing words, and they blaze forth in red ink across the whole half page. Such glaring heads compel attention and play upon the crowd's emotion. . . .

In certain sections of the United States, yellow journalism is most rampant. The practitioner of yellow journalism has a talent for picking out the picturesque and the sensational from every item of news that comes to him and twisting it to the front. "A story to be available for his purposes," said one who should know, "must have romance, sympathy, hate, gain in the first sentence, the first line, the first paragraph." . . . The yellow journals decorate their faked news with glaring scare-words, gymnastic headings, flamboyant pictures, and spicy interpretations. These irresponsible screaming sheets howl and yell and turn somersaults to catch the public eye, to get the coin of the gutter. . . .

The Sunday paper . . . is about three times larger than the weekday edition.

The Sunday paper has not only the usual editorials, the local, national and foreign news, but it also contains many special feature articles and illustrations not found in the ordinary daily issue. . . . One part is devoted to general news, one to sports and games, one to household hints, one to society and fashion, one to literature and drama, one to colored comic pictures, one to advertisements, and so on. Some Sunday papers issue a special magazine section, in which appear articles by well-known writers. . . . Still another Sunday feature, which deserves special mention, is the rotogravure section. Here you will see in beautiful green and sepia colors reproductions of the world's most pulse-stirring events, portraits of famous people, views of wonderful scenic beauty, pictures of popular favorites of the stage. . . .

The modern newspaper, which brings out from ten to twelve editions in the course of a single day, is a vast commercial enterprise, a mammoth business, like glassmaking, shoemaking, or brewing. . . . The home of such a newspaper is a skyscraper, a world in itself. Some of the largest establishments employ as many as two thousand people. Every department is specialized. On its editorial staff alone a first class city newspaper will have the following positions: editor in chief, managing editor, news editor, make-up editor, telegraph editor, sporting editor, exchange editor, dramatic editor, editorial writers, society editor, railroad editor, Sunday editor, city editor, and assistant city editor.

Scarcely fifty years ago, American editors used to ask their subscribers to bring in a load of wood, a basket of eggs, or a bushel of potatoes on subscription. The days of hand-to-mouth existence for newspaper men are gone. They now make good money out of their profession. And the chief source of their revenue is advertisements. . . . Now the advertising value of a journal is in direct ratio to its circulation. The paper having the largest circulation will naturally attract the greatest amount of advertisement. And in order to secure extensive circulation many newspapers offer themselves to the subscribers for very much less than even the actual cost of the print paper.... But herein enter the germs of corruption.... For the sake of profits a newspaper will refrain from printing specific news, which may injure the interest of its advertisers.

397. *The Sane Citizen's Art*, 1922

Sinclair Lewis, *Babbitt* (New York, 1922), 182, 187–8.

IN POLITICS and religion this Sane Citizen is the canniest man on earth; and in the arts he invariably has a natural taste which makes him pick out the best, every time. In no country in the world will you find so many reproductions of the Old Masters and of well-known paintings on parlor walls as in these United States. No country has anything like our numbers of phonographs, with not only dance records and comic but also the best operas, such as Verdi, rendered by the world's highest-paid singers.

In other countries, art and literature are left to a lot of shabby bums living in attics and feeding on booze and spaghetti, but in America the successful writer or picture-painter is indistinguishable from any other decent business man; and I, for one, am only too glad that the man who has the rare skill to season his message with interesting reading matter and who shows both purpose and pep in handling his literary wares has a chance to drag down his fifty thousand bucks a year, to mingle with the biggest executives on terms of perfect equality, and to show as big a house and as swell a car as any Captain of Industry! But, mind you, it's the appreciation of the Regular Guy who I have been depicting which has made this possible, and you got to hand as much credit to him as to the authors themselves....

But the way of the righteous is not all roses. Before I close I must call your attention to a problem we have to face, this coming year. The worst menace to sound government is not the avowed socialists but a lot of cowards who work under cover—the long-haired gentry who call themselves "liberals" and "radicals" and "non-partisan" and "intelligentsia" and God only knows how many other trick names! Irresponsible teachers and professors constitute the worst of this whole gang, and I am ashamed to say that several of them are on the faculty of our great State University! The U. is my own Alma Mater, and I am proud to be known as an alumni, but there are certain instructors there who seem to think we ought to turn the conduct of the nation over to hoboes and roustabouts.

Those profs are the snakes to be scotched—they and all their milk-and-water ilk! The American business man is generous to a fault, but one thing he does demand of all teachers and lecturers and journalists: if we're going to pay them our good money, they've got to help us by selling efficiency and whooping it up for rational prosperity! And when it comes to these blab-mouth, fault-finding, pessimistic, cynical University teachers, let me tell you that during this golden coming year it's just as much our duty to bring influence to have those cusses fired as it is to sell all the real estate and gather in all the good shekels we can.

Not till that is done will our sons and daughters see that the ideal of American manhood and culture isn't a lot of cranks sitting around chewing the rag about their Rights and their Wrongs, but a God-fearing, hustling, successful, two-fisted Regular Guy, who belongs to some church with pep and piety to it, who belongs to the Boosters or the Rotarians or the Kiwanis, to the Elks or Moose or Red Men or Knights of Columbus or any one of a score of organizations of good, jolly, kidding, laughing, sweating, upstanding, lend-a-handing Royal Good Fellows, who plays hard and works hard, and whose answer to his critics is a square-toed boot that'll teach the grouches and smart alecks to respect the He-man and get out and root for Uncle Samuel, U.S.A.!

398. *Radio City, 1936*

Edmund Wilson, *Travels in Two Democracies* (New York, 1936), 39–41.

OUTSIDE, a long aluminum-gray strip winks "Radio City" vertically in rose-red neon letters. Gray and brown mats pave the lobby, and from the ceiling shine round light-reflectors with black-blobbed bulbs in the centers, like the eyes of enormous Mickey Mice.

Inside, the Grand Foyer has a majesty which would be imperial if it were not meaningless. Against walls of henna-red, with wainscots of dried-blood-red marble, rise mirror-lengths, framed in long gray curtains and with cylindrical lusters embedded in them, to the height of the highest mezzanine; but when we look up past the chandeliers, two immense cylindrical crystal tassels, the ceiling, a reddish cartridge-copper studded with unpunctured cartridge-tops, contracts the vertiginous hall to the shape of a straight tin canteen. . . .

The Grand Lounge down in the basement suggests a cave of mystery at Coney Island. Large bright gray diamonds in the ceiling shed a sort of indoor twilight on dim gray diamonds on the floor. Diamond-shaped pillars, black and polished, reflect the lounge as a maze of lozenges. On a background of pale crinkled curtains, zigzagged with zebra stripes, a number of big, round, frameless mirrors take the pillars as polished black streaks. A dancer, dull silver, by Zorach, a giantess with legs like thick lead pipes and a rounded wad of hair like a lead sinker, kneels stiffly and stiff-neckedly turns her head.

The auditorium itself, admirable from the point of view of comfort, looks like the inside of a telescopic drinking-cup. Under magnificent looped-up portières of old gold, revealed by another curtain that opens and closes like a camera shutter and needs thirteen electric motors to work it, and to the music of a gigantic orchestra that rises all in one piece on an elevator, a veritable grandstandful of girls in green and red Indian head-dresses and equipped with tambourines and fans, sing "My Old Kentucky Home," "Dixie" and other beloved Southern melodies with a vast heart-shaped lace valentine for background.

In the center sits poor old De Wolf Hopper keeping time with one foot. It is about the only thing he can do. You feel melancholy as you see him and Weber and Fields, ineffective in the enormous theater, getting off lines which must certainly have been handed them, about the greatness of Rockefeller Center. First, you reflect, there was Weber and Fields, a show that people visited like a household; then there were the "extravaganzas," with favorite funny men and fairy-tale plots, "Blue Beard," "The Wizard of Oz," "Babes in Toyland," etc., usually framed in the gold proscenium and the blue and green peacocks of the New Amsterdam; then, later, there were the Hippodrome shows, which, though too big for personalities or plots, though lacking in human interest, had something of the excitement of a circus; then there were the Ziegfeld Follies, which, framed richly by the New

Amsterdam peacocks again, caught the speed, the intensity, the savagery, the luxury, the dazzle of New York. And now there is the Radio City Music Hall, the most elaborate theater ever built—a theater not merely too huge for personality, story, intensity, but actually too big for a show.

The performance with which the Music Hall opened scarcely survived even the first night. On such a stage, the frame, however gorgeous, was so far away from the actor that it could no longer focus interest on him: he might as well have been trying to hold an audience in the Grand Concourse of the Pennsylvania Station. Even the girls were unable to make an impression except by appearing in quantity and executing "precision" dances sug-

gestive of setting-up exercises. It would be amusing if they were really controlled by a photo-electric cell. The comedians and the singers have actually had electrical processes applied to them: though their faces may go for nothing, their voices have been swollen by loud speakers (fifty) till they devour the whole house. And they also talk into microphones for radio audiences—with an effect rather disconcerting and irritating on the audience in the theater who have paid; the theater is no longer really a theater, but merely a source of canalized entertainment; the performance is no longer your performance, but something directed at thousands of old ladies sitting around in mortgaged farmhouses, at thousands of men reading the paper on the beds of Statler Hotels.

399. *The Poet and His Place,* 1914

Ezra Pound, "Editorial," in Margaret Anderson, ed., *Little Review Anthology* (New York, 1953), 101–2.

I can not believe that the mere height of the Rocky Mountains will produce lofty poetry; we have had little from Chimborazo, the Alps or the Andes. I can not believe that the mere geographical expanse of America will produce of itself excellent writing. The desert of Sahara is almost equally vast. Neither can I look forward with longing to a time when each village shall rejoice in a bad local poetaster making bad verse in the humdrum habitual way that the local architect puts up bad buildings. The arts are not the mediocre habit of mankind. There is no common denominator between the little that is good and the waste that is dull, mediocre. It may be pleasing to know that a cook is president of the local poetry society in Perigord,—there is no reason why a cook should not write as well as a plowman, —but the combination of several activities is really irrelevant. The fact remains that

no good poetry has come out of Perigord since the Albigensian crusade, anno domini twelve hundred and nine. There being a local poetry society has not helped to prevent this.

The shell-fish grows its own shell, the genius creates its own milieu. You, the public, can kill genius by actual physical starvation, you may perhaps thwart or distort it, but you can in no way create it.

Because of this simple fact the patron is absolutely at the mercy of the artist, and the artist at the cost of some discomfort—personal, transient discomfort—is almost wholly free of the patron, whether this latter be an individual, or the hydra-headed detestable vulgus.

There is no misanthropy in a thorough contempt for the mob. There is no respect for mankind save in respect for detached individuals.

400. *The Foundation, 1928*

Raymond B. Fosdick, *Story of the Rockefeller Foundation* (New York, 1952), 140–3. Copyright 1952 by Raymond B. Fosdick.

THE Rockefeller Foundation assumed responsibility in 1928 for a far wider range of activity than had been earlier contemplated. Its work literally embraced the globe, and its branch offices in Paris, London, and the Far East reflected its augmented interests.

The new program was defined in broad terms under the heading of the advance of knowledge—later redefined to include the dissemination and application of knowledge. This became the objective that the Foundation was to follow for many years. There was a sense, therefore, in which 1928 marked a turning point in the thinking of the trustees. This was in part due to the fact that they had come to the end of an era in philanthropy, an era that was reflected in many other foundations as well. Huge sums had been spent in the endowment of medicine, public health institutes, and programs in higher education. Apart from the Foundation's contributions, the General Education Board had given over fifty million dollars on a matching basis to raise the endowments of American colleges and universities, and over ninety million for American medical schools. This type of giving could not continue without involving the rapid liquidation of the Rockefeller boards. Moreover, after the depression of 1929, it became increasingly clear that the decline in interest rates and the mounting difficulty in inducing other donors to match foundation funds made appropriations for endowments an uncertain and dubious technique. The interest rates of four and five per cent, which in the twenties and earlier could be confidently relied upon, were slashed to a point where perhaps double the amount of principal was required to maintain incomes of any fixed figure; and indeed fixed figures grew increasingly un-predictable in terms of purchasing power. A new orientation of target, program, and technique became, therefore, a vital necessity as the twenties drew to a close.

The decision of the trustees to concentrate the work of the Foundation on the extension of knowledge was based on a growing conviction that the margin between what men know and what they use is much too thin. Psychiatric institutes can be created and medical schools strengthened, but as one professor expressed it, "we haven't enough that we can confidently teach." Unless research is constantly maintained, the stock pile of knowledge becomes much too low for safety. There is a sense in which the practical applications of knowledge are the dividends which pure science declares from time to time. When pure science lags, or is interrupted by a cataclysm like war, then it is necessary to pay these dividends out of surplus; and obviously this process cannot long continue. . . .

Throughout this period, however, the trustees were always aware that research, which was the technical tool of the new program, could, in some fields at least, become sterile. They wanted to be sure that facts were tested by practical application. Some of them felt that under the impetus of the scientific method, scholarship was inclined to become overinterested in the collection of facts for their own sake, and underinterested in the problem of the philosophy implied by the facts. Those trustees wanted to be certain that the Foundation did not lose sight of what Professor Whitehead called "totality of vision"—a capacity for synthesis and integration, an ability not only to enumerate and describe but to evaluate. In a letter to one of the officers, the president of a prominent college expressed the opinion that nine-tenths of the money that foundations spent for research did not come to grips with public need. This fraction, of course, was a guess on his part, but some of the trustees were uneasy, and one of their committees reported its opinion that "large amounts of money are spent by foundations and universities alike on research projects that are unrealistic, unproductive, and often unrelated to human aspiration or need."

Another question that was raised by the trustees as the third decade of the century grew ominously black was whether the civilization which we are building can utilize the knowledge which it has. The growth of propaganda as an instrument of education, the rise of dictatorships, the arbitrary challenge to democracy as a method of social control—it was phenomena of this type which gave pause to those who believed that the primary need of our age was more knowledge.

It is interesting to note how often, during this period, the trustees gave expression to this doubt. What special branches of knowledge should be enlarged? they asked. Is all knowledge equally important? Is anybody wise enough to determine the relative significance of different types of knowledge in a social order struggling for equilibrium?

401. *The Government and the Arts, 1935*

Grace Overmyer, *Government and the Arts* (New York, 1939), 109–13, 115–16, 119–22.

FROM the standpoints both of expenditure and scope, the temporary Four Arts Projects, inaugurated by the United States in August, 1935, as a measure of unemployment relief, constitute what is probably the most extensive program for artists' rehabilitation ever undertaken by a government.

Out of the original Works Progress Administration appropriation of two billions, the Arts Projects upon their creation received an allocation of 27 million dollars to provide suitable professional work for writers, painters, musicians and actors whom economic conditions had deprived of their usual means of livelihood. By January, 1938, the original allocation for the Arts Projects had been increased to 105 million dollars, of which 87 million had been expended. . . .

The plan, however, was quickly put into operation, national and state directors were appointed, offices were established throughout the country, and before six months had passed, approximately 40,000 men and women—of whom 75 per cent were professional followers of the arts and the rest mechanical or clerical assistants—

had been enrolled in the following classifications: Art Project, 5,330; Music, 15,629; Theater, 12,477; Writers, 6,500. . . .

Begun as a human welfare movement—handicapped by temporariness, stigmatized as "relief," and dogged within by labor troubles and a thousand little human dissonances—the projects have created throughout the country the beginnings of a broad cultural awakening. . . .

In view of the former luxury status of art, the secret of this achievement is not far to seek. Pledged to avoid interference with "normal private employment," the workers on the Arts Projects have been obliged to take art into places where little, if any, art had ever gone before. . . . Through the Arts Projects, free and popular-priced dramatic and musical entertainment—most of it of good, and some of excellent, quality—and free class instruction in scores of cultural branches incidental to the musical, dramatic and graphic arts, have been brought to millions of American citizens of the economic stratum generally described as "underprivileged." . . .

Of the four million persons who, within two years, participated in activities of the new federally-sponsored Community Art Centers—combined art schools and galleries operating in eighteen states—more than half live in sections of the West, Middle West and South, in which art activities had previously been lacking; and the other half mostly in the poorer parts of cities. Of the twenty-five to thirty million persons who attended 1,700 performances by the Federal Theater between February, 1936—the date of its first play—and the beginning of 1938, fully half were youthful products of the motion-picture era, who had never before seen a performance by actors on a stage. Of the stupendous audience total of 92 million to whom, it is estimated, the Federal Music Project, through more than a hundred thousand programs, brought "living music" between October, 1935, and January, 1938, there is reason to reckon that at least nine-tenths lacked the means to attend the high-priced performances in opera houses and concert halls with which the upper tenth of American music lovers is splendidly served. . . .

Each project became a sort of road map for the cultural rediscovery of America from within. There seemed to be, on the part of project planners, a common realization that in the United States native art had been too long neglected, and foreign art too long preferred, and that the time had come at least for a national cultural stock taking. There seemed to be a common agreement that in return for support by the government, the projects might appropriately explore, interpret and exhibit the artistic creations of their countrymen, particularly those of an earlier time. . . .

In accordance with the rule that no private profit may be made out of work done on government time, all the works completed by the Art Project Proper are available, as indefinite loans, to tax-supported institutions, the recipient paying all but labor costs of the production. Assigned as loans, instead of gifts, the works remain the property of the government. They may not be sold or given away by the institution to which they are allocated. . . . More than 13,000 institutions in the first three years of the project's work received loans of 106,452 art works; and requests from hospitals, schools and other institutions far exceeded the number that could be produced. . . .

In the performance of new American works that may be described as experimental—creative efforts in unfamiliar idioms and relatively untried forms—the Composers' Forum Laboratories are fostering a purpose not served by any other agency in the country. Here the composer has not only the privilege of hearing an entire program of his own works performed with complete instrumentation, but also the advantage of appraisal and suggestions from a critical and musically enlightened audience. Forum laboratories are held in New York, Boston and Chicago, semi-monthly through the music season, and at less frequent intervals in Detroit, Milwaukee, Los Angeles and Indianapolis.

In addition to its vast performing section, this largest of the projects has maintained more than 250 music-teaching centers, in which 1,400 former private music teachers have been employed and many thousands of persons of all ages have received free class instruction which has included the playing of practically every instrument as well as singing, musical history, theory and composition. There is also a program for the retraining of music teachers, to which distinguished musicians and educators contribute instruction and lectures. . . .

The Theater Project has never, of course, been able to provide work for all the unemployed actors and stage people in the country. At the peak of its activities it had on its payroll 12,700 persons, and operated 158 companies in twenty-seven states. After the drastic cuts in project personnel in 1937 it still, with 8,500 employees, operated ninety-nine companies in twenty-two states. About half of the persons employed are actors; the others, writers, designers, theater musicians, dancers, stage hands, box-office men, ushers, maintenance workers and the necessary secretarial and accounting forces.

In 1938 the largest Federal Theater projects were in New York, with 4,011 persons; Los Angeles, with 1,289; Chicago, 768. More than a hundred separate Federal Theater plays were seen in New York City from February, 1936, to February, 1938. In the same period community drama, under the direction of project workers, was given in New York in 390 centers located in hospitals, schools and settlement houses. By March, 1938, 1,500 of the actors employed at various times on the project had returned, at least temporarily, to private jobs.

The offerings of the Federal Theater range all the way from pure drama and the classics, through local color and sociological plays, to marionette, vaudeville and circus performances. In the course of experiments with the theater as a force in education and therapeutics, the project has organized hand marionette companies to work in hospitals, with children having paralyzed hands. Experiments, the benefits of which are open to the entire theatrical industry, are also being carried on in theater forms, costuming, scenery and lighting.

402. *Rigidity and Mobility in American Life, 1930's*

F. L. Wright, *An Autobiography* (New York, 1943), 323–5, 327–30.

As SEEN in any Federal plan, catastrophe is to be made organic. The poor are to be *built in!*

Yes, the slums of today are to be made into the slums of tomorrow.

That the poor will benefit by increased sanitation may be granted at a glance. But, not only are the living quarters of the poor to be more germ-proof, but life itself where individual choice is concerned is to be rendered antiseptic. If we trust our eyes.

The skyscraper is to be let down sidewise or the flat-plane tipped up edgewise as traps to crucify, not liberate, humanity.

And the poor man's life is to become just as the rich man's office—No. 36722, block 99, shelf 17, entrance K. with a few twists and turns thrown in to distract attention from the fact. The "poor" man gets a bath-tub and a flower-box, a patch of lawn, but what Freedom to say and believe what he says, were he to say his soul is his own....

These dreams of the new city where and when no real need exists for any city at all are delightfully impartial. These new "ideals" distinguish no one, nor perceive anything except certain routine economies and the rent paying rituals sacred to a business man's civilization....

And yet, what would you? Humanity is here orderly. Decent on the surface again—rank and file—in the great war behind all wars, the great to-have and to-hold. The common denominator in this scheme is here gratuitously officered, standardized like any army, marched not only to and fro, but up and down no little less. Six stories. The common denominator (the plain citizen) on such terms would be no more able to work without the initial nominator (the capitalist) than the machine would be able to work without the human brain. No, the growing ranks of the poor themselves, they are here become the government pawn. They have become the machine itself. In theory and in fact.

"The Noble Duke of York, he had ten thousand men," they all go six floors up, and up six floors again. And none may know just why they go, so narrowly up, up, up, to come narrowly down, down,

down—instead of freely going in and out and comfortably round about among the beautiful things to which their lives are related in horizontal lines on top of this green earth. Why not spend the money on transporting them?

And is not this modern system of devising life on what we may call skyscraper terms (the skyscraper may be laid down flatwise and its occupants be not much better off) intended to reduce all but our mechanistic supervisors and the devisors who may live in pent houses or on the top floors—or those who may secure the privileges of the upper stories, to the ranks of the poor? Themselves the poor in spirit?

A free country and democratic in the sense that our forefathers intended ours to be free, means *individual* freedom for each man on his own ground. And it means that for all, rich or poor alike, as the true basis of opportunity. Or else Democracy is only another Yankee expedient to enslave man to the machine and in a foolish way try to make him like it. . . .

Meantime these United States afford increasingly great road-systems. Splendid highways are becoming ours. Telephone and power poles that everywhere mar these highways and the countryside were long ago obsolete. The old pig-tight, horse high, bull strong fence is no longer needed as modern farming goes. Electrical fencing makes it unnecessary. And these great road-systems, hastening movement toward the city at first, are facilitating reaction now. The countryside is steadily rising in importance.

Railroads, once dominant metallic lines of communication strung in competing lines across the country, are growing gradually useless except for the long haul overland. These private roads will soon be turned into great natural concrete arteries for mobile uninterrupted traffic on several levels. Clumsy heavy coaches dragged roaring along on hard rails are already obsolete. The present heavy railway no matter how amended is too cumbersome and slow for the requirements of modern mobilization, and will pass with the passing of the city.

As new and greater road-systems are added year by year they are more splendidly built. I foresee that roads will soon be architecture too. As they well may be. Great architecture.

Leading toward the city, at first to gratify a hindered or frustrated social and civil life, our great Usonian roads are working the normal way now, in the right direction, leading away from senseless urban congestion and competition to a new life and greater integrity; the Freedom of the country when man with machine leverage in his own hand takes it over. . . .

One more advance agent of reintegration, an already visible item in the coming decentralization of the City, may be seen in any and every roadside service station happening to be well located along the highways.

The roadside service station may be—in embryo—the future city-service-distribution. Each station may well grow into a well-designed convenient neighborhood distribution center naturally developing as meeting place, restaurant, restroom, or whatever else will be needed as decentralization processes and integration succeeds. Already, hundreds of thousands occupy the best places in the towns or, more significantly, pretty well outside the towns.

Eventually we will have a thousand new city-equivalents at work detracting from every small town or great city we now have. Proper integration of these would help overcome the supercentralization now trying to stand against human Freedom.

Added to many such minor stations destined to someday become beautiful countryside features there will be larger traffic stations at main intersections. There may be really neighborhood centers where there will be more specialized commerce and such special entertainments as are not yet available by every man's own fireside. They are increasingly few because soon there will be little not reaching any man where he lives, coming by space-annihilating devices such as broadcasting, television. And incessant publication, of course. The cultural quality of these new means is steadily advancing in spite of the old commercial tides of advertising now swamping them. The neighborhood garage is an "eating" place—the auto camp or "motel" are features of mostly all Western service stations. All these road-side units are increasing in numbers and in scope and scale as well as in range and desirability. . . .

Even now, a day's motor journey is becoming something to be enjoyed in itself—enlivened, serviced, and perfectly accommodated *en route*. No need to get tangled up in spasmodic stop-and-go traffic in some wasteful stop-and-go trip to town nor to any "great" city center for anything whatever except to "view the ruins." These common highway journeys may soon become the delightful modern circumstance, an ever-varying adventure within reach of everyone. Already as Cervantes said, the Road is always better than the Inn.

403. *Politics and Literature, 1930's*

Symposium, "The Situation in American Writing," *Partisan Review*, VI (1939), 26–30, 32–3, 38–44, 46, 51.

How would you describe the political tendency of American writing as a whole since 1930? How do you feel about it yourself? Are you sympathetic to the current tendency towards what may be called "literary nationalism"—a renewed emphasis, largely uncritical, on the specifically "American" elements in our culture? . . .

ALLEN TATE: The failure of proletarianism in literature and the rise of the Popular Front have doubtless accelerated the shift towards "literary nationalism"; to the literary nationalists of the twenties are added those Communists who are whooping it up for Democracy—and who are, of course, helping to liquidate themselves by also whooping it up for war. I am wholly unsympathetic towards literary nationalism of either the older or the newer variety. . . . In one phase, literary nationalism is only the sectionalism of the East and Middle West trying to set up myths for the entire country. In another phase, it can be either finance capitalism or communism cutting across the profoundly regional differentiations of the country as a whole. Literary nationalism, as I see it, is the well-intended idealism of simpletons who are preparing the way

for totalitarianism, capitalist or Marxist; I think the former. . . .

JAMES T. FARRELL: There was an energetic and healthy realistic tendency in American writing during the early years of this decade. It took a leftward turn and was informed by a critical spirit. Continual attempts were made to politicalize this tendency. Among the critics most vocal in this effort were Granville Hicks, Michael Gold, and Joseph Freeman. But these men have now abandoned everything they then asserted with such irritating dogmatism. This, plus the silence of so many of the younger writers whom they praised is, in itself, an epitaph of that effort. The attempt to politicalize literature continues under the banner of the Popular Front. But it uses a new demagogy. Under the guise of defending culture, Popular Frontism abandons literary criteria of judgment, inflates many mediocre and even commercial writers beyond their merits, re-emphasizes anachronistic literary movements such as Populism, and turns literary criticism into a welter of political sentimentalities. It heads directly into cultural and literary nationalism. I am opposed to this literary nationalism. In our day, intellect, thought, science, art must be international. Literary nationalism and Popular Frontism leads to such ineptitudes and feats of political legerdemain as the retroactive admission of Emerson, Whitman, even the late Mary Austin, into the Popular Front. It is a method of assuming literary gains in terms of inches, when losses are being sustained by miles. It collects inconsistencies all along the line as it grows, and it affords the Philistine countless excuses for his Philistinism. It substitutes conventionalizations and demagogy for serious social protest in literature. It does all this in the name of a false unity.... One of the most precious values in the world today is that of the critical spirit. The current tendency toward a cultural nationalism threatens to destroy that spirit. The present wave of literary nationalism does not merely demand a renewed emphasis on the specifically American elements in our culture. It falsifies the meaning and background of these elements, and it twists our history to fit partisan political needs of the present. It demands thinking in shibboleths and catch words which is not thinking at all. The best of twentieth century American literature describes American life, and it is many-sided. But it is critical in spirit. And that critical spirit is under attack; it is being poisoned and perverted, turned into the handmaiden of political interests, and bankrupt political programs. In consequence some writers who have been engulfed in this wave are turning themselves into literary cops. They seem, in certain instances, to be well on the way toward constituting themselves a self-appointed F.B.I. of the spirit of man, and of the spirit of a free modern literature....

KATHERINE ANNE PORTER: Political tendency since 1930 has been to the last degree a confused, struggling, drowning-man-and-straw sort of thing, stampede of panicked crowd, each man trying to save himself—one at a time trying to work out his horrible confusions. How do I feel about it? I suffer from it, and I try to work my way out to some firm ground of personal belief, as the others do. I have times of terror and doubt and indecision, I am confused in all the uproar of shouting maddened voices and the flourishing of death-giving weapons. ... I should like to save myself, but I have no assurance that I can, for if the victory goes as it threatens, I am not on that side. The third clause of this question I find biased. Let me not be led away by your phrase "largely uncritical" in regard to the "emphasis on specifically American" elements in our culture. If we become completely uncritical and nationalistic, it will be the most European state of mind we could have. I hope we may not. I hope we shall have balance enough to see ourselves plainly, and choose what we shall keep and what discard according to our own needs; not be rushed into fanatic self-love and self-praise as a defensive measure against assaults from abroad. I think the "specifically American" things might not be the worst things for us to cultivate, since this is America, and we are Americans, and our history is not altogether disgraceful. The parent stock is European, but this climate has its own way with transplantations, and I see no cause for grievance in that....

WALLACE STEVENS: I don't believe in factitious Americanism. An American has to be an American because there is nothing else for him to be and also, I hope, because it would not matter if there was. Even so, I believe in forgetting about it except as a quality, a savor....

GERTRUDE STEIN: Writers only think they are interested in politics, they are not really, it gives them a chance to talk and writers like to talk but really no real writer is really interested in politics....

WILLIAM CARLOS WILLIAMS: The political tendency of American writing as a whole since 1930 and thirty years before has been toward a discovery of the terms of a discussion and declaration in the only world it can know, that under its nose. When it has succeeded in knowing what it is talking about in those terms it may possibly begin to interest the man of alert senses (Henry Adams) who already knows the world but would be glad to see it correlated by the artist (the writer) in some new sort of creative composition. "Literary nationalism" is a confusion in terms due to bandy-legged and cross-eyed witnesses to what is before them. It hides under its blatancies the very much neglected fact that when a man sees and apprehends with his mind what is before him in America that which he sees there must perforce be American. Give stupidity any name you please, call it American, British or even German, it's still stupidity. We're not talking about that. A renewed interest in specifically "American" elements in our culture (provided they are related in the mind to general culture) would be the beginning of any basic understanding of literature among us. . . .

JOHN PEALE BISHOP: I am not unaware of the difficulties which at present confront our democracy, but I am convinced that they are not insurmountable. I share many of the misgivings as regards democracy which were owned by those who designed our government; but they do not seem to me important compared with the certainty that no other society would do for us at all. Democracy is not a magic word, which we have only to utter to have the rocks fall apart and the robbers' cave open for us, filled with all imaginable riches. It is a way of life which in the future, as in the past, will depend less upon its own virtue than upon ours.

An American writer should find American material richer than any other. But that does not mean it is richer for being American. It may be, in human terms, very poor indeed. The men and women along Tobacco Road are as American as they can be. In Erskine Caldwell's hands, they became excellent literary creatures. But even in his hands, they remain as men and women appalling in their poverty. . . .

HENRY MILLER: Having been away from the country since 1930, . . . I am hardly qualified to describe the political tendency of American writing; but had I been in America all this time I believe I would have been immune to it. I am thoroughly disinterested in politics, whether American, Chinese, or European. Politics is a pursuit which is suitable to those who have nothing better to do. Nor am I interested in the specifically "American" elements in our culture. ("Our" culture—I don't know what that means, to be frank. I didn't know we had a culture.) What interests me in human beings are those things which are above and beyond the question of nationalism. The *man* is the important thing, not what country or culture he represents.

404. *New World Dreams, 1920's*

F. Scott Fitzgerald, *The Great Gatsby* (New York, 1925), 216–18.

I SPENT my Saturday nights in New York because those gleaming, dazzling parties of his were with me so vividly that I could still hear the music and the laughter, faint and incessant, from his garden, and the cars going up and down his drive. One night I did hear a material car there, and saw its lights stop at his front steps. But I didn't investigate. Probably it was some final guest who had been away at the ends of the earth and didn't know that the party was over.

On the last night, with my trunk packed and my car sold to the grocer, I went over and looked at that huge incoherent failure of a house once more. On the white steps an obscene word, scrawled by some boy with a piece of brick, stood out clearly in the moonlight, and I erased it, drawing my shoe raspingly along the stone. Then I wandered down to the beach and sprawled out on the sand.

Most of the big shore places were closed now and there were hardly any lights except the shadowy, moving glow of a ferryboat across the Sound. And as the moon rose higher the inessential houses began to melt away until gradually I became aware of the old island here that flowered once for Dutch sailors' eyes—a fresh, green breast of the new world. Its vanished trees, the trees that had made way for Gatsby's house, had once pandered in whispers to the last and greatest of all human dreams; for a transitory enchanted moment man must have held his breath in the presence of this continent, compelled into an aesthetic contemplation he neither understood nor desired, face to face for the last time in history with something commensurate to his capacity for wonder.

And as I sat there brooding on the old, unknown world, I thought of Gatsby's wonder when he first picked out the green light at the end of Daisy's dock. He had come a long way to this blue lawn, and his dream must have seemed so close that he could hardly fail to grasp it. He did not know that it was already behind him, somewhere back in that vast obscurity beyond the city, where the dark fields of the republic rolled on under the night.

Gatsby believed in the green light, the orgiastic future that year by year recedes before us. It eluded us then, but that's no matter—tomorrow we will run faster, stretch out our arms farther. . . . And one fine morning—

So we beat on, boats against the current, borne back ceaselessly into the past.

405. *The Glory of Earth-Born Men, 1930's*

Maxwell Anderson, *Winterset* (Washington, 1935), 133–4.

TO DIE
when you are young and untouched, that's beggary
to a miser of years, but the devils locked in synod
shake and are daunted when men set their lives
at hazard for the heart's love, and lose. And these,
who were yet children, will weigh more than all
a city's elders when the experiment
is reckoned up in the end. Oh, Miriamne,
and Mio—Mio, my son—know this where you lie,
this is the glory of earth-born men and women,
not to cringe, never to yield, but standing,
take defeat implacable and defiant,
die unsubmitting. I wish that I'd died so, long ago; before you're old you'll wish

that you had died as they have. On this star,
in this hard star-adventure, knowing not
what the fires mean to right and left, nor whether
a meaning was intended or presumed,
man can stand up, and look out blind, and say:
in all these turning lights I find no clue,
only a masterless night, and in my blood
no certain answer, yet is my mind my own,
yet is my heart a cry toward something dim
in distance, which is higher than I am
and makes me emperor of the endless dark
even in seeking! What odds and ends of life
men may live otherwise, let them live, and then
go out, as I shall go, and you.

PART SEVEN

The Challenge of Totalitarianism, 1939-55

I N THE summer of 1939 the event long dreaded by many Americans finally occurred. The Nazi government of Germany, unrestrained in its ambitions and encouraged by repeated concessions, attacked its Polish neighbor. Great Britain and France, pushed to the limit of their endurance, could not now fail to honor their commitments to Poland. Total war broke across Europe.

This time there was no question as to where the sympathies of Americans were. Only the openly Fascist groups defended the actions of Hitler and his allies; and such groups lost steadily in strength as the war went on. On the other hand, a substantial number of citizens, while willing to support the Allied cause, were nevertheless convinced that the United States could ultimately best serve the interests of the free world by remaining neutral. With the experiences of an earlier world war still fresh in their minds, they secured the enactment of a series of legislative measures to prevent American involvement in any new war.

The Roosevelt administration accepted the limitations of neutrality. It was openly sympathetic to the democratic powers, and willing to use any measures short of war to assist them. But it calculated, in 1939, that open involvement would not be necessary, that France and England—with Italy neutral—would be able to bring the Germans down.

These calculations proved disastrously erroneous in the spring of 1940. Hitler then struck two decisive blows that changed the course of the whole war. One, to the North, put Norway and Denmark in his grasp; and with the other, to the West, he swept through the Low Countries and France. By the summer of that year he was unopposed on the continent of Europe.

The new situation called for a revision of American strategy. Now England alone stood between Germany and its total domination of Europe; and the administration was convinced that it was of vital interest to the United States to keep British resistance alive. To this end, the government bent every effort short of war.

The fall of France and of the Netherlands also disturbed the position in the Far East, for the rich colonies of the defeated powers lay open to the advance of the aggressive Japanese. It was no longer a question of limiting Japan's avarice; the issue was no longer China, but control of the whole Western Pacific. For more than a year American statesmen struggled unsuccessfully to arrive at some accommodation with the Japanese. The involvement of the Soviet Union in the war with Germany in June, 1941, removed the last restraint upon the Japanese, and they began to prepare the series of steps that led to the American disaster at Pearl Harbor.

In magnitude, the war was far greater than anything the United States had ever experienced before. It involved fighting in every corner of the earth, on land, on sea, and in the air. It involved the supply, on a gigantic scale, of the Russian and British allies. It called for the mobilization of immense industrial power and the recruitment of enormous sums of money through taxes and loans. At the same time it called for an immediate planning of the post-war settlement. For the disaster left by war was so monumental in scale that it would call for a complete reconstruction of Europe and Asia. That the necessary energies were found for all these tasks was evidence of the strength of the American economy and of the abiding faith of its people in democracy.

The end of the fighting brought not peace but a continuation of war under other terms. The German and the Japanese aggressors were decisively crushed; but the disordered world they left raised new problems of its own.

The American planners of peace had looked forward to a transition period in which the war-torn nations would reconstruct themselves under democratic governments. Meanwhile Germany and Japan were to be occupied; and the nations united in the war were to be organized in peace in the United Nations, to pursue their common ends and to deal with specific problems as they arose.

The difficulty sprang from the fact that the Soviet Union, though an ally, was not a democracy. It used democracy as the cloak for the spread of Communism; and in eastern Europe, it labored to create a series of satellite states. In these war-torn countries democracy failed to find defenders strong enough to resist the delusive slogans of Communism, particularly since these had the aid of the occupying Red army. A series of satellite regimes came into being, except where, as in Greece, the process was halted by the intervention of the democratic powers. Within five years of the end of the war a wholly unexpected emergency called for American intervention and aid to Europe, on the economic level through the Marshall Plan, and on the military level through NATO and a series of security treaties.

Somewhat similar forces at work in Asia were stimulated by a rising tide of nationalist hostility to colonialism. Again the friends of democracies were incapable of halting the spread of Communism without American intervention. The crisis came over Korea, where the cold war passed into open fighting. A long-drawn-out struggle produced a stalemate of sorts at the edges of the Asiatic mainland. There, too, it was necessary to devote continuing efforts to contain the spread of Communism.

The result was a continuing burden of expenditures and preparations for war, a burden difficult enough to bear in itself, and rendered more difficult still by the fact that Americans were also laboring under the threat that the atomic bomb might totally destroy civilization.

The New Deal coalition held together through the war and the early years of peace. It was strong enough to survive the raising of the war issue and of the problem of the third term in 1940. Indeed, it compelled a progressive readjustment within the Republican party, the standard-bearers of which increasingly came to accept the assumptions of the New Deal of the 1930's. But this very acceptance made it more difficult for them to conduct the kind of campaign that might attract voters away from their old allegiances.

On the other hand, the times were changing the nature of the issues. The depression was over, and in the midst of widespread prosperity the problems of the 1930's receded from men's consciousness. More important seemed the great immediate issues of peace and stability; in the election of 1952 the Republicans returned to power behind a leader who seemed to promise the security for which so many Americans longed.

All these problems were eased only by the continued capacity of the American economy to expand. The industrial adjustments of the war period had restored prosperity. But the postwar period saw no recession. Instead, all the indices pointed to continuing growth. And within the terms of that growth a striking reorganization in all the modes of production was taking place.

Prosperity lightened some of the social burdens of the cold war. The position of the minorities improved noticeably. Freedom, opportunity, and mobility seemed more characteristic of American society than for many decades earlier. At the same time there was an enormous development in education, of incalculable significance for the future. If the problems were grave, there was at least the basis for hope that the means for their solution were available.

XLV 🍃 *The Coming of War*

ALTHOUGH the overwhelming mass of Americans hoped for an Allied victory, they were still reluctant to take part in the war that began in September, 1939. Sincere isolationists believed that American participation would not ultimately serve the cause of world peace; they preferred that the United States be neutral in order to be able to assist Europe in dealing with its more fundamental problems (No. 406).

So long as it was possible to expect an Allied victory, the administration accommodated itself to popular sentiment. It left no doubt as to its sympathies, but resisted direct involvement (No. 407). But the fall of France, coming after the defeat of Norway and of the Low Countries, provoked a crisis in American policy (No. 408). Aid to Britain now became a pressing American obligation, the terms and objectives of which were ultimately fixed in a conference between the President and the Prime Minister (No. 409). These problems had already led to progressive definition of the American interest in the struggle, an interest that President Roosevelt phrased in terms of the "Four Freedoms" (No. 410). Meanwhile, the support of the Latin American states had been enlisted (No. 411).

The crisis grew more intense as Japanese activity in the Far East increased; and the American ambassador in Tokyo warned of the dangers likely to face the United States in that quarter of the globe (No. 412). Yet the Japanese (No. 413) and the American (No. 414) conceptions of an acceptable settlement were far apart and no accommodation was possible. While the negotiations were still in progress, the Japanese struck. Although there had been clear intimations of the character of their attack on Pearl Harbor (No. 415), the surprise was complete and disastrous (No. 416). The success of the Japanese conditioned the character of the whole war. But it also united Americans in the determination to fight it to a victorious conclusion (No. 417).

406. *The Wave of the Future, 1940*

A. M. Lindbergh, *The Wave of the Future* (New York, 1940), 13–14, 17–19, 22–5, 28–9, 33–4.

A VERY good case can be, and has been, built up for the "Have-not Nations" deserving more share in the possessions of the world, largely in the hands of the "Have Nations.". . . Had post-war Republican Germany been given more support and aid by the "Democracies," had reasonable territorial and economic concessions been made to a moderate government, there would have been no Naziism and no war.

I do not believe that this case, right as it may be, excuses the methods of aggression and war; but it does, to some degree, explain them. Frustration and privation explain theft; they do not excuse it. However, I am not now arguing on so literal or particular a plane. What I am trying to analyze is something far more profound and fundamental than national rights and wrongs. . . .

No, I cannot see the war as a "crusade." If I could label it at all, I would label it part of a vast revolution. I am not here defending the forms this revolution has taken: aggression, terror, class or race persecution. I oppose these as deeply as any American. But I do feel that had the world been able, by peaceful revolution, to foresee and forestall the changes, to correct the abuses that pushed behind the Communist and Fascist revolutions, we would not now have to come to them by such terrible means. . . .

I cannot see this war, then, simply and purely as a struggle between the "Forces of Good" and the "Forces of Evil." If I could simplify it into a phrase at all, it would seem truer to say that the "Forces of the Past" are fighting against the "Forces of the Future." The tragedy is, to the honest spectator, that there is so much that is good in the "Forces of the Past," and so much that is evil in the "Forces of the Future."

To make this statement is not to say that "might makes right," or that it is Germany's "turn to win," or to give any such literal and facile explanations. It is not to claim that the things we dislike in Naziism are the forces of the future. But it is to say that somehow the leaders in Germany, Italy and Russia have discovered how to use new social and economic forces; very often they have used them badly, but nevertheless, they have recognized and used them. They have sensed the changes and they have exploited them. They have felt the wave of the future and they have leapt upon it. The evils we deplore in these systems are not in themselves the future; they are scum on the wave of the future. . . .

What I question is the confident assumption that this way of life—in which I include our own here in the United States—will still be there after the war is over, even if Great Britain wins; or

that it would have continued for long, unchanged, had there been no war. A world in which there were widespread depressions, millions of unemployed, and drifting populations was not going to continue indefinitely. A world in which young people, willing to work, could not afford a home and family, in which the race declined in hardiness, in which one found on every side dissatisfaction, maladjustment and moral decay—that world was ripe for change. That it had to die in violence is the catastrophe; that it had to die in misery, terror and chaos; that it had to fall, dragging down with it much that was good and beautiful and right, spilling the blood, wasting the lives, warping the spirit of many who were needed for the reconstruction of the new world; that it had to die in war, which carries in its train those very miseries it seeks to escape.

I always hoped war could be avoided, or that an early peace would still save some part of a world I loved—that the good of a dying civilization could be bequeathed in comparative tranquillity to the new one; as, in nature, a flower dies, but the plant puts forth a new bud from the old stem. All chance for peaceful transition passes more irretrievably with each day that the war continues. The old world we loved is going, and I doubt very much that what immediately follows—if every nation blazes in the same conflagration—will be appreciably better, even in the "Democracies," than what we have witnessed in Germany lately. . . .

I cannot pledge my personal allegiance to those systems I disapprove of, or those barbarisms I oppose from the bottom of my heart, even if they are on the wave of the future. Nor do I propose the surrender of our basic beliefs. But I do feel that it is futile to get into a hopeless "crusade" to "save" civilization. I do not believe civilization can be "saved" simply by going to war. Neither can "democracy" or "liberty" or "our way of life" be saved by any such negative point of view.

If we do not better our civilization, our way of life, and our democracy, there will be no use trying to "save" them by fighting; they will crumble away under the very feet of our armies.

It seems to me that our task, instead of crusading against an inevitable "revolution," or change, in Europe, is to work toward a peaceful "revolution" here, or, rather, a reformation—to reform at home rather than crusade abroad. . . .

If one were in the war, one could not do otherwise. But we are not in the war here in America, and if we cannot take a planetary view of the world's troubles, who can? . . . The belligerents of this war can hardly help feeling hate, horror, shock, and anger. We, ourselves, cannot help feeling shock and horror; but at the same time we, in America, are in a unique position to judge the tragedies clearly. Surely our task is not voluntarily to surrender this point of vantage by climbing down into the maelstrom of war, where we can only add to the chaos; but rather to see as clearly as possible how to prevent such tragedies from happening here, and how

best to assuage the sufferings caused by them abroad. . . .

I do not believe we need to be defended against a mechanized German army invading our shores, as much as against the type of decay, weakness, and blindness into which all the "Democracies" have fallen since the last war—have fallen into, perhaps, from a surfeit of success. We are in danger—yes, not so much from bombing planes as from those very conditions which brought on trouble in Europe, and will inevitably bring on trouble here if we do not face them. Shall we turn our backs on these weaknesses, these troubles, these mistakes of our own while we try to wipe out other mistakes abroad? . . .

There is no fighting the wave of the future, any more than as a child you could fight against the gigantic roller that loomed up ahead of you suddenly. You learned then it was hopeless to stand against it or, even worse, to run away. All you could do was to dive into it or leap with it. Otherwise, it would surely overwhelm you and pound you into the sand.

407. *The Issues of Neutrality, 1938–39*

H. L. Ickes, *Secret Diary* (New York, 1954), II, 481, 703–5, 715. Copyright 1954, by Simon and Schuster, Inc. Reprinted by permission.

[SEPTEMBER 30, 1938]. In one of our private conferences the President told me that he had wanted to avoid the mistake that Wilson had made in 1914. He felt that if Wilson had expressed himself vigorously then, war might have been averted. First Wilson wanted to wait to see what Russia would do, then what France would do, and then what England would do. When he finally expressed himself, he did not allow for the difference in time between Washington and Berlin, with the result that the German troops were already across the Belgium frontier. . . .

[August 26, 1939]. The Russian-German alliance has been a great shock. It probably means a partition of Poland. Russia will not have to worry about the Ukraine, and her annexation of Bessarabia would not be disputed. Germany will probably either take outright or bring under her control Romania and Hungary. Yugoslavia will either fall to Italy or be divided. The Balkan states will probably be left as they are—buffer states between Germany and Russia but more or less under Russian influence. Greece will feel the heavy hand of Italy. What will happen to Turkey is hard to foresee, but Italy will be given control in the Mediterranean and the Black Seas. Franco will probably take Spain into the Axis powers and Portugal will be under the Axis influence. Germany will probably bring pressure upon Denmark, Belgium, and Holland and take from the latter two their great and rich colonies in Africa and the Far East. Some of these may be divided with Japan. In the meantime, Japan will probably apply itself to the dismemberment of that part of the British and French empires that impinge upon what she regards as her influence in Asia.

It is a terrible situation, but I find it difficult to blame Russia. As I see it, Chamberlain alone is to blame. I entertain no doubt that England could have concluded a satisfactory treaty with Russia months ago or even years ago. Russia was ready to join hands with England and France to fight for Czechoslovakia. That Czechoslovakia was dismembered is chargeable directly, and almost entirely, to England. Then Poland, which is now in such dire straits, wanted its slice of Czechoslovakia. Slovakia wanted to be on its own and Hitler gave it a twenty-five-year guarantee of independence and protection. Last week, in effect, he took over Slovakia and there are said to be at least 250,000 German soldiers within its borders today facing the Poland frontier. Many chickens have come home to roost, but the chief sufferer inevitably will be England because, unless a miracle happens, it seems to me that the dismemberment of the British Empire, and that of the French as well, is in sight.

England and France, with Russia, especially if Czechoslovakia had not been dismembered, could have defeated Germany and Italy. I doubt very much whether England and France can now defeat Germany and Italy with Russia sterilized. The situation today is the perfect flower of a course of British diplomacy that traces from Sir John Simon through Baldwin to Chamberlain. It is these three men, particularly Chamberlain, who are likely to be entitled to have a legend carved on their tombstones: "Here lies the destroyer of the British Empire."...

How the whole thing is going to sum up and whether, if war breaks out in Europe, we will ultimately become involved no one knows. It is all in the lap of the gods. I suspect that most people in this country believe that we would become involved and if they believe this, it is likely to happen....

[September 9, 1939]. At Cabinet on Monday we discussed the question of neutrality. It was decided to issue at once the customary neutrality declaration that follows any outbreak of war. The President was not in so much of a hurry to issue the proclamation required under the Neutrality Act. He wanted England and France to have all the opportunity possible to export munitions of war, none of which could be exported after this proclamation was once issued. We also discussed the issuing of a declaration of emergency. The President disclosed that by issuing such a declaration the Executive branch of the Government would have greatly enhanced powers. He was in some doubt whether to issue it almost at once or to wait until there was a greater evidence of public sentiment in the country.

408. *The Fall of France, 1940*

Cordell Hull, *Memoirs* (New York, 1948), I, 765–6. Copyright 1948 and used with the permission of The Macmillan Company.

BUT even more catastrophic than the news of German successes in the Low Countries were the cables Ambassador Bullitt sent the President and me on May 15. The Germans, advancing with overwhelming forces of tanks and dive bombers, had broken through the French Army at Sedan. Premier Reynaud had telephoned to Prime Minister Churchill that, since the Germans had broken through, the war might be lost in the course of a few days. In Reynaud's opinion, it would be lost unless Britain sent her fighter-plane strength to France at once. Churchill promised to recommend this to the War Cabinet, insisting to Reynaud, however, that there was no chance of the war being lost. . . .

Bullitt chanced to be with the Minister of National Defense, the former Premier Daladier, when General Gamelin telephoned the news of the Sedan collapse, endangering the whole French Army. Daladier said it was obvious that, unless God granted a miracle like that of the battle of the Marne in the First World War, the French Army would be crushed utterly. The British, he said, were criticizing the French and not throwing all they had into the fight.

On the same day, May 15, Ambassador Kennedy cabled to the President and me a striking conversation he had just had with Mr. Churchill. The Prime Minister had said he was sending the President a message on the next day that he considered the chances of the Allies' winning slight if Italy entered the war. The French were asking for more troops, but he was unwilling to send men from England because he was convinced that within a month England would be vigorously attacked. He added he intended to ask for a loan of thirty or forty of our old destroyers and also whatever planes we could spare.

The Prime Minister ended with a ringing statement, a forerunner of similar battle cries in the near future which rallied around him all those not intimidated by the Nazi might. Regardless of what Germany would do to England and France, he said, England would never give up as long as he remained a power in public life, even if she were burned to the ground. The Government, he asserted, would move to Canada, take the fleet with it, and fight on.

Kennedy, however, concluded his dispatch by asking what we could do, and saying it seemed to him that if we had to fight to protect our lives we should do better fighting in our own back yard.

The President and I were asking each other the same question in those fateful days, but we reached a different conclusion from Kennedy's. It seemed to us we should do better to keep the fighting away from our own back yard. This we could do by helping Britain and France remain on their feet. Then came the question, Exactly what could we do to help them? On the political side we had to bear in mind that, although the American people were seeing ever more clearly where their interests lay in the European war, there was still a strong isolationist sentiment in and out of Congress. Many of the isolationists maintained that the United States could go peacefully on her way whoever won the war in Europe. On the material side stood the question, Exactly what war supplies could we sell Britain and France, and how quickly could we get them to the theater of war?

Of one point the President and I had not the slightest doubt; namely, that an Allied victory was essential to the security of the United States.

409. *The Atlantic Conference, 1941*

President Roosevelt, Message to Congress, August 21, 1941, 77 Congress, 1 Session, *House Document* No. 358, reprinted in *Peace and War. United States Foreign Policy 1931–1941* (Washington, 1943), 718–19.

THE PRESIDENT and the Prime Minister have had several conferences. They have considered the dangers to world civilization arising from the policies of military domination by conquest upon which the Hitlerite government of Germany and other governments associated therewith have embarked, and have made clear the steps which their countries are respectively taking for their safety in the face of these dangers.

They have agreed upon the following joint declaration:

... The President of the United States of America and the Prime Minister, Mr. Churchill, representing His Majesty's Government in the United Kingdom, being met together, deem it right to make known certain common principles in the national policies of their respective countries on which they base their hopes for a better future for the world.

First, their countries seek no aggrandizement, territorial or other;

Second, they desire to see no territorial changes that do not accord with the freely expressed wishes of the peoples concerned;

Third, they respect the right of all peoples to choose the form of government under which they will live; and they wish to see sovereign rights and self-government restored to those who have been forcibly deprived of them;

Fourth, they will endeavor, with due respect for their existing obligations, to further the enjoyment by all states, great or small, victor or vanquished, of access, on equal terms, to the trade and to the raw materials of the world which are needed for their economic prosperity;

Fifth, they desire to bring about the fullest collaboration between all nations in the economic field with the object of securing, for all, improved labor standards, economic advancement, and social security;

Sixth, after the final destruction of the Nazi tyranny, they hope to see established a peace which will afford to all nations the means of dwelling in safety within their own boundaries, and which will afford assurance that all the men in all the lands may live out their lives in freedom from fear and want;

Seventh, such a peace should enable all men to traverse the high seas and oceans without hindrance;

Eighth, they believe that all of the nations of the world, for realistic as well as spiritual reasons, must come to the abandonment of the use of force. Since no future peace can be maintained if land, sea, or air armaments continue to be employed by nations which threaten, or may threaten, aggression outside of their frontiers, they believe, pending the establishment of a wider and permanent system of general security, that the disarmament of such nations is essential. They will likewise aid and encourage all other practicable measures which will lighten for peace-loving peoples the crushing burden of armaments. ...

The Congress and the President having heretofore determined, through the Lend-

Lease Act, on the national policy of American aid to the democracies which East and West are waging war against dictatorships, the military and naval conversations at these meetings made clear gains in furthering the effectiveness of this aid.

Furthermore, the Prime Minister and I are arranging for conferences with the Soviet Union to aid it in its defense against the attack made by the principal aggressor of the modern world—Germany.

Finally, the declaration of principles at this time presents a goal which is worth while for our type of civilization to seek. It is so clear-cut that it is difficult to oppose in any major particular without automatically admitting a willingness to accept compromise with nazi-ism; or to agree to a world peace which would give to nazi-ism domination over large numbers of conquered nations. Inevitably such a peace would be a gift to nazi-ism to take breath—armed breath—for a second war to extend the control over Europe and Asia, to the American Hemisphere itself.

410. *The Four Freedoms, 1941*

President Roosevelt, Annual Message to Congress, January 6, 1941, *Congressional Record*, 77 Congress, 1 Session, LXXXVII, Part I, pp. 45–7.

ARMED defense of democratic existence is now being gallantly waged in four continents. If that defense fails, all the population and all the resources of Europe, Asia, Africa and Australasia will be dominated by the conquerors. The total of those populations and their resources . . . greatly exceeds the sum total of the population and the resources of the whole of the Western Hemisphere—many times over.

In times like these it is immature—and incidentally untrue—for anybody to brag that an unprepared America, single-handed, and with one hand tied behind its back, can hold off the whole world.

No realistic American can expect from a dictator's peace international generosity, or return of true independence, or world disarmament, or freedom of expression, or freedom of religion—or even good business. . . .

There is much loose talk of our immunity from immediate and direct invasion from across the seas. Obviously, as long as the British Navy retains its power, no such danger exists. Even if there were no British Navy, it is not probable that any enemy would be stupid enough to attack us by landing troops in the United States from across thousands of miles of ocean, until it had acquired strategic bases from which to operate. . . . The necessary strategic points would be occupied by secret agents and their dupes, and great numbers of them are already here, and in Latin America.

As long as the aggressor nations maintain the offensive, they, not we, will choose the time and the place and the method of their attack.

That is why the future of all American republics is today in serious danger.

That is why this annual message to the Congress is unique in our history.

That is why every member of the executive branch of the Government and every member of the Congress faces great responsibility—and great accountability.

The need of the moment is that our actions and our policy should be devoted primarily—almost exclusively—to meeting this foreign peril. For all our domestic problems are now a part of the great emergency.

Just as our national policy in internal affairs has been based upon a decent respect for the rights and the dignity of all our fellow-men within our gates, so our national policy in foreign affairs has been based on a decent respect for the rights and dignity of all nations, large and small. And the justice of morality must and will win in the end.

Our national policy is this:

First, by an impressive expression of the public will and without regard to partisanship, we are committed to all-inclusive national defense.

Second, by an impressive expression of the public will and without regard to partisanship, we are committed to full support of all those resolute peoples, everywhere, who are resisting aggression and are thereby keeping war away from our hemisphere. By this support, we express our determination that the democratic cause shall prevail, and we strengthen the defense and security of our own nation.

Third, by an impressive expression of the public will and without regard to partisanship, we are committed to the proposition that principles of morality and considerations for our own security will never permit us to acquiesce in a peace dictated by aggressors and sponsored by appeasers. We know that enduring peace cannot be bought at the cost of other people's freedom. . . .

I also ask this Congress for authority and for funds sufficient to manufacture additional munitions and war supplies of many kinds, to be turned over to those nations which are now in actual war with aggressor nations.

Our most useful and immediate role is to act as an arsenal for them as well as for ourselves. They do not need man power. They do need billions of dollars' worth of the weapons of defense.

The time is near when they will not be able to pay for them all in ready cash. We cannot, and will not, tell them they must surrender merely because of present inability to pay for the weapons which we know they must have. . . .

I recommend that we make it possible for those nations to continue to obtain war materials in the United States, fitting their orders into our own program. Nearly all their matériel would, if the time ever came, be useful for our own defense.

Taking counsel of expert military and naval authorities, considering what is best for our own security, we are free to decide how much should be kept here and how much should be sent abroad to our friends who, by their determined and heroic resistance, are giving us time in which to make ready our own defense.

For what we send abroad we shall be repaid, within a reasonable time following the close of hostilities, in similar materials or, at our option, in other goods of many kinds which they can produce and which we need.

Let us say to the democracies, "We Americans are vitally concerned in your defense of freedom. We are putting forth our energies, our resources, and our organizing powers to give you the strength to regain and maintain a free world. We shall send you, in ever-increasing numbers, ships, planes, tanks, guns. This is our purpose and our pledge.". . .

The happiness of future generations of Americans may well depend upon how effective and how immediate we can make our aid felt. No one can tell the exact character of the emergency situations that we may be called upon to meet. The Nation's hands must not be tied when the Nation's life is in danger. . . .

The Nation takes great satisfaction and much strength from the things which have been done to make its people conscious of their individual stake in the preservation of democratic life in America. Those things have toughened the fiber of our people, have renewed their faith and strengthened their devotion to the institutions we make ready to protect. . . .

There is nothing mysterious about the foundations of a healthy and strong democracy. The basic things expected by our people of their political and economic systems are simple. They are:

Equality of opportunity for youth and for others,

Jobs for those who can work.

Security for those who need it.

The ending of special privilege for the few.

The preservation of civil liberties for all.

The enjoyment of the fruits of scientific progress in a wider and constantly rising standard of living.

These are the simple and basic things that must never be lost sight of in the turmoil and unbelievable complexity of our modern world. The inner and abiding strength of our economic and political systems is dependent upon the degree to which they fulfill these expectations. . . .

In the future days, which we seek to make secure, we look forward to a world founded upon four essential human freedoms.

The first is freedom of speech and expression everywhere in the world.

The second is freedom of every person to worship God in his own way everywhere in the world.

The third is freedom from want, which, translated into world terms, means economic understandings which will secure to every nation a healthy peacetime life for its inhabitants everywhere in the world.

The fourth is freedom from fear—which, translated into world terms, means a world-wide reduction of armaments to such a point and in such a thorough fashion that no nation will be in a position to commit an act of physical aggression against any neighbor—anywhere in the world.

That is no vision of a distant millennium. It is a definite basis for a kind of world attainable in our own time and generation. That kind of world is the very antithesis of the so-called new order of tyranny which the dictators seek to create with the crash of a bomb.

To that new order we oppose the greater conception—the moral order. A good society is able to face schemes of world domination and foreign revolutions alike without fear.

Since the beginning of our American history we have been engaged in change —in a perpetual peaceful revolution—a revolution which goes on steadily, quietly adjusting itself to changing conditions— without the concentration camp or the quicklime in the ditch. The world order which we seek is the cooperation of free countries, working together in a friendly, civilized society.

411. *Inter-American Assistance, 1940*

Declaration XV. *Reciprocal Assistance and Cooperation for the Defense of the Nations of the Americas.* Second Meeting of the Ministers of Foreign Affairs of the American Republics, Habana, July 21–30, 1940, *Report of the Secretary of State* (Washington, 1941), 71–2.

ANY attempt on the part of a non-American state against the integrity or inviolability of the territory, the sovereignty or the political independence of an American state shall be considered as an act of aggression against the states which sign this declaration.

In case acts of aggression are committed or should there be reason to believe that an act of aggression is being prepared by a non-American nation against the integrity or inviolability of the territory, the sovereignty or the political independence of an American nation, the nations signatory to the present declaration will consult among themselves in order to agree upon the measure it may be advisable to take.

All the signatory nations, or two or more of them, according to circumstances, shall proceed to negotiate the necessary complementary agreements so as to organize cooperation for defense and the assistance that they shall lend each other in the event of aggressions such as those referred to in this declaration.

412. *Japanese Intentions, 1940*

Ambassador Grew, Message of September 12, 1940, J. C. Grew, *Turbulent Era* (Boston, 1952), II, 1225–9.

WHATEVER may be the intentions of the present Japanese Government, there can be no doubt that the army and other elements in the country see in the present world situation a "golden opportunity" to carry into effect their dreams of expansion; the German victories have gone to their heads like strong wine; . . . they have argued that the war will probably end in a quick German victory and that it is well to consolidate Japan's position in greater East Asia while Germany is still acquiescent and before the eventual hypothetical strengthening of German naval power might rob Japan of far-flung control in the Far East; they have discounted effective opposition on the part of the United States although carefully watching our attitude. The ability of the saner heads in and out of the Government to control those elements has been and is doubtful.

Now, however, I sense a gradual change in the outburst of exhilaration which greeted the new Government on its inception. The Japanese Government, the army and navy and the public are beginning to see that Germany may not defeat Great Britain after all, . . . and now to add to that dawning realization, they see the United States and Great Britain steadily drawing closer together in measures of mutual defense with the American acquisition of naval bases in British possessions in the Atlantic and with our support of the British fleet by the transfer of fifty destroyers. They hear reports of our haste to build a two-ocean navy and of our considering the strengthening of our naval bases in the Pacific and even rumors of our eventual use of Singapore. These developments and rumors are having their logical effect on Japanese consciousness. On the one hand they tend to emphasize the potential danger which Japan faces from eventual positive action by the United States and Great Britain acting together . . . or by the United States alone. On the other hand they furnish cogent arguments for those elements in Japan who seek economic and political security by obtaining markets and sources of raw materials wholly within the control of Japan. As for Germany, the Japanese are beginning to question whether even a victorious Germany would not provide a new hazard to their expansionist program both in China and in the southward advance. Meanwhile the future position and attitude of Soviet Russia is always an uncertain factor in their calculations. These various considerations are beginning to give them concern.

High-pressure diplomacy, especially in the Netherlands East Indies, will continue, but the fact that the Japanese Government was able even temporarily to restrain the military forces from their plans for a headlong invasion of Indochina indicates a degree of caution which I do not doubt was at least partially influenced by the attitude of the United States. . . . The "nibbling policy" appears likely to continue until the world situation, and especially the attitude of the United States, becomes clearer.

In previous communications I have expressed the opinion that sanctions by the United States would set Japanese-American relations on a downward curve. It is true that our own newly instituted program of national preparedness now justifies measures which need not fall within the realm of outright sanctions. On the other hand we must envisage the probability that drastic embargoes on the export of such important products as petroleum, of which the United States is known to possess a superabundance would be interpreted by the Japanese Government and people as actually sanctions which might and probably would lead to some form of retaliation. The risks . . . will depend less upon the careful calculations of the Japanese Government than upon the uncalculated "do or die" temper of the army and navy in case they should attribute to the United States the responsibility for the failure of their expansionist plans. . . .

Having carefully set forth the inevitable hazards involved in a strong policy I now respectfully turn to the hazards involved in a laissez-faire policy.

In discussing the specific question of American-Japanese relations it is impossible to view that problem in its proper perspective without considering it as part and parcel of the world problem which, briefly, presents the following aspects:

(a) The United States and Great Britain are the leaders of a great group of English speaking nations around the world standing for a "way of life" which is being appallingly threatened today by a group of Germany, Italy, Soviet Russia and Japan whose avowed purpose is to impose by force of arms their will upon conquered peoples. In attempting to deal with such powers the uses of diplomacy are in general bankrupt. Diplomacy may occasionally retard but cannot effectively stem the tide. Force or the display of force can alone prevent these powers from attaining their objectives. Japan today is one of the predatory powers; she has sub-merged all moral and ethical sense and has become frankly and unashamedly opportunist, seeking at every turn to profit by the weakness of others. Her policy of southward expansion is a definite threat to American interests in the Pacific and is a thrust at the British Empire in the East.

(b) American security has admittedly depended in a measure upon the existence of the British fleet which in turn has been, and could only have been, supported by the British Empire.

(c) If we conceive it to be in our interest to support the British Empire in this hour of her travail, and I most emphatically do so conceive it, we must strive by every means to preserve the status quo in the Pacific at least until the European war has been won or lost. In my opinion this cannot be done nor can our interests be further adequately and properly protected by merely registering disapproval and keeping a careful record thereof. It is clear that Japan has been deterred from taking greater liberties with American interests only out of respect for our potential power; it is equally clear that she has trampled upon our rights to a degree in precise ratio to the strength of her conviction that the American people would not permit that power to be used. Once that conviction is shaken it is possible that the uses of diplomacy may again become accepted.

(d) If then we can by firmness preserve the status quo in the Pacific until and if Britain emerges successfully from the European struggle, Japan will be faced with a situation which will make it impossible for the present opportunist philosophy to maintain the upper hand. At a moment it might then be possible to undertake a readjustment of the whole Pacific problem on a fair, frank, and equitable basis to the lasting benefit of both the United States and of Japan. Until such time as there is a complete regeneration of thought in this country, a show of force, together with a determination to employ it if need be, can alone contribute effectively to the achievement of such an outcome and to our own future security.

413. *The Japanese Peace Proposal, 1941*

Draft Proposal handed by Ambassador Nomura to Secretary of State Hull, November 20, 1941, in *Peace and War*, 801–2.

1. BOTH the Governments of Japan and the United States undertake not to make any armed advancement into any of the regions in the Southeastern Asia and the Southern Pacific area excepting the part of French Indo-China where the Japanese troops are stationed at present.

2. The Japanese Government undertakes to withdraw its troops now stationed in French Indo-China upon either the restoration of peace between Japan and China or the establishment of an equitable peace in the Pacific area.

In the meantime the Government of Japan declares that it is prepared to remove its troops now stationed in the southern part of French Indo-China to the northern part of the said territory upon the conclusion of the present arrangement which shall later be embodied in the final agreement.

3. The Governments of Japan and the United States shall cooperate with a view to securing the acquisition of those goods and commodities which the two countries need in Netherlands East Indies.

4. The Governments of Japan and the United States mutually undertake to restore their commercial relations to those prevailing prior to the freezing of the assets.

The Government of the United States shall supply Japan a required quantity of oil.

5. The Government of the United States undertakes to refrain from such measures and actions as will be prejudicial to the endeavors for the restoration of general peace between Japan and China.

414. *American Proposal for Peace, 1941*

Outline of Proposed Basis for Agreement between the United States and Japan, November 26, 1941. Document Handed by the Secretary of State to the Japanese Ambassador Nomura in *Peace and War*, 810–12.

SECTION I. Draft Mutual Declaration of Policy

THE GOVERNMENT of the United States and the Government of Japan . . . affirm . . . that they have no intention of threatening other countries or of using military force aggressively against any neighboring nation, and that, accordingly, in their national policies they will actively support and give practical application to the following fundamental principles upon which their relations with each other and with all other governments are based:

(1) The principle of inviolability of territorial integrity and sovereignty of each and all nations.

(2) The principle of non-interference in the internal affairs of other countries.

(3) The principle of equality, including equality of commercial opportunity and treatment.

(4) The principle of reliance upon international cooperation and conciliation for the prevention and pacific settlement

of controversies and for improvement of international conditions by peaceful methods and processes. . . .

SECTION II. Steps to Be Taken by the Government of the United States and by the Government of Japan

The Government of the United States and the Government of Japan propose to take steps as follows:

1. The Government of the United States and the Government of Japan will endeavor to conclude a multilateral nonaggression pact among the British Empire, China, Japan, the Netherlands, the Soviet Union, Thailand and the United States.

2. Both Governments will endeavor to conclude among the American, British, Chinese, Japanese, the Netherland and Thai Governments an agreement whereunder each of the Governments would pledge itself to respect the territorial integrity of French Indochina and, in the event that there should develop a threat to the territorial integrity of Indochina, to enter into immediate consultation with a view to taking such measures as may be deemed necessary and advisable to meet the threat in question. Such agreement would provide also that each of the Governments party to the agreement would not seek or accept preferential treatment in its trade or economic relations with Indochina and would use its influence to obtain for each of the signatories equality of treatment in trade and commerce with French Indochina.

3. The Government of Japan will withdraw all military, naval, air and police forces from China and from Indochina.

4. The Government of the United States and the Government of Japan will not support—militarily, politically, economically—any government or regime in China other than the National Government of the Republic of China with capital temporarily at Chungking.

5. Both Governments will give up all extraterritorial rights in China, including rights and interests in and with regard to international settlements and concessions, and rights under the Boxer Protocol of 1901. . . .

6. The Government of the United States and the Government of Japan will enter into negotiations for the conclusion between the United States and Japan of a trade agreement, based upon reciprocal most-favored-nation treatment and reduction of trade barriers by both countries, including an undertaking by the United States to bind raw silk on the free list.

7. The Government of the United States and the Government of Japan, will, respectively, remove the freezing restrictions on Japanese funds in the United States and on American funds in Japan.

8. Both Governments will agree upon a plan for the stabilization of the dollar-yen rate, with the allocation of funds adequate for this purpose, half to be supplied by Japan and half by the United States.

9. Both Governments will agree that no agreement which either has concluded with any third power or powers shall be interpreted by it in such a way as to conflict with the fundamental purpose of this agreement, the establishment and preservation of peace throughout the Pacific area.

415. *Tokyo Gossip, 1941*

Note by Ambassador Grew, January 27, 1941, Grew, *Turbulent Era*, II, 1233.

THERE is a lot of talk around town to the effect that the Japanese, in case of a break with the United States, are planning to go all out in a surprise mass attack on Pearl Harbor. I rather guess that the boys in Hawaii are not precisely asleep.

416. *The Pearl Harbor Attack, 1941*

"Investigation of the Pearl Harbor Attack," 79 Congress, 2 Session, *Senate Document* No. 244 (Washington, 1946), 251–2.

THE ULTIMATE responsibility for the attack and its results rests upon Japan. . . . Contributing to the effectiveness of the attack was a powerful striking force, much more powerful than it had been thought the Japanese were able to employ in a single tactical venture at such distance and under such circumstances.

The diplomatic policies and actions of the United States provided no justifiable provocation whatever for the attack by Japan on this nation. The Secretary of State fully informed both the War and Navy Departments of diplomatic developments and, in a timely and forceful manner, clearly pointed out to these Departments that relations between the United States and Japan had passed beyond the stage of diplomacy and were in the hands of the military.

The committee has found no evidence to support the charges, made before and during the hearings, that the President, the Secretary of State, the Secretary of War, or the Secretary of the Navy tricked, provoked, incited, cajoled, or coerced Japan into attacking this nation in order that a declaration of war might be more easily obtained from the Congress. On the contrary, all evidence conclusively points to the fact that they discharged their responsibilities with distinction, ability and foresight and in keeping with the highest traditions of our fundamental foreign policy. . . .

The disaster of Pearl Harbor was the failure, with attendant increase in personnel and material losses, of the Army and the Navy to institute measures designed to detect an approaching hostile force, to effect a state of readiness commensurate with the realization that war was at hand, and to employ every facility at their command in repelling the Japanese.

Virtually everyone was surprised that Japan struck the Fleet at Pearl Harbor at the time that she did. Yet officers, both in Washington and Hawaii, were fully conscious of the danger from air attack; they realized this form of attack on Pearl Harbor by Japan was at least a possibility; and they were adequately informed of the imminence of war.

Specifically, the Hawaiian commands failed—

(a) To discharge their responsibilities in the light of the warnings received from Washington, other information possessed by them, and the principle of command by mutual cooperation.

(b) To integrate and coordinate their facilities for defense and to alert properly the Army and Navy establishments in Hawaii, particularly in the light of the warnings and intelligence available to them during the period November 27 to December 7, 1941.

(c) To effect liaison on a basis designed to acquaint each of them with the operations of the other, which was necessary to their joint security, and to exchange fully all significant intelligence.

(d) To maintain a more effective reconnaissance within the limits of their equipment.

(e) To effect a state of readiness throughout the Army and Navy establishments designed to meet all possible attacks.

(f) To employ the facilities, matériel, and personnel at their command, which were adequate at least to have greatly minimized the effects of the attack, in repelling the Japanese raiders.

(g) To appreciate the significance of

intelligence and other informations available to them.

The errors made by the Hawaiian commands were errors of judgment and not derelictions of duty.

The War Plans Division of the War Department failed to discharge its direct responsibility to advise the commanding general he had not properly alerted the Hawaiian Department when the latter, pursuant to instructions, had reported action taken in a message that was not satisfactorily responsive to the original directive.

The Intelligence and War Plans Divisions of the War and Navy Departments failed:

(a) To give careful and thoughtful consideration to the intercepted messages from Tokyo to Honolulu of September 24, November 15, and November 20 (the harbor berthing plan and related dispatches) and to raise a question as to their significance. Since they indicated a particular interest in the Pacific Fleet's base this intelligence should have been appreciated and supplied the Hawaiian commanders for their assistance, along with other information available to them, in making their estimate of the situation.

(b) To be properly on the *qui vive* to receive the "one o'clock" intercept and to recognize in the message the fact that some Japanese military action would very possibly occur somewhere at 1 p.m., December 7. If properly appreciated, this intelligence should have suggested a dispatch to all Pacific outpost commanders supplying this information, as General Marshall attempted to do immediately upon seeing it.

Notwithstanding the fact that there were officers on twenty-four hour watch, the Committee believes that under all of the evidence the War and Navy Departments were not sufficiently alerted on December 6 and 7, 1941, in view of the imminence of war.

417. *The Declaration of War, 1941*

A. H. Vandenberg, Jr., ed., *Private Papers of Senator Vandenberg* (Boston, 1952), 16–18.

CONGRESS declared war on Japan today—with but one dissenting vote. The Senate was unanimous. There was no other recourse—in answer to what was probably the most treacherous attack in all history.

The news of the attack on Hawaii came into Washington around 4 o'clock yesterday afternoon. I immediately issued [a press] statement. I then phoned Steve Early, White House Secretary, and asked him to tell the President that, despite all differences on other things, I would support him without reservation in his answer to Japan. Marvin McIntyre, another White House Secretary, shortly phoned me the President's thanks.

Today at 12:30 the President addressed a joint session of Congress—asking a formal declaration of a state of war. With a speed and unanimity that show how a democracy can function in crisis, the Resolution was through both Houses within one hour.

I made the only speech that was made in the Senate before the vote was taken there. I felt it was absolutely necessary to establish the reason why our non-interventionists were ready to "go along"—making it plain that we were not deserting our beliefs, but that we were postponing all further argument over policy until the battle forced upon us by Japan is won. I felt it was necessary, too, in order to better swing the vast anti-war party in the country into unity with this unavoidable decision. The Administration leaders, with typical short-sightedness, had *not* wanted it done. They wanted no speeches at all—and even tried to cut me off. . . .

But I insisted—and I was greatly pleased, when I had finished my brief statement, to have Senator Glass cross over, shake my hand, and thank me for my statement . . . and Majority Leader Barkley himself later said that, upon reflection, he was very glad that I had done exactly as I did.

We were no longer "free agents" after the infamous Japanese attack and Japan's Declaration of War on America. There was nothing left to do but to answer in kind. But I continue to believe that a wiser foreign policy could have been followed—although now no one will ever be able to prove it.

We have little or no information regarding the peace-negotiations which have been going on for ten days as a result of the visit of the Mikado's special emissary. It has all been secret—secret even from the Senate Foreign Relations Committee. Perhaps this was necessary. But I hope that some day the whole record will be laid bare. I should like to know what the price of peace in the Far East would have been. I have the feeling that it would have been necessary for us to yield but relatively little—and nothing in the nature of "appeasement"—in order to have pacified the Far Eastern situation; and certainly any such pacification, virtually taking Japan out of the Axis, would have been the deadliest blow we could have struck at Hitler. For example, Japan has been in Manchukuo for 15 years—despite our refusal to recognize her title under the "Stimson Doctrine"

(which, by the way, Britain rejected). To recognize Japan's title in Manchukuo, speaking loosely, would be simply to acknowledge an accomplished fact which will remain an accomplished fact whether we like it or not. I may frankly add that I think China is big enough so that additional territorial concessions, or trade zones, might have been arranged to the advantage of China herself in return for a guaranteed peace. This is pure speculation—except as the general notion is sustained by many conversations I have had with responsible Japs visiting America. Without condoning for an instant the way in which Japan precipitated hostilities, I still think we may have driven her needlessly into hostilities through our dogmatic diplomatic attitudes.

I fear this means a virtual end to our "lend-lease" aid to Britain et al., because we are not adequately prepared ourselves —as I have been saying for months. I fear we shall pay dearly for this lack of preparedness on our own account. I am certain it was worth infinitely much to Britain et al., to have us continue to remain out of the actual shooting war—and I doubt whether these values were appropriately assessed in determining what it was cold-bloodedly worth to all of us to take Japan virtually out of the Axis and to substantially pacify the Far East—thus permitting concentrated attention to Hitler.

But we have asked for this—and other —wars. Now we are in it. Nothing matters except victory. The "arguments" must be postponed.

XLVI ⚜ *The War at Home and Abroad*

THE GIGANTIC WAR effort called for huge expenditures of energy and resources. But it found the Americans not wanting. In strange corners of the earth and under novel conditions, the fighting men made their abilities felt (Nos. 418, 419). The organizing skill of the Americans mounted successive attacks upon North Africa, Italy, and upon the fortress of Europe itself; and the efficient use of resources earned a decisive victory against the Germans and their allies (No. 420). At the same time the Japanese advance was halted, and their soldiers pushed back toward the home islands.

The immense power needed to defeat the enemies was made possible by a total mobilization of American industrial resources. The conversion of industry toward the war effort was quick and vigorous (No. 421); and a co-ordinated development program made up the deficiency in the supply of raw materials, such as rubber, which the United States lacked (No. 422). Furthermore, it was necessary that this impressive achievement be managed with due concern for the welfare of the civilian economy and for the financial soundness of the government (No. 423).

It was more difficult to frame the terms of victory and of transition to peace. At the first stage of successful warfare, the American President and the British Prime Minister announced that they were interested only in unconditional surrender (No. 424); but this was in part, at least, an indication that they had not yet fixed upon the specific terms of peace. A long process of negotiation intervened before those were set; for it took great effort to reach agreement among the Allies. At Cairo, Teheran, Yalta, and Potsdam, the statesmen laid their plans for the treatment of the defeated enemy in Germany (No. 425) and in Japan (No. 426); and also for the creation of a new international organization to assure enduring peace (No. 427).

418. *The Dive Bombers, 1944*

Ernie Pyle, *Brave Men* (New York, 1944), 110–12.

THE DIVE BOMBERS approached their target in formation. When the leader made sure he had spotted the target he wiggled his wings, raised his diving brakes, rolled on his back, nosed over, and down he went. The next man behind followed almost instantly, and then the next, and the next—not more than a hundred fifty feet apart. There was no danger of their running over each other, for the brakes held them all at the same speed. They flew so close together that as many as twenty dive bombers could be seen in a dive all at once, making a straight line up into the sky like a gigantic stream of water.

At about four thousand feet the pilot released his bombs. Then he started his pull-out. The strain was terrific, and all the pilots would "black out" a little bit. It was not a complete blackout, and lasted only four or five seconds. It was more a heaviness in the head and a darkness before the eyes, the pilots said.

Once straightened out of the dive, they went right on down to "the deck," which means flying close to the ground. For by that time everything in the vicinity that could shoot had opened up, and the safest place to be was right down close, streaking for home as fast as they could go. . . .

The planes had to fly in constant "evasive action," which meant going right, going left, going up, going down, all the time they were over enemy territory. If they flew in a straight line for as long as fifteen seconds, the Germans would pick them off.

A pilot sat up there and thought it out this way: "Right now they've got a bearing on me. In a certain number of seconds they'll shoot and in a few more seconds the shell will be up here. It's up to me to be somewhere else then."

But he also knew that the Germans knew he would turn, and that consequently they would send up shells to one side or the other, or above or below his current position. Thus he never dared make exactly the same move two days in a row. By constantly turning, climbing, ducking, he made a calculated hit almost impossible. His worst danger was flying by chance right into a shell burst.

419. *Tank Man, 1943*

A family letter from Africa, May 15, 1943. Mina Curtiss, ed., *Letters Home* (Boston, 1944), 59–61, 65.

THE MINUTE you are in the Tank you become part of a machine, you have your certain job to do and hold your end up. You stop thinking about yourself and think of your job.

We moved out into the valley traveling in two inverted wedges VV.... As we got to the hill ... our platoon was to swing in an arc up the valley to the right of the hill, between the hill and the mountains on the right. I was to take my section up into the valley as far as I could to get at the artillery that was behind the hill.

As we moved through a large cactus patch they opened up on us with everything they had. It seemed to me that one gun picked my tank out because there were always four shell bursts after me. ... From then on it was just a question of outguessing them. The valley had a lot of small bunkers in it and we sort of jumped from behind one to another.... First they would drop four about fifty yards behind me and then four right in front of me, then it was time to move on. About this time the other tank in my section ran into a land mine and blew one track off. When that happens they are usually in a mine field and you can't help them because you'd hit one yourself. But I saw the boys bail out so I knew they could make it on foot. Now the infantry came out of the waddie on our left and swung across the valley, among us. It's not very nice to watch those boys out there run-ning in all that flying hell, but you can't watch them, you have a job to do. You can't see the guns, because they are dug in and in concrete implacements, then all at once you spot one and lay your guns on it. Over to my left I could see two tanks burning and on my right two more in the mine field. The hill was getting closer now and then and I could see the road up ahead; there's a tall cactus fence between us and the road and a large ditch also, boy, it's no time to get stuck now. Just then somebody stood up in the ditch—Our Infantry! They grinned, waved, and one of them pointed to a spot where I could get through. Thank God for the Infantry! Across the road and my friend who is shooting at me stops. I guess he can't depress his gun far enough; just then I saw a gun on my right, just next to an Arab hut, so here we go—and then I've got to get up that valley all alone now; wonder how Toth is making out in the mine field. Damn it that gun sees me and is swinging over on me, gosh it has a barrel about fifteen feet long. But just up there ahead is another bunker, we've got to get there fast. Safe for a minute but then Waitman phones up that our 75mm gun is jammed. Pawling has that 37 going like a machine gun and we are in one hell of a position. If we move from behind this bunker we'll get it sure because it's only 200 yards over to that gun. Just then Lieutenant Maloney called on the radio "Let's get the hell out of here, let's go home." So we back around and pull out just enough so I can see, the gun isn't there any more. It must be our lucky day! . . .

I'm a great believer in luck now, some one got that gun—and later I learned that after I crossed the road I was in one of their mine fields all the way. Luck—I traveled 600 yards on it. . . .

Now something about the Germans, not Hitler, but the German people themselves. They are really behind Hitler and want him, that is the majority. So you really can't blame him for all of this. They did the same things in the last war. You must destroy them or they will destroy you. They use all of the devilish, fiendish devices of war, things that we don't dare use. Personal mines, ones that bounce up and spread death for 25 yards; steel darts, that will go right through you; castorators, a nice little gadget that when you step on it it blows your groin out; Butterfly bombs;—things that you people don't realize at all.

It's a very, very horrible war, dirty, dishonest, not at all that glamor war that we read about in the home town paper we read. Someone has to remember that when the showdown comes. I know that as for myself and the other men here, we will show no mercy. We've seen too much for that. Wake up America for the real battle has not yet begun!

Mother, Dad, and Nan, and all the family, these are some of the things I have seen and done. Some of the thoughts I have had, my impressions of some things. I hope that I haven't shocked you, yet in some ways I hope I have. You are the people that run things, not us out here.

420. *Overlord, 1944*

Report by the Supreme Commander to the Combined Chiefs of Staff on the Operations in Europe of the Allied Expeditionary Force, 6 June 1944 to 5 May, 1945 (Washington, 1945), 11–12, 19, 22, 24, 25.

THE BUILD-UP of American troops and supplies in the United Kingdom continued under the direction of Lieut. Gen. John C. H. Lee. Planning for BOLERO, the name by which this logistical program was known, had begun in the United Kingdom as early as April 1942. The small original staff was divided for the North African (TORCH) operation, but expanded in 1943 and 1944 as the OVERLORD task became larger until, by D-day, the Communications Zone establishment contained 31,500 officers and 350,-000 enlisted personnel. By July 1943 some 750,000 tons of supplies were pouring through English ports each month and this amount was steadily increased until in June 1944 1,900,000 tons were received from the United States. . . . By 1 June also, the number of U.S. Army troops in the United Kingdom had risen from 241,839 at the end of 1942 to 1,562,000.

The operation of transporting supplies from the United States to the United Kingdom was facilitated by the fact that cargoes were discharged through established ports and over established rail lines. Additionally, large quantities of materials for the invasion were made directly available from British resources within the United Kingdom itself. These conditions could not, of course, exist on the Continent and plans were accordingly made to overcome the difficulties envisaged. It was recognized that the major tonnage reception on the Continent would be over the Normandy beaches during the first two months, with the port of Cherbourg being developed at an early date. Successively, it was anticipated that port development would proceed in Brittany, the major effort in that area to be an artificial port at Quiberon Bay with complementary development of the existing ports of Brest, Lorient, St.-Nazaire, and Nantes. While these were being brought into use the flow of supplies over the beaches was to be aided by the two artificial harbors. . . . As the campaign progressed, it was anticipated that the bulk of American supplies would flow directly from the United States through the Brittany ports, while the Channel ports to the north, including Ostend and Antwerp, would be developed for the British armies. These expectations, however, did not materialize, due primarily to enemy strategy and the vicissitudes of the campaign. That both the American and British supply systems were able, in spite of this, to support the armies to the extent they did is a remarkable tribute to the flexibility of their organizations and to their perseverance in a single purpose.

The importance of the steady supply of our forces, once landed, may be gauged by reference to German strategy. This was intended to insure that our supplies should never be permitted to begin flowing into the beachheads. The German philosophy was: "Deny the Allies the use of ports and they will be unable to support their armies ashore." For this reason the chain of Atlantic and Channel ports from Bordeaux to Antwerp was under orders from Hitler himself to fight to the last man and the last round of ammunition. The Germans fully expected us to be able to make a landing at some point on the Channel coast, but they were nevertheless certain that they could dislodge us before supplies could be brought ashore to maintain the troops. They had no knowledge of our artificial harbors, a secret as closely guarded as the time and place of our assault. The impossible was accomplished and supplies came ashore, not afterwards to support a force beleaguered on the beachheads, but actually with the troops as they landed. The Germans were, by virtue of our initial supply, denied the opportunity of dislodging us and were subsequently, throughout the campaign,

under sustained attack as the result of the feats of maintenance performed by our administrative organizations. . . .

June, 1944, saw the highest winds and roughest seas experienced in the English Channel in June for twenty years. . . .

On D-day the wind had, as forecast, moderated and the cloud was well broken, with a base generally above 4,000 feet. This afforded conditions which would permit of our airborne operations, and during the hour preceding the landings from the sea large areas of temporarily clear sky gave opportunities for the visual bombing of the shore defenses. The sea was still rough, and large numbers of our men were sick during the crossing. The waves also caused some of the major landing craft to lag astern, while other elements were forced to turn back.

As events proved, the decision to launch the assault at a time when the weather was so unsettled was largely responsible for the surprise which we achieved. The enemy had concluded that any cross-Channel expedition was impossible while the seas ran so high and, with his radar installations rendered ineffective as a result of our air attacks, his consequent unpreparedness for our arrival more than offset the difficulties which we experienced. . . .

The high seas added enormously to our difficulties in getting ashore. Awkward as these waters would have been at any time, navigation under such conditions as we experienced called for qualities of superlative seamanship. Landing craft were hurled on to the beaches by the waves, and many of the smaller ones were swamped before they could touch down. Others were flung upon and holed by the mined under-water obstacles. Numbers of the troops were swept off their feet while wading through the breakers and were drowned, and those who reached the dry land were often near exhaustion. It was, moreover, not possible on every beach to swim in the amphibious DD tanks upon which we relied to provide fire support for the infantry clearing the beach exists. These were launched at Sword, Utah, and Omaha beaches, and, although late, reached land at the two former; at Omaha, however, all but two or three foundered in the heavy seas. At the remaining beaches the tanks had to be unloaded direct to the shore by the LCT's, which were forced, at considerable risk, to dry out for the purpose. Fortunately the beaches were sufficiently flat and firm to obviate damage to the craft.

Despite these difficulties, the landings proceeded and on all but one sector the process of securing the beachheads went according to plan. . . .

Apart from the factor of tactical surprise, the comparatively light casualties which we sustained on all the beaches except Omaha were in large measure due to the success of the novel mechanical contrivances which we employed and to the staggering moral and material effect of the mass armor landed in the leading waves of the assault. The use of large numbers of amphibious tanks to afford fire support in the initial stages of the operation had been an essential feature of our plans, and, despite the losses they suffered on account of the heavy seas, on the beaches where they were used they proved conspicuously effective. It is doubtful if the assault forces could have firmly established themselves without the assistance of these weapons. . . .

During the next five days our forces worked to join up the beachheads into one uninterrupted lodgement area and to introduce into this area the supplies of men and materials necessary to consolidate and expand our foothold. . . .

Meanwhile, on and off the beaches, the naval, mercantile marine, and land force supply services personnel were performing prodigies of achievement under conditions which could hardly have been worse. Enormous as was the burden imposed upon these services even under the best of conditions, the actual circumstances of our landings increased the difficulties of their task very considerably. The problems of unloading vast numbers of men and vehicles and thousands of tons of stores over bare beaches, strewn with mines and obstacles, were complicated by the heavy seas which would not permit the full use of the special landing devices, such as the "Rhino" ferries, which had been designed to facilitate unloading at this stage of operations. The beaches and their exits had to be cleared and the beach organizations set up while the fighting was still in progress close by, and on either flank the unloading had to be carried on under fire from German heavy artillery. Off shore, enemy aircraft, although absent by day, laid mines each night, requiring unceasing activity by our mine sweepers. By 11 June, despite these complications, the machinery of supply over the beaches was functioning satisfactorily. Initial discharges of stores and vehicles were about 50 per cent behind the planned schedule, but against this we could set the fact that consumption had been less than anticipated. Reserves were being accumulated and the supply position as a whole gave us no cause for concern. The artificial harbor units were arriving and the inner anchorages were already in location. During the first six days of the operation, 326,547 men, 54,186 vehicles, and 104,428 tons of stores were brought ashore over the beaches. These figures gave the measure of the way in which all concerned, by their untiring energy and courage, triumphed over the difficulties which confronted them.

421. *Conversion for War, 1940–*

D. M. Nelson, *Arsenal of Democracy* (New York, 1946), 218–21, 227–8, 231–2, 235–7.

THERE could be no such thing as partial conversion in the automobile industry. Charles E. Wilson, president of General Motors, told me, as other motor magnates were to tell me later, that you do not "partly convert" a production line. You do it all the way or not at all. . . .

Consequently, converting the automobile industry was, in a sense, destroying it—and its owners did not quite see fit to demolish this industrial colossus without knowing what would take its place. In May of 1940 William S. Knudsen, predecessor of Charles E. Wilson as president of General Motors, went to Washington as Director of Production. . . . Thereafter he became the agent of the Administration in persuading his industry that the nation would, beyond question, have to prepare for war, and that the automobile firms would be obliged to do a large part of this preparing. In October of 1940, some progress began to be perceptible.

Most auto firms date their transformation to a wartime industry back to a memorable meeting which took place in Detroit on October 25, 1940. . . .

To the meeting in Detroit, October 25, 1940, Bill Knudsen, working on his idea about putting the motor industry back of airplane production, called together everyone who had anything to do with automobile manufacture: the primary producers, the parts and appliance makers, the tool and die makers. . . . So many attended that the director's room of the organization was not big enough to accommodate them. So the meeting was held in the same building but on the ground floor, in a fancy meat market, which had closed up. The guests sat on chairs supplied by undertakers.

Knudsen had brought to the meeting bits and parts of airframes and, I believe, some engine parts. Major Jimmy Doolittle . . . asked the manufacturers what they could do about reproducing the specimens which were on exhibit. They were asked to study them and deliver a verdict.

They handled, measured, and inspected the specimens, and decided that probably they could do much about reproducing them in their own plants. There was one dissenter—Charles E. Sorenson of the Ford Co. The company, he stated, would not make parts; it would make the whole plane—engine, frameparts and all—or nothing. He declared that Ford would not consider manufacturing odds and ends of parts to be shipped to a plane builder, only to have him, an alien personality, grouse that the parts didn't fit, that this or that had not been done correctly.

As a result of this most informal meeting—held together by Bill Knudsen's prestige in the industry—De Soto, Chrysler, Hudson, and the Goodyear Rubber Co. were soon building a long line of parts for Martin. The Murray Corporation was accomplishing the same for Boeing's Flying Fortress, and the Fisher Body Division of General Motors and Briggs were making parts for North American. But this was only a beginning. Within a few months, engineers and designers from the big automotive firms, and from hundreds of parts and sub-contracting concerns were swarming through the plants of the aircraft industry, making rough sketches, taking notes, and getting airplane know-how from the men who had developed it.

At this meeting, too, the American bomber program really came into being. Ford's representatives, as I have said, left the fancy meat market with the firm determination not to participate in anybody's parts program but to build complete planes. Shortly after the October 25, 1940, conference, the great Sorenson visited an aircraft plant where B-24s were being assembled. Men were crawling over fuselages, getting in each other's way, making scores of useless gestures, and occasionally hammering one another over the head. The whole procedure was a negation of mass production as Sorenson understood it, and few men alive understood it better.

While gaping at these strange antics, Sorenson is reported to have made a hurried drawing for the biggest aircraft plant in the world—Willow Run.

Later, Sorenson and his associates elaborated on the sketches, and from these grew a veritable Gargantua of aircraft production—larger than the combined pre-war plants of Boeing, Douglas, and Consolidated. It was a mile long and a quarter of a mile wide. Into this enormous cavern went 1,600 machine tools, 7,500 jigs and fixtures (some of which, I heard, were seventy-five feet long), an overhead conveyor system, and other gadgets which made possible the mass production of planes on a scale never thought possible before. This cradle of destruction seemed to spring from the ground almost as soon as the Ford Co. reached its decision. Eleven months after ground was broken at Willow Run the first four-engine Ford-made Consolidated bombers were assembled—the B-24s, which swept over the battlefields of Europe and the Pacific at a speed of more than 300 miles per hour, with a four-ton bomb load potential, and a range of 3,000 miles. . . .

The airplane industry, I have been told, disliked and feared the automobile industry because the latter was always threatening (at least in the newspapers and magazines) to make mass-production planes and to chase the "legitimate" airplane manufacturers into the Pacific. Then, inside the widespread auto industry itself, there were congeries of dislikes

and hates. The parts makers often disliked the automobile companies, because only a few of the former were able to sell the big producers and, as an added indication of dissatisfaction, they disliked one another. The little shops, the tool and die makers, disliked almost everybody, because their lot was usually precarious, with business booming in certain seasons and swooning in others. They were beholden to both the parts makers and the automobile companies.

Thus it is the more remarkable that all of these elements were able to call a moratorium on their differences, and integrate a munitions industry which astonished the entire world. They forgot that they were competitors, that they had been engaging in long-standing feuds with one another, and they became, for all practical purposes, one company, with one purpose: the production of tools for killing, of such quality and in such volume that no nation would ever dare to drop bombs on this country again. . . .

I have stressed the automotive industry's participation in the airplane program only because it affords an illuminating example of complete conversion. But the aircraft manufacturers converted also, although their conversion was a matter of quantity and quality, not a radical switch from one product to another. Their spectacular achievements, however, are not to be overlooked or minimized. Teamwork, again, seems to have been the answer. . . .

By March of 1944, more than a million engineering man-hours had been saved by the pooling of research data and production techniques alone. More than 9,000 technical reports were exchanged on the west coast. More than 20,600 items were exchanged, plus 45,000 items furnished to firms outside the Council. . . .

The plane companies worked together and with government agencies to solve the manpower problem and the results were almost incredible considering the endless diversity of skills required.

From a working force of only 48,638 persons in 1939, the army of aircraft plant employees grew to a peak of 2,102,000 in November, 1943. At this peak, aircraft plants employed 12.4 per cent of the total manufacturing employees of the entire nation.

The campaign which brought about this epochal mobilization was, itself, a masterpiece of promotion and evangelism. Women were induced to leave their kitchens. Retired workers came back into the labor market. Executives, bank clerks, laborers, worked on night shifts while holding down their regular jobs in the daytime and boys and girls worked after school and during vacation periods. Sound trucks, bands, free shows, special offices in downtown districts, special door-to-door canvasses comprised a few of the methods used to recruit workers. The plants attacked the housing and the transportation problem of prospective workers at a time when these difficulties seemed almost insoluble. The Barnum impulse which is deep in the roots of American life flared up, and the management of aircraft plants scraped close to the bottom of their local manpower barrels.

422. *Rubber, 1944*

Jesse Jones, *Fifty Billion Dollars* (New York, 1951), 414–16. Copyright 1951 and used with the permission of The Macmillan Company.

THE AMERICAN rubber program, which produced more than 700,000 tons in 1944, was operating at a rate in excess of 1,000,000 tons a year when the war ended. Compare those figures with the accomplishments of the Germans. Prior to the war the Germans were generally conceded to possess greater knowledge of synthetic rubber production than any other people. During the war their supplies of natural rubber were so extremely limited that they had to rely almost entirely upon their synthetic production. When their records became available after the surrender, we learned that their annual production never rose above 109,173 tons, that peak having been reached in 1943.

We handled the rubber situation, both natural and synthetic, in a businesslike way and got results. As a contribution to winning the war, our accomplishments in less than two years in the rubber field will stand comparison with those of any other industry. At the start we did not have the knowledge, but we went out to get it, and did, just as we did in many other fields....

Altogether, fifty-one government-owned plants were designed, constructed, and put in operation. In carrying out the program, forty-nine rubber, chemical, petroleum, and other industrial companies participated under the supervision of Rubber Reserve Company....

Our investment in these plants approximated $700,000,000. When the program really got going, expenditures for materials, utilities, services, etc., ran around $2,000,000 per day. All these plants were constructed under the auspices of... [the] Defense Plant Corporation, which leased them to the various operating companies at a nominal rental of one dollar per year. Nearly all of them were operated on a cost-plus-management-charge basis.

Since alcohol and petroleum were the principal feeder bases, the plants were built convenient to the sources of those raw materials. Twenty-one plants were in the east central states, twenty-three in the Southwest, principally in Texas and Louisiana. The remaining seven were in southern California.... Of the cost of production, 86 per cent went for materials. For alcohol more than $500,000,000 was spent, and for petroleum more than $100,000,-000. It was the predominant importance of petroleum in synthetic rubber production that motivated placing nearly half the nation's capacity in the Gulf Coast area of Texas and Louisiana. . . .

However, the whole net operating deficit of the plants up to December, 1948, had amounted to only $33,481,000. . . . The big loss—nearly $250,000,000—was for depreciation of the plants. Yet that was a very small price to pay for synthetic rubber's contribution to the victory and its guarantee that our country shall never again be wholly dependent on distant sources for its supply of such an essential article.

During the war the whole huge enterprise was administered by Rubber Reserve Company with a personnel of fewer than 300 directly assigned employees. On V-J Day there were about 24,000 employees engaged in operating the plants. Although they were working with new processes and sometimes with strange materials and machinery, they were credited by the Department of Labor in the last year of the war with the third best accident prevention record in the nation.

423. *War Finance, 1941–*

M. S. Eccles, *Beckoning Frontiers: Public and Personal Recollections.* Sidney Hyman, ed. (New York, 1951), 345–7, 349–51.

IN THE war years the maximization of war output was our supreme aim. Financing that output was a secondary consideration. Nevertheless, what was secondary was extremely important, since war has its own needs for economic stability. . . .

Those of us, then, on the financial front of the war effort had this object in view: to raise the money that was needed, but at the same time to raise it in a way that would minimize the economic instability inherent in waging global war. This being our goal, the choice of means to reach it were the following, stated in their order of preference:

First, we wanted to raise by current taxation as much money as was possible. In this way the government would transfer the purchasing power from the public to itself and thus increase its own purchasing power while reducing that of the public. . . . There were, of course, grave institutional and political blocks that made it hard to raise taxes with a speed that matched our mounting war expenditures. Nevertheless, I was among those who felt we should and could have paid more of the costs of the war out of taxes.

The Administration, the Treasury, and Congress were all shy in stating the economic facts of life to the nation. They all feared the political repercussions of a tax program that suited the needs of the hour. Many people wanted to wage a comfortable war; they wanted guns and butter, and there was a reluctance in government circles to do anything to disturb this sanguine view of how a global war could be waged. Moreover, even when some of us presented the case for stiffer taxes in terms of its effect as an inflation control measure, we were met with incredulous stares. The reaction is not hard to understand. We entered the war years with a hangover of depression psychology. For the period of eight or nine years before the war, it had been money and not goods that was in short supply; in that period we never seemed to have enough money to buy all the things that were available and that we wanted. The momentum of this belief was carried forward to the war years, and Americans found it hard to believe that in war it was goods, not money, that would be in short supply.

Nor was the tenacity with which we

clung to the belief that we could never have more money than goods very far from the truth at the beginning of the war. The enormous surplus of labor, factories, and raw materials that existed in the depression years gave us great leeway to increase production in 1940 and 1941. Despite the huge deficits accumulated in those years, no real inflationary pressures, reflecting a full use of the nation's productive plant, began to be felt until 1942. Up to that time the slack in our economic structure seemed by itself to offer security against inflation. . . .

Next in the order of preference, we felt that the part of the war cost that could not be financed through taxation should be financed by nonbank investors. That is, it should be financed by inducing the public to save as much as possible out of their current income and invest that saving in government securities. This would withdraw the money from the spending stream and reduce the public's purchasing power, and thus the inflationary pressures. Moreover, in so far as it was nonbank sources from which the money was borrowed, to that degree the securities offered by the government would not enter into the money and credit-expansion mechanism that follows when banks lend to the government—or, for that matter, to anybody. . . .

The Treasury, for its part, agreed with the general objective that the purchase of government securities should be made in the first instance and in the main by nonbank investors. They further agreed that bank buying of government securities should be limited in volume. In pursuit of these two ideas, the Treasury made new issues of long-term securities ineligible for purchase by banks. It also launched special drives to promote sales of these securities (especially savings bonds) to nonbank investors. . . .

A third general principle of war finance agreed upon by the Treasury and the Federal Reserve called for an assurance of relatively stable prices and yields for government securities. This was a radical departure from all previous war-finance experience. It was a difficult policy to maintain. It caused serious problems during the war years. It is one of the root causes of our postwar inflation problems. But it should be said that the difficulties which arose were due less to the principle itself than to the way it was applied.

The initial reasons for adopting the policy were these:

First: To encourage (in a war of indeterminate length) the prompt buying of securities by investors who might otherwise wait for lower prices and higher rates.

Second: To assure a strong and steady market for outstanding securities and to reduce speculative fluctuations in anticipation of possible changes in interest rates during a period of large deficit financing.

Third: To keep down the costs of carrying the war debt and thereby limit the growth in earnings by banks and other investors from their holdings of the public debt. Since a tremendous increase in the amount of securities offered by the government could be expected, and, further, since war expenditures and Federal Reserve operations created the money available to banks and other investors for the purchase of these securities, it would have been wrong for the government to pay increasing rates of interest for the use of these funds it helped create.

As a final tool of wartime finance, we agreed that rationing and a number of direct price controls should be used to dampen down inflation and hold it in check. But this last was to be only a supplementary source of strength.

Unfortunately, as things turned out, a weak fiscal policy—plus laggard buying of government securities by nonbank investors—plus Treasury policies that induced excessive security-buying by banks produced a situation in which the direct controls were rushed to the fore to save an economy torn by too much money and too few goods. If serious inflation was curbed during the war years—and our performance was better in the Second World War than in the First—we owe the fact to the rationing system and direct controls that were used. It took their precipitate removal at the end of the war to reveal the deeper layers of economic instability that wrong policies in the field of war finance helped to produce. In other words, it became evident that when the fiscal, monetary, and credit policy was inadequate and thus encouraged a great expansion in the supply of bank deposits and currency, direct controls only postponed and did not prevent inflation.

424. *Unconditional Surrender, 1943*

R. E. Sherwood, *Roosevelt and Hopkins* (New York, 1948), 696–9.

ALTHOUGH Roosevelt implied that he went into the press conference at Casablanca unprepared, Hopkins wrote in his description of the conference that Roosevelt consulted notes as he talked. The photographs of the conference show him holding several pages which had been carefully prepared in advance. Those pages contained the following paragraph.

The President and the Prime Minister, after a complete survey of the world war situation, are more than ever determined that peace can come to the world only by a total elimination of German and Japanese war power. This involves the simple formula of placing the objective of this war in terms of an unconditional surrender by Germany, Italy and Japan. Unconditional surrender by them means a reasonable assurance of world peace, for generations. Unconditional surrender means not the destruction of the German populace, nor of the Italian or Japanese populace, but does mean the destruction of a philosophy in Germany, Italy and Japan which is based on the conquest and subjugation of other peoples.

What Roosevelt was saying was that there would be no negotiated peace, no compromise with Nazism and Fascism, no "escape clauses" provided by another Fourteen Points which could lead to another Hitler. (The ghost of Woodrow Wilson was again at his shoulder.) Roosevelt wanted this uncompromising purpose to be brought home to the American people and Russians and the Chinese, and to the people of France and other occupied nations, and he wanted it brought home to the Germans—that neither by continuance of force nor by contrivance of a new spirit of sweet reasonableness could their present leaders gain for them a soft peace. He wanted to ensure that when the war was won it would stay won.

425. *The Future of Europe, 1945*

Crimea Conference. Statement by President Roosevelt, Prime Minister Churchill, and Premier Stalin, February 11, 1945. Department of State, *Bulletin*, XII (1945), 214–16.

WE HAVE agreed on common policies and plans for enforcing the unconditional surrender terms which we shall impose together on Nazi Germany after German armed resistance has been finally crushed. These terms will not be made known until the final defeat of Germany has been accomplished. Under the agreed plan, the forces of the three powers will each occupy a separate zone of Germany. Co-ordinated administration and control has been provided for under the plan through a central control commission consisting of the Supreme Commanders of the three powers with headquarters in Berlin. It has been agreed that France should be invited by the three powers, if she should so desire, to take over a zone of occupation, and to participate as a fourth member of the control commission. The limits of the French zone will be agreed by the four governments concerned through their representatives on the European Advisory Commission.

It is our inflexible purpose to destroy German militarism and Nazism and to ensure that Germany will never again be able to disturb the peace of the world. We are determined to disarm and disband all German armed forces; break up for all time the German General Staff that has repeatedly contrived the resurgence of German militarism; remove or destroy all German military equipment; eliminate or control all German industry that could be used for military production; bring all war criminals to just and swift punishment and exact reparation in kind for the destruction wrought by the Germans; wipe out the Nazi Party, Nazi laws, organizations and institutions, remove all Nazi and militarist influences from public office and from the cultural and economic life of the German people; and take in harmony such other measures in Germany as may be necessary to the future peace and safety of the world. It is not our purpose to destroy the people of Germany, but only when Nazism and militarism have been extirpated will there be hope for a decent life for Germans, and a place for them in the comity of nations. . . .

We are resolved upon the earliest possible establishment with our allies of a general international organization to maintain peace and security. We believe that this is essential, both to prevent aggression and to remove the political, economic and so-cial causes of war through the close and continuing collaboration of all peace-loving peoples. . . .

The Premier of the Union of Soviet Socialist Republics, the Prime Minister of the United Kingdom, and the President of the United States of America . . . jointly declare their mutual agreement to concert during the temporary period of instability in liberated Europe the policies of their three governments in assisting the peoples liberated from the domination of Nazi Germany and the peoples of the former Axis satellite states of Europe to solve by democratic means their pressing political and economic problems.

The establishment of order in Europe and the rebuilding of national economic life must be achieved by processes which will enable the liberated peoples to destroy the last vestiges of Nazism and Fascism and to create democratic institutions of their own choice. This is a principle of the Atlantic Charter—the right of all peoples to choose the form of government under which they will live—the restoration of sovereign rights and self-government to those peoples who have been forcibly deprived of them by the aggressor nations.

To foster the conditions in which the liberated peoples may exercise these rights, the three governments will jointly assist the people in any European liberated state or former Axis satellite state in Europe where in their judgment conditions require (A) to establish conditions of internal peace; (B) to carry out emergency measures for the relief of distressed peoples; (C) to form interim governmental authorities broadly representative of all democratic elements in the population and pledged to the earliest possible establishment through free elections of governments responsive to the will of the people; and (D) to facilitate where necessary the holding of such elections.

The three governments will consult the other United Nations and provisional authorities or other governments in Europe when matters of direct interest to them are under consideration.

When, in the opinion of the three governments, conditions in any European liberated state or any former Axis satellite state in Europe make such action necessary, they will immediately consult together on the measures necessary to discharge the joint responsibilities set forth in this declaration. . . .

A new situation has been created in Poland as a result of her complete liberation by the Red Army. This calls for the establishment of a Polish provisional government which can be more broadly based than was possible before the recent liberation of Western Poland. The provisional government which is now functioning in Poland should therefore be reorganized on a broader democratic basis with the inclusion of democratic leaders from Poland itself and from Poles abroad. This new government should then be called the Polish Provisional Government of National Unity.

M. Molotov, Mr. Harriman and Sir A. Clark Kerr are authorized as a commission to consult in the first instance in Moscow with members of the present provisional government and with other Polish democratic leaders from within Poland and from abroad, with a view to the reorganization of the present government along the above lines. This Polish Provisional Government of National Unity shall be pledged to the holding of free and unfettered elections as soon as possible on the basis of universal suffrage and secret ballot. In these elections all democratic and anti-Nazi parties shall have the right to take part and to put forward candidates.

When a Polish Provisional Government of National Unity has been properly formed in conformity with the above, the government of the U.S.S.R., which now maintains diplomatic relations with the present provisional government of Poland, and the government of the United Kingdom and the government of the U.S.A. will establish diplomatic relations with the new Polish Provisional Government of National Unity, and will exchange ambassadors by whose reports the respective governments will be kept informed about the situation in Poland.

The three heads of government consider that the Eastern frontier of Poland should follow the Curzon line with digressions from it in some regions of five to eight kilometers in favor of Poland. They recognize that Poland must receive substantial accessions of territory in the North and West. They feel that the opinion of the new Polish Provisional Government of National Unity should be sought in due course on the extent of these accessions and that the final delimitation of the western frontier of Poland should thereafter await the peace conference.

426. *The Future of Japan, 1945*

Proclamation at Potsdam by President Truman and Prime Minister Churchill, concurred in by Generalissimo Chiang Kai-Shek, July 26, 1945. Department of State, *Bulletin*, XIII, 137–8.

WE—THE President of the United States, the President of the National Government of the Republic of China, and the Prime Minister of Great Britain, representing the hundreds of millions of our countrymen, have conferred and agree that Japan shall be given an opportunity to end this war. . . .

The result of the futile and senseless German resistance to the might of the aroused free peoples of the world stands forth in awful clarity as an example to the people of Japan. The might that now converges on Japan is immeasurably greater than that which, when applied to the resisting Nazis, necessarily laid waste to the lands, the industry and the method of life of the whole German people. The full application of our military power, backed by our resolve, *will* mean the inevitable and complete destruction of the Japanese armed forces and just as inevitably the utter devastation of the Japanese homeland.

The time has come for Japan to decide whether she will continue to be controlled by those self-willed militaristic advisers whose unintelligent calculations have brought the Empire of Japan to the threshold of annihilation, or whether she will follow the path of reason.

Following are our terms. We will not deviate from them. There are no alternatives. We shall brook no delay.

There must be eliminated for all time the authority and influence of those who have deceived and misled the people of Japan into embarking on world conquest, for we insist that a new order of peace, security and justice will be impossible until irresponsible militarism is driven from the world.

Until such a new order is established *and* until there is convincing proof that Japan's war-making power is destroyed, points in Japanese territory to be designated by the Allies shall be occupied to secure the achievement of the basic objectives we are here setting forth.

The terms of the Cairo Declaration shall be carried out and Japanese sovereignty shall be limited to the islands of Honshu, Hokkaido, Kyushu, Shikoku and such minor islands as we determine.

The Japanese military forces, after being completely disarmed, shall be permitted to return to their homes with the opportunity to lead peaceful and productive lives.

We do not intend that the Japanese shall be enslaved as a race or destroyed as a nation, but stern justice shall be meted out to all war criminals, including those who have visited cruelties upon our prisoners. The Japanese Government shall remove all obstacles to the revival and strengthening of democratic tendencies among the Japanese people. Freedom of speech, of religion, and of thought, as well as respect for the fundamental human rights shall be established.

Japan shall be permitted to maintain such industries as will sustain her economy and permit the exaction of just reparations in kind, but not those which would enable her to re-arm for war. To this end, access to, as distinguished from control of, raw materials shall be permitted. Eventual Japanese participation in world trade relations shall be permitted.

The occupying forces of the Allies shall be withdrawn from Japan as soon as these objectives have been accomplished and there has been established in accordance with the freely expressed will of the Japanese people a peacefully inclined and responsible government.

We call upon the government of Japan to proclaim now the unconditional surrender of all Japanese armed forces, and to provide proper and adequate assurances of their good faith in such action. The alternative for Japan is prompt and utter destruction.

427. *Yalta Agreement on World Organization, 1945*

Protocol of the Proceedings of the Crimea Conference, February 4–11, 1945. Released by the Department of State, March 24, 1947. *Foreign Relations of the United States. Conferences at Malta and Yalta* (Washington, 1955), 975–7.

1. THAT a United Nations conference on the proposed world organization should be summoned for Wednesday, 25th April, 1945, and should be held in the United States of America.

2. The nations to be invited to this con-

ference should be:

(a) The United Nations as they existed on the 8th February, 1945 and

(b) Such of the Associated Nations as have declared war on the common enemy by 1st March, 1945.... When the conference on world organization is held, the delegates of the United Kingdom and United States of America will support a proposal to admit to original membership two Soviet Socialist Republics, i.e., the Ukraine and White Russia.

3. That the United States Government on behalf of the three powers, should consult the Government of China and the French Provisional Government in regard to decisions taken at the present conference concerning the proposed world organization....

Voting

1. Each member of the Security Council should have one vote.

2. Decisions of the Security Council on procedural matters should be made by an affirmative vote of seven members.

3. Decisions of the Security Council on all other matters should be made by an affirmative vote of seven members including the concurring votes of the permanent members; provided that, in decisions under Chapter VIII, Section A and under the second sentence of paragraph 1 of Chapter VIII, Section C, a party to a dispute should abstain from voting....

Territorial Trusteeship

It was agreed that the five nations which will have permanent seats on the Security Council should consult each other prior to the United Nations conference on the question of territorial trusteeship.

The acceptance of this recommendation is subject to its being made clear that territorial trusteeship will only apply to (a) existing mandates of the League of Nations; (b) territories detached from the enemy as a result of the present war; (c) any other territory which might voluntarily be placed under trusteeship; and (d) no discussion of actual territories is contemplated at the forthcoming United Nations conference or in the preliminary consultations, and it will be a matter for subsequent agreement which territories within the above categories will be placed under trusteeship.

XLVII 🦥 *The Problems of Peace*

THE NECESSITIES for wartime collaboration obscured the magnitude of the difficulties the Western democracies would ultimately encounter in dealing with the Soviet Union. All too soon American statesmen realized that their own objectives were worlds away from those of the Russians (No. 428). For the totalitarian rulers of that country, the disorder of the postwar period was an opportunity to extend Communism across their borders; and the presence of the Red Army in Europe gave them the ability to impose satellite governments on the neighboring states. Given the devastated condition of eastern Europe and Asia, indigenous forces with the will to resist were weak; only where outside aid was available could the advance of Communism be contained.

American policy was defined gradually in the face of this threat. It was most successful in Latin America, where a long period of peaceful collaboration and the good neighbor policy supplied a firm foundation for the Organization of American States (No. 429). Meanwhile, in Europe the Truman Doctrine had enunciated clearly enough the determination of the United States to resist the spread of Communism (No. 430). Its complement, the Marshall Plan, aimed to provide a sound economic basis for the free regimes of the world and thus to destroy the ground in which Communism might breed (No. 431). Through the North Atlantic Treaty Organization the United States hoped to help create a military force capable of resisting aggression in Europe (No. 432).

The measures were widely welcomed in the United States (No. 433; *see however, below,* No. 443). Yet there were no illusions; peace was no nearer at the end of the decade than just after the war. The continuing threat led to a reconsideration of attitudes toward Germany. Since unification of that country appeared remote, it was hoped that the Western sectors might develop as a democratic power and assist in the defense of the West (No. 434).

In Europe, although Communism was not pushed back, it was at least contained. That could not be said of Asia. Despite American support, the nationalist regime of China proved incapable of maintaining itself in power (No. 435). The Communists seized control of China and put all of Asia in jeopardy. Their encouragement touched off the invasion of Korea and led to the long struggle that involved the United States and the United Nations (No. 436). The Korean War, indecisive in a military sense, nevertheless maintained the principles of international morality. From that point of view, even the armistice represented a victory (No. 437). Yet in 1955 the unsettlement of all Asia remained one of the troubling elements in an unsettled world.

428. *The Russians Show Their Hand, 1945*

J. F. Byrnes, *Speaking Frankly* (New York, 1947), 71, 73, 86–7. Copyright 1947 by James F. Byrnes. Reprinted with permission.

I HAD assumed that at the end of hostilities an era of peace would be so deeply desired by those nations that had fought the war in unity that the inevitable differences of opinion could be resolved without serious difficulty.

It is true that following Yalta we had been somewhat disillusioned. . . . The Bern incident and the Soviet violation of the agreements on Poland and Rumania warned us that in the days to come we would encounter serious differences and would have to overcome deep-seated suspicion. However, fresh in our minds were the words of President Roosevelt's last message to Prime Minister Churchill, based

upon his experience with the Russians, that such difficulties would straighten out. . . .

Our paper [on Europe] stated flatly that the obligations assumed in the Yalta Declaration had not been carried out. . . . We proposed joint action in reorganizing the governments of Bulgaria and Rumania to permit participation of all democratic groups as a prelude to establishing diplomatic relations and concluding peace treaties. We also suggested that our three states should help the interim governments in holding "free and unfettered elections.". . .

Stalin's initial response to our paper was

simply that the Soviet Union had a proposal of its own to present on the subject. Molotov presented it at the meeting of the Foreign Ministers the next morning. It was devoted largely to a severe attack on Greece. Eden angrily termed the attack a "travesty of fact," pointing out that international observers, including representatives of the Soviet Union, had been invited to observe the Greek elections. Unfortunately, the same could not be said of Rumania or Bulgaria, he added. . . .

My contribution to this exchange was to repeat a statement which I was to make many times. It is one which, I fear, Mr. Molotov never fully understood or believed. "The United States," I told him, "sincerely desires Russia to have friendly countries on her borders, but we believe they should seek the friendship of the people rather than of any particular government. We, therefore, want the governments to be representative of the people. If elections are held while there are restrictions not only on newspaper and radio correspondents but upon our own governmental representatives as well, the American people will distrust any government established as a result of such an election. We do not wish to become involved in the elections of any country, but, because of the postwar situation, we would join with others in observing elections in Italy, Greece, Hungary, Rumania and Bulgaria."

This discussion contains arguments heard scores of times during ensuing months. . . . Events had shown that agreements reached in conference must be hammered out on the hard anvil of experience. We thought, however, that we had established a basis for maintaining our war-born unity. Our efforts in relation to eastern Europe had been less successful than we had hoped. We had failed to exempt Italy from reparations. We thought we had succeeded in the case of Austria. We felt we had made genuine progress in the agreements about Germany, although there was ample ground for our fears that it would be a long time before we could get the Soviets to start work on a German settlement. Nevertheless, we believed our agreement on reparations enabled us to avoid denouncing their unilateral action in removing people and property from their zone.

Certainly, no one of us suspected that the first treaties of peace would be concluded only after sixteen months of almost continuous negotiation. We considered the conference a success. We firmly believed that the agreements reached would provide a basis for the early restoration of stability in Europe.

The agreements did make the conference a success but the violation of those agreements has turned the success into failure.

429. *The Organization of American States, 1948*

Department of State, "Ninth International Conference of American States." *International Organization and Conference Series*, II (1948), Publication No. 3263, 167–74.

ARTICLE 1. The American States establish by this Charter the international organization that they have developed to achieve an order of peace and justice, to promote their solidarity, to strengthen their collaboration, and to defend their sovereignty, their territorial integrity and their independence. Within the United Nations,

the Organization of American States is a regional agency. . . .

ARTICLE 4. The Organization of American States . . . proclaims the following essential purposes:

a) To strengthen the peace and security of the continent;

b) To prevent possible causes of difficulties and to ensure the pacific settlement of disputes that may arise among the member states;

c) To provide for common action on the part of those states in the event of aggression;

d) To seek the solution of political, juridical and economic problems that may arise among them; and

e) To promote, by cooperative action, their economic, social and cultural development.

ARTICLE 5. The American States reaffirm the following principles:

a) International law is the standard of conduct of states in their reciprocal relations;

b) International order consists essentially of respect for the personality, sovereignty and independence of states, and the faithful fulfillment of obligations derived from treaties and other sources of international law;

c) Good faith shall govern the relations between states;

d) The solidarity of the American States and the high aims which are sought through it require the political organization of those states on the basis of the effective exercise of representative democracy;

e) The American States condemn war of aggression: victory does not give rights;

f) An act of aggression against one American State is an act of aggression against all the other American States;

g) Controversies of an international character arising between two or more American States shall be settled by peaceful procedures;

h) Social justice and social security are bases of lasting peace;

i) Economic cooperation is essential to the common welfare and prosperity of the peoples of the continent;

j) The American States proclaim the fundamental rights of the individual without distinction as to race, nationality, creed or sex;

k) The spiritual unity of the continent is based on respect for the cultural values of the American countries and requires their close cooperation for the high purposes of civilization;

l) The education of peoples should be directed toward justice, freedom and peace.

ARTICLE 6. States are juridically equal, enjoy equal rights and equal capacity to exercise these rights, and have equal duties. The rights of each state depend not upon its power to ensure the exercise thereof, but upon the mere fact of its existence as a person under international law. . . .

ARTICLE 9. The political existence of the state is independent of recognition by other states. Even before being recognized, the state has the right to defend its integrity and independence, to provide for its preservation and prosperity, and consequently to organize itself as it sees fit, to legislate concerning its interests, to administer its services, and to determine the jurisdiction and competence of its courts. The exercise of these rights is limited only by the exercise of the rights of other states in accordance with international law. . . .

ARTICLE 13. Each state has the right to develop its cultural, political and economic life freely and naturally. In this free development, the state shall respect the rights of the individual and the principles of universal morality. . . .

ARTICLE 15. No state or group of states has the right to intervene, directly or indirectly, for any reason whatever, in the internal or external affairs of any other state. The foregoing principle prohibits not only armed force but also any other form of interference or attempted threat against the personality of the state or against its political, economic and cultural elements.

430. *The Truman Doctrine, 1947*

President Harry S. Truman, Address to Congress, March 12, 1947, *Congressional Record*, XCIII (1947), 1980–1.

THE United States has received from the Greek government an urgent appeal for financial and economic assistance. Preliminary reports from the American economic mission now in Greece and reports from the American ambassador in Greece corroborate the statement of the Greek government that assistance is imperative if Greece is to survive as a free nation.

I do not believe that the American people and the Congress wish to turn a deaf ear to the appeal of the Greek government. . . .

When forces of liberation entered Greece they found that the retreating Germans had destroyed virtually all the railways, roads, port facilities, communications, and merchant marine. More than a thousand villages had been burned. Eighty-five per cent of the children were tubercular. Livestock, poultry, and draft animals had almost disappeared. Inflation had wiped out practically all savings.

As a result of these tragic conditions, a militant minority, exploiting human want and misery, was able to create political chaos which, until now, has made economic recovery impossible.

Greece is today without funds to finance the importation of those goods which are essential to bare subsistence. Under these circumstances the people of Greece cannot make progress in solving their problems of reconstruction. Greece is in desperate need of financial and economic assistance to enable it to resume purchases of food, clothing, fuel, and seeds. These are indispensable for the subsistence of its people and are obtainable only from abroad. Greece must have help to import the goods necessary to restore internal order and security so essential for economic and political recovery.

The Greek government has also asked for the assistance of experienced American administrators, economists, and technicians to insure that the financial and other aid given to Greece shall be used effectively in creating a stable and self-sustaining economy and in improving its public administration.

The very existence of the Greek state is today threatened by the terrorist activities of several thousand armed men, led by Communists, who defy the government's authority at a number of points, particularly along the northern boundaries. . . .

Meanwhile, the Greek government is unable to cope with the situation. The Greek army is small and poorly equipped. It needs supplies and equipment if it is to restore the authority of the government throughout Greek territory.

Greece must have assistance if it is to become a self-supporting and self-respecting democracy. The United States must supply that assistance. We have already extended to Greece certain types of relief and economic aid but these are inadequate. There is no other country to which democratic Greece can turn. . . .

We have considered how the United Nations might assist in this crisis. But the situation is an urgent one requiring immediate action, and the United Nations and its related organizations are not in a position to extend help of the kind that is required. . . .

Greece's neighbor, Turkey, also deserves our attention. The future of Turkey as an independent and economically sound state is clearly no less important to the freedom-loving people of the world than the future of Greece. The circumstances in which Turkey finds itself today are considerably different from those of Greece. Turkey has been spared the disasters that have beset Greece. And during the war, the United States and Great Britain furnished Turkey with material aid. Nevertheless, Turkey now needs our support. . . .

As in the case of Greece, if Turkey is to have the assistance it needs, the United States must supply it. We are the only country able to provide that help.

I am fully aware of the broad implications involved if the United States extends assistance to Greece and Turkey, and I shall discuss these implications with you at this time.

One of the primary objectives of the foreign policy of the United States is the creation of conditions in which we and other nations will be able to work out a way of life free from coercion. This was a fundamental issue in the war with Germany and Japan. Our victory was won over countries which sought to impose their will, and their way of life, upon other nations.

To insure the peaceful development of nations, free from coercion, the United States has taken a leading part in establishing the United Nations. The United Nations is designed to make possible lasting freedom and independence for all its members. We shall not realize our objectives, however, unless we are willing to help free people to maintain their free institutions and their national integrity against aggressive movements that seek to impose upon them totalitarian regimes. This is no more than a frank recognition that totalitarian regimes imposed on free peoples, by direct or indirect aggression, undermine the foundations of international peace and hence the security of the United States.

The peoples of a number of countries of the world have recently had totalitarian regimes forced upon them against their will. The government of the United States has made frequent protests against coercion and intimidation, in violation of the Yalta agreement, in Poland, Rumania and Bulgaria. I must also state that in a number of other countries there have been similar developments.

At the present moment in world history nearly every nation must choose between alternative ways of life. The choice is too often not a free one.

One way of life is based upon the will of the majority, and is distinguished by free institutions, representative government, free elections, guarantees of individual liberty, freedom of speech and religion, and freedom from political oppression.

The second way of life is based upon the will of a minority forcibly imposed upon the majority. It relies upon terror and oppression, a controlled press and radio, fixed elections and the suppression of personal freedoms.

I believe that it must be the policy of the United States to support peoples who are resisting attempted subjugation by armed minorities or by outside pressures. . . . I believe that our help should be primarily through economic and financial aid, which is essential to economic stability and orderly political processes.

The world is not static and the status quo is not sacred. But we cannot allow changes in the status quo in violation of the charter of the United Nations by such methods as coercion, or by such subterfuges as political infiltration. In helping free and independent nations to maintain their freedom, the United States will be giving effect to the principles of the charter of the United Nations.

It is necessary only to glance at a map to realize that the survival and integrity of the Greek nation are of grave importance in a much wider situation. If Greece should fall under the control of an armed minority, the effect upon its neighbor, Turkey, would be immediate and serious. Confusion and disorder might well spread throughout the entire Middle East. . . .

It would be an unspeakable tragedy if these countries, which have struggled so long against overwhelming odds, should lose that victory for which they sacrificed so much. Collapse of free institutions and loss of independence would be disastrous not only for them but for the world. Discouragement and possibly failure would quickly be the lot of neighboring peoples striving to maintain their freedom and independence. . . .

The seeds of totalitarian regimes are nurtured by misery and want. They spread and grow in the evil soil of poverty and strife. They reach their full growth when the hope of a people for a better life has died. We must keep that hope alive.

The free peoples of the world look to us for support in maintaining their freedoms. If we falter in our leadership, we may endanger the peace of the world—and we shall surely endanger the welfare of our own nation. Great responsibilities have been placed upon us by the swift movement of events. I am confident that the Congress will face these responsibilities squarely.

431. *The Marshall Plan,* 1947

Secretary of State George C. Marshall, Address, June 6, 1947, *New York Times,* June 6, 1947, p. 2.

IN CONSIDERING the requirements for the rehabilitation of Europe the physical loss of life, the visible destruction of cities, factories, mines and railroads was correctly estimated, but it has become obvious during recent months that this visible destruction was probably less serious than the dislocation of the entire fabric of European economy. For the past ten years conditions have been highly abnormal.

The feverish preparation for war and the more feverish maintenance of the war effort engulfed all aspects of national economies. Machinery has fallen into disrepair or is entirely obsolete. Under the arbitrary and destructive Nazi rule, virtually every possible enterprise was geared into the German war machine. Longstanding commercial ties, private institutions, banks, insurance companies and shipping companies disappeared, through loss of capital, absorption through nationalization or by simple destruction.

In many countries, confidence in the local currency has been severely shaken. The breakdown of the business structure of Europe during the war was complete. Recovery has been seriously retarded by the fact that two years after the close of hostilities a peace settlement with Germany and Austria has not been agreed upon. But even given a more prompt solution of these difficult problems, the rehabilitation of the economic structure of Europe quite evidently will require a much longer time and greater effort than had been foreseen. . . .

The truth of the matter is that Europe's requirements for the next three or four years of foreign food and other essential products—principally from America—are so much greater than her present ability to pay that she must have substantial additional help, or face economic, social and political deterioration of a very grave character.

The remedy lies in breaking the vicious circle and restoring the confidence of the European people in the economic future of their own countries and of Europe as a whole. The manufacturer and the farmer throughout wide areas must be able and willing to exchange their products for currencies, the continuing value of which is not open to question.

Aside from the demoralizing effect on the world at large and the possibilities of disturbances arising as a result of the desperation of the people concerned, the consequences to the economy of the United States should be apparent to all. It is logical that the United States should do whatever it is able to do to assist in the return of normal economic health in the world, without which there can be no political stability and no assured peace.

Our policy is directed not against any country or doctrine but against hunger, poverty, desperation and chaos. Its purpose should be the revival of a working economy in the world so as to permit the emergence of political and social conditions in which free institutions can exist. Such assistance, I am convinced, must not be on a piecemeal basis as various crises develop. Any assistance that this Government may render in the future should provide a cure rather than a mere palliative. . . .

It is already evident that, before the United States Government can proceed much further in its efforts to alleviate the situation and help start the European world on its way to recovery, there must be some agreement among the countries of Europe as to the requirements of the situation and the part those countries themselves will take in order to give proper effect to whatever action might be undertaken by this Government. It would be neither fitting nor efficacious for this Government to undertake to draw up unilaterally a program designed to place Europe on its feet economically. This is the business of the Europeans. The initiative, I think, must come from Europe. The role of this country should consist of friendly aid in the drafting of a European program and of later support of such a program so far as it may be practical for us to do so. The program should be a joint one, agreed to by a number, if not all European nations.

432. *The North Atlantic Treaty, 1949*

Signed, April 4, 1949; ratified July 25, 1949. Department of State, *Bulletin*, XX (1949), No. 507, March 20, 1949, 339–41.

ARTICLE 1. The Parties undertake, as set forth in the Charter of the United Nations, to settle any international disputes in which they may be involved by peaceful means in such a manner that international peace and security, and justice, are not endangered, and to refrain in their international relations from the threat or use of force in any manner inconsistent with the purposes of the United Nations.

ARTICLE 2. The Parties will contribute toward the further development of peaceful and friendly international relations by strengthening their free institutions, by bringing about a better understanding of the principles upon which these institutions are founded, and by promoting conditions of stability and well-being. They will seek to eliminate conflict in their international economic policies and will encourage economic collaboration between any or all of them.

ARTICLE 3. In order more effectively to achieve the objectives of this Treaty, the Parties, separately and jointly, by means of continuous and effective self-help and mutual aid, will maintain and develop their individual and collective capacity to resist armed attack.

ARTICLE 4. The Parties will consult together whenever, in the opinion of any of them, the territorial integrity, political independence or security of any of the Parties is threatened.

ARTICLE 5. The Parties agree that an armed attack against one or more of them in Europe or North America shall be considered an attack against them all; and consequently they agree that, if such an armed attack occurs, each of them, in exercise of the right of individual or collective self-defense recognized by Article 51 of the Charter of the United Nations, will assist the Party or Parties so attacked by taking forthwith, individually and in concert with the other Parties, such action as it deems necessary, including the use of armed force, to restore and maintain the security of the North Atlantic area. . . .

ARTICLE 7. This Treaty does not affect, and shall not be interpreted as affecting, in any way the rights and obligations under the Charter of the Parties which are members of the United Nations, or the primary responsibility of the Security Council for the maintenance of international peace and security. . . .

ARTICLE 9. The Parties hereby establish a council, on which each of them shall be represented, to consider matters concerning the implementation of this Treaty. The council shall be so organized as to be able to meet promptly at any time. The council shall set up such subsidiary bodies as may be necessary; in particular it shall establish immediately a defense committee which shall recommend measures for the implementation of Articles 3 and 5.

433. *On NATO, 1949*

Speech in Congress, Vandenberg, *Private Papers*, 493-4.

[THE North Atlantic] Treaty is the most sensible, powerful, practicable, and economical step the United States can now take in the realistic interest of its own security; in the effective discouragement of aggressive conquest which would touch off World War Three; in the stabilization of Western Germany; and, as declared by its own preamble, in peacefully safeguarding the freedoms and the civilization founded on the principles of democracy, individual liberty, and the rule of law. These things, Mr. President, I shall undertake to prove.

Only those without eyes to see and ears to hear can deny that these precious values—far dearer than life itself—are in jeopardy in today's tortured world. . . . This jeopardy does not stem from us. . . . It stems from embattled, greedy Communism abroad and at home; from open conspiracies which have frankly sought to

wreck the brave self-help and mutual aid which would restore independent peoples to their heritage, with our American cooperation; from kindred saboteurs in the United Nations; from those who have repelled and thwarted our American designs and aspirations for a live-and-let-live world.

I repeat: the jeopardy does not stem from us. But it inevitably involves us. Indeed, we are its heart and core. It is aimed ultimately at us. We cannot run away from it. There it is, Pact or no Pact. Every vigilant American knows this is true. We are the final target, though other independent peoples are in nearer jeopardy. We may argue ourselves out of ratifying the Pact. But we cannot thereby argue ourselves out of the jeopardy which the Pact seeks to minimize.

434. *Post-War Germany, 1952*

Speech of Secretary of State Dean Acheson, June 10, 1952, "Relations with the Federal Republic of Germany," Senate Foreign Relations Committee, *Hearings*, 2-5.

GERMANY has been occupied for almost seven years. In that time, we have sought to assist the Germans in developing demo-

cratic institutions and institutions of self-government in the towns and cities, in states, and in the Federal Government.

We have sought, and I think successfully, to conduct an enlightened occupation that looked toward peaceful and harmonious relations in the future.

But at some point in any occupation, the law of diminishing returns must inevitably come into play. It had become clear to us that the Germans who were not living under Soviet occupation had made considerable progress toward democratic self-rule, and that a prolonged extension of the occupation would have a negative and stultifying effect on the very democratic processes we were doing our best to induce. . . .

It has not been possible to conclude a treaty of peace with Germany because the Soviet Union has refused to agree to any terms for unifying Germany in conditions of freedom.

The convention before you will, however, establish approximately normal relations with the largest part of Germany. These agreements put an end to the occupation in all of Germany not occupied by the Soviet Union. . . .

The independence of the Federal Republic of Germany is established by these agreements, subject only to certain reservations made necessary by the present state of international relations. These reservations concern the stationing and security of Allied forces in Germany, including the right to proclaim a state of emergency in certain extreme circumstances, and to matters dealing with the ultimate unification of Germany and a peace settlement for Germany as a whole.

It remains our purpose to help bring about a free and united Germany, and nothing in the present arrangements will serve as a bar to the fulfillment of this aim. . . .

The new status which the Federal Republic will enjoy will grant her the greatest autonomy that is possible under present international conditions. Specifically, the occupation regime will be terminated. This means that the occupation statute will be repealed, the High Commission and Land Commissioners' offices will be abolished. Allied occupation troops in Germany will become troops for the common defense, Western Germany will regain control of her domestic and foreign affairs, and normal diplomatic relations between the Federal Republic and the Three Powers will be established.

This convention on relations with the Federal Republic was not, and could not be, prepared as an isolated document, because it does not by itself meet the full problem confronting the free people of Germany and those of other free countries. In order to provide for the security of the Federal Republic, and to enable free Germany to participate in its own defense, without recreating those military institutions and traditions that have endangered all Europe in the past, arrangements have been worked out under which the Federal Republic is joining in a European Defense Community—the common defense organization of six continental European countries. These include, in addition to the Federal Republic of Germany, France, Italy, Belgium, the Netherlands, and Luxembourg.

As a member of this community, the Federal Republic will be able to make a vital contribution to the common defense of Western Europe without the creation of a national German military establishment. The European Defense Community, with a common budget and common procurement of military equipment, common uniforms, and common training, is a very remarkable advance. It represents a voluntary merging of national power into a common structure of defense.

The principal immediate purpose of the European Defense Community is to give the people of Europe more adequate protection against the threat of aggression. In this sense, it is part of a broader effort undertaken by the entire North Atlantic Community to create the defensive strength we need to assure peace and security. . . .

Five members of the new European Defense Community are also members of the North Atlantic Treaty Organization, but the Federal Republic is not. We have therefore joined with the other members of NATO in signing a protocol to the North Atlantic Treaty which ... extends the guaranty of mutual assistance expressed in Article V of the treaty to the Federal Republic and to the forces of the Community, by providing specifically that an attack on the territory of any member of the Community, or on the Community's forces, shall be considered an attack against all the parties to the North Atlantic Treaty.

The Federal Republic will join with the other members of the European Defense Community in extending a reciprocal guaranty to the members of NATO.

Because of this necessarily close relationship, it is evident that the United States, while not a party to the European Defense Community, has a direct and abiding interest in the success and effectiveness of these arrangements.

These arrangements bear upon the defense of Western Europe and the whole Atlantic Community, which the President and the Congress have clearly indicated on many occasions is of vital interest to the security of the United States.

There must be no misunderstanding in any quarter about how we would regard any act which would affect the integrity or unity of the European Defense Community.

For this reason, we have joined with the Governments of Britain and France in a declaration which makes it clear that we would regard any such act as a threat to our own security, and that we would act in accordance with article IV of the North Atlantic Treaty.

In the Three Power declaration, we have also expressed the determination previously affirmed by the Senate to station forces, as necessary and appropriate, on the continent of Europe, including the territory of the German Republic.

435. *The United States and China,* 1949

Statement of Secretary of State, Dean Acheson, February 3, 1949, *United States Relations with China,* Department of State, *Publication,* No. 3573. Far Eastern Series 30 (Washington, 1949), xiv–xvii.

THE FAILURES of the Chinese National Government ... do not stem from any inadequacy of American aid. Our military observers on the spot have reported that the Nationalist armies did not lose a single battle during the crucial year of 1948 through lack of arms or ammunition. The fact was that the decay which our observers had detected in Chungking early in the war had fatally sapped the powers of resistance of the Kuomintang. Its leaders had proved incapable of meeting the crisis confronting them, its troops had lost the will to fight, and its Government had lost popular support. The Communists, on the other hand, through a ruthless discipline and fanatical zeal, attempted to sell themselves as guardians and liberators of the people. The Nationalist armies did not have to be defeated; they disintegrated. ...

Fully recognizing that the heads of the Chinese Communist Party were ideologically affiliated with Moscow, our Government nevertheless took the view, in the light of the existing balance of forces in China, that peace could be established only if certain conditions were met. The Kuomintang would have to set its own house in order and both sides would have to make concessions so that the Government of China might become, in fact as well as in name, the Government of all China and so that all parties might function within the constitutional system of the Government. Both internal peace and constitutional development required that the progress should be rapid from one party government with a large opposition party in armed rebellion, to the participation of all parties, including the moderate non-Communist elements, in a truly national system of government.

None of these conditions has been realized. The distrust of the leaders of both the Nationalist and Communist Parties for each other proved too deep-seated to permit final agreement.... The Nationalists, furthermore, embarked in 1946 on an over-ambitious military campaign in the face of warnings by General Marshall that it not only would fail but would plunge China into economic chaos and eventually destroy the National Government. General Marshall pointed out that though Nationalist armies could, for a period, capture Communist-held cities, they could not destroy the Communist armies. Thus every Nationalist advance would expose their communications to attack by Communist guerrillas and compel them to retreat or to surrender their armies together with the munitions which the United States has furnished them. No estimate of a military situation has ever been more completely confirmed by the resulting facts.

The historic policy of the United States of friendship and aid toward the people of China was, however, maintained in both peace and war. Since V-J Day, the United States Government has authorized aid to Nationalist China in the form of grants and credits totaling approximately two billion dollars, an amount equivalent in value to more than 50 per cent of the monetary expenditures of the Chinese Government and of proportionately greater magnitude in relation to the budget of that Government than the

United States has provided to any nation of Western Europe since the end of the war. In addition to these grants and credits, the United States Government has sold the Chinese Government large quantities of military and civilian war surplus property with a total procurement cost of over one billion dollars, for which the agreed realization to the United States was 232 million dollars. A large proportion of the military supplies furnished the Chinese armies by the United States since V-J Day has, however, fallen into the hands of the Chinese Communists through the military ineptitude of the Nationalist leaders, their defections and surrenders, and the absence among their forces of the will to fight....

A realistic appraisal of conditions in China, past and present, leads to the conclusion that the only alternative open to the United States was full-scale intervention in behalf of a Government which had lost the confidence of its own troops and its own people. Such intervention would have required the expenditure of even greater sums than have been fruitlessly spent thus far, the command of Nationalist armies by American officers, and the probable participation of American armed forces—land, sea, and air—in the resulting war. Intervention of such a scope and magnitude would have been resented by the mass of the Chinese people, would have diametrically reversed our historic policy, and would have been condemned by the American people.

It must be admitted frankly that the American policy of assisting the Chinese people in resisting domination by any foreign power or powers is now confronted with the gravest difficulties. The heart of China is in Communist hands. The Communist leaders have forsworn their Chinese heritage and have publicly announced their subservience to a foreign power, Russia, which during the last fifty years under czars and Communists alike, has been most assiduous in its efforts to extend its control in the Far East.

In the recent past, attempts at foreign domination have appeared quite clearly to the Chinese people as external aggression and as such have been bitterly and in the long run successfully resisted. Our aid and encouragement have helped them to resist. In this case, however, the foreign domination has been masked behind the facade of a vast crusading movement which apparently has seemed to many Chinese to be wholly indigenous and national. Under these circumstances, our aid has been unavailing.

The unfortunate but inescapable fact is that the ominous result of the civil war in China was beyond the control of the government of the United States. Nothing that this country did or could have done within the reasonable limits of its capabilities could have changed that result; nothing that was left undone by this country has contributed to it. It was the product of internal Chinese forces, forces which this country tried to influence but could not. . . .

And now it is abundantly clear that we must face the situation as it exists in fact. . . . In the immediate future, . . . our historic policy of friendship for China must be profoundly affected by current developments. It will necessarily be influenced by the degree to which the Chinese people come to recognize that the Communist regime serves not their interests but those of Soviet Russia and the manner in which, having become aware of the facts, they react to this foreign domination. One point, however, is clear. Should the Communist regime lend itself to the aims of Soviet Russian imperialism and attempt to engage in aggression against China's neighbors, we and the other members of the United Nations would be confronted by a situation violative of the principles of the United Nations Charter and threatening international peace and security.

436. *Invasion of Korea, 1950*

Statement of President Truman, *New York Times,* June 28, 1950.

IN KOREA the Government forces, which were armed to prevent border raids and to preserve internal security, were attacked by invading forces from North Korea. The Security Council of the United Nations called upon the invading troops to cease hostilities and to withdraw to the Thirty-eighth Parallel. This they have not done, but on the contrary have pressed the attack. The Security Council called upon all members of the United Nations to render every assistance to the United Nations in the execution of this resolution.

In these circumstances I have ordered United States air and sea forces to give the Korean Government troops cover and support.

The attack upon Korea makes it plain beyond all doubt that Communism has passed beyond the use of subversion to conquer independent nations and will now use armed invasion and war.

It has defied the orders of the Security Council of the United Nations issued to preserve international peace and security. In these circumstances the occupation of Formosa by Communist forces would be a direct threat to the security of the Pacific area and to United States forces performing their lawful and necessary functions in that area.

Accordingly I have ordered the Seventh Fleet to prevent any attack on Formosa. As a corollary of this action I am calling upon the Chinese Government on Formosa to cease all air and sea operations against the mainland. The Seventh

Fleet will see that this is done. The determination of the future status of Formosa must await the restoration of security in the Pacific, a peace settlement with Japan, or consideration by the United Nations.

I have also directed that United States forces in the Philippines be strengthened and that military assistance to the Philippine Government be accelerated.

I have similarly directed acceleration of military assistance to the forces of France and the associated states in Indo-China and the dispatch of a military mission to provide close working relations with those forces.

I know that all members of the United Nations will consider carefully the consequences of this latest aggression in Korea in defiance of the Charter of the United Nations. A return to the rule of force in international affairs would have far-reaching effects. The United States will continue to uphold the rule of law.

I have instructed Ambassador Austin, as the representative of the United States to the Security Council, to report these steps to the Council.

437. *The United Nations and Korea,* 1950–53

"Review of United Nations Charter. A Collection of Documents," 83 Congress, 2 Session, *Senate Document,* No. 87 (1954), 593–4, 596–8, 601–2.

THE Security Council, [June 25, 1950],

Recalling the finding of the General Assembly . . . that the Government of the Republic of Korea is a lawfully established government . . . "based on elections which were a valid expression of the free will of the electorate of that part of Korea and which were observed by the Temporary Commission; and that this is the only such government in Korea"; . . .

Noting with grave concern the armed attack upon the Republic of Korea by forces from North Korea,

Determines that this action constitutes a breach of the peace,

I. Calls for the immediate cessation of hostilities; and

Calls upon the authorities of North Korea to withdraw forthwith their armed forces to the thirty-eighth parallel;

II. Requests the United Nations Commission on Korea

(a) To communicate its fully considered recommendations on the situation with the least possible delay;

(b) To observe the withdrawal of the North Korean forces to the thirty-eighth parallel; and

(c) To keep the Security Council informed on the execution of this resolution;

III. Calls upon all Members to render every assistance to the United Nations in the execution of this resolution and to refrain from giving assistance to the North Korean authorities.

The Security Council, [June 27, 1950], . . .

Having noted from the report of the United Nations Commission for Korea that the authorities in North Korea have neither ceased hostilities nor withdrawn their armed forces to the 38th parallel and that urgent military measures are required to restore international peace and security, and

Having noted the appeal of the Republic of Korea to the United Nations for immediate and effective steps to secure peace and security,

Recommends that the Members of the United Nations furnish such assistance to the Republic of Korea as may be necessary to repel the armed attack and to restore international peace and security in the area.

The Security Council, [July 7, 1950], . . .

Welcomes the prompt and vigorous support which governments and peoples of the United Nations have given to its resolutions of 25 and 27 June 1950 to assist the Republic of Korea in defending itself against armed attack and thus to restore international peace and security in the area;

Notes that Members of the United Nations have transmitted to the United Nations offers of assistance for the Republic of Korea;

Recommends that all Members providing military forces and other assistance pursuant to the aforesaid Security Council resolutions make such forces and other assistance available to a unified command under the United States;

Requests the United States to designate the commander of such forces;

Authorizes the unified command at its discretion to use the United Nations flag in the course of operations against North Korean forces concurrently with the flags of the various nations participating.

The General Assembly, [February 1, 1951],

Noting that the Security Council, because of lack of unanimity of the permanent members, has failed to exercise its primary responsibility for the maintenance of international peace and security in regard to Chinese Communist intervention in Korea;

Noting that the Central People's Government of the People's Republic of China has not accepted United Nations proposals to bring about a cessation of hostilities in Korea with a view to peaceful settlement, and that its armed forces continue their invasion of Korea and their large-scale attacks upon United Nations forces there;

Finds that the Central People's Government of the People's Republic of China, by giving direct aid and assistance to those who were already committing aggression in Korea and by engaging in hostilities against United Nations forces there, has itself engaged in aggression in Korea;

Calls upon the Central People's Government of the People's Republic of China to cause its forces and nationals in Korea to cease hostilities against the United Nations forces and to withdraw from Korea;

Affirms the determination of the United Nations to continue its action in Korea to meet the aggression;

Calls upon all States and authorities to continue to lend every assistance to the United Nations action in Korea;

Calls upon all States and authorities to refrain from giving any assistance to the aggressors in Korea;

Requests a committee composed of the Members of the Collective Measures Committee as a matter of urgency to consider additional measures to be employed to meet this aggression and to report thereon to the General Assembly; it being understood that the Committee is authorized to defer its report if the Good Offices Committee, referred to in the following paragraph, reports satisfactory progress in its efforts.

Affirms that it continues to be the policy of the United Nations to bring about a cessation of hostilities in Korea and the achievement of United Nations objectives in Korea by peaceful means, and requests the President of the General Assembly to designate forthwith two persons who would meet with him at any suitable opportunity to use their good offices to this end.

The General Assembly, [May 18, 1951], Recommends that every State:

(a) Apply an embargo on the shipment to areas under the control of the Central People's Government of the People's Republic of China and of the North Korean authorities of arms, ammunition, and implements of war, atomic energy materials, petroleum, transportation materials of strategic value, and items useful in the production of arms, ammunition and implements of war;

(b) Determine which commodities exported from its territory fall within the embargo, and apply controls to give effect to the embargo; . . .

Requests the Additional Measures Committee:

(a) To report to the General Assembly, with recommendations as appropriate, on the general effectiveness of the embargo and the desirability of continuing, extending or relaxing it;

(b) To continue its consideration of general measures to be employed to meet the aggression in Korea, and to report thereon further to the General Assembly . . . ; [and]

Reaffirms that it continues to be the policy of the United Nations to bring about a cessation of hostilities in Korea, and the achievement of United Nations objectives in Korea by peaceful means, and requests the Good Offices Committee to continue its good offices.

The General Assembly, [December 3, 1952], . . .

Noting with approval the considerable progress towards an armistice made by negotiation at Panmunjom and the tentative agreements to end the fighting in Korea and to reach a settlement of the Korean question,

Noting further that disagreement between the parties on one remaining issue, alone, prevents the conclusion of an armistice and that a considerable measure of agreement already exists on the principles on which this remaining issue can be resolved, . . .

Anxious to expedite and facilitate the convening of the political conference as provided in article 60 of the draft armistice agreement,

Affirms that the release and repatriation of prisoners of war shall be effected in accordance with the Geneva Convention Relative to the Treatment of Prisoners of War, dated 12 August 1949, the well-established principles and practice of international law, and the relevant provisions of the draft armistice agreement;

Affirms that force shall not be used against prisoners of war to prevent or effect their return to their homelands, and that they shall at all times be treated humanely in accordance with the specific provisions of the Geneva Convention and with the general spirit of the Convention;

Accordingly requests the President of the General Assembly to communicate the following proposals to the Central People's Government of the People's Republic of China and to the North Korean authorities as forming a just and reasonable basis for an agreement so that an immediate cease fire would result and be effected; to invite their acceptance of these proposals and to make a report to the General Assembly during its present session and as soon as appropriate.

[August 7, 1953] The Government of the United States, as the Unified Command, transmits herewith a special report on the United Nations action against aggression in Korea, together with a copy of the official text of the Armistice Agreement concluded by the Commander-in-Chief, United Nations Command, the Supreme Commander of the Korean People's Army, and the Commander of the Chinese People's Volunteers. . . .

The Armistice Agreement has brought about a cessation of hostilities in Korea after more than thirty-seven months of bloodshed and destruction resulting from the Communist aggression. The Armistice was signed more than twenty-five months after the first indications that, due to the achievements of United Nations forces in Korea and the determination of the United Nations to bring an honorable end to the fighting in Korea, the Communist aggressors were prepared to consider ending hostilities. During these twenty-five months the representatives of the United Nations Command negotiated in good faith and made every effort to achieve an armistice. It was not until the spring of 1953 that the Communists appeared ready to settle the outstanding issues on an honorable basis. The intransigence of the aggressors was responsible for the continued loss of life and destruction and for the long delay in bringing the armistice negotiations to a successful conclusion.

In negotiating this Armistice Agreement, the United Nations Command has been guided by the basic objectives of the United Nations military action in Korea—to repel the aggression against the Republic of Korea and to restore international peace and security in the area. The Agreement leaves the forces of the Republic of Korea and of the United Nations in strong defensive positions and contains provisions offering reasonable assurances against renewal of the aggression.

XLVIII 🐝 *Realignment in National Politics*

THE THREAT of war was the most important factor that induced President Roosevelt to run for a third term in 1940. The New Deal coalition was powerful enough to overcome a long two-term tradition (No. 438), although bitterness over the break with precedent ultimately was expressed in a constitutional amendment forbidding a third presidential term (No. 439). Yet the achievements of the New Deal had already become part of the common currency of American politics. In 1940 the Republican candidate explicitly disavowed any intention of reverting to the system of 1929 (No. 440). Again, four years later, the opposition conspicuously refrained from attack upon the New Deal program of the 1930's (No. 441). To some Democrats it seemed the Republicans were stealing their issues (No. 442).

Roosevelt's death complicated the problems of national politics less than did the intrusion, after 1945, of the question of future relationships with the Soviets. In 1948 Henry Wallace argued that the responsibility for world unease was primarily American rather than Russian (No. 443). The Wallace movement evoked no public support apart from the Communists and their sympathizers. Instead, in the years after 1948, the argument was more often heard that the Communists had exercised undue influence upon American policy, an accusation that seemed to be supported by the case of Alger Hiss (No. 444). The fears and suspicions engendered by this issue poisoned the atmosphere of the years that followed. Its ultimate product was McCarthyism.

The issue was raised significantly in the presidential campaign of 1952. The necessity for defending the record of the administration compelled the Democratic candidate to speak out openly (No. 445). But Eisenhower was tempted to compromise with the right wing of his own party (No. 446). Nevertheless, McCarthyism was less significant in determining the outcome of the election than were the general problems of the Korean War and economic inflation (No. 447). And when Senator McCarthy threatened even a Republican administration, a revulsion of public opinion led to his censure and to the decline of his political influence (No. 448).

438. *The Third Term, 1940*

E. J. Flynn, *You're the Boss* (New York, 1947), 156–9. Copyright 1947 by The Viking Press, Inc.

THE 1940 Democratic convention in Chicago was not a very cheerful gathering. Political leaders thought that a mistake was being made. Never before had the third-term issue really been brought to test, and the rule with politicians is to follow precedent. They were afraid that the country would not re-elect any man to a third term. But if the President wished it they would yield.

The persons in the forefront in support of the President's ambition for a third term were largely drawn from the political machines of the country. . . . They did not support Roosevelt out of any motive of affection or because of any political issues involved, but rather they knew that opposing him would be harmful to their local organizations. The Roosevelt name would help more than it could hurt, and for that reason these city leaders went along on the third-term candidacy. . . .

Before the Chicago convention the President had talked with me about the Vice-Presidency. John Garner had announced that he would not be a candidate because he was opposed to the third term—at least for himself. It therefore became necessary to find a new man for that place on the ticket. In many conferences with the President and with the political leaders, such as Frank Walker, Edward Kelly of Chicago, Frank Hague of Jersey City, and others, a number of names were considered. . . .

After a considerable canvassing of names the President and the rest of us who had consulted with him agreed that [Henry A.] Wallace should be chosen.

To nominate Wallace in the convention, however, was a horse of another color. He had no political background whatever. His acquaintance with the political leaders was very slight. I was probably the only political leader in the country with whom he had been friendly. The rest of the leaders were not in a happy frame of mind. They were sullen and resentful, a feeling accentuated by the fact that Wallace had originally been a Republican who had changed his politics as late as 1932. . . .

But the representatives of the city organizations that had been supporting the President went to work to gather together as many votes as possible for the Wallace nomination. I was in constant communication with the President to advise him of the difficulties that were arising. The President became very nervous and upset. He resented some of the men who were persistent in urging their own candidacy. . . . Despite this antagonism Wallace was nominated on the first ballot by a vote of six hundred and twenty-seven, only seventy-six over the five hundred and fifty-one necessary for nomination. . . .

Adjournment was sullen and gloomy. Many delegates felt that the President could not possibly overcome the opposition on the third-term issue. Too, they heartily disliked the so-called New Deal group, which had played so prominent a part in the convention and its preliminaries. To make matters worse Farley did resign, and the National Committee was without a head. It was realized that there would be difficulty in selecting a new chairman and, following that, it would be very difficult to stir up enthusiasm among the organization Democrats. Further, there was a great deal of feeling that Farley had not been treated well, a feeling which he himself shared.

439. *The Third-Term Amendment, 1951*

Passed by Congress, March 12, 1947; ratified, February 27, 1951.

Article XXII

No PERSON shall be elected to the office of the President more than twice, and no person who has held the office of President, or acted as President, for more than two years of a term to which some other person was elected President shall be elected to the office of the President more than once.

But this article shall not apply to any person holding the office of President when this article was proposed by the Congress, and shall not prevent any person who may be holding the office of President, or acting as President, during the term within which this article becomes operative from holding the office of President or acting as President during the remainder of such term.

This article shall be inoperative unless it shall have been ratified as an amendment to the Constitution by the legislatures of three-fourths of the several states within seven years from the date of its submission to the states by the Congress.

440. *Republican Liberalism, 1940*

Wendell Willkie, "Some of the Issues of 1940," Address to the American Newspaper Publishers' Association, April 25, 1940, *This Is Wendell Willkie* (New York, 1940), 222–5, 230–3.

THE DEMOCRATIC process must arrive at a solution between the regulation of the people's enterprises, on the one hand, and the preservation of their independence, on the other. . . .

The great liberal movement of the early twentieth century, led by such men as Theodore Roosevelt, by the elder Robert M. La Follette and Woodrow Wilson, was the expression of an effort to make this adjustment. The last of these great leaders, Woodrow Wilson, in the program for what he called "the new freedom," thought that this adjustment had been made. Perhaps the program would have succeeded if it had been organized at a normal period in the world's history. Unfortunately, the time was not normal: the next year the world was plunged into a war. When it was over, the liberal faith, which is always one of the first casualties of war, was slow to recover. The United States was rich. People were making money. Industry was expanding so fast that there wasn't time to think about controls. A few men in business and in banking managed to concentrate in their hands an enormous amount of money and influence, and the investor, the employee and the consumer began to feel helpless before their secret manipulations.

It is clear now that the system of 1929 could not be permitted to stand. Democracy in this third phase needed more social controls. These the New Deal supplied, in a vast network of regulation. The liberal cannot object to these reforms in principle. He realizes the national character of the great American corporations and of many business and financial operations; he realizes that an extension of Federal authority is necessary to establish adequate control over these matters.

It is certainly a proper question for the defenders of the present government, therefore, to turn to him and say, "If you are opposed to this government, what powers would you take away?" ...

The answer is what it has always been. To the liberal the purpose of government is unchangeable. It is to leave men free. Whether democracy is in its first phase or its second phase or its third phase, that is the objective.

And the liberal does not see in the present Administration any will to leave men free. He sees only an attempt to increase the powers of government. For the old American principle that government is a liability to be borne by the citizens for the sake of peace, order and security, the New Deal has substituted the notion that government is an asset without which none of us can survive.... Today the government publicly proclaims the failure of the people's enterprises and has adopted the principle that progress comes from government itself....

I cannot speak for "the real powers of the Republican party." But ... I do, indeed, contend and believe that "economic opportunity and security for the great majority of our citizens are unattainable by government effort." In fact, the free enterprise system is based on just the opposite thesis. We have believed that economic opportunity and security for the great majority of our citizens will never be attainable through the government and are only attainable through free private enterprise. In the past one hundred and fifty years we have gone a long way toward proving it....

For the development of any economic enterprise three human factors are fundamental. The first is the inventor, who has the idea for a new device or a new method or a new product; the second is the investor, who has sufficient confidence in the inventor's dream to give him the necessary capital to develop it; the third is the administrator or manager, who can organize the business and keep it going....

These three types of men have constituted the triumphant triumvirate of our economic past. They are equally important to our future. Their activities, if released from government restrictions, can provide jobs enough and products enough to restore prosperity to America. But first we shall have to remove the political restrictions. The activities of the present Administration have drained the vitality and confidence from American industry. It is ironic that in view of these conditions the government should then turn upon industry and denounce it for its failure to recover and make wild charges concerning a "strike" of capital. Industry is being criticized for being unable to do what government prevents it from doing.

441. *Freedom and Opportunity, 1944*

T. A. Dewey, Speech at Des Moines, Iowa, September 20, 1948, *Vital Speeches* (New York), XIV (1948), 741–2.

I PLEDGE to you an administration which knows in its mind and believes in its heart that every American is dependent on every other American; that no segment of our people can prosper without the prosperity of all; that in truth we must all go forward together.... I deeply believe that an administration which can unite our people will have taken the greatest single step toward solving these problems. This is our most urgent need....

Let me make this one thing very clear: So far as I am concerned—so far as the

Republican party is concerned, this campaign will not create diversion among our people. Instead this campaign will unite us as we have never been united before. It will unite us so strongly that no force will again attack us and we will labor unceasingly and with unity to find common grounds of firm and peaceful agreement with all the nations of this earth.

As we chart our course for the years ahead, we must find the stars by which to sail. We must look to the fundamentals of our country. They're easy to find. Our America is not the lucky product of a rich continent discovered by a seafaring adventurer looking for a pot of gold. The roots of our country are not material. They are moral and spiritual. . . .

We believe in freedom for our neighbors across the street or across the seas —the same freedom we expect for ourselves. We believe in honesty, loyalty, fair play, concern for our neighbors, the innate ability of men to achieve; these convictions, arched over by our faith in God, are the inner meaning of the American way of life. That is why the eyes of freedom-loving people everywhere in this troubled world are turning with hope to us. That is our America for which we cannot and will not fail.

But we are in a world and in a time when these convictions are doubted and sneered at and denied. The priceless rights of freedom of speech, of assembly, of religion, of the press, academic freedom, the fundamental freedom of choice of occupation, even of the right to own a car or a home or a farm—all these are denied to many millions of regimented people throughout the world. The ideals

and the rights we hold to be good are held to be evil in those countries. No other fact about our world is of such ominous importance. . . .

We live in a world in which tyranny is on the march. The evil idea is on the march that man is not destined to be free but to be enslaved. That idea is backed by a mobilization of enormous force. Millions of families who have known freedom are in fear of evil, unfamiliar footsteps and at every moment they expect a knock on the door. Millions who still enjoy freedom live in fear that today or tomorrow some crisis or excuse will be seized upon to blot out their freedom too.

Millions of human beings, it may be tens of millions—nobody knows—are being starved and worked to death in concentration camps and at slave labor. And yet, at this very moment in the history of the world the promise of America and the truth of what America believes are being vindicated. The oppressed peoples of these lands know there is a better life. They know there is a better way. The truth about America seeps through every obstacle of iron and steel. In millions of hearts the hope that is America is flaming. That's why we in America have such a solemn obligation to love and cherish all the freedoms we enjoy; that's why we have such a solemn obligation, every single one of us, not to divide our country but to unite it for all purposes and for all time.

We are the last, best hope of earth. Neither barbed wire nor bayonet have been able to suppress the will of men and women to cross from tyranny to freedom.

442. *The Campaign of 1944*

Frances Perkins, *The Roosevelt I Knew* (New York, 1946), 119–20. Copyright 1946 by Frances Perkins. Reprinted by permission of The Viking Press, Inc.

FOR Dewey, Republican candidate in 1944, Roosevelt had little respect. He expected him to make a bad campaign and

was surprised when it turned out to be excellent, revealing preparation, thought and good advice. Dewey made a minimum of mistakes and some good plays.

The 1944 Republican platform, of course, was of great interest to us, and I remember the discussion at cabinet meeting.

One member said, "Disgusting, disgusting, so insincere and pretentious."

I replied, "Well, I think we should be grateful for that platform. It means that the New Deal has won forever. The country has adopted as a permanent program those items which, when we introduced them, were supposed to be radical, revolutionary, and temporary. Now the Republican party has adopted as its formal platform most of these items which we have called New Deal items, and have merely promised to make them better, extend them, and, of course, administer them better."

"I think you're right," Roosevelt said, "but it isn't going to be any easier to make a campaign against a man who says he is for the same things that we boast about as being our contribution."

Roosevelt in 1944 did not intend to make a real campaign. The official national decisions he had to make were all-absorbing. He was older and not so strong physically as in years past. He had no intention of taking his eyes or his mind off the war. I heard him say this over and over again.

Under normal circumstances Roosevelt would not have run in 1944. But his experience and his knowledge of our resources and plans and those of our allies made it imperative. I think there was no question in his mind, after we entered the war, that it would be necessary unless the war had finished. His hope had been that the war would be over before the next Presidential election and that his contribution in ensuing years would be in representing his government in some way in the international organization for peace. As the months wore on, it was obvious that the war would not be over in 1944, and he reconciled himself, as all of us did, to the idea that he must continue.

When he began to get reports from the field that Dewey was gaining, he changed his mind about the necessity for campaigning and announced one day at cabinet meeting that he was going to make an old-fashioned rough-and-tumble campaign. He had to go everywhere, he had to show himself, he said. "There has been this constant rumor that I'll not live if I am re-elected, and people have been asked to believe that I am all worn out and sick. You all know that is not so, but apparently I have to face them to prove it. Apparently 'Papa has to tell them.' That is the way politics go in this country, and I am going right after Dewey and make a real campaign."

443. *The Wallace Plan, 1948*

Henry A. Wallace, Testimony Before the House Committee on Foreign Affairs, February 24, 1948, printed in *The Wallace Plan* v. *The Marshall Plan* (New York, 1948), 8, 9, 18, 19, 24–5.

INSTEAD of helping European recovery, the ERP has become the blueprint of the aims of American monopoly. The American people still do not realize that the real principles of the ERP—which bear no resemblance to the principles laid down by Secretary Marshall at Harvard —reflect the aims of big bankers, the monopolists and the militarists. . . .

Big business has put its men in government from the cabinet to operating agents at lower levels of authority. . . . And they work in perfect harmony with the generals and admirals who have moved into key posts of the Administration. The President has appointed some fifty bankers, financiers and industrialists to top-notch civilian posts in government, and some thirty generals, admirals and military men.

It is these monopoly and militarist "men in government" who have dictated the terms of ERP and will administer it if it is not defeated by the articulate protest of the American people. The Harriman Committee Report—heart of the ERP—was written under the direction of W. Randolph Burgess, vice-president of the National City Bank of New York and a bitter enemy of Roosevelt's idea of a people's world bank and a people's international monetary fund. . . .

These are the men in and out of government who laid down the "conditions" for eligibility to the participating nations, who perverted the principles of self-aid and recovery into a program which in operation would subject the people of Western Europe to the control of American finance at endless expense to American taxpayers. . . . ERP is the economic side of the bankrupt Truman Doctrine. While it is being sold to the American people as a peaceful plan for cooperation and recovery, it will use the tax dollars of the American people for the benefit of private capitalists at home and abroad. It is a plan cloaked in decent language which is designed to suppress the democratic movements in Europe. . . .

A major aspect of ERP was presented to the Senate Foreign Relations Committee by John Foster Dulles when he recommended a military pact for the "defense" of Western Europe. Bernard M. Baruch went even further when he urged that the United States participate in this military alliance and that all its members pledge to "go to war" to protect their mutual interests. As ERP stands now, this means a guarantee by the U.S. and the Western European countries to back up with arms the interests of the Standard Oil trust, the Morgan banks, the duPonts, and the other American monopoly groups. . . .

I offer my plan as a realistic and complete alternative to ERP.

The operations of the UN Reconstruction Fund, modeled after UNRRA, would be directed towards restoring the industry and agriculture of the war-devastated nations of Europe and Asia and towards putting them on a self-sustaining basis as soon as possible.

The Reconstruction Fund would be administered by an agency of the UN established for that purpose, by the world community of nations and not by big business. The major emphasis of the plan I propose is on the supplies needed by war-devastated countries to repair war damage to soil, structures, and equipment, and to expand their economies—that is, to eliminate the conditions which require emergency relief.

The Reconstruction Fund should receive contributions appropriated by the Congress of the United States, as well as contributions from other nations that have the appropriate means for this purpose. Fifty billion dollars in my opinion should be sufficient to finance a ten-year world plan. Part of the appropriations from the contributing nations could be in the form of loans for capital development and part in the form of grants for emergency food, fuel and other needs.

The UN agency should be directed to give priority in the allocation of funds to those nations, including those in Eastern Europe, which suffered most severely from the aggression of the fascist Axis. Relief and reconstruction allocations should be based solely on these considerations of need and merit, without regard to the character of the political, economic and social institutions of the recipient countries. . . . The UN agency would allocate funds with scrupulous regard for the political independence of all the beneficiary nations. It would forbid political conditions on loans or grants. It would permit the people of Europe and other war-devastated areas to nationalize their key industries, to reform agriculture, to install necessary controls on foreign trade, distribution of goods and prices. It would permit the exclusion of Wall Street trusts, the refusal to purchase surplus goods dumped abroad by American big business.

The entire UN fund should be used exclusively for peaceful purposes and economic reconstruction, and no moneys should be diverted for the purchase of military supplies, armaments and war preparations. By refusing money for military supplies, armaments or war preparations, my Plan would eliminate the present American intervention in Greece, China, Indonesia, and Indo-China, which are increasingly threatening to become battlefronts of World War III. . . .

The United Nations plan would place the Ruhr under international administration and control by the Big Four—the United States, Britain, Soviet Russia and France. Its resources would be used to reconstruct Europe. The UN and the Big Four should guarantee that Germany shall never again be permitted to attain a position from which it can threaten the security of its neighbors and the peace of the world. Within this framework, the German people should be given the opportunity to restore their living standards and function within the community of nations as an independent and democratic country. By placing the Ruhr Valley under control by the Big Four, my plan would once and for all eliminate the German monopolies and controls, the most aggressive fomentors of both World Wars. . . .

Because my plan is a United Nations plan, it is a plan for cooperation between the United States and Soviet Russia. It is the economic basis for shifting from the bi-partisan policy of cold war and civil war today, and atomic war tomorrow, to a policy of progressive disarmament and friendly relations among all the nations of the world.

444. *The Hiss Trial,* 1950

Alistair Cooke, *A Generation on Trial* (New York, 1950), 340–1.

OUTSIDE on the streets we were caught again in the political reverberations that lapped out like waves from this stony center of punishment. If . . . [Hiss] was indeed innocent, it might never be proved; he had ahead of him only the long trail to the Supreme Court, that grievous distance from the wound to the hospital which makes judicial review so cruel a kindness. If he was guilty, as twenty of the twenty-four "ordinary men looking on" had judged him, then what he owed to the United States and the people who had stood by him was a dreadful debt of honor. For his conviction clinched the popular fear that those who were contriving a "clear and present danger" to the United States were determined it should never be clear and were publicly devoted to showing it was always far from present. The verdict galvanized the country into a bitter realization of the native American types who might well be dedicated to betrayal from within. It gave to ambitious politicians a license to use vigilance as a political weapon merely. It brought back into favor the odious trade of the public informer. It gave the F.B.I. an unparalleled power of inquiry into private lives that in the hands of a less scrupulous man than its present chief could open up for generations of mischief-makers an official wholesale house of blackmail. It tended to make conformity sheepish and to limit by intimidation what no Western society worth the name can safely limit: the curiosity and idealism of its young. It helped therefore to usher in a period when a high premium would be put on the chameleon and the politically neutral slob.

All this and much more flowed from the verdict of the second jury. And its suspicions were shatteringly confirmed by the confession in England of a studious, gentle traitor, one Klaus Fuchs, a physicist working in the closed circle of Anglo-American atomic secrets, who admitted to passing on the best of his knowledge to the Soviet Union. After that, no sensible man could any longer maintain that there was no threat to his country. The problem now . . . was how to protect the innocent citizen from getting pinched between the reality of the threat and the epidemic fear of it. The knowledge rumbled like thunder through our senses that in other countries men might be being sentenced for *not* having stolen State papers when they had the chance. For the principals in this case were idealists at a time when idealism, and the nature of loyalty, were undergoing an historic test. If Hiss had said he had done all this, that he had passed papers proudly to confound the Nazis, to quicken the day of deliverance of enslaved populations, he could have

been a greater Wadleigh. But because he had not stolen them, or could not or would not say he had, the defense had to argue from the impossible position that such gentle, trusted types are incapable of disloyalty. After Fuchs, we knew better. And what we were left with was not the tragic hero of a whole generation that had misjudged the endurance of national pride or the resilience of the Western tradition. What we were left with was a tragedy *manqué*.

Yet below the satisfaction of popular fears and desires, and the usefulness of arguments we happen to have at hand, lies a deeper region of the mind which holds in uncertain equilibrium the springs of self-love and self-hate; where seas of spite are able to rise and flood the low gauge of self-respect and the surrounding plains of neighborliness and patriotism. Here the real wound would fester: whether it was the false accusation, or the social betrayal of which this unhappy man had now become the public image; and somewhere in this dark region was tragedy enough, for all those who have had ideals and desires beyond, they dare to think, the understanding of their neighbors.

445. *The Democratic Program, 1952*

Adlai Stevenson, *Major Campaign Speeches* (New York, 1953), 114–16.

OUR national commitment is to a free economy—to the belief that an economic system based on freedom of choice, freedom of opportunity and freedom of decision is more productive and creative than any system devised by man. We will not abandon our free-enterprise system. We will oppose all attempts to limit its freedom whether by centralized government or by private monopoly. . . .

The foundation of any economy is its natural resources. The new technological era toward which we are moving will

make ever-growing drains upon our resources. If we are to maintain our growth we must prepare for the future prosperity of our nation and we must make those preparations today while there is still time —not twenty years from now when it may be too late.

The resources problem is partly a problem of the wise use of the things we know we have and partly the problem of discovering how to use things that have never been useful before. In the last twenty years we have recognized that our land, and what lies beneath it, is a natural patrimony. It is a reserve for all of the people, to be utilized and developed in terms of our national welfare and of the strength and of the security of the free world. . . .

This new America will be a healthier America. Our children will have a vastly increased life expectancy. To attain this goal we shall need more medical research, more hospitals, more public-health agencies, more medical schools, more doctors and nurses—and some system of protection against the economic disasters of severe illness and accident, so that adequate medical care will be available for all.

I look forward to more and better housing for our people. In the past seven years more than eight million new homes have been built. . . . This progress must be continued so that all Americans will have an opportunity to get decent housing—and public housing has a role to play in this problem.

I look forward to an America with improved education. We have made great progress in twenty years which we cannot stop until we have banished illiteracy and enlarged the educational opportunities of all of the boys and girls in this land.

I look forward to an America, my friends, which can take proper care of its aged and its invalids, and which can provide strong and expanding security for all of its workers. I rejoice in the Democratic Party's record in the establishment and the development of social security; and I endorse its pledge of a stronger system of unemployment insurance. . . .

I look forward to an America united in its national belief in equal rights for all its citizens. We can never stop in the battle against racial and religious bigotry, discrimination and fear. We must ensure equal opportunities of employment for citizens of all colors and creeds. Given our resources, given the productivity of our economic system, given the magic of the new technology, given the undeveloped potentialities of electrical, chemical and atomic power, given the wise use of our wealth in the service of our people, we have within our grasp the possibilities of an undreamed-of future.

The American faith has been a faith in the growth of our nation and in a just distribution of the wealth among all of our citizens. And that faith stands today on the verge of its most dramatic realization. We stand on the threshold. The question is whether we have the will to cross that threshold and move into the new era ahead. The struggle between faith and fear will decide the destiny of our nation. Today we stand bewildered and tormented by many fears, some real, some imaginary. There is the fear of war; there is the fear of depression; and the fear of communism; and the fear of ourselves. I would not decry these fears. Without fear we would never act in time to save ourselves, but I would warn with all of the certainty that I possess against permitting fear to seize our mind, to cloud our brain and to paralyze our will. . . .

I hold out no easy solution to the problem of peace. I reject those who tell you that we can make the Soviet danger vanish by giving one-shot solutions, whether the solution is to retreat behind our frontiers, as one of the Republican Parties suggests, or stir up insurrection in Eastern Europe, which seems to be the doctrine of the other Republican Party. But I do say that the policy of building the strength and the unity of free nations will reduce the haunting fear of war.

The fear of depression is a real fear. But this danger can be met if we have a government determined to pursue a positive policy to prevent depression and to control inflation. I have confidence in the capacity of the American people to steer an ever-expanding economy without running it over a cliff—if their leaders in government are prepared to combat inflation or depression by something more than moans, threats and incantations.

The fear of communism is a real fear. We are confronted, at home and abroad, by a vast international conspiracy. We must, at home and abroad, take measures to protect ourselves. All loyal Americans know today that communism is incompatible with American life. We have driven them out of any places of responsibility that they may have gained in our society. We will expose and identify them at every step along the way.

446. *Eisenhower and His Right,* 1952

Robert Waithman, "Eisenhower the Pawn?" *Spectator,* CLXXXIX, October 10, 1952, 462–3.

THERE never was a time in America when so many people were trying to discredit other people.... The fear of Communism, the revelation that people when afraid will believe or half-believe nearly anything, and the recurring discovery that political and literary reputations can be easily and quickly made in the business of discreditation lie behind this sorry lapse, of which in time to come Americans assuredly will be heartily ashamed. But Mr. Eisenhower is not being accused of perfidy, rascality, iniquity, or misbehavior. Few of the voters, even in these weeks of high passion and sketchy documentation, would listen with patience to any such charges against one of the great soldiers of his time, a man who has earned the admiration and gratitude of his contemporaries and whose personal integrity has never been in doubt. The assault is not upon Eisenhower's character, but upon his capacity in the existing circumstances to discharge successfully the Presidential duties.

The essence of the Democratic Party's contention is that Eisenhower has now demonstrated that he is politically too untutored and too dependent upon professional politicians with illiberal intentions to merit that national confidence. The point has been urged ... with an undertone of warning by Governor Stevenson, Eisenhower's opponent, who has suggested that the liberal Republicans who think they would be able to control Eisenhower's policies in the White House may be making the same "fatal error" as was made by the liberal Republicans who thought that they could turn the policies of the Harding administration away from the isolationism that contributed so much to the wrecking of the League of Nations....

But it was when President Truman elaborated the proposition in his famous "give-'em-hell" language that the complaint began to arise that the fight had become dirty.... When the Truman campaign-train started out, the President's advisers were in considerable doubt whether a national hero of Eisenhower's stature could be attacked in this full-bodied way without boos from the crowds. But the crowds, by and large, have been booing little, listening attentively and even, sometimes, applauding the Truman assault on Eisenhower. And what conclusions are you to draw from that? Not, it is clear, that all the elements of Mr. Truman's argument are impeccable. It can perhaps be assumed that Eisenhower's mind would be just as military if he had been a Democratic candidate as it is now that he is a Republican candidate. And when Mr. Truman goes on to accuse Eisenhower of having done "a great deal of harm" by expressing after the war the view that the Russians wanted to be friendly with the United States, he is forgetting to remember that in the era before disenchantment set in he himself once said, "I like old Joe."

On the other hand, Eisenhower has demonstrably laid himself open to Mr. Truman's scorn by shifting his ground on a variety of issues in conformity with the views of Senator Taft and his ruthless right-wing managers, who seem to have persuaded him that they and they alone can assure a Republican victory. It may not be so vital a thing that Ike expressed approval of a public power-undertaking in the west last June and has since condemned all such undertakings as Socialistic. But it is another thing that he should be demanding that the South Koreans occupy the front lines and substituting for his earlier endorsement of the decision to fight a denunciation of Mr. Truman and his Administration for having "bungled" their way into a needless war there. That is the Taft line, too. But, when Eisenhower embraces it, Mr. Truman is entitled to feel that the agonies inflicted on the nation by a courageous stand that has kept predatory Communism in check should not be exploited in the hope of winning votes.

The campaign is far enough on now to make it clear that the question whether Eisenhower, having through ignorance or inexperience surrendered the initiative to the Republican Tories, cannot now expect to be his own master in the White House, and whether he therefore should not be elected, is one of the essentials on which the voters will have to make up their minds. The decision is one that the ten million people who are outside both parties—the independent voters who might in the end decide the outcome—will have particularly to ponder.

447. *Who Elected Eisenhower, 1952*

Samuel Lubell, "Who Elected Eisenhower?", *Saturday Evening Post*, CCXXV (January 10, 1953), 27, 74, 75–8.

THE MAIN reason why the election was so supercharged emotionally, I believe, lies in the battle which millions of voters fought within themselves between two clashing sets of emotions—their dread of another depression and their frustration over the seemingly endless stalemate in Korea.

This struggle was unquestionably the decisive conflict of the entire election. Wherever I went during the campaign I found the fear of a return of "them Hoover times" was the strongest single Democratic asset. Repeatedly voters declared in effect, "I don't like lots of things in Washington, but I remember the soup lines."

On the Republican side, several issues were winning them former Democratic votes—higher prices and taxes, charges of communism and corruption in government, the sheer weariness over the Democrats' being so long in power. But what provoked the angriest condemnations of the Truman Administration from traditional Democratic voters was "the useless war" in Korea, as so many termed it.

Like two powerful wrestlers, the memory of the depression and the frustration over Korea came to grips with each other in the arena that was the voter's mind. And when the struggle was over, the back of Democratic political power in the country was broken....

In marking their ballots for Eisenhower, many persons, of course, hoped to bring their sons and husbands back home. Still, the election should not be interpreted as a vote for peace at any price. It was more a vote of impatience with the frustrating state of neither war nor peace....

In relatively few instances did the "communist" issue stand by itself as the cause of Democratic defections. In Pittsburgh, Detroit and Cleveland I sampled predominantly Catholic precincts which Truman had won tidily, but which swung for Eisenhower. All these precincts I found had been hard hit by the draft. This was especially true of Polish-Americans and Italo-Americans, who have proportionately more sons of military age than the nation as a whole, because of heavy birth rates years ago.

Disillusionment over Yalta and hatred of Russia contributed to the Polish-American break. In Milwaukee one Polish priest voted Republican for the first time in his life because "we've been too soft with Russia." This desire for a stiffer foreign policy was also reflected in the numerous Polish-Americans who favored Eisenhower "because he's a military man.". . .

The one element in the Roosevelt coalition which held most firmly was the Negroes. In every city where I checked it, their vote shows a Democratic rise over 1948. In some areas they cast staggering majorities. Ten Negro precincts in Houston, Texas, voted 97 per cent for Stevenson. . . .

Along with this break in the "big-city" coalition came another striking development of considerable significance for the future. Around New York, Chicago and Cleveland, the suburbs actually rolled up heavier majorities for the Republicans than these cities gave the Democrats—the first time since the advent of Roosevelt that the suburbs have overshadowed the cities politically. The tremendous rise in suburban population is only partly responsible. Behind this development also lay an unusual political feat which Eisenhower performed—he sharpened the sense of economic solidarity among traditional Republican voters, even while blurring it among the New Deal voting elements.

Nowhere does this feat show up more plainly than in the South. It was in Dixie's urban centers that Eisenhower rolled up his winning pluralities. For example, in Texas, which he carried by 138,000, the four counties containing Dallas, Houston, Fort Worth and San Antonio alone gave him a 120,000 plurality.

The main driving force behind this urban insurgency was a long-brewing revolt of middle-class Southerners, whose numbers have increased spectacularly as a result of the industrial boom in the South over the last two decades. Looking to business—not Government—for Dixie's future economic progress, this rising middle class has long been seeking some means of defeating the Democratic Administration in Washington. Talking with typical middle-class voters in these Southern cities I found their most frequently voiced complaints were over "destructive taxation" and "all this socialism" and "labor has too much power.". . .

All elections inspire conflicting interpretations as to what the people voted for. My own judgment is that, in addition to cleaning up corruption and communist infiltration, the election was mainly a mandate for two things—first for bringing the Korean war to a decisive end, peaceably if possible, but by war if that is the only alternative, and second, for giving the dollar a stable value.

Domestically, it was a vote to halt further social reforms and, as one Miamian put it, "to let the pendulum swing the other way a bit." But it was not a vote for a twenty-year rollback of history. To the contrary, the impression left with me was that the dominant concern of the voters was how to preserve the gains of those years. Their alarm over inflation largely reflected the fear that these gains were being imperiled by a Government which had pushed spending too far—to where all savings were losing value. . . .

Perhaps of greatest historic significance is the fact that so many persons clearly put foreign affairs above their domestic concerns, even to voting consciously against what they considered their pocketbook interest. In this respect the election may have been a remarkable vindication of the American political system.

448. *Senator McCarthy's Statement, 1954*

"Subversion and Espionage in Defense Establishments," Senate Permanent Subcommittee on Investigations of the Committee on Government Operations, *Hearings* (83 Congress, 2 Session), Part 4, December 7, 1954, pp. 205–6.

THE EXPOSURE of Communists in defense plants handling secret weapons, which may well determine whether the sons of American mothers will live or die, is in my opinion important beyond words. In view of the fact that this may be my temporary swan song as chairman of the Investigating Committee, I think that it is important to comment briefly upon certain facts.

Our committee has been held up now for approximately ten months. The President of the United States has taken it upon himself to congratulate Senators Flanders and Watkins who have been instrumental in holding up our work. There has been considerable talk about an apology to the Senate for my fight against Communism. I feel rather that I should apologize to the American people for what was an unintentional deception upon them.

During the Eisenhower campaign, I spoke from coast to coast, promising the American people that if they would elect the Eisenhower administration that they would be assured of a vigorous forceful fight against Communists in Government.

Unfortunately, in this I was mistaken. I find that the President on the one hand congratulates Senators who hold up the work of our committee, and on the other hand urges that we be patient, that we be patient with the Communist hoodlums who as of this moment are torturing and brainwashing American uniformed men in Communist dungeons.

Anyone who knows even the ABC's of the Communist war against free civilization knows that weakness and supineness will not free a single American uniformed man. If any Senator can in the future justify a vote to draft the sons of American mothers, then he must repudiate the shrinking show of weakness, and must tell those mothers that each young man who wears the American uniform carries the entire power of this nation with him when he goes to a foreign land.

Unfortunately, the President sees fit to congratulate those who hold up the exposure of the Communists in one breath, and in the next breath urges patience, tolerance and niceties to those who are torturing American uniformed men.

XLIX ✦ *The Challenge of a New Productive System*

LONG AFTER the Japanese surrender, industry still felt the stimulating effects of the war. The necessities of defense planning had given the government a far greater role in the direction and control of the economy than ever before; and peace found people disinclined to return to earlier ways. Price controls and commodity rationing dropped away; but the government continued to play an important role in the productive system, a role now justified by an expanded conception of social welfare (No. 449). An economist, surveying the situation six years after the war, still found few signs of a waning of government influence upon the economy (No. 450).

Other changes also were reshaping American industry. The capital-possessing, profit-seeking individualistic entrepreneur tended to become a figure of the past, replaced in an era of strict controls and high taxes by managers, capable of negotiating with labor and government and interested in productivity rather than in profits as such (No. 451). The war and the necessities of the post-war period also expanded industry in regions such as the Pacific Coast, the Southwest, and the Gulf states where it had not theretofore been important (No. 452).

It was true that there were indications of efforts to control and limit growth (No. 453). But, for the time being, these developments caused little economic strain. The prevailing prosperity affected every sector of society; well-being and abundance generated a mood of tolerance toward business in general (No. 454).

In part, that prosperity was due to the improvements in technology which left a larger share of the industrial product to be distributed among capitalists and laborers despite the high level of taxes. The development of automatic machines, encouraged by the war, continued through the post-war period (No. 455). But a much wider complex of factors steadily raised the output and productivity of American industry (No. 456). There were disturbing elements in the agricultural situation; but generally Americans had cause to be optimistic as they looked toward the future of their productive system.

449. *State of the Union, 1949*

President Harry S. Truman, State of the Union Message, January 5, 1949, *Congressional Record*, XCV, Part I, 81 Congress, 1 Session, 74–6.

IN THIS society we are conservative about the values and principles which we cherish; but we are forward-looking in protecting those values and principles and in extending their benefits. We have rejected the discredited theory that the fortunes of the nation should be in the hands of a privileged few. We have abandoned the "trickle down" concept of national prosperity. Instead, we believe that our economic system should rest on a democratic foundation and that wealth should be created for the benefit of all. . . .

The American people have decided that poverty is just as wasteful and just as unnecessary as preventable disease. We have pledged our common resources to help one another in the hazards and struggles of individual life. We believe that no unfair prejudice or artificial distinction should bar any citizen of the United States from an education, or from good health, or from a job that he is capable of performing. . . .

Reinforced by these policies, our private enterprise system has reached new heights of production. Since the boom year of 1929, while our population has increased by only 20 per cent, our agricultural production has increased by 45 per cent, and our industrial production has increased by 75 per cent. We are turning out far more goods and more wealth per worker than we have ever done before. . . .

But, great as our progress has been, we still have a long way to go.

As we look around the country, many of our shortcomings stand out in bold relief.

We are suffering from excessively high prices.

Our production is still not large enough to satisfy our demands.

Our minimum wages are far too low.

Small business is losing ground to growing monopoly.

Our farmers still face an uncertain future. And too many of them lack the benefits of our modern civilization.

Some of our natural resources are still being wasted.

We are acutely short of electric power, although the means for developing such power are abundant.

Five million families are still living in slums and firetraps. Three million families share their homes with others.

Our health is far behind the progress of medical science. Proper medical care is so expensive that it is out of reach of the great majority of our citizens.

Our schools, in many localities, are utterly inadequate.

Our democratic ideals are often thwarted by prejudice and intolerance.

Each of these shortcomings is also an opportunity—an opportunity for the Congress and the President to work for the good of the people.

Our first great opportunity is to protect our economy against the evils of "boom and bust.". . .

The Employment Act of 1946 pledges the Government to use all its resources to promote maximum employment, production, and purchasing power. This means that the Government is firmly committed to protect business and the people against the dangers of recession and against the evils of inflation. This means that the Government must adapt its plans and policies to meet changing circumstances. . . .

We should strengthen our anti-trust laws by closing those loopholes that permit monopolistic mergers and consolidations.

Our national farm program should be improved—not only in the interest of the farmers but for the lasting prosperity of the whole nation. Our goals should be abundant farm production and parity of income for agriculture. Standards of living on the farm should be just as good as anywhere else in the country.

Farm price supports are an essential part of our program to achieve these ends. Price supports should be used to prevent farm price declines which are out of line with general price levels, to facilitate adjustments in production to consumer demands and to promote good land use. . . .

We must push forward with the development of our rivers for power, irrigation, navigation, and flood control. We should apply the lessons of our Tennessee Valley experience to our other great river basins. . . .

The present coverage of the social-security laws is altogether inadequate, and benefit payments are too low. One-third of our workers are not covered. Those who receive old age and survivors insurance benefits receive an average payment of only $25 a month. Many others who cannot work because they are physically disabled are left to the mercy of charity. We should expand our social-security program, both as to size of benefits and extent of coverage, against the economic hazards due to unemployment, old age, sickness, and disability.

We must spare no effort to raise the general level of health in this country. In a nation as rich as ours, it is a shocking fact that tens of millions lack adequate medical care. We are short of doctors, hospitals, and nurses. We must remedy these shortages. Moreover, we need—and we must have without further delay—a system of prepaid medical insurance which will enable every American to afford good medical care. . . .

The housing shortage continues to be

acute. As an immediate step, the Congress should enact the provisions for low-rent public housing, slum clearance, farm housing, and housing research which I have repeatedly recommended. The number of low-rent public housing units provided for in the legislation should be increased to 1,000,000 units in the next seven years.

Even this number of units will not begin to meet our need for new housing.

Most of the houses we need will have to be built by private enterprise, without public subsidy. By producing too few rental units and too large a proportion of high-priced houses, the building industry is rapidly pricing itself out of the market. Building costs must be lowered.

450. *Government and Business, 1951*

Sumner Slichter, *What's Ahead for American Business* (Boston, 1951), 14–18. Copyright 1950, 1951 by Sumner H. Slichter. Reprinted by permission of Little, Brown & Co.

THE GREATEST single change in our economic institutions during the past half-century has been the expansion of the economic activities of the government. ... The government is steadily becoming a more and more important producer of goods and services and also a larger and larger consumer of goods; by means of taxes, subsidies, and various grants, the government greatly modifies the distribution of income; it regulates a growing number of prices, putting floors under some and ceilings over others; finally, it imposes an increasing number of rules that determine how economic activities must or must not be conducted.

The growing importance of the government as a producer is indicated by the fact that it now turns out about one tenth of the country's output of goods and services compared with about one seventeenth in 1929. ... In addition to the usual activities of providing security and maintaining order, the government is a large lender of money; it is in the housing business on a substantial scale; various government-owned plants produce about 20 per cent of the country's electricity; through provision of highways and airfields, the government provides much of the capital used in the transportation business; the government produces large quantities of statistics and other information that businessmen and farmers use in planning their operations and that trade unions and employers use in their negotiations.

The growing role of the government as a consumer is indicated by the fact that in 1950 it consumed over 42.1 billion dollars of goods and services, or 15 per cent of the net national product as compared with 9 per cent in 1929. A part of the purchase of goods by the government is in the nature of an investment (roads, bridges, dams, water works, school buildings) and adds to the country's productive capacity. For example, in 1949, 6.4 billion dollars of the goods purchased by the government represented new construction. During the last twenty years the government's consumption of goods has grown over twice as fast as its production of goods.

The redistribution of income by the government is shown by the rapid rise of taxes on personal income, especially on high incomes, and by the great increase in payments based on need. Taxes rose from 2.6 billion dollars on total personal incomes of 85.1 billion in 1929 to 20.4 billion on incomes of 222.4 billion in 1950. As a result of the stiff progressive income tax, the total income after taxes of all persons receiving 25,000 dollars a year or more was one sixth less in 1948 than in 1928, although the number of persons receiving incomes of 25,000 or more was almost 60 per cent greater in 1949 than in 1928.

The redistribution of income is carried further by large payments to persons in return for no services rendered—that is, on the basis of need. Between 1929 and 1949, such payments (pensions, unemployment compensation, old-age assistance, for example) increased over four times as fast as personal incomes. . . . An important effect of the large growth of payments based upon need is to make the level of personal incomes less dependent upon the level of production and employment. Today, a contraction of production and employment would have less effect upon incomes than ever before. . . .

The government regulates the prices of of an increasing number of commodities. The community has been refusing more and more to accept the prices that free markets set and has insisted that the government put floors under some prices and ceilings over others. Examples of ceilings are railroad rates, electric light and power rates, gas rates, telephone rates; examples of floors are the minimum wage of 75 cents an hour imposed by the Federal government on most concerns engaged in interstate commerce, and the many floors applied to farm products. In the fiscal year 1949–1950, a year of good employment, the government spent about 1.4 billion dollars in keeping up the prices of agricultural products.

Finally, there has been a great expansion of the areas in which the government prescribes the rules of the game. During recent years the government has undertaken to provide rather detailed rules for the conduct of industrial relations. . . . The government also regulates capital markets in considerable detail. Security issues that are offered to the public must go through an elaborate procedure administered by the Securities and Exchange Commission. The government has been attempting to develop rules regulating pricing of commodities by business enterprises. But government officials do not seem to have a clear idea of what these rules should be or what purpose they should serve.

451. *The New Management, 1951*

R. W. Davenport, *et al.*, U.S.A. *The Permanent Revolution* (New York, 1951), 78–87. Reprinted by special permission; copyright 1951 by Time Inc.

ONE of the two chief characteristics of big modern enterprise is that it is run by hired management. . . . The power inherent in the control of . . . the plant, organization and good will . . . has superseded the power inherent in . . . the stocks and bonds. Even companies whose owners are managers may be described as management-run. The Ford company, for example, behaves not as an organization solely dedicated to earning the maximum number of dollars for the Ford family, but as an organization dedicated first of all to its own perpetuation and growth.

The other chief characteristic of the big modern enterprise is that management is becoming a profession. . . . A professional manager holds his job primarily because he is good at it. Often he has begun at the bottom and worked his way up by sheer merit. Or more often he has been carefully and even scientifically chosen from a number of bright and appropriately educated young men, put through an executive-training course, and gradually insinuated into the activities for which he shows the most talent. Since even at the top he generally functions as a member of a committee rather than as a final authority, his talents are so well balanced that none of them protrude excessively. He lives on what he makes, and even when he is well paid he doesn't have much left after taxes. . . .

More important, the manager is becoming a professional in the sense that like all professional men he has a responsibility to society as a whole. This is not to say that he no longer needs good, old-fashioned business sense. . . . But the great happy paradox of the profit motive in the American system is that management, precisely because it is in business to make money years on end, cannot concentrate exclusively on making money here and now. To keep on making money years on end, it must, in the words of Frank Abrams, Chairman of the Standard Oil Co. of New Jersey, "conduct the affairs of the enterprise in such a way as to maintain an *equitable and working balance* among the claims of the various directly interested groups—stockholders, employees, customers, and the public at large." Not all pundits have understood this vital point. . . . The corporate manager . . . is part of a group that enjoys power only so long as it does not abuse it—in other words, precisely so long as it does not exercise power the way men and groups of men used to before the capitalistic transformation.

Thus it is not too difficult to define management's responsibility to the stockholder. Management . . . cannot flagrantly disregard stockholders' interests, at least not for long. . . .

But modern management exhibits also a sense of responsibility toward its employees, not only to prevent or anticipate the demands of labor unions (though this motive has often been strong) but for the simple, obvious and honest reason that a satisfied, loyal group of employees is at least as much of an asset as a modern plant or a vital piece of machinery. . . . There is a growing tendency on the part of blue-chip management to regard a job in the company as a kind of employment package, complete with pensions, savings plans, and numerous "fringe" benefits such as severance pay, maternity leave, hospitalization and medical insurance. . . .

Thus far, however, it is the modern manager's sense of responsibility to his customer and the general public that gives him his best claim to being progressive. More goods at lower cost (and prices) is the basic principle of American industry, and even companies regarded as anything but socially-minded have built themselves upon it. Many a chemical, for example, has been sold at a progressively lower price without the spur of competition, simply to encourage the market. And most modern managers do worry a good deal about the related subject of prices, monopoly, and competition. . . . The alternatives today are not monopoly or all-out competition. The Darwinian concept of all-out competition has given way to the concept of a pragmatic or "workable" competition, which, far from being the death of profits, provides, as smart companies know, the soundest way to ensure their survival. . . .

Nothing perhaps is more indicative of the corporation's awareness of its responsibilities than the growth of public-relations activities. Upwards of 4,000 companies now go in for public-relations programs. Although many of them are hardly more than publicity campaigns, more and more managers understand tolerably well that good business public relations is good performance publicly appreciated, because adequately communicated. Now the mere comprehension of a moral axiom, as all parents know, does not guarantee its observance. But its constant iteration does make the subject more and more acutely aware of its importance, and thus eventually influences his behavior. As Paul Garrett of G.M. has been saying for years, "Our program is finding out what people like, doing more of it; finding out what people don't like, doing less of it."

452. *Industry Along the Gulf, 1953*

Oscar Handlin, "Second Chance for the South," *Atlantic Monthly*, December, 1953, 54–6.

SINCE 1940 a revolution hardly noticed has been transforming a vital sector of the nation. In a great arc along the Gulf of Mexico from Pensacola in the east, through Mobile, Baton Rouge, Beaumont, and Houston, to Corpus Christi in the west, a New South has come into being. Urban and industrial, it has moved away from the agrarian past of the region. . . .

Statistics supply a dramatic indication of the magnitude of the transformation. Between 1940 and 1950, while the population of the rest of the state remained relatively stable, that of Mobile leaped upward by 64 per cent. In the same decade, Baton Rouge, from a city of 34,000, became one of 126,000. Beaumont and Corpus Christi have nearly doubled in size, Texas City and Lake Charles tripled. Houston added 212,000 to its 384,000 residents; and on the prairies rose the thriving new cities of Pasadena and Baytown, Texas. These places continue to grow, and every index of productivity and income is evidence of their capacity to expand. . . .

The history of the district . . . shows plentiful evidence of growth and prosperity. But until less than two decades ago it was growth of a very limited order. The economy was colonial; it produced a number of great staples exported to be processed elsewhere. The capital to finance and the skill to manage these enterprises came from outside the region; native labor was used only in inferior capacities. . . .

The last decades for the Gulf cities have been not merely years of rapid development; they have also been years in which the region has moved out of the colonial into a new industrial phase. It no longer simply extracts the products of the earth; it now processes and manufac-

tures them as well. Cattle still graze in the shadow of the refineries, but the whole tone of the area is urban rather than agrarian.

Driving up from Galveston toward Houston, on roads that here and there border the Bay and the great ship channel, the evidence of change is inescapable. The constant hum of unseen activity fills the air, and occasionally a remote spurt of flame is visible. Then, out of the flat, uninhabited plain, there suddenly rise the massive bulks of the new plants, in Lamarque, Texas City, La Porte, Baytown, Pasadena, and Houston. Often the great looming shapes can be seen only in distant outline; but the private roads lead down to Monsanto, Sinclair, Esso, Du Pont, Shell, Diamond Alkali, Phillips, Ethyl, Pan-American, and Republic. So too, out of Baton Rouge the same names along the Scenic Highway point to the contorted rectifiers and bulbous tanks that seem to have sprung out of a science-fiction writer's dream of the future.

A variety of factors has been responsible for the change. Since the First World War, there had been tentative experiments looking toward the production of synthetic materials from petroleum. In the 1930's these efforts reached the point at which manufacture was technologically and commercially feasible; and a new petro-chemical industry producing nylon and plastics began to thrive around the Gulf while the rest of the nation was still deep in the depression.

In the location of the new plants, there was an obvious advantage in proximity to the oil itself; and the East Texas fields providentially came in at just the right moment. In industries that operated under the open sky, a warm climate and space were also advantages, and ample supplies of natural gas enabled the region to generate power cheaply.

The outbreak of the Second World War accentuated the demand for petroleum products. Plastics and other derivatives were as necessary as the refined oil itself. Furthermore, disruption of the supply of natural rubber from the Far East forced the government to artificial substitutes, and the most convenient process derived synthetic rubber from petroleum. The urgencies of the war minimized every other consideration. The Gulf region therefore profited from the location of a number of great enterprises almost wholly supported by war orders and built with the aid of Federal capital.

Finally the political context was favorable. The New Deal had, from the start, been solicitous over the condition of the economically retarded South and had hoped industrialization might provide some relief. At the same time, Democratic Party politics ... gave a high priority to measures likely to redound to the advantage of the Gulf states. The result was a full-blown industrial revolution in little more than a decade. The handling of cotton or sugar or oil is now far less important than manufacturing.

The character of the change and the times in which it came spared the new towns many of the difficulties of transition. The petro-chemical industries do not depend upon a cheap, unskilled proletariat. The machines or, rather, the successive refining devices call for relatively little labor compared with the value of the product. Apart from the construction workers who build the equipment, the plants need mostly technicians and maintenance and service employees who are fairly well paid.

The whole development came in a period of rising prices, of union organization, and of a scarcity of manpower. Wage rates had to be favorable and working conditions good to attract newcomers, to hold them against the temptations of other employers and other regions, and to keep out aggressive labor organizers. In any case, the wage factor was relatively unimportant since the government was one of the chief consumers and all prices were rising.

The attractive power of high wage rates drew the necessary hands out of the rural countryside. Sometimes these former sharecroppers commute; from within a radius of almost forty miles, for instance, they travel daily to Baton Rouge. Often, however, they leave the farm for good; in many places, fertile acres that once grew cotton have been turned into pastures for want of tenants to till them. The supply is elastic; between jobs men can go back to the country without burdening the industrial communities in which they work.

The new hands have been a remarkably vitalizing factor in the Southern economy, not simply as wage earners but also as consumers of goods formerly beyond their reach. Every worker who left the cropper's shack for the city developed a new and stimulating desire for a host of products —for new housing, for respectable clothes, for a dependable car, and for a multitude of objects with which urban living made him familiar. The move from the farm opened up an endless series of fresh demands: a diversified diet, furniture, sheets on the beds and curtains at the windows. And dependable pay checks make all these available.

The implications of these changes, therefore, extend far beyond the workers in the new factories. Mounting demands encourage a host of service and construction industries as well as the whole range of distributive enterprises that supply the modern metropolis. The employees of the oil or rubber or chemical plants have benefited, but so have the tailors and grocery clerks, the capenters and electricians, the auto mechanics and bus drivers. In a decade, retail sales in Houston rose 279 per cent.

Prosperity also radiates to the whole

Gulf area. The migration to the cities has relieved the pressure of excess agricultural labor on the farms. Those who commute from rural homes take back wages that transform the way of life of the Southern countryside. Close connections with the city have brought new standards of consumption to the rural regions. Through the back country of Texas, Arkansas, Oklahoma, Louisiana, and Alabama, the television aerial waves triumphantly; and though its owner may still live in a dilapidated shack, a shiny car alongside shows that this population is finding the way out of its hopeless poverty.

453. *Counter-Revolution by Business*, 1949

Walton Hamilton, "The Genius of the Radical," John W. Chase, ed., *Years of the Modern* (New York, 1949), 83–9.

THE CAMPAIGN for regulation has provided its counter-revolution. For business, intent on its own advantage, did not take this turn of events lying down. If it could not stop the trespass of the state on its preserves, it could at least impose its own will upon all that came within its reach; and sooner or later it could clothe in its own livery the praetorian guard set up to keep it in order. . . . It was easier to capture an agency than to fight it; it was better to convert a control into a sanction for what the man of affairs wanted to do than to endure it.

The new strategy made its own way in the economy with amazing ease. In the learned professions, an examination was deemed necessary to test the competence of novitiates—and to protect the public. Arts not so fine could become professions by the election of the legislature; and would-be realtors, morticians and beauticians might or might not be lawfully licensed to practice by an official committee drawn from the tradesmen with whom they hoped to compete. A building code, without doubt, served the cause of public safety—but it could be made to secure the work of construction to local contractors and local labor. Inspection had once served to keep milk pure but along came pasteurization to rob it of its function. Still it had to be retained; for, through its code, an elaborate system of private government could be imposed upon the milkshed. This system limited entrance to the market to the elect, permitted the maintenance of a high price for fluid milk, while surplus milk of like kind was sold at a lower figure; and, deposing the market, converted the industry into a neat and tidy political domain.

Agencies of control, under the commission system, are ripe for capture. The interest to be regulated is compact, organized, mobile, alert to every move, able to concentrate all its forces with neatness and dispatch at its point of decision. The public interest is general, sluggish, diffused, unable to effect a united front or to move in time. It is small wonder that the American Association of Railroads has an office within the building which houses the I.C.C.; that the Milk and Sugar Divisions of the Department of Agriculture look upon their industries as constituents; that C.A.B. is intent to shield against all free enterprise its "certificated" lines. . . .

The attempt all along the line has been to convert regulation into a weapon of business enterprise. If politics meddles with business, business can take a fling at politics. . . . [The patent license] is the most brilliant of political inventions. With ease, it at once liberates an area of the economy from the rule of the market, puts it under a single political authority with no public responsibility, and allows an enterprise which would otherwise be called by a nasty name such as combination, monopoly or conspiracy, to carry on under cover of law.... A character committee scrupulously examines the credentials of all who, by applying for licenses, knock at the door of the industry. It turns down all applicants whose lack of integrity is attested by lack of funds; and in general it keeps newcomers out. A design, neat and compact enough to satisfy the most rigid planner, is frozen into the structure of the industry. Each concern occupies its appointed place within the industry. The wares to be made, the quantity of output, the capacity to produce, the price to be charged, the markets to be sold, are all set forth in detail in the license. The series of licenses constitute the law of the trade, a breach of which is not to be tolerated. A concern which exceeds its quota, applies the chisel to its price, or shows disrespect for another's preserves, becomes subject to discipline. The authority is not unversed in the fine art of reprisals; and there are formal ways of bringing the sinner to repentance. The industry's system of justice is speedy and sure. But, if, perchance, rebellion raises its head, there is a last resort. For to act in violation of the license is to invade the rights of its overlord, and exposes the offender to a suit for infringement. Thus the federal courts are called upon to underwrite and to police a private system of government....

In neatly plotted and tightly hedged domains of the corporate imperium, the freedom to adventure is gone. In putting on the ancient mask of free enterprise, the corporate estate asserts its independence of the state whose favors it regards itself free to accept. Its mark is dominion over an area of the economy and supremacy of the private law within its province. In the illustration given, that dominion was rested upon the patent grant; in examples given above, it is rested upon inspection, the building code, the license to trade or profession. It can be grounded upon a trade-mark, a public franchise or exclusive ownership of a source of supply, such as borax or sulphur.... The war years provided conditions favorable to the trend: the bulk of war orders went to large corporate estates; the little fellows, as subcontractors, became feudal retainers. The trend towards "self-government in industry," fed by government orders and subsidies, today moves faster than ever.

454. *Payroll Prosperity, 1953*

Oscar Handlin, "Payroll Prosperity," *Atlantic Monthly*, February, 1953, 30–2.

UNEMPLOYMENT as a consequential factor has disappeared. There are still seasonal rises and falls, and there have been occasional short-run declines in the number of available places. But for twelve years the labor force has kept growing and has not left any significant pools of unemployed. The 60 million jobs once regarded as visionary have long since become a reality; the worker now no longer fears idleness as a threat to his well-being.

At the same time, his earning power has changed, for the better. No matter what has happened to the purchasing power of its dollars, a phenomenal rise has carried the effective total wages of labor to a higher level than ever before.

Hourly rates everywhere have risen.... More important, total earnings have mounted. Since 1940, for example, packing house workers have found employment for an average of well over forty hours a week. The wages they take home are greater than in earlier years because they profit from a fuller work week and from extra pay for overtime, as well as from the higher hourly rate. With seasonal fluctuations largely eliminated, and with employers calling for his services through the year, the industrial laborer finds his total annual income soaring to levels beyond his fondest hopes only a few years ago.

What is more, a persistent shortage of labor has made room for numerous new employees. Women, when they wish, find hirers eager to accommodate them on a full- or a part-time basis. Well over 20 per cent of all American women of working age take such jobs, a measure of the extent to which the practice is accepted as respectable. Young people find work as soon as they like; even those who are still in school pick up vacation or part-time employment with ease, and with good pay. Such marginal hands have expanded the labor force and family incomes. The 48,-159 households of Flint, Michigan, for instance, produced 70,174 employed persons in 1950; the 219,000 households of Boston, 319,000. Data for the working class sections of the cities generally show that the ratio of employment is highest there. The resulting rise in family income offers a striking contrast to the situation ten years earlier.

The disappearance of unemployment and the rise in earning powers are unprecedented. Earlier periods of comparable prosperity, such as that during the silk shirt years of the First World War, were of short duration and affected only limited numbers of fortunate workers. The present prosperity has extended through more than a decade and has affected everyone. And in that decade the laborer's whole relationship to his work was being altered.

Less than ever before does the laborer identify himself with his job, think of himself, as an individual, primarily in terms of his position at a particular type of work in a particular plant. The riveter, the laster, the crane operator sheds the marks of his employment when he leaves the shop. The nature of his work will only slightly influence his life outside.

In part, the separation of work from life is due to long-term developments. The craftsmanship that once was the link of the laborer to his task is now disappearing. The decline in the spirit of workmanship has long since set in under the impact of mechanization that lowered the social value of skills.... The man on the assembly line finds little in his own experience that would lead him to stick to a job out of the satisfaction of doing it.

Full employment and high wages have pushed that trend to its ultimate conclusion. The mere process of holding a job is not so critical as it once was. Since the worker feels secure in the knowledge that many jobs are available and that movement is possible from one to another, the specific place he occupies at any given time is not very important in his life. Once hesitant to take the risk of shifting from one factory to another, he is not hesitant now to move from one section of the country to another, confident he will anywhere find a demand for his services.

The general rise in all earning power has also divorced the worker from the specific job by minimizing the importance of wage differentials based upon special skills. In many highly unionized industries, for instance, unskilled or semiskilled laborers are better paid than skilled craftsmen in not so thoroughly unionized plants. Often in the past ten years, cabinetmakers, bookbinders, and watchmakers have moved on to higher wages as laborers in defense plants. The mastery of a trade no longer holds the man to his job. The job, no matter what its character, is regarded as a source of income only, and the best pay attracts the worker.

Laborers are less likely to identify themselves with their work, also, because their work absorbs a smaller share of their energy and attention.

The number of hours actually spent at the machine has fallen steadily. In the hungry 1930's that decline was stimulated by the desire to spread the available work to as many hands as possible. But the featherbedding practices then introduced in some industries have persisted. The majority of New York longshoremen, for whom the work week is thirteen hours, are certainly not typical of labor in general. But in railroads, steel, and coal mining the work week has shrunk without a corresponding lowering of wages. . . . The forty-hour, five-day week has become so widely accepted that there is talk of thirty hours as the next objective.

The decline in hours, like the diminution in the value of skills, is evidence of the extent to which the worker shuts his work off into a separate category of his existence. His earning power and the demand for his labor make it possible for him to express the judgment that the tasks he performs are not, in the performance, the sources of fundamental satisfaction to him. In so far as he can, he curtails the time devoted to them because the life from which he hopes to derive pleasure and satisfaction only begins after he punches out on the clock. . . .

As a family's income rises, the nature of its expenditures changes. So long as its earnings were less than $3000 a year, the funds went almost in their entirety for food and housing. Now more dollars are available for better shelter and subsistence; in the last ten years the per capita consumption of bread and potatoes has slumped markedly while that of fruit and meat has noticeably risen. And as its earnings move across the $3000 line, the family devotes an ever-larger proportion of them to clothing, to entertainment, and to automobiles.

Such objects are not merely useful; they are the recognizable evidence of respectability. The number of potential car buyers continues to rise; but the advertisements of the least expensive vehicles stress not their low price but their resemblance to Cadillacs and Lincolns. The virtue of the Ford is not that it is cheap, but that it is "worth more," as the lady in mink says as she steps out of it in the picture. . . . Entertainment too is likely to take on middle-class forms. "I really hate to work on Saturday," writes a Pennsylvania steelworker, "because I want to go to South Bend to see the Notre Dame and University of Pittsburgh football game."

All this conforms to an old American ideal: the maximum diffusion of the goods of life among the whole population. Indeed desires often outrun the available cash. Significantly, the volume of consumer purchases has consistently been higher than the total available consumer income. The deficit has been met partly by the use of savings accumulated during the war. More important, increasingly liberal credit terms have made up the difference. The Federal Reserve Board has estimated that consumer credits in October, 1952, had soared to an all-time high of $22.3 billion from some $8 billion only ten years ago. Purchases on time are expensive and hazardous but often seem the only means of acquiring so many needed objects.

455. *Automation, 1954*

"Twenty-Five Years That Remade America," *Business Week*, September 4, 1954, p. 84.

THOUGH the assembly line was a form of mechanization, it still used people. In the twenty-five years since 1929, the dominant line of development has been in the direction of doing as much as possible without people. The art and science of going through as many stages of production as possible with as little human help as possible is called automation.

Fully automatic factories are still rare. Mainly they're confined to industries such as chemicals, petroleum refining, and some foods—industries where the product is fluid and you need only a kind of high-grade plumbing to carry the materials from one processing step to another.

But nearly every industry, in the last twenty-five years, has felt the impact of the new technology—whether it's more automatic handling of materials, more automatic feeding, loading, machining, waste disposal, or inspection. Bring each of these new techniques to the peak of automatic perfection, put them all under the same roof in interlocked production lines, run them all in a smooth flow by a system of automatic controls, and you have the engineer's dream of the fully automatic factory. This will be the next step in the growth of many industries, and undoubtedly the main line of development for the next twenty-five years.

And why all the emphasis on "Look, no hands?" Largely because labor, in the last twenty-five years, has become relatively scarce and very expensive. Wages are now up so high that in many cases a costly piece of labor-saving equipment looks like a bargain. And skilled labor—at any price —is hard to find.

Furthermore, there are some processes that machines can perform more skillfully than the most skilled worker. As products become more complicated and tolerances more finicky, as materials become more specialized and therefore more sensitive, automatic methods become more useful. They cut the chance of human error.

Also, for most jobs, machines are faster than human hands. When tremendous volumes of a particular product are needed, and especially when the time is limited (as in World War II), machines usually will do a better job. It's essential, of course, that the engineer keep a smooth flow going through the factory. It does no good to be making bolts at the rate of 5,000 an hour if the nuts to go with them are coming off the line at the rate of 2,000 an hour.

Automation has become increasingly popular as the labor force has been up-graded by better education and more income, and has been given a wider choice of jobs in a full-employment economy. It has become harder and harder to find workers for the dirty, boring, backbreaking jobs in industry. This alone has been a tremendous spur to making factories more automatic.

At the same time, automation has itself played a big part in upgrading the labor force. There simply is no longer much place in the economy for the strong back and the weak mind. For one thing, it takes a high degree of skill to run many of the new machines. For another, the problems of maintenance multiply as the machines get more complicated, and good men who can keep these machines in working order are at a premium. So the maintenance man has been graduated into a kind of junior engineer—and, like as not, he has gained his new skill in on-the-job training by industry.

But there are problems in automation too—and the closer you get to a fully automatic setup, the worse some of these problems get.

One problem is the lack of flexibility. The more automated a production line, the more it tends to become rigidly bound to turn out a standardized product. Even a small change might require junking whole banks of tools. One solution envisions tooling in interlocking blocks or gangs; sections of the line could be changed to suit a new size or product, while the main part of the line could be kept intact.

It's a tricky job, too, to keep the robot plant under control. The man running a plant loses touch with the machinery when it's remote and automatic. Control rooms have become more and more complicated; yet if something goes wrong, the engineer has to be able to spot the offender quickly among a maze of dials and measuring devices. The problem is one of human engineering—getting control systems that the human mind and the human eye can work with.

How widespread is this substitution of machines for people? You can get a good idea by looking at a single statistic—the amount of electric power used in manufacturing over the years.

Between 1945 and 1953, manufacturing production went up by 24 per cent. The number of production workers went up by 5 per cent. The number of kilowatt-hours of electric power used in manufacturing went up by 63 per cent.

456. *American Productivity, 1955*

J. F. Dewhurst, *et al.*, *America's Needs and Resources* (New York, 1955), 39–44.

ESTIMATES of private national income (i.e., value of net output of goods and services exclusive of indirect business taxes) can be made at ten-year intervals back to 1850. These dollar estimates provide a rough measure of changes in the physical output of goods and services when converted by means of a price level index into "constant dollars" of 1950 purchasing power.

Thus expressed in dollars of constant purchasing power, private national income increased from $8.8 billion in 1850 to $60.0 billion in 1900 and to $217.3 billion in 1950. The century thus witnessed a 25-fold increase in the net output of the American economy—while population multiplied less than seven times.

Private labor input in the same period increased from an estimated 26.1 billion man-hours in 1850 to 112.3 billion in 1950, or a little more than four times. These estimates of private man-hours of labor effort divided into the corresponding estimates of private national income provide a measure of output per man-hour in 1850 and at ten-year intervals to 1950.

The resulting series shows a rise from an estimated output per man-hour of 33.7 cents in 1850 to $1.93 in 1950. Thus, the productivity of labor was multiplied nearly six times during the century. Although the average increase per decade was about 18.4 per cent, the change from one decade to the next varied greatly. Generally speaking, the gains since 1900 have been greater than those during the last half of the nine-

teenth century. Between 1850 and 1900, productivity little more than doubled; between 1900 and 1950, it almost trebled.

How much productivity will increase during the 1950s nobody knows, but . . . the percentage increase from decade to decade has been showing a tendency to rise slightly. Projecting this slightly rising trend line to 1960 suggests that it would be reasonable to expect an increase of about 25 per cent during the decade, or approximately 2.3 per cent a year. . . .

The private national income that would be produced at a high level of activity in 1960, on the basis of the assumptions stated above, can now be determined by simple arithmetic. If net output (national income) per man-hour increases at the average rate of 2.3 per cent a year, it will rise by about 47 cents between 1950 and 1960—from $1.93 to $2.40. . . .

With 58.5 million persons working in private employment in 1960 and an average work week of 37.5 hours, total "labor input" would amount to 114 billion man-hours for a 52-week year. At the rate of $2.40 per man-hour, private national income at 1950 prices would amount to approximately $275 billion. This would be 27 per cent more than in 1950 and more than 31 times the amount of private national income produced in 1850.

The growth trend of private national income since 1850 is in interesting contrast to the trends of some of the "ingredients" of national income, or the factors that account for its size: employment, hours of work, total man-hours and output per man-hour. . . .

The first decade of the century appears to mark a turning point in the growth of some of these factors. Although private national income measured in constant dollars continued to rise steeply after 1910, employment grew more slowly and average hours of work declined more rapidly. This resulted in a much more gradual rise in total man-hours worked after 1910. The increase in "labor input" from 1910 to 1950 was only 22 per cent, and most of this came in the 1940s. During this period, however, private national income increased by 164 per cent because of great advances in productivity. The increase in output would have been much greater, of course, if we had not cut working time so sharply between 1910 and 1950. In other words, we have foregone a part of the potential increase in total output that steadily increasing productivity has made possible in order to enjoy a shorter work week.

The situation can be expressed more concretely by making a rough comparison of 1910 output with *potential* 1950 output. The 32.1 million persons employed in private industry in 1910 worked an average of 55.1 hours a week. With a total labor input of 92 billion man-hours and a national income of $82.4 billion (at 1950 prices), output per man-hour amounted to 89.6 cents.

By 1950, output per man-hour had risen to $1.93. The 1950 working force of 54 million, working 40 hours a week, actually produced a private national income of $217.3 billion. If the 1950 working force had put in 55.1 hours a week, total labor input would have amounted to 155 billion man-hours and private national income—at the 1950 level of productivity —to $299 billion, instead of $217 billion. This difference of $82 billion between "potential" and actual national income might be regarded as the value of goods and services not consumed in 1950 in order to enjoy the shorter work week of that year. To put the matter in a slightly different way, about 62 per cent of the potential increase in private national income over this 40-year period (i.e., the difference between $82 billion produced in 1910 and the $299 billion that might have been produced in 1950) was represented by additional goods and services actually produced, and about 38 per cent by shorter working hours and more leisure time.

L ✦ Social Aspects of War and Cold War

IT WAS DIFFICULT in the years after 1939 to escape the strains of the struggle that preoccupied the life of a whole generation. Men who had lived through the first war and the depression, now confronted the problems of a second, even greater, war. And, that was no sooner over than its rewards were threatened by a prolonged and indecisive contest round the world. That the struggle was waged under the threat of gigantic atomic power that might destroy all civilization only made the existing tensions more acute.

Under the circumstances, it was not surprising to find a failure of nerve, a loss of confidence, that made Americans long, more than ever before, for the values of stability and security. During the war these tensions had occasionally broken forth into open and ugly riots (No. 457). They were also expressed, or evaded, in the search for a traditional source of security, in a return to religion, for example (No. 458). The return was often less animated by theological than by social motives; men desired to find some secure, if limited, group within which there was shelter against the shocks of a disorderly world.

Rising religious interests occasionally created problems of the relationship of church and state; but recognition of a wall of separation between the two areas prevented group antagonism from developing (No. 459). Indeed, earlier intolerance seemed to have passed away. Relationships among American ethnic groups were more peaceful than ever before. A Committee on Civil Rights still found unsolved problems, but also noted considerable improvement in the position of Negroes and other minorities in the United States (No. 460). A decision of the Supreme Court in 1954 opened the way toward elimination of segregation in the educational system, and, presumably, in other areas of American life (No. 461). While the change was not immediately implemented, it indicated the direction of a significant trend. In the same way, although no immediate reform followed, the codification of the outmoded immigration laws in 1952 drew attention to their deficiencies (No. 462).

On the whole, indications were that Americans were successfully preserving the fluidity and mobility of their society. Recognizing that education was the gateway to careers, more students than ever sought the advantages of a college training (No. 463). And increasing attention was devoted to the content of their education—both from the point of view of presenting them with the elements of a common culture (No. 464), and from the point of view of preserving the values of individual differences (No. 465).

457. *The Los Angeles Riot, 1943*

Carey McWilliams, *North from Mexico* (Philadelphia, 1949), 248–51, 256. Copyright, 1949, by Carey McWilliams. Published by J. B. Lippincott Company.

On Monday evening, June seventh, [1943], thousands of *Angelenos,* in response to twelve hours' advance notice in the press, turned out for a mass lynching. Marching through the streets of downtown Los Angeles, a mob of several thousand soldiers, sailors, and civilians, proceeded to beat up every zoot-suiter they could find. Pushing its way into the important motion picture theaters, the mob ordered the management to turn on the house lights and then ranged up and down the aisles dragging Mexicans out of their seats. Street cars were halted while Mexicans, and some Filipinos and Negroes, were jerked out of their seats, pushed into the streets, and beaten with sadistic frenzy. If the victims wore zoot-suits, they were stripped of their clothing and left naked or half-naked on the streets, bleeding and bruised. Proceeding down Main Street from First to Twelfth, the mob stopped on the edge of the Negro district. Learning that the Negroes planned a warm reception for them, the mobsters turned back and marched through the Mexican east side spreading panic and terror. . . .

Throughout the night the Mexican communities were in the wildest possible turmoil. Scores of Mexican mothers were trying to locate their youngsters and several hundred Mexicans milled around each of the police substations and the Central Jail trying to get word of missing members of their families. Boys came into the police stations saying: "Charge me with vagrancy or anything, but don't send me out there!" pointing to the streets where other boys, as young as twelve and thirteen years of age, were being beaten and stripped of their clothes. . . . Not more than half of the victims were actually wearing zoot-suits. A Negro defense worker, wearing a defense-plant identification badge on his work-clothes, was taken from a street car and one of his eyes was gouged out with a knife. Huge half-page photographs, showing Mexican boys stripped of their clothes, cowering on the pavements, often bleeding profusely, surrounded by jeering mobs of men and women, appeared in all the Los Angeles newspapers. . . .

At midnight on June seventh, the military authorities decided that the local police were completely unable or unwilling to handle the situation, despite the fact that a thousand reserve officers had been called up. The entire downtown area of Los Angeles was then declared "out of bounds" for military personnel. This order immediately slowed down the pace of the rioting. The moment the Military Police and Shore Patrol went into action, the rioting quieted down. On June eighth the city officials brought their heads up out of the sand, took a look around, and began issuing statements. The district attorney, Fred N. Howser, announced that the "situation is getting entirely out of hand," while Mayor Fletcher Bowron thought that "sooner or later it will blow over." The chief of police, taking a count of the Mexicans in jail, cheerfully proclaimed that "the situation has now cleared up." All

agreed, however, that it was quite "a situation."

Unfortunately "the situation" had not cleared up; nor did it blow over. It began to spread to the suburbs where the rioting continued for two more days. When it finally stopped, the Eagle Rock *Advertiser* mournfully editorialized: "It is too bad the servicemen were called off before they were able to complete the job. . . . Most of the citizens of the city have been delighted with what has been going on." County Supervisor Roger Jessup told the newsmen: "All that is needed to end lawlessness is more of the same action as is being exercised by the servicemen!" While the district attorney of Ventura, an outlying county, jumped on the bandwagon with a statement to the effect that "zoot suits are an open indication of subversive character.". . .

The zoot-suit riots in Los Angeles were the spark that touched off a chain-reaction of riots across the country in midsummer 1943. Similar "zoot-suit" disturbances were reported in San Diego on June ninth; in Philadelphia on June tenth; in Chicago on June fifteenth; and in Evansville, Indiana, on June twenty-seventh. Between June sixteenth and August first, large-scale race riots occurred in Beaumont, Texas, in Detroit, and in Harlem. The Detroit riots of June 20–21 were the most disastrous riots in a quarter of a century. The swift, crazy violence of the Harlem riot resulted, in a few hours' time, in property damage totaling nearly a million dollars. The rapid succession of these violent and destructive riots seriously interfered with the war effort and had the most adverse international repercussions.

458. *Can the Churches Help?* 1943

Sidney Hook, "The New Failure of Nerve," *Partisan Review* (1943), X, 9–10.

TODAY the churches are so much of this world that their other worldliness is only a half-believed prophecy of man's inescapable destination rather than an ideal of personal and social life. As interpreters of divine purpose, they have now become concerned with social healing, with the institutions of society and with the bodies of men, as necessarily involved in the healing of individual souls. The world-order is to become a moral and religious order. Plans for the post-war world and for social reconstruction are coming from the Pope as well as from the humblest Protestant sect. They are now at flood-tide. The Churches bid well to replace political parties as sounding boards, if not instruments, of social reform.

It is characteristic of the tendencies hostile to scientific method that they reject the view that the breakdown of capitalism and the rise of totalitarianism are primarily the result of a conjunction of material factors. Rather do they allege that the bankruptcy of Western European civilization is the direct result of the bankruptcy of the scientific and naturalistic spirit. The attempt to live by science resulted in chaos, relativism, Hitlerism and war. The latter are treated as superficial evils destined to pass like all of God's trials. But the radical evil is a scientific attitude which sacrificed true understanding for prediction and individual salvation for social control.

That science was king in the social life of the Western world, that modern ills are the consequences of our attempt to live by scientific theory and practice—these assumptions border on fantasy. No convincing evidence has ever been offered for them. On the contrary, the chief causes of our maladjustments are to be found precisely in these areas of life in which the rationale of scientific method has not been employed. Where is the evidence that any Western state ever attempted to meet scientifically the challenge of poverty, unemployment, distribution of raw materials, the impact of technology? Attempts to grapple with these problems in relation to human needs in a rational and scientific spirit have run squarely against class interests and privileges which cut savagely short any inquiry into their justification. What has controlled our response to basic social problems have been principles drawn from the outworn traditions or opportunist compromises that reflect nothing but the shifting strength of the interests behind them. In either case the procedure has had little to do with the ethics and logic of scientific method. It is only by courtesy that we can call them principles at all. Drift and improvisation have been the rule. Enthusiasm for the bare results of the physical sciences—which undoubtedly did reach a high pitch in the nineteenth century—does not betoken an acceptance of a scientific or experimental philosophy of life in which all values are tested by their causes and consequences. The cry that a set of "laboratory techniques" cannot determine values in a philosophy of life betrays the literary man's illusion that the laboratory procedures of the natural sciences are the be-all and end-all of scientific method instead of restricted applications of it in special fields.

The truth is that scientific method has until now been regarded as irrelevant in testing the values embodied in social institutions. If one accepted the religionists' assumption that values can be grounded only on a true religion and metaphysics, together with their views about the ideal causation of events, it could be legitimately urged against them that the bankruptcy of civilization testifies to the bankruptcy of their metaphysics. For if science is irrelevant to values, it cannot corrupt them; and if theology and metaphysics are their sacred guardian, they are responsible for the world we live in.

459. A *Wall Between Church and State*, 1948

McCollum *v.* Board of Education (1948), 333 *U.S. Reports*, 205, 207–10, 211–16, 231–2.

MR. JUSTICE BLACK delivered the opinion of the Court.

The appellant, Vashti McCollum, began this action for mandamus against the Champaign Board of Education in the Circuit Court of Champaign County, Illinois. Her asserted interest was that of a resident and taxpayer of Champaign and of a parent whose child was then enrolled in the Champaign public schools. Illinois has a compulsory education law which, with exceptions, requires parents to send their children, aged seven to sixteen, to its tax-supported public schools where the children are to remain in attendance during the hours when the schools are regularly in session. Parents who violate this law commit a misdemeanor punishable by fine unless the children attend private or parochial schools which meet educational standards fixed by the State. . . .

Appellant's petition for mandamus alleged that religious teachers, employed by private religious groups, were permitted to come weekly into the school buildings during the regular hours set apart for secular teaching, and then and there for a period of thirty minutes substitute their religious teaching for the secular education provided under the compulsory education law. The petitioner charged that this joint public-school religious-group program violated the First and Fourteenth Amendments to the United States Constitution. The prayer of her petition was that the Board of Education be ordered to "adopt and enforce rules and regulations prohibiting all instruction in and teaching of religious education in all public schools in Champaign School District Number 71, . . . and in all public school houses and buildings in said district when occupied by public schools.". . .

The following facts are shown by the record without dispute. In 1940 interested members of the Jewish, Roman Catholic, and a few of the Protestant faiths formed a voluntary association called the Champaign Council on Religious Education. They obtained permission from the Board of Education to offer classes in religious instruction to public school pupils in grades four to nine inclusive. Classes were made up of pupils whose parents signed printed cards requesting that their children be permitted to attend; they were held weekly, thirty minutes for the lower grades, forty-five minutes for the higher. The council employed the religious teachers at no expense to the school authorities, but the instructors were subject to the approval and supervision of the superintendent of schools. The classes were taught in three separate religious groups by Protestant teachers, Catholic priests, and a Jewish rabbi . . . in the regular classrooms of the school building. Students who did not choose to take the religious instruction were . . . required to leave their classrooms and go to some other place in the school building for pursuit of their secular studies. On the other hand, students who were released from secular study for the religious instructions were required to be present at the religious classes. Reports of their presence or absence were to be made to their secular teachers.

The foregoing facts, without reference to others that appear in the record, show the use of tax-supported property for religious instruction and the close cooperation between the school authorities and the religious council in promoting religious education. The operation of the State's compulsory education system thus assists and is integrated with the program of religious instruction carried on by separate religious sects. . . . This is beyond all question a utilization of the tax-established and tax-supported public school system to aid religious groups to spread their faith. And it falls squarely under the ban of the First Amendment (made applicable to the States by the Fourteenth) as we interpreted it in *Everson* v. *Board of Education*. . . .

To hold that a state cannot consistently with the First and Fourteenth Amendments utilize its public school system to aid any or all religious faiths or sects in the dissemination of their doctrines and ideals does not . . . manifest a governmental hostility to religion or religious teachings. A manifestation of such hostility would be at war with our national tradition as embodied in the First Amendment's guaranty of the free exercise of religion. For the First Amendment rests upon the premise that both religion and government can best work to achieve their lofty aims if each is left free from the other within its respective sphere. Or, as we said in the Everson case, the First Amendment has erected a wall between Church and State which must be kept high and impregnable.

Here not only are the State's tax-supported public school buildings used for the dissemination of religious doctrines. The State affords sectarian groups an invaluable aid in that it helps to provide pupils for their religious classes through use of the State's compulsory public school machinery. This is not separation of Church and State.

The cause is reversed and remanded to the State Supreme Court for proceedings not inconsistent with this opinion. . . .

MR. JUSTICE FRANKFURTER delivered the following [concurring] opinion, in which Mr. Justice Jackson, Mr. Justice Rutledge and Mr. Justice Burton join. . . .

To understand the particular program now before us . . . , we must put this Champaign program of 1940 in its historic

setting. Traditionally, organized education in the Western world was Church education. . . . Even in the Protestant countries, . . . the basis of education was largely the Bible, and its chief purpose inculcation of piety. To the extent that the State intervened, it used its authority to further aims of the Church.

The emigrants who came to these shores brought this view of education with them. Colonial schools certainly started with a religious orientation. . . . The evolution of colonial education, largely in the service of religion, into the public school system of today is the story of changing conceptions regarding the American democratic society, of the functions of state-maintained education in such a society, and of the role therein of the free exercise of religion by the people. . . . Long before the Fourteenth Amendment subjected the states to new limitations, the prohibition of furtherance by the state of religious instruction became the guiding principle, in law and feeling, of the American people. . . .

Separation in the field of education, then, was not imposed upon unwilling states by force of superior law. In this respect the Fourteenth Amendment merely reflected a principle then dominant in our national life. To the extent that the Constitution thus made it binding upon the states, the basis of the restriction is the whole experience of our people. Zealous watchfulness against fusion of secular and religious activities by Government itself, through any of its instruments but especially through its educational agencies, was the democratic response of the American community to the particular needs of a young and growing nation, unique in the composition of its people. . . .

Separation means separation, not something less. Jefferson's metaphor in describing the relation between Church and State speaks of a "wall of separation," not of a fine line easily overstepped. The public school is at once the symbol of our democracy and the most pervasive means for promoting our common destiny. In no activity of the State is it more vital to keep out divisive forces than in its schools, to avoid confusing, not to say fusing, what the Constitution sought to keep strictly apart. "The great American principle of eternal separation"—Elihu Root's phrase bears repetition—is one of the vital reliances of our Constitutional system for assuring unities among our people stronger than our diversities. It is the Court's duty to enforce this principle in its full integrity.

460. *Civil Rights After the War,* 1947

President's Committee on Civil Rights, *To Secure These Rights* (Washington, 1947), 17–20.

IT WOULD be a grievous mistake to read this as meaning that there is nothing in our record of which to be proud. There is a great deal; enough, we believe, to warrant our conviction that no nation in history has ever offered more hope of the final realization of the ultimate ideal of freedom and equality than has ours.... There are many signs of progress and portents of still more to come....

The greatest hope for the future is the increasing awareness by more and more Americans of the gulf between our civil rights principles and our practices. Only a free people can continually question and appraise the adequacy of its institutions.

Over the past years, leaders of opinion —in public life, in our press, radio, and motion pictures, in the churches, in the schools and colleges, in business, in trade unions, and in the professions—have recognized their responsibility to act effectively in their own lives and to work to strengthen civil rights. The Committee has been much impressed by the number and work of private organizations whose chief aim is the furtherance of freedom. They have accomplished much and are entitled to a great deal of credit for their work. The existence of several groups in the South which are working for the advancement of civil rights is particularly heartening. Their courageous, unceasing efforts have already produced impressive results which surely foreshadow still further progress. We are also encouraged by the number of communities which have established official bodies to better the relations among their people and to protect the rights of their minorities.

The existence of these private agencies is a sign of the fundamental vigor of our democracy, and of our resourcefulness in devising techniques for self-help.... Almost without exception, however, all of these groups have indicated to us a belief that their own educational efforts are not enough, and that increased federal protection of civil rights is needed. They see no conflict between leadership by the national government and private local enterprise in the safeguarding of civil rights.

The past decade—particularly the war years—gives us much reason for confidence in the ability of our nation to better its civil rights record even in the midst of crisis. Equality of opportunity came closer to reality for many members of minority groups during this recent period. A few forward-looking state and local governments have acted to conserve these gains and even move ahead. New York State, in particular, has an impressive variety of civil rights laws on its statute books. A few other states and cities have followed suit, especially in the fair employment practice field. The voluntary elimination of racial bans or differentials in employment practices by many business concerns, the employment of Negro baseball players by teams in both major leagues, deserve high praise.

Similarly, one recent survey of Negro progress, made by Charles S. Johnson, and appropriately entitled "Into the Main Stream," reports that ". . . the biggest single forward surge of Negroes into the main stream of American life in the past ten years has been their movement into the ranks of organized labor." Mention should also be made of the ending of segregated schools in cities like Trenton and Gary; the lifting of restrictions against Negro doctors by hospitals in St. Louis and Gary; the establishment of interracial churches in many communities; and the employment of more than three-score Negro teachers by twenty-five white or predominantly white colleges. . . .

Some officers high in the ranks of the armed forces have shown a heartening recognition of the need to make the Army, Navy, Air Forces, and the Coast Guard more representative of the democracy whose defense they are. We must not lose sight of the fact that compared with the situation in previous wars, this one reflected sharp improvement in the utilization of minority groups.

The freedom of most of our people to seek the truth and express themselves freely is a vigorous, healthy reality. No press has ever been freer of government control than is ours. Freedom of religion, aside from discrimination against the members of one or two sects, is today remarkedly secure.

With respect to freedom of expression, it is particularly noteworthy that we were able to pass through four years of total warfare without serious inroads on this right. This was done in spite of the prediction of many that our free society would not be able to stand the strain of another war.

In the political arena, members of minority groups are increasingly taking advantage of the protection of their right to the ballot by the courts and the national government. Particularly encouraging are reports of increased voting by Negroes in many southern states, both in primary and general elections. . . .

Finally, the Committee wishes to call attention to the very substantial and steady decline in the number of lynchings which has occurred in the last two decades. From a high point of 64 lynchings in 1921, the figure fell during the 1920's to a low of 10 in 1928. During the decade of the 1930's the total climbed again to a high of 28 in 1933, although the decade ended with a low of 3 in 1939. Since 1940, the annual figure has never exceeded 6; on the other hand, there has not yet been a year in which America has been completely free of the crime of lynching. The Committee believes that the striking improvement in the record is a thing to be devoutly thankful for; but it also believes that a single lynching is one too many!

461. *Segregation and Education, 1954*

A. E. Sutherland, "Segregation and the Supreme Court," *Atlantic Monthly*, July, 1954, pp. 35–6.

THERE were worries in the five school segregation cases. Would the Court perhaps find that the Negro schools were not equal to the white, and hence that it was not necessary to decide what would be the law if they were equal? Would the Court, even if it felt that the issue was squarely presented, find distinctions between university students and grade-school pupils, and refuse to override generations of established practice of segregating children in primary schools?

These worries for those of us who wished the Negro children well disappeared a little past noon on May 17, 1954. For on that day, speaking for a united Court, the Chief Justice declared in plain words that neither in the District of Columbia nor in any one of the states does it fit with our Constitution to maintain a white public school which keeps out children whose skins are darker.

The two opinions of the Court, as is right in explaining the Constitution, are written in plain words. Mr. Justice Warren had as the center of his problem in the state cases escape from the verbal symmetry of equality in separation. If, speaking for the United States, he was to forbid any state to keep white children and black children apart in equal schoolhouses, he had to find some inequality in this treatment. He and the eight brethren for whom he spoke found it in what we all know: that excluding the Negro from schools where white children go denotes inferiority of Negro, not white. If, said Chief Justice Warren, segregation hurt McLaurin, an advanced graduate student in a university, it hurts children in grade schools the more. It generates a feeling of inferiority as to their status in the community; it may affect their hearts and minds in a way unlikely ever to be undone. Separate educational facilities are inherently unequal. . . .

Philosophically, the District of Columbia case produced an even more profound opinion. Here there was no equal protection clause to rely on. The court had to decide whether segregated schools deprive the Negro of liberty without due process of law. And the Court found it so.

> Liberty under law extends to the full range of conduct which the individual is free to pursue, and it cannot be restricted except for a proper governmental objective.

> Segregation in public education is not reasonably related to any proper governmental objective, and thus it imposes on Negro children of the District of Columbia a burden that constitutes an arbitrary deprivation of their liberty in violation of the Due Process Clause.

What lies behind the Court's concept of "proper" government? What is proper for the many to do to the few? What is right? What is truth? What is justice? Back of the decision lay ideas of the spiritual origin of individual man, and the bright hope of the eighteenth century that somehow it would turn out that all men are created equal.

Man has never succeeded in defining justice, and this is well; any definition might exclude what he would later wish to preserve. But the Supreme Court had no trouble in deciding on what was not justice; it was not justice to exclude the Negro child from the school where the white children could go. And that judgment day was a great day.

As I write, the papers are full of reports of governors calling together educational commissions to consider what shall be done; and in two or three states there are reported a few—surprisingly few—hurt and indignant utterances from public officials. This is not remarkable. For generations men have felt deeply and resentfully about this matter. People against whom any court decides are apt to be exasperated, and say things in immediate hurt which a little later they realize they do not wholly mean.

More widespread are reports of plans for the hearings in the fall, when those interested will have a chance to discuss the terms of the Court's formal decree. There is nothing very extraordinary about the Court's deferring this final crystallization of judgment. The words "Settle decree on notice" appear at the end of many opinions. A court's opinion gives general ideas about the case, discusses precedent and theory, and announces the judgment. A decree is a later, much more precise, and much less eloquent document, which tells the parties exactly what they must do. The school situations differ in each of the four states and in the District of Columbia. Even assuming a desire on the part of all concerned to put into effect the new policy at once, there would still be complicated arrangements to make. Delay and a chance for the parties to be heard about the effectuation of the judgment are not at all unreasonable.

Furthermore, it is wise. One should never forget the immense moral pressure of such a great judgment as that just announced, and its capacity to persuade men of good will who have been doubting and hesitating. No state in the Union is populated by a separate species of cruel and brutal white men, seeking by cynical devices or by sheer defiance to escape the performance of constitutional duties. One has only to travel in the present South to realize the contrary—to be convinced of the rapid increase of humanitarianism, of cultivation, of kindness, of comfort, of all the good things that go to make up a great civilization.

Announcements from thoughtful people in the southern states are sensible and heartening. . . . The most resentful statements to come from public officials are from South Carolina and Georgia. But the influence of time; the quiet example of the majority of southern states; the words of the many moderate people in the less moderate states; the admiration and respect felt for the President, who has urged that the District of Columbia proceed at once with desegregation; the immense moral pressure of the simple and unanimous opinion of the nine justices— all of these things will be working. There will be problems to solve, but foolish words will quiet down and a wiser day will come. This is a time to respect, and to have confidence in, the people of the South.

462. *The Quota System,* 1952

President Truman's Message Vetoing the McCarran-Walter Immigration and Naturalization Act, June 25, 1952. Overridden by Congress. *Congressional Record,* 82 Congress, 2 Session, XCVIII, Part 6, p. 8083.

THE GREATEST vice of the present quota system, however, is that it discriminates, deliberately and intentionally, against many of the peoples of the world. The purpose behind it was to cut down and virtually eliminate immigration to this country from southern and eastern Europe. A theory was invented to rationalize this objective. The theory was that in order to be readily assimilable, European immigrants should be admitted in proportion to the numbers of persons of their respective national stocks already here as shown by the census of 1920. Since Americans of English, Irish, and German descent were most numerous, immigrants of those three nationalities got the lion's share—more than two-thirds—of the total quota. The remaining third was divided up among all the other nations given quotas.

The desired effect was obtained. Immigration from the newer sources of southern and eastern Europe was reduced to a trickle. The quotas allotted to England and Ireland remained largely unused, as was intended. Total quota immigration fell to a half or third—and sometimes even less—of the annual limit of 154,000. People from such countries as Greece or Spain or Latvia were virtually deprived of any opportunity to come here at all, simply because Greeks or Spaniards or Latvians had not come here before 1920 in any substantial numbers.

The idea behind this discriminatory policy was, to put it baldly, that Americans with English or Irish names were better people and better citizens than Americans with Italian or Greek or Polish names. It was thought that people of West European origin made better citizens than Rumanians or Yugoslavs or Ukrainians or Hungarians or Balts or Austrians. Such a concept is utterly unworthy of our traditions and our ideals. It violates the great political doctrine of the Declaration of Independence that "all men are created equal." It denies the humanitarian creed inscribed beneath the Statue of Liberty proclaiming to all nations, "Give me your tired, your poor, your huddled masses yearning to breathe free."

It repudiates our basic religious concepts, our belief in the brotherhood of man, and in the words of St. Paul, "there is neither Jew nor Greek, there is neither bond nor free, for ye are all one in Christ Jesus." The basis of this quota system was false and unworthy in 1924. It is even worse now. At the present time this quota system keeps out the very people we want to bring in. . . .

Today, we have entered into an alliance, the North Atlantic Treaty, with Italy, Greece, and Turkey against one of the most terrible threats mankind has ever faced. We are asking them to join with us in protecting the peace of the world. We are helping them to build their defenses, and train their men, in the common cause. But, through this bill, we say to their people: You are less worthy to come to this country than Englishmen or Irishmen; you Italians, who need to find homes abroad in the hundreds of thousands—you shall have a quota of 5,645; you Greeks, struggling to assist the helpless victims of a Communist civil war —you shall have a quota of 308; and you Turks, you are brave defenders of the eastern flank, but you shall have a quota of only 225. . . .

We want to stretch out a helping hand, to save those who have managed to flee into Western Europe, to succor those who are brave enough to escape from barbarism, to welcome and restore them against the day when their countries will, as we hope, be free again. But this we cannot do, as we would like to do, because the quota for Poland is only 6,500, as against the 138,000 exiled Poles all over Europe, who are asking to come to these shores; because the quota for the now subjugated Baltic countries is little more than 700, against the 23,000 Baltic refugees imploring us to admit them to a new life here; because the quota for Rumania is only 289, and some 30,000 Rumanians who have managed to escape the labor camps and the mass deportations of their Soviet masters, have asked our help. . . .

In no other realm of our national life are we so hampered and stultified by the dead hand of the past as we are in this field of immigration. We do not limit our cities to their 1920 boundaries; we do not hold corporations to their 1920 capitalizations—we welcome progress and change to meet changing conditions in every sphere of life except in the field of immigration.

463. *A Tidal Wave of Students, 1954*

R. B. Thompson and Thomas Crane, *The Impending Tidal Wave of Students* (October, 1954), 6, 10, 12, 14, 18. Report of the Committee on Special Projects, American Association of Collegiate Registrars and Admission Officers.

THE POPULATION of the United States has doubled in the last fifty years. The number of births each year has almost doubled in the last twenty years, reaching nearly four million in 1953. The average number of births each year for the last eight years is more than a million above the average for the eight years immediately preceding. The burden of educating this unprecedented tidal wave of students when it strikes our colleges and universities will be far greater than anything we have been called upon to bear thus far. . . .

The elementary schools are, of course, the first to feel the effect of increasing enrollments. While these enrollments have grown steadily at the rate of about three quarters of a million a year for the last five years, the big increases are yet to come at the rate of more than one million per year for the next six years. For every two classrooms we had in the United States last year, another must be built within six years. Again the growth is not uniform, but by careful study and advanced planning, very exact predictions of need can be made. . . .

High schools will soon begin to feel the effect of this oncoming tide of students. Continued increasing numbers of teachers, classrooms, and added financial support will be necessary in order to extend even our present educational offerings to the larger numbers of secondary school students. This is a national problem, but it will be solved only as each community provides added facilities. It may bring the picture into clearer focus if we realize that for every three students now attending high school, there will be four in 1960 and five in 1965. . . .

The growth of higher education in the United States has been phenomenal. During the last fifty years the number of students enrolled in private colleges has multiplied more than seven times, while the number enrolled in public colleges and universities has multiplied seventeen times. No other nation has found it possible to provide so many educational opportunities for so large a proportion of its population. . . .

The tidal wave of students is sweeping through our elementary schools, approaching the secondary schools, and will engulf our colleges and universities in a few short years. These students will enter our elementary schools in ever-increasing numbers for at least six more years since the number of births in the United States has now reached an all-time peak. The sheer impact of unprecedented numbers will force us to explore every resource and exert every effort to prepare for their coming. In these years of relative peace and quiet it is difficult for us to prepare ourselves for a time when we shall be confronted with at least twice our present number of students. The fact remains that they are already born. We know the time of their coming—we can count them now.

464. *General Education in a Free Society, 1945*

General Education in a Free Society (Cambridge, 1945), 76–8. Reprinted by permission of the publishers. Copyright 1945 by The President and Fellows of Harvard College.

JUST as it is wrong to split the human person into separate parts, so would it be wrong to split the individual from society. We must resist the prevalent tendency, or at any rate temptation, to interpret the good life purely in terms of atomic individuals engaged in fulfilling their potentialities. Individualism is often confused with the life of private and selfish interest. The mandate of this committee is to concern itself with "the objectives of education in a free society." It is important to realize that the ideal of a free society involves a twofold value, the value of freedom and that of society. Democracy is a *community* of free men. We are apt sometimes to stress freedom —the power of individual choice and the right to think for oneself—without taking sufficient account of the obligation to cooperate with our fellow men; democracy must represent an adjustment between the values of freedom and social living. . . .

Josiah Royce defined the good life in terms of loyalty to a shared value. Of course when union is stressed to the exclusion of freedom we fall into totalitarianism; but when freedom is stressed exclusively we fall into chaos. Democracy is the attempt to combine liberty with loyalty, each limiting the other, and also each reinforcing the other.

It is important, however, to limit the idea of the good citizen expressly by the ideal of the good man. By citizenship we do not mean the kind of loyalty which never questions the accepted purposes of society. A society which leaves no place for criticism of its own aims and methods by its component members has no chance to correct its errors and ailments, no chance to advance to new and better forms, and will eventually stagnate, if not die. The quality of alert and aggressive individualism is essential to good citizenship; and the good society consists of individuals who are independent in outlook and think for themselves while also willing to subordinate their individual good to the common good.

But the problem of combining these two aims is one of the hardest tasks facing our society. The ideal of free inquiry is a precious heritage of Western culture; yet a measure of firm belief is surely part of the good life. A free society means toleration, which in turn comes from openness of mind. But freedom also presupposes conviction; a free choice—unless it be wholly arbitrary (and then it would not be free)—comes from belief and ultimately from principle. A free society, then, cherishes both toleration and conviction. Yet the two seem incompatible. If I am convinced of the truth of my views, on what grounds should I tolerate your views, which I believe to be false? The answer lies partly in my understanding of my limitations as a man. Such understanding is not only the expression of an intellectual humility but is a valid inference from the fact that wise men have made endless mistakes in the past. Furthermore, a belief which does not meet the challenge of criticism and dissent soon becomes inert, habitual, dead. Had there been no heterodoxies, the orthodox should have invented them. A belief which is not envisaged as an answer to a problem is not a belief but a barren formula.

How far should we go in the direction of the open mind? Especially after the first World War, liberals were sometimes too distrustful of enthusiasm and were inclined to abstain from committing themselves as though there were something foolish, even shameful, in belief. Yet especially with youth, which is ardent and enthusiastic, open-mindedness without belief is apt to lead to the opposite extreme of fanaticism. We can all perhaps recall young people of our acquaintance who from a position of extreme skepticism, and indeed because of that position, fell an easy prey to fanatical gospels. It seems that nature abhors an intellectual vacuum. A measure of belief is necessary in order to preserve the quality of the open mind. If toleration is not to become nihilism, if conviction is not to become dogmatism, if criticism is not to become cyncism, each must have something of the other.

465. *Expansion and Knowledge, 1948*

Perry Miller, "Education Under Cross Fire," Chase, *Years of the Modern*, 199–202.

THE AMERICAN educator in the year 1949 is caught in a tension of forces which play upon him with peculiar severity because upon the schools converge the issues of civilization. A shift has been insensibly wrought in the meaning of the traditions, and it is no wonder that educators are bewildered. On the one hand, the tradition of social service, which has hitherto been one with the belief in universal diffusion, is being transformed, before our eyes, into a program of restriction and limitation. But the tradition of a disinterested devotion to knowledge for its own sake, which originally had distinctly aristocratic connotations, contends for democratic freedom in the face of the democracy's hesitation. The conception of a complete receptivity to all ideas or fancies ... now insists that curtailment is death, that career must be open to talents, that everybody must be trained to the utmost of his capacity. And this conception now thrives ... upon the hard experience of the last century, which has persuaded the researcher and the teacher that a steady growth of knowledge is health, and that the slightest inhibition is fatal.

The predicament of the conscientious educator is indeed agonizing, the more so as he is convinced that it is an epitome of the whole civilization. He is the victim of historic forces that have altered their characters. Hitherto diffusion and discovery were pursued simultaneously, because they were entirely complementary: in fact, diffusion supplied the margin within which discovery could operate. But a reversal of diffusion will certainly bring the threat of a narrowing of the field for discovery. An economy of contraction—whether it be the result only of an over-production of scholars or also of the retrenchments imposed by an armed truce—is not compatible with a policy of intellectual expansion. Discovery is outgoing and improvident, and will risk any idea or experiment; retrenchment is not. Discovery requires ever-new materials to work upon; a nation frozen into a cold war will not readily supply them. America, above all nations in recorded history, has thus far embodied the reason working experimentally and experientially; it had a continent to exploit, and no limits to its wide-flung shores. So it builded schools and colleges. If it has suddenly become in effect an island economy, and the space between its coasts has violently shrunk, then the pressures will surely be exerted upon the educational system. It, along with the rest of the culture, may try to seek safety in rigidity.

If the history and experience of America mean anything, they mean that such a course foretells disaster. History is littered with the corpses of civilizations that reached the limit of expansion, dug in behind walls and moats, and there yielded to decay. There is still no evidence that America is irrevocably caught in a determined cycle of rise and decline. The instruments in our hands, the resources, the difficulties already surmounted, are immense. No society ever reached the end of its expansion with so much trained intelligence to command, with so many potentialities for understanding, and thus for transcending its predicament. American education has paid dividends so incalculable that the nation has not yet begun to tap them, and has accumulated the mightiest reservoirs of knowledge ever put at the disposal of a great power. It is not written in the stars that discovery must necessarily perish, even though it now seems possible that discoverers may have to fight for the right to discover.

In this situation, the educator, if he is to preserve his self-respect, has little or no choice. If the end of the era of indefinite expansion has indeed come, then he must stand, more firmly than ever he felt he would be called upon to stand, for the freedom of investigation, for the principle that nothing, not democracy itself, and not even the American way of life, is so sacred that it cannot be studied, analyzed, and criticized. Furthermore, the results of such criticism must continue to augment the content of education. The accumulation of knowledge cannot be arrested; the educator will be, it is assumed, loyal to his country, but he will manifest that loyalty by meticulously remaining faithful to the pursuit of learning, and to the transmission of learning to posterity, no matter how many conflicts this devotion may lead him into. Unless he is to surrender entirely his function, and to become merely an instrument of national policy, he must keep alive a passion for knowledge that is first and foremost its own excuse for being, and take the position that under present conditions, this insistence is his major responsibility to the future of democracy.

INDEX TO DOCUMENTS

A NOTE ON THE TYPE

The text of this book is set in two Linotype faces as follows: the documents in CALEDONIA, which belongs to the family of printing types called "modern face" by printers—a term used to mark the change in style of type-letters that occurred about 1800; Caledonia borders on the general style of Scotch Modern, but is more freely drawn than that letter. The introductions and comments of the editor are set in ELECTRA, also designed by Mr. Dwiggins, a face which cannot be classified as modern or old-style; it is not based on any historical model, nor does it echo any particular period or style; it avoids the extreme contrast between thick and thin elements that marks most modern faces, and attempts to give a feeling of fluidity, power, and speed.

The book was composed, printed, and bound by KINGS-PORT PRESS, INC., Kingsport, Tennessee. Designed by HARRY FORD.